W9-BCU-112

# FRIEDRICH NIETZSCHE

CURTIS CATE

THE OVERLOOK PRESS
Woodstock & New York

First published in the United States in 2005 by
The Overlook Press, Peter Mayer Publishers, Inc.
Woodstock & New York

Woodstock:
One Overlook Drive
Woodstock, NY 12498
www.overlookpress.com
[for individual orders, bulk and special sales, contact our Woodstock office]

New York:
141 Wooster Street
New York, NY 10012



∞ The paper used in this book meets the requirements for paper permanence as described in the ANSI Z39.48-1992 standard.

Cataloging-in-Publication Data is available from the Library of Congress

Printed in the United States of America
ISBN 1-58567-592-X
3 5 7 9 8 6 4 2

*To the Memory*

*of*

*my unforgotten, unforgettable*

*Elenochka*

*and of my father*

*Karl Springer Cate*

*who loved her dearly*

CONTENTS

# Acknowledgements

If punctuality, as Louis XVIII of France is reported to have said, is the courtesy of kings, then gratitude towards their predecessors or those who facilitated their task should surely be the courtesy of biographers. Let me therefore begin by expressing my thanks to the Italian scholars, Giorgio Colli and Mazzino Montinari, who, working under anything but easy conditions, when the 'Nietzsche Archives' at Weimar, like the rest of Thuringia and Saxony, were placed under the administrative control of an outspokenly proletarian régime, achieved quite remarkable results. The multiple edition of Nietzsche's published works, of his letters and the often fascinating answers they elicited, constitute a monument of painstaking scholarship for which they deserve the highest praise. As do their chief assistant for the preparation of the 8-volume paperback edition of Nietzsche's letters – *Sämtliche Briefe Studienausgabe* – Helga Anania-Hess, and the trinitarian team – Bettina Schmidt-Wahrig, Rüdiger Schmidt, and Federico Gerratana, who compiled its invaluable index.

Invaluable too, for all German-reading persons deeply interested in Nietzsche and the often dramatic tensions and vicissitudes of his physically and psychologically tortured life, is Curt Paul Janz's 3-volume biography, the work of a Swiss scholar who, having played the violin in Basel's Symphony Orchestra, was supremely qualified to appreciate Nietzsche's piano-playing talents and the vital role played by music in his life. Nor should I, in this brief catalogue of merits, overlook the significant contribution made by Ernst Pfeiffer in assembling an invaluable collection of letters – remnants, alas, of a double work of feminine destruction intended to obscure the complex truth – concerning the extraordinary 'trinitarian' embroglio into which Nietzsche, like his friend Paul Rée and the audacious Lou Salomé, plunged with (for a while) such headlong relish. (I say this in all fairness, notwithstanding the 'hard time' that Pfeiffer apparently gave Rudolph Binion during his research work on 'Frau Lou'.) And to this list of 'benefactors' one can add the name of Sander Gilman who, assisted by Ingeborg Reichenbach, compiled a priceless collection of reminiscences written by all sorts of persons who had the good fortune to meet, to befriend, or to talk with Friedrich Nietzsche.

On a more personal level I would like to thank Dr. Jochen Golz, director of the Nietzsche-Stiftung, at the Goethe-und-Schiller Archiv in Weimar, for granting me permission to do some valuable research in the Foundation's spacious library. Indebted I also am to his library assistants, and in particular to Karin Ellermann, who helped me to assemble most of the photo illustrations in this book; to Dr. Roswitha Wollkopf, of the Stiftung Weimarer Klassik, and to Elke Schwandner, of the Deutsches Literaturarchiv in Marbach-am-Neckar.

For having helped to make my sojourn in Weimar, in May 1998, so enjoyable, I would like to thank Frau Marikka Hüttman, the enterprising manager of her charmingly named 'An den Altenburg' pension.

I also owe special thanks to Professor Manfred Riedel, of the Martin Heidegger Gesellschaft in Halle, and to Professor Glenn Most, of Heidelberg and Florence, for the kindness they showed me during a visit I made to Naumburg in October 1994, at a meeting of philologists assembled to celebrate the 150th anniversary of Nietzsche's birth. I am also indebted to Frau Klee, of Naumburg's Fremdenverkehrsamt, to Suzanna Kröner, of the town's Stadtarchiv, and to Dr. Siegfried Wagner, director of Naumburg's Stadtmuseum, who managed to send me a photocopy of the nineteenth-century lithograph of the picturesque Marktplatz, which figures among the illustrations.

Among those to whom I owe a special debt of thanks, for having encouraged me to write this biography are the now deceased James O'Donnell (who had already helped with a book about the Berlin Wall crisis of 1961), and the likewise much regretted Michael Ivens, as witty a poet as he was an inspired defender of liberty in many fields; Melvin Lasky, the former editor of *Der Monat* and *Encounter*; my fellow Wykehamist and Magdalen College friend, Christopher Johnson, who took the trouble to read and even to approve my controversial Preface; my even older and no less valued friend Joseph Frank, author of a monumental work on Dostoevsky, who has shown the world what the art of biography can be in the hands of a master-craftsman of stupendous erudition; Austin Olney and Robie Macauley, enlightened editors at Houghton Mifflin, Boston, who were kind enough to offer me my first contract; and not least of all, Rob Cowley, one of the ablest red-pencil-wielders it has been my good fortune to encounter in the increasingly rare art of manuscript editing.

And how could I forget the cordial hospitality so often shown to me and my wife by Robert von Hagemeister, a rare model of Pomerian gentility, in whose lovely home near Bern entire chapters of this book were written; the kindness of his wife Annette, who once accompanied me to Lucerne for a memorable visit to the Wagner Museum at Tribschen; the generosity of his son Peter who, at a time when I was more than usually penniless, gave me a badly needed word-processor; and the charming cooperation offered to me by his vivacious daughter, Viviane, who, as an informal 'travel agent' and interpreter (for 'switzerdütch' contacts), helped me to organize my two visits to Thuringia and Saxony, and to establish fruitful contacts with Frau Jäger, of the Richard Wagner Museum at Tribschen – as also with the Lucerne photographer, Georg Anderhub, Maya Klopstein and Daniel Egloff, of Sils-Maria's Tourist-and-Information Bureau, and the equally cooperative Max Weiss, director of the Montabella photo publishing company in Saint-Moritz. Nor should I forget Joseph Gwerder, an inhabitant of Lucerne, who most kindly sent me a photcopy of an 1869 timetable for steamboat trips around the Lake of the Four Cantons, which helped me greatly in my description of Nietzsche's first trip around this beautiful lake.

For their valuable advice in matters of German semantics I am indebted to George and Beate Bailey, to Frauke Stuart, to my old Oxford friend, Rüdiger von Pachelbel, and, not least of all, to the veteran New York editor, Fred Jordan, a fine product of Viennese 'high culture' who had already helped me greatly with my biography of André Malraux. I also owe thanks to Professor Robert Harding, of the University of Pennsylvania, for valuable information in his chosen field of Anthropology.

For having had the courage to approve my initial synopsis and to obtain a contract for this book, I am most indebted to William Hamilton of A.M. Heath, as I am to his 'colleague' in New York, my old friend Tom Wallace. I would also like to express my thanks to Annie Lee for her intelligent copy-editing work on the typescript, to James Nightingale for his painstaking help in correcting galley and page-proofs and to Anthony Howard, for having inadvertently aroused me from my 'dogmatic slumbers' as to the kind of useful Index a book of this kind should have. As for their 'boss', Anthony Whittome, my long-suffering Hutchinson editor, no compliment I could possibly invent would adequately describe what I owe him for his comprehensive, gentlemanly patience.

Finally and once again, I extend my heart-felt thanks to my step-son, Professor Michael Aminoff, whose generosity over the years was quite simply boundless, to his wife Jan, who so often made us happy during our stays in San Francisco, and to my darling Elena who, with psychic prescience and the age-old wisdom of Central Asia, often said that she would never live to see the day this biography was published.

# List of Illustrations

Friedrich Nietzsche in 1882 (*photo* GSA Stiftung Weimarer Klassik)

Paul Rée (photo taken by Ferreti in Naples) (*photo* GSA Stiftung Weimarer Klassik)

Elisabeth Nietzsche (*photo* GSA Stiftung Weimarer Klassik)

Photograph taken in Lucerne in August 1882 of Lou Salomé (holding whip and 'reins'), Paul Rée, F. Nietzsche (as two 'workhorses') (GSA Stiftung Weimarer Klassik)

Nietzsche's bedroom in grocer-mayor's house at Sils-Maria (*photo* Max Weiss, Montabella Verlag, St. Moritz)

Sils Baseglia (village with steeple, next to Sils-Maria) (*photo* courtesy of Verkehrsverein Sils-Engadin)

View of Sils Lake, looking Southwest (*photo* Max Weiss, Montabella Verlag, St. Moritz)

Nietzsche with his mother in May 1892, after his mental collapse (*photo* GSA Stiftung Weimarer Klassik)

Nietzsche in 1899, etching by Hans Olde (*photo* GSA Stiftung Weimarer Klassik)

Nietzsche's sister Elisabeth Förster-Nietzsche in late middle-aged widowhood (*photo* GSA Stiftung Weimarer Klassik)

Chancellor Adolf Hitler visiting Elisabeth Förster-Nietzsche in Weimar, 1934 (*photo* GSA Stiftung Weimarer Klassik) weakness is also their strength and their charm: the charm of refreshing spontaneity. Nietzsche was not going to cheat or deceive his readers by concealing the bitter truths he had discovered or the blackest thoughts that occurred to him. The intrepidity he displayed in entitling the fifth and final book of *The Joyous Science* – 'We Fearless Ones' – was no literary pose. He had a horror of tepid thinking, even going so far as to declare, in an essay on Schopenhauer, that books that had no fire in them deserved to be burned; and the chapter he devoted in *Zarathustra* to those who 'write with their blood' was profoundly autobiographic.

That there are subtle, and sometimes even glaring, contradictions in Nietzsche's philosophy is evident to anyone who has studied it with any care. But what these flaws attest is not a love of falsehood or self-deception, but rather an unending battle to deal with the myriad enigmas, puzzles, and contradictions inherent in the mystery, or more properly, the mysteries of human Life. Indeed, it was precisely because so many varying points of view were therein expressed, so many novel 'perspectives' opened up that Nietzsche's protean philosophy began, even before his death, to exercise such an extraordinary fascination on readers and 'enthusiasts' from the most diverse walks of life. Among the seven thousand 'aphorisms' and short essays contained in a score of published books there was something for every taste and opinion – from the most conservatively and snobbishly inclined (those whom the Viennese wit Karl Kraus sarcastically dubbed the 'super-apes of the coffee-house') to the most radically-minded. Nietzsche himself was amazed to discover in 1887, one year before his mental breakdown, that among his most enthusiastic 'fans' were to be found the kinds of persons he most distrusted and abhorred: 'left-wing' socialists, revolutionary Marxists, atheistic nihilists, who, blandly disregarding everything else he had written, felt that he was one of their own kind because of his pitiless assaults on Christian hypocrisy. As Steven Aschheim noted a few years ago in his admirably researched *The Nietzsche Legacy in Germany – 1890–1990*: 'Those who predicted a quick disappearance did not realize that it was precisely the fact that there was no uniformity of opinion or binding authoritative organization that ensured Nietzscheanism's long and varied life. Its elasticity and selective interpretive possibilities constituted its staying power and facilitated its infusion into so many areas of cultural and political life.'

Many of the 'contradictions' in Nietzsche's philosophy were the consequences of his deliberately ambivalent attitude towards what is all too casually called the 'truth'. 'The truth, to be sure,' he once wittily put it, 'can stand on one leg; but with two it will walk and get around.' He was persuaded that there is no such thing as an absolute Truth, and that even in dealing with limited 'truths' the philosopher's first task is to lift each one up and turn it around, like a stone, to see what might be lurking underneath. And it was what lay below, in the nether depths of each spoken or written 'truth', that interested Nietzsche far more than the patent, superficial, often deceptive surface.

The trenchant tone of so many of his affirmations should not lead one to conclude that Nietzsche enjoyed 'laying down the law'. Dogma of any kind was something he detested, as meat for the indolent priest, poison for the genuine thinker. As he wrote in *Morgenröte* (Morning Glow), in a section (507) entitled, 'Against the Tyranny of the True': 'Even if we were mad enough to regard all of our opinions as true, we would still not want them to exist alone: I would not know why the autocratic domination and omnipotence of the truth would be desirable; it would suffice for me to know that it possessed great power. But it must know how to *fight* and have antagonists, and one must from time to time be able to *find relief* from it in untruth – otherwise it will become boring, powerless and tasteless to us, and thus make us the same.' This was one of the most succinct statements Nietzsche ever made of the 'resistentialism' that lies at the very core of his philosophy: it is not what *assists* Man that strengthens and ennobles him, but, quite the contrary, what *resists* his slothful inclinations and prejudices.

It was Nietzsche's constant endeavour to be 'multidimensional' in his thinking, his unflinching readiness to see both sides, to tackle the unpleasant *con* as well as the beguiling *pro* of every problem he examined, which so often makes his thinking seem contradictory. The man who, towards the end of his sane life, defiantly declared, 'God is a crude, two-fisted answer, an indelicacy towards us thinkers' was also the man who declared, in the magnificent opening section of *The Joyous Science*, that from time immemorial human beings had heeded the founders of moral codes and religions, even though these had repeatedly kindled religious wars, simply because in getting people to believe that they were serving the interests of God or gods, they were reinforcing a belief in the value and significance of human life and thus helping to preserve the species, which might otherwise have yielded to the suicidal extremes of pessimistic despair.

Not long ago, in a delightful book entitled *Nietzsche in Turin*, which, as she explained in her preface, was an 'attempt to befriend' him, the British author and literary critic, Lesley Chamberlain, declared that this 'strained, charming, malicious and misunderstood thinker . . .was perhaps the most original European philosopher of the nineteenth century.' We can, I think, dispense with the 'perhaps'. For good or ill, Nietzsche has proved to be the most influential philosopher since Hegel, casting his ever-lengthening shadow over the entire length of the twentieth century and beyond. I do not make this claim because of the intellectual role he is supposed to have played in promoting Nazism: a fashionable myth exploded years ago in Peter Viereck's *Metapolitics*, where German romanticism in all of its complex forms was placed in the dock and found guilty, along with its great pamphleteering poet-prophet-and-composer, Richard Wagner. I make it because no major thinker of modern times has more prophetically dissected the deepest and most dangerous 'drifts' in the permissive *laisser-aller* that has increasingly become the *modus vivendi et pensandi*, the effective, day-to-day religion – more exactly irreligion – of 'modern' men and women in the West.

If, at the risk of being simplistic – all too easy in discussing such a complex, many-sided, and subtle philosophy – one can say that the first half of Nietzsche's intellectual development (up to *Thus Spake Zarathustra*) was a desperate attempt to give written substance to his proudly proclaimed *Freigeisterei* (free-spiritedness) – essentially reserved for the 'happy few' who are brave enough to face the terrifying reality of man's cosmic insignificance in a gigantically expanding universe – the second part of his philosophical quest can be regarded as an even more desperate attempt to fill the resultant void, inasmuch as social stability, and with it civilization and culture, cannot ultimately be maintained without an instinctive, not to say atavistic, respect for Authority. Perhaps nowhere in all of Nietzsche's writings was the bitter awareness of the civil war that was raging in the darkest depths of his philosophy more poignantly expressed than in this pathetic protest, contained in a letter written (in November 1882) to Lou Salomé, the quick-witted, brilliant, precociously erudite young lady whom he had wanted to make his chief disciple: 'Surely *you* don't believe that the "*Freigeist*" is *my* ideal?'

It is one of the signal merits of Nietzsche's philosophy that he courageously recognized the inherent limitations of *Freigeisterei*, of 'free-spiritedness', free thinking. If the human mind is to be truly free and unfettered, if it is not to suffer from *Kettenkrankheit* – intellectual 'chain-sickness' – it must free itself from the ultimate and most crippling of illusions: the naive notion (so common among contemporary 'liberals' and devout admirers of the French Revolution) that Freedom or Liberty is an absolute value to which every other must pay homage. How can something as insubstantial, as a mere form of *possibility* be regarded, in any meaningful sense, as an absolute value? When what really matters is the substance. As with an empty glass or cup, it is above all else what one pours into it that counts. Freedom, by its very nature, cannot be an end in itself. It means freedom to be benevolent or nasty, brave or cowardly, generous or selfish, truthful or mendacious, magnanimous or petty-minded, honest or dishonest, polite or rude, rational or irrational.

No one understood this better than Thomas Mann who, in *The Magic Mountain* – the very title of which (*Zauberberg*, in German) he had 'lifted' from the third section of *The Birth of Tragedy* – 'personalized' these two antagonistic forces in Nietzsche's thinking by giving them human form in the persons of Professor Settembrini, the advocate of 'progress', free speech, and democracy, and Naphta, the Jesuitical apologist of Authority and Autocracy. Nothing, indeed, could have been more appropriately Nietzschean, at the conclusion of their epic debate, than Settembrini's despair over Naphta's suicide – as symbolizing the futility of dispassionate 'free-thinking' in solving the intractable problems of the modern world.

Now this, quite simply, is the situation in which we find ourselves today. The debate is as fierce and as far from being resolved as ever. It has even assumed a geopolitical dimension, as the American historian, Samuel P. Huntington, has suggested in his *The Clash of Civilizations*, and, in a purely American context, Gertrude Himmelfarb in *One Nation, Two Cultures*. And what has not changed, as Nietzsche presciently foresaw, has been the predominance in all 'Western' societies of an essentially *descensional*, downward-dragging gravitational force.

It can be argued that in an increasingly democratic age it was wishful thinking to imagine that one could reverse the trend, since the 'realistic' morality Nietzsche desperately strove to formulate was based first and foremost on aristocratic canons of good taste. As he once wrote to his sister Elisabeth, 'in this rabble-and-country-bumpkin age' he valued 'good manners' more than 'virtue', 'wit', and 'beauty'.

An intransigent enemy of egalitarianism in all of its insidious forms, Nietzsche was convinced that the democratic 'acid' at work in all Western societies was relentlessly corroding all forms of authority, respect, and veneration, and thus contributing as much as scientific rationalism to subvert religious faith. The 'democratization' of Christian belief, liturgical language, and practice – triumphantly proclaimed seven decades after his death as the Catholic Church's guiding ideal in the Vatican II Council of 1965 – far from being a form of religious 'progress', was, he believed, one more sickly symptom of a tendency to desacrilize the sacred, to demean the very notion of the Divine. Where there is no awe and mystery – as embodied, for example, in a sacred, uncolloquial language – all sense of what is sacred vanishes. Where nothing is sacred any more, there is no respect. And where there is no respect, there is no authority.

We touch here on something absolutely fundamental in Nietzsche's aristocratic attitude in judging not only religion, but so much else in daily life. This was the vitally important element of 'distance', the very foundation of awe, respect, veneration. Nothing was more repugnant to him than all forms of divine 'proximity', which he regarded as inescapably demeaning for God as well as man. In its *negative* form, that of divine vigilance, an omniscient, omnipresent, forever watching God becomes in effect a keyhole-peeper, a divine voyeur, an intrusive Big Brother. (In *Beyond Good and Evil* Nietzsche amused himself by citing an objection once made by an innocent young girl who asked her mother, 'Is God everywhere?' When the mother answered unthinkingly, 'But yes, of course,' the young daughter said, 'But don't you think that's indecent?')

Equally repugnant to Nietzsche was the positive notion of a friendly, helpful, cooperative God, ever ready to help the devout believer in moments of crisis. He rightly foresaw the grotesque absurdities to which the naive *Gott mit uns* (God is on our side) tendency in Protestantism was bound to lead. As has been dramatically proved over the past half-century – particularly in the United States, where Protestantism is still a force to be reckoned with – by the ludicrous promises made by super-salesmen of high-octane faith, such as Norman Vincent Peale (author of *The Power of Positive Thinking*), who has a cooperative God helping the 'positively-minded' believer to sell vacuum-cleaners, to run a beauty parlour, to enable a football team to win, a golfer to mashie his way out of a sandy bunker, a tireless deity who is above all super-active in the businessman's office, helping the enterprising to get ahead in the world – since there is no better recipe for success, the good Doctor assured us, than 'effecting a merger with God'. Or one could cite the no less ineffable Dr. Samuel Shoemaker, who used to cheer up members of the Pittsburg Golf Club by assuring them that 'God loves snobs as well as other people.' Or again, that arch-optimist, the Baptist faith healer, Oral Roberts, who liked to reassure his possibly worried listeners that 'Christ has no objection to prosperity'. The list of such spiritual 'boosters' could be almost indefinitely extended – in keeping with the prescription for success formulated fifty or sixty years ago by Dean Inge, the 'Red Dean' of Canterbury, who once declared: 'A religion succeeds not because it is true but because it suits its worshippers.'

It was precisely because Christianity had ceased to be harsh and exacting, as it could still be at the time of Pascal (1623–1662) – one of his 'heroic antagonists' – and had instead grown smug, complacent, soft and flabby, that Nietzsche held it in such withering contempt. Like so much else in the modern world, it had been riddled and eaten through and through by the wood-worm of democratic optimism and its categorical imperative: Christianity too must be tailored to popular wishes. Ground under in the process was the very notion of the sacred, of something to be revered precisely because it is not on our level but higher, nobler, and in the sublimest sense beyond Man's reach.

What makes a society healthy, Nietzsche believed, is an *ascensional* or aspirational force, exerting its upward pull towards an ideal of improvement or perfection, towards something higher and better, and not merely more 'successful' – success being, as he once noted, 'the greatest of liars'. Where this upward-pulling attraction (a form of respect or veneration) has lost its force or no longer exists, the prevailing social force becomes inverted and *descensional.* Those who should be exercising authority become demoralized and conscience-stricken at the mere thought of having to lead and to direct, for fear of becoming 'unjust', 'unfair', or, worst of all, 'unpopular'. The healthy notion of 'authority' is tarred and feathered and takes on the sickly hue of 'tyranny'. The result is a general flight from responsibility, a universal abdication.

This, Nietzsche foresaw with prophetic clarity, is what is happening today all over the Western world. Parents abdicate before their undisciplined children, teachers before their lawless pupils, priests before their restless, time-rationed congregations, politicians before their assiduously flattered voters – in a *modus operandi* that was codified, already a century and a half ago by the exemplary French damagogue, Alexandre Ledru-Rollin, who, when once asked where he and his party were headed, candidly replied: 'I do not know, but I am their leader, so I must follow them.' Everyone ends up giving way before something or someone, in a vertiginously descending spiral. No area of life is spared. All 'traditional' values are challenged, any trace of 'élitism' becomes instantly suspect. Ugliness, precisely because it is the opposite of the traditionally 'beautiful', is accorded an honourable status, just as what is incomprehensible (the opposite of the all-too-easy-to-understand – what the great art historian, Ernst Gombrich, had the courage to denounce as 'rubbish' or 'anti-art') – receives the stamp of profound 'significance' by cultural snobs in frantic search of 'originality'. The once elegant 'art' of *haute couture* is dragged down to the sordid level of *basse couture*, with transparently clad model-girls – the new idols of our sensation-seeking age – being forced to indulge in various forms of titillating strip-tease. The strident development of an aggressively crude 'rap' singing is another characteristic symptom of a 'mish-mash' culture which, having lost its roots and all sense of aristocratic restraint, has become 'nomadic' – another Nietzschean prediction – and reduced to importing its inspiration from other climes and continents.

It is easy to reproach Nietzsche for having, in his anathemas against pulpit preachers, contributed to the deluge by weakening the flood-gates of traditional morality. But the troubling question remains: what will happen to the Western world if the present drift cannot be halted, and to what sordid depths of pornographically publicized vulgarity will our shamelessly 'transparent' culture, or what remains of it, continue to descend, while those who care about such matters look on in impotent dismay? Perhaps, indeed, the day is not too distant when, new post-modern norms having imposed themselves through a process of Nietzschean 'transvaluation', marriage (even between 'heterosexuals') will be declared abnormal as well as deplorably 'old hat'.

Nietzsche, who was painfully aware of how much dynamite his destructive-constructive philosophy contained ('we must destroy the old before we can rebuild the new') once wrote to his friend Malwida von Meysenbug that his soul was weighed down by apprehensions 'that are one hundred times heavier to bear than la bêtise humaine (human foolishness). It is possible that for all forthcoming human beings I am a calamity, that I am *the* calamity . . .' And again, in another letter to his 'Aunt' Malwida: 'the thought still terrifies me as to how totally unsuited people will one day invoke my authority. But this is the agony of every great teacher of mankind; he knows that under certain circumstances and accidents he can become a calamity as well as a blessing for mankind. Well, I will do everything to avoid facilitating at least all too crude misunderstandings.'

This turned out to be a pious wish. Driven on by his restless inner demon – that of an *enfant terrible* – he brought out a 'very black and squid-like' book, *Beyond Good and Evil*, in the final chapter of which he trenchantly asserted that genuine culture had always been created by a powerful, self-confident aristocracy, imbued with a hardy *Herren-Moral* ('master morality'), and that the *raison d'être* of their subjects was to provide the necessary social foundation for the dominant *Herren-Caste* ('master caste'). In his next book, *The Genealogy of Morals*, he went even further by contrasting the healthy, positive, creative character of a 'master-morality' with the negative, reactive, morbidly resentful character of a 'slave-morality', which, thanks to Christianity and its bastard offspring, the French Revolution, was now becoming the dominant political religion in Europe.

That there was something foolhardy about this 'fearless' temerity, there can be no doubt. What happened, and was bound to happen, given the bombastic, bellicose '*Deutschland! Deutschland über Alles!*' super-patriotism that had fastened its grip on most of the citizens of the second Germanic Reich after Prussia' victory over France in 1870, was that Nietzsche's most uncompromising statements were seized upon by the 'unsuited followers' he had described in his letter to Malwida von Meysenbug and twisted into vicious stereotypes by a number of sub-intellectual admirers of Adolf Hitler. The aristocratic notion of a *Herren-Caste* was vulgarized and socially massified into a Germanic *Herren-Rasse* (master race); his condemnations of the cult of Christian compassion encouraged a pitiless campaign against all forms of *Untermenschen* (the sub-human opposites of the Nietzschean *Übermensch*, or superior 'overman', extolled by Zarathustra), beginning with the Slavs and the Jews; while the rampaging 'blond beast', torn out of context, provided a philosophical justification for the bestiality of the anti-Bolshevik and anti-Semitic storm-troopers of the SA and the SS. The climactic result was the triumph of four forms of tyranny Nietzsche had never ceased to denounce: the tyranny of ideology, the tyranny of the State, the tyranny of the rabble-rousing demagogue (Adolf Hitler), the tyranny of the mob.

The history of philosophy is, among other things, the history of intellectual betrayals, or, let us say, of intellectual 'twisting' performed by zealous disciples who, by concentrating on a particular strand in the Master's thinking, end up radically transforming his original intent. A classic case is that of René Descartes. In his battle against scholastic empiricism and Aristotelian 'physics', which for fifteen centuries had crippled scientific thinking and had allowed intelligent Europeans to go on assuming that the sun revolves around the earth, Descartes imprudently advocated a régime of mental cleansing, which he likened to a blackboard erasing: *a tabula rasa*. This term, used in his *Discourse on Method* as an elementary recommendation of intellectual hygiene, was intended to clean his contemporaries' brains of the cobwebs of scholastic logic-chopping which had been preventing them from thinking clearly. But in the hands of his disciples the *tabula rasa* formula was extended to cover everything. The old, *qua* old, was condemned in the name of the 'new', and Descartes's first great disciple, the fanatically Catholic Malebranche, went as far as to outlaw History as a useful guide for human beings (compared to mathematics and geometry) and as little more than a compendium of errors and superstitions: the attitude adopted by Europe's first great 'encyclopedist', Pierre Bayle (1647–1706). The past, being by definition old, had to be scrapped – the result eventually being the French Revolution, a social upheaval which would have appalled Descartes, who in matters political and religious was essentially a conservative.

Another classic case of 'intellectual betrayal' is that of Hegel. The extraordinary 'logical' system Hegel invented in order to provide a rational explanation for mankind's intellectual development – with a thesis generating an antithesis, itself superseded by a synthesis, this constituting a new thesis, etc. – was intended among other things to justify the emergence and definitive triumph of constitutional monarchy. Had Hegel, struck down by cholera in 1831, lived twenty or thirty years longer, he would almost certainly have been dismayed to see what some of his zealous disciples were bent on doing with his philosophy. In his fascinating book, *From Hegel to Nietzsche – The Revolution in 19th Century Thought*, Karl Löwith has shown how each of his principal admirers – Bruno Bauer, David Strauss, Arnold Ruge, Max Stirner, Ludwig Feuerbach – selected one particular tendency in Hegel's thought and proceeded to weave it into something radically different from what the Master would have wished to see accomplished. The most famous of these 'adapters' was Karl Marx, who took Hegel's dialectic and stood it on its head, dethroning intellectuals and making impersonal, 'scientifically' discoverable social and economic forces the real prime movers of human history.

The case of Friedrich Nietzsche is even more pathetic. To begin with, he foresaw this very process of intellectual betrayal. After noting, in the 281st 'aphorism' of *Human, All Too Human*, how difficult it is for one-track-minded pedants to understand a thinker who plays on several strings, he added: 'It lies in the very nature of the higher, *many-stringed* culture that it will always be falsely interpreted by the lower one' – a prediction which, if one changes 'lower' into 'lowest', was more than fulfilled by his Nazi admirers. What Nietzsche did not foresee, however, was that the person who became in many ways the most influential of his intellectual betrayers, who posed for years as the 'supreme authority' on his writings, who used left-over notes to concoct a posthumous 'crowning work' with the inflammatory title *The Will to Power* (ready-made to encourage 'misreaders' to regard it as an apologia for the political 'will to power' of a dangerously militaristic Germanic Reich), and who took it upon herself to write a 3-volume biography about him, would be . . . his sister Elisabeth! A sister who had already infuriated her brother by marrying a notorious anti-Semitic agitator, and who, with the same pig-headed disregard and disrespect for everything he had so profoundly thought and fought for, transformed Nietzsche into an apologist of totalitarian tyranny by courting Mussolini ('Zarathustra's most splendid disciple') and, later, by welcoming to her home in Weimar an authentically Teutonic *Übermensch* named Adolf Hitler.

CHAPTER I

# A Strongly Pastoral Tradition

*– 'Ah, our good, pure Protestant air!'*

History, and not least of all the history of philosophy, is full of subtle ironies. One of the strangest is the fact that the most iconoclastic of modern philosophers, the one who did more than anyone since Martin Luther to challenge the established Church, should have been born in a village of Saxon Thuringia, in the Lutheran heartland of Germany – a mere seventy kilometres from the great Reformer's birthplace at Eisleben, eighty kilometres from Erfurt, where he began his university studies, and less than 120 kilometres from the castle of Wittenberg, on whose chapel door the anti-papal rebel posted up his ninety-five theses in October 1517, 327 years before Friedrich Nietzsche's appearance on the scene.

Even if, as the familiar dictum has it, no one is more apt to become an ardent atheist than a once ardent believer, no one can reasonably claim that Luther's most uncompromising modern critic could have been born only in this particular part of Germany, and that he should necessarily have been a Protestant vicar's son. Nietzsche himself regarded these 'accidents' as due to 'blind' chance or fortune, or what he later called 'Fatum'. He will always remain an enigma for neo-Freudians, since contrary to the standard X-pattern of attraction, he adored and idolized his father and never suffered from a mother complex. His rebellion against Christianity and all anthropomorphic religions was an intellectual, not a psychological phenomenon.

Geography may, however, have played a role in Friedrich Nietzsche's intellectual development in a more subtle way. The Saale river valley, where he spent fourteen decisive years of youth and adolescence, happens to be the northernmost wine-growing region of Germany. Konrad Adenauer, a man of dry wit, once remarked that there were three distinct Germanies: the Germany of the schnapps-drinkers of Prussia, the Germany of the beer-drinkers of Bavaria, the Germany of the wine-drinkers of the Rhineland. Of the three, only the wine-drinkers were sober enough to rule the country. Would Nietzsche have agreed? Possibly. At the age of twenty this disillusioned scholar decided that beer-drinking was an uncouth, mind-clouding, ego-inflating pastime collectively indulged in by raucous super-patriots and an impediment to clear thinking. It was thus perhaps not altogether an accident that this abstemious devotee of Dionysos, who developed an admirable clarity of style, should have been brought up in a pleasant valley whose relatively sober, thrifty, hard-working inhabitants paid temperate homage to Bacchus.

With its vaguely Japanese sound and its distinctly un-Japanese spelling, the name Nietzsche strikes us as a bit exotic. The letter combination *ietz*, which links it to other Middle-German or Saxon names like Leibniz, Choltitz, Tirpitz, suggests a Slavic origin (comparable to the *ice* – pronounced *itze* – combination one finds in Czech names), while the final *sche* is unmistakably Teutonic. The most illustrious bearer of the name was proudly persuaded that his was not only a hybrid but also an aristocratic genealogy. During the winter of 1883–4, when the thirty-nine-year-old philosopher was hibernating on the French Riviera, he met a Pole who showed him a document entitled, '*L'Origine de la famille seigneuriale de Nietzke*'. Nietzsche, who had by then developed a virulent abhorrence of many aspects of German life and culture, needed no further persuading that his father's family was of Polish origin. His cousin, Max Oehler, who later investigated his parental genealogy, clambered back 200 years without finding a trace of Polish ancestry in the family tree, but this in itself means little; for, like neighbouring Silesia, this part of Saxony was inhabited by indigenous Slavs long before the Germanic tribes began their colonizing *Drang nach Osten* (push towards the east) in the ninth and tenth centuries AD. The name is anything but rare; and variations like Nitsche, Nitzke or Nitze abound all over central Germany.

Far from being of noble stock, Friedrich Nietzsche's ancestors on his father's side were modest Saxon townsfolk – butchers and cottagers who lived in and around Bibra, some eleven miles north-west of the cathedral city of Naumburg. The first to achieve any prominence was Christoph Nietzsche (1675–1739), a public notary who got himself appointed tax inspector for the *Kurfürstentum* (elector-principality) of Saxony. The decisive step in this slow social ascension was taken by his son, Friedrich August Ludwig, who was Nietzsche's grandfather. Instead of serving the state, he decided to serve God, an even surer way for a person of humble origin to move up in the world. In Protestant Germany the pastor was usually the most important person in any village community, having to act as teacher for the young as well as spiritual guide for adults. Those who displayed unusual promise could even climb out of their rural rut. By publishing several dissertations on moral and religious subjects, Friedrich August Nietzsche earned himself an honorary degree in theology from the university of Koenigsberg and, a little later, a promotion to the rank of Superintendent for Eilenburg, an important town situated some fifteen miles north-east of Leipzig, on the main high road towards the Elbe.*

Friedrich August Nietzsche's first wife died in 1805, seven weeks before the battle of Austerlitz, which put a final end to the first Germanic *Reich* (or Holy Roman Empire). She left seven children behind her, as well as a husband who was in no mood to remain single for the rest of his days. Four years later he married a widow named Erdmuthe Krause. The ecclesiastical connection was thus notably strengthened; for her father had been an archdeacon, while her eldest brother, after occupying a chair in theology at Koenigsberg, succeeded the celebrated philologist-philosopher Johann Gottfried Herder as Superintendent of the Stadtkirche in Weimar.

The times were not propitious for peaceful family life, for Saxony, in 1812–13, was again invaded by foreign troops, who emptied the wine-cellars and lecherously fondled the womenfolk, as first Prussian and then French soldiers had done in Goethe's Weimar before and after the Battle of Jena, seven years before. Erdmuthe Nietzsche, who had already given birth to two daughters (Rosalie and Auguste), was pregnant once again in October 1813, when the great Battle of the Nations near Leipzig sealed Napoleon's doom. A few days before this historic clash, she gave birth to her third child, an infant son named Karl Ludwig. The father was already a ripe fifty-seven, whereas the mother was only thirty-three and destined to live long enough to be able to tell her grandson Friedrich many dramatic stories about those tumultuous times.

Like his father, Friedrich August, the young Ludwig Nietzsche was brought up to be a clergyman. At the age of seventeen he was sent to Halle, an old salt-mining town situated twenty-one miles north-west of Leipzig which had made a name for itself as a seat of religious learning. Most German priests, in the early nineteenth century, could boast a rigorous intellectual training, and German universities were second to none in Europe in the thorough grounding they offered in theology, Greek and Hebrew history, classical philology and biblical exegesis. Although not as famous as Jena, where Fichte, Hegel and Schelling had taught philosophy during the twelve golden years (1794–1806) which had preceded the Napoleonic invasion, Halle's university had also known a period of greatness at the turn of the century thanks to Germany's foremost theologian, Schleiermacher, and to two extraordinary scholars,

*In the Lutheran Church a Superintendent had several subordinate priests to aid him in his tasks. A General-Intendent had several churches to supervise in a town where there was no cathedral. The next highest rank was that of bishop.

Friedrich August Wolf and his disciple Philipp August Boeck, who between them had founded the science of classical philology.

At Halle Ludwig Nietzsche was a pious, hard-working student who won a prize for eloquence after preaching an inspiring sermon. His subsequent career might well have been nondescript but for a stroke of luck which later greatly impressed his son, the future philosopher. After her husband's death in 1826, Ludwig's mother went to live with one of her brothers at Altenburg, some twenty miles south of Leipzig. The town's most notable landmark, aside from a Renaissance town hall, was a fortress perched on top of a mass of outjutting porphyry rock which had long belonged to the Wettin family, the hereditary rulers and Prince-Electors of (Upper) Saxony. The forbidding castle had received a baroque facelift in the 1720s, enabling its princely owners to assume the gracious *mode de vie* of an eighteenth-century court – one of the umpteen princely courts which made the map of Germany resemble a harlequin patchwork costume of proud, semi-independent sovereignties.

When the twenty-one-year-old Ludwig Nietzsche returned from Halle to Altenburg, the little principality had officially ceased to be Saxon and had been incorporated into the powerful kingdom of Prussia, along with most of Saxon Thuringia. This was the punishment that the victorious Prussians, at the Congress of Vienna, had imposed on the irresolute Saxon ruler, Frederick Augustus III, who had rashly sought to aid Napoleon during the Leipzig campaign of 1813. Too small to pose a threat, the diminutive duchy of Altenburg was allowed to retain its ducal court and its *Landwehr* (local militia). Asked to tutor the children of a *Landwehr* captain, Ludwig Nietzsche soon attracted the attention of the reigning Duke Joseph, who decided that this accomplished young man who knew Latin, Greek, some French, and played the piano well was ideally suited to supervise the education of his three daughters, Therese, Elisabeth and Alexandra.

After seven years of princely tutoring, Ludwig Nietzsche decided to strike out on his own. In 1842 he was appointed by the Royal Chancellery in Berlin to be parish priest for Röcken, Michlitz and Bothfeld, three villages situated about fifteen miles south-west of Leipzig near the site of the historic battle of Lützen, where the Swedish warrior-king Gustavus Adolphus had met his death in 1632. The Röcken parsonage, a large three-storey house with a tall tiled roof and small, crocodile-lidded dormer windows, was big enough to accommodate a family, enabling the twenty-nine-year-old pastor to move into it with his mother, Erdmuthe, and his two unmarried sisters, Rosalie and Auguste.

On one of his routine visits to the parsonages in nearby villages, Ludwig Nietzsche drove his mother and two sisters down the Leipzig highway as far as the village of Pobles, where they called on the local priest. Still a robust, red-cheeked, energetic man for all his sixty-five years, David Ernst Oehler inhabited a hilltop house from which, looking out over fruit and vegetable gardens, one could view the rolling hills and plains across which had been fought the memorable Thirty Years War clash of Lützen and the more recent and even bloodier battles of Gross Görschen and Leipzig (May and October 1813). The front courtyard, framed by coach-houses, horse-stalls, cowbarns and a kiln for baking bread, looked more like a farm than a vicarage. For to feed his brood of eleven children the rural pastor of Pobles spent as much time hunting game, ploughing fields, milking cows and tending hogs as he did leading services, preaching sermons and giving Bible lessons to his flock.

The son of a master-weaver from the nearby town of Zeitz, David Ernst Oehler had improved his social status by marrying the well-to-do daughter of a landed squire, Wilhelmine Hahn, thanks to whose solid dowry the household could include a coachman and a cook. A spartan upbringing had kept the children in good health, and none more so than the seventeen-year-old Franziska. Why she, rather than one of her three older and still unmarried sisters, caught Ludwig Nietzsche's fancy is not clear. She later told her mother that she reminded him of the Princess Elisabeth he had tutored at Altenburg. She was a pretty, dark-haired girl, with a somewhat angular forehead, protruding brows and large brown eyes. There was a disarming air of innocence about her which was enhanced by the unaffected liveliness of her speech. Her education, compared to that of the Altenburg princesses, was distinctly spotty. She had picked up some rudiments of Latin, geometry and logic, but her father's efforts to teach her French – an 'indispensable' language, he kept repeating – had been conspicuously unsuccessful. She was a healthy, outdoor kind of girl who liked to get up early in the morning, who took her prayers and religious duties seriously, and who, as Ludwig Nietzsche soon discovered, had a sweet-sounding voice for poetry recitations and quite a good ear for music.

If the twenty-nine-year-old Ludwig Nietzsche was attracted by the seventeen-year-old Franziska Oehler, she was no less impressed by the visiting pastor and the unrustic elegance of his black attire. His years spent at the princely court of Altenburg had clearly left their mark – on his manners as on his mode of dress.

The Oehlers – and particularly the father, David Ernst, who liked to liven up the evenings with song-*fests* – were also impressed by the visiting pastor's musical talents, which he exhibited by playing piano pieces and by fanciful improvisations on the keyboard. This too was a gift Friedrich Nietzsche was to inherit, and even to develop into an audience-astounding art.

Three months after their betrothal, Ludwig Nietzsche and Franziska Oehler were married at Pobles. The date chosen was his thirtieth birthday: 10 October 1843. At the Röcken parsonage it took the shy young bride some time to feel at home in her new surroundings. She felt awed in the presence of Ludwig's mother Erdmuthe, a somewhat frail, quiet-mannered lady of sixty-three, whose pallid features were strikingly offset by handsome dark eyes and coal-black hair, two locks of which were curled over her temples under the rim of the ruffled bonnet she always wore. Although her word was law in all domestic matters, she left the daily chores to her daughter Auguste, who was assisted by a kitchen maid named Mine. This arrangement suited Ludwig's other, slightly older sister, Rosalie, who, being of a more high-strung and intellectual cast of mind, preferred to devote her time to charitable causes, Church problems, and even politics, which she followed by subscribing to the Berlin newspaper *Vossische Zeitung*.

Franziska had not been in Röcken for more than five months when she realized that she was pregnant. She came close to presenting her husband with a rare birthday gift, but five days later she was finally delivered of an infant son. There was much rejoicing in the village, for the date – 15 October – was also the birthday of their sovereign, King Friedrich Wilhelm IV. In honour of this auspicious coincidence, the newborn child was named Friedrich Wilhelm Nietzsche.

The young Fritz, or 'Fritzschen', as he was called, showed no early signs of being an infant prodigy. He had fair hair, was wilful, and, when thwarted in his desires, would roll over on his back and kick his little legs in the air. He was even slow to learn to speak. His most remarkable characteristic was an acute sensitivity to music. Whenever his father began to play the piano, little Fritz would drop whatever he was playing with and listen with rapt attention. That his father was the only person in the community able to extract such lovely sounds from this wondrous instrument raised him above ordinary mortals and enveloped him in a celestial aura of infant adoration.

In July 1846, twenty-one months after her first delivery, Franziska Nietzsche gave birth to a daughter. She was given three first names – Therese Elisabeth Alexandra – in honour of the three Altenburg princesses her father had tutored. The middle name – Elisabeth, or its diminutives, Lisbeth and Lieschen – quickly eclipsed the others, doubtless because Elisabeth von Altenburg had been Ludwig Nietzsche's favourite charge.

The young Fritz does not seem to have been affected by the jealous ill-will many firstborn children show to the 'invasion' of a newcomer. Friedrich Nietzsche's adolescent recollections of these golden years at

Röcken dwell on other matters. He fondly recalls the old moss-covered church, the powerful impression made on him by the sound of Easter bells, the fright that overcame him each time he crept into the sacristy and was confronted by the superhuman figure of Saint George with his terrible spear, as portrayed in a wall-carving of the dimly lit chamber. He describes the elms and poplars, shading the neighbouring farmsteads and the grass-covered orchard, which, like the cellar, was often flooded when the winter snows began to melt. Inside the parsonage, the one room mentioned is the upstairs study with its rows of books, illustrated albums and learned tomes, where the little Fritz liked to tarry. Its principal occupant, his father, is portrayed in the stilted language of an adolescent as a model priest, 'arrayed in all the virtues of a Christian . . . and respected and beloved by all who knew him. His fine manners and lively mind embellished the many social gatherings to which he was invited and made him everywhere liked at his very first appearance.' About his mother and sister there is hardly a word. Yet we know, from a letter written to him on the occasion of Fritz's seventh birthday, that his sister Elisabeth – who had been nicknamed '*Plapperlieschen*' ('Prattle-lisbeth') by her godfather – grew up to be as garrulous as her slightly older brother tended to be fitful, meditative and withdrawn.

Theirs, on the whole, was a quiet life, like that of their peasant neighbours. Only once was their rustic peace disturbed: in March 1848, when carriages rolled dustily past on the Leipzig–Weissenfels highway filled with cheering travellers, who waved their hats and the black-red-gold banner which had become the symbol of Germanic unity and freedom. The 'monstrous' February Revolution in Paris had triggered dozens of similar uprisings all over Germany, not least in Berlin, where cannon-fire and cavalry charges were needed to overpower the barricades. Lacking artisans' guilds and an urban proletariat, Röcken was spared these social upheavals and the heady cries of '*Freiheit! Gleichheit! Brudersinn!*' ('Liberty! Equality! Fraternity!'). A few Prussian hussars were briefly billeted in the village, before trotting on to hotter points of discord. But when Ludwig Nietzsche read a newspaper account of how, to appease the noisy crowds milling around in front of his royal palace in Berlin, the Prussian monarch had donned the red cockade of the revolutionaries, he broke down and wept. The former Altenburg tutor probably thought that King Frederick William IV was going to be swept from his throne, like Louis XVI of France, and that Germany in its turn was going to experience the excesses of mob rule. The pastor's fears were exaggerated. The tumults of the spring were soon forgotten. His wife gave birth once again – this time to a son who was baptized Joseph, in honour of the Duke Joseph of Altenburg whom Ludwig Nietzsche had once served.

The joy occasioned by this new family addition was short-lived. In the late summer of this same year (1848) 'black clouds billowed up, the lightning flashed and damaging thunderbolts fell from the heavens', as Friedrich Nietzsche later described the onset of catastrophe. His father was beset by nervous seizures, which caused him to sink back into his armchair and to stare fixedly in front of him without uttering a word. As his fits and spasms grew more frequent and severe, priests from neighbouring parishes had to come over to officiate at Sunday services. The doctors summoned to examine him declared themselves baffled. Finally, a noted Leipzig physician diagnosed the ailment as 'softening of the brain'. On 29 July 1849, a bare ten months after his first seizure, Ludwig sank into a deep, coma-like sleep.

The funeral, celebrated three days later, made an indelible impression on the sensitive Fritz, who later described it in some detail: 'The ceremony began at one in the afternoon, under the noisy pealing of bells. Oh, never will I forget the sombrely sung melody of the hymn, "Jesu, meine Zuversicht!" The notes of the organ boomed through the church's vaults. A large number of kinsfolk and acquaintances had gathered, most of them priests and teachers from the neighbourhood . . . The coffin was then lowered, the priest's muffled words rang out, and he, the dear father, was removed from all of us, bereaved. The earth lost a believing soul, Heaven received a beholding one.'

This traumatic experience was soon followed by another. One night, in late January 1850, the five-year-old Fritz had a weird dream. He found himself opening his bedroom window, surprised by the night-time sound of organ notes coming from the nearby church. Looking out over the adjacent cemetery, he saw his father's grave suddenly open and a white-shrouded figure rise from it and disappear into the church. The bells kept tolling eerily as the white figure reappeared, carrying something under his arm. The grave opened once again, the white figure sank from sight, the organ fell silent. At which point he woke up.

The next morning Fritz's younger brother, Josephchen ('Little Joseph'), hitherto an alert and vigorous child, was seized by convulsive cramps. An hour or two later, notwithstanding the frantic ministrations of his mother and the two aunts, the child died – a few weeks before his second birthday.

Although she was entitled to a widow's pension of 30 thaler a month, with an additional 8 thaler per child, Franziska Nietzsche could not go on occupying the Röcken vicarage for ever. Grandmother Erdmuthe decided that they must move to Naumburg, where she had many friends who could help them to find suitable lodgings. Their furniture and personal belongings were trundled out into the courtyard and piled on to various carts, several of which were sent ahead with Erdmuthe, Aunt Rosalie and the maid.

His last evening at Röcken, with the melancholy evensong of the Angelus echoing over the dark fields as the moon rose in a star-filled sky, remained such a vivid memory that ten years later Friedrich Nietzsche could describe it as though he had left the village just the day before. Unable to sleep, he got up after midnight and went down into the courtyard, where loaded carts and carriages were dimly visible in the pale glow of a coach-house lantern. 'How painful it was to tear oneself from a village where one had enjoyed happiness and sorrow, where there were the graves of one's father and tiny brother, and where the local inhabitants always greeted one with love and friendliness. As the first light of dawn spread out over the fields, the carriage rolled out on to the highway and took us to Naumburg, where a new home awaited us. Farewell, farewell, dear Father's house!'

## CHAPTER 2

# Naumburg

Situated near the confluence of two small, sluggish rivers (the Unstrut and the Saale), Naumburg in 1850 was a picturesque old town still solidly surrounded by the dark-stoned medieval ramparts its German margraves and bishops had erected, centuries before, to protect this outpost of the Holy Roman Empire in a region inhabited by Slavs. Announced by the chimes of the Rathaus tower bell, the wooden doors of its five towered gates were closed at 10 p.m. and not reopened until five o'clock the next morning, so that anyone venturing out after dark had to hurry home in time, for fear of being shut out for the night.

For the five-year-old Friedrich Nietzsche all this was new and strange. He was overawed by the unfamiliar sight of long cobbled streets, of steep-roofed burgher houses, some adorned by ascending rows of mouse-eyed dormer windows, of fountains in the broad marketplace, dominated on one side by the domed Wenzelskirche (dedicated by the town's Slavic inhabitants to the memory of Good King Wenzeslaus of Bohemia) and on another side by the square mass of the town hall, with its quaint façade and gaily painted Renaissance doorway (rust-red pillars, yellow lions), over which had been sculpted the armorial crests of the city's patron saints, Peter and Paul, adopted early on by the patrician bishops of Naumburg. But nothing, not even the expressive beauty of the dozen statues honouring Naumburg's aristocratic founders in an extraordinary western apse inside the four-towered cathedral, impressed the young country boy as much as the unfamiliar sight of townsfolk often brushing past each other in the narrow streets without a word or sign of recognition.

The lodgings into which the Nietzsche family moved, on the Neugasse (New Street), belonged to a Naumburg burgher who worked as a dispatcher for the recently completed railroad linking Naumburg to Weissenfels and Leipzig. Above them, on the topmost floor, lived a cartwright and his wife, next to a workshop full of lathes, spoked wheels, metal rims and vices, which the young Fritz was soon climbing the stairs to admire. He felt at first like a caged bird in these new urban surroundings, where his mother and he had to walk for an hour to reach the house inhabited by his father's half-sisters, Line and Fredericke.

The latter – Aunt Riekchen, as she was familiarly known in the Nietzsche household – was married to a lawyer, Bernhard Dächsel, at this time attached to the *Oberlandesgericht* (district court) of Naumburg. As the young Fritz's male guardian, he felt that the rudimentary instruction in reading and writing he had been receiving from his mother was inadequate. This was also Grandmother Erdmuthe's opinion. And so, a few months after their arrival in Naumburg, the almost six-year-old Fritz was enrolled at the *Knaben-Bürgerschule*, an elementary day-school frequented by the sons of relatively modest families.

As an elementary school the *Knaben-Bürgerschule* left much to be desired. In the following year, 1851, the family 'elders' decided to entrust Fritzchen to the care of a candidate priest named Weber, in whose house a score or two of privileged pupils were given special tutoring in Latin, Greek and religious subjects. An affable pedagogue, this soon-to-be-ordained clergyman did not overburden his young charges with massive assignments of homework. Particularly pleasant were the summer outings, when he and the pupils of his Institute sallied forth through one of the town's old gates and trudged along the banks of the sleepy Saale river as far as Grosseck and Schönburg, a typical robber baron's castle built by one of medieval Saxony's more resilient heroes, Ludwig der Springer.

With two of his fellow pupils in particular, Fritz, now seven, soon struck up a youthful friendship. The first, a somewhat frail boy named Wilhelm Pinder, lived with his father, a legal counsel for the Royal Court of Appeals, and his grandmother in one of the city's most celebrated homes – a green-stuccoed house facing the broad marketplace, where both Frederick the Great and Napoleon were said to have lodged during their sojourns in the city. A good friend of Erdmuthe Nietzsche, Grandmama Pinder was one of Naumburg's leading ladies, and her house was a gathering-place for all those in the cathedral town who were at all interested in literature, art and theology.

Young Fritz's other friend was Wilhelm Pinder's first cousin, Gustav Krug, whose tall, imposing father, one of Naumburg's privy counsellors, was an accomplished musician. He had composed a number of quartets and prize-winning sonatas, and so beautifully could he play on his exceptionally fine drawing-room piano that Fritz would often tarry in front of his house during the warmer months, rooted to the spot by the sublime sound of Beethoven chords cascading out through the open window. Felix Mendelssohn had been one of his friends, as were the celebrated Müller brothers, a pair of virtuoso fiddlers whom the young Gustav Krug was brought up to emulate by being taught to play the violin.

Although Nietzsche at first felt a greater affinity for the more reticent Wilhelm Pinder than for the impetuous Gustav Krug, the three of them soon became inseparable companions, who vied with each other joyfully during the winter by sledding down the city's snowy paths towards the railway station, and, in the spring and summer, by building imitation earthworks to honour the Russian defenders of Sebastopol during the Crimean War.

In October 1854 – after a happy summer spent near Halle, where an uncle who had married one of his mother's sisters taught him to ride horseback and catch mice – Friedrich Nietzsche was admitted to the fifth (lowest) form of the *Domgymnasium* (cathedral high school) after passing an oral exam in Latin. Still painfully shy, the ten-year-old boy was at first dismayed by the sombre, narrow-windowed classrooms overlooking the cathedral cloister, the severe mien of the teachers and the haughtiness of the older third-formers, who swaggered about with canes and were allowed to smoke an occasional cigarette.

There was a notable improvement in the quality of instruction the next year, when, like his friends Wilhelm Pinder and Gustav Krug, the *Quintaner* (fifth-former) moved up to the *Domgymnasium*'s fourth form. Its *Ordinarius* (responsible teacher) was an inspiring pedagogue blessed with the chrematistic name of Silber. He was also more demanding in his assignments, and young Nietzsche now had to work overtime to prepare for his next classes in German versification and elementary Greek. He was used to getting up at five o'clock in the morning, a habit instilled in him by his country-bred mother; but there were times when he had to work at home until 11 p.m. or later: not a healthy regimen for a young boy who had inherited his father's weak eyesight.

The summer of 1855 was overshadowed by the illness and death of his paternal aunt Auguste, followed a few months later by that of her heartbroken mother, Erdmuthe Nietzsche, who died in early April of 1856. She was given an elaborate funeral, attesting to the high esteem in which the venerable lady was held by so many Naumburg friends. Once again the young Fritz shed bitter tears, recalling the engrossing hours he had spent listening to his grandmother's vivid reminiscences of the tumultuous events of 1806–13: events that had inspired a surprising admiration for Napoleon in one who considered herself a German patriot.

Erdmuthe Nietzsche's death was followed by a change of residence for her daughter-in-law and grandchildren. Reluctant to go on living under the same roof with her querulous, hypochondriacal sister-in-law, Rosalie Nietzsche, Franziska left the railway dispatcher's lodgings and moved her children into a house belonging to a pastor's widow like herself. Fritz was now eleven, and was given a bedroom of his own, on one wall of which he could hang the rapiers he had acquired for fencing practice. Particularly agreeable for the country-loving lad was the spacious garden, full of fruit trees, which extended behind the house as far as the recently rebuilt and redecorated Mary Magdalene church. The view from the house's upstairs windows, framed on one side by the towered gateway of the Marientor and extending beyond the tree-lined highway as far as the hillside vineyards to the north, was equally enchanting.

In addition to a glass-paned cabinet where Fritz could stack his books, the living-room acquired a new piano. Since her own limited ability could not be compared with her late husband's keyboard talents, Franziska Nietzsche had taken lessons from a choirmaster before having him take over the musical education of her Fritz, who had inherited his father's piano-playing gift. The family move to Naumburg thus turned out to be a blessing. Thrilled as well as drilled by the finest piano-player in the city – a woman, as it happened – Fritz found plenty more to inspire him in the musical atmosphere of Gustav Krug's family and in the choral recitals inside Naumburg's cathedral. The director of the cathedral choir was an excellent musician named Wettig, who had married a former opera singer. From the *Domgymnasium*'s classrooms it was but a step to the cathedral, into whose echoing semi-darkness Fritz would creep to hear the soaring voices. The impression made on him by the *Dies Irae* and the heavenly Benediction of Mozart's *Requiem*, during the autumn rehearsals leading up to All Saints' Day, was so overwhelming that, as he later wrote, it penetrated 'to the very marrow' of his bones. Music again overpowered all his other interests during the summer months of 1856. At Pobles, where he went for the long vacation, he spent the days picking and eating cherries, and the long twilit evenings listening to his priestly uncles (married to his mother's sisters) or other guests playing Beethoven sonatas and a four-handed version of his 2nd Symphony.

At the Naumburg *Domgymnasium* the obedient, hard-working Friedrich Nietzsche moved up steadily from year to year. But shortly after his thirteenth birthday on 15 October 1857, which brought him a new crop of Beethoven scores (gifts from Gustav Krug and Wilhelm Pinder), he began to suffer from blinding headaches – an affliction that was to plague him on and off for the rest of his life. His mother, alarmed by the strain to which he had put his eyes by working long hours in the evening by weak oil-lamp or candlelight, kept him at home and away from the *Domgymnasium* until the pains had subsided – with the result that Fritz skipped most of a semester.

What he may have lost scholastically through this unexpected vacation he made up for in literary output. Almost every morning he would leave Naumburg through the nearby Marientor and walk past ploughed lands or fields of stubble as far as the hillside vineyards of the Spechzart, where the vintners had recently celebrated the annual Oktoberfest grape harvest with folksongs and dances, firecrackers and musket shots. These morning walks stimulated his poetic and musical imagination. The result was a short play entitled *Die Götter von Olymp*, which his friend Wilhelm helped him to write and which was actually staged in the Pinder drawing-room, with the Olympian gods decked out in gleaming breastplates, shields and cuirassiers' helmets, while the goddesses (including Elisabeth Nietzsche and two Pinder sisters) intoned their verses in silver-studded satin garments borrowed from mothers, aunts and cousins. Gustav Krug having fallen ill, the role of Jupiter was assumed *in extremis* by Wilhelm's father, who looked absurdly outsize as he fought with a smaller, long-haired Titan (Fritz Nietzsche). He managed, however – to howls of laughter from the audience – to succumb to the titanic *coup de grâce* with convincing heroism.

Quite different in subject-matter was another dramatic brain child called *Orkadal*, a Merovingian orgy of banquets, duels, spooks and witch-like apparitions, for which the young bard composed a frenzied, four-hand piano overture. Less fortunate than its more classical predecessor, this neo-Gothic extravaganza never made the boards.

Early in 1858 Nietzsche resumed his regular class attendance at the *Domgymnasium*. By working overtime and ignoring Church holidays, he was able to pass his exams and gain promotion to the prestigious third form. The rainless heat of the final weeks was dreadful, but he made it out every day for an invigorating plunge in the Saale's cool waters.

Most of the ensuing holidays were spent at Pobles, where Fritz helped Grandmother Wilhelmine, his mother Franziska, and the usual host of aunts, uncles, and cousins celebrate Grandfather Oehler's seventy-first birthday by bombarding the evening sky with a cannonade of fireworks. These periodic returns to the teeming parsonage-farm of Pobles, which felt more like home than the rented lodgings in Naumburg, inevitably recalled the 'golden years' of his infancy at Röcken. This time they inspired thirty manuscript pages of youthful reminiscences which he laboriously wrote out with a scratching quill pen from 18 August to 1 September. Entitled '*Aus meinem Leben*' ('From My Life'), this auto-biographical fragment is, if we except a few surviving poems, the first significant manifestation of Friedrich Nietzsche's literary gifts. The style is often stilted, the portrait of his father ('the perfect image of a country clergyman') is too idyllic, there are occasional lurches into the purple prose and the meteorological excesses of the romantic *Sturm und Drang* school, but what emerges is a vivid account of his youthful years. There are poetic evocations of the 'ethereal' joys of winter skating ('gliding with winged feet over the crystalline surfaces of frozen ponds and streams'), there is an ecstatic hymn of praise to honour Christmas – with the angel-decorated pine tree, the glowing, red-cheeked apples (reminders of Adam and Eve's banishment from the Garden of Eden), etc. – followed by the question: why, on our birthdays, do we feel so much less 'penetrated with joy' than at Christmas time? Answer: because Christmas 'does not concern us only, but all of mankind, poor and rich, small and great, the lowly and the highly placed'.

No less striking, in this fragment of youthful reminiscence, is the critical self-analysis to which Nietzsche subjected his early experiments in poetry writing. 'A thought-lacking poem, one that is overburdened with images and phrases,' he reasoned, 'is like a red-cheeked apple which has a worm inside it. Empty phrases should be totally missing from a piece of poetry . . . A model in this respect are Goethe's poems in their profound, clear-as-gold thoughts. The young . . . seek to disguise their lack of ideas behind a scintillating, brilliant style. Does not poetry in this respect resemble modern music? So too presently will a poetry-of-the-future [*Zukunftspoesie*] emerge from what now is. One will begin speaking in the most peculiar images; one will shore up confused thoughts with dark, but sublimely sounding proofs; in short, one will write works in the style of *Faust* (second part), but precisely the thoughts of this work will be missing. *Dixi*!!' he concluded imperiously.

The term *Zukunftspoesie* (poetry-of-the-future) was inspired by the *Zukunftsmusik* (music-of-the-future) which Franz Liszt had been promoting for a number of years in nearby Weimar as a post-Romantic philosophy of music, one aimed at combating the idea that great music had come to a final, culminating end with Beethoven. Young Nietzsche had heard this controversial subject being discussed by grown-ups at the home of his friend Gustav Krug, and his reaction to this music-of-the-future was one of instinctive, adolescent hostility. He had developed a hero-worship for the great composers – Mozart, Haydn, Bach, Beethoven, Schubert, Mendelssohn (those 'pillars of German music') – and an 'inextinguishable hatred for all modern music and all that is not classical', as he noted in this remarkable autobiographical fragment, in which for the first time he tried to formulate an anti-histrionic criterion of artistic 'decadence'.

> God has given us music so that we should first of all be led upwards through it . . . its main designation is that it leads our thoughts to higher things, that it elevates us, even shakes us. This is above all the purpose of church music . . .Who does not feel a quiet, clear peace steal over him when he hears the simple melodies of Haydn? Music often speaks to us more penetratingly with notes than poetry in words . . . But if music is used solely for enjoyment or to make a public exhibition of itself, it is sinful and harmful. Yet one now finds this frequently, indeed, almost all of modern music bears traces of it . . .
>
> Above all, this so-called music-of-the-future of a Liszt or Berlioz seeks to display as many singular spots as possible . . .

Friedrich Nietzsche was only thirteen years and ten months old when he wrote those lines. His adolescent tastes in musical matters were still dominated by moral criteria ('sinful', 'harmful', etc.). Little could he guess, at this early point in his life, that a determined effort to shatter the tyrannical sway of such moral prejudices in almost every field of human thought and activity was to become the central aim of his existence.

CHAPTER 3

# A Formidable Scholastic Fortress

– *'Was not one of the three Muses named Meleti (care, diligence)? Heaven knows, without honest industry nothing but weeds sprout from the finest disposition.'*

The summer holidays were already drawing to a close, in September 1858, when Franziska Nietzsche was informed that her son's scholastic achievements at the Naumburg *Domgymnasium* had so impressed the rector of the Pforta boarding-school that he had decided to offer him a scholarship. The news came as an immense relief to Ludwig Nietzsche's widow, who had struggled hard against her brother-in-law, the lawyer Dächsel, and Erdmuthe Nietzsche to keep her Fritz from being sent to an orphans' school at Halle. Friedrich Nietzsche's next six years of schooling now seemed financially assured.

The establishment of Latin schools in all important communities had been decreed in Saxony as early as 1528 through an ordinance drafted by Luther's colleague, Schwarzerd ('Black-earth'), better known to posterity by his Hellenic pseudonym, Melanchthon. The result of similar measures in other parts of Germany was a thorough grounding in the Greek and Latin classics which, by the end of the eighteenth century, put secondary education and university studies in other European countries to shame, causing Madame de Staël to remark: 'What is called study in Germany is truly admirable, fifteen hours a day of solitude and labour during years on end seem to them a normal mode of existence.'

One of the institutions that had contributed much to the maintenance of these high standards was the Pforta school, near Naumburg. Originally a Cistercian monastery bearing the Latin name, Porta coeli (Gate of Heaven), it had been transformed in 1543 into a '*Prinzenschule*' by the Protestant Prince-Elector Moritz of Saxony. Situated slightly south of the Saale river in a wooded valley extending from the western edge of Naumburg to the narrow gorges of Kösen, Pforta or Schulpforta, as it is known to this day, consisted of some sixty acres of gardens, orchards, groves, buildings and cloisters, protected from the outer world by a thick twelve-foot-high wall, which formed an almost perfect rectangle. A branch canal of the Saale flowed through the middle of the enclosure, separating the vegetable and other gardens, the 'household' barns and workshops and most of the teachers' houses from the school buildings and quadrangles. The philosopher Fichte had studied here, as had the poet

Klopstock and the historian Leopold von Ranke, and at the time Nietzsche entered it, Pforta was generally regarded as the finest preparatory school for classical studies in Germany.

At first the former Naumburg day-student was dismayed by the communal nature of this scholastic 'prison', with its 180 boarders and twelve teachers-in-residence. The dormitory to which Nietzsche was assigned, one of six dormer-windowed chambers situated on the topmost floor underneath the sloping roofs, contained thirty beds, while the *Stube*, or study-room, where he kept his books and did his classwork, had two tables, the surface of which he had to share with seven other students.

The daily programme, like Pforta's scholastic curriculum, was far stricter than anything the young Fritz had so far experienced. The dormitory doors were opened at 4 a.m. to allow the 'early birds' to get a head-start in the rush towards the washroom. At five o'clock the main school bell began pealing and the dormitory inspector (a first-former) would shout, 'Get up! Get up! Quick! Quick!' – ready to impose a penalty on any laggard who took his time crawling out from under his goose-feather 'puffy'. Seniors and lower-formers were given one minute in which to drag themselves from their iron-sprung bedsteads, to seize their individual towels and toothbrush mugs and to hurry down two flights of stairs to the crowded washroom. Here close to 180 heaving and shoving bodies queued up in front of fifteen available basins. Teeth were brushed over a central trough, into which the dirty water was emptied. They then returned upstairs to their dormitories, climbed into their clothes and repaired to their respective study-rooms – fifteen in all, lining both sides of a long, central corridor. Most of these *Stuben* contained three tables, each large enough to accommodate four students apiece. Some had four tables, and a few (like Nietzsche's) had only two. Each table was presided over by a *Primaner* (first-former).

At 5.25 (in the winter months it was one hour later) the first bell was sounded for morning prayers. At the sound of a second bell, the boarders trooped out of their study-rooms and down to the chapel. A brief roll-call followed, with each upper-form 'inspector' guaranteeing the presence of all in his pew. The organ then throbbed and pealed, the *Hebdomarius* (teacher responsible for that week's roll-calls and other duties) read a short passage from the New Testament, and after a recitation of the Lord's Prayer in Latin and a second stanza of hymn-singing, the students returned to their *Stuben*, where jugs of warm milk and bread rolls awaited them.

Punctually at six o'clock the school bell tolled again and the students repaired with their books to their respective classrooms for an hour of instruction. This was followed by a *Repetierstunde*, or hour of study (from seven till eight), by two more hours of instruction (eight till ten), by another hour of study (ten till eleven), and a final hour of instruction (eleven till twelve). At the stroke of twelve the students gathered up their books, returned to their study-rooms, collected their individual napkins, and then hurried down to the cloister, forming up, two abreast, in 'tables' of twelve students. Preceded by the *Hebdomarius*, they marched into the refectory and took their places at the tables assigned to them. There was another head-count, the names of those absent were noted, one of the first-form 'inspectors' said grace, and all present responded with a brief '*Gloria tibi trinitas!*' The midday meal consisted almost invariably of soup, beef, a vegetable, a fruit, and the twelfth part of a bread loaf. The students were then offered forty minutes of free time, during which they could go for walks or play games in the school gardens, use their pocket money to buy fruit from a woman vendor, or check with the *Pfortenbote* (Pforta-messenger) for incoming mail. At a quarter to two they were summoned back to their classrooms by the ringing of another bell. The afternoon classes lasted until ten minutes to four, when the students were treated to a snack (bread rolls and butter, with bacon dripping or plum jam). They then returned to their study-room, where the responsible upper-formers tested the lower-formers with a *docimastica* (a Greek dictation or a mathematical problem) for close to one hour. There were two more hours of study from five to seven p.m., after which the students marched back into the refectory for supper – soup and buttered bread, accompanied by cheese, potatoes, pancakes or herring, depending on the day of the week. The evening meal completed, the students were again allowed into the school gardens, which were divided into six parts, one for each form. Here they could amuse themselves as they liked until 8.30, when they reassembled for evening prayers. By nine o'clock, after another toothbrush session in the crowded washroom and a concluding roll-call inspection, all were supposed to be in bed – save only for the first-form supervisors, who were allowed to stay up for another hour to make up for the time they had lost in the afternoon tutoring the lower-formers.

It was an exacting schedule, with five hours of classroom instruction and another five of preparatory studying every day. Little time was left over for physical exercise, even though a special hall was now reserved for gymnastics and the boarders were supposed to do a certain amount of rope-climbing, parallel-bar-swinging, and obstacle-vaulting in their *Turnjacken* and *Turnhosen* – gym costumes developed by an East Prussian drill-master, Friedrich Ludwig Jahn, who had coined the four famous F's – *frisch, fromm, fröhlich, frei* (brisk, devout, joyful, free) – as vital ideals for every genuine German patriot.

To judge by his letters, Nietzsche did not have too much trouble adapting himself to this rigorous schedule. Accustomed as he was to rising before dawn, he could often complete his ablutions well ahead of the pack. He was also consoled by the proximity of Naumburg, which made it possible for him to meet members of his family in the nearby hamlet of Almrich during the Sunday afternoon walk period, when Pforta students were allowed to leave the school for several hours.

Writing in early November to his friend Wilhelm Pinder – who, like Gustav Krug, was continuing his studies in Naumburg – Fritz was forced to admit that the teaching he had received at the *Domgymnasium* had been laxer and 'a bit too free'. He had been forced to give up Homer, while his Pforta teachers pitilessly reviewed his knowledge of Latin and Greek declensions and had him familiarize himself with scores of anecdotes and fables. Pinder's answering letter, in which he described the four-handed piano-playing with which 'Lehmann and Uncle Krug' had celebrated Gustav's birthday (16 November) – performing Berlioz's *Waverley* overture, Schubert's *Phantasie*, a Beethoven quartet, and Berlioz's *King Lear* overture – must have made Fritz turn green with envy at the thought of the entertainment he was missing.

Fritz's requests for Christmas gifts, expressed in letters to his mother and Pinder, included piano extracts from Mozart's *Requiem*, Haydn's *Creation* and *The Seasons*, Niendorff's edition of the *Niebelungenlied* (12.5 silver *grosschen*), and Karl Immermann's *Münchhausen*, for which one had to pay all of 1 thaler (then worth 30 silver *grosschen*).

After twelve joyful days of vacation (22 December 1858 to 2 January 1859), Nietzsche returned to Pforta, where he was soon lamenting the onset of a midwinter thaw, which had wrecked the student skaters' ice-rink. In early February he wrote again to Wilhelm Pinder to say that he was now reading Ovid's *Pentheus* and *Bacchus*. He had been much impressed by the 'magnificent, elegant' descriptions to be found in Lucian's humorous dialogues making fun of Greek mythology. He and his classmates were through with arithmetic and were now tackling geometry and the properties of the triangle: a revealing indication of how underrated at Pforta were the sciences. In May and June his mythological ruminations, inspired by his study of the fascinating Prometheus myth, were only slightly disturbed by the distant rumble of artillery and the tramp of marching feet as Napoleon III's French soldiers swept into northern Italy and routed their Austrian opponents at Magenta and Solferino. The members of the Germanic Bund – which still numbered thirty-seven states and principalities – looked on apprehensively, and even Naumburg was affected by pre-war movements, as trains were requisitioned for the transport of infantry and horses. Behind the walls of his scholastic fortress Nietzsche, who (like other third-formers) was not allowed to read newspapers, had to glean what he could from his mother about the momentous events taking place in the great, outer world.

Boarding-school life grew steadily more agreeable as winter mellowed into spring, and spring gave way to summer. There were games of bowls almost every evening in the gardens, while nightingales and other birds filled the air with their rhapsodic trills and pipings – inspiring the young composer-bard to put a few more verses to music, in a merry May-Song madrigal.

Nietzsche began the midsummer vacation of 1859 in early July, leaving Pforta on foot and walking cheerfully home through the intervening woods. After spending a few days in Naumburg he decided to visit Jena, where an uncle, Emil Schenk, who had married one of his mother's sisters, was now mayor of Germany's most famous university town. Warmly welcomed by his aunt and uncle, Fritz felt quite at home in this picturesque old town, whose narrow streets wound their way up the mountainside to the fortressed peak of the Fuchsturm. He was impressed by the wall tablets he kept encountering, indicating that in this Gothic house or that, Luther, Goethe, Schiller, Winckelmann the classicist or Klopstock the poet had once lived. But the high point of his stay was a beer-drinking *Fest* to which he was taken by his uncle, a veteran member of the Teutonia fraternity. Jena, though it had known wilder days, was still an academic cockpit for student duellers, stoically prepared to expose cheeks and chins to the sabre slashes of their fellows.

So pleasant was the memory of this visit to Jena that Nietzsche subsequently wrote two fairly detailed accounts of it. The second, longer version was added as a kind of appendix to a diary he began keeping in early August and which offers us a vivid, day-to-day account of his life at Pforta over a period of three weeks. There are frequent references to the torrid heat and visits to the nearby 'swim-establishment' – for whenever the temperature rose to 30° C the students were allowed to go for a collective swim in the Saale. As he surveys this year's poetic crop – eight poems so far composed, or barely one per month – he has to admit that they are 'ordinarily very ordinary'. He is fascinated by the larger-than-life figure of Alexander the Great, and in particular by the number of 'excellent tragedies' various episodes in his dramatic career could inspire. He reads a bit of *Don Quixote* in Ludwig Tieck's translation, is much taken by the dauntless hero of La Mancha, but feels misgivings about his exalted exemplarity.

Towards the end of August Nietzsche's diary-keeping zeal began to flag, as more and more of his spare time was claimed by the challenge of the end-of-semester exams. He passed them all, obtaining a straight 1 in German, Latin verse and Latin dictation, with a 2b in mathematics and a 2a for his Greek dictation: enough to put him at the head of his class.

Nietzsche's first semester in the upper third form was marked by a sudden interest in botany and biology, probably inspired by a biography of Alexander von Humboldt, whose compendium of scientific knowledge (*Kosmos*) had become such an international bestseller in the 1850s that more copies of it were said to have been sold than of any other book except the Bible.

Christmas, a few weeks later, brought its usual crop of presents. They included the works of Heinrich von Kleist, piano excerpts from Gluck's *Iphigénie en Tauride*, and the score of Beethoven's A Major Symphony. But this festive winter season was darkened by the demise of his grandfather, David Oehler, who died of influenza shortly before Christmas. Four months before, when a host of uncles, aunts and cousins had gathered at Pobles to celebrate the pastor's seventy-second birthday, Fritz had had a disturbing dream, in which he had seen his grandmother seated disconsolately in the courtyard of the farmstead vicarage, now reduced to a pile of roofless walls and tumbled timberwork.

Though less dramatic than this oneiric premonition of disaster, David Oehler's death marked the end of another period in Friedrich Nietzsche's life. The joyful summer and winter holidays he, his mother and sister had known at Pobles were now a thing of the past. Just as they themselves had had to abandon the Röcken parsonage in 1850, so Grandmother Wilhelmine Oehler now had to vacate the Pobles vicarage, so that another pastor could move in.

## CHAPTER 4

# Three Naumburg Bards

*– Without music life would be a mistake. The German even thinks of God as singing songs.*

Notwithstanding a new attack of blinding headaches in mid-January of 1860 – almost certainly a psychosomatic symptom of profound melancholia over the 'irretrievable loss' of Pobles and all it had represented in Christmastide and midsummer festivities – Nietzsche, after ten days of confinement in the Pforta sickroom, was soon able to make up for lost study-time and to regain his position at the head of his class. He derived scant enjoyment from the chores associated with this honour – for example, having to keep order during classroom breaks – but he had no choice in the matter. His classmate, Paul Deussen – a Rhinelander who had found it difficult to adapt himself to Pforta's stringent discipline – was one day quietly chewing a chunk of breakfast roll during an intermission when he saw the weak-sighted Nietzsche staring up and down the aisle in search of a victim to be reprimanded. His myopic gaze finally settled on Deussen, whose refractory behaviour had often been condemned as shameless by his colleagues. Walking up to his bench, he bent down and told the startled, silently munching classmate not to talk so loudly to his neighbour!

Eager to get away from Naumburg and its familiar vicinity, Fritz decided to spend a good part of his midsummer holiday visiting his Uncle Edmund Oehler, who was now serving as the parish priest of Gorenzen, a forest-surrounded town not far from Luther's birthplace at Eisleben, on the south-east fringe of the Harz mountains. He found his mother's brother, a bachelor, comfortably installed in a large, many-roomed vicarage and well cared for by a friendly *Frau* who had left Naumburg to cook and keep house for him. Everything about the place delighted Fritz: the many barns and stables, the front courtyard fountain with its crystalline drinking water, the huge fruit and flower filled garden, an upstairs library crammed with fascinating books, and, not least, an aeolodicon (or harmonium), which his uncle taught him how to play, using his feet to operate the bellows-treadles. With Wilhelm Pinder, who joined him several days after his arrival, Nietzsche did a lot of hiking. One hike took them to a hilltop from which, using a spyglass, they could see the cross on the distant Josephshöhe and the misty hump of the Brocken, whose legendary witch-, elf- and demon-haunted heights had been immortalized in Goethe's *Faust*.

Their imaginations fired by these peregrine excursions into Germany's legendary past, Fritz and his friend Wilhelm decided to found a literary society, whose members (which is to say, themselves) would meet once a year in some suitably romantic spot in order to read and listen to their poetic or scientific lucubrations. The place best suited for this annual rite seemed to be the topmost floor of the old Schönburg keep, with its sweeping robber-baron's view of Naumburg and the Saale river valley. The name finally chosen after considerable argument – the 'Germania' Society – probably owed a lot to the 'Teutonia' fraternity, to which Nietzsche had been introduced the previous year by his uncle, Emil Schenk, in Jena.

Gustav Krug was promptly let into the secret, and on 25 July the three resolute 'Germanians' bought a bottle of red Naumburg wine and marched out to the ivy-covered ruins of the old Schönburg fortress. After clambering warily up its weak-runged ladders until they reached the summit of the keep, they made a solemn vow that here, every year, they would meet to share and discuss their latest literary, critical or musical inventions. The bottle of Naumburg wine was then emptied and tossed from the dungeon's heights into the waters of the Saale.

It was later decided that all three would meet more often to discuss their respective contributions, to be produced at the rate of one per month and reviewed or criticized at quarterly 'synods'. With that the three enthusiasts went to work – Pinder on the description of a trip up and down the Rhine, Krug on the overture to an opera entitled *Gudrun*, Nietzsche on the overture and first chorus of a Christmas oratorio.

By the time these works were completed, in middle and late August, Fritz had returned to his scholastic fortress. Here he was offered an agreeable surprise: a new, less primitive washroom had been installed during the five-week summer vacation, making it possible to brush one's teeth over individual basins rather than over a common trough.

The final semester exams, in September, gave Nietzsche little trouble. With Paul Deussen and other classmates, he moved up into *Untersekunda*, as the lower second form was known to the classicists of Pforta, who were encouraged to speak Latin on all possible occasions. The daily drill was tedious, but the *Ordinarius* for the lower second form was a stimulating teacher named Corssen, who could make even Livy sound exciting.

In late November Nietzsche received a long letter from Gustav Krug, whose birthday presents this year had included a biography of Liszt, various music scores, and a visit to Leipzig, where he had heard Bach's *Christmas Oratorio* sung by the famous Thomaskirche choir. After criticizing Fritz's latest 'Germania' offerings (two 'shepherd choruses' for his Christmas oratorio), Krug described the mighty impact made on him by Richard Wagner's *Tristan und Isolde*. The overture and first three scenes had just been analysed in an article published in the autumn issue of the *Neue Zeitschrift für Musik*. The overture of this new opera struck the young Naumburg connoisseur as being even more beautiful than that of *Lohengrin*, and he was convinced that Wagner was right in wishing to rid opera of the conventional, 'characterless' recitative. Those lines were written in late November of 1860 by an adolescent of almost exactly Nietzsche's age. Wagner, who had finished the third act of *Tristan und Isolde* in August of the preceding year, was now in Paris overseeing the rehearsals for the French première of *Tannhäuser*, and nobody had yet seen *Tristan* actually performed. Yet here was a young teenager who was able to discuss its overture and opening scenes with some degree of competence, simply on the basis of the score – now being offered for sale at the (for Krug) astronomic price of 36 thalers – and what a Leipzig critic had to say about it.

The start of the new year (1861) was clouded by the death of King Frederick William IV of Prussia. No longer could Friedrich Wilhelm Nietzsche look forward to the traditional festivities and firework displays which up until then had enlivened his 15 October birthday. The heirless monarch was succeeded by his sixty-three-year-old brother, Wilhelm, whose partly balding pate was offset by a snowy avalanche of Santa Clausian beard. At Pforta, rector and teachers were so dismayed by the uncertainty of the times that they agreed to relax the rules that had hitherto banned the reading of newspapers within the school precincts.

As the time approached for his confirmation, scheduled for early March, the sixteen-year-old Fritz seems to have been more than usually preoccupied by the question of religion and the place it should occupy in art. Whereas Gustav Krug was now trying to compose a fugue inspired by Liszt's Faust Symphony, Nietzsche worked doggedly at his Christmas oratorio. Refusing to share his friend's growing enthusiasm for Wagner, he sat down in mid-January and penned a long epistle, in which he rejected the conventional notion that the oratorio, in the realm of sacred music, was what opera was in the universe of the profane. This seemed to Nietzsche unacceptably disparaging, since an oratorio did not provide a musical accompaniment for a scenic or theatrical spectacle. Precisely because it appealed solely to the sense of hearing and was 'infinitely simpler and more sublime', he considered oratorio music to be superior to opera. This first, negative reaction to Wagner's claims to be producing a truly new, all-embracing form of art confirms Paul Deussen's contention that Nietzsche at this time was still an ardently Christian believer – as was Deussen himself. Indeed, so gripped were both of them by religious exaltation during the weeks immediately preceding and following their confirmation that Deussen, who knelt next to Nietzsche during the altar ceremony, later claimed that both were possessed by a 'super-terrestrial cheerfulness' and sense of personal abnegation.

The month of March 1861 may indeed have marked a spiritual apogee in Nietzsche's life. From then on the relentless tug of worldly temptations, scholarly criticism, philosophical doubt and the 'stormy passions' which Gustav Krug found so admirably expressed in Richard Wagner's music pulled the fervent adolescent in an entirely different direction.

In terms of physical well-being the late winter of 1861 was once again a season of suffering for Nietzsche. In mid-January his headaches, this time induced by rheumatism of the neck, returned with a vengeance. Finally yielding to the advice of his benevolent tutor Robert Buddensieg, he retired to the Pforta sickroom. Here leeches were applied to his earlobes and he was bled, in the belief that this standard cure (for almost every ailment) would work wonders. All it did was to aggravate the impatient sufferer's desire to escape from this régime of enforced idleness by being allowed to go for long walks in the nearby woods. Scholastic diligence as well as migraine-enduring fortitude enabled him to make up for lost study-time, and once again he came out of the end-of-semester exams in March at the head of his class. A Latin essay he wrote some weeks later was considered so faultless by the strict (though stimulating) Professor Corssen that it was awarded a straight 1 (A) grade.

Gustav Krug by this time had managed to get hold of a copy of the score for the overture and first act of *Tristan und Isolde*, bits of which, during the Easter holidays, were performed on the Krugs' drawing-room piano for the recalcitrant Fritz's enjoyment. Not long after his return to Pforta he was informed by his music-loving friend that the second and third acts of *Tristan* – parts of which were now being played on the Krugs' drawing-room piano – were *wunderschön*, though the start of Act II was not easy to understand. Frustrated in his attempt to compose a 'quasi fugue' inspired by Liszt's Faust Symphony, Gustav Krug shamefacedly substituted a poem entitled 'Barbarossa' as his April contribution to the Germania Society. Pinder fulfilled his monthly obligation with a straightforward analysis of the main characters in Goethe's play *Goetz von Berlichingen*. Nietzsche, for his part, left his fellow-members open-mouthed by producing a German translation of six Serbian folksongs! He followed up this feat by also delivering a new fragment of his unfinished oratorio: an 'Annunciation to Mary' with a fugal development, which struck Krug as being 'the best and *most Lisztian*' thing his friend Fritz had yet composed.

If the sixteen-year-old Nietzsche was still holding out against the black magic of Richard Wagner's music, he was clearly succumbing to the dazzling orchestral effects of Franz Liszt's descriptive music. His September contribution to the Germania Society was an analysis of his Dante Symphony, while Fritz's November offering, entitled 'Serbia', though composed for two pianos, was the first in a series of 'symphonic poems', inspired by Liszt's Hungaria. After a disappointing summer vacation – spoiled by Franz Liszt's cancellation of an eagerly awaited *Tristan und Isolde* première in nearby Weimar – Nietzsche returned in early August to Pforta, where he had to endure heatwave temperatures of 35°C. He was much upset by the illness and death (from typhus) of Robert Buddensieg, whose task it had been to supervise his book borrowings, purchases of pen-nibs, paper, notebooks and pocket-money allowances. But he was fortunate in the choice of the teacher chosen to replace him – an able Latinist named Max Heinze, who, later, as a university professor, offered Nietzsche friendly help and support in the world of Leipzig publishing.

The September exams gave Nietzsche little trouble. He received a straight 1 for good behaviour, 'industry' and Latin; a 2A in Religion, Greek, German, French and History; a 2b in Hebrew and Mathematics. With the start of the new semester he was promoted to the upper second form. He celebrated this promotion and his seventeenth birthday on 15 October 1861 by composing a remarkable apologia of Hölderlin (1770–1843), the most spurned of German Romantic poets.

To take up the cudgels for a 'heretic' who had dared to contrast German 'barbarism' with the cultural greatness of ancient Greece was a singularly bold venture for a young boy of Nietzsche's age. A student of theology who had gone to Jena to be near Schiller and to listen to Fichte's lectures in philosophy, Hölderlin had become a rabid admirer of ancient Greece: a country ideally located geographically between the cold, harsh latitudes of the north, which had retarded the cultural development of the Germans and other Nordic peoples, and the oppressively hot, debilitating climates of the south, which had paralysed African and other tropics-dwelling peoples through an excess of heat and light. Whereas Goethe had finally condemned the excesses of the French Revolution, Hölderlin had chosen to express his sentiments about the recent convulsions by writing a tragic poem about Empedocles, a fifth-century BC sage and faith-healer who had been expelled from the Sicilian city of Acragas (the modern Agrigento) for having dared to challenge the conventional myhology and to have claimed that, as a daemon (banished deity or 'fallen angel'), he was a mortal reincarnation of the gods, whose blessed company he would regain after a final stage of purification on earth. When the same citizens who have earlier banished him from their city flock out to the grotto where the philosopher-hermit has taken refuge, to offer him a crown and supreme authority over them, Hölderlin's Empedocles replies: '*Dies ist die Zeit der Könige nich mehr*' ('This is no longer the time of kings'). And if there was one line in this elegy that must have shaken Nietzsche to the core it was the philosopher-hermit's pathetic lament:

*Allein zu sein, und ohne Götter, dies – dies ist er, ist der Tod.*

(To be alone, and without gods, this – this it is, is Death.)

As Nietzsche noted: 'Empedocles's death is a death from godly pride, scorn for men, world-satiety, and pantheism. The entire work has always shaken me most deeply each time I have read it; there is a godly majesty in this Empedocles.'

Indeed, there was. And so indelible was the impression that Hölderlin's Empedocles made on Nietzsche that he was one of the poetic models who later inspired his Zarathustra – the iconoclastic prophet-sage who vexes his contemporaries by daring to mention the unmentionable and to proclaim the sacrilegious truth that 'God is dead!' From the heights of religious fervour he had known at the time of his confirmation, it had taken the Pforta second-former little more than six months to begin a vertiginous, soul-shaking descent towards the cheerless desert of a godforsaken world.

That Hölderlin could have contributed so much to pushing one of Pforta's students in this particular direction, none of its teachers could then have suspected, including the man who was regarded as its number one authority in questions of German literature: August Koberstein. The prestigious professor (author of a standard *History of Literature*) knew that Hölderlin had given his German countrymen translations of Sophocles of a matchless grandeur; but this was not enough to overcome the prevailing prejudice against a poet who had spent the last years of his life in a state of mental derangement bordering on insanity. And so, to the 2a grade he was willing to accord Nietzsche's paper, Koberstein added: 'I would nevertheless like to offer the author this friendly advice, to restrict himself [in future] to a healthier, clearer, more German poet.'

The score of Schumann's *Paradies und Peri* figured alongside Seybt's translations of Shelley's poems and an English edition of Byron among Fritz's first requests for Christmas gifts. But his classroom studies as an upper-second-former – in Greek, Plato, Homer, Herodotus; in Latin, Livy, Cicero, Sallust; in (old) German, the *Nibelungen* saga; in Italian, Dante; in French, Racine's *Athalie* – now included a lot of history. In late November he wrote to his sister to say that he had developed a great interest in history, thanks in part to Becker's *World History* (particularly the volume dealing with the German Reformation). He now wished to improve his knowledge by acquiring Barrau's *History of the French Revolution*. Its two volumes must have struck him as quite incommensurate with the tempestuous scope of that watershed decade (1789–99), for he added a postscript, saying that he would prefer receiving Arndt's six-volume *History of the French Revolution*, available in a Berlin edition for 3 thaler.

Krug's efforts to compose a Faust Symphony had meanwhile run into such difficulties that for two successive months (October and November 1861) he was unable to make his contribution to the Germania Society. In December, when the three friends met in Gustav's home for one of their quarterly gatherings, he had to plug the embarrassing gap with a short essay on Germany under its medieval emperors. Wilhelm Pinder's contribution to this 'synod' was a paper in which he argued that music was originally derived from poetry: a controversial thesis to which Gustav Krug took immediate exception. The minutes for this meeting, as drawn up by Krug, make somewhat comic reading towards the end; for when he had to move from a discussion of these musical problems to Nietzsche's contribution – an essay devoted to Byron's dramatic works – he was forced to forgo all comment, either pro or con, because he was insufficiently acquainted with the Scottish poet's works.

The incident graphically illustrated the cultural advance that Nietzsche, as a result of his wide-ranging curiosity and superior schooling, was relentlessly gaining on his two less intellectually gifted friends. Compared to the 'clear-as-gold' composure of Goethean poetry, Byron, so Fritz claimed, was a volcano, now spewing lava, now in repose, his noble head unclouded by billowing pillars of smoke as it serenely surveyed the blooming fields at his feet.

It is worth noting that the word *Übermensch* (superman) and the adjectival *übermenschlich* (superhuman) both occur in his discussion of *Manfred*. As it had on so many other nineteenth-century Romantics, this poem made a mighty impact on the seventeen-year-old Pfortensian, who regarded it as one of the 'idea-richest' works ever penned by man: a poem which, notwithstanding its static, monologue form, 'spellbinds the reader with its magic power and can plunge him into a state of the deepest melancholy'. Byron's Manfred, with his Hamlet-like perplexity before the obscure significance and value of Man's transient existence, was to be, along with Hölderlin's Empedocles, one of the spiritual forerunners of the Nietzschean 'superman'.

Nietzsche's next contribution to the Germania Society proved much more controversial. It was a positive appraisal of Louis Bonaparte's meteoric rise from the status of exile and outsider to his dominant position as President and then Emperor of the French. Fritz's views had obviously undergone a dramatic change since his youthful Naumburg days when, parroting the anti-French sentiments of his compatriots, he had casually dismissed the first Napoleon as a kind of 'paper eagle'. The change in viewpoint was almost certainly influenced by Machiavelli's *Il Principe*, which Nietzsche was now studying in the original text. This shameless apologia for a man whom most Germans regarded with a mixture of dread and detestation was too much for Wilhelm Pinder. He accordingly drafted a rebuttal, which met with Gustav Krug's approval when it was presented to the Germania Society in February 1862.

When the three friends met again in March for another quarterly 'synod', Pinder's contribution, devoted to a poem of Hölderlin's, turned out to be his last. Krug's, on Wagner's *Rheingold*, was followed in April by a general summing-up of the society's activities since the beginning of the year, after which he too lapsed into silence. While Nietzsche continued, with almost clockwork regularity, to churn out musical, poetic, or critical essays, his friends Gustav and Wilhelm defaulted on every one of their commitments over the next fourteen months, leaving the third to trudge on stubbornly, alone.

## CHAPTER 5

# The Final Years at Pforta

*– To improve one's style means to improve one's thought, that and nothing more!*

The year 1862 was with little doubt the most creative of the six years Friedrich Nietzsche spent at Pforta. But it began badly for the chronically afflicted migraine-sufferer, who experienced five bad days in January and an even longer spell of blinding headaches in February – enough to send him back to the sickroom, where once again he was bled by leeches.

In addition to rheumatic and arthritic pains brought on by the wintry cold, Nietzsche was probably affected by an intense inner crisis which had been steadily building up inside him. He was no longer the ardent Christian he had been nine months before, and if there was one thing he had learned from his theological and other studies, it was that the fundamental beliefs on which Christianity reposes – the existence of God, the immortality of the soul, the 'divinity' of Christ, the 'inspiration' of the 'Holy Ghost' – are all assumptions which, lacking incontrovertible proof, will always remain problems.

Nietzsche's April contribution to the Germania Society, entitled 'Fate and History', took this sobering realization as its starting-point. 'I have tried to deny everything,' he confessed. 'Oh, to tear down is easy, but to build up again!' This tearing down was no simple matter, since it is not easy to eradicate the prejudices one has been taught in one's youth and has accepted blindly as the truth. 'We have been influenced without having had the strength in us to oppose a counter-force, without even realizing that we have been influenced.'

The idea the incipient philosopher was trying to express is that it is misleading to speak of a theoretical freedom of the will if the individual who is supposedly exercising that freedom is in reality obeying all sorts of hidden forces, impulses, and motivations – of an intellectual as much as a genetic character. The existential environment in which a growing individual finds himself is made up of internal as well as external forces, which he must oppose and combat if he is ever to achieve more than an illusory freedom of choice. The idea, here exposed for the first time in embryonic form, was later to blossom into the Nietzschean concept of *Selbstüberwindung* (self-overcoming): the constant battle every human being must wage against one's hidden, inherited, unconsciously prejudiced, and thus inferior 'self' in order to become that rarest of products

– a truly free-spirited individual. 'Fate', as Nietzsche put it, 'is the endless power of resistance to our free will. Free will without fate is as little conceivable as spirit without matter, Good without Evil. For it is the opposite that establishes the quality.'

The same idea was expressed in even more forceful terms in a somewhat shorter meditation composed during this same spring of 1862, under the title, 'Freedom of the Will and Fate':

> In freedom of the will, for the individual, resides the principle of separation . . . of absolute limitlessness. Fate, however, places Man back in organic connection with the development of the whole and compels him, in that it seeks to dominate him, to the free development of a counter-action. Absolute, fateless freedom of the will would make of Man a God, the fatalistic principle reduce him to an automaton.

Thus, at the age of seventeen, Nietzsche had already stumbled on the truth, which was to be popularized by the French Existentialists three-quarters of a century later, that 'Man is condemned to be free.' He is also condemned to be mortal. Which is why Nietzsche could also write (to his friends Wilhelm Pinder and Gustav Krug), in a letter obviously inspired by Emerson, whose essays he had just discovered: 'That God should have become man indicates only that man must not seek his salvation in infinity but found his heaven on earth. The illusion of a supraterrestrial world has led the minds of men to a false attitude towards the earthly world; it was the product of an infancy of peoples . . . Only through grave doubts and battles does mankind become manly; in itself it experiences "the beginning, the middle and the end of religion".'

Wilhelm Pinder, to judge by his nonchalant reply, failed to grasp the import of these sentences, which implied that religions, like everything else in life, are mortal.

By the spring of 1862 Nietzsche had succumbed to the thrall of three competing Muses: Clio (history), Calliope (epic verse), and Euterpe (music and lyric poetry). His readings in Germanic mythology, under August Koberstein's guidance, had led him to the fourth-century (AD) figure of Ermanarich, a powerful Ostrogothic king who had once ruled over a large part of what is now known as the Ukraine. Ermanarich, according to a Roman historian, had committed suicide in 370 AD in despair over his inability to save his kingdom from being overrun by the invading Huns. A different account of his death had been chronicled by a Byzantine monk (Jordanes), who, though he wrote in Latin, was himself of Gothic origin and thus inclined to view their exploits and sufferings in a more sympathetic light. The differing versions of Ermanarich's tragic death, as developed in ancient German, Danish, and Anglo-Saxon sagas, could thus be traced back to two separate historical sources – which made them virtually unique in the literature of German and Scandinavian mythology. Extraordinary too was a savage act of cruelty directly linked to the circumstances of Ermanarich's death: for before dying, the aged king had ordered his wife – Suanahild or Swanhild – to be torn apart by wild horses.

Nietzsche's encounter with this strange tale of elderly impotence, alleged suicide and uxorial cruelty happened to coincide with his discovery of Liszt's *Dante* Symphony and *Hungaria* compositions. During the three-day Michaelmas holiday, in late September of 1861, he composed a first sketch, curiously entitled 'Serbia'. It was followed in November by a second symphonic poem, although actually written for two pianos. In both sketches the thematic material was inspired by the Ermanarich saga. But in the process of composition Nietzsche found himself trying to express the folk-feelings of a Slavic rather than of a Germanic people; and by February 1862, when he delivered three more 'Hungarian Sketches' (including a 'Triumphal March' and 'Wild Dreams') to the Germania Society, the Slavs had become Magyars and the scene of the Ermanarich tragedy had been moved from the regions of the Dniester and the Don to the great plains of central Hungary.

The plot he was now trying to describe in music – with a lovely young bride, Swanhilde, being brought to the castle of the old, 'lightning-eyed' Ermanarich by his son, the hot-blooded and impetuous Radwe – bore a tell-tale resemblance to the story of Isolde being brought by the young Tristan to the court of her future husband, the considerably older King Mark. None of Nietzsche's teachers were at all aware of a hidden Wagnerian influence when they awarded his Ermanarich 'saga' a 2a mark as the best poem written by a member of his class.

The Ermanarich poem was followed not long afterwards by a Latin essay, which caused a sensation at Pforta. The subject was: 'For what reasons did Cicero go into exile?' Displaying the same nonconformist audacity he had earlier shown in praising Hölderlin, Nietzsche produced a withering critique of the great Roman writer's motivations. Readier to laud originality than had been the more conventional Koberstein, Professor Steinhart, to whom it was submitted, gave Nietzsche's essay a straight 1a – a higher mark than this stiff grader had been willing to grant to any Pforta student in many years.

In early July Fritz joined his mother at Gorenzen for the summer vacation, which at Pforta began on the first day of the month and ended abruptly on 4 August. His Uncle Edmund (Oehler) gave him a large upstairs room where he could read books, write poems, compose music, or play on the piano undisturbed. Rising early, as usual, Nietzsche continued to labour on his 'Ermanarich Symphony', to which he had added two new fragments – some Hungarian marches and a 'Hero's Lament'. He also wrote a few poems, of which three – one about Louis XV, another about imprisoned Girondistes, the third about Saint-Just (the intransigent apologist of the Terror of 1793–4) – were inspired by his study of the French Revolution. The egalitarian doctrines of the revolutionaries prompted him to reread the Gospels; for the agenda for these holiday weeks include this significant note: 'To consider Jesus as a popular orator . . . The Sermon on the Mount and its purpose.' Thus, during this fruitful summer of 1862, when he was not yet eighteen, was sown the first seed of a thought, linking the slave-morality of the early Christians to the hate-filled resentments of the French Jacobins of 1789 – which, twenty-four years later, blossomed forth dramatically in *Beyond Good and Evil* and *The Genealogy of Morals*.

Nietzsche's August contribution to the Germania Society was another Hungarian Sketch. Its Lieder-like title – '*Still, mein Herz*' (Be still, My Heart) – confirmed Gustav Krug's opinion that there was a strong Schumann influence at work in Fritz's musical inventions. The young symphonic poet was finding it increasingly difficult to pour such compositions into a Lisztian mould. This may explain a new bout of violent headaches to which he succumbed a fortnight after his return to Pforta. After a week spent in the sickroom he persuaded the school doctor to let him go to Naumburg for a few days of total rest, during which he stoically denied himself all forms of musical and intellectual stimulation. The cure seems to have worked. There was in any case little time left over for extra-curricular composing now that the end-of-semester exams were nigh. Once again Nietzsche passed them with flying colours. On 25 September he broke the good news to his mother: he was now a *Primaner* as well as *Primus*, having moved at the head of his class from the upper second to the lower first form.

The resultant excitement brought on another bout of headaches, fortunately short-lived. A few days later Fritz went home for the short Michaelmas holiday, happier and seemingly healthier than ever. Most of these three carefree days were spent in a wild 'Wagner orgy' – as Elisabeth Nietzsche later described them. Gustav Krug had persuaded his two Germania colleagues to invest all of the society's funds in the purchase of a good part of the monumental *Tristan und Isolde* score (three times longer than Beethoven's longest symphony). Since Krug's father had remained a stubborn classicist in musical matters, it was on the Nietzsche piano that the two enthusiasts now sought to plumb the orchestral subtleties of the score. Having never heard a Wagnerian opera performed, they kept losing the melodic line in an ocean of harmonic chords, though they struggled manfully to keep it afloat by singing, or rather bawling, at the top of their voices. Nietzsche, who had by now shed his earlier reservations, was so smitten by the *Tristan* score that he took it back to Pforta – to the dismay of his friend Gustav, who complained that he was being unfairly deprived of this 'magnificent Wagnerian opus'.

With the approach of Christmas Nietzsche put in his usual requests for presents. Since he would soon be receiving special instruction in English from a modern-languages teacher, he asked his mother and sister for a five-volume edition of the complete works of Byron, his 'favourite English poet'.

That Nietzsche, at Pforta, was already a trenchant idealist, there can be no doubt. Years later, his classmate Paul Deussen wrote that 'the appreciation, perhaps over-appreciation, of everything great and beautiful, and a corresponding disdain for everything that served purely material interests, was already present within me; but this glowing spark was kindled by daily intercourse with Nietzsche into a flame for everything ideal, one that was never to be extinguished even after we had gone our separate ways'.

This idealism, however, was accompanied by a taste for prankish mockery, which the adult Nietzsche was later to raise to the level of an art. Deussen and a few others had already banded together in the lower second form to indulge in clandestine smoking and drinking, and particularly to criticize excessive *Strebertum* (zeal) on the part of scholastic eager beavers. Nietzsche was one of the most zealous of these anti-zealots, condemning exhibitions of studiousness which he was forced to indulge in privately. He and Deussen even teamed up with a gifted cartoonist named Guido Meyer to form a *Dreibund* of 'anti-zealots' – a short-lived experiment in 'Triple Alliance' mockery which came to grief when the rebellious Meyer was expelled from the school because, as a mere second-former, he had 'illegally' entered an Almrich tavern.

Nietzsche's performance during the end-of-semester exams of March 1863 were as outstanding as ever, and once again he emerged from them at the head of his class. The ebullient *Primaner* celebrated his return to Pforta after the Easter holidays by going on a binge with a fellow first-former. At a tavern they visited at Kösen each emptied four full mugs of beer – more than the abstemious Nietzsche (who usually drank a glass or two of soda water) had ever consumed at a single sitting. As the two joyous tipplers tottered their way back towards the school, probably giving tongue to bawdy songs, they were surprised in this unseemly condition by one of their Pforta teachers, who had the two inebriates haled before the teachers' synod. Nietzsche was demoted from his position as *Primus* to third place in his form, and a full hour was docked from the time allotted for his next Sunday outing.

In June Nietzsche ended the Germania Society's death agony by drafting a brief post-mortem for the benefit of his defaulting friends. Wilhelm Pinder and Gustav Krug were now too busy preparing for their final exams at the Naumburg *Domgymnasium* (due in the spring of 1864) to have time for extra-curricular creativity. Fritz's terminal exams were not so close; for on being admitted to Pforta as a lower-third-former he had been put back by a full semester. His present studies were not unmitigated drudgery, for by now he was deep into Plato's *Symposium* – a dialogue which caused him such intense delight that he was soon calling it his 'favourite poetic work'.

The main event of this summer took place in August, after his return to Pforta. During the hot months its students were traditionally allowed at least one *Bergtag* – a 'mountain day' or outdoor jamboree, complete with refreshments and dancing, which took place in a clearing on one of the nearby hills. The weather on this occasion was exceptionally fine and Fritz enjoyed himself dancing with Anna Redtel, the sister of a third-form student it was Nietzsche's duty as a senior to drill in certain subjects. A short, sweet, even 'ethereal' Berliner (as Elisabeth Nietzsche later described her), she had accompanied her mother on a visit to Kösen and its curative waters. Anna Redtel, Fritz soon discovered, was not only a charmingly light-footed dancer, she was also a musically talented young lady. No more than this was needed to fan the flames of his romantic temperament. He made frequent trips to Kösen, where he called on Frau Redtel and her daughter and spent hours of blissful proximity seated next to the music-loving Anna as they played four-handed piano pieces. Throwing financial caution to the winds, he hired a Naumburg clerk to copy out a number of his piano compositions in a neat, unsmudged script. They were then carefully folded into an elegant black portfolio, adorned with a gold vignette. Anna Redtel wrote a thank-you note, to tell him how touched she had been by this gift and how much she had enjoyed the 'lovely hours' they had spent together. With that she returned to Berlin, where Privy Councillor Redtel was impatiently waiting to recover the feminine members of his brood, while a disconsolate Friedrich Nietzsche returned with a sigh of frustrated longing to his studies.

These agreeable distractions did not keep the industrious Fritz from passing his September exams, and he was accordingly promoted to the *Oberprima* (upper first) form. The presents he requested for his nineteenth birthday in October included the score of Schubert's *Grand Duo à quatre mains*, but the hours he could devote to music were growing steadily shorter. Although Pforta had a music room, where Nietzsche's classmate

Carl von Gersdorff often went to watch him *phantasieren* (give free rein to his fantastic keyboard improvisations) during the 7–7.30 p.m. intermission period, its curriculum was not designed to encourage the flowering of musical talent. In Nietzsche's case it soon claimed a victim: the abortive 'Ermanarich Symphony', which the pseudo-Lisztian composer finally abandoned, in a hopelessly disarticulated state, in the autumn of 1863.

In its place there was born a sixty-three-page treatise on the Ermanarich sagas, which was completed in November. To explain the extraordinary distortions to which the actual circumstances of Ermanarich's death were later subjected by Germanic and Scandinavian chroniclers, Nietzsche came up with an ingenious solution. The 'fair-as-a-sunbeam' Suanahild, he claimed, had not been Ermanarich's wife but the wife of one of his courtiers. The latter, a member of an Alan tribe, had betrayed the great Ostrogothic king by going over to the conquering Huns, who were already devastating his mighty kingdom. To avenge himself, the irate Ermanarich had ordered the traitor's wife to be seized and torn apart by wild horses – this being, as one of the Grimm brothers had pointed out, the punishment traditionally reserved for acts of treason. Suanahild's brothers had then avenged their sister's hideous death by attacking the aged king, who had had his arms and legs hacked off by his furious enemies.

Nietzsche's first major effort in the field of comparative philology would have done credit to an older scholar. Already apparent was the keen analytical insight he was later to display in seeking to unravel the transformations – or 'transvaluations', as he called them – which moral and other values undergo when the underdogs of yesterday become the overlords of the morrow. But at Koberstein's table in the refectory the normally taciturn historian of literature amazed Carl von Gersdorff by praising this young Nietzsche, who had so ably combined scholastic thoroughness with analytical acuity and mastery of style.

At the end-of-semester exams in March 1864 Nietzsche was awarded a straight 1 in Religion and German, a 2a in Greek and Latin. In French, Physics and History he could only obtain a 2b, while in Hebrew and Mathematics he slipped down to a lacklustre 3. His friends Wilhelm Pinder and Gustav Krug also passed their exams, graduating from the Naumburg *Domgymnasium* with the *Abitur* (qualifying certificate), which gave them the right to attend a university. They had both decided to study law, and after the Easter holidays they left for Heidelberg, from which they were soon sending back glowing reports of its marvellously free and cosmopolitan atmosphere, the seductiveness of the French and other girls frequenting its student taverns, the indescribable beauties of the Neckar valley, the eloquence of the university's lecturers, etc., in the hope that they could prevail on Fritz to join them there in the autumn. Nietzsche however, resisted the temptation. He had decided not to follow his father's and several of his uncles' example by going to Halle, because he wanted to get away from Saxony. Heidelberg would have been a perfect choice had it boasted a first-class philological faculty. Unfortunately this was not the case.

Nietzsche chose to devote his *Abiturient* thesis to an obscure Greek philosopher, Theognis of Megara, about whom little is known, save that he was a sixth-century (BC) contemporary of Heraclitus, wrote verses for the edification of young men, and was an intransigent aristocrat who extolled the virtuous and nobly born (for him practically synonymous) and denounced the 'vile' and 'cowardly' for not treating the cruel vicissitudes of life with lofty, calm-spirited contempt. Fritz was determined to get his Theognis thesis out of the way as soon as he could. The speed he displayed was impressive. He had decided to devote all five weeks of his summer vacation to its composition, but he actually wrote it in five days. 'I have just finished lunch and, as is my custom, I am drinking some warm water after the meal,' he reported on the first day (Monday, 4 July) to Wilhelm Pinder, after completing the first five pages. 'The Latinity is farcical and I have already laughed several times over the many short questions.'

Rising fairly early, as usual, he paused to drink a cup or two of coffee with his mother and sister at 7 a.m., adding a musical *Morgengruss* (morning greeting), which he improvised on the piano for their enjoyment. 'After this,' as he wrote to Paul Deussen, who had returned for his own vacation to his Rhineland home, 'I betake myself to my room. There is a big table there completely covered with partly opened books; a cosy grandfather armchair; I myself clad in my beautiful dressing-gown. I write. At about 1 o'clock I sit down to table with Mother and Sister, drink my hot water, play a wee bit on the piano, and drink coffee. Then I write some more. At six o'clock tea and supper are brought to me in my room; I drink and eat and write. It gets dark. I rouse myself, look at the clock: half past eight. I dress at full speed, leave our house, and hasten in the dusk of the in-stealing night to the Saale. It is cool, cold, hence bracing. The river gurgles, all is still, the mist and I rest on the water . . .' etc.

His output, by the end of the first day, was seven foolscap pages. But with each passing day the pace seemed to accelerate. By Tuesday evening he had completed sixteen, by Wednesday twenty-seven pages. By Friday he could jubilantly inform Deussen that he had filled forty-two pages, which, properly copied out in less closely spaced lines, would probably total sixty pages.

According to his sister Elisabeth, Fritz composed a number of poems during this summer when he should have been concentrating on his mathematics. Nothing could induce him, however, to change his insouciant attitude – with the result that he was barely able to obtain a mark of 'satisfactory' in this subject during his final Pforta exams, held in August and September. But for the high grades of 'excellent' for his superior achievements in Latin and German, he would not have been granted his *Abitur* and he would have been obliged to repeat his final semester, or abandon all hope of going to a university. As it was, he had to submit to the additional test of an oral examination in most subjects. His French, once again, was considered merely adequate, while his knowledge of Hebrew grammar was found to be defective.

Great was the rejoicing in the Nietzsche household in Naumburg on 4 September, therefore, when Fritz informed his mother and sister that, his poor subjects notwithstanding, he had been granted the coveted *Abitur* and could now go on to Bonn for the next academic year. Three days later he delivered a brief valedictory speech while one of his Pforta classmates tolled the knell traditionally rung for departing graduates. He then joined six other *Abituriente* in the wreath-festooned stagecoach. There was a crack of the whip and a ritual flourish of trumpets as they were carried off to Naumburg's railway station and from there, after tearful farewells, to their homes in different parts of Germany.

## CHAPTER 6

# With the Beer-drinkers of the Rhine

*– To be a good German means*
*to de-Germanize oneself*

Nietzsche, after graduating from Pforta, had five free weeks to do with as he pleased. The first two were spent in Naumburg, in his mother's new home: a pleasantly sun-filled corner house situated at the southern end of the Weingartenstrasse, within yards of the old medieval ramparts. Here a room was made available for Fritz's classmate Paul Deussen – the once refractory Rhinelander who had later managed through strict self-discipline and industry to become about the best Greek and Latin scholar in the class. On 23 September, after a painful parting from his weeping mother, Nietzsche headed west with his friend. The trip was punctuated by three stops: the first at Elberfeld, east of Düsseldorf, where they spent the night with one of Deussen's aunts, and where, the following morning, Nietzsche had to sustain a heated argument with a fanatically Pietistic lady, who tried to persuade him that theatrical productions were 'the work of the Devil'; the second at Königswinter, on the Rhine, where a fun-loving Deussen cousin plied the two Pforta alumni with white wine and then persuaded them to join him in a crazy horseback ride up the rocky slopes of the legendary Drachenfels (dragon cliffs); the third and longest with Deussen's parents, five brothers and three sisters, all comfortably housed in a rustic parsonage not far from Koblenz, which reminded Nietzsche of his Oehler grandfather's farmhouse-vicarage at Pobles.

On 16 October Paul and Fritz set out for Bonn, travelling this time in a downstream direction. After visiting a dozen boarding-houses Nietzsche found himself an upstairs room with three west-facing windows in a corner house on the busy Bonngasse, belonging to a Holstein wood-turner. The rent was 5 thalers a month, which was what Deussen had to pay for his room nearby. For another 5 thalers a month the wood-turner's wife was willing to provide a lunch, and for the first few weeks in Bonn Deussen and Nietzsche took their midday meal together.

Determined though he was to lead a sober, thrifty life, the music-loving Fritz could not bear to do without a piano. He accordingly had an upright installed in his room, where it occupied a place of honour beneath a portrait of his father. The cost of hiring it aggravated Nietzsche's financial plight, which was so desperate that two weeks went by before he could pay the university's registration fee of 7 thalers.

In Naumburg it had been decided that Fritz would have to make ends meet on a monthly allowance of 20 thalers. But with his disdain for pecuniary matters Nietzsche had left Naumburg without claiming 25 thalers in scholarship money he was still entitled to receive from Pforta. The circuitous trip to Bonn had cost more than had been planned. 'Without 30 thalers a month I can't possibly get by,' he wrote the day after he had settled in – the first of many plaintive letters to his mother.

In his next letter Fritz surprised his mother with the news that he was going to join the Franconia *Burschenschaft*, one of Bonn's four student fraternities. First established in 1815 by young Germans recently returned from the 'wars of liberation' against Napoleon's armies of occupation, the *Burschenschaften* had originally been intended to instil a sense of patriotism and to 'elevate' the provincial climate of German university life. Forty years later, in recalling their first weeks in Bonn, Paul Deussen wrote that the 'patriotic fooling around' that the *Burschenschaften* indulged in appealed but little to 'cosmopolitans' like Nietzsche and himself. But this is not the impression one gets from the letters Fritz was sending home to Naumburg. Nietzsche at this time was an ardent German patriot, and in joining a student fraternity he naïvely assumed that he was gaining admission to a kind of debating club where the great issues of the day could be argued out in an intellectually stimulating atmosphere.

Like the other fraternities, the Franconia had established its 'seat' in a local *Kneipe* (tavern), where a room was reserved for its 'tavern-evenings'. Deussen and Nietzsche were soon lured here by a Pforta alumnus named Stöckert. Five other Pforta graduates were also invited along for the occasion, and as each entered the tavern chamber and sounded off his name, he was received with cheers and a collective raising of beermugs.

If Nietzsche felt any misgivings about this boisterous initiation, he did his best to hide them. In his letters to Naumburg there was not a trace of criticism but, on the contrary, an outpouring of enthusiasm for the fraternity's 'cultural' activities: a good example being a Franconia outing to nearby Plittersdorf, where the red-gold-and-white-capped students joined the red-faced villagers in jolly rounds of prancing and dancing.

It was not, of course, to drink beer or to take part in the Rhinelanders' *Oktoberfest* libations that Nietzsche and Deussen had chosen to come to Bonn; it was above all to attend the lecture courses of its two leading philologists, Otto Jahn and Friedrich Ritschl. Jahn, who had been appointed rector of the university six years before, was a fifty-one-year-old North German who had spent a year at Pforta before going on to study philology at Kiel, Leipzig and Berlin. An unusually versatile man, he had made a name for himself in the field of archaeology, had helped Theodor Mommsen and others found the *Litterarisches Centralblatt* (a weekly survey of scholarly publications), and had been one of the promoters in Leipzig of the Bach Gesellschaft, dedicated to collecting and editing the great composer's many scattered manuscripts.

Ritschl, the second academic luminary, was a fifty-eight-year-old Thuringian now serving as dean of Bonn University. Unlike Jahn, a relative newcomer, Ritschl had been teaching at Bonn for the past quarter of a century and had contributed greatly to the prestige of the university's philology department as the founder-editor of the *Rheinische Museum für Philologie*.

In Naumburg, Franziska Nietzsche must have been beset by doubts on reading her son's glowing accounts of his extra-curricular activities. Of studies and lectures there was hardly a word, while he covered pages with descriptions of jolly outings to nearby towns and historic sites – like the excursion to Sieburg he undertook with his fellow Franconians, who marched through the town with loud huzzays before dancing themselves into a state of perspiring exhaustion.

Accompanied by his landlady and her daughter, the newcomer from Thuringia paid a visit to the local cemetery, pausing respectfully for a moment by the grave of the patriotic poet Ernst Moritz Arndt before laying a specially purchased wreath on the tombstone of Robert Schumann. Music loomed large during these early weeks at Bonn. Not content to resume his piano-playing, Nietzsche got himself admitted to the local *Gesangverein* (glee club). The inspiring proximity of Beethoven's birthplace was enough to arouse his dormant muse. The result was a dozen Schumannesque *Lieder*, which he composed in late November and early December. Parodying Offenbach's controversial satire on the Olympian gods (Orphée aux enfers), he composed a skit entitled '*Die Franconen im Himmel*' ('The Franconians in Heaven'), which won him the nickname of 'Gluck' from his fraternity colleagues. Deussen, who was rapidly turning into a pipe-smoking polyglot, was given the name of '*Meister*': a tribute to his astonishing proficiency in Hebrew and Greek and a new interest in Sanskrit.

Unable to afford the train fare to Naumburg for the brief ten-day break, Nietzsche spent his Christmas holidays in Bonn, with a few Franconians from Prussia. The one major distraction during the lonely holidays was a visit to the opera house, where he saw Weber's *Freischütz*. It pleased him no better than had *Oberon*, and, as Fritz wrote to his mother and sister, 'the being-sucked-down-into-hell scene struck me as laughable'.

Nietzsche's first New Year resolution was not exactly heroic for one long used to getting up at five o'clock in the morning. He decided to rise at six, rather than at eight a.m., as he had been doing for the past few weeks, doubtless to recover from the hangover effects of frequent tavern-evenings with his fellow Franconians. The score of Schumann's *Manfred* (a Christmas present from his Aunt Rosalie) kept him busy at the keyboard for hours at a stretch. Nor could he resist the temptation of visiting the theatres of Cologne – where he heard the famous Austrian soprano Jenny Bürde-Ney sing the part of Valentine in Meyerbeer's *The Huguenots*, saw the noted actor Karl Devrient play the lead role in Schiller's *Wallenstein*, and saw Friederike Gossmann perform in four light comedies (including Shakespeare's *The Taming of the Shrew*).

By the end of January 1865 he was 55 thalers deep in debt, as he informed his mother in a callous birthday letter. Adolescents should be allowed to sow a few wild oats – so, at least, Nietzsche felt. It was annoying to have 'philistines', as he called his creditors, hammering daily on his door with uncouth demands for quick repayment. Hard-working and abstemious though he was by upbringing, he was determined to be one of the boys, to the extent that this was possible for someone who was not gregariously inclined. He wanted to prove himself a 'man' as well as an aesthete and a scholar, if only to avoid a belated attack of Faustian regret when he was too old and spent to indulge in erotic adventures.

Such adventures, for members of the Franconia fraternity, were frowned upon within the town limits of Bonn but tacitly admitted beyond them. Many were the Franconians who therefore journeyed to Cologne to pay carnal homage to the Devil in the old cathedral city. Nietzsche too found himself heading in the same direction, although the motivation was probably less specific. In February 1865, according to Paul Deussen, to whom he later related the incident, Fritz was accosted in Cologne by a sightseeing guide who, instead of taking him to a restaurant, led him to a house of ill-repute. Here the still-virgin undergraduate found himself surrounded by half a dozen sinuous creatures thinly draped in spangled tinsel and gauze. Unnerved by their bold, questioning eyes, Nietzsche stood for a moment speechless. Then, spotting a piano, he went up to the keyboard and struck several loud chords. They were enough to break the tense spell, giving him the strength to flee.

By the middle of February Nietzsche was so penniless that he wrote to Naumburg to say that he was seriously thinking of not returning to Bonn for the second semester. He was giving up the monthly hire of a piano in order to economize, but he desperately needed 80 thalers to tide him over the next two months. He then casually listed a few more *Kunstgenüsse* (artistic treats) he had recently indulged in: a magnificent concert evening with the famous Italian soprano Adelina Patti; Jenny Bürde-Ney in Beethoven's *Fidelio*, 'to say nothing of the lovely concerts given by the Bonn Gesangverein'.

This was too much for his normally indulgent mother, who replied with a stern reprimand. The impenitent spendthrift declared himself profoundly 'shocked' and 'indignant' over the 'wormwood' flavour of this letter, but Franziska Nietzsche's epistolatory broadside seems to have had some effect. For in late February Nietzsche surprised his university friends by forgoing the pre-Lenten carnival in Cologne, preferring the rustic peace of the Deussen home at Oberdreis (where he spent a few days) to the masked hubbub of the Rhineland.

Three weeks later, when he returned to Naumburg for the Easter holidays, his mother and sister had trouble recognizing Fritz's puffy cheeks and beer-bloated face. This first, physical surprise was mild, however, compared to the spiritual shock that followed. The devout Franziska, who habitually wore a black or dark-hued dress, as befitted a parson's widow, had always expected her son to follow in the footsteps of his father and his Oehler uncles, most of whom had gone to study theology at Halle in preparation for the ministry. (Most of Franziska's sisters had also married clergymen.) But now Fritz informed her that he was fed up with theology. He felt no religious vocation, nor could he go on paying lip-service to myths and fairy tales – such as the Immaculate Conception, the 'dogma' of the Holy Trinity, the Resurrection of the Body, etc. – with which generations of disciples and believers had undertaken to glorify the figure of Jesus Christ. His philological training, both at Pforta and at Bonn, had taught him a great deal about the myth-making process, to which the Christian religion, like others, had succumbed. Any lingering doubts he might have had about the real, historical Jesus (as opposed to the legendary miracle-worker and semi-divine Son of God) had been dispelled by David Friedrich Strauss's new *Life of Christ*, a copy of which he had brought along to show to his mother and his sister.

It is difficult for us, who live in a radically secular, critical and scientific age, to appreciate the tremendous furore which the first edition of Strauss's *Das Leben Jesu* aroused when it was published in 1835. So scandalously provocative did this microscopic analysis of the Gospels seem to Strauss's contemporaries that it went through four editions in five years and helped to spawn more than forty books and treatises.

Unlike France, which had been exposed much earlier to the anti-dogmatic spirit of Cartesian rationalism, to the hammer-blows of Pierre Bayle (the sworn enemy of religious superstitions), to the anti-clerical mockery of Voltaire and the free-thinking of the eighteenth-century Encyclopedists, the German-speaking regions of Europe had remained fundamentally unaffected by atheism through the first three decades of the nineteenth century. But the critical spirit of the Enlightenment, epitomized in the tolerant humanism of Goethe and the cynicism of

Frederick the Great, had profoundly affected German thinking, not least of all in the realm of theology. Indeed, if there was such a thing as an official German theology during the eighteenth century, it was probably provided by Leibniz's disciple Johann Christian Wolff, whose *Theologia Naturalis* (published in 1737) sought to end the fratricidal struggle between Reason and Faith by propounding the notion that revelation was essentially an extension of human knowledge.

Any attempt to rationalize Christianity is bound to involve one in an effort to rationalize the Bible – to explain its ambiguities and contradictions and to decide which parts are truly relevant and of everlasting worth and which are merely anecdotal or spurious. The patriarch of rationalistic theology in Germany was the Heidelberg professor Heinrich Gottlieb Paulus (1761–1851), a disciple of Kant as well as of Spinoza, who bluntly affirmed the basic principle of Deism: that it would be ungodlike, unworthy, and indeed 'insane' for God in all the majesty of His infinite wisdom and bounty to interfere with the *Gesetzmässigkeit* (law-abiding regularity) of natural events by momentarily suspending the operation of His universal laws so that a miracle could be performed. Accordingly, in his *Life of Christ*, Paulus sought to explain away the miracle of Jesus walking on the waters of the Sea of Galilee as the product of an optical illusion suffered by disciples who were half blinded by shimmering sunlight or possibly misled by wisps of fog.

By the time this book appeared (in 1828), Paulus's rationalistic theology had already been overtaken by a new school of 'scientific' theology, which argued that if religious faith was to survive in the 'development period of Christianity' which mankind was now entering, many of the traditional beliefs that had sufficed for the sixteenth and seventeenth centuries – such as those of the Trinity, of Christ's divinity, of the Holy Ghost, etc. – would have to be jettisoned. The proponents of this school were partly influenced by Hegel's view of history, according to which Christianity was a manifestation of the World Spirit achieving 'self-consciousness' as it proceeded onward and upward towards Philosophy (the highest stage of human development, in which 'concepts' replaced 'images' and 'symbols'). They were also influenced by Lessing's contention that Christianity was a perfectible religion, which could be improved by rigorously separating the wholesome wheat from the unnutritive chaff. In theory this wish to create a dynamic, as opposed to a static, inflexible religion was admirable, but who was to decide how much of the New Testament needed to be pruned and how much of it retained as basic and uncorrupted Christianity? Such was the situation – a kind of four-sided battle between traditional supernaturalists, anti-rational Pietists, mediation theologians eager to reconcile the Lutheran and Calvinist branches of the Protestant Church, and straightforward rationalists – when David Friedrich Strauss burst on to the scene. A native of Württemberg who had been trained for the Protestant ministry by a Hegel-influenced theologian, he had gone to Berlin at the age of twenty-three to study under Hegel, arriving just in time to attend the eminent philosopher's last lecture. Strauss then returned to southern Germany to continue his theological studies under Ferdinand Christian Baur, who had turned Tübingen into a centre of neo-Hegelian analysis. Three years later Strauss published his first book: a *Life of Christ*. Although 1,480 pages long, this two-volume book created a sensation, making its author famous, or more exactly infamous, overnight.

The novelty of Strauss's *Das Leben Jesu* lay in the fact that he was the first to apply the full force of Kantian and Hegelian analysis to the contents of the Gospels. Before we undertake to examine the nature of 'things as they are', Immanuel Kant had warned, we must begin by examining our way of viewing those things. Such, in effect, was the 'Copernican revolution' Strauss now sought to bring about in the field of New Testament research by focusing his critical attention less on the biographical subject-matter (the life of Christ) than on the ways in which it was presented by his disciples. Far from being 'historical' chronicles, the Gospels were products of a partly deliberate, partly unconscious myth-making process. Their 'truth' was not factual but propaedeutic. They were meant above all to 'elevate' and inspire. Thus the myth of the Immaculate Conception and of Jesus's semi-divine birth formed the triumphal archway through which believers were invited to approach the life of Christ, while the myth of the Resurrection was the grand exit-gate at the conclusion of this exalting narrative.

This myth-making process began from the moment Jesus died. Contrary to what so many people had been taught to believe, not one of the Gospels was the work of an actual eye-witness, not even that of St John, which – so Strauss claimed – was the least reliable of the four Gospels, having been composed some time later to sustain a dogmatic-Hellenistic interpretation.

The new *Das Leben Jesu*, which David Strauss published in 1864 and which was the one that Nietzsche read at Bonn and brought back with him to Naumburg, was a substantially shorter work than the first, epoch-making edition. Albert Schweitzer, in his *Search for the Historical Jesus*, considered it vastly inferior to the first, and far less satisfactory as a work of art than Ernest Renan's *Vie de Jésus*, which had appeared in Paris in 1863. Be that as it may, this new *Life of Jesus*, deliberately intended for laymen, made an immense impression on Nietzsche. The preface alone was heady stuff, for it contained a blistering attack on theologians: a caste with a vested interest in its own conservation. 'What we must recognize,' insisted Strauss, a *persona non grata* who had been banished into academic limbo for three decades by these same doctors of theology, 'is that if Christianity ceases to be a miracle, the ecclesiastics will no longer be able to be the agents of the miracle they liked to serve. They will have to limit themselves to teaching . . .' In short, to save itself in an increasingly godless age Christianity must become scientific.

Such was the explosive book Nietzsche brought home to Naumburg and which he brandished before the startled faces of his mother and uncles to justify his decision to give up the study of theology. We have little detailed information about the tenor of the arguments, but the debate was surely long, heated, bitter. Already displaying that intransigence which later made him famous, Nietzsche remained adamant and refused to make concessions simply to have peace and quiet at home. He further saddened his mother by refusing to accompany her to the usual Sunday service and Holy Communion. His sister Elisabeth, whose principal desire at this point was to be well esteemed in Naumburg's stuffy, provincial, and snobbish society, was no less upset. Later, after Fritz had returned to Bonn, she wrote her brother a long reproachful letter in which she tried to defend their mother's and uncles' point of view: one asserting the importance of believing in an age of general doubt.

'As far as your basic principle is concerned,' Fritz wrote in reply, 'that the Truth is always on the side of the Difficult, I grant you this in part. However, it is difficult to conceive that 2 x 2 is not 4; is it therefore truer?

'Do we in our research seek repose, peace, happiness? No, solely the Truth, even if it be exceedingly deterring and ugly . . . Here men's ways diverge,' he concluded. 'If you wish to aspire to peace of soul and happiness, then believe; if you wish to be the disciple of the Truth, then search.'

The idea, here expressed, that religious belief is essentially facile, comforting and shallow compared to the rocky road the philosopher must tread in his arduous pursuit of the truth seems to have made a great impression on Elisabeth, who had long been awed by her brother's superior intellect. Soon she too began to voice doubts about the absolute veracity of the Gospels, to the dismay of her pious mother, distressed to see her daughter become an *Überkluge* – an overly smart young girl.

When Nietzsche returned to Bonn for the start of the second semester, he put a formal end to his theological studies by registering as a student in the Faculty of Philology. He found the little university town at its loveliest, with the no longer bare-branched lindens in full aromatic bloom, the fruit trees erupting into springtime bouquets of white and pink, the undulating hills now a tender green. The Rhine, free of the chunks of ice that had clogged it in January, was more inviting than ever – not only for paddle-steamer excursions but also for rowboat outings with congenial friends.

In an effort to mend his spendthrift ways Nietzsche gave up his piano and desisted from further composing. But he could not deny himself the pleasure of ordering a new tailor-made suit, which cost him 17 thaler: enough to generate a new plea for funds from his mother and his guardian, Bernhard Dächsel. The cool spring mornings soon grew uncomfortably warm in his west-facing room; but this torrid calamity was an academic blessing, since it prompted Fritz to begin his daily life at dawn and to attend his first lecture (in philosophy) at the early hour of seven.

In mid-May Nietzsche received a moving letter from his friend Carl von Gersdorff, who had gone to study law at Göttingen. His elder brother, now an officer in the Prussian army, had persuaded him to join the Saxonia *Burschenschaft*, but Gersdorff had been appalled by its barbaric beer-swilling drink-*fests*, in which 'that wretched, brown, sticky shudder-substance' stimulated an artificial jollity. For wishing to quit the fraternity he had been sternly rebuked by both brother and father, and to escape the damning charge of cowardice he had exposed his face to the sabre slashes of uncouth boisterers, while reading Manzoni's *I Promessi Sposi*.

Nietzsche, replying on Ascension Day (25 May), chose to play the part of Devil's advocate. He expressed admiration for the 'moral strength' his friend Carl had shown in plunging resolutely into the 'almost muddy, turbid waters' of fraternity life, arguing that 'he who as a student wishes to get to know his time and his people must sport a fraternity's colours. The fraternities and their organizations represent in the sharpest possible way the type of the next generation of men.' Which did not mean that one should stifle one's sense of indignation at exhibitions of drunkenness. Despite the insufferable 'beer-materialism' of certain members, he had decided to stick it out, having, he claimed, 'learned a great deal' from the fraternity and the 'intellectual life that is to be found therein'.

Nietzsche was clearly doing violence to his better judgement. But he was probably flattered by the prospect of soon having to deliver a speech on Germany's patriotic poets, as though this would suffice at one stroke to elevate the fraternity's tavern-evenings to a higher intellectual level.

June in any case proved to be a particularly eventful month for Nietzsche. On the 2nd he travelled to Cologne to take part in a Lower Rhine music festival. Dressed in black tails and with a red-and-white silk ribbon strung across his waistcoat, he joined the 182 sopranos, 154 altos, 112 tenors, and 172 basses in the Gürzenich Hall, where with extraordinary gusto they sang Handel's *Israel in Egypt* under the skilful direction of the celebrated orchestra conductor Ferdinand von Hiller.

This three-day music festival in Cologne – 'certainly the finest thing I have experienced this year' – marked the high point of this second semester. From then on Fritz's letters to Naumburg sounded an increasingly critical note, which even the bright blue skies of late June failed to temper. 'Recently,' he wrote in a letter describing the distinctly cool welcome offered by the stoutly Catholic inhabitants of Cologne to the stoutly Protestant King Wilhelm I and his spike-helmeted Prussian generals, 'we, that is the Franconians, celebrated a joint get-together with two other fraternities, Marchia and Helvetia. *Hei!* What bliss! *Hei!* What has the *Burschenschaft* not achieved! *Hei!* Are we not Germany's future, the nursery-grounds of German parliaments!' To which he added pointedly, 'It is difficult withal, says Juvenal, to write no satires.'

The ironic tone of this paragraph makes it clear that Nietzsche had by now lost all of his earlier illusions concerning the 'instructive, uplifting' role that these beer-drinking and sabre-swinging fraternities could play in German university life. But he was no less determined to drink this particular potion to the lees. After one more beer-swilling session he hied himself to Bonn's baroque town hall and cobbled marketplace and there accosted a member of a rival Allemann fraternity, with whom he struck up a lively argument about some literary topic. Nietzsche then courteously asked him if he would be willing to cross sabres with him in a duel.

When Paul Deussen learned that his friend was going to 'have it out' with another fraternity member, he was understandably concerned, given Nietzsche's short-sightedness, corpulence and inexperience in this kind of toe-to-toe combat. He accompanied Fritz to a remote barn, beyond the limits of the town, where the Allemannians and the Franconians traditionally hacked at each other's faces, and watched with trepidation as the swords were ritually crossed and then flashed above the duellists' heads. The bout lasted a scant three minutes and was brought to a halt when Nietzsche opened a gash in his adversary's forehead while he himself received a cut on the bridge of his nose. Deussen bundled his bleeding friend into a carriage and had him driven back to his lodgings, where he was put to bed and treated with cold compresses. A couple of days later the intrepid sabre-swinger returned to his lectures and seminars as though nothing had happened, although his nose now bore a scar which was to remain with him for the rest of his life.

Nietzsche's decision to leave Bonn, which he had found prohibitively expensive, was taken long before this epic encounter. His decision to go to Leipzig, finally taken in mid-May, was almost certainly influenced by an unavowed desire to be closer to Naumburg, where it would be easier for him to plead his case for more money. But the decision was reinforced by two other considerations. The first was Carl von Gersdoff's wish to give up the study of law, which he had found unbearably tedious, and to move from Göttingen to Leipzig to study German literature. The second was the realization that Leipzig University, whose Faculty of Philology had suffered a major decline since the days of the great Gottfried Hermann (1772–1848), was going to acquire a new academic star in the person of Friedrich Ritschl.

Nietzsche's final weeks in Bonn were anything but happy. He was racked by rheumatic pains, toothache and splitting headaches, induced by drenching downpours and the Rhine valley's unpleasantly humid, soggy climate. The last days were spent in a frenzy of letter-writing, trunk-filling and debt-settling activity, as he packed up his books and clothes prior to the boat and train trip home. The evening of his departure he was accompanied to the pier by a new friend and fellow-Franconian, Hermann Mushacke, rather than by Paul Deussen, who had refused to follow Fritz's example in giving up theology.

Not long after his return to Naumburg Nietzsche received an amusing letter from Mushacke, describing the end-of-semester tribulations of the remaining Franconians, reduced to playing hide-and-seek with their philistine creditors, who had them dogged by spies and watchful birds of prey. In his reply Nietzsche admitted that he had squandered a good part of the year in worthless activities. In particular his sojourn in the Franconia *Burschenschaft* struck him as being a *faux pas*. 'There I transgressed my own principles, not to give oneself over to things or to people until I have got to know them . . . I am far from being an unconditional supporter of the Franconia . . . I consider their capacity for political judgement to be very limited, and only active in the heads of a few. I find their behaviour outwardly plebeian and repulsive . . . With my studies', he added, 'I must also, all things considered, be dissatisfied, even if I attribute much of the blame to the fraternity, which thwarted my lovely plans. Precisely in these days do I notice what wholesome relief and human elevation are to be found in continuous, urgent work. Such relief I seldom found in Bonn. I can only contemplate with scorn the works I managed to complete during this Bonn period – these being an essay for the Gustav Adolf Club, one for a fraternity evening, and one for the [Otto Jahn] seminar. Abominable!' concluded Nietzsche in disgust. 'I am ashamed when I think of this junk' – so inferior in quantity, no less than in quality, to his creative efforts at Pforta.

CHAPTER 7

# Arthur Schopenhauer's Fateful Spell

*– A philosopher may be recognized by the fact that he avoids three glittering and noisy things: fame, princes, and women – which is not to say that they do not come to him.*

Two days after his twenty-first birthday – celebrated in Berlin during a visit to Mushacke's family – Nietzsche boarded the southbound train with his friend Hermann, who had also decided to pursue his philological studies in Leipzig. They reached their destination in the late morning of 17 October, and after wandering through the crowded streets of the old inner city, they stopped to have lunch at Reiss's restaurant, recommended to them by Mushacke's father, who had once been a Leipzig student. They spent the afternoon tramping up and down stairs in street after winding street, disgusted by the odours and the dirt they encountered everywhere. Finally they were guided by a second-hand bookseller to an alleyway cheerfully named Blumengasse (flower alley), where, well protected from street noises by a house and adjoining garden, Nietzsche was shown a study and bedroom 'eminently' fitted for a scholar.

The next morning, when the two friends went to register as students in philology, they and other newcomers were harangued by the rector, who warned them that the ways of genius are unique and that they should not try to model their university behaviour on that of their illustrious predecessor, Goethe. (The great poet had registered as a student in this same university exactly one century before – on 18 October 1765!)

A few weeks before, replying to a Pforta alumnus, Raimund Granier, who had gone to Würzburg to study medicine, Nietzsche had vehemently denounced the 'outrageous philistinism' of the student fraternities. 'This unexaltedness, this ponderous clumsiness, this humdrum, pedestrian mentality, this arid sobriety which reveals itself most hideously in drunkenness – Ye Gods, how glad I am to have escaped from this shrieking wilderness, this hollow plenitude, this senescent youth!' Now, to ensure himself against possible backslidings, he penned a formal letter to his Franconia colleagues in Bonn, announcing his resignation from the fraternity. 'I do not hereby cease to hold the idea of the *Burschenschaft* in high esteem,' he pompously explained. 'I must, however, openly admit that its presently manifested form pleases me but little . . . I therefore bid it farewell. May the Franconia soon surpass the level of development in which it now finds itself. May it ever number among its members only such as are of sound mentality and good manners.' The last two sentences were greeted in Bonn with indignation, and Friedrich Wilhelm Nietzsche was informed by return post that he had been expelled from the fraternity.

On 25 October he attended Ritschl's inaugural address, delivered in Latin in a hall overflowing with students and others who were curious to hear and see the newcomer who had acquired a national notoriety, thanks to his academic clash with Otto Jahn.

The main event of this autumn, far more momentous for Nietzsche's intellectual development than Ritschl's lectures on the tragedies of Aeschylus, was his discovery of Schopenhauer. One day in late October he was browsing in his landlord's second-hand bookshop when he chanced upon a volume of Schopenhauer's *Die Welt als Wille und Vorstellung* (*The World as Will and Representation*). He leafed through it casually, then began reading with rapt attention. There was something about the style, so much more readable than the methodical demonstrations of Immanuel Kant or the abstruse terminology of Hegel, there was something so congenial about the tone, that Nietzsche found himself transfixed.

Back in his lodgings he sat down on the sofa and began to read, enthralled. 'Here every line shouted renunciation, negation, resignation, here I saw a mirror in which I spied the world, life, and one's own mind in frightful grandeur,' Nietzsche later described this moment. So powerful was the spell that for several weeks he gave himself up to an orgy of self-criticism, self-contempt and self-hatred, recorded in a journal filled with self-accusing lamentations (which he later destroyed). He even subjected himself to a kind of Lenten penance, snuffing out his oil-lamp at 2 a.m. and allowing himself a scant four hours of sleep before rising again at six to continue his feverish reading. A nervous excitement possessed him, and, as he later admitted, 'who knows what degree of folly I might have attained had the enticements of life, of vanity, and the constraints of regular studies not acted against it'.

Had Nietzsche's discovery of Schopenhauer simply been a personal infatuation, it could be dismissed as a singular idiosyncrasy. But the fact that so many of his friends also succumbed to the spell can only mean that Arthur Schopenhauer's pessimistic *Weltanschauung* filled a vaguely sensed void for the confused and leaderless generation that grew up in the 'swamp-air of the fifties' (as Nietzsche later described it), when the ground was littered with the fragments of the Hegelian system. But to understand why this was so, one must go back for a moment to consider what exactly had been happening in the field of European philosophy, that things should have come to such a pass.

When René Descartes set out to revitalize and renovate the practice of philosophy in the first half of the seventeenth century, he was confronted by an awesome question: how was it that the ancient Greeks, who had been so intellectually curious and inventive for several centuries, should suddenly have ceased to be great innovators in the fields of geometry, logic and philosophy?

What had fatally stunted the further growth and development of Greek science and philosophy, Descartes finally decided, was not an external calamity, like the Roman occupation of the Hellenic world, but rather an internal malignity so profoundly buried in the depths of Greco-Roman thinking that it had escaped all critical attention. This malformation was due to the tyrannical triumph of Aristotle – and this for two reasons. The first was the emphasis Aristotle had placed on the empirical nature of thought, later summed up in the celebrated maxim, '*Nihil est in intellectu quod non fuit prius in sensu.*' What indeed could seem more reasonable than this common-sense statement to the effect that our thoughts need image-contents ('There is no thought without an image,' Aristotle had declared) and are derived from sense impressions? But, as Descartes realized, what seems obvious can turn out to be the opposite of the truth. Nothing is more 'self-evident' to one who relies on everyday experience and the testimony of his eyes than the 'fact' that the sun revolves around the Earth. So the Greeks had believed – with the single exception of the Alexandrian astronomer Aristarchus of Samos (third century BC) – and after them the Romans, the Goths, and all of the medieval scholastics had been no less persuaded of this 'elementary truth', right up until the moment when an obscure Polish-German monk named Copernicus had dared to defy common sense by suggesting that the Earth, which Aristotle and all of his successors had declared to be the centre of the universe, was in fact no more than a humble satellite of the sun.

The second fatal legacy of the Aristotelian school was a passion for classification which had become an end in itself, stultifying the further development of philosophy for close to twenty centuries. Unlike his teacher Plato, who was of a more abstract cast of mind, Aristotle was a naturalist with a keen interest in biology. The logic he created, the first to deserve the name and the most influential there has ever been, was thus primarily designed with an eye to classifying the innumerable things and beings existing in the world into neatly defined genera and species. Syllogisms – like the classic one that states: 'All men are mortal; Socrates was a man; therefore Socrates was mortal' – were logical exemplifications of this system of universal classification. The beautiful simplicity of these syllogisms was at the same time their gravest defect. Like Plato's Ideas, they were magnificently self-sufficient, so that no new truths could be derived from them. Philosophy, under the pressure of this internal thrust, thus turned into a science of verbal definitions: that particularly degenerate form of philosophizing which came to be known as 'scholasticism' – which is what it still was in Descartes's day.

What had begun as an admirable endeavour to classify and organize the varied phenomena of the universe thus ended up an ossified system. As time passed it came to be regarded as axiomatic, simply because Aristotle had suggested it, that just as each genus is a whole that admits of no partial or intermediate category (the genus 'animal' being totally distinct from the genus 'plant' or the genus 'mineral', etc.), so the four sciences that were recognized by the Greeks – arithmetic, geometry, astronomy and physics – each formed an essentially distinct, self-ordering and independent whole. Thus astronomy, the 'science of celestial phenomena', was declared to be radically different from physics, the 'science of sublunary phenomena'. Although no astronomer could operate properly without reference to certain geometric notions, any more than a geometer could work without the use of certain arithmetical notations, the axiom of the 'incompatibility of [different] genera' remained the official dogma for close to 2,000 years. The splendid springtime of science, which had flowered in ancient Greece, was thus frozen in the bud. Arithmetic having been defined once and for all as a self-contained 'science of numbers', the Greeks could go on lazily using six dots – ::: – to signify the 'oblong number' that we (thanks to Arabs and Persians) express by the figure 6 – with the result that Greek mathematics, Euclid and Archimedes notwithstanding, never advanced beyond the kindergarten stage.

Aristotle being, as Descartes pointed out in his *Discourse on Method,* considerably more intelligent and universally minded than his successors, vaguely realized at one point that the overriding validity of genera and species might have to yield to a higher category or imperative of thinking. It occurred to him, while he was developing his logic, that the principle of negation is of universal validity and no respecter of persons or species. An affirmative proposition, though positive, may well be false; conversely, a negative proposition may be true. For example, the proposition 'A horse is an animal' is true; but the no less affirmative statement 'A horse is an animal that flies' is false. But if we give this second proposition a negative twist by saying, 'A horse is not an animal that flies', it becomes true again. And the same process can be applied, virtually *ad infinitum,* to any particular species and genus.

Had Aristotle grasped the full import of this realization, he would have applied his curiosity to the methodical search for other overriding imperatives or rules of logical thinking to which even genera and species must pay homage. Instead, he proceeded on his way without giving further thought to the matter. And the astounding thing is that for the next 2,000 years most philosophers followed tamely in his footsteps, even when they disagreed with other aspects of his thinking. Thought being, like the universe it seeks to comprehend, a highly complicated activity, post-Aristotelian dialectics gradually developed into an intellectual Tower of Babel, in which random definitions (like 'Man is a rational biped') were piled on top of each other and raised to the level of 'axioms' of universal validity. With truly philatelic zeal the medieval scholastics kept collecting new particular 'truths' and 'species', and inventing new pseudo-principles to justify them.

The first task of the modern philosopher, Descartes accordingly decided, was to break with this 2,000-year-old tradition by reimposing the primacy of deductive over inductive thinking. This, essentially, is what philosophy had been for Plato. But whereas Plato tried to find the 'truth' in universal forms of unchanging Being (Beauty, Justice, Courage, Friendship, Love, the Good, the Bad, etc.), Descartes decided that it must be looked for in processes of 'correct thinking'. It was not through external observation that he had managed to simplify the numerical and algebraic systems (already greatly streamlined by certain predecessors), nor had any appeal to the senses enabled him to invent analytical geometry. These were cerebral inventions, 'pure' creations of the mind. It was here, in the *terra incognita* of human intellection, that one had to look for that *mathesis universalis* – that system of universal mathematics which he foresaw as applicable to all realms of human endeavour (a visionary anticipation, which has been fully realized in our time through the development of the two-digit system of computer mathematics); and it was here, in the mysterious recesses of human consciousness, that one must look for the basic rules of sound cognition which could lead subsequent thinkers and scientists to the fruitful discovery of new truths.

The twenty-one *regulae ad directionem ingenii* (rules for the guidance of the mind), which Descartes formulated at a relatively young age (probably before his thirtieth year), were neither as simple nor as systematic as could have been desired from the man who proclaimed that the philosopher must begin his search for the truth with 'clear and distinct ideas'. Not until half a century after his death were they first published, Descartes having prudently decided that he could not risk a head-on clash with the Inquisition, still a formidable power in seventeenth-century Europe, as Galileo's trial in 1632 had made dramatically clear. It was thus left to Descartes's greatest disciple, Gottfried Wilhelm Leibniz, to simplify and systematize these guiding rules for fruitful cognition. From his study of

Descartes's posthumous papers Leibniz reached the conclusion that the first and all-important task of philosophy must be the formulation of general principles valid for all forms of knowledge.

The most significant of these principles for the future evolution of European philosophy was the principle of 'sufficient reason'. This principle, which simply states that every event must have a cause, was of course no invention of Leibniz's, having been known to the Greeks, and not least of all to Aristotle. But Leibniz greatly simplified its application by disentangling 'material' causes from the medieval jungle of 'formal', 'motivational' and 'final' causes with which it had been mixed up in Aristotelian scholasticism. Every event must have a cause, and also be preceded by a previous condition or event, itself caused by another, and so on back *ad infinitum*. These successive stages in the causal 'chain' succeed but do not contradict each other, which is why the 'truths of Reason' – the 'necessary' truths of logic, geometry or mathematics – do not apply to them. The realm of physical (and thus historical) events is a realm of 'contingent' truths – at any rate for human beings, with their limited life-spans and intellectual faculties. Only God, in His infinite wisdom and longevity, can comprehend the totality of the chains of 'contingent' events – from the tiniest, most infinitesimal units of being (which Leibniz called 'monads') up through a series of gradations to those that are gifted with consciousness (the higher forms of animal life) and finally self-consciousness (human beings).

The first to realize how fateful for philosophy was this distinction between 'necessary' and 'contingent' truths was another fervent admirer of Descartes – the Scotsman David Hume, who made a special trip to La Flèche, in the Touraine (where Descartes had received his early schooling), before embarking on his deliberately anti-deductive *Treatise of Human Nature* (which dates from 1739). If Descartes can be called a revolutionary because he launched a frontal assault on Aristotelian scholasticism, Hume can be called a counter-revolutionary for having sought to reverse the trend. The distinction between 'necessary' and 'contingent', he argued, was absolutely basic, but Descartes, Leibniz, Spinoza and their followers had seriously overreached themselves in seeking to apply the kind of deductive thinking to be found in geometry or logic to everyday events. Leibniz, in particular, was mistaken in regarding the law of sufficient reason as absolutely binding on all events in the universe. If a man holds a glass of water in his hand and relaxes his grip, the glass, to be sure, will fall to the ground. But the realization that this is 'bound' to happen does not repose on any Euclidean axioms or other deductive systems of demonstration; its rests solely on observed experience. Things happen as they do not because they obey some preordained principle proclaimed by man, but simply because that is the way events occur, that is how objects behave. Causality, in other words, derives its force not from any deductive process but from habit and anticipation, from the repeated observation that if one does x, then y will follow.

That there was a grain of truth in this contention, there can be no doubt. Had it been otherwise, Hume's *Treatise of Human Nature* could never have aroused Immanuel Kant from the 'dogmatic slumbers' in which he had been quietly plunged for the first years of his philosophical life, under the soporific spell of Leibniz's disciple Johann Christian Wolff, for whom there was absolutely nothing in the universe that could not be deduced from the infinite wisdom and bounty of Almighty God. But Kant, a much slower but deeper thinker, soon realized that Hume's corrosive empiricism, while perhaps helpful for the study of morals and history (which is what really interested Hume), could be absolutely fatal for science. The behaviour of human beings may be unpredictable, but this is not the case with the objects of the physical sciences. When Newton formulated the laws of universal gravitation, he was not codifying past experience; he was revealing laws that are valid for all time – which is to say, valid for the future as much as for the past. These laws may be regarded as *a posteriori* in being derived from observed phenomena, but in their application they are essentially *a priori*, in regulating and thus anticipating actually observed events.

It would be difficult to imagine two more diametrically opposed systems of thought than those of Leibniz and Hume. If allowed to develop independently of each other, there was no telling what might happen, but the barren result was likely to be the outbreak of another civil war in the field of philosophy, not unlike that which for centuries had opposed Platonists and Aristotelians. To stave off this calamity, Kant undertook the Herculean task of constructing an elaborate new philosophy, combining the best elements of what was available in a determined attempt at architectural synthesis.

Kant began by accepting the notion, implicit in both Hume and Leibniz, that the events of the phenomenal world must be considered from the point of view of human consciousness. What lies beyond the realm of sense perception is transcendental and not, *sensu strictu*, accessible to human 'knowledge', even though the human mind can seek to probe the mysteries of this 'beyond' through intuitive speculation. All philosophizing from the point of view of God – the perspective that Descartes, Leibniz and Spinoza had instinctively adopted – was thus outlawed as inherently non-philosophical, or, to be more precise, non-epistemological. This was a gigantic step, for it relegated theology to the realm of the 'beyond', about which we can speculate but never 'know'. It removed God from the central position in philosophy which He had occupied for the previous 1,500 years.

Having made this essential restriction – with little doubt the most restrictive 'statute of limitations' ever issued in the history of philosophy – Kant could come to grips with the main problem confronting him. How, he asked, is a science like physics possible, since it involves the application of *a priori* laws to *a posteriori* (i.e. observed and observable) events? The answer to this question, one of extraordinary complexity, was essentially the contention that *a priori* laws can be applied to *a posteriori* events because both are conditioned by human consciousness. Since our knowledge of the world is limited to observed and observable phenomena, we must begin with these, as Hume and the British empiricists had insisted. But this concession to sense perception, which Descartes so distrusted (and rightly so, in Kant's opinion), was offset by the reminder that human 'apprehension' (the composite term philosophers use to designate the reception of sense impressions) involves intellection. Experience, furthermore, is 'open' in the sense that possibly experienced sense impressions are as vitally important as those actually experienced in the formulation of judgements about the world surrounding us. When someone gropes in a dark room fingering different objects, it is not the fingertips but the brain that tell him or her that the object touched is a lamp, a desk, a chair, a book, or whatever it may be. These acts of recognition are not sensual but intellectual, and it is in this sense that the human understanding may be regarded as imposing a certain 'order' on diversified sense impressions – what Kant called the 'manifold of apprehension'.

Since these scattered sense impressions, which the brain resolves into 'things' or 'beings' of one form or another, are all we limited beings can 'know', it makes no sense to speak of the 'essential being' of, let us say, a table or a tree. We cannot know their 'essences', what they are 'in themselves'; we can only judge them in terms of their phenomena, of the way they appear to us. But these acts of judgement are inescapably cerebral. In this way each human being imposes 'order' on the chaotic inflow of disparate sense impressions. This is the primordial, 'legislative' function of the human mind. And what is true of simple objects is no less true of the universe at large. Newton, in formulating the laws of universal gravitation, was simply extending this process and imposing a cosmic order on phenomena as disparate and seemingly disconnected as the movements of the planets and the falling of an apple to the ground. Which is why Kant could quietly proclaim, in one of the more breathtaking sentences of the *Critique of Pure Reason*, that the human understanding was the 'legislator of the universe'.

Since our knowledge of the universe is limited to its phenomenal appearance, it follows that we do not know the 'real nature' of causality any more than we know the 'real nature' of time and space. Kant chose to regard the latter as the 'forms' of human apprehension, while causality was relegated to a somewhat less compulsory status as a mere 'category' of human thinking. (Essentially, this amounted to saying that it is virtually impossible to think of an event in the abstract – i.e. as not taking place in a given temporal and spatial context – whereas it is possible to regard an event as a kind of accidental happening, taking place for no particular reason.) But Kant, who was not a Newtonian for nothing, was no less persuaded that all events in the physical universe are determined *a priori* and thus subject to the universal sway of causality. The behaviour of human beings is as precisely conditioned by causes as the behaviour of plants, animals and inanimate objects, even if the human motivations, when viewed from the outside, remain obscure. In the realm of observable phenomena there is thus no such thing as Free Will, for that would imply 'lifting' the universal efficacy of causality – something that Kant, as a Newtonian, could not bring himself to do.

There is, however, one area that lies outside the world of phenomena and where, as a result, the iron law of causality no longer holds: this is that mysterious entity known as one's 'self' and which Kant called the Transcendental *Ich*, or Ego. The 'knowledge' that each human being has of himself may be as limited and fragmentary as the knowledge he has of external objects, but of one thing he is absolutely sure: that he (or she) is a certain, particular being and that he (or she) experiences this 'is-ness', this awareness of existence, from the inside. This inner awareness is so primary that it antecedes and transcends phenomenal experience (our impressions of the outer world, which are all causally determined). In this inner realm one is no longer 'phenomenon' but 'noumenon'; one is reality itself and not simply its appearance. Here the individual is metaphysically free and can exercise real freedom of choice. This in turn is the basis of Man's moral being. For without the freedom to sin and act wrongly, morality could not exist.

This attempt to rescue free will from the 'tyranny' of universal causality – of which the 'predestination' of St Augustine and Martin Luther were different formulations – can only be described as gigantic. But it did not satisfy everyone. Any philosophy that uses human consciousness as the ultimate touchstone of the 'truth' is bound to run into self-generated problems. No one knew it better than Descartes, who was the first to elevate human consciousness to this exalted status, but who, because he distrusted purely sensuous perceptions, was often plagued by the fear that the world as we know it, far from resembling its appearance, might be the devilish *trompe l'œil* work of an 'evil genius' bent on deliberately deceiving us. Kant thought he had solved this particular problem by dismissing such doubts as idle speculation, since the only world we can ever know is that of our sensuous experience. But within half a dozen years of the publication of his third great *Critique* (the *Critique of Judgement*), one of his earliest champions, the Jena professor Karl Leonhard Rheinhold, was already proclaiming the need for an even more fundamental *Elementar-philosophie*, designed to reconcile the 'antagonistic' realms of 'sense perception' and 'understanding' which in Kant's philosophy were still opposed to each other. Another of his disciples, Johann Gottlieb Fichte, who had made a special trip to Koenigsberg in 1791 to pay homage to the Master, then outdid Rheinhold by declaring that the 'real' world is not the world of phenomena but the noumenal (non-phenomenal) world where human beings are free to do (or not to do) their duty, the world of sense experience being a kind of 'stage' for the 'objectivation' of this moral drama.

Had Kant been born one generation earlier, it is just conceivable that his philosophy might have been spared the fate that overtook it. As it was, his three great *Critiques*, published between 1781 and 1790, appeared at a moment when Germany was succumbing to an orgy of *Sturm und Drang* romanticism. To many of its younger spirits, inebriated by the heady feeling that Germany at last was experiencing a belated Renaissance, Kant's cautious rationalism seemed singularly tame stuff. By the time he died, in 1804, virtually all of his successors, including those who professed to be his disciples, were busy throwing his metaphysical caveats to the winds in their zeal to construct idealistic systems of their own.

The most ambitious and all-embracing of these systems was the one that Hegel spent a quarter of a century constructing from 1805 until his death in 1831. What Newton had done for physics, Hegel set out to do for history, by undertaking to reveal the hidden laws that had governed the development of the civilized world in the fields of art, religion and philosophy. It was mental laziness to assume, as so many had done before him, that historical events occur for no particular reason and that the human understanding cannot, from the jungle of recorded facts about the past, discern some guiding thread or pattern, some kind of inner logic or causal necessity.

For Hegel, human history, beginning with the earliest origins of civilization in the Orient (China, India, Persia, ancient Egypt, etc.) was essentially the history of ideas or principles that had worked out some of their potentialities in the realms of art, law and politics, religion and philosophy. The 'objectification' of each idea or principle produced a legacy which had to be continued, opposed or surmounted in the short run, but which also continued to exert a long-term influence as a distant source of inspiration for later generations. For this reason philosophy was the supreme form of intellectual activity, being the most reflective and self-conscious about the 'lessons' of the past.

Now if the philosopher-historian (or philosopher of history) can fruitfully bring the full power of the 'legislative' faculty of the human understanding to bear upon the seemingly meaningless accumulation of facts about the past, it is because this mass of historical data is understandable and, by extension, rational. No motive force or determining principle can be found where none exists. The 'real world', which is to say the world of historical phenomena, was thus declared to be intelligible and rational, giving rise to the celebrated Hegelian maxim: 'The real is rational, and the rational is real.' Kant, in his *Critique of Judgement*, had indicated that the *a priori* principle of 'purposiveness' (*Zweckmässigkeit*) alone makes the study of the natural sciences meaningful. Hegel's task, as he saw it, was to extend this same principle to the study of the human past, and to do so in the boldest and most 'positive' manner possible. Thus was born the idea of a *Weltgeist* (world spirit), a kind of cosmic Ego or Subject unravelling its successive attributes in limited time and space and thus 'objectifying' and 'realizing' itself through an essentially logical process of development.

That this stupendous system of logical interpretation owed a great deal to Spinoza's pantheism has often been pointed out. It also owed something to Leibniz and Descartes, authors of the notion that self-awareness is an intellectual privilege reserved for beings of a higher order. Nor was this debt to these great predecessors in any way an accident. Hegel was the last of the great rationalist philosophers, perhaps the most rationalistic of them all. Even Leibniz had not dared to apply syllogisms and other processes of dialectical analysis to the study of human history. Nor had Kant, for whom logic was the 'forecourt of the sciences', no more. But Hegel set out to demonstrate that deductive logic could render the human past intelligible. The result, as the historian Franz Schnabel pointed out, was a 'spiritual monism, to which Hegel was unwilling to have the word "pantheism" applied. For Spinoza God was still Nature.' For Hegel, on the other hand, God was Idea, Thought, Reason – summed up in the trinitarian word, *Geist*, meaning Mind, Spirit, Ghost.

King Frederick William III of Prussia, who was not exactly a model of speculative intelligence, probably understood very little of this philosophy. But it flattered his vanity to have an authentically German thinker (even if he originally came from Swabia) installed as State Philosopher at the University of Berlin, which he had founded and which bore his royal name, rather than have to import a brilliant foreigner, as Frederick the Great had done with Voltaire. It also suited the King's purpose – at a time when he and his chief minister Altenstein were trying to reconcile the Lutheran and Reformed branches of the Protestant Church by creating a new 'synthetic' liturgy for the officially rebaptized 'Evangelical' faith – to see the power of the state exalted and religion (relative to philosophy) down-graded and secularized in the name of historical 'realism'.

Never, at any rate, has a system of philosophy contributed more to the systematic study of history. Never during his lifetime has a philosopher been able to exercise the kind of intellectual tyranny and sway which Hegel wielded from the moment he was named professor of philosophy in Berlin in 1818 down to his death in 1831. Nor has any modern system of thought, after reaching such a pinnacle of prestige, suffered such a speedy and shattering collapse within a few years of its apogee. Two decades after his death the mighty edifice he had built looked like a monumental ruin, watched over by one faithful disciple, his biographer Karl Rosenkranz, while 'right-wing' Hegelians and radically minded 'Young Hegelians' or 'Hegelians of the Left' quarrelled with each other as to how best the remaining pieces could be 'preserved' or dismantled and rebuilt into neo-Hegelian or anti-Hegelian structures of their own.

Human history being ceaseless movement and change, Hegel sought to develop a dynamic logic better equipped to grapple with the problems of the past than the static logic of Aristotle, which was based on the Eleatic notion of eternal, unchanging Being. In this new analytical system the emphasis was placed on the process of Becoming, and the principle of contradiction, which had so fascinated Leibniz, was subtly transformed into a principle of substitution, or, more exactly, of supersession. The blossom, to take an illustration used by Hegel himself, does not 'contradict' the bud, nor the bud the seed; each supersedes the other without, however, being more nor less 'real'. For the total 'reality' of the flower, from birth to death, embraces all of the successive stages of growth, which are implicitly included in the synthetic 'concept' of the flower. But this kind of process, which in botany takes place in a relatively short span of time, can in human history take centuries to work itself out; and until that process has exhausted all its potentialities, any concept formulated about it is necessarily incomplete, fragmentary and thus partially 'false'. Not until the Middle Ages were over could the concept 'Middle Ages' be properly formulated and acquire its truly total significance. Even a genius like Leonardo da Vinci, living through the second half of the fifteenth and into the first years of the sixteenth century (1452–1519), could not comprehend the real 'concept' of the Renaissance, because he was living in the middle of this historical process, which was not completed until half a century or more after his death.

Had Hegel been an Englishman and thus pragmatically inclined, he would have sought to escape from this dilemma by admitting that in matters historical we must often content ourselves with 'half-truths'. But this as an intransigent rationalist he could not bring himself to do. Philosophy for him consisted above all in the formulation of synthetic 'concepts' covering the totality of the events therein contained. This rugged honesty on his part proved fatal for the future of his system of philosophy, for it meant in effect that one could not really understand the age in which one lives – the present – precisely because the present is unfinished. His system of intellectual concept-forming could be applied only to the past. In the very last of his works – his lectures on the *Philosophy of History*, which were published after his death by his students – he was forced to exclude America from his interpretation of World History (as he called it) because American civilization was in a formative stage, which meant that it was not conceptually intelligible. It would be like trying to guess what a blossom was going to look like from a mere examination of the seed. The same was true of science, which was likewise in an early, formative stage and headed in an obscure, unpredictable direction.

Now a system of philosophy is inevitably judged by contemporaries not according to the amount of truth or 'truths' (always a matter of controversy) it seems to contain, but according to the solutions it proposes for the problems of the present and the immediate future. As long as Hegel was alive, his awe-inspiring prestige sufficed to silence any doubts his followers might harbour about a system that was so exclusively concentrated on the past. But the moment he died, the magic spell was broken and the inadequacy of his essentially backward-looking, past-oriented system became increasingly apparent. There was here a basic 'fault' that had to be repaired. Hegel's philosophy had to be 'updated', as we would say today in the language of journalism; it had to be amplified in such a way as to provide an analytical tool for the understanding of the present and the future. There is nothing a disciple likes to do more than fill out and, if possible, improve the legacy that has been left him. Hegel having made many 'converts' to his way of thinking, a number of them undertook to 'modernize' his system of historical interpretation by applying it to the burning problems of the day. The most brilliant of these 'updaters' was Karl Marx, who eliminated the idealistic 'superstructure' and set out to demonstrate that the motive forces in human history were not Ideas but economic forces and the age-old struggle between oppressive overlords and exploited underdogs.

When a thinker takes liberties with the work of a predecessor – as

Hegel had done with Kant's cautious philosophy – he runs the risk of being called back to order by a later thinker. This was the role assumed by Arthur Schopenhauer, who was half a generation younger than Hegel. In 1818, the very year of Hegel's appointment to the chair of philosophy in Berlin, Schopenhauer, who had just turned thirty, persuaded the Leipzig publisher Brockhaus to bring out *Die Welt als Wille und Vorstellung*, after declaring (in a letter) that it was an entirely new system of philosophy and one which would prove to be 'the source and occasion for hundreds of other books'.

The starting-point in Schopenhauer's treatise, which was designed to provide a rigorously down-to-earth and realistic contrast to the 'cloud-castle' fantasies that had been thrown up by Fichte, Schelling and Hegel, was a resolute attack on Kant's notion of causality. Kant, he asserted, had been mistaken in regarding causality as a mere 'category' of human thinking. It was, on the contrary, as fundamental as the consciousness of time and space and thus an inherent 'form' of apprehension. Sense impressions, Schopenhauer argued, cannot exist by themselves. If one sees a puff of smoke or hears a distant sound, it is in each case because the sensation has been caused by some external happening. No sense impression can be had without relation to some external object or event, and this relationship is one of cause and effect. Without causality, apprehension through sense impressions would be impossible.

Philosophers often devise ingenious arguments for a specific purpose, and this was clearly the case with Schopenhauer. Once he had sunk his teeth into this 'soft spot' in Kant's philosophy, he refused to give up. With the obstinacy of a Scottish terrier he clung to this *idée fixe* from the moment he first conceived it right down to his dying day in 1860. He spent the rest of his life proclaiming his admiration for Immanuel Kant, so misunderstood by others, but his own interpretation of the great Critiques was deliberately designed to magnify the defeatist element in Kant's thinking: the explicit admission that human knowledge is limited and imperfect. The door Kant had sought to keep open, so that one could slip from the world of causally determined phenomena into the 'noumenal' world of Freedom, was resolutely closed: the result being one of the most uncompromisingly pessimistic and deterministic philosophies ever elaborated by a major thinker.

Since causality, Schopenhauer argued, is an inherent 'form' of apprehension, human thoughts are as causally connected as our sense impressions when viewed by the thinking Subject as cerebral 'phenomena'. Human awareness being limited to the world of phenomena, one cannot, as it were, penetrate behind the veil of existence – what the Hindus call the 'veil of Maya'. One cannot comprehend oneself as Subject, whether as body or as mind; one can only be aware of bodily or cerebral 'phenomena', caused by physical sensations or mental impulses. The Subject – the Transcendental Ego or 'Thing in itself' of Immanuel Kant – is consequently unknowable. It lies outside the bounds of time, space and causality, which apply to phenomena.

Even 'concepts' – which Hegel had placed at the apex of his system as the goal and supreme product of philosophical thinking which at that point ceases to be mere Understanding and rises to the level of Reason – even 'concepts' are no more than 'representations of representations', cognitive reflection being not primary but derivative. Schopenhauer thus went back to the British empiricists, who had sought to derive all thinking from sense impressions, in reaffirming the primacy of perception over thought and logic. But he carried this trend even further than John Locke or David Hume by deliberately denigrating logic. For logic, he boldly asserted, 'can never be of practical use, but only of theoretical use for philosophy. For although it might be said that logic is related to rational thinking as thorough-bass is to music, and also as ethics is to virtue . . . or as aesthetics is to art, it must be borne in mind that no one ever became an artist by studying aesthetics, that a noble character was never formed by the study of ethics, that men composed correctly and beautifully long before Rameau, and that we do not need to be masters of thorough-bass in order to detect discords. Just as little do we need to know logic in order to avoid being deceived by false conclusions . . . Aesthetics and ethics also, though in a much lesser degree, may have some use in practice, though mainly a negative one, and hence they cannot be denied all practical value; but for logic not even this can be conceded. It is merely knowing in the abstract what everyone knows in the concrete . . . ' And so on.

This of course was a frontal assault on Hegel's system of thinking, in which the attempt to understand the world and the past through logic and reflection was considered the highest form of intellectual activity. It was also an attack on philosophy itself, since the truly creative activities of the human mind – those finding expression in poetry, music, art and sculpture – were declared to be primary activities, compared to such 'reflective' and thus secondary occupations as philosophizing and writing books of history. Schopenhauer made no bones about it, bluntly declaring in a sentence which betrayed his deep-seated misogyny (derived from an almost pathological hatred of his mother): 'All this inevitably follows from the nature of Reason, which is feminine, receptive, retentive, and not self-creative.' Even science – which he had studied at Göttingen (as a student of medicine and biology) – was not spared, since it dealt with the world of phenomena and could never penetrate to the strange, dark, mysterious essence or inner nature of things. The scientist was thus compared to the man 'who goes round a castle, looking in vain for an entrance, and sometimes sketching the façades. Yet this is the path that all philosophers before me have followed.'

What then was the internal nature of this 'castle' Schopenhauer seemed so intent on penetrating? The answer was that it was the region of the Will, an obscure, restless, unknowable force which is present in every human, and indeed in every living creature. In reality, Schopenhauer was no more able to illuminate the interior of this 'castle' than had been the philosophers before him whom he claimed to be improving on. But instead of bewailing this fatality, he derived an almost neo-Gothic relish from the recognition of this impenetrable opacity, of this unfathomable mystery at the centre of all existence. No one could ever know what this pulsing, ever-present Will consisted of; all one could do was observe its strivings and manifestations – in the movements of one's muscles, sensations of thirst and hunger, sexual urges, etc. Human beings might fancy that they were free to control this surging Will, but this was simply an illusion, since in fact each of us is motivated by this universal, arcane inner force, to which we give the vague name of 'character'. Spinoza had once observed that 'if a stone projected through the air had consciousness, it would imagine that it was flying of its own will. I add merely that the stone would be right,' Schopenhauer unflinchingly asserted.

For the unknown and unknowable 'thing in itself', which lies behind phenomena, Schopenhauer thus substituted 'force in itself'. Basically, this was a universal, cosmic force, of which plants, animals, and human beings were partial exemplifications. It was also a blind, totally amoral force, whose individual objectifications were quite capable of combating and devouring each other. Indeed, the higher manifestations of this universal, pulsing Will-to-live could not exist without feeding on lower forms. 'Thus everywhere in nature we see contest, struggle, and the fluctuations of victory . . . Animals have the vegetable kingdom for their nourishment, and within the animal kingdom again every animal is the prey and food of some other . . . Thus the Will-to-live generally feasts on itself, and is in different forms its own nourishment, till finally the human race, because it subdues all the others, regards nature as manufactured for its own use.'

This description of the struggle for survival, which Schopenhauer first conceived during the second decade of the nineteenth century and then amplified in a longer edition of his magnum opus in 1844, might have been written by Charles Darwin. Indeed, the third edition of *The World as Will and Representation*, published one year before the author's death, appeared in 1859 – the same year as *The Origin of Species*. In emphasizing the universal struggle for existence and survival of all living creatures, and in propounding the idea that Nature proceeds more or less blindly through a process of trial and error in slowly and painfully evolving new and more complex forms of life, Darwin seemed to offer detailed confirmation for Schopenhauer's sombre view of the Universal Will in action. The rise of Darwinism in Germany thus contributed substantially to what some were soon calling a 'Schopenhauer revival'. To be sure, the belated attention accorded to his philosophy during the final decade of his life owed much to the sudden twilight that had descended on German philosophy and literature after the deaths of Hegel and Goethe in 1831 and 1832. In the kingdom of the blind, as the saying has it, the one-eyed man is king. But this disenchanted *Weltanschauung*, which exalted aesthetic contemplation and Buddhistic renunciation as the sole means of escape from the woes and sufferings of the human and terrestrial condition, seemed to be tailor-made for a puzzled and disoriented generation of young men who had seen the Idealist philosophers toppled from their pedestals and who were thus left to choose between a crass, atheistic materialism and a naïve belief in the infinite mercy and divine goodness of Divine Providence.

Schopenhauer's mighty impact on Friedrich Nietzsche may be judged by the letter he wrote to his mother and sister on 5 November 1865, in which he made short shrift of the biblical and Kantian injunction: 'Do thy duty!' 'Fine, my honoured ones, I do it or strive to do it, but where does it end? How am I to know that everything I have to carry out is my duty? . . . There are only two roads, my dear ones. Either one exerts and accustoms oneself to being as limited as possible and screws one's mental wick down as low as possible, in which case one seeks riches and enjoys the pleasures of this world; or one realizes that life is wretched, one realizes that the more we wish to enjoy it, the more are we the slaves of life, and then one relinquishes the goods of life, one practises abstinence, one is frugal towards oneself and kindly towards all others . . . in short, one lives according to the strict demands of early Christianity, and not of the present, sweetish, diluted kind. Christianity is not something one can "get along with", as it were *en passant*, or because it is fashionable.'

In her letter of reply to this latest manifestation of her son's 'inner disruption and discontent', Franziska Nietzsche could not help adding that to 'such views and developments' she much preferred a 'straightforward letter-chatter . . . Give up your heart to the true dear God and Lord,' she enjoined him, 'and all the worldly wisdom you will perhaps find in thick tomes, when contemplated with such heart and eyes, will become disgraces.' Further on in the same letter she rebuked her son for having proudly declared, in a moment of sublimely Schopenhauerian renunciation, that he could get along in Leipzig without a scholarship, by giving private tutoring lessons. Franziska Nietzsche may have known nothing about Schopenhauer, but she knew her son well enough to be certain that this scorn for money was an adolescent pose and that he would soon be making another appeal for funds. And sure enough, on the very Sunday (12 November) on which she penned her letter of mild remonstrance, Fritz wrote from Leipzig to say that he needed 10 more thaler (over and above his monthly allowance of 40 thaler).

Nietzsche does not seem to have been guilty of undue extravagance during his first months in Leipzig – unless one regards his musical activities as an expensive luxury. He himself considered music a vital necessity, and if challenged about this 'imperious' need, he could now quote Schopenhauer to the effect that musical enjoyment was the deepest, most total, the most self-obliterating form of aesthetic rapture. He introduced himself to Carl Riedel, the director of a choral group, who asked him to recruit other singers among his university friends.

During this autumn the Carl Riedel ensemble advertised its 'modernity' by devoting a series of ten matinées exclusively to the *Zukunftsmusik* of Liszt, Berlioz and Wagner. After one of these concerts, held on a Saturday morning in early December, Nietzsche took the train to Naumburg with his fellow philologist Hermann Mushacke, his old Pforta friend Carl von Gersdorff, and an Oehler cousin named Rudolf Schenkel, who was studying law at Leipzig. To entertain these young men, Fritz's mother and sister had organized a dance evening, to which Wilhelm Pinder's sisters and a number of Naumburg 'beauties' were invited. Schenkel, an uncomplicated *bon vivant*, had a jolly time dancing with the girls; Gersdorff was agreeably surprised by the intelligence of Gustav Krug's sister Clara; even the taciturn Mushacke seemed to enjoy himself. The one person who did not enjoy the evening was Friedrich Nietzsche, whose sullen mood was as black and chilling as the tails he wore for the occasion.

Fortunately for everyone, this mood of Schopenhauerian gloom did not last for more than a few weeks. By early January of 1866 Nietzsche was almost his old, combative self again – the surest proof of it being the founding of a Philological Club, which he helped to launch with three other undergraduates, and which from then on held its weekly meetings in a *Bierstube* or in the vaulted dining-room of the Löwe (Lion) restaurant.

If this Philological Club helped Nietzsche to combat his mood of world-rejection, so too did the old city of Leipzig. No city in Germany could boast as many bookshops or publishing houses, and whereas Berlin and Bonn had acquired universities only fifty years before, Leipzig had had a university since the year 1409.

Nietzsche's life by this time had settled into a well-established routine.

From his morning lectures he would repair for lunch to Mahn's restaurant, located near Leipzig's main theatre on the broad, tree-lined Blumenberg. From there he and his friends would move on to the Café Kintschy, to drink coffee and devour the daily newspapers, conveniently made available on wooden racks. The evenings were usually spent in Simmer's recently opened *Weinstube*, and it was here on Saturdays that Fritz would get together with his friends Hermann Mushacke and Carl von Gersdorff to indulge in Schopenhauerian discussions about life and the world. Spurred on by Nietzsche, whose library now included the two volumes of his essays, *Parerga* and *Paralipomena*, Mushacke and Gersdorff had also succumbed to the embittered sage's misobiotic spell. With the zeal that often accompanies adolescent revelations, the three sought to make converts among their fellow students. With those of a more thoughtful disposition they tended to succeed. Others refused to 'see the light' – like Nietzsche's cousin, Rudolf Schenkel, whose *joie de vivre* was too robust to be affected by metaphysical misgivings.

The third and most decisive factor in Nietzsche's battle with his pessimistic daemon was the encouragement he began to receive from his principal teacher, Professor Friedrich Ritschl. Emboldened by the surprising acclaim that had greeted a paper he had read to his Philological Club colleagues (devoted to Theognis of Megara), Nietzsche added some erudite marginal comments and then handed the text to Ritschl after attending one of his lectures. A few days later Ritschl summoned Nietzsche to his house, had him sit down in his study, asked him a few questions, and then told him that never before had he encountered such a sureness of approach and such a mastery of analytical technique in a third-semester student. If he was willing to do more work on his Theognis paper, then he, Ritschl, would gladly guide him in his research and help him to get his treatise published.

The twenty-one-year-old student could hardly believe his ears. That same afternoon, when he accompanied several of his friends to the Gohlis Castle park, in Leipzig's northern suburbs, he felt himself floating on a cloud of joy.

CHAPTER 8

# Philologist and Cannoneer

*– How fine bad music and bad reasons sound when one marches forth against an enemy!*

Shortly after the Easter holidays of 1866 Nietzsche moved from his humble lodgings on the Blumengasse to a bigger and quieter abode on the Elisenstrasse, consisting of a single high-ceilinged room with a fine oriental carpet, a large mirror and the usual accessories (bed, wash-basin, table, bookshelves and two chairs). For a monthly rent of 4½ thaler the owner even offered his tenant a morning breakfast of two cups of warm milk and tasty bread rolls.

Nietzsche, at the start of his second Leipzig semester, was frankly bored – by the lectures on Greek history and Roman law he had to attend as much as by the scholastic drudgery demanded by his research on Theognis. As he wrote to Hermann Mushacke, who had decided to spend this second semester in Berlin, the only professor who enthused him was Friedrich Zarncke, whose lectures on German literature he and his rebellious friend Gersdorff (supposedly studying law) found most rewarding.

Fortunately there was no dearth of distractions, for Leipzig's musical and theatrical offerings were particularly rich during this late spring and early summer. Nietzsche was able to applaud Karl Devrient in the roles of Hamlet and Count Wetter von Strahl (in Kleist's romantic play *Kätchen von Heilbronn*), as well as Theodor Wachtel's tenor performances in Verdi's *Il Trovatore* and Rossini's *William Tell.*

Overshadowing these scholastic grievances and cultural delights was the looming crisis in German affairs, which exploded into civil war in June. Ever since 1864, when Prussia, under Bismarck's masterful guidance, had put an end to Denmark's sovereignty over the north-western provinces of Schleswig and Holstein, friction had been growing between Berlin and Vienna over the status of the two liberated duchies and the future of the Germanic confederation. Determined to control the military security and thus the foreign policy of the North German states, Bismarck in April 1866 had signed an agreement with the Kingdom of Piedmont designed to stir up trouble for the Habsburgs in northern Italy. The Austrians responded by persuading a majority of the states represented in the Germanic parliament in Frankfurt to mobilize the confederate army against Prussia. This decision, voted on 14 June by a majority of nine to six, precipitated Prussia's withdrawal from the Germanic Bund and the initiation of hostilities on several widely scattered fronts.

For the Germans, still divided into a score of separate kingdoms, duchies and principalities, this was a civil war, with all of its fratricidal stresses and clashes of loyalty. Some – like Nietzsche's friends Hermann Mushacke and Wilhelm Pinder, who were pursuing their university studies in Berlin – were not too much affected. But at Tübingen, in the South German (and thus pro-Austrian) state of Württemberg, Paul Deussen found himself isolated in the midst of anti-Prussian students, who would have had him interned as a prisoner of war if the authorities in his home state of Nassau had called him up for military service. Persuaded that the Germanic civil war was going to be a long one, Carl von Gersdorff had left in a hurry for Berlin, where his brother-in-law, a captain, had him posted to the artillery battalion of a Prussian Guards regiment.

But for his poor eyesight Nietzsche too would have liked to volunteer. He had become an ardent admirer of Bismarck and even a 'rabid Prussian' (as he wrote to his mother) – unlike his cousin, Rudolf Schenkel, who was no less radically Saxon in his loyalties. Saxony's nominal ruler for the past dozen years had been King Johann I, a scholar-poet who had translated Dante, but the real power behind the Dresden throne was one of Nietzsche's *bêtes noires*: the anti-Prussian Count Beust, who had made this largely Protestant country the ally of Catholic Austria and Bavaria. In Saxon Leipzig Nietzsche thus found himself momentarily cut off (with an interruption in mail deliveries) from his mother and sister in Prussian Naumburg. Having severed all links with the Franconia fraternity, Nietzsche lacked a student cap to fling into the air when, in late June, the Duke of Mecklenburg's Prussian soldiers made their triumphal entry into Leipzig without a shot being fired. But at Kintschy's coffee-house, which was transformed overnight into a pro-Prussian camp – unlike Mahn's restaurant, which remained sullenly Saxon – the jubilant Fritz made no attempt to conceal his satisfaction. He marvelled more than ever at Bismarck's breathtaking audacity, even though, like Gersdorff, he frankly doubted the Chancellor's ability to found a 'united German state in this revolutionary fashion'.

Nietzsche was soon pleasantly surprised. Using trains to move their troops with unprecedented rapidity, along with a fast-firing breech-loaded cannon – the *Zündnagelgewehr* (needle-igniting gun), which Gersdorff was being taught to load and fire on his Spandau training grounds – the Prussians inflicted a major defeat on the Austrians at Sadowa, in northern Bohemia. News of this decisive victory reached Leipzig on 5 July, whereupon the new City Commandant hoisted the black and white Prussian colours over the balcony of his hotel.

Within the university there was hardly an interruption in the regular curriculum of seminars and lectures; and whereas Dresden seemed to have become a ghost town, with local actors playing to empty houses, Leipzig's theatres remained jam-packed throughout these weeks of critical transition.

On his return from a brief visit to his family in Naumburg, Nietzsche was informed by Professor Ritschl that two other scholars were preparing to publish papers on Theognis of Megara. Instead of a lengthy treatise, which would take too long to complete, his friendly mentor advised him to rework his material into a longish essay, which he would arrange to have published in his prestigious journal of philology, *Das Rheinische Museum*. Hard-pressed though he was by this new challenge, Nietzsche still found time for evening visits to the theatre. In a mid-August letter sent to Gersdorff, who was irked by the anti-intellectual prejudices of Prussian army officers and non-coms, Nietzsche expressed the hope that his friend Carl could get himself posted to Leipzig, so as to be able to awe the burghers and, even more, their *Bürgerfrauen* with the splendour of his uniform. 'That one can live pleasantly in Leipzig you have already experienced; and we can look together for better lodgings, free from certain terrors.'

Just what these 'certain terrors' were, Nietzsche did not say. We know nothing about the lodgings Gersdorff occupied during his first Leipzig semester, but it is just possible that they were located near a brothel, where students went take the edge off their adolescent lust. Nietzsche, after his first frightening glimpse of such an establishment in Cologne, seems to have returned more resolutely to the attack. There is even reason to believe that he contracted syphilis and had to make several visits to a Leipzig doctor, to be cured of this humiliating ailment. There is here a mystery that will probably never be elucidated, but which helps to explain Nietzsche's later mental breakdown in his forty-fourth year.

Before the tumultuous summer of 1866 was over, Germany was struck by another cholera epidemic, almost as virulent as the one of 1831, which had put a sudden end to the life of Hegel. In Naumburg one of Franziska Nietzsche's ground-floor tenants came down with the disease. Elisabeth was hastily dispatched to some relatives at Oelsnitz, while Fritz and his mother took refuge in a hotel in the watering-spa of Kösen. Here he was annoyed to discover that there was no instrument on which to try out the major themes of Richard Wagner's *Die Walküre*, of which he had recently obtained the piano score.

For Nietzsche the other major occurrence of this late summer was his discovery of Friedrich Albert Lange's *Geschichte des Materialismus* (*History of Materialism*). Schopenhauer had revealed what a highly personal philosophy could offer him in its uncompromising nonconformity, but Lange was the first to provide him with a panoramic view of philosophy – from its origins in ancient Greece down to the mid-nineteenth century.

The mysterious nature of matter had been one of the fundamental problems of philosophy ever since the Thracian thinker Democritus first formulated his atomistic theory in the fifth century BC. Embracing both materialism and its metaphysical opposite, anti-materialism, Lange's *History of Materialism* was in reality an 800-page history of philosophy – one which can still be regarded as one of the best of its kind and which Nietzsche, still a novice in such matters, could be pardoned for hailing as 'the most significant philosophical work to have appeared in the last few decades'.

The central theme of Lange's work was the contention that the Materialistic view of life and the universe, which had burst upon the German scene with such volcanic force during the fourth and fifth decades of the nineteenth century, was no more than half the truth, albeit an essential component of it. The same was true of the Idealistic view of life and the universe, which Plato did so much to formulate and his disciples to propagate in later times. The first is the product of the microscopic working of the human intellect, while the second illustrates the unifying function in human thought. The first is essentially geared to empirical investigation, the second carries us into the realms of art and religion. As long as the Materialistic philosophers were able to offset and combat the Idealists, science and constructive thinking flourished in ancient Greece. But the triumph of neo-Platonic and Pythagorean modes of thought, eventually generating forms of mystical abstractionism, helped to kill the creative thought and science of the Hellenic world.

One of the many merits of Lange's *History of Materialism* was his comprehensive knowledge of contemporary scientific as well as philosophical writings: topics about which Nietzsche knew relatively little. The history of philosophy, Lange claimed, was basically unintelligible if separated from the history of science; and one of the great disservices that the Hegelians', the Fichteans', and the Schellingians' love of visionary speculation had rendered to the serious study of philosophy was to discredit it in the eyes of German scientists and pseudo-scientific popularizers of Materialism. Only a profound ignorance of Immanuel Kant's philosophy had enabled the dietetic physiologist Jacob Moleschott to propound a purely chemical explanation of all living substances in his *Kreislauf des Lebens* (*Life's Cycle*), published in 1852. For among other things Moleschott had failed to grasp the scientific significance of Kant's 'thing in itself'. 'When worm, chafer, man and angel perceive a tree, are there then five trees?' Lange asked. His answer was: 'There are four representations of a tree, presumably very different from each other.' It was precisely to preserve the materiality of matter – as opposed to the limited perspective of the viewing agent – that Kant had elaborated his concept of the unknowable 'thing in itself'.

Lange was even more critical of Ludwig Büchner, an outspoken materialist and science popularizer whose *Kraft und Stoff* (*Force and Matter*) had created such an uproar when first published in 1855 that its author had been forced to give up his teaching post at Tübingen. 'Philosophical expositions that cannot be understood by every educated man,' Büchner had decreed, 'are in our opinion not worth the printer's ink used to produce them.' This, Lange claimed, was an entirely new and shallow conception of philosophy, which had never claimed to be the property of all or to be accessible to every educated mind – 'at least not without profound and thoroughgoing preparation. The systems of a Heraclitus, an Aristotle, a Spinoza, a Kant or a Hegel demand the most strenuous exertions . . . That these works were worth more to our forefathers than the ink they were printed with is obvious, for otherwise they would never have been printed, paid for, praised, and often even read.'

All of this was profoundly congenial to Nietzsche, whose emphatic 'anti-materialism', already evident at Pforta, had been reinforced by Schopenhauer's resolutely unfashionable and anti-popular philosophy. Here too Lange's *History of Materialism* had a great deal to offer. The notion that all animals had enjoyed an independent existence from the very beginning of time was, Lange showed, a superstition as old as the legend of Noah's ark. Darwin's *The Origin of Species*, on the other hand, was no piece of mythology. It did not deal in Articles of Faith, which have no lawful place in science, but offered a comprehensive explanation for the evolution of all living beings based on observed similarities in different species. The struggle for animal existence had been going on for centuries and millennia, yet only in recent times had this basic fact begun to receive serious attention from the seekers of the truth.

After quoting a passage from *The Origin of Species*, Lange continued: 'The struggle for a spot on earth, the success or non-success in the persecution and extermination of other life, determines the propagation of plants and animals. Millions of spermatozoa, eggs, young creatures hover between life and death in order that single individuals may develop themselves . . . For Nature luxuriant propagation and painful destruction are two opposedly working forces which seek an equilibrium . . . Nay, even in the intellectual world it seems to be Nature's method that she flings a thousand equally gifted and aspiring spirits into wretchedness and despair in order to form a single genius, which owes its development to the favour of circumstances. Sympathy, the fairest flower of earthly organisms, breaks forth only at isolated points, and is even for the life of mankind more an ideal than one of its usual mainsprings.'

From Schopenhauer Nietzsche had already absorbed the pessimistic view that the world is a cockpit of conflicting appetites without end or discernible purpose. Now, thanks to Charles Darwin and his apologist, Friedrich Albert Lange, this pessimistic view was given a scientific foundation. The idea of an anthropomorphic God or Creator of the Universe, Lange felt, must be rigorously combated by all contemporary philosophers and scientists if modern man was ever to rise above the level of childish superstition and achieve intellectual maturity. It only remained to show that even this view of life was insufficiently realistic to be truly adult, and that human sympathy, which Schopenhauer had extolled as the salutary antidote to individual selfishness and self-absorption, was not 'the fairest flower of earthly organisms', as the socialistically minded Lange had claimed, but a manifestation of childish sentimentality. Such, in its origins, if not in its conclusions, was to be Friedrich Nietzsche's 'realistic' philosophy.

When Nietzsche returned to Leipzig in late October, he found many of the city's houses bedecked with the black-red-gold banner of German nationalism, while other windows sported the white and green colours of Saxony: a manifestation of the divergent sentiments of its inhabitants, torn between the aspirations of German patriotism and a detestation of the conquering Prussians, who had now made themselves the undisputed overlords of northern Germany by annexing Hanover, Schleswig-Holstein, Hessen, Nassau, and the hitherto free city of Frankfurt. Although Saxony, like Bavaria, had been allowed to retain its monarch, it was now *de facto* a vassal of Prussia; and, as the more realistic of Leipzig's citizens grudgingly admitted, 'Now we have two kings.'

One day, during one of their weekly meetings at his house, Ritschl asked Nietzsche if he might be interested in preparing a paper on the sources that the third-century AD chronicler Diogenes Laertius had used for the compilation of his ten-volume history of Greek philosophy. This was a challenge Nietzsche was happy to accept, particularly when he learned that the subject chosen by the Leipzig University authorities for the 1867 prize essay in Latin was '*De fontibus Diogenis Laertii*'. Whereas Theognis of Megara had proved to be a philological dead-end, Diogenes Laertius was a central figure for modern man's understanding of antiquity, for much of what we know about the lives of the Greek philosophers is due to Laertius, who was writing at second or third hand, centuries after the deaths of the thinkers whose achievements he did his best to chronicle. Nietzsche accordingly set to work on this new subject with a view to winning the Latin essay prize. At Naumburg, where he spent Christmas with his family, he drafted a preliminary outline in German, having decided that this was the surest way of achieving an elegant, unpedantic clarity of style.

Nothing in Schopenhauer had more delighted Nietzsche than his vigorous denunciations of pedantry. The determined Hegel-hater had spent most of his adult life excoriating academic pedants, and in his introduction to the second edition of *The World as Will and Representation* he had bluntly asserted that most professors of philosophy were money-grubbing mediocrities who were more interested in 'nourishing the outer man' than in pursuing the arduous truth. When, in April 1867, Fritz received a letter from Paul Deussen, in which his Pforta friend told him that he had returned from Tübingen to Bonn in the hope of securing a pedagogical post, he immediately upbraided him: 'Are you really determined to jump with both feet and as fast as possible into a teacher's job? I have the contrary wish: to remain free of external shackles for as long as possible . . . What I like most is to find a new point of view or several, and to collect material for them. My brain is irritated when its maw is stuffed to overflowing . . . Most of our learned scholars would be worth more as scholars if they were not too learned.'

Among Nietzsche's fellow philologists at Leipzig the student who came closest to combining rigorous scholarship with novelty of insight was Erwin Rohde, a somewhat bashful northerner from the Hanseatic city of Hamburg. Their particular interests and judgements often differed greatly, generating heated arguments. But Nietsche appreciated his friend's stubborn defence of his opinions and the ironic scorn he felt for the pedagogical vanities of teachers and student colleagues. To this must be added a final cementing factor: a joint veneration for Schopenhauer, often ascending to mystic heights of hero-worship.

Erwin Rohde thus filled the void left in Nietzsche's university life by the departures of Mushacke and Gersdorff. The two 'Prussian patriots' spent many evenings together at a local rifle club, where they indulged in target practice. They also took riding lessons in a Leipzig manège, and as Fritz wrote to his mother and sister in June, the resultant 'shaking-up is very beneficial for the under-belly. One is thirsty and hungry and enjoys a sounder sleep than other people.'

Having completed his Diogenes Laertius prize essay and given it to the examining judges, Nietzsche left Naumburg in late September to attend a big meeting of classical philologists at Halle. On the station platform he was informed by a lieutenant commanding the local artillery regiment that new rules had just been issued for the selection of conscripts. Young men wearing size 8 glasses – Nietzsche's size – were now considered suitable for military duty. On 5 October he made a quick trip to Berlin in a vain attempt to gain admission to a Guards Regiment; and on his return to Naumburg he reported for duty with the 2nd Battery of the 4th (Mounted) Field Artillery Regiment.

The first weeks of training as a lowly cannoneer were quite strenuous. The day's training began at 5.30 a.m. and ended at 6 p.m., with a half-hour break for lunch at midday. Nietzsche bore this sudden change of fortune with philosophical good humour. He spent a lot of time in the stables, learning how to feed and curry a horse and to muck out the dung-filled stalls. There was the inevitable foot-drill and parade-ground training; and other hours were devoted to gun-crew practice in loading, unloading, sighting, elevating, firing, and ram-rodding the new breech-loaded guns of the Prussian army. The pleasantest hours were spent in the riding ring, where a blanket was thrown over the horse's back and he had to trot, gallop, and control his mount without the aid of saddle, stirrups, or riding crop, through the pressure of thighs and the stimulus of spurs.

In this new 'adversity', too, his morale was sustained by his favourite philosopher. As he wrote to Erwin Rohde in early November, 'hidden beneath the belly of my horse I whisper, "Schopenhauer, help me"; and when I come home exhausted and bathed in sweat, I am comforted by the picture on my desk' – a picture of Schopenhauer which Rohde had sent to him from Hamburg – 'or I open the *Parerga*, which are now, along with Byron, more congenial to me than ever.'

The scholar-turned-cannoneer's enthusiasm for riding soon got him into serious trouble. With the onset of spring, in mid-March of 1868, he and his fellow trainees were able to leave the ring and gallop their horses around the large exercise ground. As the ablest rider among the new recruits, Nietzsche was given the most unruly of the battery's horses to mount. Mastering this nervous steed was not easy, particularly during jumping practice, as the novice horseman soon discovered. Unbalanced by his fiery charger's sudden spurt in going for a jump, he ended up on the horse's neck, his chest hitting the pommel of the saddle with full force. He went on riding as though nothing had happened, despite the pain he felt on one side of his ribcage and in the centre of his chest. But the next day he fainted twice and had to be put to bed. The following morning he could hardly move his arm, while the throbbing in the middle of his chest was agony. His chest was bandaged, cold compresses were applied to his feverish forehead, and in the evening he was given morphine for the pain.

After ten days of acute suffering, the local doctors finally decided to make some surgical incisions in the centre of his hideously inflamed chest. From it they drew several cupfuls of infected pus. This crude operation brought the sufferer considerable relief, making it possible for Nietzsche to sit up and even to get out of bed. But as he wrote to Erwin Rohde on 3 April, he was still as 'feeble as a fly, as spent as an old maid, and as skinny as a stork'.

One day in late May a tiny piece of fractured bone came out with the pus. Nietzsche had not simply torn several chest muscles; in landing heavily on the pommel of his saddle, he had cracked his sternum. After several weeks of hesitation the military authorities yielded to the entreaties of Franziska Nietzsche and agreed to let the stricken cannoneer go to Halle, to be examined by a famous surgeon named Volkmann. Nietzsche may not have thought that his last hour was approaching – to judge at any rate from the relatively sanguine letter he wrote to Carl von Gersdorff on 22 June – but before leaving Naumburg he had himself photographed in a mock military pose. Those who knew him well could not but laugh at the sight of this short-sighted scholar with the steel-rimmed spectacles standing proudly erect with out-thrust chin, his right hand resting on the grip of his sabre, while his left hand was hidden behind the spiked helmet placed on the table next to him. With his hair rising in a wave and his curving Viking moustache, he looked so much the prototype of arrogant Prussian militarism that this farcical pose later misled many readers to believe that it faithfully portrayed the philosopher-warrior's real sentiments.

From Naumburg Nietzsche first travelled to Leipzig, where he spent five nights – two of them in a hotel, three others with a student friend. He received a particularly warm welcome from Friedrich Ritschl and his intelligent Jewish wife, who invited him to a hearty Sunday lunch and engaged him in a long discussion of musical matters – partly inspired by Schopenhauer, partly by Richard Wagner. Nietzsche then took the train to Halle, from where he had himself driven in a cab through pelting rain to the nearby health resort of Bad Wittekind. The next day his gloomiest forebodings seemed confirmed. At the *table d'hôte* luncheon, inside the palatial Kurhaus, he found himself seated next to a deaf-and-dumb man and 'two hideous specimens of female malformation'. But he was more than relieved to be informed shortly afterwards by a surprisingly jovial Dr Volkmann that he could eat and drink anything he liked and that his festering wound could probably be cured, without surgical intervention, through salt-water baths and medically soaked bandages.

Nietzsche's cure at Bad Widdekind lasted through the entire month of July. He took frequent baths in the Kurhaus pool and for the first two weeks he paid daily visits to Dr Volkmann's fine house in Halle, where his wound was several times (and most painfully) disinfected with iodine. For intellectual stimulation he could fall back on Schopenhauer's precious

*Parerga and Paralipomena* essays, which his sister Elisabeth in Naumburg had been asked to wrest from the hands of Wilhelm Pinder, whom Fritz was now trying to convert to the new faith. And what a faith it had become! For, compared to the 'factory workers' of philology, Schopenhauer was an intellectual demigod, indeed . . . the greatest philosophical demigod to have arisen during the last 1,000 years!

Having brought along the score of Wagner's *Die Meistersinger*, Nietzsche could also devote many spare hours to composing. 'Female influences' were once again at work, as he admitted cryptically to Erwin Rohde, who had retured to his home in Hamburg. The first of these inspirers seems to have been Ritschl's stimulating wife, Sophie, who had taken issue with Nietzsche's old enthusiasm for Schopenhauer and his new admiration for Richard Wagner. In a letter written to Rohde on 6 August, after his return to Naumburg, Fritz was a little more specific in noting, in a terse inventory of his recent activities: 'Wittekinder Badekur und-cour'. But who the lady was to whom he had been paying court, he did not say.

One year before, in late October of 1867, shortly after the start of his military service, Nietzsche had learned that his essay on Diogenes Laertius had won the coveted first prize and that Ritschl himself had praised it in glowing terms in a Latin oration delivered in Leipzig before a packed auditorium. Ritschl had moreover decided to have the essay published in two successive issues of *Das Rheinische Museum für Philologie*.

In March 1868 a new horizon had opened up before Nietzsche when Friedrich Zarncke had asked him to review a recently published book on Hesiod's *Theogony* for the *Litterarisches Centralblatt*. Although hindered by the bandages around his chest and shoulders, he managed in mid-April to send off his first review article, soon followed by others. Two weeks later he sent Ritschl a short essay on the *Hesychianum* as a 'kind of epilogue' to his 'Laertius work'. It was followed in mid-May by another essay, devoted to one of Nietzsche's favourite pieces of Greek lyric poetry: the celebrated dirge that Simonides of Chios (*c.* 556–469 BC) had composed about Danaë and Perseus on the stormy waters. Both were accepted for inclusion in *Das Rheinische Museum für Philologie*, which thus carried something by Nietzsche in all four of its quarterly numbers in 1868.

The high hopes aroused in Ritschl by his perusal of Nietzsche's Theognis paper in February 1866 had not been disappointed; and it was now clear to him, as to others in the field of classical philology, that the young Friedrich Nietzsche was a rising star.

## CHAPTER 9

# A Momentous Encounter

*– Ah, this old magician, how much*
*he imposed upon us!*

As he approached the end of his twenty-fourth year, Friedrich Nietzsche was as undecided as ever about his immediate future. For months he had been toying with the idea of spending a year in Paris. His term of military service had forced him to postpone this tempting project, which at one point had been conceived as a four-student pilgrimage (with Carl von Gersdorff, Hermann Mushacke and Erwin Rohde), undertaken in a missionary spirit to bring the Schopenhauerian gospel to the unsuspecting innocents who were still wallowing in a bog of unenlightened optimism along both banks of the Seine.

In the meantime there was the pressing question of the autumn semester. Should he go to Berlin to join his friends, Hermann Mushacke, Paul Deussen and Carl von Gersdorff, or should he stay on and take his Habilitation exams at Leipzig University, to which, stoutly Prussian though he was, Nietzsche was by now very much attached?

The answer to this question was found for him by a colleague who was untroubled by such conflicts of loyalty, since his family came from the vicinity of Saxon Dresden. Ernst Windisch was a gifted philologist who, like Deussen, had branched off from Greek to study Sanskrit and Hindu literature. In this field he showed such promise that his teacher, Professor Hermann Brockhaus, had decided to let him teach a course in Sanskrit grammar during the autumn semester. In June, during a brief trip to Naumburg, Windisch pointed out to the convalescing cannoneer that he had everything to gain by remaining in Leipzig. Nietzsche had already made a name for himself in university circles, and he was familiar enough with the strengths and weaknesses of the various professors in his field to be able to select a subject for his doctoral dissertation about which they knew relatively little. He had impressed the noted medievalist Professor Friedrich Zarncke, who had welcomed his contributions to the *Litterarisches Centralblatt*, and this was merely a beginning. For if he stayed on in Leipzig, Windisch could arrange to have Nietzsche meet Hermann Brockhaus, whose wife, Ottilie, was a close friend of the Ritschls as well as being one of Richard Wagner's sisters.

Nietzsche finally yielded to these persuasive arguments. Although the old university city was no longer the great musical centre it had been during its eighteenth-century 'golden age' (1723–50), when Johann Sebastian Bach had served as organist and choirmaster of the celebrated Thomasschule, or even what it had been more briefly in the mid-nineteenth century (1835–47) as a result of the combined genius of Felix Mendelssohn and Robert Schumann, Leipzig had remained in the eye of the musical storm that had been sweeping Germany for more than two decades thanks to the *Neue Zeitschrift für Musik*, which Schumann had launched in 1834. Under his editorship and that of his successor, Karl Franz Brendel, who taught musical history and aesthetics at the Leipzig Conservatory, this biweekly publication had become the leading mouthpiece of *Zukunftsmusik* in Germany – the daringly orchestrated 'music of the future' which Berlioz and Liszt had been championing in their symphonic works and which Wagner was supposed to be illustrating in his operas. It was in the pages of this avant-garde review that Hans von Bülow, who had gone to Weimar in 1851 to study piano-playing under Liszt, had published some of his fieriest articles in defence of *Tannhäuser* and other Wagner operas, thereby arousing the equally vehement hostility of another Leipzig publication, *Die Grenzboten*, which the novelist Gustav Freytag had turned into a bastion of anti-Wagnerian polemics.

Years before, Wagner, though himself a 'native son', had infuriated many Leipzigers by his bold suggestion that the Conservatory be moved from the old university city to the Saxon capital at Dresden as part of an ambitious scheme of musical and operatic reform. A number of Leipzig's leading musicians had been no less outraged by a vicious attack, entitled '*Das Judentum in der Musik*' ('Jewishness in Music'), which Wagner had written to denigrate his arch-rival, Meyerbeer, and his 'sycophantic' admirers. The publication of this inflammatory article in Karl Brendel's *Neue Zeitschrift für Musik* had stirred up such an uproar in September 1850 that his professorial colleagues, most of whom were Jewish, had signed a petitition asking for Brendel's dismissal from the Conservatory.

The simmering pro-Wagner, anti-Wagner controversy had, in this year of 1868, reached new and epic heights thanks to the production of *Die Meistersinger*, which had had its long-awaited première in Munich on 21 June. The composer's presence in the royal box, next to King Ludwig II of Bavaria, was more than unusual. Such favour bestowed on a mere commoner and, even more, on an erstwhile radical who had had to flee from Saxony after the abortive revolution of 1849 created a sensation.

Any doubts Nietzsche had previously harboured about Wagner's compositions were dispelled by his close study of the *Meistersinger* score during his five weeks at Bad Wittekind. He was overwhelmed by the richness of this new, 'truly national opera' about the mastersingers of medieval Nürnberg, just as Liszt had been by its 'incomparable sap, audacity, vigour, abundance, verve and *maestria*'.

It was in a resolutely pro-Wagnerian mood that Nietzsche returned to Leipzig shortly after 15 October – a real 'red-letter day', since his twenty-fourth birthday coincided with the end of his term of military service and the official start of his adult 'maturity'. Once again he was aided by Ernst Windisch, who arranged to have him lodged and boarded in a corner-house on the Lessingstrasse belonging to a professor who answered to the comic name of Biedermann (a *Biedermann*, in German, designates someone who is of a smug, middle-class respectability). Though a Leipziger born and bred, Friedrich Karl Biedermann had supported Prussia's unification policy in the Frankfurt parliament of 1848–50: a 'national-liberal' stance that had not endeared him to his half-brother, the fiercely anti-Prussian Count Beust, who had for so long directed the foreign and domestic policies of Saxony. Now in his fifty-sixth year, Biedermann was riding higher than ever as editor of the liberal newspaper, the *Deutsche Allgemeine Zeitung*, and as the brother-in-law of Leipzig's Lord Mayor, a gentleman with the no less inspiring name of Koch.

The Lessingstrasse house was thus one of Leipzig's most distinguished homes. From his spacious second-floor study Nietzsche had a fine view of the promenade, where the city's most important burghers liked to stroll or drive past in their equipages. Among the many guests who found their way to the Biedermanns' dining- and drawing-rooms were not only politicians, journalists and authors, but even pretty actresses – like the bright-eyed Suzanne Klemm, whom Nietzsche on one memorable evening was given the pleasant duty of escorting home. Thus, quite effortlessly, the young student found himself projected into the mainstream of Leipzig's cultural life. Impressed by his knowledge of music, no less than of the classics, Professor Biedermann commissioned Nietzsche to 'cover' certain university lecture courses and city concert evenings for the *Deutsche Allgemeine Zeitung*.

Little could Nietzsche guess, as he left Leipzig's Stadttheater on the evening of 5 November 1868, that circumstances were propelling him towards the most momentous encounter of his life. Inside the Biedermanns' house he found two letters waiting for him. One was an invitation to some sort of function in Professor Georg Curtius's house, the other was a letter from Erwin Rohde (now working on his doctoral dissertation in Hamburg), who was much upset by the offhand way in which Ritschl had rejected an article he had submitted for possible publication in his *Rheinisches Museum*.

On Saturday morning, around noontime, Nietzsche went to Ritschl's house to remonstrate with the professor on Erwin Rohde's behalf. This chore completed, he returned home, where he found a note waiting for him from his friend Ernst Windisch: 'If you would like to meet Richard Wagner, come to the Café Théâtre at a quarter to 4.' At the Café Théâtre Windisch told him that Wagner had recently turned up in Leipzig on a secret visit to his sister, Ottilie Brockhaus. Among the few who had been made privy to the secret was Sophie Ritschl, a good friend of the Brockhauses. After hearing Wagner play the lead theme from *Die Meistersinger* for the benefit of those present, she had told him that she was familiar with this music, having heard it played and explained to her by a bright young philologist who had developed a passion for his music. Intrigued, Wagner had expressed a desire to meet this learned connoisseur. Windisch, who was immediately contacted, told them that Nietzsche could not make it the following evening (Friday, 6 November) since he had to deliver an eagerly awaited paper at the Philological Club. Whence the suggestion that the two of them come to call on Saturday afternoon.

From the Café Théâtre Windisch took his friend to the Brockhauses residence. Here Nietzsche was introduced to the professor and his wife. Her brother Richard, however, was not present. Wagner had suddenly decided to go out for a walk, and to maintain his precious incognito he had discarded his usual beret in favour of an extraordinary broad-brimmed sombrero (his famous 'Wotan hat'), pulled down low over his eyebrows. Nietzsche was accordingly invited to return the following evening to meet the man whose music he so admired.

What ensued was more like a scene from vaudeville than grand opera – but, Nietzsche later reflected, sufficiently out of the ordinary to fit the occasion. He had recently ordered a new set of evening clothes – just what was needed to make the most favourable impression on the brilliant company he expected to find assembled in Professor Brockhaus's salon. He spent the next morning – a dismal, sleet-swept Sunday – waiting for the tailor to make his promised appearance with the goods, while distractedly listening to a university colleague (Wilhelm Roscher) explaining why he wanted to write a dissertation about 'Aristotle's concept of God'. The light was already beginning to fade, and still there was no sign of the tailor. Accompanying Roscher out into the rain, Nietzsche hurried to the tailor's shop, where he found an apprentice putting the final touches to his finery. Yes, he assured him, it would all be ready in three-quarters of an hour and delivered, as promised, to the house on the Lessingstrasse.

Back at his lodgings, Nietzsche waited with mounting impatience for the tailor to appear. Finally, through the window, he made out a dripping form standing forlornly before the garden gate. The iron doors being locked, Nietzsche shouted to him to come around to the side entrance, but his words were drowned out by the splashing of the rain. Soon the whole house was in an uproar. A door-key was finally found and a little old man, carrying a parcel, was allowed to come in.

'It was half past six,' Nietzsche later described the scene in a letter to Erwin Rohde,

> time to put on my things and to finish my toilet . . . Fine, the man has my things, I try them on, they fit. But then [there is] a confounded, unexpected turn [of events]. He presents the bill. I accept it politely. But he insists on being paid upon receipt of the goods. I express astonishment and seek to make him understand that it is not with him, as one of my tailor's workmen, that I must deal, but with the tailor himself, to whom I gave the order in the first place. The man grows more insistent, so does the passing time. I seize the clothes and begin to put them on; the man seizes them and keeps me from putting them on. Violence on my side, violence on his side! A scene. I fight in my shirt, for I am determined to get into my new trousers.
>
> Finally a display of dignity, solemn threats, the cursing out of my tailor and his assistant's assistant, vows of revenge, while the little man disappears into the distance with my things. End of Act 2. Brooding on the sofa in my shirt, I eye a black suit and wonder if it is good enough for Richard.
>
> Outside it is pouring rain.
>
> Quarter to eight. At half past seven I have an appointment with Windisch, we are to meet at the Théâtre café. I rush out into the dark, rainy night, also a small black figure, without tailcoat but in a keyed-up, novelesque mood. Fortune smiles upon me, even the tailor scene has something monstrous and unroutine about it.

When the two young men were ushered into Ottilie Brockhaus's comfortable drawing-room, Nietzsche was amazed to find that they had been invited to a small, strictly family evening. He and Windisch were the only guests. Wagner, after the usual exchange of civilities, asked Nietzsche how he had become so well acquainted with his compositions, repeatedly cursing the wretchedness of the performances (save for the famous Munich productions) each time one of his operas was mentioned. Nietzsche was much amused by the fun poked at various conductors, as they pleaded with their orchestras: 'Gentlemen, let us have some passion . . . my dear ones, shtill a bit morre passion!' – made all the funnier by Wagner's skilful imitation of the Leipzig dialect.

The entertainment that evening exceeded Nietzsche's fondest hopes. Never happier than when he could show off his talents to a select circle of admirers, Wagner sat down at the piano, both before and after dinner, and proceeded to accompany himself while he sang different *Meistersinger* roles. Nietzsche was astounded by the composer's overflowing exuberance. As he later wrote to Erwin Rohde: 'He is indeed a fabulously lively and ardent man, who talks very fast, is very witty, and makes a company of this very private kind right merry.'

At table Wagner engaged his young admirer in a long conversation about academic matters, and Nietzsche was thrilled to hear him go into rhapsodies over Schopenhauer – to whom, he said, he owed so much, the only philosopher who had ever understood the real nature of music. What were the university professors saying about him? When Nietzsche referred caustically to a recent congress of philosophers in Prague, Wagner made open sport of these 'philosophical vassals'. Nor was there any let-up in the entertainment as the evening advanced. Wagner ended it by reading some recently written passages from his autobiography, including a scene from his Leipzig student days so vividly described that Nietzsche was later moved to laughter each time he thought of it.

When the time came to say goodbye, the fifty-five-year-old composer took his twenty-four-year-old admirer by the hand, pressed it warmly, and invited him to visit him in Switzerland, so that they could continue their talk about music and Schopenhauer. In the meantime, he enjoined Nietzsche to make his operatic music better known to his sister Ottilie and other relatives: an educational mission the young philologist-musician was only too happy to assume.

## CHAPTER 10

# From Leipzig to Basel

*– Not for nothing has one been a philologist,*
*perhaps one is such still, that is to say*
*a teacher of slow reading.*

His encounter with one of the century's great composers and the discovery that he too was a fervent Schopenhauerian exacerbated the growing discontent with his university studies which for months had been simmering and stewing inside Friedrich Nietzsche. The deeper he delved into the nooks and crannies of classical philology, the more he began to question the ultimate utility of this industrious burrowing. Beyond a display of scholastic ingenuity, had he really contributed anything to his contemporaries' understanding of Greek and Roman antiquity and its relevance to present-day problems through his painstaking analysis of the sources Diogenes Laertius had used in compiling his ten-volume survey of the lives of the Greek philosophers? And was it really that important to know, or more exactly to claim through the skilful marshalling of the available evidence, that Homer and Hesiod were contemporaries – the subject he had chosen for his doctoral dissertation? The answer in all honesty was no. But it was the kind of answer no aspiring philologist could make without prejudicing his academic future.

The truth was that Nietzsche was fed up with classical philology. He had accepted this academic discipline as a kind of *pis aller* in order to free himself from the coils of theology, with which his devout mother and his pious aunts and uncles had sought to trap and tame his intellectual energies – it being understood by all of them that the direst fate that could overtake the refractory Fritz would be a hazardous career as a man of letters without a remunerated post to sustain him. This had been Schopenhauer's wilfully chosen lot, that of a rugged individualist who had had the good luck to be born the son of a prosperous Danzig merchant. But such a luxury the impecunious Friedrich Nietzsche could simply not afford.

Although, at the relatively young age of twenty-four, he could not clearly perceive what he was destined to be, he already knew what he was not going to become. No matter what happened, he was not going to turn into a rut-minded specialist, an academic pedant like Valentine Rose, whose 'porcupine style' of writing (in an essay devoted to Anacreon) he had recently deplored in a review written for Zarncke's *Litterarisches Centralblatt*. Fritz's letters to his friends, during this momentous autumn of

1868, were full of withering comments about the *Kleinkrämer* (petty grocer) triviality of so much plodding, philological research. Far more, he explained to Erwin Rohde, was to be gained by predatory stalking and the sudden 'leap-like comparison of concealed analogies and the ability to handle paradoxical questions'. To which Rohde responded with a zoological simile of his own by comparing academic life to a stagnant swamp in which stale, bloated frogs could prosper but in which the hardy river-water pike (a creature like themselves) was bound to languish and grow limp.

About the non-academic aspects of his life Nietzsche could not complain. He was invited to a big reception by Professor Hermann Brockhaus and his wife Ottilie, who told him many fascinating things about her brother, Richard Wagner. At Kintschy's café, he followed the daily goings-on in the Leipzig theatre world, now galvanized to new heights of feverish activity by its bustling new director, Heinrich Laube. At the Biedermanns' well-frequented residence on the Lessingstrasse he was given several opportunities to talk to the actress Suzanne Klemm and her sister, and in early December he was even able to lure the 'blue-eyed' siren up to his second-floor study for an hour of sheer *gelos* and *glukutis* (laughter and sweetness).

Determined to free himself as soon as possible from tedious philological drudgery, he had boldly decided to write his doctoral dissertation while preparing for his Habilitation exams, to be taken at Eastertime. Then at last he would be free to go to Paris for a year of scholastic dissipation.

All thought of soon jettisoning philology was, however, abandoned on 10 January 1869 when Nietzsche was summoned to Ritschl's house and given the incredible news that Professor Adolf Kiessling, who had decided to move to Hamburg, had proposed that Nietzsche be considered as a possible successor to his chair of classical philology at the University of Basel. Ritschl, under whom Kiessling had studied at Bonn, had backed up this suggestion with an extraordinary letter of recommendation in which he had written that never in all his thirty-nine years of teaching had he met a young man who was 'so mature so early and so soon as this Nietzsche'. He was the only student from whom Ritschl had accepted an article for publication in the *Rheinisches Museum für Philologie* before the completion of his third university year. 'Should he, God grant, live long, then I prophesy that he will one day stand in the front rank of German philology.' Nietzsche, Ritschl had added, was the 'idol and (without wishing it) the leader of the entire young generation here in Leipzig, which (quite numerous) cannot wait for the moment to hear him as a lecturer'.

Impressed by these superlatives and by Nietzsche's essays in the

*Rheinisches Museum*, Professor Wilhelm Vischer, who headed the City of Basel's Educational Council, had asked Ritschl to find out if the twenty-four-year-old 'prodigy' would accept the post of professor extraordinarius (i.e. without tenure) for a salary of 3,000 Swiss francs a year: a job which, in addition to university lectures and seminars, involved six hours of instruction every week in Greek grammar and literature to the senior class of the local *Pädagogium* (a kind of advanced high school).

This astounding offer, made to a young man who had neither passed his Habilitation exams nor written his doctoral thesis, threw Nietzsche into a state of feverish excitement. Fate, unpredictable Fate, had intervened to alter the expected course of his life. Instead of going to Paris, he now seemed destined to go to Basel – within easy train distance of Lucerne, from which town Richard Wagner had recently sent him a friendly note of New Year's greetings. An entirely new horizon of experience had suddenly opened up before him, and so alluring were the prospects that Nietzsche spent an entire afternoon walking up and down Leipzig's promenade, singing *Tannhäuser* melodies and praising the invisible divinity that had decreed that he and his composer-idol would soon meet again.

It was six days before he could calm down sufficiently to finish the letter he had begun writing to Erwin Rohde before receiving Ritschl's summons. In a letter written to his mother and sister the next day (17 January) there was not a word about this dramatic new development. Most of it was devoted to describing Fritz's active social life in Leipzig. The climax was reached four days later (21 January) when Nietzsche made a quick trip to Dresden to attend the Saxon capital's première of *Die Meistersinger*. This 'supreme artistic indulgence' made such an impression on the young Wagner enthusiast that throughout the performance, as he wrote to Erwin Rohde, 'I had the overwhelming feeling of suddenly being utterly at ease and at home, and my other activities seemed to me like a distant fog from which I was delivered.'

On 12 February Nietzsche was officially informed by Wilhelm Vischer that he had been appointed to succeed Adolf Kiessling as professor of classical philology and that he was expected to take up his duties in Basel with the start of the second semester immediately after Easter. At last able to spread the good news, Fritz penned a series of short notes on a dozen visiting cards, adding underneath his printed name: 'Professor extraord[inary] of Classical Philology at Basel University.' The two cards sent to Naumburg (one to his mother, the other to Friedrich August Wenkel, the cathedral prelate who had succumbed in his turn to the Schopenhauerian spell) carried a brief but significant parenthesis – '(with a salary of 800 thalers)' – after the professorial title.

The good tidings, and not least of all that additional scrap of information about his future emolument, brought tears of bewildered happiness to Franziska Nietzsche's eyes when she opened Fritz's letter. Lisbeth, still in bed, was aroused from her slumbers. A congratulatory telegram was immediately dispatched to Fritz in Leipzig. Franziska Nietzsche spent the rest of the day writing letters to her mother, various sisters and brothers, Fritz's former guardian, Bernhard Dächsel, and a Fräulein von Grimmenstein, who was asked to convey the astonishing news to Princess Therese of Altenburg and her sisters.

In Leipzig the news was only slightly slower in making the rounds. Overnight Nietzsche became something of a social lion in university circles, where professors' wives vied with each other in their eagerness to invite him to their tables. In the greater world of Leipzig entertainment he now had a standing invitation to frequent Heinrich Laube's elegant salon, where the playwright's wealthy wife maintained a generously 'open house' from 5 to 6.30 every afternoon.

Relieved to be exonerated from the obligation of having to pass the normal Habilitation exams and to complete a doctoral dissertation, Fritz said goodbye to his Leipzig friends in late March. The sadness he felt in leaving a city he had come to like was compounded by the realization that the relatively carefree student days were over and that henceforth his life would be ruled by 'the stern goddess, Daily Duty . . . May Zeus and all the Muses preserve me from being a philistine, an *anthropos amousos* [museless individual], a herd-man!' he wrote to Carl von Gersdorff. Thanks to the great mystagogue Schopenhauer, he was reasonably sure he could avoid over-concentration on minutiae and any 'shameful backsliding' away from the Idea.

After two relaxing weeks spent in Naumburg with his mother and his sister, Fritz boarded the train for Cologne, Heidelberg and Basel. On 19 April he reached the old Swiss city, where he was shocked to discover that the landlady had already rented his predecessor's lodgings to another tenant, who was not moving out until the end of June. For his first ten weeks in Basel Nietzsche was thus forced to inhabit a 'hideous hole in the wall', which his embarrassed sponsor, Dr Wilhelm Vischer, had found for him at no. 2 Spalenthorweg, near one of the three surviving Gothic gates. From here it was a fifteen-minute walk up through a maze of narrow, climbing streets to the Münsterplatz, on the crest of the central hill, where the *Pädagogium* was located, not far from the red-sandstone cathedral. The university's new lecture hall was situated nearby, on the lower part of the Rheinsprung, a steep street leading down to the old wooden bridge, built on solid stone foundations (with a chapel in the middle of it!), which at that time was Basel's one and only bridge across the Rhine. Only slightly more distant (just over a mile) was the main railway station, and more pertinently Recher's Hauptbahnhof restaurant, where for the first few weeks Nietzsche had his midday meal with two other faculty members, both of them Germans like himself.

The few letters he found time to write during this first semester make it clear that he had trouble adapting himself to Basel's stuffy society, which, like that of many Italian city-states, was dominated by a few patrician, albeit stoutly bourgeois families. With some 30,000 inhabitants, Basel was far smaller than Leipzig, which already numbered 100,000 souls, and the same was true of its university, which could boast only four faculties and 120 students, most of them theologians. Whereas in Leipzig forty students of the classics could turn up for a meeting of the Philological Club, in the University of Basel there were seven registered philologists.

The university's classical philology faculty, Nietzsche soon discovered, owed its existence to Wilhelm Vischer, a member of the city's wealthy silk ribbon manufacturers' aristocracy, who had won his academic spurs as a pupil of three great German scholars: the historian Barthold Niebuhr, the archaeologist Friedrich Welcker and the philologist August Boeck. Vischer's dream all along had been to raise the study of the Greek classics, hitherto neglected in favour of Latin studies, to a respectable level, in the hope that Basel could one day turn out first-class philologists capable of staffing the faculty, rather than have to rely on imported German talent. In 1867, when he became the canton's Minister of Education, Wilhelm Vischer had had to give up his university lecturing. The burden of all higher Greek studies was thus placed on the shoulders of one man: first Kiessling, now Nietzsche. The other two members of the classical philology faculty (Franz Gerlach and Jakob Mähly) were both Latinists.

Nietzsche's weekly schedule involved thirteen hours of instruction. His work day began at 7 a.m. with a one-hour lecture devoted (for the first three days of the week) to the history of Greek lyric poetry, and (from Thursday to Saturday) to Aeschylus's play *Choephoroi* (*The Libation Bearers*). Monday was the day chosen for the seminar. On Tuesdays and Thursdays Nietzsche had to give two hours, on Wednesdays and Fridays one hour of advanced Greek instruction to the senior-form students of the Basel *Pädagogium*.

His inaugural address, devoted to Homer's personality, was finally delivered before a packed auditorium on 28 May and seems to have been well received. If it failed to disarm the hostility of the septuagenarian Gerlach – an aged sourpuss who had long resented the ascendancy of his former pupil Vischer – it sufficed to convince others that Vischer had been well advised to pin his hopes on this unusually young philologist. But the immediate consequence of this academic breakthrough was to increase the pressure of Nietzsche's social obligations, as professors' wives and others hastened to invite him to dinners and garden parties. These distractions inspired varying degrees of boredom. In a letter written to his sister the day after his inaugural address, almost all the persons named whose company Fritz found tolerable were German. The only Swiss, other than Vischer, meriting a mention was the historian Jacob Burckhardt, whom Fritz described in this and other letters as being an intelligent and gifted individual.

What Nietzsche most missed in Basel was the stimulating theatre and concert life he had first encountered in Cologne and later relished in Leipzig. The old patrician town lacked a concert hall that could stand comparison with the famous Gewandhaus, while its stage offerings were so wretched that Nietzsche stigmatized Basel as being a place that was 'hostile to the Theatre-Graces'. In Leipzig he had been surrounded, stimulated and consoled by a circle of young friends – Hermann Mushacke, Carl von Gersdorff, Heinrich Romundt, Wilhelm Roscher, Ernst Windisch – but in Basel he had no close friends or colleagues who were at all close to his age. The historian Jacob Burckhardt was twenty-six years older.

The result was to throw Nietzsche back upon himself and to encourage that natural propensity to anti-social solitude which Schopenhauer's philosophy had done nothing to discourage.

## CHAPTER II

# Tribschen

*– Over* our *sky there never passed a cloud.*

There was another reason for Nietzsche's unconvivial aloofness in Basel. This was the relative proximity of Lucerne, or more exactly of Tribschen, a lakeside promontory situated just beyond the town's south-western limits. It was here that Richard Wagner had chosen to settle, far from the politicians and the court intrigues, the malicious gossip and the theatre 'riff-raff' which had driven him from Munich several years before. That the composer should have taken the trouble to send Nietzsche a New Year's greeting card, inviting him to visit him at any time, was flattering enough; that it should have reached him a bare week before the first inkling of the Basel professorship made it seem that much more portentous, causing him to write to Erwin Rohde, on the 12 February note accompanying his professorial visiting card: 'Long live free Switzerland, Richard Wagner and our friendship!'

Nietzsche let three weekends pass without making any effort to strike out in the direction of Lucerne. The fourth happened to be the Whitsun weekend, which meant that he could enjoy a class-free Monday before returning to the university. And so early on the Saturday morning of 15 May 1869 Nietzsche headed for Lucerne, only a couple of hours away by train. He had decided to take a paddle-steamer trip around the Vierwaldstättersee (the Lake of the Four Cantons) and to visit a number of historic spots associated with the founding of the Swiss Confederation and the heroic exploits of William Tell. But when he reached Lucerne, he was told that the next sightseeing steamer was not due to leave for several hours, giving him time to make it to Tribschen and back in a hackney-cab.

As he approached the squat, three-storey country house Wagner had rented on the lake's western shore, he heard the sound of a piano. Someone inside was insistently repeating the same plaintive chord. It was Wagner, who was working (as Nietzsche later discovered) on the third act of his *Siegfried* opera. Not wishing to interrupt the Master's work of composition, Nietzsche handed his visiting-card to a servant. Wagner, who had little use for formality, came out to greet Nietzsche on the doorstep and, after hearing the young philologist's weekend plans, invited him to come back for lunch on Monday.

Returning to Lucerne, Nietzsche boarded the paddle-steamer, which took him and other sightseers along the mountainous eastern shore of the lake to the little town of Brunnen. Here he was able to admire the Mythenstein – an eighty-foot eruption of clifflike rock rising like a petrified geyser from the water's mirroring surface. The little pleasure-boat's next stop was Rütli, revered by the Swiss as the spot where, in November 1307, thirty-three hardy souls from the three cantons of Uri, Schwyz and Unterwalden had sworn to liberate their lands from Habsburg domination. Farther on, Nietzsche disembarked to visit the celebrated Axenstein, beneath whose towering cliff-face William Tell, in the year of grace 1388, sprang from Landvogt Gessler's storm-rocked boat and made it safely to the foaming shore. Later that evening he had a jolly time with three university professors from the Zürich law faculty at the Pension Imhof in the village of Flüelen, near the foothills of the Gitschen glacier and the two-horned saddle of the Uri-Rothstock.

On Whit Sunday afternoon Nietzsche boarded the last, pre-nightfall steamer and travelled back along the lake's eastern and northern shores to Lucerne, where he spent the night at the Rössli (Little Horse) Hôtel. From here, on Monday morning, he set out again for Tribschen.

It would have been difficult, even on such a scenic lake, to have found a more beautifully located house than the one Wagner had chosen – with its tall tiled roof, its quaint dovecot windows, overhanging eaves and shuttered windows. Planted on a lakeside knoll and surrounded by tree-filled parkland, an extensive vegetable and flower garden full of rose-beds and cherry-trees, as well as lush pastureland where cows with hollow bells beneath their sagging throats could be heard as well as seen contentedly munching the green grass, it commanded a spectacular view across the waters of the lake. To the east, visible from the windows of the drawing-room, were the summits of the 6,000 ft Rigi mountain mass, and, to the south-east, the three knuckles of the fist-like Bürgenstock. And if one turned towards the south-west, one could see the bony shoulder of the often cloud-wreathed Pilatus, from whose craggy, cleft-rent heights – according to a legend Schiller had helped to popularize – a conscience-stricken Pontius Pilate was supposed to have leapt to his death some time in the middle of the first century AD.

If the lakeside scenery was spectacular, so too were the ground-floor rooms of this beautifully located house, which Wagner had remodelled and lavishly refurnished. A modern interior decorator might raise an eyebrow at the wealth of silk, satin and damask hangings that had been used to decorate these chambers; but Nietzsche, being closer to the luxuriant tastes of the period, found them furnished in a manner that was both 'princely' and 'ingenious'.

The 'gallery' leading from the square dining-room to the larger, oblong salon, for example, was draped in violet velvet to bring out the whiteness of the marble statuettes, which represented figures from different Wagner operas (Tannhäuser playing his lyre, Tristan draining the magic love potion, young Siegfried holding the fatal ring between his fingers, etc.). The salon itself was swathed in tawny Cordovan leather imprinted with gold arabesques. Its most obtrusive ornament was a grand piano, placed near the French window, which was reflected in the huge, ornately framed mirror hung over the mantelpiece. Goethe and Schiller (specially commissioned portrait copies) gazed at each other from facing walls, assisted in their silent contemplation by two Ludwigs – Wagner's stepfather, Ludwig Geyer (a respected painter as well as actor and playwright), and the young King of Bavaria. Two busts – one of Wagner, the other of King Ludwig II – filled two corners of the room, while a third was graced by a watercolour in which the Bacchic god Dionysus was shown receiving instruction from the Muses.

Finally, there was the south-facing Green Room – the name given to the Master's silk-curtained sanctum where, surrounded by shelves of handsomely bound books and watched over by another portrait of his black-haired, lustrously blue-eyed patron (Ludwig of Bavaria), Wagner did his composing on a specially designed desk-piano, equipped with sliding panels and drawers for score-sheets, pencils, pens and other writing materials.

The main centres of attraction during Nietsche's first visit to Tribschen were, in addition to Wagner, the other members of the household – which is to say, Baroness von Bülow and her four young daughters (ranging in age from eight to two). That Richard Wagner, whose estranged wife had died three years before, had found somebody to keep house for him in his Swiss retreat was now fairly common knowledge in Munich, and doubtless also in Leipzig, where Nietzsche must have heard the matter discussed at the homes of Wagner's sister, Ottilie Brockhaus, and of her friends, the Ritschls. That this *maîtresse de maison* was also Franz Liszt's daughter Cosima, and that she was still officially married to the conductor Hans von Bülow, Nietzsche must have known before coming to Tribschen. He may not have realized that the two younger of her four daughters were not her husband's but Richard Wagner's. But the best-kept secret of all – that she was now eight months pregnant – must have come as a complete surprise.

Unlike her elder sister Blandine, who had inherited much of her father's youthful radiance and charm, Cosima Liszt had never been a beauty. Her long nose, making hers a somewhat equine face, was matched by a long, lanky body, which contrasted most curiously with Richard Wagner's short, stocky frame. Her redeeming features were a pair of soft blue eyes, golden hair and a deep, resonant voice, which Nietzsche, who was sharper of ear than of eye, must have found most beguiling. Even now, in pregnancy, she moved with the exquisitely mannered poise she had absorbed from her mother's aristocratic circle in Paris and from the two Petersburg governesses who had been assigned the task of 'perfecting' her education. But what must have struck him most on the occasion of this first encounter was the notable disparity in age between the Master and the Mistress of the Tribschen household. Richard Wagner was now in his middle fifties, while the person he had chosen as his consort was more than twenty years his junior. This in itself was an extraordinary commendation; for Nietzsche could not for a moment have imagined that a genius like Wagner would have chosen to spend his old age with someone who was witless. Which explains why, in the one letter (written a few days later to Erwin Rhode) in which he did more than simply note her presence at Tribschen, Nietzsche used the term *gescheuten* (meaning 'shrewd' as well as 'sensible') to describe Cosima von Bülow. She struck him, in other words, as being a model of feminine adaptation: clever enough to keep up with Wagner's exuberant conversation, yet shrewd enough to restrain any desire to compete with him in this particular domain.

We unfortunately know little of what was discussed over the luncheon-table at Tribschen on this Whit Monday of 1869. But Nietzsche reinforced the favourable impression he had already made on Wagner during their first meeting in Leipzig the previous November. For months the composer had been living in a state of almost total seclusion. But now, in the person of this short-sighted but intent young professor of philology, was someone who could teach him a thing or two about classic Greek authors – Homer, Sophocles, Aeschylus, Plato – whom Wagner loved but could only read (as he often did in the evening to Cosima) in German translations. A learned scholar, moreover, who was willing to apply the insights of the present to the understanding of the distant past – which is what Nietzsche had done by quoting passages from Wagner's recently published work *Opera and Drama*, to illustrate certain points he wished to make in his university lectures on Aeschylus's *The Libation Bearers*.

Since their first meeting Nietzsche had managed to see two performances of *Die Meistersinger*: the Dresden première of 21 January and a later performance in Karlsruhe on 18 April. Although Wagner had received telegrams and letters from various relatives, friends and musical acquaintances describing the audiences' enthusiastic response, Nietzsche was the first person able to provide him with an eye-and-ear-witness account of how the opera had been performed in both places. He could do so, furthermore, as a musical connoisseur who had carefully studied the score and who, as Cosima noted approvingly in her diary that evening, 'has a thorough knowledge of R's works'.

Whereas the Dresden and Karlsruhe premières had been notable successes, *Die Meistersinger* had been received with boos and whistles when it was first performed in Mannheim. The main reason for this was the recent publication, in 'updated' pamphlet form, of Wagner's provocative essay, '*Das Judentum in der Musik*'. Depressed by the lack of success his operas were enjoying, Wagner had decided to dust off this twenty-year-old pamphlet and to add a preface explaining its genesis. What had prompted this action was the bitter realization that neither in Berlin nor in Vienna – the two most important musical centres in the German-speaking world – did the powers that be seem at all eager to follow King Ludwig II of Bavaria's example by staging *Die Meistersinger*, despite the triumphal success that this innovative opera (the first great comic opera with a German libretto to have been composed since Mozart's *Magic Flute*) had enjoyed in Munich. Ever prone to ascribe to sinister 'plots' and 'cabals' the lack of recognition accorded to his operas, Wagner decided that once again baleful Jewish influences were responsible.

We do not know if Nietzsche, during his Leipzig years, had read the original 'Jewishness in Music' essay – an extraordinary philosophical mish-mash (composed of elements borrowed from Herder, Hegel and Schopenhauer) with which Wagner had sought to demonstrate how Jewish composers (which is to say, Mendelssohn and Meyerbeer), aided and abetted by Jewish press lords and financiers, had contributed to the degeneration of German music that had set in after Beethoven's death. But the question of 'sinister' Jewish influences was certainly discussed over the luncheon table at Tribschen. For in the thank-you letter he wrote to Wagner a few days later, Nietzsche made a pointed reference to 'obtrusive Jewry' (*vordringliches Judentum*), placing it next to 'philosophical drivel' (as churned out by Hegelians and neo-Hegelians) as one of the root causes of Germany's present woes.

If Nietzsche had not already read the controversial pamphlet before visiting Tribschen, Wagner must have given him a copy from the stock he had just received from the Leipzig printer. He also gave his guest a little-known photograph of himself, and, as a final mark of favour, he had his coachman drive them to the Rössli inn, where he took leave of his guest, warmly pressing his hand and telling him to come back soon.

This was anything but a glib farewell formula. Four days later Nietzsche received a note from Cosima von Bülow. Next Saturday (22 May), she wrote, was Richard Wagner's birthday. It would give him great pleasure if Nietzsche could join them for a one o'clock lunch, stay on that afternoon, and even spend the night at Tribschen, if he didn't mind being put up in a tiny bedroom. Nietzsche had to refuse, because of a Saturday morning lecture. This contretemps gave him one more reason to curse the 'loathsome' chains of his 'Basel dog-house'.

Nietzsche's ecstatic 'bread-and-butter' letter, in which he thanked his hosts for having made it possible for him to link 'the best and most sublime moments' of his life to the name of Richard Wagner and to place him alongside his 'great spiritual brother Arthur Schopenhauer', made a most favourable impression at Tribschen. Ten days later Wagner wrote to Nietzsche suggesting that he pay them another visit the following Saturday (5 June), stay over all of Sunday, and return to Basel on Monday morning – something 'any artisan can do, all the more so then a professor'. After which he added these two flattering sentences, which not only admitted Nietzsche to the select circle of the 'blessed few' who could appreciate his artistic creations, but which virtually placed him above all the rest: 'Many blissful experiences with fellow Germans I have not yet been able to enjoy . . . May you rescue my not altogether unwavering faith in what I – along with Goethe and a few others – call German freedom.'

This friendly letter was written on the spur of the moment, perhaps in a local café or inn during one of Wagner's regular walks into Lucerne. A few days before, Cosima had told him that she wanted to keep all of her four daughters with her the better to supervise their education, rather than send the eldest two to their father in Munich. To accommodate the two additional children, two new bedrooms had to be installed on the house's third floor. All the hammering, plastering, painting, papering, curtaining and cushioning this had involved, with the carpenters and other workmen tramping up and down the stairs, had begun to get on Wagner's nerves. This may well explain his sudden 3 June invitation to Nietzsche, in whose stimulating company he sought relief from these domestic upheavals.

Such was the situation at Tribschen on Saturday, 5 June, when suddenly and quite literally out of the blue – for a bright sun was shining above the blue-green mountains and the sparkling waters of the lake – a servant came in to say that Professor Nietzsche had arrived. Much embarrassed, Wagner hurried upstairs to ask Cosima if they shouldn't beg off, given the advanced state of her pregnancy. But Cosima felt that this would be unforgivably rude, and that it would be better to let the young professor stay, now that he was here.

Neither Richard Wagner nor Cosima seem to have realized just how advanced her condition really was. The governess who took care of the two oldest daughters was off visiting her parents, and a new, pig-headed maid was giving Cosima a lot of trouble. The lady of the house being forced to remain upstairs, Nietzsche this time had Wagner all to himself. The waiting at table during the evening meal left much to be desired – Cosima later apologized for the 'neophyte-confusion' – but Nietzsche, being accustomed to a humbler style of life, was not one to complain.

When host and guest finally took leave of each other around 10 p.m., neither suspected that this was destined to be one of the most memorable nights in all of Richard Wagner's six-and-fifty years. At one o'clock in the morning, while Nietzsche was asleep in his little third-floor bedroom, Cosima crept downstairs to inform Wagner (now relegated to a makeshift ground-floor bedroom) that she was in labour. Throwing a dressing-gown over her shoulders, he accompanied her upstairs to her bedroom. At two o'clock Vreneli, Wagner's faithful housekeeper, was woken up and told to go with her husband Jakob Stocker (who acted as valet and coachman) to fetch the midwife, who turned up at 3 a.m. One hour later, while Wagner paced nervously to and fro in the adjacent salon, Cosima gave birth to a tiny son, to whose shrill, protesting cries the overjoyed father was soon listening with rapturous delight. At that moment, as though it had all been planned and orchestrated in advance, the first rays of the rising sun, emerging from behind the mountain mass of the Rigi on the other side of the lake, lit up the orange wallpaper and Cosima's blue jewel-box, suffusing the entire room in a rosy glow. A little later Wagner, and probably the normally early-rising Nietzsche too, heard the church bells of Lucerne across the intervening water, calling the faithful to matins.

Not until twelve o'clock on this memorable Sunday, 6 June, could Wagner come downstairs to join his house-guest and later the four children for the midday meal. The Master of the House, whose crowning wish – to be the father of a son (duly named Siegfried) – had just been fulfilled, was in a radiant mood as he announced the news. But Nietzsche, realizing how inopportune his presence was at this awkward moment, cut his visit short in the middle of the afternoon and returned to Basel, feeling 'astoundingly refreshed' by this renewed contact with a genius.

Cosima's recovery from her ordeal was rapid. The very next day she wrote Nietzsche a brief letter, thanking him for the book he had brought her to read and enclosing the manuscripts of two Wagner essays, which he was asked to bring back on his next visit. Although this letter amounted to a standing invitation to visit Tribschen whenever he wished, Nietzsche discreetly let seven weeks go by before returning to Lucerne.

In early July he was at last able to move out of his dingy hole on the Spalenthorweg into the little two-storey house where his predecessor, Adolf Kiessling, had lived. Two weeks later the university went into its midsummer recess. Nietzsche spent the first week of this vacation visiting

Interlaken and the foothills of the Bernese Oberland. One year before, as he wrote to Sophie Ritschl, he had been convalescing at Bad Wittekind, on the Saale, whose humble cliff-faces now seemed ludicrous compared to the towering mass of the Jungfrau. But how right she had been in her prediction that he could make up for the loss of Leipzig by being able to visit Richard Wagner!

In a letter written the next day to his sister Elisabeth, he struck a different, plaintive note. Switzerland's more scenic spots were hideously expensive. At Grindelwald a single room cost 2½ francs a night; breakfast cost 1½, lunch (without wine) 4 francs, supper 3 francs, service 1 franc – a total of 12 francs a day. This was more than twice what it cost him to live in Basel, where his rent was 50 francs a month, and where thirty midday meals cost him roughly the same sum.

Four days after writing this letter, Nietzsche again turned up at Tribschen, where he was received with the usual cordiality and invited to spend the weekend. Cosima, like Wagner, found his company most agreeable. That evening (Saturday, 31 July) Wagner gave Nietzsche a batch of manuscripts to take up to his third-floor bedroom. They included some curious short stories he had written about his younger days in Paris, philosophical essays, outlines for plays, and an exposition 'On The State and Religion' which Wagner had written in 1864 for the young King of Bavaria.

Nietzsche spent the next morning reading this unpublished material, which further enhanced Wagner's gigantic stature in his eyes. As he later wrote to his music-loving friend, Gustav Krug (now a lawyer in Naumburg), 'this man, about whom no judgement has yet been made which fully characterizes him, displays such an unbounded and faultless greatness in all his qualities, such idealism in all his thinking and willing, such an unattainably noble and warm-hearted humanity, such a depth of life-seriousness, that I always have the feeling of standing before one of the Elect of the Centuries. If right now he is so happy, it is because he has just finished the third act of his *Siegfried* and is already movng on with an exuberant sense of power to the composition of *Götterdämmerung*.'

After lunch on this same Sunday (1 August), Nietzsche climbed into a carriage with Wagner, Cosima and her three oldest daughters to be driven to the village of Hergischwyl, four miles to the south. Here he took leave of his hosts, who had tried in vain to persuade him to accompany them to a rustic beer, cheese and skittles *Fest*. The sun had reappeared after the downpours of the previous day and Nietzsche had decided to climb the 6,000-ft Pilatus and to spend most of Monday on the summit before returning to Tribschen for another night. He made it to the summit and spent the night in a primitive *Berghotel*. Early the next morning the mountain seemed to explode in a dazzling electric storm, and so window-shaking were the detonations of thunder that down at Tribschen Wagner's servants began to ask themselves, 'Just what is Professor Nietzsche up to?' as though he were Jupiter Almighty. The spectacular view of the lake and the surrounding peaks was blotted out by clouds. But the frustrated sightseer found ample consolation in the 'majestic' views Wagner had expounded in his essay, 'On the State and Religion'. Its thesis was that the theatre – more exactly a new cultural trinity composed of Music, Theatre and Opera – should replace religion as the main educative force in contemporary society.

On Tuesday the skies cleared again. But Nietzsche by this time was so deeply buried in Eduard von Hartmann's *Philosophy of the Unconscious* that he made no effort to leave his mountain top. Wednesday came and went, without his reappearing at the Wagner house – to Cosima's and everyone else's surprise.

Basel, currently deserted by most of its faculty members, seemed more than usually friendless when Nietzsche returned there on 5 August. 'Ah, dear Friend,' he wrote a few days later to Erwin Rohde (now vacationing in Sorrento), 'I have little pleasure and must chew my cud in solitude.' He missed his Leipzig friends, just as he missed his mother and his sister at Naumburg, now even more inaccessible than it had been when he was a student in Bonn. A single, second-class train fare from Basel cost 73 Swiss francs – an astronomical sum for someone who had so far received only one-quarter (750 francs) of his annual salary.

On Friday, 27 August, Wagner was taking his afternoon walk into Lucerne, accompanied as usual by his two dogs – Kos (an ageing Dobermann Pinscher) and Russ (a big black Newfoundlander) – when he bumped into his sister Ottilie, who had just arrived from Leipzig with her husband, Professor Hermann Brockhaus, and their two daughters. Wagner invited them to lunch the next day at Tribschen. Then, going to the post office, he sent off a telegram to Nietzsche: 'Brockhauses lunching tomorrow (Saturday) at 2 o'clock at my home, very much request your presence, in return promise complete freedom for Sunday afternoon' – i.e. his guest would then have him all to himself, to talk about whatever topic it might please them to tackle.

To give Nietzsche time to make it to Lucerne by train after the conclusion of his Saturday morning lecture, Wagner had delayed the usual lunchtime by an hour – itself a rare mark of esteem. Cosima, in a recent letter, had promised that 'never again would there be any confusion' in the Tribschen household (comparable to previous weekends), but there was a new commotion on this particular Saturday afternoon when the postman delivered a batch of telegrams from Munich, indicating that the

*Rheingold* dress rehearsal – which Liszt, Saint-Saëns, Karl Klindworth, Manual García, Turgenev, Pauline Viardot-García and other celebrities had come to Munich to see – had been a ludicrous fiasco.

The commotion was compounded the next morning by other telegrams, requiring telegraphic replies from an irascible Wagner. In the midst of the uproar, as Cosima noted that evening in her diary, was Professor Nietzsche, '*immer angenehm*' (always agreeable). Knowing nothing about what was going on in Munich – where Wagner's protégé, the twenty-six-year-old Hans Richter, was hell-bent on succeeding Hans von Bülow as full-time orchestra conductor – the young philologist from Basel innocently supposed that all this tumult was generated by genuine artistic issues rather than by a battle of wills fought out through intermediaries between Wagner and King Ludwig of Bavaria.

Today, when so much more is known about the seamy side of Richard Wagner's supremely egocentric and self-indulgent character, it is easy to smile at the ingenuousness of his young admirer, who in a letter to Paul Deussen could describe his opera-composing hero as the '*greatest genius* and the *greatest man* of this age, absolutely incommensurable!' and declare in another letter, written to Erwin Rohde, that what he had seen and heard at Tribschen was quite simply indescribable. 'Schopenhauer and Goethe, Aeschylus and Pindar still live.'

That these encomia were a bit inflated is undeniable. But many others before Nietzsche had succumbed to the magnetism of those piercing blue eyes ('as blue as the Lake of Lucerne', eyes blending 'the most beautiful shades of sapphire', as Judith Mendès described them during this same summer of 1869) and had been overwhelmed by the torrential flow of speech. Ernest Newman, his biographer, claimed that his face was so expressive and his histrionic gifts so marked that had he chosen the stage for a career, Richard Wagner could have become the greatest actor in Europe. Franz Liszt, who had met many exceptional persons during his virtuoso concert tours, was so impressed by his first encounters that he too resorted to superlatives in describing Wagner's versatile personality, and not least of all his voice, which in moments of supreme excitement resembled the 'shriek of a young eagle . . . A great and overwhelming nature, a sort of Vesuvius, which when in eruption scatters sheaves of fire and at the same time bunches of roses and elder. It is his habit to look down on people from the heights.' Although those lines were written in 1853, time had done little to subdue this elemental force – as can be seen from the impression Wagner made on the Alsatian music critic Edouard Schuré, who turned up at Tribschen on the birthday weekend of 22 May (the one Nietzsche had missed). After describing the sucked-in mouth, the thin, sensual, sardonic lips, the wilful, pointed chin, the determined, domineering forehead, a ravaged face bearing 'the traces of passions and sufferings capable of exhausting the lives of many a man', he added that 'his manner was no less surprising than his physiognomy. It varied between absolute reserve, absolute coldness, and complete familiarity and sans-gêne . . . When he showed himself, he broke out as a whole, like a torrent bursting its dykes . . . His gaiety flowed over in a joyous foam of facetious fancies and extravagant pleasantries; but the slightest contradiction provoked him to incredible anger. Then he would leap like a tiger, roar like a stag. He paced the room like a caged lion, his voice grew hoarse and the words came out like screams; his speech lashed about at random . . . Everything in him was gigantic, excessive.'

In 1883, not long after Wagner's death, Hans von Bülow, whose marital life had been irreparably shattered, as though by the searing passage of a comet, was still so much under the spell that he could write: 'This century has seen three famous men – Napoleon, Bismarck and Wagner – who are not to be held accountable for what was human in them, or indeed for anything.'

Friedrich Nietzsche never went quite so far, but when he too looked back over the most memorable moments of his existence, he did not hesitate to declare that he could dispense with all the other friendships of his life, but that 'for nothing in the world would I part with the days at Tribschen, days of trust, of gaiety, of sublime confidence – of *profound* moments . . . I do not know what others have experienced with Wagner: over *our* sky there never passed a cloud'.

## CHAPTER 12

# An Intoxicating Friendship

> *– A strong and well constituted man digests his experiences (deeds and misdeeds included), as he digests his meals, even if he has to swallow some tough morsels.*

Although Basel was only a couple of hours away by rail from Lucerne, the six trips Nietzsche made to Tribschen during the summer of 1869 did nothing to improve his precarious financial situation. At the university professors were paid their salaries in two annual instalments: the first in early January, the second six months later. But these payments were remuneration for services rendered. Nietzsche, who had begun to teach in April, was thus paid one half of his semi-annual instalment (750 Swiss francs) in early July. This had to last him until the following January, when he would receive the full semi-annual payment of 1,500 francs. By late August Fritz was so 'strapped' that he wrote to his sister Elisabeth and asked her to dig into the investment fund that had been established for them by their mother (from various inheritances and annual gifts made by the Altenburg princesses) and to sell a state bond.

The sale of this bond, which brought in 81 thalers (slightly more than 300 Swiss francs), again aroused Franziska Nietzsche's misgivings about her son's 'extravagant', financially carefree ways. In early September she sent him a pained letter, saying that all their friends and relatives in Naumburg had fondly imagined that Fritz was living frugally and putting aside savings from his professorial salary. This remonstrance was not made to impress a fervent Schopenhauerian who shared his intellectual mentor's anti-materialistic contempt for 'sordid' questions of money. But several weeks later Franziska punished her 'spendthrift' son by curtly informing him by telegram that their scheduled trip to the Lake of Geneva was cancelled.

'Vacation' is too strong a word for the two laborious weeks which, by way of penance, Fritz was now forced to spend in Naumburg. He used them to fulfil a rash promise made to his benefactor, Friedrich Ritschl, by completing the indexing of the first twenty-four years of the *Rheinisches Museum für Philologie*. He spent some pleasant hours with Gustav Krug, regaling his friend with lyrical descriptions of their hero, Richard Wagner, but his happiest moments were spent in Leipzig with Ritschl and his intelligent wife, Sophie.

On 19 October Nietzsche was back in Basel, after spending two freezing nights in unheated train compartments. He was happy to regain his cosy lodgings on the Schützengraben road, with their warm stove, double-windows, red-upholstered sofa and worn horsehair rug. But when the semester began he received a shock. Eight undergraduates had signed up for advanced instruction in Latin, but the far more interesting course devoted to pre-Platonic philosophy had attracted no more than 'three *dumb* students' (as he put it in a letter to Friedrich Ritschl).

On Saturday, 13 November he made another pilgrimage to Tribschen, where he was more than ever *persona grata*. (A few days before, Wagner had picked up the five-month-old Siegfried and had laughingly told Cosima that when the time came for the young boy to sally forth into the world and 'to taste adversity, have fun, and misbehave himself' – for under no circumstances did he want him to become a dreamer, like King Ludwig of Bavaria – he would send him away to be taught by Nietzsche . . . 'and we shall watch from afar, as Wotan watches the education of Siegfried'.) Cosima was appalled by Nietzsche's reports of the incredible things that were being said or written about them in Naumburg, Leipzig and Basel. According to one story, inspired by the Gallery of Great Men, Wagner spent hours admiring himself in the mirror, in an effort to persuade himself that he was the poetic equal of Schiller and Goethe; according to another story, the Tribschen house had been transformed into an oriental palace, filled with luxurious silks and satins and a pasha-style harem. This time, however, Sunday was undisturbed by incoming telegrams and concluded with a lovely evening walk along the western shore of the lake as a sinking sun inflamed the rosy mountain mass of the Rigi against a soft, translucent sky.

Each return to Basel, after weekends such as these, made Nietzsche's academic life seem more pedestrian and tedious. 'Of social gregrariousness,' as he wrote to his mother, 'I now have even less than in the past half-year. And thereby I notice how little I need it.' On the walls of his study he now had two pictures of Schopenhauer to inspire him; and it was enough to contemplate that turbulent shock of white hair, those determined eyes and pursed lips to be reminded (as he wrote to Gustav Krug) that 'without isolation there is nothing Noble or Lofty to be obtained; where all go, meanness follows alongside'.

On 24 December Nietzsche again left for Tribschen, this time invited to spend all of the Christmas holidays with Richard Wagner, Cosima and the five children. As Christmas gifts from Cosima, Wagner received an edition of Kant's *Complete Works* and, as a crowning surprise, the portrait of Wagner's Uncle Adolf (a gifted translator and essayist) which Nietzsche had managed to wrest from a maidservant in Leipzig. From his house-guest he received a copy of a rare Schopenhauer photograph, into the frame of which a Naumburg wood-carver had engraved the Wagner coat of arms. Nietzsche's gift for Cosima – a combined birthday and Christmas present, since she was born on 25 December – was a printed copy of his inaugural address at Basel, retitled 'Homer and Classical Philology'.

Cosima spent the afternoon of Christmas Day with Nietzsche reading Wagner's poetic sketch for a 'Parzival' opera, after which they were treated by the Master of the House to a 'sublime' dissertation on the 'philosophy of music', which was supposed to supplement and even to supplant the educational functions of Church and State. During the next few days there were skating expeditions out on to the frozen lake, where 'Herr Nützsche' amused the children with several spectacular falls. Indoors, while Wagner continued to labour on his essay about orchestra conducting, Nietzsche and Cosima spent hours conversing together in the upstairs study, now christened the *Denkstube* ('think-room') in honour of the pensive professor from Basel, even though it was intended to be a classroom for the children.

For several months, under the confluent influences of Schopenhauer's philosophy and Wagner's writings on opera, Nietzsche had been giving serious thought to the role played by music in the development of Greek drama. Music and the theatre, which today are naturally regarded as fully independent and separate forms of art, did not originally enjoy this distinction – music being essentially an accompaniment of dance movements, while dramatic acting was a feature of religious commemoration and myth-narration. A similar dislocation was evident in the gradual shift from poetry to prose – exemplified in ancient Greece by the contrasting figures of Aeschylus and Aristophanes, and in modern times by the difference between the epic verse tragedies of Shakespeare, Corneille and Racine, and the critical prose comedies of Molière, Beaumarchais and Marivaux. Although Goethe and Schiller had sought to revive the noble traditions of verse dramas, the nineteenth-century stage was being increasingly invaded by satirical or didactic prose plays – like those of Karl Gutzkow and Heinrich Laube in Germany, or those of the two Alexandre Dumas (father and son) and George Sand in France. The spirit of critical dissection, which Immanuel Kant had done so much to exalt, was everywhere in the ascendant, and this phenomenon promised to be as fateful to Europe's future intellectual development as had been the emergence of Socratic dialectics for the culture of ancient Greece.

Such, pared down to essentials, was the double theme Nietzsche had decided to expound in two lectures. The first, devoted to 'Ancient Music-Drama', was delivered in Basel on 18 January 1870 before a 'mixed public' composed for the most part of middle-aged 'mothers' (as he put it in a letter to Wagner), whose desire to 'broaden' their minds seems to have been baffled by the complexity of the subject. The second lecture, delivered two weeks later on 1 February, was more provocative, arousing (as Nietzsche later explained to Paul Deussen) varying degrees of 'hatred and fury' among certain members of the audience. Basel's thirty-eight-year-old professor of philosophy, Gustav Teichmüller, was incensed by the presumption displayed by his twenty-five-year-old colleague in maintaining that Socrates's questioning dialectics, like the satires of his contemporary Aristophanes, were a symptom of cultural decadence, a kind of analytical acid which had eaten into the very core of high Greek culture, as represented by its epic poets and tragedians, thereby precipitating its decline and eventual extinction.

Both Wagner and Cosima, to whom Nietzsche sent the text of his second lecture (on Socrates), were startled by the audacity of his assertions. Even in his most Schopenhauerian moments Wagner had never dared suggest that logic could poison the wells of art. In an admiring and remonstrating letter he expressed the fear that his young friend was going to break his neck if he boldly persevered in such categorical affirmations. Cosima, in a much longer, almost 'maternal' letter, frankly doubted that a single one of his Basel listeners, with the exception of Jacob Burckhardt, possessed a sufficiently profound understanding of the nature of music to be able to follow the subtle thread of Nietzsche's reasoning. At Tribschen, at any rate, the text of his public lecture had made such a forceful impression on the Master (Richard Wagner) that in a joyous burst of inspiration he had added a bold violin accompaniment to the Siegfried-on-the-Rhine horn motif in the *Götterdämmerung* overture. Nietzsche's stimulating influence had even begun to affect their choice of authors for the usual evening session; for, after finishing *The Frogs*, Richard Wagner and Cosima had begun to read Aristophanes's *The Acharnians*.

On 7 February Wagner again wrote to Nietzsche, to say what a fine thing it was that they could write such letters to each other. 'I now have nobody with whom I could take things up as seriously as with you, the Unique One [i.e., Cosima] excepted.' He was often surprised by the happy mood that came over him as soon as he stopped his critical writing and returned to his composing. Believing, as he did, in the division of labour, he wondered if Nietzsche couldn't assume some of his intellectual burden, thus incidentally helping to fulfil his own vocation. 'Look how wretchedly I have fared with philology, and on the other hand what a good thing it is that you have fared about as well with music. Had you become a musician, you would have been approximately what I would have become if I had stubbornly stuck to philology. Yet philology – as a meaningful disposition – is something I have in my bones, it even guides me as a "musician".' In short, Nietzsche, with his superior, inside knowledge of classical philology, could help bring about a 'great "Renaissance", in which Plato embraces Homer, and Homer, imbued with Plato's Ideas, will at last become a greater-than-ever Homer'.

What the 'Master of Tribschen' was proposing was that the young philologist from Basel should become the philosophical theorist and exponent of Wagnerian aesthetics. By lucidly analysing the fate that had overtaken ancient Greek culture, above all in the fields of poetry and drama, Nietzsche could provide him with a philosophical foundation for his own views as to what had gone wrong with modern European culture, increasingly corroded by 'vulgar realism', and which he proposed to combat through the inspirational medium of the *Gesamtkunstwerk*: the 'complete art work' (i.e. Wagnerian opera), in which the artificially alienated arts of verse, song, acting and music were to be heroically blended into a newer and higher aesthetic totality. Gluck, while aspiring to create a 'heroic' opera style, had sought his models in the world of Greek antiquity rather than in the old Nordic and Germanic sagas, which had inspired several of Shakespeare's greatest tragedies. It was in this less exploited realm of mythology that Wagner had searched for the subject-matter of his operas: mythological treasures which (as Nietzsche had discovered at Pforta) were as worthy of philological investigation as the epic world of Homer. This was what Wagner meant when he said that he had philology in his bones. He had sought to explain his vision of what an authentically 'Germanic' opera style should be in a number of essays. But, being more of a creative than of a critical temperament, he was willing to admit that Nietzsche could supply a historical-analytical depth which his own unscholarly theorizings of the past had lacked.

On 9 April Nietzsche was informed by the university authorities that he had been appointed Professor Ordinarius (with tenure) for services well rendered during his first academic year. Shortly afterwards, his mother and Elisabeth arrived in Basel to spend the Easter holidays with Fritz. The devout Franziska refused to leave the city until after the conclusion of the Good Friday service; and not until the next day could her impatient son finally drag her and Lisbeth away by train to the northern shore of Lake Geneva. Here, in a chalet-pension perched on a hillside above Montreux, they spent several sunny weeks admiring the photogenic silhouette of the Dents du Midi and the snowy crest of the more distant, unusually cloud-free Mont Blanc.

Towards the end of April Fritz had to cut short his vacation and hurry back to Basel. The number of students enrolled in the Faculty of Classical Philology was increased from nine to fourteen, but the ironic satisfaction that the new Professor Ordinarius derived from this significant promotion was soured by the news that because of the ill-health of one of his two Latin-teaching colleagues (Mähly) he would have to double the number of his Latin classes at the *Pädagogium*. Nietzsche's workload was now an exhausting total of twenty hours a week.

Although his mother and sister, after their return from Montreux, could now keep house for him, theirs was an embarrassing presence as far as new trips to Tribschen were concerned. Nietzsche had to deny himself the pleasure of celebrating Richard Wagner's fifty-seventh birthday (22 May 1870) with the Master, though he honoured the occasion with the timely dispatch to Lucerne of a dozen rose-bushes.

In late May Erwin Rohde, who had spent a studious year perusing ancient manuscripts in Italian libraries and museums, turned up in Basel. Fritz, though overworked, persuaded him to prolong his stay. After a three-day Pentecostal excursion to Interlaken, Wengernalp and Lauterbrunnen, in the Bernese Oberland, Nietzsche wrote to Cosima to say that he would be coming to visit them on Saturday, 11 June, accompanied by his friend Erwin Rohde. Rohde's was by now a familiar name at Tribschen, thanks to extracts from his letters (expressing enthusiasm for Schopenhauer and Wagner) which Nietzsche had read aloud to his hosts during previous visits. More than ever Wagner was persuaded that it was among members of the 'third generation' that at last he was finding admirers capable of understanding his operatic ambitions. Save for one or two fellow geniuses, like Hector Berlioz and Franz Liszt, the generation he himself belonged to had been unable to appreciate his visionary conception of an all-embracing 'art-work-of-the-future'. The next generation, composed of those who had matured during the two revolutions of 1830 and 1848, had been too much influenced by Meyerbeer to feel much more than a dumb, semi-comprehending appreciation for Wagner's works. Like Schopenhauer, whose genius had not been recognized until he was already a white-haired old man, Wagner had had to wait for a third generation – those, like Nietzsche and King Ludwig of Bavaria, who were now roughly twenty-five years old – to produce young persons of sufficient seriousness to be able to admire his artistic creations. Erwin Rohde was clearly one of them – as was Carl von Gersdorff, whose enthusiasm for Wagner's works had been rewarded by the issue of special tickets enabling him to attend performances of *Die Meistersinger* in Berlin.

In bringing Rohde to Tribschen, Nietzsche knew that he had nothing to fear. Rohde's 'manly earnestness', his pertinent observations, the 'friendly feelings piercing through the stern features' (as Cosima later described them) made a favourable impression on Wagner, while the copy of a Dürer engraving ('Melancholie') which, at Nietzsche's request, he had picked up in an Italian art shop as a present for his hostess made him *persona gratissima* with the Mistress of the House. Nietzsche had also brought along the manuscript of the first of his two public lectures (the one delivered on 18 January), which he was asked to read aloud in the evening. Wagner took immediate exception to the title – 'Ancient Music-Drama' – probably because he felt that Nietzsche was according an importance to the musical component in the evolution of Greek tragedy which it really did not possess, compared to modern operas. But to the substance of Nietzsche's lecture, and particularly to its demonstration of how the chanting and dancing chorus had, like a temple frieze, provided the original narrative kernel from which the character-portraying actors had later developed, Wagner could only listen with the fascination of a neophyte.

At luncheon the next day, an unusually ebullient Wagner made fun of professional musicians, whom he likened to 'wild beasts, not educated creatures, very close in fact to actors'. In Munich, Kapellmeister Wüllner was now rehearsing *Die Walküre* with Ludwig of Bavaria's active encouragement. For Wagner this production was one more act of artistic desecration, since this 'music-drama', aside from being the truncated fragment of a greater whole, was going to be offered to 'the lounging opera public, accustomed solely to the trivial'. What he wanted was a theatre of his own, a Temple of High Art, where his works could be performed by specially trained singers and instrumentalists and offered to select audiences of connoisseurs who had had the good taste to hold themselves aloof from the 'shallow entertainments' that were currently the stock-in-trade of German theatres and opera houses.

With these exalted aspirations Nietzsche by now was quite familiar. What he did not know, until this Sunday luncheon, was that Wagner had found the ideal spot for his projected Temple of High Art. It was located in the north-eastern corner of Bavaria, at Bayreuth, a modest town which had acquired an exquisite eighteenth-century castle and a magnificent opera house built by Frederick the Great's sister Wilhelmine. This unforeseen development came as a shock. Tribschen for the past year had been Nietzsche's greatest consolation. It had not occurred to him that Richard Wagner, having lavished so much care on its expensive decoration, could regard this tranquil 'island of the blessed' as a mere stepping-stone to something grander.

In a thank-you letter sent to Cosima, along with a green-bound copy of his two Basel lectures (written out in longhand by a hired scribe),

Nietzsche made no secret of his troubled ruminations. All things considered, he wrote, it might be best if he were to give up his professorial activities for a year or two and join their artistic 'pilgrimage' into the Fichtel mountains, near the little city of Bayreuth.

## CHAPTER 13

# A Bitter Taste of Warfare

*– In pain there is as much wisdom as in pleasure; it is, like the latter, one of the forces that best preserve the species.*

On 6 July 1870 Carl von Gersdorff wrote from Berlin to say that he was planning a mountain-tour of Mont Blanc, Monte Rosa and the Bernese Oberland and that he would be passing through Basel to see his dear friend Fritz. Like Sophie Ritschl, who had brought her daughter to Switzerland for a month of fresh Alpine air, Gersdorff had not the slightest inkling of the thunderclap that was about to break over their heads. Nor was Nietzsche any more prescient. The pressure of academic work kept him so busy that on 17 July, when Napoleon III's France declared war on Bismarck's Prussia, he was taken completely by surprise.

Like his friend Gersdorff in 1866, Nietzsche feared the worst. This war between the continent's two leading military powers might drag on for years and destroy what was left of European civilization. 'Our whole threadbare culture is slamming headlong into this most frightful of demons,' he wrote to Erwin Rohde, who had returned to his native Hamburg. 'What are we going to endure! Friend, dearest Friend, we saw each other once again in the sunset-glow of peace . . . What now are all our aims! . . . What a wasteland!' This time, instead of the usual signature ('your dear friend, F.N.'), he signed ironically '*Der treue Schweitzer*' (the true Swiss patriot).

As a German who had renounced his Prussian citizenship to be able to teach in Switzerland, Nietzsche could remain neutral, at any rate in theory. But if there was one thing he detested, it was neutrality. It was the reproach he was already levelling at liberalism and liberals: a tepid philosophy for tepid souls devoid of any deep-rooted, personal convictions, ever ready to compromise, to swim with the prevailing current, to dilute whatever remained of their beliefs in a bouillon of tasteless 'moderation'. The idea that he could remain neutral at such a moment was enough to make him squirm in an agony of self-reproach. How could he, who had recently written to his friend Gersdorff to condemn the '*Zeitverflachung*' – the 'flabbiness', or, more exactly, the 'flabbification' – of the present age, look at himself in the mirror without breaking into a sarcastic laugh at the sight of that Bismarckian bush of a moustache which, instead of bristling with defiant determination, now seemed to droop over his lips like seaweed?

A day or two later Fritz and his sister managed to get away from the sweltering hornets' nest of Basel, the two main stations of which were now crammed with French and German tourists who were trying to elbow and cane their way on to trains bound for their bellicose homelands. At Lucerne they boarded a paddle-steamer, which took them past the poplar-studded promontory of Tribschen to Brunnen, on the lake's eastern shore, where they had themselves driven up a steep, winding road to a large hotel on top of the Axenstein cliff. Here, with more than 100 other clients (many of them British) who were not going to let the outbreak of hostilities upset their summer plans, Nietzsche spent a fretful week wondering what to do next. He felt ashamed whenever he contemplated the unruffled beauty of the fingered lake, slumbering peacefully amid the cushioned recesses of its cliffs and evergreen and emerald mountain slopes, for if ever there was a time when he should have been in the field with an artillery battery, it was now. On the other hand, he had no burning desire to contribute actively to the destructive havoc which a 'war of national embitterment' could wreak on European civilization.

On 28 July he and his sister descended from their scenic heights and took the little lake-steamer back to Lucerne. The mother of one of Nietzsche's Basel colleagues had invited Elisabeth to spend a few days at her suburban villa on Lucerne's eastern fringe, separated from Tribschen by half a mile of intervening water. Taking leave of his sister, Nietzsche proceeded on alone to Wagner's house, which was in an unusual state of tension. Wagner had interrupted work on *Götterdämmerung* in order to write an essay on that most Germanic of composers, Beethoven, the hundredth anniversary of whose birth was due to be celebrated in December. This had done nothing to temper his pro-German militancy – an attitude in which he was fully supported by Cosima, who cared little for her brother-in-law, Emile Ollivier (husband of her deceased sister Blandine), the parliamentary leader of an ultra-nationalistic, sabre-rattling party which had done so much to plunge France into war. All of Wagner's Francophobic resentments, the bitter fruit of his unhappy years in Paris (where, in 1861, *Tannhäuser* had practically been booed and hissed off the stage of the Paris Opéra), now came pouring out in cascades of condemnation. The French deserved to be chastised for the insolent arrogance they had shown in thinking that they could issue ultimata to the King of Prussia and have him bow and scrape before them like a bewigged Versailles lackey. Everything about this foppish Gallic race was degenerate. They gave themselves grand airs, they took it for granted that French language and culture were superior to all others, they talked endlessly of *la gloire* – the bygone 'glory' of Louis XIV and Napoleon. Like the Bavarians, who at least had had the good sense to join the Prussians in this righteous, 'cleansing' war – cleansing because it promised to rouse the sluggish Germans from their provincial torpor – the French had been thoroughly corrupted by the Jesuits. They were a race of mendacious hypocrites, ever ready to accuse others of dishonesty in order to cover up their own talents for scheming and dissembling, etc., etc.

Nietzsche, to judge by Cosima's terse diary notations, kept his opinions to himself. Unlike Wagner, he had never been to France, nor was he as familiar with French literature and culture as was Cosima, who, though born in Italy, had been brought up in Paris. With their contention that the French were a decadent people, compared to the less united but also less corrupted Germans, he was prepared to agree. But that there was a strained tendentiousness in their anti-Gallic vehemence must have become apparent to him in the evening, when, to their considerable embarrassment, Cosima and Wagner had to play host to three of his most fervent French admirers: the young Judith Mendès, a bubbling, blonde beauty who had inherited her father Théophile Gautier's poetic volubility; her more discreet husband, the writer Catulle Mendès; and their inseparable travelling companion, an effete specimen of French nobility named Jean-Marie Villiers de l'Isle-Adam, whose rhetorical verse plays Richard Wagner could not endure. The three ardent Wagnerophiles had recently travelled to Munich, where they were deterred in extremis from attending the *Walküre* rehearsals by the threat of instant excommunication from the Master, who regarded any encouragement given to this 'misbegotten' enterprise as tantamount to high treason.

The next morning Nietzsche once again had Cosima to himself – until Wagner appeared with some manuscript pages of his Beethoven essay, which he read aloud to both of them. After lunch Nietzsche and Wagner's young protégé, Hans Richter, walked down to the boat-shed and rowed across the intervening stretch of water to the villa where Elisabeth was staying. They then rowed her back to the Tribschen promontory, where she was introduced to the Master and Mistress of the House. The visit went off without a hitch. Elisabeth struck Cosima as being a 'nice, modest girl', while Fritz's sister found Richard Wagner and the Baroness 'delightful' and the four girls, and particularly the one-year-old Siegfried, 'fascinating'.

The next morning Nietzsche took leave of his kind hosts. Not knowing what to do next, he had agreed to spend the rest of his midsummer holiday with his sister in the Maderanerthal, a valley full of romantic rocks and waterfalls, hemmed in one one side by the Grosse Windgälle and on the other by the 10,000-ft-high Oberalpstock, some distance to the south and east of the lake. Here, at an altitude of 1,300 metres and in a hostelry boasting the robust name of Alpenklub, Nietzsche found the inspiration he needed to undertake an analytical description of the 'Dionysian *Weltanschauung*' – a first draft version of what became the first two sections of *The Birth of Tragedy*.

Among the other clients of the Alpenklub was a Hamburg landscape painter named Adolf Mosengel, who had also come to this cascade- and cliff-filled valley in search of inspiration. He too was conscience-stricken by the thought that he was sitting out the war while the students at Kiel and other German universities were volunteering in droves for military service. On 6 August news reached them that German troops had scored a major victory over the French at Weissenburg, in Alsace.

Two days later Nietzsche wrote to Wilhelm Vischer in Basel asking the city's education board to grant him leave of absence for the second half of the summer semester, to enable him, as he put it rather pompously, to fling the 'tiny mite' of his personal capacities into the 'donations-box of the Fatherland', thereby accomplishing his German duty. Cosima immediately wrote him a letter of sensible remonstrance. Present-day Germany was not, as in 1813, overrun or threatened by a French invasion. His dilettantish exertions as a carer of the sick and wounded would probably bring less practical relief than hundreds of cigars. 'You are a scholar,' she reminded Nietzsche, 'and it seems to me that this you must remain as long as it is not a disgrace to be a scholar, that is until our dear land is threatened . . . '

Nietzsche, however, was in no mood to heed sound advice. On 10 August he and his sister left the romantic Maderanerthal and returned to Basel, where they learned that the city's education board had granted Nietzsche's request for temporary leave of absence, provided that he restrict his participation in the war to medical care for the wounded. Fritz and his sister then travelled eastward to Lindau, on the northern (German) shore of Lake Constance. Here they found the painter Mosengel, who had decided to join an excellent *Felddiakonie* (auxiliary medical unit) which had been improvised by the University of Erlangen's Faculty of Medicine. Most of the volunteer assistants were students from other faculties and thus inexperienced neophytes, like Nietzsche and Mosengel. The latter, as 'out-of-towners', were lodged at a Hôtel Wallfisch, but otherwise their treatment was the same. They were assigned to a clinic full of wounded Prussian and French soldiers, where they learned how to administer chloroform for operations, paint and bandage wounds, and accomplish other rudimentary tasks of bedside care.

On 22 August the professor-doctor in charge of the clinic left for Saarbrücken with fifteen assistants. Other *Felddiakonie* teams, led by professor-doctors or qualified medical students, had already been dispatched to various military units in the west. But everything had been improvised in such haste that they had been sent ahead without the financial means to support themselves in the field. Nietzsche and Mosengel were accordingly instructed to catch up with these different teams and to distribute badly needed funds and letters recently received from home. This proved to be an impossible assignment, so rapid had been the German advance into Alsace. From Karlsruhe the two 'paymasters' were sent forward to Weissenburg, site of the first big Prussian victory, and from there they were forced to hike for eleven tiring hours to the battlefield of Wörth, still nauseatingly strewn with hundreds of decomposing corpses.

In each Alsatian village, houses had been requisitioned and turned into *Lazarethen* (camp hospitals), but the care provided for the sick and wounded was primitive in the extreme. Though German-speaking, the peasant population seemed more sullen than elated over their recent 'liberation'; but their ill-feigned hostility was cowed by the strictness of the curfew and martial law ordinances, the slightest infringement of which was punished by execution before a Prussian firing-squad.

From Haguenau for some miles south there were no further signs of combat, but at Bisweiler, where Nietzsche and Mosengel spent nine cold hours in a railroad cattle-car, they and the Prussian cavalrymen who were travelling with their horses in the same goods-train saw tongues of fire and billowing columns of smoke on the horizon – rising from beleaguered Strasbourg.

Their progress from this point on was relatively swift and uneventful. On 30 August their goods-train reached the famous porcelain-manufacturing centre of Lunéville, and two days later they caught up with the headquarters of the Prussian Southern Army, now established in the Lorraine capital of Nancy.

Nietzsche, throughout this period, had been sending back reports to Tribschen describing the harrowing scenes he had witnessed. On 2 September – the day on which Napoleon III and the besieged French army surrendered to the Prussians at Sédan – Cosima wrote to Nietzsche in Nancy to say that she and Richard Wagner had been married on 25 August in Lucerne and that their son, Siegfried Richard, could now be formally baptized under his father's name. On the day the letter was sent, Nietzsche and Adolf Mosengel were dispatched northwards to a little town near Metz. Here Nietzsche ran into a colleague from Basel University who had volunteered for service as a medical assistant. A goods-train filled with wounded soldiers was about to leave for Karlsruhe, and since they were desperately short-handed, he asked Nietzsche and his painter friend to accompany them. Mosengel was given five soldiers to look after, Nietzsche, in another straw-carpeted cattle-car, had to care for six. All were serious cases, with fractured bones and festering wounds. All of them, moreover, suffered from dysentery, and two of them were already in the throes of diphtheria. To keep them from being soaked by the pouring rain outside, the doors of the cattle-car had to be kept shut. The stench was revolting.

For three hellish days and nights, during which he hardly slept a wink, Nietzsche had to feed and water his groaning charges, unbandage and rebandage their wounds, and try to relieve their suffering as best he could. At Karlsruhe the wounded soldiers were unloaded on to stretchers and carted off to a field hospital. Nietzsche by this time was so ill and exhausted that he could barely make it back by train to Erlangen, where he and Mosengel had to report to their superiors. An examining physician found that Nietzsche in his turn had contracted diphtheria as well as dysentery. He was consigned to his bed at the Hôtel Wallfisch, and for the next two weeks Mosengel looked after him, gradually nursing him back to health with opium, tannin and other enema ablutions.

By 19 September Fritz had sufficiently recovered his strength to be able to return to his home in Naumburg. He felt frustrated, as a former cannoneer, to have contributed so little to the German victories in the field. As he remarked in a letter to Friedrich Ritschl, 'If I had been with my battery, I would have participated practically and perhaps even passively in the great days of Rézonville, Sedan, and Laon. But my hands were tied by my Swiss neutrality.' Warfare, as he had learned the hard way, was as full of paradoxes as peace, and what he had seen of it 'in the rear' was not only less heroic but even more gruesome than what he would have experienced at the front.

## CHAPTER 14

# Wild Hopes and Fantasies

*– But it is still better to be foolish from happiness than foolish from unhappiness; better to dance ponderously than to walk lamely.*

On 21 October, six days after his twenty-sixth birthday, Fritz said goodbye to his mother, his sister and his Naumburg friends and dutifully returned to Basel – another harrowing train-trip marked by recurring fits of vomiting. He continued to be plagued by post-dysentery upsets during the next couple of weeks, largely taken up with the correction of his *Pädagogium* students' end-of-term exam papers. This tiresome chore completed, he had to prepare his lecture courses for the next university semester. The first, devoted to Hesiod's *Days*, required little work. Far more innovative (in challenging accepted theories) was his second lecture course – devoted to the metric schemes employed by the epic and lyric poets of ancient Greece. He was very disappointed, therefore, when he discovered that, whereas the routine course on Hesiod could attract eleven students, the more interesting course on ancient Greek versification interested only five.

Once again he was having to make a radical revision of his ideas and was finding it a painful process. In Bonn he had joined a fraternity in the hope that he could recapture the spirit of heroic idealism that had inspired the *Burschenschaft* movements during the anti-Napoleonic 'wars of liberation' of 1813–14 – only to discover that the beer-imbibing and song-chanting reality differed radically from his exalted expectations. This time he had plunged into a war against another, far less gifted Napoleon, whose swift collapse had robbed the hostlities of all heroic grandeur. A war fought to unite the disparate German principalities, grand duchies and kingdoms was one thing; but a war of conquest fought to humiliate the French by leaving their country maimed betrayed a warped longing for national revenge, which boded ill for the future.

In late October Nietzsche could still write to Friedrich Ritschl to express his indignation over the prevailing atmosphere in Basel, most of whose leading citizens, though German-speaking, were now emphatically pro-French. But this was the last letter in which such sentiments appeared. Nine days later (7 November) he confided to Carl von Gersdorff, whose 4th Prussian Guards Regiment was now encamped with other German units a few miles to the north-east of Paris, that he regarded contemporary

Prussia as 'a most dangerous power for culture', and Bismarck as a cynical opportunist, ready to 'solve' the thorny problem of religious instruction in the newly conquered provinces of Alsace and Lorraine by soliciting the cooperation of the Pope, the same incorrigible Pio Nono (Pius IX) who had persuaded the recently concluded Vatican Council to approve the dogma of papal infallibility.

Unlike Wagner, Nietzsche had been able to see for himself just how hostile many Alsatians were to the substitution of Prussian for French rule. And what was true of many Alsatians was even truer of the French-speaking inhabitants of eastern Lorraine, which Bismarck, under pressure from the generals of the Prussian General Staff, was now bent on annexing. It was this exorbitant ambition which was needlessly prolonging the war: a war that many moderate French politicians would have been ready to end overnight if offered reasonable terms.

The clearest expression of Nietzsche's misgivings is to be found, curiously enough, in a letter written on 23 November by his friend Carl von Gersdorff, whose Guards unit had now moved to the village of St Brice, north-west of Paris. Gersdorff too had been appalled by the horrors of this war. But throughout he had sought to retain a cool, detached, philosophical view of these turbulent happenings, thanks to several Schopenhauer volumes he had brought along with his military gear. Because of the grievous blows they had suffered and which had helped to sober them up and to shake them out of their 'raving hate-frenzy', the French were now perhaps better prepared to receive the Schopenhauerian gospel than (as Gersdorff put it) 'our victory-drunk Fatherland, where the intoxication of victory does not allow the distress of war to become sufficiently apparent'. Now, as in 1814 and 1815, the German book market was likely to be swamped with 'war stories, regimental histories, battalion narratives, etc.; phrases about Prussia's mission, about Prussia's private God, about the Finger of God in all of its magic omnipresence will blossom forth in all their glory'.

This extraordinarily lucid letter, so different in tone from the chauvinistic hue and cry which the historians Heinrich von Treitschke and Sybel and a large part of the German press had taken up, reached Nietzsche a good two weeks after 26 November, when he made another weekend trip to Tribschen. From Cosima's diary we know that during the Saturday afternoon she (at the piano keyboard) and Hans Richter (playing the viola) offered him some musical entertainment, and that in the evening Richard Wagner regaled them by reading a satirical skit he had written about the French, entitled '*Nicht kapituliert*' (doubtless because the besieged Parisians were still stubbornly holding out and refusing to surrender). Richter, who had been asked to compose the orchestral accompaniment for this club-footed brainchild, had been so embarrassed that he had forthrightly declined the assignment. Nietzsche probably felt the same way, but knowing into what sudden fits of fury Wagner could fly over the slightest criticism, he prudently held his peace.

Two weeks later Nietzsche wrote to his mother and sister to say that his health was better, even though his doctor still found it necessary to paint his throat. In addition to his teaching activities, which consumed fourteen hours of each week, he now had to attend faculty meetings, and even meetings of the university's governing board, which had just elected a new rector (Heusler) and a new secretary – himself. These irksome obligations had, however, one advantage: they offered Nietzsche an inside view of the university's administrative problems. It was thus that he learned, on 12 December or thereabouts, that Gustav Teichmüller, the younger of Basel's two professors of philosophy, was leaving the university at the end of the semester and moving on to Dorpat, in East Prussia.

A day or two later Nietzsche received a particularly gloomy letter from Erwin Rohde, complaining about the petty clique-mindedness and 'scholarly philistinism' of his Kiel University colleagues, about the 'blood and ever more blood' that was being 'heaped up' (in France) in corpse-like mounds of 'distress and misery'. The only solution, as he saw it, was to seek refuge in one's work and stuff one's ears with wax in order not to hear the 'disharmonious howl' of these storm-swept times, when the World Will once again was in 'wrathful motion'.

This letter, a bleak specimen of Schopenhauerian moodiness, elicited a prompt reply from Nietzsche. Their present tribulations were part of that apprenticeship in suffering they would have to endure for another year or two before they could throw over the pedagogical 'yoke' and found a 'new Greek Academy' – along the lines of Wagner's Bayreuth project. Indeed, Fritz was already preparing a 'great *adhortatio*' for all those souls who were not completely smothered and swallowed up in this *Jetztzeit* ('now-time') infatuation: a favourite Schopenhauer term which Richard Wagner liked to brandish every time he was irritated by the trivial 'mediocrity' of the present age.

What Nietzsche had in mind was the kind of cultural 'haven', the kind of 'enchanted Island of the Muses' that Wagner now envisaged for Bayreuth, and which, as a starter, could be established in Basel. All this, Fritz assured his doleful friend, was no 'eccentric whim'; it was quite simply a necessity. There can be no doubt that he meant it. For, after writing to Rohde, Nietzsche wrote another letter to their friend Heinrich Romundt, the frustrated playwright-turned-philologist who had vainly tried to found a local Schopenhauerian society during his final year at

Leipzig. After graduating from the university, he had landed a job tutoring the refractory son of a professor of physiology. Nietzsche now suggested that Romundt give up this demeaning job and come to Basel to teach philosophy – first as a *Privatdozent* (unpaid instructor-tutor) and later, after passing the exams, as a fully-fledged university lecturer.

When Nietzsche left Basel for Tribschen on Christmas Eve, it was in a mood of soaring expectations. Wagner had sent him a last-minute telegram inviting him to attend the final rehearsal of a 'Tribschen Symphony', scheduled for 3 p.m. on this Saturday, 24 December, at the Hôtel du Lac, in Lucerne. Unknown to Cosima, fifteen instrumentalists had been rounded up by Wagner's protégé Hans Richter, and had been given two initial rehearsals in Zürich. But this time the Master himself was going to put them through their paces. Nietzsche was thus being admitted as a privileged spectator into the very workshop of genius.

Cosima, who had been kept in the dark about these doings, was not inordinately surprised to see Nietzsche turn up around five o'clock in the same sleigh as her husband. This time the house-guest's gifts, presented that same evening after the Christmas-tree candles had been lit, were an Albrecht Dürer engraving (*Knight, Death, and Devil*) for Wagner, and for Cosima a carefully transcribed copy of Nietzsche's latest meditations, '*Die Entstehung des tragischen Gedankens*' ('The Genesis of Tragic Thought').

Because of the continuing war in France, Cosima and Richard Wagner had agreed not to give each other Christmas presents and to reserve their 'donations' for suffering soldiers and more particularly for the wounded in the field. Cosima's surprise was thus total when, around half past seven the following morning, she was awoken by the soft, insistent, slowly welling sound of music – and what music! – coming, it soon dawned on her, not from some enchanted dreamland but from the landing, staircase and vestibule of the Tribschen house, where had been posted the fifteen instrumentalists from Zürich and the fair-haired Hans Richter, who had been learning to play the trumpet in order to be able, when the crucial moment came, to blare forth the robust *Siegfried* theme. What Cosima was hearing was the private première of the *Tribschen Idyll* (known to us now as the *Siegfried Idyll*), a musical love-poem into which Wagner had woven all sorts of highly personal allusions to his and Cosima's six-year-old romance.

The surprise concert concluded, Cosima's five children crowded into her bedroom to wish her a happy birthday, followed by Wagner, who handed her the score of his 'Symphonic Birthday Greeting'. Nietzsche, who had been watching and listening down below in the vestibule, missed this moving scene, but he was again a privileged spectator when the *Idyll*

– already dubbed '*Treppenmusik*' ('Staircase music') by the children – was replayed in the drawing-room.

The next evening, after the players had packed up their instruments and left, Wagner entertained the assembled company by reading extracts from Nietzsche's Christmas present to Cosima, 'The Genesis of Tragic Thought'. Nietzsche had set out to explain why Goethe and Lessing, ardent Hellenophiles though they were, had never properly understood the Greeks and their culture; they had appreciated the Apollinian aspect, as exemplified in the narrative epic, where events were externally described, but they had overlooked the deeper Dionysian impulse in Greek culture: the recurrently felt need to lose oneself in the mysterious, sub-rational flux of life, a need that could only truly be satisfied in dance and music. Although Wagner was by now familiar with these two antipodal terms – in his public lecture on 'Socrates and Tragedy' Nietzsche had already described the great dialectician as being the embodiment of 'Apollinian clarity' – he had never seen or heard the distinction between the Apollinian and the Dionysian so sharply drawn as a kind of epic struggle between two antagonistic propensities. The distinction struck him as being so profound and enlightening that in early January, after his house-guest had returned to Basel, he spent several days elaborating on it in conversations with Cosima – Goethe, for example, in creating the characters of Faust and Mephistopheles, clearly had a Dionysian streak in him, whereas Schiller was a pure Apollinian, etc. Indeed, he declared, apart from the historian Constantin Frantz (who had opened his eyes to the true, profound nature of German culture), Nietzsche was the only living person who had contributed a positive enrichment to his views on life and art.

Nietzsche's return, after these happy Christmas holidays, to the pedagogical 'servitude' of Basel was more than usually dismal. The first blow to his soaring hopes was delivered on 29 December by Erwin Rohde, who in another gloomy letter doubted his capacity and even his 'right' to abandon his university post and bid farewell to classical philology. The second blow to Nietzsche's hopes was delivered one day later by a friend and former colleague, Gustav Schönberg, who wrote from Freiburg to say that Professor Jonas, at Stettin, on whom they had pinned high hopes as a fellow Schopenhauerian, was not a candidate for Teichmüller's professorship at Basel. The third and final blow came from Heinrich Romundt who, in a long, hand-wringing letter written on the first day of the New Year (1871), went to tortuous lengths to explain why, though he had been reading Berkeley and Hume as well as Kant and Schopenhauer, he just didn't feel himself sufficiently prepared to move to Basel and set himself up as a *Privatdozent* in philosophy.

The three negative responses, added to the feeling of abysmal let-down he experienced each time he returned from the euphoric heights of Tribschen to the classroom drudgery of Basel, plunged Nietzsche into a state of deep depression, finally culminating in a nervous breakdown. On or around 21 January, after three weeks of silence, he informed his worried mother that he was suffering from stomach upsets, sleepless nights, too little exercise, severe eye-strain and 'intolerable weather'. He was overworked, he felt at times completely fed up with the 'whole professorial business', he was frustrated by the feeling that the best years of his life were being consumed in 'excessive school-mastering'.

While all this was true, it was only part of the truth. The rest of it was revealed a few days later in a letter addressed to Wilhelm Vischer, in which he said that his doctors had diagnosed his ill-health as being due to overwork. He himself had begun to wonder why this kind of strain manifested itself regularly in the middle of each semester, and the conclusion he had reached was that it was due to the inner conflict that kept arising between his teaching duties and his personal desire to concentrate on certain philosophical problems and to think them through to comprehensive solutions. 'This juxtaposition of *Pädagogium* and University is one I can hardly endure in the long run because I feel that my real task, my philosophical task, to which if necessary I must *sacrifice every profession*, suffers and is indeed degraded to the status of a secondary activity.' Then came the crucial sentence in this letter, set apart, like a paragraph, from the rest: 'With this in mind I take the liberty of asking you to grant to me the *philosophical professorship* which is being vacated by Teichmüller's departure.'

What Nietzsche was proposing, as he went on to explain, was in effect a double operation. While he took over Teichmüller's chair of philosophy, Erwin Rohde – the most qualified of the young philologists he had come to know and potentially a 'real ornament' to any university faculty – should be summoned from Kiel to take over his own professorship of classical philology.

That there was something outlandish in this extraordinary proposition, Nietzsche must have realized even as he was drafting the letter. For while it was true, as he took pains to point out, that he had a thorough knowledge of Plato and Aristotle and had even proposed a lecture course devoted to Greece's pre-Platonic thinkers, he had never specialized in philosophy, still less written a doctoral dissertation on some philosophical subject. His claim to have studied Kant and Schopenhauer 'with special predilection' meant little, while the only sponsors he could name as being able to vouch for his intense interest in philosophical investigations must have caused Vischer to shake his head in wonderment. The first was

Erwin Rohde, who had met Vischer during his two-week stay in Basel the previous May and June. But he was no more an authority in the field of philosophy than was Nietzsche's second sponsor: an admirably good-natured and good-neighbourly scholar named Franz Overbeck who had come to Basel the previous semester, had found lodgings in the same house at 45 Schützengraben, and had so disarmed the often reclusive Nietzsche that they now regularly took their evening meals together. Although his rising forehead, calm manner and thoughtful air were made to inspire confidence, the thirty-three-year-old professor of critical theology was far too modest to make any claim to philosophical omniscience, nor had he bothered during his six years at Jena to attend many of Professor Kuno Fischer's scintillating lectures on the history of philosophy.

Nietzsche's agonized despondency had, by late January, plumbed an absolutely shattering depth. On 6 February he informed his mother that his state of ill-health, now marked by dreadful insomnia, stomach, intestinal and haemorrhoidal pains, had so deteriorated that the two university doctors who had examined him had put him on a Karlsbad water cure. He needed a change of scene and it was imperative, he wrote, that he leave Basel and seek the 'more southern air' of Italy.

Nietzsche was almost certainly suffering from an ulcerated stomach, brought on by the nervous tension which Wilhelm Vischer's silence (about his request for Teichmüller's philosophical chair) had raised to a peak of intolerable acuteness. His tormented state of mind was clearly reflected in this letter, in which, like a pleading child, he asked if his mother or his sister could accompany him southwards – only to add that he could perfectly well make the trip alone!

Later that same day he sent a terse telegram to his sister: 'Awaiting you here until Thursday, together to Lugano, I unwell. If not, telegraph.' An exchange of letters followed, but Fritz was adamant. His sister had to come and nurse him back to health and keep him company, as she had done the previous summer in the Maderan valley, and that was all there was to it.

The upshot of all this epistolatory and telegraphic wrangling was that an increasingly embittered and insistent Fritz finally got his way. Although the wintry cold in Naumburg had been even fiercer than in Basel, with the thermometer registering -24°C, Lisbeth dutifully boarded the unheated train on Sunday, 12 February, and spent a freezing night and day wrapped in furs and rugs in order to join her sick brother. On Tuesday morning, 14 February, Nietzsche, warmly enveloped in a fur coat Franz Overbeck had kindly lent him, left Basel with his sister. At Lucerne they moved from the train to the little steamboat, which took them down the lake's south-eastern shore to the terminus at Flüelen, where they spent the night. In the same hotel they were introduced to a gentleman with the implausible name of Mr Brown. He was none other than Giuseppe Mazzini, the Italian patriot who had still not abandoned hope, after half a dozen abortive uprisings, of establishing a republican regime in one of the peninsula's city-states.

Two days later they reached Lugano, after a difficult climb in a small horse-drawn sleigh up to the summit of the 6,000-ft high St Gotthard Pass and a perilously rapid descent, around repeated hairpin bends. For most of their stay at the Hôtel du Parc, the garden and terraces were covered with snow, and only too often the glaucous waters of the lake and the grey-white mountainsides were hidden by fog or drizzle.

On 1 March, the day on which the new German Kaiser, Wilhelm I, made his triumphal entry into Paris, Nietzsche reported to his mother that he was glad to be in Lugano, where life was tolerable, whereas in Basel it had become unendurable. His haemorrhoids were better, his intestines were no longer upset, and with time, he hoped, sleep would return.

Once again this was only part of the truth. One of his main reasons for wishing to get away from Basel was to have time to weld the disconnected fragments he had been working on – his two public lectures, the 'Dionysian *Weltanschauung*', 'The Genesis of Tragic Thought', etc. – into a coherent whole, so as to be able to have them quickly published under the title, *The Origin and Aim of Greek Tragedy*. He could thus substantiate his claim to be a bona fide philosopher and reasonably aspire to be Gustav Teichmüller's successor. This desperate gamble was anything but sleep-inducing.

On 2 April – by which time the snows were melting and little snakes and lizards could be seen sunning themselves on the rocky mountain paths – Fritz and his sister said goodbye to Lugano and returned by post-chaise to the Lake of the Four Cantons. Leaving his sister at Weggis, on the southern rim of the Rigi mountain mass, Nietzsche the next morning boarded the 8.15 steamboat and one hour later turned up at Tribschen, looking 'very run down', as Cosima noted in her diary.

Nietzsche's main reason for making this surprise visit was to solicit Richard Wagner's and Cosima's approval for the long 'essay' he had just put together on *The Origin and Aim of Greek Tragedy*. But it was more than a day before he could begin his reading. Wagner had just composed a *Kaisermarsch* to honour Wilhelm I's accession to the imperial throne of the second Germanic *Reich*, as well as a five-stanza poem (praising the German army besieging Paris) which he had sent to Bismarck at Versailles. He had also prepared the text of an address ('On the Destiny of Opera') that he was due to deliver in three weeks' time before the Academy of

Sciences in Berlin, as well as a detailed account of how he proposed to have the four *Ring* operas performed in a gigantic *Bühnenfestspiel* (stage-festival-play). The reading, reciting, singing and playing of these various Wagnerian creations took up a good part of the day. The bombastically pro-German and anti-French tone of the poem can hardly have pleased Nietzsche, but he was thrilled to discover that Wagner had quietly adopted his 'Apollinian-Dionysian' contrasts for his Berlin Academy address. About Wagner's and Cosima's reactions to Nietzsche's own brainchild we know little (from the terse comments in her diary) beyond the fact that the reading took three days, that it seemed commendably full of Wagner's own ideas fashioned into something new, and, when finished, would be dedicated to Richard Wagner.

On Easter Sunday Nietzsche left Tribschen to return to Basel. After two more sleepless nights he learned the bitter truth, probably from the lips of Wilhelm Vischer. Basel's educational authorities had found a suitable occupant for the vacant chair of philosophy in the person of Rudolf Eucken, a former pupil of Teichmüller's who had studied under him at Göttingen before going on to Berlin to receive further instruction from Friedrich Adolf Trendelenburg, the sexagenarian patriarch of Aristotelian studies in Germany. Eucken, furthermore, had written a doctoral dissertation on the use of prepositions in Aristotle's *Metaphysics* – which meant that his credentials were impeccable.

That evening, in writing to Erwin Rohde, Nietzsche made no effort to conceal his disappointment from the friend he felt he had betrayed. 'What idiocies I committed! And how sure I was in all my schemes! I cannot hide behind the bed-screen of my sickly state; obviously it was an idea born of a sleepless night of fever, and with it I thought I had found a healing remedy against sickness and nerves.'

## CHAPTER 15

# *The Birth of Tragedy*

*– A people – as for that matter an individual – is to be valued only to the extent that it is able to impose the stamp of eternity on its experiences.*

To lighten Nietzsche's academic burden, the university authorities agreed to limit his schedule for the next semester to a single lecture course and a seminar. The seminar included selected readings and exercises in Greek and Latin authors, while the three-hours-per-week lecture course was boldly devoted to an exposition of Nietzsche's ideas as to what the science of philology should be. The preparation of this latter course consumed only part of the three weeks that were still left before the start of the new semester on 1 May 1871, giving him time to complete the text on which he had worked in Lugano.

On 20 April Nietzsche sent the opening section of the manuscript, now entitled *Music and Tragedy*, to a Leipzig printer, Wilhelm Engelmann. His purpose, as he made clear in the accompanying letter, was to explain the origins of Greek tragedy in an entirely new and non-philological manner, and more specifically to 'elucidate Richard Wagner, the strange enigma of our present time, in his relationship to Greek tragedy'. The letter, like the manuscript, elicited no response. They had reached Leipzig during a book fair and were allowed to gather dust while Engelmann busied himself with more urgent matters.

Being kept on tenterhooks like this did nothing to improve Nietzsche's precarious state of health. Although the haemorrhoids and the gastric spasms gradually disappeared, he continued to be plagued by insomnia, which the comforting presence of his sister and the kind-hearted Franz Overbeck could not allay. His thoughts, more than ever, were concentrated on Richard Wagner and the one-month tour of German cities that he and Cosima had begun in mid-April and which took them as far as Berlin, where Wagner read his paper to members of the Academy and had a private talk with Bismarck.

On 15 May he and Cosima turned up in Basel, where Nietzsche and Wagner's nephew, Friedrich Brockhaus (now a professor of law at the university), were invited to spend the evening with them. The trip, they were informed, had been a great success, even though an on-the-spot inspection had revealed that the Bayreuth theatre, with its pretty *amoretti* and numerous rococo shells, was too much of an eighteenth-century extravaganza to suit Wagner's requirements – which meant that a new opera house would have to be built from scratch. The cost of constructing such a theatre was likely to reach the astronomical sum of 300,000 thalers – twelve times more than the 25,000 thalers that King Ludwig of Bavaria had reluctantly agreed to contribute. To raise the balance, an undaunted Richard Wagner and his influential Berlin friends had decided to form a nationwide society of patrons, each of whom agreed to purchase a *Patronatschein* (sponsor's certificate) for 300 thalers.

One week after this stimulating evening Wilhelm Vischer invited Nietzsche to accompany him to Lucerne to attend a teachers' conference. The date being 22 May, Nietzsche excused himself during the afternoon and made a quick trip to Tribschen to congratulate Richard Wagner on the occasion of his fifty-eighth birthday. The visitor was offered a re-enactment of that morning's birthday surprise: a carefully composed family tableau in which the children and Cosima assumed theatric poses around the bust of the Master and the statuettes of Wagner opera heroes, which had been arrayed around in the drawing-room. Nietzsche returned the compliment by informing his hosts that he was planning to found a 'Reformation-Journal' aimed at promoting the 'Art of the Future' and the Bayreuth scheme.

Two days later the 'Professor', as Cosima Wagner usually referred to him in her diary, made a second visit to Tribschen. Wagner this time accompanied him to the railway station, and before they parted he insisted that Nietzsche return the following Saturday (27 May) with his sister for the three-day Whitsun holiday. By this time, however, the hypersensitive Fritz was seriously upset by the bloody turmoil in Paris, where a band of revolutionary 'patriots', outraged by Adolfe Thiers's and his bourgeois government's meek acceptance of Bismarck's peace terms, had occupied the city hall and many other public buildings. The *Communards* – a mixed crew of republican extremists, Proudhon anarchists, Blanqui egalitarians and followers of Karl Marx's First International – had chosen this inopportune moment to establish a new proletarian régime, even more radical than the one that Danton, Robespierre and Marat had set out to establish in the early 1790s. Two French generals had been shot, the archbishop of Paris and scores of priests and other prominent figures had been seized as hostages, a Committee of Public Safety had been formed to mete out exemplary 'justice' to the 'enemies of the people', and on 16 May a gang of revolutionary hotheads had brought the Napoleonic Victory Column crashing down on to the pavement of the Place Vendôme in a fanatical attempt to expunge the memory of the country's pernicious imperial past. While the Prussians and other German forces, who had surrounded the capital with an iron ring of guns and bayonets, maintained a watchful neutrality, French army regulars loyal to the Thiers government in Versailles were sent in to put an end to the orgy of looting and vengeful destruction. It seemed, from newspaper reports reaching Basel, as though all of Paris was on fire, as the furious revolutionaries put the torch to buildings they were forced to evacuate. The Palace of the Legion of Honour, Richelieu's Palais-Royal, the Tuileries Palace, which both Napoleons had made their official Paris residence, had all been gutted, and now came the news that the Louvre, with its priceless library and art collections, was ablaze. Paris was going up in smoke, in a self-inflicted conflagration as senseless and destructive as that of Nero's Rome.

The news left Nietzsche absolutely shattered. 'What does it mean to be a scholar, over and against such an earthquake of culture!' he wrote on 27 May in a pathetic letter to Wilhelm Vischer. 'How atomically minute one feels! One employs one's entire life and the best of one's strength, the better to understand and the better to explain a period of culture: how does this vocation look when a single, wretched day is enough to reduce the most precious documents of such periods to ashes? This is the worst day of my life.'

At noon of this same Saturday Friedrich Brockhaus turned up at Tribschen alone. Poor Nietzsche, he informed his uncle, was crushed by the dreadful news from Paris and was feeling so rotten that he was staying behind in Basel. Determined to shake him out of his depression, Wagner went to the Lucerne post office and sent off a two-sentence telegram enjoining Nietzsche to keep his recent promise or risk offending the entire family.

This imperious summons from the 'Emperor' of the Tribschen household had the desired effect. The next day Fritz and his sister Elisabeth turned up in time for the Whit Sunday lunch. Wagner took him to task for getting so needlessly worked up over the burning of all those buildings and art treasures in Paris, which, though damaged or destroyed, could be rebuilt or replaced. He added, 'If you are not capable of painting pictures again, you are not worthy of possessing them.' The latest turn of events had confirmed Wagner in his conviction that the less emotive but profounder Germans were superior to the French

Fritz and his sister had meanwhile discovered a little hotel at Gimmelwald, a remote village high up in the foothills of the Jungfrau, where they could spend the mid-July summer recess for the modest price of 4 Swiss francs a day for room and board. Here they were joined by Fritz's old Pforta friend, Carl von Gersdorff, who had recently been most honourably released from his Prussian Guards unit with the rank of reserve lieutenant and as a Knight of the Order of the Iron Cross.

During the two weeks spent in the 'sublime mountain wilderness' of

Gimmelwald, Fritz received a letter from Heinrich Romundt in Leipzig, informing him that he had retrieved Nietzsche's manuscript from the still undecided publisher, Engelmann. The text had created a sensation with all (including Ritschl) who had read it. However, there was a general feeling that the basic distinction Nietzsche had tried to draw between the Apollinian and Dionysian aspects of human life had not been properly developed. This helpful criticism may well have precipitated a meteoric 'shower of illuminating thoughts' of a kind Nietzsche despaired of experiencing in the Basel 'lowlands'. The crisp mountain air was also a wonderful tonic for his nerves. So too was the prospect of being able to introduce his friend Carl to Richard Wagner, who had kindly made free tickets available to him for performances of *Die Meistersinger* in Berlin. On 30 July the two friends turned up at Tribschen, where Gersdorff made a most favourable impression, exhibiting (as Cosima noted that evening in her diary) 'all the noble and earnest characteristics of the North German'.

The next three days were spent in pleasant boat-trips on the lake, walks with the children through the nearby woods, and long conversations about the 'Art of the Future' and Bayreuth. Nietzsche once again struck Cosima as being the 'most gifted of our young friends', but this time she noted in her diary that 'a not quite natural reserve makes his behaviour in many respects most displeasing. It is as if he were trying to resist the overwhelming effect of Wagner's personality.' For one who had long since subordinated her entire life and being to the care and cult of this temperamental demigod, the slightest sign of reticence smacked of heresy.

Seven weeks later Nietzsche took the night train to Frankfurt, where he picked up his sister Elisabeth, and on 28 September they were reunited with their mother in Naumburg. The three-week holiday that followed was a particularly happy one, even though Elisabeth now found her home town terribly provincial compared to the 'merry' city of Basel, to many of whose patrician-professorial homes she had been granted privileged access thanks to her brother's university position.

During the second week of October Fritz went to Leipzig, where he was joined by Erwin Rohde and Carl von Gersdorff, who made the trip from faraway Kiel and less distant Berlin for this *réunion à trois*. The annual trade fair was in full swing and the city was overflowing with commercial travellers, but nothing could temper their juvenile delight in being able once again to frequent Mahn's restaurant and the Kintschy café, and to have themselves photographed in a state of sagging ebriety.

Nietzsche returned to Basel in unusually high spirits. The most important thing in life was to remain faithful, come what may, to a lofty ideal, and, as Goethe had put it:

*im Ganzen, Guten, Schönen*
*resolut zu leben.*

(to live resolutely in the Whole,
the Good, the Beautiful).

For the past twelvemonth the daemons – the spirits presiding over their respective destinies – had repeatedly thwarted their plans and expectations, but there was no reason to be daunted by their persistent malice. Gersdorff and Rohde, to whom Nietzsche wrote shortly before his departure from Naumburg, were accordingly exhorted, at the solemn stroke of ten o'clock the next Monday evening (23 October), to empty half a glass of red wine and then, with a cry of '*Khairete Daimones!*' ('Spirits, hail!'), to toss the rest of the precious liquid 'into the black night'.

The triangular oath seems to have been executed, more or less simultaneously, in the three geographic points of Kiel, Berlin and Basel. Erwin Rohde, having no open window through which to heave his half-glass of wine, propitiated the 'deities' in Jesuitical fashion by surreptitiously spilling some of it out under his tavern table. Gersdorff's performance left even more to be desired; finding himself at the appointed hour short of red wine, the former Guards officer and presently reluctant lawyer popped the corks from several beer bottles, much of whose foaming contents spilled out on to his study floor before he could wet the pavement of the Alexandrinenstrasse. Nietzsche, better prepared for the solemn moment, hied himself to the house of the fifty-three-year-old historian Jacob Burckhardt, who must have been a bit startled to find himself invited to take part in such a demon-appeasing rite. In earlier centuries, he pointed out, emptying a glass of wine out into a Basel street could have led to prompt arrest for indulgence in 'sorcery'. This being a less stringent age, Burckhardt good-naturedly agreed to empty a beer-glass full of Rhône wine into the street below, to the Dionysian cry of, '*Khairete Daimones!*'

The toasted spirits lost no time responding. An hour and a half later, when a less than sober Nietzsche returned to his house on the tree-lined Schützengraben, he found a shadowy figure waiting for him by the garden gate. It was Paul Deussen, whom he had not seen since the day they had said goodbye to each other on the Bonn dockside six years before. Deussen had obtained a brief leave of absence from his *Gymnasium* teaching post at Marburg to pay a quick visit to Montreux, where a wealthy Russian lady (recommended by Nietzsche) was looking for someone to tutor her thirteen-year-old son in Latin, English and German. Delighted though he was to see him, Nietzsche, who was in a 'fiery' state of wine-induced intoxication, could not understand why his former Pforta schoolmate should be in such an absurd rush to return to his pedagogical 'yoke' and so loath to telegraph some ingenious excuse to his high-school superiors in Marburg to justify an additional day of truancy. In a vain effort to undermine Deussen's sense of magisterial duty, he spent several ghostly hours walking him back to his hotel through a circuitous succession of dark, gaslamp and moonlit streets.

The episode offers one more illustration of Nietzsche's bristling rebelliousness against the constraints of academic life – which for the first part of this winter semester he seems to have found reasonably tolerable, probably because of his success in persuading six university students to follow his three-lectures-a-week course on Plato's dialogues. His morale was also given a big lift in mid-November when he learned that someone at last seemed prepared to publish his little book, now titled *Die Geburt der Tragödie* (*The Birth of Tragedy*), with the explanatory subtitle, *Aus dem Geiste der Musik* (*Out of the Spirit of Music*). During the jolly week they had spent in Leipzig, Gersdorff, Rohde and Nietzsche had called on Ernst Wilhelm Fritzsch, the owner of a musical weekly who had published a number of Wagner's pamphlets and who was now bringing out an edition of the composer's *Collected* (prose and poetry) *Works*. Fritzsch was frankly baffled by the manuscript pages Nietzsche entrusted to his care. Knowing next to nothing about classical philology, he turned the pages over to an associate, who helped him edit the *Musikalisches Wochenblatt*. There things might have remained, more or less dormant, had Wagner, at Nietzsche's request, not written Fritzsch a strong letter of recommendation.

On 18 November Nietzsche received word from Fritzsch that he was willing to publish his text and could even have it ready by Christmas, provided he received the rest of the manuscript without delay. Nietzsche, however, had decided to add ten new sections to the text, in order to expand the Apollinian-Dionysian and pseudo-Schopenhauerian analysis of the development and decline of ancient Greek dramatic art, applying it to modern times and, more specifically, to the 'serious German problem' posed by Wagner's conception of what operatic art should be. Not until the second week of December could Nietzsche send off the many added pages – too late to have the book printed and ready to be presented to Richard Wagner as a Christmas gift.

Wagner and Cosima were meanwhile pursuing their ambitious project. To galvanize the Wagner Clubs that had sprung up in a score of German cities, an enterprising music dealer named Emil Heckel had volunteered to organize a special Wagner concert series in Mannheim, which the Master was to conduct in person. On 9 December Wagner was forced to leave Tribschen and make another urgent trip to Munich and Bayreuth. Cosima, after writing three times to Nietzsche in the hope that he could accompany her to Mannheim, sent him a last-minute telegram on 16 December, asking him to join her that evening in Basel. Cosima's diary indicates that she turned up in Basel at 9 p.m. and spent that evening with Nietzsche and Wagner's nephew, Friedrich Brockhaus. The next day, Sunday the 17th, she continued her train-trip to Mannheim. On Monday she watched Wagner rehearse the overture to Mozart's *Magic Flute* and Beethoven's 7th Symphony. The 'indescribable impression' made on her by the two performances was, however, spoiled by the appearance in her theatre box of Alexander Serov's widow (the 'hideous-as-night' apostle of feminine 'emancipation'). The next entry in Cosima's diary reads: 'Tears that our communion in music can be disturbed by such ugly faces! Arrival of Prof. Nietzsche, who has literally run away from Basel.'

After completing his Monday morning lectures and classroom work Nietzsche had surreptitiously left Basel, probably with the connivance of Franz Overbeck, who was instructed to explain that his colleague had suddenly fallen ill. One thing is certain: he was in Mannheim for the two climactic days of Tuesday, 19 December, when he watched Wagner rehearse the overtures to *Lohengrin*, *Tristan und Isolde* and *Die Meistersinger*, and Wednesday the 20th, when he attended a morning rehearsal of the *Idyll*, the gala 6 p.m. concert, and the subsequent banquet given in Richard Wagner's honour. Nietzsche was given a room not far from the Wagners' suite, on the same first floor of the Europäischer Hof, he was introduced to Wagner's friends and relatives, as well as to local dignitaries, and he was treated throughout as a musical connoisseur and one of the Master's most respected devotees. No wonder he later resorted to superlatives in evoking those two glorious days, compared to which, as he wrote to Erwin Rohde, all previous musical experiences paled into insignificance.

Just how Nietzsche managed to explain his sudden two-day absence to his Basel University colleagues, we do not know. But on Thursday evening (21 December) he and Friedrich Brockhaus joined Cosima and Richard Wagner for dinner during their brief stopover in Basel. Wagner, able to relax at last after three nerve-racking days, gave his guests a spirited account of how, in Bayreuth, the municipal authorities had offered him gratis a plot of ground for the construction of the new festival opera house and had renamed it '*Richardshöhe*' (Richard's Heights) in his honour. A new date had been set for the laying of the foundation stone – 22 May 1872 – chosen to coincide with the composer's fifty-ninth birthday.

Nietzsche was warmly pressed to join them once again at Tribschen for the Christmas holidays, but he declined the invitation, saying that he had to remain in Basel to 'collect his thoughts' and to prepare six public lectures on the urgently needed reform of German educational institutions, which he intended to deliver early on in the New Year.

There was another reason. He wanted to surprise Cosima with a combined birthday and Christmas gift: a four-handed piano composition entitled 'New Year's Eve Echo, with procession-chant, peasant dance and midnight bells', which he had been inspired to write, in a moment of 'Dionysian' exaltation, by the example of his Naumburg friend Gustav Krug, who had not allowed his mind-numbing law studies to stifle his love of musical composition. Nietzsche's *Nachklang einer Silvesternacht*, which he and Franz Overbeck had been practising for some weeks on his little piano, had to be copied out twice – one copy being destined for his mother and sister in Naumburg, while the other went to Tribschen. This second copy was delivered to Cosima on Christmas Day, along with a 'fine' letter from its author-composer. To judge by the terse mention in her diary, the surprised recipient was more pleased by the letter than by the long composition (which, properly played, lasted twenty minutes), even though she graciously wrote, on New Year's Eve, to thank the friendly '*mélomane*' (music-lover) and to say how much his presence had been missed around the Christmas tree at Tribschen.

A nagging uncertainty as to just how this birthday gift was going to be received added to authorial jitters about his friends' reaction to his firstborn book, brought on another spell of nervous stomach upsets in early January 1872. Nietzsche's publisher, Ernst Wilhelm Fritzsch, had prudently decided to limit the first print-run of *The Birth of Tragedy* to 800 copies. A first batch of printed copies, including five that Nietzsche had had printed on fine-vellum paper, reached Basel on 29 December. Two of the fine-vellum copies, destined for Wagner and Cosima, were immediately taken to a workshop to be given de luxe bindings, while a third copy was sent ahead to Tribschen with an apologetic letter, addressed to Richard Wagner, in which Nietzsche said that every page of the book bespoke his gratitude to the Master.

Letter and book reached Tribschen on the morning of 3 January 1872. By noon of that day Wagner had already read the Preface and the first sections with intense admiration. He told Cosima how pleased he was to have lived long enough to be able to read such a book, adding that in his estimation of human beings Nietzsche came immediately after Cosima and before the painter Franz von Lenbach, who had just completed two more portraits – one of Franz Liszt, the other of Wagner himself – for Tribschen's Gallery of Great Men. Cosima, Wagner informed her, was his priestess of Apollo: she represented the Apollinian element, he the Dionysian, but they had made a pact, and from it had sprung Fidi (their son, Siegfried). Indeed, so stimulated was he by Nietzsche's text that in the afternoon he shut himself into his Green Room and began to work on the third act of *Götterdämmerung*, causing Cosima to write in her diary that this 3 January was a 'thrice-blessed day'.

That evening Balzac and Jacob Grimm, who had recently provided the material for the out-loud reading sessions, were pushed aside to make way for *The Birth of Tragedy*. Increasingly taken by the text, Wagner wondered how the arbiters of contemporary taste in Germany were going to react to this 'splendid' book; but on the basis of what he had read, he was now determined to establish a journal in Bayreuth and to have Nietzsche edit it.

Both Richard and Cosima Wagner were persuaded that it was a watercolour by Bonaventura Genelli (*Dionysus being educated by the Muses of Apollo*), now prominently displayed in the so-called Gallery of the Tribschen villa, which had provided Nietzsche with the crucial creative spark for *The Birth of Tragedy* – much as, more than twenty years before, it had inspired Wagner's visionary pronouncements in *Die Kunst und die Revolution* (*Art and Revolution*) and *Das Kunstwerk der Zukunft* (*The Artwork of the Future*). In both of those essays, written in the post-revolutionary year of 1849, Wagner had extolled Greek tragedy as 'the deepest and noblest' achievement ever reached by 'our human consciousness', compared to which contemporary theatrical productions were cheap artefacts of frivolous entertainment served up by profit-motivated stage-managers for the exclusive enjoyment of a rich, self-satisfied clientèle, and which had about as much to do with a true, popular 'art' capable of satisfying the hungering, frustrated masses as a libertine's passing fling with a prostitute had to do with genuine love. Indeed, in the first of those two essays Wagner had given free rein to the political-intellectual contradictions in his complex personality as a prince-detesting 'radical' by praising Aeschylus's noble conservatism, in effect the apogee of Greek dramatic art; going on to describe his 'defeat' at the hands of the young Sophocles and of the 'revolutionary' Pericles as being nothing less than the 'first step downwards from the heights of Greek tragedy, the first moment in the dissolution of the Athenian state'. Two intertwined themes which Nietzsche, partly inspired by his conversations with the Master, undertook to disentangle and to develop into a theory of cultural decadence in *The Birth of Tragedy*.

The central thesis of Nietzsche's book, a rich bundle of many strands of thought, was that it was the hardy genius of great poet-dramatists like Aeschylus and Sophocles, inspired by the exemplary epics of their illustrious predecessor Homer, which had made it possible for the Greeks to tame what had originally been a wild bacchanal honouring the Wine-god Dionysus and to transform this frenzied cult into a superior form of art, which ever since then had borne the name of Tragedy. What had made this artistic synthesis possible was not merely a sense of Apollinian restraint – 'Apollinian' because exercised in the spirit of Apollo, God of the Arts – which Aeschylus and Sophocles had displayed with such consummate mastery; it was due no less to the primitive, primeval force of basic human instincts that had found its uninhibited expression in the singing and dancing rituals of Dionysus's devotees. But for the volcanic power of this Dionysian force, erupting from the dark, instinctual depths of the human psyche and which Schopenhauer had associated with a primal, universal, indomitable will-to-live, Greek tragedy could never have existed. The result, instead, would have been a pallid pantomime, a caricatural representation of the more superficial aspects of human existence.

The 'classic' view of Greek culture, which both Goethe and Schiller had so eagerly embraced in their younger years, was the one that the famous archaeologist and art historian Johann Winckelmann had elaborated in the eighteenth century. A fervent admirer of the plastic arts of antiquity, Winckelmann had hailed the masterpieces of Greek architecture and sculpture as the exemplary products of a gifted people who had elevated the cult of Beauty, Harmony, Serenity to unprecedented heights, leaving behind them a legacy which the less gifted Romans had preserved and which, after the 'dark night' of the Middle Ages, had inspired the artists of the Italian Renaissance.

'The inevitable effect of the beautiful is freedom from passion,' the young Schiller had boldly proclaimed, inadvertently providing Schopenhauer with an idea he later developed into an aesthetic philosophy. But to this idyllic conception of 'harmonious' Greek culture Schiller, who was above all a dramatist, had added a new twist. The beguiling idea that the citizen of Athens, not to say Hellenic man, was perfectly at home with Nature (unlike the medieval Christian, perpetually at war with carnal desires) was superimposed on the notion that Jean-Jacques Rousseau had sought to popularize, in *The Social Contract* and *Emile*, according to which Man is born naturally good as well as free but is later corrupted and enslaved by the vices of Society. For Schiller, the model human being whose individual instincts were in perfect harmony with the collective constraints of society, was the exuberant, life-loving citizen of Athens. Winckelmann's all too idyllic vision of 'Greek cheerfulness' was thus given added depth, and indeed an entirely new dimension, by Schiller's subsequently developed distinction between the 'naïve' art of the epic poet Homer, realistically embracing the intricately intertwined human and divine worlds of Greek mythology, and the more intellectualized 'sentimental' art of lyric poetry, in which cosmic concerns are subordinated to individual thoughts and feelings.

In *The Birth of Tragedy* Nietzsche, with the help of Schopenhauer, undertook to continue the intellectual exploration Schiller had begun but left unfinished. There were at least four elements in Schopenhauer's philosophy that had greatly impressed both Wagner and Nietzsche, not least of all in their appreciation of Greek culture. The first was an emphatically non-optimistic attitude to life which made full allowance for everything in human existence that is inescapably harsh, cruel, self-centred, ugly, sordid and mean, and which viewed human beings as they are and not primarily as they ought to be.

The second element in Schopenhauer's philosophy that had enthused Wagner, as it had Nietzsche, was his dialectical division of human activity into two basically different forms of behaviour: on the one hand, active willing, selfish striving and doing, and, on the other hand, serene, passive, soul-uplifting contemplation, capable, in its supreme moments, of attaining a sublime state of self-forgetting bliss, a 'seventh heaven' of sheer rapture.

The third element in Schopenhauer's philosophy that had fascinated Wagner, as it had Nietzsche, was the Frankfurt sage's robust approach to sex. It was high time for philosophers, he had proclaimed, to stop beating about the bush and to call a spade a spade. In a vitally important chapter of the enlarged version of *The World as Will and Representation*, a chapter entitled 'The Metaphysics of Sexual Love', Schopenhauer had casually dismissed what all previous philosophers – including Plato (in *The Banquet* and *Phaedrus*) – had written on the subject of love as deplorably superficial. He had gone on to identify the sexual instinct with the arcane 'will-to-live' at work in all human beings (as indeed in animals) for the preservation of the species. However, guided by a quest for beauty, this sexual urge could attain the heights of passion, a blinding force imperiously defying all accepted restraints, laws and prohibitions, giving rise to tragic (or tragicomic) situations, which for thousands of years had provided poets with material for their odes and sonnets.

Although Schopenhauer had, *en passant*, condemned this erotic force of attraction as being 'on the whole a malevolent demon' – not for nothing was he a mother-detesting bachelor – his portrayal of this compelling, universal, and totally amoral urge, common to all living beings, was not entirely negative, since it was biologically justified as the 'will-to-live' implicit in all acts of procreation for the perpetuation of the species. After asserting that human beings are sexually attracted to each other by certain qualities – often the very ones each of the two partners lack – Schopenhauer added, quite arbitrarily, that the will or character of the future child was inherited from the father, while the element of intellect was inherited from the mother. Today such a brash suggestion would make any serious biologist smile or even laugh. But the notion appealed to Richard Wagner, a forceful individualist whose adult life had been dominated by a monumental effort to impose his characteral will in the world of operatic music. Equally pleased was Cosima – surprised to find that a notorious misogynist like Schopenhauer could offer such a generous genetic 'compensation' to members of the 'fair sex'.

The fourth element in Schopenhauer's philosophy that had enthused Wagner, as it had Nietzsche, was, as we have seen, his elevation of music to a superior status as 'the most powerful of all the arts', as the one that speaks most directly and movingly to the soul, without any necessary addition of visual images, spoken or written words. Schopenhauer's affirmation with respect to opera, that 'it might perhaps appear more suitable for the text to be written for the music than for the music to be composed for the text', was precisely the mode of composition Wagner had adopted for the four operas of his *Ring* series, in which the musical outline for each scene had preceded his subsequent elaboration of the verse libretto.

For Nietzsche this affirmation of the artistic supremacy of music was intellectually even more challenging. It prompted him to suggest, in *The Birth of Tragedy*, that the lyric poetry of ancient Greece had originally been musically inspired. It also led him to assert that the starting-point of Greek tragedy was not the orally declaiming chorus, still less the individual actors (all disguised in masks), but the chanting and dancing chorus dressed up as satyrs.

Although *The Birth of Tragedy* was peppered with Schopenhauerian concepts – terms like Will, Representation, the *principium individuationis* (the egotistical principle of self-awareness and self-interest) – the end result turned out to be the opposite of the Frankfurt sage's gloomy *Weltanschauung*. Nietzsche himself must have been dimly aware of this extraordinary metamorphosis; for, in a letter written to his musically minded friend Gustav Krug on the last day of this stimulating year (31 December 1871), he forthrightly declared: 'Sadness is not made for men but for animals, says Sancho Panza. When Man gives way too much thereto, he turns into an animal. I now avoid, as much as possible, this "animality" in music. Even pain must be enveloped in such an aura of dithyrambic ravishment that to a certain extent it drowns therein: the feeling I have, to take the loftiest example, in the third act of *Tristan*.'

The ancient Greek, to be sure, 'knew and felt the terrors and horrors of existence': horrors powerfully recorded in the 'terrible lot of the wise Oedipus' (who kills his father and marries his mother), the family curse placed on the descendants of Atreus (which 'drove Orestes to matricide'), the dire punishment imposed by Zeus on the overly intelligent Prometheus, the stealer of heavenly fire, long condemned to having his liver pecked at by a vulture. But with a courage born of despair, of a willingness to face the bitter facts and thus to ovecome the tragic absurdity of life, the ancient Greeks had invented an 'Olympian divine order of joy' to supersede what had originally been the 'Titanic divine order of terror' – much, Nietzsche added, 'as roses burst from thorny bushes'. In this Olympian world there was no trace of 'asceticism, spirituality, or duty; here what speaks forth is nothing but a lush, triumphant existence, in which eveything, whether good or bad, is deified. And so the spectator may stand quite astounded by this fantastic excess of life, asking himself how, with the help of what magic potion were those high-spirited men able to enjoy life so much that wherever they looked, there was Helen, the ideal image of their own existence "floating in sweet sensuality" and quietly smiling back at them.'

This, obviously, was music to the ears of the sybaritic Richard Wagner who, having among other things helped to beget two daughters out of wedlock, had never paid much heed to the joyless asceticism underlying Schopenhauer's philosophy. And he must have felt like cheering when he came upon a sentence in which Nietzsche implicitly condemned the imaginary 'after-world' of Christianity (so resolutely rejected by Feuerbach), writing of those mischievously scheming, plotting, quarrelling Olympians: 'Thus do the gods justify the life of man, inasmuch as they themselves live it – the only satisfactory theodicy.' In that single sentence, though Wagner could not have guessed it, was already compressed in embryonic form the wilfully 'amoral', heaven-and-hell-rejecting philosophy which Nietzsche was later to elaborate in *Human, All Too Human*, *Beyond Good and Evil*, and many other works.

In his preface to *The Bride of Messina*, Schiller had described the ancient Greek chorus as being 'a living wall . . . which Tragedy constructs around itself in order to close it off completely from the real world and to preserve its ideal terrain and its poetical freedom'. What Schiller had not said, however, was that this semi-circular human wall was originally composed of satyrs. In Nietzsche's words: 'The satyr, as the Dionysian chorist, lives in a religiously acknowledged reality under the sanction of myth and cult. That tragedy should begin with him, that his should be the voice of the Dionysian wisdom of tragedy, is for us just as strange a phenomenon as is in general the genesis of tragedy from the chorus . . . With this chorus the profound Hellene, uniquely susceptible to the tenderest and deepest suffering, consoles himself, having dared to look stout-heartedly into the terrible destructiveness of so-called world history, as well as at the cruelty of nature . . . Art saves him, and through Art he saves Life.' Early on in his book, Nietzsche had compared the Dionysian baccanals to the singing and dancing crowds that used to surge through the streets of German towns during the Middle Ages in honour of St John and St Vitus. 'There are some who, from obtuseness or lack of experience, turn contemptuously or condescendingly away from such phenomena as from "folk-diseases", with a smug sense of their own healthy-mindedness. But such poor souls have no idea how corpse-like and spectral this 'healthy-mindedness' of theirs looks when the glowing life of the Dionysian revelers roars past them.'

Indeed, by the time he was through with the ninth section, Nietzsche had made it abundantly clear to anyone at all acquainted with Schopenhauer's thinking that he had retained the verbal labels while radically altering the contents. He had also launched an assault against prudishness and puritanical hypocrisy, against the ascetic, life-punishing, life-denying aspects of Christianity. Over and against Schopenhauerian resignation and the 'glory of passivity', he explicitly extolled the 'glory of activity', as magnificently portrayed in Aeschylus's *Prometheus*: 'Man, rising to Titanic stature, battles to carve out his culture and forces the gods to ally themselves with him because in his personal wisdom he holds their existence and their limitations in his hands.' In other words, the notions of God, gods and the Divine are all human inventions; and with their potential downfall – the term '*Götterdämmerung*' (twilight of the gods) figures in the text – Man is forced to become more Promethean and more sacrilegious than ever, finally rising to Titanic heights . . . those later occupied by the Nietzschean *Übermensch* (Superman).

Long before Wagner had finished reading *The Birth of Tragedy* he dashed off a short note to the author: 'A lovelier book than this one of yours I have never read! Everything is magnificent!' He added that he would be writing at greater length once his initial excitement had abated. The evening reading session was again devoted to Nietzsche's book, which, as Cosima noted in her diary, gave Wagner 'ever-growing satisfaction', although they were already beginning to wonder 'where the public for it is to be found'. This time Wagner was moved to declare that his love for Cosima was both 'Dionysian and Apollinian'. And so it went. Two evenings later they finished the last chapters. 'This is the book I have been longing for,' said Wagner.

His enthusiasm is easy to understand. The final (recently added) sections of the book were little more than a prolonged denunciation of contemporary shallowness (an age dominated by journalists, critics, priestly 'dwarfs' and bird-brained salon gossipers) and a panegyric to the 'glorious, intrinsically healthy, primeval power' of the not yet completely corrupted German spirit and to its sublimest manifestations in the 'Dionysian' music of Beethoven and Wagner. The joy Wagner now experienced did not much differ from the thrill of 'recognition' he had felt years before, as far back as 1853, when he had first opened the pages of Schopenhauer's *The World as Will and Representation* and had found it expressing ideas and sentiments that had long lain dormant within him. Firmly convinced, as many Romantic and post-Romantic Germans were, that the deep-thinking, deep-feeling, metaphysically inclined Germans were the predestined cultural successors of the profound sages and tragedians of ancient Greece, Wagner immediately perceived the propaganda capital for his Bayreuth scheme and the 'art-work-of-the-future' that he could derive from this 'authoritative' book, written by someone who was a respected professor of classical philology. He accordingly asked Nietzsche to send a copy of *The Birth of Tragedy* to Ludwig of Bavaria, and another, accompanied by a letter, to the King's personal secretary, Count Lorenz Düfflipp. Other copies were dispatched to Ludwig's chamberlain, Max von Baligand, to the influential Marie von Schleinitz in Berlin, and to the ravishing Marie Mukhanoff, whose incomparable violet eyes and swan-like figure had fired the poetic genius of Alfred de Musset, Théophile Gautier and Heinrich Heine.

Still other copies were sent to Cosima's former husband, the orchestra conductor Hans von Bülow, and to her father, Franz Liszt. The first, writing in late January from Dresden, regretted that his present virtuoso concert tour had not afforded him the time to give the book the attention it deserved, but he hoped to convey his impressions to the author in person when he passed through Basel in March. The second let a month go by in order to give *The Birth of Tragedy* a second reading. His reply was finally written on 29 February of this leap year, 1872. As a steadfast Catholic believer, Liszt had to admit that he had never been particularly drawn to ancient Greek culture and idolatry. Nietzsche's exegesis of the Apollinian and the Dionysian, of myth in relation to tragedy, he had found truly 'serious and penetrating' in their construction and set forth in 'an amazing light and in magnificent language. Nor have I elsewhere found as beautiful a definition of Art – "the beguiling completion and perfection of a destined-to-live-on existence" – and statements like – "A people, as indeed an individual, is to be valued only to the extent that it is able to impose the stamp of eternity on its experiences" – find an echo in the deepest soul.'

About the response of the 'creatively inclined', Nietzsche had never had much doubt. But the specialists, as he had feared, were to take a more jaundiced view.

## CHAPTER 16

# The End of an Idyll

*– 'And with no one perhaps have I ever laughed so much.'*

On Saturday, 20 January 1872, Nietzsche made another visit to Tribschen. Wagner had decided that the surest way of making the foundation-stone ceremony, now planned for 22 May, a resounding event would be to assemble a national orchestra, made up of 100 hand-picked instrumentalists drawn from all parts of Germany, and 300 singers, whom he proposed to conduct in a majestic performance of Beethoven's 9th Symphony. Much of the afternoon was taken up with a discussion of Nietzsche's plans for extending the spirit of this cultural renaissance to the vitally important field of education. For if, in this glowing vision of the future, it went without saying that the artistic crucible of Bayreuth would generate the sacred fire and provide a model of musical and theatrical perfection, it was no less essential that gifted disciples, like Nietzsche, should carry the torch of their enthusiasm from this new Olympus of the Arts to other provinces of national activity. It was in this cultural context that *The Birth of Tragedy* had been conceived. In the eyes of its author it was anything but a self-sufficient whole; it was more like a prologue, the first in a series of explanatory works intended to revive interest in the heroic-tragic past of ancient Greece as a stimulus and model for the present. The second broadside in this campaign – for he conceived of it in military terms – was to consist of six public lectures, 'On the Future of Our Educational Establishments', the first of which Nietzsche had already delivered the previous Tuesday (16 January) to an audience of 300 students, professors, and more or less distinguished citizens in the jam-packed hall of Basel's Academic Society.

That evening, as a kind of intermezzo, Nietzsche sat down before the drawing-room piano and played his *Sylvesternacht* composition 'very beautifully', as Cosima noted in her diary. (What Wagner thought of the composition, as distinguished from its keyboard interpretation, she did not say.)

Upon his return to Basel Nietzsche was agreeably surprised by a delegation of students from four university fraternities who called on him at his Schützengraben house. Word had reached them that Greifswald University (on North Germany's Baltic coast) had offered him its chair of classical philology and that he had immediately turned it down. To manifest their gratitude for his loyalty to Basel, so unusual in a German professor, they wanted to organize a torchlight procession in his honour. A few days later the university's governing board made known its own appreciation of his decision to remain in Basel by raising his annual salary to 4,000 Swiss francs in recognition of his 'outstanding services'.

On 23 January, the day after the torchlight procession was proposed and politely declined, Carl von Gersdorff wrote to Nietzsche that Berlin was a 'new Jerusalem' filled with self-styled Wagner Club founders, headed by a local cigar manufacturer, who were more interested in fancy banquets, oysters and champagne than they were in Richard Wagner, whose *Ring* cycle operas they wanted to have performed in Germany's new imperial capital rather than in provincial Bayreuth. Nietzsche had probably not yet received this sarcastic letter when, quite unexpectedly on 24 January, Wagner turned up in Basel. Two days before, he had been thunderstruck to learn that the two men who had volunteered to collect a large number of patronage subscriptions to finance the construction of the Bayreuth Festival Theatre – Baron Loën from Weimar, Baron Cohn from Dessau – had so far collected a mere fraction of the needed funds. Without money the entire Bayreuth enterprise was doomed. The man best qualified to replace the two lacklustre money-raisers was Emil Heckel, who had organized the recent Mannheim concert, and Wagner was now on his way to see him. After which he was travelling on to Berlin. Nietzsche, sensing the depth of the Master's dismay, sought to cheer him up, saying that he was prepared to make any sacrifice, even that of his university position, to help the imperilled cause. He followed this up, after Wagner's departure, with a hurried letter to Gersdorff, beseeching him 'to do, to see, and to feel everything that can be of value to him [Wagner] in so important a moment'.

In his letter of 23 January Gersdorff had assured Nietzsche that he was doing all he could to arouse local interest in *The Birth of Tragedy*. But he was exasperated by the suspicion that, save for his artist friends, who would immediately understand it, it might take years, even decades, to overcome the prevailing dull-wittedness of the rest.

In Basel Nietzsche's little book was greeted with feelings of more or less uncomprehending stupefaction. Probably no more than a handful of its worthy burghers were acquainted with Schopenhauer's ideas about music – as a universal language capable of directly expressing the innermost 'quintessence' of life (joy, pain, sorrow, gaiety, merriment, peace of mind, etc.) – but even those who had read the two pertinent chapters in *The World as Will and Representation* seem to have been reluctant to accept Nietzsche's sweeping affirmation, in the second part of *The Birth of Tragedy*, that pre-Wagnerian opera had fatally corrupted modern music by promoting an idyllic rather than an elegiac tendency. It had thus managed to 'divest music of its Dionysian world-mission and to impress on it a playfully formal and pleasant character: a change comparable to the metamorphosis of the [tragic] Aeschylean man into the cheerful Alexandrian'. The one notable exception was the historian Jacob Burckhardt, who realized that, stripped of its Schopenhauerian and Wagnerian exaggerations, Nietzsche's tragico-musical interpretation of Greek cultural history was more illuminating in its insights than the classic vision of the ancient Greeks as a race of serene, beauty-and-harmony-loving optimists. But Burckhardt's open-mindedness was not shared by most of his university colleagues; and, as Nietzsche wrote to Erwin Rohde towards the end of January, 'What I have had to hear about my book is quite incredible . . . for in such voices I divine the future that lies in store for me. This life will still be very difficult.'

Rohde, meanwhile, had not been idle. To give *The Birth of Tragedy* some badly needed publicity, he had written a short 'masterpiece' of a review which he had sent to Friedrich Zarncke, editor of the *Litterarisches Centralblatt.* The editor who had once been so favourably disposed towards Ritschl's 'wonderboy' had recently been appointed Rector of Leipzig University. He was now less than ever prepared to alienate the university's classical philologists, two of whom were bitterly opposed to Ritschl and his 'conjectural' methods of analysis – which Nietzsche, in *The Birth of Tragedy*, had just raised to new, dizzying heights of tightrope artistry.

As Rohde had feared, the review article was rejected. In denigrating 'theoretical-Socratic' culture and the decadent 'Alexandrian' civilization of which modern Europe was the heir, Nietzsche had packed his little book with more intellectual dynamite than any ordinary philologist cared to handle. The relatively young, unknown Hermann Hagen, who taught classical philology at Bern, could write an exultant fan letter, extolling *The Birth of Tragedy*'s 'fiery, jubilant, dithyrambic tone', but Nietzsche could expect no such praise from those of an older, more traditional cast of mind. As Nietzsche wrote to Erwin Rohde, the 'regeneration' of the Germanic spirit called for nothing less than the destruction of the '*Lumpenkultur*' of the present. A war to the knife? Or a war with muskets and artillery? The answer was now clear: it would be '*Kampf auf die Kanone!*' – a war fought with cannon!

There was one philologist, however, whom Nietzsche was not prepared to dismiss as a tiresome micrological grubber – Friedrich Ritschl, whose star pupil he had once been. Troubled by his enigmatic silence, Nietzsche could restrain himself no longer. On 30 January he wrote to express his amazement at not having received so much as a 'tiny word' from his old friend and mentor about his recently published book, which was a 'sort of manifesto'. He had written it, 'full of hope for our science of antiquity, full of hope for the essential nature of Germany . . . ' For he was determined, as he was making clear in a series of public lectures he was now delivering on 'The Future of our Educational Establishments', to make himself 'the master of the younger generation of philologists, and I would regard it as a disgraceful symptom if I did not succeed in this'.

Ritschl's first reaction to *The Birth of Tragedy*, noted in his diary after a cursory perusal on the last day of 1871, was a two-word comment: '*geistreiche Schwiemelei*' (idea-rich giddiness). After receiving Nietzsche's letter he took another look at the book, and in mid-February he wrote him a long, frank letter, in which, as though by prescient anticipation, he condemned many of the trends of thought so forcefully expressed in Nietzsche's later works. 'So decidedly do I belong by my entire nature to the historical tendency and to a historical consideration of human affairs that never could the world's salvation appear to me to be found in this or that philosophical system; that never too could I characterize the natural withering away of an epoch or of a phenomenon as "suicide"; that I cannot regard the individualization of life as a backward step, nor can I believe that the spiritual life-forms and potentialities of a people, no matter how rarely gifted and to a certain degree privileged by nature and historical development, constitute an absolute standard for all peoples and for all times, any more than one religion suffices, has sufficed, or will suffice for different ethnic individualities. You cannot possibly require the "Alexandrian" and the scholar to condemn knowledge and to see in art alone the world-transforming and liberating power of salvation. The world is something different to each and every one of us; and inasmuch as we can no more overcome our "individuation" than a plant with individualized leaves and blossoms can return to its root, each people must in the economy of life live itself out according to its aptitudes and its particular mission.'

Nietzsche was pleasantly surprised by this candid critique – the calm, considered, and far from acerbic tone of which made it clear that he could still count Ritschl among his friends. He was even more agreeably surprised, however, by the extraordinary impact that *The Birth of Tragedy* had made on Cosima's former husband, Hans von Bülow, who finally reached Basel on 27 March. The forty-one-year-old conductor and piano virtuoso had been so beguiled by its unpedantic freshness and stylistic sparkle that he had bought scores of copies from the Leipzig publisher, distributing them to acquaintances in all of the Austrian, German and Swiss towns through which he passed during his present concert-tour.

*

It was Nietzsche's conviction, one shared by Wagner, that contemporary German 'culture' had undergone a radical decline because the cultivation of the humanities, which had inspired and sustained the spectacular florescence of German thought and letters during the 'golden age' of 1780–1830, had later been superseded by an ever-growing interest in science, historical scholarship and encyclopedic erudition. Friedrich Albert Lange, whom Nietzsche had read with such adolescent zest while still a boarder at Pforta, had remarked on the phenomenon in his *History of Materialism*, saying that it was as though the German genius, after erupting in a dazzling outburst of creative endeavour in the fields of poetry, drama and philosophy, had by 1831–2 (the years of Hegel's and Goethe's death) completely burnt itself out as far as the arts were concerned, its remaining strength being channelled into zoological investigations, laboratory experiments and physicochemical research.

Schopenhauer, though well aware of this phenomenon, had made no attempt to explain it. Human genius, he was convinced, was something exceedingly rare and accidental, due to what he liked to call the 'parsimony of Nature', which was impenitently aristocratic, being content to manufacture millions of humdrum individuals for each truly original or brilliantly creative being it brought forth. Whether it was a scientific or philosophical intellect or a truly innovative musical, poetical or artistic talent made no difference. Such persons were rare, their great works were like eye-opening 'revelations', and there was no point in trying, like Hegel, to demonstrate that their appearance at this or that particular time or place was more or less preconditioned by what had happened before.

This, however, was precisely the kind of explanation that Wagner and Nietzsche were determined to provide for Germany's classic age and its aftermath. In this respect, though they swore allegiance to Schopenhauer, both were unwitting followers of Hegel. Some reason or complex of reasons had to be found to explain this swift cultural decline. How had it come about that a people who up until the middle of the eighteenth century had been looked down upon by the more 'civilized' inhabitants of Spain, Italy, France and Britain had in the short space of fifty years been able to produce playwrights of the stature of Goethe, Schiller and Heinrich von Kleist, poets as original as Klopstock, Hölderlin, Novalis, and Heine, philosophers like Kant, Fichte, Schelling, Hegel, composers like Mozart, Beethoven and Schubert? Between 1780 and 1830 hardly a year had passed without the appearance of some new masterpiece in the fields of poetry, drama, music or philosophy. Europe, as Madame de Staël had had the wit to realize, had seen nothing comparable since the Renaissance, and though there were no German painters or sculptors who could stand comparison with the great Italian masters of the fifteenth and sixteenth centuries, in philosophy and music the Germans had left the Italians and everyone else very far behind.

But then, quite suddenly, the creative spark seemed to have flickered out. From the inspiring heights the level of cultural output had suffered a precipitous drop. To be sure, Heine's last great poem – *Deutschland, ein Wintermärchen* (*Germany, a Winter Tale*), a biting satire of contemporary German life – was written in the early 1840s, while the second volume of Schopenhauer's *The World as Will and Representation* appeared in 1844, followed a few years later by two volumes of essays (*Parerga* and *Paralipomena*); but those works rose up like isolated pinnacles in a cultural wasteland, overgrown with the weedy products of the 'Young Germany' school (Ludwig Börne, Karl Gutzkow, Heinrich Laube, Wolfgang Menzel, Theodor Mundt, etc.), the inferior, politically motivated poetry of Franz Dingelstedt, Ferdinand Feiligrath, Hoffmann von Fallersleben (author of 'Deutschland! Deutschland über alles!') and the 'realistic' novels of Gustav Freytag, Friedrich von Spielhagen and Berthold Auerbach.

What, then, was the explanation for this decline? To this question Wagner had two ready answers. In the field of music, Mendelssohn, Schumann and his particular *bête noire*, Meyerbeer, had deliberately chosen to tread the low road rather than the high road of art by turning their backs on Beethoven and by composing shallow, sentimental music of a deliberately entertaining kind. Elsewhere, the spirit of poetic idealism that had fired Germany's classic age had been relentlessly undermined by down-to-earth realism and the materialism of an increasingly influential middle class, whose prosaic tastes were being flattered and corrupted by money-grubbing bankers, Jewish newspaper owners, carping critics, narrow-minded 'ink-slingers' (a favourite Schopenhauer term) and other dispensers of *Jetztzeit* ('now-time') mediocrity. This cultural climate had had a particularly devastating effect on German stage productions. As Nietzsche had put it in *The Birth of Tragedy*, 'the tendency to use the theatre as an institution for the moral education of the people, which was still taken seriously in Schiller's time, is already reckoned among the unbelievable antiques of a superannuated form of education'.

All, however, was not lost. For Wagner was persuaded that with the help of altruistic souls – like King Ludwig of Bavaria and the ever-widening circle of Wagnerian enthusiasts – this baleful trend could be reversed. To keep contemporary Germany from sinking further into the morass of mediocrity, like its decadent neighbour, France, appeal had to be made to what was most deep-rooted in the German psyche. The age-old Germanic virtues of steadfastness, perseverance, honesty, courage, loyalty, seriousness of work and purpose had to be summoned up from the dormant depths of the Teutonic consciousness. This, no less, was the heroic task of spiritual 'salvation' to which the *Nibelungen* opera cycle and the music-and-drama training centre of Bayreuth was to summon Germany's cultural élite.

In the twenty-third section of *The Birth of Tragedy* Nietzsche had argued that a deliberate return to poetic myth – the kind that had inspired the personally drafted librettos of Richard Wagner's operas – was necessary to offset the growing influence in modern German life of the critic, as opposed to the creative artist. But to alter this hypercritical, art-sapping and destroying climate, one had to start at the grass roots, at the level of German high-school (*Gymnasium*) education.

It was to this momentous subject that Nietzsche now addressed himself in a series of public lectures he began delivering in Basel. It did not take him long to realize that he had underestimated the magnitude of the task he was setting himself. Indeed, the rest of Nietzsche's creative life attests an increasingly desperate effort to achieve the unachievable. For it is not enough to decry the spiritual and intellectual maladies of the present to be able to form and reform the future.

The two dominant trends in contemporary German education, Nietzsche pointed out in his first lecture, were aimed, on the one hand, at broadening the scope of instruction (to embrace new subjects not included in the old 'classical' curriculum) and, on the other hand, at narrowing the focus of investigation to specific fields of study. The first aim was motivated by a desire to produce useful, 'common-currency' human beings to satisfy the economic needs and dogmas of the present; the second aim, basically antithetical to the first, was prompted by the steady advance of specialized knowledge in various scientific disciplines. The two antagonistic trends had combined to bring forth a 'sticky' stream of intermediate beings possessing a smattering of knowledge about many things who sought to cement together the disjointed spheres of the sciences, the fine arts, politics, economics and so on with the 'glue' of daily journalism. The scholar of yore had thus been replaced by the journalist, by the 'servant of the present' (another Schopenhauerian expression), who had become the cultural pace-setter of society, instead of the 'great genius', who had once been revered because he was an atemporal model, a 'leader for all times, a saviour from [the tyranny of] the moment'.

In the second lecture, delivered on 6 February, Nietzsche trained his guns on the German *Gymnasium* or high school, which, he said, was now a debased caricature of what it had originally been intended to be when established at the time of the Reformation: a place where students were given a thorough grounding in Greek and Latin for their possible admission to a university. A glaring symptom of this debasement was the substitution of 'newspaper German' (*Zeitungsdeutsch*) for the older, classic German of the great prose writers of the eighteenth century. In the lower *Gymnasium* classes many students were now encouraged to show off their 'originality' and to develop a 'free personality' by writing critical essays about those 'great masters' long before they had acquired a sufficient understanding of the grammatical, syntactical and other rules that went into the making of a fine prose style.

Nietzsche, as one can see, had no use for progressive education – the philosophical roots of which go back, via Heinrich Froebel (a native Thuringian, like himself) and Johann Pestalozzi to Jean-Jacques Rousseau. He rightly sensed that this democratic dogma – even 'little ones' (like Rousseau's *Émile*) must be 'liberated' from pedagogical oppression and allowed to 'express themselves' – encouraged scholastic indolence, intellectual indiscipline, sloppiness of thought, style and speech. Developing a literary style – a matter the ancient Greeks and Romans had always treated with the utmost seriousness – was anything but easy. It required rigorous self-discipline, the kind of obedience to rules (*Gehorsam*) and habit-forming (*Gewöhnung*) which alone can turn a slovenly sloucher into a smartly marching soldier.

In the third public lecture, delivered on 27 February, Nietzsche began by restating a basic Schopenhauerian tenet – that geniuses are rare – and then went on to declare that popular education and the 'emancipation of the masses from the rule of the great individual' were certain to lead to a 'Saturnalia of barbarism'. Posterity, whether one likes it or not, judges the educational level of a people by its lonely, 'on-striding' heroes and by the manner in which they are recognized, encouraged and acclaimed, or abused, locked up and destroyed by the 'stealthy-footed' or 'limp-winged' mass. This was followed by several remarkable paragraphs which went considerably beyond Schopenhauer in warning that popular education could even prove to be a dangerously destructive force if it disturbed the 'healthy unconsciousness', the 'sound-sleepingness' of a people. For, without the 'curative beneficence' of this underlying somatic calm, no culture could survive the shattering tension and excitements aroused by its own activities and its violent intrusions into the lower depths of collective consciousness. The lecture ended with a sharp critique of the modern state, and in particular of the 'barbaric' determination of the modern Prussian state to subordinate a greatly expanded educational system to its political aims and self-aggrandissement.

In the fourth public lecture, which was no less Schopenhaueian in tone, Nietzsche asserted that 'real education' (*Bildung*) – 'this tender-footed, pampered, ethereal goddess' – which was reserved for the cultivation of rare geniuses and those willing to help them, should not be confused with utilitarian instruction (*Erziehung*), 'that useful maidservant' which was designed to help human beings in the struggle for existence and to train future administrative officials, salesmen, army officers, farmers, doctors and technicians. Institutions like the *Realschulen* and the higher *Bürgerschulen*, which offered practical or technical instruction for specific crafts and trades, had their rightful place in society; but they no more deserved to be called 'educational establishments' (*Bildungsanstalten*) in the highest and proper sense of the word than did the shamefully debased *Gymnasium*, or for that matter – the subject of his fifth lecture – the contemporary German university.

On Sunday, 18 February, roughly midway between the second and third of these public lectures, Nietzsche made another surprise visit to Tribschen. Wagner gave him a detailed account of his recent trip to Berlin, where with the help of the 'indispensable' Carl von Gersdorff he had relieved the cigar manufacturer Bernhard Löser and the 'Court Jew' Baron von Cohn of further responsibility for selling Patronat certificates and had placed the collection and administration of all Wagner Club funds in the hands of the Bayreuth banker Friedrich Feustel. It had been a stroke of 'practical genius' to have settled on this small and 'uncorrupted' Bavarian town as the site and centre of his artistic plans rather than to have chosen the detestable 'New Jerusalem' (Berlin) of the north. 'There is much discussion of the reform of educational establishments, also of the German character,' Cosima noted in her diary.

One month later, the Thursday before Palm Sunday, Wagner's nephew, Friedrich Brockhaus, brought written copies of the first four of Nietzsche's lectures to Tribschen, where they were read several days later on successive evenings. The day the first two were read (Saturday, 23 March), Nietzsche delivered the fifth public lecture before another hall-packing audience at Basel's Academic Society. His target this time was the summit of the educational pyramid – the German university, which was criticized for a multitude of sins: too much freedom accorded to immature students, allowed to select lecturers they wished to listen to, often with only half an ear; an over-emphasis on 'historical education'; a flabby attitude of 'philosophical neutrality'; a general unconcern for art and style, and a tendency to dispense 'pseudo-culture' and to turn out a degenerate species of self-satisfied *Bildungsmensch* ('educated individual').

Nietzsche (in a letter to his mother and sister) felt that the success of his lectures had been 'extraordinary – emotion, enthusiasm, and hatred – nicely combined'. Jacob Burckhardt, who attended all five lectures, later wrote to a friend that he and all the others were waiting impatiently to hear what kind of solution Nietzsche was going to provide to the 'questions and complaints so boldly and broadly tossed out. . . . You should have heard them! In places it was quite enchanting, but then a sadness again made itself heard, and just how the *Auditores humanissimi* should draw comfort from the matter, I do not see. One thing we surely had: a man of lofty aptitude, who takes and dispenses everything from first hand.'

The subject of the sixth and culminating lecture was probably discussed during the long Easter weekend (28 March–1 April) which Nietzsche spent at Tribschen. Wagner was in a mood of deep despondency, almost ready to abandon the Bayreuth undertaking and to move with Cosima and the children to the warmer climate of Italy. While the response to the grandiose 22 May concert had been most gratifying – the entire Karlsruhe orchestra had volunteered to perform Beethoven's 9th Symphony under his direction, and in Leipzig several hundred members of Carl Riedel's choral ensemble were on their knees, begging to be admitted to the giant choir – Wagner had been much upset by a recent letter from Ludwig of Bavaria's personal secretary informing him that the Bayreuth Festival Theatre was going to cost 900,000 thaler – three times more than the 300,000 thaler originally foreseen. The project, once again, seemed doomed.

Nietzsche, who had already informed his Leipzig publisher that he would soon have the text of his six public lectures ready for printing as a second book, now began to wonder if this would suffice to save the Bayreuth cause. On 11 April he wrote to Erwin Rohde to say that he was seriously thinking of vacating his chair of classical philology in the autumn and of arranging to have Rohde succeed him for the winter semester. He himself was going to undertake a tour of the 'German fatherland', delivering lectures on the projected *Nibelungen* 'stage-festivals', since, as he put it, 'each must do what is his duty and, in the case of conflict, do what is more than his duty'. Well aware of the prestige that a German university professor enjoyed in the eyes of the general public, Wagner had never encouraged Nietzsche's readiness to 'sacrifice himself for the cause' by abandoning his chair of classical philology. But Rohde too had his doubts about Nietzsche's latest '*combinazione*'. Much as he appreciated his friend's generous offer to step down in his favour, he had just heard that he was likely to be offered a professorship in classical philology at Kiel.

Rohde's sobering letter, which reached Basel around 15 April, brought Nietzsche back to earth with a jolt. His friend's politely worded remonstrance added nervous stress to the head-cold and end-of-semester weariness from which he was already suffering. To complicate matters, his Leipzig publisher, Fritzsch, did not seem to think that he would be helping him much by bringing out his second book. There was also the troubling question of the sixth and final lecture in his 'Educational

Establishments' series, which Nietzsche had yet to deliver to an audience he had left in a state of intrigued suspense.

To find the quiet he needed to think over these various problems Nietzsche left Basel on 16 April – the first day of the brief inter-semester recess – and headed for the Lake of Geneva. This time he was accompanied by Dr Hermann Immermann, the university's new professor of physiology. At Vernex, near Montreux, they were joined a few days later by Fritz's Naumburg friend Wilhelm Pinder, who had decided to celebrate his recent admission to the bar by making a trip to Switzerland.

In his haste to get away from Basel Nietzsche had forgotten to inform his Tribschen friends of his vacation plans. Nor did he realize just how close to the final departure date Cosima and Richard Wagner were. On Saturday, 20 April, after receiving an urgent telegram from Friedrich Feustel in Bayreuth, asking him to go to Darmstadt to consult the noted stage-scenery expert Karl Brandt, Wagner sent a telegram to Basel asking Nietzsche to come to Tribschen the next day. Franz Overbeck, who had remained behind in the Schützengraben house, relayed the telegram to Vernex, where it arrived too late for Nietzsche to be able to heed the summons.

The next day, while Wagner and Cosima waited in vain for his arrival at Tribschen, Nietzsche wrote from Vernex to say that he had gone to the Lake of Geneva to restore his health and peace of mind, much troubled by metaphysical and other problems. His letter did not reach Tribschen until Monday afternoon – by which time Wagner had bid a last farewell to the Tribschen house he had furnished with such loving and lavish care, leaving Cosima to join him a few days later with the children in Bayreuth. In Basel he was much put out to discover that Nietzsche had left without a word, and, having no one else to talk to, he spent nine boring hours wandering through Basel's old streets while waiting for the northbound train to leave.

Two days later Cosima sent Nietzsche the copies of his Basel lectures, which he had absent-mindedly left behind at Tribschen, along with a recent issue of the Italian-language *Rivista Europea* containing a brief reference to *The Birth of Tragedy* – the first printed mention to have appeared anywhere. Wagner, she wrote, had been greatly touched by the 'profound, significant, gripping' Open Letter which Erwin Rohde had addressed to him, but he had not had time to answer it. He had barely managed to finish the pencil sketch for the third act of *Götterdämmerung*, and he would need two full months of peace to ink in the pages of the score. How and where he would ever find the time to complete this vital task, she didn't know, but the thought of these endless distractions was enough to make her want to 'weep like a child' or like the poor, heartbroken housekeeper Vreneli Stocker, who, having recently given birth to a baby daughter, was staying on at Tribschen while the others travelled to Bayreuth. 'And so we are now leaving,' wrote Cosima, 'and we are going to try, like Amphion, to move the stones [through music], in order to tame and enchant, as Orpheus once did the beasts . . . Today I went out for a few minutes in the garden and experienced in my beloved enclosure one of those Tribschen evenings whose peaceful blessedness will never again illuminate my soul – "So Fare Ye well, you silent house!" – no one will be missing from the caravan, not even the dog's barking, for Rus is coming with us.'

Nietzsche needed no further urging. Taking hasty leave of his companions at Vernex, he reached Tribschen the next evening. The trees in the garden could not have looked more lovely – clusters of white blossoms softly powdered against the tender green of the leaves – but inside the house everything and everyone seemed in mournful disarray. The potted palms were still there in the vestibule where he had once listened with enchantment to Cosima's birthday *Idyll*, but in the drawing-room the busts had been crated, and the damask walls, bereft of their framed Lenbach paintings, were now dismally bare. Stripped of its figurines, engravings and butterfly cases, the Gallery was now an empty passageway, weirdly lit by the polychrome quiltwork of light filtering in through the stained-glass windowpanes. Cosima, who had spent the day filing and arranging Wagner's papers, was worn out. The usually playful children were unusually subdued. Only the watchful mountains, visible beyond the salon terrace, seemed to be unmoved.

The next day Nietzsche helped Cosima with the packing. Later he accompanied her on foot into Lucerne, from which they returned in a taxi-sailboat to the little wharf on the edge of the poplar-studded promontory. That evening, to console her, he sat down before the keyboard and played her some piano pieces.

On Saturday (27 April), after a last walk to the lakeside village of Winkel, Nietzsche took his leave, so deeply moved that he hardly knew what to say. 'Tribschen has ceased to be,' he wrote four days later to Carl von Gersdorff. 'We wandered around as though through ruins, there was emotion everywhere, in the sky, in the clouds; the dog would not eat, the servant family, whenever one spoke to them, kept breaking into sobs. Together, we packed away manuscripts, letters and books – ah, it was hopelessly sad! What haven't they meant to me, these three years I have spent in the vicinity of Tribschen, and during which I made 23 visits there! Without them, what would I be now!'

## CHAPTER 17

# Future-philosophy and After-philology

*– And no one lies as much as the man who is indignant.*

If April 1872 marked the end of one period in Friedrich Nietzsche's life, the ensuing month of May proved no less momentous in ushering in another. It began with the news, transmitted in a seven-word Latin telegram, that Erwin Rohde had been appointed professor of classical philology at Kiel, and it ended with a flurry of publicity about *The Birth of Tragedy*.

Although Nietzsche was sadly aware that life in Basel would no longer be the same now that Cosima and Richard Wagner had left Switzerland, he was still determined to do everything he could to shorten the distance that separated him from Bayreuth. There could be no question of his missing the foundation-stone ceremony planned for 22 May. The same went for Erwin Rohde and Carl von Gersdorff. The latter, having bought a certificate of patronage, was automatically entitled to one of the 700 seats in the small auditorium of Bayreuth's rococo theatre, where Beethoven's 9th Symphony was to be performed. But Wagner had to use his personal influence with the local organizers to obtain places for 'his' two professors (Nietzsche and Rohde).

This year Richard Wagner's birthday fell on a Wednesday, immediately after the long Whitsun weekend, which began on Saturday, 18 May, and extended on through Monday the 20th. By taking a late-night train on Friday evening Nietzsche made it to Bayreuth by the early afternoon of Saturday the 18th, well in advance of the first rehearsal, due on Whit Monday. Cosima and Richard Wagner, with the five children and a governess, had established temporary residence in a hotel charmingly called the Fantaisie (the name given to the nearby *Schloss* and its vast tree- and peacock-filled park). It was here or in an inn called the Goldene Pfau (Golden Peacock) that Nietzsche spent this and the next four nights, along with Carl von Gersdorff, the enterprising Emil Heckel of Mannheim and Hans Richter, who had taken a two-week leave of absence from his Budapest orchestra to be present at this inaugural. 'Cheerful, congenial atmosphere, we all belong together,' Cosima noted that evening in her diary.

The next day it began to rain, but nothing could dampen the enthusiasm of those who had travelled from near and far to be present for the great event. Wagner had to spend most of this wet Whit Sunday at the railway station, greeting incoming musicians and helping them to find carriages, of which there was a dire shortage, to take them to their respective hotels and lodgings. Erwin Rohde did not reach Bayreuth until that evening – after Gustav Krug and King Ludwig of Bavaria's exuberant chamberlain, Max von Balligand, who startled everyone by letting out a bellow of recognition and joyously embracing Nietzsche.

On Monday morning Fritz and his young friends (Rohde, Gersdorff, Krug) were among the privileged guests allowed to witness the first rehearsal with the orchestra players, who treated Wagner to a 'fine and touching welcome' when he appeared before them. There was another fatiguing rehearsal in the afternoon, this time with the chorus of 300 singers, which left Wagner so exhausted that he retired to bed early that evening. The company at the Fantaisie was further swollen by a number of new arrivals – including Ernst Dohm, the former editor of the satirical *Kladderadatsch* weekly (one of the rare journalists for whom the normally press-hating Wagner felt any sympathy), and the small, starry-eyed and determinedly idealistic Malwida von Meysenbug, who had shared many of the revolutionary enthusiasms of Richard Wagner's younger years.

On Wednesday morning – Wagner's birthday – the rain set in again, as unrelentingly as on the previous Sunday. Nietzsche, as a special mark of favour, was granted a seat in Wagner's carriage. Many of the faithful, lacking carriages, had to trudge through the mud to the hillside excavation site, now marked by tall flagpoles, where the foundation stone for the new opera house was to be lowered into place. A dripping band then struck up the '*Huldigungsmarsch*' (the 'March of Homage' Wagner had written some years before for his royal Bavarian benefactor). The foundation stone was slowly lowered into place, along with a little casket containing a telegraphic message from King Ludwig II of Bavaria (hailing 'this day, which is so significant for all of Germany') and a four-line poem of Wagner's calling on this precious stone to preserve the secret which, for many centuries, was to be made manifest to the world. Wagner then took the hammer and struck three resounding blows, saying, 'Bless you, my stone, long may you stand and firmly hold!'

Inside the Margrave's rococo theatre, where it had been decided in extremis to hold the rest of the morning's ceremonies, the stage, though the largest in Germany, was soon so crammed with singers that some of them had to occupy the front rows of the orchestra. The address that followed was surprisingly modest. The new theatre building, of a simple but radically new design, Wagner explained, would afford future audiences an unprecedented opportunity to appreciate the full significance of what they saw and heard. Although many people were already talking of a National Theatre in Bayreuth, he himself refused to use the term. How could one speak of a 'German theatre' when one worthy of the name did not yet exist? What had sustained him in this enterprise was the support of 'the friends of my particular art . . . ' By the time Wagner was through, as Cosima noted that evening in her diary, 'even the gravest of the men' present had tears in their eyes.

No less moving was the afternoon performance, in the same rococo theatre, of Wagner's *Kaisermarsch* and Beethoven's 9th Symphony, the choral parts of which were sung with extraordinary fervour. 'Quite magnificent,' Cosima later noted in her diary, 'everyone feeling himself freed from the burden of mortal existence; at the conclusion sublime words from R. [Richard Wagner] on what this celebration means to him.'

Erwin Rohde returned to Kiel feeling that he had just said goodbye to his real home (Bayreuth) and that it was more than ever his duty to add his 'weaker strength' to his friend's as a companion-in-arms 'in this battle for the highest good'. Nietzsche himself felt numbed by those exalting four days – which inspired two fine thank-you letters to his Bayreuth hosts, prompting Cosima to comment in her diary: 'Certainly few people have so much feeling for our sufferings and joys as he.'

The next day – Sunday the 26th – Berlin's leading daily, the *Norddeutsche Allgemeine Zeitung*, which was now solidly committed to the Wagner cause, published a fairly long review of *The Birth of Tragedy*, which its author, Erwin Rohde, had hoped to see printed before the Bayreuth inaugural. Although not quite so rhapsodically worded as the article he had vainly submitted to Friedrich Zarncke's *Litterarisches Centralblatt*, this review was just as uncompromising in declaring that the 'cruel consistency' of Socratic thought had slain ancient Greek mythology, and that in modern times 'we are seeing the fruits ripen of a purely logical ethics, which will bring us the vandalism of the socialist barbarians'. The only antidote to this 'malady of the times' was a cultural renaissance fired by the kind of 'art-enthusiasm' which, at Bayreuth, was now providing the firm foundation for a 'pantheon of the German nation'.

Cosima Wagner, who read Rohde's article on that same Sunday in the company of Malwida von Meysenbug and her foster-daughter, Olga Herzen, was not impressed. 'Not suitable for the general public,' was her diary comment. Nietzsche, however, was overjoyed. 'Friend, Friend, Friend, what have you done! . . . ' he wrote ecstatically to Rohde. 'Slowly without seeing those printed characters which I read with ever growing astonishment, I plunged into the emotional abyss of Bayreuth and finally I hear that this voice, which rings out so solemnly and deeply, is that of my friend. Ah, dearest Friend, what have you done! . . . I am molten hot.

Fight, fight, fight! I need war,' he concluded. After which he dashed off a letter to the publisher, Ernst Wilhelm Fritzsch, asking him to have fifty copies of Rohde's article printed up in pamphlet form.

Nietzsche's pugnacious challenge to his enemies was not long in being answered. On the last day of this momentous month of May 1872 Carl von Gersdorff wrote to Fritz from Berlin to say that he had picked up a copy of a recently published pamphlet written by a former Pforta schoolmate. The pamphlet, entitled *Zukunftsphilosophie!* (*Philosophy-of-the-Future!* – an ironic allusion to the *Zukunftsmusik*, or Music-of-the-Future, to which Wagner, like Berlioz and Liszt, was supposed to be addicted), was, as the subtitle made clear, a 'rejoinder' to *The Birth of Tragedy*. Its author, Ulrich von Wilamowitz-Möllendorff, who was four years younger than Nietzsche, was an up-and-coming scholar who had decided to ingratiate himself with the leading classical philologists in Berlin by writing an ill-tempered rebuttal. In it he mocked Nietzsche's tone – at times a 'pulpit style', at others a form of *raisonnement* akin to that of the 'papering slave of the day' (Schopenhauerian terminology for 'journalist'). He took him to task for pretending to have a deeper understanding of the nature of drama than Aristotle and Lessing, not to mention Shakespeare, Goethe, Schiller and Calderón. He claimed that Nietzsche had never read Winckelmann (who had praised the critical spirit as essential to the proper appreciation of art); he had misunderstood Homer and entertained erroneous ideas about Archilochus's lyric poetry. He ridiculed the notion of an artistic alliance between Apollo and Dionysus as being tantamount to a union between Nero and Pythagoras; and he ended by declaring that, whatever Nietzsche might choose to do next, he should step down from his academic chair and stop trying to lead 'Germany's philological youth' astray from the straight and narrow path of ascetic, 'self-denying toil'.

For Gersdorff this shrill attack on *The Birth of Tragedy* was the 'angry cry of the theoretical man, who for the first time sees his own reflection in its true features and, horrified, would like to smash the mirror'. Rohde, writing five days later (5 June) dismissed Wilamowitz's diatribe as the work of a jealous, 'pamphleteering ragamuffin and his clique' – by which he meant the professional philologists of Berlin University, who had little use for Friedrich Ritschl and his 'Leipzig school'.

Wagner's reaction to the Wilamowitz pamphlet was no less violent. Indeed, he was so incensed by this 'newest example of "nastiness" – but, alas, so typical of the times!' – that he drafted a stinging rebuke. It took the form of an 'Open Letter' addressed to Friedrich Nietzsche, professor of classical philology at the University of Basel. He began by recalling how, as a young student at the Kreuzschule in Dresden, he had been fascinated by Greek mythology, largely thanks to the classes of an inspiring teacher. But later, at the Nikolaischule and the Thomasschule in Leipzig, his youthful enthusiasm for classical studies had been blighted by deadening drillwork, and he had later forgotten almost all of the Greek he had learned. Notwithstanding this linguistic handicap, he had probably retained a greater respect for Greek antiquity than Mendelssohn and other musicians who were familiar with the language. After taking a Schopenhauerian swipe at the journalistic jargon – often worthy of 'a Wisconsin stock-market news-sheet' – which was now pervading every field and undermining the German mother-tongue, he noted that classical studies had fallen into such disrepute that theologians, lawyers and doctors no longer wished to have anything to do with them. Whereas the theological faculties continued to turn out priests, the law faculties to produce judges and barristers, and the medical faculties to provide doctors, Germany's faculties of philology now produced nothing but philologists, a closed caste of scholarly Brahmans who were of no use to anybody but themselves.

The great merit of Nietzsche's 'thoughtful treatise', Wagner went on, lay precisely in the fact that *The Birth of Tragedy* had not been written in scholarly language nor laboriously weighed down with ungainly footnotes, but addressed to a non-specialist reading public about matters of fundamental importance. 'This time we had a text, but not footnotes; we gazed out from the mountain heights over the broad, spreading plains without being disturbed by the brawling of peasants in the tavern below.' Such a brawling peasant, obviously, was this Wilamowitz-Möllendorff, whom Wagner compared to a bull on the loose – one it would be better to avoid, it being absurd, as Socrates had pointed out, to kick back when struck by a donkey's hoof – and who was then likened for his clumsiness in writing to 'a Berlin street-corner loafer staggering from beer to schnapps'.

Cosima, to whom Wagner read this 'Open Letter', found it 'quite masterly'. He then sent it to Carl von Gersdorff in Berlin, who arranged to have it published in the *Norddeutsche Allgemeine Zeitung*. Its appearance, in the Sunday, 23 June edition, delighted Nietzsche – as it did his sister Elisabeth (who once again was looking after him in the Schützengraben house), their kindly neighbour Franz Overbeck, and Fritz's old Leipzig friend Heinrich Romundt, who had finally agreed to set himself up in Basel as a *Privatdozent* (unofficial instructor) in philosophy. Elsewhere, however, Wagner's 'Open Letter' confirmed a sentiment now widespread in many German faculties – that Nietzsche was a *Spassphilolog* (philogical joker).

In generously rushing into print on his admirer's behalf, Wagner inadvertently complicated the task that Nietzsche had set himself in delivering a series of public lectures on the future of Germany's educational establishments. A key word in those lectures was *Zucht* – a word of multiple connotations meaning 'breeding' (of animals as well as of human beings), 'culture' (of pearls, silkworms, bacteria, etc.), 'cultivation' of plants, and, above all, 'discipline' or 'drill'. It was, Nietzsche had suggested, because high-school teachers were no longer insisting on strict grammatical drill and linguistic self-disciplining (*Selbstzucht*) in order to allow the 'free personality' of their students to express itself that the German educational system was now failing in its task and opening the gates to a floodtide of semi-educated barbarism. But it was precisely this joyless, mind-numbing emphasis on grammatical drill – this '*tödlich falschen Zucht*' (this 'lethally false disciplining'), to quote his own words in the 'Open Letter' to Nietzsche – that had killed the young Richard Wagner's enthusiasm for the serious study of the language and literature of the ancient Greeks. The man Nietzsche most admired as the epitome of genius, Richard Wagner, was thus the living refutation of the merits of that strict linguistic disciplining Nietzsche felt was needed to arrest the general *laissez-aller* of German school life. He was the proof that human genius is refractory to strict rules and regulations and that it cannot be artificially produced or cultivated by any amount of hothouse education (as Immanuel Kant had noted in his *Critique of Judgement*). Here, at the very outset, was a massive contradiction which had somehow to be resolved before Nietzsche could make a convincing claim to have completed his ambitious enquiry into what was wrong with Germany's educational establishments. His inability to solve this dilemma explains why he did not deliver the sixth and climactic public lecture, and why his letters during the summer and early autumn of 1872 stressed his need to think these problems through more thoroughly.

Save for a brief illness in mid-June Nietzsche enjoyed this semester more than any he had previously known in Basel. Particularly gratifying was his lecture course on the pre-Platonic philosophers, for which ten university students had signed up (for him a record number). Equally stimulating were his walks with Jacob Burckhardt, whose lectures on Greek cultural history he was not allowed (as a fellow professor) to attend, but the gist of which he could gather from their conversations. With friends like Overbeck and Romundt to keep him company, while his sister kept house for him in what they jokingly called the 'Gifthütte' (the 'poison-brewers' lodge', an appellation derived from the name of a famous Basel tavern, the Gifthüttli), Fritz no longer suffered from the feeling of being an 'outsider'.

His high spirits were further buoyed by a feeling of aesthetic kinship, as a respected member of an ever-growing 'family' of Wagnerian enthusiasts, many of whose leading members he had met in Bayreuth. When he learned that Hans von Bülow was going to conduct two performances of *Tristan und Isolde* in Munich, he asked his conductor friend to reserve him several seats and then persuaded Carl von Gersdorff to join him there in June. The long weekend (Friday to Sunday, 28–30 June) that Nietzsche spent in the Bavarian capital was a sheer delight, and the two performances of *Tristan* – 'the most prodigious, purest, and unexpected' creation he had ever encountered – left him 'swimming in sublimity and happiness' (as Fritz later described this unique experience to Erwin Rohde). Almost as enjoyable were the pleasant hours Nietzsche and Gersdorff spent with Malwida von Meysenbug and her inseparable companion Olga, the younger of Alexander Herzen's two daughters. In Florence, where she now resided, the fifty-year-old Malwida had befriended a number of German exiles who shared her enthusiasm not only for Richard Wagner's operas but also for *The Birth of Tragedy*, which she had praised to every 'kindred soul' she met.

In mid-July there was almost Dionysian jubilation among the 'poison-brewers' of the Schützengraben house in Basel when Franz Overbeck came up with a spicy, one-word title for the detailed anti-Wilamowitz rebuttal that Erwin Rohde had been diligently preparing: *Afterphilologie*. When used as a prefix, *After* in German means 'pseudo' – as in *Aftergelehrsamkeit* (pseudo-scholarship). But in this case *Afterphilologie* also contained a double play on words. When thought of in the English sense, *After* was a subtle retort to Wilamowitz's ironic title, *Zukunftsphilosophie* (*Philosophy-of-the-Future*). But the prefix also contained a scabrous overtone, since *After*, when used as a substantive in German, means 'anus'. The title of Rohde's rebuttal thus cleverly suggested that Wilam-ohne-Witz ('William-without-wit', as Nietzsche now dubbed him) had written a pamphlet that was not only half-baked, but, as one might more crudely put it, a 'half-arsed' exercise in critical philology.

Just four days after Overbeck and his 'poison-brewing' friends had concocted their pungent title for Rohde's essay, Nietzsche wrote to thank Hans von Bülow for having offered him access in Munich to 'the most sublime artistic impression' of his life with his two performances of *Tristan und Isolde*. Bülow had unwittingly become his doctor and Friedrich Nietzsche his 'patient'; for, as he explained, without a periodic cure of good music capable of rescuing him from philology, he was likely to start whining and moaning 'like tom-cats on the rooftops'. As an example of the 'atrocious music' this 'patient' was capable of inventing, Nietzsche enclosed a copy of a 'Manfred Meditation' he had written in a deliberately anti-Schumann style, with discordant dissonances intended to evoke the Byronic hero's soul-shattering doubts and feeling of vertiginous despair.

Replying almost by return post (on 24 July), the pianist-conductor made no secret of his embarrassment at having to pass judgement on such a work, produced by someone he admired as a 'creative-genius representative of science'. Nietzsche's 'Manfred Meditation' struck Bülow as being 'the most extreme in fantastical extravagance, the least uplifting and most anti-musical thing it has been given to me to see as score-paper notations in a long time. More than once I had to ask myself: is all this a joke, did you perhaps intend a parody of the so-called Music-of-the-Future? Is it with conscious intent that you express an uninterrupted scorn for all rules of tonal connection, from the higher syntax to the usually accepted orthography? . . . ' and so on.

A number of writers, including Wagner's biographer Ernest Newman, have concluded from this that Nietzsche's musical talents were negligible and that in matters of composition he was a rank amateur. But this was neither Richard Wagner's nor Cosima's opinion. Both had been impressed by Nietzsche's *Sylvesternacht* composition when they had heard him play it for them at Tribschen. Franz Liszt too was impressed when he was asked to play it during his five-day visit to Bayreuth in October of this same year. When Cosima repeated what Hans von Bülow had said about Nietzsche's music, Liszt gently shook his white-haired head, saying that Bülow's judgement seemed to him too 'despairingly' extreme.

In late August Malwida von Meysenbug wrote from Heidelberg to say that she, her foster-daughter Olga Herzen, and the latter's fiancé, a young French historian named Gabriel Monod, would be passing through Basel at the end of the month. Of all the friendships Nietzsche was to make during his creative lifetime, perhaps none – that with Richard Wagner alone excepted – was more surprising than this one, with a middle-aged spinster who was twenty-eight years his senior. If Wagner's relationship to Nietzsche can be called 'paternal' – and Wagner made no bones about it, going as far as to say that Nietzsche represented a missing generational link between himself and little Siegfried (who in age was more like a grandson) – then Malwida von Meysenbug's relationship can with equal propriety be termed 'maternal'. The photographs and portraits we have of her reveal a serene and pleasant rather than a strikingly handsome face, marked by a long, straight nose, a strong chin, and somewhat wistful eyes, framed by hair that was pulled back over the ears from the central parting and usually covered by the kind of lozenge-shaped lacework one sees in pictures of Queen Victoria. The last but one of ten children born to a German of Huguenot origin who had been made a *Freiherr* (baron) by the

Prince-Elector of Hessen-Cassel, Malwida von Meysenbug had been brought up in a strictly conservative and Lutheran tradition, which had proved painfully constricting for her ardent, idealistic nature. Greatly influenced by the *philosophes* of eighteenth-century France and by the anti-authoritarian nationalism of the 'Young Germany' movement, she had espoused the cause of working-men's and women's rights and had even spent some months in Hamburg as a member of a 'free community' of dedicated revolutionaries. She had thrown herself heart and soul into the revolutionary turmoil of 1848, and, like Wagner, whose early works (*Art and Revolution*, *The Art-work of the Future*) she had avidly read, she had later taken refuge abroad. In London, which after the Napoleonic coup d'état of December 1851 became the haven of many crestfallen revolutionaries, she had supported herself by teaching German and doing translations and had befriended the Hungarian patriot Louis Kossuth, the no less anti-Habsburg Giuseppe Mazzini, and above all the recently widowed Alexander Herzen ('the most arresting Russian political writer of the nineteenth century', as Isaiah Berlin once called him), who had asked her to supervise the education of his daughters. It was also in London, where she attended many of his Philharmonic concerts in the spring of 1853, that Malwida von Meysenbug had first met Richard Wagner, whose unpopular cause she and Olga Herzen had later courageously espoused by trying to silence the whistling and jeering barbarians of the Jockey Club during the three tumultuous performances of Tannhäuser at the Paris Opéra in March 1861. Long before this, however, she, who had begun her life as a Goethean art and nature lover, had followed Wagner's example by becoming a fervent Schopenhauerian.

During Malwida von Meysenbug's brief stay in Basel Nietzsche was impressed to discover that it was she who had translated into forceful German Alexander Herzen's fascinating memoirs – which seemed startlingly new and 'noble' to someone who abhorred all forms of revolution. Like the broad-minded Franz Overbeck, who had been brought up in St Petersburg and Paris and who spoke fluent French and English as well as Russian, Malwida von Meysenbug was a polyglot capable of broadening Nietzsche's intellectual horizon. Before leaving Basel she surprised him yet again by giving him a Swiss-French edition of her reminiscences, candidly entitled *Mémoires d'une idéaliste*.

Early in September Franziska Nietzsche came to spend a few days with her son and daughter in Basel. As a special treat they offered her a weekend visit to the Lake of Lucerne and the Rigi mountain mass, where the short-sighted Fritz gave everyone a fright by missing his step and almost tumbling into a ravine. When his mother left Basel on 11 September, he told her that he would try to make it to Naumburg for the inter-semester holidays at the end of the month. But on the 27th he suddenly changed his mind, overwhelmed by the autumnal beauty of a cloudless day. No, Fritz informed his startled sister, he wasn't going to Naumburg after all! Instead, he was going to take advantage of this rare spell of 'golden' weather by leaving immediately for Zürich, moving on from there to Chur and over the Splügen Pass to Chiavenna and Lake Como in Italy.

The trip began auspiciously, for Nietzsche made it to Basel's eastern railway station with half a minute to spare. But after the sun had set he began to suffer from the cold in the unheated carriage compartment. The hour-after-hour rumbling of the iron wheels brought on painful headaches, and when, a full day and night later, he was at last able to dismount at Chur, he barely had the strength to drag himself to the nearest hotel. However, four hours of sound sleep sufficed to rid him of his migraine, and later he felt so refreshed by a long walk up the cliff-enclosed gorge of the thundering Ragiusa torrent that on reaching the small thermal hotel at the head of the valley he ordered a bottle of Asti Spumante, to supplement the glasses of soda-water which the inkeeper and his wife kept thrusting upon him.

Early the next morning he boarded the post-coach that was to take him over the mountains into Italy. The ride was one of the most breathtaking Nietzsche had ever experienced. 'I will write nothing about the tremendous splendours of the *Via mala*,' he later wrote to his mother. 'It is as though Switzerland up till now were utterly unknown to me. This is my natural landscape, and when we neared Splügen, I was overcome by the wish to remain here.'

The little village of Splügen, located at the confluence of two mountain torrents and the junction of two roads – one leading south-west to the San Bernardino Pass, the other due south to Chiavenna – was then no more than a cluster of slate-roofed peasant chalets perched on a mountain slope which gradually rose in an increasingly vertical cliff-face towards the sky. Being much higher than the verdant meadows and hill-cloaking evergreens of the gentle Lake of Lucerne, it was closer to the treeline and the 'eternal snows'.

'This high-Alpine valley [c. 5,000 ft] is absolutely my delight,' Nietzsche wrote to his mother. 'Here there are strong, pure gusts of air, hillsides, and cliff-boulders of every shape, with mighty snow-mountains posted all around; but what please me most are the splendid highroads, over which I walk for hours, sometimes towards the Bernardino, sometimes towards the summit of the Splügen Pass, without having to watch my step; and wherever I look around, there is something magnificent and undreamed-of to be seen . . . At noon, when the post-coaches arrive, I eat with strangers. I don't need to speak, nobody knows me, I am all alone and could sit and go for walks for weeks on end. In my little room I work with fresh vigour, that is, I jot down and gather together random thoughts for my main subject for the moment, [the] "Future of Educational Establishments".'

The rest of the trip was less exalting. Finally deciding to leave this highland hamlet, Nietzsche took the daily post-coach over the zigzagging Splügen Pass to Chiavenna and Lecco, on Lake Como. It had been his intention to go all the way to Venice, but by the time he reached Bergamo he was so depressed by the greyness of the overcast sky, the dampness of the air, and his unfamiliarity with Italian, that he turned around and travelled back over the mountains.

He was back in Basel on 11 October, four days before his twenty-eighth birthday. His abortive 'descent into Italy' had cost him quite a sum and earned him a reproachful letter from his lonely, widowed mother. Nor had the exhilarating solitude of Splügen provided him with enough inspiration to complete his lecture series on Germany's educational establishments.

Shortly afterwards, the Leipzig publisher Ernst Wilhelm Fritzsch brought out Erwin Rohde's *Afterphilologie* rebuttal to Ulrich von Wilamowitz-Möllendorff's attack on *The Birth of Tragedy*. In forty-eight pages bristling with polemical as well as analytical barbs, the brash 'pipsqueak' from Berlin was ridiculed as a Pasquillant, dismissed as a 'critical windbag', and subjected to a withering counter-critique designed to show up artful misquotations and other errors and lacunae. Nietzsche, who had recently been singled out for special mention in Berlin's *Nationalzeitung* as the only person in the baggage-train of Richard Wagner's 'literary lackeys' to be the holder of a university post, was overjoyed by Rohde's trenchant tone, as were Franz Overbeck and Heinrich Romundt. Wagner, to whom the forty-eight-page booklet was dedicated, was also delighted, remarking, after he had read it to Cosima, 'Yes, there we find ourselves in quite good company.'

If, subjectively, the publication of Rohde's counter-attack was a stimulating tonic for Nietzsche, its objective benefits were less evident. By the time it appeared, Friedrich Nietzsche was on the blacklist of most of Germany's classical philologists. The prevailing sentiment in most German philological faculties had been voiced in Bonn by Ritschl's successor, Hermann Usener: *The Birth of Tragedy* was 'plain nonsense', and anyone crazy enough to write such a book was 'scientifically dead'. In Basel it came too late to make Nietzsche feel any less an outcast. At the start of the winter semester, a score of students who had been planning to pursue their studies of the classics at Basel preferred to transfer to other universities.

A few months before, fifty-three students had enrolled for Jacob Burckhardt's lectures on Greek cultural history. At the start of this winter semester (1872–73) forty students had signed up for Rudolf Eucken's lecture courses on Aristotle, while twenty registered for one of Heinrich Romundt's *Privatdozent* courses in philosophy. But only two students were willing to sign up for Nietzsche's lecture course on Greek and Roman rhetoric. His projected lecture course on Homer, like the one-hour-a-week seminar, had to be abandoned. His classes at the Basel *Pädagogium* were not affected. But his professorial status was now practically reduced to that of an upper high-school teacher. Such was the measure of his fall from academic grace.

## CHAPTER 18

# A First Essay in Polemics

*– The aggressive pathos belongs just as necessarily to strength as vengefulness and rancour belong to weakness.*

To make amends for his sudden flight to Splügen, Fritz decided to spend the coming Christmas and New Year's Day of 1872/3 in Naumburg with his mother and his sister. In so doing he inadvertently opened a rift in his hitherto untroubled relations with Richard Wagner, which from then on was to grow ever wider with the passage of the years.

The forced abandonment of one of his two lecture courses left Nietzsche with more time to deal with the problems posed by the new book he wanted to publish on 'The Future of Germany's Educational Establishments'. But the more he pondered the problem, the more it dawned on him that in tackling this momentous subject, he had promised more than he was able to deliver. As he put it in a letter to Malwida von Meysenbug, to whom he had sent copies of his Basel lectures, 'On reading this, one contracts a parched throat, with at the end nothing to drink.'

The reform of any educational system – in practice this means the importance attributed to the various subjects taught – can never be more than a partial cure, since the pedagogical principles underlying the current curriculum are themselves a reflection of the 'conventional wisdom' or *Zeitgeist* of the moment. Schopenhauer had instinctively understood this in repeatedly deploring the popular *Jetztzeit* ('now-time') cult of facility, which had downgraded Greek and Latin to the level of 'dead' languages, with the result that there were now 'well educated' and truly 'modern' men who could no longer read, write or speak Latin, as any truly educated European had been able to do in the age of Erasmus (1466–1536). Scientifically, Germany might be moving forward, but culturally it was moving backward, encouraged by university professors whose primary interest was to 'keep abreast of the times' by conversing and writing in colloquial journalese.

Shortly before or after Christmas Wagner wrote or sent a telegram to Nietzsche, inviting him to attend a slightly delayed celebration of Cosima's birthday in their at last properly furnished Bayreuth home. Exactly how Nietzsche replied to this flattering invitation, we do not know, for, like Wagner's message, the reply has disappeared. We know, however, from Cosima's diary that Nietzsche sent her a note of birthday greetings, which reached her on Christmas Day, and that it was soon followed by a New Year's Day 'gift' of five embryonic 'Prefaces' to 'Five Unwritten Books' – which were so sketchily composed that they caused more head-shaking than joy when they reached Bayreuth in early January and were read out loud by Richard Wagner. 'Prof. Nietzsche's manuscript also does not restore our spirits,' Cosima noted in her diary. 'We wish he would confine himself principally to classical themes.' This last sentence revealed how little Wagner and Cosima really understood of what was going on in Nietzsche's mind, with regard to his future vocation. It had not yet occurred to either that Nietzsche's deepest ambition was nothing less than to become another Schopenhauer. Nor did either of them feel that this dubious New Year's Day gift made up in any way for Nietzsche's failure to visit them in Bayreuth.

Nietzsche's reluctance to make it to Bayreuth for New Year's Eve is easy to understand. He had reached Naumburg just three days before Christmas and he would have to leave his home town on 31 December, effectively cutting his holiday to eight days and nine nights. He knew that this would be a bitter disappointment to his mother and his Naumburg friends, for of those eight short days, one was largely spent on a hurried trip to nearby Weimar (to attend a performance of *Lohengrin*, which Fritz had not yet seen staged), while another afternoon took him to Leipzig for an important meeting with his and Wagner's publisher, Ernst Wilhelm Fritzsch. More difficult to fathom were Nietzsche's reasons for choosing to return directly to Basel via Erfurt and Frankfurt, rather than by the slightly longer railway route that would have taken him from Naumburg to Nürnberg, with a stopover in Bayreuth. He may have hoped that his birthday present for Cosima would elicit a telegram of congratulations, and had surmised, from her silence, that the gift had not been appreciated.

Richard Wagner took Nietzsche's *Nichtkommen* (non-arrival) very badly. He felt that he had paid his young friend a compliment by inviting him to join Cosima and himself for their first New Year festivities in Bayreuth. The composer's feeling of admiring affection for the brilliant young professor from Basel had over the past three years assumed an almost paternal intensity, as he had recently made clear in two extraordinary letters. In the first, written in late June 1872, he had solemnly declared: 'Strictly speaking, you are, after my wife, the sole windfall that life has brought me; now, however, Fidi [his son Siegfried] has also been added thereto; but between him and me I feel I need a link, which you alone could form, somewhat as a son is to a grandson . . .' In a second, much longer letter, dated 24 October, Wagner had written: 'I now look at my son, my Siegfried: the youngster grows sturdier and stronger by the day, and is as ready to fight with his pranks as with his fists . . . For me he is a sheer marvel, and at my wife's side I have chased away despair, so much hope has the little fellow given me . . . The young boy makes me think of you, my Friend, and out of sheer family egotism he fills me with the greedy desire to see all the hopes I have pinned on you fulfilled to the letter: for the young boy – ach! – needs you.'

In making this extraordinary confession, Wagner was clearly thinking of his own slipshod education, in which his study of Greek and Latin had been sadly neglected. Even as he wrote those revealing lines, he must have realized how selfishly unrealistic was this fond hope that Nietzsche could somehow oversee his son's education and thus make sure that 'Fidi' received a thorough grounding in the classics. Had he and Cosima remained at Tribschen and thus close to Basel, such an ideal might conceivably have been realized – with the young Siegfried becoming one of Nietzsche's *Pädagogium* and later university students. But, reluctant though he was to admit it – Wagner had always been a man who wanted to have his cake and eat it too – the move to Bayreuth had knocked the props out from under this frail fancy. And while Nietzsche, as recently as October, had still been considering the possibility of having Rohde replace him as professor of classical philology at Basel – an 'honour' his friend Erwin had strenuously rejected – neither Richard Wagner nor Cosima were at all eager to see Nietzsche give up his academic chair. It was his professional renown as one of Germany's most promising professors of classical philology that had made *The Birth of Tragedy* such a significant event, just as it was Erwin Rohde's recently acquired prestige as an associate professor of classical philology at Kiel that had given his subsequent duel with Wilamowitz-Möllendorff a truly national dimension.

It was in a moment of despondency, brought on by various financial setbacks and the realization that the planned four-opera *Ring* cycle could not now be staged before 1875, that Wagner had invited Nietzsche to celebrate the first days of the New Year with him and Cosima in Bayreuth. He wanted among other things to discuss what kind of periodical was needed to publicize Bayreuth and the 'art-work-of-the-future' undertaking, and how much Nietzsche should be paid for his editorial work and personal contributions. Nietzsche's mere presence, he felt sure, would act as a stimulating tonic. All the more bitter, therefore, was the 'Emperor's' disappointment when his most cherished disciple failed to show up.

Wagner was still seething with frustration over this 'slight' when, on 7 January, the day chosen for a belated celebration of Cosima's birthday, Carl von Gersdorff unexpectedly arrived from his parents' home in Silesia.

Wagner was too busy entertaining the banker Feustel and other Bayreuth notables to be able to discuss the matter with Nietzsche's friend. But Gersdorff sensed from the tone of their voices how much Richard Wagner and Cosima had been saddened by Nietzsche's odd absence.

In mid-January Richard Wagner and Cosima left Bayreuth on another fund-raising concert tour, which took them to a slightly less hostile Berlin and then on to a distinctly more enthusiastic Hamburg. Not until 12 February, four days after their return to Bayreuth, was Cosima at last able to sit down and write Nietzsche a long, embarrassed letter of apology for her long silence. In it she frankly admitted that it had taken her a long time to tell him the honest truth: that the 'Master' had been hurt by his 'not-coming' and by the manner in which he had informed them of his 'not-coming'.

Nietzsche was both surprised and upset by this letter, which also contained a lucid critique of his five prefaces. In a letter written in early March to Gersdorff, Fritz expressed his bewilderment that Wagner should have been so offended. 'I cannot conceive how someone could show more loyalty and be more deeply devoted to W[agner] in all important matters than I am . . . But in small, minor, secondary matters and in an abstention from more frequent personal cohabitation, which for me can be called an almost "sanitary" necessity, I must preserve my freedom in order really to be able to maintain my loyalty in a higher sense.'

Gersdorff lost no time replying (this time from Rome) with a letter of intelligent remonstrance. In this delicate matter Wagner had had every right to feel offended. 'Wagner is of a most delicate tenderness in matters of the heart, and you have a weighty status. But don't forget how much he values you and how little joy such a solitary soul derives from his daily intercourse with human beings. And so in future, travel from Naumburg via Eisenach and Lichtenfels to Bayreuth, etc., and everything will go much better.'

Wagner in the meantime had written Nietzsche a gentle rebuke: 'Today for the first time I was able to sleep through the night undisturbed by loathsome conditions. Many are the pleasures I have had to forego. There are moments when I lose myself in reminiscences, and then you also appear before me – as it were between me and Fidi. But it doesn't last long, and then Wagner Clubs and Wagner concerts revolve around me in a lovely circle. Therefore – patience! As I must also have with you!'

Having decided to shelve his unfinished series of lectures on Germany's educational establishments, Nietzsche now began to prepare another book: one devoted to the relatively obscure pre-Socratic philosophers of ancient Greece. Little was (and still is) known about those early philosophers. Unlike many of the works of Plato and Aristotle, mere fragments have survived of what Thales, Anaximander, Heraclitus, Parmenides, Anaxagoras, Empedocles and Democritus actually wrote and said. Much the same fate had overtaken the works of their great contemporararies, Aeschylus and Sophocles, whose surviving plays – seven for the first, eight out of more than 100 for the second – were but a tiny portion of their total output. But those plays had at least survived more or less in their entirety, whereas the 'works' of Thales and his successors were no more than fragments. Indeed, in some cases the only remnants were summaries recorded by later scholars or historians, like Diogenes Laertius. This, Nietzsche felt, was a gross injustice rendered to the pioneers of Greek free-thinking who, at a time when the mythical fables of Creation – with Uranus fathering the Titans before being castrated by his son Cronos, who in his turn was killed by his son Zeus – were beginning to lose their credibility, had manfully striven to provide their countrymen with less fanciful explanations of the universe and of Man's place in it. To begin the study of Greek philosophy with Socrates, as was then the tendency in German universities, was, Nietzsche felt, ridiculous. In reality, Thales, Anaximander, Heraclitus, Parmenides and the rest were the true creators of what had come to be known as 'philosophy' – which is to say Man's conscious effort to comprehend the world in which he lives without resort to poetic flights of fancy. How much easier it had been for Socrates, a relative latecomer, to criticize and even to ridicule what his speculative predecessors had struggled so heroically to build!

In dragging those little known Greek thinkers from the dark wings of 'pre-philosophy' out on to the bright centre of the stage, Nietzsche once again was flouting the conventional wisdom of the academic world in which he lived. Heraclitus, in particular, was singled out for praise as a supremely 'realistic' thinker, who had unflinchingly accepted the ceaselessly changing, mutable nature of human and animal life, the perishability of all things, whereas the 'ice-cold' Parmenides, in a pathetic search for philosophical certainty, had rejected everything in the world that was 'incipient, lush, blossoming, illusory, attractive and vital' as quintessentially transient, untrustworthy and ultimately unreal, inventing a kind of 'counter-universe' of permanent, unchanging but also 'empty' certitude – later transformed by Plato into an idealistic world of everlasting 'universals'.

Schopenhauer, while full of praise for great poets, writers, sculptors and composers, whose works had a 'timeless' value far exceeding the momentary 'victories' of soldiers, politicians and so-called 'statesmen', had never ceased to regard 'genuine' philosophers – so rare a species that not more than one or two usually appeared in any century – as exemplary human beings. This too was Nietzsche's feeling. Made painfully aware of his shortcomings as a musician each time he studied a Wagnerian score or listened to the Master play out a new theme on the piano, he knew that his vocation was to be a thinker. What puzzled him was how exactly to meet this challenge. The creative artist needs no theoretical justification. His works, even when insufficiently recognized during his lifetime, outlive his death and become part of an artistic legacy for future generations. But what of the philosopher? Was Nietzsche's predestined role simply to be a critic of society, as Socrates had been in Greek antiquity, and Schopenhauer in modern times? Was his role essentially a negative one, compared to the positive creations of the artist? Nietzsche fancied he had found an answer to this troubling question in assigning to philosophy an essentially curative role. Which is why, in writing to his friends Erwin Rohde and Carl von Gersdorff, he spoke of calling his new book *Der Philosoph als Artz der Cultur* (*The Philosopher as the Physician or Doctor of Culture*). If a society was sick – and it was Fritz's conviction that this was very much the case with contemporary German society – then it should be the philosopher's task to try to cure its culture.

Nietzsche was hoping to have his new book finished before the start of the new semester, so as to be able to offer it as a gift on the occasion of Richard Wagner's sixtieth birthday, due to be celebrated on 22 May. But on 24 March he was thrown off his stride by a letter from Erwin Rohde, in which his friend informed him that he was travelling south to Heidelberg on the 27th to stay with Professor Otto Ribbeck, one of the few classical philologists in Germany who had supported him in his duel with Wilamowitz-Möllendorff. Rohde's salary as assistant professor at Kiel was so meagre that he lacked the means to pay the train fare as far as Basel, but he wondered if they couldn't arrange to meet for a day or two in Stuttgart or Karlsruhe? Nietzsche replied with a telegram suggesting that, instead of Stuttgart or Karlsruhe, they converge on Bayreuth. Another telegram was dispatched to Bayreuth, to ask if he and his friend Erwin Rohde could visit the Wagners during Easter week. It elicited a joyous response from the composer.

The two friends reached Bayreuth during the afternoon of Palm Sunday (6 April), shortly after the unexpected arrival of the Munich architect and sculptor Lorenz Gedon, who had agreed to decorate the interior of the new house Wagner had decided to have built for himself and his family. Nietzsche and Rohde were also invited to visit this new mansion, which, though still far from finished, was praised by Gedon for its excellent design.

The next day the two visiting professors were taken by Wagner to visit the barely begun opera house, the construction of which had been repeatedly delayed by lack of money. The afternoon was enlivened by the visit of the local dean, who got into a spirited argument with Wagner, claiming that the only solution to the Jewish problem in Germany would be through intermarriage and assimilation; to which the composer retorted that German blood was simply not strong enough to withstand this 'alkali'. The end result was likely to be a mongrel race, such as the French had become when the hardy blood of the Norsemen and the Franks had been diluted with Latin blood from the south.

Nietzsche and Rohde, to judge from Cosima's diary, prudently held their peace. That evening Nietzsche was invited to read the first handwritten pages of his new manuscript, devoted to the pre-Socratic philosophers. Cosima found what she heard 'new and interesting', and this seems to have been Wagner's opinion too, for the next evening Nietzsche was again asked to continue his reading. The absence of any further comment in Cosima's diary makes it clear that the Master of the House found this material far less exciting than *The Birth of Tragedy*. This is hardly surprising. *Philosophy in the Tragic Age of the Greeks* – the title Nietzsche had chosen, *faute de mieux* – was not primarily concerned with either drama or music, and it had no direct bearing on Wagner's present preoccupations. Loath as he was to admit it to anyone but Cosima, Wagner secretly regretted leaving the tranquillity of Tribschen, where he had been able to compose most of the *Ring* series. Here in Bayreuth he was so harassed by letters he had to answer from the presidents of Wagner Clubs reporting on the troubles they were having, by fund-raising concert and lecture tours explaining the noble aims of the Bayreuth enterprise, that he had not yet found the time to complete the orchestration of *Götterdämmerung*.

By Wednesday morning Wagner had grown so glum and irritable that he told Cosima that he could not stand 'continual conversation'. This was probably less a critique of *Philosophy in the Tragic Age of the Greeks* than an expression of frustrated exasperation at the slow progress being made; for most of this day was devoted to discussing ways of promoting the Bayreuth 'ideal'. Beyond the fervent hope that Nietzsche would somehow manage to edit the periodical he wished to launch, Wagner had nothing concrete to suggest. Nor for that matter did Nietzsche, or the taciturn Erwin Rohde. Dedicated Wagnerians though they were, both were university professors, had no desire to become 'propagandists' in any popular sense, and, like Wagner himself, they shared Schopenhauer's contempt for *Jetztzeit* (now-time) journalism. Indeed, by evening the prevailing gloom was such that Wagner had to sit down at the piano after dinner and play the conclusion of *Götterdämmerung* before their cares, as Cosima put it in her diary, could 'vanish into thin air'.

Maundy Thursday (10 April) happened to be the birthday of Wagner's elder daughter, Isolde – the celebration of which kept Cosima busy for most of the day. The next day, Good Friday, Wagner decided to defy the elements by taking his guests out for a carriage drive to the Eremitage Castle, which Frederick the Great's sister had built for herself a century before. Overhead the thunder rolled, while eerie flashes of lightning briefly illuminated the baroque walls. Only a furious wind and racing clouds were missing to make it look like a scene from *Die Walküre.*

That evening Nietzsche was again asked to read something from his latest work, but it elicited no reaction from the Master of the House. To liven things up, Wagner went to the piano and sang several of his favourite Karl Loewe ballads. This musical intermezzo so excited Nietzsche that he asked his hosts if he could play something he had composed. The permission could not be politely refused. The composition – it may have been a streamlined version of a four-handed piano piece wittily entitled 'Monodie à deux', which Nietzsche had recently sent to Florence as a wedding gift for Olga Herzen and her bridegroom, Gabriel Monod – caused more embarrassment than pleasure. As Cosima noted that evening in her diary: 'We are vexed by our friend's music-making pastimes.'

Four days after his return to Basel, Nietzsche wrote Wagner a humble letter of apology, regretting that his recent visit to Bayreuth had brought his 'dearest Master' so little relief from his present cares. 'I beg you to adopt me simply as a disciple, wherever possible pen in hand and with a notebook before him, as a disciple moreover with a very slow and far from versatile ingenium.'

Nietzsche had, however, found a remedy for his mood of despondency: a feeling of indignant rage. In the long letter she had sent to Nietzsche in early February, Cosima had told him how surprised she and Richard Wagner had been, during their trip through northern Germany, by the enthusiasm everywhere aroused by a recently published book entitled *Der alte und der neue Glaube* (*The Old and the New Faith*). Its author was the same David Strauss who, thirty years before in his *Life of Christ*, had undertaken to 'demystify' the life of the founder of Christianity by stripping away the legendary accretions added by later disciples, in order to present his German readers with an account that was as historically accurate and credible as possible. Strauss's new book, of a distinctly less critical and more popular kind, struck both Cosima and Wagner as being 'shallow', but this had not kept it from going through five editions in less than a year.

The mere fact that Strauss's new book had become so popular in so short a time made it automatically suspect to Nietzsche as one more example of *Jetztzeit* (now-time) mediocrity. Before leaving for Bayreuth he had been incensed to learn from his friend and neighbour, Franz Overbeck, that Strauss, in advocating an up-to-date, positive, progressive and optimistic Christianity, had dismissed Schopenhauer's pessimistic *Weltanschauung* as the rotten product of a 'putrefying brain'.

It was not until he reached Bayreuth and heard Cosima and Richard Wagner expressing their profound distaste for David Strauss's new brand of agreeably 'modernized' Christianity that Nietzsche decided that he too must read this 'worthless rubbish'. He may even have begun to do so during his train-trip back to Basel. One thing is certain: within four days of his return he had read Strauss's *The Old and the New Faith* from cover to cover. It filled him with a fury which wrenched him overnight from his spirit of dejection. As he wrote to Wagner on 18 April, Strauss's book had amazed him 'by the obtuseness and meanness of the author as much as of the thinker'.

One week later Nietzsche wrote a second letter to Wagner, to say that his friend Franz Overbeck had run into trouble with a just completed manuscript on the subject of the 'Christianness' (*Christlichkeit*) of contemporary theology. Overbeck's 'shocking' thesis was that it was impossible to reconcile Christian theology, which had evolved over the centuries as a distinctly intellectual interpretation of the Gospels, with the primitive faith of Jesus's disciples, who had lived in a naïve expectation of the end of the world and of a 'second coming'. But what had particularly annoyed his publisher was Overbeck's critique of David Strauss's best-selling apologia of a popular, positive and painless Christianity. He had refused to publish such an iconoclastic work for fear of offending 'German public opinion'. Nietzsche now wondered if Wagner could recommend Overbeck's heretical 'masterpiece' to his publisher, Ernst Wilhelm Fritzsch. Wagner, who had heard Nietzsche praise his friend's independence of mind and his antipathy for factional 'Protestant clubs' and 'theological party-men', urged Fritzsch to publish Overbeck's book. If it caused readers to froth at the mouth and aroused an uproar like the one provoked by *The Birth of Tragedy*, so much the better. He added: 'As regards your Straussiana, I feel but one torment – that I cannot wait for it. *Also: heraus damit!*' So, get it out – as fast as possible!

Nietzsche had not waited for this word of encouragement to add his own firebrand to the controversial blaze. Like a hungry dog gnawing away at his sole remaining bone (as he put it in a letter to his mother and sister), Fritz used the few remaining days of his post-Easter vacation to work on his polemical onslaught on David Strauss. By 5 May he could write to Erwin Rohde that the first draft was virtually finished. He hoped to have it ready in time to be able to send it to Bayreuth as a gift for Richard Wagner's sixtieth birthday on 22 May. But shortly after the start of the second university semester and the resumption of his tedious *Pädagogium* classes, Nietzsche began to suffer blinding eye-aches which made it impossible for him to work at night by lamplight.

On 18 May Gersdorff reached Basel, after a brief stopover in Florence to see Malwida von Meysenbug. During his tour of Sicily Carl had contracted malaria, but the bouts of shivering fever and intestinal inconveniences it had caused him were mild compared to the blinding torments now affecting his friend Fritz. With each passing day Nietzsche's agonizing eye-aches grew more intense. By the time his sister Elisabeth reached Basel on 5 June, he could no longer read or write letters, even to close friends like Erwin Rohde, Cosima or Richard Wagner. He was forced to wear dark glasses every time he ventured out of the Schützengraben house, and much of his time was spent indoors in a room with the curtains carefully drawn to reduce the daylight to a minimum. If his friend Carl had not generously volunteered to stay on and help Fritz with the laborious writing, reading and correcting of the partly dictated manuscript, Nietzsche could never have finished his anti-Strauss polemic.

It was also the selfless Gersdorff who took the manuscript on 20 June and personally delivered it into the hands of Ernst Wilhelm Fritzsch. Having by now sold out of the first edition of *The Birth of Tragedy*, with a second printing expected soon, Fritzsch welcomed Nietzsche's new text. He was even ready to offer the 'most honoured' professor from Basel a long-term contract for a series of *Unzeitgemässe Betrachtungen* ('Untimely' – in the sense of inopportune, out-of-step, anti-fashionable – 'Meditations'), of which the anti-Strauss polemic was to be the first.

By early July Nietzsche's condition had deteriorated so drastically that his doctor friend, Professor Immermann, told him that he would have to cease his *Pädagogium* classes before the end of the school year and undergo a cure of total rest in some secluded mountain village. On or around 7 July, Fritz and his friend Carl left Basel and headed south-eastward past Zürich and its long lake over the same railway route Nietzsche had used nine months before to reach Splügen. They found what they were looking for some distance west of Chur, in a beautifully wooded mountain region. Perched on a hillside overlooking the village of Flims, their balconied chalet-*pension* offered them a splendid view of the tiny Lake Camau and the soaring cliff-face of the appropriately named Flimserstein, rising like a petrified geyser from the tranquil deep-green waters. At an altitude of 1,000 metres the crisp, resin-scented air was intoxicatingly pure and bracing, while the surrounding woodlands, with their firs and larches, offered Nietzsche the shade he needed for his daily walks down to the lakeside, where he, Carl von Gersdorff, and (for a while) Heinrich Romundt splashed around late in the afternoon, after the conclusion of an after-lunch siesta.

Nietzsche's rest cure began at 5.30 a.m. when a glass of fresh cow's milk was brought to his bedside by a maid. Stretched out in bed, he spent the next hour and a half quietly digesting it, before rising and getting dressed. The rest of the day, between meals of healthy Swiss food, was spent in walks over wooded paths to clearings and patches of greenery, where, comfortably reclining on soft banks of moss, Carl and Heinrich took turns entertaining their friend by reading extracts from the 'greatest and best authors' (as Gersdorff put it in a letter to the absent Rohde): Goethe, Plutarch, the despondent Leopardi and the verse librettos of three *Ring* operas – *Die Walküre*, *Siegfried* and *Götterdämmerung*. Alpine thunderstorms, with sudden gusts of wind and drenching rain, alternating with bursts of scorching sunshine, added a Wagnerian depth to the beauties of an ever-changing landscape; and neither the pounding on an ill-tuned piano in the leafy 'reading-room', nor the flies buzzing over steaming dishes in the dining-room could spoil the bucolic charm of this tranquil vacation.

On 8 August the first bound copies of Nietzsche's anti-Strauss booklet were brought to the chalet-*pension* by the postman. Forgetting the usual afternoon siesta, Fritz and his two friends made their way down to the lakeside, and, using a knife, they commemorated this exciting moment by inscribing the letters U.B.I. F.N. 8./8. 1873 (*Unzeitgemässe Betrachtung* I. Friedrich Nietzsche. 8 August 1873) into a slab of slanting marble. They then swam out to another protruding slab of rock, where a longer series of initials (with C.G. for Carl von Gersdorff, and H.R. for Heinrich Romundt) were carved into the cliff-face. After swimming back to the shore, the three friends emptied a bottle of wine over the first inscription. 'The evening was celestially pure and clear,' reported Carl von Gersdorff the next day to Erwin Rohde: so pure indeed that in his ears Nietzsche may well have heard the softly descending and upward-soaring notes of Wolfram's '*Abendstern*' prayer in *Tannhäuser*, invoking the benediction of an evening star the short-sighted Fritz could not distinctly see.

If the first days of the autumn semester were relatively calm, it was the lull that often precedes a storm. For before a month was up Nietzsche could report, in the first long letter he had been able to write since the second half of May, that the firstborn of his 'Untimely Meditations' had stirred up an 'indescribable' uproar in Switzerland: 'a crazily hostile newspaper literature has arisen against me, but it has been *read* by everybody'.

In the very first paragraph of this remarkable essay Nietzsche made it clear that he was not motivated by any personal animus, even though the use of the word *Bekenner* (Confessor) in the title – 'David Strauss, the

Confessor and the Writer' – was unmistakably sarcastic. This opening paragraph is worth quoting in its entirety – for the elevation of the thought no less than for its calm defiance, just three years after Prussia's crushing triumph in its war with France, of the 'conventional wisdom' of the moment.

> Public opinion in Germany seems almost to forbid that one should talk of the evil and dangerous consequences of the war, and above all of a victoriously concluded war. All the more willingly, however, will those writers be heard who harbour no more important opinion than that known as 'public' and who are therefore militantly zealous in extolling the war and in jubilantly noting the mighty phenomena of its impact on morality, culture, and art. Nevertheless, let it be said: a great victory is a great danger. Human nature endures it with more difficulty than a defeat; indeed, it even seems easier to obtain such a victory than to endure it in such a way that no greater defeat should result from it. But of all the evil consequences which the latest war with France has left in its wake, the most nefarious perhaps is a widespread, indeed a universal mistake: the mistake made by public opinion and all who publicly opine, that in this conflict German culture also triumphed and must therefore be crowned with laurel wreaths commensurate with such extraordinary happenings and successes. This illusion is exceedingly pernicious: not because it is an illusion – for some errors are most salutary and fruitful – but because it could transform our victory into a total defeat: *the defeat, the extirpation of the German spirit on behalf of the 'German Reich'*.

Even if, Nietzsche went on, deciding to puncture this illusion at the outset, the Franco-Prussian War had been a war between two cultures, it was no reason to indulge in jubilation or self-glorification. The 'subjugated culture' (i.e. of France) – a brief concession to the Francophobic Wagner – might indeed be of little worth; in which case the victory obtained over it was not much to boast about. For the fact of the matter was that French culture had survived the débâcle of 1870, while the Germans were as dependent on it as before. The German virtues that had made their victory possible – 'strict military training, natural courage and endurance, superior leadership, the cohesiveness and obedience of those led' – had nothing whatever to do with culture. As for the 'hardy and imperturbable' courage of the Germans, it remained to be seen if they would have the strength of mind and purpose to apply it against the 'internal enemy' – which is to say, against 'that highly ambiguous and in any case unnational "educatedness"' (*Gebildeheit*) which in Germany was erroneously mistaken for 'culture'. But with each passing day, it seemed to Nietzsche, the prospects of such an 'inner battle' on behalf of a genuine German culture were growing dimmer, so solidly entrenched in their self-satisfaction were the close-knit clique of jingoistic, punch-drunk 'journalistic hacks and manufacturers of novels, tragedies, songs, and history books' who were now preening themselves like peacocks before the mirror of their self-esteem and expecting the world to pay homage to their status as 'classic authors'.

None of this, as regards substance, was radically new. Schopenhauer, particularly in his *Parerga* essays, had trenchantly denounced the formless mish-mash of German 'culture', forced to import everything from the cut of clothes to architectural styles from France. He had ridiculed the pompous pedantry of German 'chair philosophers' and so-called 'scholars' who could no longer express themselves in Latin, and the shallowness of journalistic scribblers who were butchering the German language. He had even, in a diatribe on 'Philosophy at the Universities', castigated the 'philistinism' of Hegel and his disciples for their pernicious deification of the State. But what Schopenhauer had not done and which Nietzsche now proceeded to do, with a polemical verve not seen in Germany since the days of Heinrich Heine, was to combine the two notions of *Bildung* (education) and *Philister* (philistine), thus creating a kind of hybrid centaur dubbed the *Bildungsphilister*: the 'educated philistine', the current prototype of the supposedly 'cultivated' German.

Unlike the truly great creative souls of Germany's eighteenth and early nineteenth centuries – men like Goethe, Schiller, Lessing, Lichtenberg, Hölderlin – all of whom were *Suchende* ('seekers' after truth and beauty), the contemporary *Bildungsphilister* was a smug, self-satisfied 'finder' who did not have to do any more searching, since he had already found what he considered to be 'true' and 'beautiful'. Goethe had had the modesty to declare that German culture was still so embryonic and formless that it might take the Germans a couple of centuries before they could honestly claim that they had ceased to be barbarians. The contemporary *Bildungsphilister*, on the other hand, having elevated these 'glorious' predecessors to the rank of immutably 'classic' authors, could then calmly appropriate and make them his personal cultural property, to be interpreted for his petty purposes and according to his petty standards. In this way, with the help of Hegel's 'deification of everydayness', the *Bildungsphilister* had created for himself a cosy nest of *Philisterglück* (philistine happiness), one well cushioned with smug certainties in which there was no need to exert oneself unduly, since everything of genuine worth had already been discovered, or more exactly 'revealed' by one of the current age's great 'confessors' – David Strauss.

It was only towards the end of the second section (out of a total of twelve) that Nietzsche for the first time mentioned Strauss as being a 'truly *satisfait* [example] of our educational conditions and a typical philistine'. And it was not until the beginning of the third section of his essay that Nietzsche actually began to dissect the 368 pages of Strauss's 'catechism' – *The Old and the New Faith* – with an increasingly tigerish ferocity. He ridiculed the author's fatuous pontifications about everyone and everything (Haydn, Beethoven, Kant, Schopenhauer, etc.); his equally fatuous propagation of a 'Religion of the Future' in which Darwinian evolution could be happily married to the teaching of the Gospels, thus ensuring everlasting spiritual contentment for future generations.

It is impossible in a few words to do full justice to this juicy essay. But let me cite this passage as an example of Nietzsche's polemical verve at its most savage: 'For the worm a corpse is a lovely thought, and the worm is a horrible one for every living being. Worms dream of their heaven in a fat body, professors of philosophy by grubbing around in Schopenhauer's entrails, and as long as there are rodents, there has been and will be a rodent heaven. Our first question – How does the new believer dream of his heaven? – is thus answered. The Straussian philistine makes his home inside the works of our great poets and musicians as does a termite, which lives while it destroys, admires while it devours, adores while it digests.'

By the time Nietzsche had completed his own work of critical destruction, virtually every aspect of Strauss's 'cultural philistinism' had been ruthlessly exposed and ground to dust. Strauss, the self-ordained apostle of a comfortable, progressive, sentimentally 'humanized' Christianity, in which the Darwinian lion could lie quietly down with the evangelical lamb; Strauss, the advocate and apologist of a mind-numbing scholastic rat-race (in Nietzsche's eyes a new form of 'cultured' barbarism); Strauss, the insolent spokesman of the scholastic community's 'aesthetic infallibility'; Strauss, in religious matters the self-proclaimed revealer of the 'silent assent' of most Germans (an interesting anticipation of Richard Nixon's 'silent majority'); Strauss, the less than inspired prophet of a 'new' faith that was so radically new and different from the old that he himself could not coherently distinguish them and had to leave those striving to do so to their own devices; Strauss, whose secret ambition was to be a German Voltaire, not to say a French Lessing, and wherever possible, both at once; Strauss, the sarcastically dubbed 'Magister who tripped so lightly past the dizzying abysses of fundamental problems greater geniuses have dared to face'; the new Strauss, so different from the 'strong, upright, straitlaced' scholar-author of *The Life of Christ* ('whom we found so sympathetic'), yes, the new Strauss, who had betrayed his past by assuming the role of 'naïve' genius and 'classic' author, and who for that very reason had ended up a ham actor and an unworthy stylist – all were pitilessly mocked and raked over the coals.

It only remained for Nietzsche to deliver the *coup de grâce* by meticulously analysing what Schopenhauer would have called the *Lumpen-Jargon* (the rags-and-tatters slang) of this 'classic' writer. A dozen pages were devoted to pinpointing the many stylistic lapses of Straussian prose – with sloppy usages, the faulty placing of adjectives and prepositions, wrong choices of prefixes and grotesquely mixed metaphors. After which, Nietzsche concluded, in a tone of defiance that was also a programme for the future: 'Germany's philistine culture will, of course, be infuriated when one speaks of painted idols, there where it sees a living God.'

## CHAPTER 19

# The Uses and Abuses of History

*– The errors of great men should be revered as more fruitful than little men's truths.*

In mid-October of 1873, when he celebrated his twenty-ninth birthday, Nietzsche's eye- and headaches were still so blindingly acute that every third day he had to take to his bed and remain in his room with the curtains drawn. He was not allowed to read by lamplight, nor had his doctor yet permitted him to resume his classroom teaching. And it was at this moment, when he was reduced to a state of near impotence, that he received an 'invitation' from Emil Heckel's Wagner Club committee in Mannheim, asking him to draft an 'Appeal to the German People' explaining the national significance of the Bayreuth enterprise.

Incapacitated though he was, Nietzsche dragged out the rough draft of an 'Appeal' he had prepared a few months before, probably intending to present it to Richard Wagner for his sixtieth birthday. On Wednesday, 22 October, he spent a hectic morning revamping the text with the aid of the invaluable Heinrich Romundt. At 1 p.m. the text was completed and promptly taken to a local printer to be typeset. By Saturday evening the printed pamphlets were ready. A copy was immediately dispatched to Richard Wagner in Bayreuth, another sent to Erwin Rohde in Kiel.

In a desperate attempt to keep his Bayreuth enterprise from foundering for lack of funds, Wagner had invited representatives from all the major Wagner Clubs in Germany to an informal conference in Bayreuth on 31 October – celebrated throughout Protestant Germany as 'Reformation Day', because it was on that day in 1517 that Martin Luther had nailed his ninety-five theses to the chapel door of Wittenberg's castle.

In his accompanying letters to Rohde and Wagner, Nietzsche had stressed his basic intent: to 'enrage the Evil-minded and to assemble and inflame the Good Ones through this anger'. In the text he had followed this prescription to the letter by adopting, from the first sentence on, a tone of censorious admonition: 'We want to be heard, for we speak as warners; and the voice of the warner, whoever it may be and wherever it may resound, is always in the right.' For, as Nietzsche went on, it was these warners – he meant of course the promoters of the Bayreuth cause – who were bent on defending 'the welfare and honour of the German spirit and of Germany's good name'. Over and against these altruistic, far-sighted souls Nietzsche pitted, in scathing contrast, the *Unwissenden* – the narrow-minded 'ignoramuses' who, wilfully or through short-sighted inadvertence, refused to appreciate the significance of Richard Wagner's efforts to drag German 'culture' out of its swamplands of mediocrity.

Even for Erwin Rohde this was pretty strong medicine. Much as he sympathized with the sentiments expressed, convinced though he was that the 'lukewarm, dissatisfied Germans' deserved the kicks that Nietzsche was administering, this was no way to persuade them of the error of their ways.

Wagner's reaction was both positively enthusiastic and reluctantly negative. Of a naturally combative temperament, he was delighted by the trenchant tone of Nietzsche's text. It thrilled him almost as much as had a second reading of the anti-Strauss booklet, which had moved Wagner to pay the author this extraordinary compliment: 'I swear to God that I regard you as the only one who knows what I want!' But, as Wagner had learned from experience, if the Bayreuth enterprise was to be effectively promoted, it would have to be with the kid gloves of the diplomat rather than through the polemical punches of a prizefighter.

Two days later, on 30 October, Nietzsche reached Bayreuth. On his way to the Wagners' house he met the composer and Cosima. As they walked back to their rented house – the Wagners' new home, like the future Festspiel opera house, was not yet finished – Nietzsche told them that his anti-Strauss essay had made him a host of new enemies, notably in Leipzig, where a local 'ink-slinger' had written an article in the notoriously anti-Wagnerian *Grenzboten*, denouncing Nietzsche as a dangerous radical and sworn enemy of German culture – with the comic result that certain hotheads of the communistic First International had decided that the iconoclastic Basel professor was at heart a revolutionary and one of their own.

The next morning Nietzsche joined Wagner and Cosima for breakfast. His 'very fine' Appeal was read and approved by the Master, enthused by the elegance of Nietzsche's style and the fervent elevation of his thought. He brushed aside all reservations – at any rate for the moment. For, as Cosima noted that evening in her diary: 'Is it wise to issue this – but of what use is wisdom to us? Only faith and truth can help.'

A great deal of faith was needed on this particularly dismal 'Reformation Day'. Overnight the pure blue sky and bright autumn sun had disappeared, replaced by sheets of rain which poured down from the grey clouds as densely as they had during the foundation-stone ceremonies on 22 May of the preceding year. The sorry handful of Wagner Club representatives who made a ritual visit to the recently roofed opera house had to slog through mud and puddles, while water dripped from their top hats. Inside the Bayreuth Rathaus it was so dark that oil-lamps had to be lit to enable the assembled Wagnerophiles – far fewer than expected – to read the printed copies of his 'Appeal to the Germans', which Nietzsche had brought with him from Basel. Just as Rohde had feared, the text was deemed far too bold to be signed by a mass of sympathizers. Adolf Stern, a professor of literature from Dresden, was asked to draft a shorter, more acceptable text.

That evening, at a small banquet given at the Gasthaus zur Sonne, Nietzsche, as a special mark of 'imperial' favour, was seated between Cosima Wagner and Malwida von Meysenbug, the only two ladies present.

The next morning there was another meeting of Wagner Club delegates, this time in the house of the banker Friedrich Feustel. A brief, innocuous and (as Nietzsche described it) 'optimistically dyed' text, prepared by Professor Stern, was unanimously approved as being likely to attract rather than repel potential signatories. This was followed by a 'cheerful' as well as exclusive lunch *à cinq* to which Nietzsche and Emil Heckel were alone invited by the Wagners, along with Malwida von Meysenbug, who was beginning to regret her valiant decision to serve the Wagner cause by moving from sunny Florence to wintry Bayreuth. At dinner that evening, which was also attended by Professor Stern, Wagner told amusing stories before expounding on one of his pet themes: his quest for the authentic 'roots' he felt must be discovered in order to establish the linguistic purity of a German language that had been fatally corrupted by the importation of foreign words. Nietzsche amused the company by graphically describing a visit made to Basel by a crazy widow of unbelievable ugliness, Rosalie Nielsen, who, after reading *The Birth of Tragedy*, had developed a wild passion for the author, persuaded that she was a feminine incarnation of Dionysus. After returning to Leipzig, she had tried to buy out Ernst Wilhelm Fritzsch and to take over his publishing company: a move that had alarmed Nietzsche, particularly after he had discovered that she had close ties with the Marxist International!

Nietzsche's description of this mad virago's 'Dionysian' irruption into his Schützengraben lodgings in Basel so amused Wagner that later, after the guests had left, he sat down and composed nine verses of amusing doggerel expressing his appreciation for Nietzsche's unflagging loyalty and the harassing troubles it had caused him:

*Schwert, Stock und Pritzsche*
*kurz, was im Verlag von Fritzsche*
*schrei', lärm' oder quietzsche*
*das schenk ich meinem Nietzsche, –*
*wär's ihm zu was nütze!*

(Sword, stick and bat
From Fritzsche's firm, in short,
Shouts, noise or shrieks
I hereby give to my Nietzsche
May it all be of use to him!)

Throughout the autumn and early winter of 1873 Nietzsche was almost permanently unwell, suffering not only from acute eye-aches every time he tried to read for more than an hour or two, but also from nausea, stomach upsets and even vomiting – almost certainly due to his hyper-nervous condition in moments of difficult creativity. As his doctor friend, Professor Immermann, one day said to him, knowing in advance that it was an impossible prescription: 'Be more stupid and you will feel better.'

By this time Nietzsche's university seminar (on Plato and the pre-Socratic philosophers) and his *Pädagogium* classes had become such a matter of routine that they required little preparation. Even so, only through a great effort of will power and the aid of his devoted friends, Heinrich Romundt (who did much of the writing) and Franz Overbeck, could he complete most of his second *Unzeitgemässe Betrachtung* (Untimely Meditation) between his birthday (15 October), which he had to 'celebrate' in bed, and the start of the Christmas holidays. Radically different in tone from his anti-Strauss polemic, though written in an anti-Hegelian spirit, this second 'essay' was devoted to a searching enquiry into the 'Utility and Disadvantage of History for Life'.

On 10 December Carl von Gersdorff turned up in Basel, after completing a three-month artistic tour of cities in central and northern Italy. He and Fritz then went over the first draft, page by page. On the 18th Gersdorff left Basel, taking with him a number of chapters which he generously volunteered to rewrite in his far clearer script once he had reached his parents' home in Silesia. From Bayreuth, where Wagner and Cosima were delighted to welcome 'this excellent man, who is utterly lacking in vanity, always open, truthful and serious' (Cosima's description in her diary), he moved on to his parents' home near Görlitz, where he was happy to report on his birthday (26 December) that he had finished the recopying.

Nietzsche, who went to Naumburg to spend the holidays with his mother and sister, began the tenth and final chapter the day after Christmas. Four days later he made a quick trip to Leipzig, where he signed the contract Fritzsch had prepared and was glad to see the neatly written manuscript pages that Gersdorff had sent to the publisher from Silesia.

In the concluding, hastily added chapters of *The Birth of Tragedy*,

Nietzsche had tried to explain why a better understanding of the origins of Greek drama could enable one to appreciate what Richard Wagner was seeking to achieve with his 'global' conception of opera as the 'art-work-of-the-future'. But this left unanswered the deeper question of what benefit the study of antiquity could be to nineteenth-century Europeans. And behind this question loomed an even greater one: one that Schopenhauer, anti-Hegelian though he was, had not bothered to tackle. What use to human beings, and above all to creative human beings, is a knowledge of the past, the study of history? In a long letter written in Genoa during a tour of Italy, Heinrich Romundt had criticized Schopenhauer, pointing out that while his descriptions of the state of deep contentment reached by human beings in moments of aesthetic rapture, when the surging 'will' is totally at rest, provided a satisfactory explanation of aesthetic appreciation, they offered no insight into artistic creation. Schopenhauer had emphasized the essentially passive, contemplative aspects of human existence, but his philosophy shed no light on the mysterious processes of artistic creativity. It was this lacuna in Schopenhauer's philosophy that Nietzsche now decided to fill by devoting the second of his 'Untimely Meditations' to the question of the role that knowledge of the past plays in determining the behaviour of active, creative human beings.

In the brief foreword to this ten-part book Nietzsche acknowledged his debt to the greatest of German poets by quoting from a letter Goethe had written to Schiller in December of the fateful, revolutionary year of 1789: 'Besides, I hate everything that merely informs me, without increasing or directly stimulating my activity.' The man who had made this confession was the same who later had had Faust, in his first encounter with Mephistopheles, redefine the opening lines of the Gospel of St John: 'In the beginning was the Act.' History, Nietzsche roundly declared, deserved to be scorned if it was merely regarded as a form of luxury and an excess of knowledge to be used for the enjoyment of 'spoiled idlers wandering about in the garden of Knowledge' rather than as something 'we need for Life and Action'.

One of the things Nietzsche had already come to realize, thereby anticipating Freud, Adler and Jung, is that an individual's attitude towards his past is essentially ambivalent. It can act as a stimulus, as a source of inspiration, or, on the contrary, as a depressant, inducing a condition of passive resignation, morbid discontent, resentful rejection and revolt. The first of these varying attitudes that were singled out for analysis Nietzsche called the 'monumental'. The landscape of the past, as one looks back over it, presents one with a jagged panorama, what Nietzsche called a 'mountain range' (*Höhenzug*) of exemplary human beings, whose lives and deeds in different spheres of activity provide inspiration for Doers and Strivers (men of action, politicians, generals, creative artists and scientists), Preservers and Admirers (teachers, administrative officials, museum curators), Sufferers and Consolers (sages and saints). But those who seek inspiration from these gigantic figures of the past – here Nietzsche was clearly thinking of Wagner – find themselves perpetually warring against the stuffy habits of the small and petty-minded; they are depressed by the damp 'valley air' which stiflingly obscures everything that is great. Such petty beings 'want only one thing: to live at any price . . . And yet there are always a few who are aroused, who with a backward glance at the greatness of the past, are so fortified by its contemplation that they feel supremely happy . . .' The 'lesson' they draw from the contemplation of the past is that 'he lives most beautifully who pays little heed to existence'.

Emerson had said much the same thing, in describing the hero as one who is 'negligent of expense, of health, of life, of danger, of hatred, of reproach, and [who] knows that his will is higher and more excellent than all possible antagonists'. But Emerson had not had a Schopenhauer to contend with. For before he had finished with this crucial paragraph, Nietzsche made it clear that his thinking differed radically from Schopenhauer's. The kernel of the aristocratic-Hellenic ideal, partly revealed in *The Birth of Tragedy*, had now burst open the pod of Schopenhauerian pessimism. The attitude of passive resignation before the cruel vicissitudes of life, which Schopenhauer had implicitly approved, was now assigned to the 'petty man' whose short-sighted, downcast gaze is focused on his immediate needs, and witheringly contrasted to the 'Olympian laughter' and 'sublime scorn' of the upward-gazing creator. 'Fame in this most transfigured form is, however, something more than the delicious bite of vanity, as Schopenhauer called it; it is a belief in the fellowship and continuity of the Great Ones of all times . . . '

In what way exactly, Nietzsche then asked, could a 'monumental' appreciation of the past, of classical antiquity and other 'rare' periods, serve the contemporary individual? The answer was simple: it helped people to realize that because Greatness was once possible, it could well exist again. Then, hammering home the central theme around which the book was constructed, Nietzsche suggested that it was quite feasible to imagine that one hundred truly productive souls, 'brought up in a new spirit', could rid Germany of the pedantry (*Gebildeheit*) that was currently the fashion, since the entire culture of the Renaissance had been 'carried on the shoulders of one hundred men'.

Having thus briefly described the positive élan that a 'monumental' attitude to the past can arouse, Nietzsche pointed out the inherent dangers: the temptation to ignore vast areas of human history in order to concentrate exclusively on certain facts or figures; a tendency to indulge in a hero-worship that was indistinguishable from mythical fiction; a readiness to deceive oneself through a resort to false historical analogies; a state of mind that worked enthusiasts up into a frenzy of fanaticism, encouraged visionary hotheads and scoundrels to destroy empires, assassinate princes, ignite wars and revolutions.

What Nietzsche was presenting here, in a highly condensed and sketchy form, was a non-Hegelian dialectic of his own. Just as in broad daylight every material object casts a shadow, so every truth is shadowed by its darker opposite, every apparent blessing by its corresponding curse. Whence, as the ancient Greek philosophers had realized early on, a need for balance in passing judgement on human events. Nothing over the centuries had proved to be more hostile to genuine creativity than those perennial parasites, the arbiters of 'good taste'; but at the same time nothing was more beneficial to the welfare of stable societies than a conservative feeling of respect, or what Nietzsche called an 'antiquarian' attitude towards an honoured past. Indeed, in describing the love, the fidelity, the 'piety' that the inhabitants of a town feel towards the past of their community – with its walls, its towered gateways, its town-council regulations, its folk festivals – Nietzsche was clearly recalling the feeling of close community he had known during his younger years in Naumburg and which was still clearly felt in the larger, more patrician city of Basel. And what was true of town and city was also true of the entity known as one's country. For no worse fate could befall a people than to lose a feeling of fidelity towards its past and to abandon itself to a 'restless cosmopolitan searching and choosing of what is New, forever New'.

Veneration of the past, as something to be preserved unchanged, could, however, all too easily become a mummifying, dead-weight force, crushing the life out of creative enterprises. This was why, alongside of the 'monumental' approach to the past, capable of inducing heady fevers of intoxication, and the 'antiquarian' attitude of cultural conservatism, there was needed a third attitude towards the past which Nietzsche chose to call 'critical', but which – and it was a huge but – had to be employed 'in the service of Life'. To be truly creative, 'Man must from time to time have the courage to shatter and to decompose the past in order to live. This he does by hauling the past before a court of justice . . . ' But, Nietzsche unflinchingly added, 'it is not Justice that sits in judgement here; still less is it Mercy which hands down the sentence; but solely Life, that dark, driving, insatiably self-craving power. Its verdict is always unkind, always unjust, for never is it derived from the pure fountain of Knowledge.'

By this subtle feat of intellectual legerdemain Nietzsche in a couple of sentences accomplished a triple revolution. He gave the negative word 'critical' – previously used to condemn the rationalism of Socrates, the 'gravedigger' of 'great' Hellenic culture – an entirely new, positive connotation. He made it clear that he felt more sympathy for Goethe's life-enhancing paganism than for Schopenhauer's life-denying pessimism. Finally, in praising 'Life, that dark, driving, insatiably self-craving power', he reinterpreted Schopenhauer's negative notion of the Will as a dark, driving force to be resisted by Man's intellect into a positive creative urge anteceding the acquisition of knowledge and the regulatory control of the Intellect.

Anyone who, like Heraclitus, develops a philosophy based on the inevitability of Change and on the vital importance of Becoming (as opposed to static Being), must be prepared to accept the socially destabilizing, and indeed destructive, consequences. 'For it then becomes clear how unjust is the existence of any privilege, any caste, any dynasty, and how much this thing merits its disappearance.' But the consequences, Nietzsche (a bitter foe of revolutions) hastened to add, are dire. 'Then is the past regarded critically, then does man seize the knife and hack away at the roots, then are all forms of piety trampled under foot. It is always a dangerous process, notably for Life itself; and men or times who serve Life in this way, by judging and destroying the past, are always dangerous and endangered men and times.'

Having weighed the advantages and dangers of three basic attitudes towards the past, Nietzsche could now do what he had wanted to do from the beginning: open fire on everything he most disliked in contemporary German culture and behaviour: academic pedantry, fact-cluttered historiography, bogus 'objectivity', pedestrian 'everyman wisdom', the insolent claim to have a right to judge earlier periods of human history according to the yardsticks of 'contemporary triviality'. For, 'as judges you must stand higher than those who are to be judged'. In extolling the handful of gifted individuals who can reach the sublime level of 'objective' history writing, Nietzsche did not wish to belittle the earnest efforts made by the 'wheelbarrowing', 'shovelling' and 'sifting' labourers who lacked the genius to be truly great historians. They will always remain the indispensable journeymen and hod-carriers who place themselves in the service of the master. But, Nietzsche noted, aiming one more punch at his favourite foe, 'A great scholar and a great blockhead – can easily be combined beneath the same hat.'

Only those capable of forward-looking vision, possessed indeed of an almost oracular capacity to divine the shape of the future, could, Nietzsche argued, become truly great historians. One of the great crimes committed by Hegelianism had been to 'depoetize' and demean the study of history by making it retrospectively rational. Any historical enquiry, unless linked to some forward-looking hope, was bound to end up being destructive. Once a religion is subjected to meticulous historical and scientific analysis – one that is bound to expose all sorts of false, crude, inhuman, absurd and violent realities – it is doomed. For – and here Nietzsche was anticipating the bitter truth Dostoevsky later enunciated in *The Legend of the Grand Inquisitor* – a scientifically analysed religion loses that 'atmosphere of pious illusion in which everything that wants to live can only live . . . only in love, however, shaded by the illusion of love, can Man create, namely in an unlimited belief in what is just and perfect'.

Again using Goethe as his sword and shield, Nietzsche repeated the great poet's realistic dictum: 'He who destroys illusion in himself and in others will be punished by Nature, the sternest of tyrants.' But this was what Protestant theologians had been doing in an attempt to 'liberalize' and 'modernize' Christianity. It had not occurred to them that they were thus undermining the very religion they were seeking to buttress 'scientifically'. For, Nietzsche added: 'Everything living needs to be enveloped in an aura of mystery; when one removes this protective covering, when one condemns a religion, an art or a genius to gravitate like a star without an atmosphere, then no one should any longer be surprised to see it quickly dry up and become unfruitful.'

The essential difference between the late medieval Christian and the modern Hegelian was that the former was naïvely persuaded that, when the great moment came, Justice would be exercised by the Son of Man. Hegel and his disciples, on the other hand, had usurped this divine privilege, arrogating to themselves a secular right to sit in judgement on the past, simply because they constituted the latest and thus best-informed generation in a historical process that was close to 2,000 years old. By creating a kind of 'wandering God', revealing himself in successive stages of history, Hegel had implanted in his disciples a pernicious adulation of the 'power of history', an idolization of actuality, thereby developing in them a head-bowing, 'Chinese-mechanical' attitude of puppet-like submission and readiness to say yes to 'any power, be it that of a government, of public opinion, or of a numerical majority'. And, in prophetic words that were to be fulfilled sixty years later, Nietzsche added: 'Since every success carries within itself its rational necessity, since every event is the triumph of the logical or of the 'Idea' – quick, get down on your knees and kneeling climb every rung on the step-ladder of success!'

Nothing, furthermore, had more encouraged the presumptuousness of Hegel's followers than the extension of scientific knowledge far back beyond the earliest origins of 'human history' 6,000 years ago. The historico-biological realization of the enormous distance Man had travelled from the earliest species of animal down to the contemporary *Homo sapiens* had filled him with a feeling of 'swelling elation' at having reached such a breathtaking 'summit', the be-all and end-all of the world-historical process. The superb Hegelo-Darwinian could now exclaim: 'We are the goal, we are the goal, we are completed Nature!'

'Oh, excessively proud European of the nineteenth century, how you rave!' thundered Nietzsche. 'Just measure for a moment the heights [you have reached] as a scientific knower with the depths [to which you can descend]. To be sure, on the sunbeams of science you climb upward to the heavens, but [you descend] also downwards to chaos . . . The ground beneath your feet pulls you back into uncertainty. For your life there are no more props, merely the filament of a spider's web, which each new clutch of knowledge tears asunder.'

But no, Nietzsche continued, after ridiculing Eduard von Hartmann, a neo-Hegelian 'parodist' who, in his much acclaimed *Philosophie des Unbewussten* (*Philosophy of the Unconscious*), had brashly asserted that soon geniuses would no longer be a 'necessity' for a stage of the world-historical process that was 'more important and progressive' than the present age. For the time would surely come when the emphasis on 'mankind history' would once again be shifted away from the masses to 'isolated individuals, who form a bridge over the torrent of Becoming. The latter do not perpetuate a process, but rather live timelessly and simultaneously . . . they live like the Republic of Geniuses, of which Schopenhauer once spoke: one giant calls to another across the bare intervals of time and, undisturbed by the noisy chatter of the dwarfs who crawl away beneath them, carry on their lofty intellectual conversation.' No, Nietzsche defiantly concluded, enunciating a credo that was to blossom forth later in his vision of the 'Overman' (*Übermensch*), the goal of humanity cannot lie at the end of the road, but only in its loftiest examples!'

It must be admitted that Neitzsche's anathemas against the dominance in German schooling of the historical-scientific spirit were more forcefully and compellingly expressed than were his vague recommendations for teaching the next generation of Germans how to 'learn from life'. His two prescriptions were, first of all, an 'unhistorical' ability to forget the past and to confine oneself to a limited *horizon* (underlined by Nietzsche), and, secondly, a 'suprahistorical' capacity to disregard transient movements in order to concentrate on realities that are eternal – as in *Art* and *Religion* (again underlined by Nietzsche). The trouble with *science* was that it was fundamentally unsettling. It possessed a volcanic, telluric force – Nietzsche even coined a new word, *Begriffsbeben* (concept-quake), to describe the earthquaking effect it had in undermining security and peace of mind. In ceaselessly pushing back the horizons of knowledge, science left Man alone, like a hapless mariner afloat on a 'timeless, boundless sea of luminous waves'. But when it came to spelling out what the next generation of Germans should 'learn from life', all he could recommend was that those young rebels throw overboard all the shopworn 'party-words' and hackneyed notions that presently encumbered academic talk in Germany.

What, in this limp conclusion, Nietzsche was in effect recommending was a 'philosophy of life' – a *Lebensphilosophie*, as the slightly older Wilhelm Dilthey later called it – in which rational thought or Reason was downgraded from the heights to which it had been raised from Descartes's time down to that of Hegel, and subordinated to the imperatives of that exhilarating but also potentially explosive mystery known as life. And in pointing out that Man cannot live by science alone, he was already sounding the note of existential anguish which was to be echoed so insistently in the works of his philosophical successors of the twentieth century.

CHAPTER 20

# Forging a Philosophical Hammer

*– A book that has no fire in it deserves to be burned.*

Nietzsche returned to Basel on the fourth day of the new year, 1874, half frozen from hours spent in an unheated train compartment during the overnight train-trip from Naumburg. He managed to cross the slippery, snow-covered Rhine bridge leading from the railway station to the old patrician town without mishap and was glad to regain the cosy warmth of his Schützengraben lodgings, where he shared an evening meal with a disconsolate Heinrich Romundt. Rudolf Eucken, whose chair of philosophy Nietzsche had once hoped to occupy, was moving on to the University of Jena, and Romundt, now as ostracized a Schopenhauerian as his friend Fritz, knew that he had not a chance in the world of being selected for the vacant post.

In Naumburg two weeks of maternal care and a simple diet, beginning every morning with warm cow's milk (the best remedy for his frequent stomach upsets and ulcerous condition), had greatly helped to calm his nerves. In Basel Fritz gave up his habit of lunching at a nearby tavern, offering himself instead a late 11.30 'breakfast' of soup and two ham sandwiches, with 'vegetarian' bread and a simple meat dish in the afternoon: a diet which seems to have worked wonders for most of 1874.

Five days after his return to Basel, Nietzsche received the corrected galley proofs of the first chapters of *On the Utility and Disadvantage of History for Life*, sent by the publisher to Erwin Rohde in Kiel. By mid-February the first printed copies were ready to be sent to several privileged recipients. Jacob Burckhardt responded with a letter of thanks in which he modestly confessed that his 'poor head' had never been able to ponder so deeply the 'ultimate foundations, aims and desired qualities of historical science' as Nietzsche had done. Cosima and Richard Wagner were put off by the difficult beginning, in which Nietzsche laboriously explained that human happiness, like the bucolic contentment of a ruminating, 'non-historical' cow, is best achieved when one lives solely in the present, untroubled by the burden of past reminiscences. But their initially negative opinion soon changed as they read on into the more specifically anti-Hegelian and anti-Eduard von Hartmann sections. As Cosima wrote the next day: 'We continue with our friend's book and delight in it – great courage, great fervour, very acute judgement. R[ichard]'s example has opened his eyes to the triviality of the modern world' – an affirmation that blandly ignored Schopenhauer's immense contribution to Nietzsche's intellectual disoccultation. By the evening of 24 February the entire book had been read, giving rise the next day to a discussion between Wagner and his wife, who noted that 'the fiery wit with which it is written is quite astonishing'.

On the 27th Wagner wrote to Nietzsche that he had found his book so stimulating that it could have given rise to lengthy expatiations quite unsuitable for a single letter. He would have to leave it to his wife to write a proper commentary. In the meantime he wanted Nietzsche to know that his 'great affair' (the Bayreuth venture) was going to be realized after all. The inauguration was now planned for 1876; for a full year of rehearsals would be needed in 1875 before the *Ring* series could be properly performed in all of its splendour. 'Our house will be ready in May: your room will then be ready. I hope you will come to rest here, the countryside hereabouts is mountainous.' The letter ended with the promise that Cosima would be writing soon, although for the time being her eyes were giving her trouble.

Not until 20 March had Cosima's eyesight sufficiently improved to enable her to write Nietzsche a many-paged commentary which, by its sheer length, was an extraordinary compliment paid to the author. She and Richard Wagner had initially been startled and impressed by the profundity of the thoughts Nietzsche had expressed, but both nevertheless feared that the 'difficulty' of this essay would make it 'inaccessible to most'.

Erwin Rohde, in a long letter written four days later, was more critical. He took Fritz gently to task for not developing his arguments sufficiently, leaving the puzzled reader 'to find the bridges between your thoughts and your sentences'. He advised his friend to read 'the finest' English essayists; for, notwthstanding their 'dreadful common-sense style', they marvellously understood 'the difficult art of logical exposition without resort to peremptory insistence'.

Wagner, curiously enough, had reached much the same conclusion. For, after rereading Nietzsche's little book in early April, he told Cosima that this second 'Untimely Meditation' was 'the work of a very significant person, and if he ever becomes famous, this work will one day earn respect. But it is very immature. It lacks plasticity, because he never cites examples from history . . . This work has been brought out too quickly.'

Erwin Rohde's judicious critique, combined with the bitter realization that his tedious *Pädagogium* classes, extending several weeks beyond the conclusion of the university's winter semester, would make it impossible for him to spend the Easter holidays in Naumburg with his mother and sister, plunged Nietzsche into a state of deep dejection. In a letter of congratulation (on the last-minute rescue of the Bayreuth undertaking) sent to Cosima Wagner in early April he made no attempt to conceal his despondency. This letter has unfortunately disappeared; but to judge by the tenor of Richard Wagner's prompt and Cosima's later reply, it contained a litany of complaints – about the 'morose, Calvinistic' atmosphere of Basel, the kind of 'useless life' he was leading, with virtually no students willing to sign up for his more or less boycotted lectures, etc.

Wagner's reaction, when Cosima read him this melancholy letter, was both realistic and cynical: 'He should either marry or write an opera, though doubtless the latter would be such that it would never get produced, and so would never bring him into contact with life.' Wagner then took time out from the laborious completion of his *Götterdämmerung* score – now constantly interrupted by the need to test the vocal and musical aptitudes of the singers and instrumentalists he wanted to recruit for the inaugural Festival performances of 1876 – to write Nietzsche a brutally frank as well as friendly letter. Without beating about the bush, the former philanderer and uninhibited seducer deplored the excessively masculine atmosphere of the Schützengraben household, with its Nietzsche–Overbeck–Romundt trio: a closed male world of afternoon tea and philosophical conversations in the evening which he, Richard Wagner, never given to hypochondria, had never known in his youth. 'But it seems that it is women that these young gentlemen lack: that means of course, as my old friend [Johann] Sulzer once remarked, "from where to take and not to steal?" At a pinch, however, one can always steal' – which, of course, was exactly what Wagner himself had done by stealing Cosima away from her conductor-husband, Hans von Bülow. 'I mean that you must marry, or else compose an opera. The one will help you as well or as ill as the other. But I regard marriage as the better of the two.'

In the meantime, Wagner had a 'palliative' to suggest – of a kind he himself had never been offered in his lifetime: that their young friend come to spend the entire summer with Cosima and himself in their new 'Wahnfried' home. He reproached Nietzsche for having intimated some months before that he was going to spend the summer holidays on some 'very high and isolated Swiss mountain . . . Doesn't that sound like a painstaking defence against any kind of invitation from us? . . . why do you spurn what is most urgent? – Gersdorff and the entire Basilicum' – i.e. Fritz's Basel friends Overbeck and Romundt – 'could have a good time here. A lot is going on: I am having all my *Nibelungen* singers passed in review; the stage-set decorator paints, the machinist rigs the stage: we are all here together. But – one knows that in this as in other ways there is something strange about Friend Nietzsche! . . . Ach! My God! Marry a rich wife! Why must Gersdorff be the only male among you! Then you can travel and enrich yourself . . . and compose your opera, which however will certainly be shamefully difficult to produce – What kind of Satan made you only a pedagogue!'

Nietzsche did not immediately reply to this extraordinary letter, at once friendly and paternal, frank and callously uncomprehending. Generous though it unquestionably was, there was something outlandish in Wagner's proposal that Nietzsche come to spend all of his summer holidays in Bayreuth. His sarcastic reference to the 'very high and isolated Swiss mountain' on which Nietzsche proposed to perch during the summer vacation displayed a callous disregard for his young friend's intellectual need for peace, solitude and sublime scenery in which to pursue his meditations. What had made each visit to Lucerne a sheer, untroubled delight was the relative seclusion of the Wagners' house at Tribschen, far from the beaten track of effusive admirers, insincere bankers, busy-body 'well-wishers' and unreliable 'promoters' of every kind. It was precisely for this reason, as Wagner himself was honest enough to admit in his more lucid moments, that he had been able to complete most of the *Ring des Nibelungen* operas during his six years in Switzerland. But if there were three things that were totally lacking in Bayreuth, they were peace, quiet and seclusion. At Tribschen, where he was a rare, privileged and highly valued visitor, Nietzsche had had Wagner virtually all to himself. But in Bayreuth, which the composer was bent on making the musical capital of Germany, if not of Europe, Nietzsche knew – from Carl von Gersdorff's descriptions, Cosima's letters, and now from the Master's own admission – that he would have to share Wagner's time-rationed friendship with a ceaseless succession of singers, instrumentalists, scenery designers and stagecraft engineers in a residential mansion which, though it contained a special guest-room for himself, would be in a state of permanent commotion.

Equally gratuitous was Wagner's common-sense suggestion that Nietzsche find himself a wife, and, if possible, a rich one. This had become a matter of increasing concern to Fritz's mother, particularly since his Naumburg friends Wilhelm Pinder and Gustav Krug had each found a 'suitable' fiancée and were due to be married in the autumn. But Fritz had already seen enough of the world to know that the road to marital felicity is full of pitfalls, and that a hastily concluded marriage could easily become as cramping and oppressive as his *Pädagogium* drudgery. Nor was Richard Wagner ideally fitted to offer advice; for his first marriage to a pretty, charming but intellectually disappointing actress (Wilhelmine Planer) had quickly proved disastrous.

In late May, Carl von Gesdorff, who had left his Silesian ploughlands and hen-coops (where he was learning to be a farmer) to pay a birthday visit to Richard Wagner in Bayreuth, wrote Fritz a long letter describing the new 'Wahnfried' house in glowing terms. Wagner had installed him in the guest-room just vacated by his musical assistant, Hans Richter. Cosima had shown Gersdorff the gloomy letter Nietzsche had written to her in early April, and they had discussed his case at length. He fully supported the advice Wagner and also Cosima had given Nietzsche about the need to be well married. It took two to make a good match possible; but, Gersdorff asserted glibly, 'there are no lack of women; finding the right one is your business'.

Fritz thanked his friend Carl for his vivid description of the Wagners' new Wahnfried home. But the thought that Gersdorff and the 'Bayreuthers' (i.e. Wagner and Cosima) were going to constitute a 'marriage-deliberation-committee' to determine his future welfare struck him as being 'truly heavenly'!

Nietzsche, in the meantime, had partly completed his third 'Untimely Meditation'. All it needed, as he wrote to Erwin Rohde on 10 May, was a shower of 'warm, fruitful rain' and it would shoot up overnight like a 'growth of asparagus'.

In the rough plan – for thirteen 'Untimely Meditations' – he had conceived at Flims, the topic of 'The Philosopher' had been accorded the third place in the line-up. But in February, exasperated by a new Reichstag law imposing a 'voluntary' one-year period of military service on all young Germans, Nietzsche had thought of pushing 'The Philosopher' to one side while he fired off a broadside against the progressive militarization of the German *Reich* and the undermining of its shaky culture. As he explained to Rohde: 'That I am somewhat dilettantish and immature in my outbursts I know well, but that is the way it is and I must first eject the whole polemical-negative stuff; I must first untiringly sing away the entire gamut of my hatreds, up and down the scale . . . so that "the vault resounds". Later . . . I will fling all polemics behind me and think about a "good work".'

Nietzsche's spur-of-the-moment burst of rage against the Reichstag's militaristic legislation cooled, however, almost as fast as it had erupted. In mid-May he informed Erwin Rohde that he was reverting to his original plan: the title of his new 'Meditation' would be *Schopenhauer among the Germans*.

Early in July Nietzsche suffered a major loss when his venerable university mentor, Wilhelm Vischer, died of kidney and bladder trouble. No matter who the city of Basel's governing council chose to succeed him, Nietzsche knew that he could no longer expect the friendly tolerance and protection he had been accorded by his warm-hearted benefactor and the members of his family. His conspicuous failure as an 'unwanted' professor of philology was bound to become an embarrassment for everyone. For once again only four university 'cripples' had been willing to sign up for his lecture course on Aeschylus's *Choephoroi* (*The Libation-Bearers*), one of whom turned out to be a thirty-year-old upholsterer who had started learning Greek at the age of twenty-nine!

His sombre mood, aggravated by an unpleasant heatwave which affected his delicate nervous system and provoked new stomach upsets, might easily have touched rock-bottom when he received a letter from Ernst Wilhelm Fritzsch, in Leipzig, informing him that his publishing firm's financial situation was now so dire that for the time being he could not pay Nietzsche any overdue royalties nor undertake the immediate publication of the third 'Untimely Meditation'. However, just two days before (10 July), by a fortuitous coincidence, Nietzsche had received a letter from Ernst Schmeitzner, an enterprising Saxon from Schloss-Chemnitz (near Dresden), who was about to launch a new firm specializing in the publication of books in the fields of philosophy, aesthetics and 'beautiful literature'. Would Nietzsche let him bring out one of his books? Nietzsche replied that he would gladly send him a new manuscript, entitled *Arthur Schopenhauer*, which he expected to finish during the month of August.

On 19 July Nietzsche left the unpleasantly hot city of Basel and, accompanied by Heinrich Romundt, headed once again for the high Alpine regions of eastern Switzerland. At the Hôtel Lukmanier, in Chur, where they spent the night, they ran into a group of holidaymakers whom they had met the previous summer and who were now returning to verdant Flims. Among them was a pretty girl from Basel, Berta Rohr, who so charmed Nietzsche that for a moment he felt tempted to alter his plans, follow her to Flims and there propose to her. But in so doing he knew he would forfeit the solitude and peace of mind he needed to complete his third 'Untimely Meditation'. And so, putting duty before pleasure, Fritz continued southward, instead of turning west. The last stretch of the trip was again accomplished by post-chaise, this time up the narrow valley of the torrential Albula river leading to the highlands of the Engadine.

Situated near the mountain mass of the Piz Ela, the village of Bergün, where Nietzsche and Romundt had chosen to seek refuge from the heat of Basel, overlooked a broad, rocky valley, offering them a far grander panoramic view of the surrounding mountains than they had known amid the pine and larch groves of Flims. For a price of 6 francs per night, they found that they were virtually the only boarders in a mountain hostelry briefly visited each day by 100 post-chaise travellers – 'chloritic and weak-nerved folk from all over the world', as Fritz described them contemptuously in a letter to his mother – who were on their way to or returning from the fashionable watering-spa of St Moritz. Around noon their restful solitude was noisily interrupted by a sudden influx of hungry strangers, with forty of whom, seated around a single table, Nietzsche and Romundt had to share the midday meal.

Invigorated by the crisp Alpine air, which, as he wrote to his mother, stimulated luminous thoughts 'which one does not find in the depths and in the summer sultriness of cities', Fritz was able to complete most of his Schopenhauer essay before descending from the highlands in mid-August. He was encouraged by an intelligent letter from the Schloss-Chemnitz publisher, Schmeitzner, who wrote that he would be happy to continue publication of the planned series of 'Untimely Meditations'. Nietzsche's spirits were also cheered by a letter from Franz Overbeck, who from his parents' home in Dresden reported that he was going to offer Schmeitzner a new, iconoclastic book in the field of Church history. He ended by wishing his friend well, adding, in the Wagnero-Siegfriedian language now favoured by the inmates of the 'Baumann cavern', the hope that Fritz had by now successfully completed his 'forging of the philosophical hammer'.

A year and a half before, in February 1873, Fritz's former friend and admirer Professor Friedrich Ritschl had written from Leipzig to Wilhelm Vischer in Basel to say that he shared the chairman of the governing council's concern for Nietzsche's academic welfare. But the problem now seemed to Ritschl insoluble. 'It is truly wondrous how two souls simply live next to each other in this man. On the one hand, the strictest methods of well-schooled scientific research . . . On the other hand, this fantastic-rhapsodic, overly brilliant, excessively head-over-heels-into-the-unintelligible, Wagnero-Schopenhauerian, art-mystery-and-religious, giddy enthusiasm. For it is not too much to say that he and his co-adepts Rohde and Romundt, who are totally under his magical influence, are out to found a new religion. Both orally and in writing I have made no secret to him of what I am intimating here. The end of the story is that mutually we lack understanding for each other. For me he is too dizzily high, I for him am too much of an earth-bound caterpillar creeper. What angers me most is his impiety towards his real mother, who suckled him on her breasts: Philology.'

Had Friedrich Ritschl been able to foresee to what dizzying heights of matriphobic impiety his former star pupil was going to elevate himself in his third 'Untimely Meditation', his disapproval would have been even more harshly phrased. The heady Alpine air of the Engadine may have had little to do with it, for the most virulently polemical pages had been written even before Fritz reached Bergün. But what is certain is that this time, in launching a frontal assault on academic scholarship, Nietzsche was burning his bridges as never before.

From the point of view of varied content, *Schopenhauer as Educator* was less original than its predecessor, *The Utility and Disadvantage of History for Life*. Though slightly longer (111 printed pages), it was, however, less diffuse (with only eight, instead of ten sections) and better constructed, rising steadily towards a powerful polemical crescendo.

This third 'Untimely Meditation' began with a remarkable paragraph which, behind its quietly enunciated basic theme, possessed the tranquil power of a Brahms symphony. When asked what human quality he had everywhere discovered among the many lands and peoples he had visited, a much travelled globetrotter would probably answer, 'Laziness'. Others might disagree, regarding Fear as a more basic motivation. They would be right, for in fact the two are intimately related. For what after all is indolent conformism but a fear of what one's neighbour may think if one defies convention and doesn't think like the rest, or, as Nietzsche more forcefully put it, 'like the herd' (*herdenmässig*). With most human beings the readiness to think and act conventionally like the rest is simply the result of convenience, sloth, the laziness of habit. 'When a great thinker scorns human beings, it is their laziness he scorns; for it is because of this that they resemble factory products and appear insignificant and unworthy of being consorted with and taught. The man who does not wish to belong to the mass needs only to cease being complacent towards himself; let him follow his conscience, which tells him: "Be yourself! For everything you are now doing, intending, and desiring is not at all you."'

But what exactly is the nature of this 'self', to which Socrates had appealed in issuing his famous exhortation, 'Know yourself', in the name of self-truthfulness and authenticity? Nietzsche, who spent the next fifteen years wrestling with this question, did not yet have an adequate answer. But, as he made clear in the ensuing paragraphs where he excoriated vacuous individuals – mere 'publicly opining pseudo-persons' (*öffentliche meinende Scheinmenschen*) – of one thing he was already convinced: this mysterious human 'self' was not something fixed and static, it was a dynamic process of change and, wherever the effort was made, of self-guiding and self-improving. As he put it, resorting to poetic imagery: 'Nobody can build for you the bridge over which you must cross the river of life, no one other than yourself . . . There is in the world but one way over which nobody but you can pass. Where does it lead? Ask not, but follow it. Who was it who spoke the sentence: "A man never rises higher than when he does not know whereto his way may lead him"?'

The answer was Cromwell, whose remark Emerson had quoted in one of his essays. If Nietzsche did not identify the source, it was because the beginning of this third 'Untimely Meditation' was impregnated through and through with the anti-conformist sentiments the sage of Concord had so forthrightly expressed in several of his essays, and particularly in *Self-Reliance*, in sentences like this: 'These are the voices we hear in solitude, but they grow faint and inaudible as we enter the world. Society everywhere is in conspiracy against the manhood of every one of its members . . . Whoso would be a man, must be a nonconformist.'

But the fundamental question, which Emerson in his all too impressionistic manner had simply alluded to – what is this mysterious thing we call the 'self', and how can one be faithful to oneself? – was one Nietzsche was determined to tackle more seriously. And so, addressing an imaginary young man who was poised on the threshold of adult life, Nietzsche asked: 'What up till now have you really loved, what has pulled your soul upwards, what has governed and at the same time made it happy? . . . Compare these objects, noting how each one completes, broadens, surpasses, and reveals the other, and how they form a step-ladder up which till now you yourself have been climbing; for your true being does not lie deeply concealed within you, but immeasurably high above you, or at any rate above what you usually regard as your "I".'

Human life, in other words, if it is not to be passive, imitative, 'horizontal', presents each individual with a chance for upward striving and fulfilment of one's potential, superior 'self', and thus of one's 'destiny' or 'vocation'. It should thus be the task of the educator to reveal to the young the fundamental potential and basic material of one's being, 'something completely unteachable and untrainable, but in any case difficult of access, hamstrung, and paralysed. Your teachers cannot be anything but liberators', whose paramount task it should be to remove 'all the weeds, the rubbish, the vermin' – i.e. conventional notions, opinions, beliefs – 'that threaten to choke the life out of the tender buds; it is a radiation of light and warmth, a loving whisper of nocturnal rainfall . . . To be sure, there are other ways of finding oneself, of emerging to oneself from the stupor in which one usually lives as in a turbid cloud; but I know of no better way than to recall one's trainers and teachers. And so today I will recall one whom I am proud to call my teacher and trainer, Arthur Schopenhauer – in order later to honour others.'

As the title of this new 'Meditation' suggested, it was with Schopenhauer's lifelong struggle to propound a highly individual and unpopular philosophy that Nietzsche was primarily concerned. When it suited his purposes, he did not hesitate to propound his own ideas, even when they were flagrantly at variance with those of a thinker he was holding up as a model of philosophical integrity. At one point, donning the mantle of a hortatory prophet, Nietzsche boldly proclaimed that the 'new philosophers' of the future would have to begin living a 'true, ruddy, healthy life' before trying to exercise their 'legislative' function as the pace-setters of current thinking, and that it must be their duty to promote 'the mightiest furtherance of life, of the Will to Live' (*Willens zum Leben*), if they were to drag German culture from its present state of exhaustion: an affirmation that could only be interpreted by connoisseurs as a blatantly anti-Schopenhauerian prescription – above all for thinkers.

Not surprisingly, this third 'Untimely Meditation' became a highly personal apologia for Nietzsche's most deeply felt convictions and antipathies. And since the very notion of 'popularity' and of what was currently *zeitgemäss* ('timely', 'fashionable') covered a multitude of evils, Nietzsche could yield with relish to his favourite sport of spearing everything he most detested in the contemporary world – from the arrogant optimism displayed by the idolators of the new Germanic *Reich*, to the brain-stuffing of overawed students by fact-crammed teachers of history, and the abysmal decline of a once vigorous but now effete Christianity.

Once again his chief *bête noire* was the scholar and university professor – or what Schopenhauer, in a celebrated essay, had ridiculed as the 'chair-professor'. Schopenhauer, Nietzsche declared, was one of those rare sages who had written not for others, but solely for himself. He had said what was on his mind, much as a father might speak to a son, in a simple, unaffected style quite different from that of the 'narrow-chested, angular scholar' and of the literary poseurs who liked to add a touch of 'courtly grace' and an 'excessively silvered pseudo-Frenchiness' to their laborious pontifications. Like great artists, who tended to live 'more boldly and honestly' than academic pedants – Richard Wagner being a supreme example – Schopenhauer had not cared two hoots about the sentiments of the 'learned caste' or the 'cultural needs' of State and Society. Such sages, Nietzsche declared (thinking of Empedocles, but also, prophetically, of himself), were dangerous, for the simulation needed to protect their innermost thoughts from external contamination generated within them a melancholy bitterness capable of sudden, volcanic eruptions. 'From time to time they avenge themselves for this violent self-hiding, for this forced restraint. They come out of their cave with a terrible glare; their words and deeds are explosions, and it is possible that they themselves perish. Thus, dangerously, did Schopenhauer live.'

This, of course, was a highly personal conception of the sage. There have been many philosophers over the past two and a half millennia, but few have felt the need, like the legendary Sicilian Empedocles, to end their careers by throwing themselves into the crater of a volcano. The placid Kant was clearly not one of them. But, unflinchingly faithful to his own volcanic temperament and logic, Nietzsche did not hesitate to criticize the great Immanuel for having been too much of a conformist, a philosopher who had remained a university professor and a defender of established religion to the end of his days.

Walter Bagehot, in a recent essay, had described the difficulty that eccentric characters have in living in an all too 'normal' society, citing the poet Shelley as an example of someone who had become increasingly melancholic and sick and unable to go on living in England. In Germany, Hölderlin and Kleist had similarly suffered from their 'unusualness', unable to hold out in the 'climate of so-called German upbringing'. For, Nietzsche continued, 'only men of iron, like Beethoven, Goethe, Schopenhauer and Wagner are able to stand fast; but the traces of exhausting struggles and exertions can be read in wrinkled features and furrowed brows'.

After painting an almost apocalyptic picture of the present-day world – with the 'receding waters of religion' leaving behind them 'swamps and stagnant ponds', with nations that were splitting up and getting ready to tear each other to pieces, while the 'learned classes' had ceased to be 'lighthouses and asylums' in the midst of an increasingly secularized world which was tottering towards barbarism – Nietzsche held up three thinkers who, for good or ill, had provided their successors with quite different models of behaviour. The first and most popular was Jean-Jacques Rousseau, whose message of emancipation had unleashed earth-shaking revolutions and socialistic upheavals which were continuing to convulse the planet. The second, Goethe, a 'contemplative man in the grand manner', had created too noble an ideal of manhood ever to become truly popular. Because the image of Goethean man was a bit lacking in fire, in 'muscularity and natural wildness', there was needed a third, correcting model, the model of a man capable of getting angry with the way things are and towards which they are moving. Such was the image of Schopenhauerian man. 'He who would like to live in a Schopenhauerian manner would probably more resemble a Mephistopheles than a Faust – that is, for our weak-sighted modern eyes, which always see a sign of evil in negation. But there is a form of negation and destruction which is precisely an outpouring of that powerful longing for deliverance and salvation, of which, amid the profane and thoroughly secularized people that we are, Schopenhauer was the first philosophical teacher.'

This important passage, an apologia for his own incendiary iconoclasm – Nietzsche in an attack on tepid thinking had even asserted that books that 'have no fire in them' deserve to be burnt! – was followed by a quotation from Schopenhauer in which the gloomy sage had asserted that happiness in this tragic world was impossible and that the closest Man could come to it was with a 'heroic career. Such a life is led by whomsoever in any way and circumstances fights against overwhelming odds for the coming benefit of all, and finally triumphs, but is badly or not at all rewarded.' This was also Nietzsche's heroic conception of what his future life as an iconoclastic thinker was going to be. It would be fearless, fought without optimistic illusions against overwhelming odds, and, initially at least, be unrewarded.

Having thus paid passing homage to the pessimistic 'realism' of Schopenhauer's philosophy, Nietzsche could emulate his model's example by mercilessly criticizing and assailing everything and everyone he and his intellectual hero most cordially detested in the contemporary world: beginning with the egotism of the moneymakers – the *Erwerbende*, literally the 'acquirers', curiously resembles Tawney's 'acquisitive society' – interested in manufacturing as many pragmatically minded 'current' men as possible, like mint-manufactured coins, and the equally pernicious egotism of the State, so deplorably glorified by Hegel.

The primary aim of a truly sound, healthy educational system, Nietzsche asserted, repeating the point he had already made in *The Utility and Disadvantage of History for Life*, should be to facilitate the emergence of geniuses: more specifically of what he called 'the most sublime order of philosophers, artists and saints' – an aim that could only be promoted by the 'liberation' rather than by the intellectual shackling of the student. But this noble aim was now being systematically perverted by the selfishness of the modern State, interested only in the manufacture of useful, law-abiding, 'money-earning' citizens.

When Nietzsche went on to describe the character of those who were the dispensers of education – the 'learned ones' (*die Gelehrten*) – this third 'Untimely Meditation' rose to a polemical climax. The disciple now exceeded his Master (Schopenhauer) in the vehemence of his assault. Indeed, it would probably be hard to find in all of philosophical literature a more withering review of the petty foibles and vanities of academic scholars. By the time he was through, Nietzsche had listed no less than thirteen failings – in addition to a dishonest desire to make a name for oneself in one's chosen field, as opposed to the sincere pursuit of the truth. These failings and foibles, listed as succinctly as possible, were – or perhaps one should say are – as follows: (1) a stubborn addiction to conventional wisdom causing the scholar to adhere to axiomatic 'truths' (like the medieval scholastics in their battle against Copernicus); (2) an excessive, magnifying-glass concentration on a tiny area of knowledge, inducing a condition of intellectual myopia for everything beyond its ken; (3) an insipid, demeaning tendency to judge everything, and particularly the motivations of the great historical figures of the past, according to one's own petty standards, with the consequent glorification of the present ('A mole is happiest in a mole-hill'); (4) intellectual aridity – for, like the mule overlooking the abyss, the pedant never feels the thrill or fright of intellectual intoxication; (5) a touching modesty, carried to the point of a self-effacing willingness to remain a pathetically crawling creature rather than a winged explorer; (6) a feeling of corporative gratitude expressed by scholars towards the teachers and masters who made possible their admission to the 'worthy halls of Science', but who – here Nietzsche was clearly thinking of Hegel and his followers – only too often become a calamity for the Master thanks to the absurdity of their exaggerated imitations; (7) a rut-minded addiction to routine combined with a herbalistic passion for collecting data and drawing up indices which make them formidable workhorses; (8) a flight from boring inactivity on the part of plodding pedants who prefer to have their thinking done for them by the books or manuals they read; (9) a bread-and-butter concern for one's welfare and advancement, causing the scholar to 'belch forth profitable' truths and theses, likely to find favour with the academic powers that be; (10) a clan-like respect for the work of other scholars who, it is hoped, may be moved to reciprocate a comparable admiration; (11) academic vanity, based on a jealous desire to cultivate one's tiny plot of knowledge, particularly if this invaluable 'research' can be stretched to justify expensive trips abroad for purposes of excavation, etc.; (12) a delight in 'play-thinking' – that is, in the dreaming-up of scientific 'puzzles' requiring ingenious solutions, but which are basically as superficial as crossword puzzles; and finally (13), but this time expressed as a desideratum, a normally absent desire for intellectual equity which, when accidentally ignited like a spark 'in the soul of a scholar, is enough to fire and consume his life and endeavours so that he knows no further rest and is forever driven from the tepid or frosty mood in which ordinary scholars go about their daily work'.

No sooner had Nietzsche completed his devastating list of petty faults and failings than, like a magician pulling a rabbit out of his top hat, he suggested that if all or most of these elements were powerfully shaken up and mixed, there could emerge, like a chemical compound, a completely transfigured being, 'the servant of the truth': a scholar devoted to an 'extrahuman and superhuman occupation' – a pure, disinterested, dispassionate search for knowledge. But after evoking this rare possibility, Nietzsche hastily pushed the rabbit back into his conjuror's top hat, reiterating his contention that the average scholar was quintessentially unproductive and incapable of being a genius – which is why at all times geniuses and scholars had disliked and feuded with each other.

After adding yet another category – the 'devotees of forms', by which were meant the arbiters of contemporary taste – to the three other 'powers' – the money-grubbers, the imperious State, the learned scholars – that were busily promoting a highly bogus pseudo-culture, Nietzsche sombrely predicted that if things continued along their present course, the next millennium might bring forth one or two 'fancy notions' (*Einfälle*), the mere enunciation of which would be enough to make 'the hair of every presently living person stand on end': a piece of doomsday prophecy dramatically confirmed less than 100 years later by the triumph in Europe of Communism and Nazism.

Nietzsche completed his work of 'affirmative' destruction by categorically declaring that anyone possessed of a genuine *furor philosophicus* would have no time left over for any kind of *furor politicus* – a sweeping affirmation implicitly outlawing the politically *engagé* intellectual. A scholar, he asserted no less trenchantly, could never become a philosopher; for the first requirement of a philosopher was to be a 'true man' – such as Socrates had once been, and implictly Spinoza (who had refused a university post in order to continue his private meditations), but which Kant had not been, having never attempted to extricate himself from his academic chrysalis. Nietzsche then listed six qualities that went into the making of a genius – these being 'free manliness of character', a precocious knowledge of human beings, an absence of scholarly education (a requirement which, strictly interpreted, would have excluded Nietzsche himself from this category), no patriotic 'constriction' (*Einklemmung*), no penchant for bread-winning, no links with the State. In a word, as he continued in the same forthright and fearless fashion: 'Freedom, and ever again freedom: that wonderful and dangerous element in which the Greek philosophers could grow up.'

Indeed, Nietzsche defiantly suggested, here too walking in Schopenhauer's footsteps, the wisest thing the State could do would be to abolish all academic chairs of philosophy, forcing their present holders in an atmosphere of *sauve-qui-peut* panic to seek refuge and livelihood elsewhere: in rural vicarages, as schoolteachers, as authors of books for young boarding-school girls, as journalists – ah, how are the mighty fallen! – or as truly useful ploughmen of the fields, while the vainest among them headed for an imperial, royal or ducal court.

If, Nietzsche concluded, contemporary rulers paid so little attention to philosophy, it was because in the hands of its present practitioners it had become a fleshless spectre, unworthy of respect or consideration. He ended with a long quotation from Emerson, whose influence on the composition of this essay was almost as great as that of his demigods, Schopenhauer and Goethe: 'Beware when the great God lets loose a thinker on this planet. Then all things are at risk. It is as when a conflagration had broken out in a great city, and no man knows what is safe, or where it will end. There is not a piece of science but its flank may be turned tomorrow; there is not a literary reputation, not the so-called eternal names of fame, that may not be revised and condemned . . . The things which are dear to men at this hour are so on account of the ideas which emerged on their mental horizon, and which cause the present order of things, as a tree bears its apples. *A new degree of culture would instantly revolutionize the entire system of human pursuits*.'

Schopenhauer was by no means forgotten. But Nietzsche was here announcing his own red-hot, revolutionizing and unmistakably Vulcanic, hammer-and-tongs philosophy.

CHAPTER 21

# A Tense Apotheosis

*– My greatest experience was a recovery.*
*Wagner is merely one of my illnesses.*

On 2 August 1874 Nietzsche left the now fog and rain swept heights of Bergün and headed northwards for Bayreuth. At Glarus, in central Switzerland, he spent an exasperating afternoon under pelting rain and thunderstorms vainly waiting for a Florentine admirer (Emma Guerrieri-Gonzaga) to turn up. This first contretemps was followed by a second when, after crossing Lake Constance on a paddle-steamer, the short-sighted Fritz lost a travelling-bag in a railway station where he had to change trains. It contained a precious volume of Emerson's *Essays* and a personally autographed edition of Wagner's prose outline for the *Ring des Nibelungen* operas. These two mishaps so upset Nietzsche's high-strung nervous system that when he finally reached Bayreuth, suffering from acute stomach pains and colic, he immediately retired to his hotel bedroom.

Informed by a hotel attendant that Professor Nietzsche had arrived, but was ill, Richard Wagner left his work-desk and hurried over to the Gasthaus zur Sonne. His energetic appearance in Nietzsche's bedroom had an electrifying effect on the travel-weary 'invalid'. Though still feeling unwell, Nietzsche let the forceful composer move him from the inn to the Wagners' new home, where, as at Tribschen, 'his' guest-room was waiting to be occupied. Here, as Cosima later noted in her diary, the visitor soon recovered – 'and we spend a cheerful evening together. But what he tells us about the newspapers and about university people is horrifying.'

In the new 'Wahnfried' home Nietzsche was a privileged house-guest, along with the composer, pianist and conductor Karl Klindworth, who was preparing a piano version of the second act of *Götterdämmerung*. He was present at all the midday and evening meals and, as Cosima's diary makes vividly clear, on more than one occasion the honoured guest from Basel did not hesitate to express opinions markedly at variance with those of the Master of the House – to the latter's intense annoyance.

A few quotations from Cosima's invaluable diary tell the story. At lunch on Thursday, 6 August, Wagner discussed the poems he had been receiving for a 'Bismarck Hymn' he was planning to write in honour of the 'Iron Chancellor'. The conversation then shifted to the financial misfortunes of Wagner's and Nietzsche's now penniless publisher, Fritzsch. Nietzsche said that he had been approached by another publisher (Ernst Schmeitzner) in Schloss-Chemnitz, who was willing to continue publication of his 'Untimely Meditations'. As Cosima noted: 'both N[ietzsche] and Prof. Overbeck are accepting his offer, since they could not hope to find another publisher in the whole of Germany; indeed, if they were to give up their professorships, they would probably be without bread, for not even a position as private tutor would be open to them. The *Neue Freie Presse* [of Vienna] introduces an article by Karl Hillebrand on Nietzsche's book about History with the remark that it is only out of respect for their distinguished contributor that they pay heed to the work of an author who has sufficiently branded himself through his attack on Strauss, etc.'

That evening, after dinner, Wagner entertained his guests by playing a piano version of the Rhinemaidens scene in the third act of *Götterdämmerung*. When he had finished, Nietzsche, who had brought it with him from Bergün, showed Wagner the score of a *Triumphlied* (*Song of Triumph*) that a new composer from Hamburg, Johannes Brahms, had composed to honour the recent unification of the second Germanic *Reich* and which he had personally conducted during a gala concert given in Basel to celebrate the fiftieth anniversary of the founding of the city's *Gesangverein* (Glee Club). The reaction was immediate and sarcastic. As Cosima recorded in her diary: 'R[ichard] laughs loudly at the idea of setting such a word as *Gerechtigkeit* [Justice] to music.'

Two days later, after an early morning walk in the nearby palace gardens and a lunch-table discussion of the 'vices and abominations of Sparta', there was a sudden change in the congenial atmosphere when Wagner sat down at the piano and put Brahms's *Triumphlied* to the test. The more he played, the angrier he grew, vehemently expressing (as Cosima dutifully recorded in her diary) 'dismay over the meagre character of this composition which even Friend Nietzsche has praised to us: Handel, Mendelssohn and Schumann, wrapped in leather. R[ichard] very angry, he talks about the longing one day to find in music something that expresses Christ's transcendence, something in which the creative impulse, an emotion which speaks to the emotions, can be seen.' There was no further talk of Brahms; and that evening, after playing a number of piano pieces by Auber, Wagner formally buried Brahms's composite-leather *Triumphlied* by playing his own, infinitely more pompous and 'superior' *Kaisermarsch*.

Throughout the ensuing 'Klindworth–Nietzsche week', as she termed it, Cosima was kept busy by various visits from female singers and others, so that she had no time to make daily diary entries. But the two sentences recording Nietzsche's departure on 15 August, after having caused Wagner 'many difficult hours', clearly indicate that the relations between the Master of the House and his once revered and revering guest were now strained. 'Among other things, he [Nietzsche] maintains that the German language gives him no pleasure, and that he would rather talk in Latin, etc.'

Nietzsche's unusual epistolatory silence after this ten-day visit to Bayreuth confirms what Cosima's diary all too succinctly suggests. Not a word about it to his mother or his sister, not a line about Bayreuth in the letter he finally wrote on 24 September (six weeks after his return to Basel) to Carl von Gersdorff.

Nietzsche had begun recording his increasingly critical perceptions of Richard Wagner's strengths and weaknesses in one of his notebooks early on in this year of 1874. They were partly inspired by Wagner's articles and essays, by a penetrating analysis of his operas, and by his many conversations with the composer. Here are some samples:

> – If Goethe was a transplanted painter (i.e. someone who became a poet because insufficiently talented to be a painter) and if Schiller was a transplanted orator, Wagner is a transplanted actor.
>
> – None of our great musicians in his twenty-eighth year was as bad a musician as Wagner.
>
> – In *Tannhäuser* he seeks a series of ecstatic states in order to motivate an individual: he seems to imply that the natural man reveals himself in such states.
>
> – In *Meistersinger* and in parts of his *Nibelungen* he reverts to self-control; he is greater therein than in self-uncontrolledness. Restraint serves him well.
>
> – As an actor he wanted to imitate Man only at his most effective and truest: in the highest emotion. For his extreme nature discerned weakness and untruthfulness in all other states. There is an extraordinary danger for the artist in emotional portrayal. That which intoxicates, the sensually ecstatic, the sudden surprise, the urge to be profoundly stirred at any price – dreadful tendencies!
>
> – Not to be forgotten: it is a theatrical language that speaks forth in Wagner's art; it doesn't belong in a room, in camera. It is a form of language, and it cannot be thought of without a strong element of coarsening, even of the noblest elements. It must work at a distance and cement folk chaos – for example, the *Kaisermarsch*.

> – The tyrant acknowledges no individuality other than his own and that of his most trusted friends. Great is the danger for Wagner, when he refuses to acknowledge Brahms, etc; or the Jews.

After describing Wagner's lack of finesse in his dealings with the King of Bavaria, and the heap of troubles he had needlessly brought down on his head by his short-sighted support of the revolutionary movement in Saxony in 1849, Nietzsche added: 'Third, he insulted the Jews, who in Germany today possess most of the money and the press. When he did this, there was no vocational reason for it: later it was revenge.'

And finally – this remarkable paragraph, which shows that even as he was beginning to write his Schopenhauer essay and was already drawing up plans for another devoted to Richard Wagner, Nietzsche had parted philosophical company with both and no longer believed that their respective visions of the world could offer much hope for the future:

> – Wagner's art is overflying and transcendental,
> what should our poor German wretchedness do with it.
> It reeks of a flight from this world, it denies it,
> it does not transfigure this world. This is why it
> has no direct moral effect, but only indirectly, a
> quietistic one. We see him busy and active only in
> preparing a site in this world for his art: but of
> what concern to us is a Tannhäuser, a Lohengrin, a
> Tristan, a Siegfried? But this seems to be the lot
> of Art in such a present-time; it draws part of its
> strength from a dying religion. Whence the alliance
> between Wagner and Schopenhauer . . . Schopenhauer's
> 'Will to Life' here receives its artistic expression:
> this ecstasy, this despair, this tone of pain and
> desire, this accent of ardour. Seldom a ray of
> sunshine, but a great deal of magical wizardry
> in the lighting.

Worn out by weeks of nerve-racking tension, insomnia and end-of-semester weariness, Nietzsche was glad in late September to get away from Basel and enjoy a two-week hiking tour in the mountains south-east of Lucerne. He was accompaned by Heinrich Romundt and by one of his brightest university students, Adolf Baumgartner, the son of a Mulhouse (now Mülhausen) manufacturer who had regretted the forceful incorporation of Alsace into Bismarck's Germanic *Reich.*

On 6 October Nietzsche returned to Basel, four days before the start of the autumn-winter semester. He felt depressed by his new academic schedule. In addition to seven hours of university lecturing, it included a completely new course covering the entire history of Greek literature, which he had to prepare for the senior class of his *Pädagogium* students. The academic burden – a total of thirteen hours a week, with seven hours of preparatory work every day – was a heavy one; and, as he wrote to Carl von Gersdorff, he was now kept busy from 8 a.m. till 11 p.m. and sometimes until midnight, allowing him no time to write a fourth 'Untimely Meditation'. For his thirtieth birthday – joyfully celebrated in the 'Baumann cavern' by its three philosophical 'owls' (Fritz, Franz and Heinrich) – Nietzsche received thirty author's copies of *Schopenhauer as Educator* from his new publisher. Ernst Schmeitzner had in the meantime travelled to Bayreuth, where he had so favourably impressed the Master of 'Wahnfried' that Wagner was now urging him to buy up Fritzsch's publishing company.

The author of the third 'Untimely Meditation' did not have to wait long for the first written reaction. It came from Marie Baumgartner, the mother of Nietzsche's favourite student, Adolf. She had read *Schopenhauer as Educator* at a single sitting, between breakfast and midday, and had been particularly impressed by the author's feeling for Beauty and by his ability to convey it 'in such movingly beautiful words'.

Richard Wagner responded two days later (21 October) with a lively telegram: 'Deep and great. Boldest and newest in the presentation of Kant's [ideas]. Truly comprehensible only to the devilishly possessed.'

Five days later Cosima Wagner dipped her pen into the inkwell in her turn. Whereas *The Utility and Disadvantage of History for Life* had left her disappointed and perplexed, 'this is my Untimeliness [*Unzeitgemässe*],' she exulted. 'Feelings, thoughts, sudden inspirations, cognition, penetrating insight and sound knowledge aroused my astonishment, and once again I was warmed by the glowing fire of enthusiasm pervading everything, as I was by *The Birth of Tragedy*. And how beautiful and singular is your language here!!'

From London on 1 November, Cosima's former husband, Hans von Bülow, wrote in his turn to express his delight. He had been particularly struck by Nietzsche's ironic juxtaposition of 'public opinions' and 'private indolences' – '*privaten Faulheiten*', which in German suggests 'private states of lazy rottenness'. 'Brilliant!' commented Bülow. 'That is again a winged word comparable to the *Bildungsphilister*, and surely so in those very circles of the most extensive popularity. Bismarck should quote it some time in Parliament.'

These favourable reactions to his third 'Untimely Meditation' explain

Nietzsche's state of unusually good health, so remarkably prolonged that this turned out to be the best twelve months he had known in years. The daily régime of cold-water baths to which, at Wagner's urging, he had been subjecting himself, may have had something to do with it; but the main cause was the absence of nervous strain due to the urgent need to complete a new 'Untimely Meditation'. Indeed, so intellectually relaxed was Fritz that when he went home to Naumburg for the Christmas holidays, he left his academic books and papers behind, taking along instead all of his musical compositions, which he amused himself rewriting and improving.

His return trip from snowbound Naumburg in a freezing train compartment laid him low for several days, as it had the previous January. But he soon recovered, and by early February of 1875 he could report to Erwin Rohde that he had finished with Greek lyric poetry and could now introduce his *Pädagogium* students to the masterpieces of Greek drama: a subject he knew by heart.

Nietzsche's spirits during the cold winter weeks were cheered by the exciting prospect of being able to attend the elaborate *Ring des Nibelungen* rehearsals that Wagner was planning to hold in Bayreuth during the summer months of 1875. His relations with his artistic idol seemed at this moment more cordial than ever; for at Cosima's request Fritz's sister Elisabeth had agreed to spend a few weeks in the 'Wahnfried' home looking after the four daughters and little Siegfried, while Cosima accompanied her husband on an orchestra-conducting and fund-raising trip to Vienna.

Meanwhile Nietzsche had been using his rare moments of spare time to work on his fourth 'Untimely Meditation'. In the first outline for thirteen controversial essays that he had drawn up with Gersdorff and Romundt at Flims in August 1873, the third essay, devoted to 'The Philosopher', was to be followed by a fourth, devoted to the *Gelehrter* – the Learned Man or Scholar. But by the time he had completed his devastating dissection of scholastic pettiness in the sixth section of *Schopenhauer as Educator*, Nietzsche realized that for the time being he had exhausted the subject. He therefore decided to move on to the next of his thirteen themes – originally listed under the generic term of 'Art'. Just as in his third 'Meditation' he had singled out Schopenhauer as a heroic model of what a genuine, free-thinking philosopher should be, so now he picked Richard Wagner as a gigantic prototype of the creative artist in action.

Some of this essay was written during the Mardi Gras carnival celebrations, which began this year on 15 February, and which Nietzsche spent in a Lucerne hotel, in search of peace and quiet and meditative inspiration. As he wrote to Richard Wagner, 'Right now I have taken flight from the drumming din of Basel; I could stand it for four hours only, then I rushed away and now I find myself in Lucerne, in thickest snow and snowfalls.'

Two weeks later Fritz wrote to Erwin Rohde that he had made such progress that his fourth 'Untimely Meditation' would be ready by Easter. Most of this letter, however, was devoted to the psychological shock, a veritable 'earthquake of the soul', that he had just experienced with the third of the philosophical 'owls' of the 'Baumann cavern', Heinrich Romundt. The fellow philologist from Leipzig University days who had so enthusiastically embraced Schopenhauer's philosophy and who, heeding Nietzsche's advice, had bravely set himself up in Basel as an independent tutor in philosophy; the loyal friend who, during Fritz's blinding eye-aches, had for hours on end laboriously copied out his dictated letters; yes, this seemingly solid companion had suddenly abjured everything Schopenhauer had advocated and combated, preferring to sink back placidly into the cushy comfort of religious dogma – that of Roman Catholicism. 'Ah, our good, pure Protestant air!' Nietzsche wrote to Erwin Rohde. 'Never have I felt more strongly my innermost dependence on the spirit of Luther up till now, and this unhappy fellow now wishes to turn his back on all those liberating geniuses?'

Nietzsche, like Wagner, had long since ceased to go to church on Sundays, and, like Cosima, who felt that it was her maternal duty *faute de mieux* to bring up her children in the Evangelical faith, he had no use for the platitudinous sermons, proffered by poorly educated clergymen, that had come to occupy such prominence in the Protestant liturgy. He still admired Luther for having boldly denounced the practices of a thoroughly corrupted Church, just as he admired Luther's hard-headed earthiness in daring to challenge convention – for it had never been more than a convention – of priestly celibacy by himself marrying a wife and begetting children. It was in this sense, and in this sense only (for there were many things about Luther he disliked), that Nietzsche could place the great religious rebel alongside of Schopenhauer as a 'liberating genius'. And it was precisely at this moment when the Vatican, in a fit of intellectual folly, had proclaimed the grotesque dogma of papal infallibility that Heinrich Romundt, deaf to the arguments of friends and oblivious of everything that Schopenhauer had stood and fought for in the realm of free thinking, had chosen to throw himself like a child into the soft, welcoming bosom of the Catholic Church!

Even before this crisis provoked new gastric upsets, Nietzsche's eyes were again causing him trouble, so onerous was the academic burden he had to bear in preparing his university lectures and his *Pädagogium* course.

'Work, nothing but work!' he lamented in mid-April to his sister Elisabeth, who had returned to Naumburg after spending a month in Bayreuth looking after the five-year-old Siegfried and Cosima Wagner's daughters.

On 14 May, after a brief 'Easter vacation' spent as the sole client of the proudly perched Hôtel Victoria, near Bern, Nietzsche received a letter from his new publisher, Ernst Schmeitzner, informing him that about 350 copies (out of a print order of 1,000 copies) of *Schopenhauer as Educator* had so far been sold. Unfortunately, not one of the Paris publishers to whom he had written about Marie Baumgartner's French translation of the Schopenhauer text had bothered to reply. His long, friendly letter ended with a simple question: could Nietzsche send him the manuscript of his fourth 'Untimely Meditation' soon, so that he could start printing the book in June?

This gentle reminder that, according to their agreement of the previous July, the author of the 'Untimely Meditations' was to provide the publisher with a new essay at intervals of about nine months, in order to assure the series a profitable regularity, had a shattering effect on Nietzsche, unleashing a psychosomatic crisis of extreme gravity. For the next six weeks, despite the consoling presence of his sister, he suffered acute eye-aches and headaches, and convulsive stomach upsets, some of them so protracted that blood came up with the vomit.

Nietzsche's friend, Professor Immermann, seemed to be at his wits' end as to how to deal with this new crisis, which could not be attributed to cerebral over-excitation during a tense period of literary creativity. He began by prescribing the daily absorption of a sinister 'Höllenstein' solution – the latest 'miracle drug' in the apothecaries' arsenal – and when this treatment failed to work wonders, the frustrated professor prescribed massive doses of quinine. One shudders in imagining the acute abdominal spasms that this *traitement de cheval* must have generated in 'attacking' Nietzsche's stomach ulcers. The vomiting, sometimes going on for hours on end, was often so convulsive that Nietzsche felt that his last hour had come and yearned for nothing so much as a quick, 'easeful death'.

On 28 June, after receiving a letter from Fritz describing his nightmarish Höllenstein and quinine 'cure', Carl von Gersdorff wrote to his friend in Basel: 'I don't wish to shake your confidence in the medical treatment but it nonetheless sounds to me as though I[mmermann] has been experimenting dangerously with your poor stomach. For quinine I wish you a good appetite . . . '

Fritz had asked his friend Carl to write to Cosima Wagner and to explain that for reasons of poor health he (Nietzsche) would be unable to make it to Bayreuth for the long-awaited August rehearsals. But Gersdorff refused. He was convinced that a week or two of pure Alpine air would work the wonders that medical quackery had so signally failed to achieve in Basel. 'Wouldn't it be possible,' he suggested, 'with the help of a doctor's attestation, for you to take off before the start of the vacation? . . . Since your nerves are so sensitive and in particular cause your body to be excitedly affected by every kind of emotion, it seems to me that forbidding you to go to Bayreuth is downright absurd and dangerous, for I fear that this painful renunciation could impair the good effects of a water-cure.'

The complex truth that Gersdorff had stumbled on was that if, as Professor Immermann was persuaded, an excess of intellectual activity could provoke acute headaches and stomach upsets, so too could its opposite, creative inactivity, particularly when combined with a frustrating sense of inability to realize and enjoy one's fondest hopes and expectations.

If Fritz had followed his friend Carl's advice, had returned to Flims and resumed the simple milk-cure régime he had adopted two years before, he might have overcome this latest crisis and been able to make it to Bayreuth. But the humble village of Flims unfortunately did not boast a medical expert in stomach upsets. Instead, when the summer vacation began on 16 July, Nietzsche, meekly bowing to Immermann's wishes, boarded a train bound for the Black Forest town of Bonndorf, near which, in a kind of forest clearing at Steinabad, a Dr Wiel ran a hotel-clinic for persons suffering from gastric abnormalities.

An amiable septuagenarian, Dr Joseph Wiel had established his reputation as a gastric 'specialist' by writing medical 'cookbooks' prescribing strict dietary régimes which he had personally elaborated in a kind of kitchen-laboratory. The one prescribed for Nietzsche was curious in the extreme, but, alas! only too typical of the medical 'science' of the day. After carefully examining Nietzsche's belly, he decided that his patient was suffering from 'chronic stomach catarrh'. The cure he prescribed involved an early morning use of a cold-water-injecting clyster – that all-purpose instrument of anal torture which Molière had so mercilessly lampooned in several of his comedies. Next, the amiable Dr Wiel prescribed a dietary régime of four small meals a day, almost exclusively composed of meat. They were preceded in the morning by some Carlsbad fruit salts and accompanied for the midday and evening meals by a glass of Bordeaux wine. As Nietzsche wrote to Marie Baumgartner three days after his arrival at Steinabad, 'no water, no soup, no vegetables, no bread'. And, as an ultimate refinement, the application to the earlobes of blood-sucking leeches!

The consequences of this odd régime – enough to make any

contemporary gastroenterologist groan with horror – were not surprising. Two days after his arrival Nietzsche was again beset by violent headaches and fits of vomiting. Even the tiny morsels of meat prescribed by the good doctor provoked an almost instant feeling of nausea. Nietzsche finally told the doctor that he had had enough of this exclusively meat diet, but what the amiable 'culinary artist' prescribed instead we unfortunately do not know from Fritz's letters to family and friends, including Franz Overbeck, Carl von Gersdorff and Erwin Rohde, all three of whom were planning to converge on Bayreuth in early August.

If the four weeks Nietzsche spent at Steinabad failed to restore him completely to good health, they at least afforded him a refreshing period of rest. A swimming pool had been built in the middle of the hotel gardens, and into its cold water, which was shunned by the rest of Dr Wiel's less hardy patients, Nietzsche plunged every morning at six o'clock. But for those early morning dips and long walks through the soggy, rain-soaked forests, he would probably have returned to Basel as ill as when he had left. For, as the fateful date of 1 August approached and passed, he began to receive letters from his enthusiastic friends, describing the rehearsals in Bayreuth. With the arrival of each letter, written by friends who deeply regretted the absence of the connoisseur who had personally introduced them to Richard Wagner, Fritz suffered an intense half-hour spasm of frustration and regret. Manfully he sought to master the emotions seething within him by striding along dark forest paths and listening in his mind to the rich orchestral evocations of the 'flowing gold' of the Rhine, the rippling and splashing of the Rhinemaidens, the shrill, whirring wing-beat and wind-borne flight of the valkyries, such as he imagined them to sound – for what he knew of the *Ring des Nibelungen* operas was solely derived from piano extracts and from his study of the orchestral scores.

On 13 August, when Nietzsche returned to Basel, his mood was one of resignation. He would have to learn how to live with his high-strung nervous system for the rest of his days. To take care of him during his first weeks of illness, Fritz had persuaded his sister Elisabeth to come to Basel, a city she much preferred to provincial Naumburg. The time had come, however, to abandon the crowded quarters of the 'Baumann cavern' and to find more spacious accommodation in a nearby house on the Spalentorweg. Here he had an entire floor to himself, as well as part of an upper floor for Elisabeth: in all, six rooms, partly filled with furniture sent by train from Naumburg, in addition to a kitchen, a cellar and a housemaid-cook.

In persuading 'Lieschen' to keep house for him, Fritz was in effect using his sister as a kind of substitute wife. Ever since his thirtieth birthday, celebrated the previous October, he had been giving much thought to marriage, but the melancholy conclusion he had reached was that his chances of finding an 'adorable creature' capable of adapting herself to his intellectual tastes, working habits, and periodic illnesses were very slim. His less complicated friend, Carl von Gersdorff, had been vainly wooing the daughter of a Prussian nobleman, but he had had the good sense not to lose his head as well as his heart – unlike Erwin Rohde, who had developed an infatuation for a young girl who seemed unworthy of such an honour.

Although consoled by the comforting presence of Elisabeth, whose eminently practical temperament accorded so well with his own, during the final months of 1875 and the first months of 1876 Fritz continued to suffer periodic relapses, with gastric upsets and blinding eye-aches, which his sister sought to alleviate by reading him German translations of Walter Scott novels. His Christmas was the most excruciatingly painful he had known in years, with feverish headaches which Professor Immermann did his best to cool every morning by applying ice-pads and pouring pitcherfuls of cold water over his suffering patient's head.

In early January of 1876 the university authorities reluctantly agreed to relieve Nietzsche of his onerous *Pädagogium* course in Greek literature for the remaining months of the winter semester. He had abandoned Dr Wiel's 'miracle-working' four small meals a day régime and was now living almost exclusively off milk – the best remedy for his ills, along with lots of sleep and Walter Scott. Even this proved insufficient, and by mid-February his head- and eye-aches had become so acutely painful that he had to interrupt his university lecturing as well.

It had become increasingly evident to Nietzsche that in rashly agreeing to provide his publisher, Schmeitzner, with a new 'Untimely Meditation' at regular intervals of eight to nine months, he had promised more than he could deliver. Profound thinking, he had come to realize, is radically different from the quick thinking of the lawyer or politician; it is the result of slow, prolonged rumination. As he had explained to Carl von Gersdorff shortly before Christmas: 'I am training myself to unlearn the haste of knowledge-wanting; this is what all scholars suffer from and they thereby deprive themselves of the marvellously soothing calm of every hard-won insight.'

In early February Fritz's spirits rose when he learned that Erwin Rohde had been appointed full professor of philology at Jena. But this good news, tempered by Erwin's passing reference to his 'unlucky' damsel (who had just given birth to a baby boy!), failed to impede another relapse, so paralysingly painful that for days Nietzsche could neither read nor write.

Shortly afterwards Carl von Gersdorff turned up in Basel, in time to catch a brief glimpse of Franziska Nietzsche, who had travelled all the way from Naumburg to visit her son and daughter. Long chagrined by her son's agnostic waywardness and the rare visits he now made to his home town, the widowed mother was saddened to see her beloved Fritz disappear with Gersdorff a day or two after her arrival in Basel. Their destination this time was the Lake of Geneva and Montreux, near which, in the village of Veytaux, they took up residence as the only boarders in a cheap pension optimistically called La Printannière. The weather during the late winter of 1876 was anything but spring-like, with plenty of rain, sleet, fog and furious gusts of wind which churned up the frothing waters of the lake. But heedless of the rain and several days of snowfall in mid-March, the two friends spent five to six hours every day tramping through the snowy slush past the castle of Chillon, which Byron had celebrated in a famous poem. The evenings were spent in front of a blazing fire, where Nietzsche and Gersdorff (who did the reading) entertained themselves with Manzoni's *I Promessi Sposi*.

On 29 March Carl said goodbye to his friend Fritz, who had decided to stay on as the Veytaux pension's only client. The less than cheering news Gersdorff brought to Franziska and Elisabeth Nietzsche during his brief stopover in Basel was that Fritz had not yet recovered his good health and had suffered several serious relapses. So concerned was Gersdorff that he wrote several letters on the subject to Franz Overbeck, who had gone to Zürich to spend the inter-semester holidays with his fiancée.

It is difficult, I think, to exaggerate the psychological impact that this 'happy event' – Overbeck's betrothal, announced in early January – had had on Friedrich Nietzsche. Franz Overbeck was clearly succeeding where Carl, Fritz and Erwin Rohde had so far failed. On 4 April Overbeck wrote to Nietzsche from Zürich in an effort to cheer him up. He too was not happy at the prospect of soon having to return to Basel, and of being separated for a while from his beloved Ida. 'I can only say to you, find yourself one like her and let this aim too . . . incite you to good health.' There followed a description of his fiancée's keyboard talents, ably developed by an expert pianist, Robert Freund, who had once been a pupil of Tausig and Liszt.

Nietzsche received this letter shortly before he left Veytaux for Geneva, where he wanted to meet a Countess Diodati, who was said to have finished a French translation of *The Birth of Tragedy*, and the director of the Geneva Orchestra, Hugo von Senger, a rabid Wagnerian he had met several years before in Munich. The Countess, he discovered, had lost her mind and had been confined in a local lunatic asylum. Senger, however, greeted Nietzsche warmly and introduced him to a number of German-speaking friends and admirers. Among the friends were two young ladies from Riga who, after their family had moved to Switzerland, had come to Geneva to study piano-playing with Senger. The older of the two sisters, Mathilde Trampedach, was twenty-three years old. Slim, with dark blonde hair and green eyes, she had delicate features and looked as though she had just stepped out of a Fra Filippo Lipi portrait.

The two sisters were staying in a Geneva pension run by an English lady when one bright morning Hugo von Senger turned up, accompanied by Nietzsche. Seated in the sun-bathed verandah, the two girls had trouble distinguishing the features of the 'famous' stranger, for Nietzsche was unwilling to lower the thick green parasol he held over his head to shade his eyes. Mathilde Trampedach was impressed, however, by the intelligent vivacity of the two men's conversation, as Senger and Nietzsche discussed their favourite poets, shifting from Shakespeare to Byron, from Shelley to Longfellow. When Nietzsche confessed that he was unfamiliar with Longfellow's poem 'Excelsior', Mathilde Trampedach volunteered to write out the German translation.

Several days later Hugo von Senger invited the two young girls to join him and Nietzsche for a carriage drive along the lake-shore as far as the Villa Diodati (where Byron had once lived). The conversation, this time focused on the Byronic theme of oppressed peoples, aroused such keen interest in the sharp-witted Mathilde Trampedach that she broke in to say how odd it seemed to her that men should spend so much time and energy pining for a purely external lifting of constraints, while remaining astonishingly unaware of how inwardly constricted they still were. As she raised her eyes at the end of her little speech, she was struck by the intensity of Nietzsche's penetrating gaze.

Before leaving Geneva, Nietzsche returned to the English pension in what seemed to Mathilde Trampedach a playful mood. Sitting down abruptly at the piano, he unleashed a tempest of surging chords, which rose to a stormy crescendo before gradually subsiding into joyful harmonies and soft sounds. Having completed his brief 'concert', the visitor appeared to be at a loss as to what to say. Shortly afterwards he took his leave, with a deep bow over Mathilde's extended hand.

Later, after discussing the matter with the older and already twice married Hugo von Senger, Nietzsche sat down in his hotel room and wrote Mathilde Trampedach an extraordinary missive. To call it a 'love letter' would be misleading. As a marriage proposal it was more like an ultimatum. 'Gather together all the courage of your heart,' he began, 'and be not frightened by the question I hereby address to you: are you willing to become my wife? I love you and for me it is as though you already belonged to me. Not a word [to anyone] about the suddenness of my inclination! At least there is no blame in the matter, nothing therefore needs to be excused. But what I would like to know is if you feel as I do – that we have not been strangers to each other, not for an instant.'

What Nietzsche did not realize in making this extraordinary proposal was that the young Mathilde Trampedach was already secretly in love with her talented piano teacher, Hugo von Senger, whose third wife she later became. But she was so flattered by the iconoclastic professor's amorous overture that she also preserved his second, this time apologetic letter, in which he wrote: 'You are sufficiently magnanimous to forgive me, I sense it in the gentleness of your letter, which I honestly did not deserve. I have suffered so much from reflecting on my terrible, violent manner of behaving that I cannot be grateful enough for this gentleness.'

The six days Nietzsche spent in Geneva, where he was 'lionized' by a number of admirers, seem to have done more than the restful month he had spent near Byron's castle of Chillon to restore a feeling of self-confidence he had largely lost since his nervous breakdown of the previous May. He wrote to Erwin Rohde on Good Friday to say how invigorated he had been by the three-volume edition of Malwida von Meysenbug's *Memoirs of an Idealist*, which he had just finished reading. But it was to Carl von Gersdorff that he was the most explicit in describing all that his visit to Geneva had brought him. 'When we see each other again, I will talk to you about Ferney and Voltaire's home (to which I brought my genuine homage), of the luminous and yet wonderfully mountain-close and freedom-breathing Geneva . . . of the Concert Populaire, at which for my sake Berlioz's *Benvenuto Cellini* overture was played . . . of the banker Köckert (a former virtuoso), . . . of the discovery that I am supposed to be a great piano-player, of countless moralistic conversations. Above all, what I have discovered in particular: the only thing that people of all kinds recognize and before which they bow is the high-minded act. Towards everything in the world [one should take] no step towards accommodation! One can have the greatest success only when one remains true to oneself.'

In resolutely denouncing all attempts at compromise and 'accommodation' with mediocrity and (human) mediocrities – a cardinal pillar of Richard Wagner's 'philosophy' – Fritz had his own as much as Carl von Gersdorff's marital initiatives in mind. '*At no price* a conventional marriage (like all the marriages . . . which have been proposed to you by others). We do not want to start wavering on this point of purity of character! Ten thousand times better to remain alone forever – that is now my watchword in this matter.'

His self-confidence restored by his stimulating week in Geneva, Nietzsche, after his return to Basel, lent the unfinished manuscript of *Richard Wagner in Bayreuth* to a young musician named Heinrich Köselitz. A fervent admirer of *The Birth of Tragedy* and the three 'Untimely Meditations', Köselitz had been encouraged by the publisher Ernst Schmeitzner to move from Leipzig to Basel, where he could broaden his intellectual horizon and understanding of the world by attending Friedrich Nietzsche's and Franz Overbeck's lectures. The twenty-one-year-old student's gift for composition was matched by a seemingly boundless veneration and a degree of self-sacrificing devotion which soon made him a welcome visitor to Nietzsche's Spalentorweg apartment. Granted the rare privilege of reading the unfinished manuscript on Wagner, Köselitz was so enraptured that he insisted that this essay must be published. He even volunteered to copy the entire text, so as to make it more legible for the printers.

By the time Köselitz had finished copying out the text, it was too late to have this new 'Meditation' ready to be offered as a birthday present for Richard Wagner. Nietzsche was nevertheless determined to have it appear in print before the start of the Inaugural Festival ceremonies in Bayreuth. Thanks to Köselitz's diligent copying and proof-correcting – for Nietzsche's eyes were again causing him intense pain – two luxuriously bound *Festexemplare* ('Festival copies') of the ninety-eight-page essay were ready to be sent to Richard Wagner and Cosima by 9 July.

Harassed though he was by frantic last-minute preparations and rehearsals, which he personally conducted, Wagner took a hasty look at this unexpected gift. 'Friend!' he wrote in a three-sentence letter. 'Your book is prodigious! But where have you found out so much about me? Now come quickly, and thanks to the rehearsals get used to the impressions!' (To be made on Nietzsche by the four *Ring* operas.)

Similar advice was offered on this same Thursday, 13 July, by Malwida von Meysenbug, who had left Rome with the firm intention of spending two full months in Bayreuth. In a thank-you letter expressing her immense appreciation for Nietzsche's 'unsurpassable' essay on Wagner, she urged him to advance the date of his arrival (in early August) and to come immediately to Bayreuth in order to watch the rehearsals. 'I fear,' she wisely explained, 'that if you come only for the performances, it will be too much, too overpowering for you. With the rehearsals, during which one loses oneself more in the details, with long rest periods in between, one is more slowly gripped and gladdened and prepared for the mighty impression of the whole.'

Nietzsche's spirits were greatly cheered at the start of the new semester by the high number of students who had signed up for his university courses: twenty students for one lecture course, ten for another, and the same number for a seminar. In June, moreover, he was pleasantly surprised when the university's governing council agreed to grant him a year of absence, beginning at the conclusion of the summer semester, in October 1876: a sabbatical year he intended to spend, at her generous and 'motherly' insistence, with Malwida von Meysenbug in southern Italy. But the nervous strain aroused by his last-minute addition of three sections to *Richard Wagner in Bayreuth*, combined with an agonizing uncertainty as to how the great composer would react to this 'gift' and supreme token of his veneration, brought on a rapid deterioration of his health. As he wrote to Erwin Rohde on 7 July, '. . . once again, for the past 3–4 weeks, I have been faring miserably and . . . I must drag myself along up until and above all through Bayreuth.'

His dear friend Erwin inadvertently compounded Fritz's psychological torments by choosing this moment to announce his engagement to the daughter of a lawyer from the Baltic seaport of Rostock. Nietzsche immediately responded with a letter of congratulation written from the 'bottom of his heart', but which also sounded a plaintive note as to his own uncertain future. 'So will you in this year of Grace 1876 build your nest, like our Overbeck' – due to be married in Zürich on 8 August. 'For me,' he added wistfully, 'it is otherwise, Heaven knows it or knows it not . . . Perhaps there is an evil fissure in me . . . I hardly know how to explain it.' But the thought of losing all of his dearest friends and of remaining a solitary bachelor was such a melancholy prospect that during the following night of 18 July he composed a poem, which began:

*Es geht ein Wandrer durch die Nacht . . .*
*Er schreitet zu und steht nicht still,*
*Weiss nicht, wohin sein Weg noch will . . .*

(There goes a wanderer through the night . . .
He strides along and stands not still,
Knows not whereto his path will lead . . . )

and which, no less poignantly, ended with this verse:

*Leb wohl, Du armer Wandersmann!*

(Fare you well, poor wanderman!)

On Saturday, 22 July, Nietzsche surprised his sister and even more Franz Overbeck, who had been hoping that Fritz and Elisabeth could attend his wedding in Zürich on 8 August, by abruptly leaving for Bayreuth. He reached the overcrowded town on Sunday afternoon without a word of warning to Richard and Cosima Wagner, who only learned of his arrival the next day. He had arranged to be put up by a well-to-do Bayreuther in the very centre of the busy town, but he found the sweltering heat singularly oppressive in the low-ceilinged lodgings placed at his disposal. As he reported to his sister on Tuesday, 25 July '*fast habe ich's bereut!*' ('I almost regretted it!' – i.e. having come here, a typically Nietzschean pun on the word 'Bayreuth'). 'For up till now I was miserable. From Sunday noon till Monday night, headaches, today relaxation, but I can hardly guide my quill . . . On Monday I was at the rehearsal – [of the first act of *Götterdämmerung*] . . . I did not like it at all and I had to get out . . . I spend each day with Fräulein von Meysenbug, who has a lovely cool garden. There I also eat lunch, until you come and take over the running of *our* household . . . Here it is insanely hot. Just had a thunderstorm.'

Three days later he wrote again to his sister, to say that he was feeling better, that from early morning on he was spending each day in Malwida von Meysenbug's cool garden, was drinking lots of milk, and taking daily baths in the local river. 'In the meantime I have seen and heard the entire *Götterdämmerung*, it is good to get used to it, now I'm in my element.'

King Ludwig of Bavaria, he went on, was expected to arrive that evening. Wagner had sent him a copy of the fourth 'Untimely Meditation' and, as Fritz informed his sister, 'He sent a telegram about my essay, [saying] that it had enchanted him.' Then, after naming a number of familiar faces, Nietzsche added: 'I must however very much control myself and have refused all invitations, even from the W[agner]s.'

These wise precautions did not suffice to stave off a relapse, due to an unsettling combination of torrid heat, crowded streets, and the ceaseless arrival of counts, dukes and princes – what Nietzsche in *Ecce homo* later called 'the entire loafing riff-raff of Europe' – who understood little or nothing of Wagner's music and whose main motivation was the idle curiosity aroused by 'one more sport'. By 1 August – the day on which Franz Liszt arrived to lend his moral support to his gifted son-in-law and daughter, and almost two weeks before the first full performance of *Das Rheingold* (which did not occur until 13 August) – Nietzsche could stand it no longer. In a letter to his sister, who despite his entreaties was taking her time leaving Basel, Fritz complained of 'enduring headaches, although not of the worst kind, and exhaustion. Yesterday I could only hear *Die Walküre* in a darkened area' – presumably of the orchestra. 'Any kind of seeing impossible. I long to get away, it is too senseless for me to stay. I dread each of these long art-evenings; and yet I do not stay away . . . This time you must also do the hearing and seeing for me . . . I have had enough.'

When Elisabeth Nietzsche reached Bayreuth a couple of days later, even Malwida von Meysenbug could not tell her exactly where Fritz had gone. Not until Monday, 7 August, when she finally received a letter from her brother, did she discover that he had found the calm and well-shaded coolness he needed in the charmingly named town of Klingenbrunn (tinkling fountain), in the thick-forested region of the Bayerischer Wald, south-east of Bayreuth. He had had only one very bad day, which had forced him to remain in bed, and he was still tormented by constant headaches – 'as at certain times in Basel.'

The only reason he offered for his panicky flight was the Giessels' 'dreadful' apartment in the busy centre of Bayreuth, which he had found intolerably stifling and uncomfortable. That there might have been other, deeper, aesthetico-philosophical reasons for his sudden disappearance Fritz did not bother to explain to his practically minded sister. But after receiving a plaintive letter from Elisabeth, who felt very lonely and out of place in the cosmopolitan, 'Franco-Russian circle' of Wagner admirers that had formed around Malwida von Meysenbug and the two Herzen sisters, Fritz finally changed his mind and returned to Bayreuth. His sister had thoughtfully brought along some eye-soothing sprays and lotions, but what must above all have prompted Nietzsche to come back, in addition to the fatal, narcotic lure of Wagner's lush orchestral music, was the unique opportunity of being able to participate in a sublime moment of musico-spiritual communion with his dearest friends – Erwin Rohde, Carl von Gersdorff, Franz Overbeck.

To judge from two letters later written by Elisabeth, Fritz, during his two weeks in Bayreuth, where the mid-August temperature mercifully cooled, greatly enjoyed himself in the company of his closest friends, even though his eyes continued to cause him pain. So too did Erwin Rohde who, emboldened by his recent betrothal, 'turned on the charm' and paid outlandish compliments to every lady he met.

Carl von Gersdorff also enjoyed himself. He was smitten, not only by Wagner's overpowering music, but also by a young Italian countess with the sirenic name of Nerina Finochietti, with whom he fell madly, insanely, desperately in love. Wagner's sensuous, erotically sublime as well as tragic music, particularly in his portrayal of Siegfried and Brünnhilde, put the apprentice farmer into an appropriately romantic mood, so sweeping him off his feet that he decided to stay on through the third and final cycle of performances (27–30 August).

Nietzsche, who probably left Bayreuth on Sunday, 27 August, just as the third *Ring* cycle was about to begin, seems to have been only dimly aware of the giddy 'madness' that had suddenly overpowered his friend Carl. For he himself had suffering eyes only for another lovely blonde creature, named Louise Ott. An inhabitant of Strasbourg who had moved to Paris with her Protestant husband after the German *Reich*'s annexation of Alsace and Lorraine, she was a rabid Wagnerian as well as a gifted singer and connoisseur of German and Russian music. Their brief 'romance', if such it can be called, seems to have been as momentarily intense as it was platonic. She was fascinated by the mysterious depth of Nietzsche's gaze as well as by the elegance and diction and the exceptional 'nobility' of his thinking, devoid of all trace of platitudes. He for his part felt that he had met a kindred soul, capable of fully sharing his most elevated thoughts and feelings.

'Everything was dark around me when you left Bayreuth,' he wrote to her three days after his return to Basel, 'it was as though someone had removed the light. I first had to pull myself together, but that I have now done, and you can take this letter in your hand without apprehension. We want to hold fast to the purity of the spirit that brought us together,' he added, for as a doting mother she had come to Bayreuth with her little son Marcel.

To this Louise answered three days later from Paris: 'How good it is that a true, healthy friendship can spring up between us, so that we can think of each other so directly from the heart without our conscience forbidding it. Thus can we still reciprocally give each other the best of ouselves: heart and mind! Your eyes, however, can I not forget: your deep, loving gaze still rests upon me, as it did then . . .' After saying how happy she would be to receive his 'Untimely Meditations', and thus be able to know him better, she added, faintly conscience-stricken, 'In this way our exchange of letters can proceed quite simply. Make no mention of your and my letters – Everything that has so far come to pass will remain between us – it is our sanctuary, for both of us alone.'

CHAPTER 22

# Winter in Sorrento

*– Sickness itself can be a stimulant to life: only one must be healthy enough for this stimulant.*

At Bayreuth Malwida von Meysenbug had renewed her generous suggestion that Nietzsche spend the first part of his sabbatical vacation with her in southern Italy. It had also been agreed that he would be accompanied by one of his former students in classical philology, Albert Brenner, a delicate young scholar-poet from Basel who had been sent to Rome by his worried parents to be cured of adolescent moodiness and fits of suicidal despair. Having a companion to help him was an elementary travel precaution, for Nietzsche's eyesight had by now so deteriorated that he could hardly see. The drastic treatment prescribed by his ophthalmologist, Professor Schiess – atropine eyedrops, derived from the deadly nightshade plant – seems to have aggravated rather than alleviated the head- and eye-aches, and to have been equally ineffective in warding off the serious relapses, which now recurred with painful regularity every eight to ten days.

His sister Elisabeth having decided to return to Naumburg after a year-long stay in Basel, Fritz moved back to his old bachelor lodgings on the Schützengraben, where his favourite student, Adolf Baumgartner, now occupied the quarters previously inhabited by Franz Overbeck. From Bayreuth, Overbeck had taken his young bride, Ida, to his parents' home in Dresden. In his absence it was a real joy for Nietzsche to be able to share his lunches and dinners in the 'Baumann cavern' with Dr Paul Rée, a twenty-seven-year-old admirer who three years before had been persuaded by Heinrich Romundt to leave Leipzig and to come to Basel to follow Nietzsche's lectures in classical philology. The son of a well-to-do Pomeranian landowner of partly Huguenot and partly Jewish descent, Rée had defied his father's wishes by turning his back on law and choosing to obtain a doctorate in philosophy. An ardent Schopenhauerian, he had developed a keen interest in Darwinism and modern science, as well as in the sceptical 'rationalism' of eighteenth-century French thinkers, whose predilection for aphoristic brevity had inspired a short book, entitled *Psychologische Beobachtungen* (*Psychological Observations*), which Rée had had published anonymously in Berlin.

On 26 September Nietzsche wrote to Malwida von Meysenbug that he would be accompanied by Dr Rée (whom she had met at Bayreuth), a scholar of independent means whom he described in laudatory terms as having an 'altogether clear head' and a 'considerate, truly friendly soul'. Five days later Nietzsche followed his friend to Montreux, where Rée's affluent mother was spending the summer. After which, the two 'philosophers' – one a rebellious professor of classical philology, the other a wayward doctor who had run away from law – spent two restful weeks enjoying a lovely autumn in the town of Bex, situated directly beneath the glistening white teeth of the Lake of Geneva's most photogenic mountain, the Dents du Midi.

Shortly before his departure for the south, Fritz sent a postcard to his sister saying that he had just finished his fifth 'Untimely Meditation'. This brash claim was a gem of wishful thinking. For, far from having finished it, he had merely begun an interminable 'Meditation' that was to keep him occupied for the next twelve months and finally assume monstrous proportions.

Although he dared not say so openly, Nietzsche for some time past had begun to regret that Wagner, in his search for operatic subjects, should have interested himself almost exclusively in Germanic and Scandinavian myths – something that had inevitably made him, as he had boldly intimated towards the end of *Richard Wagner in Bayreuth*, 'not the prophet of a future, such as he would perhaps like to appear to us, but the interpreter and transfigurer of the past'. By that Nietzsche meant of course the Germanic past. Great as was Wagner's proclaimed admiration for Greek antiquity, he had never seriously used it as a source of inspiration – as had, for example, his great predecessors, Gluck and Mozart. Nor was this all. The more Nietzsche pondered the problem posed by Greek antiquity and the lessons it could usefully transmit to nineteenth-century Europe, the more he became convinced that Schopenhauer, though a staunch admirer of the Greek and Latin classics, had uncritically adopted the classically 'pagan', at once moralistic and sentimental, interpretation of Greek culture and civilization, basically derived from Christian ethics. In *The Birth of Tragedy* Nietzsche had praised the Greeks' robust and affirmative *ja-sagend* ('yes-saying') acceptance of life as it is, not least of all in its Dionysian and erotic aspects. But so blinding had been his readers' faith in Schopenhauer that nobody, and not even he himself, had fully realized how basically un-Schopenhauerian and 'heretical' his views on this subject already were.

It was certainly no accident, Nietzsche realized, if, at the end of the seventieth section of the first volume of *The World as Will and Representation*, partly devoted to Christian teachings regarding *grace*, the *denial of the will*, *salvation*, Schopenhauer should have concluded by asserting that his own system of ethics 'fully agrees with the Christian dogmas proper, and, according to its essentials, was contained and present in these very dogmas. It is also just as much in agreement with the doctrines and ethical precepts of the sacred books of India, which again are presented in quite different forms.'

Now if there was one thing that had been proved by the long, trimillennial history of India, it was that the denial of human individuality, which is the root concept of both Hinduism and Buddhism, is not conducive to the production of great literary and artistic geniuses. If India, with the *Mahabharata* and the *Ramayana*, had produced great epic poems roughly equivalent to the *Iliad* and the *Odyssey*, India had never produced an Aeschylus or a Sophocles, nor a Phidias, a Praxiteles, a Botticelli, a Michelangelo, a Leonardo da Vinci, a Shakespeare or a Goethe, a Rembrandt or a Rubens, to say nothing of a Bach, a Mozart, a Beethoven or a Richard Wagner. It was the Greeks who had discovered and exalted human individuality, the very principle of which (*principium individuationis*) Schopenhauer had repeatedly condemned. This more than any other was the reason why Greek antiquity, rediscovered by the poet-philologists and 'humanists' of the Renaissance, had bequeathed to the entire continent a priceless artistic legacy, on the noble ruins of which a good part of European culture had been built.

Although Nietzsche probably still considered himself a Schopenhauerian when he wrote the first chapters of his fourth 'Untimely Meditation', he must have half realized that Wagner was the living refutation of Schopenhauerian dogma. His entire life, from youth on, had been a stubborn and ultimately victorious affirmation of individual will power, of the overpowering desire and instinct to create and possess, welling up from the dark, mysterious depths of his inner being (what Carl Jung, in the next century, was to call the 'creative unconscious'). Far from being something to be combated as fundamentally self-deluding, it had been a positive force, a healthy will, just as had been the composer's '*Drang nach Macht und Ruhm*' – his drive for power and fame, specifically praised in *Richard Wagner in Bayreuth*.

Already, in the second section of *The Utility and Disadvantage of History for Life*, Nietzsche had dared to flout a basic principle of Schopenhauerism by asserting that ambition and the desire for fame, prompted by a desire to emulate the great geniuses of the past, was 'something more than the delicious bite of self-esteem . . . it is the belief in the fellowship and continuity of the great ones of all times'. Healthy emulation, in the form of *agon* (competitive struggle), had been one of the causes of the admirable creativity of the ancient Greeks. This was something Schopenhauer had never properly understood or attempted to explain, just as he had never truly appreciated the evolutionary processes of human history. In his lifelong battle against Hegel's dialectical exaggerations, he had in fact rejected history as a subject worthy of serious philosophical investigation. Over and against Hegel's monumental system Schopenhauer had erected his own anti-historical, essentially static, life-denying and individuality-hostile view of life and the world. A view which, because of the stylistic elegance of its exposition and the special place it accorded music as the most soul-stirring of the arts, had mesmerized its devotees – among them Nietzsche and Cosima and Richard Wagner. They had touched the magic bark, they had drunk of the fatal potion, not realizing that it was a life-denying drug that had paralysed their intellectual faculties. Nietzsche and his friends had become neo-Schopenhauerians, just as most of their contemporaries were self-deluding neo-Christians, proclaiming their fidelity to a faith, the harsh implications of which they casually chose to disregard.

Nietzsche, however, was now determined to free himself of this magic thrall. It was to begin this painful reappraisal that, after attending the dress rehearsals of the four *Ring* operas, he had fled from the stifling heat of an overcrowded Bayreuth to the cool, wood-surrounded peace of Klingenbrunn. Nietzsche may well have been overwhelmed by the magnitude of Wagner's music – his orchestras were three times the size of Mozart's. Disappointed because neither the harassed hostess of 'Wahnfried' nor the frantically busy composer could devote a moment to discussing the strengths and weaknesses, the bold analogies with Greek antiquity, and not least of all the challenging finale of *Richard Wagner in Bayreuth*, he was understandably upset. But none of these highly subjective reactions explain his brusque 'flight' to Klingenbrunn, still less the curious title he chose for his fifth 'Untimely Meditation' – '*Die Pflugschar*,' 'The Ploughshare'. But the meaning was obvious to anyone who had read *Schopenhauer as Educator* with any care. In that essay Nietzsche had defined the goal of genuine education, and consequently of philosophy, as being one of 'liberation, a removal of all the weeds, the rubbish, the vermin' – i.e. of conventional notions, opinions and beliefs – 'that threaten to choke the life out of the tender buds' of original and truly honest thinking. In undertaking a radical re-examination of the Schopenhauerian dogma which for years had blinded him, and in clearing out the luxuriant, arch-romantic underbrush that was encumbering his prose and smothering the tender shoots of the unpalatable truths that were germinating inside him, Nietzsche needed an instrument mightier than a hoe: nothing less than a ploughshare, with which to upturn and reseed the weed-and-thistle-infested field of his thinking.

★

On 19 October Nietzsche boarded the train for Geneva, while Paul Rée got off at Montreux to spend a day with his mother. In Geneva Nietzsche picked up Albert Brenner, and together they boarded the evening train that was to take them through the new Mont Cenis tunnel to Turin, and from there on to Genoa. He found himself sharing a first-class compartment with two exceptionally intelligent ladies – Claudine von Brevern and her slightly younger travelling companion, Isabella von der Pahlen, with whom Nietzsche struck up a long, lively conversation.

In Genoa the travellers identified themselves, exchanged addresses, and ended up staying in the same hotel. Exhausted by the long nocturnal conversation, Nietzsche retired to his bedroom and probably remained there until the arrival of Paul Rée. When he heard that the two ladies were about to leave Genoa by train, he asked Rée to accompany him to the railway station. But on the way he was smitten by such a violent headache that he almost fainted and had to ask Rée to take him back to the hotel. In a hurriedly written note addressed to Claudine von Brevern, Nietzsche apologized for having, as he put it in curiously martial terms, had to beat a shameful retreat 'like a defeated army. Nevertheless, I cannot fail to express to you in writing my joy about a meeting which let me see a double drama: a lofty *already reached* culture and a lofty striving for culture' – an elegant compliment intended to flatter the vanity of the older, more experienced lady and the eagerness to learn of the young neophyte who was visiting Italy for the first time.

This chance encounter with two remarkable ladies was one more manifestation of a deep-seated hope which, with Nietzsche, had acquired the force of an *idée fixe*. Much as he valued solitude – his musical 'Hymn to Friendship' had significantly preceded the later 'Hymn to Solitude' – he enjoyed the company of friends and not least of all of disciples. Determined to free himself from the life-denying thrall of Schopenhauerian pessimism, he was now as eager to form a circle of courageous 'free thinkers' as he had once been, with the help of Erwin Rohde and Heinrich Romundt, to form a close-knit community of disciples for the propagation of the Schopenhauerian gospel. At Bayreuth, where the question had been seriously discussed, Malwida von Meysenbug had enthusiastically welcomed the idea of establishing a 'cloister for free spirits', recalling how, years before in Hamburg, inspired by the teachings of Friedrich Froebel, she and other ardent feminists had founded an institution designed to emancipate and educate members of her sex. Nietzsche, feeling little sympathy for the word *Kloster* (monastery), preferred to regard it as an ideal 'community', as a 'school for teachers' whose first task it should be to educate themselves.

As he had written on 22 September to the captivating Louise Ott, who had so charmed him in Bayreuth: '. . . this new frienship is like new wine, very pleasant, but maybe a bit dangerous. For me at any rate. But also for you, when I think of the kind of Freigeist you ran across there. A man who each day wishes nothing more than to lose some comforting belief . . .'

In all, the steamboat voyage from Genoa to Naples lasted three days. At Livorno, where there was a long stopover, Nietzsche and Albert Brenner had time to make a quick visit to Pisa, where they were able to admire the leaning tower and catch a second glimpse of Claudine von Brevern and Isabella von der Pahlen.

Back on board and to his considerable surprise, Nietzsche was not seasick. As he wrote to his sister shortly after his arrival in Naples, 'I also prefer this way of travelling to train travel, which for me is utterly dreadful.' He was disagreeably surprised, however, by the teeming dockside, with its noisy throng of gesticulating urchins and insistent *facchini* who swarmed around him and his two companions in their eagerness to seize their trunks and suitcases and lug them to the waiting cabs. That evening, to cheer him up, Malwida von Meysenbug took Nietzsche and his two friends out for a carriage drive along the shore to Pausilippo. The sight of ash-grey clouds billowing up over the summit of Vesuvius, all crimsoned in the rays of the sunken sun against a pale blue and violet sky, was so beautiful that Nietzsche's ill-humour quickly disappeared.

The next morning they left Naples and travelled to Sorrento, to which they had been preceded by Richard and Cosima Wagner and three of the children. Not far from the Hôtel Vittoria, where the composer was staying, Malwida von Meysenbug had rented a villa. Nietzsche, like his two companions, was given a large, high-ceilinged bedroom on the first floor, from which he could step out on to a broad terrace offering him a magnificent view over groves of orange, lemon and olive trees to the Bay of Naples beyond. The self-sacrificing Malwida occupied the second, less luxurious floor, along with her housemaid, while downstairs there was a large dining-room and a living-room where all could gather for lunch and dinner and discussions in the evening. Fritz wrote next day to his sister in Naumburg, 'I have just come back from my first sea-bath; the water, according to Rée, was warmer than the North Sea in July . . . Sorrento and Naples are beautiful, people don't exaggerate . . . '

The previous afternoon (Friday, 27 October) Malwida had taken her three house-guests to the Hôtel Vittoria to call on Richard Wagner and his wife. Exhausted by eight frantic weeks spent rehearsing and overseeing the difficult performances of the *Ring des Nibelungen* operas, the composer had decided to offer himself several months of relaxation in Italy. The week-long stay in Venice, however, had been spoiled by the upsetting news, transmitted by the Bayreuth banker Feustel, that they were now saddled with debts totalling 120,000 marks. A repetition of the Bayreuth Festival in 1877 now seemed out of the question.

On 23 September, Wagner had sent Nietzsche a terse telegram from Venice, asking him to have two pairs of silk waistcoats and trousers sent to him by express delivery to Bologna by his favourite tailor in Basel. In the long reply he had dictated to Heinrich Köselitz, Nietzsche said how pleased he had been by Wagner's urgent request, so reminiscent of the 'errands' he and Cosima had often imposed on him during the lovely Tribschen years. 'I now have time to look back over the past, distant as well as close, for I do a lot of sitting in a dark room, because of an atropine-cure for the eyes which it was felt I needed after my return home.' The rest of this letter contained a pathetic description of Nietzsche's nervous seizures, some of them lasting for thirty agonizing hours and recurring regularly at intervals of four to eight days. 'Complete rest, mild air, walks, dark rooms – that is what I expect from Italy; I dread having to see or hear anything there.' By which he meant anything resembling operas or plays.

This plaintive letter can hardly have pleased Wagner who, though not insensitive to the physical sufferings of others, now realized that the almost blind professor could not possibly become the robust promoter of his 'art-work-of-the-future' on whom he had once pinned such hopes. That this was also Cosima's feeling can be judged by the brevity of the one-sentence comment in her diary on Malwida von Meysenbug's first visit to the Hôtel Vittoria with Dr Rée 'and our friend Nietzsche, the latter very run down and much concerned with his health'.

On Saturday, 28 October, Cosima reported having seen Malwida, whose birthday it was, but there was no mention of Nietzsche. Two days later Cosima took her children to the Villa Rubinacci, while Wagner remained behind at the Hôtel Vittoria. Again there was no mention of Nietzsche. He may have succumbed to one of four severe seizures he suffered during his first fortnight in Sorrento. This would explain why on All Saints' Day, (1 November), when the weather turned so wet and blustery that Wagner called it 'All Fiends' Day', Paul Rée came to the Hôtel Vittoria alone. He would have done better not to have come at all; for, as Cosima recorded in her diary, his 'cold and precise character does not appeal to us; on closer inspection we come to the conclusion that he must be an Israelite'.

The following morning, All Souls' Day, the weather cleared and, as Cosima noted in her diary, 'the evening we spend with our friends

Malwida and Prof. Nietzsche'. In the final volume of her memoirs, published twenty years later, Malwida von Meysenbug recalled how unnaturally stiff Nietzsche seemed during these meetings with Wagner in Sorrento, displaying a gaiety that was more forced than spontaneous. Cosima, who had long since noticed the wariness Nietzsche often displayed in the presence of the 'Master', interpreted his paradoxical remarks as facile provocations and symptoms of poor judgement. As she wrote six months later to her friend Malwida: 'I believe there is in Nietzsche a dark productive substratum of which he himself is quite unconscious; it is from this that whatever is significant in him springs, but then it alarms him, whereas everything he thinks and says, which is brilliantly lit up, is really of not much value. It is the tellurian element in him that is important; the solar element is insignificant, and rendered even disquieting and unedifying by its struggle with the tellurian.'

Cosima's harsh judgement, though not devoid of psychological insight, shows how little she understood the deeper trends in Nietzsche's philosophical preoccupations, and in particular his increasingly critical attitude towards the excesses of *Sturm und Drang* romanticism, of which Richard Wagner's monumental operas were superlative baroque examples.

On Monday, 6 November, when the decision was made to 'leave this beautiful place tomorrow', Richard and Cosima Wagner spent the evening with Malwida. Again there was no mention in Cosima's diary of Nietzsche; any more than there was the next day, when the Wagner family left Sorrento, accompanied as far as Naples by Malwida von Meysenbug.

Just as Wagner's flight from Bayreuth failed to bring him the peace of mind he had hoped to find in Italy, so Nietzsche's much longer 'flight from Basel' offered him scant relief from the recurrent eye-aches and headaches he so desperately craved. More loving care and motherly attention could not have been lavished on him by Malwida von Meysenbug and her efficient housemaid-cook, Trina. Indeed, during the first cold-weather days Nietzsche, who was hyper-sensitive to changes of temperature, was allowed to do his dictating (to Albert Brenner) in the only room in the house that boasted a warming porcelain stove.

The daily régime, beginning with a 7 a.m. cup of warm milk, soon followed by a pot of tea for breakfast, could not have been more wholesome. As Paul Rée reported to Fritz's sister Elisabeth two weeks after their arrival: 'After the [breakfast] tea he dictates something' – new additions to his fifth 'Untimely Meditation' – 'and then he usually goes for a walk before lunch. The lunch, thanks to the loving care of Fräulein von Meysenbug, this clever and angelic lady, is always simple and plentiful.

After lunch there is a long, general siesta, then we all go together for a walk. Your brother has recently been able to take walks lasting for hours up mountain paths, and this surely is in large part the reason why he has been spared headaches since the latest, brief, but nevertheless severe attack.'

The condition of Nietzsche's eyes throughout his seven-month stay in Sorrento was such that all he could bring himself to write (with but one or two exceptions) were postcards. In mid-November, after learning that his maternal grandmother had died, he wrote a longish letter to his now orphaned mother to express his sorrow. He added that he was being wonderfully looked after, not least of all by Trina, the housemaid-cook, who had become a very efficient *Krankenwärterin* (sick man's nurse).

Daily life at the Villa Rubinacci soon settled into a calm routine. On the days when he was not bedridden and suffering from blinding headaches, Nietzsche spent the morning dictating new paragraphs and aphorisms to his devoted disciple Brenner. He had decided to alter the title of his fifth 'Untimely Meditation' from the heavy-booted '*Die Pflugschar*' ('The Ploughshare') to the more graceful '*Der Freigeist*' ('The Free Spirit'). Some of these aphorisms were inspired by the stimulating evenings when, before or after dinner, Malwida and her three house-guests gathered in the spacious living-room. Seated on one side of the blazing fireplace, with Albert Brenner on the other, she would listen to Paul Rée read from some chosen book or text, placed under an oil-lamp on a table in the middle of the room. Nietzsche, to protect his fragile eyes, was seated far from the fireplace, but, his hearing being as acute as ever, he frequently intervened to comment on a just-read passage.

Along with the many books that had accompanied them from Basel were handwritten notes that Adolf Baumgertner and another student had taken while attending Jacob Burckhardt's lectures on Greek culture and civilization. Nietzsche's running commentaries on these lectures, as read out loud by Paul Rée, made such an indelible impression on Malwida von Meysenbug that years later, in a burst of lyrical reminiscence, she wrote that 'never has this most glorious of periods in the development of mankind been more luminously and completely described than by these two men, each of them having a perfect knowledge of Greek antiquity'.

Burckhardt's edifying lectures were followed by readings from Xenophon, Plato's *The Laws*, and Thucydides, who again aroused Malwida's rapturous enthusiasm. In early December Voltaire was given pride of place, soon followed by Diderot and, as an antidote to the eighteenth-century rationalists, by the arch-Romantic French historian Jules Michelet.

It is difficult now to appreciate the intellectual delight that such reading sessions could arouse. (As Cosima's fascinating diary reveals, those spent with Richard Wagner were extraordinarily varied and enriching.) And it would be a grave error to believe that, because the readings at the Villa Rubinacci were devoted to 'classic' authors and subjects, they were in any way stuffy and pedantic. Malwida von Meysenbug's memoirs make it clear that they were, on the contrary, constantly enlivened by the wry wit that spiced and peppered so many of Nietzsche's letters. Not to be outdone, Paul Rée, while reading, would often straight-facedly skip a few pages just to see if his 'audience' was still awake and listening – which, to judge by the ensuing protests and laughter, it usually was.

Christmas, in particular, was celebrated in a spirit of Nordic gaiety, with candles, a decorated Christmas tree, and gifts for each house-guest presented with a humorous verse or two composed by Malwida. Nietzsche was given a fan to shield his eyes when drawing closer to the fireplace, as well as a red headdress, which ( Albert Brenner claimed) made him look like a Tartar because of the sun-tanned features and the bristling moustache. 'May it protect the forehead of the friend, the seat of such noble thoughts,' ran Malwida's charming note.

So extraordinarily harmonious was this cohabitation between a foster-mother and her three adopted 'children' that it revived in the good Malwida, an impenitent idealist, the desire to set up the kind of model school that she and and other kindred souls had founded years ago in Hamburg to further the 'emancipation' and education of young women. The many letters she had been receiving from admiring female readers of her memoirs confirmed her in the belief that, with the help of talented 'professors' like Friedrich Nietzsche and Paul Rée, it would be possible to establish a 'kind of haven for missionaries' (as she later put it) where young men and women would be encouraged to 'develop the noblest faculties of the mind' before going out into the great world 'to sow the seeds of a new and higher culture'. The scheme generated such fervour among the inmates of the Villa Rubinacci that exploratory excursions were made to nearby grottoes, some of them so large that they resembled vaulted churches, within whose cool interiors, well protected from the torrid summer sun, future 'disciples' could gather to listen to the inspired lectures of their 'teachers'. For to Malwida, as to Nietzsche – both of them in this respect still ardently Schopenhauerian – it went without saying that no such school or 'colony' of teachers could possibly thrive in the fetid air of a modern city.

Enthused by Malwida von Meysenbug's and her brother Fritz's descriptions of this ideal community or 'monastery' of 'free-thinking apostles', the practically minded Elisabeth had leapt at the idea of setting up just such a '*Klösterchen*' (little convent) in a manor-house located near the village of Arlesheim, south of Basel. Shortly before leaving for the south, Fritz had gone one better by proposing that the self-sacrificing Heinrich Köselitz, to whom he had been dictating new aphorisms for his fifth 'Untimely Meditation', be appointed 'Perpetual Secretary' of this new musico-philosophical academy. In a letter written to a young Berlin admirer, Reinhard von Seydlitz, Nietzsche had explained that in his ceaseless search for real friends he operated like a corsair pirate, ever on the lookout for new captives, 'but not in order to sell these men into slavery, but in order to sell myself with them into freedom'.

Granted a privileged look at Paul Rée's new philosophical opus – a precise, analytical refutation of the concept of 'free will' – the poetically minded Albert Brenner instinctively recoiled in horror. Yet the fond hope refused to die, sustained by the deceptive harmony of the Villa Rubinacci. It was revived in mid-December when out of the blue Nietzsche received a letter from Claudine von Brevern, expressing the hope that the 'Herr Professor' could come to visit Rome or at least write to her, so that 'our brief acquaintance could acquire lasting value through the exchange of a few thoughts'. In a short accompanying note the younger Isabella von der Pahlen extended the invitation to the author of *Memoirs of an Idealist* (Malwida von Meysenbug). Since Nietzsche was in no condition to move to Rome, or even to write the kind of letter that the older of his two former train companions was hoping to receive, he asked his publisher, Ernst Schmeitzner, to have copies of the second and third 'Untimely Meditations' sent to Claudine von Brevern, and copies of the first and fourth sent to Isabella von der Pahlen in Rome.

In early January (1877) Nietzsche was informed by Heinrich Köselitz and his friend Paul Widemann that, disregarding their objections, Ernst Schmeitzner had agreed to become the publisher of a new journal designed to propagate Wagner's views. It was to be edited by the music critic Richard Pohl (an old Wagner friend) and by Hans von Wolzogen, an affluent young baron who had recently manifested his ardent Wagnerophilia by publishing an explanatory pamphlet on the *Nibelungen* myth. These two gentlemen and others of the same 'characterless' ilk, Köselitz claimed, had 'nothing new to say'. With this harsh judgement Nietzsche, in his reply, expressed complete agreement: 'R.W[agner] has not learned to fear' – a reference to the innocent young Siegfried, who has to sally forth into the great, wild world to discover what fear is – 'nor unfortunately has he also learned to wait. I was hitherto hoping that in four years enough men' – i.e. persons like Erwin Rohde, Franz Overbeck, the talented Albert Brenner, who had almost finished a remarkable short story, the pianist and musicologist Carl Fuchs, Louis Keltenborn (the most musically talented of his Basel students), Heinrich Köselitz, and perhaps even Paul Rée – 'would have come together in order to be able to begin the undertaking in a grander style'.

This, of course, was a vain hope. It was totally unrealistic to imagine that Wagner, hounded as he was by impatient bankers demanding the prompt reimbursement of their loans, could quietly wait for another four years before launching the propaganda organ he now needed more desperately than ever. Wagner's wilful and domineering character being what it was, it was also wishful thinking to suppose that he would ever allow Nietzsche and his 'free-thinking' friends to use this new periodical for the airing of their bold views as to how contemporary Germany's cultural 'Reformation' should be realized in practice.

Shortly before Christmas, Nietzsche had written a birthday-greetings letter to Cosima Wagner, in which, after saying that 'post-Bayreuth' had seen all the hopes of 'pre-Bayreuth' fulfilled, he added: 'Once I have straightened things out with Philologica, a more difficult [task] awaits me: will you be amazed when I confess that I have almost suddenly become aware of a disagreement with Schopenhauer which has slowly been growing within me? I am not on his side in almost all general propositions; already when I was writing about Sch[openhauer] I noticed that I am far removed from every kind of dogmatism; for me everything depended on *Man*.'

To this distinctly elegiac letter, which contained a moving paragraph inspired by the recent death of his influential sponsor Friedrich Ritschl, Cosima replied on New Year's Day of 1877 with a much longer letter of her own, in which she expressed her astonishment that Nietzsche, in his quarrel with Schopenhauer, should be laying the emphasis on Man. 'Every doctrine, even the most sublime and the most coherent, can only, it seems to me, be an allegory to which the philosopher adheres just as the poet does to his characters . . . It would fascinate me to hear what objections you have against our philosopher. Wouldn't you like to dictate your letters to me via Brenner?'

Nietzsche made no attempt to reply to this cordially expressed letter. Open-minded though Cosima tried to sound, the mere fact that she used the word *Lehre* (doctrine) to describe such systems of thought and referred to Schopenhauer as 'our philosopher' meant that Nietzsche, in announcing his fundamental disagreement, had overstepped the bounds of what was intellectually permissible. It would have required pages and pages to explain what was wrong and 'incoherent' in Schopenhauer's philosophy, and for this he had neither the energy nor the inclination.

On 1 February, Paul Rée, who had dutifully been supplementing Nietzsche's laconic postcards with longer letters to Naumburg to keep his mother and sister informed of Fritz's health and activities, wrote to say that the past six weeks had been exceptionally good, with but two bad days.

Unfortunately, one of Nietzsche's eyes had suddenly become even more short-sighted, with an impression of 'shimmering' which caused the letters on any page before him to 'collide' and to form into lumps. Though Rée was persuaded that this was the result of a cold, his friend had been forced to give up all kinds of reading and writing.

At the suggestion of his Basel ophthalmologist, Heinrich Spiess, Nietzsche travelled to Naples, where his eyes were examined by a Professor Schrön, from the university's medical faculty. He returned to Sorrento almost in high spirits, convinced, as he wrote to his mother and sister on 18 February, that Sorrento had a well-established reputation as an ideal place for eye cures. Professor Schrön had subjected him to the first truly meticulous examination he had ever undergone, had dismissed as nonsense the idea that he might be suffering from *Kopfkatarrh* ('head-catarrh', one of his sister's favourite notions), and had given him a clearer idea of the origin of the trouble – though what this was Fritz did not tell his mother.

The Mediterranean sun had by this time disappeared, and for most of the next five weeks Sorrento was lashed by fierce winds and rain, while the summit of Vesuvius turned white with snow. 'If only I could believe that things were gradually getting better,' he wrote to his mother on 26 March. 'But the very serious condition of the eye has gone, that is good.'

At the end of March Reinhart von Seydlitz, whom Nietzsche had lured southward by sending him a lyrical description of the quiet walks one could take through groves of orange trees, pines and cypresses so thickly leafed that all one could *see* of the soundless wind storming overhead was the violent swaying to and fro of the pine-tops, turned up in Sorrento with his attractive Hungarian wife. Lodged nearby, they were welcome additions to Malwida's 'convent of free spirits' – particularly since Albert Brenner now had to return to Basel for the summer semester, while Paul Rée headed for Jena, where, he felt, the Darwinistic axioms underlying his recently completed second book, on *The Origin of Moral Feelings*, would be received with less hostility than in philosophically arch-conservative Basel.

On 10 April Malwida von Meysenbug accompanied Paul Rée and Albert Brenner to Naples, where they were to take the north-bound train to Rome and on up the peninsula to Switzerland. Astonishingly enough, she, the incorrigible idealist, had developed a maternal fondness for the 'positivistic' Paul Rée, who, with a consummate sense of diplomacy, had shown himself to be the most attentive of her three house-guests.

Abandoned for three days to the competent care of Malwida's house-maid and cook, Trina, Nietzsche felt so depressed that he fell ill almost immediately. As he wrote to Rée shortly after Malwida's return from

Naples, 'Several days in bed, always bad, until today [17 April]. Nothing is more desolate than your room without Rée. We speak and are silent a great deal about the Absent One . . . In the evening we play merels . . . Seyd[litz] lies ill in bed; we could mutually serve as "humane medical orderlies" [*humaner Krankenwärter*] for each other, by simply changing our periods in bed. Dearest friend, how grateful I am to you! You must never be lost to me again!'

Since Malwida von Meysenbug also had trouble with her eyes, there were no more reading sessions in the evening. But the two friends were never at a loss for topics of conversation – one of them being the kind of woman Nietzsche should marry. Here Malwida, who in her younger days had been abandoned by the man who was supposed to marry her, saw eye to eye with Fritz's mother, for whom this vital question had become an obsession. Unfortunately, the quiet, 'monastic' life led by the foursome in Sorrento had done nothing to further the realization of this 'holiest of hopes'. But this had not kept Fritz's busybody sister from frequently returning to the subject in her letters. In Sorrento, he explained in a letter written to Elisabeth on Easter Sunday (31 March), he had discussed the possibility of marrying Olga Herzen's older sister Natalie with her foster-mother, Malwida von Meysenbug. But she was already thirty years old, barely three years younger than himself, and, he argued, 'it would be better if she were 12 years younger'.

The troubles that had befallen Erwin Rohde and Carl von Gersdorff, when they had yielded to amorous passion, had provided warning examples not to be followed. Even a marriage based on 'reason' was no sure recipe for marital felicity. The finest but also rarest example of an exceptionally happy marriage, one which ceaselessly haunted Nietzsche's imagination, was that of Richard Wagner and Cosima Liszt, the miraculous result of a chance meeting in Berlin in 1853.

In her answering letter, sent from Naumburg in mid-April, Elisabeth chided her brother for being too exacting in his conception of an 'ideal' marriage. She herself had nothing against Natalie Herzen, as she had made clear when they had discussed the matter in Bayreuth, but she personally favoured the 'little Köckert', the daughter of a Geneva banker whose wife was an ardent admirer of Nietzsche's. When he read extracts from his sister's long letter to Malwida, the self-styled 'idealist' proved that her two feet were solidly planted on the ground by exclaiming, 'Good, but rich!' – causing both of them to laugh. The idea of helping Nietzsche solve this critical marriage problem enthused the generous Malwida, now more than ever persuaded that if he resumed his professorial duties in Basel, it would irremediably undermine his health and eyesight. To ward off this calamity, she proposed to invite several 'choice beings' of the fair sex –

Elise von Bülow from Berlin, Elisabeth Brandes from Hanover, etc. – to come to Switzerland in the summer. Once his choice was made, Nietzsche could celebrate his marriage in the autumn. He would then bring his bride south to Rome – 'which place is equally suited for health, company, and my studies', as Fritz explained to his sister.

Even as he penned these lines, Nietzsche must have realized how close these projects were to wishful thinking and the stuff that dreams are made of. For, as he added, 'I still find the intellectual qualities best united in Nat[alie] Herzen. You have accomplished wonders in idealizing the little Köckert [girl] in Geneva. Praise, honour, and glory to you! It is however doubtful; and [the] fortune?' For although Natalie's brother Alexander, a professor of physiology at the university, owned a villa in Florence, the Herzens were not wealthy.

Beneath his signature on this letter, Fritz identified himself ironically by adding – 'in future (if I am still alive in another year) a Roman'. Rome, only slightly less torrid during the summer months than Naples and Sorrento, could not possibly provide a satisfactory habitat for his delicate constitution. For now, with each passing day, the heat, like the sunlight, grew uncomfortably more intense.

'Dearest Friend,' Nietzsche wrote to Paul Rée on 7 May, 'tomorrow I am leaving. From sheer necessity, for since your departure things have gone from bad to worse, every three days I have to remain in bed. Now I'm going by the shortest route (by sea) to Pfäffers' – a small watering-spa near Ragaz, in eastern Switzerland – 'in which I have a certain confidence.'

The trip from Sorrento to Naples was made in the company of his new friend Reinhart von Seydlitz and his Hungarian wife, who took care of the dockside porters and saw to it that all of Nietzsche's trunks and suitcases, containing his precious notes and books, were safely stowed on board the steamship that was to transport him to Genoa. The voyage up the Tyrrhenian coast was as stormily rough and rainy as the southbound trip had been calm and enjoyable. Nietzsche, again suffering from acute headaches, was so violently seasick and disgusted that he was forced during two days and nights to change his place eight times to escape the nauseating odours, the small talk and the sight of table companions who kept 'tucking it in' with Rabelaisian gusto. 'Everything in the ship,' as Nietzsche later described it to Malwida, 'rolled noisily back and forth, the saucepans jumped and came to life, the children screamed, the storm howled; eternal sleeplessness was my lot, as the poet would say.'

Nor did the nightmare cease when the steamship finally docked at Genoa. Without a companion to help him through the customs, Nietzsche absentmindedly forgot to register his trunk and suitcase for transport by railroad to Lugano. He thus found himself, short-sighted as he was, encumbered by his baggage and having to argue with a small horde of porters as well as with a cab-driver who wanted to take him to the wrong hotel and who even threatened to 'dump' him, bag and baggage, in front of a wretched *trattoria*.

In his hotel bedroom, still wracked by headaches, he barely had strength enough to scribble a brief thank-you note to Reinhart von Seydlitz: '"He had *aes triplex* [triple bronze] *around his chest*, who for the first time travelled on the sea," says Horace; I had only *aurum triplex* [triple gold]; that's how horrible it was! Today [I'm] a broken man in all respects; morally too, for I am visibly distrustful, keep every moment counting my belongings, suspect my fellow creatures, and can't properly imagine that the sun is shining down on me – which is also not the case.'

The next morning (11 May) he plucked up his courage and, though it was still raining, he walked over to the Palazzo Brignole to have a look at its paintings. The sight of a noble member of the Brignole family proudly seated on his war-horse was so invigorating that it dispelled his headaches and renewed his shattered self-confidence; inspiring him to write two days later to Malwida von Meysenbug that he personally revered 'Van Dy[ck] and Rubens more highly than all the painters in the world'.

The tedious train-trip from Genoa to Milan was enlivened by the presence in his compartment of a young, *molto simpatica* ballerina named Camilla who was much amused by the German professor's curiously Latinized Italian. From Como he travelled on alone over the new Gotthard railway line to Lugano. The train was greeted at the Swiss frontier by pelting rain and a single, blinding flash of lightning, followed by a deafening thunderclap. 'I took it as a good omen,' he later wrote to Malwida, 'nor will I deny that the closer I got to the mountains, the better grew my health. At Chiasso my luggage disappeared on two different trains, there was hopeless confusion, and then again the customs. Even the two umbrellas followed opposite tracks. But I was helped by a good porter, the first to speak to me in *schweitzerdeutsch*; just think, I heard it with a certain feeling of emotion, I noticed all of a sudden that I am far happier living among the German Swiss than among Germans. The man took such good care of me, he ran back and forth in such a paternal fashion – all fathers are a bit clumsy – and finally everything was back together and I travelled to Lugano. The Hôtel du Parc's carriage was waiting for me and here I really wanted to shout for joy, so good is everything, I wanted to say, this is the best hotel in the world.'

After briefly watching an 'improvised' ball, frequented by simple English men and women, whose polite antics amused him, Nietzsche went to bed and, as he reported to Malwida, had a long, sound sleep: and this morning I see all of my beloved mountains in front of me, pure mountains of remembrance . . .

It now suddenly occurs to me that it has been years since I wrote so long a letter, and also that you will not read it.

Simply see in the *fact of this letter* a sign of my feeling better. If only you can decipher the end of this letter!

I think of you with heartfelt love, several times every hour; as a gift I was offered a good chunk of motherly being, I will never forget it.

My best greetings to Trina the Good One.

More than ever I am relying on Pfäffers and the high mountains . . .

Your gratefully devoted
Friedrich Nietzsche
Third Report of Odysseus.

## CHAPTER 23

# A Book for Free Spirits

*– A very common error – having the courage of one's convictions; rather it is a matter of having the courage for an attack on one's convictions.*

From Lugano Nietzsche travelled north and eastward up and over the sinuous San Bernardino Pass to Chur, and from there, twenty kilometres farther on, to the watering-spa of Bad Ragaz, not far from the borders of the Grand Duchy of Liechtenstein. On Whit Sunday (20 May, 1877) he was joined by Franz Overbeck, who, like Jacob Burckhardt, had been alarmed to learn that their good friend intended to give up his Basel professorship at the conclusion of his sabbatical year in September. A decision of this gravity, Overbeck felt, should not under any circumstances be hastily reached; for once he had resigned his chair of classical philology, there was not a hope in the world that the university authorities would be willing to take him back even if his health and eyesight dramatically improved. Knowing only too well how financially dependent he still was on his university salary, Nietzsche agreed to postpone his decision.

The three and a half weeks spent at Ragaz were anything but happy, notwithstanding the invigorating mountain air, plenty of pine forests, and the standard water-cure prescriptions of a local doctor. On 6 June, after suffering a three-day relapse partly due to the oppressive heat, Nietzsche wrote to Malwida von Meysenbug that he was moving up into 'the heights' – to an isolated village with the charmingly Helvetian name of Rosenlauibad, perched on the northern flank of the great Bernese Oberland mountain range, which stretches from the 2,780-metre Engelhorn down past the Eiger, the Mönch, and the Jungfrau to the Breithorn to the south-west. 'An air-and-milk-cure resort' was the way it was described in a guidebook. 'Lovely ladies' salon with piano. Most of the rooms covered with carpets; baths in soft alkali-sodium water. Only shortly after sundown does the air usually exceed the freshness of May, while the evenings are remarkably mild far into the night . . . Comfortably reached via Thun, Interlaken, the Brienner Lake, Meiringen.'

Far from helping to solve Nietzsche's troublesome 'marriage problem', this summer turned out to be a maddening 'comedy' of frustrated hopes, crossed purposes and ill-planned rendezvous. In Florence, where Malwida von Meysenbug stopped on her way to Switzerland, Natalie Herzen made it quite clear that she was not at all interested in marriage. Another of Malwida's 'candidates', a young lady supposedly named von Bülow who had written her a 'fan' letter after reading her *Memoirs of an Idealist*, turned out to be a plebeian Fräulein Bütow who had read none of Nietzsche's books. After being uncomfortably jostled and jolted on the rocky road leading northward from Chiavenna over the Splügen Pass, the luckless Malwida spent a hot, frustrating week in the noisy beer-drinking town of Seelisberg, on the Urnersee (the south-eastern extension of the Lake of Lucerne), vainly waiting for Richard and Cosima Wagner to appear (after a disastrous trip to London).

In the end, Olga Herzen Monod, her husband Gabriel and their two children actually made it up to Rosenlauibad, where for two days they were offered a spectacular view of the glistening peaks and summits of the Bernese Oberland and a welcome escape from the sweltering heat of the lower-lying Lake Thun. But the ill-planned 'rendezvous' of the 'Sorrentiners' and their friends at Äschi, near the western shore of Lake Thun, proved a miserable fiasco. The talented Albert Brenner, who had just had his short story published in a German monthly, remained conspicuously absent. Paul Rée had to hurry off to his parents' home in Prussia because of some sudden financial crisis. When Malwida von Meysenbug reached Äschi, instead of the peace and tranquillity that had been promised her, she found a little town so crammed with summer holidaymakers that she and her faithful maid, Trina, had to move the next morning to an expensive hotel in Thun, at the northern end of the lake.

The unluckiest of the lot, in terms of fond hopes and foiled intentions, was Nietzsche. As he wrote to Malwida on 1 July, he had casually let an entire year go by 'unused'. He now had only a couple of months left in which to 'win a wife', and yet he had long known that 'without this' (i.e. a wife) 'an alleviation of my suffering is not to be reckoned with'. After his sister had returned to Basel to prepare their new apartment, Fritz spent two ruinously expensive as well as roasting days having himself driven around Lake Thun in vain search of Malwida, before returning almost penniless to Rosenlauibad, where, thanks to a special month-long arrangement with the hotel manager, he was able to survive on 7 or 8 Swiss francs a day.

At Meiringen, on his way back, he ran into a Frankfurt doctor, Otto Eiser – a rabid Wagnerian and also a fervent admirer of Nietzsche, all of whose books he had brought along for himself and his wife to read during their summer vacation in the Bernese Oberland. After briefly questioning him and subjecting Nietzsche's eyes to a cursory examination, Eiser prescribed some bromkalium powder to be dissolved in water three times a day, adding that in his opinion the treatment Professor Schrön had recommended to him in Naples was too 'homoeopathic'.

The most enjoyable moments at Rosenlauibad were spent in the company of another 'wayward' Sorrentiner, the jovial Reinhart von Seydlitz, who had impressed Malwida von Meysenbug by his gift for pencil drawings. After tracking down Malwida on the shores of Lake Thun, Don Rinaldo (as he now called himself) brought along not only his Hungarian wife but also his baroness mother (a great admirer of Nietzsche's books). The four days the couple managed to spend in the remote Alpine village seem to have been particularly joyous, the dark-skinned Irene von Seydlitz displaying the agility of a chamois in clambering around or leaping over crevasses on the nearby glacier.

Too penniless to be able to accept the Seydlitzes' friendly invitation to join them at Interlaken, Nietzsche barely had enough money left to pay for the post-chaise trip to Brienz, a second-class steamboat ticket to Interlaken, and a third-class railway ticket to Basel. On 1 September he found everything prepared and waiting for him in the new apartment that his efficient sister Elisabeth had rented for the coming autumn and winter on the Gellertstrasse, a pleasant street lined with modern villas located near the St Alban's Gate, on the southern periphery of Basel.

A private 'house-warming' was celebrated six days later with a memorable luncheon attended by Malwida von Meysenbug, the young Albert Brenner (with whose parents she was staying), and by Reinhart and Irene von Seydlitz. The finally realized 'rendezvous of the Sorrentiners' (only Paul Rée was missing) occasioned such gaiety and bacchanalian merriment, more soberly prolonged by the arrival in the evening of the stimulating Jacob Burckhardt, that the following day Nietzsche had to pay the price for excessive intellectual excitement with another nervous seizure. Writing that evening from the hotel where he and his wife were staying, a contrite Reinhart von Seydlitz asked to be forgiven for his truly 'German' lack of moderation, adding almost rhapsodically, 'But why, why, was it so wonderful to be with you!' Like 'Aunt Malwida', who was much upset because the other 'Sorrentiners' were not prepared to return with her to Rome, Don Rinaldo couldn't help wondering when they would meet again.

Thanks to Franz Overbeck's intervention and the support of the influential Jacob Burckhardt, the university's governing council had agreed to grant Nietzsche a 'temporary' exoneration from his *Pädagogium* obligations. His academic workload for the autumn semester was thus reduced to five hours of lecturing (on Thucydides and the lyric poets of ancient Greece) and a one-hour-a-week seminar on Plato's *Phaedo*. Fritz's sister Elisabeth took over the task Paul Rée had assumed in Sorrento – by reading to her brother in the evening. For, as Nietzsche had explained in a letter written to Franz Overbeck shortly after leaving Rosenlauibad, on the basis of careful chronometric testing, 'I have roughly one and a half hours of eyesight to spend each day . . . If I read or write for longer than that, I have to atone the same day with pains and several days thereafter with the old familiar seizure.'

In early October Nietzsche finally yielded to the entreaties of Dr Otto Eiser, who in several letters had insisted that he come to Frankfurt as his house-guest and undergo a 'thorough examination' of his eyes. In Frankfurt he was carefully examined not only by Dr Eiser, but also by an eye specialist, Dr Gustav Krüger. The gist of the report that Eiser sent to Basel on 6 October was that Nietzsche's headaches and nervous seizures (he even used the word 'paroxysms') were primarily caused by the eyes and irritation of the optic nerve. A 'careful application' of 'galvanic currents' could be recommended, but all remedies of a 'heroic kind' (such as clysters, etc.) were to be avoided. Particularly dire was the stern prescription, underlined to stress its capital importance: an *absolute avoidance of reading and writing for years to come*. Blue-lensed spectacles were recommended by Dr Gustav Krüger, and, in general, the patient should avoid 'every form of extreme physical and intellectual exertion'.

The stark implications of this medical report were so shattering that they unleashed in Nietzsche, long obsessed by the feeling that he was slowly going blind, a major paroxysmic relapse. In the letter accompanying Dr Eiser's detailed report, which he sent on 17 October to Carl Burckhardt, the new chairman of the university's governing council, Nietzsche asked to be exonerated from all further teaching obligations at the *Pädagogium*.

One of the first to be informed of these medical diagnoses of approaching blindness was Cosima Wagner, to whom, on 10 October, Nietzsche sent a copy of a speculative essay that Dr Otto Eiser had recently written about the *Ring des Nibelungen* operas. All he could now hope for was the retention of 'the faint glimmer of eyesight I still have. Thus is approaching a sombre time for painful decisions. So far I have not been lacking in courage; therein I think I have learned something from Wagner.'

In her answering letter, written twelve days later, Cosima thanked Nietzsche for having sent her Dr Eiser's interesting analysis of the *Ring* operas, particularly since the doctor had constructed the 'edifice of his commentary' on a solid Schopenhauerian foundation. 'How joyfully I would have welcomed it if at the same time you had been able to give me consoling news of your state of health!' Of their friends, the only one who seemed to have been spared anxiety about the future was Franz Overbeck, who had recently written to say how happily married he was. After which she added: 'We now have Herr von Wolzogen with us, he will very probably settle here with his wife, which in every respect is agreeable to us.'

Although the concluding sentences could not have sounded more cordial – 'May you fare well, best Friend, how much patience you must now display! It hurts me to think of it' – this was destined to be the last of the close to eighty letters Cosima had written to Nietzsche over a period of seven years. It was also, inadvertently, one of the most pain-inducing. For it confirmed what Nietzsche had already heard: that in order to cooperate more closely with Richard Wagner in the editing of his new journal, Hans von Wolzogen (whom Nietzsche regarded as insufficiently musical and a second-rate writer) had decided to move with his family to Bayreuth and to build himself a house not far from the Wagners' 'Wahnfried' mansion. In his letter of 10 October to Cosima, Nietzsche had referred to himself as '*dem Abgeschlossenen*' (the recluse). But from now on he knew that he could just as aptly described himself as '*dem Ausgeschlossenen*' (the excluded one). As he had explained to his sister Elisabeth in the middle of the summer, 'Wagner's proximity is not for the sick, that was also shown at Sorrento.'

Although there was a lot of truth in this remark, Nietzsche was being unfair to Wagner. The moment Wagner heard that Nietzsche, now reduced to near-blindness, had recently seen three excellent doctors who had all rendered the same verdict – a total cessation of all reading and writing activities – he put two and two together and decided that one of them was probably Dr Otto Eiser, an active Wagnerophile and the author of the essay Nietzsche had just sent to Cosima. Hans von Wolzogen was asked to write to Eiser in Frankfurt to find out if, by any chance, Professor Nietzsche had recently come to see him, and if so, if he could tell anything about the conclusions of the medical examination. This totally unexpected request from the Master of 'Wahnfried' elicited a long explanatory letter from his fervent admirer Dr Eiser, detailing the deplorable carelessness of the doctors Nietzsche had been dealing with in Basel. Particularly interesting for Wagner was the mention of the visit Nietzsche had made to Professor Schrön in Naples, who, like Malwida von Meysenbug (as Cosima had recently learned), had strongly urged Nietzsche to get married. On 23 October Wagner, who had long felt that there was something pathologically abnormal in the celibate life Nietzsche had been leading, sat down and wrote a long letter of his own to Dr Eiser, saying as he did so to Cosima, 'He [Nietzsche] will more likely listen to the friendly advice of a doctor than to the doctoring advice of a friend.' Perhaps Eiser could succeed where he himself had manifestly failed, in imperatively urging Nietzsche to get married. The conclusion he had reached – for he had noticed similar symptoms in other high-strung men – was that the root cause of Nietzsche's nervous disorders was a perversion of the sexual drive. Wagner, like Professor Schrön before him, was probably close to the bitter truth: one almost certainly compounded by the paralysing inhibitions generated by Nietzsche's brief but traumatic experiences in the brothels of Cologne and Leipzig.

The Christmas season, with all it conjured up in memories of happier, bygone times along with the approaching death of another year, had long been a painful time for Nietzsche. That of 1877 was no exception. He was nagged by the guilty realization that he had funked the marriage issue – as 'Aunt Malwida' had gently scolded him in a letter written in August, 'Just as then you were too fast [in proposing to Mathilde Trampedach], so now, I fear, you are too slow.' It was in any case in a moment of 'black' despondency that Fritz wrote a letter of harsh remonstrance to his friend Carl von Gersdorff, which began with a kind of Schopenhauerian parody of Calderón de la Barca's gloomy affirmation (in *La Vida es sueño*) that 'Man's greatest crime – is to have been born.' Nietzsche's version: 'The greatest triviality in the world is death; the second greatest is to be born; then in third place comes marriage.' From the very beginning of his romance with Nerina Finochietti, Gersdorff had assumed the heroic pose of a 'saviour' bent on rescuing an unhappy daughter from the clutches of an unworthy father. This had not kept this heroic saviour from entering into sordid negotiations over dowry questions with a man who was beyond doubt a 'wretched scoundrel'. When the idealistic Malwida von Meysenbug, who had at first encouraged this chivalrous endeavour, discovered the dreadful truth – that in Florence the Finochiettis were considered a disreputable family (Nerina's mother, for example, had been sleeping with the cook!) – and felt duty-bound to inform Gersdorff's parents, Carl and Nerina had begun bombarding Malwida with angry letters, accusing her of slanderous allegations. That Nerina should have dared to smear 'the purest soul among German women' with the 'dung of her suspicions' was, Nietzsche wrote, proof enough that she was as morally tainted as her parents. 'I would find it disgraceful and dishonourable for a German nobleman to let himself become the instrument, the police-agent in the service of that ungrateful person, I would find it sufficient grounds to break off all personal relations did I not know that he has been acting in a state of blind infatuation. But on behalf of Fräulein von Meysenbug I hereby forbid this blind man from now on sending further letters to this person.'

The pompous language, so unusual in Fritz's letters, betrayed his embarrassment at having to issue an ultimatum that was likely to fall on deaf ears. It did. In his answering letter, sent from Berlin in late December, his friend Carl repeated his accusations against Malwida von Meysenbug (a mendacious intriguer) and stubbornly insisted, 'I am acting and have been acting as someone who knows what he is doing, not as one who has been blindly infatuated.'

In using unusually harsh language with his old Pforta friend, Nietzsche was displaying the same kind of 'realism' that had motivated some of the more uncharitable observations which, with the help of Heinrich Köselitz, he had been recording in 'Woman and Child', the seventh chapter of his new book. Examples:

> Some men have sighed over the abduction of their wives, most, however, because no one wanted to abduct them (aphorism 388).
>
> If married couples did not live side by side, good marriages would be more frequent (aphorism 393).
>
> Sometimes stronger spectacles are all that is needed to cure a man in love; and anyone having sufficient power of imagination to envisage what a face or form would be like twenty years hence might perhaps traverse life quite undisturbed' (aphorism 413).

The laborious work of compilation was by now so far advanced that on 3 December Nietzsche was able to inform his anxious publisher, Ernst Schmeitzner, that his new book would be called *Menschliches, Allzumenschliches* (*Human, All Too Human*). It would carry as a subtitle: 'A Book for Free Spirits', and it would honour the memory of Voltaire by referring on the frontispiece to the centennial commemoration of his death, due to be celebrated on 30 May 1878. Schmeitzner, who had already heard from Heinrich Köselitz that this new book would probably run to 300 pages and be about three times as long as its predecessors, wanted to use a smaller type format in order to reduce the printing costs. But Nietzsche insisted that the same type must be used as with his previous books. Since it was almost certainly the author's fate to become blind, he wished to read what was printed 'while I have a shimmer of eyesight left'. He yielded, however, to Schmeitzner's strenuous objection to his initial proposal that the book be published anonymously.

Nietzsche's reasons for wishing to preserve the 'secret' of the authorship of *Menschliches, Allzumenschliches* were explained in an apologetic letter he began drafting in early January of 1878 for Richard and Cosima Wagner. First of all, he was choosing anonymity to keep this radically new book, in which he had expressed his 'innermost feelings about human beings and things', from harming the efficacy of his earlier works. Secondly, he wanted to keep his personal 'dignity' from being publicly and privately 'besmirched' – something that was bound to affect his fragile health. Third and most importantly, he wanted his book to arouse a factual discussion among his many intelligent friends without their feeling obliged to conceal or temper their judgements and opinions for fear of hurting the feelings of the author.

In the end, Nietzsche never sent this letter to Bayreuth, realizing with what hostility his new, 'subversive' book was likely to be received by Richard and Cosima Wagner. The title of the very first of its 638 aphorisms – 'The Chemistry of Concepts and Feelings' – was bound to irritate Wagner, just as Paul Rée's cold, analytical approach to philosophical problems had prompted Malwida von Meysenbug to chide him at Sorrento for being no more than a 'chemical combination of atoms'.

The actual contents of this first aphorism – it would be more accurate to call it a 'section', for it filled more than one printed page – was not something the composer could reasonably quarrel with, at any rate as regards the first sentences. For the past 2,000 years, Nietzsche began, the basic concern of philosophers had been to explain 'how something can emerge from its opposite' – order out of chaos, the rational from the irrational, feeling from what is unfeeling and dead, logic from the illogical, disinterested contemplation from greedy desire, altruism from egotism, truth from errors. Ever since Descartes (not specifically mentioned by Nietzsche) had tranquilly declared in the opening sentence of his *Discourse on Method* that 'Common sense is the best shared thing in the world', European philosophers – whether rationalists like Leibniz, Kant and Hegel, or anti-rationalist empiricists like David Hume – had assumed that Man, *Homo sapiens*, is an essentially rational being. The result had been what Nietzsche called a 'metaphysical philosophy', which, like 'popular conceptions', assumed a miraculous origin for 'more highly valued things' rather than trying to look for their origins in what was sub-rational. 'Historical philosophy' – to Wagner's ear this could not but sound dangerously Hegelian – 'could no longer be thought of as separated from natural science'; it was founded on the idea that there are in reality no opposites, and that, strictly speaking, there is no such thing as an 'unegotistical activity' or a 'fully disinterested contemplation' – two fundamental notions on which Schopenhauer had constructed his philosophical system.

In the second section, entitled 'The Hereditary Defects of Philosophers',

Nietzsche deplored the tendency of thinkers from time immemorial to judge 'Man' in terms of their own limited experience, as though he were an eternal, unchanging reality. In stressing the error of disregarding the immensity of the evolutionary past and in concentrating solely on the past 4,000 years of human history as representing a reliable 'norm', Nietzsche was in effect adopting a Darwinistic (as opposed to Hegelian) approach to the fundamental problems of philosophy, similar to that which had brought his friend Paul Rée into open conflict with the conservative teachers of philosophy at Jena. All of modern teleology – the assumed 'purposiveness' or 'final goal' of human evolution, which Kant had discussed in his *Critique of Judgement* and which Hegel had elevated to the status of quasi-religious dogma – was founded on this kind of flawed thinking. For, Nietzsche roundly declared, 'everything is becoming; there are no eternal facts: just as there are no eternal truths. Which is why the historical philosophy is from now on badly needed and with it the virtue of modesty.'

The third and somewhat longer section, enigmatically entitled 'Estimation of Inconspicuous Truths', was, Nietzsche knew, even more likely to infuriate Wagner. Not only did it implicitly criticize all forms of religious belief but – O heresy of heresies! – it dared to place science on a level even higher than art. 'It is the hallmark of a higher culture,' Nietzsche began, 'to place a higher value on small, inconspicuous truths that have been found through a rigorous method than on happy-making and dazzling mistakes, derived from metaphysical and artistic epochs and human beings.' Here again, though there was no mention of his name, the 'small, inconspicuous truths' were those Descartes had in mind when, in the third chapter of his *Discourse on Method*, he had described the deep contentment he had experienced 'in every day discovering by it [i.e. his philosophical method] certain truths which seemed to me quite important, although generally unknown to other men': in short, the 'inconspicuous truths' of modern science that had enabled Descartes to simplify arithmetical enumeration and to develop analytical geometry, Leibniz to invent the infinitesimal calculus, which had permitted Newton to formulate the laws of universal gravitation, Lavoisier to found the science of chemistry, Faraday and Clerk-Maxwell to enunciate the basic principles of electromagnetics, of which the recently invented magnetic telegraph (often used by Nietzsche) was a highly practical derivative. Invariably such innovators had been greeted by the scorn and sarcasm of the conventionally minded; but, as Nietzsche resolutely added, 'What is painfully achieved, certain, lasting, and thus rich in consequences for every additional piece of knowledge is nevertheless what is higher; to adhere to it is manly and displays courage, simplicity, moderation. Gradually not only the single individual but all of humankind will be elevated to a higher evaluation of durable, lasting bits of knowledge and will have lost all belief in inspiration and in the miraculous transmission of truths.'

The regrettable fogginess of the language used to praise the advances of modern science and to condemn religious superstitions clearly shows how embarrassed Nietzsche personally felt at thus 'breaking new ground', he who in his previous books had tended to belittle scientists and in particular scientific 'specialists', men who in their own way could be as narrow-minded as academic philologists. Had he been content to stop here, he could still have been regarded as reasonably Schopenhauerian, since Schopenhauer had consistently maintained that Philosophy, as Man's rational attempt to understand the world in which he lives, was superior to Religion, which remained a necessary consolation for the insufficiently intelligent masses. But in the rest of this third section Nietzsche broadened his attack on the religious superstitions of the past by comparing the 'severe thinking' of Descartes and his successors to the serious 'elaboration of symbols and forms' indulged in by the medieval scholastics, pointedly adding: 'This has changed; the seriousness of the symbolic has become the hallmark of the lower culture.' Since all of the *Ring* operas, as well as the composer's latest brainchild, *Parsifal*, were based on medieval symbols – the curse attached to riches, the importance of the sworn oath or pledge, the sanctity of the Holy Grail, etc. – this amounted in effect to a demotion of Wagnerism and a challenge to the Master's claim to be promoting a genuinely 'futuristic' form of art.

It is true that in a later 'aphorism' (no. 6) Nietzsche stressed the latent antagonism existing between the 'specialized fields of Science and Philosophy. The latter, like Art, wants to give the deepest possible significance to life and activity; in the former one seeks knowledge and nothing more – whatever may come of it.' Yet the fact remains that, though he ridiculed the 'high-flying metaphyscics' to which philosophers resorted in order to justify its usefulness, Nietzsche did not hesitate (in aphorism no. 4) to liken 'objects of religious, moral and aesthetic feeling' to the superstitions of astrology, according to which 'the starry sky rotates around the lot of man; the moral man, however, assumes that what lies closest to his heart must also be the essence and heart of things'.

The key word here, even though for once it was not italicized, is 'must' – which implies some kind of moral imperative, an implicit subordination of the cosmos to the will of Man. For one of the fundamental aims of *Human, All Too Human* – and for Nietzsche this was nothing less than a Copernican revolution or, as he later explained to Malwida von Meysenbug, 'the crisis of [his] life' – was to criticize as childish and irrational all forms of anthropomorphic, homocentric religion.

★

It is impossible to summarize the extraordinarily rich and varied contents of *Human, All Too Human* in a few words. Each of its aphorisms, as Walter Kaufmann judiciously pointed out, is like a finely polished diamond, reflecting the sparkle and increasing the effulgence of the others. Nietzsche was not the first to have used this particular form of exposition for his philosophical musings. He had been preceded by the German satirist Georg Christoph Lichtenberg (1742–99), the hunchbacked 'toad' of Göttingen whose pessimism (anticipating Schopenhauer's) had been equalled in Italy by the hunchbacked poet Leopardi (1798–1837); by a number of French moralists – La Rochefoucauld, Chamfort, Vauvenargues, Voltaire – and of course by the pre-Socratic philosophers (Heraclitus, etc.) of ancient Greece. If he had finally chosen this form of expression in *Human, All Too Human*, it was essentially for three reasons. He did not want to produce a work of 'systematic' philosophy comparable to those of Kant or Hegel or even, for that matter, in the far more readable form of Schopenhauer's. He wanted to make his unconventional thoughts and observations as pithy and challenging as possible, even at the risk of presenting them in unfinished and paradoxical fragments – the 'truths' he was bent on revealing being often contradictory. And finally, he wanted to have his book published while he could still see and before he had become totally blind.

This explains the book's unusual length, compared to the modest dimensions of his previous works. Although Nietzsche was convinced that deep thinking is necessarily slow, solitary thinking, it is no exaggeration to say that *Human, All Too Human* was a book 'written against the clock' by a man in his early thirties who was never able to forget that his father had died of 'softening of the brain' at the age of thirty-six. It was also the product of a man whose imaginative faculties, abetted by an extraordinarily retentive memory, never stopped churning out new ideas. In Sorrento it had become a source of amusement for Malwida von Meysenbug, Paul Rée and Albert Brenner: in the garden near their villa there was a certain tree under whose leafy foliage Fritz liked to tarry; it soon came to be known as the *Gedankenbaum* (thought-tree) because every time he stood under it for a minute or two Nietzsche was visited by a new, illuminating inspiration.

Of the nine chapters into which Nietzsche 'poured' his random thoughts, at least four had figured in the plan for thirteen 'Untimely Meditations' he had first conceived with Carl von Gersdorff and Heinrich Romundt at Flims in the summer of 1873 and which he had later several times modified in his notebooks.

They were: Chapter III ('Religious Life'); Chapter IV ('On the Soul of

Artists and Writers'), Chapter VIII ('A Glance at the State'); Chapter IX ('Man alone with Himself'). The new ones, in addition to the introductory chapter, were: Chapter II ('On the History of Moral Sentiments'); Chapter V ('Characteristics of a Higher and Lower Culture'); Chapter VI ('Man in Society'); Chapter VII ('Woman and Child').

The main purpose of the first, introductory chapter ('Of First and Last Things') was to question the very notion of metaphysics, whether religious or philosophical – that is to say, the existence of another world lying 'beyond' or 'behind' the phenomenal world of Man's everyday experience. Nietzsche made this quite clear in section 5 ('Misunderstanding the Dream'), in which he suggested that it was thanks to the dreams he had when asleep that primitive man had conceived the notion of a second real world as something actually existing – the result being the popular belief in an afterlife, the age-old division of body and soul, and, generally speaking, the existence of extraterrestrial gods.

If, as we shall see, such affirmations came as a shock to Nietzsche's friends, it was because it seemed to them that he had suddenly abandoned the cause of poetry and art and gone over to the camp of the crass materialists, like Ludwig Büchner and Ernst Haeckel. Nietzsche, however, was far too conscious of the extent to which the naïve, mythological belief in the gods of Olympus had marvellously enriched Greek culture to assume that the mere suppression of such superannuated beliefs could provide a satisfactory solution to Man's spiritual problems. As he put it in section 20: 'An assuredly very high degree is attained when Man overcomes superstititions and religious conceptions and fears and no longer believes, for example, in sweet angels or original sin, and has even learned not to speak of the salvation of souls. Even at this stage of liberation he must exert all the energies of his level-headed intelligence to surmount metaphysics. Then, however, a *retrogressive* movement is necessary; he must grasp the historical, and even psychological justification of such representations, he must recognize how the great advancement of humanity has come from there and how Man, without such a retrogressive movement, would rob himself of the finest achievements of humanity in the past.'

Although here again the language was more allusive than explicit, it is fairly clear that Nietzsche here had in mind the retrogressive, revival-of-the-classic-past aspect of the Renaissance, which proved to be so artistically enriching for modern Europe. This retrogressive movement could also assume an artistically less satisfying and yet comprehensible form, as Nietzsche pointed out in a typically 'pro' and 'con' interpretation (Section 26, 'Reaction as Progress').

> There occasionally appear gruff, violent, onsweeping and nonetheless backward souls who once again conjure up a past phase of humanity: they serve to prove that the new tendencies that they oppose are not strong enough, that they lack something; otherwise they would more firmly have resisted those conjurors. Luther's Reformation, for example, shows that in his century all the impulses in favour of intellectual freedom were still uncertain, tender, juvenile; science could still not raise its head. Indeed, the entire Renaissance appears as a first spring which was almost completely snowed under. But in our century too Schopenhauer's metaphysics has proved that even now the scientific spirit is still not strong enough; it was thus that the entire world-outlook and human-feeling of the Christian Middle Ages could celebrate a resurrection in Schopenhauer's doctrine, notwithstanding the long-since accomplished destruction of all Christian dogmas. A lot of science rings forth in his doctrine, but it is not this that dominates, but rather the old, familiar 'metaphysical need' . . . I believe that without Schopenhauer's help nobody could now so easily do justice to Christianity and its Asiatic kinsmen . . . only, on such an essential point, after we had corrected the historical conception that the Age of the Enlightenment had brought us can we again raise the flag of the Enlightenment – the flag with the names of Petrarch, Erasmus, Voltaire. Out of Reaction we have thus made Progress.

Schopenhauer, had he still been alive, would probably have been startled to find his 'retrogressive' metaphysics being interpreted as a necessary antidote – Hegel would have called it an 'antithesis' – to the overly negative, Church-hating agnosticism of Voltaire and the French Encyclopedists. But having thus accorded Schopenhauer's philosophy its rightful place in the evolving history of ideas, Nietzsche, in the next section (no. 27), quickly added the necessary corollary – by arguing that to help people make the 'violent, perilous leap' from 'religion to a scientific attitude', art should be used to relieve minds 'overloaded with feelings . . . From art it is then easier to pass over to a truly liberating philosophical science.'

Without daring to suggest that art can be a valid substitute for religion – the perilous leap that the agile André Malraux was later tempted to make – Nietzsche was here establishing a hierarchy of cultural values in which Schopenhauerian metaphysics was superior to Christianity, Wagnerian music superior to Schopenhauer's metaphysics because less mentally constricting, while his own *Freigeisterei* (free-thinking) was superior to all three as a truly 'liberating' conception of life and the world unburdened by medieval torments, pessimistic premisses, and neo-Gothic symbolism.

Those wishing to attain this higher stage of philosophical awareness must, Nietzsche continued (in section 28), learn to discard hackneyed terms like 'optimism' and 'pessimism'. Why should any rational being wish to proclaim himself an 'optimist' and claim that the world is the work of a 'good' God, and indeed that ours is the best of all possible worlds (a reference to Leibniz's *Theodicy*, mercilessly lampooned by Voltaire in *Candide*), since he no longer needs the hypothesis of a God? And what is the point of insisting that the world is a sorry place ruled by Evil, where pain is more prevalent than pleasure, indeed a 'shoddy construction' and the manifestation of an 'evil will to life' (the neo-Zoroastrian notion which Schopenhauer had in a sense revitalized) unless it was to provoke the theologian? But who, Nietzsche asked, brandishing the polemical axe that had made him so feared, disliked, and famous, who today needed to get worked up about theologians – except the theologians? The world, clearly, was neither 'good' nor 'bad', and it was high time to stop using such shallow, shopworn terms which, even when applied to human affairs, were often quite unjustified.

No illusion could be greater, Nietzsche went on (section 29), than to believe that the more Man elevates himself above the rest of the animal world, to the point of considering himself a genius of the species, the closer he comes to grasping the real 'essence' of things. Essentially deceptive the phenomenal world may be – this had been one of Heraclitus's profoundest observations – but it is one that is full of meaning, of which art and religion are precious blooms, a world that is 'deep, wonderful, carrying happiness and unhappiness in its bosom'.

Nietzsche's fundamental aim, as he had declared in the opening lines of *Human, All Too Human*, was to explain how certain things can emerge from their opposites: the rational from the irrational, truths from errors and untruths, logic from the illogical. And what interested him in this process of emergence, and which philosophers for the past 2,000 years had too often taken for granted and neglected, was the illogical substratum or hidden root from which the supposedly logical bloom or blossom had sprouted. In a dramatic reversal of priorities that had dominated European thinking from Descartes down to Kant and Hegel, he indicated that the study of what is illogical in life and human beings should precede the study of what is seemingly 'logical'. Thinkers might be reduced to despair by this consideration, but they would have to recognize the bitter truth that, as he put it in aphorism 31, 'the illogical is necessary to Man and a great deal of good is derived from the illogical. It is so solidly anchored in passions, daily speech, Art, Religion, and, generally, in everything that confers value to life, that one cannot uproot it without irreparably harming those lovely things.' No matter how great might be one's personal experience of another human being, it is insufficient to give one a 'logical right to an overall appreciation. All estimates are hasty and must be so' – simply because no one can live without passing judgement, without feeling affection or aversion. 'We are from the outset illogical and thus unjust beings and can recognize this: this is one of the greatest and most insoluble disharmonies of existence.'

All of this was 'tame stuff' compared to the often 'shocking' contents of the two chapters that followed: Part II ('Concerning the History of Moral Sentiments') and Part III ('Religious Life') – much of which aroused consternation among Nietzsche's neo-Schopenhauerian as well as ardently Wagnerian friends. What had made Schopenhauer so acceptable to most of them, beginning with Cosima Wagner, was a kind of residual Christianity and an emphasis placed on human compassion as a form of 'selflessness' – comparable to aesthetic and in particular musical rapture – which permitted the human individual to escape for a moment from the deep-seated tyranny of the pulsing, surging, selfish will. Even as he was writing his essay on Schopenhauer, it had begun to dawn on Nietzsche that there was a glaring contradiction in a philosophy that condemned the selfishness inherent in individual behaviour while at the same time extolling human genius, which had almost invariably involved a superlative assertion of one's individuality above and very often against the collective mass of less gifted human beings. Human sentiments, far from being simple feelings, are complex realities often involving highly varied, more or less subconscious, and unlovely motivations, and this was as true of 'compassion' as of other virtues. In every act or expression of compassion, as La Rochefoucauld and other French moralists had pointed out, there was a latent element of vanity and self-esteem: one of vanity in wishing to appear 'benevolent' and 'kind-hearted' in the eyes of others, one of righteous self-satisfaction in appeasing a latent sense of guilt – that *Gewissensbiss* (the 'bite' or pang of conscience) which, Nietzsche believed, was one of the baleful psychological legacies of Christian teaching.

It was these psychological considerations, Nietzsche asserted in the first three 'aphorisms' of Part II, which French moralists had bravely tackled but which German philosophers had tended to ignore, that he was now bent on exploring. Here, summarized as succinctly as possible, are some of his 'shocking' observations:

> Aphorism 41 ('The Immutable Character'): That the [human] character is unchangeable is not in a strict sense true; rather, this popular proposition merely means that during the short lifetime of a man the effective

> motivations cannot scratch deeply enough to destroy the inscribed characteristics of many thousands of years. If one could conceive of a man eighty thousand years old, one would find in him an absolutely changeable character: so much so that a crowd of different individuals would progressively develop out of him. The brevity of human life leads to many mistaken affirmations as to the qualities of Man.
>
> Aphorism 43 ('Cruel men, as retarded human beings'): Human beings who now are cruel must appear to us as stages of earlier cultures that have survived; the mountain of humanity here reveals deeper formations which often remained concealed . . . They show us what we once were and they cause us fright; but they themselves are no more responsible for this than a piece of granite is for being granite.
>
> Aphorism 49 ('Benevolence'): . . . Cordiality, affability, the courtesy of the heart are ever-flowing emanations of the altruistic instinct and have contributed far more powerfully to civilization than those famous manifestations that are called pity, charity, and self-sacrifice.
>
> Aphorism 50 ('Wishing to arouse Compassion'): In the most remarkable passage of his 'Self-Portrait' (first printed in 1658) La Rochefoucauld is certainly close to the truth when he warns all those who are governed by Reason against compassion, advising them to leave this to common folk who thrive on passions (because they have not been formed by Reason) and to come to the aid of someone who suffers and to intervene vigorously when confronted by a misfortune; whereas pity, according to his (and Plato's) judgement, weakens the soul. Clearly, one should *show* pity but avoid *having* it.

This warning was particularly valid for parents and others who have to deal with obstreperous children who 'cry and scream in order to be commiserated and who therefore wait for the moment when their condition attracts attention'. One has only to live for a while with the sick and mentally depressed, Nietzsche went on, now leaving La Rochefoucauld far behind,

> and to ask oneself if eloquent complaints and whimpers, the making-a-show of one's misfortunes are not intentionally pursued in order *to hurt* those present; the sympathy that the latter then express is a consolation for the weak and suffering in that they realize that at least they still possess *one power* despite their weakness: the *power of hurting*. The unfortunate one derives a kind of pleasure in the feeling of superiority that the manifestation brings

> him; his imagination is exalted, he is important enough to be able to make the world suffer. The thirst for pity is thus a thirst for self-satisfaction, at, to be sure, the expense of his fellow beings . . .

Indeed, even in the most innocent conversations in society people were moved to prove their superiority by delivering pin-pricks and indulging in witty and often cutting repartees. This unconscious self-assertion and desire to harm was as natural and stimulating an element of social life as was its ever-ready remedy: good-will.

Aphorism 56 ('Victory of Knowledge over the radically Evil'): The notion of 'sin' has no philosophical foundation, any more than does the notion of 'virtues', even though for enormous spans of time human beings lived under the dominion of such assertions. There has always been something shaky and unsure about moral concepts such as Good and Evil, the Moral and Immoral. The wise man is the one who can learn to live with things as they are – this was the Epicurean ideal Nietzsche was to uphold for most of his sane life – and not try to excommunicate and extirpate desires. The person who thus learns to live quite happily with himself will no longer be tormented and impressed by terms such as 'hellfire and damnation' and 'sinfulness' – evanescent notions that falsify one's view of life and the world.

Even more shocking for many of Nietzsche's contemporaries were the sobering 'home truths' he proceeded to unfold in Part III of *Human, All Too Human*, devoted to 'Religious Life'. Here, as elsewhere, he went back to the very beginnings of religion in the firm conviction that this is the only way to reach the fundamental truths by a process of what might be philosophico-palaentological, or even geological exploration. What is essentially lacking in any religious conception of the world is a firm belief in natural, which is to say scientific, causality. The underlying aim of all primitive religions is to propitiate the mysterious forces of nature, regarded as benevolent or evil spirits in more or less human form.

The conclusion Nietzsche drew from this examination of religious belief (far more detailed than this brief summary suggests) is that the basic aim of any religious cult is to influence and exorcise Nature for the benefit of Man, and thus to 'impose on it a legality that it does not from the outset have, whereas in the present age one seeks to know the laws of Nature in order to adhere to them. In short, the religious cult rests on conceptions of magic existing between Man and Man; and the magician is older than the priest.' But Nietzsche would not have been Nietzsche – which is to say an ardent admirer of the ancient Greeks – had he not immediately added the following sentences to this somewhat derogatory description of religion as being little more than superstitition:

> But it [the religious cult] likewise rests on other, nobler ideas; it presupposes the cordial relationship between Man and Man, the existence of goodwill, gratitude, the answering of requests, treaties between enemies, guarantees and claims for the protection of property. Even on the lowest levels of civilization Man in his relation to Nature is not necessarily the will-less servant thereof: at the Greek stage of religion, particularly in its relation with the Olympian gods, one can conceive of a co-existence of two castes, one more distinguished and powerful, the other less distinguished; but both in their origins somehow belong together and are a single species, they need feel no shame towards each other. That is what is so refined and noble in Greek religiousness.

But what, by way of contrast, is one to think of Christianity? The blunt, brutal answer was given in section 113 ('Christianity as Antiquity'), in which Nietzsche pulled no punches:

> When, on a Sunday morning, we hear the old bells boom, we ask ourselves: is this possible? All this for a Jew who two thousand years ago was crucified, who said he was the Son of God. There is no proof for such an affirmation. Christianity, assuredly, is an upthrusting piece of antiquity . . . A God who brings forth children with a mortal woman; a sage who exhorts one to stop working and to cease sitting in judgement, but to look for signs of the impending end of the world; a form of justice that accepts the innocent as vicarious victims; someone who enjoins his disciples to drink his blood; prayers [made] for miraculous interventions; who commits sins against a God which a God atones; fear of a Beyond, of which Death is the gateway; the symbolic figure of the Cross in the middle of an age that no longer understands the meaning and the shame of the crucifixion – how dreadfully all this reeks, as though issuing from the sepulchre of the very ancient past! Can one believe that such things are still believed in?

Most of the ensuing 'aphorisms' were amplifications and embroideries, along with a few caveats, of the points made in this devastating section. Nietzsche's quarrel with Christianity, as he made clear in the next section (114), was that it was based on a 'sickly excess of feeling', on what he called a deep, psychological 'corruption of heart and mind; it wants to destroy, shatter, stun, intoxicate, there is only one thing it does not want: a *sense of measure*, and for this reason it is in the deepest sense barbaric, Asiatic, undistinguished, un-Greek'.

Because Christianity was based on such a nexus of absurdities, it was in the final analysis an unworkable religion. The inevitable result had been the emergence in modern times of what he called (aphorism 116) the

'*Alltags-Christ*', the everyday Christian: a pitiful figure who simply paid lip-service to such concepts as a vengeful God, the omnipresence of sin, the perils of everlasting hellfire and damnation – beliefs which, if taken at all seriously, would force him to become a priest, an apostle, or a hermit. In a word, what Nietzsche most disliked and despised in any human being – a smug hypocrite.

## CHAPTER 24

# The Wanderer and His Shadow

*– The truth, to be sure, can stand on one leg;*
*but with two it will walk and get around.*

On 30 December, one day before the end of the year 1877, Reinhart von Seydlitz wrote to Nietzsche from Salzburg to say that he and his wife had spent Christmas Eve reading the recently published prose outline of *Parsifal.* He had not yet recovered from the shock. With the sole exception of the temptress and later repentant Kundry (a kind of medieval Mary Magdalene), everything in this new opera, compared to those that had preceded it, seemed to him 'dry, lifeless, alien'.

Four days later Nietzsche received a personally autographed copy from the composer who, after offering his 'dear friend Friedrich Nietzsche' the most cordial greetings and wishes for the New Year, signed himself 'Richard Wagner, Oberkirchenrat' ('Senior Consistorial Adviser'). The irony of this self-conferred title was obvious, given Wagner's ambiguous attitude towards religion; for, if the one-time admirer of Ludwig Feuerbach had agreed in 1870 to a Christian wedding, it was, as Nietzsche knew, above all to please Cosima. Nietzsche's reaction to the *Parsifal* outline – the tale of a 'poor fool made wise through pity' and thus combining two human qualities he despised (foolishness and pity) with the 'wisdom' he revered as an ideal – was every bit as negative as Seydlitz's. 'More Liszt than Wagner, spirit of the Counter-Reformation,' he commented in a letter to his friend; 'for me, who am accustomed to what is Greek and generally human, everything is too limited to Christian times; sheer phantastical psychology, no flesh and much too much blood (particularly in the communion scene . . . ) and then I don't care for hysterical women' – a reference to Kundry. 'Much that is tolerable for the inner eye will be unendurable when performed: think of our actors, praying, trembling and with ecstatic throats . . . But,' Nietzsche added, more than ever torn between admiration and annoyance, 'the situation and their consequences – does it not partake of the highest poetry?'

This spontaneous reaction to the *Parsifal* story reveals how deeply torn and tormented Nietzsche was by his mixed feelings towards his former hero. But this intellectual cleavage was by no means limited to Richard Wagner and his operas. It was a fundamental cleavage, an almost unbridgeable contradiction between the scientific 'realism' he was advocating in *Human, All Too Human* and the imaginary, dreamlike 'unreality' of poetry and music, and not least of all of religion – without which, as he had admitted in aphorism 29 ('Inebriated by the Scent of Blossoms'), human life would be dismally impoverished. Nothing could have been more embarrassing for Nietzsche than the New Year 'gift' Wagner had sent him. He could not say what he really thought of this operatic story without offending the composer, nor could he indulge in mendacious praise without soon being unmasked as a hypocrite by the scathing remarks he had made in *Human, All Too Human* about Christianity and excessively emotional expressions of pity. Confronted by this excruciating dilemma, Nietzsche decided to say nothing. A silence Wagner could only interpret as a mark of discourteous ingratitude.

Nietzsche's waning hopes of finding an effective cure for his headaches and nervous seizures were revived in early February 1878 by the arrival in Basel of a new professor of pathology and therapy named Rudolf Massini. With the professor's emphatic endorsement, Nietzsche reqested and obtained the university governing council's consent to be permanently relieved of all further teaching obligations at the *Pädagogium*: a dispensation (reducing his academic workload from twelve to six hours a week) which would make it possible for him to continue his university lecturing and seminar work. Even so he suffered another major relapse towards the end of the month – one so serious that he had to interrupt his lectures and undertake one more 'cure', this time at the famous Black Forest spa of Baden Baden.

Here, on 22 March, he was joined for a couple of days by his sister and by the self-sacrificing Heinrich Köselitz, who had been helping Nietzsche with the proofreading of *Human, All Too Human.* Although upset by the news that his former publisher, Ernst Wilhelm Fritzsch, had quietly sold 400 copies of a second edition of *The Birth of Tragedy* without paying him a pfennig in royalties, Nietzsche on the whole responded well to the invigorating air of Baden Baden. His long walks through the snow-whitened pine forests gave him back an appetite he had totally lost in Basel.

Reluctantly declining Reinhart von Seydlitz's friendly invitation that he come and stay with him and his wife in the lovely baroque city of Salzburg, Nietzsche in early April headed northwards in order to perform a token 'penance' for his increasingly long absences from his home town by spending the Easter holidays with his mother and sister in Naumburg. On 16 April he finally met his new publisher, Ernst Schmeitzner, in Leipzig. Their lively conversation lasted an hour and a half – one hour more than had been planned – and was followed, just as Nietzsche had feared, by another nervous relapse. But the time spent with Nietzsche was so stimulating that in his letter of apology, written four days later,

Schmeitzner said that for him this particular Tuesday had been a real '*Feiertag*', a holiday of celebration.

A more timorous publisher might have developed cold feet and shown himself reluctant to publish some of Nietzsche's more blatantly anti-Christian aphorisms. But Schmeitzner showed no such qualms or hesitations. On the contrary, though he had been an admirer of Wagner's operas, he now regretted having disregarded the advice of his friends Köselitz and Widemann, who had vainly urged him not to become the publisher of the *Bayreuther Blätter*. Wagner and his editorial factotum, Hans von Wolzogen, seemed to think that someone who had been granted the extraordinary privilege of publishing a pro-Wagner monthly should be willing to carry on without earning a penny of profit. They were also forcing him to publish intolerably long-winded articles. Schmeitzner had decided to avenge himself by inserting a notice advertising Nietzsche's *Human, All Too Human* in the fourth (April) issue of the *Bayreuther Blätter*.

On 20 April Schmeitzner sent Nietzsche the last corrected proofs, and three days later the publisher began sending out gift copies to twenty-seven privileged recipients. The first to respond by letter was Reinhart von Seydlitz. Writing from Salzburg to his 'Dear Surpriser' (Nietzsche), he, 'the good letter-writer' (described in aphorism 319 as someone who writes no books, thinks a lot, and lives in an unsatisfactory society) expressed his thanks for No. 163 (a description of how through hard work and painstaking attention to details a reasonably talented person could become a good novelist), whereas his wife had shuddered at the bleak 'probability of remaining a bachelor', which seemed to be the chosen lot of the 'philosopher of the morning', condemned to a life of wandering outside the city gates (final aphorism, 638). However, the husband who two and a half years before had accepted the challenging tests of marriage – described in aphorism 406 as depending on one's ability to maintain a conversation with one's wife right into old age – had been doing his best to console her.

This playful, tongue-in-cheek reaction to *Human, All Too Human* – aggravated by Seydlitz's gentle reproach that all too often the carefully concocted 'fruits of thought' dangled before the reader's nose were theatrically whisked away and replaced by others, leaving him frustrated – cut Nietzsche to the quick. He was further exasperated to learn that Seydlitz had recently met Hans von Wolzogen, editor of the *Bayreuther Blätter*, and had even been tempted by the 'crazy' idea of following his example and of establishing residence in Bayreuth.

From the moment of his first meeting with Reinhart von Seydlitz, during the Bayreuth Festival of August 1876, Nietzsche had been hoping against hope that his new friend would prove himself to be someone worthy of joining the elect company of 'free spirits' he wanted to gather around him. This hope had now been dashed by 'Don Rinaldo'. In his letter of reply he wrote that if his friend could but feel what it had meant to him to be able to express publicly for the first time an ideal and a goal 'that otherwise no one has, which almost no one can understand', then he would understand why 'in this year, as soon as my profession gives me freedom, I need solitude . . . Accept this, please, without discussion.'

The second person who reacted promptly, after a hasty perusal of *Human, All Too Human*, was Nietzsche's warm-hearted translator, Marie Baumgartner, the mother of Adolf, his favourite student of philology. Writing on Sunday, 28 April, she said that she had spent all of the previous Friday reading his new book and that it was a day she would never forget. While outside and overhead the lightning flashed and the thunder rolled, drenching the village of Lörrach (north of Basel) in a deluge of rain, the storm of mixed emotions aroused within her was no less tempestuous. 'I can only say to you that – like the thunderstorm – I trembled alternatively from admiration and fright; that never yet have I experienced with you such feelings of respect-fear; that today it seems as though something has died within me – I must have a little time to endure the sorrow, to recover my breath, the grief came so suddenly.' But, having said this, she bravely added that Nietzsche had written a magnificent book, which would probably achieve a bit of what he wanted and which she was determined to read again.

The single paragraph Malwida von Meysenbug devoted to Nietzsche's new book, in a letter sent from Rome on 30 April, made it clear that she had not had time to give it a thorough reading. But she was happy to see that the many lonely walks and the *Gedankenbaum* at Sorrento had brought forth such lovely fruit, and that Nietzsche had dedicated *Human, All Too Human* to Voltaire – a free-spirited act which was certain to vex his enemies.

In early May Nietzsche heard from Ernst Schmeitzner, who had just made a brief, three-day visit to Bayreuth. In the course of a conversation Richard Wagner had casually remarked that he had read a few lines of *Human, All Too Human* and had then laid the book aside 'in order not to alter the beautiful impression made by his [Nietzsche's] previous works'. (Cosima's diary reveals that in fact several attempts to read the book were made before both gave up.)

Radically different was the enthusiastic reaction of Paul Rée, whose copy of *Human, All Too Human* had been accompanied by this extraordinary handwritten compliment: 'To you it belongs – to the others it is being given. F.N.' In a rhapsodic letter sent from his Prussian home at Stibbe, Rée wrote that he had leapt on the contents like a hungry beast of prey. The successive aphorisms in this 'Book of Books' had aroused thousands of half-forgotten reminiscences. 'What a man you are! – precisely not One Man, but a conglomerate of men; whereas each one of your so differently constructed friends struggles to prop up his talent – the only one he really has . . . you have all of these different talents . . . I particularly revelled in "Christian holiness and asceticism". If the Germans don't now become friends of psychologists, I will emigrate to France.'

Nietzsche immediately replied that Paul Rée's was the first truly laudatory letter he had so far received; for, with the sole exception of Jacob Burckhardt, who had praised *Human, All Too Human* as a 'sovereign' book, it had aroused 'annoyance, misunderstanding, and estrangement. But I feel rejuvenated, like a mountain bird that sits far up, near the ice and looks down upon the world. If we but hold together . . . some solid carpentry work will be accomplished on the House of Science, for which both of us will one day be praised.'

On 30 May, the date marking the centennial anniversary of Voltaire's death, Nietzsche, to his delighted surprise, received a small bust of the great free-thinker, accompanied by an anonymous card charmingly phrased in French: 'l'âme de Voltaire fait ses compliments à Frédéric Nietzsche' (Voltaire's soul pays its compliments to Frederick Nietzsche).

Ernst Schmeitzner's relations with Wagner had in the meantime deteriorated drastically. Unwilling to forgive the publisher for having had the nerve to insert a laudatory notice advertising *Human, All Too Human* in his *Bayreuther Blätter* monthly, the composer had indicated that he was going to find himself another publisher. Three weeks of claims, counter-claims and recriminations had followed, leaving Schmeitzner so fed up and exhausted that, as he wrote to Nietzsche on 30 May, he had often found himself sighing, 'Lucky is the one who had nothing to do with Wagner! . . . I have in truth become the tiny grain that has landed between the two millstones of Wagner and your book. But I will not let myself be ground to dust.'

In this conflict of opinions most of Nietzsche's friends shared Wagner's negative feelings, but with this important difference: they at least took the trouble to read *Human, All Too Human*. In a remarkable letter written from Ancona, on the northern tip of Lake Maggiore, where she had stopped to rest before going on to Munich and then Paris, Malwida von Meysenbug showed that her warm, maternal feelings towards Nietzsche were accompanied by an acute psychological understanding of his personality. The sentence on the postcard he had sent to her in Rome, in which he had said that 'the crisis of life is there', had been ringing in her ears ever since she had read it. This was Nietzsche's moment of

Gethsemane, in which he had to decide whether to accept or reject the chalice. 'You will drink the chalice of solitary souls, bravely, unrefused, of that I am certain. But,' she went on, with prophetic perspicacity, 'you will pass through many phases in your philosophy, of that too I am certain. You are not born to analysis, like Rée; you must create artistically and in spite of everything balk at unity' – she meant by unilaterally adopting a purely scientific view of life and the world – 'and thus will your genius lead you back again to the same as in *The Birth of Tragedy*, only with no more metaphysics . . . You cannot, like Rée lay out legs and arms and say this is how Man is put together . . . ' etc.

The idea that the ultra-rationalistic, logically minded Paul Rée was the 'evil genius' who had led Nietzsche astray was expressed far more bluntly by Reinhart von Seydlitz in a plaintive letter sent from Salzburg on 19 June. He was still digesting *Human, All Too Human*, but he confessed that he had not found in it much trace of the free-spirited 'Ideal' of which Nietzsche had so often spoken at Sorrento. 'Everything,' he added, concocting a clever pun, 'is much too réeal.'

The same charge, in a less casual manner, was made by Fritz's old friend Erwin Rohde. Writing from Jena on 16 June, Rohde confessed that he had found the book so rich and varied in its contents that he had so far read only half of it; but his overall impression was that its 'medicinal herbs' had been allowed to spring up too haphazardly. He had even felt as though he was being ejected from the hot caldarium of a Roman bath into an 'ice-cold frigidarium . . . Can one in this manner rip out one's soul and accept another in its place? Instead of Nietzsche suddenly become Rée? I still stand dumbfounded before this miracle and can neither be happy nor have a definite opinion about it; for I don't yet properly grasp it.'

Rohde felt no sympathy for the kind of intellectual amputation his friend Fritz seemed bent on practising on himself in advocating a supposedly 'truthful' practicality of behaviour. He was particularly critical of the notion of 'non-responsibility' – Man, because of his predetermined heritage, cannot be regarded as truly responsible for his actions in any deeply moral sense: an untenable notion which Nietzsche seemed to have borrowed from Paul Rée's *Origin of Moral Sentiments*. In a key aphorism (no. 39) entitled 'The Fable of intelligible freedom', Nietzsche had argued that notions like 'good and bad', imposed first of all on Man's actions, then on his motivations, and finally on the individual regarded as an essential whole, were highly arbitrary and based on the fundamental error of the 'freedom of the Will'. Schopenhauer, confronted with this problem – human beings, like everything else in the universe, are subject to the iron laws of causality – had tried to wriggle out of this awesome dilemma by claiming that there was one area in which human freedom nevertheless exists: there where the individual feels regret or repentance, and experiences what Nietzsche preferred to call the 'bite of conscience'. Since the ability to act otherwise implies freedom to do so, Schopenhauer had argued that in terms of acting – *Handeln* or *operari*, as he had termed it – Man is causally determined; but on the level of *Sein* (fundamental being) or *esse* he was acting freely, since here the individual found himself in the realm of the universal Will. This conclusion, Nietzsche pointed out, meant in effect that the individual's Will is there prior to his existence. All of this was quite arbitrary. 'Freedom of the Will' was simply an illusion. It is 'because Man regards himself as free, not because he truly is free, that he feels repentance and pangs of conscience'.

In thus stressing the human being's dependency on inherited as well as historical and contemporary social factors, Nietzsche was clearly taking issue with Jean-Jacques Rousseau's fatuous affirmation that 'Man is born free but is everywhere in chains.' But the counter-claim that Man, being determined or influenced by factors other than his supposedly 'free will', cannot be regarded as 'responsible' for his actions or his 'character' was one that Erwin Rohde could not accept. Like Franz Overbeck, he knew that this could not but undermine the very basis of morality. (This has in fact happened in recent times, with lawyers and psychiatrists urging clemency for their 'sick' clients on the grounds that their crimes were motivated by irrational drives for which they cannot be regarded as rationally responsible.) Even if all human beings were 'ghastly egotists' – and Rohde added, 'I know, my dear friend, how much more I am like this than you!' – nobody should wish to 'tear out the sting or thorn [of conscience] which warns us that selfish we *should* not be'. In short, he preferred to adhere to existing standards of morality, with all of their necessary prohibitions, and to continue to 'honour what is Good, about which, acording to Rée, there should be no more talk'.

Just as no chemist can measure the true artistic value of a splendid painting through a purely chemical analysis of the materials used, so Rohde, here speaking as an impenitent Schopenhauerian, had no faith whatsoever in an 'Age of Wisdom'; for wisdom, unsuited to the unripe brains of 99.8 per cent of human beings, isolates the wise man, and for this reason no culture can ever be built upon it.

This said, Rohde appreciated the serious tone of *Human, All Too Human*, which he had found 'unspeakably rich' in the topics covered and in the philosophical approaches used. Particularly agreeable to Rohde was to find in so many of the thoughts expressed 'the old, unchangeable Nietzsche, uncorroded by any Réeish rumination', which had made his heart beat faster in the love and admiration he had always felt for his friend.

Pleased to see that Erwin Rohde should have taken the trouble to write him a long, serious, and above all honest letter of criticism and appreciation, Fritz replied that both of them were not standing on such a 'rickety platform' of friendship that a mere book could topple and overturn it. He felt, however, like a man who has prepared a huge banquet, but from which 'at the sight of all those good dishes the guests flee . . .'

'Incidentally,' he added, 'in my book look for me and not for friend Rée. I am proud to have discovered his splendid qualities and aims, but on the conception of my "Philosophia in nuce" he has *not had the slightest* influence: it was all ready and in good part committed to paper when I came to know him better in the autumn of 1876. We found ourselves on the same level . . . the advantages on both sides very great (so much so that R[ée] with kindly exaggeration autographed his book [On the Origin of Moral Sentiments] "To the father of this work, most gratefully from its mother!").'

No less interesting was the plaintive letter sent to Nietzsche by Mathilde Maier, a highly intelligent friend of Richard and Cosima Wagner who, like Malwida von Meysenbug, had remained unmarried. An admirer of *The Birth of Tragedy* and of his 'Untimely Meditations', she had in March 1874 vainly asked Nietzsche to help her launch a Women's Wagner Club in her home city of Mainz. In the long letter she now wrote to him in mid-July, the forty-five-year-old Wagnerophile made no attempt to hide the intellectually shattering effect that Nietzsche's book had had upon her. It had cost her sleepless nights. Had Nietzsche simply been one more crass nineteenth-century materialist, it would not have mattered. But that a mind like his, 'so ideally constituted, and with, I believe, such an unusually strong and pronounced metaphysical need, should by quite different roads end up with the statement: the Philosopher of the Future will be identical with Natural Science, could not but leave me deeply shaken'. That men like Nietzsche should no longer believe in the illusions needed to sustain a 'world of everything that is dear and sacred to us' was serious enough, but it seemed to her even more important that women should remain religious. 'I who suffered the loss of faith at an unusually early age . . . would give anything to see the female sex retain the comforting illusion, not only for the effect that this would have on education, but for the welfare of women themselves. What a foundation of serene repose it would continue to be for the female mind, and thus to sustain the family! Because love in all its forms constitutes the essential central point in a woman's life, her lot without faith will be far harder than that of the man, for Love without the protective bulwark of Faith becomes an almost incessant torment. Will it then still be possible to save something, to preserve something? Cosima is an admirable, truly an almost inconceivable example.'

To this extraordinary letter – precisely the kind he had been hoping to receive from attentive readers of his book – Nietzsche replied with a far shorter but no less fascinating one of his own. He could not help it, he wrote, he was obliged to cause his friends distress by at last explaining how he had saved himself from distress. 'That metaphysical obfuscation of everything that is true and simple, the struggle *with* Reason *against* Reason, which would fain see in everything a marvel and an absurdity – and with it a corresponding baroque art of extravagance and glorified lack of moderation – I mean Wagner's art – these were the two things that finally made me sick and sicker and which could have alienated my good temperament and talents . . . Now I am shaking off what does not belong to me – human beings, friends and foes, habits, comforts, books. I now live and will live for years to come in solitude until, fully ripened and ready, I *may* (and then probably *must*) return to society as a philosopher of *Life*.'

This was by no means the end of this epistolatory fencing-match. It was prolonged by two more reproachful letters from Mathilde Maier, in which she expressed her amazement that Nietzsche could consider Wagner's music to be 'baroque', and by a sharply worded reply: 'Few can be as surely convinced of Wagner's greatness as I; because few *know* so much about it. Nevertheless, from having been an unconditional supporter I have become a conditional one . . . Finally, a thesis: the true Wagnerians are good, very good people, but *not at all* musicians (like you!) and all are more or less obscurantists (I am thinking of your first letter). Now laugh and remain good. Your F.N.' As a postscript Nietzsche added: '(For Heaven's sake) read J. Burckhardt's Cicerone on the subject of baroque style!!!'

Nietzsche's assertion that, with the sole exception of Paul Rée, *Human, All Too Human* had aroused nothing but annoyance, misunderstanding, and estrangement on the part of letter-writers turned out to be a hasty exaggeration. This iconoclastic book dismayed many of his friends who felt, as Nietzsche wrote to Paul Rée in late July, as though he had 'emptied the milk-pot' over their heads; but it did not undermine his friendships with Erwin Rohde, Franz Overbeck, Marie Baumgartner, Malwida von Meysenbug and Reinhart von Seydlitz. There were, moreover, at least three persons who, in Nietzsche's conflict with Wagner, sided with the philosopher against the composer. The first was Henrich Köselitz, who had emigrated to Venice in search of 'Mediterranean' inspiration for the non-Wagnerian opera he wanted to compose. The second was Carl Fuchs, a former piano virtuoso and gifted musicologist who had recently abandoned Schopenhauer and who now wanted to subject the four *Ring* operas to a meticulous analytical dissection. The third was Nietzsche's new publisher, Ernst Schmeitzner.

As late as early May of 1878 Schmeitzner still naïvely believed that, as the publisher of the *Bayreuther Blätter*, he could raise the literary level and the sycophantic contents of this propaganda organ by proposing more objectively minded and imaginative contributors – Nietzsche being one of those he had in mind. But by the end of the month he had reached the sobering conclusion that this was out of the question. Schmeitzner who, if not a 'free-thinker', was roughly speaking a 'liberal', was so outraged by what he encountered in Bayreuth that on 26 May, when the conflict between composer and publisher was working up to a first crescendo, he wrote to his friend Köselitz (now far removed from the field of battle in distant Venice) that he was fed up with the 'wash-rag' Wolzogen and the 'accursed yes-men' surrounding Wagner. 'They all stink of church air,' he wrote. 'Frau Wagner goes to church, he too, "even if not often", as he usually expresses it. Wagner is not reading Nietzsche's book . . . He said to me that people only read Nietzsche in so far as he clings to him [Wagner] . . . He got off some really nasty remarks about Nietzsche that I shall never forget . . . You should have heard in Bayreuth the constant grumbling against the Jews and "Snap up" (Bismarck). Lucky is he who has nothing to do with Wagner!' After which he noted: 'Quite another sort of man is Nietzsche.' Recalling their meeting four weeks before in Leipzig, he added: 'From the outset I was struck by the love and warmth of this man.'

The ensuing battle of wills, fought out between Schmeitzner and Wagner's pliant factotum, Hans von Wolzogen, raged on for another month. But on 1 July Schmeitzner was able to inform Nietzsche that he had won a partial victory: he was still the publisher of the *Bayreuther Blätter*, which would 'remain what it has been so far' – that is, the kind of highly prejudiced *Parteiblatt* (partisan news-sheet) with which Nietzsche had indicated he would never have anything to do.

In mid-July, yielding to Franziska Nietzsche's insistent pleas, Fritz's sister Elisabeth returned to Naumburg to look after their widowed mother. Most of the furniture that had been sent from Naumburg four years before to furnish their joint apartment in Basel was now transported back by rail to Thuringia. Loath as he was to admit it – was not a life of solitary wandering the lot of evey genuine 'free spirit'? – Fritz missed his sister's devoted company and care.

Equally depressing was the rainy weather which pursued him when, at the end of the semester, he left the sultry city in search of pure mountain air. His choice this time fell on an Alpine hotel situated on a mountain top, at an altitude of 6,600 feet, above the town of Grindelwald. The view, southward towards the snow-covered Jungfrau, was spectacular when, all too infrequently, the skies cleared and the solitary hotel was not shrouded in fog, pelted by rain, or blinded by a blizzard.

Here Nietzsche received a letter from Schmeitzner, warning him that Wagner had just written another article ('The Public and Popularity') for the August issue of the *Bayreuther Blätter.* Though Nietzsche was not mentioned, the composer had ridiculed a book described as being '*Menschliches und Unmenschliches*' ('Human and Inhuman'), had denounced the 'historical school' of thinking to which Nietzsche, after abandoning Schopenhauer, now in effect adhered, and, without daring to attack Darwin, had praised religion and damned logical analysis as the mortal enemy of art.

By the end of the third week on his mountain top Nietzsche could stand the lonely wind and rain-swept heights of his hotel no longer. From Grindelwald he moved to lower-lying Interlaken, where he continued to devise new aphorisms for an 'annexe' he wanted to add to *Human, All Too Human.* Here he adopted the daily baths and long walks through the woods régime he had followed the previous October at Baden Baden. Ten days later he informed his mother and sister (once again by postcard) that he had regained his appetite and was sleeping soundly.

That same day (3 September) he wrote to his publisher that he had at last been able to read Wagner's article on 'The Public and Popularity' and had found it even meaner in its personal cracks than Schmeitzner had indicated. (In it Nietzsche was lampooned as a typically German professor who had written a book refuting the views of a 'predecessor' (i.e. Schopenhauer), in order to make a name for himself, as a scholar whose knowledge of the real world was limited to the immediate vicinity of his academic chair, and who, like Goethe's Faust, might well end up cursing the sterile accumulation of unproductive knowledge.) One week later he sent another postcard to Schmeitzner, who for financial reasons was forced to continue publishing the *Bayreuther Blätter* (with its 1,400 subscribers). Nietzsche politely declined the publisher's offer of a free annual subscription. Why, he asked, 'should I be forced to absorb monthly doses of Wagnerian angry drivel? Henceforth I would like to feel pure and clear about him and his greatness: I must keep his All-Too-Humanness at arm's length.'

In another postcard written three days later (13 September) Nietzsche thanked Marie Baumgartner for the sympathetic (even if shocked) letter she had written to him about *Human, All Too Human.* What an exception hers had been among all the letters he had been receiving for months past! 'Most disown me three times in one breath and then crow like cocks.'

On 17 September Nietzsche left Interlaken and returned to the humble bachelor's apartment which his practically minded sister had found for him on the Bachlettenstrasse, in a southern suburb of Basel. The apartment's greater distance from the university, where he had to go for his lectures, was one of its notable avantages; it required a long walk (now for health reasons a daily necessity) to the old city centre and back.

An even longer walk took Nietzsche through Basel and on northwards to the village of Lörrach, where his delight at being received with open arms by the warm-hearted Marie Baumgartner was so emotionally upsetting that it precipitated another nervous fit: one so serious that he had to send a telegram to Franz Overbeck in Zürich announcing a delay in his arrival.

During his brief stay in Zürich, in the luxurious villa of Overbeck's in-laws, Nietzsche's exquisite manners and the surprising softness of his voice charmed Overbeck's mother-in-law (Louise Rothpletz) as well as his wife Ida. While Nietzsche was full of praise for the masterly way in which Bismarck had presided over the recently concluded Berlin Congress (devoted to the explosive future of the anti-Ottoman Balkans), he felt misgivings about the concessions the German Chancellor seemed prepared to make in not ruthlessly outlawing all communist and socialist movements, some of whose revolutionary hotheads were blamed for having recently tried to assassinate Kaiser Wilhelm I.

We know little about Fritz's three-week stay (4 September to 17 October) in Naumburg, where his mother had at last bought the corner house on the Weingartenstrasse (which she had previously been renting) and had had it enlarged to accommodate several rent-paying lodgers to cover the annual mortgage costs. Fritz's health throughout his stay remained so delicate that arguments about *Human, All Too Human* were carefully avoided and visits from Naumburg friends discouraged.

In Basel, throughout the autumn–winter semester of 1878–79, Nietzsche continued to be plagued by headaches and paroxysmic seizures, recurring at weekly intervals, and even, towards the end of November, every three days. He needed all the fortitude he could muster to continue his university lectures – Greek lyric poets (three hours a week), Thucydides (two hours), Plato's *Phaedo* (a one-hour seminar). He was encouraged by his growing prestige as a teacher – thirteen students for his main lecture course! As he wrote to his mother and sister, 'Ah, if only you knew what a blessing, in spite of everything, my lectures are!'

The first days of December were the coldest but also the loveliest winter week Nietzsche had yet spent in Basel, with the white rooftops and the steeple of St Margaret's church glittering in the frosty sunshine, while the sagging branches of the trees in the nearby botanical garden seemed about to break under the weight of foot-high coverlets of snow. But Christmas once again was a season of physical torment, with one paroxysmic seizure following another right up to the end of the year.

All autumn he struggled to finish the work he had begun on his lonely mountain top in the Bernese Oberland. But frequently he was forced to limit himself to spells of composition and reading lasting no more than fifteen minutes each. This time, moreover, there was no Heinrich Köselitz to help him. In despair he appealed to the devoted Marie Baumgartner, who felt deeply honoured to be entrusted with the chores of copyist. The work was completed on the feast-day of St Sylvester (31 December 1878), enabling Nietzsche to send off the manuscript as a New Year's Day 'surprise' to Ernst Schmeitzner in Chemnitz.

This 'prolongation' of *Human, All Too Human* contained another 394 aphorisms (later increased to over 400) of 'Mixed Opinions and Maxims'. Nietzsche's intention was to have them added to the previous 638, so that together they could constitute a single, uninterrupted series. But Schmeitzner objected that this was not a practical solution, since 200-300 copies of the initial print order of 500 had already been sold. *Vermischte Meinungen und Sprüche* would have to be published separately as a companion volume to *Menschliches, Allzumenschliches*; but, being shorter, it could be sold at an advantageous price of 4 marks per copy.

The good news that Heinrich Köselitz had kindly volunteered to check the manuscript and galley proofs in Florence, where he was presently spending a few weeks, did little to reduce Nietzsche's nervousness over the final state of his new book. From early February of 1879 on, his violent headaches were accompanied by a cramp which forced him to keep his right eye closed for hours at a time. The steady deterioration in his health made it more and more difficult for him to complete his weekly quota of five lectures and one seminar hour. In early March he suffered a major shock when he discovered that, without asking his permission, Schmeitzner had used the last two pages of *Mixed Opinions and Maxims* to advertise Paul Rée's *The Origin of Moral Sentiments* with a sentence of rash praise lifted from one of Nietzsche's letters to the publisher. This contretemps and a few glaring errors made by the typesetters unleashed several severe seizures, forcing him to cease all his lectures.

On 22 March, after informing his 'so-ready-to-help comrade' Heinrich Köselitz, that he needed 'mountain air, solitude' and could not make it to Venice, as he had hoped, Nietzsche left Basel and headed for Geneva. He had originally intended to cross the Savoy mountains into France and to proceed southward towards the Mediterranean. He was restrained, however, by the fear of putting too great a distance between himself and Basel at a moment when the first copies of *Mixed Opinions and Maxims* were reaching a number of privileged recipients. Instead, he decided to stay on in the 'luminous' city of Geneva at a lakeside hotel which (he hoped) would offer him a lovely view of the Alps as well as wholesome shower-baths.

Not until 30 March, after the sun had reappeared in a bright sky reflected in the sparkling blue waters of the lake, did his spirits begin to rise – even though, as he wrote to his mother and sister, so far he had known '*more torture* than recovery. If only I could be master of my stomach!' His life, 'on the edge of the abyss', he added, was 'three quarters pain and one quarter exhaustion!'

These fits of nausea and vomiting were almost certainly psychosomatic symptoms of nervous anxiety over his friends' reactions to his new book. No one could now accuse him of not having written a 'Nietzschean' book, since it had been almost a year since he had seen Paul Rée. Many of its 408 aphorisms had been designed to answer objections raised against the more controversial, ill-understood, or insufficiently developed affirmations of *Human, All Too Human.*

In aphorism 17, entitled 'The Happiness of the Historian', Nietzsche ironically compared the 'poor in spirit' who, like himself, gloried in the 'paradise of change, with spring and autumn, winter and summer', to the subtle metaphysicians and *Hinterweltler* ('behind-the-real-worlders') who could offer only a grey, frosty otherworld of endless mists and shadows – an allusion to the nebulous unreality of the asphodel fields of Greek antiquity or of Dante's *Paradiso.* But he who can walk in the 'light of the morning sun' and whose heart and mind is constantly rejuvenated by the study of history can justly regard himself as far happier than the metaphysician since, instead of one 'immortal soul', he has many mortal souls to keep him company. This aphorism was Nietzsche's retort to Wagner, the present-day critic of the 'historical school' of science who, years before, had been an admirer of Ludwig Feuerbach, the brash post-Hegelian philosopher who had proclaimed that ideas should descend from the abstract 'heaven of their colourless purity' down to the realm of sensuous corporeality.

Although in this new book Kant's name was rarely mentioned, any more than it had been in the first volume of *Human, All Too Human*, one of its central purposes was to denounce everything that was false and artificial in contemporary Christianity, and ultimately derived from that *Pflichtgefühl* (sense of duty) which Kant had invested with the sanctity of dogma in his *Critique of Practical Reason*. A spontaneous feeling of affection for other human beings is one thing; it can even be considered a 'virtue' in the noblest sense of that word. But a 'love of one's neighbour' generated by a sense of moral duty is intrinsically hollow, fraudulent, inauthentic, one of the myriad forms of righteous self-deception to which human beings are so prone.

Nietzsche had already made the point in aphorism 589 of *Human, All Too Human* ('The Day's First Thought'). Repeating what he had once written to Malwida von Meysenbug, he had declared: 'The best way to begin each day is, on waking up, to think of how one can give joy to at least one person on that day. If this could do as a substitute for the religious habit of prayer, others would greatly gain from this change.'

In the seven devastating sections (136–142) that had preceded the magnificent conclusion to the third chapter of *Human, All Too Human* (devoted to 'Religious Life'), Nietzsche had undertaken a pitiless psychological analysis of the medieval Christian practices of self-flagellation, the mortification of the flesh, the morbid frustrations induced by sexual abstinence – the sensual 'phantasies of many Christian saints were dirty to an extraordinary degree' – the schizophrenic battle fought against one's inner 'demon' by naïve believers so haunted by the fear of eternal damnation that they came to regard the very act of procreation as inherently sinful, and other metaphysical aberrations. What interested Nietzsche, however, was not simply the extent to which such anti-carnal hallucinations could generate pathetically tormented human beings; it was the element of histrionic vanity, of a desire to appear pious, devout and 'good' in the eyes of others that so often underlay practices of deliberate self-abasement – 'humility' being regarded as an exemplary Christian virtue. It was also a desire to give oneself 'a good conscience' and thus to please or at least to console oneself. In other words, one more form of hidden self-centredness lurking behind the benevolent mask of 'altruism'.

If doing good out of a sense of duty was not particularly commendable, preaching it was even more suspect. This was the distinction Nietzsche sought to establish in his new book (aphorism 92) between *Christentümler* (Christianizers) and *Christen* (Christians). What was one to think of pulpit preachers who praised 'God and His saints' in order, by comparison, to belittle and vex the 'sinners' they were haranguing, or who, going to the other extreme – here Nietzsche was thinking of Victor Hugo and his Christian cult of 'Humanity' – had raised Man, or more exactly Mankind in the aggregate, to such a pinnacle of adulation that God and his saints could not but take offence? 'I would like it if at least you learned Christian manners,' was Nietzsche's concluding admonition, 'since the good breeding of the Christian heart is so lacking in you.'

As this last sentence makes quite clear, Nietzsche's fundamental quarrel with Christianity was that it was overly emotional and histrionic, ostentatiously mawkish and sentimental. Like Wagner's music, it was profoundly un-Greek, in that it lacked a sense of measure, of serene moderation – such as was to be found, for example, in the philosophy of Epicurus. One could apply to Christianity the dictum that Goethe, in his conversations with Eckermann, had applied to art: 'I call classic what is healthy, and romantic what is sick' (alluded to in aphorism 221 of *Human All Too Human*). Unlike Judaism and Islam, both of them essentially 'heroic-epic' religions (aphorism 95), Christianity was fundamentally a 'lyrical' religion which, not content to elevate Love to the status of a mystical ideal unattainable for the many, had made a cult of suffering, sinfulness and spiritual anguish rather than exalting good health. Anticipating Karl Kraus's later dictum that 'Psychoanalysis is a remedy for the illness of which it is itself the cause', Nietzsche, in aphorism 68 ('The Evil Qualities of Compassion'), returned to one of his favourite themes: that the 'virtue' of compassion was in effect the remedy Christianity proposed for the spiritual torments it caused by regarding Man as an inherently sinful being. 'Compassion' – in German *Mitleiden* (literally, 'suffering with') – 'has its own shamelessness for travelling companion: for while it would like to help at any cost, it exhibits no embarrassment as to the means of healing or the nature and cause of the malady, and practises glib quackery on the health and reputation of its patient.' On the other hand, '*Mitfreude*' ('with-joy' or 'shared joy' – aphorism 62) was an aristocratic quality cultivated by those who (like Carl von Gersdorff before he had succumbed to his Nerina-madness) are naturally generous, kind-hearted, and, as the French put it so gracefully, *de bonne compagnie*.

Again displaying the ferocious frankness that had shocked so many readers of *Human, All Too Human*, Nietzsche summed up his feelings on the subject towards the end of his new book in a pithy aphorism entitled 'Counter-propositions' (385): 'The most senile thing that has ever been thought about Man is contained in the famous proposition: "The I is always detestable"; the most childish in the even more famous "Love thy neighbour as thyself". Knowledge of what human beings are ceased with the first, with the second it has not yet begun.'

The price that the Christian world was paying for this lack of realism was a pervasive hypocrisy, as omnipresent in Germany as elsewhere. 'I may be mistaken,' Nietzsche wrote in aphorism 299, 'but it seems to me that in present-day Germany a double form of hypocrisy has become for everyone the duty of the moment: one demands Germanness [*Deutschtum*] for reasons of imperial-political interest and Christianity for reasons of social anxiety, both of them, however, solely in words, attitudes, and in particular in knowing how to keep quiet.'

In writing these lines Nietzsche was in effect replying to Richard

Wagner who, in a recent article published in his *Bayreuther Blätter* ('*Was ist deutsch?*' – What is German?), had once again extolled the age-old 'Germanic virtues' of honesty, profundity, seriousness of purpose, perseverence, and contrasted them to the superficiality, the frivolity, the insincerity, the unreliability of the French and other Latin peoples.

In aphorism 323 ('To be a good German means to de-Germanize oneself') Nietzsche went even further, well aware that he was walking in the footsteps of the cosmopolitan Goethe:

> National differences, where they are to be found . . . are merely variations in different *stages of civilization*, having only a tiny degree of something permanent (and even this not in any strict sense). This is why all arguments about the national character impose so few demands on anyone working for the *transformation* of convictions, which is to say, of culture. If, for example, one takes everything that already *has been* German, one will have to improve the theoretical question – what *is* German? – by raising the counter-question: 'What is German *now*?'; and every *good* German will find a practical solution to it precisely by overcoming his German characteristics. When, specifically, a people advances and grows, it each time bursts the girdle that was binding its *national* prestige; if it stays put, it atrophies and winds another girdle around its soul. The ever hardening crust forms around it a prison whose walls grow steadily thicker. If a people has something very solid about it, this is the proof that it will petrify and that it would like to become a *monument*: which is what, from a certain moment of time on, happened to Egyptian civilization. He, therefore, who wishes the Germans well should for his part see how more and more he can outgrow what is German. *The orientation towards what is un-German* has for this reason always been the hallmark of superior beings among our people.

This blunt, anti-nationalist affirmation was not made to please Richard Wagner and his Bayreuth devotees; any more than were half a dozen other aphorisms of the same ilk: (144) in which the 'baroque style', which had so outraged Mathilde Maier, was portrayed as ending an artistic movement, not as starting a new one; (171) in which music was described as being a relative 'late-comer' in the history of every culture; (159) in which the 'moral ecstasy' and 'minimal debauches' of (Germany's) 'new music' were likened to sickness, etc.

Those who, in reading *Human, All Too Human*, had concluded that Nietzsche had been so analytically 'Réeified' as to have lost his former poetic touch were quietly proved wrong in the concluding aphorism (408) of *Mixed Opinions and Maxims*. Ernst Schmeitzner regarded this '*Hadesfahrt*' – this 'Journey down into Hades' – as a brilliant apologia in which Nietzsche, by briefly alluding to his intellectual battles with his earlier convictions, paid homage to the thinkers who had stimulated as well as annoyed him and with whom, therefore, he would continue to wrestle:

> I too have visited the Underworld, like Odysseus, and will still go there ever more often. Not only rams but my own blood have I sacrificed in order to be able to converse with certain of the dead. Four pairs it was who did not shun me, the sacrificer: Epicurus and Montaigne, Goethe and Spinoza, Plato and Rousseau, Pascal and Schopenhauer. With these must I argue, when I have long wandered alone; by them will I be told if I am right or wrong, and to them will I listen when among themselves they point out what is right and wrong. Whatever I may say, whatever I conclude, whatever I may think through for myself and others, it is to those eight that I raise my eyes and see their own trained upon me. May the living forgive me if sometimes *they* appear to me like shadows, so pale and peevish, so restless and oh! so lusting after life; whereas those others seem to me alive, as though now, *after* death, they could never more tire of life. What counts is *this everlasting vivacity*: of what concern is 'everlasting life' and, in general, life itself!

One of the first to thank Nietzsche for her gift copy of *Mixed Opinions and Maxims* was Malwida von Meysenbug. From her 'sunny nest' in Rome 'Aunt Malwida' wrote to say that she had heard from his sister Elisabeth that Nietzsche could no longer write long letters or maintain an elaborate correspondence. Her own frail eyesight had so far kept her from giving his new book a thorough reading, but its publication was in itself a hopeful sign. 'You are heading upwards towards a sublime goal, I understand it well: freedom and the peace therein of the sage, for whom even suffering becomes an asset. It is fine and moving to think of the lonely wanderer, who unflaggingly struggles up the rough path towards the heights where one breathes the pure ether of thought. Yes, my friend,' she couldn't help adding, her profoundly Christian ideals having remained unchanged, 'much will then again become clear and valued which was once dear to you and which today, because of the necessary one-sidedness of the path, you no longer perceive at all or in the proper light.'

Of Nietzsche's three-week stay in Geneva we know little, beyond the fact that the water-cure and daily-baths régime he adopted at the Hôtel Riche-Mont, where he occupied a fifth-floor room overlooking the lake, brought him scant relief from blinding headaches and spells of nausea. 'If only I were blind!' he wrote to Franz Overbeck in Basel. 'This silly wish is now becoming my philosophy. For I read and should not do so – just as I should not think – and yet I think.'

His Palm Sunday (6 April) was brightened by the arrival of a remarkable letter of appreciation from Jacob Burckhardt, in which the historian expressed his 'new astonishment at the free plenitude' of Nietzsche's mind, as revealed in his new book. 'I, as is well known, have never penetrated into the temple of genuine thinking, but have all my life dallied in the outer court and halls of the peribolus, where reigns the graphic in the broadest sense of the word. And now in your book, even for as negligent a pilgrim as I am such a wealth of treasures is offered on every side. There where I cannot tread, I watch with a mixture of fear and pleasure how sure-footedly you wander over the dizzying knife-edge cliff-crests, and try to picture to myself what it is that you must see in the breadth and depth below.'

The longer Nietzsche stayed in Geneva, the more bitter and outspoken became his 'Baselophobia' (his hatred of Basel). 'I have opinions of all sorts about the most varied regions of Switzerland,' he wrote to Overbeck on 11 April. 'There is general agreement that Basel has a bad, depressing, headache-inducing air. For years there I have *never* had an *absolutely free* [i.e. of aches] head, as, for example, I have had here for several days. As a result, I endure reading and writing for only twenty minutes. Ergo: *Academia derelinquenda est.*'

So basically unaltered was Nietzsche's condition when he returned ten days later to 'abominable, detrimental Basel, where I lost my health and shall lose my life!' (as he put it in a letter to his mother and sister) – with one paroxysmic fit following hard on another – that he was unable to deliver his first scheduled lecture. On 2 May Nietzsche dictated a letter adressed to the chairman of the university's governing council, asking to be relieved of all further academic responsibilities. The request was endorsed by his ophthalmologist, Professor Heinrich Schiess, and backed up by a letter from Rudolf Massini, in which the professor of pathology and therapy certified that Nietzsche was incapable of continuing his lectures.

Alerted by a telegraphic dispatch from Franz Overbeck, Elisabeth reached Basel on 10 May. Acting with her customary energy, she whisked her brother away from Basel to a castle near Bern, where Fritz spent a week of almost blissful repose. Elisabeth then returned to Basel to oversee the selling and disposal of her brother's furniture and the packing and safeguarding of his precious books, notebooks, random papers and letters (of which more than 1,000 had been carefully preserved). Nietzsche, heading in the opposite direction, moved on to Zürich, where he spent a night in the mansard bedroom-study which Overbeck's kind mother-in-law, Louise Rothpletz, had prepared for him in her spacious 'Falkenstein' villa. Worried about her guest's immediate future, she generously proposed to help the 'errant fugitive' keep body and soul together by sending him parcels containing various edible goodies. His books, she reassured him, could be stored in the Rothpletz villa. To satisfy his intellectual needs she promised to buy and send him a copy of John Stuart Mill's autobiography and of Gibbon's *Decline and Fall of the Roman Empire*.

Nietzsche's next destination was Wiesen, a village near Davos (1,450 metres above sea-level) which had been recommended to him by Köselitz's friend Paul Widemann. 'Pain, loneliness, walks, bad weather – such is my daily round,' he wrote on a postcard sent to Franz Overbeck on 8 June. 'No trace of excitement. Rather, a kind of unthinking, dazed feeling-rottenness' – aggravated by the jarring news (from Schmeitzner) that so far no more than 120 copies of *Human, All Too Human* had been sold.

Nietzsche's intention from the start had been to move on to the upper Engadine and to the fashionable water-cure and baths resort of St Moritz, located at the north-eastern end of a long, lake-flooded valley which, at an altitude of 1,800 metres, was the highest in Switzerland. Two considerations held him back: fear of being engulfed in a wave of summer tourists from Germany and Basel, fear of the exorbitant prices he would be forced to pay in this most expensive of Swiss resorts. But in mid-June he was agreeably surprised by a letter from the city of Basel's governing council informing him that the university had decided to pay him a retirement pension of 1,000 Swiss francs per annum for the next six years. This good news was soon followed by another welcome surprise, relayed to him by Franz Overbeck, who had been handling his financial affairs in Basel: the city's Academic Society, of which he had once been an active member, had decided to match the governing council by offering him an annual pension of 1,000 Swiss francs, also for six years. Heartened by these two windfalls, Nietzsche left Davos on 12 June, travelling by post-chaise to Tiefencastel and on up the Julier river valley and over the Julier Pass to Silvaplana and Campfer. Here he found a trunk, full of clothes and books, which Overbeck had dispatched from Basel. From the moment he set foot on the long broad valley, with its necklace of lovely, mirror-smooth lakes, its pine forests, and the upper Engadine range of mountains to the south separating Switzerland from northern Italy, he felt that this was the place where a physical recovery might be possible. 'But now I have taken possession of the Engadine and am as though in *my* [twice underlined] element, altogether wondrous,' he wrote to Franz Overbeck. 'I am related to this [kind of] nature. I now sense the relief. Ah, how longed-for it has been in coming!'

To Elisabeth he wrote on 24 June, 'Dear Sister, St Moritz is perhaps after all what is right. It is as if I was in the Promised Land. A permanently sunny October' – the month of his birthday, temporally located midway between the fierce heat of midsummer and the bitter cold of midwinter. Ten days later he wrote again to his sister to say that notwithstanding the outrageous '*highland*-prices' – each egg here cost him 20 centimes! – St Moritz was what was 'right' for him, even though it had brought no immediate improvement in his physical condition. To his mother in Naumburg he wrote that the 'woods, lakes, the finest footpaths, as they must be laid out for someone almost blind like me, and the most bracing air – the best in Europe – make me love this place. Yet I am ill here, as elsewhere, just as I was in the autumn in Naumburg; having to lie down and stay in bed every second day. But I endure it here much better, whereas elsewhere, particularly in Basel, I was on the very verge of desperation.'

As ill-luck would have it, this proved to be the cloudiest, rainiest and even snowiest summer the inhabitants of St Moritz had ever known. But there was another more personal reason for Nietzsche's continuing nervous upsets and seizures. His vainly sought 'empty-mindedness' – more exactly 'devoid-of-thought-ness' (*Gedankenlosigkeit*) – did not last long. Deliverance from the academic burdens of his life brought him such joyful relief that he was unable to stem the torrent of thoughts, arguments, and aphorisms with which he wanted to round out, buttress and complete what he had left unsaid in *Human, All Too Human* and *Mixed Opinions and Maxims*. Before he knew it, he had filled six small notebooks and run out of pencils. The excitement generated by these feverish moments was aggravated by the excruciating efforts he later had to make to develop these sudden illuminations into intelligible arguments and aphorisms: efforts which regularly brought on blinding headaches and nervous fits.

Sustained by the dried plums and prunes, the tins of tongue, the packets of cornmeal, the jars of fish which the generous Louise Rothpletz kept sending him from Zürich, Nietzsche spent three months holed up in a little house – the hotels of St Moritz being much too expensive. By mid-August his feeling of solitude had grown so unbearable that he sent a pathetic postcard to Overbeck, who, sensing his friend's profound despondency, left his wife's family in Zürich and journeyed all the way to St Moritz. He found Nietzsche lodged in a tiny room and in such a state of prostration that he could not leave his bed and accompany Overbeck on his walks up and down the valley.

Nietzsche's decision to undergo a one-month water-cure before leaving St Moritz – made possible by the University of Basel's decision to add another 1,000 Swiss francs to his annual retirement pay by tapping a special endowment fund, thus raising the total income to 3,000 francs a year – struck Overbeck as eminently sensible. But he strongly advised his friend Fritz not to subject himself to another stringent régime of total solitude.

On hearing the bad news from Chemnitz, Overbeck had already given Nietzsche his frank opinion on the subject: he and Ernst Schmeitzner had committed a practical blunder in bringing out a big book like *Human, All Too Human* in a single volume; they would have done far better had they spread out the contents over four or five slim books, which could have been sold in far greater quantities and at one-third of the prohibitive 10-mark price. Nietzsche said nothing about the new collection of aphorisms he had been compiling, realizing how dismayed his friend Franz would be to hear that this third book was going to be almost as long as *Mixed Opinions and Maxims*. He did, however, ask Overbeck, on his return to Zürich, to write to Köselitz in Venice to find out if he could devote two or three hours a day to reading to or taking dictation from him – the intimation being that he might be moving on from St Moritz to Italy. Nietzsche, however, had other plans. He had decided not to go to Venice, where even the Lido, notwithstanding Köselitz's idyllic description and several drawings, could not offer him enough space for his daily walks. On 11 September he sent Köselitz a long letter, announcing the dispatch of a new manuscript which, lacking the strength and courage to do the job himself, he asked his 'disciple' to transcribe into a more legible script. For the time being he would not be coming to Venice. His still fragile state of health led him to believe that he could best be cared for by his mother in Naumburg.

A brief note, sent from Venice on 12 September – the Italian mail service in 1879 was three times as rapid as today's – acknowledged receipt of the manuscript. On 22 September, the day after his arrival in Naumburg, where he received a warm welcome from his overjoyed mother, Nietzsche sent his 'devoted disciple' a postcard indicating his whereabouts. Köselitz, working at a tempo which left Nietzsche open-mouthed with admiration, had in the meantime completed almost half of the rewriting, and by 4 October everything he had so swiftly transcribed was already in Nietzsche's hands. In a brief note of thanks he marvelled at the speed at which Köselitz had worked, blessing him for this 'inconceivability of the deed'. His mind was now completely at rest. 'You will not believe,' he added in a second, longer letter, 'how faithfully I have been adhering to the programme of devoid-of-thoughtness [*Gedankenlosigkeit*], and I have solid grounds to be faithful, for "behind the thought lies the devil" of a furious attack of pain.'

That same day (5 October) Nietzsche wrote to Schmeitzner in

Chemnitz to say that he could at last reply to the question the publisher had put to him in the spring: would he have another manuscript to give him by the end of the year? The answer was yes, and his friend Köselitz in Venice could tell him exactly what he thought of this new text. Its title, *Der Wanderer und sein Schatten* (*The Wanderer and His Shadow*) was to be followed, on the frontispiece, by an explanatory sentence to the effect that this was a 'Second and Final Supplement to the previously published collection of thoughts "Human, All Too Human". A Book for Free Spirits.'

The title, for any well-educated German, immediately evoked Goethe's poem, *Der Wanderer*, a dialogue in verse form between a traveller and a lady met in Italy. It also recalled Adalbert von Chamisso's *Peter Schlemihls wundersame Geschichte* (*The Wondrous Story of Peter Schlemihl*) – the delightful tale of a young man who relinquishes his shadow in exchange for a well-filled purse, but who later, after recognizing the folly of his ill-got gains, strides around the world in seven-league boots.

What Nietzsche more specifically had in mind – the kind of questioning dialogue that the human mind carries on with the body to which it is inseparably attached – had already been suggested by Schopenhauer in the 54th chapter of *The World as Will and Representation*, with this sentence: 'As the Will is the thing in itself, the inner content, the essence of the world, whereas Life, the visible world, the phenomenon, is only the mirror of the Will, this world will accompany this Will as inseparably as a body is accompanied by its shadow.'

CHAPTER 25

# From *Morgenröte* to Messina

Judgements of the Weary
*– They hate the sun, find steep the grade,*
*And love trees only for their shade.*

Less austere than the first sections of *Human, All Too Human* – whose opening paragraphs (devoted to a 'chemical' analysis of concepts and feelings) had so shocked Malwida von Meysenbug, Marie Baumgartner, Richard and Cosima Wagner and many others – the concluding volume began with a light-hearted dialogue between the Wanderer and his Shadow. When the Wanderer suggests that Man's inseparable shadow is his vanity, the Shadow retorts that human vanity is neither silent nor humble enough to ask for permission to speak, as he had done. The Wanderer reassures his inseparable companion, expressing his delight that his discreet Shadow should for once be talking, thus making possible a conversation between them. Shade, he adds, is every bit as necessary as light – to bring out the 'beauty of a face, clarity of speech, firmness of character. They are not opponents; rather they hold themselves affectionately by the hand, and when the light disappears, the shadow slips stealthily away.'

This was, more poetically expressed, a restatement of one of Nietzsche's cardinal convictions, expressed in the very first paragraph of *Human, All Too Human*: that Truth springs from Error (its opposite), just as surely as the Good emerges from the Bad, and that the philosopher's first task is, like the gardener's, to concern himself as much with the soil and the hidden roots (of Untruth, 'Evil', Ugliness) as with the blossoms (of Truth, 'Goodness', Beauty, etc.).

The 350 aphorisms and brief essays of *The Wanderer and His Shadow* that followed were once again an intermittent monologue in which Nietzsche recorded his random meditations as they occurred to him with little regard to any pre-established plan. The central theme was stated almost at the outset (section 5), when he renewed his attacks on metaphysical and religious beliefs – this time by stressing how the attention focused on otherworld fantasies had kept human beings from dealing in an honest, healthy way with the everyday realities that are of the most immediate concern to their well-being.

> There is a hypocritical disregard for all things that human beings really and truly take most seriously, *all the closest things* [of life]. It is said, for example,

> 'One eats only in order to live' – an execrable *lie*, like the one that speaks of the procreation of children as being the real intent of sensuality. Conversely, the high esteem felt for 'the most important things' is almost never entirely sincere; priests and metaphysicians have, to be sure, accustomed us to a hypocritically exaggerated *way of talking* about such matters, but have not changed the general feeling that these 'most important things' are less important than the other scorned closest things.

More than a century has passed since those words were written, and today this critique of theological 'high-mindedness' and otherworldly metaphysics sounds distinctly quaint, so radical has been the shift in modern society from a world of puritanical 'propriety' to one in which the 'closest things' of life – everything from eating habits and gastronomy to cosmetics, athletic sports, physical fitness, medical care, domestic comfort, entertainment and erotic pleasure – now dominate all else, relegating religious preoccupations to the periphery of daily existence. But it would be a grave mistake to conclude from this that what Nietzsche was recommending was unbridled paganism. For reasons that will become apparent later on, he would have been apalled by the rampant hedonism and (particularly in 'pop' music) the 'Dionysian' vulgarity of the twentieth century's noisy fin de siècle.

What Nietzsche was denouncing was an insidious love of abstractions indulged in by priests, teachers and idealists of every kind, who were not only bent on persuading children that what mattered in life was (as he put it in aphorism 6) 'salvation of the soul', but also 'service of the State' (i.e. of the second Germanic *Reich*). His model of sagacity was Epicurus, who, though he had inspired the word 'Epicurean', had preached a life of exemplary simplicity, in which sensual pleasure had its rightful, moderate place. This 'soother of the souls of late antiquity' (section 7) had found the sensible spiritual solution for the all too theoretical questions and the 'divine anguish' that were tormenting his contemporaries. If there are gods, he had argued, they are far too busy with their own affairs 'to be concerned with us' – an eminently sensible attitude which relieved the 'believer' of having to 'prove' the contrary: that gods not only exist but are permanently concerned with lowly human beings.

What had been admirable about Epicurus was his calm refusal to adopt a single dogmatic attitude regarding imponderable questions for which other hypotheses might provide a better answer. This was *Freigeisterei* – tolerant 'free-mindedness' – in its most admirable form. It implicitly rejected every form of anthropocentric naïveté based on the self-infatuating notion that Man is the measure of all things and the central hub around which everything in the universe – including the preoccupations of the gods, or of a single God – revolves. If human beings had been more intelligent and quick-witted, it would long since have dawned on them that if a God had really created the world, He would also have created Man to be 'the ape of God, a constant source of merriment in its all too lengthy eternities'.

In penning these irreverent lines, Nietzsche was clearly thinking of Voltaire and of his satirical treatment of Leibniz (Pangloss), the rational apologist of an omniscient creator of the 'best of all possible worlds' – a world whose 'perfection' was marred by plagues, floods, droughts, incessant wars, exactions, cruelties, injustices, crimes and natural calamities of every kind. The no longer innocent Candide, in finally deciding to retire from a hopelessly strife-torn world in order to cultivate his little garden, had in fact adopted an eminently Epicurean attitude to life. But Nietzsche, in going Voltaire one better by portraying Man as the 'ape of God', was also challenging what might be called the 'moral naïveté' of Pascal, Immanuel Kant and, not least of all, of Jean-Jacques Rousseau. That of Pascal, the anguished, hand-wringing Christian, so benumbed by the 'cold immensity' of the universe that he had taken out a kind of spiritual insurance policy against the uncertain future by opportunistically 'betting' on the existence of God. That of Kant, so wonder-struck by the celestial glory of the star-lit heavens that he had wanted to subject morality to the kind of regulatory 'laws' Newton had formulated for universal gravity. And finally that of Rousseau, whose Romantic sentimentalism about the natural goodness of Man had exercised its fatal thrall on the normally sober Kant and popularized a totally unrealistc conception of Man and Mankind, thereby generating enormous social and political upheavals.

Immanuel Kant had once declared that two things in particular had led him to believe in the existence of God: the star-spangled magnificence of the heavens and the divine simplicity of the moral law – what he called the Categorical Imperative. But Kant, essentially an eighteenth-century thinker, had been born in 1724 – 120 years before Nietzsche – and in that span of time the tireless, pioneering research of the astronomers had been relentlessly pushing back the 'boundaries' of space. For, as Nietzsche observed in section 14:

> Our uniqueness in the world! Ah, it is far too implausible a thing! The astronomers, much of whose work lies beyond their earthly scope, give us to understand that a drop of life in the world is of no significance for the total character of the huge ocean of becoming and perishing; that countless stars have similar conditions for the production of life as does the Earth . . . that life on each of these stars, compared to the duration of its existence, has

> been no more than a mere instant, a mere flaring-up, with long, long intervening spans of time – hence in no way the goal and final intent of their existence. Perhaps the ant in the forest likewise imagines that it is the goal and intent of the forest's existence, much as we do when in our fond fantasies we almost instinctively link the extinction of mankind to the extinction of the Earth.

The conclusion Nietzsche drew from this sobering realization of just how infinitesimal man really is in the cosmic context of an astronomically expanding universe was that human beings should stop worrying themselves needlessly about such distant matters. The trouble with human beings was that they demanded certainties – certainties which inevitably took the form of religious beliefs. But, Nietzsche resolutely declared (in section 16): 'We do not at all *need* these certainties about the outer and most distant horizons in order to live a full and excellent human life; any more than the ant needs them in order to be a good ant . . . ' Like Epicurus, human beings should learn to be indifferent to such 'ultimate realities', leaving them to the scientific specialists.

If Epicurus, mentioned no less than three times, can be called the venerated hero of *The Wanderer and His Shadow*, Jean-Jacques Rousseau was clearly the adversary with whom Nietzsche most wished to cross swords. For it was he who, in proclaiming (in the second paragraph of *The Social Contract*) that 'Man is born free, and everywhere he is in chains', had done more than anyone to conjure up a visionary image of Man as being 'the eternal *miracle worker*, whether he acts well or badly, the astounding exception, the super-animal, the demigod, the sense of Creation, the One-who-cannot-be-wished-away-by-thought, the key word for solving the cosmic riddle, the great ruler over Nature and despiser thereof, the being' – here Nietzsche had quietly moved on from Rousseau to Hegel – 'who calls his history *world history – Vanitas vanitatum homo!*' (aphorism 12).

The mere fact that Rousseau could write a sentence beginning 'Man is born free . . . ' was proof enough that he had blindly swallowed the philosophical doctrine of 'freedom of the will'. The visceral antipathy Nietzsche had developed for this notion was not simply due to the influence of Schopenhauer, or even of Spinoza (praised as 'the purest sage' in aphorism 475 of *Human, All Too Human*), both of whom had condemned this facile 'assumption'; it was the psycho-intellectual consequence of his own all too human feeling of abject dependence on a body and a brain whose painful tantrums he was unable to control. This was a physical condition he had inherited from his father, who had died of 'softening of the brain' at the age of thirty-six: a fate Nietzsche felt and feared might soon overtake him too. None of the crucial elements that had dictated or diverted the course of his life – his modest middle-class origins as the son of a Protestant vicar in the Lutheran heartland of Thuringia, the convenient proximity of Naumburg to Pforta, his chance meeting in Bonn with his mentor Friedrich Ritschl, who had later arranged to have him appointed assistant professor of philology at Basel at the incredibly young age of twenty-four, his accidental discovery of Schopenhauer and his even more fortuitous and fateful meeting with Richard Wagner in Leipzig: proof of the immense role that the Tykhee or Tyche (the 'good fortune' of the Greeks or the Fortuna of the Romans) had played in his life, as in that of others – none of these were vital factors that he had personally chosen, any more than were his weak eyesight, his superior mind and memory, and his 'temperament', which, as scientific knowledge progressed, might one day be satisfactorily explained through the chemical analysis of one's blood.

The alpha of any human life, therefore, is not Freedom, as Rousseau had so frivolously proclaimed, but rather its opposite: bondage or at least dependence – on hereditary, social, linguistic, national, geographic and temporal factors. This bondage or dependence, as Nietzsche explained in aphorism 9, could take many forms. With one it might be the sway of difficult-to-resist or unresisted passions; with another, the passive habit of heeding and obeying; with a third, the imperious desire to be logical and accurate; with a fourth, a capricious love of mischief and light-hearted escapades.

It is not because one feels independent that one truly is so, Nietzsche pointed out in an aphorism (10) significantly titled 'Feeling No New Chains'. No human illusion is more insidious than the naïve belief that one is normally aware of one's effective dependence on unwilled factors. Man would be closer to the truth and more honest with himself if he realized the opposite: that he always lives in a state of multiple dependence, but regards himself as free when and wherever 'from long-standing habit he *no longer feels* the pressure of the chains'.

Stated in other words, what is loosely called 'freedom' is not an abstract birthright to which every human being is entitled by virtue of being human. It is, above all, a psychological reality, enjoyed or experienced when a human being's actions (often not the case) accord with his innermost wishes.

On one important point only did Nietzsche find himself in agreement with Rousseau: the capital role played by feelings of envy in human society. But whereas Rousseau, in this respect a good 'Christian', considered it an unmitigated evil and a pernicious agent of social disharmony and discord, Nietzsche regarded envy as both a blessing and a curse. Like the good 'Eris' imagined by Hesiod, it can act as a social leaven, an upward-oriented drive of healthy emulation, whereby the ordinary individual strives to improve himself by salutary imitation and a profound admiration felt for exemplary models of behaviour and creativity. Envy can also become a social curse when it assumes a sickly, malignant form of jealousy and resentment against everything that is in any way superior, 'nobler', uncommon or 'élitist', expressing itself most violently in a revolutionary longing to destroy everything of generally accepted value in a fundamentally 'wicked' and unjust world.

Rousseau's gravest intellectual crime in Nietzsche's eyes was to have introduced a strong element of romantic sentimentalism into what should have been a serene, sober, realistic study of what human beings really are and of how human societies are really formed. The idea that 'all men are born free' was as much a product of sentimental wishful thinking as was the notion of the 'natural goodness of man' in an idyllic 'state of nature', or the equally fatuous notion that human beings, contrary to what everyday experience shows us, are fundamentally equal. In his *Social Contract*, first published in 1762 and which had since become the political bible of all 'republicans' and revolutionaries, Rousseau had elaborated a highly fanciful account of how in a state of nature quintessentially 'free' human beings had for their collective benefit contracted to form communities of human beings who had voluntarily surrendered their individual freedom for the cohesion and welfare of the whole. The historical truth, Nietzsche claimed in section 22, was radically different from this romantic fancy. Human communities were originally founded as a means of self-defence by persons who felt weak and who lived in daily fear of external attack. Their willingness to serve a strongman – like the medieval baron, for example – by providing him with food and retainers was due to their preference to pay tribute or 'taxes' on a regular basis rather than to be permanently exposed to the arbitrary ransoms exacted by brigands. It was the strongman's duty to establish a favourable balance, in which his power and prestige were at least equal to and, if possible, superior to that of the brigand and highwayman.

For Nietzsche this notion of 'balance' or equilibrium of forces was of paramount importance for understanding the formation of civic society and the evolution of justice. Far from being based on abstract principles that defied easy definition, justice in primitive societies was simply a legalized system of revenge. Not retaliating promptly in self-defence was regarded as a sign of weakness or of cowardice. The Old Testament Law of Talion recognized this implicitly by proclaiming the need to exact a punitive balance: an eye for an eye, a tooth for a tooth. As societies developed, the swift riposte – a fist replying to a blow, a duel fought to avenge one's sullied honour – was replaced by a delayed-action form of revenge in which the law court, representing the collective interest of society, undertakes to punish the criminal offender by imposing a punishment at least equal to the gravity of the offence. The purpose of the punishment is to preserve society from *further* damage by a process of *intimidation* (both words italicized in the next-to-last line of section 33). Implicitly, this realistic explanation of justice as a form of legally sanctioned revenge condemned Jesus Christ's unrealistic injunction: 'Whosoever shall smite thee on thy right cheek, turn to him the other also.'

In a remarkable section (no. 28, 'What is arbitrary in the meting out of Justice') Nietzsche in effect anticipated the abuses that were bound to arise from an overly sentimental view of human guilt and responsibility, according to which it is the criminal who is punished for his wrongdoing rather than the act itself. If, Nietzsche pointed out, the criminal's past was taken into consideration, then it could be argued that it was not simply the criminal who was guilty, but his parents, his teachers, even society itself. Nothing was more pernicious than this supposedly 'fair' attempt to incorporate the past in the judicial process. For 'if one is not prepared to admit the absolute exoneration of every guilt, one should stop at the individual case and not look back beyond it . . . Therefore, you Free-willers, draw the necessary conclusion from your doctrine of "Freedom of the Will" and boldly decree: "*No act has a past.*"'

Nietzsche was unquestionably right in thus foreseeing the tangled knots into which the convenient argument of 'attenuating circumstances' could tie judicial procedures in our day. But, contrary to what he intimated here, it has not been the believers in free will but the unwitting neo-determinists – the psychiatrists, the 'social scientists', the 'social-welfare experts', and clever lawyers – who have done the most to confuse and upset the contemporary judicial process by arguing in case after case that the committers of crimes cannot rightfully be considered guilty since through no fault of their own they were the helpless victims of their wretched upbringing, family neglect, a dismal social environment, as well as of psychopathic tendencies they could not control.

The same kind of pernicious sentimentalism, Nietzsche believed, now enveloped and obscured the basic human reality of death and its willed companion, suicide. Already, in aphorism 94 of *Mixed Opinions and Maxims*, he had written that the 'two greatest judicial murders of world history are, to put it bluntly, disguised and well-disguised suicides'. To anyone familiar with Nietzsche's previous works it was clear enough that it was Socrates, forced by his Athenean judges to drink his cup of hemlock, and Jesus Christ, deliberately risking the supreme punishment of crucifixion, who were here referred to. The desire to live eternally and the inability to die (aphorism 187 of *The Wanderer and His Shadow*) is a symptom of 'sentimental senility'. He now boldly tackled this thorny problem in a prophetic little essay (section 185, 'On rational Death'), which is worth quoting at length, in view of the controversial heat that has been generated in our day by 'pro-life' fanatics and the equally hysterical denouncers of human 'euthanasia'.

> What is more reasonable – to let the machine stop when the work demanded of it is achieved, or to let it run on until it stops of itself, which is to say until it is ruined? Is not the latter a squandering of maintenance costs, a misuse of the strength and attentiveness of those who are called upon to serve? . . . Is not a kind of disregard for the machines thereby actually propagated, that many of them should so uselessly be maintained and serviced? I am speaking of involuntary (natural) and of voluntary (rational) death. Natural death is the truly *irrational* death, independent of all Reason, whereby the wretched substance of the skin determines how long the kernel should last or not; whereby, therefore, the atrophying, often sick and stupid jailer is the master who determines at which point his noble prisoner should die. Natural death is the suicide of Nature, that is, the destruction of the rational being by the irrational thing to which it is attached. Only from a religious point of view can it appear the other way round, since, quite rightly, the higher Reason (of God) gives its order, to which the lower Reason (of man) has to submit. Natural death, outside of religious-mindedness, is not worth glorifying. The wise ordering and disposing of Death belongs to that now almost inconceivable and immoral-sounding Morality of the Future, whose morning glow [*Morgenröte*] it must be an indescribable joy to perceive.

In probably none of the other 349 aphorisms and longer sections of this book did Nietzsche come closer to explaining why he had chosen to call it *The Wanderer and His Shadow*. This short, pithy essay is of capital importance too for a proper understanding of his philosophy. His refusal to accept abstract notions like the immortality of the individual soul and the even more incredible 'resurrection of the body' in no way blinded him to the essential physiological duality of mind and body which – except for a handful of modern behaviourists and illogical positivists – philosophers from time immemorial have accepted as one of the basic realities of the human condition. Like the notion of the Holy Trinity, inherited from the Greek Pythagoreans, the dogmatically proclaimed 'resurrection of the body' was all too clearly part of the carnal legacy of ancient, or more exactly of imperial Rome; but its pagan origin, so conveniently forgotten by contemporary Christians, did not make this doctrine any less suspect. It was simply, as Schopenhauer had already pointed out, one more symptom of Man's childish propensity to magnify his own importance in the cosmic scheme of things by arbitrarily conferring on his perishable body the anti-natural attributes of a visionary immortality.

Just as the desire to live eternally and the inability to die were symptoms of 'sentimental senility', so war, Nietzsche unflinchingly added (in aphorism 187), was a remedy for pitifully exhausted peoples. He was careful to add, however, that 'the more fully and vigorously one lives, the readier one is to give one's life for a single good sentiment. A people that lives and feels in this way' – was he perhaps thinking of Switzerland? – 'does not need wars'.

This was, in effect, an extension of aphorism 444 of *Human, All Too Human*, in which he had written: 'It can be said to the detriment of war: it makes the victor stupid, the conquered one malicious. And in favour of war: it barbarizes in both just mentioned consequences, making things more natural; for culture it is a form of sleep or hibernation, from which Man emerges stronger – for good or evil.'

This was a characteristic example of Nietzsche's insistence on presenting both sides – the good, bright, shining side, and the bad, dark, mysterious side, the advantage and disadvantage of any problem he discussed. War, considered from the strictly cultural point of view, was an unmitigated bane; but, from a non-cultural point of view, although strong and bitter medicine, it could prove a healthy stimulus for an effete and will-less nation or society. (A classic example, although Nietzsche did not live to see it, was Great Britain in 1940.)

As someone whose whole philosophy was aimed at achieving a 'higher and nobler' degree of culture, not least of all in his native Germany, Nietzsche could not but deplore the increasingly bellicose nationalism which was now threatening to tear Europe to pieces. The only way out of this vicious circle, he now declared, lapsing for once into idealism, would be for one of these powers – he was clearly thinking of imperial Germany, militarily the most powerful – to announce proudly, '*We shatter the sword,*' and to follow up on this noble gesture by destroying its weapons altogether. If it was ever to be destroyed, the 'tree of military glory' would have to be felled at one stroke, by a single thunderbolt; 'but the lightning comes, as you know well, from the cloud and from on high'. In other words, the blow would have to be delivered (though he went unnamed) by Germany's supreme warlord, Kaiser Wilhelm I.

If this was wishful thinking – which, alas, it was! – quite different in the prophetic accuracy of its analysis was the next section (285), concerning a possible reconciliation between the seemingly irreconcilable concepts of property and social justice. Contemporary Socialists, Nietzsche pointed out, were in effect proposing to have the Seventh Commandment – 'Thou shalt not steal' – changed to 'Thou shalt have no property'. In Greek antiquity attempts had often been made to divide up property into equal plots of land, and the consequence had invariably been to arouse new jealousies and to sow the seeds of strife between supposedly equal landowners. When the alternative solution – the handing over of the land to the community – was tried, the consequences were equally catastrophic, hastening the deterioration and the destruction of the arable land. The reason was simply that Man is naturally careless about everything he does not personally possess, and is unwilling to make any sacrifice to preserve it, behaving with the irresponsible disregard of an exploiter, a robber, or a wastrel. Plato's claim that human selfishness would disappear if private property were eliminated was fanciful nonsense; for with selfishness all cardinal virtues would disappear as well. Plato's utopian 'basic theme' (*Grundmelodie*), which 'the Socialists continue to sing', was based on an inadequate knowledge of human beings. 'He lacked the history of moral sentiments, an insight into the origin of the good, useful qualities of the human soul. Like all of antiquity, he believed in good and evil, as one believes in white and black, as a radical difference between good and evil men, between good and evil qualities.'

Nietzsche's conclusions were equally categoric. If the ownership of private property was to inspire more confidence and become more moral, measures would have to be taken to encourage easy access to small property ownership, while steps were taken to limit sudden, effortless enrichment. All branches of trade and commerce favouring the accumulation of great fortunes, and notably the handling of money – in today's parlance, banking and stock-market speculation – should be removed from the hands of private individuals and private companies; and, not least of all, those who owned too much should be regarded, along with those who possessed nothing, as inherently dangerous to the welfare of society.

If Nietzsche's realistic warnings about the dire consequences to agricultural output that could be expected from the collectivization of the land were later fulfilled to the letter, with devastating consequences from which ex-Soviet Russia and many of its former 'satellites' are still trying to recover, his recommendations regarding banking and stock-market speculation sound surprisingly 'socialistic' for a thinker who never ceased to promote a vision of an 'élitist' society. Like Schopenhauer, who despised every form of money-grubbing – one of the things that had made his biologically 'advanced' philosophy seem so archaic and 'untimely' –

Nietzsche regarded financial and industrial matters as regrettable necessities. So far as we know, he had never read Adam Smith's *The Wealth of Nations*, nor taken the trouble to read any of Karl Marx's works, other than the relatively brief Communist Manifesto, whose seriousness he automatically discounted as the work of an admirer of Jean-Jacques Rousseau and a wayward disciple of Hegel. Here too his thinking was dominated by a fundamental concern for proper balance and equity, and by a dislike of extremes, so perilous to social stability. Whence what might be called his double anathema: one aimed at restricting the accumulation of vast fortunes and even the voting rights of the over-privileged 'haves', which could only exacerbate popular feelings of injustice, the other aimed at eliminating the 'have-nots' by improving the lot of the dispossessed, ever ready, out of sheer desperation, to heed the incendiary calls to action of revolutionary hotheads.

Anti-utopian and anti-Platonic though he was, he could still not help dreaming of an ideal form of 'free-spirited' democracy radically different from that monarcho-parliamentary 'centaur' – the increasingly ultra-nationalistic, sabre-rattling Bismarckian–Wilhelmian *Reich*. Had he not been so prone to idealism, how could Nietzsche ever have believed, even for a moment, that the necessary 'reformation' of Germany's backward culture could possibly be accomplished through the black magic of Richard Wagner's 'art-work-of-the-future'? Old intellectual habits, as he knew better than most, die hard.

On 18 October Nietzsche took his new manuscript to Leipzig, where he met Ernst Schmeitzner and his friend the musician Paul Widemann at the Stadt Rom café. Their lively conversation brought Nietzsche up to date on the latest goings-on in Bayreuth, where the pliant 'wash-rag', Hans von Wolzogen, continued to edit the increasingly antisemitic *Bayreuther Blätter*. But so mentally stimulated was Nietzsche by this enjoyable encounter that his headaches returned with a vengeance, forcing him to spend the night in a hotel room and most of the following Sunday stretched out limply on a sofa.

Galley and then page proofs of *The Wanderer and His Shadow* were soon on their way to Heinrich Köselitz in Venice and to Nietzsche in Naumburg. On 12 December Schmeitzner informed him that the printing of the book was about to begin and that the first gift copies would be on their way to the privileged recipients one week later. It seemed to him incredible, Nietzsche wrote in reply, that he could have begun *The Wanderer and His Shadow* in St Moritz on 21 June and could now see it in published form less than six months later.

The first to express gratitude for her gift copy was, once again, his devoted friend and translator, Marie Baumgartner, who only wished that she could write French as beautifully as he wrote German. What most struck her about this book was a new tone of 'wonderful calm', with no attempt made to achieve 'desired effects' through forced juxtapositions.

To Erwin Rohde, who wrote shortly before Christmas from his new academic post at Tübingen, Nietzsche's new book evoked a host of vivid memories – of their student days in Leipzig, of Fritz's 'night-time piano fantasies', of 'all the hours and days spent in the shadow of Wagner'. He could not but admire the 'courage, clarity, and finesse', and the noble loftiness of thought Nietzsche had here displayed, far removed from 'every earthy coarseness and triviality'. In comparison, Rohde's placid professorial routine and quiet domestic existence, with a contented wife and a 'crawling, crowing' little rascal of a son, seemed singularly uninspired.

Writing from distant Rome, Malwida von Meysenbug expressed her delight over this unexpected gift. It had come as a relief to know that 'the Friend not only wanders, but finds his sole happiness in an active exchange with his thoughts'. But the brevity of the letter, like the ensuing silence, made it clear that she was in no hurry to read this latest Nietzsche opus.

Meanwhile Fritz's health had been deteriorating rapidly, so excessive had been the strain imposed on his weak eyes by the imperatives of proof-reading. His sister Elisabeth, who could have helped him, was at this moment keeping house for a friend near the Swiss town of Chur. The first week of December was mostly spent in bed, with fits of vomiting accompanying the violent headaches. Heavy snowfalls made it difficult for him to maintain his daily routine of long, nerve-calming walks, and shortly after Christmas he suffered a major three-day collapse, during which he actually passed out. 'Never,' Fritz wrote to his sister on 28 December, 'have I observed such a *regular* worsening of my condition as in the past three months.' The next day, in a note thanking Elisabeth for the handsome trunk she had thoughtfully given the 'errant fugitive' for Christmas, he added sadly: 'During the past year I had *118 serious* nervous-attack days. Lovely statistic!'

In early January of 1880 Nietzsche wrote to the Frankfurt doctor Otto Eiser that his existence had become a '*frightful* burden'. He could presently not read, nor write as much as he would like, nor even to listen to music. Pills, powders and pharmaceutical solutions had all proved to be useless. Soon, he continued, he would go south, to begin his 'walk-taking existence. My *consolation* are my thoughts and perspectives. Here and there along my bypaths I scribble something on a scrap of paper, I write nothing on a desk, friends decipher my scribblings. The latest' – he meant *The*

*Wanderer and His Shadow* – 'follows herewith, accept it kindly, even if it is perhaps less welcome to your mode of thinking'.

Nietzsche was not mistaken in suspecting that this third and outspokenly anti-romantic volume of *Human, All Too Human* would be no more congenial to the good doctor's conventionally Wagnerophilic taste than its two predecessors; for in his thank-you letter Dr Otto Eiser said not a word about the contents.

Before leaving for the south in search of warmth and sunshine, Nietzsche felt the need to send a few explanatory words to his 'older sister', Malwida von Meysenbug. 'Have you good news from the Wagners?' he could not help asking. 'For three years now I have heard nothing from them: *they* too have abandoned me, and I knew long ago that from the moment W[agner] would notice a rift in our endeavours, he would no longer stick by me . . . I think of him with lasting gratitude, for to him I owe some of the most powerful incitements to intellectual self-perseverance. Frau W[agner], as you know, is the most sympathetic woman I have met in my life. But to all association and to a resumption of relations I am quite unsuited. It is too late.'

On or around 10 February (1880) Nietzsche finally said goodbye to his mother, who had done her best to keep him entertained during the long autumn and winter evenings by reading him German translations of stories and novels by Bret Harte, Mark Twain, Gogol, Lermontov, Edgar Allan Poe and even George Eliot (*Adam Bede*). Travelling directly south to Munich and then, with a detour around the Bavarian Alps, to Innsbruck, he proceeded by stagecoach over the Brenner Pass and on downhill to Riva, an enchanting mountain-surrounded town situated near the northern tip of Lake Garda. Here, despite the rain, he found just what he was looking for: a lakeside hotel surrounded by a garden full of yews, cypresses and evergreens, with, nearby, an olive orchard and even a grove of oak trees, where he could take long walks well shaded from the western sun.

On 23 February the impecunious Heinrich Köselitz turned up in Riva, after receiving a bank order for 200 marks discreetly sent to him by Paul Rée, who was appalled by the 'friendless' solitude that Nietzsche was imposing on himself in this small Italian town. Three weeks later the music-loving ex-professor of philology and his piano-playing 'disciple' left for Venice. Here Köselitz found Nietzsche a room heated by a porcelain stove, near the Piazza San Marco. The city was still beflagged by post-carnival banners, and although there was a chill in the morning air, Nietzsche could enjoy a cup of coffee in the afternoon, seated outside and listening to the violins of the Café Florian, and watch the fluttering pigeons alight on the flagstones of Europe's most famous pedestrian square.

Towards the end of March he moved from his cramped lodgings in the noisy centre of the city to a large room located in the eastern district of Castello, which, instead of facing the bright, sun-reflecting lagoon, looked out northwards towards the graveyard island of San Michele. 'My room,' as he wrote on a postcard to his mother, 'is 22 feet high, 22 feet wide and 23 feet long, with lovely marble, a splendid stairway, alongside of the strangest poverty.' Having decided that this 'find' would be his habitat for several months, he asked his mother to send him a trunk containing a number of badly needed books, including Herbert Spencer's *Matters of Ethics* (in German translation), two volumes of Stendhal, and a large volume concerning Byron. Thus intellectually provisioned, Nietzsche's life in Venice soon settled into a regular, generally nerve-soothing routine. After a long, bracing walk in the morning along the north-facing sea-front and a spartan lunch, he was usually joined at 2.15 p.m. by Köselitz, who spent the next hour and a half reading out loud, or sometimes taking dictation. A second reading session took place in the evening from 7.30 to 9 o'clock.

By adopting a simple diet of risotto and calf's meat, in addition to the frugal supper of porridge, Nietzsche managed to survive his first six weeks in Venice without a single stomach upset. But, as he wrote on 3 May to his sister Elisabeth (who had by now returned to Naumburg) 'the intellectual diet is an unbelievably difficult thing for a productive man, and I have to atone for each offence' – he meant of 'free-thinking' and hurried note-scribbling – 'with a nervous seizure'. These notes were intended for a new book, which was given the provisional title of *L'Ombra di Venezia*, thus paying homage to the welcome shade he had found in this city of 400 bridges and three times that number of dark, narrow, well-paved streets.

It was all too good to last – the inexpensive food (two to three times cheaper than in Basel), the calm, sleep-filled nights in an airy, high-ceilinged bedroom, the daily reading sessions and conversations with the 'unexcellable' Köselitz. For, after the rains had set in in early June, the bracing sea breezes lost their freshness, the climate turned sultry, the temperature began to rise. It was time to find a cooler habitat for the torrid summer months. But where?

The proximity of the Dolomites, visible above the flatlands of the Veneto when a cloudless wind was blowing from the north or east, convinced Nietzsche that the mountainous Tyrol or the thickly wooded hills of Carinthia would provide him with a surer refuge for the summer than Corfu or Corsica. Unfortunately, the elements refused to cooperate and what the hypersensitive 'fugitive' everywhere encountered was the dismal drizzle – what the Austrians call *Schnürlregen* ('string-rain') – which led him to reject every town or resort he visited. In despair, Nietzsche headed north, finally ending up in the Bohemian watering-spa of Marienbad. Here, after five sleepless days and nights 'on the road', he collapsed into a modest hostelry, the Hermitage, conveniently surrounded by woods where he could take long walks.

If only because of the hideously expensive prices (three to five times higher than those of Venice) Nietzsche did not want to spend more than a few weeks in this all-too-fashionable resort. In fact, notwithstanding the cost and the spa's 'fatal waters', which he forced himself to drink, he stayed on for two full months. His long, lonely walks through the woods of Marienbad unleashed another flood of fruitful ruminations, similar to the torrent that had submerged him the previous summer in St Moritz. His restless mind had been stimulated by several books on morality sent to him by Franz Overbeck, and by two valuable studies of Brahmanic and Buddhist beliefs and practices written by a brilliant young Basel philologist, Jacob Wackernagel. He had also received a collection of Sainte-Beuve 'portraits' of eighteenth-century French thinkers, recently translated by Ida Overbeck and published by Schmeitzner in Chemnitz, which fortified his conviction that the new anti-metaphysical, non-Christian 'morality' he was bent on developing would continue the pioneer work the French rationalists had begun before being overtaken by the twin disasters of the political revolution of 1789 and the Romantic 'counter-revolution' that had followed it.

In an unusually long letter written to Köselitz on 20 August Nietzsche declared that right now he was in a 'harvest, yes, in a harvest-festival mood'. To his devoted 'disciple', who had recently confessed how difficult he had always found it to establish a sympathetic rapport with others, Nietzsche wrote that Köselitz need have no fears, since in this respect he was made of stronger stuff than himself. 'I for my part suffer terribly when I am deprived of sympathy; and for me, for example, nothing stands comparison with what I endured when in recent years I lost the sympathy of Wagner . . . How often have I dreamed of him, and always in the stillness of what was then our trusting being-together. Never was a nasty word uttered between us . . . and with nobody perhaps have I ever laughed so much. All that is now past and gone – and what is the use of proving oneself right against him in many matters?'

All in all, he was as satisfied with Marienbad as he had been with Venice. 'I live incognito, like the humblest of cure-takers, on the registry for foreigners I am listed as "Herr Teacher Nietzsche". There are many Poles here and – this is truly wondrous – they take me absolutely for a Pole, they accost me with Polish greetings and do not believe me when I explain that I am Swiss.'

On 31 August Nietzsche finally left Marienbad for Naumburg. During the five weeks he spent with his mother and sister, he was unusually sullen and morose; and, as he later wrote to Köselitz, not once during his stay in his home town did he dip his quill into an inkwell. Normally Fritz should have stayed on in Naumburg long enough to celebrate his thirty-sixth birthday with his family on 15 October. But one week before, he abruptly decided to leave for the 'sunny south' (Italy) before the onset of the autumn cold. The result of this impetuous decision was another nerve-racking trip. By the time the train reached Frankfurt, he was vomiting. Farther south at Heidelberg he had to interrupt his journey and spend a day and night in bed. In Basel he spent a few refreshing hours with his dear friends Franz and Ida Overbeck, but the respite was brief. During the trip through the Gotthard tunnel he suffered a major paroxysmic fit and had to spend three days in rainswept Locarno trying to recover. At Stresa, near the other, southern extremity of Lake Maggiore, which he reached on 14 October, he spent three fretful weeks waiting for the trunk he had asked his sister to send on to him from Naumburg and cursing the relatively flat lakeside town, which offered him none of the well-shaded walks he had enjoyed in mountain-protected Riva.

Almost certainly it was the fear of putting too great a distance between himself and his invaluable transcriber and proofreader, Heinrich Köselitz, at a time when he felt a new book germinating inside him, which caused Nietzsche to abandon a projected trip to southern Italy. Instead, he headed west, probably with the idea of finding a mild winter haven somewhere along the Italian or French Riviera. He was still undecided when he reached Genoa on or around 12 November, after one more harrowing train-trip – 'a jumble of nervous seizures and mishaps' (as he wrote on a postcard to his mother and sister) probably involving misdirected luggage he had trouble retrieving from railway dispatchers. But the first four days, spent laboriously moving from one unsatisfactory lodging-place to another, left him tired but full of admiration for the great seaport which had given the world stout-hearted mariners like Christopher Columbus and Andrea Doria.

He finally found what he wanted: a humble mansard room located at the top of a house on a quiet street lined with old Genoese palazzi, which he had to climb 164 steps to reach. The cobblestones were so unworn by horses' hooves and rumbling carriage wheels that tufts of grass could be seen sprouting between them. Between periodic seizures and relapses that would have daunted a normal sufferer, as he wrote to Franz Overbeck in Basel, his irrepressible 'foolishness' caused him to go on pursuing 'quite unbelievable things from the moment I wake up, and I believe that never has the dawn [*Morgenröte*] illuminated any garret-dwellers anywhere with lovelier and more desirable things . . . I live as though the centuries were nothing, and I pursue my thoughts without thinking of newspapers or the date.'

The only trouble with his garret, with its good bed and a dormer-window view over the great maritime city, was that it had no stove. But so unbelievably mild was the weather throughout November and for most of December that at first this was no inconvenience. To his amazement the busy seaport, where 10,000 ships docked every year, afforded him an extraordinary degree of quiet and the creative seclusion he needed from the teeming world below him. Genoa had, moreover, what horizontal Venice so notably lacked: great cliffs rising up behind the city, up which he could climb over winding paths and on whose crests he could sit down and admire the grandiose panorama or even stretch out, with a parasol to shade his head and eyes, and let himself be sun-warmed 'like a lizard'.

If his physical sufferings in Genoa were more acute than they had been in Venice, it was essentially because once again he was in the prenatal throes of cerebral 'labour'. By 25 January 1881 the birth-pangs were over and on a postcard sent to Köselitz he announced the launching of his 'Genoese ship', which was already on its way to Venice in a separate package. His devoted 'disciple' replied enthusiastically that the honour granted him of again transcribing Nietzsche's almost illegible script made him 'the happiest of men'.

By working at a furious tempo, Köselitz was able to send the transcribed text back to Genoa two weeks later. On 9 February it was Nietzsche's turn to express his delighted amazement. 'To see the beauty and the manly gracefulness of this your manuscript – is to feel as one does after a Roman-Turkish bath, not only washed clean but also rejuvenated and improved.'

Köselitz, in sending back the rewritten text, had suggested that one of Nietzsche's shortest aphorisms – the Hindu verse from the Rigveda's 'Hymn to Varuna': 'There are so many dawns that have not yet shone' – should be placed up front on the title page of the book. Nietzsche wondered if they would not do well to scrap the provisional title, *Die Pflugschar* (*The Ploughshare*), which he had resurrected *faute de mieux*, and instead give this new work a more evocative, more luminous title: *Eine Morgenröte* (literally, 'a morning redness' or, in current English, 'a dawn') – to symbolize the glowing dawn of a radically new form of thinking about moral judgements it was his desperate ambition to develop. Finally he gave the title a more timeless dimension by eliminating the indefinite article. It thus became, more simply – *Morgenröte*: *Morning Glow*.

On 23 February, 1881, Nietzsche wrote to Ernst Schmeitzner in Chemnitz to ask if he would be prepared to publish another work of his, entitled *Eine Morgenröte*, the text of which their friend Heinrich Köselitz had just transcribed for him into a legible script. The usual small advance of 300 marks would permit him, in Genoa, to live a 'by no means ascetic existence' for a period of five months.

The first pages of the manuscript did not actually leave Venice until 16 March. In the meantime the conscientious proofreader had met and befriended Carl von Gersdorff, who was now trying to make his mark as a portrait painter. His passionate romance with Nerina Finochietti was not yet finished, but what remained, so it seemed to Köselitz, more resembled dying embers than hot flames. Eager though Nietzsche was to see his old friend Carl again, he declined Köselitz's proposal that he come to Venice, explaining that his precarious state of health made it impossible for him to maintain a normal conversation for any length of time. The self-sacrificing composer then suggested that they join forces for the laborious proofreading at Recoaro, which had been recommended to him by a Venetian pharmacist as an agreeably cool resort town situated on the southern slopes of the Tirolian Alps.

At Recoaro Nietzsche had a hard time recovering his health after one more dreadful train-trip – this time from Genoa to Vicenza. His one consolation, in a small mountain town he did not like, was the orchestral score for Köselitz's 'comic' opera (based on one of Goethe's poems) which seemed to him a work of genius. 'Friend K[öselitz],' as he wrote to Franz Overbeck on 18 May, 'is a musician of the first rank,' his work being a 'new and individual marvel of beauty, in which none of the living [composers] can match him' – an outlandish compliment which must have made Overbeck wonder how such a genius – the equal, no less, of Richard Wagner and Johannes Brahms! – could have lived poorly for so long without his extraordinary talents being recognized by anyone . . . except Friedrich Nietzsche.

The four weeks spent at Recoaro proved to be a trying time for both 'master' and 'devoted disciple'. Nietzsche was almost constantly ill, fretfully frustrated by the slowness with which a new Leipzig printer (Teubner) kept sending them the proofs of *Morgenröte*, and by the absence of nearby forests for the well-shaded walks his head and eyes so badly needed. Köselitz, for his part, was so engrossed by his work of orchestral composition that he spent much of each day in his bedroom.

Not until 17 June, three weeks after his return to Venice, was Köselitz at last able to send Nietzsche the final proofs, directly dispatched to him from Leipzig. He now regretted having recommended Recoaro as a quiet 'retreat', and he sensibly suggested that his revered 'Master' cross the Alps and return to the Engadine, which he had found so propitious for his health two years before. Nietzsche, whose nerves had been severely shaken by frequent thunderstorms caused by warm Adriatic air colliding with the cooler air of the Alps, had already reached the same conclusion. On 19 June he instructed Schmeitzner to send the first printed copies of his book to the post office at St Moritz. Four days later he wrote despairingly to Köselitz: 'Where is the land with a lot of shade, an eternally blue sky, an *equally* strong sea-wind from morning till evening, without thunderstorms? Thither, thither will I betake myself! Even should it be outside of Europe!'

By the time Nietzsche left Recoaro, on 25 or 26 June, he was suffering from paroxysmic seizures and vomiting every day. But he had no choice in the matter: it was a matter of life – the several more years he needed to complete his philosophical 'mission' – or death brought on by suicide in the darkest moment of depression. He was in no condition to travel, but travel he did. Once again the trip was agony, aggravated by a missed train connection, which almost doubled the travel time as well as the cost. When he finally reached St Moritz, he was so downhearted, not least of all by the disagreeably high prices – anywhere from 90 to 180 Swiss francs per month for a simple room – that after three hours he boarded a stagecoach and headed aimlessly down the valley in a south-westerly direction. At one of the stops he struck up a conversation with a young Engadiner who had just spent some months in Naples as an apprentice hotel-manager. Distressed by the plight of this patently sick, short-sighted and impecunious professor, he had him dismount at the south-western end of Lake Silvaplana and then accompanied him to the village of Sils-Maria, where he found a relatively cheap room for him above a grocery in a simple, two-storey house, owned by the mayor, which was conveniently located near a thick pine-tree forest.

It took Nietzsche an entire week to recover from the nerve-racking torments of this trip – a recovery delayed by a three-day paroxysmic seizure brought on by a heavy thunderstorm. Not until 7 July, on the eve of his sister's thirty-fifth birthday, did he feel sufficiently fit – for here too he could not write for more than a quarter of an hour without having to lie down and give his eyes a rest – to pen a long letter to Elisabeth. Yes, there could be no doubt about it, of all the places and resorts he had tried – Naumburg, Basel, Geneva, Baden Baden, Marienbad, Sorrento, the Italian lakes and a dozen different spots in the Swiss Alps – it was here 'in the Engadine that I feel far and away the best on earth: to be sure, the seizures befall me here as they do everywhere else, but [they are] far milder and more human'. To Heinrich Köselitz he wrote that with the help of a 'serious and kindly Swiss man', he had found 'the most delightful corner of the earth . . . Such quiet have I never known, and all fifty conditions of my poor life seem here to be fulfilled.'

On 15 July he sent a brief letter to Marie Baumgartner, intended to announce or 'accompany' the gift copy of *Morgenröte* which the printer was sending her from Leipzig. Unfortunately we do not know just how she or Franz Overbeck responded to this new Nietzsche book. For, like all the letters sent to Fritz by his mother and sister during the spring, summer and autumn of 1881, theirs too later disappeared (probably lost in a wayward suitcase during one of Nietzsche's later peregrinations). Only one such letter did survive, penned by Nietzsche's friend and admirer Jacob Burckhardt. 'I am still in the casual leafing-through and nibbling stage in your enormously rich book,' the eminent historian wrote on 20 July. 'A lot of it, as you surmised, goes against my grain, but my grain is not necessarily the only true one. Above all and particularly I am grateful to you . . . for the bold perspectives from which you view the essence of antiquity; about some of them I had the beginnings of an inkling, but you see clearly and thereby much more and farther. For the capital section "*On so-called Classical Education*" you will find many persons sharing your feelings.' For the rest, speaking as an old man (twenty-six years his senior), Burckhardt had to admit that he was seized by vertigo every time he saw Nietzsche moving without a trace of dizziness along the mountain precipices.

Because it was later overtaken and overshadowed by briefer and more stridently anti-Christian works, *Morgenröte* (*Dawn, Daybreak* or *Flush of Dawn*, depending on whose translation one is using) has remained to this day one of Nietzsche's least known and least read books. His belief, expressed in an 11 June letter to his mother and sister, that this new opus would make the 'not so lovely name' of Nietzsche *immortal* was fanciful exaggeration. Essentially it was one more stepping-stone in his arduous attempt to define and analyse the general problems and principles of a new, less incoherent, less idealistic, more rational and realistic system of morality, which it might take decades and even centuries to be fully elaborated by his successors for the benefit of increasingly sceptical Europeans who, no matter what they pretended, had in reality 'lost the faith'.

That there was a lot of spur-of-the-moment chaff in this new book, no dispassionate reader can deny. But it also contained a great deal of philosophical wheat, as well as nuggets of sheer gold, which cannot be ignored if one is to have a coherent *vue d'ensemble* of Nietzsche's thinking, notably concerning fundamental problems of morality and Christian values. Two examples of 'sheer gold': an eloquent encomium of the former Roman slave, Epictetus, stoically refusing to adopt the servile irrationalism of Christianity (section 546, 'Slave and Idealist'), and (132) a remarkable analysis of the insidious way in which Auguste Comte's moral imperative, *vivre pour autrui* (to live for others) – the final gasp of an 'over-christized Christianity' – was inexorably undermining human individuality and sanctifying its necessary adaptation to the collective welfare of society.

Nietzsche's main quarrel with Plato was that in his neo-Socratic search for a 'more truthful' set of principles than the ramshackle 'morality' to which his fellow Athenians continued to adhere for reasons of slothful convenience, he had invented a series of abstract ideals – notions like 'good' and 'bad', 'just' and 'unjust', 'true' and 'false' – which were supposed to have existed from time immemorial and to possess an immutable, everlasting validity. This *modus cogitandi*, Nietzsche felt, was every bit as arbitrary as had been the vanity of primitive Man in deciding that inanimate objects too should be accorded human genders – such as 'masculine' and 'feminine'. Why should *die Sonne* (the German word for 'sun') be regarded as feminine, whereas in Latin languages, *il sole*, *el sol*, *le soleil* were all masculine? Words like 'good' and 'evil', 'honest' and 'dishonest', 'truthful' and 'mendacious' were man-invented, shorthand abbreviations applied to individual relationships that were exceedingly complex. For in everyday reality there is no such thing as an absolutely 'good' or 'evil' man (or woman), just as no human being is always 'honest', 'upright' and 'truthful', or, conversely, totally and invariably 'dishonest', 'sly' and 'mendacious'. Even the bravest of men can, on occasion, display symptoms of cowardice.

What Plato had in effect developed was an essentialy unhistorical system of morality. But, Nietzsche claimed, this was the surest way of not understanding the very roots of morality. Just as *Sittlichkeit* (morality) in German is derived from the word *Sitte* (custom), so the English word 'morality' (or the French '*moralité*') is derived from the Latin *mos, moris*, meaning usage or custom (a meaning preserved in English in its plural form of 'mores'). Any profound, penetrating, 'scientific' study of a system of morality must therefore begin with a study of the ancient primitive customs, superstititions and prejudices out of which it slowly evolved and whose distant origins in time modern human beings have come to forget.

Here, even more than in *Human, All Too Human*, Nietzsche kept stressing the extent to which human beings, far from being a completely separate and superior species, are related to the animal and even to the vegetable world of Nature. The apprehensions engendered by having to live in often hostile surroundings caused primitive human beings to project their fears and sense of weakness on to objects as varied as thunder-clouds, beasts of prey, rivers, forests and poisonous plants. If *Besonnenheit* (prudence or circumspection) was so highly prized in the moral systems of ancient Greece and Rome, it was because this was essentially an ancient instinct inculcated by the need to remain constantly alert and on the qui vive in a perilous environment far removed from the 'good Nature' so fondly and fatuously imagined by Jean-Jacques Rousseau. Even the search for the 'truth', which might at first seem so ethereal and altruitsic, is, Nietzsche claimed in one of his most penetrating insights (section 26), at heart a search for personal assurance and security, which Man shares with animals. This was why Socrates, in Plato's *Republic*, listed *phronesis* (prudence or caution) as one of the four cardinal virtues – alongside courage, fairness and a sense of moderation.

What is called 'civilization', Nietzsche declared in aphorism 16, is based on the recognition that 'any custom is better than no custom'. But the coercive force or power that custom possesses does not stem from any immediately perceived utility – here Nietzsche was parting company from the neo-Darwinian Utilitarians, like Thomas Huxley and Herbert Spencer; it derives its social power, its 'sanctity', its 'indiscutability', from its age and aura as a venerable custom handed down from generation to generation as 'the way things are and should be'. Rational though a moral system may seem to be in its elaboration, its roots are buried in the humus of the irrational – metaphysical concepts such as the supreme authority of a single God, or the wilfulness and caprices of various gods and goddesses, as in the polytheistic systems of ancient Greece and Rome.

Because of the veneration insinctively accorded to ancestral Custom or Law, any 'free-doer' or free-thinker (*Freitäter* or *Freidenker*) who dares to challenge the established conventions of morality is automatically regarded as suspect and is vigorously combated. (Three classic examples are Socrates, Jesus Christ and, later, Martin Luther.) Generally speaking, such free-doers and free-thinkers have always been regarded as 'evil men'. However, if their attempts at ethical reform are not immediately crushed and stamped out, they are gradually transmuted and metamorphosed with the passage of time from 'evil' into 'good men'. (This did not happen with either Socrates or Plato, but it did happen with Jesus Christ, and also with Martin Luther.) This was the first, embryonic formulation of what later became one of the cardinal principles of Nietzsche's philosophy: the transformation or 'transvaluation' – *Umwertung*, which in German suggests both an 'overthrow' and a 'reversal' – of existing values into something radically different.

Even more explicitly than he had already done in *The Wanderer and His Shadow*, Nietzsche condemned all forms of romantic affectivity, excessive emotionalism and spiritual hysteria – whether exhibited in states of religious ecstasy or in the 'beside-oneself' intoxication induced by artistic rapture (as, for example, under the influence of Wagnerian opera, clearly implied though not specifically mentioned). This was one of the respects in which Christianity had turned its back on the tranquil wisdom of the Greek philosophers, who almost to a man had warned against all forms of passion. In Christianity the emphasis, from the very start, had been placed on an emotive love of God, a cringing fear of God, a fanatical faith in God, the blindest kind of hope in God (aphorism 58).

What, among other things, permitted the ultimate triumph of Christianity – one of the most implausible phenomena in all of human history – was its extraordinary ability to assimilate different moods and intellectual currents during the twilight years of a declining Empire. Nietzsche's passing tribute to this genius for assimilation (in section 60) is worth quoting at some length, if only to dispel the shallow, stereotypic notion that he was not only viscerally but blindly anti-Christian.

> Christianity swallowed up and absorbed into itself the entire spirit of countless subjugation-hungry souls, of all those subtle and gross enthusiasts of self-abasement and devotion. Out of a rustic loutishness . . . it grew into a *sophisticated* religion . . . It gave wit to the people of Europe and did not simply make them theologically cunning. It was in this spirit, allied to power and very often with the deepest conviction and integrity of devotion, that were perhaps *carved out* the subtlest figures that human society has so far seen: the figures of the higher and highest Catholic clergy, particularly where they were sprung from a distinguished lineage from the outset and brought with them the innate grace of gestures, commanding eyes, fine hands and feet. Here the human face attains that spiritualization which emanates from the constant ebb and flow of the two forms of happiness (the sense of power and the sense of devotion) once an elaborate style of life has tamed the beast in Man. Here a form of activity that consists of blessing, of forgiving sins and representing the divine, ceaselessly maintains alive a feeling of a superhuman mission in one's soul, *yes, and also in one's body*. Here rules that noble scorn for the frailty of the body and the welfare of good luck, which is to be found in born soldiers; one takes one's *pride* in one's obedience – the distinctive trait in all aristocrats; one finds one's idealism and one's excuse in the huge impossibility of one's task. The powerful beauty and subtlety of the Princes of the Church have always provided the people with the *truth* of the Church; a contemporary brutalization of the clergy (as happened in Luther's time) always brought with it the opposite of faith . . .

All this, of course, was only one part, and a very small part of the story. For nothing during the early years did more to promote Christianity than that fateful penchant human beings so often display for short-cuts and short-term 'solutions' on the road to personal 'perfection'. The great promoter of this short-cut to perfection was the first 'Christian' (as Nietzsche called him in section 68), St Paul, but for whose tireless exhorting, scolding and excoriating, the cult of Jesus Christ would have been limited to a small, obscure sect of humble Jews in the Roman province of Judea.

The unusually long portrait (more than three printed pages) that Nietzsche drew of St Paul is one of the psychologically most incisive that has ever been written about the apostate Pharisee from Tarsus. Paul was depicted as having been a violent, harsh, pitiless, sensual, melancholy man who one day realized that he was incapable of carrying out the stern precepts of the sacred Law of the people of Israel, the 'bar' of which had been placed so high that it could not be attained by ordinary Jews. His extraordinary achievement was to have thrown overboard most of the Judaic ballast weighing down the new cult. Traditional Judaism had never had a clearcut notion of an afterlife; and the remarkable thing, as Nietzsche took pains to point out, was that for generations the prospect of terminal oblivion had sufficed to act as an effective deterrent for those tempted to stray from the path of virtue. The notion of an afterlife, as something other than the final triumph on earth of the long-awaited Messiah, had begun to infiltrate Judaism during the years of the captivity in Egypt, and it had similarly made inroads from the north and east with the Iranian notion of Paradise (a word of Persian origin meaning a 'green enclosure' or 'garden').

Unknown to the early Christians, who naïvely believed that the Kingdom of God was at hand, the notion of hellfire and damnation was one of the many religious superstitions that had sprouted and run wild over the vast length and breadth of the Roman Empire. In third-century Greece Epicurus had tried to combat all forms of fanciful belief in an imaginary afterlife; and in Rome, two centuries later, the poet Lucretius (a contemporary of Julius Caesar) had vainly sought to do the same for his countrymen. But by the second half of the first century AD his poetic admonitions were all but forgotten, and it was precisely this bold 'theft' from pagan mythology (of an imaginary afterlife in the 'Elysian fields', etc.) which helped to make Christianity so popular among the masses of the Roman Empire.

Over and against the *tedium vitae*, the *aere perennius* (more durable than bronze) inexorability of a relentlessly expanding Roman Empire, Paul, with the visionary zeal of the fanatic, offered his listeners and the readers of his epistles the radiant prospect of an afterlife in which the righteous would join God and the heavenly host of angels and archangels, of cherubim and seraphim. All that was needed was faith in Jesus, the Son of God, and hope in the prospect of eternal life. In this respect too the first-century Christian differed radically from the sober sage of ancient Greece. The future, for the ancient Hellenes, was something infinitely mysterious and unpredictable, sometimes forecast by the seers and priestesses of Apollo. It was something no rational human being could hope to control. But it was precisely this power of controlling the future which St Paul offered to his fellow Christians with his extravagant promises of future 'salvation' through faith and hope.

This elevation of an imaginary Kingdom of God above the dismal reality of everyday existence naturally depressed the status of the latter in the eyes of the 'faithful'. The tribulations of the Jews and others became the living proof of their faith, of their righteousness. Suffering was thus accorded a positive connotation – a favour it had never enjoyed in ancient Greece. With the passage of the years the Kingdom of God failed to materialize on earth – as the earliest disciples had naïvely expected – whereupon Christians began to doubt the innate mercy and benevolence of an Almighty, All-seeing God and began to envisage Him, as had the Old Testament prophets – 'great haters', as Nietzsche had previously noted – as a jealous and wrathful God, as prepared to punish as to bless. And thus there arose, alongside the radiant vision of an extraterrestrial Kingdom of God, reserved for the 'righteous', the sombre menace for 'sinners' of an infernal 'underworld' of hellfire and damnation, to which was added the Greek attribute of 'everlasting'.

The anathema placed on carnal desire and the general denigration of the flesh that resulted from an over-exaltation of the immortal 'soul' inherent in each human being resulted, however, in the very reverse of what was intended. Passions, Nietzsche noted in section 76, become evil and perfidious when they are regarded in an evil and perfidious manner. In this way Christianity came to regard Eros and Aphrodite – major powers capable of being idealized – as hellish kobolds and forgers of hallucinations, arousing conscience-stricken torments in believers whenever they were seized by sexual excitements. Was it not dreadful, Nietzsche exclaimed, anticipating Freud, to see perfectly regular and necessary impulses transformed into a source of inner wretchedness – all the more pernicious for being kept secret and thus more deeply rooted? And is it not the trait of petty souls to regard the enemy as being necessarily evil? But this demonization of Eros had a comic outcome:

> . . . the 'devil' Eros gradually became more interesting to human beings than all the angels and the saints, thanks to the covert whispering and secretiveness of the Church in all erotic matters. It has had the effect, quite

obvious down to our own times, that the *love story* has become the sole real interest that is common to all circles of society – an exaggeration that would have seemed incomprehensible to antiquity, and which in later times will doubtless provoke laughter.

In one of the concluding aphorisms of Book I – entitled 'At the Death-Bed of Christianity' – Nietzsche roundly declared that 'truly active human beings' no longer took Christianity seriously. Middle-class intellectuals had so watered down its interdictions that it had become a tender, cushion-soft moralism. No matter how 'advanced' Europe might consider itself to be, in religious matters it had not yet attained the free-minded naïveté of the ancient Brahmans: those wise sages who, 4,000 years ago, had reached the conclusion, first, that the priests are mightier than the gods, and, second, that it was in religious customs and practices – prayers, ceremonials, sacrifices, songs and metrical chants – that resided the power of the priests (aphorism 96). One step further – the gods were tossed aside, 'what Europe must sometime also do. Yet another step, priests and intermediaries were no longer needed, and along came the teacher of the *Religion of Self-Redemption*, Buddha – but how far Europe still is from this stage of culture!'

One of Nietzsche's most persistent reproaches against Christianity was that it had developed into a doctrine of implicit self-abasement, thus robbing Man of what should be his self-reliant dignity and independence. Thanks to the very notion of human sinfulness the all-perceiving, omniscient God of the Christians had been transformed into an omnipresent, intrusively obnoxious keyhole peeper, a divine 'Big Brother'. In an aphorism deceptively entitled 'The Shame of the Bestowers' (464), Nietzsche minced no words in expressing his profound disgust at this inescapably belittling notion of divine intrusiveness. For if, as was naïvely believed, God was everywhere omnipresent in Nature, then 'everything is again unfree and apprehensive. What? Never to be allowed to be alone with oneself? Never more to be unwatched, unprotected, not held on a leash, unspoiled and uncoddled? When there is always someone else around us, what is best in courage and goodness in the world is made impossible.'

Five years later, when he added a preface to *Morgenröte*, Nietzsche compared his philosophical labours to those of a miner or even of a mole, actively burrowing beneath the bright blooms and verdant foliage of moral injunctions and ideals, in order to reveal the covertly self-centred, egotistically self-flattering impulses that often underlie the most 'altruistic' motives. Social intercourse, far from being a kind of happy forum in which individuals strive to be genuinely kind and benevolent towards each other, is in reality an arena of ceaseless friction, contest and competition, in which individuals, usually without realizing it, seek to manifest a superiority over others; for even the simplest argument is a battle of conflicting opinions in which each partner wishes to 'prove' that he or she is 'right' and the other 'wrong'. This striving for superiority, which Nietzsche did not hesitate to call a desire for *power*, could, like its opposite, the desire to conceal one's sense of weakness and inferiority, assume the weirdest and most deceptive forms. For example (aphorism 351), in conversations people often lay traps, not out of any innate nastiness but simply to derive pleasure from a display of their own superior cleverness or subtlety. Many 'kind' persons (aphorism 215) devote themselves to charity and 'good deeds' essentially to enhance their self-esteem and to make others feel ashamed of their selfishness, thereby secretly humiliating them and establishing over them their own moral superiority. (The tragically short-lived Diana, Princess of Wales, is a classic example of this inner need for psychological 'compensation'.)

Similarly, not to appear or feel inferior is one of the most constant concerns of every individual. Simply trying to justify oneself (aphorism 372) is almost an admission of weakness. Indeed, Nietzsche claimed (aphorism 377) that it was to conceal and overcome a profound sense of weakness that the Jews invented the 'Love thy enemies!' ideal; just as it was those who had been most abominably wanton who glorified chastity. In its extremest form, self-hatred – what Nietzsche's successor, Alfred Adler, later called the 'inferiority complex' – could induce human beings to flee from a sense of their own failings by displaying a suspect 'charity' to others. For, as Nietzsche added (aphorism 516), it is precisely this – 'to flee and hate one's ego and to live in others and for others, which people have hitherto so thoughtlessly as well as confidently termed "*unegotistical*" *and consequently* "*good*".' A form of self-abasement, of shame, of flight from one's own culture which, by the end of the second Christian millennium, was encouraging many abject excesses in the hallowed name of 'multi-culturism'.

The three midsummer months Nietzsche spent in the village of Sils-Maria were, in terms of health and weather, more tempestuous than calm. July, by Engadine standards, was unusually hot, with successive thunderstorms, each of which laid him low with another nervous seizure. August was no better, with dramatic changes of temperature and, in the middle of the month, a wintry snowfall and such an onset of cold that in his small, unheated, pine-walled room Nietzsche suffered a chilblained finger and had to write to his mother and sister in Naumburg, begging them to send him a pair of gloves and thick woollen stockings. In a letter written to

Heinrich Köselitz he observed wrily that, instead of coming to the Engadine, he would have been better advised to go to Paris for the big Electricity Exposition – not, however, as a spectator but as a prize exhibit, 'for in this particular I am probably more receptive than any other person, to my ill luck'. September brought little relief, with alternating days of rain, snow and thunder.

His changes of mood were as unstable as the weather, varying from tearful rapture, when he felt himself 'uplifted' by some luminous thought during his long walks through the woods, to moments of deep gloom brought on by the feeling that he had been abandoned by his friends, several of whom (like Erwin Rohde) had not bothered to write him thank-you letters for their gift copy of *Morgenröte.*

Persuaded that his was a very special case, about which he knew more than any of the more or less 'quack' doctors he had consulted in the past, Nietzsche followed his own dietary régime. It now included meat as well as macaroni for the midday meal, and in the evening two raw egg-yolks and a plateful of polenta – the standard supper fare for local farmers and shepherds. As ever an 'early bird', he got up at five o'clock in the morning and began the day by washing himself from head to foot with cold water from the porcelain jug and basin in his room. When not forced to remain in bed, he spent five or more hours walking through the dense pine forests. From 7 to 9 p.m. he sat in the dark to give his eyes a rest – as he had done at Genoa where, as he wrote to his mother on 24 August, he was always back home 'every evening without exception from six o'clock on; never theatre concerts, etc. You cannot imagine how thriftily, indeed how *stingily* I have to husband my *intellectual* powers and my time, so that such a suffering and imperfect being as myself can nonetheless bear *ripe fruit* . . . '

The 'ripe fruit' were five more 'chapters' (i.e. collections of aphorisms and brief essays) he wished to add as a second, follow-up volume to *Morgenröte*. He could not write for more than fifteen minutes at a time without having to lie down to rest his eyes. Forced to ration the time devoted to reading, he forwent the pleasure of reading music scores or works of fiction, restricting himself to books on scientific subjects. The one exception was a book Kuno Fischer had devoted to Spinoza, in whom Nietzsche now belatedly discovered a kindred soul who had rejected the Cartesian notion of free will, all teleological notions concerning the future of mankind, and who had bravely defended individual egotism and challenged traditional notions as to what in daily life is truly 'bad'.

In the last letter addressed from Sils-Maria to Heinrich Köselitz, on the eve of his return to Genoa on 22 September, Nietzsche wrote that the past three months had been dangerous times during which '*Death* stared down on me, I suffered terribly all summer long. Whereto should I [now] turn! That a sky with long months of purity has become a *vital requirement* for me, I now fully realize . . . Just think, in all, up here, I have had 10 endurable days, and the bad days brought me woes as ghastly as any I suffered in Basel.'

The uncomfortable downhill trip from the Alpine highlands to Genoa was once again prolonged agony, which left Nietzsche so weakened that not until 4 October (five days after his departure from Sils-Maria) could he muster the strength to send a postcard to his mother and sister, saying that he had made it safely to the great seaport. In Genoa he was suffering, but in a way that made it "*humanly possible*" to live, whereas life in the Engadine had been sheer 'cruelty to animals . . . I can live only near the sea.' To Franz Overbeck he wrote that he was back 'in my city of Genoa, the most unmodern that I know and at the same time brimming over with life – totally unromantic in a way, and yet uncommon to a degree: so I will go on living here under the protection of my *local* patron saints – Columbus, Paganini and Mazzini, who *together* represent their city well'.

Unfortunately his three heroes were unable to control the elements, which throughout the month of October blew and blustered and erupted into drenching thunderstorms, causing him incessant suffering. But then, without warning, the unruly elements calmed down, the dark clouds vanished, a bright Mediterranean sun dried out the wet city. The weather was now so mild that in the evening he could sit in a vineyard with, below and around him, sea, mountains, villas. The surest sign of improved health and spirits was a renewed interest in operatic music – aroused by Rossini's *Semiramide* and Bellini's Romeo and Juliet opera (*I Capuletti ed I Montecchi*), which so enchanted him that he saw and heard it four times.

Eager to show the new, handwritten sections of *Morgenröte II* to his invaluable copyist and proofreader, Nietzsche invited Heinrich Köselitz to visit him, offering to pay the train-trip to Genoa and back. Köselitz, who was now trying desperately to write another comic opera – this time along the lines of Cimarosa's *Matrimonio segreto* – was, however, unwilling to leave Venice. He thus deprived himself of the pleasure of attending the Genoese première of Bizet's *Carmen*. In a letter written to his devoted admirer on 28 November, Nietzsche resorted to superlatives in an effort to convey the impression of surprise and novelty he had just experienced: 'A truly French talent for *comic opera*, not in the least disoriented by Wagner, on the contrary a real disciple of H[ector] Berlioz. I had [not] thought that *something like this* was possible! It looks as though the French are on a better path in dramatic music; and they have a head-start over the Germans in one essential point: with them passion is nowhere near as *reiterated* (as for example are *all* passions with Wagner).'

Hard on the heels of this musical 'discovery' came the good news, transmitted with a personally signed betrothal card, that Carl von Gersdorff had freed himself at last from his woefully misfitted passion for the volatile Nerina Finochietti and was now engaged to marry a young lady named Martha Nitzsche – a distant Saxon relative whom Fritz had met years ago at her parents' home near Leipzig. Nietzsche wrote to congratulate the bridegroom-to-be for having in such a *grandiose* manner ended the 'eclipse' that had long darkened their friendship. That same day (18 December) he sent Köselitz a postcard announcing the good news. 'Wish me good luck and *bright* weather!' he added. For in the absence of a badly needed typewriter, which he had ordered from a Copenhagen manufacturer, he would have to pick up his pen and laboriously write out the manuscript pages of a new work intended to add five more chapters to the already published five of *Morgenröte*.

Köselitz's prompt response – once again offering to provide author, publisher and printer with a legible text – was such heartening news that the next day Fritz penned an unusually long and cheery pre-Christmas letter to his mother and sister in Naumburg. Genoa had turned out to be his 'happiest find in terms of health and intellectual undisturbedness'. Its streets, no matter how steep or suburbanly located, were magnificently paved with smooth and solid stones. 'I have a very bright, *very high* room – that has a good effect on my mood . . . Close by there is a charming garden, which is open to the public, with thick woodlike greenery (even in *winter*), waterfalls, wild animals and birds, and splendid vistas over sea and mountains.'

A miserable Christmas, marred by a major paroxysmic fit, probably due to excessive inspiration, was followed by an extraordinary spell of fine weather – no wind, no clouds, no rain! – which made the month of January 1882 the most wonderful Fritz had ever enjoyed. One Genoese old-timer assured him that he had never seen anything like it in more than three-score years. It was so unseasonally mild that Nietzsche could sit out of doors in the morning without feeling at all cold, and by the end of the month the peach-trees were bursting prematurely into blossom – to the consternation of fruit-growers who knew that a touch of frost could wipe out their annual crop.

Buoyed by the splendid weather, Nietzsche by the middle of the month had virtually completed the third of the planned five chapters of *Morgenröte* II. On 28 January he sent the manuscript – Books VI to VIII – to Köselitz in Venice. Writing the next day to Franz Overbeck in Basel, he explained that to complete the final two he needed '*fresh* strength for it and the *deepest* solitude (Dr Rée is coming next week). Perhaps in some wood this summer, I may find a month that will give me both.'

On 4 February Paul Rée reached Genoa, bringing with him a Danish typewriter, which had been slightly damaged in its loosely assembled wooden casing during a bumpy trip on successive trains. A Genoese mechanic was summoned to repair the damage. Writing the next day to Fritz's sister Elisabeth in Naumburg, Rée said that never since their first meeting in Basel in 1872 had he seen her brother looking so well and in such high spirits. He was living in a cosy room which, though situated in the heart of the city, was wonderfully quiet since it overlooked a monastery past which no carriages were allowed to pass.

The afternoon of Rée's arrival in Genoa Nietzsche took him down to the shore, where they stretched out – like 'two sea-urchins' – on the sun-warmed sand. To his surprise, Rée found Genoa almost as beautiful as Naples. 'We were afraid,' he added in his 5 February letter to Elisabeth, 'that the unusual amount of talking might have somewhat upset him for today, but this morning he came to see me' – in a nearby house, where Fritz had found a room for him – 'looking as healthy and cheerful as yesterday. We are to meet again at two o'clock, go down to the sea, and this evening Sarah.'

The 'Sarah' in question was none other than France's most celebrated actress, Sarah Bernhardt, who had agreed to enliven Genoa's carnival season by playing the tragic role of Marguerite Gautier in the younger Alexandre Dumas's *La Dame aux Camélias*. To the bitter disappointment of Nietzsche and his friend, the Genoa première was a lamentable fiasco. 'After the first act,' as Fritz wrote to his mother and sister, 'she fell down as though dead. After an embarrassing hour of waiting she went on playing, but in the middle of the third act she burst a blood vessel on the stage – and then it was all over . . . Nonetheless she played again the very next day and on the following evenings with huge success . . . She reminded me' – and this, coming from Fritz, was the acme of high praise – 'of Frau Wagner.'

If Nietzsche did not try a second time to see Sarah Bernhardt play the role of Dumas's consumptive beauty at the Carlo Felice theatre, it was because the next morning the all too familiar symptoms reappeared: he suddenly felt weak, and in the afternoon he fainted. That night he succumbed to a paroxysmal seizure, which forced him to remain in bed all of the next day. The fifth day he managed to get up, but he had to lie down again in the afternoon. 'In short,' as he wrote to his mother and sister on 10 February, 'we must still learn to be together. It is much too agreeable to converse with Dr Rée.'

This severe attack, according to Paul Rée, was the only serious one of its kind during the five weeks he spent in Genoa. Throughout, as Rée reported to Elisabeth, her brother's mood was 'a cheerful one. In appearance he looks like a stripling; his landlady refused to believe that he is closer to 40 . . . Actually, his constitution is quite extraordinary, and to me incomparably tough. One day of travel exhausts me more than a three-day seizure your brother. As soon as it is over, he can again take long hikes, and is mentally fresh and alert.'

Towards the end of Rée's stay, Nietzsche took him up Genoa's curving coast as far as Monte Carlo, in whose famous casino, as Fritz reported to his mother and sister on 4 March, he did not play while 'Rée at least did not lose. It is as regards position, natural beauty, art, and human beings, the paradise of hell . . . This entire coast is unbelievably expensive, as though money had no value,' added the relatively impecunious Fritz.

His claim that Rée had lost no money at the roulette-wheel was a glib falsehood, designed to conceal the embarrassing truth from Franziska and Elisabeth Nietzsche, who were likely to pass on the news to Paul Rée's mother, with whom both were now on friendly terms. For by the time he left Genoa, Paul Rée was so 'strapped' that he had to borrow some money from Nietzsche to pay for the train fare to Rome, which he had been invited to visit by their former Sorrento hostess, Malwida von Meysenbug.

Among the many subjects discussed during Rée's five weeks in Genoa, two were of urgent concern to Nietzsche. The first was the problem of his next 'refuge' – a cool, temperate spot offering plenty of shade for his daily walks, where he could spend a not too torrid summer. The other problem that was troubling Nietzsche concerned his weak eyesight. The Danish typewriter, even after it had been repaired, offered him scant relief, since he had to squint even more closely at the unfamiliar keyboard and the inserted paper to make sure that he was hitting the right key with his index or other fingers. 'This machine,' as he typed to Franz Ovebeck, 'is as delicate as a small dog and causes a lot of trouble – and some amusement. What my friends must invent for me is a *Vorlese-Maschine*' [a reading-out-loud-machine] 'otherwise I am bound to fall behind and will no longer be able to provide myself sufficiently with intellectual nourishment. Or rather: I need to have a young person nearby, who is sufficiently intelligent and well educated to be able to *work* with me. Even a two-year marriage would serve this purpose – in which case of course a couple of other requirements would have to be taken into account.'

There was more in this than whimsical irony. It was a question Nietzsche must have discussed with Paul Rée – he who at Sorrento had so dutifully performed this service, reading to him, to Malwida von Meysenbug, and to the consumptive Albert Brenner during those pleasant evenings by the fireplace, throughout the autumn, winter and early spring of 1877–8. Heinrich Köselitz had performed the same service during the fifteen weeks Nietzsche had spent with him in Venice in the spring of 1880. But Köselitz, who seemed in no hurry to return his latest manuscript, had made it quite clear that for the next six months at least he could not devote more than an hour per day of his precious time to anything other than the Italo-German or German-Italian 'comic opera' he was anxious to complete.

Although in the end nothing had come of the fond dream that Nietzsche, his sister Elisabeth, Paul Rée and Malwida von Meysenbug had once harboured of founding a creative 'colony', 'monastery', or 'Epicurean garden' of 'free spirits', the months spent at Sorrento had lingered on as a kind of beautiful ideal with all of them – and not least of all with Paul Rée. Had it been otherwise, the extraordinary events that now occurred could not have taken place nor be rationally explicable.

From the moment Paul Rée reached Rome in mid-March he began bombarding Nietzsche with letters about Malwida von Meysenbug and her beautifully located apartment on the via della Polveriera, overlooking the Capitol and the more distant Colosseum. (These letters later disappeared, so that one can only guess what they contained from Nietzsche's brief replies.) 'Aunt Malwida', who received Rée with motherly solicitude, was delighted to learn that Nietzsche, despite his sufferings, seemed in extraordinarily good health and looked astonishingly young and vigorous. When Rée explained their friend's present predicament – his anxious search for a cool, well-forested 'refuge' where he could spend the summer – the good Malwida recommended Pieve di Cadore, a lovely old town in the foothills of the Dolomites, where the painter Titian had spent the first years of his life. Rée promptly transmitted the recommendation. But much of his letters were devoted to an extraordinary creature he had met in Malwida von Meysenbug's salon, where friends of hers met regularly to discuss literary topics. She was a talented young poetess from the Russian capital of St Petersburg who had spent a year as an auditor at the University of Zürich studying philosophy, psychology and theology. Lively, sharp-witted, she had amazed Rée by the iconoclastic audacity of her opinions on almost any subject. She was totally unaffected by any religious or moral prejudices – she had long since lost her faith in the god of her pulpit preachers – and yet seemed to be eagerly seeking some new kind of ideal on which to pin her hopes. In short, she was an extraordinary phenomenon, a creature of the kind they had long since thought did not exist, an authentic feminine *Freigeist* who, when Rée and Malwida had begun talking about Nietzsche, had exclaimed: 'That's somebody I must meet!'

On 21 March Nietzsche, using the Danish typewriter to make his letter more legible, wrote to Malwida von Meysenbug to say how pleased he had been to learn that she had never ceased to believe that he would one day enter a 'second existence'. He hoped that she would live for many, many years, long enough to derive enjoyment from his writing; but he himself could not accelerate the pace nor alter the 'curve' described by the trajectory of his life. 'I must go on being *young* for a long, long time, even though I am already approaching the forties.'

To Paul Rée he wrote immediately afterwards to say that he had received the 30 francs that Rée had sent him as an initial reimbursement for the cost of the railway fare to Rome. After which he added: 'Give this Russian lady my greetings if this makes any sense: I long lustily for souls of this species. Yes,' he went on, resorting once again to the predatory language he had used in his first letter to Reinhart von Seydlitz, 'I will soon be on the prowl for such [souls]. Marriage is quite another matter – I could only agree at the very most to a two-year marriage, and this only with respect to what I have to do in the next ten years.'

Two days later Nietzsche sent a postcard to Rée, first to thank him for having more than reimbursed him for the travel fare to Rome, secondly to report that the typewriter, for baffling reasons, was no longer working as it should, and finally to admit that he had just spent several wretched days (headaches, vomiting, etc.). 'Ah, this damned cloud-electricity!' he lamented. 'Should I really be crazy enough to approach the *mountains* again?' he asked, clearly thinking of Pieve di Cadore, in the foothills of the Dolomites. 'Life by the seaside is what for me is easiest to endure. But where is the sea-spot that has enough *shade* for me! è una miseria!'

To Heinrich Köselitz he wrote the next day to say that he was leaving Genoa the following week and that he would not be troubling him again for another two months. 'Thank God – you will say.' To his sister Elisabeth he sent one more postcard on 27 March, saying that the weather was now so damp and his typewriter so sticky that the letters seemed to have dissolved into illegible blobs. 'I will write, *as soon as I have* a fixed summer domicile; but that will perhaps take quite a long time!'

The 'long time' proved much shorter than Fritz had envisaged. His next postcard, written four days later, was sent from – of all places – the ancient seaport of Messina, strategically located near the treacherous straits once haunted by the six-headed, dog-barking Scylla and the equally monstrous water-spouting Charybdis, for whose possession Greeks, Persians, Carthaginians, Romans, Saracens, Norman crusaders, German emperors and Spanish monarchs had successively fought over the centuries, and from whose magnificent, sickle-shaped harbour Don Juan of Austria (and incidentally a certain Miguel de Cervantes) had sailed forth with a mighty European fleet to defeat the Ottoman Turks at the battle of Lepanto in the year of grace 1571.

CHAPTER 26

# Lou Salomé

*– Overly intellectual men need marriage, but resist it as much as they would a nasty medicine.*

We know little about Nietzsche's voyage from Genoa to Messina – except that it was made on a brig or schooner bound for Sicily, of which he was the only passenger. Disconcerting to his friends though it was, this 'bold leap' was not a totally irrational caprice. The musicologist and biographer Curt Paul Janz has suggested that the restless philosopher was drawn towards Sicily by the powerful attraction of a 'magnet' – in the person of Richard Wagner, who, having, like Malwida von Meysenbug, discovered that the winters in Bayreuth could be unpleasantly harsh, had decided to spend the Christmas season of 1881 and the first weeks of 1882 in the orange-and-lemon-scented city of Palermo.

Like Byron, like Goethe's Wilhelm Meister, Nietzsche was gripped by a powerful *Wanderlust*, a psychic antidote to his all too sedentary existence. He felt a Dionysian need to free himself from the mental stranglehold of critical cogitation and to give vent to his 'creative' genius, which – now that he had abandoned musical compositions – expressed itself spontaneously in verse.

The first of these light-hearted poems was a seven-stanza ballad honouring a small brig, *Das Engelchen* (*The Little Angel*), in which the lilting overtones, built around the word *Mädchen* (maiden or girl) were more sentimental and erotic than angelic. Heading for Messina, where the 'free-spirited' trajectory of his life might possibly intersect Richard Wagner's, was his way of tempting fate, of surprising everyone, including himself, in a word of 'living dangerously' – as he had recently put it in an aphorism ('Well preparing men') that was destined to become a fateful watchword for future generations.

His sudden, southward 'lunge' resulted in a narrow miss. By the time he reached Messina, probably on the last day of March, the Wagners had come and gone – on their way to Rome. Nietzsche in any case would have been in no condition to meet them. As he wrote to his mother and sister on 1 April, the marine voyage unleashed a nervous fit that 'fully resembled sea-sickness: when I came to, I found myself in a pretty bed by a quiet cathedral square; in front of my window a pair of palm-trees . . . I must, after the bad experiences of the last few years, make the attempt to live by the sea also in the summer.'

Of the three and a half weeks Nietzsche spent in the imposing baroque city of Messina we know only slightly more than we do about his marine voyage from Genoa. It was here that he completed most of the fourth part of *Morgenröte* II, which he finally decided to turn into a separate work, entitled *Die fröhliche Wissenschaft* – literally 'the joyous science', or 'joyous knowledge' in the older, broader meaning of the German word, and for which he himself later chose the sprightly Provençal title of *la gaya scienza*.

To Heinrich Köselitz he sent a postcard on the 8th, saying that he had reached the 'rim of the earth' – there where, according to Homer, '*happiness* is supposed to dwell'. Never in his life had he been so pampered and coddled and in such a friendly fashion by his 'fellow townsfolk' as during the past week. On another postcard, sent the same day to Franz Overbeck, he announced a bit too confidently: 'Reason has *triumphed*.' Recent summers in the mountains had convinced him that 'getting closer to the clouds' aggravated his physical condition, so he was now going to try to spend a *summer by the sea*.

There was one thing Fritz neglected to mention on his postcards to his mother and sister and Franz Overbeck, for it would have punctured his absurd claim that Messina was ideally suited to the exacting demands of his precarious health: there was only one place in the city where he could take long, well-shaded walks. He candidly admitted this 'drawback' in a postcard sent to Paul Rée, who immediately replied from Rome to express his stupefaction over Nietzsche's whereabouts. And not only his own, but that of the young Russian prodigy, who was so eager to meet and talk to Nietzsche that she had been planning to return to Zürich via Genoa. 'She is,' added Rée, 'an energetic, unbelievably clever being, with girlish, even childish qualities.' Rome, in the month of May, Rée concluded, 'would not be for you. But the Russian girl you must absolutely get to know.'

Writing from Basel on 20 April, Franz Overbeck had frankly doubted that Fritz would be able to hold out for long in the 'half-Punic zone' where his nomadic friend had chosen to pitch his tent for the summer. And, sure enough, within days a hot wind, blowing out of the sub-Carthaginian desert, drove the bold wanderer from the friendly city of Messina. It chased him through the Straits of Messina and up the Calabrian coast all the way to Naples, where, finally yielding to the magnetic gravity of two dear friends (Paul Rée and 'Aunt Malwida') and to the astral attraction of a mysterious new 'star', Friedrich Nietzsche bowed his head to Fate and boarded a train for Rome.

The bewitching siren about whom Paul Rée had written to Nietzsche in such ecstatic terms was named Lou Salomé. Like Paul Rée and Malwida too, she was partly of French Huguenot descent. Born in February 1861 – and thus sixteen years younger than Nietzsche, eleven years younger than Rée, she was the pampered daughter of a Baltic German who in the pro-German climate of St Petersburg – both Nicholas I and Alexander II had German wives as well as mothers – had risen to become a general and a well-paid senior official in the Tsarist Army's General Staff. A timid, introverted, headstrong child, she had been brought up in conditions of cosmopolitan affluence with the assistance of a French and of a Russian governess. She worshipped her handsome father – an 'affectionate tyrant' and god-on-earth figure – as much as she detested her mother, Louise, who vainly sought to discipline her. At the German school she was forced to attend, she was a listless student, who soon rebelled against the Pietistic Lutheranism of the teachers. When, with the start of puberty, she lost her faith in God, altogether too silent and remote to satisfy her narcissistic craving for a truly intimate god-on-earth, she felt lost and abandoned.

Such was the fragile, high-strung, anxious creature who after her father's death in 1878 had been urged by a sympathetic aunt to go and listen to the controversial sermons of an ultra-liberal theologian, Hendrik Gillot, who held forth at the Dutch Evangelical Reformed Chapel on the Nevsky Prospect. Strongly influenced by Hegel, Gillot, who like the Salomés was of French Huguenot descent, had developed a four-stage philosophy of religious evolution, culminating in Christianity – more exactly in the 'authentic' kind that Jesus had taught, according to which the Kingdom of God is within one and not, as his disciples had come to regard it, a form of 'salvation' promised to devout believers in a blissful afterlife. The moment she laid eyes on this inspired Dutchman – with his flaxen hair, his sensual mouth and 'the eyes of a demonic apostle' (Rudolph Binion's description) – the seventeen-year-old Lou Salomé was transfixed. She sought him out and he, quickly sensing the intensity of her burning interest in religious and philosophical problems, became her spiritual mentor, her psychological father-confessor. She learned Dutch in order to be able to read Immanuel Kant's *Critiques* in Gillot's annotated copy; he taught her to revere Spinoza's altruistic love of God, a pure love so untainted by any trace of selfishness that it demands no token of affection in exchange. Not long after her confirmation, carried out at her insistence in Gillot's Dutch home town of Haarlem, the headstrong Lou had experienced a dramatic spiritual 'let-down'. Spinoza had taught her the value of self-reliance. Since Hendrik Gillot was married and inaccessible – or was he? for in her erotico-religious fantasies she began to discern in his keen interest the mirror-image of her own unassuaged desires – she realized that from now on she would have to live for herself without the help of her theological mentor or even of his God. Hendrik Gillot, however, had ignited within her an intellectual fire, a burning thirst for knowledge and experience, which could no longer be extinguished. Disregarding her mother's warnings, she continued frantically reading and studying, developed insomnia, heartaches, coughs and what seemed to be a form of incipient consumption, with occasional bleeding in the lungs. Seriously alarmed, Louise Salomé had finally decided that she would have to leave the harsh northern climate of St Petersburg and take her daughter south and westward to the more temperate climate of Switzerland. In the autumn of 1880 Lou Salomé was accordingly registered and allowed to attend lectures as a female auditor at the University of Zürich. Here she studied Hegel and supplemented her precocious erudition by reading extracts from the Hindu *Rig-Veda*, the pre-Socratic philosophers of ancient Greece, Confucius and the *Tao-teh-king*, the German mystic Jakob Böhme, Goethe and Victor Hugo. She also joined a literary circle presided over by Gottfried Kinkel, an elderly professor of art and archaeology who, like Malwida von Meysenbug, had been an ardently republican supporter of the revolutionary movements of 1848. He it probably was who drew the young Lou Salomé's attention to Malwida von Meysenbug's *Memoirs of an Idealist* which, since its first appearance in 1876, had become a bible for young women seeking ways to further the cause of feminine emancipation. When Louise Salomé decided to take her ailing daughter over the Alps to various resort towns in Italy, it was to Kinkel that the young Lou wrote, asking him for a letter of recommendation to Malwida.

Still chaperoned by her mother, Lou Salomé reached Rome in early February of 1882, in time to celebrate her twenty-first birthday amid the joyful tumult of the carnival season. Desperately anxious to free herself from irksome maternal surveillance, she lost no time delivering Gottfried Kinkel's letter of introduction to Malwida von Meysenbug's elegant villa. The good Malwida responded by inviting her and her mother to tea. Impressed by the young Lou's poetic gifts and effusive enthusiasm for her own 'respectable' form of idealism, Malwida was happy to have the young poetess join her 'literary circle'.

It was into one of these exquisitely refined literary soirées, attended almost exclusively by polite, high-minded ladies, that on 17 March Paul Rée had suddenly burst – like a gust of wind blowing open a window. Or so it seemed to the delighted young Lou Salomé. Here at last was something startlingly new, unsettling, different! Years later she could still vividly recall the scene: a sudden tinkle of the doorbell, answered by the faithful Trina, hurrying to the entrance and then returning to whisper a mysterious message into her mistress's ear. 'Whereupon Malwida hastened over to her lovely old desk, quickly gathered together some money and took it with her. When she returned to the room, she was laughing, but the fine black-silk kerchief was still fluttering from excitement on her head. Next to her walked in the young Paul Rée: a friend of hers of many years standing (whom she loved like a son), who, having just arrived post-haste from Monte Carlo, wanted to repay the waiter from whom he had cadged the money for the trip, after he had quite literally and utterly gambled away everything.'

It was of course absurd to imagine that a man who had just gambled away all his money playing the roulette wheel could have persuaded a mere 'waiter' at the Monte Carlo casino to lend him the money needed to pay the train fare to the distant city of Rome. But what one wishes to believe can easily 'colour' an eye-witness's experience of an unexpected happening, and the 'tall tale' in this case was what the bored Lou Salomé wanted to believe. How wonderfully reckless, bohemian, even Russian it all was! A man capable of gambling away his money in Monte Carlo and then persuading the croupier to finance his train-trip to Rome was someone worth knowing, a gift from the gods!

Lou Salomé virtually admitted as much in the next paragraph of her memoirs, which were written in the early 1930s, half a century after this memorable evening of March 1882.

> This funny, sensational prelude to our friendship disturbed me astonishingly little . . . In any case I was immediately drawn to his [Paul Rée's] sharply cut profile and his deep-set eyes, in which at that moment could be glimpsed a touch of humorous contrition mixed with a touch of benevolent superiority.
>
> That same evening, as daily from then on, our eager conversations ended only after we had left Malwida's Via della Polveriera and had wended our way slowly back to the *pensione* where my mother and I were lodged. These walks by moon and starlight through the streets of Rome soon brought us so close together that a wonderful plot began to develop within me, whereby we could prolong them after my mother, who had brought me south from Zürich to convalesce, had returned home. To be sure, Paul Rée at the start committed a grave blunder by unfolding another plan to my mother, which made it infinitely more difficult for me to obtain her consent. I first had to make him understand that my love-life was 'closed for the duration of my life' and what my totally unbridled thirst for freedom impelled me to undertake.

The 'other plan' which, according to this account, Paul Rée is supposed to have unfolded to Lou's mother was nothing less than a proposal to marry her daughter. It seems highly unlikely, given Paul Rée's anything but impulsive character, that he ever made such a bold overture. The haste he furthermore displayed in writing to Nietzsche in Genoa, to tell him about this extraordinary Russian girl who shared his, and indeed their practical idealism, even going as far as to mention a possible marriage – not for himself, but for Nietzsche – would seem to disprove it. Nor is this all. Paul Rée, as he had once confessed in a letter to Nietzsche, had emerged 'disgusted' from his first love-affair; and it may well have been this reassuring weakness in his character which, no less than the sardonic wit, unconventional agnosticism and gentleness of manner, made him such an agreeable companion for the high-strung, amorously schizophrenic Lou Salomé, torn between a romantic desire to 'live life to the fullest' and an equally passionate and prohibitive determination not to be dominated by any man – unless, miraculously, he turned out to be of the rare 'man-god' species.

The extraordinary 'solution' Lou Salomé proposed for this philosophico-psychological dilemma was so scandalously unconventional that it could not but shock her mother and the prudish idealist Malwida von Meysenbug. Candidly admitting that it had first occurred to her as a kind of 'nocturnal dream', Lou Salomé later described her plan as being constructed around a 'pleasant work-study full of books and flowers, flanked by two bedrooms, with, coming to and fro between us, work comrades forming a merry and serious circle'. Although there was no mention of Nietzsche's name at this early stage of her account of this extraordinary scheme, it seems certain – from Rée's haste to communicate this astonishing 'good news' to his friend in Genoa – that Nietzsche from the outset was envisaged as being the very first of the carefully chosen 'work comrades' (*Arbeitskameraden*) to be invited to join this idyllic haven of intellectual intercourse and mutual enrichment, this 'Epicurean garden' of philosophical delights.

Paul Rée was thrown into such a dither of excitement by this extraordinary scheme that he came to see Malwida von Meysenbug about it, saying that for Lou's sake as well as his own he would have to hasten his departure from Rome. Malwida treated him to a stern lecture: she would bitterly regret seeing such a promising 'mental relationship' prematurely terminated, and she persuaded him to stay on. Then, after a 'heart-to-heart' talk with Lou Salomé, whose 'practical idealism' still struck her as a 'most noble occupation', Malwida wrote to Rée to say that she wanted to have no part in the execution of the Lou Salomé, scheme. 'It is always dangerous to tempt fate; that way one exposes oneself to mishaps, and what could at present and in retrospect remain pure, clear, and beautiful turns discordant and turbid.' Which, as we shall see, was exactly what happened – and, one is tempted to add, was fatally bound to occur.

Even more alarmed by this crazy scheme dreamed up by her fantast of a daughter was Louise Salomé, who wrote to Hendrik Gillot in St Petersburg, asking him to write to Lou in order to bring her back to the path of 'reason'. His letter of remonstrance has disappeared, but not Lou's indignant response. Bits of it are worth quoting, for they admirably transcribe the narcissistic determination of this wilful young lady to defy convention, no matter what the consequences might be. Who was he, she pointedly asked, to dismiss her plan as 'sheer fantasy' – a plan she intended to carry out with the aid of men who 'almost explode' with genuine intelligence and keenness of understanding? Her former mentor was quite mistaken in thinking that she was too young to be able properly to judge 'far older and superior men like Rée, Nietzsche and others . . . one knows immediately or not at all what is essential (and in *human* terms the essential for me is Rée *alone*). Rée is not completely won over, he is still a bit perplexed . . . Malwida too is against our plan, and that pains me, for I love her tremendously . . . I will most certainly construct my life according to myself, come what may . . . Happier than I am now can nobody be, for the fresh-pious-joyous war which may well break out does not frighten me at all, on the contrary, let it break out! We shall see if the 'insurmountable barriers' that the world has erected won't turn out to be as harmless as streaks of chalk.'

Those fighting words were penned on 26 March, just nine days after her first encounter with Paul Rée and more than three weeks before Nietzsche finally reached Rome. The alliterative combination of adjectives she used – *frisch*, *fromm*, *fröhlich* (fresh, pious, joyous) – to describe the war she intended to wage against puritanical conventions was a sarcastic adaptation of the four ideals, *frisch*, *fromm*, *fröhlich*, *frei* (fresh, pious, joyous, free), which in the early decades of the century a super-patriotic firebrand, Friedrich Ludwig Jahn, had advocated as the four essential pillars upon which a 'healthy' Germanic ethos or 'folkdom' (*Volkstum*) should be constructed.

Such was the situation when Nietzsche reached the Eternal City, so nervously upset and exhausted by the rhythmic pounding of the railway-carriage wheels beneath him that, on reaching his *albergo*, he had to spend the rest of the day in bed. The next day, 26 April, he turned up at the Villa Mattei, on the Via della Polveriera, where Malwida von Meysenbug was overjoyed to greet the 'vagabond son' she had not seen in close to four years. Nietzsche, likewise profoundly moved, told Malwida that it was years since he had enjoyed such a 'happy hour'. 'The poor man,' she went on in a letter

Nietzsche, aged 13, at the time of his confirmation

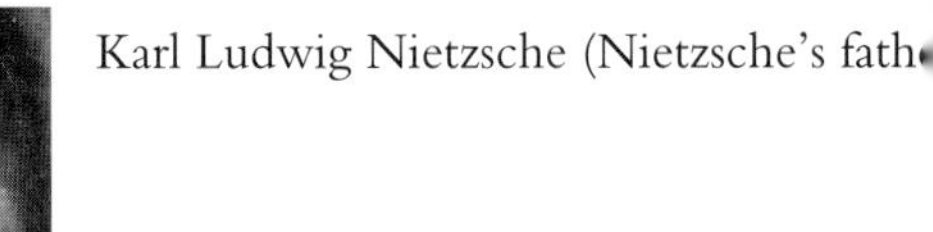

Karl Ludwig Nietzsche (Nietzsche's fath

Vicarage at Röcken

Franziska Nietzsche (Nietzsche's mothe

Elisabeth Nietzsche
(Nietzsche's sister)

Wilhelm Pinder

Rudelsburg Castle

Naumburg's Marktplatz (Markt)
(nineteenth century lithograph)

Carl von Gersdorff

Nietzsche (wearing glasses) as student graduating from Pfort (1864) (Photograph by G. Schultze, Naumburg)

Nietzsche holding a sabre, striking a military pose

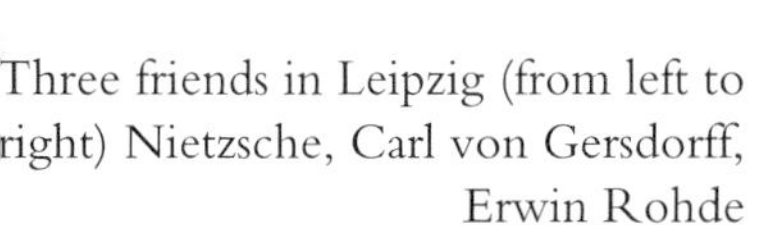

Three friends in Leipzig (from left to right) Nietzsche, Carl von Gersdorff, Erwin Rohde

Nietzsche as a student at Leipzig

Arthur Schopenhauer

Friedrich Ritschl.
Nietzsche's favourite Professor of Philology

Nietzsche, (third from left, back row) with members of the Philological Club he helped found in Leipzig

Cosima Wagner, drawing by Franz von Leubach

View from Wagn
house at Tribschen
over the Lake of
Four Cantons tow
the Bürgenst

Richard Wagner

w of Wagner's house
'ribschen

Malwida von Meysenbug

Heinrich Köselitz (alias 'Peter Gast'), composer and expert proofreader

ranz Overbeck (Professor of Theology)

Ida Overbeck (his wife)

Franziska Nietzsche's corner house on The Weingartenstraße in Naumburg

Lou Salomé

Friedrich Nietzsche in 1
(probably an engraving
made from a photograpl

Paul Rée (photograph taken by Ferreti in Naples)

Elisabeth Nietzsche

Photograph taken in Lucerne in August 1882 of Lou Salomé (holding whip and 'reins'), Paul Rée, Friedrich Nietzsche (as two workhorses)

Nietzsche's bedroom in the grocer-mayor's hc
(now a museum) in Sils-M

Sils Baseglia (village with steeple) next to Sils-Maria

View of Sils Lake, looking Southv

ietzsche with his mother in May 1892, after his mental collapse

Nietzsche in 1899, etching by Hans Olde

Nietzsche's sister Elisabeth Förster-Nietzsche in late-middle-aged widowhood

Chancellor Adolf Hi
visiting Elisabeth Först
Nietzsche in Weimar, 1

written the next day to her foster-daughter, Olga Herzen Monod, 'is truly a saint, endures his dreadful sufferings with heroic courage, has thereby grown even gentler, indeed almost jolly, and continues to work, even though he is almost blind, cannot read nor write (only with a machine), has absolutely nobody who helps and takes care of him, and very little money. He was enchanted by my [drawing-] room, which seemed to him miraculously beautiful compared to the wretched little rooms he has inhabited for the past four years. He looks quite well, only from his lovely eyes can one see that he has lost his power of sight.' Two days later Malwida wrote again to her foster-daughter in Paris to say that Nietzsche had returned to the villa and spent three hours talking to her. She had been amazed to discover how 'fresh and eternally effervescent' was his mind, despite his sufferings. 'He has spent almost his whole time here in bed, and has seen nothing of Rome save for the Villa Mattei and St Peter's.'

The momentous excursion to St Peter's had been carefully stage-managed by Paul Rée, who like an impatient alchemist had been waiting for weeks to see what kind of chemical reaction would take place when the softly smiling but inwardly incandescent Lou met the deceptively reserved iconoclast. Seated on a prayer-stool, Paul Rée pretended to be busy taking notes and recording his impressions of the huge basilica with what Lou Salomé later facetiously described as a combination of 'fervour and piety'. In the penumbral light of the great baroque interior the short-sighted Nietzsche had trouble making out the features of the young girl who stood waiting for him, with her auburn hair primly parted over the middle of her head, the deep-seated blue eyes at once inquisitive and fearful, and the equivocal smile that flitted around her often tight-pressed lips, in an attitude of hesitant defiance. To his sharper ear there was something a bit rasping and not particularly appealing about her voice when, finally, she opened her mouth to speak.

Well may the young Lou Salomé have been daunted by the oracular solemnity of Nietzsche's greeting: 'From what stars have we fallen here to meet?' Her first impression, she later wrote, was that of someone who, 'arriving from the desert and the mountains, wears the frockcoat of everyday people', but whose studied reserve was a mask donned to conceal his inner thoughts. 'For the superficial observer there was nothing particularly striking about him; this man of medium height, in his extremely simple but also carefully worn clothes, with a tranquil expression on his face and brown hair that was brushed back plainly, could have gone unperceived. The fine, extremely expressive lines around the mouth were almost hidden by a big, down-combed moustache; he had a soft laugh, a noiseless way of speaking, and a cautious, thoughtful way of walking, which caused a slight stoop in the shoulders . . . ' She was struck by Nietzsche's small, 'delicately modelled ears, of which he said that they were "true ears for hearing the unheard". There are men who to an unavoidable degree exhibit intelligence, no matter how much they twist and turn and hold up their hands before their revealing eyes (as though the hand was no less of a betrayer).' This was true of Nietzsche's 'incomparably beautiful and finely wrought hands and which he himself believed betrayed his intelligence. His eyes too betrayed him. Although half-blind, they had none of the searching, blinking quality which make so many short-sighted persons look unconsciously intrusive . . . His defective eyesight lent his features a very special kind of magic, for instead of reflecting changing impressions from outside, all they rendered was what was going on deep down within him.'

Although nervously upset by the train-trip from Naples, Nietzsche had reached Rome in an unusually sprightly mood. During his sun-blessed weeks in Messina he had given free rein to his poetic fancy by finishing a number of poems he had begun in Genoa. Now, for the first time in his life, he, who had hitherto proudly refused to contribute essays to any periodical carrying articles by others, had decided to send them to Ernst Schmeitzner for inclusion in the new monthly (*Internationale Monatsschrift*) which the Chemnitz publisher had launched at the beginning of the year. Nietzsche had also completed the fourth part of what was originally intended to become *Morgenröte* II, but which he now wanted Schmeitzner to publish as the concluding section of a separate new work, *Die fröhliche Wissenschaft* (*The Joyous Science*) – the title of which was intended to provide a challenging contrast to the 'gloomy' science of Christian theology, and indeed of theology in general. In the first aphorism (no. 276) of the now renumbered Book IV – entitled 'Sanctus Januarius' in honour of the unbelievably clement month of January he had spent in Genoa – he had boldly declared that for the rest of his lifetime he would continue to 'learn more and more', notably as regards the latest advances of science (though this was not specifically stated), and that his aim from now on would be to regard as 'beautiful that which is necessary in things – thus will I be one of those who make things beautiful. *Amor fati*: may that from now on be my love.'

When Nietzsche had written his apologia for accepting life and the world, with their pleasures and displeasures, as they are rather than as one would fancifully like them to be or not to be, he had stoically assumed that it was his predestined lot to remain a bachelor for the rest of his days. He was far too 'fragile a thinking animal' – this or similar phrases abound in his letters – to make a happy marriage possible. It would be asking too much of any wife to have to play the role of nurse (during his 'dark' moments of suffering) as well as of housewife – as his sister Elisabeth had so successfully managed to do for several years in Basel. But the pleasant memory of this sisterly solicitude had left behind it an aroma of regret. Had it been otherwise, Nietzsche could not conceivably have responded to Paul Rée's plea that he come to Rome immediately to meet a most extraordinary 'Russian girl' by saying that he was prepared to envisage the prospect of a 'two-year marriage'.

Nietzsche's first encounter with this 'energetic, unbelievably clever being' came very close to being a fiasco, so unimpressive did he find Lou Salomé. The meeting was arranged in a great hurry, before the nervously upset traveller had fully recovered from the dreadful discomforts of his trip from Messina. Both Paul Rée and Lou Salomé were afraid that her impatient mother might whisk her away from Rome before the 'Herr Professor Nietzsche' – the title alone was a guarantee of respectability – had a chance to 'present his respects' to Madame Salomé. To ward off this calamity, Rée was asked by the 'high-commanding Fräulein Lou' to intercede with her mother and to suggest that they all meet up again near Milan. The plot to move the stage of future meetings from Rome to the Italian lakes seems to have been hatched by Lou with astonishing determination and celerity. But the timetable was upset by another nervous attack, which laid Nietzsche low on the eve of his and Rée's planned departure for Milan. He may not even have been in a condition to 'present his respects' to Lou Salomé's mother at the appointed hour.

Not the least curious aspect of this extraordinary plot – hatched by the twenty-one-year-old Lou Salomé as a way of emancipating herself from maternal tyranny – was the major role played in its initial stages by the simultaneously prudish and 'progressively minded' Malwida von Meysenbug. In a long and singularly revealing letter written to her 'protégée' in late May, 'Aunt Malwida' confessed that it had been years since she had experienced such a deep feeling of tenderness for a young girl – as an astonishing 'resurrection' or reincarnation of her own idealistic youth. It was her belief that the natural intermingling of the sexes was 'the only [form of] progress and the *only* thing worth striving for, so that people can freely and openly consort with each other, but precisely without that form of intercourse which, even when it was no more than a kind of momentary excitement' (in other words, the gallantry and flirting that were fashionable in the eighteenth century) was the kind of 'levity and coquetry of the old society' that she was bent on reforming. For young girls to go on walks at night with young men – a pointed reference to Lou Salomé's and Paul Rée's moonlit strolls through the streets of Rome – was unseemly behaviour to be avoided at all costs, if, as Malwida hoped, they (i.e. including herself) were to provide an example to the world of persons who remaind faithful to a fundamental principle of upright behaviour. In impenitently Schopenhauerian language Malwida exhorted her young protégée to remain faithful to the high ideals she should be exemplifying in her conduct. 'You seem to me to be what I have so long wished to see, a lofty, pure apostle of our new faith, and such I would like to see you preserved. Consorting with noble men is agreeable and enhancing, but let it always remain on the tender borderline, there where the Will does not exercise its urgent drive . . . We need such pure, lofty figures equally removed from the unrestraints of nihilism as from the prudishness of the old world.'

Not for nothing had the good Malwida styled herself an 'idealist'. Vehemently opposed though she was to Paul Rée's 'basically false' (*grundfalsch*) philosophical views, she retained the hope that somehow he might still be intellectually influenced and sufficiently converted to become, along with Nietzsche, one of the pillars of a new circle of noble, idealistic souls rejuvenated by the presence – truly a godsend! – of this exceptionally gifted young virgin. In this way the 'spirit of Sorrento' could live on – even if she herself, for reasons of health and her sedentary fondness for Rome, could no longer play the role of a benevolent 'Mother Superior'.

Indeed, but for Malwida's high-minded exhortations, Paul Rée's envisaged flight from Lou Salomé and Rome would just as surely have been followed by Nietzsche's. For Nietzsche, clearly, was as much thrown into a 'dither' by the sudden intrusion into his bachelor existence of this unstable and destabilizing feminine element as was his friend Paul Rée.

Because of the delay caused by Nietzsche's latest nervous seizure he and Paul Rée were preceded rather than followed to Milan by Louise Salomé and her headstrong daughter. The rendezvous took place, more or less exactly as Lou had hoped and planned, at Orta, a town situated on a small lake of that name, narrowly separated by a mountain range from the southern extremity of Lake Maggiore.

The following day the foursome travelled up the lake to the foot of the *Monte sacro*, where a jealous Paul Rée was left behind to keep Madame Salomé company, while Lou followed Nietzsche up the mountainside. On the summit of the sacred mount, long revered by the Franciscans, Nietzsche subjected the eager, nervous, palpitating Lou to a rigorous cross-examination. She was an attentive listener and her intelligent replies seem to have impressed Nietzsche. Lou Salomé later reported to Malwida von Meysenbug that, to her surprise, she had found the supposedly god-scorning Nietzsche to be someone of a profoundly 'religious nature' (like herself). Years later, when questioned about this physical as well as spiritual 'ascension', she smiled enigmatically and said: 'Did I kiss Nietzsche on the Monte sacro? I no longer know.' Questions of this kind are crude, and Lou Salomé by then was posing for posterity.

When the two 'mountaineers' descended to the lakeside, hours later than expected, it was almost dark. Lou's worried mother treated her daughter to a tongue-lashing for disrespectful and unseemly behaviour, while Paul Rée sulked and made no attempt to conceal his annoyance over his exclusion from this philosophical 'initiation'. To soothe his ruffled feathers Lou, speaking of Nietzsche, gave him an answer worthy of La Gioconda: 'His very laughter is a deed.' Lou, her contrition notwithstanding, was radiant; and so too was Nietzsche, although, being the very opposite of an extrovert, he was careful not to betray his inner excitement. For the first time in his life he had found someone capable of becoming what he had assumed to be impossible: a feminine disciple, someone he could form and 'elevate' to the ideal of his dreams. Lou for her part had good reason to exult: she had overcome the exacting philosopher's initial reservations – so much so that he now seemed ready to accompany her and Paul Rée wherever they might choose to establish a 'trinitarian workshop' or philosophical 'Academy'.

The next day, when Nietzsche had to leave them to make a quick trip to Basel, it was agreed that they would meet again in Lucerne. Availing himself of Ida Overbeck's standing invitation, Nietzsche turned up quite unexpectedly at Franz's house on the Eulergasse and spent five days 'incognito' with his dear friends. Host and hostess were amazed by his healthy looks and suntan and their guest's newly found robustness and vitality – so different from what they had known in the past that not once during his stay did Nietzsche suffer a nervous fit. Seated at his usual place – a chair with its back to the living-room's white porcelain stove – he kept them up each evening until midnight, talking and listening, explaining his plans for the future, getting up every now and then to play the piano. He spoke of his desire to lead a less solitary life, one more 'open to contact with things and human beings'. In the young Lou Salomé he had found a feminine *alter ego*, someone who, like himself, had wrestled and suffered with an intense, youthful love of God. How candid he was in speaking about her, it is impossible to say; for, as Ida Overbeck observed years later in a long essay of reminiscence, Nietzsche in his conversations preferred to be allusive rather than exhaustive. 'He knew how to listen and take in, but never revealed himself completely or clearly. To hold himself back in concealment was for him a necessity; it was not truly a distrust towards others, rather it was a distrust towards himself and the response he encountered.'

In none of Nietzsche's books had there been the slightest suggestion that *Freigeisterei* (free-spiritedness) could be equated with the doctrine of 'free love' that the disciples of Claude-Henri de Saint-Simon, the intellectual father of French Socialism, had begun propounding in the 1820s. A philosopher who yielded to erotic passion would be betraying his vocation as a thinker. But – to quote Ida Overbeck again: 'A non-marital spiritually passionate relationship was an ideal he always cherished. Passion there was, but at the same time the wish not to let himself be swept away by it. It gave him reassurance that Rée should be the third member in the trio, and he expected much from this helpful, selfless being.'

On 8 May, during a stopover in Lucerne on his way to Basel, Nietzsche had written a note to Paul Rée, which ended: 'The future is completely sealed, but not "dark". I must absolutely speak once again with Frl. L [Fräulein Lou], in the Löwengarten, perhaps? In boundless gratitude your friend N.' The cross-examination on the *Monte sacro* had not been enough, and Nietzsche wanted to make sure that his astonished rapture had not got the better of his reason. Lou Salomé was just as eager to see Nietzsche, since without his cooperation her scheme for a 'trinitarian' study-group – a twenty-one-year-old student girl 'chaperoned' by two older 'instructors' – could not possibly be realized. Any form of marriage would end what little 'independence' Lou possessed – in the form of a modest annual allowance she had been granted in her father's will to cover her unmarried years. Besides, she had no intention of becoming anybody's slave, not least of all in an intimately physical sense.

Both she and Paul Rée were waiting on the platform for Nietzsche as the train from Basel puffed to a halt in the railway station of Lucerne. From the station they proceeded to the Löwengarten – a public park bounded on one side by an upjutting cliff-face, next to which the Danish sculptor Bertel Thorvaldsen had carved a monumental lion. Exactly what happened at this point in their stroll is anything but clear – except that Paul Rée was once again forced to allow Lou Salomé and Nietzsche to have a brief conversation alone. All she herself was willing to admit, in writing the story of her life fifty years later, was that Nietzsche, dissatisfied by the 'intervention Paul Rée had made on his behalf in Rome, wanted to explain himself with me, something he did near the Löwengarten in Lucerne'. The intimation clearly was that Nietzsche, after having made a first 'request for her hand' via Paul Rée in Rome, was now personally repeating his marriage proposal. It clearly suited her narcissistic vanity to have the world believe that the great philosopher had on two separate occasions made known a desire to marry her. But if such had really been the case, why had Nietzsche not made this 'second proposal' during the hours they had spent together on the summit of the *Monte sacro*? Reading between the lines of a singularly laconic prose, Lou's biographer Rudolph Binion concluded that in the Löwengarten she was apprehensively expecting a formal marriage proposal, which she was determined to repulse, if possible without hurting Nietzsche's ultra-sensitive masculine pride. To her intense relief, but also secret mortification, no marriage proposal was made.

The feeling of relief was understandably shared by Paul Rée, who once again for a moment had been forced into the unhappy position of what Stendhal used to call the *terzo incomodo* (the importunate third party). This probably explains the post-crisis gaiety of this particular afternoon, which reached its climax when an impish Lou prevailed on a reluctant Paul Rée, morbidly self-conscious about his unimpressive looks, and an obliging Nietzsche to pose for a local photographer. The extraordinary trio – or 'trinity', as the mischievous Lou preferred to call it – were thus immortalized for posterity against an Alpine backdrop featuring the snow-covered Jungfrau. In the foreground a resolute, clean-shaven Paul Rée lightly touched the shaft of a small cart with his left hand, while Nietzsche (who had removed his glasses) stared off into the distance; Lou, seated in the cart, held a small whip (with a sprig of lilac) in her right hand and, in her left, the two ends of the thin cord which, tied around their elbows, symbolically harnessed the two 'work-horses' to the rack-waggon's happy driver.

From Basel Nietzsche had brought along a copy of *Schopenhauer as Educator*, which he now gave Lou to read as a preliminary introduction to his philosophical ideals and aspirations. The maxim she had inscribed on the cover of her knick-knack box – 'Strive to live quietly and to produce with your own hands' (from St Paul's first Epistle to the Thessalonians) – was replaced by Goethe's stirring exhortation, which, years before, Nietzsche, Gersdorff and Rohde had adopted as their own:

> From half-measures weaned
> And in the Whole, the Good, the Beautiful
> Resolutely let us live.

In exchange, Lou gave him a poem entitled 'To Pain' (spiritual as well as physical), which so perfectly echoed his own feelings on the subject that even two months later Nietzsche could not read it without tears coming into his eyes.

Before leaving Lucerne, the three *Freigeiste* made plans to spend the summer in the Engadine, in whose healthy Alpine air Lou, it was hoped, could get rid of her persistent cough. She herself wanted to attend one of the first *Parsifal* performances at Bayreuth in late July. In the meantime, she would visit Rée's family home at Stibbe (near the Baltic coast of West Prussia) in order to be 'properly' presented and found 'acceptable' by his mother.

On 16 May Nietzsche boarded the train for Basel, from where he was going to travel on to Naumburg, while Paul Rée accompanied Lou and her mother to Zürich. Fritz was eager to have Franz and Ida Overbeck meet the extraordinary creature he had described to them in such rapturous terms, to see if they could share his enthusiastic hopes and feelings about this feminine 'disciple'. Unfortunately, the recent emotional excitements now took their toll, and when he reached the Overbecks' house he was suffering from such an acute migraine attack that he had to lie down for an hour and had trouble explaining to Ida Overbeck the exact nature of the 'trinitarian' *Bund* (pact) which he, Paul Rée and Lou were so eager to establish.

From Zürich, that same day, after saying goodbye to Lou and her mother, Paul Rée travelled westward to Basel. At the station, between a change of trains and while waiting for Nietzsche to join him – for it had been agreed that they would travel part of the way northward together – Rée, who up till then had shown scant interest in members of the fair sex, wrote Lou an unmistakably amorous letter, already using the second person singular '*Du*' form reserved for close friends or intimate relationships. Speaking as an 'Epicurean' and as an 'egotistical moralist', he assured her that 'you are the *only person in the world I love*'. In effect this meant that he was transferring to Lou 'all the love I am withholding from other persons'. Since the 'other persons' included Nietzsche, Rée added that this might sound like a 'dubious' affirmation; but their trio, being constructed according to the Goethean maxim of living resolutely 'in the Good and Beautiful', was 'fire-and-bomb-proof'. This was of course a fatuous assertion; for, if only for conflicting reasons of health and sentimental attraction, the three 'workhorses' in this curious troika were bound to start pulling in different directions.

Rée's mother, who had long wanted to see her son Paul married, like his sister, was delighted by the prospect of having Lou Salomé come to stay with her at Stibbe. Indeed, she was almost prepared to 'adopt' her into the family. But, Rée wondered in the almost daily letters he now sent to Lou in Zürich, could this be arranged without giving their hypersensitive friend Nietzsche the impression that he, Paul Rée, was subtly trying to pull Lou away from him?

One of the suggestions that had been made by the three 'resolute' but not particularly 'good' or 'beautiful' plotters in Lucerne was that Lou, after stopping at Basel to meet the Overbecks, should continue by train to Naumburg, to be formally presented to Nietzsche's mother and sister, before travelling on from there to the Rées' family home near the Baltic. Geographically this made sense, but psychologically it was a sure recipe for disaster. As soon as he reached Naumburg, with its staid, stolidly Lutheran atmosphere, Nietzsche began to get cold feet. His pious mother, who had long vainly hoped that her beloved Fritz would get married, was certain to bristle at the idea that her son was preparing to consort with an 'emancipated' young girl, sixteen years his junior, who had not the slightest intention of marrying him, while Lou's superior intelligence was likely to arouse Elisabeth's furious jealousy.

Their mother having left on one of her periodic trips to visit relatives, Fritz found his sister Elisabeth running the house on the Weingartenstrasse with her usual energetic efficiency. The housemaid-cook, Alwine, was amazed how jolly the 'Herr Professor' now seemed to be – in marked contrast to the sullen taciturnity he had displayed during his last trip to Naumburg in the autumn of 1880.

The six months Fritz had spent in Genoa, followed by the three sun-blessed weeks in Sicily, had been extraordinarily productive, while the irruption into his sedentary existence of Lou Salomé – of whom he prudently said not a word to his sister – had had a galvanic effect on his creative energies. Once he had recovered from the fatigue and migraine torments of his train-trip to Naumburg, Nietzsche sent his publisher eight poems, entitled '*Idylls from Messina*', which a delighted Ernst Schmeitzner had quickly printed up and published in the May issue of his recently launched *Internationale Monatsschrift*. The title, *Die fröhliche Wissenschaft* (*The Joyous Science*), of Nietzsche's new work also made him feel 'very excited'. But there remained the irksome problem of preparing a legible manuscript. Elisabeth's 'girlish' handwriting seemed to her brother ill-suited to the adult seriousness of the contents. She then hired the services of a Naumburg shopkeeper, who had recently gone bankrupt. Since he was unable to decipher much of the scribbled manuscript, Elisabeth and Fritz took turns dictating the text to an unsatisfactory and often shocked 'scribe'.

On or around 25 May Nietzsche wrote to Lou Salomé in Zürich, giving her the Overbecks' exact address in Basel. In order to be more independent, he explained that he had 'remained silent' (i.e. had said nothing to his mother and sister about their 'trinitarian' scheme). 'The nightingales have been singing all night long in front of my window. Rée,' he went on, in the same charitable mood, 'is in all matters a better *friend* than I am and can be; take careful note of this difference.' But then, yielding to an irresistible temptation, he couldn't help concluding: 'When I am all alone, I often, very often pronounce your name – to my greatest pleasure.'

Could it be that the short-sighted, thirty-seven-year-old professor was also falling in love with the auburn-haired siren from distant Petersburg? In Zürich, where (with her mother) she was still champing at the bit, Lou must have read and reread this short but revealing letter a dozen times. It doubtless pleased her narcissistic vanity to realize that Friedrich Nietzsche, initially so solemn, withdrawn and austere, was now beginning to melt – just as had Paul Rée and Hendrik Gillot before him. From the start her feminine instinct had told her that Rée was someone she could dominate without too much trouble, but Nietzsche was clearly made of sterner, more forbidding stuff. Or was he? Perhaps the exterior, like the bristling moustache and many of his more trenchant aphorisms, was but a mask concealing an incongruously soft, diffident interior – one as tender as the curious softness of his voice?

A day or two later Nietzsche received a copy of the Lucerne photograph. Her mother, Lou informed him, had decided to go to Hamburg to attend a wedding celebrated by some German cousins. From Hamburg they were moving on to Berlin, where they would spend several weeks. Her mother, accompanied by the youngest of Lou's three brothers, was then returning by Baltic steamship to Petersburg. Lou, however, had insisted that their train-trip from Zürich should be interrupted at Basel, to give her time to call on Franz Overbeck and his wife.

Early on Whit Sunday morning (28 May) Nietzsche wrote to Ida Overbeck to say that Lou Salomé would be reaching Basel on Tuesday afternoon. He wanted her and Franz to know that he and Paul Rée shared the '*same feelings*' (doubly underlined) for their 'brave and high-hearted friend' (Lou), that he and Rée had '*very great confidence*' in each other. He was sure that the 'revered Frau Professor' (her title as the wife of a professor) understood the essential goal he was bent on attaining: the moulding of the malleable young Lou into a replica of himself.

Having thus asked Ida Overbeck to make his personal intentions quite clear to the young Lou, Nietzsche next wrote to his 'dear Friend', as he called her (in marked contrast to the far more intimate 'My Dearest' or 'My dear Lu' – deliberately respelled – which Paul Rée was already employing), to say that he now proposed to go *immediately* to Berlin, a city surrounded by 'lovely dense woods'. If, as he hoped, he could find a 'worthy' forester's house or even a vicarage tucked away in the huge Grunewald forest, he would ask Lou to come and spend a couple of days there with him before returning to Paul Rée's home at Stibbe. 'For, sincerely, I *very much* want for once to be completely alone with you as soon as possible. Solitary souls, such as I am, must first slowly get *accustomed* to the persons who are dearest to them: [please] make allowances for me in this matter, or rather be a tiny bit obliging. Should it, however, suit you better to travel farther afield, we can find some secluded refuge in the woods not far from Naumburg . . . thereto, if you wish, I could summon my sister. (So long as all the summer plans are dangling in the air, I will do well to maintain a complete silence towards my family – not out of any delight in secrets but because of a "knowledge of human beings").'

To Paul Rée, Nietzsche wrote the next day, explaining his latest plan for moving to Berlin's Grunewald forest. From there he proposed to accompany Lou to some wooded village in Thuringia. Had Rée, he asked, given her his Bayreuth Festival ticket for the first *Parsifal* performance? His sister Elisabeth would be there from 24 July on. 'Things have been going well for me,' he continued, referring to his health, 'and I am jolly and industrious . . . I often laugh about our Pythagorean friendship, with the very rare 'φίλοις πάντα κοινὰ' [*filois panta koinà* – everything in common among friends]. I have a better conception of myself, in being really capable of such a friendship. But it remains ridiculous, doesn't it?'

Ridiculous it was – as none knew better than the cynical Paul Rée who, throughout the second half of May, did not bother to write to Nietzsche while continuing to bombard Lou Salomé in Zürich with almost daily letters (and even telegrams) in which he barely concealed his exultation at the thought that, whereas his mother was ready to welcome Lou with open arms at her home near the Baltic, in Naumburg his 'fearless' friend Nietzsche had not dared to breathe a word to his mother and sister about the captivating Lou for fear of bringing the roof down on his head. An indolent 'dallier' Rée might be – he who so far had produced two slim philosophical volumes, while the industrious Nietzsche had already published nine books and was busy preparing a tenth – but in the fine art of courtship and repeatedly manifested solicitude (for Lou's state of health) he had stolen a long march on the inhibited ex-professor.

Of Lou Salomé's brief stopover in Basel, we know relatively little – beyond the fact that after spending a lively hour with Franz Overbeck and his wife, the wilful Lou persuaded her mother to stay overnight in the old university city, in order to attend a lecture by Jacob Burckhardt (whom she wanted to meet!) and to spend another hour with the Overbecks the next day. Franz Overbeck was so intrigued by this feminine phenomenon that he sent Nietzsche an eight-page report on his and his wife's impressions. It is more than regrettable that this invaluable letter has disappeared. Nietzsche, who received it in Naumburg in early June and who had to keep its contents secret from both his mother and sister, wrote to Franz, shortly after recovering from another nervous attack, that it was the kind of letter one receives once in a lifetime, and that it was something he would never forget. He was happy to find that his 'plan, which must shimmer *very fantastically* for uninitiated eyes', had encountered such a profoundly human as well as friendly understanding from both Overbecks. But the mirage-suggesting imagery of his language made it clear that Nietzsche was trying above all to overcome nagging doubts as to his personal ability to 'forge' the future and to achieve the seemingly impossible.

Writing on 4 June from Hamburg, where she was bedridden once again, Lou was less expansive about her brief visit to Basel, simply letting Nietzsche know that the Overbecks had received her most cordially and that they had had a long 'chat'. She could not, however, arrange to meet Nietzsche alone in Berlin's Grunewald forest for the good reason that at the insistence of her mother and brother she first had to be presented formally to Paul Rée's mother. A private meeting with Nietzsche would have to take place after the *Parsifal* première in Bayreuth.

The arrival of the mysterious letter from Hamburg – about which Fritz was unwilling to say anything to his mother and sister, beyond the fact that it was from an 'admirer' – may well have caused a lifting of eyebrows among the womenfolk of the Weingartenstrasse. In his reply Nietzsche mentioned the eight-page letter he had received from the Overbecks, which was full of 'love and admiration' for Lou as well as of 'much concern and anxiety for us both'. The good news was that 'such stout and level-headed friends' had displayed sufficient 'human under standing' to regard the hardy trio's plan as 'advantageous'. This said, Franz and Ida Overbeck were outstanding exceptions, and Nietzsche considered it vitally important to say nothing about their plan to their closest relatives and friends.

On or around 9 June Nietzsche at last received a letter from Paul Rée. With Lou due to arrive soon, it was going to be a full house, with, alas, not a free bed for Nietzsche. In his letter of reply Nietzsche said that he had recently been ill, but had managed nonetheless to complete his 'uneditable' (meaning 'illegible') manuscript: a piece of news that must have filled the indolent, unproductive Rée with a sense of shame. Fräulein Lou, Nietzsche assumed, would be staying with Paul and his mother until she left for the festival in Bayreuth. But what were to be their plans thereafter? He himself was thinking of heading towards Vienna in early July, perhaps stopping on the way for a 'summer' halt at Berchtesgaden.

Nietzsche had hardly finished this letter when he received another from Lou Salomé, who was still in Hamburg. Malwida von Meysenbug had just sent her a stern letter of remonstrance, expressing her profound misgivings over the trio's naïve plans to spend the winter in Vienna – particularly for Nietzsche's sake. 'How can he listen to lectures? Any more than he can deliver them. And the very bad weather in Vienna – after he has had infallible proof that the South alone makes his sufferings endurable.' It was 'unpractical folly' to be carried away by enthusiasm for a scheme that could only end in disaster. 'Poor N[ietzsche], how one would love to grant him this, and yet I consider it nothing short of presumptious even to try it. And finally, the Trinity! Firmly convinced though I am of your neutrality, the experience of a long lifetime and knowledge of human nature tell me that it cannot work without one heart thereby suffering cruelly in the noblest case, and in the worse an alliance of friendship being destroyed . . . What we want,' continued the impenitent idealist, 'can only work on a larger basis through joint studying in universities, etc. It will not work in an isolated togetherness, nature doesn't let itself be mocked, and the shackles are there even before one is aware of it.'

Lou took these warning words to mean that the triad, to be workable, needed to be enlarged. To this suggestion Nietzsche reacted negatively, explaining to Lou that he had trouble seeing who were the persons who *necessarily* had to be *initiated* into their little circle. For him, who liked seclusion, the worst thing that could happen would be to be exposed to gossiping and 'European prattle . . . whatever ensues, we want to endure it *together*, and *together* every evening toss the entire kit and caboodle' – he meant of conventional ideas – 'into the water.'

It was all very well to have sent Lou a copy of *Human, All Too Human* as an inspiring example of just how bold and iconoclastic he could be. For in Naumburg his health had seriously deteriorated, and as he confessed to Lou, 'I very much need mountains and high forests: not only my health, but even more "*die fröhliche Wissenschaft*" [*Joyous Science*] are driving me into solitude. I want to finish it.' Would she therefore object if he now headed for Salzburg (or Berchtesgaden) before moving on to Vienna?

From an attitude of bold insistence Nietzsche had suddenly moved, in the space of a few sentences, to an admission of weakness, culminating in this pathetic confession: 'I am in all matters of action inexperienced and unskilled; and for years I have *never* had to explain or justify any action before human beings. I am only too happy to leave my *plans* in concealment . . . Nature however gave each being different weapons of defence – and to you it gave a splendid openness of will. Pindar once said, "*Become* the one that you *are*!" Truly and devotedly F.N.'

Lou's answer to this letter has unfortunately been lost. It elicited a short thank-you note from Nietzsche, in which he complained of the 'dreadful existence of *renunciation*' he was forced to lead and which he found as hard to endure as an 'ascetic life-strangulation'. Lou immediately sent him a letter intended to cheer him up. She regretted that she would not see him until the summer, since she was now leaving Hamburg for Berlin, while Nietzsche was presumably headed for Salzburg or Berchtesgaden. When, indeed, would they see each other again?

This letter, which reached Naumburg on Thursday, 15 June, pierced Nietzsche like an arrow, unleashing a violent commotion within him.

'For the past half-hour,' he scribbled in reply, 'I have been melancholy, and for the past half-hour I have been asking myself why so? – and find no other reason than the announcement made in your lovely letter that we shall *not* see each other in Berlin. Now see what sort of man I am! Therefore: tomorrow morning at 11.40 I will be in Berlin at the Anhalter Station. My address is: Charlottenburg, near Berlin, poste restante. My hidden motive is 1) – – – and 2) that in a few weeks I may accompany you to Bayreuth, assuming that you find no better escort. – That's what is called a *sudden* decision!'

For some time past Nietzsche had been secretly suffering from the painful realization of how glaringly different, not to say diametrically opposed, was his sedentary and relatively sheltered life, compared to the 'resolute' form of living ('in the Whole, the Good, the Beautiful') Mazzini had adopted in accordance with Goethe's stirring maxim. It was the kind of bold existence he himself was now advocating in even stronger terms, with his encouragement to 'live dangerously' (in the 283rd aphorism of his new book). And it was to prove to himself, if to no one else, that he could at times be a 'man of action', even ready to hurl himself into the 'lion's mouth', that he decided to undertake this 'mad' trip to Berlin.

The trip was made on Friday, 16 June. A Swiss forester had once assured Nietzsche that the huge, partly lake-flanked Grunewald forest provided the fortunate Berliners with a labyrinth of well-shaded walks and was one of the urban causes of the celebrated 'Berliner Luft' – the great city's unusually pure and healthy air. On this particular Friday, however, it was raining so hard that Nietzsche's first afternoon visit to the Grunewald forest was a drenching disappointment. The next morning the sun was shining, but Nietzsche, who loved woods above all for their mossy tranquillity and the sense of silent eternity they seemed to breathe, was dismayed to find the forest teeming with boisterous holidaymakers, who had generously littered the ground with their sordid breakfast remains. Not knowing in exactly which hotel Lou Salomé was staying with her mother and brother, he made no attempt to find her. Even if he had known, it is by no means sure that he would have mustered the courage to present himself, since it would have aroused the suspicions of Madame Salomé and of Lou's brother, and have seriously compromised the trio's plans for the future.

Without wasting any further time on this 'detestable forest', Nietzsche beat a hasty retreat to Naumburg. The next day he wrote to Paul Rée that Germany's 'cloud-weather' had afflicted him with a kind of 'sickliness', with the result that his 'reason' had ceased to be 'reasonable'. He had travelled to Berlin to see the Grunewald forest, which he never wished to see again, and Lou, whom he had not seen at all. What, he went on, were the latest plans for the period after Bayreuth?

The letter to Rée was accompanied by another to Lou, in which Nietzsche mentioned the 'little, apparently very silly trip to Berlin', which had taught him a thing or two about the Grunewald forest as well as about himself. But he had since recovered from the fatigue of the trip and had fallen back into his fatalistic 'submission to God's will', firmly believing anew that everything *must* necessarily turn out to his best advantage. 'I would so much like to work and study with you soon, and I have prepared lovely things – fields in which *sources* are to be discovered, assuming that *your* eyes want to discover sources (mine are no longer fresh enough for that!). You know however that I want to be your *teacher*, your guide on the path to scholarly *production*?' Once again he asked about any plans she might have made for the summer period after the Bayreuth Festival. 'My trip,' he concluded, 'once again taught me about my unspeakable clumsiness as soon as I feel *new* places and people around me –: I believe that the blind are more reliable than the half-blind. My wish as regards Vienna is now to be deposited like a piece of luggage in a tiny room of the house in which you wish to live. Or in the house next door, as your true friend and neighbour F.N.'

This pathetic request to be allowed a humble nook in the future 'philosophical workshop' they were planning to set up in Vienna must have troubled Lou as much as it flattered Paul Rée's tormented ego, constantly jerked up and down by a love-hate feeling of admiration for his 'free-thinking' friend Nietzsche and a simmering resentment of his crushing intellectual and productive superiority. He could not but note with a feeling of secret satisfaction the flagrant contradiction between what had so far been Nietzsche's masterful insistence that he be allowed to spend a few days with Lou *alone*, and this sudden, fawning readiness to admit that in their future 'trinitarian workshop' he would, from the masculine point of view, meekly accept a minor, subordinate, almost dog-like role. This was not the robust language to be expected from the kind of man-god-on-earth Lou secretly craved to meet (and also feared as a challenge to her intellectual 'freedom'); above all not from a philosopher who, from *Schopenhauer as Educator* on, had praised self-reliance and condemned every form of spiritual and intellectual servility. Nietzsche's reference to 'sources' also had an ominous ring – as though his principal objective (and his particular, candidly admitted form of 'egotism') was to use Lou as a kind of secretarial assistant for his own research purposes. Moreover, what exactly were his dark, deep-seated, 'Dionysian' motivations in undertaking the hasty trip to Berlin? Did he by any chance fancy that he could take her by storm?

If Nietzsche's fluctuating plans and even actions at this moment were so contradictory, impulsive and confused, it was partly because he was once again under great self-imposed stress. Unlike the otiose Paul Rée, whose growing fondness for Lou provided him with a convenient excuse for taking time out from his 'philosophical labours' to drive her in the family carriage aound the countyside, Nietzsche was now desperately trying to prepare a legible manuscript for his new book. His exasperation with the unsatisfactory 'scribe' his sister Elisabeth had hired for the job of copying had reached such a pitch that on 19 June he wrote to Heinrich Köselitz in Venice to ask his devoted disciple if he could possibly complete the job of copying and proof-correcting? 'The torture of putting the ms together, with the help of an old bankrupt merchant and sorry ass, was extraordinary: I have once again conspired to let such a thing befall me.'

He was now waiting in Naumburg for the 'sundry *essential* to happen or to be prepared' – looking on in astonishment at the 'strange toss of the dice' while he waited and waited. 'From the autumn on,' he continued, without offering any explanation, 'I am beginning a new *student-time*: I am going to the University of Vienna. Will you be coming to Vienna? Ah, I cannot tell you how I manage it, not having you nearby. The hermit-like seclusion of life is far too great and will become ever greater,' he concluded in a tone of resignation – as though glumly aware, but without openly admitting it, that the bold 'trinitarian' experiment, into which he had been thrust by the imperious 'dice-toss' of Fate, was doomed to failure.

## CHAPTER 27

# *Incipit tragoedia*

*– 'Love is the danger of the loneliest, love of everything, if only it is alive! Laughable, verily, are my folly and my modesty in love!'*

It was, ironically enough, Elisabeth Nietzsche, from whom he had tried to hide the truth, who finally helped lift her tormented brother off the horns of the dilemma on which he was psychologically impaled. For years she had been trying to persuade Fritz to spend his summers in the cool shade of the Tautenburger Wald, a dense Thuringian forest situated nine kilometres from Jena and a little more than twenty kilometres south-west of Naumburg. But after he had discovered the high Alps Fritz had stubbornly refused this 'convenient' solution to his annual search for summer shade and coolness. Not until the excruciatingly painful summer spent at Sils-Maria in 1881, when his peace of mind had been repeatedly shattered by thunderstorms and nerve-racking discharges of electricity, did he begin to have second thoughts about the infallibility of the 'Alpine-highlands' solution to this recurrent problem. Now that the 'second phase' of his life's work – the one he had begun with *Human, All Too Human* – was virtually over, he could offer himself a period of intellectual repose, by accepting his sister's suggestion that he spend the summer in the Tautenburg forest, before moving on in the autumn to attend lectures on scientific subjects at the University of Vienna.

On 22 June, when they met in Leipzig, Nietzsche was at last able to give his publisher, Ernst Schmeitzner, the first three parts of *The Joyous Science*. They were accompanied by a 'Bacchanalian rout' of sixty-three tongue-in-cheek 'aphorisms' in verse form, in which he made witty fun of everything: narrow-minded souls, health-obsessed pessimists, Seneca ('*primum scribere, deinde philosophari*'), the lover who has lost his head, Lucifer, Feuerbach's shocking contention that 'Man created God' (rather than the other way round), ponderous scholarship, poetic vanity, his own book, *Human, All Too Human*. In one of them, irreverently titled 'Ecce homo', he summed up his incandescent nature in six short lines:

*Ja! ich weiss, woher ich stamme!*
*Ungesättigt gleich der Flamme*
*Glühe und verzehr' ich mich.*
*Licht wird Alles, was ich fasse,*

*Kohle Alles, was ich lasse:*
*Flamme bin ich sicherlich.*

(Yes, I know wherefrom I came!
Unsatiated like the flame
I glow and thus consume me.
Light will all be I conceive,
Coals everything that I do leave:
Flame am I assuredly.)

If Nietzsche could have foreseen all the proofreading troubles he was going to have with an inefficient postal service, he would have had second thoughts about the advisability of choosing this Tautenburg forest retreat. But it was to the little castle of Dornburg, overlooking the sluggish Saale river at the western fringe of the forest, that the seventy-nine-year-old Goethe had retired for two months after the death of his kind patron, Grand Duke Carl August of Weimar, in the summer of 1828; and Nietzsche could already imagine the pleasure it would give him to accompany the poetically minded Lou from the tiny hamlet of Tautenburg to the Schloss where, in search of peace and solitude, the ageing bard had composed three beautiful romantic poems. It was probably during the relatively short trip from Naumburg to Dornburg, made on Sunday, 25 June, that Fritz at last told Elisabeth about Lou Salomé. Her mother was returning to her native Petersburg, and Fräulein Lou was going to spend a few weeks with Paul Rée's mother at Stibbe, from where she was due to go on to Bayreuth for one of the first *Parsifal* performances. Since Elisabeth was planning to attend the first dress rehearsal on 24 July, she would be able to meet the young Russian 'student', as well as renew her acquaintance with Malwida von Meysenbug, who had warmly endorsed the idea that Nietzsche should provide Lou Salomé with some solid grounding in philosophy and theology – two subjects in which the gifted poetess was passionately interested. Fritz at this point was clearly taking liberties with the truth; but, after all, what 'sacrifices' must one not be prepared to make in pursuing a 'lofty' goal, particularly when an irresolute 'man of thought' has to transform himself into a resolute 'man of action'! Almost certainly Elisabeth felt flattered to be assigned the task of personally 'examining' the young poetess during her stay in Bayreuth. An adoring admirer of her brother, she had long thrilled at the idea of helping to found a 'colony' or *Kloster* (monastery) of 'free spirits', and although this latest scheme seemed a bit restrictive, since Paul Rée was not being invited to Tautenburg, she accepted Fritz's laborious explanations: it was *indispensable* that Lou

Salomé undergo a philosophical 'cram-course' in order to be properly 'initiated'.

The cosy single-windowed room that the resourceful Elisabeth had found for her brother in the sylvan hamlet of Tautenburg was located in a farmhouse. For Lou Salomé, clearly, something grander was required. To give her planned stay every semblance of propriety, overtures were made to the parish priest, who regularly rented out certain rooms in his vicarage to transient visitors. Brother and sister seem to have derived a mischievous delight in getting the unsuspecting priest to cooperate in a plot hatched by the heretical author of *Human, All Too Human*.

The day after his arrival Nietzsche wrote to Lou Salomé to say that his sister had found an 'idyllic litle nest' for him in the middle of the lovely woods of Tautenburg a mere half-hour from the Dornburg Schloss, where the 'ageing Goethe enjoyed his solitude'. If Lou had no better plans for the month of August, his sister Elisabeth would be glad to accompany her from Bayreuth to Tautenburg.

In answer to a letter Lou had sent him from Berlin regarding his exact intentions, Nietzsche now sought to reassure her: '*Never* have I hitherto thought that you should "read aloud and write" for me; but it has been very much my wish that I should be your *teacher*. Finally, to tell the entire truth: I am looking for persons who could be my heirs; I carry about within me something that is not at all to be found in my books – and for that I am looking for the finest and most fertile soil . . . See in this my *selfishness*!' After saying how his soul overflowed every time he thought of her frail health, Nietzsche added with naïve sincerity: 'And then, I am always happy to know that you have Rée and not just me as a friend. To think of you both strolling and talking together is for me a true delight.'

On 3 July, after suffering another severe seizure, due to thunderstorms and rainy weather, Nietzsche wrote again – this time to thank Lou Salomé for agreeing to come to Tautenburg. Her letter, like a shower of 'birthday gifts', had reached him along with a package full of cherries from his sister and the first forty-eight pages of *Die fröhliche Wissenschaft* (*The Joyous Science*), which he had received from the printer. He had just sent off the final part of the manuscript to his publisher, and now at last he could heave a great sigh of relief. Thus was completed 'the work of 6 years (1876–82), my entire "*Freigeisterei*"! Oh, what years!' he went on. 'What torments of every kind, what solitude and weariness with life! . . . Heaven preserve me from follies! But from now on, when *you* will advise me, I shall be *well* advised and need not fear myself.'

The celebrated Tautenburger Wald, though offering plenty of dense forest shade, unfortunately proved to be no more thunder-and-lightning-proof than had been the Engadine; and before the second week of July was over, Fritz was writing plaintive letters to his mother to say that he was suffering from repeated headaches and even nervous seizures. In one notable respect, moreover, the Tautenburg forest proved to be a singularly perilous 'refuge'. Within days of his arrival, the word had spread that a 'famous philosopher' was spending the summer here. Out of gratitude for the honour thus paid them, the members of a local 'Embellishment Club' (*Verschönerungs-Verein*) insisted on having benches placed at various spots along the paths he regularly followed, so that he could rest during his long walks.

As an expression of his gratitude for Heinrich Köselitz's self-sacrificing willingness once again to assume the tiresome chore of proofreading, Nietzsche decided to let him in on the secret that was beginning to transform his life. The author of the poem, 'To Pain', of which he had sent the struggling composer a copy early in July, was his 'friend Lou . . . the daughter of a Russian general, and twenty years old; she,' he went on, in language that bore a remarkable resemblance to what he would have liked to say about himself, 'is as sharp-witted as an eagle and as brave as a lion' – while being at the same time a 'girlish child, who has perhaps not long to live'.

So totally at variance with Nietzsche's previous cult of solitude was this new scheme for communal living in the same house in Vienna – with, furthermore, a virgin in her twenties! – that Köselitz could not but be astounded. To reassure his often misanthropic disciple, Nietzsche hastened to add in unusually stilted language: 'Dear Friend, you will surely do us the honour of excluding the notion of a liaison from our relationship. We are *friends* and I will regard this girl and this trust in me as sacred . . . Incidentally, she has an incredibly sure and candid character and knows exactly what *she* [doubly underlined] wants – without asking the world and worrying herself about the world. And all this for you and for nobody else,' he added. 'But if *you* could come to Vienna, it would be lovely!'

Almost certainly this was sincerely meant and not simply a casual invitation. Eager as he was to be Lou Salomé's principal teacher, Nietzsche would not have minded incorporating Köselitz, who had a girlfriend in Vienna, into a wobbly *ménage à trois*. Of all Nietzsche's close friends, Köselitz alone had dared to offer him positive criticism regarding the style and contents of *Human, All Too Human* and the books that had followed. As his often long letters had made clear, he knew far more about scientific matters than Erwin Rohde, Franz Overbeck, Carl von Gersdorff or even the 'positivistic' Paul Rée. However, Köselitz can hardly have been reassured by the last sentence of Nietzsche's letter: 'Finally, who so far have been my most valuable human-*finds*? You – then Rée – then Lou.' Flattering though it was to be ranked as the philosopher's most highly prized 'find', a dark horse – more exactly, a dark filly – capable of moving up so fast in the hierarchy of Nietzschean friendships was an unsettling omen for the future.

Now that the painful stress of proofreading was begining to subside, Nietzsche could at last write a letter of explanatory justification to Malwida von Meysenbug. His recently finished tenth book in effect completed the 'thought-chain' of works he had begun composing at Sorrento. He would not be bringing out any more books during the next few years, for his intention was to resume his life as a student – in Vienna. His life from now on would be devoted to a 'higher goal', to developing a '*heroic* mode of thought' . . . although certainly not in any 'religious-resigned form'. Should Malwida happen to come across any other persons capable of achieving *this* particular form of thinking – like the 'young Russian . . . a truly heroic soul' she had recently discovered – then he begged her to let him know. 'I wish to acquire in her a disciple, an heiress and thought-perpetuator.'

Having thus expressed his chronic fear of an early death, Nietzsche devoted an illuminating paragraph to the erotically repressed abnormality of this hyper-intellectualized *ménage à trois*: 'By the way, Rée should have married her (in order to remove the many difficulties of her situation); and I for my part did not fail to approve it. But it now seems to me a vain endeavour. He is in one deepest respect an unshakable pessimist . . . The thought of the propagation of mankind is something he cannot endure . . . All of this, *privatissime*!' Because he was writing to a sexagenarian spinster in an age of Victorian 'respectability', Nietzsche had to resort to euphemisms to intimate that Paul Rée was one of those unfortunate males who find sexual intercourse repellent.

The two final paragraphs of this revealing letter were devoted to the coming Festival in Bayreuth. Nietzsche was very satisfied, he explained in a sudden display of petulant defiance, 'not to *have to* listen to the *Parsifal* music'. With the exception of two portions, he frankly did not like 'this "style" (this laborious and overloaded bits-and-pieces work)' – any more than he cared for 'the monstrous pretensions and *Cagliostricity* of its creator'.

No matter how strenuously he might proclaim his indifference to Richard Wagner's religiously inspired music, the truth was that deep down within him Nietzsche envied his sister and Lou and Malwida and the other friends who would be converging on Bayreuth. He virtually admitted as much in a letter sent to Lou Salomé at Stibbe on 16 July, just ten days before the planned première: '. . . and yet, if I could quite spectrally be near you, murmuring this and that into your ear, then I could stand the *Parsifal* music (otherwise for me it is unendurable)'.

One of the problems Nietzsche had been turning over in his mind was just how, if Lou Salomé was to be properly initiated into his ways of thought and thus become a reliable disciple and perhaps even the 'heiress designate' of his philosophy, she was to be 'liberated' from the bewitching spell of Richard Wagner's music. Her musical talents were not on a par with her poetic gift, and she could not properly read a complicated music score. It occurred to Nietzsche that the easiest way to effect a cure of anti-Wagnerian disintoxication would be to offer her a dose of Henrich Köselitz's non-Wagnerian music – extracts, for example, from the first act of his 'modernized' version of Cimarosa's *Matrimonio segreto*, which the aspiring (and perspiring) composer had offered to send to him from Venice. But given his poor eyesight, Nietzsche was afraid that he himself might be unable to play the piano version with sufficient dexterity to impress the young Lou. But precisely at this moment Fortune or Fate – the same arcane force or deity that had caused Lou Salomé's vital trajectory to cross his own – seemed to intervene again by arranging a providential encounter with a talented young piano-player. He was a Berliner named Arthur Egidi, who had come to spend a few days in the Tautenburg forest before going on to Bayreuth. He and Nietzsche had struck up a conversation while waiting inside a lecture-hall pavilion for a sudden cloudburst to abate outside. A half-hour of discussion – during which the young Egidi boldly declared that, just as Gluck was followed by Mozart, so Wagner too could be followed by another great composer – sufficed to convince Nietzsche that here was another heaven-sent 'find'.

Fritz's sister by this time had left Naumburg for the *Parsifal* première. It had been arranged that she would pick up Lou Salomé in Leipzig and accompany her to Bayreuth, where Elisabeth had found rooms for both of them in the same house. At first all seemed to go well. The older Elisabeth and the much younger Lou pretended to like each other from the start, and by the time they reached Bayreuth, they were already using the familiar, second person singular '*Du*' form of speech with each other. But within one week this highly constrained 'friendship' had turned into outright enmity.

There were several reasons for this. Because she had once acted as interim governess for Cosima's children, Elisabeth Nietzsche had remained *persona grata* with the Wagners. But this was not a sentiment shared by many rabid Wagnerophiles, who could not forgive Nietzsche for his apostatic abandonment of the 'sacred' cause and his blasphemous attacks against their philosophical demigod, Schopenhauer. In Bayreuth Elisabeth found herself meeting persons who had no reason to like her.

Lou Salomé, on the other hand, suffered from no such handicaps. Quite the contrary. She was overjoyed to find herself suddenly consorting, as a member of the privileged 'élite', with so many celebrities. Her youth and intellectual vivacity, compared to Elisabeth's middle-aged plainness, set her apart as a remarkable 'phenomenon'. One of those she charmed was the painter Paul Zhukovsky, a close friend and neighbour of the Wagners in whose rented house Malwida von Meysenbug was staying. The half-Russian, half-German son of a famous poet and literary editor, Zhukovsky, after finishing a huge family portrait of Cosima's children (which now graced the entrance-hall of the 'Wahnfried' mansion), had been asked by Wagner to help prepare the complicated décor and stage-sets for the *Parsifal* performances. The thirty-seven-year-old painter and the twenty-one-year-old poetess hit it off immediately, carrying on long conversations about Petersburg, Russia and Germany – dutifully recorded in a diary, extracts of which Lou took a 'sincere' (but also malicious) pleasure in sending to an increasingly perturbed and jealous Paul Rée, at Stibbe.

Another 'victim' of her charm and intellectual temerity (and likewise a house-guest of Zhukovsky's) was Heinrich von Stein, who for some months had served as the erudite tutor of the young Siegfried Wagner. Lou Salomé was initially dismayed by Stein's ardent enthusiasm for Schopenhauer, which seemed to her too trenchant, inflexible and dogmatically 'infallible'. But after being told off by Paul Rée, who urged her to display more tolerance towards 'persons of merit' and to respect Heinrich von Stein's 'fiery soul' – which attested a deep, authentic interest in metaphysical problems – Lou shed her initial coldness and engaged Stein in such vigorous discussions that the captivated agnostic finally invited her to visit him in Halle, where he was studying to obtain a doctorate in philosophy.

As a special treat and almost certainly with the warm encouragement of her dear friend Malwida, Cosima Wagner agreed to receive the unknown Lou Salomé and the familiar Elisabeth Nietzsche, who had once taken such good care of her children. During their '*privatissime*' audience the mistress of 'Wahnfried' expressed a 'sincere affection' for Elisabeth's brother, which was not altogether feigned; for with the passage of time she too, like her husband, had come to regret the ending of the stimulating conversations they had so much enjoyed at Tribschen.

Exactly what Lou Salomé thought of the *Parsifal* première we do not know. But since she was tone-deaf, she was almost certainly less impressed than the Wagnerophilic Elisabeth, who was so excited and overwhelmed by the scenic and sonic spectacle that she wrote to her brother to say that 'even a deaf man would have been enthused by the performance'.

On 28 July, the date chosen for the second *Parsifal* performance, Fritz wrote to his sister urging her and Lou to stay on, pointing out that 'if one doesn't come away from Bayreuth with a couple of *high* moments, there was no point going to B[ayreuth].' He also urged Elisabeth not to leave before the 30th, when Franz Overbeck and his wife would be reaching Bayreuth. Elisabeth was only too happy to heed this last piece of advice. At some point during their brief meeting she stunned Ida Overbeck by the vehemence of her complaints against 'Fräulein Salomé' – a philosophical upstart who had not bothered to read Fritz's books and who ought to be sent back to school.

Elisabeth's growing irritation was not simply due to jealousy aroused by Lou Salomé's 'astounding dialectical virtuosity' and a genuine talent for 'hair-splitting sophistry' (as Malwida's friend, Resa von Schirnhofer, later described it); she was outraged to discover that Lou, with a tactless mixture of adolescent conceit and brazen effrontery, had been showing Malwida's friends the 'amusing' Lucerne photograph of herself, seated in the little cart by her two harnessed 'workhorses', who were ready to go wherever it might please her to lead them.

Blissfully unaware of the storm that was brewing in Bayreuth, Nietzsche on 1 August wrote to Köselitz in Venice to say that he need not bother, after all, to send him piano-score extracts from his *Matrimonio segreto*, since the young Berlin piano-player Arthur Egidi was leaving for Bayreuth on the 7th and would thus no longer be around to play Köselitz's music for the educational enlightenment of Lou Salomé. 'The old wizard,' he added, speaking of Wagner, 'has again [scored] a huge success, with the sobbing of old men, etc.' What he did not say to Köselitz, who might have taken it as a sign of intellectual 'weakening', if not an outright betrayal of the 'new', non-Wagnerian music they were supposed to be promoting, was that the daily reports that Egidi was bringing him of the festival performances had so ignited Nietzsche's curiosity that he felt tempted to accompany the young Berliner to Bayreuth.

Nietzsche had hardly begun to hatch this little plot when a telegram informed him that Elisabeth was leaving Bayreuth and would be back in Naumburg in a matter of hours. Fritz immediately took the train to Naumburg, and may even have been waiting at the railway station for the arrival of his sister, so as to be able to discuss the crisis in Bayreuth *à deux*, rather than in the presence of their easily shocked mother. Elisabeth minced no words in giving vent to her indignation: she was fed up trying to guide an unmanageable young girl and was not prepared to act as a nursemaid for this brazen hussy who was now bedridden with a cold. Fritz immediately sent Lou a telegram, expressing concern over her health and suggesting that, once recovered, she come to Jena rather than to the depressing, rain-sodden Tautenburg forest.

In her letter of reply, written in Bayreuth on 2 August and sent to Naumburg, where she was reasonably sure that Elisabeth would read it, Lou took pains to thank Nietzsche's sister, 'who now is almost mine', as though innocently unaware of any trace of dissension between them. She was quite ready to come to Jena, from where they could easily reach the Tautenburg forest as soon as the first ray of sunshine pierced the clouds. She was as eager as ever to see Nietzsche again and to begin the 'industrious quiet-life' (*arbeitsames Stillleben*) they had planned for the month of August. Their plans for spending the winter in Vienna, however, would have to be abandoned, for reasons she would explain to him orally when they met.

There were at least two reasons for this change of plan. Ida Overbeck, who had volunteered to find Lou a place to live in Vienna, had been sharply rebuffed by a strait-laced lady, who had made it quite clear that she was not going to have two unmarried men and a young girl living next to and consorting with each other under one roof. In imperial Vienna, with its strict court etiquette, such things were simply not done. Malwida von Meysenbug, for her part, was every bit as negative. Vienna, she pointed out, was an impossible place to spend the winter for Nietzsche and Lou, since for reasons of health both clearly needed the winter sunshine of the Mediterranean.

In his telegram to Lou, Nietzsche had promised to follow up with an explanatory letter. Exactly what he wrote, we do not know. Like other evidential elements in this complex philosophico-erotic imbroglio, this piece of the jigsaw puzzle is unfortunately missing. But his letter must have contained a stern rebuke, even if couched in polite language, at the disloyal way in which Lou had been behaving at Bayreuth by casually consorting with rabid Wagner-lovers who detested Nietzsche, by showing around the Lucerne photograph which ridiculed Paul Rée and himself, and by brazenly declaring that these two 'captive' men were ready to follow her wherever she chose to go. This was no way for a real friend to behave; and since Lou had apparently decided that they should not go to Vienna, it would be better if they simply forgot their plans for spending the winter together.

Lou's at once furious and plaintive retort – furious because Elisabeth was stirring up trouble between them, plaintive because Nietzsche was scrapping their 'lovely' winter plans and filling her, ill and bedridden as she was, with grief – has also disappeared. All that has survived is a fragment from an apologetic letter which a melancholy Nietzsche wrote to Lou after his return to Tautenburg on 4 August: ' . . . I wanted to live alone. But then the dear bird Lou flew across my path and I thought it was an eagle. And I wanted to have the eagle near me . . . Do come, I am suffering too much for having made you suffer. We will endure it better together.'

Identical images were used in a letter Nietzsche wrote on that same day to his close confidant Heinrich Köselitz: 'One day a bird flew past me; and I, superstitious as are all solitary persons who stand at the turning-point of their street, believed I had seen an eagle. Now the entire world is trying to prove to me that I am mistaken – and there is polite European gossip about it' – i.e. in Bayreuth's 'high society'. It was not only from Elisabeth's glowing description of *Parsifal* that Nietzsche had gathered that the 'old wizard' had surpassed himself in the art of orchestration; it was also from Arthur Egidi, whom he had been meeting almost daily during his walks through the Tautenburg woods. Wagner had decided to have the premiére of *Parsifal* performed on 26 July, followed by eighteen other presentations extending through much of August. It was to see one of these performances that Arthur Egidi was going to leave Tautenburg on 7 August to join friends of his in Bayreuth. On the 5th, when Egidi accompanied Nietzsche to Dorndorf station, where 'the fabulous philosopher' wanted to pick up the incoming mail and final proofs of his new book, the young Berlin pianist was under the impression that this friendly, music-loving connoisseur would be travelling with him two days later. This may have been Nietzsche's intention, his way of acting in a 'heroic-idyllic' spirit by arriving in Bayreuth incognito to surprise the ailing Lou and also to see and hear *Parsifal* performed. But the next day (Sunday, 6 August) Egidi received word that, alas, the Herr Professor was feeling too unwell to be able to accompany him to Bayreuth. This may well have been the truth. But it is also possible that Nietzsche had just learned that Lou Salomé had left Bayreuth and was now on her way to Jena.

During his brief stay in Naumburg Nietzsche had found time to write a two-paragraph letter to Jacob Burckhardt. He explained that he was relying on his highly honoured friend's 'prejudiced good-will' in having a gift copy of his new book sent to him. Were it otherwise, Burckhardt would have every right to mock *The Joyous Science* – 'it is far too personal, and everything personal is truly *comic*.'

One day in Genoa Nietzsche had begun rereading *Morgenröte* and had been appalled. This book, which he had written in the hope that he had so completely mastered his physical torments that nowhere in it could a trace of his sufferings be found, was nevertheless full of harshness and asperity. Despite the rosy title, *Morgenröte* (*Morning Glow* or *Flush of Dawn*) was not a joyous book. Its fourth chapter was almost grim in denigrating 'altruism' and stressing the importance of selfishness in the constitution of strong, healthy, self-reliant, free-thinking, unbigoted individuals, while the fifth and highly autobiographical final chapter was larded with barbed allusions to the incomprehension of his readers, including (though none were named) most of his friends. Strive as he might and striven though he had, the nerve-racking thunderstorms and unstable weather encountered at Recoaro in the Dolomites and then at Sils-Maria had got the better of his intentions.

It would be simplistic to suggest that Nietzsche's exclusive aim at this point was to write a 'cheerful' or 'joyous' book. None of his books, from *Human, All Too Human* on, had had a single aim. All of them had been marked by a chaotic plethora of mini-essays on a large number of subjects, which made them all what they have since remained: among the most seminal, overly rich and not easily digestible books ever written by a philosopher. *The Joyous Science*, in this respect, did not differ from its predecessors. Nietzsche, furthermore, had been too profoundly irritated by the fashionable tendency of so many contemporary philologists to idealize the ancient Greeks and their 'cheerful', inherently 'optimistic' culture to wish to eliminate all trace of the tragic from his purposefully '*ja-sagende*' (yes-saying-to-life) philosophy. His quarrel with Schopenhauer was not that he had emphasized this aspect of human existence; it was that Schopenhauer had passively and pessimistically accepted it, instead of trying to combat the tragic mode and mood. Damning the world and in a sense all of creation for being an eternal cockpit of misery and incessant strife was a highly idiosyncratic and sentimental, not a truly rational reaction. It was one more proof of the extent to which Schopenhauer had remained an incorrigible romantic, and also neo-Kantian in implicitly applying the moral criterion of 'good' and 'evil' to natural phenomena: which is why his philosophy, despite his personal interest in biology, was radically unscientific. It was one more deplorable example of the 'anthropocentric fallacy': the tendency to view natural phenomena from a short-sighted, narrowly human rather than from a cosmic perspective. How childish and unrealistic it was, for example, to regard the predatory, carnivorous instincts of so many animals as inherently 'cruel' and 'bad'! If the vital instinct to survive – what Nietzsche later called the 'will to power' – is inherently 'bad', then the universe itself is flawed, and the Zoroastrians were right to regard the world as the creation of an evil 'God of Darkness', and Satan (as St John put it) as 'the Prince of this World'.

The conclusion Nietzsche had reached at this point in his thinking was that the 'Creator' of the universe – what Spinoza had astutely called *Deus sive Natura* (God or Nature) – had not let himself be influenced by such petty considerations. There was every reason to believe that what the moralists considered 'evil' was, in terms of durable survival over centuries and millennia, essentially 'good', life-preserving, and far more prevalent. This was the basic subsoil from which the 'Good' or the 'Beautiful' – those floral embellishments of human life – had sprung. And, just as what is 'good' in human life can only appear and distinguish itself against a background of circumambient 'badness' or 'evil', so joyfulness can only thrive and cease to be mere raucous and superficial mirth in a context that is inherently and inescapably tragic: the plight of infinitesimal man in an ever-expanding, frighteningly huge and inhuman universe. Nietzsche may not have heard of Horace Walpole's famous dictum – 'The world is a comedy for those who think, a tragedy for those who feel' – but he was one of those rare thinkers whose capacity to feel was as strong as his capacity to think. Human existence, he was persuaded, is inescapably tragicomic, or comico-tragic, depending on how one looks at it: comic because of the presumptious vanity of short-lived mortals, tragic in the awesome context of cosmic 'eternity'.

In the first sections of *Morgenröte*, Nietzsche had gone back over a number of millennia to seek the origins of moral sentiments in the anthropological fears and defence mechanisms of primitive societies. Now, in the long opening paragraph of *The Joyous Science*, he went much farther back to contemplate Man's fate in the context of biological evolution. When, at Pforta, the young Fritz had first heard of Charles Darwin and his theories, he had instinctively scoffed at the idea that human beings might be descended from apes. But that was before he had read *The Origin of Species*, or had devoted any serious attention to this and other scientific subjects. Since then it had dawned on him that Darwin, with his theory of biological evolution stretched out over an enormous passage of time, had dealt to all forms of anthropomorphic religion a blow far more deadly than the one Copernicus had dealt to medieval Christianity. In dethroning the earth from its central position in the solar system, Copernicus had left unshaken the conviction that the universe is basically 'harmonious' and God-ordained. Kepler's later discovery that the planets revolve around the sun in elliptical orbits rather than in perfect circles had not basically affected the quaint Pythagorean notion of the 'music of the spheres' or the deep-rooted belief in a pre-established 'celestial harmony' which was shared in different ways by Leibniz and Spinoza before being given a rigorous scientific explanation in Isaac Newton's laws of universal gravitation. Like Voltaire (who had devoted a book to his scientific hero), Immanuel Kant too had remained throughout his long life an admirer of Newton; and, although he had been unable in his first great *Critique* (*of Pure Reason*) to provide teleology – the

*Zweckmässigkeit* or purposiveness of human existence – with a firm a *priori* foundation comparable to what he had done for mathematics and physics, in his third *Critique*, devoted to 'Judgement', Kant had offered teleology an honourable position alongside his discussion of aesthetic problems. But it was precisely this belief (also shared by Hegel) that mankind, as the highest stage of biological development, was moving steadily forward towards a distant goal of 'perfection' that Charles Darwin had shattered by concluding, from his laborious empirical investigations, that biological evolution does not proceed according to any pre-established plan but thanks to chance mutations. 'Natural selection' – a terminological misnomer, as Darwin discovered too late to remedy this verbal error – was in effect 'unnatural' in that it did not follow any clearly defined plan, but proceeded by trial and error, with certain species managing to survive, while those incapable of adapting to an unfavourable environment succumbed. The motive force of biological evolution was not the precise, mathematically minded, perfection-seeking God of Descartes, Leibniz and Spinoza, but a kind of blind, groping deity, the fumbling force of Chance.

It is easy to understand the relish with which Nietzsche embraced this basic Darwinian concept. This new notion of Chance as one of the motive forces of all biological development was simply the scientific equivalent (and to that extent a confirmation) of the ancient Greek concept of Fate or Fortune. What Nietzsche liked about Darwin's theory was its scientific impartiality, its calm annihilation of the fairy-tale fable of the Creation of the World, as related in the Book of Genesis, and its serious attempt to view the huge span of biological evolution from a non-anthropocentric, non-man-centred point of view. Man, according to this theory, was as much the product of fortuitous accidents as were any of the 'lower' species.

What Nietzsche did not like about Darwinism, on the other hand, was what one of Darwin's most influential propagandists, the sociologist and philosopher Herbert Spencer, had contributed: the notion of the 'survival of the fittest'. While it seemed to sum up admirably the essence of Darwin's thesis, this shorthand formula in effect begged the question. Survival of the fittest, fine; but 'fittest' for what? Fittest to survive? If this was the be-all and end-all of human existence, it was not much to boast about. Indeed, in terms of logic it was something of a vicious circle, not to say a tautology. For if there was one thing that human history proved, it was that it was often those who were the least fitted to survive in a strictly physical sense – geniuses who had died prematurely, like Raphaël and Giorgione, like Mozart, Schubert and Chopin, club-footed limpers like Byron and Talleyrand, or high-strung epileptics like Alexander the Great, Julius Caesar and Mohammed – who had contributed the most to human culture. In any purely utilitarian evaluation of the process of human evolution – and for Nietzsche, Spencer was the very prototype of the English utilitarian – it did not really matter what sort of human beings were produced, provided that they demonstrated their capacity to survive. Such a 'philosophy' could only end up implicitly justifying the mass perpetuation of idiots and brutes, of 'rudimentary human beings', of *Dauermenschen* (made-to-last human beings), who were in reality as bereft of true human worth and individuality as were those Chinese – a race of multiplying 'survivors', if ever there was one – who, as Nietzsche had commented in several notes dating from 1881, spent their time taking opium, gambling and frolicking with women.

Precisely because Nietzsche's attitude towards Darwinism was ambivalent, at once admirative and critical, the unusually long paragraph he devoted to the subject in the opening section of *The Joyous Science* was as subtle and complex as any he ever wrote. Its basic propositions may be summarized as follows:

1. There is no basic, unquestionable teleological purposiveness to human existence, for in the cosmic context of the universe the human being is as 'boundlessly wretched' as the fly or the frog.
2. For this reason life is essentially tragic.
3. Human beings, by exhibiting a desire to live, have helped to perpetuate the species.
4. Even 'evil' men have contributed to the survival of the species – by fighting, using guile to overcome enemies, force, craft and cunning to tame certain animals, etc. If, from the very beginning of their history, human beings had been uniformly 'good', the human species could not possibly have survived.
5. Because of their need to believe that there must be a sense of purposiveness to their brief lives – in which respect they differ from other animals – human beings at all times have heeded the founders of moral codes and religions, even though such persons have regularly kindled religious wars and battles over moral evaluations. In getting people to believe that they were serving the interests of God, they were in fact promoting a belief in the value of human life and thus helping to preserve the species, which might otherwise have yielded to the suicidal extremes of pessimistic despair.
6. Even better than religious dreaming, however, is Man's capacity to laugh at the vanity of human existence – an ability which in the long run has invariably eroded and undermined the doctrines of the *Zwecklehrer* (final-goal teachers).
7. Given Man's need to believe in the purposiveness of existence,

'serious' faith-dispensers keep popping up and imperiously declaring: 'There is one thing that must absolutely not be laughed about any longer!'

8. There thus results a permanent conflict between the comic and the tragic. Or, as Nietzsche put it, 'not only laughter and the joyous wisdom but also the tragic, with all of its sublime irrationality, belong to the means and necessities of the preservation of the species'.
9. All religious beliefs consequently have their day, but also experience a rebirth, according to what Nietzsche called 'this new law of ebb and flow'.

The question left hanging in the air at the end of this subtle introduction was: on which side was Nietzsche in this perennial conflict between the comic and the tragic? His answer, given in section 2 (entitled 'The Intellectual Conscience'), was equally subtle and further proof that here, as in so much else, he was not going to be a narrow-minded partisan fanatically determined to view everything in black and white terms. Most human beings, he pointed out, do not worry too much about matters of final ends and morality. They take life as it comes. In other words, they are intellectually lazy – as he had already indicated at the start of his third 'Untimely Meditation', devoted to Schopenhauer. To this vast majority even the 'most talented of men and the noblest of women' belong. But at this point Nietzsche let fall the hammer that was already beginning to make him famous. What, he roundly declared, did he care about the kind-heartedness, the delicacy, even the genius of such persons if they harboured but tepid feelings about faith and moral judgements, and above all were not possessed by a deep-seated longing for certainty – which, in the final analysis, is what 'separates superior from inferior persons'? After which he added – and this must have come as a surprise to those of his readers (the vast majority) who had given his books a superficial reading – that he personally preferred a 'hatred against Reason', which he had found among certain pious persons, to the indifferent lukewarmness of the rest; for among the haters could at least be found 'a bad intellectual conscience'. (Precisely the kind that had been so splendidly and pathetically exemplified by that sublimely anguished, scientifically minded, passionately despairing Catholic, Pascal.)

Since it was neither kind-heartedness, nor delicacy, nor even genius that set truly superior persons apart from the rest, what quality was it that distinguished such persons from ordinary human beings? An initial answer to this question was provided in the third section ('Noble and Common'), in which Nietzsche once again expressed his strong distaste for 'utilitarian' ethics, according to which the value of any human action lies in the benefit of its results rather than in the 'purity' of the intention: 'To commonplace beings all noble, magnanimous feelings seem purposeless and thus first of all implausible.' The ability to 'shelve' rational 'common-sense' for the sake of a noble aim – such, for example, as a passionate pursuit of knowledge at the cost of one's health and honour (here Nietzsche was obviously thinking of himself) – was something that 'normal', practically minded persons could never understand. But it was such 'passion-possessed' souls – Columbus setting out on his 'crazy' voyage to discover a more direct, western route to distant Cathay, Galileo risking his academic reputation by forthrightly defending Copernicus's 'heretical' views about the solar system – who were truly 'noble', and their sceptical, 'practically minded' critics who were truly 'common'.

In the fourth section ('That which preserves the species') Nietzsche developed the thoughts embryonically suggested in the first two sections. Inasmuch as all societies are made up of more or less dormant masses, they must be periodically aroused from their passive slumbers by 'strong' and 'evil' men capable of arousing latent passions. These periodic disturbers of the peace, who arouse men against men, who defy piety but who also found new religions and systems of morality, are invariably regarded as 'evil' because they overturn the established boundary-markers and trample old-fashioned pieties underfoot. 'Good' men have traditionally been those whose roots are so deeply buried in the soil of a prevailing culture that they bring forth ripe fruit and are recognized as great cultivators of the mind. (Goethe, not named, was one such 'good' man.) But after a while the fertile land becomes exhausted and the 'ploughshare of evil' must be used to overturn it. By the 'ploughshare of evil', Nietzsche clearly had in mind the reformative, and even more the revolutionary processes – Christianity was one of them – which periodically are needed to keep societies from becoming stagnant and unproductive: as was the case for thousands of years in ancient Egypt, and for centuries in the history of modern China. It is 'evil' in the sense that every revolution is destructive of established society and values, but at the same time a beneficial, man-made evil, comparable on a far shorter time-scale to the mutations that had played such an important role in the long process of biological evolution. This was in effect – even if at this point little more than suggested – a cyclical theory of historical development, similar to the one that Boris Pasternak – to that extent a neo-Nietzschean – was to develop in his novel *Dr Zhivago*.

In reality, Nietzsche declared, 'evil instincts are every bit as purposive (*zweckmässig*), species-preserving, and indispensable as the good – their function alone is different'. The 'proof' of this peremptory statement was not offered until fifteen aphorisms further on – after Nietzsche had 'digressed' by discussing the inordinately hurried pace of modern life, which left people no time to think; the vital importance of unconscious drives and instincts, so blithely ignored by Descartes and his successors (four remarkable sections in which Nietzsche anticipated not only Freud, but Carl Jung's notion of the 'collective unconscious'); and Jeremy Bentham's utilitarian ideal of 'the greatest happiness for the greatest number' (unfavourably compared to the Stoics' more sober ideal of minimizing unhappiness).

> Examine the lives of the finest and most productive men and peoples and ask yourselves if a tree, which should proudly grow high in the air, can do without bad weather and storms; whether inclemency and outer resistance, whether hatred, jealousy, stubbornness, distrust, harshness, greed and violence do not belong to the *favourable* circumstances without which no great increase even in virtue is possible? The poison that is the undoing of weaker natures is invigorating for the strong – which is why he does not call it a poison.

It was from this small, highly concentrated acorn of a thought that Nietzsche was to develop his philosophy of 'strength through adversity' and its complementary opposite, 'degeneration through facility and comfort'. An approach to the problems of existence, both individual and collective, which in the twentieth century his most important successor, José Ortega y Gasset, adapted and improved in his own 'resistentialist' philosophy, and which Arnold Toynbee (who may not have realized that he was a neo-Nietzschean) later applied to six millennia of human history with his notion of 'challenge and response'.

In at least two respects Nietzsche's thinking had not basically changed since he had begun expounding it in *The Birth of Tragedy* and in his first 'Untimely Meditations'. The value of any civilization or culture depends on the number of geniuses and masterpieces it is capable of producing; and its ability to do this depends on a fragile balance, on a state of intellectual instability due to the perennial conflict between a destructively life-enhancing Dionysian force or frenzy, and a counter-force of artistically preserving Apollinian control. The old heady wine was now being poured into newly labelled bottles, but the age-old antagonism was basically the same: between the periodically erupting and disrupting masculine thirst for revolutionary change, and the feminine desire to preserve the embellishments and also the spiritual values of civilization.

This question of 'masculine' and 'feminine' influences in European history was highly speculative. What was anything but speculative and for

Nietzsche a burning question was the question of how aristocratic values were going to survive in increasingly middle-class and industrialized societies. Schopenhauer's response to this question had been to condemn businessmen out of hand as incurably uncouth, and the industrialization process and the growth of huge over-populated cities as deplorable developments. But this was merely an opinion, and, being unsupported by any attempt at social or psychological analysis, little more than a personal prejudice.

Nietzsche's own approach to this portentous question was curiously hesitant, more resembling a brief skirmish with the theme than a frontal assault. First of all, one had to begin by ridding oneself of a näive belief in the 'innocence' of youth, and particularly of young adolescents. Anyone wishing to formulate a 'realistic' aristocratic ethos had to pay heed to certain basic, often unpleasant sociological and psychological realities. One of them, expressed in aphorism 38, was the inherent volatility of young men, expressed in words that might have been written yesterday, rather than close to 120 years ago:

> When one thinks of how much force is contained in young men's need to explode, it is no wonder just how unsubtle and undiscriminating they show themselves to be in choosing this or that cause: what attracts them is the spectacle of the zeal enveloping the cause and, as it were, the sight of the burning fuse – not the cause itself. Subtle seducers understand this well and carefully emphasize the prospect of the explosion and disregard the reasons favouring the cause: for it is not with arguments that one can win over these powder-kegs!

Here, as elsewhere, Nietzsche was stressing the importance of deep-rooted, unconscious drives and motivations. What he called *Schadenfreude* (joy in destruction) was simply one particular manifestation of a more general desire for or 'will to power'. When a child takes a toy to pieces, it is in effect showing that it can do with it as it pleases, that the destroyer is more powerful than the object being destroyed. (This might seem to be so elementary as not to deserve mention. But entire generations of young boys and girls have recently been brought up – it would be more accurate to say 'brought down' – by Dr Benjamin Spock and other 'experts', according to the notion that young children must be allowed to 'express themselves' no matter what – on the unspoken assumption, inherited from Jean-Jacques Rousseau's *Émile*, that the unthwarted, unpunished child is, like the socially uncrippled adult, naturally good.)

Two aphorisms farther on (40, 'On the lack of noble forms'), Nietzsche contrasted the greater willingness of soldiers to obey a military 'chief' to the grudging reluctance of industrial workers to obey a 'boss'.

> It is singular that submission to powerful, frightening, indeed terrible persons, to tyrants and army leaders, is felt to be far less painful than this submission to unknown and uninteresting persons, such as all magnates of industry are: the worker normally sees in the entrepreneur nothing more than a crafty, blood-sucking, misery-exploiting dog, whose name, shape, habits, and renown are matters of total indifference to him. Manufacturers and big entrepreneurs have so far probably been all too lacking in those forms and distinctive traits of the *superior race*, which alone make *persons* interesting; had they in their looks and gestures the distinction of the hereditary nobility, there might perhaps be no socialism of the masses. For the latter are basically prepared for *slavery* of every kind, provided that the one who is above them constantly legitimizes himself as superior, as *born* to command – through distinguished form! The commonest man feels that refinement is not something that can be improvised and that one must honour in it the fruit of lengthy periods – but the absence of the superior form and the notorious vulgarity of manufacturers, with their plump, red hands, leads him to think that chance and good luck alone have raised this one above the others. All right, he concludes, let *us* for once try chance and luck! Let's now toss the dice! – and socialism begins.

This is, to put it gently, a quaint explanation of how 'socialism begins' and, even more, began; but it is typically Nietzschean in being, above all else, aesthetically inspired. What Nietzsche disliked about businessmen and industrial magnates were the bad manners, the swaggering self-importance, the loud-mouthed vulgarity. In this respect, as in so many others, he differed from Karl Marx, whose dislike was essentially moral. For, as the Russian philosopher Nicolas Berdyayev shrewdly noted long ago, the very notion of human 'exploitation' as something evil is a moral, not a 'scientific' criterion. Whereas, furthermore, Marx believed that industrial labourers could work in joy once they had freed themselves from the yoke of heartless capitalistic exploiters, Nietzsche regarded every kind of involuntarily accepted work as a form of slavery (section 42). It was his firm conviction, based on a profound study of the past, that no society can survive without 'slaves' – whether they be called serfs, farmhands, charwomen, garage mechanics, cooks, restaurant or hotel waiters, factory workers, street cleaners, garbage collectors or whatever. It was as much an illusion to think that the workers of the world could obtain real 'freedom' from drudgery as it was to believe that human beings are truly 'equal' by virtue of some innate 'right' which is flagrantly violated every day by

Mother Nature in all animal societies. Charles Darwin, in this respect, had shown himself to be more realistic than Karl Marx.

Another (negative, not to say 'plebeian') sign of the times, for Nietzsche, was what had been happening in the domain of 'repression of passions' (aphorism 47). In France, during Louis XIV's 'grand siècle', serious efforts had been made to regard all 'outbreaks of passion' as inescapably 'common', worthy of the bourgeois and the peasant. During the ensuing, eighteenth-century reign of Louis XV, the public display of passions in words and gestures became so inhibited that they assumed a supremely elegant, superficial, playful guise – even an insult could be accepted and returned with exquisitely courteous words. However, Nietzsche went on, the nineteenth century seemed bent on displaying and promoting the very oppposite:

> Everywhere, in daily life and in the theatre and not least of all in everything that is written, I see the relish caused by all *cruder* outbreaks and gesticulations of passion: there is a demand for a certain conventionality of passionate ardour – but not above all for passion itself! Nevertheless it will thereby finally be attained, and our descendants will have a *genuine savagery* and not merely a savagery and unmanneredness of forms.

Here, as in so many respects, Nietzsche's prophetic premonitions have been horrendously over-fulfilled and realized; and today hardly an evening passes without the television screen offering us the visual and sonic copulation of hysterical emotionalism and sentimental frenzy in a wild orgy of brutish 'passion', which would have left the soft-spoken author of *The Joyous Science* speechless with disgust.

Nobility of birth, for Nietzsche, was no guarantee of noble-mindedness. Genuine noble-mindedness, like genuine courage, seeks no honours, and manifests itself in a spontaneous magnanimity – a form of *noblesse du coeur*, as Nietzsche had already called it – which can be cultivated to the point of becoming a 'second nature', but which cannot be imposed from outside through a categorical imperative or universal norm of behaviour binding on all theoretically similar human beings. Nothing, in fact, for Nietzsche was further removed from genuine 'noble-mindedness' than the arrogant posturing of smug aristocrats who regarded their superiority as a birthright and who mistook the external trappings of 'respectability' for true 'nobility' of thought and sentiment, sufficient to set them apart from the rest of humankind. Like the 'altruism' displayed by so many, this was one more form of self-delusion, a hollow mask concealing a lack of genuine inner warmth and the kind of disinterested courage that 'seeks no honours'.

Real courage, here as elsewhere, begins with an unflinching readiness to face the often harsh realities of life, rather than to flee from them by brushing them under the carpet and treating them as 'unmentionable'. Nietzsche made this quite clear in section 71, devoted to 'Feminine Chastity', some of which is worth quoting in his own trenchant words:

> There is something quite astonishing and monstrous in the education of genteel women, indeed nothing perhaps is more paradoxical. Everyone is agreed on one thing, to bring them up as ignorant as possible in erotics and to instil in their souls a profound feeling of shame about such matters and an extreme impatience and fearful flight at the mention of these things. Only here, strictly speaking, is a woman's entire 'honour' at stake: what otherwise would one not be prepared to forgive her! But about this they must remain ignorant to the very depths of their being – they should have neither eyes nor ears nor words nor thoughts for this, their particular 'evil': indeed, here even knowledge is evil. And then! To be hurled with a ghastly lightning-flash into the reality and the knowledge through marriage – and furthermore through him whom they most love and revere: to surprise love and shame in contradiction, indeed, to have to experience rapture, sacrifice, duty, compassion and fright because of the unexpected proximity of god and beast and Heaven knows what else! – all this in one man! It would be difficult to improve on this tying of the soul into knots! Even the compassionate curiosity of the wisest connoisseur of human beings is insufficient to figure out how this or that woman manages to find this solution of the riddle in this riddle of a solution, and what ghastly deeply penetrating suspicions must be stirred up in the poor soul that has thus been unhinged . . .

No one who has taken the trouble to read this paragraph can honestly accuse Nietzsche of having been a misogynist or despiser of womankind. His poignant description of the excruciating spiritual and physical torments suffered on their wedding night by so many poorly prepared virgins antedated what Simone de Beauvoir had to say on the subject in *The Second Sex* by close to seventy years. Today, of course, this excoriation of Victorian prudery sounds distinctly 'old hat'. But now that the pendulum of 'propriety' has swung to the opposite extreme, it is by no means sure that Nietzsche would have approved of the 'sex education' that is now so generously offered to young schoolchildren, and which has robbed the first fumbling initiation and eroticism in general of the alluring mystery that once enveloped it. Indeed, he might well have agreed with Karl Kraus's mordant comment: 'Sexual education is that hard-boiled procedure thanks to which youth, for hygienic reasons, is denied the right to satisfy its curiosity unaided.'

If there was one significant respect in which *The Joyous Science* differed from its predecessors, it was in a greater abundance of poetic passages, rising at times to heights of lyrical intensity, in which Nietzsche did not hesitate to mock his own brand of idealism, and also Richard Wagner's. As in this aphorism (59) boldly entitled, 'We Artists!'

> It is enough to love, to hate, to desire, in fact to feel – and immediately the spirit and power of the dream descend upon us, and with wide-open eyes and insensitive to all dangers on the most perilous paths, we clamber on to the rooftops and towers of the fantasmagorical, and with no trace of vertigo, as though born to climb – we sleepwalkers of the day! We artists! We concealers of naturalness! We moon-and-god-struck addicts! We deathly quiet and tireless wanderers, up on the heights, which we do not perceive as heights but as our level plain, as our security!

In all, more than half a dozen sections of *The Joyous Science* were inspired by Richard Wagner. In one of them (99), titled 'Schopenhauer's Disciples', Nietzsche did something he had never dared to do before: he subjected Wagner's veneration of Schopenhauer to a severe critique, pointing out that this adoration had not only blinded the composer to the importance of other philosophers, but had even blinded him to the significance and achievements of modern science. It was, he claimed, what was most mysterious and irrational in Schopenhauer's philosophy – elements that would have fascinated Cagliostro – which had held Wagner in their thrall ever since he had first discovered him. 'Schopenhauerian', for example, had been Wagner's indignation over the corruption of the German language, even though Wagner's own style suffered from all the 'inflated sores and swellings' the sight of which used to make Schopenhauer so raving mad. Indeed, Wagnerism, among German-writing Wagnerians, was beginning to prove itself as dangerous as any kind of 'Hegelry' had ever been. Schopenhauerian too had been Wagner's hatred of the Jews, to whom he was unable to grant credit for their greatest deed: for the Jews were the 'inventors of Christianity'. This said, Nietzsche continued, it would be unfair to judge Wagner according to his writings, influenced as they were by a philosophy he had borrowed from another.

> Let us remain true to Wagner in what with him is *real* and original – and particularly let us, his disciples, remain true to what is real and original in ourselves . . . It matters little that, as a thinker, he is so often wrong; fairness and patience were never *his* forte. It is enough that his life should be right and maintain itself rightly for itself . . . We too should be free and fearless

and likewise grow and blossom out of ourselves in innocent self-centredness!

'*Frei und furchtlos*' – free and fearless! It was in this hardy as well as sanguine spirit that Nietzsche launched into the fourth and final book of *The Joyous Science*, dedicated to 'Sanctus Januarius'. It was preceded by a short eight-verse poem in which the wintry, two-faced saint was portrayed piercing the ice over Nietzsche's soul with his 'flaming spear', and it began with a gentle leg-pull of Cartesian metaphysics: 'I still live, I still think; I must still live, for I must still think. *Sum, ergo cogito: cogito, ergo sum.*' A charming way of suggesting that, contrary to what Descartes and so many other philosophers took for granted, the throbbing, urgent reality known as Life is even more primary and demanding than is Thought.

It is no more possible to do full justice to this fourth and final book of *The Joyous Science* than it was with the three that preceded it. But there is one 'aphorism' (283, titled 'Well preparing human beings') which deserves to be quoted *in extenso*, so fateful was the impact it later had on future generations of 'disciples', particularly in Germany:

> I welcome all advance signs of the start of a more manly, more warlike age, which will above all restore courage to a place of honour! For it should pave the way for a still higher epoch and muster the strength that it will one day need – an epoch that carries heroism into [the field of] knowledge and which *wages war* on behalf of thoughts and their consequences. To this end many better preparing and braver men are now needed who cannot spring up out of nothing – just as little from the sand and slime of present-day civilization and big-city education: men who with silent, solitary determination know how to be content and constant in their invisible activity: men who have an inner inclination to seek in all things that which is *to be overcome*: men to whom cheerfulness, patience, simplicity, and a scorn for major vanities are as natural as magnanimity in victory and indulgence towards the petty vanities of all who are defeated: men with a sharp, free judgement regarding all victors and the part played by chance in every victory and renown: men with their own festivals, their own work days, their own times of mourning, well practised and assured in matters of command, and equally ready, on occasion, to obey, and to be equally proud in either case, as though serving their own cause: more exposed and endangered men, more productive men, happier men! For, believe me – the secret for reaping the greatest fruitfulness and the greatest enjoyment from existence is called – *living dangerously*! Build your cities near Vesuvius! Send out your ships to hitherto unexplored seas! Live in constant warfare with the likes of you and with yourselves! Be brigands and conquerors, so

> long as you cannot be rulers and possessors, ye seekers after knowledge! The time will soon be past when it will be enough to live hidden in the woods like bashful deer! Knowledge will finally stretch out its hand for that which is its due – it will want *to rule* and *possess*, and you with it!

Dangerous words! And a dangerous recipe for living! For although the war Nietzsche was here extolling was an intellectual war waged against all forms of religious and metaphysical obscurantism, a war fought on behalf of science and to free the modern mind for the gigantic tasks that lay ahead, and in no way a nationalistic war to further pan-German or any other militaristic cause, this was how this particular 'Call to Arms' was later interpreted by hundreds of thousands of patriotic numbskulls, who read their own narrow-minded, fanatical meaning into this inflammatory exhortation.

Did Nietzsche sense that this might happen? At this point of his life, probably not. But of one thing at least he was already convinced: the battle between the comic and the tragic, between the cosmic and the human, between Science and Religion, had only just begun. And it was by no means certain that in this mighty clash the forces of Reason would ultimately triumph, so agonizing was the void that the loss of religious certainty was already opening up in many modern souls. Already in the 125th aphorism, sombrely named 'The Madman', Nietzsche had described an old man wandering about in broad daylight with a lantern and angrily apostrophizing everyone he meets: 'Whither has God gone? I will tell you. We have killed him – you and I! We are all of us his murderers!'

Even Socrates, the heroic prototype of the rationalist, the fearless debater, the joyous Socrates who had lived out his life 'before all eyes like a soldier' (aphorism 340), had been unable to keep himself from saying, on his deathbed, 'Oh Crito, I owe a cock to Asclepius' (the Greek god of medicine), thus revealing that he too had been a sufferer – Nietzsche could have added, like himself – and superstitious to boot. Try to laugh as one might at the 'comedy' of human existence, the tragic sense of life always triumphs in the end. Which is why, quite logically, he ended *The Joyous Science* with a final section (342) titled '*Incipit tragoedia*' ('The tragedy begins'). A tragedy – for Nietzsche the man as well as Nietzsche the thinker – which was about to be as soul-shattering as any he had so far experienced.

## CHAPTER 28

# Storm and Stress

*No! Life has not disappointed me! With each passing year I find it more real, more desirable, more mysterious – ever since the day when I was overcome by the great deliverer, the thought that life should be an experiment for the seeker after knowledge – and not a duty, not a fatality, not a swindle!*

It is impossible to say just when this 'liberating' thought (expressed in the 324th aphorism of his recently completed book) took possession of Nietzsche. But it may have 'crystallized' after his first meetings with Lou Salomé in Rome. Now, after several setbacks (with Erwin Rohde and Heinrich Romundt), he fancied that at last he had found someone capable of becoming a reliable disciple. All the greater, therefore, was the shock administered to him by his sister when, after her return from Bayreuth, it dawned on him that the 'experiment' into which he was so 'heroically' plunging might end up in inglorious defeat.

Because of the rainy weather, which made the Tautenburg forest so damp and forbidding for someone afflicted with a chronic bronchial cough, Fritz and his sister had decided that, until the skies cleared, it would be better if the delicate Lou Salomé spent a day or two in Jena with their good friend Heinrich Gelzer, a historian and Byzantine scholar who had previously taught at Basel.

When Lou reached Jena, on 6 or 7 August, she was in an angry as well as anxious mood. She had been reluctant to leave Bayreuth, where Paul Zhukovsky and Heinrich von Stein were urging her to stay on, like Malwida von Meysenbug, who no more liked the idea of Lou's spending two weeks alone with Nietzsche than did a morbidly jealous Paul Rée. But this was the price Lou knew she had to pay to be able to realize the 'trinitarian' scheme on which she had set her ardent heart and mind.

Nietzsche was not present when Lou reached the Gelzers' house in Jena, but his sister was. And almost immediately the sparks began to fly. Still inwardly fuming over Nietzsche's reproachful letter and the blow he had delivered to her hopes by telling her that their 'winter plans' were shelved, Lou turned on Elisabeth once they were alone and gave shrill vent to her fury. Her brother, she said, was a madman who didn't know what he wanted and was out above all to exploit her! He had first wanted to use her as a kind of secretary and reader, but he had soon realized that he had much more to gain by exploiting her brilliance as an exponent of his philosophy. She had agreed to this in good faith, but now, by deciding to scrap their winter plans, he was placing her in an acutely embarrassing position, since people were certain to conclude that she had proved herself to be an inadequate 'student'. When Elisabeth began to protest, Lou lost her temper and told her that she was not going to be exploited by anyone; not even by her brother, a mean egotist whose 'lofty' plans for an intellectual 'cohabitation' concealed the most sordid intentions. She had learned enough about men to see through their 'high-minded' intentions, having twice already suffered this kind of experience. Elisabeth heatedly retorted that this may well have been the case with the Russian men Lou had frequented, but that her brother's intentions were pure. Lou scoffed: 'Who was the first to sully the plan for communal living with the basest intentions? Who was the first to begin talking of an intellectual friendship when he saw that he couldn't have anything else? Who was the first to think of a free union? It was your brother!' In German a *wilde Ehe* (a 'wild' or 'savage marriage') has a far stronger connotation than a 'free union' in English, and was thus particularly shocking to the provincial, puritanical Elisabeth Nietzsche. 'Yes,' repeated Lou, 'it was your noble, pure-minded brother who first had the filthy intention of a wild marriage!'

The furious altercation was interrupted by the appearance of Clara Gelzer, who was so alarmed by the shouting that she hurried up the stairs to find out what was going on. But this was by no means the end of this verbal duel. Since the Gelzers were leaving the next day for Basel, Lou could not remain in Jena, even for a night. Nietzsche, who turned up in the early afternoon, accordingly accompanied Lou and his sister to Tautenburg that evening. While he was busy talking to the parish priest, who had agreed to put up both 'ladies' in his vicarage, Lou, relishing her 'free-spirited' lack of inhibitions, said to the prim Elisabeth: 'Don't think for a moment that I have designs on your brother or am in love with him! I could sleep in the same room with him and harbour no seditious thoughts.' When the horrified Elisabeth repeatedly asked her to stop this 'obscene talk', Lou said to her with a sneer, 'Come now, with Rée I say things that are far more obscene.' Outraged to hear that it was from Rée himself that Lou had learned that Nietzsche had thought of a 'wild marriage', Elisabeth told the 'shameless young hussy' that she was going to write to her mother to find out if this was really so. At this Lou flew into a rage and uttered such 'dire threats' that Elisabeth did not dare to repeat them later in a long letter of explanation to Clara Gelzer.

The least that can be said is that this bold experiment in 'philosophical initiation' got off to a sticky start. It might have ended the very next morning when Elisabeth, after a sleepless night, told Fritz some of the things Lou had said to her the day before. Nietzsche promised to take the matter up with Lou, which he apparently did – not (as Elisabeth had hoped) by sending the 'upstart hussy' back to Stibbe, but by making Lou understand that she would have to treat his sister with more respect during her stay in Tautenburg, or face the prospect of never seeing him again. Her bluff called, Lou capitulated, being artful enough to realize that Nietzsche only half trusted his easily shocked sister, whose enthusiasm for *Freigeisterei* had never been more than verbal.

The result was an uneasy truce, which lasted throughout Lou Salomé's three-week stay at Tautenburg. While Elisabeth wandered off into the woods to weep and bewail the fate that had overtaken her brother, Nietzsche was allowed to climb the stairs in the vicar's house and to console the 'naughty' Lou, who even allowed him to kiss her hand twice – so at least she reported in another instalment of the 'diary' which, here at Tautenburg, as previously in Bayreuth, she dutifully dispatched every other day to Paul Rée at Stibbe.

As soon as the weather improved, Lou's cough disappeared and she and Nietzsche began to take long walks through the dense pine forests, pausing to watch the squirrels that kept warily hopping back and forth over the moss and the sun-streaked paths. To Lou's delighted surprise, Nietzsche, normally so 'reclusive', was happy to have her at his side for hours on end. Theirs soon became a delicious solitude *à deux*. While Elisabeth disappeared into the woods to continue her unhappy moping, Nietzsche and Lou – he with his inseparable parasol, she with her auburn hair covered by a hunting-cap – could sit beneath the linden trees adjoining the local inn and enjoy their luncheon out of doors. Sometimes, to be altogether free of Elisabeth's importunate presence at the vicarage, Lou would remain in Nietzsche's ground-floor bedroom talking and debating until midnight, with her red scarf casually wound around the lampshade on his little table to shield his sensitive eyes – much to the annoyance of Herr Hahnemann, the farmer, who had to escort her back to the vicarage when he would have preferred to be in bed for another brief night of sleep before rising at dawn for the harvest.

There was no dearth of things to talk and laugh about – among them the prudishness displayed by the frequently absent Elisabeth and the curious sounds made by the 'poltergeists' each time Nietzsche climbed the stairs to Lou's bedroom in the vicarage. Lou had brought along the rough draft of an essay on 'Woman', which was subjected to a severe critique because of the 'execrable' style of its first part. Nietzsche codified his recommendations in a ten-point memorandum entitled 'The Theory of Style', in which he explained that a good style must be 'alive', it must sound as natural as normal speech, it must express feeling, and it should approach poetry, without trangressing the limits between poetry and prose. He also offered her a list of thirteen themes or aspects of womanhood that merited further investigation – including (no. 12) the condition of pregnancy, which (he claimed) had over the centuries determined the 'essence' of a woman's being.

To prepare her for this 'cram-course' in philosophical 'initiation', Paul Rée in his Prussian home near the Baltic had begun compiling a list of aphorisms in what he dubbed the 'Stibbe Nest-Book' – Stibbe, since her mother had returned to Petersburg, having become for his *Schneckli* ('little snail', in German-Swiss baby-talk vernacular) Lou's normal home, habitat and protective 'shell'. Lou joyfully adopted the aphoristic 'mode', in which brevity of wit and challenging paradoxes count for more than philosophical profundity. By the time she reached Tautenburg, she had become quite adept. (Sample: 'To keep life from becoming a burden, one must not shoulder it but place it beneath one's feet' – to which Nietzsche appended, 'and make a pedestal of it'.) He added six aphorisms of his own – one of which he later developed in *Beyond Good and Evil*: 'The immense expectation with regard to sexual love spoils woman's vision for all further perspectives.'

Nietzsche was so enthralled by his new companion's quick-wittedness that on 20 August he wrote to Heinrich Köselitz that Lou, who was staying another week at Tautenburg, was '*the intelligentest of all women*. Every five days we have a small tragicomic scene. Everything I wrote to you about her is nonsense, and probably also what I have just written.'

The first of the four bound copies of *Die fröhliche Wissenschaft*, which Nietzsche had just received, was immediately dispatched to Köselitz (with the author's personal thanks for his invaluable proofreading services). Another was offered to Lou. She probably received the gift with a feeling of relief, for there is reason to suspect that she had not read *Schopenhauer as Educator* (which Nietzsche had lent her in Lucerne) or *Morgenröte* (which he had had sent to her in Zürich) with any close attention. A quick reading of the final part of this new, positive, '*ja-sagend*' ('yes-saying') book prompted Lou to give Nietzsche a poem she had begun months before: *Gebet an das Leben* – 'A Prayer to Life', in which she had imagined herself lustily embracing life and trying 'in the scorching heat of battle' to find the 'solution to the riddle of your being'.

Towards the middle of the month Lou began to feel bored with this all too 'studious' and sedentary existence, so different from the stimulating social life she had enjoyed at Bayreuth. In a letter to Paul Rée she expressed a longing to see the world and savour all it had to offer. Replying from the North Sea island of Helgoland, where he was undergoing a brief salt-water 'cure', Rée said that he was leaving Hamburg on 25 August and would spend the night of the 26th in Berlin, where he proposed that Lou join him. He was eager to see his darling again – particularly since Nietzsche had been behaving like a 'bridegroom' in kicking up a fuss over the goings-on in Bayreuth. 'You do not need to befriend him more, do you hear, *Schneckli*!'

The proprietary tone of this injunction probably flattered Lou's vanity more than it irritated her deep-seated determination to preserve her feminine 'independence'. She had, in any case, no desire to prolong her stay at Tautenburg, for she had won her 'wager' with herself. Her winter plans once again included an enthusiastic Nietzsche, who had agreed that the three members of the 'unholy trinity' should next assemble in Munich, before moving on to Paris – a proposal that had been warmly approved by Malwida von Meysenbug.

On Sunday, 27 August, the day after Lou Salomé's departure, Nietzsche took the train alone to Naumburg. His sister Elisabeth refused to accompany him, saying that her eyes were so swollen from tears and weeping that their mother would have a shock on seeing her and demand an explanation. Fritz argued with her briefly. She was making a mountain out of a molehill, she didn't understand Lou and her candid *Freigeisterei*. What did he care what the world thought of him and Lou Salomé, since at Tautenburg nothing 'scandalous' had happened between them!

In Naumburg his mother was delighted to see her Fritz again, but surprised that their 'Lieschen' should not have come home with him. Nietzsche, at his most evasive, explained that Elisabeth had decided to remain at Tautenburg, a place she dearly loved, in order to enjoy a bit of solitude. To Paul Rée, now returned to Stibbe, he asked if he had received his gift copy of *Die fröhliche Wissenschaft;* and to Lou, in a letter enclosed in the same envelope, he explained that he had only spoken 'a little' to his sister Elisabeth, 'but enough to dispatch the newly popping-up spectre back to the *nothingness* from which it came'. He was once again possessed by the 'daemon' of composition, and he was putting her poem, 'A Prayer to Life', to music in the hope that his friend Louise Ott in Paris could sing it for them with her 'wonderfully strong and expressive voice'. Finally, he pleaded with Lou to '*become what you are*', explaining that 'first one needs to emancipate oneself from one's chains, and finally one must emancipate oneself from this emancipation. Each of us, even if in very different ways, has to toil against the chain-sickness, even after he has smashed the chains.'

This was a reminder that the cause of feminist 'emancipation' could, like any other kind of dogma, end up shackling the minds of its most fervent advocates. It was also a reminder of his own mission in life: to avoid becoming a blind advocate of scientific knowledge, whose praises he had tried to sing in his latest book.

Nietzsche's stay in Naumburg lasted little more than one week, in an atmosphere of steadily mounting tension. Fritz continued his embarrassed equivocations, which were finally torn to shreds by a plaintive letter addressed to their mother in which, without mentioning Lou Salomé by name, Elisabeth wrote that at Tautenburg she had seen her brother's philosophy 'come to life' and had been profoundly shocked. It was a philosophy that exalted Evil rather the Good she had been brought up to revere. She had been so profoundly shocked by what she had witnessed that, had she been a Catholic, she would have retired immediately to a convent and spent her time in prayer in order to atone for the mischief that was being committed.

Franziska Nietzsche now demanded that her son come clean and tell her the whole truth, finally calling him a liar and a coward who had dishonoured the memory of his father. In a rage Fritz went upstairs to his bedroom, packed his trunk, and told his trembling, weeping mother that he was taking the train to Leipzig and going on from there to Paris for the winter.

From Leipzig Fritz wrote a letter to Elisabeth (still sulking at Tautenburg) to say that she had not the slightest idea of how much 'joyful confidence' (in himself and the future) this blessed summer had brought him. Even Lou had profited from her stay at Tautenburg. Paul Rée had written from Stibbe that, intellectually speaking, she had 'grown several inches' taller.

To Franz Overbeck in Basel he wrote at even greater length on the same day (9 September) that this 'long, rich summer' had proved to be a 'testing time' in which for once he had managed to bridge 'the hideous chasm between willing and fulfilling'. The 'daemon of music' had again possessed him, but nothing had been more profitable than his conversations with Lou. 'Our intelligences and tastes are to the deepest degree *related* – and, on the other hand, the contradictions are so great that we are for each other the most instructive objects and subjects of observation. I have not yet known anyone who knew how to extract such a mass of *objective insights* from her own experiences, and knows how to draw so much from everything she has learned.' Indeed, he went on, working himself up into a state of rapture, he wondered if such a degree of '*philosophical frankness*' had ever existed anywhere between two human beings!

After the good news came the bad. For, alas, his sister Elisabeth had turned into a deadly enemy of Lou, 'she was filled with moral indignation from start to finish and now claims to know what there is in my philosophy'.

The next day Nietzche sent a postcard to his mother, giving her his new address in Leipzig. He had suffered a major migraine attack, two sleepless nights, and severe eye-aches, but despite the strains of apartment-hunting, he had managed to overcome his physical woes and was now lodged with a schoolteacher named Janicaud, who lived near the suburban Rosenthal park.

Before heading for the Naumburg railway station, he had found time to write to Lou, saying that Köselitz in Venice had found the music he had composed for her poem, ' A Prayer for Life', not only 'Christian', but even 'Christian-warlike', as though he had written a 'Crusaders' March' full of strident dissonances suggesting the clang and clash of shields. 'It now looks as though my *return* to "human beings" is going to have the devastating result that I will *lose* the few I could still be said in any way to possess.'

The second-floor room Nietzsche had rented – for the 'studentish' price of 15 marks per month – was not quite as 'quiet' as he had indicated in his letter to his mother. For the schoolteacher-landlord had several small children whose noisy romping in the corridor often prompted the 'Herr Professor' to open his door and stare at them sternly through his thick-lensed glasses. At his request a tall-backed 'grandfather's armchair' was installed by his desk, over which Nietzsche could gaze out through the window at the poplar-fringed meadows and the sturdy green-leafed oaks of the Rosenthal park.

Here, as he had done in Genoa and at Sils-Maria, he brewed his own tea before getting down to work in the morning. The one notable difference in his daily routine – now that he had decided to abandon his previous hermit-like solitude and to try a 'return to human beings' – was his regular visit every afternoon to the Kintzschy Café, where he could meet old friends like Heinrich Romundt or Max Heinze, his former tutor at Pforta, later professor of philosophy at Basel, and now university rector: one of the few members of Leipzig's academic community who still dared to be seen talking to the 'scandalous' author of *Human, All Too Human* and the heretical books that had followed.

Nietzsche's fear that he was about to lose his few remaining friends turned out to be excessive. Within ten days of his arrival in Leipzig he received no less than four letters of congratulation for *The Joyous Science* – sent to him by Carl von Gersdorff and Marie Baumgartner (both of whom felt that it was the least negative and most cheerful book he had yet written), by the Swiss novelist Gottfried Keller and by Jacob Burckhardt. The sixty-four-year-old Burckhardt, who modestly likened himself to an 'aged waggoner' who had trouble bumping his way over the high roads and by-roads of history *sans malheur* (without mishap), was lavish in his praise for the 'immense and more or less compressed wealth' of insights into the most diverse historical subjects offered in this book; indeed, he regretted that the study of history could not be enriched by others possessing Nietzsche's penetrating perspicacity.

On the last day of September Lou Salomé and Paul Rée turned up in Leipzig, intending to stay several weeks before moving on to Paris, where (so Malwida von Meysenbug claimed) the winter weather was far more clement than in Germany. Paul Rée's mother had agreed to accompany them to Paris in order to reassure Lou's worried mother in St Petersburg. For the moment there was no further talk of Lou's bold scheme for a harmonious 'cohabitation' under one roof, and since Nietzsche had already found a 'nest' for himself in a Leipzig suburb, this aspect of her 'trinitarian' project was quietly shelved.

Nietzsche at this point was innocently riding the crest of the wave. Despite the rift with his sister, everything seemed to be working out wonderfully well. As he wrote to his mother on 1 October, with an urgent request for a warm dressing-gown – for the weather had suddenly turned cold – for him this was continuing to be a 'festival-year', and to his delighted surprise he was being 'spoiled' by everyone, just as he had been in Messina. Max Heinze's wife was allowing him to use her husband's library; Heinrich Romundt had delayed his departure in order to see his friend Rée again; Carl von Gersdorff was expected to turn up at any moment with his recently wedded wife. Carl Riedel, the director of a famous Leipzig choral group, had warmly greeted Nietzsche and indicated that four of his singers might be ideally suited to perform a sung version of the music he had composed for Lou Salomé's 'A Prayer for Life'. 'Peter Gast' (Heinrich Köselitz's musical pseudonym) was travelling all the way from Venice to help his enthusiastic sponsor, Nietzsche, 'sell' him and his compositions not only to Arthur Nikisch, the highly respected conductor of the Leipzig City Orchestra, but also to the musical publisher Ernst Wilhelm Fritzsch.

Knowing how intrigued Lou was by poltergeists, fortune-telling and all forms of 'spiritism', Nietzsche took her and Paul Rée to attend a public display of the 'telepathic' gifts of a famous medium who proposed to conjure up 'dead spirits' (the 'Russian nun', the 'small child', etc.) and have them 'communicate' with her. The performance was such a wretched piece of hocus-pocus that Nietzsche lost patience after half an hour and did not bother to offer the assembled company one of the three 'physiological', psychological, or 'moral' theories he had prepared to explain away these 'extrasensory' phenomena.

On 18 October the 'trinitarians' attended a big 'Wagner concert', at which extracts from the composer's operas, including *Parsifal*, were sung by several 'stars' who had performed during the recent Festival at Bayreuth. But Nietzsche's hope that his 'friend' Lilli Lehmann (whom he had met at Bayreuth) would leave Berlin, where her performances in Bizet's *Carmen* had created a sensation, and come to Leipzig soon evaporated.

This was only one of several disappointments which gradually turned this initially 'radiant' month of October into one of bleak melancholy. Even before Heinrich Köselitz reached Leipzig on the 13th, Nietzsche had been told by Arthur Nikisch that he had not had time to look at Peter Gast's neo-Goethean *Singspiel* fantasy ('Jest, Ruse and Vengeance'), being overwhelmed with work preparing performances of Schumann's *Manfred* and Wagner's *Meistersinger.* The choirmaster, Carl Riedel, proved equally evasive in (not) deciding what to do with Nietzsche's musical version of Lou Salomé's 'A Prayer to Life' – judged by Köselitz to be closer in spirit to the 'philosophy of the knights of the Holy Grail' than to the *joie de vivre* so cheerfully expressed in the introductory verses of *Die fröhliche Wissenschaft.* This latest Nietzsche opus, as his publisher, Ernst Schmeitzner, had warned him, was likely to be as 'unsellable' to an indifferent or hostile reading public as had been *Morgenröte.*

Even more troubling than these setbacks was Nietzsche's realization that Lou Salomé's 'trinitarian' experiment in 'fruitful philosophical cohabitation' was fast turning into a dishonest 'triangle', in which none of the partners any longer dared to express what was really on his or her mind when they were together. The first signs of impending collapse had begun to appear at Stibbe, after Lou's return from Tautenburg. Galvanized by three weeks of intimate exposure to Nietzsche's stimulating company, Lou had plunged back feverishly into a new round of 'studies', including a close, attentive reading of *Human, All Too Human.* This display of intellectual industry, accompanied by an incisive critique of the new 'book' on which he was supposed to be 'working', undermined the little self-confidence he still possessed and plunged Paul Rée into a state of deep depression. After a long argument one evening, during which Lou took him to task for being so dispirited and listless, Rée wrote her an apology saying that for years he had fought against an adversary more powerful and terrifying than any she had had to face: a love of gambling and of night-time, bohemian loafing in the streets of Berlin – which had slowly become an ineradicable feature of his character. 'Although I am a protection and support for you in life, you are too honest in spite of everything to go on wanting this if the innermost and deepest sympathy between us is in the slightest bit upset. But this it is. For . . . inertia now lies deep in my nature . . . Therefore,' Rée had concluded, 'let us walk towards our tombs by separate paths.'

To these gloomy words Lou had reacted with her customary energy. Just as she had modified Paul Rée's first pessimistic maxim in the 'Stibbe Nest-Book', changing 'Every happiness dies of itself' into 'Every happiness survives itself', so now she wrote below Rée's pathetic confession, 'No, certainly not! Let us live and strive together until you have *retracted* this.'

From that moment on Lou Salomé knew that she had a life-giving task to fulfil. She had to bring a 'dead man' back to life as gently as only a woman could, appealing to his 'better self', to the active intellectual he had once been and still occasionally showed himself capable of being. This flattered her vanity and simultaneously aroused the martial spirit that had found expression in 'A Prayer for Life' – a poem that had prompted Köselitz to write to Nietzsche from Venice: 'More and more I am scared of this Fräulein Lou. I can stand this kind of feeling in a woman even less than in a man. I cannot fully endure this abrasive use of warlike expressions and even less the yearning for the pain of life. Is this young Fräulein sick?' It was a good question, and one that may have touched Nietzsche to the quick. For there is little doubt that it was Lou Salomé's frailty and what he assumed was an incipient form of consumption which from the start had made this 'fellow sufferer' particularly sympathetic to Nietzsche.

The dilemma now facing Lou was in reality insoluble, reluctant though she was to admit it. The masculine 'saviour' she had latched on to in Rome, in order to free herself from her mother and the tyranny of domestic life in Petersburg, was a self-crippled and self-crippling intellectual who needed her at least as much as she needed him. But, precisely for this reason, he resembled a broken stick, likely to snap under the slightest strain. And Nietzsche's overpowering presence, as Rée had candidly admitted more than once to Lou, was just such a strain. It 'crushed' him, it caused his mind to 'falter'.

As long as they had been alone, in purely masculine company or with a benign 'aunt' like Malwida von Meysenbug, whose heart neither yearned to possess, Paul Rée and Nietzsche had been able to get along reasonably well. But, as Malwida had quite rightly feared (while paradoxically trying to promote a non-cohabitational, purely platonic 'trinity'), the intrusion of an alluring young lady with whom both men – whatever they might consciously think or imagine – had gradually fallen in love, was bound to turn the 'trinity', whether holy or unholy, into a vicious triangle. Each wanted to be her exclusive 'protector': Paul Rée by offering an alternative home and 'shell' for his fragile, high-strung *Schneckli*, Nietzsche by raising this 'intelligentest' of women to new, unheard-of heights of philosophical genius as his feminine disciple. Was it pure accident if he was now in his thirty-eighth year – the same age as Abélard when he had first met the nineteen-year-old Héloïse? Was this not his predestined task, his superhuman Fatum? He would show a sceptical, shallow, superficial world that miracles could still be accomplished in the genuine 'liberation' of exalted womanhood with the help of a contemporary Héloïse far more credible and full of fire and genius than the sentimental creature of Jean-Jacques Rousseau's romantic imagination.

Of Lou's two 'suitors', which in effect they had become, it was clearly Paul Rée who represented the lesser danger. He was not trying to found a philosophical school, he was not looking for disciples. This, however, was Nietzsche's avowed aim. Lou's long walks and daily talks with Rée at Stibbe had convinced her that Paul had no physical claims on her body, that he was quite capable of being an 'undemanding' and 'comfortable' companion. But with Nietzsche, no matter how 'noble-minded' he might claim to be, she had no certain assurance, or more exactly self-assurance. For there is little doubt that her furious outburst and 'obscene talk' at Jena and later at Tautenburg with Elisabeth, were aimed not only at Nietzsche for his masterful insistence on having Lou to himself for several weeks of 'philosophical initiation', but also at herself for being exposed to and having to struggle against temptation.

Her dilemma was pointedly expressed in at least three maxims penned in the 'Stibbe Nest-Book': 'The sensual moment is the last word of love for the woman, the first for the man'; 'The greater the intensity between two human beings, the stouter are the barriers that are needed'; and finally: 'Spiritual proximity between two human beings seeks to express itself physically – but the physical expression devours the spiritual proximity.' If she were ever to succumb to temptation – one reason why Paul Rée was such an indispensable 'protector' – she was bound to become Nietzsche's physical as well as intellectual slave: an explosive situation almost certain to provoke the very hatred that an overpowering 'love' was supposed to banish for ever.

Lou's schizophrenic sentiments on this subject were clearly revealed in a longer, highly private note written for herself during her five weeks in Leipzig: 'Just as Christian (like every) mysticism attains crude religious sensuality at its highest ecstasy, so the most ideal form of love again becomes sensual in ideality precisely thanks to the great untensing of feeling. A disagreeable point, this revenge of the human – I do not like feelings there where, in the process of circulation, they again merge into each other, for that is the point of false pathos where truth and sincerity of feeling are lost.

'Is it this that is estranging me [from] N[ietzsche]?'

The answer to this question was almost certainly yes. And not the least extraordinary aspect of this intellectual love-affair between Lou Salomé and the author of *Human, All Too Human* is the length of time it took Nietzsche to realize the extent to which Lou's erotic psychology had been warped by her sex-resisting Christian upbringing.

In Leipzig Heinrich Köselitz was struck by Nietzsche's habit of coming to see him each day before going to visit Lou Salomé and Paul Rée. It was almost as though he was seeking encouragement and invigoration before each encounter, and all the stranger in someone who struck him as being 'not quite there'. At Nietzsche's insistence he went to call on the young lady who had managed to work the ex-professor up into such a state of nervous euphoria, but was told that Lou was ill. The next day he was luckier and, like Malwida von Meysenbug, Franz and Ida Overbeck before him, he was bowled over by this feminine phenomenon. 'She is truly a genius,' he wrote in a letter to a girlfriend in Vienna, 'and of an utterly heroic character; in height a little taller than me, with a well-proportioned figure, fair-haired with the face of an old Roman patrician. Her ideas make one realize that she has ventured to the farthest horizons of the thinkable, morally as well as intellectually – as said: a genius, in mind and spirit.'

Lou, for her part, may not have had as flattering an opinion of Köselitz, even though Nietzsche had been trying to persuade everyone he could buttonhole in the Leipzig musical world that this 'Peter Gast' was a new Italo-German or German-Italian Mozart, combining the finest virtues of both peoples. But when Lou expressed a desire to see Köselitz again, the misanthropic composer prudently declined.

Since Köselitz made no claim to be a 'thinker', this was no great loss as far as Lou's long-range ambition was concerned – which was to attract around herself as many brilliant minds as possible. One such was Ludwig Hüter, a young student of philosophy and admirer of Malwida von Meysenbug whom she had recently met in Berlin. On 14 October she wrote to Hüter (who later described Lou as being 'beautiful and emotionally bewitching') to say that she and Paul Rée would soon be arriving in Berlin and staying for a 'fairly long time' with Rée's mother, who was going to spend the winter in the German capital. There was no mention of Nietzsche in this letter nor, oddly enough, of any plan to go on from Berlin to Paris. One thing it clearly attested: Lou's determination to widen the threesome's small philosophical 'circle' by attracting other 'talents'.

Another of these coveted 'talents' was the erudite Heinrich von Stein, the prototype of the 'blond, imposing . . . German, very serious, yet very friendly', as Cosima Wagner had noted in her diary when he had first come to Bayreuth to tutor the young Siegfried in October 1879. Lou, who had enjoyed her dialectical duelling with him during the *Parsifal* festival in August, had not forgotten his invitation that she visit him in Halle. Paul Rée was now dispatched to the old university town, where Stein had set himself up as a private tutor in philosophy, and two days later (24 October) Lou followed up with a letter – written 'in the name of our trinity, that is Nietzsche, Rée and myself' – imploring him to come to see them in Leipzig. An open-minded admirer of Nietzsche's writings, Stein found the invitation too tempting to resist. Unfortunately, on the day he picked for a brief visit to Leipzig (31 October), Nietzsche was absent. He may have travelled to Naumburg to effect a reconciliation with his mother who, greatly relieved to discover that her Fritz was living alone with a respectable schoolteacher and not in a 'wild-marriage' state of concubinal sin with the perverse Fräulein Lou, had sent him a fancy cake for his thirty-eighth birthday on 15 October. When, on his return to Leipzig, Nietzsche learned that Heinrich von Stein had briefly come and gone, he sent him the proofs of his new book and expressed the hope that they might meet one day in Halle to discuss *The Joyous Science*. 'I have been told that you, perhaps more than anyone else, have devoted yourself heart and soul to Wagner and Schopenhauer. This is something *priceless*, assuming that it has its time.' This was a reiteration of the *Kettenkrankheit* (chain-sickness) warning he had already issued to Lou Salomé. To be a passionate admirer of Wagner and Schopenhauer when one was still relatively young was a sure sign that Stein was one of those rare, 'nobler' souls Nietzsche had described in *The Joyous Science* who belong to a superior species because they take art and the mysteries of human existence with the utmost seriousness. But this was only a first step on the rocky, uphill road to personal improvement, and it could easily prove to be paralysing, mind-numbing and enchaining were it also to be the last.

To Nietzsche's dismay, an uncomfortably cold October passed over into an even harsher November without anything having been decided about a future move to Paris. Not until the eve of her and Rée's departure for Berlin (on 5 November) did Lou bother to ask Nietzsche to write to her sceptical mother, who did not like the idea of her daughter going to spend a few months in Paris, even if chaperoned by Paul Rée's mother. In his letter of 'forceful' recommendation – to judge by Madame Salomé's reply from Petersburg – the glowing picture Nietzsche painted of Lou's strenuous striving towards 'intellectual perfectionment' was more alarming than reassuring, since she was persuaded that the principal source of her daughter's frailty was cerebral over-exertion, which had completely undermined her health. To Franz Overbeck in Basel Nietzsche wrote that

Lou's state of health struck him as being so 'pitiable' that he was persuaded that she had an even shorter time to live than he had thought when he had first met her in May. Which is why, unlike Madame Salomé, he felt that Lou should develop her intellectual capacities and 'blossom forth' in print before expiring prematurely in a poetic swan song.

This letter, which ended with another rhapsodic tribute to Heinrich Köselitz's musical genius, had begun on a distinctly sombre note, in which, because of the 'northern overcast', the cold weather, and his doubts about his ability to endure the noise and tumult of Paris, Nietzsche confessed that never had he lived through 'so many melancholy hours as during this Leipzig autumn'. The truth was that Lou Salomé's departure, without his knowing when or where they would next meet, had left him shaken and depressed.

'What melancholy!' Nietzsche wrote to Lou in Berlin on 8 November. 'I didn't know until this year how very mistrustful I am. Particularly of myself . . . You wanted to say something to me?' – presumably the apology he had been expecting for Lou's rude outbursts at Jena and Tautenburg, but the words at the moment of their parting on the station platform had remained unspoken. 'Your voice pleases me most when you implore. But it isn't heard often enough. I will be eager and expectant. Ah, this melancholy! I am writing nonsense. How *shallow* human beings seem to me today! Where is there still a sea in which one can truly *drown*! I mean a human being.' But what he meant, of course, was a woman.

Did his sixth sense tell him that he might never make it to Paris? That he might never see his Lou again? . . . In his letter to Overbeck, written five days after Lou Salomé's and Paul Rée's departure for Berlin, he made it clear that Genoa, with all the implicit perils of loneliness from which he had tried to free himself by returning 'to the world of men', was already pulling him southward towards the 'sunnier' Mediterranean. He had admitted as much in the two-stanza poem he had inscribed in Lou's gift copy of *The Joyous Science*:

*Freundin – sprach Columbus – traue*
*Keinem Genueser mehr!*
*Immer starrt er in das Blaue,*
*Fernstes zieht ihn allzusehr!*

*Wen er liebt, den lockt er gerne*
*Weit hinaus in Raum und Zeit –*
*Über uns glänzt Stern bei Sterne,*
*Um uns braust die Ewigkeit.*

STORM AND STRESS

(Darling –quoth Columbus – never
Trust another Genoese!
Across the brine he stares forever,
Over the distant deep blue seas!

His loved one lures he from afar
Through space and time's immensity –
Above us star shines next to star,
Around us roars eternity.)

CHAPTER 29

# *Finita è la commedia!*

> – The love of one sole being is a barbarism;
> for it will be employed to the detriment
> of all the rest. So too the love of God.

On 7 November or thereabouts (for his letter was undated) Nietzsche wrote to Louise Ott, who had so charmingly consoled him during the first Bayreuth Festival of 1876, to say that he was coming to Paris and would love to see her again. Another letter went off the same day to a Basel jurist, Dr August Sulger, who was asked if he could help Nietzsche find a single room in Paris for a half-blind 'hermit and thought-worm' (*Gedankenwurm*) and even meet him at the station? Both responded affirmatively. Indeed, Louise Ott was so overjoyed by this unexpected 'resurrection' that she had a bouquet of flowers sent to Nietzsche in Leipzig. But on 15 November, little more than one week later, he wrote again to say that he would not be coming to Paris now.

Since their departure from Leipzig on 5 November Nietzsche had not received a word from Lou Salomé or Paul Rée, and this casual behaviour in what was supposed to be a closely knit intellectual community cut the hypersensitive 'trinitarian' to the quick.

From Leipzig, where the first wintry snows were already falling, Nietzsche took the train to Basel, to 'help' Franz Overbeck celebrate his forty-fifth birthday on 16 November. Here he spent three anxious days vainly waiting for letters to be forwarded to him by his Leipzig landlord, Herr Janicaud, or Heinrich Köselitz. He told his Basel hosts that his 'idyll' with Lou Salomé was finished, without explaining what had gone wrong. Lou's health was so fragile – like his own – that she was as ill-suited to look after him as he was to take care of her. She had, however, found an ideal 'sick-watcher' in the person of Paul Rée, on whom Nietzsche lavished such extravagant praise that Ida Overbeck finally exclaimed, 'But you are describing Daniel Deronda!' – the hero of a George Eliot novel Nietzsche had never heard of. Knowing next to nothing about what had happened in Leipzig, she did not realize at the moment of parting, when Nietzsche took her hand and said sadly, 'Now I am going into complete solitude,' that he had abandoned as hopeless his short-lived endeavour to 'return to the world of men'.

If Nietzsche heard the nasty rumour that was already circulating in Basel's academic circles – about the 'mistress' he had brought back from

Italy and whom he had been 'sharing' with a friend of his in Leipzig – it was certainly not from the Overbecks. They were the only persons in Basel who had had a chance to form their own opinions of Lou Salomé, and, knowing how sensitive Nietzsche was about such personal matters, they would never have dreamed of bringing up the subject. But what infuriated Nietzsche was to discover that his sister Elisabeth, in her rightous zeal as the self-appointed guardian and preserver of her brother's 'sullied reputation', had taken it upon herself to 'set the record straight' not only by denying the ugly rumour – the surest way of giving it some credence – but also by exposing Lou Salomé as a scheming adventuress whose main ambitions in life were to marry a rich husband and to establish a spurious reputation as a 'brilliant intellect' by shamelessly stealing ideas and thoughts from others.

From Basel Nietzsche travelled in an unheated train compartment through the freezing Gotthard tunnel to Milan, and from there on to Genoa, where, to his dismay, he found that in his absence the landlady had rented his little room to another tenant. Unable to find suitable lodgings in the cold, rainswept city, he journeyed down the Ligurian coast to Portofino and to Santa Margherita, where he ended up renting a bleak, chilling, stoveless room. For four days he was paralysed by violent headaches and fits of vomiting, and not until 23 November could he find the strength to write to Köselitz in Leipzig and to Overbeck in Basel, giving them his new address.

He also sent a postcard to Paul Rée, who replied with a reproachful note expressing his and Lou's regret that he should have chosen to 'abandon' them. In his answering letter to Rée, Nietzsche wrote that, quite the contrary, he had imagined that he and Lou would be quietly pleased to get rid of him for while. 'A hundred times during the past year, from Orta on, I felt that you were "paying too dearly" for your friendship towards me. I have already received more than my fair share of *your* Roman "find" (I mean Lou) . . . Every proximity makes me so insatiable – and all in all I am an insatiable man.'

Nietzsche was on his way to the post office with this letter when he had second thoughts. He decided to add another, directly addressed to Lou. 'Take this as a token of trust, of my *purest* determination to establish confidence between us . . . And now, Lou, sweetheart,' he went on, 'sweep the heavens clean! I now want nothing but pure, bright sky: otherwise I will struggle on, no matter how hard the going. But a solitary soul suffers dreadfully from a suspicion concerning several persons he loves . . . You perhaps know *how* unbearable I find every desire to blame, every accusation and having-to-defend-oneself . . . In you I feel each stirring of a *higher* soul, these stirrings alone are what I love in you. I will gladly renounce all intimacy and nearness if only I could be sure of this: that we feel *at one* there where menial souls do not reach.' After which he added, in what was clearly a thrust aimed at Paul Rée's cold, sceptical, all too analytical rationality which, Nietzsche felt, was already eating like a corrosive acid into Lou's ardent, enthusiastic, vibrant soul: 'Intelligence? What is intelligence to me! What is knowledge! All I value are *impulses* – and I would swear that therein we have something in common . . . Don't you let yourself be deceived about me – surely *you* don't believe that "the *Freigeist*" is *my* ideal? I am –' he stopped, then added, 'Forgive me! Dearest Lou, be what you *must* be.'

Having to justify his 'unpardonable flight' in abandoning the 'trinity' was excruciatingly painful for Nietzsche, who wrote to Köselitz on 3 December that he never wanted to relive what he had gone through in recent weeks, that he had been so frozen by the cold, rainy weather at Santa Margherita that he had moved to the Albergo della Posta, in nearby Rapallo, where as the only client he had been given a bedroom with a stove.

What Nietzsche had been vainly awaiting was some sort of apology from Lou for her irresponsible behaviour at Bayreuth and the crude charges she had levelled against him to his sister at Jena and Tautenburg. But from Paul Rée's home at Stibbe no apology was now forthcoming. Quite the contrary. Her furious letters of reply to Nietzsche later disappeared, as did Paul Rée's more temperate missives, perhaps destroyed by Nietzsche's sister, anxious to 'tilt the balance' in his favour by eliminating all trace of the adversaries' arguments. However, the tenor of their contents can be guessed from Nietzsche's protests. The sudden collapse of her 'trinitarian experiment' infuriated Lou, who took it as a personal affront, as a vote of non-confidence in her intellectual brilliance and capacities, as an act of 'disloyalty' and 'betrayal'. Just as she had done in Rome, in heatedly replying to her former mentor's (Hendrik Gillot's) remonstrances against her crazy project of 'philosophical cohabitation', just as she had done at Jena and Tautenburg in giving Nietzsche's dumbfounded sister a 'piece of her mind', so now Lou took the offensive, accusing Nietzsche of intellectual dishonesty, in having led her to believe that his philosophy was one thing, only to discover, on closer acquaintance, that it was quite different. The insinuations were less crude, but the general tone was every bit as vehement.

'M[y] d[ear] L[ou],' wrote Nietzsche in one of his protesting letters, 'do be careful! If I now reject you, it is a terrible verdict on your entire being . . . If you give free rein to everything that is deplorable in your nature, who then can still frequent you? . . . In me you have the best of advocates, but also the most implacable of judges! I *want* you to judge yourself and to determine your punishment. These are all things one has to overcome – in order to overcome oneself . . . ' In another letter, the rough draft of which has survived, he wrote: 'Yes, I was angry with you! But why dwell on this detail? . . . I ascribed to you *higher* feelings than to other p[eople]: it was this, and this alone, that attached me to you so quickly . . . some sort of deep-seated misfortune in your upbringing and development has momentarily crippled your good-will thereto. – Just think: that sort of cat-egotism that can no longer love, that vital feeling for nothingness which you acknowledge in yourself are precisely what I find most repulsive in human beings: worse than any kind of evil . . . 'At that time in Orta I had envisaged the prospect of leading you step by step to the very last consequence of my philosophy – you are the first person I had regarded as fit for it . . . But what I wanted to do here, now, with my physical strength still in a poor condition, went far beyond anything previously done. A laborious building and upbuilding! It never occurred to me to ask you first of all for your consent: you were not supposed to notice how you had got involved in this work. I trusted those higher impulses I believed to be in you.

'I thought of you as my heiress –'

Having gone this far in his confession, Nietzsche decided that he might as well be just as frank about the man who had become Lou's closest companion and 'protector': 'As far as Friend R[ée] is concerned, I felt what I have felt each time (even after Genoa): I cannot watch this slow ruin of an extraordinary being without growing *furious*. This absence of a *goal*! and in addition this scant craving for the means, for work, this lack of diligence, even of scientific conscientiousness. This perpetual dissipation! If only it had at least been a dissipation due to delight in extravagance! But it has so much the air of a bad conscience. Everywhere I perceive the errors of upbringing. A man should be brought up to be a soldier, in one sense or another. And a woman to be the wife of a soldier, in one sense or another.'

For much of this cold, dismal December Nietzsche thus poured out his heart in a litany of grievances, which he first prepared in rough-draft form. Some of them may never have been posted as laboriously copied-out letters. Save for a single remaining fragment of a page sent from Rapallo shortly before Christmas, none of these reproachful letters survived Lou Salomé's later work of destruction, since she knew that the telling criticisms of her character and behaviour they contained would forever tarnish the exalted image of herself she was bent on bequeathing to posterity as Nietzsche's one-time friend, admiring critic and intimate interpreter. But if there is one thing that surprises in this devastating catalogue of grievances, it was the indulgence Nietzsche was prepared to show towards the young Lou Salomé right up until the end, when the final scales fell from his love-blinded eyes.

The most striking proof of this indulgence was provided in a letter to Malwida von Meysenbug, who had written to Nietzsche shortly after her return to Rome to thank him for her gift copy of *The Joyous Science* and to say how much she and the Gabriel Monods had regretted his failure to turn up in Paris. In his reply Nietzsche wrote that Malwida's kind letter had moved him to tears. 'You wanted to know what I think of Fräulein Salomé? My sister regards Lou as a poisonous reptile, which must be destroyed at all costs – and behaves accordingly. Now for me this is a thoroughly exaggerated point of view and utterly abhorrent to my heart. On the contrary, I would like nothing more than to be useful and beneficial to her, in the highest and most unpretentious sense of the word . . . Her cleverness is extraordinary: Rée claims that Lou and I are the cleverest of [human] beings – from which you can see that Rée is a flatterer . . .

'But I beseech you *with all my heart* to preserve the feeling of tender sympathy you have had for Lou – indeed, to do more!

'Do not be upset,' he concluded. 'I am basically a soldier and even a kind of "sleight-of-hand conjuror of self-overcoming" (so Friend Rohde recently called me, to my astonishment). Dear Friend, is there not a single human being in the world who loves me?'

By the time this letter was written Nietzsche had drawn up a long list of grievances against the less than innocent virgin he had rashly wanted, like a God-Creator, to mould in his own 'heroic' image. But this devastating indictment was also a critique of his own misjudgement and of his monomaniacal folly in placing his character-reforming hopes too high.

'Whether I have suffered much is for me nothing compared to the question whether, dear Lou, you will find yourself again or not – I have never consorted with such a wretched p[erson] as you.' This trenchant assertion was 'illustrated' by a series of terse marginal annotations about her:

rich in the utilization of what she knows
without taste, but naïve in this lack . . .
Without any delicacy of feeling for taking and giving
without sentiment and incapable of love
in emotion always sickly and close to insanity
without gratitude, shameless towards the benefactor . . .
incapable of politeness of the heart . . .

without shame, always undressed in thinking, powerful in particulars against herself . . .
not 'stout-hearted'
crude in matters of honour
monstrously negative . . .
Character of the cat – the beast of prey that installs itself as a pet . . .
cruelly perturbed sensuality
superannuated child-egotism as a result of sexually stunted growth and retard . . .
without love for h[uman beings], but love of God
Need for ostentation
sly and full of self-control with regard to the sensuality of men

The most acute of these insights into Lou's complex personality was with little doubt this one – 'without love for human beings, but love of God'. As Nietzsche had already observed in one of his notebook jottings: 'Religion as a spiritual release of erotic needs is something irreplaceable for all women in whom the satisfaction of the sexual drive has been forbidden by moral custom and shame.' In Lou's case the intellectual rejection of religion had in no way reduced the erotically inhibiting force of its agnostic, God-rejecting surrogate. But the most revealing of these psychological comments was, as far as their author was concerned, the very last: 'sly and full of self-control with regard to the sensuality of men'. Since Paul Rée by his own admission was the most unsensual of men, this reproach could refer only to Nietzsche himself. It was an unmistakable admission of masculine frustration. It made mincemeat of his exalted claim to have been pursuing a sublimely pure, altruistic, self-ennobling grand design with Lou Salomé. The all too human Friedrich Nietzsche was clearly not a eunuch. Like Pygmalion, he had become enamoured of his tempting idol and had unconsciously desired – the most powerful human instincts being subconscious – to sleep with the alluring creature he wished to reshape into a nobler, superior, more perfect human being. For this purpose he had implicitly usurped the divine prerogatives of Zeus, a Zeus who did not even have to assume the disguise of a teacher-professor, since this is what he himself had long been. Paternally as well as fraternally inspired, it was an incestuous love and doubly monstrous in its pretensions, since Nietzsche's avowed aim was to 'elevate' Lou by refashioning her in his own 'heroic' image.

When a man begins to reproach a woman for being too erotically alluring, it is a sure sign of masculine simple-mindedness, since this is and has always been Woman's birthright. This was not the kind of argument that the essentially passive Paul Rée would have wished to use against the hypersensitive Nietzsche, since his part in this heated three-cornered battle of words seems to have been to try to pour oil on troubled waters rather than add fuel to the flames – like the more indignant, combative and directly assailed Lou. But the longer the battle lasted, the more hypochondriacal, incoherent and excessive Nietzsche's letters became. As in this one to Paul Rée, concerning Lou: 'I have never doubted that somewhere in some heavenly way she will cleanse herself of the filth of those disgraceful actions' (i.e. Lou's behaviour at Bayreuth and Jena). 'Any other man would have turned away in disgust . . . Compassion played this trick on me' – a reference to Lou's frail state of health and her artfully expressed fear, 'I have not long to live, I will soon die.'

'I for my part don't need to be ashamed of myself in this entire matter,' Nietzsche continued, 'the strongest and most heartfelt feelings I had this year were for L[ou], and there was nothing in this love that belongs to the erotic. At most I could have made the d[ear] G[od] jealous.

'Strange! I thought an angel had been sent to me when I turned back to h[uman beings] and to life – an angel who would mollify a great deal that had grown too hard in me through pain and solitude, and above all an angel of Courage and Hope for everything I have *before me* – Meanwhile, it was no angel.'

With the younger, more vehement, and more 'guilty' Lou Salomé Nietzsche sought (in vain) to be more circumspect. 'My sole reproach against you today' – an understatement, if ever there was one – 'is that you were not frank with me at the proper moment. In Lucerne I gave you my w[ork] on Sch[openhauer] – I told you that contained therein were my fundamental convictions and that I believed that they could become yours. You should then have read them and said No! – in such matters I detest *superficiality* – it would have spared me much trouble.'

Lou's retort to this probably contained a charge of '*folie des grandeurs*', of megalomania, eliciting this pained response:

'But L[ou], what sort of letters are you writing! They are what petty, vengeful schoolgirls write . . . Do understand this: I want you to *raise* yourself up before my eyes, not that you should further belittle yourself. How can I forgive you unless first of all I again discover in you the being for whose sake you can at all be forgiven!

'No, m[y] d[ear] L[ou], we long since passed the stage of "Pardon". I cannot pluck a "Pardon" out of my sleeve, after the injury had four months in which to burrow into me.

'Adieu, m[y] d[ear] L[ou], I will never see you again . . .

'Adieu, d[ear] L[ou], I have not read your letter to the end, but I already read too much.'

This should have ended this acrimonious debate. Instead, it dragged on for a few more days, as the two main protagonists in this battle of conflicting wills and offended egos continued to tilt against each other. Emotions, as Nietzsche confessed to Lou Salomé and Paul Rée in a pathetic letter written a few days before Christmas, were 'devouring' him, a well-inoculated, antisentimental *Freigeist* though he might claim to be. 'A dreadful compassion, dreadful disillusionment, a dreadful feeling of wounded pride – how can I endure it any longer? Is not compassion a feeling out of hell? What should I do? Every morning I despair of lasting out the day. I no longer sleep: what good does it do to hike 8 hours [a day]! Whence come these fierce emotions! Oh for some ice! But where is there still some ice *for me*! This evening I will take so much opium that I will lose my reason: where is there a h[uman] b[eing] one could still *revere*!'

After taking a huge dose of opium, Nietzsche noted with surprise that, instead of making him lose his understanding, it seemed to have cleared his mind. 'Incidentally,' he wrote to Rée, 'I was really ill for weeks on end . . . Ask Lou to forgive me *everything* – she will yet give me an opportunity to forgive her. For thus far I have forgiven her nothing. One forgives one's friends with far greater difficulty than one forgives one's foes . . . Could it be that Lou is a misjudged angel? And that I am a misjudged donkey?

'In opio veritas: Long live Wine and Love!' – he meant of course for others, for in both so far he had been remarkably abstemious.

The 'horrible' year 1882, which had begun so auspiciously in Genoa under the smiling auspices of 'Sanctus Januarius', was not yet over. Fritz was so furious with his mother and sister for the sanctimonious tone of the Christmas letters they wrote to him that he sent them back to Naumburg, saying that if they continued to pester him with letters of that kind, he would return them unopened.

To Franz Overbeck he wrote on Christmas Day from Rapallo, to say that nothing had hurt him more in his recent tribulations than the 'hostile judgements' of his relatives, who seemed to have joined forces with his enemies in wishing to 'ruin his reputation' – an accusation directed above all against his smug, sententious sister rather than against his simpler, pious mother. The 'chunk of life' he had just lived through was the 'toughest' he had so far had to 'chew', and he might still possibly 'choke to death' on what he had been forced to swallow. 'If only I could sleep! – but the strongest doses of my soporifics help me as little as do 6–8 hours of hiking. If I don't discover the alchemist's artifice, in order to make *gold* out of this dung too, then I am lost. Here I have the *loveliest* opportunity to prove that for me "all experiences are useful, all days holy, and all men divine!"' – a quotation from Emerson that he had used on the frontispiece of *The Joyous Science*.

'All men divine!' Nietzsche commented acidly. 'My distrust is now so great: from everything I hear I feel a contempt for me. For example, in a recent letter from Rohde' – a letter that had expressed higher praise for *The Joyous Science* than for its immediate predecessors – 'I am willing to swear that, *but for* the accident of our previously friendly relations, he would now be passing judgement on me and my aims in the most contemptuous manner.'

On reading such a sentence, Overbeck, who had long been urging Erwin Rohde to write more frequently to his old friend and fellow philologist, could only shake his head in dismay. Nietzsche's 'convalescence' from the deep wound inflicted by the young Lou Salomé on his hypersensitive psyche would obviously be a long one.

In one of the maxims she had coined for her 'Stibbe Nest-Book', Lou had written with pertinent perspicacity: 'The friend gives, the lover demands'; and also: 'Just as in love we idealize the loved one, so in it too do we idealize ourselves. It induces in us a striving for ennoblement as well as for dissimulation.' Both of these shrewd observations now clearly applied to Nietzsche. His claims on Lou had ceased to be those of a 'friend' – the original intent of the 'trinitarian' scheme – and had become those of a plaintive lover. In the process the blinding 'nobility' of the ideal had occulted the latent power of dissimulation and selfish possessiveness of the ardent psyche. As Nietzsche wrote to Paul Rée during the last week of December, in a final, despairing effort to extract an apology from his 'friend' Lou for her outrageous behaviour and, implicitly, for not being the kind of person he wanted her to be and to become: 'In the meantime all I see is that she is bent on amusement and entertainment . . . She took it very badly that I should have denied her the right to the term "heroism of knowledge", but she should be honest and say, "I am infinitely removed there from." In heroism it is a question of self-sacrifice and duty and indeed a daily and hourly one, and consequently that *much more*: the entire soul must be full of one thing, and life and happiness insignificant in comparison. Such a character I thought I had perceived in Lou . . .

'In the spring I thought I had found a p[erson] who was capable of *helping me*: for this obviously there was needed not only a good intellect but a morality of the highest order. Instead of this I discovered a being who wants to amuse herself and who is shameless enough to believe that the most outstanding minds on earth are good enough for that.

'For me the result of this confusion has been that more than ever I lack the *means* to find such a p[erson] and that my soul, which was *free*, will be tortured by a host of revolting memories. For the entire dignity of my life's task has been called into doubt through [a] superficial, immoral, light-hearted and callous being like Lou, and also my name . . . has been besmirched.'

So ran the last two revealing paragraphs of the initial draft of a letter Nietzsche may have rewritten slightly before sending it to Paul Rée. What implicitly he had wanted Lou Salomé to do was to suppress and sublimate her erotic impulses as his devoted spiritual and intellectual servant. This was a monstrously egocentric ambition, but one justified (as with all religious or philosophical 'reformers') by the exalted nature of the aim. Her predestined role, as the high priestess of a new 'sub-rational' philosophy of which he was at once the Apollo, the Dionysus and the Homer, was to be a sublime model of feminine superiority, a kind of inverse Virgin Mary – in the sense that she was his spiritual daughter rather than he her son – one blessed furthermore with the supreme intelligence of a St Teresa of Avila. It was a late romantic dream, as fanciful as anything Wagner had invented in *Parsifal*, one which could only have blossomed in the feverish brain of a man who had lived for years like a hermit, out of touch with the noisy, throbbing, intellectually disturbing and all too 'vulgar' world of everyday reality. For even as a dream it was hopelessly unrealistic and 'anti-historical'. St Teresa had had her San Juan de la Cruz, but both were genuine mystics – which neither Nietzsche nor Lou Salomé were. Nor had St Teresa or San Juan ever tried to live in any kind of physical proximity. Never too had that glorious 'sinner' Abélard asked of his beloved Héloïse the heroic abnegation Friedrich Nietzsche was in effect demanding of Lou Salomé. Both, in suppressing and sublimating their erotic impulses, were supposed to prove to an incredulous world that they could attain the superhuman heights of *Selbstüberwindung* – self-mastery, self-overcoming. They were to be the living martyrs of a new, heroically agnostic faith, which did not need any metaphysical 'superstructure' or imaginary props to glow and burn with the incandescent heat of a suprarational enthusiasm. It was an ideal prescription for a permanent crucifixion of the senses, for the superimposition of additional physical torments on two persons who were already the unwitting victims of their high-strung temperaments; and it was simply incredible that a thinker who, in *Human, All Too Human*, had pitilessly exposed all that was perverse, sickly, misshapen and unhealthy in medieval asceticism should not have realized how insidiously sado-masochistic in its inspiration was this 'noble' design for sublime cohabitation in which each sufferer could not but rack the other with the hell-on-earth torments of carnal desire.

Eros, once again, had not missed the mark; and with a single arrow he had reduced the short-sighted Nietzsche to a (fortunately short-lived) condition of intellectual blindness.

## CHAPTER 30

# The Birth of Zarathustra

*– He who no longer finds what is great in God will find it nowhere – and must either deny or create it.*

Nobody at this low point in his career, and probably not even Nietzsche – who felt that from the euphoric heights of Orta and the *Monte sacro* in early May he had been precipitated by mid-November to the dark depths of the 'abyss' – could guess that within a few weeks he would rebound and reach a new zenith in an astonishing 'eruption'. But this is what happened. It was a triumph of will power, of *Selbstüberwindung* (self-overcoming), as he called it, and it offered dramatic proof that, as he had written to Franz Overbeck, the 'watch-spring' of his overly tensed, 'machine-like' brain had not snapped and that he still possessed enough of the magic powers of the alchemist to be able to transform the 'dung' of misfortune into verbal 'gold'.

Climatic factors again played a major role in this amazing resurgence. During the first two weeks of January 1883 Rapallo was so lashed by wintry gales and rain that never in his life had Nietzsche felt so frozen as in his small, seaside *albergo*. He was forced to spend much of his time in bed, racked by blinding headaches and fits of vomiting. His nights and days were haunted by ghastly memories of the humiliations recently inflicted on him – first, by his mother, with her reproach that he had 'disgraced his father's tomb', then by a brazen 'adventuress', Lou Salomé, who used ideas as others use crossword puzzles for purposes of mental stimulation and amusement.

But then, suddenly, the skies cleared, he was able to sleep at night and, as he wrote to Heinrich Köselitz (who had gone back to Venice), he again became 'master of himself'. His energies galvanized by a warm sun and blue skies, which made his morning walks past the pine trees overlooking the lovely bay so enjoyable, his spirits cheered by a friendly letter from Malwida von Meysenbug, inviting him to come to Rome, where she had found a young lady who was ready to take dictation from him, Nietzsche poured out his intimate thoughts and ironic lamentations in a new manuscript, the first draft of which was completed in ten days. On 1 February he wrote to Köselitz that he had finished a 'quite small book: roughly one hundred printed pages. But it is my best, and with it I have rolled a heavy stone from off my soul. Nothing of mine has been more serious and nothing gayer; my heartfelt wish is that *this* colour – which need not at all be a mixed colour – should be the colour of my "nature".'

His latest brainchild, he then announced, framing the words inside a rectangle, would carry the title: *Thus Spake Zarathustra: A Book for Everybody and Nobody.*

'With this book,' Nietzsche went on, he had 'entered into a new *Ring* – a subtle intimation that, like Wagner's *Rheingold*, this was merely the first of a new 'cycle' of works. 'From now on in Germany,' he added, 'I shall be reckoned among the mad. It is a wondrous kind of "moral predication".'

To Franz Overbeck he wrote the same day, saying that with this, his *best* book, he had taken the 'decisive step' for which he had lacked the necessary courage the previous year. All that was now needed were total solitude and a few days of fine 'tuning' – something that required the most delicate 'hearing' (a revealing indication of the importance Nietzsche attached to matters of euphony).

His euphoria was short-lived. The radiant weather, which had enabled him to enjoy fourteen consecutive nights of sleep, again turned wet and cold, plunging him back into an 'abyss' of despair so dark and deep that, as he wrote to Franz Overbeck on 10 February, he was persuaded that he had not long to live and was almost ready to take his life with a pistol.

Three days later Nietzsche wrote to Ernst Schmeitzner that he could now offer him something that might be 'useful': a small work (barely 100 pages) entitled *Also sprach Zarathustra* (*Thus Spake Zarathustra*). 'It is a "work of poetry" or a "Fifth Gospel" or something for which there is as yet no name: far and away the most serious and also the gayest of my products, and accessible to everyone' – he added, to reassure his publisher, who had often complained that Nietzsche's books were not written for the 'general public'.

To speed things up, Nietzsche may have decided to post the registered parcel from Genoa. There, after picking up the evening edition of a local paper, he learned that Richard Wagner had died the previous afternoon (Tuesday, 13 February) in Venice. Nietzsche immediately dashed off a postcard to Köselitz, asking for more details as to the cause of the composer's sudden death. In his lengthy reply, written two days later, Köselitz indicated that Wagner had died of asthma, compounded by a heart attack.

Several days passed before Nietzsche could bring himself to write the letter of condolence he had to send to Cosima Wagner. His agonies of indecision as to just how to express his sympathy without sounding like a hypocrite were dramatically revealed in the tortuous first draft, in which no less than three times he repeated the same heavy-handed compliment (for Cosima) – 'the best-esteemed woman who is close to my heart'. This was clearly a bold statement of admiration. Equally bold was the sentence in which he wrote of Wagner: 'We were never enemies in minor matters' – which he may have omitted from the final version.

What Nietzsche could not say to Cosima was (as he put it in a letter to Köselitz) that Wagner's death, although a momentary shock, had also come as a relief to him, since it ended the bitter enmity between them. 'It was hard for six long years to be the adversary of the man one most admired, and I am not crude enough for *that*. Ultimately, it was the ageing Wagner I had to resist: as regards the authentic Wagner, I will to a good extent become his heir (as I have often said to Malwida).' Not, that is, as Wagner's musical 'heir' (clearly a preposterous claim), but as the promoter of a 'higher German culture' which (prior to Bayreuth) had been Wagner's great ambition. 'Last summer,' continued Nietzsche, 'I found that he had taken from me all the persons there might be some point in trying to influence in Germany and was beginning to draw them into the confused, desolate hostility of old age' – a wild reproach probably directed at his most disappointing friend, Erwin Rohde (a Wagner-loving philological specialist who had made no serious attempt to rise to a higher level of intellectual 'comprehension') and also at his publisher, Ernst Schmeitzner, whose monthly *Internationale Monatsschrift* was now vying with Wagner's *Bayreuther Blätter* in the vehement frequency of its antisemitic articles.

To Cosima Wagner's close friend Malwida von Meysenbug, Nietzsche was no less candid in expressing his sense of relief at Wagner's death, the news of which had so terribly affected him that he had taken to his bed. Wagner, he explained, 'offended me to a *deadly* degree – I will say it to you nonetheless! – his slow backsliding and slinking towards Christianity and the Church I felt to be a personal slur against me . . . Had he lived longer, what else might not have arisen between us!'

The next day, 22 February, Nietzsche informed Köselitz that he was returning to his old lodgings on the Salita delle Battestine, in Genoa. In a letter sent to Overbeck in Basel he rolled out the same grievances against Wagner, after declaring that he had been far and away 'the *most complete* man' he had ever met. Whence the immensity of his later disillusionment. After which he added, as another example of a bitter disappointment: 'Lou is far and away the *cleverest* person I have known. But etc. etc.'

His return to his old lodgings in Genoa brought Nietzsche no immediate relief from his migraine, stomach upsets and insomnia. So weakened by weeks of nervous sleeplessness was his normally robust constitution that he came down with a severe attack of influenza, which Genoa's 'best doctor' undertook to combat with daily doses of quinine. In a letter to Franz Overbeck, in which he mentioned his feverish condition – intense nocturnal sweating, immense fatigue, a total absence of appetite – he went further than he had ever done before in describing his strained relations with his family. 'I do not like my mother, and hearing my sister's voice causes me displeasure; I have always been ill when I was with them.'

By 9 March a heavy snowfall was blanketing the old city, accompanied by incongruous thunderclaps and flashes of lightning, further delaying Nietzsche's slow 'recovery'. His two consolations were the intelligent letters he kept receiving from Heinrich Köselitz (mostly devoted to musical matters) and a book that Paul Deussen, now a respected Sanskrit scholar, had recently brought out on the Hindu Vedânta system (as expounded in the *Brahma-Sutra*). In mid-March he wrote to his old Pforta schoolmate: ' . . . And not least of all, dear Friend, do I value the fact that you have not forgotten how to work industriously. Was not one of the three Muses named Meleti (care, diligence)? Heaven knows, without honest industry nothing but weeds sprout from the finest disposition' – a critique aimed at the indolent Paul Rée (not named). 'Looked at closely, even the finest artist should not differ from the hand-worker. I hate the riff-raff who will have nothing to do with handicraft and who look upon intelligence with the fastidiousness of the gourmet.' Thanking Deussen for having elucidated what had long motivated his distrust of Hindu thinking, he added: 'I read page after page with total "malice" – you could not wish for a *more grateful* reader, dear Friend.

'Quite by chance, a *manifesto* of mine is being printed up which says Yes! with roughly the same eloquence as your book says No! What a laugh. But perhaps it will pain you . . . '

By 22 March the snow was melting, but a listless Nietzsche was still bedridden. Unable to take stimulating walks, he was filled with a 'black melancholy', even though (as he wrote to Overbeck) he had found a *trattoria* where he could stuff himself and add a bit of flesh to his emaciated body. Four weeks had passed since he had sent his manuscript to his publisher, who seemed in no hurry to bring out this new, short opus.

Three days later (Easter Sunday), he sent Schmeitzner a furious letter of reproach. This angry outburst elicited an apologetic reply. But it was not until early April that Nietzsche learned the truth: the Leipzig printer, Teubner, had shoved the *Zarathustra* manuscript aside in order to meet a rush order for 500,000 hymnals, which had to be delivered in time for Easter. The realization that his fearless *Zarathustra*, the 'madman' who had the nerve to proclaim to the somnambulists around him that 'God is dead!' should have been momentarily smothered beneath the collective weight of 500,000 Christian hymnbooks struck Nietzsche as downright 'comic' – even though, as he wrote to Schmeitzner in a forgiving letter, it had cost him five nervous 'weeks of fever and quinine-eating' in the 'damp, windy, frozen city' of Genoa.

The first, rapturous response to Nietzsche's latest offspring came from his devoted 'disciple', Köselitz, to whom once again the proofs were sent from Leipzig to be read and corrected. 'The magnificent expression of your intelligence, the power of your language, the richness of invention down to the tiniest detail, the fiery glow and majesty of your feelings leave me astounded, they excite me, make me tremble all over . . . Nothing comparable exists . . . ' He expressed the hope that this extraordinary book would one day be as widely distributed as the Bible: something that would probably not take place until the start of the twenty-first century. In the meantime it would provide many readers with fortitude and courage: a prediction that was to be fulfilled far sooner and more dramatically than Köselitz anticipated during the sombre years of the First World War.

Markedly different was the reaction of the typesetters in Leipzig, who were so frightened by what they read that they came close to rebelling. In a letter written to thank his publisher, Schmeitzner, for having stood by him in this matter, Nietzsche refused to alter a single word, no matter how nervous his God-is-dead-proclaiming *Zarathustra* might make the Saxon 'state'. He didn't care two hoots about the Leipzigers' fears – they could even lump him together with the anarchists as an unsavoury individual! 'What is certain is that I foresee European anarchies and earthquakes on a monstrous scale. All movements are headed in that direction – your anti-Jewish one included.'

Nietzsche was so elated by Köselitz's ecstatic praise for his new opus that he sent on his letter to Malwida von Meysenbug in Rome, saying that with *Zarathustra* he had taken a 'decisive step . . . Do you want a new name for me? Church parlance has one: I am . . . the *Antichrist*.' After which he added with a chuckle, 'But let's not forget how to laugh!'

The good Malwida, who unlike her friend Cosima Wagner was more idealistically than religiously inclined, wrote back immediately to say how delighted she was by the good humour evident in Nietzsche's letter. Like Franz Overbeck, who had been trying to find some way of combating Fritz's love of solitude by luring him back to Basel, she gently upbraided him, pointing out that while solitude was a necessary condition for creativity, to be truly productive it was necessary from time to time to 'have a glimpse of the world, of its plight, its needs, and its knowledge. Christ went into the wilderness in order to become capable of dying for the misery of the world; the Antichrist, it seems to me, should sally forth among human beings in order to complete the work of salvation in which the former failed' – an extravagant compliment tailor-made for Nietzsche, who had long regarded himself as a profoundly 'moral' human being: one who, as he had written in aphorism 292 of *The Joyous Science*, detested 'preachers of morality' because, like political demagogues, they cheapened genuine religious feelings by pandering to the mass tastes of their congregations with promises of 'happiness through virtue', 'tranquility of soul', and other spiritual panaceas in their shameless quest for 'popularity'.

Towards the end of April Nietzsche found a conciliatory letter from his sister waiting for him at Genoa's central post office. In his reply Fritz said that he was pleased that Elisabeth had decided to stop 'waging war' against her brother. He had just survived the hardest and 'sickest' winter he had ever lived through – with four months of insomnia and nightly sleeping-pills and a long bout of malaria-like influenza. But now that he was recovering from his disastrous attempt to 'return to the world of men' he wanted to restore a bit of 'order' in his old relationships – by meeting his sister, in Rome.

Nietzsche's second, month-long stay in Rome could hardly have been better timed. He arrived on 4 May and, as he wrote to his mother nine days later, the nearby mountain crests were still powdered with snow, and the spring air was so crisp that not once had he so far been able to put on a pair of the handsome white trousers he wore (somewhat old-fashionedly) during the warm summer months. His sister had found him a quiet, spacious top-floor room – something the often cramped garret-dweller particularly appreciated – on the Piazza Barberini, with a Swiss landscape-painter and his family, who treated the Herr Professor with a respect bordering on reverence. 'Aunt Malwida' again greeted her 'wayward son' with open arms, as she had done the previous May, and was tireless in introducing him to members of the German colony in Rome. One of them was Franz von Lenbach, Richard Wagner's favourite portrait painter, who later told friends that Nietzsche's luminous and deeply brooding eyes were the most beautiful he had ever seen on a man.

Towards the middle of May Nietzsche received a brief note, accompanying a letter of credit in French francs, in which Ernst Schmeitzner referred casually to the financial 'perplexities of the publisher', from which he was presently trying to extricate himself. In his letter of thanks for the advance royalty payment (all he could expect to receive) Nietzsche was unable to conceal his astonished irritation: 'Of Zarathustra I hear not a word. Inconceivable! Is he still alive? Or have Teubner [the Leipzig printer] and his lads finished him off at last, perhaps because of his "strong expressions"?'

This sarcastic letter elicited no immediate reply. The temperature had now begun to rise, and with it Nietzsche's urgent need to find a cooler habitat for the summer. The architectural marvels that his sister and Malwida dragged him to admire left him cold – as too familiar or (in his present state of mind) too distracting. As he wrote to Franz Overbeck, the only objects that had spoken to his soul 'as to a brother or a friend' were an antique bust of Epicurus, another of Brutus, and three landscapes by Claude Lorrain. 'Yesterday,' he noted with disgust, 'I even saw men kneeling at the top of the sacred steps . . . I hope that *Zarathustra* has meanwhile come into your hands. I myself know nothing about him, after completing the correcting. May he make his way in the world *alone*!'

Nietzsche's own 'way' at this moment was more undetermined than ever. He and Elisabeth kept searching for mountain resorts in Italy where he could spend the hot summer months. In early June he made a quick exploratory trip to Aquila and Terni, in the rugged Abruzzi mountains north-east of Rome, several of whose peaks and plateaux are more than 8,000 feet high; but here too the 'flaming sword of the sirocco' (as he wrote on a postcard to his sister) relentlessly pursued him.

Finally, on 14 June, Fritz and his sister said goodbye to the hospitable Malwida and travelled northward by train up the long shank of the Italian peninsula, headed for Milan. Fritz, in a merry mood, amused himself composing comic verses which Elisabeth found so funny that they could hardly stop laughing. Believing himself to be the butt of this unseemly mirth, an irate Englishman climbed down at the next stop in search of a quieter compartment. At Milan they parted. Elisabeth wanted to see Lugano, while Fritz headed for Bellagio, at the centre of the root-shaped Lake Como. The grey, pitted waters were barely visible through sheets of pouring rain. After weeks spent in stimulating company, Fritz confessed to his sister (who had moved on to Basel): 'I now almost shrink from solitude: but I long ago learned to clench my teeth.'

There was no let-up in the rain, which pursued *Zarathustra*'s 'father' up the shore of Lake Como to Chiavenna, and from there north-eastward up the Mera river valley, gradually turning into icy sleet as the stagecoach lumbered its way up and over the Maloja Pass to the plateau of the Silser lake. Within two hours of his arrival the village of Sils-Maria had disappeared in a swirl of blinding snow. Half frozen, Nietzsche sought refuge in the Hôtel Edelweiss, where he spent the next three days nursing headaches in a bedroom well heated by a porcelain stove.

In the grocer's house, to which he moved on the fourth day, he was warmly received by Herr Durisch, the owner, his wife and their little daughter, Adrienne. Nietzsche was relieved to find that he did not have to leave the house to buy biscuits, corned beef, tea, soap and almost everything he needed – except the good Naumburg ham and sausages his thoughtful mother sent to him, along with jars of honey. 'Here in my unheated room,' he wrote home on 21 June, 'I feel worse off than in the coldest January days on the Genoese coast.' But these were transitory hardships, for 'the region and the entire nature of the Engadine again please me *exceptionally*, it remains my favourite region'.

The coldness of his small, stoveless room was not the only thing that bothered Nietzsche. His soaring spirit felt crushed by the lowless of the ceiling – a feeling which, with Nietzsche, was close to claustrophobia and explains the thrill he had experienced in Venice, in Messina and in Rome by being able to occupy a high-ceilinged bedroom.

In a long letter to Carl von Gersdorff, whose mother had recently died, he wrote that Sils-Maria was his 'rightful home and breeding ground', perfect for the incubation of everything he could feel inside him waiting to burst forth. 'I would like to have enough money to build myself an ideal dog-house: I mean a chalet with two rooms, and moreover on a peninsula that juts into the Silser lake, on which once stood a Roman castle. In the long run I cannot live in these peasant houses as I have done so far: the rooms are low-ceilinged and oppressive, and there is always a lot of noise and disturbances. Otherwise, the inhabitants of Sils-Maria are fond of me and I cherish them. I eat my meals at the Hôtel Edelweiss, a truly excellent Gasthaus: naturally alone, and at a price that is not altogether out of proportion to my meagre resources. I have brought along a big hamper of books with me' – books sent on to him from Rome at a 'huge' cost of 87 Swiss francs.

To Heinrich Köselitz Nietzsche wrote on 1 July that he had returned to his 'beloved Sils-Maria in the Engadine, the place where one day I will die; in the interim the finest instincts for "living on" are at work within me. On the whole, I am remarkably unsettled, perturbed, full of questioning – it is cold up here, that maintains and strengthens me.' If he felt so unsettled and perturbed, it was because he had just heard from his publisher that none of the printed copies of *Thus Spake Zarathustra* had so far left the printer's workshop in Leipzig. As Nietzsche remarked acidly to his composer friend in Venice: 'Such are the results of the "very important negotiations" and the constant trips of the Chief of the alliance anti-juive, Herr Schmeitzner: so "the publishing company must wait a bit": this he writes. It is truly laughable: first of all the Christian obstacle, the 500,000 hymnals, and now the Jew-hating obstacle – these are altogether "experiences of the founders of religion".' In other words, what he was now personally experiencing was a 'classic' repetition of the inveterate hostility that all great religious reformers – from Buddha to Jesus Christ, from Mohammed to Martin Luther – had encountered in challenging conventional procedures and beliefs and in daring to propound new rules of personal conduct.

The German word Nietzsche used to describe his highly unsettled state was *schwebend*, which literally means 'hovering'. It was not casually chosen. He had long liked to compare his ambitious 'upward striving' and 'soaring thought' to the lofty flight of the eagle, able to overfly petty human problems with a broader, more panoramic, more 'cosmic' perspective. Never did this feeling grip him more powerfully than here in Sils-Maria, during his long lakeside and forest walks in the bracing air of the Engadine highlands. For days, not to say weeks, he had felt the glow of his creative fire gathering pressure within him. Now, yielding to an instinctive force he seemed powerless to control, he was ready once again, like the eagle – or, perhaps one should say, like the legendary owl of Minerva – to make the deadly swoop on the 'unsuspecting prey' that lurked in the deep, dark depths of his 'creative unconscious'.

The idea of creating a striking prophet-figure to be the spokesman of his deepest and 'darkest' thoughts about morality, metaphysics and so much else was anything but a sudden 'illumination'; it was more like the Dionysian upsurgence of an intellectual tendency he had never been able nor made much effort to repress. As the very title of *Morgenröte* (*Morning Glow*) had suggested, Nietzsche conceived his mission as a thinker to be that of the herald of a new 'dawn' in philosophical thinking, the prophet of a new, more honest, less visionary morality, purged and purified of a vast accretion of moral, political, social and metaphysical prejudices and misconceptions which had reduced the vast majority of his contemporaries to a collective condition of sheep-like stupidity.

Nor was the choice of Zarathustra to be his mouthpiece in any sense haphazardly inspired. The idea that the world is a place of constant conflict and warfare between antagonistic forces had been expressed, early on, by the first Greek philosophers – and notably by Heraclitus, who had claimed (as Nietzsche had once written) that 'the strife of the opposites gives birth to all that comes to be; the definite qualities which seem permanent to us express but the momentary ascendancy of one partner. But this by no means signifies the end of the war; the contest endures through all eternity.' However, the man who had done more than any other to develop this idea of a fundamental 'cleavage' in human affairs, elevating it to the status of a religious cosmology, was not a Greek; he was more probably a Mede (an ancestor of present-day Kurds) who had lived and preached his new conception of the world in the mountainous regions of what is now Iranian Azerbaijan and northern Iraq, or possibly in Bactria (northern Afghanistan) some time between the eighth and sixth centuries BC. In an attempt to simplify the complexities of Hindu polytheism, with its plethora of gods, evil spirits and demons, Zarathustra – or Zoroastes, as he was later called by the Greeks – had propounded a new conception of the universe as being the work of a Creator-God of Light named Ahura, further dignified by the attribute of 'Mazda' ('the Wise'), who from the very outset had been opposed by a deadly foe known as Angra Mainush, the God of Darkness. After being expelled from the Kingdom of Light, this anti-god of Darkness had continued to wage war against the celestial order of Ahura Mazda, with the aid of countless devils and demons, as the Lord not merely of the 'Underworld' but of the Earth itself. The fascination exercised throughout the Middle East by this singularly clear-cut, black-and-white *Weltanschauung* can hardly be exaggerated, even though Zoroastrianism never established itself as a major religion for any length of time. However, the figure of Satan (which originally meant 'adversary'), like the angels and demons that began to infiltrate the later, pre-Christian stages of Judaism, was almost certainly of Zoroastrian–Persian origin; and it was as an unwitting neo-Zoroastrian that the author of the Fourth Gospel (of St John) could refer to this malignant God of Darkness as the 'Prince of this world'.

If, in its archaic biblical style and language, Nietzsche's new work differed markedly from its predecessors, in the essential respect of attempting to define what is truly noble, self-enhancing and upward-striving in Man, *Thus Spake Zarathustra* was not radically different; thematically it was a continuation, but elevated, to a 'higher', more poetic, less literal plane. Its purpose was to proclaim that, even in a godless world, life is worth living. Thus, in writing to his old Pforta friend Paul Deussen, Nietzsche could declare that his new work was a "*ja-sagend*" (yes-saying) book, quite different in spirit from the passive acceptance, from the sense of cosmic resignation (human beings as the helpless victims of the eternally revolving 'wheel of life') expressed in the Hindu *Rig-Vedas*.

There were also highly personal reasons for the special affinity Nietzsche felt for the figure of Zarathustra. Pliny, repeating an ancient legend, had written that on the very day of his birth Zarathustra had laughed, thus establishing his spiritual kinship with the dancing gods of Hindu mythology. For, Nietzsche felt, if one must believe in gods, let them at least dance and not pontificate like German theologians and pulpit preachers! At a crucial moment in his life, Zarathustra, like Nietzsche, had turned his back on the world – 'out of love of wisdom and righteousness' – and had chosen to live a hermit's life in the 'wilderness', keeping himself alive on cheese (not unlike the sour-milk diet Nietzsche had recently adopted). When Zarathustra finally returned among his fellow men as the reforming prophet of a new faith, he had – like Nietzsche with his iconoclastic books – aroused the fury of a sacerdotal caste of sorcerers and magicians, as stolidly entrenched behind their conventional beliefs and privileges as were the Protestant and Catholic priesthoods in Germany and Switzerland. Like Nietzsche too, Zarathustra had regarded life as being an incessant battle against lies and evil; and the fact that in the end his teachings had not triumphed was a point in his favour, for it was this that had kept him from establishing what, in aphorism 507 of *Morgenröte*, Nietzsche had stigmatized as the 'Tyranny of the Truth'. When a single, universal, overly pretentious 'truth' is invested with the aura of dogma, it becomes in the very nature of things tyrannical and thus mind-numbing. As he had noted in a paradoxical maxim: 'The believing human being is the opposite of the religious human being.' In other words, the 'believer', comfortably ensconced in his 'respectable' convictions, is the opposite of the truly religious soul, forever racked by doubt, who has to fight a daily spiritual battle to preserve his faith.

Zarathustra, in this respect, is not only a great dissenter; he is also a great doubter. That so little was known about the real Zarathustra was, for Nietzsche's purposes, an additional asset. He could with relative impunity place all sorts of highly provocative and paradoxical affirmations in the mouth of his 'prophet' which did not necessarily reflect his own far from 'final' thoughts on this or that subject. He could even have his artificially resuscitated Zarathustra dispense a form of 'wisdom' that was in certain particulars the opposite of what the real Zarathustra had expounded. Forcibly wrenched from his obscure historical context and transposed two and a half millennia later to the present age, this new Zarathustra could be presented as a wiser prophet: one who, like Nietzsche, had managed to overcome his earlier simplistic illusions through strenuous cogitation and a painful *Selbstüberwindung* – a 'self-overcoming' of his earlier 'prejudices' and misconceptions.

In a biography covering the entire span of Nietzsche's life and works, it is impossible to do justice to the extraordinary prose-poem he had begun at Rapallo and was about to continue at Sils-Maria. All one can do is pick out a few salient points and relate them to the deepest trends in his thinking and to the recent, searing circumstances of his life. So let us begin with a commentary on the introductory sections, which 'set the scene' for the prophet's later 'speeches' or discourses. Zarathustra has just stepped forth from his cave, in which he has been living for ten years, to greet the sun. Like Jesus, he was born near a lake and left his home at the age of thirty – not to preach, like the great Galilean, but to think. For Nietzsche this was a capital distinction: his Zarathustra is not only an older, he is also a wiser man – like Siddharta or Gautama Buddha (the 'enlightened one'), who lived to a ripe old age. As the prophet of a radically new, non-Christian system of values, this 'reincarnated' Zarathustra is, in the profoundest sense, a philosophical adversary and to that extent an 'anti-christ'. Later, in *Ecce homo*, Nietzsche pointed out that his *Zarathustra* was a long hymn of praise to solitude. He could have added that his hero's ten years of solitary cogitation in the mountains corresponded to his own ten years of philosophical meditations – from *The Birth of Tragedy* in 1872 to *The Joyous Science* of 1881. In January 1883, when Nietzsche began his *Zarathustra*, he was three months into his thirty-ninth year, and thus only one year younger than his prophetic *alter ego*.

So much for the analogies. But let us return to the 'story'. Zarathustra decides to 'descend' from his mountain heights into the world of men – much as Nietzsche had chosen to abandon his hermit-like existence in 1882 after meeting Lou Salomé in Rome. The symbolic overtones in this 'descent' are extremely subtle. The German word *Untergang* is rich in suggestive connotations: it can refer to the setting of the sun, to an eclipse of the moon, to the fatal foundering of a ship, to a decline or downfall (as in Oswald Spengler's apocalyptic *Decline of the West*), and even to a total 'extinction'. This 'descent' of Zarathustra's from his solitary mountain thus bears a symbolic resemblance to Jesus Christ's 'descent' from Heaven into the world of men, as was made quite clear in this sentence: 'But lo! This goblet again wishes to be empty, and Zarathustra again wishes to become a man. Thus began Zarathustra's downfall' – *Untergang* again. The 'predestined' downfall of the prophet whose heretical teachings are rejected by most of his contemporaries and who must empty the 'cup of bitterness' to the dregs. As had happened to Jesus Christ. And as, recently, had happened to Nietzsche, whose return to the 'world of men' had ended in disaster.

On his way down Zarathustra meets a saintly old man who is surprised that Zarathustra, who used to bring ashes up into the mountains, should now be bringing fire down into the valleys. Fire-worship was one the practices of the ancient Persian magicians, but the allusion here was also to Prometheus, the overly bold mortal who stole the dangerous fire of knowledge from the Heaven of the Olympian gods and who was duly punished for this sacrilege. For this new act of daring, the aged saint warns, Zarathustra runs the risk of being denounced as an 'arsonist' (*Brandstifter* or 'fire-igniter' – another Nietzschean pun, since the German word *Stifter* is the term used to designate the 'founder' of a religion). When Zarathustra explains that he is going down into the valley because 'I love men', the holy man replies that he loves only God, human beings being too imperfect. Zarathustra then continues on his way, amazed that the old man has not yet heard that '*God is dead!*'

Having enunciated one of the book's main themes, Nietzsche went on to formulate a second, no less striking leitmotiv. Zarathustra reaches a town, 'the Motley Cow' – in colloquial German *Kuhdorf* ('cow-village') has the pejorative meaning of a 'one-horse town' . . . was Nietzsche perhaps thinking of Naumburg? – where a large crowd of people have gathered in the marketplace to watch a tightrope-walker. Zarathustra proceeds to harangue them, beginning his speech with these mysterious words: '*I teach you the Overman.* Man is something that must be overcome. What have you done to overcome him?' He then takes the townsfolk to task for wanting to see an ebbing of the 'great floodtide' (i.e. of scientific knowledge and intellectual progress) and for being readier to return to an animal condition than interested in striving to 'overcome' Man. 'For what is the ape for men? A laughing-stock and a source of painful shame. I have made my way from worm to man' – a veiled reference to Darwin's theory of evolution – 'and there is much in you that is still worm. Once upon a time you were apes, and even today Man is more ape than any ape.'

These peremptory affirmations sound strange to an Anglo-Saxon ear; as indeed the term *Übermensch* (which the noted American scholar Walter Kaufmann rightly translated into English as 'overman') must have sounded odd to Nietzsche's contemporaries. What exactly did the author mean in coining this new substantive, hitherto normally used in German in the adjectival superlative form of *übermenschlich* (superhuman)? Nietzsche offered no clear answer to this question. Instead, he chose to portray the *Übermensch* (the future paragon of human perfection) with a series of impressionistic brushstrokes: as the goal towards which mankind should be (but was not in fact) headed; as someone who remains 'true to the earth', who does not delude himself with otherworldly fancies, who pays no heed to the baleful, 'poison-mixing' despisers of the human body; as one whose soul is so vast and all-embracing that, like the sea, it can absorb and dilute every kind of filth; as one who does not seek an easy life of stolid happiness and comfort, who is not tepid and faint-hearted but more closely resembles 'lightning and folly'.

Nietzsche then offered his readers one of his most striking metaphors to define Man and human life, as enunciated by Zarathustra: 'Man is a rope, strung between animal and overman – a rope strung over an abyss.' As for life, it is a 'perilous there-over, a perilous on-the-way, a perilous looking-back, a perilous shuddering and standing-still. What is great in Man is that he is a bridge and not a goal: what can be loved in Man is that he is a *going-over* and a *going-under*' – in German, an *Übergang* and an *Untergang*. A 'going-over' for those who make it safely to the other side (and thus achieve their 'destiny'); a 'going-under' for those who do not make it, and, more generally, the fate that awaits all mortal beings, for whom the end of the road is death. There follows a list of all those Zarathustra particularly loves (too long to be repeated here), which culminates with those he likens to heavy raindrops heralding the approaching storm – such as (though not specifically named) John the

Baptist and Jan Hus. He then adds: 'Behold, I am the herald of the lightning, and a heavy raindrop from the cloud: this lightning, however, is called [the] Overman.'

After listing those he loves, as the human raw material out of which a genuine 'overman' can be created, Zarathustra lists those he most despises, lumped together into a collective prototype designated as '*der letzte Mensch*' – the last or latest man: a Nietzschean euphemism for the contemporary human being, who has made the Earth grow smaller, thanks to his talents for reproduction (contemptuously compared to those of the flea-beetle), and also – here he was aiming the arrows of his irony at revolutionary egalitarians – because this type of human being 'longs for the herd without the shepherds. Everybody wants to be equal and alike, everybody is equal and alike: whoever feels differently goes voluntarily to the madhouse.'

In the marketplace the response of the crowd is loud and unequivocal: they want the 'last man' for a model. Meanwhile the tightrope-walker has begun his balancing act, advancing along a taut rope strung between two towers. He is overtaken by a jeering acrobat, who leaps over him, causing his rival to lose balance and fall to the ground. To Zarathustra, who kneels down beside him, the dying tightrope-walker says that he had long known that this would be his fate: sooner or later the Devil would trip him up, and he would surely drag him down to hell. Zarathustra reassures him: there is no Heaven and no Hell. 'Your soul will be dead even before your body.'

Shouldering the dead tightrope-walker, Zarathustra carries him outside the town gates, where the grave-diggers mock him, accuse him of trying to cheat the Devil of his due, and refuse to bury this 'dead dog'. Later, after a long, wearying walk through a nearby forest, Zarathustra lies down and enjoys a long, refreshing sleep. He is greeted, when he awakes at dawn, by a fresh, consoling thought. In the town he had made a stupid mistake in addressing himself to the people, to the common 'herd', whose dog and shepherd he wanted to become. This was an affront and a usurpation that the jealous 'shepherds of the flock' (i.e. the upholders of traditional religious and moral values) would never tolerate. Whom, after all, did these 'shepherds' most detest? The answer was: the sacrilegious upsetters of the Tablets of the Law, the tablets of established values – here too the allusion to Jesus Christ (and his conflict with the conservative members of the Sanhedrin) was transparent. Yet who, verily, was this 'breaker, this criminal' (in German, '*den Brecher, den Verbrecher*', another Nietzschean play on words) – if not the 'creator' of a new set of values? What the genuine creator needs are neither the dumb herd nor the blind believers; what he needs and must hereafter seek are 'fellow creators' (*Mitschaffende*). 'Wreckers' such as he will always be regarded as despisers of Good and Evil, whereas in truth he and those ready to follow him will become 'fellow harvesters and fellow celebrants'. As he buries the corpse of his first 'disciple' – this passage in German is of potent lyrical beauty – Zarathustra 'says unto his heart' that henceforth he will show his fellow creators, harvesters, and celebrants 'the rainbow and all the [upward-leading] steps to the overman'.

It is not difficult to discern in Zarathustra's burial of his first 'disciple' an allegorical allusion to the recent loss of Nietzsche's designated 'heiress', Lou Salomé. And sure enough, as Zarathustra, his doleful task completed, looks up into the air, he sees an eagle soaring in wide circles above him, with, gently coiled around its neck, 'not as a prey but as a friend', a serpent. 'They are my animals!' exclaims Zarathustra, overjoyed by the sight. 'The proudest animal under the sun, and the cleverest animal under the sun.'

The eagle, of course, was the far-sighted bird of prey to which Nietzsche liked to compare himself. But what of the serpent? Here the German text is unambiguously clear. The eagle's 'friend' (*Freundin*) is specifically feminine (as is the word *Schlange* – snake or serpent), and is furthermore described as being '*das klügste Tier unter der Sonne*' ('the cleverest animal under the sun'). The word *klügste* was the same superlative Nietzsche had used when, writing from Rapallo to his friend Franz Overbeck, he had written that, just as Wagner was the 'most complete' (*vollste*) human being he had ever known, so Lou (Salomé) had been the 'cleverest' (*klügste*).

Even more poignantly autobiographical was the concluding lament in this final introductory section:

> Would that I could be more clever! Would that I could be clever, like my serpent, through and through!
>
> But there I beg for the impossible; so I beg my pride that it should always accompany my cleverness.
>
> And if one day my cleverness abandons me – ah, how it loves to fly away! – may my pride go on flying with my folly.

And so began Zarathustra's downfall.

Of the twenty Zarathustran 'speeches' that followed, few attained the clarity and lyrical beauty of the explanatory preface. Five of them, however, deserve special mention.

In the first 'speech' or discourse, entitled 'Of the Three Transformations', Zarathustra–Nietzsche began by describing allegorically the three stages through which the human Mind or Spirit must pass on its way to creative perfection. It must first become a camel, waiting to be laden (i.e. burdened with knowledge, traditional beliefs and prejudices, conventional 'wisdom') before having to choose from a number of possible courses: everything from an arduous upward climb towards the heights to a peaceful grazing off the grass of knowledge, or a bold plunge into 'the dirty waters of the truth', etc. During a second metamorphosis the human Spirit must become a lion in order to confront the Dragon of Tradition and Conventional Morality and to liberate itself in a struggle that is unavoidably negative and destructive. In its third and final metamorphosis, the Mind or Spirit must attain the playful innocence of the child, uncrippled by any notion of sinfulness, in order to launch a healthy 'new beginning' and to proclaim a '*heiliges Ja-sagen*' (a 'sacred yes-saying') to Life and its challenges.

Zarathustra's seventh discourse, innocuously titled 'On Reading and Writing', began with two trenchant sentences, destined to become world-famous, in which Nietzsche opened fire more fiercely than ever on those (the vast majority of human 'scribblers') who are half-hearted, lukewarm and prudently uncommitted in their thoughts and feelings: 'Of all that is written I like only that which one has written with one's blood. Write in blood: and you will find that blood is spirit.'

There followed, in swift, staccato sentences, a cannonade of personal injunctions, antipathies and anathemas aimed, among other things, at universal 'education' and the cult of propaedeutical facility; and, after the cannonade, an encomium of lightness, so beautifully exemplified by butterflies that the mere sight of them can reduce Zarathustra to tears of joy. He then exclaims, expressing Nietzsche's deepest thinking: 'I would believe only in a god who knew how to dance. And when I saw my devil, I found him serious, thorough, profound, solemn; it was the spirit of gravity – through it all things fall. Not by wrath but by laughter does one kill. Come, let us kill the spirit of gravity!'

In Zarathustra's tenth discourse, Nietzsche renewed his spirited defence of 'free thinking' in language reminiscent of his exhortation that one should learn to 'live dangerously'.

> If you cannot be the saints of knowledge, at least be its warriors. They are the companions and forerunners of such sainthood.
>
> I see many soldiers: would that I saw many warriors. 'Uniform' one calls what they wear: would that what they thus conceal were not uni-form.

Subtle 'free-thinking' caveats like this one could easily be overlooked by casual readers, impressed above all by the bellicose tone of other exhortations:

> Not to work do I call you but to combat. I call you not to peace but to victory. May your work be a fight, may your peace be a victory. War and

> courage have accomplished more great things than love of one's neighbour. It was not your pity but your courage that so far saved the luckless.

This hymn of praise to courage and exertion was in no sense intended as approval of the increasingly bellicose climate of contemporary Europe, at a time when the great sabre-rattling powers of the continent were introducing ever longer terms of compulsory military service. For, in Zarathustra's next discourse ('On the New Idol'), Nietzsche went further than he had ever gone before in stigmatizing the modern State as 'the coldest of cold monsters', as a 'hellish artifice and a horse of death, clanking in the finery of divine honours', etc.

Two of Zarathustra's 'speeches' had to do with women and were clearly influenced by Nietzsche's recent blistering experiences with Lou Salomé. In the thirteenth, devoted to 'Chastity', he began by once again expressing his Schopenhauerian dislike of great cities:

> It is bad to live in great cities: there too many are in lustful heat. Is it not better to end up in the hands of a murderer then in the dreams of a woman in heat? And behold these men: their eyes say it – they know nothing better on earth than to lie with a woman. Mud lies at the bottom of their souls; and woe to all if their mud also has spirit!

Did this mean that Zarathustra was advocating sexual abstinence? No. 'Chastity for some is a virtue but for many also a vice. They abstain, to be sure; but the bitch sensuality leers forth enviously from everything they do.' Like a bloodhound, she pursues one 'up to the very heights of virtue', politely knowing how to 'beg for a piece of spirit when a chunk of meat is refused her . . . Those for whom chastity is burdensome should be counselled against it: that it should not become a road to hell – that is, to the slime and lustful heat of the soul.'

The concluding lines in this Zarathustran discourse sounded an entirely different note and were clearly inspired by a model of womanhood quite different from Lou Salomé – by the good 'Aunt Malwida', the ageing spinster *malgré elle* who years before had been 'jilted' by the man she wished to marry.

> Verily, some are chaste through and through: they are gentler of heart, are fonder of laughter and laugh more heartily than you. They also laugh at chastity and ask, 'What is chastity? Is chastity not folly? But this chastity came to us, not we to it. We offered this guest hostel and heart: now it lives with us – may it stay as long as it wishes.'
>
> Thus spake Zarathustra.

In what was perhaps the most provocative of all these discourses ('On little old and young women'), Nietzsche had Zarathustra recall a conversation he had recently had with a little old woman, who had challenged him to speak his mind about her sex. In a series of lapidary sentences Zarathustra then speaks his mind:

> Everything about Woman is a riddle, and everything about Woman has one solution: it is called pregnancy. Man for Woman is a means: the goal is always the child. But what is Woman for the Man?

The answer to this question is twofold. A 'real', full-blooded man wants two things in life: danger and play. What he therefore seeks in woman is a 'dangerous plaything'. Nietzsche then had Zarathustra declare: 'Man should be educated for warfare, and woman for the relaxation of the warrior: everything else is folly.'

But if the woman for the man is a plaything, this is by no means a dishonour. Let her be 'pure and delicate, like a gem that is irradiated by the virtues of a world that is not yet there. May the radiance of a star sparkle in your love! Let your hope be: "May I give birth to the overman!"'

Fine sentiments, fine words! the old crone tells Zarathustra after listening to his expatiations. As a token of her gratitude she then offers him this 'tiny truth': 'You are going to women? Do not forget the whip!'

This was a typically Nietzschean leg-pull, one more example of the prankishness which often prompted him to make provocative statements in order to shock staid readers. The 'tiny truth' about the whip was no invention of his. It had been suggested by a novelette of Turgenev, which his sister Elisabeth had once read to him in Naumburg: the strange story of a lovely young girl who, when offered the choice between a brutal father and a gentle son, obdurately prefers the former. This said, this 'joke' concealed a hard core of personal bitterness, and the not-to-be-forgotten whip was clearly associated in Nietzsche's mind with the sound thrashing Lou Salomé deserved for having so artfully transformed him for months into a lovesick buffoon.

The next to last of the prophet's twenty-one 'speeches' – each of which ends with the same sentence, 'Thus spake Zarathustra' (a variation of the Sanskrit formula, *iti vutta kam*, 'Thus spoke the saint') – was devoted to that most ultimate and definitive of human realities: Death. It was in some ways the most portentous of these discourses, in anticipating a problem – that of old age and longevity – which in our time has assumed increasingly monstrous and dangerously insoluble proportions. The speech began with three arresting sentences: 'Many die too late, and a few die too early. The doctrine still sounds strange: "Die at the right time!" Die at the right time: so teaches Zarathustra.'

That Raphael, Mozart, Schiller, Schubert and Chopin had all died prematurely, before being able to complete what they still had to offer to the world, no one could seriously question. But, Nietzsche pointed out, such geniuses were relatively few, compared to the many who 'die too late'. Zarathustra's imperious injunction was one of those recommendations it is easy to make but difficult to put into practice. Even Nietzsche at this point recoiled from drawing the logical conclusion: that the solution for those who have 'overlived their time' and who are a burden to society is a form of discreet suicide.

Nietzsche had not yet found his way out of this dilemma. Faced with this awesome problem, all Zarathustra can do is beat about the bush with facile anathemas like this one: 'Of course, how could someone who has never lived at the right time die at the right time? Would that he had never been born! Such is the advice I give to the superfluous' – which is to say, to the vast majority of human beings, viewed from the lofty perspective of the 'overman', of the truly creative and innovative genius.

What then could be a valid example of a truly 'consummating death', which acts 'on the living as a spur and a solemn pledge'? The unspoken answer was: Socrates's exemplary death. Already, in the 94th aphorism of *Human, All Too Human* II (*Mixed Opinions and Maxims*), Nietzsche had asserted that the two greatest 'judicial murders' in the history of the world had both in reality been 'well-disguised suicides'. Socrates had preferred to empty his cup of hemlock rather than retract his 'erroneous' and 'youth-corrupting' arguments, while Jesus Christ had arranged to meet his disciples on the Mount of Olives, fully aware of the deadly risks he was taking. But how could such shining examples be followed by ordinary folk, by the great mass of human beings whom Zarathustra had superciliously dismissed as 'superfluous'? To this question Zarathustra–Nietzsche had no clear answer. All he could do was to lavish scorn on those beings who, having lived too long, cling to life like yellow-wrinkled, late autumn apples.

> Cowardice is what keeps them on their branches. All too many live and all too long do they hang from their branches. Would that a storm came and shook all this worm-eaten rot from the tree! Would that there came preachers of quick death! They would be the proper storms and shakers of the trees of life! But I hear only slow death preached, and patience with all that is earthly. Ah, you preach patience for what is earthly? But it is what is earthly that has too much patience with you, you blasphemers!

Nietzsche here was boldly attacking what has come to be the more or less official 'line' on euthanasia (a word which in ancient Greek meant 'a quiet and easy death') by both the Protestant and the Catholic Church. That word in Nietzsche's day had not yet been semantically disembowelled and corrupted, as has happened in our own, more tragic, post-Hitlerian age. But his prophetic 'sixth sense' warned him that this urgent subject too was likely to be shunned as morally 'indecent', too shameful to be discussed, and publicly muzzled, as had so often happened in the past, by a mind-numbing taboo. Meanwhile, what greater humbuggery could there be than to preach the 'sanctity' of a spent life – when a 'toothless mouth' can no longer utter the slightest 'truth' – on the part of those who promise an escape from suffering into 'everlasting life' and the miraculous 'resurrection' of an imperishable body?

Leaving the reader to draw (or not to draw) his own conclusion, Nietzsche now chose to honour the memory of Socrates's exemplary companion in the noble art of self-sacrifice:

> Verily, he died too early, that Hebrew whom the preachers of slow death do honour: and for many since then a calamity it was that he should have died too soon. And yet, he knew naught but the tears and the melancholy of the Hebrew, together with the hatred of the Good and the Righteous – the Hebrew Jesus: thus a longing for death overcame him. Would that he had remained in the wilderness and far from the Good and the Righteous! Perhaps he would have learned to live and love the earth – and laughter too! Believe me, my brothers, he died too soon; he himself would have retracted his teaching had he reached my age! Noble enough was he to recant! But he was still too immature. Immature is the young man's way of loving, and immature his hatred of Man and Earth. Heavy is his mind and still fettered are the wings of his spirit. But in man there is more of the child than in the youth, and less melancholy: he better understands both life and death. Free for death and free in death, a sacred Nay-sayer when the time for Yes is over: thus understands he death and life.

Fine thoughts! Provocative but also inconclusive thoughts which, wrapped in the rich raiment of biblical expression, left this grave problem unresolved.

## CHAPTER 31

# 'Oh, my son Zarathustra!'

*– The poison that is the undoing of a weaker nature is invigorating for the strong – nor does he call it a poison.*

Whereas the lovely fortnight of bright blue skies in the second half of January had enabled a sunshine-stimulated Nietzsche to finish the first draft of his *Zarathustra* in just ten days, the second part, or *Zarathustra* II, as he was already calling it, was written over a slightly longer period of two weeks, despite erratic variations in the unusually cold weather. The crisp mountain air of Sils-Maria, however, proved as mentally invigorating as had been the bright sunshine and sea-breezes of Rapallo. By early July the work was virtually completed. In a pre-birthday letter sent to his sister on the 6th, Nietzsche wrote that once again he was as nervously ill as he had been for four long weeks in the spring thanks to the foot-dragging equivocations of his Chemnitz publisher and Leipzig printer. He beseeched Elisabeth to intervene and to make Schmeitzner understand that for him it was a matter of life or death to know if he was prepared to bring out the second *Zarathustra* volume without delay. More than five months had passed since he had sent him the laboriously copied-out manuscript of *Zarathustra* I, but not one of the privileged recipients had received what was supposed to be an Easter present.

It was precisely at this moment, when he was 'swinging' between a euphoric sense of exhilaration (at having so swiftly given birth to a second *Zarathustra* 'child') and a sense of anguished urgency about his new book's fate, that Nietzsche was rudely jolted by several letters from his busybody sister. With the simple-minded zealotry so often displayed by those who are 'more royalist than the king', Elisabeth had decided to conclude her private war against that evil-minded temptress, Lou Salomé, and her no less sinister 'partner in mocking derision', Paul Rée, by writing a letter to Rée's mother intended to 'open' the poor woman's eyes to the kind of abject creature her son really was. Its main accusation – that it was the foul-mouthed Paul Rée who had warned Lou Salomé that Nietzsche's 'idealistic' teaching was simply a mask concealing lewd inclinations – left Nietzsche stunned and staggered. In the final section of *Zarathustra* I, entitled 'The Gift-Giving Virtue', he had set out to rectify the misleading impression, derived from a casual reading of his books (by persons like Elisabeth), that he favoured human egotism and selfishness in praising self-reliance, self-esteem, self-love and self-improvement, when what he was extolling was rugged individuality, the 'sublime' ability to rise above praise and blame, and (as he had already written in *The Joyous Science*) the magnanimity to overcome a demeaning thirst for revenge by showing mercy and forgiveness towards one's enemies.

Elisabeth's offensive was astutely timed to take advantage of her brother's momentary weakness in having to implore her energetic intervention with his publisher, Schmeitzner, who, yielding to her epistolatory threats, sent Nietzsche a telegram assuring him that *Zarathustra* II would, without delay, be sent to another, less lethargic printer. In his present state of dependency all Fritz could do was to offer his sister his sarcastic congratulations: 'The letter to Frau R[ée] is, in literary terms, your finest performance yet; but may Heaven see to it that never again should *such* occasions arise in which you have to distinguish yourself in literary matters!'

What particularly infuriated Nietzsche was to discover, at this late date, that his sister had told him only a part of the shocking things Lou Salomé had said to her in her angry outbursts at Jena and Tautenburg during the previous August, and that it was from Paul Rée himself that Lou had learned of Nietzsche's plans for a 'wild marriage'. In a fit of rage he now wrote Rée a furious letter, accusing him of being a sneaking, insidious, mendacious fellow and the very opposite of what a real 'friend' should be. He ended by saying that he would like to teach Rée a 'lesson in practical morality' with a couple of pistol-shots – for in such matters 'my Herr Doktor Rée, clean hands alone are suited but not slimy fingers'.

This letter, though copied out, may not have been sent. It ended with two savage sentences in which Nietzsche quoted from a letter Paul Rée had written to him in which he had called Lou Salomé 'his calamity: quel goût! This sterile, dirty, evil-smelling she-ape with the false breasts – a calamity!'

By the time he got around to writing to Ida Overbeck, who had kindly sent him some tea and vegetable soups in powder form, Nietzsche's fury had begun to cool. 'My sister wants to get her revenge on that Russian girl – well, all right, but up till now I have been the victim in everything she has done . . . In reality, without the *aims* of my work and the *implacability* of such aims I would no longer be alive. To such an extent is my saviour called Zarathustra, my son Zarathustra!'

Soon Nietzsche was assailed by feelings of remorse at having resorted to such intemperate language, utterly unworthy of a thinker who, in *Zarathustra*, had defined the superior human being as one who was sufficiently self-assured to be 'above praise or blame'. To what a level of abject 'lowness' had he now, under the influence of blind passion, suddenly descended!

In another long, explanatory letter to Ida Overbeck, Nietzsche went even further in distancing himself from his sister's warlike feelings towards the 'villainous' Lou Salomé. 'Quite apart from the idealistic light in which she was presented to me (as a martyr of knowledge almost from childhood on and more a heroine than a martyr), for me she is and remains a being of the first rank . . . As regards the energy of her will and the originality of her mind she was suited for something great; even though in terms of practical morality she may well belong in a prison or a lunatic asylum. *I miss* her, for all her bad qualities: we were different enough so that something useful always had to emerge from our conversations, I have never found anyone so free of prejudice, so bright and prepared for *my* kind of problems. Since then it is as though I had been condemned to silence or to a humane hypocrisy in my *dealings with all human beings.*'

Altogether this was not a happy summer for Nietzsche, much as he loved the Upper Engadine. It was so extremely cold that the nearby mountains remained snow-covered down the foothills as far as the valley floor. Foreign visitors and even the hardiest of old-timers were beginning to complain. In a letter written to his sister towards the end of July, to thank her for having intervened so energetically with Ernst Schmeitzner, Fritz remarked wrily that his misguided publisher might well be bankrupted by the additional cost of printing up *Zarathustra* II, after having so recklessly squandered on antisemitic agitation everything he had earned from the sale of Nietzsche's books.

Recently, he had endured a 'day of hell', followed by a nervous collapse, when he was informed by the manager of the Hôtel Edelweiss that the entire Rée family were expected to turn up in Sils-Maria that very afternoon. Drenched to the skin by a cloudburst, he had hurried to the post-station to book a seat on the next day's stagecoach headed for Chur . . . only to disover a few hours later that the family name of the newcomers had been wrongly registered.

In making this candid confession Nietzsche was quietly puncturing his wild talk about exchanging 'bullets' and fighting it out, pistol in hand, with Paul Rée, his brother Georg, or any other 'scoundrel' who dared to sully his good name and reputation. But once he had recovered his composure, he made up for this momentary loss of nerve by sending off his insulting letter to Georg Rée. What he did not know was that Paul Rée and Lou Salomé had decided to spend a few weeks at Schuls, in the Lower Engadine (north-east of St Moritz) and that Lou had sent one of her new admirers, a young Berliner named Ferdinand Tönnies, from there to Sils-Maria to see if he could meet and effect a reconciliation with the author of *Human, All Too Human.*

Emboldened by the painful events of the previous autumn and winter, Franz Overbeck had written Nietzsche a letter of friendly admonition, reminding him that as a writer he had overstepped 'every *accepted* mean', adding for good measure that his aphoristic mode of expression in books that were too long and diffuse had been enough to tax the patience of the most devoted reader. This may also have been the private feeling of Heinrich Köselitz, who, as Nietzsche's most devoted 'disciple', had so far been too humble, wary and discreet to express any serious reservations. But when Nietzsche informed him that he had just completed a second *Zarathustra*, to remedy certain defects in Part I, Köselitz, who in the last of three ecstatic letters of congratulation had described *Zarathustra* I as being 'the most beautiful book of post-Christian times', plucked up his courage and offered his 'Master' a paragraph of sound criticism: 'I am delighted that Zarathustra's mood was merely temporary; for me there was too much thunderstorm-violet in him . . . I believed that a scorn for others was justified only in the lower regions of the valuable man – there where from time to time he yields to popular excitements; as a wise man he must always have present to mind the conditions of his own, highly individual existence – whereby he will always reach the conclusion that he and the entire world complement themselves.'

To clarify what he meant, Köselitz pointed out that in haughtily disregarding those he contemptuously called 'superfluous', Zarathustra was in fact destroying himself. A teacher, to be a teacher, must have disciples or at the very least persons who are willing to listen to him; and to be a teacher at all one is dependent on a host of other more or less inivisible but actively present persons. Even Epicurus could not have survived on his meagre diet of goat-cheese, with or without his disciples, had there not also previously existed a mass of goatherds and shepherds in the mountains, to say nothing of wood-choppers, boiler-makers, miners and waggoners, potters and cutlers, carpenters and joiners, etc.

To Köselitz's intense relief, Nietzsche's response to this down-to-earth criticism was anything but hostile. He was grateful that *Zarathustra* I should have been given such a careful perusal by someone who not only knew how to 'read between the lines' but understood what 'should stand between them', and to whom therefore Zarathustra was honour-bound to reply. The only trouble with Köselitz's notion of 'complementary human beings' was that in searching for persons capable of comprehending 'solutions, aims and justifications' in life, Nietzsche had so far found '*no one of this kind*'.

The first proofs of *Zarathustra* II reached Sils-Maria in early August, dispatched by a new Leipzig printer, Naumann, whose typesetters were so unfamiliar with Nietzsche's pen-jabbing scrawl that the printed text was full of errors. Not a single copy of the first part of *Thus Spake Zarathustra* had so far left Leipzig, and the reason, Nietzsche had begun to suspect, was that Schmeitzner was by now so debt-ridden that he could not pay the printer, Teubner. This raised a troubling question: if he could not pay for the first, how on earth could Schmeitzner finance the printing of the second *Zarathustra*?

On 26 August Nietzsche wrote to Franz Overbeck that he had developed a 'veritable hatred' for his sister Elisabeth, who had kept quiet at the wrong time and had then begun to speak up at the wrong time, making him the victim of a 'pitiless feeling of revenge'. He had almost finished correcting the proofs of *Zarathustra* II, about which Heinrich Köselitz had just written from Venice to say that its impact on him had been immensely strong:' . . . it has bowled me over, I am still lying on the floor.'.

No wonder Köselitz was bowled over! At times wielding his Apollinian spear like a Jupiterian thunderbolt, at times roaring with the 'tenderness of a lion' – the images are his – Nietzsche in twenty-two new Zarathustran discourses expanded the range of his literary virtuosity to include oneiric, dream-like elements, stiletto-sharp anathemas, devastating formulations of arguments previously developed less succinctly, light-hearted 'scherzos', and passages of poetic prose which rose to heights even he had never previously striven to attain.

In the second discourse, for example, deceptively titled the 'Blessed Isles' – where truly free spirits, unshackled from crippling taboos, can live happily with the notion that God is merely a 'conjecture' invented by man, Zarathustra–Nietzsche suddenly let fly with a vengeance:

> God is a thought that renders crooked all that is straight, and revolving everything that stands. How so? Time would vanish, and everything transient would merely be a lie?
>
> To think thus is whirl and dizziness on limbs, and even nausea for the stomach: verily, I call it the whirling sickness thus to conjecture.
>
> Evil I call it and inimical to Man: all this teaching about the One and the Full and the Unmoved and the Sated and Imperishable.

Here Nietzsche was not only attacking Parmenides and the Platonic notion of everlasting and immutable 'ideals', as well as the Schopenhauerian notion of the cosmic 'Whole'; he was also, great admirer of Goethe though he was, attacking the Christian notion of Eternity, as intoned by the 'chorus mysticus' at the end of the second part of *Faust*:

*Alles vergängliche*
*Ist nur ein Gleichnis*

(Everything perishable
Is merely a parable)

Corrected by Zarathustra, the old formula is turned upside down and now reads, '*Alles unvergängliche – das ist nur ein Gleichnis*' (Everything imperishable – that is merely a parable). To which he adds, for good measure: 'And poets lie too much' – a dig at Plato's ideal 'Republic', from which poets should be banned as inventors and propagators of misleading myths.

Nietzsche's ironic *modus scribendi* – with mild chapter titles and introductory lines leading softly up to the hammer-blow – was perhaps nowhere better illustrated than in the fifth Zarathustran discourse, devoted to his pet foe, the 'Virtuous':

> With thunder and heavenly fireworks must one speak to slack and sleeping senses. But softly speaks the voice of Beauty: it steals only into the most wide-awake souls.
>
> Softly today did my shield quiver and laugh: that is the sacred laughter and quivering of Beauty.
>
> About you, ye Virtuous Ones, my Beauty did laugh today. And so came her voice to me: 'You still want to be paid!'
>
> You want to be paid, ye Virtuous Ones! Is it reward for virtue, Heaven for Earth, and Eternity for your today that you would have?
>
> And now you are angry with me, that I teach that there is no reward and no paymaster? And verily, I do not even teach that virtue is its own reward.
>
> Ah, that is my sorrow: reward and punishment have been lied into the very heart of things – and now too into the very foundation of your souls, ye Virtuous Ones!
>
> But like the snout of a boar will my word rip up the foundation of your souls: a ploughshare will I be for you.

Never before, perhaps, had Nietzsche so scathingly denounced the sordidly commercial bargaining (through prayers) for a good-deal-with-God aspect of Christianity than in this initially soft-pawed Zarathustran 'pounce'.

In the seventh Zarathustran discourse, 'preachers of equality' – a 'secretly vengeful' species (of Marxist and other revolutionaries) – were compared to tarantulas, and the 'will to equality' denounced as the 'tyrannomania of impotence'.

> They resemble enthusiasts: but it is not the heart that enthuses them – but revenge. And if they become cold and subtle, it is not wit but envy that makes them cold and subtle . . .
>
> From every one of their complaints sounds forth vengeance, in every word of praise there is a sting; and to be a judge seems to them sheer bliss.
>
> But I counsel you, my Friends: distrust all in whom the drive to punish is powerful!
>
> These are folk of a sorry sort and stock; the hangman and the bloodhound peers forth from their faces.

Before he finished describing this vengeful species, Zarathustra–Nietzsche painted an apocalyptic picture of the revolutionary convulsions into which the world would soon be plunged:

> Over a thousand paths and bridges shall they press towards the future, and ever more war and inequality shall there be sown between them: so does my great love speak!
>
> Inventors of images and spectres shall they in their enmities become, and with their icons and spectres shall they yet with one another fight the highest fight!

At the time these words were written, neither the Roman fasces, nor the Bolshevik hammer-and-sickle, nor the Nazi swastika had yet been raised above the cheering heads of the vengeful masses; but had he lived long enough to witness the future he had so clairvoyantly foretold, Nietzsche would not have been one whit surprised.

Completely different in spirit – for Nietzsche, like a Chinese cook, was deliberately mixing the sweet and the sour – were three central chapters, all called 'songs'. In the first ('The Night-Song'), which he had composed one night in May while looking out over the dark city of Rome from his loggia balcony on the Piazza Barberini, Nietzsche wrote his own hymn to Love and Solitude, his own highly individual Song of Songs.

> Night it is: now more loudly do all leaping fountains speak. And my soul too is a leaping fountain.
>
> Night it is: only now awake the love-songs of the lovers. And my soul too is the love-song of a lover.
>
> Something unstilled, unstillable is there within me that would loud be heard. A craving for love is within me, which itself speaks the language of love. Light am I; ah, that I were night! But this is my solitude, that I am girt with light.

> Ah, that I were dark and nocturnal! How I would suck at the breasts of light! . . .
>
> I know not the happiness of those who receive; and oft have I dreamed that even stealing must be more blessed than taking.
>
> This is my woe, that my hand never rests from giving; this is my envy, that I see expectant eyes and the illuminated nights of longing.
>
> Oh, wretchedness of all who give! Oh, darkening of my sun! Oh, craving after craving! Oh, ravenous hunger in satiety!
>
> etc.

This was followed by a 'Dance Song', improvised by Zarathustra when, with his disciples, he comes upon young girls dancing in a meadow. In this 'mocking song' – designed to make fun of the 'Spirit of Gravity, my highest and mightiest devil, of whom it is said that he is the "Lord of the world"' (German pedantry being thus identified with Angra Mainush, the Zoroastran God of Evil) – Nietzsche invented an amusing dialogue between himself, Life and his 'wild Wisdom', which owed much to the 'Unholy Trinity' of the previous year. For the jealousy expressed by Wisdom recalled Paul Rée's proprietary feelings, while Life, armed with a golden fish-hook and maliciously conscious of her powers, was a poetic transfiguration of Lou Salomé.

The third and last of Zarathustra's *Lieder* ('The Tomb-song') – an elegiac lamentation over the loss of all his youthful loves and illusions – was a pathetically autobiographical confession. Brought up to believe (by Emerson, not named) that one should regard all human beings as 'divine' and all days 'holy', Zarathustra–Nietzsche lists all the 'dirty ghosts' that had killed the innocent happiness of his youth, and which, like the Furies of Greek antiquity, had been hounding him ever since. The 'dirtiness' of these 'spectres' may have been inspired by Nietzsche's hallucinating memories of experiences in the brothels of Cologne and Leipzig, just as the 'owl-monster' flung across his path might refer to Schopenhauer, that great philosophical misleader, or, possibly, to Lou Salomé, in whom Nietzsche had first espied a 'happy bird of omen'. There was an unmistakable allusion to the intellectual ostracism to which he had been subjected by his family and so many of his friends in this terrible sentence: 'All disgust I once vowed to renounce, but then you' – i.e. the Furies – 'transformed those close and closest to me into putrid boils.' They (the Furies) had similarly exploited his sense of pity by sending him the 'incurably shameless' – persons like Paul Rée and Lou Salomé. He had wanted to dance, as he had never danced before; whereupon 'they' had persuaded his 'favourite singer' to strike up an 'eerie, dreary tune' and to tootle into his ear like a 'gloomy horn'. Here Nietzsche may have been recalling the bitter blow dealt to his musical pride and 'creative' hopes by Hans von Bülow's blistering critique of his '*Manfred Meditation*'; but the 'favourite singer' could only have been Richard Wagner, who had not only displayed a testy indifference to Nietzsche's musical lucubrations, but had added insult to injury by going on to compose a religiously inspired *Parsifal*.

In terms of philosophical substance, as opposed to literary virtuosity, the most important of these Zarathustran meditations was with little doubt the twelfth, devoted to 'Self-overcoming'. Here for the first time Nietzsche began to develop a theme – the 'will to power' – that was destined to become the most radically upsetting, 'subversive' and controversial of all his contributions to contemporary thinking. Addressing himself to the 'wisest ones' (i.e. philosophers and theologians), Zarathustra–Nietzsche began by ruthlessly tearing away the benign illusions that envelop and embellish the 'will to truth':

> You first wish to *make* all things thinkable: for you doubt with well-founded mistrust if it is already thinkable.
>
> But it must yield and bend for you. Thus your will wants it. It must become smooth and subject to the mind, as its mirror-image and reflection.
>
> This is your entire will, you Wisest Ones, a will to power; and so too when you speak of Good and Evil and of valuations.
>
> You would still create the world before which you can kneel; such is your ultimate hope and intoxication.

The key word here, which Nietzsche was careful to underline, is 'make' – in German *machen*, the first cousin of *Macht* (might or power). Philosophical thinking, in the very nature of things, is an attempt to make (a subject or whatever) intelligible to others; and that means to propose, and only too often to impose a particular interpretation of the world and of life or thought for the guidance of the less intellectually minded, of 'non-thinkers', of 'the unwise'.

In making this point Nietzsche was not simply thinking of Hegel and his neo-Hegelian disciples and successors, who had imposed their particular interpretation on centuries and entire millennia of human history, in a wilful effort to comprehend the past and to predict and, in a sense, to dictate the future evolution of mankind; he was also thinking of the theologians who impose a vision of the world before which all men not only can but should kneel. Karl Marx had brazenly declared that religion was the opiate of the masses. But in a far deeper sense religion could be said to be the opiate of the 'wisest', the opiate of the theologians, and indeed the opiate of all conservative philosophers who proclaim that things are thus and so and that the wise one is he who, as the saying has it, 'does not kick against the pricks'.

At the centre of Schopenhauer's conception of the world was the notion that in all forms of organic life a kind of cosmic life-force or Will is at work, primarily intended to assure (through procreation) the survival of the species. Giving this basic concept a new, fateful twist, Nietzsche now substituted 'the struggle for mastery' for the 'struggle for survival'. Even in the act of procreation there is an element of domination and an element of submission. (When unwilling and resisted, the act is known as 'rape'.) And what is true of the sexual act is, no matter what the 'moralists' might claim, true of all human relations. Human beings do not approach each other in a purely passive or neutral spirit. Instinctively, and most of the time unconsciously, each individual, whether male or female, tries to size up 'the other' in an effort to determine if and in what way he or she might be superior or inferior. This was why Envy, long regarded by Church fathers as one of the seven cardinal sins, is neither intrinsically good or evil. It can, as Nietzsche had already pointed out in *Human, All Too Human*, incite admiration and prove an emulative spur to self-improvement; or it can turn into the mean, sickly, arachnoidal kind of jealous hatred Zarathustra had described in his discourse, 'On the Tarantulas'. The bitter truth, which so many shallow moralists and political windbags were doing their utmost to blur, is that no two human beings are absolutely equal and identical – this is even true of twins – and that psychological factors of superiority and inferiority are present and active in all human relationships. As Nietzsche had his 'second' Zarathustra declare in three trenchant maxims: Everything that lives, obeys. Secondly, he will be commanded who cannot obey himself. And thirdly, commanding is harder than obeying. He who commands must bear the burden of all who obey, and this burden can all too easily crush him.

Nietzsche had not yet formulated a 'law of psychological compensation', but it was already here in embryonic form, even though draped in somewhat laboured neo-biblical language:

> Where I found the living, there I found the Will to power; and even in the will of those who serve did I find the will to be the master . . .
>
> And just as the smaller yields to the greater, that it may have pleasure and power over the smallest, so even the greatest too submits and for the sake of power risks life . . .
>
> And where there are sacrifice, and service, and amorous glances, there too there is the will to be master. Along stealthy paths does the weaker steal into the castle and even into the heart of the mightier and there steals their might.

As has been proved over and over through the centuries by sycophants and Court intriguers, by royal 'favourites' and the mistresses – the very word pays homage to their power – of countless kings.

Moral values, Zarathustra points out towards the end of this important discourse, do not impose themselves by magic but by a 'will to power'; nor are they in any sense eternal.

> Verily, I say unto you: Good and Evil that are not transitory – do not exist . . .
>
> With your values and your words about Good and Evil you use force, you High Esteemers; and this is your hidden love and the splendour, trembling, and overflowing of your soul . . .
>
> And he who must be a creator in Good and Evil must verily first be a destroyer and shatterer of values.
>
> Thus the highest Evil belongs to the highest Good: but it is creative.

Stated in simpler, less exalted, and less elliptic terms, neither the pomp and ceremony of the established Christian Church, nor the trembling of its greatest thinkers (like Pascal), nor the overflowing love and fervour of its saints could mask the decisive fact that its authority was established through acts of force in its overthrow of the established values of the Greco-Roman world. In much the same way the established values of a presently moribund Christianity must be shattered and replaced by something higher through acts of creative destruction. Acts which Zarathustra, in his very first speech, had likened to the 'lion' stage of individual development.

The other major theme unveiled in *Zarathustra* II concerned the irreversibility and the consequent acceptance of the past – what Nietzsche had already called '*amor fati*'. Here he was confronted with a cruel dilemma which he had to 'bridge' or overcome if his entire philosophy was not to collapse into a heap of contradictions. Zarathustra, as he had made amply clear, was a prophet of destruction as well as of creation: the baleful present, weighed down by its cargo of superannuated myths and hypocritical allegiances to moral slogans which few still took seriously, had to be swept out and cleansed and replaced by a more honest, self-reliant, science-respecting and joyously life-enhancing future. But in so 'preaching', wasn't he too succumbing in his turn to a form of revolutionary idealism? Or, stated differently: when is a revolutionary desire to alter an existing situation a wholesome, healthy, positive inclination, and when is it, quite the contrary, a sickly, psychologically warped, morbid and negatively inspired 'drive'? Wagner, who had begun his life as an ardent supporter of revolutionary change – he had had to flee from his native

Saxony as a result – had answered this question with a nationalistic 'solution': the particular genius of the Germans was a genius for reform, as heroically exemplified by an essentially 'constructive' Martin Luther, whereas the genius of the French was essentially critical and destructive, as had been made quite clear by the atheistic *philosophes* of the eighteenth century, the fanatical regicides of the Great Revolution and the crazy hotheads of the Paris Commune in 1871.

Nietzsche, however, was too much an admirer of the Italian Renaissance – the first serious attempt made to free Europe from the grip of the ascetic, life-denying excesses of the Middle Ages – to be able to look upon Luther as a national hero. During his long walks at Sils-Maria it had occurred to him that the spirit of revenge which fires the revolutionary's desire to overthrow the existing order also colours and warps his attitude towards the past. The past, fatally 'marred' by all sorts of social injustices and inequalities, is judged and found guilty for not having been what *morally* it should have been. But since the past is something that cannot be changed, the resentful revolutionary settles his scores with the 'wicked' past by wreaking his revenge on the present, often mutilating it so recklessly and creating such social havoc that a strong-willed 'saviour' is needed to try to put the fractured pieces together again. (Cromwell was one example, Napoleon another.)

What would happen, however, if one were to adopt a radically different approach to the past, and, instead of childishly gnashing one's teeth in impotent rage because it had not been what it *should* have been, one adopted a higher, supra-moral viewpoint and accepted the past and all it had to offer – for better or for worse, whether good or evil – as it had actually happened. Essentially this was the attitude Spinoza had adopted, since a God-permeated world could not intrinsically be bad. It was also the 'unbiast' attitude that Hegel, much influenced (like Goethe) by Spinoza, had adopted and justified in one of his most famous formulations: 'The real is rational.'

There is no point in tearing one's hair or shedding tears over the more dismal and barbaric moments of human history; this is a sentimental attitude, unworthy of any serious student of the development of mankind. Hegel, however, had remained at heart a deist, his *Weltgeist* or 'world spirit' simply being a historical dynamic transmogrification of the divine. If he had to choose between the two, Nietzsche was readier to choose Hegel, the *bête noire* of his earlier years, rather than Karl Marx and his revolutionary 'rabble'. And if God was removed from the picture as an anachronistic accessory, was this not a saner course, one more worthy of a 'sage', than to indulge in wild flights of fancy as to what the past should have been? This, in effect, is the course chosen by Zarathustra who, in his twentieth discourse ('*Von der Erlösung*' – which can be translated by 'On Redemption' or by 'Deliverance'), informs his disciples that he is 'wandering among men as though among the fragments and limbs of men' – i.e. of intellectually disarticulated human beings, torn apart by the contradictory tugs of past loyalties and futuristic hopes and aspirations.

> The Now and the Past on earth – ah, my Friends – that is *my* most unendurable lot; and I would not know how to live were I not also a seer of what must come.
>
> A seer, a willer, a creator, even a future and a bridge to the future – and, alas, also a cripple on this bridge: all that is Zarathustra.

As he explains to his disciples: 'And how could I endure being a man if Man were not also a poet and solver of riddles and the redeemer of chance!' And the answer Zarathustra has found for these riddles is this: 'To redeem all who have lived and to transform every "It was" into "Thus I wanted it" – that alone would I call salvation.'

To the awesome question – how is Man to escape from the implacable constraints of the human condition? – Nietzsche's initial answer was: through sheer will power, by choosing not to think or act like a slave, not to be slavish in any way, either by servile imitation or by submitting passively to the sway of prevalent beliefs and prejudices. The individual Will, which Schopenhauer had branded as the great, omnipotent enslaver, the pulsing, surging life-force which makes every human being the slave of his senses, was thus transformed by Nietzsche into the great saviour and redeemer of human existence. As Zarathustra explains to his disciples: 'Will – that is the liberator and joy-bringer.' But having made this portentous affirmation, Zarathustra is forced to add: 'But now take this to heart: the Will itself is still a prisoner' – above all of an irreversible past.

> That Time does not run backward, that is his wrath; 'that which was' – such is the name of the stone he cannot move.
>
> And so he hurls stones out of wrath and ill-humour and wreaks vengeance on him who does not, like himself, feel wrath and ill-humour.
>
> And thus did the Will, the liberator, become a cause of grief; and upon all who can suffer he wreaks his vengeance because he cannot go backwards.

The essence of this spirit of revenge, Zarathustra continues, is a morbid desire to punish; and since the past could not be punished, it took it out on the present – so much so that life came to be regarded as a form of punishment, of 'original sin'.

> And now cloud upon cloud rolled up over the spirit, until madness preached: 'Everything passes away, therefore everything deserves to pass away. 'And this itself is justice, that law of time, that it must devour its own children,' so preached madness.

In those two sentences, ostensibly so simple, Nietzsche was simultaneously criticizing the gloomy pessimism of Ecclesiastes, for whom life on earth was a 'vale of tears'; the teaching of the neo-Platonists, who had implicitly condemned the imperfections and the transient nature of life on earth, unfavourably compared to the eternal 'beauties' of Heaven; Calderón de la Barca's gloomy reflection (*in La vida es sueño*) that 'Man's greatest offence / Is to have been born' (one of Schopenhauer's favourite verses); Mephistopheles's claim in *Faust* that his eternal right to deny is justified, since 'everything that comes into being deserves to perish', and, finally, the cannibalistic ferocity of the French revolutionaries of the Robespierre Terror of 1793–4, which later prompted the poet Lamartine to write that 'like Saturn, the Revolution could in its turn devour its children'.

'I led you away from such fables when I taught you: "The Will is a creator",' Zarathustra now proudly declares to his disciples. 'All "it was" is a fragment, a riddle, a dire accident – until the creative Will says, "But such I wanted it."' But then Zarathustra continues with evident humility:

> And when will this happen? Is the Will already unharnessed from its own folly? Has the Will already become a liberator and a joy-bringer for itself? Has it unlearned the spirit of revenge and all gnashing of teeth?

Even those familiar with Nietzsche's mode of thinking may well have been mystified by these concluding sentences. What exactly was Zarathustra–Nietzsche trying to say? To accept the past in its entirety, with all its horrors and cruelties as well as its most beautiful moments and creations, is this truly an act of intellectual 'liberation'? Is Man, no matter how unprejudiced, open-minded and 'free-spirited' he may strive to be, not condemned to pass judgement on the past, to consider certain periods luminous and creative, others abysmally brutish, bestial and barbaric? Is not Man – in German, *Mensch*, a word etymologically derived from 'measurer, he who measures' – condemned by his very nature to be an evaluator (a *Wortschätzer*), one who must weigh the relative value, non-value, or anti-value of the present, and to indicate, if such be his philosophical ambition, what should be the dominant values of tomorrow? Above all, how was one to reconcile the 'naïve' notion of Freedom of the Will – casually taken for granted by Descartes and laboriously codified by Immanuel Kant with his *deux ex machina* invention of the 'noumenon' (the human individual regarded as wondrously freed from the iron chains of phsyical causality) – with the deterministic notion (dear to Spinoza and which Nietzsche had inherited from Schopenhauer) that in our thoughts and actions we are all of us dominated by mysterious tendencies, inclinations and drives of which we are only dimly aware?

This was the heavy philosophical stone that Zarathustra had not tried to remove from his path. Was it because Zarathustra had so far found no satisfactory answer to the baffling riddle of 'free will'? Perhaps. Which is probably why, at the end of this puzzling discourse, Nietzsche generously gave the last word to a listening hunchback, who complains that the language the prophet-sage has been using with him and his fellow hunchbacks is not the same as the one he had been using with his disciples. And why, the hunchback adds for good measure, 'does Zarathustra speak to his disciples otherwise than to himself?'

## CHAPTER 32

# 'Midday and Eternity'

*– 'Praised be that which hardens! I do not praise the land where honey and butter flow!'*

Realizing that he would have to make a trip to Naumburg in September – that fruitful season of the year when it was neither too hot nor cold – Fritz decided to give his sister Elisabeth a piece of his mind, in another attempt to get her to understand that his latest book did not in any significant respect represent a radical departure from his earlier works. 'Every word of my *Zarathustra* is victorious scorn and more than scorn for the ideals of this age; and behind almost every word there is a personal experience, a self-overcoming of the first rank. It is absolutely necessary that I be *misunderstood* [twice underlined]; even more, I must see to it that I be badly understood and despised. That it was my "closest" relatives who had to begin it, I realized last summer and autumn, and I was thereby made splendidly aware that I was following *my* path.'

Consciously or unconsciously Nietzsche at this point was alluding to Jesus Christ, he who had warned those ready to follow him that they must be ready to risk every form of opprobrium, including a painful separation from their families. 'What,' he went on, 'is all this fuss over these Reées and Lous! How can I be their *enemy*! And even if they did me harm – I have derived enough *profit* [twice underlined] from them . . . And when I complain, then the whole world believes it has a right to vent its tiny bit of power-feeling [*Machtgefühl*] on me as upon a suffering being; it's what is called soothing words, pity, good advice, etc.'

The four weeks Nietzsche spent in Naumburg proved to be almost as dismal and upsetting, although for other reasons, as the preceding three months at Sils-Maria. His two main consolations were the belated distribution of printed copies of *Zarathustra* I and a warm letter of appreciation from Carl von Gersdorff, who had found the book 'absolutely splendid. What a path [you have travelled] from *The Birth of Tragedy* to this. You are a good tiller of the soil, who does not see behind him, or like a good mountain climber. Many people will feel dizzy from being on your heights, but up there the breezy air is full of ozone.'

Meanwhile, a new storm was brewing – one in which, quite unexpectedly, Fritz found himself not opposed to but allied with his pious mother. Among Franziska Nietzsche's friends in Naumburg was the widow of a former Superintendent of the Protestant Church named

Förster who had once been the direct superior of her father, David Ernst Oehler, the energetic vicar-farmer of Pobles. After her husband's death Frau Dr Förster had chosen to settle with her ailing daughter in Naumburg, where she was occasionally visited by her two sons, Paul and Bernhard. An ardent admirer of Richard Wagner, Bernhard Förster was one of those who, after Prussia's victory over France in 1870–1, had become a rabid super-patriot. In Berlin, where he was an instructor at the famous Friedrich Gymnasium and the State *Kunstschule* (school of art), his intellectual heroes were Ernst Hasse, a former Prussian army surgeon who was helping to found a Pan-German League aimed at encouraging the establishment of German colonies in Africa, South America and Eastern Europe, and Adolf Stöcker, a former army chaplain who did not hesitate to preach antisemitic sermons from the pulpit of the formerly Royal-Prussian and now Imperial-German cathedral. Like them, Bernhard Förster shared the lyrical vision of German might which the historian and Reichstag deputy Heinrich von Treitzschke was beginning to propound in his monumental *History of Germany in the Nineteenth Century*, according to which 'Might is Right', political feebleness was a 'sin against the Holy Ghost', the Catholics were 'deficient in true Germanism' while the Jews were agents of 'decomposition' and the 'misfortune' of Germany.

In January 1877, when Nietzsche was in Sorrento, Bernhard Förster spent a few days in Naumburg with his mother. From the moment of their first meeting Elisabeth was impressed by this handsome Berlin school-teacher, who told her how much he admired her brother's second 'Untimely Meditation'. She was delighted to find someone – a rarity in provincial Naumburg – who could carry on a 'serious' philosophical conversation with her, and during their second meeting (as Elisabeth reported in a gushing letter to her brother) 'we talked and talked like two books'. Intellectually, they were on much the same level. Above all, they shared the same Wagnerian enthusiasms and were regular readers of the Master's increasingly nationalistic and anti-Jewish propaganda organ, the *Bayreuther Blätter*. From Eastertime of 1877 on, this 'kindly' Berliner, who had also adopted a Bismarckian moustache, made periodic visits to Naumburg to visit his mother, his ailing sister and the beautifully fair-haired Elisabeth Nietzsche, a radiant specimen of Aryan womanhood.

By 1880 Bernhard Förster had begun to make a name for himself as a vehement antisemitic agitator, but this does not seem to have bothered Elisabeth. In April an article chock-full of platitudes that Förster had written extolling Richard Wagner and his music was published in the *Bayreuther Blätter*, prompting the composer to remark with a sigh of sarcastic resignation: 'I am like a phantom, what people say about me does not concern me, whether it be good or bad.' Emboldened by this journalistic 'breakthrough', Förster, whose dream was to become a respected member of the select 'Bayreuth circle', wrote to Wagner asking him to sign a petition that was to be presented to Bismarck with the request that the Chancellor take stern measures against Jewish plutocrats and others who were taking over the Berlin press and 'corrupting' established religious values. Wagner, annoyed by this busybody intriguer, replied tartly that ever since he had signed a misbegotten manifesto against vivisection, he had sworn never to add his signature to a petition.

In the late autumn of 1882 Bernhard Förster was involved in a bloody brawl, provoked by antisemitic insults and well publicized in the Berlin press. Förster was dismissed from the two schools where he had been teaching. All this alarmed the devout Franziska Nietzsche – it was not commendable Lutheran behaviour! – while on the contrary it aroused the sympathy of her daughter Elisabeth, for whom from then on Bernhard Förster was a an unjustly punished 'martyr' for his political opinions.

This much publicized affair occurred at a particularly critical psychological moment in Elisabeth Nietzsche's life. An almost incestuously ardent admirer of her brilliant, sick and often helpless brother, Elisabeth had spent four years taking care of him in the bigger, more cosmopolitan, intellectually more exciting city of Basel, before being obliged to return to provincial Naumburg to look after her lonely, widowed mother. For years Elisabeth had dreamed and throbbed at the idea of helping her brother found a 'colony' or 'cloister' of kindred Wagnernophilic Schopenhauerians, of which (as Fritz had once suggested) she was ideally suited to become the efficient 'quartermaster'. But, as the years had gone by, the bright dream had faded and her brother, after dramatically rejecting Schopenhauer and then Wagner, had begun to develop a blatantly anti-Christian and wilfully 'egotistical' philosophy, which had bewildered most of his friends and which she herself found detestable. In September 1882 she had made a desperate efort to 'save' her brother in the hope that she might after all be able to bring him back to his senses and to the adoption of a more 'reasonable' philosophical 'line'. But the result had been a disastrous fiasco when a furious Fritz had packed his trunk and left in a huff for Leipzig.

In January 1883 Elisabeth had candidly admitted in a long letter to Heinrich Köselitz that she had recently 'been completely wrenched from the path of my life . . . I must now try to build a new kind of life-happiness, but oh, it is so difficult . . . To love and admire my brother, to be active for him – that was the task and centre of my life . . . There is something moving and sublime when unselfish, noble human beings extol egotism . . . But when a creature like this Frl. Salomé, of whom her own mother says that for as long as she has lived, she has never thought of anybody but herself, her personal advantage, and her amusement, starts to laud egotism, it is downright impudent, and it was every bit as impudent when, after she had lied to me on several occasions, she declared scornfully: "What then is a lie? Nothing, absolutely nothing."'

No less revealing was the paragraph that preceded this frank confession, and which revealed to what extent Elisabeth's growing inability to serve, guide or influence her brother had now caused her, out of acute frustration, to transfer her psychic energies from her brother to someone else. 'A friend of ours, a Dr B. Förster, was living here for a while and is full of splendid admiration for Wagnerian undertakings. We gorged ourselves every now and then on compassion, heroic self-denial, Christianity, heroism, vegetarianism, Arianism, southern colonies, etc. etc. All this is so sympathetic to me and with these notions I find myself so much at home . . . Right now Dr Förster has written an excellent article on National Education, it should appear in the first quarterly number of the *Bayreuther Blätter*, and I would beg you to read it. It is such a pity,' she added, 'that these lovely views on education can never be realized, since Dr Förster is going on 1 February to Paraguay and who knows if one will ever see him again.'

Embarrassed by the bloody brawl in which Bernhard Förster was involved, his colleagues of the 'German People's Party', which he had helped to found, had encouraged him to leave the 'polluted' atmosphere of Berlin for a while and to further the noble cause of pan-Germanism by establishing a 'model' German community in South America. Nietzsche's reaction to the news was an ironic compliment. 'I sincerely congratulate Dr Förster,' he wrote to his sister in late July, 'for having at the right time left Europe and the Jewish question behind him.' Not until he reached Naumburg in early September did he realize that Elisabeth had fallen in love with this German 'colonizer' and was exchanging letters with him, much to the distress of her mother, who now feared that this Paraguay 'venture' might be an irresistibly tempting challenge – at once marital, managerial and ideological – for her restless, strong-willed daughter.

The moment he crossed the threshold of the pleasant corner house at the southern end of the Weingartenstrasse, Fritz was asked by his anxious mother to help her talk 'Lieschen' out of this absurd '*Marotte*' (passing whim). She did not have to ask him twice. Nietzsche's detestation of all forms of super-patriotic 'Germanism' was as strong as his antipathy for antisemitism: it was one more form of collective hysteria and the kind of un-Goethean provincialism he had denounced long ago in *Human, All Too Human* in a 'scandalous' anathema ('To be a good German means to de-Germanize oneself'). But the more Franziska Nietzsche and her son upbraided 'Lieschen' for her evident sympathy for the antisemitic sentiments and pan-German projects of Bernhard Förster, the more the stubborn Elisabeth dug in her heels and defiantly defended them.

It was probably the seething rage aroused within him by the realization that his once 'devoted' sister had now joined the hate-driven and vengeful 'rabble' Zarathustra had recently flayed which kept Nietzsche from travelling to Leipzig for a potentially explosive meeting with his antisemitic publisher, Ernst Schmeitzner. For not until 18 September, more than ten days after his arrival in Naumburg, and then only because Schmeitzner had sent him a postcard commending the 'sunshine' he had found in *Zarathustra* II, did Nietzsche bother to write to his publisher asking him for a statement concerning book sales and earnings, along with the advance royalty payment due to him now that the printing of the second volume was completed. He added sarcastically that if his 'Zarathustra-sunshine' failed to 'illuminate' his readers, it would be through no fault of his. 'There now reigns in our lovable Germany the loveliest darkening of all skies; I will make a point of again removing myself from this cloud-misery as soon as possible.'

Schmeitzner, who had no idea that Nietzsche had returned to Naumburg, promptly replied that he had just sent the first bound copy of *Zarathustra* II to Sils-Maria. For the 110 printed pages of this second volume (at a price of 40 marks for every sixteen pages) he owed Nietzsche 300 marks – which, being presently short of cash, he proposed to pay him early in October. 'The two *Zarathustra* volumes will, let us hope, again incite your readers more keenly to buy your writings.' He tactfully refrained from reminding Nietzsche that he had warned him long ago that prospective buyers might be put off by the inordinate length of the five 'aphorism volumes', which had made the sales price of each prohibitively expensive.

Early in October Fritz said goodbye to his mother and sister and took the train to Frankfurt, where he ran into Ida and Franz Overbeck, who were returning from a visit to relatives in Dresden. They had not been travelling for much more than an hour on the southbound train when Nietzsche suffered a nervous seizure, with splitting headaches and nausea, and had to dismount at Freiburg and drag himself to a hotel, where he spent a miserable night vomiting up his entrails. The next morning he continued manfully on to Basel where, crippled by a violent headache, he spent an entire day in the bedroom that the hospitable Overbecks were always happy to have him use.

From Basel, two days later, Nietzsche travelled on to Genoa, where he was dismayed to discover that his old lodgings on the Salita delle Battestini had been rented out by his landlady to another tenant until mid-October. Informed that Malwida von Meysenbug had stopped at La Spezia during her return from her annual trip to Paris, he hurried down the Ligurian coast, only to discover that the good 'Aunt Malwida' had just left for Rome.

Eight days later he travelled back to Genoa, where his old room was now free. But, as he wrote to Heinrich Köselitz on 22 October, his nervous seizures were recurring at ever shorter intervals, leaving him utterly exhausted and depressed. On a postcard sent that same day to his mother and sister, Fritz wrote that he had taken up temporary residence in Genoa, until he could find someone to accompany him to Spain. Italy, from Spezia southwards, was impossible – because of the sirocco.

The idea of going to Spain had been encouraged by Nietzsche's discovery, in the guide and travel books he kept consulting, that Barcelona had a sunnier climate than Genoa. The stubbornly Italianophilic Köselitz had made it clear that he disliked Spain, but recently Nietzsche had received two rapturous letters from a romance-language scholar of Silesian origin named Paul Lanzky, who, after reading *Human, All Too Human*, had decided that its author was far and away the most important of contemporary German philosophers. Ready to clutch at any straw in his desperate search for a disciple, Nietzsche had written to ask if Lanzky could not accompany him to Barcelona or Murcia, where, he claimed, there were 220 cloud-free days in every year: a surprising invitation to which his thirty-one-year-old admirer responded by inviting Nietzsche to visit him at Vallombrosa, near Florence, where he had become half-owner of a hotel catering to pilgrims wishing to visit the nearby Benedictine monastery.

Nietzsche was still feeling so unwell that he spent most of the first week of November holed up in his little room, too listless and demoralized even to want to climb to the summit of the nearby ridge. He vented his ill-humour on his sister, who with her customary effusiveness had been recommending new pharmaceutical remedies against his fits of vomiting. Although full of praise for the style of *Zarathustra* I, Elisabeth regretted that Fritz had not made his position clearer regarding 'egotistical' as opposed to 'unegotistical' behaviour. Fritz retorted that he was his own best doctor, and that Elisabeth, as his sister, should stop using words like 'egotistical' and 'unegotistical'. He then treated her to a lecture on the future direction of his thinking: 'Above all, I distinguish between *strong* and *weak* human beings – those whose vocation is to rule from those who are called upon to serve, to obey, [to show] "devotion". What disgusts me about *this* [twice underlined] *age* is the unspeakable feebleness, unmanliness, impersonalness, changeability, good-naturedness, in short the weakness of "*self*"-*seeking*, which would still like to drape itself as "virtue". What has so far *done me good* has been the sight of human beings of a *long will* – who can remain silent for decades . . . but who are honest enough to believe in nothing but their *self* and their will, and thus to *imprint* it on human beings for all, yes, for all time.

'What drew me to R[ichard] W[agner] was *this*; similarly Schopen[hauer] lived exclusively in much the same feeling . . . And pardon again, if I add that last year I believed I had found a being of this kind, namely Frl. S[alomé]; I *ruled her out* [twice underlined] for myself when I finally found out that all she wanted was to make herself *comfortable* in her own cosy way, and that the superb energy of her will was directed at such a *modest aim* . . . Do you realize that in any age there are hardly 5 human beings who possess this quality and who have at the same time enough intellectual acumen to be able to express it. (Napoleon was one of them.) . . .

'Read Shakespeare: he stuffs his plays with such strong men, rough, hard, powerful Men-of-Granite. Of *such* is our age so poor – and of strong human beings who might have *enough* intelligence for *my* thoughts.'

In a letter written to Malwida von Meysenbug in early November, he confessed that never in his life had he felt so lonely. 'All the experiences of the past year have taught me this *one thing*: there is nobody who wishes to go with me along my path – nobody yet *sees* this path.'

The same plaintive note regarding the depressing lack of intellectual or spiritual 'fellow-travellers' was sounded in a pre-birthday letter sent to Franz Overbeck, in which he informed his friend that on 16 November, during a visit she was due to make to Basel, his sister Elisabeth would be bringing him a gift copy of *Zarathustra* II. 'Read it as the second part of *four* – i.e. understand that a great deal therein will only acquire its necessity in the *meaning of the whole*.'

Genoa, he went on, had lost its previous charm. He now found it too noisy, the long walks out to the surrounding ridges too tiring. 'To get well, I need *new first*-hand impressions . . . Basically there is nothing I more need than human beings (as, for ex. in Rome); but the other fact of the matter is that it is only *by the seaside* that I can still hold out.'

In his prompt letter of reply Franz Overbeck reported that he had recently reread *Zarathustra* I. Although he was still unable to overcome certain basic misgivings, he was 'sufficiently struck by many lofty beauties to understand why you are of the opinion that never so far have you achieved anything of a loftier kind.'

This letter probably reached Genoa after the belated arrival of a letter from Jacob Burckhardt, mistakenly sent to Rome. It was perhaps the most laudatory letter the eminent historian had yet written to his former university colleague about any of his books. 'This time it is no longer fixed individual observations, as in your recent writings, but a mighty resounding speech about life in its entirety, from one mouth.' It was Burckhardt's impression that among Germans, to whom it was addressed, Zarathustra would arouse both enthusiasm and vexation. 'Of the latter there can hardly be a dearth since, honoured Sir and Friend, this time you make it particularly difficult for [us] mortals' – a subtle allusion to Zarathustra's speech 'On Free Death' and 'superannuated' human beings – 'but the book will forever and again attract those it irritates. For me it was a quite special delight to hear someone announce from the watch-tower placed far above me what horizons and depths he espies. I thereby discover how superficial all my life long I have been and shall also remain in my kind of relative narrowness, for in my [declining] years one no longer changes, at most one grows older and weaker.'

During the last week of November Nietzsche left Genoa and travelled up the curving Riviera coast past Ventimiglia, Menton and Monte Carlo as far as the fortified fishing port of Villefranche. He had learned from the guidebooks that the French Riviera, better protected from various winds by the soaring Alpes Maritimes, rising dramatically up from the Mediterranean littoral, enjoyed an annual average of 220 clear, cloudless days, or roughly twice as many as Genoa, particularly during the crucial winter months. Realizing, however, that at Villefranche he would be as lonely as he had been the previous January at Rapallo, Nietzsche moved on to nearby Nice – or Nizza, as its Italian inhabitants had gone on calling it after 1860, when it had been peacefully wrested from an impotent Kingdom of Sardinia and made part of the French Empire by Napoleon III.

Nietzsche was at first put off by this large seaside resort, with the elegant balconied hotels that had been opened up or were being built to accommodate an ever-increasing flood of affluent sun-lovers from Great Britain, Germany and Russia, whose cabriolets, calèches and handsome equipages kept ceaselessly, and for Nietzsche too noisily, klop-klopping up and down the long, faintly palm-shaded Promenade des Anglais. But next to this fashionable sea-front and façade was a teeming town of well-shaded streets, of blood-red, tangerine-orange and rose-hued house-fronts which had remained refreshingly Italian. 'Nizza, as a *French* city, I find disagreeable and almost a stain in this southlandish splendour,' he wrote to Köselitz on 4 December; 'but it is still an Italian city – there, in the older part . . . and when people have to speak, *Italian* is spoken; and then it is like a Genoese suburb.'

The second-storey room Nietzsche rented for 25 francs – only 3 francs more than what he had been paying for his Genoese garret – was located in a *pensione* that could not have been more cosmopolitan. As he wrote to his mother and sister shortly after moving in, he found himself sharing meals in the dining-room with a Prussian general and his daughter, the wife of an 'Indian' prince implausibly named 'Lady Mehmet Ali', likewise accompanied by a daughter, a 'magnificently costumed Persian', who was seated at Nietzsche's table, along with a number of Russian and British travellers.

Nietzsche was so surprised to find that this part of Nice was less expensive than he had expected, with modest restaurants where the food was better than in Genoa and the wine incredibly cheap, that he urged Köselitz to leave Venice. Köselitz replied shamefacedly that he was more penniless than ever, owed more than 100 Swiss francs to various Venetian creditors, and could not interrupt his work on his *Matrimonio segreto* opera score.

This depressing news, probably abetted by bad weather, upset Nietzsche's nervous stomach, which had a way of acting up when he had to share his meals with others. So, much to his regret, he said goodbye to the 'colourful dinner-table company' of the cosmopolitan *pensione* and moved to a quiet villa, where his German landlady cooked special meals for him and a jovial Spanish lodger who treated Nietzsche like a '*fratello*'. She even installed a small stove in his bedroom which, as Fritz wrote to his mother and sister in a Christmas Day letter, offered him 'if not the pleasure of warmth, at least that of thick smoke'.

January – the 'Sanctus Januarius' which two years before had inspired the fourth and final part of *The Joyous Science*, and one year later the first volume of his *Zarathustra*, once again proved to be a 'blessed' month – thanks to Nice's bright blue, cloudless skies. On 18 January 1884 Nietzsche surprised his publisher with a piece of 'good news': the final part of his *Zarathustra* 'trilogy' was finished, and all that was needed was the laborious copying out of a legible script.

This achievement was all the more remarkable since it was interrupted by a row with his German landlady, so that the harassed author had to seek new refuge in a Swiss-run 'Pension de Genève'. From here Nietzsche wrote to Franz Overbeck on 25 January that he had finished *Zarathustra* III. He could hardly believe that the trilogy had been completed in just one year – 'strictly speaking in the course of 3 x 2 weeks. The last two weeks were the happiest of my life: never have I travelled with such sails over such a sea.'

By 6 February all of *Zarathustra* III had been painstakingly copied out. 'You now have the most future-rich book in your publishing firm – I know very well what I am saying and am in no wise mad or vain,'

Nietzsche wrote to Ernst Schmeitzner. The manuscript, he explained to his publisher, should as usual be sent along with the page-proofs to Köselitz in Venice. Above all, '*presto, presto*! – for it concerns the finale of my symphony,' and he did not want the printing to be held up once again by '500,000 hymn books and other devilry!'

Two weeks later he wrote to Erwin Rohde who, shortly before Christmas, had written from Tübingen to say how impressed he had been by the new and 'freer form of presentation' Nietzsche had adopted with his *Zarathustra*. 'I think that with this new form – which is capable of many variations and metamorphoses – you have begun to find your authentic form. Even your *language* has for the first time found its fullest resonance . . .' In his letter of reply Nietzsche wrote that, having completed his long sea-journey – not for nothing had he lived for years in the 'city of Columbus' – he would soon be able to send Rohde the second and third parts of *Zarathustra*, which offered 'a kind of abyss of the future, something ghastly, particularly in its blissful happiness. Everything therein is my own, without model, comparison, predecessor; who once has *lived* therein returns to the world with another countenance.'

The 'confession' that followed may have sounded extreme and vainglorious to the sober '*homo litteratus*' that was Rohde, but it was an appraisal which, I think it fair to say, few German critics would dare to contest today. 'I fancy that with this *Z*[*arathustra*] I have brought the German language to its perfection. After *Luther* and *Goethe* a third step still needed to be taken; look well, old Heart-Comrade, [to see] whether force, suppleness, and euphony have ever thus been [put] together in our language. Read Goethe after one page of my book – and you will feel that that "undulating quality", which was peculiar to Goethe as a draughtsman, was not alien to the language-sculptor. I have the advantage over him of a severer, more manly line, without, like Luther, ending up among the louts. My style is a *dance*; a game of symmetries of every kind, and a leaping-over and mocking of these symmetries. That even goes for the choice of vowels' – a reference to Nietzsche's masterly use of alliterations to give each verbal climax a maximum of sonic 'punch'. 'Incidentally, I have remained a *poet* to the very limit of this concept, although I have already industriously *tyrannized* myself with the opposite of all versifying' – i.e. logical analysis. Then, thinking with a sigh of envy of Erwin Rohde's happy family life, with a wife, a young son and daughter, he added: 'Ah, my friend, what a mad, secluded life I lead. So alone, alone! So without "children"!' By which he meant, of course, disciples.

By early March Nietzsche was beginning to suffer from his own brand of 'spring fever': a form of nervous anxiety caused by the steady increase of bright sunlight, which was harmful to his eyes, and his search for a place where he could settle for several months before moving up to Sils-Maria and the Upper Engadine in June. Nice, in terms of climate, was perfect. Never had his health been better, his spells of sickness occurring only when the sky was overcast. But along with a shortage of well-shaded walks, Nice lacked good libraries and the musical entertainment Venice had to offer. He therefore asked Köselitz if he couldn't find a room for him somewhere along the 'Canale grande', from which he could admire its 'long multicoloured stillness' – gondolas being, by implication, more silent than carriage wheels and horses' hooves.

All doubts about Köselitz's reaction to the latest batch of page-proofs, sent to him from Leipzig, were dispelled by his disciple's reply, written on 25 March '*Zarathustra* is ever more magnificent; he [sic!] is the most sublime book there is. You are the first to have discovered this combination of Reason and Pathos (which people have always regarded as deadly foes). You must truly look back with delight at this type, the Zarathustra, which indeed you yourself almost are. I am glad to be living close to such great happenings.'

It would be hard to improve on Heinrich Köselitz's succinct formulation: that what made *Zarathustra* III so 'sublime' was this extraordinary 'combination of Reason and Pathos'. It must be added, however, that this was both its strength and its weakness. As a highly subjective confession of Nietzsche's philosophical doubts, torments and aspirations, the third volume was in many places as eloquent as the second part. But towards the end the tragic Pathos clearly got the better of sober Reason. To the extent that there is something inescapably pathetic about all forms of Dionysian exuberance – not for nothing in ancient Greek mythology was Dionysus a suffering god who was torn to pieces (before being reconstituted by his earth-goddess of a grandmother), as were his devotees, the maenads – it can be said that the 'grand finale' of the *Zarathustra* 'symphony' was quintessentially Dionysian, rather than Apollinian, even though it was intended to be a powerful affirmation of Nietzsche's positive, anti-Schopenhauerian, *ja-sagend* attitude to life and the cosmos. The result, in any case, was something unique in the history of modern philosophy: a prose poem rising and descending to lyrical heights and depths, full of anger and sweetness, light and sombre darkness, joyful gaiety and sadness.

Almost all of Nietzsche's favourite themes were at one point or another reiterated, sometimes in trenchant phrases calmly stolen from the Bible and refashioned. Thus, for example, as Zarathustra in the opening chapter ('The Wanderer') climbs the mountain from which he wants to view the sea and the ship that is to carry him to the 'blessed isles' (of philosophical serenity) – this being in a deeper sense his 'road to greatness' – he reflects: 'He who has always spared himself much will in the end grow sickly from too much self-sparing. Praised be that which hardens! I do not praise the land where butter and honey flow!' This was a restatement, in more poetic form, of Nietzsche's 'resistentialist' conviction that where everything is easy, where there are no obstacles, where there is no resistance, nothing but mediocrity can result.

The injunction 'Praised be that which hardens!' is followed by a beautiful description of that 'dark monster', the restless night-time sea tossing in its sleep, with Zarathustra sighing, 'Alas, that my hand has not strength enough! Happily, in truth, would I like to deliver you from evil dreams!' And the tender note (so typical of Nietzsche, where everything is hot and cold, hard and soft, sweet and bitter) that follows shows once again how much *Thus Spake Zarathustra* owed to Lou Salomé and to Nietzsche's 'loss' of almost all his friends:

> 'Oh you loving fool, Zarathustra, delirious with trust! But thus were you always: always came you trustfully to every terrible thing.
>
> 'Every monster would you stroke. A whiff of warm breath, a tuft of soft shagginess on the paw – and at once you were ready to love and lure it.
>
> '*Love* is the danger of the loneliest, love of every thing, *if only it be alive*! Laughable, verily, are my buffoonery and my modesty in love!'
>
> Thus spake Zarathustra and laughed a second time: but then he thought of the friends he had left behind – and, as though he had wronged them with his thoughts, he was angry with himself for his thoughts. And presently it came to pass that the laugher wept – from wrath and longing Zarathustra wept bitterly.

This tender lament was followed by a second chapter – a long parable entitled 'On the Vision and the Riddle' – which in nightmarish intensity surpassed everything Nietzsche had so far written. One evening, in the 'cadaverous dusk', Zarathustra was climbing up a rocky mountain path when he felt the 'spirit of gravity' suddenly perched on his back in the loathsome form of a lame creature, half dwarf, half mole. This 'spirit of gravity, my devil and arch-enemy' who was insidiously dripping lead into his ear, 'leaden thoughts' into his brain, was clearly much more than the German pedantry Nietzsche had condemned in *Zarathustra* II. It was above all the downward tug or inertia – in Nietzschean physics inertia too is a force – which keeps each individual from becoming the superior human being he (or she) could be. The dwarf mocks Zarathustra's insistence on climbing ever higher, whispering into his ear that, though he may be a 'stone of wisdom', every stone that is thrown upwards inevitably falls down again. Zarathustra's answer to this nagging taunt (here the dialogue must be condensed) is to say that Courage is what makes Man a man, and Man the most courageous of all animals. Finally they reach a gateway which, like that of Janus, has two faces. From it stretch out two straight roads – one of them (symbol of the past) stretching backwards to eternity, the other (symbol of the future) stretching forwards also to eternity. Both seem to contradict each other, their point of conflict being this gateway, marked 'Instant', but is this 'contradiction' itself eternal? 'Everything straight lies,' is the dwarf's mocking comment. 'Every truth is crooked, time itself is a circle.'

It was almost as though this 'devil and arch-enemy' (the Spirit of Gravity) was here expressing Zarathustra's deepest apprehensions: that each 'instant', far from being unique, might be a repetition of something that had previously happened, and not only a repetition, but an identical repetition – with the same gateway, the same black spider crawling in the eerie moonlight, the same painfully ascending mountain-climber and far-seer, the same mocking, downward-dragging dwarf.

Zarathustra's gloomy meditation is interrupted by the sudden, blood-chilling howl of a dog, barking at the full moon, as though it had seen a ghost. The devil-dwarf and the gateway disappear, and, a moment later, in the nightmarish décor of 'wild cliffs' Zarathustra approaches the howling, whining, leaping hound and understands the reason for this hysterical barking: a young man with a hideously distorted face is sprawled out on the ground and into his open mouth a heavy black snake has thrust its head. Seizing the snake, Zarathustra vainly tries to wrench it from the poor shepherd's throat. Nietzsche described this gruesome moment with a vividness worthy of Dostoevsky:

> My hand tore at the snake and tore – in vain! It could not tear the snake out of the throat. Then a cry went forth from me: 'Bite it! Bite it! Bite its head off! Bite it!' – thus out of me there cried my horror, my hatred, my disgust, my compassion, all my good and evil cried out of me in a single cry.

Like a good story-teller Zarathustra at this point leaves his spellbound listeners in anxious suspense. Can they find an answer to the 'riddle' of this nightmarish vision, a vision of the future? What kind of man is this into whose throat 'everything that is heaviest and blackest' will crawl? Finally – Zarathustra here resumes his lurid tale – the young shepherd heeded his frantic cries, clenched his teeth, bit off the snake's head and spat it out of his mouth. He then sprang to his feet – 'a shepherd no longer, a man no longer – one transfigured, radiant, and who *laughed*! Never yet on earth has a man laughed as *he* laughed!'

For anyone familiar with Nietzsche's thinking the symbolism was fairly obvious. The hideous black snake that had crept into the unwary shepherd's mouth was hateful metaphysics and fire-and-brimstone Christianity, everything that had been poisoning human happiness for centuries; and the freed, 'delivered' shepherd who had plucked up enough courage to bite off the snake's head was the joyous, jovial, guilt-freed man of the future. But was this what Nietzsche really meant by this symbolism? The answer is no, not entirely. But, like the clever writer he had become, he decided to keep his reader on tenterhooks until the moment came to 'solve' the riddle in the book's dramatic finale.

So Zarathustra takes the reader by the hand and leads him on a kind of treasure-hunt over mountain paths and past dizzying abysses, fraught with anathemas and soaring hopes, laments and exhortations. His disciples (Lesson 3) must learn to resemble wind-blown trees, hardened by the storm-winds of adversity, shunning a facile search for 'happiness' and ready to expose themselves to every form of misfortune. Let them worship the sun, as he does (Lesson 4, a lovely poetic Hymn to Sunlight) and learn to hate clouds that sully their souls and turn them into slack, half-hearted, wishy-washy, spineless individuals. Over all things, they should realize, there stands 'the heaven Accident, the heaven Innocence, the heaven of "By Chance", the heaven of "high spirits".' During an inspection trip on firm land, Zarathustra is surprised to find that the human beings, like the houses, have all grown smaller. Their goal is the soft life, comfort, a cringing desire to serve the strong. These 'new men' are clever, they have clever fingers but no fists. They seek a 'small happiness' in life, they have turned the wolf into a dog and Man into man's favourite domestic pet. Their ideal is *Mittelmässigkeit* – mediocrity.

Maliciously leading his reader astray (in 'On the Mount of Olives'), Zarathustra–Nietzsche writes a mocking ode about the 'snow-bearded Winter Heaven' (inspired by his cold nights in Nice), which turns into a hymn honouring silence and the 'ice' under which he has learned to hide his deepest thoughts. Continuing his travels on his way back to his mountain cave, Zarathustra reaches the gateway to a 'great city', where a 'foaming fool' launches into a Schopenhauerian diatribe against all the stinking ills and iniquities to be found in any metropolis. (Nietzsche at his polemical best: 'Here is hell for a hermit's thoughts: here great thoughts are boiled alive and shrivelled through cooking. Here all great feelings rot . . . Does this city not steam with the fumes of the slaughtered spirit? Do you not see the soul strung up like limp, dirty rags? And yet out of these rags they make newspapers!' etc.)

Zarathustra finally halts the 'foaming fool's' Jeremiad by saying that his hatred emanates from the 'swamp-air' of the city. Why doesn't he take to the woods, go till the soil like an honest ploughman, or go to sea like a hardy mariner? The trouble with the 'foaming fool's' diatribe is that it is motivated by hog-like resentment and revenge. And in a prophetic anticipation of what might happen with his own philosophy, Zarathustra–Nietzsche takes the 'foaming fool' to task for the harm he is doing to his thoughts by so shamelessly vulgarizing them.

And so the meditative meanderings continue. Zarathustra's next 'lecture' is devoted to the 'Apostates', to those who, instead of following his agnostic lead, had decided to revert to their old religious beliefs. This chapter was partly inspired by a talented but highly unstable Viennese poet named Siegfried Lupiner, who, after a year or two of giddy veneration for Nietzsche's writings, had let himself be converted to Catholicism and had gone on from there to become an antisemite.

An entire essay could be written about those Nietzsche had in mind in mocking not only 'apostates', but would-be 'disciples', arch-Catholic mystics, pious songsters and hymn-writers, 'light-shunning' obscurantists expecting a selfish gratification of their prayers, and cult-forming practitioners of 'spiritism'.

At one point Zarathustra recalls a conversation he once overheard between two night-watchmen discussing God's existence:

> 'For a father, he doesn't worry enough about his children: human fathers do this better!'
>
> 'He's too old! He no longer cares any more about his children,' thus answered the other night-watchman.
>
> 'Does he then have children? Nobody can prove it, if he himself doesn't prove it! I've long wished he'd prove it thoroughly for once.'
>
> 'Prove? As though *He* had ever proved anything! Proving is something he doesn't like; he's very fussy in wanting people to *believe* in him.'
>
> 'Yes! Yes! Faith, faith in him makes him holy. That's the way it is with old folks! It's also true of us!'

And what was Zarathustra's reaction? A mighty laugh, one the Germans call *Tod-Lachen* (death through laughter), which so shook and 'twisted' Zarathustra's heart that it seemed to want to break and, not knowing where to go, 'sank into the diaphragm'.

In composing this chapter Nietzsche must have wondered with a chuckle how his dear friend Franz Overbeck, the open-minded theologian, was going to react to such 'impieties'. As he wrote to him from Nice in the same 6 February letter in which he described himself as being a 'most dangerous' friend: 'How I would like to *laugh* with you and your dear venerable wife (and *laugh* myself to *death* about myself!!!).'

But inevitably, after the cosmic laughter must come the tears . . . and concerns that are deadly serious. Zarathustra has another dream, in which the world appears to him as a ripe, golden apple, with a 'cool, soft, velvet skin'. He is asked (in a parody of the Paris of Greek mythology) to place it in the scales and to weigh the world and more particularly the three most maligned and accursed things on earth – for 'he who taught to bless also taught to curse'. These are: *Wollust* (voluptuous lust), *Herrschsucht* (lust for power), *Selbstsucht* (selfishness).

Let us leapfrog over the half-dozen forms that *Wollust* (voluptuous desire) and *Herrschsucht* (the desire to dominate) can assume. Selfishness (*Selbstsucht*), the third and last of the maligned 'Evils', seems to have defied precise exemplification. Instead, after praising the sacred, wholesome selfishness that wells forth from a 'powerful, beautiful, triumphant, refreshing soul', linked to a body that is 'lithe and persuasive', like that of a dancer, Zarathustra proceeds to list everything that is most contemptible and hateful for this kind of selfishness, beginning with every form of cowardice, self-pity, servility, 'nit-witted pedantry and priestly foolishness'. For all such, Zarathustra continues darkly, 'the day is now at hand, the change, the Sword of Judgement, *the great Midday*: there much will be revealed. And whoever blesses the Ego [Ich] as wholesome and holy and selfishness as blessed, verily speaks forth what he, a prophet, knows: "*Behold, it comes, it is near, the great Midday*!"'

But what does this 'great Midday' consist of? And when will it occur? The chapters that follow make it clear that what Nietzsche had in mind was a day of sun-filled Revelation, untroubled by any lingering metaphysical and religious clouds and superstititions, when truly modern Man would at last be freed from his servile subservience to a self-created myth: one which, in moving from the many to the single, from the prankish polytheism of the ancient Greeks to the rigid monotheism of Judaism, Christianity and Islam, had 'put the clock back' and slowed the groping, limping 'progress' of human enlightenment. But this bright, sun-blessed Midday or High Noon could not be reached without a prior work of destruction: the 'lion stage' of individual development projected on to the stage of world history, such as it had been briefly outlined in the very first of Zarathustra's 'speeches'. Pending the arrival of this radiant, fog-darkness-and-superstitious-gloom-dispelling Midday of revelation, Zarathustra is shown seated, like a new Moses, among the ruins of ancient tablets (of Christian morality) and the half-built tablets of a new, liberating *Weltanschauung*.

Of the thirty sections that compose this long chapter ('On the Old and New Tablets') two deserve special mention. First of all, the 5th, in which spontaneous joy is regarded as the prerogative of 'noble souls', as opposed to the thirst for happiness – vulgar hedonism – of the 'rabble'.

> One should not want to enjoy where one does not give enjoyment. And – one should not *wish* to enjoy. Enjoyment and innocence in particular are the most bashful things: both do not wish to be sought. One should *have* them, but better still should one *seek* blame and suffering!

In the 12th section Zarathustra–Nietzsche makes it clear that genuine nobility (more exactly, 'nobleness') has nothing to do with aristocratic privileges and particularly with those that are inherited, thus acquired without effort, and which wear a false appearance of permanence. (Nietzsche, for this reason, felt little sympathy for diehard 'conservatism'.)

> Not that your species became courtly at Courts, and that you have learned, as multicoloured as flamingos, to stand for hours in shallow ponds. For *knowing* how to stand is a merit of courtiers; and all courtiers believe that blessedness after death includes – *permission* to be seated!

And so, slowly, after many fascinating digressions, we are led forward to the grand finale, where the riddle of the hideous vision is to be revealed. Paradoxically, but there was a logic in this 'counter-truth', it is not Zarathustra but the animals summoned to his cave who, wishing to revive him after seven days of prostration, intone, like a Greek chorus, the sobering truths:

> Everything goes, everything returns; eternally revolves the Wheel of Being.
> Everything dies, everything reblossoms, eternally runs the Year of Being . . .
> In every Now Being begins; around every Here rolls the sphere There.
> The centre is everywhere. Crooked is the path of Eternity.

This conception of the world as an unending cycle was no invention of Nietzsche's, even if the 'abysmal' inexorability of this thought had occurred to him one day as he was walking along the edge of the Sils lake near Sils-Maria. It was a reiteration in his own words of the age-old wisdom of Hindu India – according to which no living being dies, but through a process of *karma* is doomed to be reborn in a never-ending cycle of reincarnation. For, from the inexorably turning Wheel of Life there is no escape, save for those – the Brahmans, the supremely wise and righteous – whose souls are at long last blissfully dissolved into the all-embracing Spirit-of-the-Universe of Brahma. This was the pessimistic view of life which his old Pforta schoolmate Paul Deussen seemed to have adopted and justified in his book on the Vedânta teachings; and it was precisely this kind of Schopenhauerian pessimism – for Schopenhauer too had felt a weakness for Hinduism – that Nietzsche was most determined to combat.

This explains Zarathustra's 'smiling anger' and his rebuke to his well-meaning animals, likened to 'joking fools and barrel-organs' grinding out the same old hackneyed themes and refrains. The truths that his animals were mouthing were no more than half-truths, and it was what was not said that was deeper, more disturbing, more 'abysmal'. For the hideous truth that Zarathustra had so far stifled, which he had been unwilling to pronounce when coaxed and challenged by his voiceless 'it' in the 'Stillest Hour' conclusion of the second volume, the ghastly truth that had crawled into his mouth and throat like a black serpent, and which, like the tormented shepherd of his nightmarish vision, he had with difficulty bitten and spat out, was not simply the depressing notion that Life is an eternal repetition, an eternal recurrence of what had happened before, but that this repetition brings with it the eternal recurrence and reappearance on earth of those whom, in *Zarathustra* I, the poet-prophet had called the 'superfluous ones' (a term Nietzsche had prudently avoided in the next two books): which is to say – mediocre human beings. Man, St Augustine had proclaimed, was born with a stigma, the stigma of original sin, for which he must atone and strive to overcome for all of his life on earth. Rousseau had brashly tried to claim the opposite: that Man, uncontaminated by the evils of social coexistence, is born free and good. Both of them were wrong. For Man in the collective aggregate was above all born – mediocre.

In the opening chapter of *Human, All Too Human*, Nietzsche had propounded what might be called the Theme or 'Law of Salutary Opposites'. It is from the root-soil of Evil that must spring the Good, just as a beautiful bloom rises from dirty soil or manure, Truth from the well-trodden ground of Falsehood, and Wisdom, like Neptune, from the restless seas of folly. Without evil there would be no struggle to be good; without cowardice, no struggle to be brave; without ugliness, no effort to create the beautiful; without falsehood, no need to search for the truth. Life would become as lax, boring and insipid as the sexless, spineless, eternally harp-lulled Heaven of devout believers. And so Zarathustra–Nietzsche continues:

> It was not to *this* torture-cross that I was nailed, in that I knew: Man is evil – but I shouted, as no one had yet shouted:
>
> 'Alas, that the worst in him is so small! Alas, that the best in him is so small!'
>
> The great disgust with Man – *this* choked me and had crawled into my throat; and what the soothsayer said: 'Everything is the same, nothing is worth-while, knowledge chokes.'
>
> A long twilight limped before me, a deathly, weary, death-drunk sadness, which spoke to me with a yawning mouth:

> 'Eternally will he return, the man you are tired of, the little man' – so yawned my sadness and dragged his foot and could not go to sleep . . .
>
> 'My sighing sat on human tombs and could no longer rise; my sighing and questioning croaked and choked and gnawed and wailed by day and night:
>
> 'Alas, Man returns ever and again! The little man returns eternally!'
>
> 'Naked had I once seen them both, the greatest man and the smallest man: all-too-like one another, even the greatest all-too-human!
>
> 'All too small the greatest! that was my disgust with Man! And eternal recurrence also of the smallest! – that was my disgust with all existence!
>
> 'Alas! Disgust! Disgust! Disgust!' Thus spake Zarathustra and sighed and shuddered; for he remembered his sickness.

Logically, Zarathustra at the end of this speech should have felt free and mercifully delivered of the bitter truth that had been poisoning his mind and his existence: as jovial as the snake-delivered shepherd of his vision. And in a sense this is how this third book ends. First, with a lovely ode Zarathustra composes for his melancholy soul; then with a new 'Dance Song', parodying the earlier 'Dance Song' in the second volume, in which Zarathustra carries on a monologue and then a dialogue with Life, portrayed as tempting and capricious, as taunting and repelling as Lou Salomé; and finally, with a one-line response after each of the twelve chimes that are to usher in the great 'Midday' or High Noon:

> *Doch alle Lust will Ewigkeit – will tiefe, tiefe Ewigkeit!*
>
> (But every pleasure wants Eternity – wants a deep, a deep Eternity!)

CHAPTER 33

# Knights and Ladies of the *Gaya Scienza*

*– Raise up your hearts, my Brothers, high, higher!*
*And do not forget your legs! Raise up your legs*
*too, you good dancers; and, better still,*
*stand on your heads!*

On 30 March 1884 Nietzsche sent a postcard to Heinrich Köselitz in Venice: he had corrected the final page-proofs of *Zarathustra* III and ended his 'symphony' with a finale linking it to the start of the trilogy – to form a circle which, he hoped, was not a '*circulus vitiosus*'. The postcard had hardly been dispatched when he had to write another one, postponing his departure for Venice. He had just received a letter from a friend of Malwida von Meysenbug named Resa von Schirnhofer, an erudite young Austrian, now studying philosophy at the University of Zürich, who expressed a wish to meet him. Nietzsche's response was prompt and sympathetic. He had still not abandoned the idea of somehow founding a 'colony' of kindred souls, and this sudden appearance of someone who might possibly 'fit in' seemed one of those blessed accidents that an unpredictable Fortune kept strewing across his path.

On 3 April the twenty-nine-year-old Resa von Schirnhofer found the thirty-nine-year-old cave-dwelling 'hermit' (as he had described himself in his welcoming letter) waiting for her as she stepped down from the Genoa 'express' on to the platform of Nice's railway station. Overawed at first by the intimidating presence of such a formidable thinker, the young student of philosophy was relieved to find that Nietzsche was a man of 'exquisite sensibility, tactful and of a disarming politeness in his way of thinking and manners' towards persons of the fair sex.

During the next ten days the 'dear, half-blind professor' devoted much of his time to this unusually intelligent young lady, who, having already written a short treatise on Spinoza and Schelling, had not let herself be overly impressed by Lou Salomé's 'dialectical virtuosity' when they had met a year and a half before at the *Parsifal* première in Bayreuth. She was surprised by the keen interest Nietzsche displayed in her dreams and obsessions, which he urged her to record. Many of one's strangest and most original thoughts occurred at night, and Nietzsche had found that if he didn't write them down immediately on a notebook by his bed, by the next morning they had flown away – for ever!

One radiant morning he took her on a tram-ride to the suburbs and then on foot up the nearby Mont Boron. Near the top they were buffeted by the cold, cloud-chasing Mistral wind, which stimulated Nietzsche's 'dithyrambic' joviality – each gust seeming to lift him up and to release him from the ponderous 'gravity' he had mocked in his *Zarathustra.* After being prevented by French sentries from reaching the fortified summit, they sat down by a plain wooden table beneath the pergola of a humble *osteria,* from where they could enjoy a splendid panoramic view of the littoral, with its beautifully sculpted bays and creeks. Stimulated by the Vermouth di Torino he ordered for them both, Nietzsche began improvising comic verses, making fun of the '*bewachte Berg*' (well-guarded mountain), from which they had been 'routed' by humourless soldiers.

He also took her to watch a local bullfight – a sorry imitation of a Spanish *corrida de toros.* There were no mounted picadors to infuriate the bulls, nor were the 'matadors' allowed to kill their 'victims', which were only too happy at the end of each 'dance of death' to make a hasty exit from the dusty arena through suddenly opened side-doors. The two spectators could hardly stop laughing. No less ludicrous, given the tame nature of the 'sport', were the snatches of 'heroic' music from *Carmen* which burst forth from the trumpets and drums of the band between each 'round'. Resa von Schirnhofer was amazed at the electrical effect that these simple, pulsing rhythms had on Nietzsche; they seemed to whip him into a state of ecstatic jubilation, just as had the fierce gusts of the mistral.

By no means as 'half-blind' as he claimed to be, Nietzsche took Resa one day for a long walk along the beach, as far as the promontory and its parapet, from which, he explained, one could sometimes see a tiny black point rising from the blurred surface of the sea – Corsica's highest mountain top. He spoke at great length of Napoleon, for whom he felt a boundless admiration because of his exemplary 'strength of will', as well as a sense of kinship because of his unusually slow pulse rate: sixty throbs per minute – the same as his own heartbeat.

During their long conversations at the Pension de Genève, Nietzsche astonished her by his knowledge of French literature. He urged her to read the memoirs of Saint-Simon and Hippolyte Taine's masterly treatment of the French Revolution and its aftermath in his *Origines de la France contemporaine.* As a token of his gratitude for her visit he gave her all three volumes of *Thus Spake Zarathustra,* as well as a copy of *Le Rouge et le Noir,* written by that master of 'intimate dissection', Henry Beyle, better known by his pen-name of Stendhal. Shunned by his contemporaries, Beyle had predicted that he would not begin to be appreciated until forty years after his death – a presentiment Nietzsche shared about his own works.

★

On 21 April Nietzsche finally left Nice for Genoa and Venice. Heinrich Köselitz had been unable to find him lodgings on the Grand Canal, and had instead found a room for him in the same house he inhabited in the San Canciano district. About the seven weeks Nietzsche spent in this 'Oriental-Gothic' city we know little. They were essentially an interlude, a moment of idleness between one intellectual 'pregnancy' and the next.

For Köselitz, on the other hand, Nietzsche's arrival on the scene had the disruptive force of a whirlwind. After listening to his friend play out the various melodies and arias of his *Matrimonio segreto* score, Nietzsche made Köselitz understand that his orchestration was too complex. It was madness to imagine that he could persuade an Italian theatre manager or orchestra conductor to accept a work bearing the same title as Cimarosa's famous opera (*The Secret Wedding*). The title was accordingly changed to *Der Löwe von Venedig* (*The Lion of Venice*), and an unhappy (but later grateful) Köselitz was browbeaten into accepting the inevitable. His musical future, as the Saxon introducer of a 'lighter', less overpowering, post-Wagnerian opera style, lay in Germany, not in Italy.

Meanwhile Nietzsche was wondering what his next philosophical work should be. In Nice he had shown Resa von Schirnhofer a recently published book, *Inquiries into Human Faculty and Development*, by Francis Galton (Charles Darwin's first cousin), who had already made himself famous with a book on *Hereditary Genius* (1869). Convinced that the worth of a society should be judged by its ability to produce individual geniuses rather than a multitude of humdrum human beings, Nietzsche was fascinated by what Galton was soon to call the science of 'eugenics'.

In Nice Nietzsche had been visited a number of times by an agnostic Jewish physiologist, Josef Paneth, with whom he had had long conversations about Spinoza, religion and science. But when, after his return to Vienna, Paneth expressed a wish to write a review of the first two *Zarathustra* volumes, Nietzsche wrote from Venice to discourage him. 'Regard me rather as someone who has unfurled his flag and leaves no further doubt about himself . . . Fifty years later, perhaps, there will be some (or one – for that a genius would be needed!) who will begin to see the light as to what through me has been accomplished.'

If, however, his works were so misunderstood during his lifetime, what guarantee was there that after his death they might not be hideously misinterpreted by fanatical 'devotees' – the species of 'blind disciples' he had denounced in *Human, All Too Human*? This sombre foreboding was all too prophetically expressed in a long letter Nietzsche wrote to Malwida von Meysenbug, in which he informed her that his publisher was sending her the two final *Zarathustra* volumes. This, he explained, was no gift, since these volumes demanded a 'relearning' of the contemporary reader's 'dearest and most honoured sentiments' (regarding Christian sentimentality on the subject of 'compassion'). 'Who knows how many generations will first have to pass in order to bring forth a few human beings who fully grasp in all its depth what I have done! And then, I am still terrified by the very thought of what sort of unqualified and totally unsuited persons will one day feel themselves called upon to invoke my authority. But that is the torment of every great teacher of mankind: he knows that in certain circumstances and fortuitous happenings he can become a calamity for mankind, as well as a blessing.' A premonition that was to be dramatically confirmed in Germany some thirty years after Nietzsche's death, and in Italy even sooner.

Just what Malwida thought of the *Zarathustra* trilogy, there is no way of knowing, for her thank-you letter subsequently disappeared. But one month later, replying to a letter in which the 'good Malwida' claimed to have discovered a young enthusiast who seemed ideally suited to act as reader and private secretary, Nietzsche explained that almost every time someone capable of helping him had been proposed, it was he himself who had ended up having to help the other. 'My task is immense; but my determination no less so. What it is I want, that will my son Zarathustra not say but rather advise; perhaps even have one guess . . . I will push mankind towards decisions that decide the entire future of mankind, and it can happen that one day entire millennia will take their highest vows in my name.' A spontaneous outburst of megalomaniacal Zarathustraism which must have made Malwida shake her head, dismayed.

In mid-June Nietzsche left the sea-borne city of the Doges and headed for Basel, while Heinrich Köselitz returned to his native Saxony, to try his luck with the musical overlords of Dresden. The two weeks Nietzsche spent in Basel were anything but happy. More than ever he felt himself an outcast among his former academic colleagues – 'it was as though I was living among cows,' he later wrote to Köselitz. Even Jacob Burckhardt, whose opinion he so valued, seemed embarrassed when they met. Not knowing what to say about the third and (for his sober Basel-patrician taste) the darkest, most fanciful, and weirdest of the three *Zarathustra* volumes, he asked Nietzsche if by any chance he was thinking of trying his hand at play-writing?

His oculist, Professor Schiess, could offer him no miracle remedy, except seawater baths and – more sleep, more rest, less reading! Glumly realizing that he would soon be forty years old without having acquired a single disciple, Nietzsche surprised Overbeck by coming up with a new variation of the old 'colony of kindred souls' idea. In Nizza (as he invariably called it) he would treat a select audience of listeners to a series of lectures on philosophical subjects: a preposterous proposal for which he later apologized as being due to depression brought on by the noxious sultriness of 'Basel air'.

From Basel Nietzsche moved on to the uncomfortably hot, sunbaked city of Zürich. Here he wanted to re-establish contact with Resa von Schirnhofer and meet a student friend of hers, Meta von Salis. A twenty-eight-year-old student of philosophy at the University of Zürich, Meta von Salis had decided to follow the pioneering example of her great-grandfather, Ulysses von Salis, who had been a personal friend and follower of the Swiss pedagogic reformer Pestalozzi. She was a determined foe of the kind of 'future *Hausfrau*' education that was still the general rule in most Swiss and German boarding-schools for girls. Her bible was *The Memoirs of an Idealist* and her model of truly enlightened and emancipated feminine behaviour was its author, Malwida von Meysenbug, who had invited her to spend the winter of 1878–9 in Rome, where Nietzsche's books were frequently discussed in Malwida's and her sister's 'literary circle'.

Years later Meta von Salis wrote that, like those that followed, her first meeting with Nietzsche had been a 'halcyonic' moment, which had cast a 'golden shimmer' over the rest of her life. Like her friend Resa, she too was struck by the non-German aspect of Nietzsche's sunburnt face, which did not look at all professorial. Even stranger at first seemed the gentle softness of his melodious voice and the extraordinary tranquillity of his mode of speech, full of calm self-assurance and with no trace of affectation. Particularly engaging was his smile, which had something touchingly childlike about it.

When Nietzsche asked her why she was so eager to obtain a doctorate, Meta von Salis replied that the title itself meant nothing, but that in the interests of 'feminism' she was determined to prove that women are not necessarily dumb creatures destined to be *Hausfraus* and could, through hard work and concentration, also obtain university degrees – at any rate in Zürich, since in Basel the admission of women to lecture halls was still officially forbidden. Nietzsche was delighted. This, he explained, was the essence of his philosophy, since no one could know in advance what he (or she) really was. He quoted two of his aphorisms: the first (336) from *Morgenröte*, 'How do we know whereto circumstances *could* drive us?'; the second (9) from *The Joyous Science*: 'All of us have secret gardens and plantations within us . . . we are all smouldering volcanos which will have their hour of eruption; – how close or distant that is, no one of course knows, not even the good Lord.'

When the time came to say goodbye to this enterprising student of philosophy (who went on to learn Greek and Sanskrit on her way to a doctorate) Nietzsche took Meta von Salis's hands in his own – a gesture he reserved for those whose company he had particularly enjoyed – and expressed the hope that they would soon meet again.

The next day he was glad to leave the torrid, heat-drugged city of Zürich and to travel southward by train as far as Chur, and from there by stagecoach over the mountains and the Julier Pass to Silvaplana and its luminous lake. He found his little resin-scented, pine-panelled bedroom, above Sils-Maria's one and only grocery shop, just as he had left it: well shaded by the fir trees beyond the single window, and with a small library of books which had been carefully preserved for his return.

Although he felt like a 'conqueror', in looking back over his achievements, he confessed to Franz Overbeck towards the end of July that he was 'stuck back' in his problems; 'my theory, that the world of Good and Evil is merely an apparent and perspectivistic world, is such a novelty that it takes my breath away . . . There should be somebody,' he added sadly, 'who "lived for me", as they say; then you, my dear Friend, would be spared a great deal. The evenings, when I sit all alone in this narrow, low-ceilinged, little room, are lumps that are hard to chew.'

With a spartan rigour which never ceased to amaze his landlord-grocer, Nietzsche would get up every morning when the faintly dawning sky was still grey, and, after washing himself with cold water from the pitcher and china basin in his bedroom and drinking some warm milk, he would, when not felled by headaches and vomiting, work uninterruptedly until eleven in the morning. He then went for a brisk, two-hour walk through the nearby forest or along the edge of Lake Silvaplana (to the north-east) or of Lake Sils (to the south-west), stopping every now and then to jot down his latest thoughts in the notebook he always carried with him. Returning for a late luncheon at the Hôtel Alpenrose, Nietzsche, who detested promiscuity, avoided the midday crush of the *table d'hôte* in the large dining-room and ate a more or less 'private' lunch, usually consisting of a beefsteak and an 'unbelievable' quantity of fruit, which was, the hotel manager was persuaded, the chief cause of his frequent stomach upsets. After luncheon, usually dressed in a long and somewhat threadbare brown jacket, and armed as usual with notebook, pencil and a large grey-green parasol to shade his eyes, he would stride off again on an even longer walk, which sometimes took him up the Fextal as far as its majestic glacier. Returning 'home' between four and five o'clock, he would immediately get back to work, sustaining himself on biscuits, peasant bread, honey (sent from Naumburg), fruit and pots of tea he brewed for himself in the little upstairs 'dining-room' next to his bedroom, until, worn out, he snuffed out the candle and went to bed around 11 p.m.

This year Nietzsche was lucky in finding two kindred souls who usually avoided the crowded *table d'hôte* hour and who sometimes joined him for a late luncheon at the Hôtel Alpenrose. The first was Helen Zimmern, a cultivated Londoner with a fluent knowledge of German who had translated Schopenhauer into English. Often, after lunch, she and Nietzsche would walk along the edge of Lake Silvaplana and as far as the outjutting slab of rock, near Surlej – his 'Zarathustra-stone', as he now called it – where in 1881 he had one day been overwhelmed by the visionary 'truth' of 'eternal recurrence'.

The other unusual visitor whose company Nietzsche particularly enjoyed was an elderly Russian spinster, Mademoiselle de Mansuroff, a former lady-in-waiting to the Tsarina in Petersburg who had come to Sils-Maria to recover from a nervous breakdown. He was as thrilled to discover that she had been a gifted pianist who had studied under Chopin as the old lady was to find a partner with whom she could share her precious reminiscences.

The two 'high moments' during Nietzsche's three months at Sils-Maria were occasioned by brief visits made to the Upper Engadine by 'lowlandish' admirers. The first was Resa von Schirnhofer, who had just completed a hiking tour in the Austrian Alps. Nietzsche led her along the southern bank of Lake Silvaplana to show her the 'Zarathustra-stone', located at a lovely spot where, as she later recalled, 'the dark green lake, the nearby wood, the high mountains, the solemn silence together weave their magic'. Seated on the 'sacred stone', she listened, spellbound, as Zarathustra–Nietzsche poured forth a 'dithyrambic' torrent of thoughts and images, followed by a humble account of how amazed he had been by the bursts of inspiration that had produced the three *Zarathustra* books, so rich and overpowering that his cramped writer's hand could hardly keep pace with his torrential thoughts.

During her visit the sky clouded over and she then caught a glimpse of a radically different, joyless, suffering Nietzsche, pathetically crippled by one of his nervous seizures. When, after vainly waiting for a whole day for him to appear at the Hôtel Alpenrose, she went to the grocer's house to find out how he was, she was taken upstairs to a tiny dining-room. Suddenly a door opened and a haggard, wild-eyed, almost white-faced Nietzsche appeared. Leaning against the door-jamb, he told her that he could not sleep, that the moment he closed his eyes he found himself surrounded by a fantastic whirl of flowers which kept clasping and entwining themselves about him as they blossomed upwards and outwards in a never-ending luxuriance of changing shapes and colours. He stopped, and looking at her intently with his deep, dark, and now fearful eyes, he asked her in a soft, disturbingly insistent voice, 'Do you think that this condition is a symptom of incipient madness? My father died of a brain illness.' Not until later did it occur to Resa von Schirnhofer that these hallucinations were probably caused by the chloralhydrate 'sleeping powders' which, as he had explained, he had obtained at Rapallo and elsewhere on the Italian Riviera to combat insomnia, by writing out his own prescriptions and signing them 'Dr Nietzsche'.

The other 'high moment' during this summer of 1884 came with the visit to Sils-Maria of Heinrich von Stein, who had recently obtained a doctorate in philosophy with a dissertation on the pantheistic Renaissance mystic Giordano Bruno, who had been seized, tried and burnt by the Inquisition in 1600 for having dared, among other things, to endorse the heretical heliocentric theories of Copernicus. That the young 'philosopher' from Halle, a fortress of German theological teaching, should have chosen such an exemplary 'free spirit' as the subject for his thesis made him immediately sympathetic to Nietzsche. Nor had he forgotten the enthusistic letter Stein had sent him, saying how 'dumbfounded' he had been by *The Joyous Science*. Stein, furthermore, was an agnostic – something that had initially shocked the devout Cosima Wagner. Writing from Venice on 22 May – Wagner's birthday, no less! – Nietzsche had thanked Stein for his German translations of several Giordano Bruno poems. He could not make it to the Bayreuth Festival, simply because 'the Law that is over me, my task, leaves me no time for it. My son Zarathustra may have revealed to you what is at work within me; and if I obtain everything I want, I shall die with the awareness that future millennia will pin their highest vows to my name.'

When Heinrich von Stein reached Sils-Maria on 27 August, Nietzsche was feeling so much 'under the weather' and paralysed by headaches that he remained bedridden for most of that day. But on the 28th, displaying an astonishing ability to 'bounce back', Nietzsche spent the entire day with his visitor, taking him for long walks through the woods and along the lakeside, while they talked and talked about everything – from Homer and the plays of Sophocles and Aeschylus (one of which Stein had partly translated into German) to the philosophy of Heraclitus. They talked, of course – how could such a monumental subject be avoided? – of Richard Wagner and his operas. They also talked about Lou Salomé, who, Stein told Nietzsche, had just written a first novel, *Der Kampf um Gott* (*The Fight over God*). As for Paul Reé, he had recently spoken of his continuing love for Nietzsche – in spite of everything that had occurred.

With disarming frankness (or was it irony?) Stein confessed that there were no more than twelve sentences in the *Zarathustra* trilogy he had really understood. He did, however, express his enchantment over 'The Other Dance-Song' in *Zarathustra* III, much of which, to Nietzsche's amazement, he was able to recite by heart. (That Stein should have taken this trouble was certainly no accident: the enticing, mocking, capriciously repelling Life – 'supple snake and slippery witch' – in this prose poem was clearly inspired by Lou Salomé, and this was Nietzsche's imaginative response to her 'Hymn to Life'.) Pleased to see that he could get the ultra-serious Baron to laugh at his jibes and witty formulations, Nietzsche was even more delighted to obtain Stein's tentative endorsement of the *idée fixe* the lonely 'hermit' was still desperately pursuing. After his ailing father had died, Stein intimated that he would be willing to come to Nice to help found a non-academic philosophical circle, or what (in a letter to Köselitz) Nietzsche preferred to call a 'Knights and Brothers Fraternity of the *gaya scienza*' – whose members would be required to take a ritual oath honouring the gusty, cloud-dispelling Mistral (wind)!

Four days after Heinrich von Stein's departure, Nietzsche wrote to Resa von Schirnhofer – very much a prospective member of the *gaya scienza* 'club' – to say that at Sils-Maria the frost had set in with a biting, 'blue-finger cold', which was adversely affecting his health. Heinrich von Stein's visit, however, had done him a world of good – 'at last a man with a fundamentally *heroic* disposition, beautifully brought up in R. W[agner]'s entourage to *reverence*, completely different from the way people are now brought up (that is, to talk and chatter about everything to everybody).'

To Köselitz, in a letter written the same day, he admitted that his health had not been good – 'it was better in Venice, and even better in Nice. Every ten days a good day: so says my statistic, to the devil with it! . . . No one to read to me! Every evening seized by melancholy in this low-ceilinged room, shivering with cold, and waiting 3–4 hours for permission *to go to bed*.'

Nietzsche's original intention had been to leave as soon as possible for Nice. But a cholera epidemic in northern Italy now made the rail-trip via Genoa impossible. His sister Elisabeth had just written to say that she must absolutely see him for some mysterious reason she was unwilling to divulge. Meanwhile, Köselitz had informed him that the director of the Dresden Opera had insisted that, if *Der Löwe von Venedig* (*The Lion of Venice*) was to be staged in Germany, it would need a German libretto. The frustrated composer had since been laboriously working on it in a small house adjoining his father's home near Dresden.

Realizing from his letters that the despondent Köselitz was psychologically in no condition to impress any theatre director or orchestra conductor in Dresden, Nietzsche decided to take matters into his own hands. This would be the 'noblest' way to repay his faithful 'disciple' for the many services rendered in the past – for, as Emerson had so wisely noted, the best way to have a friend is to be one.

His 'autumn offensive' was launched with a sudden burst of 'lion-hearted', not to say Zarathustran energy. Nietzsche began by writing to Friedrich Hegar, previously the first violinist and now the conductor of

Zürich's Symphony Orchestra, whom he had first met in Richard Wagner's house at Tribschen on the occasion of a *Sylvesternacht* (New Year's Eve) concert in December 1870. On 20 September he wrote to Köselitz, asking him to send him the score of his Goethean *Singspiel* composition, 'Jest, Ruse, and Revenge', which he wanted to show to Hegar. Köselitz replied that his *Singspiel* extravaganza was 'absurdly orchestrated' and could not possibly impress Hegar. Instead, he was sending Nietzsche the score of his *Lion of Venice* overture.

On 24 September Nietzsche said goodbye to his friendly landlord-grocer, Herr Durisch, his wife and their little daughter Adrienne, who were probably all relieved to see the 'Herr Professor' cart away 104 kilograms of books, which, after being loaded on to the stagecoach at Maloja, were later dispatched by train from Chur to Zürich. He found the lakeside city pleasantly sun-warmed, one radiant autumn day now following another in an uninterrupted 'Nizza-like' succession. Friedrich Hegar offered him a 'festive' welcome, and when he discovered how much the former Wagnerophile loved Bizet's lively music, he had Robert Freund, a former pupil of Franz Liszt and a friend of Ida Overbeck's parents, play piano excerpts from *L'Arlésienne* for him on the grand stage of the empty concert hall. The score of *The Lion of Venice* overture reached the Pension Neptun on 29 September, and the next afternoon Nietzsche took it to Hegar.

That same day Zarathustra's 'father' went to call on Gottfried Keller, Switzerland's most famous author, who, Robert Freund had assured him, was an admirer of Nietzsche's works. Their meeting in Keller's house seems to have been something of a *dialogue de sourds* – a 'dialogue of the deaf', as the French say of persons talking at cross-purposes. The next afternoon, when they went for a walk, Freund asked Nietzsche how it had gone. Very well, answered Nietzsche – except that he had been appalled by Keller's atrocious German. Several days later, when Freund asked the sixty-five-year-old novelist if Herr Nietzsche had called on him, Keller replied in his gruff Zürich patois, '*Ich glaube dä Kerl ischt verruckt*' ('I believe the fellow's crazy').

Fritz had meanwhile been joined by his sister Elisabeth. The important news she wished to communicate was that she had decided to marry Bernhard Förster and to help him run his 'pan-German colony' in distant Paraguay. Nietzsche, who regarded smouldering resentments and rancour as vices of petty, mean-minded souls, felt that the time had come to forgive his sister for her meddlesome interference in his affairs. Elisabeth, for her part, having so effectively helped to 'rout' Fritz's 'enemies', could afford to appear magnanimous; and having more affinity for poetry than for philosophical complexities, she was full of gushing praise for what Fritz had achieved with his *Zarathustra* trilogy. She may even belatedly have begun to grasp that what her brother meant by *Selbstsucht* – the 'search for oneself' that each individual should undertake in order to discover and maximize his or her 'dormant' capacities – had nothing whatever to do with *Eigenliebe* ('self-love' and selfishness). Later, in writing the story of her brother's life, Elisabeth claimed that seldom had she seen Fritz in such a merry mood, constantly improvising poems and saucy remarks about the people they kept meeting which made her laugh until the tears came into her eyes.

It was from this moment on that the previously dismayed Elisabeth, who in the autumn of 1882 had so bitterly denounced Fritz's 'new' philosophy (the one he had begun expounding with *Human, All Too Human*) as utterly 'detestable', underwent a radical conversion. Her brother's prestige – at least with certain Zürichers – his energetic *savoir-faire*, the skill he displayed in promoting Heinrich Köselitz's cause with Friedrich Hegar and other influential musicians, revived her fervent hero-worship. This was Zarathustra the gift-bringer, Zarathustra the persuasive, Zarathustra the sublime, transported from the realm of philosophico-poetic fiction to real life. As she wrote to Fritz not long after her departure from Zürich in luridly purple prose: 'Whoever sees you as I have now seen you is filled with enthusiasm in brandishing the torch of immortality. You are like a conqueror, mighty, magnificent!!'

This feeling, more soberly expressed, was shared by Heinrich Köselitz, who had been slaving away at his German libretto while waiting for news from Zürich. It was not long in coming. On 8 October Nietzsche informed him that the preliminary copying-out of the orchestral score (for the instrumentalists) was virtually finished, and that the *Lion of Venice* overture would soon have its first rehearsal in Zürich's *Tonhalle* (concert hall). Ten days later, on Saturday, 18 October, Nietzsche wrote at last to say that they had won the first round. Köselitz's *Lion* overture had been granted its first full concert-hall rehearsal.

This was the moment Köselitz had been anxiously awaiting. He showed Nietzsche's 'victory letter' to his sceptical father who, now at last persuaded that his son was more than a dilettantish amateur, agreed to finance a trip to Zürich. On or about the 26th Peter Gast, the incognito composer of *The Lion of Venice*, reached Zürich, where Nietzsche spent the next few days introducing him to Friedrich Hegar, his orchestral assistant, Weber, the pianist Robert Freund and others. Galvanized by his influential sponsor's enthusiasm, a no longer despondent Köselitz soon regained his self-confidence and agreed to stay on in Zürich, so as to be able to make the necessary revisions in his excessively 'naïve' music.

On 7 November Nietzsche finally left Zürich and its sparkling lake, reasonably assured that his protégé Peter Gast was going to make his mark at last ás the prioneering promoter of a more vivacious style of post-Wagnerian music. This time he did not stop at Basel, but travelled straight on to Genoa and from there to Mentone (he refused to call it by its French name of Menton), where, close to the Italian border, someone he had met in Zürich had recommended a German-run pension. This turned out to be a mistake for several reasons. At the Pension de Genève in Nice the 'half-blind professor' was by now an almost pampered figure, but at the Pension des Étrangers in the far smaller town of Mentone Nietzsche found himself without a single acquaintance to talk to, without a theatre or concert-hall where he could satisfy his craving for music. Mentone had another disadvantage: it was too well protected by its curving shield of mountains and thus windless. He missed the refreshing gusts of the northern 'Mistral' wind, which he had so enjoyed in Nice and whose praises he now sang in a breezy poem sent to Köselitz in Zürich, a 'dance-song' he wanted his composer-friend to put to music:

> *Mistral-Wind, du Wolken-Jäger*
> *Trübsal-Mörder, Himmels-Feger,*
> *Brausender, wie lieb' ich dich!*
>
> (Mistral-wind, you strong cloud chaser,
> Sorrow-strangler, sky-brush sweeper,
> Roaring, raging, how I love you!) etc.

At Sils-Maria Nietzsche had told Heinrich von Stien that he wanted to found an informal colony of kindred souls in some sunny Mediterranean town, like Nice, unaffected by the African sirocco. Stein, in a moment of high-altitude exhilaration, had enthusiastically endorsed the 'colony' idea. Clearly, the 'community of kindred souls' idea, discussed at Sils-Maria, was, for Nietzsche, no passing fancy. Stein understood this well. In his letter of reply he thanked Nietzsche for the unforgettable 28 August they had spent together. There was nothing he himself more craved than 'genuine, free life', but for the time being he would have to remain holed up in his little Berlin garret, with easy access to various university and other libraries. Moreover, it was Stein's conviction that only with the active cooperation of their friend Malwida von Meysenbug could Nietzsche succeed in forming such a longed-for 'circle' or community – but, alas, Malwida was by now so solidly attached to her Roman home that she would certainly be unwilling to move to Nice.

Overcome by melancholy as he pondered these 'insoluble' problems, Nietzsche on 26 November left Mentone and went to Nice to find new lodgings for himself at the Pension de Genève. He found a letter waiting for him, written by his German-expatriate admirer Paul Lanzky, who had left his hotel at Vallombrosa, near Florence, and come to Nice in the hope of finding Nietzsche. After vainly waiting for four weeks, he had left for Corsica, just two days before Nietzsche's arrival.

The realization that he had wasted two weeks in Mentone, thanks to a misguiding 'well-wisher' in Zürich, and had thus been cheated out of a trip to Corsica with Lanzky so upset Nietzsche that he suffered another nervous seizure. This did not keep him from communicating the good news of Lanzky's arrival to Resa von Schirnhofer, who was now continuing her university studies in Paris. His letter to Resa ended with a typically Nietzschean piece of doggerel, expressing his exasperation with German-speaking 'well-wishers':

*Geht die Welt nicht schief und schiefer?*
*Alle Christen treiben Schacher,*
*Die Franzosen werden tiefer –*
*Une die Deutschen – täglich flacher.*

(Does the crooked world not grow more crooked?
All Christians huff and haggle,
The French grow ever deeper –
And the Germans – daily flatter.)

Paul Lanzky, whom Nietzsche met at the Nice dockside and escorted back to the Pension de Genève, was something of a disappointment. He was clearly no Heinrich von Stein, with an impressive intellectual past and strongly held opinions of his own. Like Köselitz, he was too much of a fervent 'disciple'; but, unlike Köselitz, he could not provide Nietzsche with musical entertainment. Not least of all, he was tense and solemn and lacked Resa von Schirnhofer's delightful ability to laugh. As Fritz ruefully admitted to his mother and Elisabeth the day after Lanzky's arrival: 'He has a notion of *who* I am. But on the whole, to express myself in French: *il m'ôte la solitude, sans me donner la compagnie.*' (He deprives me of solitude without giving me company.)

The New Year season – this time from 1884–5 – was, as had so often happened in the past, a prolonged torment for Nietzsche with repeated vomiting caused by poor weather and the standard *pension* fare. 'Someone get me a cook!' he sighed in a letter to his mother and sister. He was fed up with the rumblings of passing carriage-wheels, and fed up with the fellow boarder of his *pension*, with their uncouth manners and petty table talk. 'Herr Lanzky,' he went on, 'is a considerate man and *very* devoted to me – but [it's] the same old story: when I need someone to entertain me, I always end up having to entertain. He remains silent, sighs, looks like a cobbler and knows neither how to laugh nor to be witty. In the long run, insufferable.'

Even the 'good' Heinrich von Stein no longer found favour in his eyes, having indicated once more that he could not presently leave Berlin to join Nietzsche in Nice. With the 'high-minded' baron clinging like an oyster to his academic post in Berlin, with Resa von Schirnhofer now studiously occupied in Paris, with an ailing Malwida wanting to hurry back to Rome, while Köselitz was immobilized for the foreseeable future in Zürich, and with but a single unsatisfactory 'disciple' to sustain him in Nice, Nietzsche once again was left to chew the cud of the bitter truth: his fond idea of founding a noble 'brother-and-sisterhood' of high-minded souls in the *douce Provence* of the troubadours was already withering on the vine without having known a spring.

## CHAPTER 34

# 'Very Black and Squid-like'

*– 'Has he not created the world in his own image, namely as stupid as possible?'*

Altogether, this was not a pleasant winter for a mercurially sensitive Nietzsche, marked as it was in January 1885 by below-zero temperatures, a heavy snowfall and a furious three-day storm, with howling winds and waves which played havoc with the palm-trees lining Nice's Promenade des Anglais. Nevertheless, intermittent spells of bright blue skies sufficed to inspire new *Zarathustra* scenes, parables and odd encounters – with magicians, soothsayers, beggars, two kings, a retired pope, a braying ass, the 'ugliest man', and even a 'wanderer and his shadow' (for there was nothing Nietzsche more enjoyed doing than making fun of himself). Included were a number of satires of the New Testament and in particular the Sermon on the Mount. ('Except we turn back and become as cows we shall not enter the Kingdom of Heaven. For one thing should we learn from them, the chewing of the cud,' and so on.) These, as Nietzsche wrote to Köselitz in mid-February, were intended to provide his *Zarathustra* series with a 'sublime finale', in the form of a 'divine blasphemy', composed in the jovial 'mood of a buffoon'. Yes, but a buffoon with a wicked sense of humour – as in this cruel jibe, simultaneously mocking the prophet Isaiah and Leibniz: given the multitude of fools there are on earth, one could logically ask, 'Did He [God] not create the world in his own image, as stupid as possible?'

There was, however, a major snag. Who in Germany would dare publish such a sacrilegious book? The answer was – no one. At any rate for the time being. How many of the 'happy' or (to parody Stendhal) of the 'unhappy few' who had read the three *Zarathustra* volumes had really understood them? All things considered, this was perhaps not such a bad thing, given the highly personal nature of this philosophical confession. As Fritz wrote to Gersdorff on 12 February, 'the word "publicity" and "public" with regard to my entire *Zarathustra* sounds to me approximately like "whorehouse" or "street-walker".'

The solution to this dilemma, Nietzsche decided, was to have the final book of the *Zarathustra* series privately produced by Constantin Naumann, whose typesetters and designers had done a fine job of printing with the first three volumes. It would be a highly limited edition, designed to preserve his sacrilegious 'buffoonery' for the delectation of posterity and, in the interim, of a handful of 'connoisseurs'. Since he himself was anything but affluent, he asked his friend Carl if he could not help cover the expense with a loan – which he promised to repay once he had managed to extract 6,000 francs' worth of debts owed to him by his foot-dragging publisher, Schmeitzner. The letter to Gersdorff had hardly been posted when Nietzsche received heart-warming news from Franz Overbeck, who for years had been handling his financial affairs. In Basel both the Academic Society and the Heusler Foundation had agreed to continue their annual pension payments of 1,000 francs beyond the six-year time-limit originally foreseen. No decision had been taken by the university's governing council, but another 1,000-franc payment had already been included in the latest budget. For the time being there was no decrease in Nietzsche's annual pension payments, totalling 3,000 francs.

In early March Paul Lanzky finally left Nice and returned to Florence, dismally aware that increasingly he had been getting on Nietzsche's nerves. One week later the manuscript of *Zarathustra* IV was dispatched to Constantin Naumann in Leipzig, with the request that he have it printed up in a highly limited edition of twenty copies. One set of proofs was to be sent to him in Nice, while another, accompanied by the manuscript, was dispatched to Heinich Köselitz's *pension* in Zürich.

Köselitz, more ne'er-do-well than ever, had, however, just left Zürich after vainly trying to persuade Friedrich Hegar and other prominent musicians to perform several of his less ambitious compositions. Although put out by this sudden, but alas so typical 'flight', Nietzsche finally decided to join his devoted 'disciple' in Venice. It had the immense advantage over all the other Italian cities he had visited of having dark, well-paved streets and alleyways where, weak-sighted as he was, he ran no risk of being run over by a passing carriage. His eyes, despite a pair of dark-lensed spectacles, were now constantly watering and, to his acute embarrassment, tears he could not control often rolled down his cheeks.

Venice, which Nietzsche reached on 10 April proved a bitter disappointment. Köselitz had found him wretched lodgings – a far cry from the high-ceilinged bedroom he had found so pleasant several years before. 'Oh Genoa and Nizza!' he complained in a long letter written to his sister after moving to another house. What he needed for his eyes was a wonderful 'deep wood', but where was he to find it – now that thickly forested Vallombrosa (near Florence) had become so popular that rental prices had risen dramatically?

Elisabeth meanwhile had been bombarding him with gushing letters, rapturously describing her deep love for Bernhard Förster. The wedding of the two rabid Wagnerians was due to take place in Naumburg on 22

May – the late composer's birthday. How wonderful it would be if Fritz could be there too, to act as her 'best man'! This of course was wishful thinking, for no force in the world could have moved Nietzsche to bestow a public seal of approval, above all in Naumburg, on his sister's marriage to a man he continued to regard with deep misgivings as an antisemitic 'agitator'. Equally fanciful was Elisabeth's reiterated plea that Fritz at last get married. What impudence it was to imagine that a 'man of his rank' could find someone capable of loving him, for that meant of knowing who he really was: he who, after belatedly discovering what Man really is, had to his great regret come to despise Richard Wagner and Arthur Schopenhauer and now regarded the founder of Christianity as 'superficial'!

Still, this was no time to pick a quarrel with his sister. She had just done him a service by persuading their uncle, Bernhard Dächsel, an experienced lawyer, to open legal proceedings against Ernst Schmeitzner: a move that had so upset Schmeitzner's father that he had offered to guarantee eventual repayment of the 5,600 marks owed to his 'favourite author' by the now bankrupt publisher. Even before receiving this welcome news, Nietzsche had asked Naumann to print forty (instead of twenty) copies of *Zarathustra* IV. He could now afford to pay the modest cost (284 marks) out of his own pocket.

On 6 June Nietzsche left Venice and made his way up into the Alps via the familiar route to Chiavenna, and from there up the Mera river valley and over the Maloja Pass to Sils-Maria, where once again he was warmly welcomed by the friendly grocer Herr Durisch, his wife and their young daughter Adrienne.

During the first three weeks the entire Engadine steamed and stewed beneath a torrid sun in an unprecedented heatwave. Nietzsche cursed the stifling, low-ceilinged smallness of his upstairs bedroom, while also blessing the presence of an 'excellent' old lady named Luise Röder-Wiederhold, whom Köselitz had befriended in Zürich and who had agreed to come to Sils-Maria to take dictation from the 'half-blind professor'. Although not exactly a 'suffragette', she was a 'modern-minded' woman, like Malwida von Meysenbug, whose heart had throbbed and fluttered during the heady revolutionary days of 1848, which had rocked so many of the capitals of post-Metternichian Europe. At times the impenitent idealist had trouble stifling her simmering objections, and, as Nietzsche reported to Resa von Schirnhofer (still studying in Paris), the old lady was displaying an 'angelic' patience in putting up with his 'atrocious "anti-democratism"'.

Now that he had enjoyed his poetic fling and had rounded out his *Zarathustra* 'quartet' with a 'sublime' extravaganza, it was high time,

Nietzsche had decided, to get back to 'serious' philosophizing by writing a kind of prose commentary on the themes that had been all too cryptically expounded in *Zarathustra*'s discourses and parables. The composition of this 'serious' work seems at first to have caused Nietzsche serious intellectual dissatisfaction. He was afflicted by blinding headaches and was finally felled by a week-long seizure. After the 'angelically' patient Frau Röder had returned to Zürich in early July, Nietzsche made no attempt to conceal his feeling of relief. This experiment, he wrote to Köselitz, was not one he was ready to renew. Everything he had dictated to Frau Röder was 'worthless'. He had found her unstable, and too prone to weep over her present lot. 'But worst of all: she has no manners, and swings her legs. Nevertheless, she helped me to get through a bad month, with the very best of dispositions.'

This question of 'good manners' was for Nietzsche anything but a minor matter. They were an essential ingredient, not only of what he felt that women could and should display, but also of what should characterize the truly 'superior' male. In a letter written to his sister on 5 July he had undertaken to defend Meta von Salis against the accusations of aristocratic arrogance that had been levelled against her, not only by Frau Röder and Heinrich Köselitz, both of stoutly bourgeois origins, but also, more surprisingly, by her nobly born Austrian friend Resa von Schirnhofer. Personally, he had found Meta von Salis 'by no means unsympathetic', Fritz explained to his sister, 'above all because she appreciates good manners, and, albeit somewhat stiffly Swiss, practises them herself: something which in this rabble-and-country-bumpkin age means more to me than "virtue", "wit", and "beauty". In this respect an aged and much suffering Englishwoman, about whom I spoke to you last autumn, affords me ample pleasure; and should you somewhere yet discover a wonder-beast [*Wundertier*] of elegance in wit and gestures, do please, dear Sister, let me know: there are few things left that still afford pleasure to your brother.'

This old, 'much suffering' Englishwoman was a widow, Mrs Emily Fynn, who had chosen to settle in Geneva. Together with her daughter, a talented painter of Alpine flora, she had become such an inseparable companion of Chopin's former pupil, Mademoiselle de Mansuroff, that the three now formed a close-knit 'trio'. More than once Nietzsche had urged her not to read his books; and as a reward for this 'discretion', her 'swan-like' poise and movements were soon to be singled out as a rare English virtue by a bespectacled ex-professor of classical philology who was by no means as 'half-blind' as he often seemed.

The problem of what separates what is 'noble' from what is 'common' or 'vulgar' had begun to preoccupy Nietzsche long before he made a first attempt to contrast these forms of behaviour in the third aphorism of *The Joyous Science* (entitled in German '*Edel und gemein*'). The more he pondered the matter, the more it occurred to him that *edel* (the German word for 'noble') was not the term he should be using for the kind of human qualities and behaviour he was bent on extolling. Because *edel* was the adjectival form of *Adel* (the German word for 'nobility'), it suggested qualities that were inherited rather than individually acquired and earned through a long, rigorous process of *Zucht* ('drill', 'discipline'), or what Nietzsche preferred to call *Selbstüberwindung* (self-overcoming). Better suited for what he had in mind was the German word *vornehm*: thanks to the prefix *vor* (denoting 'in front of', 'ahead of') and the root term *nehm* (from *nehmen*, to 'take' or 'place'), it suggested displacement, distancing, in short 'distinction' and 'distinguished': both derived from the Latin word *stigma* (brand-mark), denoting a separation from the herd. It was certainly no chance coincidence if, in the same letter in which he mildly criticized Frau Röder's lack of good manners, Nietzsche treated her sponsor, Heinrich Köselitz, to a highly personal lecture on what he considered *vornehm* to mean. 'Distinguished, for example, is the firmly maintained appearance of frivolity, whereby a Stoic toughness and self-constraint are masked. Distinguished is slow-moving in all matters, likewise the slowly moving eye. We find it difficult to admire . . . Distinguished is . . . the conviction that one has duties towards one's equals and that one proceeds towards others with discretion; that one always feels as someone who has honours to bestow . . . that one is capable of *otium* [leisure], and is not merely busy, like hens that cackle, lay eggs, cackle again and so forth, and so forth.' If Nietzsche had not stopped here, for fear of exhausting the patience of his 'dear Friend', he would have offered Köselitz an embryonic preview of the ninth and concluding chapter (entitled '*Was ist vornehm*?' – 'What is distinguished?') of the new book he was preparing.

In August the oppressive heat gave way to cold and often breezy weather. There was a notable improvement in Nietzsche's unstable health, which he had been trying to 'tame' by maintaining a strict diet of milk, rice pudding, beefsteak, raw eggs and honey. With the conclusion of the harvest, when the green fields decked themselves out in a yellow, ochre and a light brown patchwork of 'Mediterranean colours' and the air became wonderfully dry, Nietzsche once again felt quite at home.

Much as he dreaded the prospect of making another visit to 'cloud-covered' Germany, Nietzsche was by now resigned to his 'fate' for two imperious reasons. By continuing to disregard his mother's repeated pleas that he return to Naumburg, he would be displaying a callous lack of magnanimity unworthy of a 'man of distinction', at a moment when she was about to lose her only daughter. He was also nagged by a sense of guilt towards his sister Elisabeth, whose marriage he had snubbed, and whom he might not see again for years after she had left with her husband Bernhard Förster for distant Paraguay early in 1886. The second reason was the critical situation in which he now found himself as a writer who no longer had a publisher.

On or around 20 September Nietzsche left Sils-Maria, reaching Naumburg the next day for a joyful reunion with his mother and sister. His brother-in-law, Bernhard Förster, was momentarily absent, having left on one more propaganda tour of public speeches, this time in Westphalia, where (as Nietzsche reported to Franz Overbeck) he was 'alternately *ranting* and riding his two favourite horses (Paraguay and antisemitism)'.

In Leipzig, to which Fritz promptly hied himself in order to foil his mother's latest 'plot' – to have him married to the daughter of his former military commander – he was dismayed to discover the enormous inroads that antisemitism had made, not only among local Saxons but also in the more 'distinguished' ranks of the Prussian nobility. Schmeitzner had clearly been 'bending with the wind' – something that had not endeared him to Leipzig booksellers, many of whom were Jewish, nor saved him from bankruptcy. His latest 'coup' was a plan to sell his entire stock of unsold books, including thousands of volumes authored by Nietzsche, to a Chemnitz rogue named Erlecke, who was going to dispose of them at a public auction. The price Schmeitzner was demanding to save these volumes was 14,000 marks! In a rage, Nietzsche hired the services of a clever Jewish lawyer named Kaufmann who, by ordering Schmeitzner's father to honour his pledge, managed to extract close to 6,000 marks from the bankrupt publisher.

On 14 October Fritz made a two-day visit to Naumburg, to celebrate his forty-first birthday with his mother, his sister Elisabeth and her husband, Bernhard Förster, whom he now met for the first time. Assuming his most affable mask, he was hypocritical enough to praise the couple's Paraguayan venture, even though privately he shared his mother's deep misgivings. For if 'Lieschen', brought up in provincial Naumburg, knew little about milking cows and raising hens, her husband, a former schoolteacher from Berlin, knew even less.

On 1 November Fritz was accompanied to the Leipzig railway station and given a moving send-off by his weeping mother. In gloomily overcast Munich, where the sun had not been seen for more than a week, he spent a pleasant morning with Ida Overbeck's mother and a lively evening discussing the merits of Japanese art with an ebullient Reinhard von Seydlitz, before being plied by Seydlitz's sprightly wife Irene with beefsteaks and a bottle filled with tea to help him endure the tedious train-trip to Milan and Florence.

In Florence, Nietzsche visited the local observatory, where an aged stargazer with snow-white hair and beard astounded him by reciting a number of aphorisms from *Human, All Too Human.* Shepherded by the obliging Paul Lanzky, he moved on to beautifully wooded Vallombrosa – where Milton, among others, was said to have found inspiration for his description of paradise. Nietzsche took an instant dislike to this 3,000-foot-high 'sanctuary', where the prices were too high and the sleet too depressing for his hypersensitive metabolism. Hardly pausing for breath, he took hasty leave of the crestfallen Lanzky and boarded a train for Genoa, where the clouds were just as thick and the streets just as wet and slippery. By 11 November he was back in Nice, as happy as a 'Hamletian mole' could be. 'It was *highly worthwhile* to be able to test almost simultaneously the air of Leipzig, Munich, Florence, Genoa and Nizza,' Fritz wrote on a postcard to his sister. 'You cannot imagine by how *much* Nizza has triumphed in this competition. My lodgings as before are at the Pension de Genève, petite rue St Etienne . . . My table partner is a bishop, a Monsignore, who speaks German.'

Two weeks later his feelings had not changed. From what were probably cramped quarters at the Pension de Genève he had quickly moved to a 'perfect' second-storey bedroom which was twenty feet long, fourteen feet wide and fourteen feet high – what a change from the low-ceilinged 'hermitage' of Sils-Maria! – and which, in addition to a high-backed 'Voltaire' armchair, contained a bed three times as big as the one he used in Naumburg. The southward view from the eight-foot-high window was spectacular – out over the Square des Phocéens (named after Greek mariners who had founded Marseille 2,000 years before) towards a cluster of warmly red-stuccoed houses, huge eucalyptus trees, mountains and a shimmering expanse of Mediterranean water. All of Nietzsche's previous grievances against this pretentious, carriage-crammed imitation of Paris had vanished overnight, and, as he wrote to Heinrich Köselitz, 'The air [here] is incomparable, its stimulating power (like the bright plenitude of the sky) is not to be found anywhere else in Europe.'

In Leipzig Nietsche had been told by Constantin Naumann, in whose sound judgement he had ever-growing confidence, that none of the three *Zarathustra* volumes had sold more than 100 copies. This sobering news made Nietzsche realize how much time he had wasted during the summer in the hope of bringing out a second, 'improved' edition of *Human, All Too Human.*

The normally painful Christmas season passed without a major seizure, even if Nietzsche's solitude at times was distinctly melancholic. He no longer needed sleeping tablets, preferring in the evening to drink a hot grog or a bottle of Munich's Kindl-Bräu beer to assure him a restful night. On Christmas Day he had himself driven out in a carriage to the lovely promontory of Saint-Jean-Cap-Ferrat, from where he returned on foot, ending up in a park where young soldiers were playing bowls. 'Fresh roses and geraniums in the hedges, and everything green and warm: not at all Nordic!' as he wrote in a New Year's letter to his sister Elisabeth and her husband. After emptying three large glasses of sweet white wine, he felt '*a bitzeli betrunken*' (Switzerdütsch for 'a wee bit drunk'). In which mellow condition he had himself driven the rest of the way in to Nice, where he was offered a 'princely' dinner at the Pension de Genève, in a dining-room aglow with a large Christmas tree and candles.

Stimulated by an 'everlasting' succession of bright, sun-blessed days, he soon made up for the time he had wasted during his three summer months at Sils-Maria. In mid-January 1886 he wrote to Hermann Credner, one of the editors of the 'respectable' Veit publishing company in Leipzig, to ask if he would be interested in bringing out a new Nietzsche book: a second, follow-up volume to *Morgenröte*, carrying the subtitle 'Thoughts on Moral Prejudices', which he had written for 'intellectual daredevils and gourmets'. Credner's response to this overture was not unfavourable. He was even prepared to pay Nietzsche an advance of 40 marks for every sixteen pages of printed text, with an initial print order of 1,250 copies. The only trouble was that he had never read *Morgenröte*. When he finally obtained a copy, he was appalled to discover that Schmeitzner had been trying to sell the book at the prohibitively high price of 10 marks per copy, thus effectively limiting its distribution to 'admirers'.

On the 15th Nietzsche's sister left Hamburg with her husband, after receiving a melancholy letter from Fritz frankly regretting that she had become involved in this Paraguay venture which was going to tear her out of her traditional European context and plunge her and her husband into a brutal society of tough, uncouth farmers and bush-whackers, primitive peasants and 'embittered and corrupted Germans' – a prophecy destined to be fulfilled almost to the letter. To this sad, reproachful letter from her 'poor lamb' of a brother, the headstrong Elisabeth did not bother to reply directly. Instead, she sent a note to Irene von Seydlitz – the kind of 'frisky female' Fritz seemed to fancy – asking her to find a suitable wife for her brother.

Thanks to two woollen shirts his brother-in-law had thoughtfully given him as a present, Nietzsche was able to survive many freezing nights in an unheated room during an exceptionally cold winter. On 27 March he informed Hermann Credner that he had virtually completed the tiresome chore of copying out a legible script for his new book, which he had decided to rename *Jenseits von Gut und Böse* (*Beyond Good and Evil*). He followed up several days later with a second letter of explanation, acompanied by two poems – the first of which, a hymn of praise to the 'Mistral' wind, was intended to 'introduce' the book, while the second summed everything up with a verse finale. This 'poetic licence', aggravated by certain demands concerning type and page format (about which Nietzsche was very fussy), failed to impress the humourless Herr Credner, who had meanwhile been dismayed by some of the daredevil 'temerities' he had encountered in *Morgenröte*. Vexed by the Leipzig publisher's baffling silence and not knowing what else to do with his new, 'frightening' book, which (as he wrote to Köselitz) had flowed out of his soul like 'very black, almost squid-like' ink, Nietzsche in late April sent the manuscript to his old Pforta tutor Max Heinze, begging him to deliver it personally to Hermann Credner. He then left Nice and moved to Venice, where in Köselitz's absence he occupied the composer's apartment in the San Canciano district.

After nine lonely days (1–9 May), during which he suffered intense eye-aches – for here too the sunlight was now too bright – he headed for Munich, in the hope of seeing Reinhart von Seydlitz and his vivacious wife Irene. Quickly responding to Elisabeth Förster's 'hint' in her farewell letter from Hamburg, Irene von Seydlitz had written to Nietzsche in February to say that nothing would please her more than to find him a suitably rich wife, if he could only come to Munich to facilitate her task. To this generous offer Nietzsche had replied (tardily from Venice) that, alas, he was the kind of man who 'is stretched taut in his problem – in his "task", might one say? – as in a lovely, old-fashioned instrument of torture: once one has "withstood" it, well, one is *kaputt* for a longish time. For example, now: a manuscript with the malicious title "Beyond Good and Evil" is one result of this winter; the other – lies here in Venice, I myself, perhaps beyond good and evil, but not beyond disgust, boredom, malinchonia and eye-aches.' Four days later the tardy letter-writer turned up in Munich, only to discover that Reinhart and his wife had left for Berlin, where Seydlitz was busy organizing a big exhibition of Japanese art.

When, to the intense delight of his lonely mother, Fritz reached Naumburg on 12 May he learned that she had recently been visited by a Chemnitz 'editor' named Albert Erlecke, who was interested in buying up the large stock of unsold Nietzsche books still in Schmeitzner's possession. It did not take Nietzsche long to discover that Erlecke was a disreputable charlatan who had several times been fined for publishing obscene books. The same could not be said of the more experienced, reputable and nonchalant Hermann Credner, who had not bothered to answer Nietzsche's recent letters or acknowledge receipt of the manuscript of *Beyond Good and Evil*. Nietzsche sent him a telegram and a sharply worded letter ordering him to send the unwanted manuscript to Naumburg without delay.

In early June he moved to Leipzig to take personal charge of operations. He had already asked his trustworthy printer, Naumann, to provide him with an estimate of what it would cost to have his new book – roughly the same length as *The Joyous Science* – typeset and published at his expense with a print order of 1,000 copies. The estimate was higher than expected, but Nietzsche had no choice but to accept.

On 5 June he sent a telegram to Köselitz, asking him to come to Leipzig to help him with the proofreading. Two days later he asked Paul Widemann to join them, in the hope that together they could persuade Schmeitzner to reduce the 'outrageous' price – more than 12,000 marks – he was still demanding for the remaindering of his stock of unsold Nietzsche books.

For one whole week, during which the temperature soared to 30° Celsius in the shade, Nietzsche suffered agonies in the normally cool bedroom he once again rented from the schoolteacher Herr Janicaud, near Leipzig's Rosenthal Park. This was a physical torment he had feared and was consequently prepared for. What surprised and dismayed him was the distraught behaviour of Erwin Rohde, who had rashly chosen to leave Tübingen, where he had been so happy, and to come to Leipzig, where he had immediately quarrelled with his fellow philologists. After just six weeks of lecturing Rohde had persuaded the university authorities at Heidelberg to offer him a position, which he had accepted with alacrity. But the academic strains under which he was labouring were such that, as Fritz reported to his sister in distant Paraguay, he had been unable to have a heart-to-heart talk or exchange a single 'rational word' with his old friend.

On 27 June Nietzsche could at last leave Leipzig, after persuading the director and several leading instrumentalists of the Gewandhaus orchestra to perform 'Peter Gast's' latest brainchild: a septet for piano, string instruments and woodwinds. He had also introduced the struggling composer to the music publisher Ernst Wilhelm Fritzsch. When Fritzsch heard that Nietzsche was having trouble with Schmeitzner, he offered to buy up his stock of unsold copies for an 'acceptable' price.

By early July Nietzsche was back again in his 'hermit's cell' at Sils-Maria, after making a two-night stopover in Chur, where he read more page-proofs and treated himself to a long, headache-dispelling walk through thick pine woods. Meanwhile, in Leipzig, Ernst Wilhelm

Fritzsch found it difficult to strike a 'reasonable' bargain with Schmeitzner. The main reason became glaringly evident when Schmeitzner finally sent Nietzsche an itemized listing of all unsold copies in his possession. Of the thirteen books Nietzsche had so far produced, only two – *The Birth of Tragedy* and the fourth 'Untimely Meditation' (*Richard Wagner in Bayreuth*) – had gone into a second edition; and of these second editions no more than one-quarter had been sold. The other Untimely Meditations had been relatively successful – almost 800 copies sold of the 'sensational' David Strauss essay. But the results for Nietzsche's later books had been increasingly catastrophic. Barely one-half of the printed copies of the first volume of *Human, All Too Human* had been sold, less than one-third for *Human, All Too Human* II, and only one-fifth for *The Wanderer and His Shadow*. Exactly 216 copies (out of a print order of 1,000) had been sold of *Morgenröte* and even fewer (212) of *The Joyous Science*. None of the three *Zarathustra* volumes, though shorter and more cheaply priced, had even reached the 100-copies-sold mark. All told, Schmeitzner still had 9,723 copies of unsold Nietzsche books on his hands!

Nietzsche's irritated response to this bad news was to place the blame squarely on Schmeitzner, who had stopped distributing review copies of his books to literary critics. But his reaction also showed that Schmeitzner had not been entirely wrong in criticizing Nietzsche's 'absolute blindness for the simplest business matters' in an angry letter written on 3 April. Both were in fact to blame for what had happened: Nietzsche for having blithely disregarded Schmeitzner's warning that books of the inordinate length of *Human, All Too Human* would be difficult to sell; Schmeitzner for having nevertheless agreed to publish them, at the risk of bankrupting himself.

Ernst Wilhelm Fritzsch's interest in the unsold copies of his books now seemed to Nietzsche an auspicious omen. On 14 July he wrote to Overbeck that Fritzsch seemed to welcome this chance of becoming the publisher of Nietzsche's *Complete Works*, just as he had become Richard Wagner's exclusive publisher – a 'neighbourliness' which did not trouble him in the least. 'For, all things considered, R[ichard] W[agner] was the only one, or at least the first, who had a feeling of what I was after. (Of which Rohde, for example, to my regret, seems not to have the faintest notion, to say nothing of a sense of duty towards me).'

Since his arrival in the Engadine, as Fritz wrote to his mother on 17 July and again on the 22nd, he had been constantly unwell, suffering stomach upsets and insomnia, feeling dissatisfied, 'intellectually frustrated' and exhausted. He also complained of being poorly fed – even though he had just received a lovely cheesecake made 'in the Russian manner' with sour cream, sent to him from the Hôtel Alpenrose by the now inseparable

Anglo-Russian 'trio: the aged Mrs Emily Fynn, her flower-painting daughter and the ailing Mademoiselle de Mansuroff, who had once been Chopin's pupil.

This year the 'trio' had virtually turned into a quartet, thanks to the arrival of an intelligent polyglot who divided her time between London and Florence. 'How odd!' Nietzsche wrote on 20 July to Köselitz, who had praised what he had dared to write on the 'Woman's Question' in *Beyond Good and Evil*: 'Refuse to admit Women's Emancipation as one may try to do, an exemplary model of a little literature-woman has just turned up here, Miss Helen Zimmern (the one who made Schopenhauer known to the English) . . . Jewish, naturally. It is fantastic to what extent this race now has the "intellectuality" of Europe in its hands (today she talked to me at length about her race).'

Nietzsche's stomach upsets, headaches and insomnia were, once again, psychosomatic symptoms of the nervous stress that invariably gripped him between the moment when he had sent off a manuscript and the moment when he received the first bound copies from the printer. This time, however, the feeling of joyful relief was twofold. On 4 August he received the first copies of *Jenseits von Gut und Böse (Beyond Good and Evil)*, and to his delight he found that Naumann's competent printers had made only one minor typographical error. The next day he received a telegram from Ernst Wilhelm Fritzsch informing him that he had won his battle of wills with Schmeitzner and was now the lawful owner of all unsold copies of Nietzsche's books.

In announcing this good news to Overbeck, Nietzsche warned him that he would soon be receiving a gift copy of *Beyond Good and Evil*. In almost pathetic terms he begged his dear friend to muster all the strength of his 'patient and one hundred times proved good-will' and not to be 'embittered or estranged' by what he read. If he found the book unbearable, at least he hoped that Franz would find a hundred details in it that were not. Perhaps in places it might project 'elucidating rays of light' on his *Zarathustra* – 'an incomprehensible book because it goes back to genuine experiences I share with no one. If only I could give you some idea of my feeling of *solitude*! No more among the living than among the *dead* do I have somebody to whom I feel related.'

In early February, when Nietzsche had boldly proposed an initial print order of 1,250 copies – 250 more than the standard order of 1,000 copies he had repeatedly negotiated with Schmeitzner – it was in the confident conviction that, in *Beyond Good and Evil*, he had produced a résumé of his basic thinking which was more tightly constructed than the ramshackle volumes of the *Human, All Too Human* type. Those works had been products of compulsive haste brought forth by an author in a hurry who was haunted by the dread that he had not long to live. But now that he had survived for five full years beyond the fateful age of thirty-six, when his father had died, Nietzsche felt that he could slacken the hectic pace and devote more time to painstaking composition. While personal experience had taught him that illuminating thoughts hit one like 'lightning flashes' – the three *Zarathustra* 'miracles' had been the products of cerebral thunderstorms – he had also reached the conclusion that deep thought is the product of slow thinking, and even of slow, attentive reading: something he had learned from his studies in philology and which he was soon to compare, in a lovely preface, to a 'goldsmith's art and expertise in the fashioning of the word'.

Divided into nine parts, like *Human, All Too Human*, *Beyond Good and Evil* was two-thirds shorter, with 296 short essays and aphorisms, compared to the 638 of the other. The gigantic tree which, in the earlier work, had thrown out limbs and branches in all directions had this time been pruned, and the 'sprigs', no longer allowed to sprout at random, had been concentrated into a decorative cluster of 123 short-stemmed but often piquant 'Maxims and Interludes', placed in the middle of the whole.

Later (in *Ecce homo*) Nietzsche defined the primary purpose of this new book as being a scathing 'critique of modernity': a critique of a relentless process of democratization, of a tendency to exalt compassion and pity that was becoming increasingly pathological, of a cult of facility and painlessness, which were corrupting European civilization and encouraging the development of a sheep-like, 'herd-animal' mentality.

The very title, *Beyond Good and Evil*, summed up what had long been a cardinal tenet of Nietzsche's *Freigeisterei:* the ability any truly 'free-spirited' thinker must display to rise above the level of moral and other prejudices which, partly thanks to Plato (Sections 1,2,3), lie concealed in contrasts such as 'true' or 'false', 'good' or 'bad', 'beautiful' or 'ugly', 'useful' or 'useless', and which are embedded in the grammatical structure of everyday speech (Section 24). In a 'multicoloured' world that is full of nuances, to judge everything in black and white terms is to display the simple-minded 'faith of governesses' and to blind oneself to the 'the brighter and darker shadows and tonalities of appearance . . . ' (Section 34). In this sense, genuine *Freigeisterei*, as he had explained to Lou Salomé, was marked by a resolute determination to 'break one's chains', not to be a prisoner of dogma, nor to manifest a doglike fidelity to a single thinker, fatherland, scientific discipline, passion, love (even of God), or to 'higher human beings' – by which he probably meant Richard Wagner, and Arthur Schopenhauer as well (Section 41).

Here, summarized as succinctly as possible, are some of the major themes that run like leitmotivs through this book, gradually ascending towards the culminating chapter and the vital question already posed by Zarathustra: '*Was ist vornehm?*' (What is 'noble'? What is 'distinguished'?)

Charles Darwin and the British Utilitarians, like Spinoza before them, were mistaken in believing that a desire for self-preservation is the most basic of all drives. Self-preservation is merely a consequence of a more fundamental 'will to power', which is synonymous with life itself (Section 13). Even an occupation as seemingly inoffensive as philosophizing is in reality an intellectual 'will to power' (Sections 6 and 9): one which is also expressed in books. To this extent every thinker, like every writer or artist, is inescapably histrionic (Section 8). The deepest, sincerest, purest thoughts thus germinate in the 'stillest hour' of solitude, when the philosopher is conversing with himself and not trying to influence the multitude (the concluding section, 296).

The natural corollary to the 'will to power' that is manifested and exercised by 'leaders' (in German, 'Führer) – not always of the best variety and who might indeed represent a 'frightening danger' for the future (Section 203) – is a general willingness to obey. When this healthy balance ceases to exist, massive discontent and unhappiness result.

A philosophy valid for every human being is of little value, and the badly needed 'philosophers of the future' will avoid this tyrannical assumption. Why? Because 'what can be common is always of little worth' (Section 43). Or, as Nietzsche had already declared, in a singularly 'black and squid-like' anathema: 'Books for all the world are always foul-smelling books: the stench of the petty populace [*Kleine-Leute-Geruch*] clings to them. Where the people [*das Volk*] eats and drinks, even where it reveres, it usually stinks. One should not go into churches if one wishes to breathe *pure* air' (30). Indeed, a moral system valid for all is basically immoral. Why so? Because it implicitly rejects the vital need for a *Rangordnung* ('Order of Rank'), on which in the past all healthy cultures have been based (221). Psychology – pointing 'the way to fudamental problems' – is more important than Logic (Section 23): something long since recognized by the French, but which has not yet penetrated the lumbering German brain. The distinctive mark of youth is lack of moderation and reckless impulsiveness in the expression of feelings. The adult man learns to temper his judgements and to 'put a bit of art into his sentiments' (31). A piece of age-old wisdom which the 'ultra-modern', progressively minded adult of today has recklessly chosen to ignore.

Although the notion of the 'soul' was killed by Descartes (Section 54), belief in the Cartesian cogito ('I think, therefore I am') has lingered on in the naïve belief that 'I can will' this or that. But this too is a myth. 'I think' is a typically egocentric form of vanity, since ideas 'occur' to one and nobody can will them into existence (Sections 16 and 17).

While *Freigeisterei* – free-spiritedness and the ability to rise above the normal level of prejudice and faith – is an essential quality in those who are at all philosophically inclined, religion in the past has proved itself to be an invaluable asset in permitting an incipient ruling caste to establish its dominion over subjects who are offered spiritual solace, 'manifold peace of heart', and contentment with their humble lot. Nietzsche was even willing to admit that 'asceticism and puritanism are almost unavoidable means of education and ennoblement when a race seeks to establish its mastery over its rabble origins and works its way up towards its future domination' (Section 61).

But having made this 'utilitarian' concession, Nietzsche hastened to add, in the next section (62), that religions become dangerous when they cease to serve a sound philosophical purpose and become supreme and *sovereign*, choosing to forget that all societies are ruled by minorities, and espouse the cause of the *suffering majority*. Nothing had contributed more to the 'deterioration of the European race' than this wilful forgetfulness, this refusal to recognize 'the abysmal chasm in the Order of Rank which separates man from man' – displayed by those who, in coining the slogan 'equal before God', had ended up producing a 'diminished, almost ludicrous type, a herd-animal, something obliging, sickly and mediocre . . . the European of today'.

What is true of religion is no less true of morality. In a mini-masterpiece of an essay (Section 188), Nietzsche pointed out that Morality, like genuine Art, is a form of necessary tyranny imposed on the lawlessness and extravagance of Nature, and consequently is the very opposite of *laissez-aller*. The stern restrictions and constraints imposed by every strong morality – by Stoicism, Puritanism, as in the severe Catholicism of Pascal's Port-Royal – were not fundamentally different from the strict rules and disciplines that have made languages what they are: necessary instruments of grammatical coercion offering freedom of expression along with solid strength; just as what made poetry possible was 'metrical compulsion, the tyranny of rhyme and rhythm'. These 'laws' and 'principles' may seem arbitrary and capricious – as certain utilitarian blockheads and freedom-loving anarchists now claim – but it is they that made possible music, dance, 'rhetoric and persuasion' (*Reden und Überreden*), poetry and the arts in general. What fashioned the 'European spirit' over the centuries was precisely this discipline and drilling (*Zucht and Züchtung*, two key words in the Nietzsche lexicon), imposed within the framework of 'guiding rules' laid down by ecclesiastical authorities or noble courts, or according to Aristotelian precepts.

In this process of disciplining and rearing, a great deal of 'strength and spirit' was suppressed and stifled; but that is how it is with Nature in her prodigal and *indifferent* magnificence, 'which is infuriating but distinguished' (*vornehm*). 'Unfair', 'unjust', even 'immoral' this might seem, but, Nietzsche added, harking back to an idea he had already expressed in his second Untimely Meditation, Nature it is that teaches us to hate all forms of *laissez-aller*, excessive freedom, and 'which implants the need for limited horizons, for the most immediate tasks – which teaches the *narrowing of perspectives* and thus in a sense stupidity as a condition of life and development. "Thou shalt obey – someone and for a long time: otherwise thou shalt come to grief and shalt lose all respect for thyself." Such was the 'moral imperative' of Nature: one far more all-embracing than Kant's Categorical Imperative, since it applied to peoples, races, ages, social classes and to the entire animal species known as 'Man'.

This was not, however, the direction that 'modern man' was now taking, even though the Bible, and in particular the admirable Old Testament (artificially glued to the New Testament in a supreme 'sin against the Spirit'), was still enveloped in an aura of awe and veneration (Section 52). But this residual veneration was more and more an anomaly in an age that was now contesting every form of authority – and not least of all the patriarchal authority of a God who no longer seemed capable of expressing himself clearly to his 'flock' (53).

Typical of the 'drift' was the ever-growing hue and cry, voiced not least of all by 'male flatheads' for the 'emancipation of women' (Sections 238 and 239). The result was certain to be the defeminization of the 'weaker sex'. For what, Nietzsche now declared in more trenchant terms than ever before, from time immemorial and in all 'higher cultures' had always characterized Woman was her fear of Man. When she loses her 'protected' status, she ceases to be a companion and becomes a rival. The 'woman as clerk' ideal – today we would call it the 'woman in the office' – was a sure sign of the extent to which a new industrial ethos was now subverting and corrupting age-old aristocratic and military values. Traditionally, when men were still men, they had looked upon Woman as a 'delicate, curiously wild, and often agreeable domestic animal which had to be maintained, looked after, protected, and spared'. This essentially 'slave-like' condition was taken for granted, since no 'higher culture' has been able to exist without an element of slavery. But a legion of 'imbecilic women-friends and women-corrupters among the learned asses of the male sex' were now doing their damnedest to have women defeminize themselves and to imitate all the fashionable stupidities presently displayed by European men and European 'masculinity' – by dragging them down to the level of 'general education' and encouraging them to become newspaper-readers and political meddlers. And, Nietzsche added, no less trenchantly with a passing tribute to the 'utility' of religion, 'Here and there they even want to make of them free-thinkers and female literati; as though a woman without piety would not be something utterly abhorrent or ridiculous for a profound and godless man.' The lamentable consequence of this curiously transvestite trend, so typical of 'modern ideas', was easy to predict: Woman would lose her magic spell and become (like so much else) a boring creature.

In Europe and America, a species of bogus 'free spirits' had arisen who were preaching an easy-going, pain-avoiding, pain-eliminating 'philosophy', which had found favour with the 'herd'. Theirs was the cult of facility, of the 'green-pasture happiness of the herd'. They preached and promised security, lack of danger, cosy comfort, and their two great maxims were 'Equality of Rights' and 'Pity for all who Suffer'.

The dominant and indeed the only tolerated type in Europe was now the 'herd-animal', who had to be pampered by 'leaders' smitten by a guilty conscience. So much had they abdicated their ancestral responsibilities and right to rule that they now felt obliged to invoke elements other than themselves – ancestors, a constitution, venerable laws, even God – to justify their authority, even going as far as to curry popularity by claiming to be the 'first servants of their people' or 'instruments of the common weal' (Section 199). The 'lambs and sheep' had taken over and were preaching and practising a 'morality of fearfulness', which had so corroded the exercise of Justice that the very notion of punishment was now increasingly called into question (201).

In this general climate of aristocratic abdication and bourgeois *laissez-aller*, in which the last vestiges of moderation and tasteful refinement were being thrown to the winds, Nietzsche could not help wondering where European culture would end up in its mad haste to unburden itself of all 'old-fashioned restraints . . . A sense of *measure* is alien to us, let us admit it; our thrill is precisely the thrill of the infinite, the unmeasured. Like the rider on his snorting, onward-galloping steed, we let fall the reins before the infinite, we modern men, we semi-barbarians – and only attain *our* highest bliss there – *where we are also most in danger*' (Section 224). A particularly dangerous arch-romantic 'yearning for the infinite' which, forty years later, was to flex its muscles, fill its lungs and proudly proclaim itself to a stunned, sheepish, and increasingly supine Europe as – German National Socialism!

In the eighth chapter, entitled 'Peoples and Fatherlands'(*Völker und Vaterländer* – the alliteration was deliberate), Nietzsche devoted seventeen successive essays of comparative description to three of Europe's leading peoples: the Germans, the English, the French, with a surprising fourth insertion – the Jews.

In a digression intended to make clear that the fate of Europe mattered to him more than the characteristic virtues and weaknesses of its individual nations, Nietzsche (Section 242) returned to his pet theme: the present levelling and 'democratization' of society was producing a type of 'useful, hard-working, deft and highly adaptable herd-animal type of man' – something that was likely to give rise to 'exceptional human beings of a most dangerous and attractive species'. Why so? Simply because the democratization of Europe was bound to mass-produce highly malleable and will-less human beings who needed to be ruled; and the strong men who undertook to rule them, being uninhibited by age-old (i.e. aristocratic) restraints, would become formidable despots. In short, as Nietzsche summed it up, 'the democratization of Europe is at the same time an involuntary arrangement for the rearing of *tyrants* – taking the word in all of its meanings, even in the most spiritual sense'. A sombre prediction that was dramatically fulfilled within the next fifty years by the appearance on the European stage of four of the most awesome tyrants the continent had ever seen: Lenin, Mussolini, Hitler, Stalin.

Before finishing with his fellow Germans, Nietzsche singled out a particularly obnoxious national vice: the 'nervous fear', mixed up with political ambition, which had fastened its grip on the German spirit, a rampant xenophobia which had exhibited a whole variety of sickly symptoms – 'anti-French stupidity', anti-Jewish, anti-Polish prejudices, Christian-romantic, Wagnerian, Teutonic, and not least of all Prussian obfuscations and petty 'befuddlements', of which the *Reich*'s two most famous and super-patriotic historians, Heinrich von Sybel and Heinrich von Treitzschke ('historians with thickly bandaged heads') were egregious examples. As for that sinister 'political infection' of the German brain, antisemitism, this is what Nietzsche had to say on the subject:

> I have yet to meet a German who was favourably disposed towards the Jews . . . That Germany has ample *enough* Jews, that the German stomach, German blood has trouble (and for a long time will still have trouble) absorbing this quantum of 'Jew' – as the Italian, the Frenchman, and the Englishman have done, thanks to a stronger digestive system: that is the clear affirmation and language of a general instinct which one must heed and according to which one must act. 'Let no more Jews be admitted! And, lock the doors, particularly towards the east (and also to Austria)!' thus commands the instinct of a people whose characteristic type is still weak and indeterminate, so that it could easily be blurred, could easily be extinguished by a stronger race. The Jews, however, are beyond all doubt the strongest, toughest, and purest race now living in Europe; they know how to prevail under the worst conditions (even better than under favourable conditions)

> thanks to certain virtues which today one would like to brand as vices – thanks above all to a resolute faith that does not need to feel ashamed in the presence of 'modern ideas' . . .

Nietzsche's conclusion was that it would be much fairer and far more useful to expel the antisemitic bawlers, rather than the Jews, who were supposedly bent on taking over the country. Indeed, the Germans could benefit by imitating the example of the British aristocracy. The officers of the Mark of Brandenburg (the Prussian heartland, around Berlin), so well trained to command and obey, could not but benefit from intermarriages, which would have the signal advantage of providing them with the 'genius of money and patience', to say nothing of 'wit and intellectuality' (*Genie des Geldes und Geduld . . . Geist und Geistigkeit* – five alliterative Gs, all capitalized in German) of which at present they were singularly lacking.

It is regrettable that Nietzsche should have shown himself less indulgent towards the English. Had he known that the motto chosen for the first 'public school' to have been established in England (at Winchester, in 1382, more than 100 years before Pforta) was 'Manners Makyth Man', he who valued good manners above all else might have been less severe and intemperate in his judgements. But he was unquestionably right in considering the English, as represented by their most famous thinkers – Bacon, Hobbes, Hume, Locke – as not being a 'philosophical race'. The trouble with British empiricism was that, willy-nilly, it elevated 'common sense' and everyday 'sense data' to the status of valid criteria for judging Truth or Falsehood. Nietzsche's quarrel with Hobbes was influenced by some disparaging remarks the misanthropic philosopher had made on the subject of malicious wit; and it was this that prompted Nietzsche, in one of his wildest moments of misjudgement, to describe the Englishman as being 'gloomier, more sensual, more strong-willed, and more brutal than the German', and, as the more vulgar, also the more pious of the two.

What Nietzsche found most objectionable about the English was the stubbornness with which they clung to their religion. John Wesley and his 'Methodists' had, with typically 'English clumsiness and peasant seriousness', sought to popularize and demean the 'language of Christian gestures' through prayers and psalm-singing. They had made it acceptable to a 'herd of drunks and rakes', before inventing the Salvation Army in a kind of 'penitential spasm', which, all things considered, might be regarded by some as 'the highest achievement of "humanity".'

And how could Nietzsche forget that it was an Englishman, Jeremy Bentham, who had coined the shallowest, the most simplistically arithmetical of recipes for human happiness – 'the greatest good for the greatest number'? It was his successors, and in particular three 'respectable but mediocre Englishmen' – Darwin, John Stuart Mill and Herbert Spencer – who with their 'profound averageness' had become the great 'depressors of the European spirit'. Generally speaking, it was the 'damnable Anglomania' for modern ideas, of which the French had become the unwitting 'apes' and 'victims', that had undermined the great French culture of the sixteenth and seventeenth centuries. For, Nietzsche insisted, enunciating an unfashionable proposition of 'historical fairness' to which any lucid person should hang on to 'with his teeth': 'European *noblesse* – of feeling, tastes and mores, taking the word in every higher sense – is the work and invention of France; European vulgarity, the plebeianism of modern ideas, that of England' (Section 253).

The toughest blows in this 'very black and squid-like' book were reserved for the first sections of the ninth and final chapter, entitled '*Was ist vornehm*?' (What is distinguished?). The harsh truth, Nietzsche roundly declared, from which almost everyone in an increasingly squeamish age was now recoiling, was that every enhancement and elevation of the type 'Man' had so far been the work of an aristocratic society: of a society displaying a 'long ladder in the Order of Rank' (*Rangordnung*) based on an implicit recognition of a '*pathos of distance*', of significant differences between man and man, one therefore requiring a certain degree of slavery. In an absolutely egalitarian society, in which all human beings enjoy the same status, there is no inner incentive for the individual to strive to 'improve himself' and to attain a higher level of 'manhood', since the longed-for 'goal', for the 'common man', has, at any rate in theory, already been reached.

The truth, Nietzsche continued, is harsh, and anyone brave enough to look facts in the face should not yield to 'humanitarian illusions'. Every higher culture that has so far existed on earth resulted from an initial act of aggression. Men with a 'still natural nature', which is to say 'barbarians in every frightful sense of the word, men of prey still possessing an unbroken strength of will and lust for power, hurled themselves upon weaker, better mannered, more peaceful races, perhaps of traders or cattle-raisers, or upon old, decaying civilizations whose last signs of vitality were flickering out in brilliant fireworks of wit and depravity'. After which Nietzsche, at his most intrepid, added a dangerous sentence ready made for misinterpretation by unsophisticated, uncouth readers: 'At the outset the distinguished caste was always a barbarian caste; their predominance was primarily due not to their physical but to their psychic strength – they were *more completely* men (which at every stage amounts to saying "more completely beasts").'

At this point Nietzsche should logically have tackled the momentous question he had raised: by what subtle civilizing processes does an initially barbaric caste of crude, rough-hewn warriors transform itself into an elegant and distinguished aristocracy? Instead, shying away from a frontal confrontation with this complex question, Nietzsche chose to leap right over it, moving without transition from the beginning (how a dominant caste forcibly imposes itself) to the end (how and why an aristocratic élite declines and finally perishes). Nietzsche had not yet read Alexis de Tocqueville's masterly treatment of the subject in his book, *L'Ancien Régime*, but he had read the first volume of Hippolyte Taine's *Les Origines de la France contemporaine*, Madame de Rémusat's reminiscences of the revolutionary upheavals of 1789–94, during which her aristocratic father had been guillotined, and not least of all the Duc de Saint-Simon's memoirs, in which he had scathingly condemned his fellow noblemen for allowing themselves to be lured and effectively divested of their traditional powers, disarmed and imprisoned by '*le Roi Soleil*' (Louis XIV) in the 'golden cage' of Versailles. The final stage in a long process of aristocratic abdication was reached on the fateful 4 August 1789, when a number of French noblemen had gathered in the Jeu de Paume (the indoor tennis-court) at Versailles and had solemnly forsworn their ancestral privileges, divesting themselves of their titles in a collective, self-sacrificing spasm of 'social suicide' probably unique in the millennial annals of aristocratic rule. Every time he thought of this episode, Nietzsche was reminded of his father, breaking down and weeping in the spring of 1848 when he learned that, to curry favour with the noisy mob massed in the square below, King Frederick William IV of Prussia had appeared on the balcony of the Stadtschloss in Berlin with, pinned to the royal chest, the tricolour cockade of the German revolutionaries.

The extraordinary mass abdication of 4 August 1789, Nietzsche now wrote in Section 258 of 'What is Distinguished?', had simply been the final episode in a centuries-long process of 'corruption', whereby the nobles of France had step by step surrendered their lordly prerogatives and allowed themselves to become an ornament and showpiece, and thus a function of the monarchy. For what is absolutely vital in any good, thriving aristocracy is that it should not feel itself to be a mere function, whether of a monarchy or of a commonwealth, but its very *raison d'être*, its supreme significance and justification. The basic belief of any truly healthy aristocracy, Nietzsche declared without beating about the bush, was not that it should exist for the advantage and benefit of society as a whole, but, quite the contrary, that society should exist for its sake, as the necessary foundation and framework of a social system in which members of a select élite could fulfill their 'higher tasks' and thus attain a superior form of being.

This blunt, two-fisted apologia for aristocratic rule flagrantly contradicted the conventional wisdom of 'modern times'. For the main thrust of all 'rational' (as opposed to theological) political thinking from Thomas Hobbes on had been to justify monarchical rule as a necessary constraint needed to maintain the fragile cohesion of the commonwealth, which is to say of society; so that even this most 'aristocratic' form of government was justified on essentially utilitarian grounds. Having briefly explained how an aristocratic caste arises and then declines, Nietzsche undertook to provide both phenomena with a realistic, unsentimental rationalization – by bluntly declaring that 'Life itself is *essentially* appropriation, injury, the overcoming of what is alien and weaker, subjugation, harshness, the forcible imposition of one's own forms, incorporation and, at the very least and mildest, exploitation' – a term which (thanks to Karl Marx and his followers) had come to acquire a stupidly 'slanderous' connotation. Any truly living body – and this was true of every healthy aristocracy – 'will have to be an incarnate will to power, it will want to grow, enlarge itself, attract, and acquire predominance – not because of any morality or immorality, but because it *is alive* and because life *is* precisely will to power'. In the course of his comparative studies of various systems of morality, Nietzsche went on (Section 260), he had come to realize that, despite all sorts of variations, there have always existed two basic types that are radically distinct. The first, he robustly asserted, is a *master-morality* (*Herren-Moral*), the second a *slave-morality* (*Sklaven-Moral*) – although, he hastened to add, in all higher and mixed cultures attempts have been made to reconcile the two, only too often giving rise to misunderstandings, not only in society in general but within the individual. The salient characterteristic of a master-morality is self-confidence and a feeling of superiority, so natural and instinctive that 'good' is virtually synonymous with 'noble' (or 'distinguished' – in German '*vornehm*'), and 'bad' with 'contemptible'. 'Profound respect for age and tradition – all law reposes on this double respect – a prejudiced faith regarding ancestors and disregarding those to come is typical of the morality of the powerful.'

Diametrically opposed to the basic traits of the 'master-morality' were the characteristics of the 'slave-morality'.These were rooted in a general lack of confidence and a 'pessimistic' suspicion of everything 'superior' in human behaviour.This suspicion and distrust, on the part of those who feel themelves to be abused, oppressed, and thus 'unfree', is directed against everything regarded as 'good' by the 'master-caste', the real creator of all values. Compassion, the obliging hand, the warm heart, patience, industry, humility, friendliness are honoured, for these are the most useful qualities for the suffering and oppressed.

It was this fundamental antagonism between two diametrically opposed attitudes to life which, Nietzsche argued, had given rise to the famous contradiction between what is 'good' and what is 'evil'. In a 'slave-morality' the 'evil man' is the one who arouses fear; in a 'master-morality', on the contrary, it is precisely the 'good man' who inspires fear and wishes to inspire fear, while the 'bad' man is regarded as contemptible.

Even in the original German, the distinction Nietzsche was trying to establish was too succinctly expressed to sound wholly convincing. (Which is why he had to write another book to reinforce his arguments.) But the truth he was trying to 'unearth' and expose from underneath successive accretions of 'modern ideas' was made quite clear, further on in Section 262, in which Nietzsche reiterated one of the cardinal tenets of his 'resistentialist' philosophy. What makes possible a dominant type of human being is hardship (what Arnold Toynbee later called 'challenge'). Any breeder of animals knows that the species will degenerate if it is left untrained, is overfed and coddled. The same is true of Man, and also of human societies.

A sure touchstone of 'distinction' or 'nobility' is the instinct for reverence, Nietzsche pointed out in Section 263, which made crystal clear how far removed this 'god-destroyer' was from any vulgar form of atheism.

> The way in which reverence for the *Bible* has so far on the whole been maintained in Europe is perhaps the best bit of discipline and refinement in manners that Europe owes to Christianity: books of such profundity and ultimate significance require for their protection the external tyranny of authority in order to acquire those thousands of years of *duration* that are needed to exhaust and unriddle them. Much is gained once the feeling has finally been inculcated in the great multitude (of flatheads and high-speed intestines of every kind) that they should not touch everything; that there are sacred experiences before which they should take off their shoes and draw back their unclean hands – this is almost their highest ascension towards humanity. Conversely, nothing is more nauseating among so-called educated persons and believers in 'modern ideas' than their lack of modesty, the casual impertinence of eye and hand with which they touch, lick, finger everything; and it may well be that today a *relatively* greater degree of distinction in taste and respectful tact is still to be found among simple, lowly folk, and particularly among peasants, than among the newspaper-reading demi-monde of the intellect, of the well educated.

Among other sections in this final chapter (which is full of surprises), two at least deserve special mention. In Section 268 (one of his most incisive)

Nietzsche pointed out that a language, in the very nature of things, is a convenient form of communication developed for the common weal and designed to be intelligible to all. This is its strength, but also, alas, its 'weakness'. For no greater, more effectively insidious form of collective constraint has ever been invented. Precisely because it acts as a linguistic common denominator, it favours the mass rather than the individual. Which is why enormous counter-forces are required to thwart this 'natural, all-too-natural progressus in simile, the steady development in man of what is similar, ordinary, average, herd-like – and *common*!'.

In Section 287 Nietzsche came very near to contradicting one of the fundamental 'truths' enunciated in *Thus Spake Zarathustra* by arguing that what characterizes the 'noble' or 'distinguished' man is not his actions or his 'works' but the faith he has in himself. This was an allusion to the old Lutheran and Calvinistic formula, according to which profound Christian faith is more important for the salvation of the soul than good, utilitarian works here on earth. Walter Kaufmann, in his commentary on this passage, pointed out that this conception of nobility was derived from Aristotle's *Nicomachean Ethics*, in which the Greek sage had declared: 'The good man ought to be a lover of self, since he will then act nobly, and so benefit both himself and his fellows; but the bad man ought not to be a lover of self, since he will follow his base passions, and so injure himself and his neighbours.' What Kaufman neglected to add was that this conception of human beings as being essentially 'good' or 'bad' was one of those 'static' notions, introduced into Greek philosophy by Parmenides and raised to sublime heights by Plato, which Nietzsche had spent most of his adult life combating. The central thrust of *Thus Spake Zarathustra* had been to portray human life as a process of becoming, of self-improvement and 'self-overcoming', of striving up the 'ladder of existence' towards one's 'superior self', which lies not within but above one. This was a universal truth, applicable to every human being, to commoner and nobleman alike. Or, for that matter, to kings – and their fawning courtiers, whose obsequious postures Nietzsche had sarcastically compared to the static stance of flamingos, placidly balancing on one leg.

Here, clearly, in the dark, subterranean depths of his labyrinthine philosophy, there lurked a Minotaurian malaise, an infernal tension caused by this unresolved conflict between a basically static notion of aristocratic stability, needed for the maintenance of every 'higher culture', and a dynamic conception of individual self-improvement. No one was more painfully aware of this logical 'flaw' than Nietzsche, who was to spend the rest of his rational life trying to bridge this 'abysmal' contradiction.

## CHAPTER 35

# The Genealogy of Morals

> *– 'I suffer: someone must be to blame for it'*
> *– so speaks every sickly sheep.*

The first public reaction to *Beyond Good and Evil* caused Nietzsche considerable embarrassment. A critical broadside entitled 'Nietzsche's Dangerous Book' appeared in two successive issues of Bern's leading daily, *Der Bund*, a newspaper much read by the clients of the Hôtel Alpenrose at Sils-Maria – which this year included twenty-six visitors from Basel and ten university professors. Making no secret of his democratic preferences, its editor, Josef Viktor Widmann, was reminded of the black warning flag that blasters had put up at the entrance to the St Gotthard tunnel when the dynamiting had begun.

> It is entirely in this sense that we speak of the philosopher Nietzsche's new book as a dangerous book. In this designation we level no trace of a reproach against the author and his work, any more than the black flag was a reproach to that explosive material. Even less would it occur to us to hand the lonely thinker over to the pulpit ravens and the altar crows through the indication of the dangerousness of his book. Intellectual, like material explosives, can serve very useful ends; it is not necessary that they be misused for criminal purposes. But where such material is stored, it is well to say quite clearly, 'Here lies dynamite!'

Although Nietzsche's first reaction to this article was jubilant – 'one cannot think of a greater enticement to buy than what this article provides', he wrote to Constantin Naumann in Leipzig – he was soon assailed by misgivings when he heard of the speculative gossiping that the *Bund* article had aroused among his 'friends' and acquaintances at Sils-Maria. 'There are truths that should only be "spoken into one's ear",' he wrote to the French historian Hippolyte Taine, to whom he sent a gift copy of his new book, 'spoken out loud they would not be heard'– by which he meant 'understood'. To Jacob Burckhardt, the privileged recipient of another gift copy, he wrote more explicitly to say that to speak out on the subject of how Man can be 'made greater' (rather than 'better' or 'more human') was perhaps 'the most dangerous gamble there is, not with regard to the one who takes the risk, but with regard to those to whom he talks of such matters'.

Replying a few days later, Burckhardt expressed his astonished admiration. But once again he had to admit that he had little knowledge of philosophy. Though fascinated by many of the arguments presented – regarding the claims of contemporary 'herd-men', the author's explanation that democracy was the heir of Christianity, his description of the future 'strong ones of the earth' – the book was way above his 'poor old head' and made him feel 'utterly dim-witted'. Nietzsche was more impressed by Taine's reaction, which was less nebulous in its praise for the book's lively literary form, its 'passionate style', its paradoxical surprises, made to open the eyes of readers 'willing to understand', its large quantity of 'new ideas' and the 'infinitely suggestive' eighth essay (devoted to national characteristics).

Nietzsche, meanwhile, had not been idle. To help Fritzsch peddle the thousands of unsold copies of his books he had recently acquired from Schmeitzner, he decided to write explanatory prefaces in order to provide them with 'wings' for new 'flights'. The first one ('Attempt at a Self-Critique'), written for *The Birth of Tragedy*, was remarkable for its unsparing severity in judging this first, 'immature' book, out of which, nonetheless, had evolved all of his later, outspokenly anti-Christian, anti-pessimistic, anti-romantic and life-exalting philosophy. Looking back at this 'impossible' book, 'marked by every defect of youth', Nietzsche unflinchingly stigmatized it as 'badly written, ponderous, embarrassing, image-crazy and image-jumbled, sentimental, sweetened here and there to the point of effeminacy, uneven in tempo, with no will towards logical cleanliness, very convinced and therefore disdainful of proof . . . ' etc.

Working with his customary speed, Nietzsche had completed the first two prefaces – to *Human, All Too Human* and *The Birth of Tragedy* – by the end of August, and was already preparing a third, for *Morgenröte*, when, in early September, he was agreeably surprised by the unexpected arrival of Meta von Salis. After the recent death of her father, she had taken her widowed mother on a trip to Italy, accompanied by a copy of *Beyond Good and Evil*, which she had read without being overly exasperated by the author's disparaging remarks about 'emancipated' women. During a walk to one of his favourite spots, a grassy, larch-shaded promontory overlooking the gently rippling surface of Lake Sils, where part of *Zarathustra* II had been composed, she told him that she had just finished reading *Beyond Good and Evil*. This was a book, he commented, that had to be read 'with clenched teeth'. To which the stoic Meta replied that throughout she had kept her own well clenched.

One of the last to leave the increasingly frigid Upper Engadine, along with his luncheon partner, Helen Zimmern – whose interesting table talk moved him to write to his mother, 'Heaven have mercy on European understanding, if ever one wanted to remove from it Jewish intelligence!' – Nietzsche on 25 September said goodbye to the friendly Durisch family who had been his landlord hosts for another summer season. By 20 October he was back in Nice, after spending several weeks at Ruta Ligure, a village perched 1,200 feet above the little fishing town of Portofino, on the lovely Ligurian coast south of Genoa, where his disappointing 'disciple' Paul Lanzky again robbed him of solitude without giving him company. To his delighted surprise, the living quarters at the Pension de Genève had been considerably expanded by the acquisition of a nearby villa. Not only was it quieter, but here he could occupy a large, high-ceilinged bedroom and work without suffering from the claustrophobic feeling of oppression which had often spoiled his summers at Sils-Maria.

Six days later he wrote to Reinhart von Seydlitz, in answer to a sprightly letter regretting Nietzsche's failure to turn up in Munich. 'What a melancholy autumn! Everywhere leaden weights, nobody who brightens me up a bit – and nothing round-about me but my old problems, the old raven-black problems!' He wondered if his friend Reinhard had read *Beyond Good and Evil*: a kind of commentary on his *Zarathustra*, written for persons of the most 'extensive erudition', like Jacob Burckhardt and Henri (it should have been Hippolyte) Taine. Unfortunately, even they did not share his sense of distress (at the way the world was going), nor his determination to do something about it. '*This* is solitude. I have nobody who might have my No and my Yes in common with me! . . . Have but a bit of patience: I will still come to Munich. Perhaps there is there a very merry feminine creature with whom I can laugh? Laughter is something I must catch up on.'

In the meantime Nietzsche had completed his preface to *Morgenröte*. As he remarked in a lovely concluding section, the preface was not being added five or six years too late, since the book, like its author, was in no hurry, both being 'friends of the *lento*'.

By 15 November he had finished a preface for Fritzsch's new edition of *The Joyous Science*. He further embellished the book by adding a terminal garland of bitter-sweet verses, as a pendant corresponding to the sixty-three poems adorning the beginning. The title chosen – '*Lieder des Prinzen Vogelfrei*' ('Songs of Prince Free-bird') – suited Nietzsche perfectly. *Vogelfrei*, in the German Middle Ages, was the term used to designate an 'outlaw'; which is what in the eighth decade of the nineteenth century this 'dangerous' *Freigeist* had now become for literary critics and professors of philosophy.

While he was at it, Nietzsche decided to take a much larger step – by adding an entire fifth book to the four he had so joyfully completed during the sun-blessed Genoese January of 1882. The rainy weather, which had often depressed him during the first part of November, had by now changed to brilliant sunshine. This acted like a spur, even though the solar rays could not penetrate the windowpanes of his relatively cheap, north-facing room, where, in the absence of a stove, it was often so cold in the early morning that his numbed, bluish fingers could hardly hold his pen. All of which, as he wrote to Malwida von Meysenbug, encouraged his 'ice-cold thoughts', further stimulated by moonlight so brilliant that it made the feeble gaslamps in the street below blush red with shame.

In late December, after completing the tedious copying out of a legible text, Nietzsche sent the fifth book of *The Joyous Science* to his publisher Fritzsch in Leipzig. This new addition was boldly entitled '*Wir Furchtlosen*' ('We Fearless Ones'). It was accompanied by a robust quotation from France's illustrious general, Turenne (1611–75), addressing his ageing body: '*Carcasse, tu trembles? Tu tremblerais bien davantage, si tu savais où, je te mène.*' (Carcass, you tremble? You would tremble much more if you knew whither I am taking you.')

If a single theme could be said to dominate the whole – for, like all of his works since *Human, All Too Human*, this was a rich fruit cake of a book stuffed with juicy plums and bitter-sweet surprises – it was Nietzsche's reiterated contention that the philosopher's way of viewing life and the world differs radically from that of the ordinary human being – for whom 'knowledge' is not a search for what is odd and strange, but precisely the reverse, based on an anxious desire to reduce everything strange or upsetting to the reassuring status of something well known and familiar (Section 355).

The grave spiritual crisis into which Europe was now plunged was due to the fact that the world, which for a long time had seemed 'reasonable', had been shown by the inexorable advances of science to be 'non-divine', 'non-moral', even 'non-human' (*ungöttlich, unmoralisch, unmenschlich*) – to the dismay of contemporary Man, by nature a 'revering animal'. Having lost his traditional faith and sense of spiritual security, he had become embittered. Distrust, ever since Descartes, had become the dominant attitude of philosophers, while on a lower, popular level the feeling that something had gone wrong, that the world was out of joint and not what we *would like it to be* – ah, the eternal vanity of human beings! – had bred pessimism. In its most radical form this pessimism had turned into a rejection of all values, or what was now known as 'nihilism' (Section 346).

The second major theme or emphasis in 'We Fearless Ones', and clearly intertwined with the first, was Nietzsche's insistence on regarding religious and other forms of faith – for even science reposes on faith – in terms of *health* and a positive, affirmative and ultimately joyous acceptance of life on this earth. The two leading religions of the world, Christianity and Buddhism, were, he claimed, products of a monstrous 'weakening of the will' (Section 347): Buddhism by promising (with the concept of *nirvana*) a short-cut escape from the reincarnational miseries of the ceaselessly revolving Wheel of Life, Christianity by promising an escape from a cruel and unsatisfactory world into an imaginary afterlife of eternal bliss (Section 353). The genuine 'free spirit', on the other hand, is the one who knows how to 'dance on the edge of the abyss'.

Judged by the first of these two central criteria (the viewpoint of the philosopher, as opposed to that of the 'man in the street'), Protestantism was basically a vulgar, simplistic, 'good-hearted' revolt on the part of northern Europeans, and particularly of uncouth Germans, against the sophisticated complexity of Roman Catholicism – which, though a disfigured relic, was the last great offfshoot and achievement of the Roman Empire (Section 350). This revolt – the work of a fanatical monk (Martin Luther) filled with hatred for the 'superior' men of the Catholic hierarchy in Rome – was nothing less than a peasant insurrection (*Bauernaufstand*) against the established order in Europe. By allowing a priest to marry, Luther, that 'impossible' monk, had dragged him down from his traditional pedestal as an exceptional human being, different from ordinary mortals and invested with the aura of the 'superhuman' (*übermenschlich*), thus fatally undermining his authority and prestige in the eyes of his 'flock': a process of social levelling which later had been carried to its baleful conclusion by the intemperate hotheads of the French Revolution (Section 358).

Nor was this all. By banning the practice of 'confession', Luther had robbed devout parishioners of a discreet listener, of a 'friendly ear' into which they could pour out their petty secrets, cares, nasty thoughts and vices, thus flushing out the spiritual garbage that had accumulated within and leaving their souls replenished with clean water (Section 351). For in no respect did the humble parish priest sacrifice himself more stout-heartedly than in gratuitously providing this 'private healthcare' (*nicht-öffentliche Gesundheitspflege*). (If Nietzsche were alive today, he would probably say that the essential difference between the traditional father-confessor and the modern psychoanalyst is that the former was a benevolent 'amateur' who imposed no charge for his services.)

After expressing the fear that modern Europe, like post-Periclesian Greece, was likely to see the triumph of a new type of pliable, spineless, essentially histrionic type of human being – out of which 'building material' no stable society could possibly be built (Section 356) – Nietzsche, as though to reassure himself that this might not after all be the continent's inevitable fate, launched into an extravagant encomium of

Napoleon, the initiator of a 'classic age of warfare' which, he speculated, might again make possible a 'virilization' of Europe – in which Man, with a macho M, would once again assume his rightful place as the overlord and master of 'the merchant and philistine' (362). This was wishful thinking of the shallowest kind – as Nietzsche, a 'veteran' of the Franco-Prussian War, should have been the first to realize. For if that war had proved one thing, it was that modern warfare, in becoming more industrialized, was relentlessly divesting itself of the colour and pageantry it had still possessed at Austerlitz and Waterloo. In sober reality, the soldier – more precisely the spike-helmeted general and field-marshal of the German General Staff – was already establishing his supremacy not over and against the 'merchant and philistine', but with the active connivance of the manufacturers of arms and explosives (Krupp, etc.) and, later, of the raucous philistines of National Socialism – to the deadly detriment of the unified Europe it had been Napoleon's dream to forge.

Another actor of genius was Richard Wagner, whose personality and music were now subjected to the most critical analysis Nietzsche had yet attempted (Section 368). He frankly admitted that his objections to Wagner's music were physiological, since he personally preferred music that was light-footed, which could bound, leap and dance in captivating tempo and thus rid him of his melancholy. Nietzsche made no bones about it: he was not a theatre-lover and had little fondness for the convulsions and 'moral ecstasies' so much enjoyed by 'the people' (*das Volk*) and so generously offered to them by the 'gesticulating hocus-pocus of the actor'. Wagner, in this respect, was the opposite of Nietzsche – quintessentially a man of the theatre and an actor, and indeed 'the most enthusiastic mimomaniac there has ever been', and this even as a musician. For while Wagner had propounded the thesis that 'the drama is the aim, the music is always merely the means thereto', in practice, in everything he wrote, the 'attitude' was the aim, 'the drama and also the music merely *its* means'.

Nietzsche, as he made clear one year later by devoting an entire book to the subject, had merely scratched the surface of the problem posed by the hypnotic thrall, by the collective, black-magic *envoûtement* of Richard Wagner's music, and by the dangerously mind-numbing and mind-poisoning clouds of incense that assiduous thurifers continued to dispense from the hallowed shrine of Bayreuth, which, as Thomas Mann later noted, was already becoming the 'Lourdes' of this new musico-religious movement. And since, speaking as an iconoclastic 'cynic', Nietzsche had dared to challenge the new cult, he felt that the time had come to clarify his own position regarding the entire romantic movement – of which Wagner and Schopenhauer had been such outstanding proponents and he himself, during the early years of his philosophizing, an overly näive admirer (Section 370). For what was 'Romanticism'? Essentially, Nietzsche answered, a cult of suffering indulged in either by persons overflowing with a superabundance of vitality, or by those who suffer from an impoverishment of vitality and who seek in art and philosophy tranquillity, silence, self-forgetfulness, or drunkenness, even folly.

In an eloquent lamentation (Section 377), which was at once defiant, proud and angry, Nietzsche placed himself among 'the homeless ones' (*Die Heimatlosen*), who could find no ideals offering them real shelter, who had no wish to 'conserve' and to return to the past, 'children of the future' who could feel the perilously thin ice beginning to crack under their feet, 'free-thinkers' who had no faith in Progress and who were deaf to the 'future-voiced sirens' (*Zukunftssirenen*) of the marketplace who sang of 'equal rights', of a 'free society' in which there would be 'no masters and no servants'. In a tone as uncompromising and intransigent as the one he had employed in the final chapter of *Beyond Good and Evil*, he bluntly declared that he and fearless souls like himself regarded themselves as conquerors: they loved war and adventure, they dreamed of a need for new orders of society, and even of a 'new slavery' – for each new 'strengthening' of the type 'Man' had always been accompanied by a new kind of slavery. No, he and his 'fearless fellows' did not feel at home in an age that claimed the dubious honour of being the 'most human, the gentlest, the most righteous that the sun has ever seen'. These self-flattering words were simply a mask designed to hide the bitter reality: that those ideals were symptoms of weakness, weariness, waning strength.

'We homeless ones,' he concluded in a ringing peroration, were too much descended from an ancient mixture and intermingling of races to be prepared, as 'modern men', to indulge in the 'racial self-admiration' and ill-bred obscenity (i.e. xenophobic hatred of Frenchmen and Jews) that were now being paraded around as the distinctive hallmark of the German mentality.

> We are, in a word, and it should be our word of honour! – *good Europeans*, the heirs of Europe, the rich, gift-encumbered but also lavishly duty-bound heirs of thousands of years of European culture: as such those who have outgrown and become estranged from Christianity, and this precisely because we have grown *out* of it, because our ancestors were Christians of the most reckless Christian probity, who willingly sacrificed their blood and possessions, social standing and fatherland on behalf of their faith. We – are doing the same. But why so? For our unbelief? For every kind of unbelief? No, my friends, you know better than that! The hidden *Yes* in you is stronger than all the *No*'s and *Maybe*'s which have made you and your times

> so ill. And should you put out to sea, you emigrants, what will also compel you is – a *faith*!

Having reached these heights, all Nietzsche could do was, like Zarathustra, descend . . . back downhill into the valley. Which he did most gracefully, with an epilogue that was as gay, laughing and light-footed as anything he had ever written. While he was slowly penning the final question-mark suspended over his book, he was surprised by gales of impish laughter: emerging from the underbrush, the hobgoblins of *The Joyous Science* were now tugging playfully at his ears and calling him back to order. 'Away, away with this raven-black music!' Instead, they invited him to take advantage of the bright morning sunshine and the fresh green grass and to join them in a dance of joy, which, even to the accompaniment of a rustic bagpipe, was merrier than the 'toad-like croakings, the tombstone-voices and the marmot-whistlings with which so far you have been regaling us in your wilderness, Mr Hermit and Musician-of-the-Future! [*mein Herr Einsiedler und Zukunftsmusikant*!']

It was an appropriate finale for a book he himself preferred to call, in the language of the errant minstrels of Provence, *la gaya scienza* – and beneath whose joyous title on the frontispiece Nietzsche had mischievously added the four rough-hewn lines that were inscribed above his bedroom door at Sils-Maria, as a warning to ponderous pedants and humourless intruders who might be tempted to tramp up the wooden stairs to importune him:

> *Ich wohne in meinem eignen Haus,*
> *Hab Niemandem nie nichts nachgemacht*
> *Und – lachte noch jeden Meister aus,*
> *Der nicht sich selber ausgelacht.*
>
> (Alone I live in my own house,
> Have nothing copied of anyone
> And – every master have I mocked
> Who at himself could not poke fun.)

In early January of 1887 Nietzsche, after visiting no less than forty different houses, finally found himself a sunny, south-facing room on the rue des Ponchettes, not far from the battlements of Nice's old promontorial castle. Two weeks later, unable to resist the temptation, he made a trip to Monte Carlo to hear the overture to Wagner's *Parsifal* performed by a local orchestra. The fully sung and acted opera would probably have exasperated him; but its introductory orchestral condensation left him stunned with admiration. As he wrote a day or two later to Heinrich Köselitz: considered from a purely aesthetic viewpoint, had Wagner ever composed anything *better*? 'The very highest psychological awareness and certitude with regard to what should be said, expressed, *communicated*, the shortest and most direct form thereof, every nuance of feeling reduced to the epigrammatic; a clarity of music as descriptive art which makes one think of a coat of arms magnificently embossed; and finally, a sublime and extraordinary feeling, experience, eventfulness of the soul at the very heart of the music, which honours Wagner to the highest degree . . . [together] with a cognizance and penetration which cuts through a soul as with knives – along with compassion for what is being looked upon and judged. With *Dante* one finds something similar, otherwise not.'

The second major surprise of this winter was Nietzsche's discovery of Dostoevsky. One day he was browsing in a bookshop when he came upon a book entitled *L'Esprit souterrain*, a French translation of Dostoevsky's *Zapiski iz podpolya* (*Notes from Underground*). The title intrigued Nietzsche, who had often compared his philosophical spade-work to the underground burrowing of a mole. A couple of pages sufficed to persuade him that this was something special. He experienced a sensation of intense, joyous surprise, not unlike the feeling of ravishment that had gripped him when, as a twenty-one-year-old Leipzig University student, he had first stumbled on Schopenhauer. As he wrote on 23 February to Franz Overbeck, he, an 'uneducated fellow' who read no newspapers and had never heard of Dostoevsky, had instantly been smitten. 'The instinct of kinship (or how should I call it?) immediately spoke up, my joy was extraordinary.' Not since the day, eight years before, when he had accidentally picked up Stendhal's *Le Rouge et le Noir*, could he recall a book that had given him such a thrill. 'They are two stories,' he went on, about *Notes from Underground*, 'the first, really a piece of music, very strange, very un-German music; the second a stroke of genius in psychology, a kind of self-derision of the *Gnothi sauton* 'Know thyself' [written in Greek letters]. 'Incidentally,' he continued – and this coming from the normally Hellenophilic Nietzsche was the acme of praise for this 'unknown' Russian novelist – 'these *Greeks* have much on their conscience – faking was their real handiwork, all of European psychology suffers from Greek *superficialities*; and without a bit of Jewishness, etc. etc. etc.'

Encouraged by Overbeck, Nietzsche read *Humiliated and Oppressed* with a feeling of grudging admiration. He then read *The House of the Dead*. This moving description of Dostoevsky's years of imprisonment in Siberia so impressed him that in early March he wrote to Köselitz to say that it was 'one of the most "human" books' that had ever been written.

The third surprise of this winter was an earthquake, which during the early hours of 24 February emptied Nice's hotels and pensions of their panic-stricken clients. Nietzsche, as befitted a man who had recently classed himself among the 'fearless', refused to be rattled and insisted on making a nocturnal tour of the city to see how others were reacting. To Reinhart von Seydlitz he wrote almost gleefully: 'We are living in the most interesting expectation of *perishing*. Thanks to a well-intentioned earthquake, which made not only all dogs howl far and wide. What a pleasure it is when the old houses above one rattle like coffee-grinders! When the inkwell declares its independence! When the streets fill up with terrified half-clothed figures and shattered nervous systems!' Nice, he reported, seemed to have been transformed overnight into a military bivouac. 'I found all my men and lady friends pitifully stretched out under green trees, well towelled and blanketed, for the cold was piercing, and thinking with every tiny tremor that the end of the world had come.'

In the evening, when he turned up for his usual dinner at the Pension de Genève, he found the *table d'hôte* deserted, the frightened clients preferring to have their food served to them outside in the spacious garden. With the notable exception of a pious old lady, who was persuaded that the 'good Lord' should not do her any harm, he himself, as he reported to his friend Reinhard, was the 'sole *cheerful* human being among grub-like creatures and "feeling breasts"'.

Far less amusing, indeed distinctly sobering, was the news Nietzsche received at this moment from his publisher, Constantin Naumann. Despite his earnest efforts to interest the press by sending out more than fifty review copies of *Beyond Good and Evil* to newspapers and periodicals, only sixty-five copies had so far been sold. In his letter of reply Nietzsche admitted that this bad news about *Beyond Good and Evil* had not been exactly reassuring. But he remained persuaded that this book, like his other works, would gradually attract readers by a kind of slow, 'subterranean' process.

By the third week of March the Pension de Genève was virtually empty, the number of its unnerved, earthquaked clients having shrunk from sixty-eight to a mere six, including Nietzsche. The top storey, in one of whose rooms he had written two of his books, was now so tottering and fissured that the pension's owners had decided to have the entire storey dismantled and a new roof built to protect the lower floors.

Once again for Nietzsche the time had come to move on – to some intermediate 'haven', neither too unpleasantly bright and hot, nor too cold, where he could survive the difficult spring weeks before moving up, during the torrid summer months, to the cool plateau of the Upper Engadine. This time he decided to try Canobbio, on the western shore of

Lake Maggiore, which had been recommended to him as a 'heavenly' spot where he would be well cared for in a villa run by a reliable Swiss couple. The train-trip from Nice was a nightmare, interrupted at Laveno by blinding headaches which forced Nietzsche to dismount and spend a 'terrible ice-cold' night vomiting. At Canobbio he was greeted by a cloudless blue sky and by sunshine that was almost too bright, causing his eyes (as he wrote to Köselitz) to react with a plaintive 'No', while the '*inner* eyes' of his mind rejoiced with an ardent 'Yes'. The first week was a sheer delight, as Nietzsche travelled up the lake's western shore in search of a place where he could enjoy the beauties of the landscape (rightly prized by Stendhal) in untroubled solitude. 'This spot,' he wrote to Köselitz on 12 April, 'is lovelier than any spot on the Riviera, more moving – how can I have been so late in making this assessment?'

He had hardly dispatched the postcard to the maestro in Venice when his 'enemies, the clouds' gathered over the lovely mountainsides and the headaches returned to torment him. Two days later, in a moment of deep dejection, he wrote one of the gloomiest, 'raven-black' letters he had ever written to Franz Overbeck in Basel. He was fed up with Sils-Maria, just as he was with Nice, where he had recently been visited by a young German-American admirer (Heinrich Adams) who wanted Nietzsche to teach him how to 'become a philosopher'! In both Nice and Sils-Maria he was now too well known. In neither could he any longer find the solitude he needed to tackle his 'problems down below'; for, to a frightening degree, he was 'a man of the depths; and but for this underground work I would no longer endure life'. The conclusion he had reached, after examining what others in Europe were writing, was that his 'philosophical position' was '*far and away* the most independent' – so much did he feel himself to be the 'heir to several millennia'. But no one in Europe had any inkling of the terrible decisions he was turning over and over in his mind, and to 'what a wheel of problems' he was now tied. Nor did anyone realize 'that with me a *catastrophe* is being prepared, whose name I know, but will not utter'.

Unable to join Heinrich Köselitz in Venice, where there was not a free room to be rented because of the lavish celebrations for the official unveiling of a monument honouring united Italy's first king, Vittorio Emmanuele, Nietzsche left the no longer 'idyllic' haven of Canobbio on 28 April and headed northward via Bellinzona and the St Gotthard tunnel to Zürich. He reached the sultry lakeside city that evening in such a state of prostration that he barely had strength enough to drag himself and his luggage to the Pension Neptun. On Friday, 29 April, he wrote a pathetic letter to Franz Overbeck in Basel. He was suffering terribly from the 'slack, flabby' air and a painful excess of sunshine, and his repeated fits made it impossible for him to come to Basel. Could his dear friend not make a quick trip to Zürich, where he would gladly have him put up for Saturday night at the Pension Neptun – naturally at his expense?

Overbeck's weekend visit offered Nietzsche one of the few pleasant moments he was able to enjoy during ten dismal days spent in Zürich waiting for the final proofs of 'We Fearless Ones' to be sent to him from Leipzig. He called on Friedrich Hegar and his wife, but, realizing that it was a lost cause, he made no attempt to alter the orchestra conductor's negative opinion of 'Peter Gast's' *Lion of Venice* opera. Meta von Salis was fortunately in Zürich, but she was so busy trying to finish her doctoral dissertation and to help her sister refurnish an apartment recently gutted by a fire that all she and Nietzsche could do during their brief meeting was to compare notes on the unexpected heroism that normally timid souls or even crippled persons can display in moments of crisis. Particularly frustrating for Nietzsche was the absence of another of his and Malwida von Meysenbug's admirers, Resa von Schirnhofer, who had not yet returned from Paris. Not until 6 May, a couple of days before his departure from Zürich, was he at last able to meet the 'emancipated' young lady who, like Meta von Salis, was also actively pursuing her university studies. The year she had spent in Paris had not been wasted. In addition to a number of interesting French authors, she had, thanks to Natalie Herzen, discovered Dostoevsky, whose *The House of the Dead* had moved her tremendously. She was struck by a kind of hesitation, by something oddly 'fluctuating' in Nietzsche's remarks about his own works, amounting almost to an apology for having given her and others the impression that he was a reckless destroyer of all values; whereas in fact he was merely 'on the way' towards something completely new, not fully known in advance, and which was likely to be fraught with surprises, even for himself.

On 8 May Nietzsche finally left Zürich, travelling south-eastward over the now familiar railway route to Chur and its thick pine forests. Here, cheaply lodged in a schoolteacher's suburban house, he spent the next four weeks waiting for the moment when he could ascend to the Upper Engadine 'without freezing to death'. The surly 'airlessness' of Zürich was now followed by a spell of cold, almost wintry rain – which did nothing to improve Nietzsche's sombre mood. He was still seething with annoyance over the behaviour of his latest young admirer, Heinrich Adams, who, not content to pursue him from Nice to Zürich, had had the gall, being momentarily penniless, to ask Nietzsche to settle the bill for his bedroom at the Pension Neptun. In another gloomy letter to Franz Overbeck he complained that he had nothing to console him, 'neither man, nor book, nor music', adding that he was fed up with 'young folk' who were attracted to his 'literature', when it was obvious that this was no literature for youths.

Almost identical words, about importunate 'young folk', were used in a letter to Erwin Rohde, who was nevertheless asked if he could have Adams, a great admirer of Rohde, attend his lectures in classical philology at Heidelberg. Nietzsche ended this generously inspired letter by casually remarking that his sole consolation was '*old* men, such as J[acob] Burckhardt or H[ippolyte] Taine: and even,' he added ironically, 'my friend Rohde who has *long not been old enough* for me . . . But "sometime the day will come" etc.' Stung to the quick, Rohde riposted with an angry letter in which he rashly declared that Taine was vastly overrated and that personally he had found his books singularly 'devoid of content'. This stupid remark elicited a sharp rejoinder from Nietzsche. He would allow no one to speak to him in this disrespectful manner of Taine, a 'brave pessimist' who was moved by an imperious sense of mission in dealing with 'fundamental problems (and not as arbitrarily, as casually as you, like most philologists, do with philology)'. On 23 May Nietzsche ended this epistolatory duel with a letter of apology for his angry outburst. But Taine and Burckhardt, he explained, were the only two persons who over the years had had a warm-hearted and sympathetic word to say about his writings; he had thus come to regard them as his only readers. 'We are in fact basically assigned to each other as three thoroughgoing nihilists; although I myself, as you may perhaps surmise, still do not despair of finding the hole and the exit through which one comes to "something". When,' he concluded, 'one gets stuck like that in one's deep mine-works and digs, one becomes "subterranean", for example distrustful. It spoils one's character: proof – my latest letter.'

On 1 June Nietzsche was at last able to send back the corrected page-proofs of 'We Fearless Ones' to Fritzsch in Leipzig. His wish to avoid Sils-Maria, now too 'popular' for his taste, and to go to Celerina, north-east of St Moritz, was thwarted by the high price for room and board demanded by a local innkeeper. And so, around 10 June, Nietzsche boarded the stagecoach and travelled up the Albula and Julier valleys and over the pass to Silvaplana, and from there south-west along the lake-shore to Sils-Maria. He was warmly welcomed by the grocer-mayor, Herr Durisch, his wife and their little daughter Adrienne, who congratulated him on being the first foreign visitor to reach the village.

Here, as in Chur, the month of May had been exceptionally cold and snowy, so that the mountainsides were still beautifully clothed in gleaming white, while just outside his window Nietzsche could see the crusty remains of an avalanche. Beset by headaches, aggravated by a twelve-hour fit of vomiting and a serious cold, which made him break into a feverish sweat every time he made the slightest physical effort, he was in no condition for the first few days to enjoy the beauty of the landscape and felt far too weak to undertake long walks. And yet, as he wrote to Overbeck on 17 June, he was glad to be here again and above all '*to be*'. For to have been forced to suffer what he had had to endure over the past few years, after pouring out his 'innermost soul' in *Zarathustra*, to have heard not the slightest sound of a response, and to know that from now on he would have to endure a solitude a thousand times more total than before, was a terrifying prospect enough to kill the strongest of mortals. Although 'mortally wounded', he was amazed to find himself still alive.

This mood of deep depression was brought on by the news that at the Easter Book Fair in Leipzig, Constantin Naumann had been able to sell no more than 114 copies of *Beyond Good and Evil* – the book 'condensing' his philosophy on which Nietzsche had pinned such high hopes that he had wanted to expand it to double the size once the first edition had sold out! To be reduced to this, to the status of a nonentity, after all these years of . . . fruitless effort! As he wrote to Köselitz on 22 June, he had slumped into a state of 'literal décadence'; he felt so utterly limp and will-less, despite the 'sublimely blue and *green-meadowed* weather', that he was overcome with shame.

But if he was such a failure as a philosopher, he was by no means finished as an 'artist'. Let music once again be his salvation! Displaying the extraordinary resilience and ability to 'bounce back' which had so astounded Heinrich von Stein during his 1884 visit to Sils-Maria, Nietzsche now completed a kind of pagan oratorio (for choir and orchestra) he had begun in 1882, based on Lou Salomé's 'A Prayer for Life'. On 24 June he sent the score to Fritzsch in Leipzig, explaining that he had composed it in order to survive oblivion and as a hymn designed to be sung 'in memoriam' (i.e. after his death).

The envelope had hardly been posted when he was stunned by the news that Heinrich von Stein – Siegfried Wagner's erstwhile tutor, who had made such a promising start in the field of philosophy – had died. Quite unexpectedly, of a heart attack. It seemed too incredible, too abnormal, too 'unjust' to be true! For Stein was a healthy fellow and six years younger than himself. 'I really loved him,' Nietzsche wrote sadly to Köselitz. 'It seemed to me that he had been saved up for my old age. He belonged among the few human beings in whose *existence* I found real joy; he also had a great confidence in me. He even said to me that in my presence thoughts occurred to him that otherwise he would not have had the courage to find; I "liberated" him. And how up here we *laughed* together! He had a reputation for not laughing . . . He was far and away the finest species of man among the Wagnerians: so far at least as I have known them. This affair causes me such pain that over and over I *do not believe it*. How lonely I feel! Eventually the good Malwida [von Meysenbug] will die off too – how many will then be left? I am afraid *to count*.'

Nietzsche's health by this time had at last begun to improve. One reason, in addition to the glorious weather, was that for the first two weeks he had Sils-Maria – with its two luminous lakes, his favourite paths and mossy nooks, the lovely cliff-walled valley of the Fex with its tumbling brook and its glistening white glacier – all to himself. But all of a sudden the rustic calm was disturbed by the clop-clopping of horses' hooves as carriage after carriage unloaded its cargo of summer visitors. By early July, when Meta von Salis reached the village with a friend, Sils-Maria's two hotels were completely filled and they had to be lodged in an old stone house, gaily window-boxed with flowers, near the bridge spanning the Fexbach.

Never had the village, with its surrounding meadowland, looked more beautiful. An unusually cold May, with an abundance of late spring snow, followed by a hot and radiant June, had encouraged a luxuriant blossoming of Alpine flora. Wild flowers were everywhere to be seen, lining the paths through the fields, peeping out in red, Alpenrose profusion from bushes and underbrush, peppering the soggy mountain meadows with brown *Nigritellen* blooms, and dotting the stern cliff-faces of the Fextal valley with tufts of white and yellow saxifrages and edelweiss.

It was so hot that from midday onwards most of the clients of the two hotels preferred to remain indoors. But almost every morning, when he was feeling well, Nietzsche would cross the little Fexbach bridge and take Meta von Salis and her friend for a brisk walk to one of his favourite haunts, returning well before noon for his luncheon, so as to avoid the midday crush and scramble around the *table d'hôte*. Sometimes in the late afternoon, when the lucent waters of Lake Sils were fired with streaks of salmon red and scarlet in the golden glow of sunset, the three of them would go out boating. Such moments offered Nietzsche refreshing relief from his strenuous labours, particularly since his friends of the Anglo-Russian trio – Emily Fynn, her daughter and the piano-loving Mademoiselle de Mansuroff – had this year decided to desert the humble Alpenrose and to spend the summer in a luxurious hotel at Maloja, at the south-western extremity of the lake.

To mitigate the sweating discomfort caused by the midday heat, particularly difficult to bear in his low-ceilinged bedroom, Nietzsche normally rose at 5 a.m., when the morning air was freshest, and he was usually able to complete three to four hours of work before the time came for his morning walk. Thanks to this exacting regimen he was able to accomplish a great deal: far more than he had disconsolately thought would be possible during the first, gloomy days of June. Naumann, in his 'bad news' letter of 22 February, had suggested that what was needed to stimulate the flagging sales of *Beyond Good and Evil* was 'sharp controversy' as well as 'witty reviews'. Witty reviews Nietzsche could not provide, but sharp controversy he was ready to supply. He would take the 'left-over' material he had wanted to add to a second, enlarged version of *Beyond Good and Evil* and turn it into a deliberately polemical book.

On 17 July, barely two weeks after beginning, Nietzsche informed Naumann, who must again have been astounded by the 'half-blind' professor's prolixity, that he had completed a small *Streitschrift* (polemical pamphlet) intended to amplify and elucidate *Beyond Good and Evil*. The title he had chosen was *Zur Genealogie der Moral* (*On the Genealogy of Morals*).

More compact, strictly disciplined, and less diffuse than any of the books he had written since the four 'Untimely Meditations', the text Nietzsche now sent Naumann consisted of two essays, each composed of a number of sections. At the risk of being simplistic – all too easy in analysing Nietzsche's writings – one could say that the first, titled '"Good and Evil", "Good and Bad"', was essentially an exercise in linguistic etymology applied to moral values, while the second essay, '"Guilt", "Bad Conscience" and the Like', was an attempt to develop an 'anthropology of morals'.

Nietzsche began, in the first essay, by expressing a grudging admiration for 'English psychologists' – by whom he meant Herbert Spencer, John Stuart Mill and other proponents of 'Utilitarianism' – who had at least tried to bring notions like 'good' and 'bad' down to earth from the imaginary empyrean where they had been placed by Plato and after him by Christian theologians. But these would-be 'historians of morality' had arbitrarily decided that the notion of 'good' in primitive societies was derived from a sense of utility, of what was useful for the survival of the community as a whole. 'Good' actions, and particularly 'unselfish', altruistic actions were deemed 'good' from the point of view of those who benefited from them. But in so doing, Nietzsche argued, these British 'psychologists' were yielding to sentimentality. In reality the criterion of what is 'good' was not based on 'others', on those to whom 'goodness' is shown. It was invented by a dominant caste, imbued with the 'pathos of distinction and distance', in contradistinction to what members of the dominant caste regarded as 'bad' – as low-minded, mean and 'vulgar' (in German, *pöbelhaft*, 'rabble-like' – a favourite word with Nietzsche, the pejorative force of which is attenuated by the usual English translation of 'plebeian'). What was 'good', in those distant times, was what the ruling caste decided was 'good' and imposed on the rest of society. Only when aristocratic values began to lose their force and were challenged by the 'herd-instinct' of the ruled, did 'good' come to be associated with 'unselfish', 'unegotistical', and the term 'bad' with 'selfishness'.

This was followed by a fascinating etymological analysis (sections 4 and 5) of various adjectives invented by aristocratic ruling classes to distinguish the 'good', the 'noble', the 'brave' – the Sanskrit *arya*, the Greek *esthlos* and *agathos*, the Latin *bonus*, the German *gut*, the Gaelic *fin* – from their 'bad', 'common', 'craven' opposites: the German *schlecht* (bad), the Greek words *kakos* and *deilo* (the 'vile' or 'craven' antithesis of *agathos*), the Latin *malus* (derived from the Greek *melas*, meaning 'dark' or 'black', an adjective applied by the blond conquerors to the darker-skinned, darker-haired inhabitants of pre-Aryan Italy) etc.

How then did the term 'good', closely associated with nobility and courage, come to have an entirely different connotation? Nietzsche's answer (section 6) was that this semantic transformation was essentially the work of priests, and in particular of triumphant priesthoods, for whom robust manliness, virility and courage were less important than 'cleanliness' and 'purity'. There was always, he claimed, something unhealthy in such priestly aristocracies. The 'cures' – everything from the avoidance of meat, fasting and sexual abstinence to the autohypnosis of fakirs and the Buddhistic concentration on nothing – were more dangerous than the 'maladies' they were supposed to cure. This said, he added a typically Nietzschean caveat: 'With the priests everything becomes more dangerous, not only cures and healing remedies, but also arrogance, revenge, perspicacity, profligacy, love, the desire to dominate, virtue, illness – but it is only fair to add that it was only on the soil of this *essentially dangerous* form of human existence, the priestly form, that Man actually became *an interesting animal*, that only here in a higher sense did the human soul acquire *depth* and become evil – and these are the two basic respects in which Man has so far proved his superiority over other beasts.'

Now applying the criterion of 'underdog' or 'slave resentment' which he had unveiled in *Beyond Good and Evil*, Nietzsche went on to contrast the 'knightly-aristocratic' mode of valuation – with its healthy love of war, adventure, hunting, dancing and war-games – with the sickly ethos of the priests, born of hatred and a sense of impotence. For, he declared roundly, 'the truly great haters in the history of the world have always been priests, and likewise the most ingenious haters'. Already, in *Human, All Too Human*, Nietzsche had called the Jews 'great haters,' but now, throwing caution to the winds with an intrepidity that was to earn him the title of the 'Thunderer of Sils-Maria', he went much further:

> All that has been done on earth against 'the nobles', the mighty', 'the overlords', 'the power-wielders' is as nothing compared to what *the Jews* did against them: the Jews, that priestly people who were only able to obtain satisfaction against their enemies and conquerors through a radical revaluation of the latter's values, that is, by an act of the most *spiritual revenge*. This befitted a priestly people, this people of the most deeply repressed priestly vengefulness. It was the Jews who with awe-inspiring logical consistency dared to invert the aristocratic value-equation (good = noble = powerful = beautiful = happy = beloved of God) and who clung to it with the teeth of the most abysmal hatred (the hatred of impotence), saying 'the wretched alone are the good ones; the poor, the helpless, the lowly are alone the good ones; the sufferers, the have-nots, the sick, the ugly are also the only devout ones, the only God-blessed, for them alone is blessedness – whereas you, you who are powerful and noble, are to all eternity the evil ones, the cruel, the lustful, the insatiable, the godless, and forever will you be the unblessed, the accursed and the damned!'

In short, as he had already pointed out in section 195 of *Beyond Good and Evil*, it was with the Jews that there began the 'slave revolt in morality', a revolt with 2,000 years of history behind it which had gradually vanished from sight precisely because it had ended up victorious.

Out of this tree trunk of Jewish vengefulness and hatred (section 8) there had sprung up an extraordinary flower, a new love, deeper and more sublime than any seen before: the love that Jesus of Nazareth brought to the poor, to the sick, to sinners, as a sublime 'Redeemer'. A phenomenon so utterly unheard-of and fantastic that it acted as the most dangerous kind of spiritual bait. Thus, through an extraordinary paradox which had the semblance of a defeat, Israel had triumphed again and again over all nobler ideals. The consequence of this long-drawn-out process (section 9) was that the entire Western world was now suffering from 'blood poisoning'; everything was being 'Jewified' (*verjüdelt*) or Christianized or 'mobified' (*verpöbelt*) – no matter how one chose to call it, the visible result was there: '"The masters" have been disposed of, the morality of the common man has triumphed.'

For a man who detested antisemitism, because it was the hate-induced product of morbid jealousy, this was strong and dangerous language, quite likely to be misinterpreted (as indeed happened). But this was a risk, Nietzsche felt, that any fearless philosopher and *Freigeist* had to be prepared to take. Particularly since what was most important in this etymological investigation into the origins of morality still remained to be said. For the fundamental difference between a truly noble morality and its opposite is that it is a positive, confident, self-created, self-affirming system of values emanating from a feeling of abundant strength, whereas a 'slave morality' is a form of negative reaction against a reigning system of values, an expression of a deep-seated *ressentiment* (Nietzsche invariably used the French word, derived from his study of the French Revolution) harboured by jealous human beings consumed by the repressed hatred and desire for revenge of the impotent. The hallmark of the 'man of *ressentiment*' (i.e. of the plotting revolutionary) is that his 'soul *squints*', that he loves obscure hideouts, secret paths, back doors, and in general everything that is covert, sly and 'underhand' (section 10). And, Nietzsche added, expressing his pessimistic fear that the modern world might go the way of ancient Rome and witness the triumph of the weaker over the stronger, 'a race of such men of *ressentiment* will necessarily become *cleverer* in the long run than any noble race; it will honour cleverness to a far greater degree'. In short, whereas 'bad' (*schlecht*) was originally the term used by a dominant aristocracy to designate lowly, common, vulgar human beings, the word 'evil' (*böse*) was the term that clever common folk had pulled from 'the witches' cauldron of unsatisfied hatred' to stigmatize everyone and everything that was in any way noble or superior.

That the proud and domineering forgers of a noble system of values were anything but saints, Nietzsche was quite ready to admit. The traditional constraints of veneration, of courtesy, of loyalty, which they accepted as a matter of course, as time-honoured custom *among themselves* (members of the dominant caste), they were not prepared to accept in dealing with others, with 'strangers' of every kind. Their behaviour was then no better than that of 'unleashed beasts of prey', of 'exultant monsters', quite capable of emerging from a 'revolting' rampage of murders, house-guttings, rapes and tortures with a feeling of exhilaration and spiritual equanimity, as though it were 'no more than a students' fling'. Indeed, Nietzsche fearlessly and, it must be said, recklessly added that underlying all noble races one could not but recognize 'the beast of prey, the magnificent *blond beast* lustily prowling in search of spoils and victory; from time to time an explosion is needed from this inner core, the animal must break out again, must return to the wilderness – the Roman, Arabic, Germanic, Japanese aristocracies, Homeric heroes, Scandinavian Vikings were all alike in [satisfying] this need'.

These dangerous words, which certain Nazis were to take quite literally as a philosophical justification for their bestial behaviour, were written at Sils-Maria during the month of July 1887. And the question that arises is why Nietzsche felt the need to hammer home this point (in the crucial 11th section) and even to repeat the expression '*blond-Bestie*' a little further on, in referring to the 'deep, icy mistrust that the German arouses as soon as he comes to power', this being the psychological aftermath of 'that inextinguishable horror with which for centuries Europe watched the raging of the blond Germanic beast'. Clearly embarrassed, Walter Kaufmann, in commenting this passage in his book on Nietzsche, claimed that the 'blondness' here was not derived from any notion of Aryan racial superiority – Nietzsche regarded such theories as sociohistorical claptrap – but referred to the tawny 'blondness' of the Lion, the animal chosen in Zarathustra's first speech to symbolize the second, essentially destructive stage in human development, in which necessary destruction precedes a new creativity. This association of 'blond' colour and tawny beast may well have existed in Nietzsche's mind; but the point he was stressing here concerned *historical* facts, at any rate as he interpreted them, with relation to what most interested him: the past, present and future of Europe. No one can reasonably deny that the Vikings who sailed down the rivers of Russia and founded the first principality at Kiev, that the Norsemen who colonized the region of ancient Gaul which to this day is known as Normandy, that the Danish Angles and the Saxons of the lower Elbe who invaded Britain, to say nothing of the Visigoths, the Ostrogoths, the Lombards, who rampaged over southern Europe, along with the Vandals, who also wreaked havoc on North Africa, were bestial ruffians, whose wild behaviour in looting and raping Nietzsche had been careful to describe as '*scheusslich*' (revolting). But – and it is odd that Nietzsche did not stress this fundamental point – it was their virility as warriors which saved Europe after the collapse of the Roman Empire, from becoming an effete theocracy, run by Christian priests, who would have been unable to keep this 'western tip of Asia' – an expression used by Nietzsche long before Paul Valèry made it famous in 1919 – from being 'Mongolized' or overrun by Ottoman Turks. Instead of proud castles and palaces, products of an aristocratic 'will to power' based on the healthy emulation of rival families, all an inert Europe would have been able to display would have been churches and monasteries, or their ruins, next to mosques in over-abundant numbers. For what had saved Europe from this fate was not Christian charity and meekness but martial force – of the kind that had been used by the legions of the Roman Empire to establish and maintain a *pax romana*: something so awe-inspiring and prestigious that centuries later a Frankish king, Charles, later called the Great (*Carolus Magnus* or 'Charlemagne'), had decided to resurrect it by having himself crowned *imperator* or Caesar (in German *Kaiser*, in Russian *Tsar*), with a retinue of 'princes' (from the Latin *princeps*, the 'first' in any field) and 'dukes' (derived from the Latin *dux*, meaning 'leader'). But if Nietzsche did not choose to make this point, it was probably because it would have weakened his basic contention: that in the long, millennial conflict between Rome and Judea, Judea versus Rome, it was (as he declared in section 16) Judea – which is to say, Christian values, supposedly born of love but in fact the product of 'underdog' resentment – that had triumphed.

This brings us back to Nietzsche's concept of *amor fati* (love of fate), first enunciated in the fourth part of *The Joyous Science*, as a wise encouragement to accept the world as *it is* and not as *we would like it to be*, or to have been. What we experience as 'the world' or 'life' is not simply the fleeting present; it is also the remembered past, which alone offers us a reliable guide for the future – provided that its 'lessons' are properly interpreted and not distorted by visionary fantasies or moral prejudices. In *Zarathustra* II Nietzsche had denounced the tendency to reinterpret and rewrite the 'savage' past in accordance with the standards of a soft, squeamish, effeminate and not least of all revolutionary pseudo-Christian 'morality'. The feudal order, based on 'outrageous inequalities' and 'injustice', was for these reasons fundamentally 'evil', 'unprogressive'. The turbulent fifth to eighth centuries AD, when the lawlessness was at its height, had accordingly been denigrated as the 'Dark Ages'. Nothing was more childish and insidiously pernicious than this peremptory condemnation of the past by 'modern' and thus 'superior' human beings for not having been what it should have been (a smug, self-righteous sitting in judgement on the past which Nietzsche had criticized in his second 'Untimely Meditation'). Whether this denigration of vast areas of human history was the work of morally shocked Christians or of Jacobin revolutionaries, the basic motives were the same: those of 'men of *ressentiment*', determined to pull the 'wicked' past from its pedestal and down to their own, gloriously 'modern' level of mediocrity.

That the Jacobin revolutionaries of 1789 who had destroyed the *ancien régime* in France were hate-filled 'men of *ressentiment*' hardly needed to be proved. Still draped in the sacred garments of pious hypocrisy, on the other hand, was the popular illusion that Christianity was still, as it had always been, a religion founded on Faith, on Love, on Hope. 'In faith of what? In love of what? In the hope of what?' Nietzsche asked, in a section (15) whose ferocity matched his devastating critique of St Paul in *Morgenröte*. For what among other things did the Christian hope of future bliss in Paradise consist of? Nothing less than the prospect of a visual feast, of a truly 'celestial' delectation offered to the 'good' and the 'righteous' on the Day of Judgement – of seeing the wicked roasting and writhing and agonizing in Hell. As none other than Thomas Aquinas, that compendium of medieval Christian wisdom, had proclaimed in his *Summa Theologiae* – 1,000 years after Tertullian (160–220 AD), St Augustine's predecessor as the most influential theologian since St Paul, had described these infernal 'delights' in *De Spectaculis*. To say nothing of what the early Christians had been promised in the Book of Revelation – a 'book of hatred' which, Nietzsche added, in keeping with the 'deep consistency of the Christian instinct', had been attributed to John, the disciple of infinite love.

Yes, Nietzsche went on, there could be no doubt about it. In the millennial struggle between Rome and Judea, Judea had triumphed. Centuries later, at the time of the Renaissance, it looked for a moment as though the miraculous had occurred and that the old Roman virtues were about to be resurrected. But once again Judea triumphed – thanks to that fundamentally vulgar, plebeian (*pöbelhaften*) German and English movement of *ressentiment* known as the 'Reformation'. This, however, was merely a foretaste of what was to come. For, as Nietzsche concluded, Judea triumphed yet again, and in a deeper and more decisive sense, with the French Revolution:

> The last form of political gentility [*Vornehmheit*] in Europe, that of the seventeenth and eighteenth *French* centuries, collapsed under the weight of the folk-insincts of *ressentiment* – never before had greater jubilation, had more clamorous enthusiasm been heard on earth! To be sure, in the middle of it all something tremendous, something totally unexpected occurred: the antique ideal stepped forward *incarnate* and with unheard-of splendour before the eyes and conscience of mankind – and once again, more strongly, simply, insistently than ever, there resounded, over and against the old mendacious resentment-slogan of *the supreme rights of the majority*, and in opposition to the desire to lower, to debase, to level, to hasten the twilight of humanity, the terrible and enchanting counter-slogan of the *supreme rights of the fewest*! Like a last signpost indicating *another* road, there appeared Napoleon, the most singular and late-born man there ever was, and in him the *noble ideal in itself* became a flesh-and-blood problem – just think what a problem it is: Napoleon, this synthesis of *inhuman monster* and *superhuman man* [*Unmensch und Übermensch*].

In the second essay Nietzsche set out to do what Paul Rée had failed to achieve with a short book published in 1885: provide a rational explanation for the historical origins of two related sentiments – the sense of 'guilt' and that of 'bad conscience' – which had played such a paramount role in the development of modern man. This anthropological explanation for such deeply rooted sentiments was totally at variance with the prevailing belief, popularized by Christianity, that human beings, from the time of the Creation on, were all born with an innate 'conscience' and instinctive notion of 'good' and 'bad'. If Nietzsche's reasoning at times was fuzzy and speculative, it was because he was exploring a *terra incognita*;

for in 1887 the twin 'sciences' of anthropology and ethnology (devoted to the serious study of aboriginal and 'primitive' societies) were not yet born. Pioneers like Franz Boas, James Fraser, Bronislaw Malinowski, Margaret Mead and Ruth Benedict, to name but those, all belong to the twentieth century; and what Kant had written under the heading of 'Anthropology' was no more than random observations culled from books about human beings and forms of behaviour in various climes and countries.

Nietzsche's 'prehistorical' investigation was greatly influenced by the German word for 'guilt' (*Schuld*), which also means 'debt'. One of his theses – for as usual there were many separate strands, tied into a bundle – was that the notion of 'guilt' in primitive societies was intimately associated with the notion of indebtedness, not only towards human 'creditors' but also towards one's ancestors and gods.

Let us, for the sake of brevity, concentrate on this single strand of thought, arbitrarily disregarding the many interesting things Nietzsche had to say on the nature, necessity, efficacy and ineffectiveness of punishment, and not least of all self-punishment (essential to the development of culture – a fascinating anticipation of Freud's famous essay on *Civilization and its Discontents*). In primitive societies punishment was not meted out to the committer of a crime because he was deemed 'guilty'; it was meted out instinctively, much as an angry parent slaps a child. The wrong committed was thus righted. The notion of 'personal responsibility' – meaning that the wrong-doer was 'free' and could have acted differently – appeared fairly late in the development of primitive societies (section 4). Punishment for failure to pay debts was dire. The creditor (a power-wielder) could seize a debtor's belongings, his wife, and even exact the amputation of certain parts of his body as 'payment'. Roman law made a great advance when it limited such abuses, watering down the punishment to make it more symbolic than real (5). The 'guilty one' had to be made to suffer in order to please the offended party. This association of *guilt* and *suffering* seems to have been a feature common to most primitive societies, attesting a deep-seated enjoyment of cruelty in human beings (6 and 7). As communities grew more secure, the collective wrath against malefactors became attenuated. Out of this there grew a system of 'justice' and a penal system based on *compositio* – the settlement of grievances between the offended party and the 'offender'. The 'creditor' became more humane; being richer, he could afford to be more lenient and ready to 'forgive'. In its loftiest form this process of 'self-uplifting' assumed the lovely name of 'grace' (*Gnade*) or mercy. This was the 'privilege of the mightiest, even better, his "beyond the law"' (10). Eugen Dühring's contention that the roots of Justice are to be found in reactive feelings of revenge was pernicious nonsense. Vengeance is a personal sentiment, whereas Justice is necessarily collective. Its supreme expression is the Law, which prescribes what is permitted or forbidden as a general rule, valid for all (11).

In primeval times all tribal communities tended to revere their ancestors and in particular the 'founders' of their tribe. They felt that they owed them a debt of thanks for having displayed the heroism and tenacity needed to survive (section 13). These debts were settled through various sacrifices: offerings of food, the slaughtering of animals, even human sacrifices. As the tribe grew stronger, so did the stature of the legendary 'founders', whose prestige kept growing until they became colossal figures, demigods, and finally gods. Along with basic concepts such as 'good' and 'bad', which were imposed on them by the master-caste of 'rulers', the great majority of subjects inherited this sense of indebtedness to certain deities and, finally, after the establishment of universal empires (like those of Alexander the Great and Julius Caesar) to a single, autocratic God. Applying psychological insight to several millennia of human history (in section 21), Nietzsche argued that the consciousness of a 'debt' to be paid, of a 'duty' to be performed, inextricably intertwined with a feeling of 'bad conscience', had grown and spread inside Man like a malignant polyp, finally culminating in the notion of a 'debt' so huge that it could never be repaid, of a 'guilt' so profound that it could not promptly be expiated and discharged. Man, symbolically represented by Adam, was thus burdened with the curse of 'original sin'. Nature itself became tainted and diabolized, human existence came to be regarded as something worthless, from which one should above all seek escape (as in Buddhism). Thus far this process of malediction had only concerned the 'debtor'. But then Christianity, through a 'stroke of genius', offered a tormented humanity temporary relief by extending the 'debt-awareness' process to the 'creditor' – by imagining 'God sacrificing himself for the guilt of mankind, God having payment made to himself, God as the only one who can redeem man for what has become irredeemable for man himself – the creditor sacrificing himself for his debtor, out of love (can one believe it?), out of love for his debtor!'

Nietzsche by this time was back on his warhorse and not prepared to relent until he had transfixed and speared the writhing dragon of Christianity (an unparalleled 'madness of the will in psychic cruelty', etc.). It only remained for him to deliver the *coup de grâce* by holding up a different model of religious thought and behaviour: that of the ancient Greeks, whose Olympian gods were mirror-images of 'nobler and more high-handed men', in which 'the animal in man felt itself to be deified and did not lacerate itself, did not rage against itself'. In *Human, All Too Human* Nietzsche had already declared that the notion of 'sin' was a pernicious invention of semitic thought. Now he claimed that the ancient, 'lion-hearted' Greeks had kept this inhibiting, tormenting, joy-destroying notion of 'bad conscience' at arm's length by having their gods regard the misdeeds of mortals not as 'sinful' but as acts of foolishness, of momentary 'disturbances of the mind'. In this way the ancient Greek gods had helped to exonerate the misdeeds of human beings, being themselves the causes of evil and thereby assuming responsibility not for the punishment but – something far nobler and more distinguished – for the guilt.

Exactly when 'modern man' would finally put an end to this 'conscience-vivisection', to this self-inflicted 'cruelty to human animals', Nietzsche could not say. But in the culminating section (24), which rose to a Zarathustran crescendo, he expressed his sublime conviction that one day a new saviour, a '*redeeming* man of great love and scorn', would surely appear to deliver mankind from 'the great disgust, the will to nothingness, nihilism'; and at the 'bell-stroke of midday and the great decision' he would 'restore its goal to the earth and hope to Man, this anti-Christian and anti-nihilist, this victor over God and nothingness' – yes, '*he must one day come*'.

## CHAPTER 36

# The Marvels of Turin

*– Wagner is bad for youths;*
*he is calamitous for women.*

In early September Nietzsche was granted a treat as rare as the one that Heinrich von Stein had offered him in 1884 – when his old Pforta friend Paul Deussen turned up at Sils-Maria, accompanied by a 'small wife', with whom he was going to travel on to Greece, the Aegean islands and Turkey. Close to thirteen years had passed since the two philologists had last seen each other in Basel, and what a difference that interval of time had effected in their respective careers! While one of them (Fritz) had become an anti-Schopenhauer iconoclast, the other (Paul) had become a renowned Sanskrit scholar and the first Schopenhauerian to be appointed to a professorial chair in philosophy – at the University of Berlin.

For Nietzsche it was a joy to take his visitors on a guided tour of his favourite Alpine spots. But Deussen could not help noticing how much his friend had changed. Gone was the 'proud posture, the elastic gait and the fluent speech of yore'. With one shoulder slightly lower than the other, Nietzsche seemed to have trouble 'dragging himself along' and finding the proper words for what he wanted to say. This may not have been one of his 'good days', for at one point he waved at some passing clouds and said, 'I must have blue sky overhead to be able to collect my thoughts.' What most distressed Deussen, however, was the visit he was allowed to make to Nietzsche's 'den', which he found in a state of deplorable disorder – with eggshells and a coffee-cup next to toilet articles and manuscript pages, loosely scattered over the rustic table and, beyond an upright boot-jack, over the sheets of an unmade bed.

When the time came to say goodbye, a grateful Nietzsche insisted on accompanying Deussen and his wife all the way to the Maloja post-chaise station; and when they embraced, his old friend Paul, who had never imagined that such a thing could happen, was surprised to see tears in Fritz's eyes.

On 20 September, after hastily adding a fascinating third essay (on various forms of 'ascetic idealism' and how they had helped or hindered artists to create and philosophers to overcome the suicidal despair of nihilism) and sending the amplified text of *The Genealogy of Morals* to Naumann in Leipzig, Nietzsche left the chilly highlands of the Upper Engadine and descended via the familiar route and railway stations of

Chiavenna and Como to sea-borne Venice. Despite an electrifying thunderstorm over Lake Como, the trip was relatively painless, while the Adriatic air of Venice seemed to him on arrival of an 'elastic limpidity'. He found his favourite *maestro* (Heinrich Köselitz, alias 'Pietro Gasti') luxuriously lodged, fed and cared for by a noble Venetian family, and so completely recovered from his previous morosity that he was delighted to help Nietzsche correct the proofs of his new book.

Nightmarish, in comparison, was the next train-trip (from Venice to Nice) – brutally interrupted by a breakdown in a dark tunnel between Milan and Genoa, which unleashed violent headaches. But these were soon dispelled by the 'intoxicating' air of Nice and the warm welcome he received at the Pension de Genève. For a special price of 5½ francs per day (2½ francs less than the cheapest rate for others) he was given a north-facing room where it was often so cold that Nietzsche suffered 'blue fingers' in the morning. Heeding his mother's sensible advice, he finally hired a small stove: or what (in a letter to Köselitz) he called a 'fire-idol' and around which, once lit, he 'leaped and pranced' in a dance of pagan jubilation.

On 14 November Nietzsche wrote to Jacob Burckhardt, asking to be forgiven for sending him a gift copy of one more book (*The Genealogy of Morals*), filled with 'nut-cracking' problems on which he might break his teeth. He did so, however, out of deep veneration, since he regarded him, along with Hippolyte Taine, as one of his 'only two readers'. Had this letter been written two weeks later, Nietzsche could have raised the figure of his 'real' readers from two to three. For before the month of November was over he received a moving letter of thanks – for gift copies of *The Genealogy of Morals* and *Beyond Good and Evil* – from Georg Brandes, a Danish literary critic who had made a name for himself in northern Europe as the author of a many-volumed study of the nineteenth century's principal literary trends. With a beguiling candour which made it clear that he had read Nietzsche's two latest books, as well as *Human, All Too Human*, without recoiling in horror, Brandes declared that he had found in the books 'the breath of a new and original spirit. I do not yet fully understand what I have read; I do not always know towards what issue you are headed. But there is much that accords with my own thoughts and sympathies – the contempt for ascetic ideals and the deep indignation against democratic mediocrity, your aristocratic radicalism. Your scorn for the morality of compassion is something I have not yet been able to fathom. In the other book [*Beyond Good and Evil*] there were reflections on women in general which do not concord with my personal ways of thought. You are so completely differently constituted from myself that I find it difficult to share your feelings. Despite the universality in your mode of thinking and writing you are very German. You belong to the few people with whom I would like to talk.' To which he added, about himself,'Though no longer young, I am still one of the most eager-to-learn and inquisitive of men. You will therefore not find me closed to your thoughts, even when I think and feel differently. I am often stupid, but never in the least narrow-minded.'

It is easy to imagine the thrill with which Nietzsche read and reread this extraordinary letter. Here, clearly, was an authentic *Freigeist* who was not afraid to speak his mind, to praise and to avow perplexity, and who, in just two words – *aristocratic radicalism* – had grasped the very essence of his philosophy. Fate, which had treated him so harshly, was now at last beginning to relent, confirming what he had long suspected: that, in accordance with the adage – 'a prophet is not without honour save in his own country' – the recognition he so desperately craved would come to him first of all from non-Germans. As had happened with Jacob Burckhardt, who was Swiss; with Hippolyte Taine, who was French; and now with Georg Brandes, 'the intellectually most brilliant Dane there now is, i.e. Jewish' – as Nietzsche later described him to Heinrich Köselitz.

In his long reply, written on 2 December, Nietzsche thanked Brandes for having joined the select circle of his admirers. His expression – 'aristocratic radicalism' – was the 'cleverest word' he had read about himself. 'Just how far this mode of thought has brought me, how far it will still carry me – I almost dread to imagine. But there are paths that do not allow one to turn back; and so I go forward, because forward *I must.*'

Thus began a fascinating exchange of letters, which was more mutually enriching for both correspondents than any Nietzsche had so far maintained with any of his friends. Ernst Wilhelm Fritzsch was asked to send the latest editions of all the earlier works (with their new prefaces) to Brandes; and, as a supreme token of his trust, Nietzsche had Köselitz take a copy of *Zarathustra* IV from the secret stock he kept in Venice and send it to Copenhagen.

The four months Nietzsche spent in Nice, from early December of 1887 to the end of March 1888, were the happiest he had yet known at the Pension de Genève. For the first time in eight successive winters he was spared the 'blue-fingered' torments of early morning frosts, thanks to the crackling benevolence of his 'fire-idol' stove. There was also a notable improvement in the quality of the food he was offered in the *pension*'s dining-room, where his most stimulating conversational partner was a Baroness Plänckner. Related to a court chamberlain serving with the Crown Princess Victoria, she kept Nietzsche well informed of the frail health of imperial Germany's greatest political hope for the future: the anti-Bismarckian Crown Prince Friedrich, who spent this winter at nearby San Remo, trying to recover from a throat-cancer operation.

Thanks to a strict diet – no wine, no beer, no alcoholic spirits, no coffee – thanks to long walks (one hour in the morning, three in the afternoon), and thanks to many bright, cloudless days, Nietzsche's physical sufferings (with headaches and fits of vomiting) were relatively mild. But, as he confessed to his mother in mid-February, spiritually he was a 'brave' but also 'sick animal', apt to display a 'ridiculous and wretched vulnerability' to shamelessly superficial reviews of his books. Equally upsetting was the 'unbearable tension' from which he suffered 'night and day, brought about by the *task* that lies upon me and the absolute ill-will of all my previous acquaintances towards the solution of such a task'.

The daunting task Nietzsche had imposed on himself was nothing less than the completion of a four-volume work intended to supply the crowning arch or dome to the philosophical 'temple of the future' he wanted to erect, of which (as he had once written to Malwida von Meysenbug) the *Zarathustra* 'trilogy' was merely an ornamental 'entrance-hall'. This new series, as later planned, was to appear under the overall title, 'The Will to Power' (*Wille zur Macht*) – with, as a subtitle, *An Attempt at a Revaluation of all Values*. Each volume was to consist of three parts, thus resembling *The Genealogy of Morals*. In the first, entitled 'What is Truth?', Nietzsche proposed to analyse the 'psychology of error', to judge the relative worth of 'truth' and 'error', and finally to demonstrate how the 'will to truth', when properly understood, helped to justify the positive 'yes-value of Life'. In the second book, devoted to 'The Origin of Values', he proposed to deal, more thoroughly than ever before, with 1) his old enemies, the 'metaphysicians', 2) the '*homines religiosi*' (by which Nietzsche meant persons who are genuinely religious and not merely robed or bearded 'dispensers of the faith'), and 3) 'The Good Ones and the Improvers' – a diatribe against Christian optimists naïvely bent on improving a 'wicked' world. (A fragment of his thinking on this question was later incorporated into *Götzen-Dämmerung – Twilight of the Idols*). The third book, aggressively titled 'The Battle of Values', would begin with 'Thoughts on Christianity' (later developed by Nietzsche in *The Anti-Christian*); would continue with a study of the 'physiology of Art' (i.e. an analysis of 'healthy', as opposed to 'sickly' art); and would be rounded out with a 'History of European Nihilism'. The series would then rise to a majestic climax with a final volume ('The Great Midday'), the first part of which hammered home the unpalatable truth that every genuine culture and civilization depends on an accepted *Rangordnung* (Order of Rank) between power-wielders and subjects. The second chapter would describe the two 'ways' or 'paths' (i.e. upwards or downwards) human beings could choose to follow in life. Then, in the third and culminating chapter, Nietzsche would elucidate what he had all too allusively suggested in *Zarathustra* III, with his mystical concept of 'eternal recurrence'.

Even for a philosophical *alpiniste* like Nietzsche, this was quite a programme. No wonder there were times when he felt that such a project would require five, six or more years of preparation! A 'History of European Nihilism' – more or less the theme that Albert Camus later tackled in *L'Homme révolté*, – was all by itself an enormous mountain, requiring a great deal of homework and reading – oh, his poor eyes! – which a sociologically ill-informed Nietzsche had yet to accomplish. Indeed, in a letter written shortly before Christmas of 1887, Georg Brandes had gently chided Nietzsche for his 'irate' snap judgements on complex social phenomena such as socialism and anarchism. 'The anarchism of Prince Krapotkin,' he pointed out, 'is not stupid. Even the name does not really fit. Your intelligence, which as a rule is so dazzling, here seems to me to fall a bit short, where the truth lies in the nuance.'

Throughout the cold but sunny winter weeks Nietzsche wrestled with his self-imposed 'task', torn between an impatient desire to 'get on with the job' and a monitory feeling that, in trying to go too fast, he would undermine the solidity of what he was trying to build. So disturbing were these contradictory forces that he kept altering the initial outline of March 1887. He even decided to scrap the overall title, *Der Wille zur Macht* (*The Will to Power*), realizing that in the super-patriotic climate of the Second *Reich*, with its intoxicating '*Deutschland! Deutschland über Alles!*' rhetoric, his four-volume magnum opus would be misinterpreted as a philosophical endorsement of Bismarck's *Blut und Eisen* (blood and iron) policies. Finally, on 13 February 1888, at the end of a long letter to Heinrich Köselitz, he added, almost as an afterthought: 'I have readied the first draft of my "Attempt at a Revaluation": it was, all in all, sheer torture, also I definitely don't yet have the courage for it. Ten years later I will do it better.'

In March, as the warm sunshine of Provence grew steadily brighter and more painful for his eyes, a worried Nietzsche again began casting around for an 'ideal' place to spend the springtime months of April, May and early June. Zürich, despite the friendships he had made there, had turned out to have a climate that was as unpleasantly sultry as that of Basel. The Italian lakes he had found too windless. Venice, though ideal in many ways, offered insufficient space for long, bracing walks. Did Köselitz, to whom he wrote on 21 March, know of any other spot that offered a solution to this annual springtime dilemma, which was beginning to cost him sleepless nights?

Replying on the 30th, Köselitz suggested that Nietzsche try Turin, which, even in summer, enjoyed refreshingly cool nights. It might provide a good 'intermediate station' between hot seaside Nizza and the cool highlands of the Engadine. Without wasting a moment, Nietzsche decided to follow this advice. The guidebooks assured him that Turin was a clean, quiet city, beautifully laid out and offering its inhabitants long, well-shaded walks. Moreover, it was fairly easy of access; for if one boarded the 6 a.m. train for Genoa, one could be in Turin by 6.30 that evening.

Early on Easter Monday (2 April) he set out on what he fancied would be a relatively short train-trip. Instead, it turned out to be the most confused and catastrophic of any he had so far undertaken. At Genoa he had to change to another train. Just what happened next is not clear. Probably aided by a porter, he had his hand luggage stowed away in a compartment and then wandered off, perhaps in search of refreshment. Returning, he absentmindedly climbed into the wrong train and soon found himself headed in the wrong direction towards the town of Sampiedarena, not far from Genoa. This mishap so unnerved him that he suffered a breakdown and had to spend the next two days in a hotel bedroom, while telegrams were dispatched to various points asking the stationmaster to recover the wayward bags. Fortunately the heavy trunk, stuffed as usual with many books, had been registered in Nice and made it safely to its destination, where it was patiently waiting to be reclaimed by its owner when, utterly exhausted and feeling stupid, the 'half-blind' professor finally reached Turin, the proud capital of the kings of Sardinia, Piedmont and Savoy who had contributed so much to the *Risorgimento* and the recent unification of Italy.

It was three more days before Nietzsche was sufficiently recovered from these nerve-racking upsets to be able to write a long letter of thanks to Heinrich Köselitz in Venice. And in what glowing terms! 'But *Turin*!' he began ecstatically. 'Dear Friend, may you be congratulated! Your guess is after my own heart. This is really and truly a city I can *now* use!' – even though he had been greeted on his arrival by intermittent showers of icy rain. 'But what a dignified and serious city! Not at all a huge city, not at all modern, as I had feared . . . ' Instead, a princely residence dating from the seventeenth century. Here 'aristocratic *tranquillity*' had been preserved in everything. There were no squalid suburbs. Instead, he had found an admirable 'unity of taste, even extending to colour (the entire city is yellow, or reddish-brown). And for feet, as well as for eyes a classic spot! What security, what pavements, to say nothing of the omnibuses and the trams, whose installation here verges on the miraculous!'

And on it went . . . Here he had been treated with the most extraordinary respect and officially registered as an '*ufficiale tedesco*' (German official), whereas in Nice he had merely been entered in the foreigners' registry as a '*Polonais*'. And then what grave and ceremonious squares! And a palace style totally lacking in pretension! The lovelist cafés he had ever seen! Not to mention the grandiose arcades, so badly needed for pedestrians in such a variable climate – 'only they are spacious, they are not oppressive. And the evenings on the *bridge over the Po*: Magnificent! Beyond Good and Evil!!'

Not far from the Royal Castle, on the Piazza Carlo Alberto (named after the father of the present King of Italy) Nietzsche found what he wanted – in a corner house belonging to a newspaper and bookstall vendor named Davide Fino, who was also the superintendent of the public writing-room. The fourth-storey room he was offered – in a house that boasted a piano! – was small but so well situated that from its tiny balcony Nietzsche could see the green hills of *la collina* to the south-east, and, on clear days, the Alps to the north-west. All for a moderate price of 25 francs per month: which, as he wrote to Franz Overbeck on 10 April, enabled him to eat his main meal – usually a *minestra* (soup) with a meat course – in an elegant restaurant.

Here, even more than in Nice, he felt that he had found another home, where the dry Alpine air was so 'sublimely clear' that the entire city seemed to shine with extraordinary effulgence. A few paces from his front door, as he wrote enthusiastically to Resa von Schirnhofer, was the grandiose Palazzo Carignano, in which the present King of Italy (Vittorio Emmanuele II) had been born! Farther on, beyond a café, where in the evening he could savour a delicious *gelato*, was the Carignano Theatre, which was now offering its opera-loving audiences 'a most respectable *Carmen*'. But what most amazed the newcomer was the multitude of arcades and vaulted passageways, far more extensive than those of the Piazza San Marco in Venice, where he could walk for hours, well protected from the sunlight or, in wet weather, without being touched by a drop of rain.

This fortuitous change of habitat galvanized Nietzsche's creative energies, which in Nice had begun to flag. So too did his exchange of letters with Georg Brandes, who was so impressed by his perusal of Nietzsche's books that he had decided to deliver a series of lectures about them to the professors and students of Copenhagen University. Astonished that a non-German should wish to honour a '*vir obscurissimus*' like himself, Nietzsche wrote Brandes a long letter of appreciation, accompanied by a biographical summary of his life and works, in which he stressed the 'indescribably close intimacy with Richard and Cosima

Wagner' and the 'boundless trust' that had existed between them during the years spent at Tribschen, near Lucerne.

This nostalgic reminiscence, added to a fascinating discussion of the conflicting opera styles of the Italian *opera buffa* 'comedies' of Niccolò Piccinni and the more rigorously theatrical 'French style' of Gluck, which he had been carrying on with Köselitz, now prompted Nietzsche to push aside the formidable problems confronting his attempted 'revaluation of all values' and to compose something in a lighter, gayer, less 'raven-black' vein. If only as a kind of intermezzo. This, after all, was what Wagner had done when, interrupting his laborious work on the monumental *Ring* series, he had composed Germany's first great comic opera, *Die Meistersinger.*

'I am in a good mood, working from early morning to evening,' Nietzsche wrote on 20 April in another letter to Köselitz, as full as ever of rhapsodic praise for this 'capital discovery' (Turin), where booksellers peddled books in three languages, and where, in an excellent *trattoria*, for 1 franc and 25 centimes (half the price he had to pay at Sils-Maria) he was offered a tasty meal of risotto, a sizeable roast, vegetables and bread. Turin, moreover, was nothing less than a '*Musik-Ort*' (music-spot), boasting twelve theatres, an *accademia philharmonica*, a Lyceum for Music, twenty-one officially registered composers, and a multitude of teachers for different instruments. Yes, he continued, 'a small pamphlet on music keeps my fingers busy, I digest like a demigod despite the fact that at night the carriages rattle past: all of them indications of Nietzsche's eminent adaptation to Torino'.

Ten days later, in one more rhapsodic letter to Köselitz – this time praising the Café Nazionale, where for 20 centimes for a cup of coffee, 30 centimes for a hot chocolate or ice cream, one could listen to a concert played by an excellent small orchestra – Nietzsche wrote that he had worked non-stop, achieving more in a couple of weeks than during his entire winter in Nice. In this 'captivating, light, carefree' air even the 'dullest thoughts' developed wings. The proof? Despite the insidious temptation, he had not gone to see *Carmen* performed and had spent only one evening at the theatre!

While the fresh Alpine air had a lot to do with this industry, no less stimulating was the news from Copenhagen, where Brandes reported that his lectures on Nietzsche and his works were filling a packed auditorium of 300 listeners. '*Sic incipit gloria mundi*' – was Nietzsche's ironic comment on a postcard which transmitted the good news to Paul Deussen in Berlin.

To Brandes himself he wrote that it had been years since he had known such fruitful weeks, fired by an energy which, for an hour or two each day, enabled him to contemplate from above the 'monstrous' multitude of problems confronting him. Such was his good mood that he had been amusing himself hanging a 'tiny tail of buffoonery to the most serious things. Whence comes all this? Is it not to the good *north-winds* I owe this, the north-winds which do not always come from the Alps – for occasionally they also come from *Copenhagen*!'

By early June even the fresh air of the Alps could no longer keep the temperature from rising to a hot 31°C. It was time to leave for the cool highlands of the Engadine. After saying goodbye to the *molto simpatico* Davide Fino, to his wife and two daughters (with the younger of whom he liked to play four-handed compositions on the downstairs piano), Nietzsche boarded the train, which, thanks to a new rail connection, could now take him more directly via Como to Chiavenna.

After crossing the Maloja Pass he was confronted by an extraordinary spectacle. His beloved valley seemed to be steaming, as a wave of hot air melted unprecedented heaps of snow, in some places six feet high, which had accumulated during the preceding weeks. At Sils-Maria, where once again he was the first foreign visitor to arrive, the landlord-grocer, Herr Durisch, told him that they had suffered twenty-six avalanches, which had wreaked havoc on the pine and larch forests, felling many trees.

The unusually hot and sultry weather was so upsetting that not until 10 June, four days after his arrival, could Nietzsche muster the strength to write a letter to his mother, to thank her for the ham she had so thoughtfully sent to him from Naumburg. More than ever he was shocked by the 'sky-high' prices of the Upper Engadine – even at the modest Hôtel Alpenrose they were now charging 2 francs 25 centimes – twice what he had had to pay in Turin – for the simplest midday meal.

On 14 June he wrote to Heinrich Köselitz in Venice, to say that since yesterday the skies had cleared and his lovely valley had regained all its diverse colours, making it a *perla perlissima* of beauty. But hardly had he posted this long letter than the clouds again gathered, and it began to snow, and then to rain – this time so uninterruptedly that there was no let-up in the wet weather before the middle of July. But for the 'good work' he had accomplished during the eight wonderful weeks in Turin, Nietzsche could never have sent Constantin Naumann the manuscript of his new book on 26 June. As it was, the text was so disorderly that his publisher did not know what to do with it. On 12 July Nietzsche asked him to send back the manuscript. For five weeks, he explained, he had been suffering from nevous exhaustion, constant headaches and fits of vomiting, brought on by 'the *abominable* weather', which had so affected his handwriting that he too could not decipher it. Once he had recovered his strength, he promised to rewrite the entire text 'with the greatest possible clarity'.

That same night the temperature dropped below zero. This sudden, midsummer touch of frost, bringing with it several star-filled nights and bright, sun-warmed days, galvanized him once again. Four days later he was able to send the rewritten text back to Naumann in Leipzig – with the usual request: that, once typeset, the manuscript be sent, along with a set of proofs, to Heinrich Köselitz who, having recently left Venice, had returned to his father's home near Dresden.

The next day, 17 July, after surviving one more dreadful storm, he was at last able to let the black cat out of his magician's bag. The 'small pamphlet' he had begun writing in Turin was, he informed Köselitz, to carry the title: *Der Fall Wagner: Ein Musikanten-Problem* (The Case of Wagner: A Musicians' Problem). 'It is something jolly, with a foundation of almost too much seriousness,' Nietzsche explained.

Köselitz's response was uncritically ecstatic – thus reassuring a nervous Nietzsche that he had not overstepped the bounds of propriety. 'Only though your eyes,' he wrote back on 31 July, 'could the realities and idealities of Wagner be viewed in such a striking fashion, only from your heights can this refreshing, cleansing gale blow.' Only Nietzsche could 'with a flaming sword interrupt the daily increasing "stupidification"' (*Verdummung*) wrought by Wagner's admirers. But after this heroic flourish, Nietzsche's most faithful disciple had to conclude, somewhat sheepishly: 'Even you will hardly be able to hold back the torrent of nonsense; but one day one will at least know that the preacher of the right road [to be followed] was there and remained unnoticed.'

## CHAPTER 37

# The 'Cave-bear' of Sils-Maria

*– When trodden on, the worm curls up. That is wise. It thereby reduces the likelihood of being trodden on again. In the language of morals: humility.*

During the second week of August the skies cleared and for the first time in months of wintry weather, marked by rain, wind and snow, the village of Sils-Maria at last enjoyed a tardy summer. Nietzsche could return the two extra blankets that Frau Durisch, the grocer's wife, had kindly lent him to keep the 'Herr Professor' from freezing during the chilling nights, and it was in a joyous 'summer mood', as he wrote to his mother, that he was now enjoying 'the most beautiful colours I have ever seen here' – offered in profusion by soft, snow-powdered mountains, dark green firs and larches, silvery lake waters veering in hue from emerald green and turquoise to sombre black and (at sunrise and sunset) rose, scarlet red and crimson, under a sky that was 'completely pure as in Nice'. Meta von Salis chose this auspicious moment to leave the family castle at Chur and to spend two weeks at Sils-Maria, where the thirty-three-year-old 'Fräulein Doktor' – the first woman ever to obtain a degree from Zürich University – accompanied the forty-three-year-old 'cave-bear' on long walks, and even volunteered to row her curious mentor to a tiny, insect-rich island near the Chasté peninsula, on the Silser lake.

After ten days of fine weather the rains returned and, as Nietzsche wrote to the blue-eyed Meta not long after her departure, the Hôtel Alpenrose had already lost half its clients. Proud though he was of his anti-Wagner 'pamphlet', it had been written almost entirely in Turin, and, compared to what he had achieved at Sils-Maria in 1887, this summer had been a 'washout'. All summer long, when he was not correcting proofs or adding postscripts to *The Case of Wagner*, Nietzsche had been wrestling with a new text, eventually entitled *Der Antichrist* (*The Anti-Christian*), which was intended to be part of the first volume in a collection of four books attacking established values under the overall heading of '*Umwertung aller Werte*' (*Revaluation of all Values*). Its composition proved to be particularly laborious, partly because of the dismal weather, partly because of a feeling that this renewed attack on Christian idealism and hypocrisy – in German *Antichrist* has the double meaning of 'anti-Christian' and 'Antichrist' – might appear vindictive unless it was preceded by an 'intermediary' work attacking a number of conventional notions or shibboleths: everything from the stereotypic view of Socrates as one of the 'pinnacles' of Greek philosophy, to the real nature of what philosophers called 'Reason'.

This new burst of inspiration overpowered Nietzsche during the final week of August, when Sils-Maria was again blessed by blue skies and lovely weather. On 7 September he wrote to Meta von Salis that his earlier report on this 'washout' of a summer had been overly pessimistic. For some days now, 'driven by the spirit' (of inspiration), he had been getting up at two o'clock in the morning to jot down the thoughts that kept racing through his head. Often he would hear Herr Durisch, his landlord-grocer, stealthily unbolt and then relock the front door as, armed with a hunting rifle, he set out to see if he could bag himself a chamois. Unforgettable in particular had been 3 September, when he had sat down to write the Preface to his *Revaluation of all Values*. 'I then went out – and behold! the most beautiful day I have seen in the Engadine, blue in lake and sky, a clarity of air, absolutely unprecedented.'

That same day he informed his Leipzig publisher, Naumann, that he had a surprise in store for him: 'far and away the cleanest' manuscript he had yet sent him, entitled *Müssiggang eines Psychologen* (*The Leisure Idleness of a Psychologist*). He wanted to have him bring out the new work – a worthy 'twin' to the 'rollicking farce against Wagner' – as quickly as possible; for it would look ridiculous to have something as 'cheerful' and 'charming' published after the grim seriousness of his next major work (*The Revaluation of all Values*), which he was planning for the next year (1889).

Constantin Naumann's heart-warming response to this unforeseen 'surprise' arrived in a parcel containing ten printed copies of *Der Fall Wagner* (*The Case of Wagner*), which he asked Nietzsche not to start sending out to friends before 22 September, to give him time to arrange for an orderly distribution to booksellers and to carefully selected newspapers and periodicals. The 'piquant' title, advertised in the booksellers' bulletin, had aroused such unusual curiosity that the first edition (with a print order of 1,000 copies) would already be exhausted if he chose to satisfy all of the incoming requests.

By the time this good news reached Sils-Maria the clear blue skies had disappeared, beclouded by drenching downpours of raindrops mixed with sleet. 'In 4 days alone 220 millimetres have fallen (whereas the monthly average here is usually 80 mm),' Nietzsche wrote to Köselitz on 12 September. The lakes, he reported on a postcard to Meta von Salis, had overflowed, almost inundating the highway from Silvaplana to Maloja. The Chasté, peninsula – that magic spot on Lake Sils on which he had fondly hoped to build a 'hermit's hut', the 'meeting-place of Italy and Finland' and of every imaginable tone of silver – was now 'an *entire* island'. The grassy Samaden valley had disappeared beneath a third, smaller lake. Worst of all, the torrential waters roaring down the gorges of the Mera river had flooded the flatlands beyond Chiavenna, interrupting railway traffic to Colico, on Lake Como. Once again Nietzsche found himself the 'victim' of his 'enemies', the clouds.

Momentarily immobilized, he used his final days in the muddy village of water-surrounded Sils-Maria – soon dried out by a reappearing sun – to write letters to various friends and relatives, announcing the publication of his 'musically problematic' anti-Wagner 'pamphlet' and the completion of a new book of philosophico-psychological meditations. To his influential Danish champion, Georg Brandes, who had shamefacedly admitted that he was not musically talented, he wrote on 13 September to reassure him that, as a 'Herr Cosmopoliticus', he was 'much too European-minded not to *hear* one hundred times more' what *The Case of Wagner* had to say 'than my so-called compatriots, the "musical" Germans'. He announced the forthcoming publication of yet another book, entitled *The Leisure Idleness of a Psychologist*, candidly admitting that both were simply 'relaxations', and thus implicitly a momentary retreat from the formidable challenge posed by his essential objective, the *Revaluation of all Values*, which was certain to create an unprecedented uproar. ('Europe will have to invent a new Siberia to which to send the originator of this assassination-attempt on values.')

With Jacob Burckhardt, who had been so dismayed by the *Zarathustra* extravaganza, Nietzsche was more circumspect. He made no mention of his long-range plan to open fire on all established canons of morality, but he was more explicit in explaining why he had a 'right' and perhaps even a 'duty' to speak out clearly on the subject of Wagnerism. 'The movement is now more than ever haloed in the aureole of sanctity. Three-quarters of all musicians are half or fully persuaded, theatres from St Petersburg to Paris, from Bologna to Montevideo now live off this art, recently too the young German Kaiser [Wilhelm II] designated the whole matter as a national affair of the *first rank* and placed himself at the head of it: reason enough for one to be *allowed* to step out into the arena . . . '

To the jocose Reinhart von Seydlitz, Nietzsche wrote in a less solemn vein to say that the entire summer had been a meteorological 'scandal'. The little church of Sils-Maria had acquired a new set of bells, an enterprising angler had hauled a monstrous 30 lb trout from a nearby lake, and a Herr Baedeker from Leipzig had (along with his wife) honoured the Hôtel Alpenrose with his summer-long, three-star presence. He could not, alas, come to Munich, but his friend would soon be receiving a gift copy of *The Case of Wagner – A Problem for Musicians*, more or less complementing what another 'back-stager', Hans von Bülow, was bringing out on the same subject. Paul Deussen – who, to Nietzsche's grateful stupefaction, had recently persuaded a number of Berlin friends to make a joint donation of 2,000 marks to cover the publishing costs of future books – was informed that he too would soon receive a copy of the anti-Wagner 'pamphlet'. It would be followed by a 'very strong and subtle expression of my entire *philosophical heterodoxy*:' these two works being gentle preliminaries to the 'immeasurably difficult and decisive task which, *if it is understood*, will split the history of mankind into two halves'. A piece of neo-prophetic bombast which his old Pforta schoolmate probably shrugged off with a smile. The level of *tolerance*, Nietzsche went on, was going to be 'downgraded through value-determinations of the first rank to mere cowardice and weakness of character. To be a *Christian* – to name but one consequence – will from then on be *indecent*.' The first book of this new, explosive series *(The Anti-Christian)* was already half finished.

On 20 September Nietzsche was at last able to say goodbye to his friends in Sils-Maria – the sympathetic Herr Durisch and his family, the gruffer manager of the Hôtel Alpenrose, who did not realize that they would never again lay eyes on this hard-working, hard-hiking, often solitary luncher. For the first time in years he did not suffer a nervous seizure during the tiring train-trip, even though, near the flooded town of Como, he had to climb down from the railway carriage and cross a narrow wooden bridge by torchlight before travelling on to Milan, where he spent the night. He reached Turin feeling worn out, but also overjoyed by the warm welcome offered to him by his landlord, Davide Fino, his wife, his son Ernesto and the two daughters. Nothing, to his delight, had changed – neither the crisp, invigorating quality of the air nor the leafy elegance of the tree-lined avenues and river-bank, along which he liked to stride during his daily 'promenade'. The fare in the *trattorias* was as good and inexpensive as ever, and on the nearby *piazza* he could sit outside savouring a delicious *gelato* in front of the tiny theatre, admire the crepuscular silhouette of the medieval *castello*, and watch the 'public' crowd in to listen to Edmond Audran's *La Mascotte* – whose 'pretty, sprightly, tiny melodies' (as he wrote to Köselitz) he found relaxing, compared to the loathsome music of Johann Strauss's *Zigeunerbaron* (*Gypsy Baron*), which combined two execrable characteristics ('the animal and sentimental') of German vulgarity.

Of the score of letters Nietzsche wrote during his last two weeks at Sils-Maria, the most important was the one he sent to Heinrich Köselitz on 12 September, announcing the completion of his manuscript. This new book, he explained, was 'roughly twice as strong' as *The Case of Wagner.* He wanted to have it published now to allow for an interval of time before he brought out the *Umwertung* (*Revaluation* or *Overturning*) series – which was going to be a work of '*rigorous* seriousness and one hundred times removed from [liberal] tolerances and amiabilities'.

This letter did not catch up with Köselitz until the 20th; for in the meantime he had left his parents' home near Dresden to spend a few weeks near the Baltic coast on the estate of a music-loving Pomeranian nobleman whom he had met in Venice. Nietzsche's 'disciple' took immediate exception to the new work's unassuming title, altogether unworthy of an ardent admirer of the great Napoleon: 'You have brought your artillery up on to the highest mountains; have cannon such as have never before been seen, and need only shoot blindly in order to scare the daylights out of the surroundings. The tread of a giant, enough to make the mountains tremble in their depths, is no longer an idle stroll. In our age, moreover, idle leisure usually comes *after* work . . . Oh, I beg you, if an incapable man may beg: a more resplendent, lustrous title!'

Five days after his return to Turin – by which time he was again working at full tempo, simultaneously correcting proofs and continuing his composition of *The Anti-Christian* – Nietzsche sent Köselitz his grateful agreement: the title must be changed. Instead of the tame *Müssiggang eines Psychologen* (*The Leisure Idleness of a Psychologist*), he was choosing *Götzen-Dämmerung* (*Twilight of the Idols*) or 'How one Philosophizes with the Hammer'.

This was the most ingenious title Nietzsche had yet invented for any of his books. It was an 'eyecatcher' in subtly lampooning Wagner's *Götterdämmerung* (*Twilight of the Gods*) while suggesting that this was one more iconoclastic book written by a *Freigeist* whose favourite 'sport' was attacking fashionable 'idols' and shibboleths in every field.

Köselitz was unquestionably right in pleading for a change of title. The added subtitle, however, exceeded his expectations. The 'hammer' image was misleading, even though, in the brief, brilliant Foreword, written on the last day of September, Nietzsche gave the word a musical connotation by comparing it to a 'tuning-fork' used to test the 'off-key' hollowness of the 'idols' he was impenitently attacking. For if *Götzen-Dämmerung* was in places a sarcastic masterpiece, it was because Nietzsche was using a French rapier rather than a Siegfriedian hammer to lunge at everything he most disliked. Astonishing variety as well as incisive brevity marked this new opus, which, to employ a different simile, resembled a five-course meal concocted with the finesse of a first-class Torinese chef.

It began with a first course of forty-four highly spiced *antipasti* (entitled 'Maxims and Arrows'), many of them as pungent as they were provocative. (Examples: 'Idleness is the beginning of all psychology. What? Could psychology be a vice?' 'Can an ass be tragic? – to be crushed to death by a burden one can neither bear nor throw off? . . . The case of the philosopher.') The *antipasti* were followed by several *entrées*: a new attack on Socrates, criticized this time as a typical *décadent* rabble-rouser and buffoon who used the 'offensive' weapon of dialectics to undermine the aristocratic values of ancient Athens, accompanied by another assault on Platonic and other forms of 'idealism', unfavourably compared to Heraclitus's courageous acceptance of a permanently changing world. No less than three *pièces de résistance* were offered to gourmets with a strong stomach for philosophical fundamentals. 'Morality as anti-Nature' was another Nietzschean assault on Christian asceticism and the short-sighted attempt to 'kill the passions', as propounded by the 'holy lunacy' or 'diseased reason' of the priest. 'The Four Great Errors' included the logical error of mistaking the effect for the cause, and the by now familiar condemnation of the doctrine of 'freedom of the will'. In 'The Improvers of Mankind' Nietzsche developed one of the basic theses expounded in *The Genealogy of Morals*, by contrasting the positive 'breeding' of aristocracies to the negative 'taming', 'castration' and emasculation of the strong by insidious 'underdogs'. Example: 'Christianity, growing from Jewish roots and comprehensible only as a product of this soil, represents a *reaction* against the morality of breeding, of race, of privilege – it is the anti-Aryan religion *par excellence*.'

'What the Germans Lack', originally planned as an *entrée*, now became a kind of sauerkraut or coleslaw salad, generously spiced with anti-Teutonic vinegar. Sample: 'Learning to think: our schools no longer have any idea what this means . . . that thinking has to be learned in the way dancing has to be learned, as a form of dancing . . . Who among Germans still knows from experience that subtle thrill which the possession of intellectual light feet communicates to all the muscles! . . . The German has no *fingers* for *nuances* . . .' (etc.).

The dessert course was presented as the hit-and-run 'Excursions of an Untimely Man'. These intellectual 'raids' were among other things Nietzsche's muscular response to Rousseau's arch-romantic *Rêveries du promeneur solitaire*. The diversity of its fifty-one items beggars description. In the very first aphorism, if such it can be called, Nietzsche, whirling the cape of sarcastic derision, delivered a series of deft *estocadas* to his pet dislikes: his 'impossibles: Seneca: or the toreador of virtue. – Rousseau: or the return to nature *in impuris naturalibus* [in natural dirtiness] . . . Dante: or the hyena which *versifies* in graves . . . Victor Hugo: or the Pharos in the sea of absurdity . . . Michelet: or the enthusiasm which strips off its jacket . . . ' And so on. After which, Ernest Renan, the French literary critic Sainte-Beuve, George Eliot, Thomas à Kempis, Thomas Carlyle, George Sand ('this prolific writing cow'), Schopenhauer, Immanuel Kant all received their deserved or undeserved comeuppances – Emerson alone managing to survive upright and erect amid the corpses littering the sand.

From famous persons Nietzsche moved on to popular issues – as in section 34 (Christian and Anarchist):

> Whether one attributes one's feeling vile to others or to *oneself* – the Socialist does the former, the Christian, for example, the latter – makes no essential difference. What is common to both, and *unworthy* in both, is that someone should be to *blame* for the fact that one suffers – in short, that the sufferer prescribes for himself the honey of revenge as a medicine for his suffering . . .

Here is another example, equally pertinent to the grave problems of today. Section 38 (My Conception of Freedom):

> The value of a thing sometimes lies not in what one attains with it, but in what one pays for it – what it *costs* us. I give an example. Liberal institutions cease to be liberal as soon as they are attained: subsequently there is nothing more harmful to freedom than liberal institutions. One knows, indeed, *what* they bring about: they undermine the will to power, they are the levelling of mountain and valley elevated to a moral principle, they make small, cowardly and smug – it is the herd-animal that triumphs with them every time. Liberalism: in plain words, herd-animalization . . . As long as they are still being fought for, these same institutions produce quite different effects; they then in fact promote freedom mightily . . . The man who has *become free* – and how much more the *mind* that has become *free* – tramples on the contemptible sort of well-being dreamed of by shop keepers, Christians, cows, women, Englishmen and other democrats . . .

Potent stuff – at any rate for 'newcomers' who had not yet read *The Genealogy of Morals*.

Shortly after his return to Turin, Nietzsche received a first reaction to *The Case of Wagner* – from Carl von Gersdorff. As a former Wagner enthusiast who had managed to escape from 'Klingsor's Castle' (i.e. Bayreuth), he was overjoyed by the 'cold stream of cognition' that Nietzsche had let loose against 'the burning Wagner fever which lifeguard trumpeters have fanned to a fiery glow in our wives, young maidens, and young men'. Never had a book been more timely. For while he could not reproach Germany's 'fiery young Caesar' (Emperor Wilhelm II) for having recently aired his enthusiasm – 'at the age of twenty-nine one is ripe for Wagner' – Gersdorff could only hope that he would eventually come to regard this rapt condition as a 'process of disease' and use the prestige of his mighty office to help 'promote better results from good dispositions'.

At the end of this cordial letter Gersdorff wrote that, though his wife was not a Wagnerian, he was not going to let her read Nietzsche's new book, for 'she should not misunderstand you, and I would like to see the woman who could understand you'. The 'proof' of this uncharitable remark was not long in coming. One week later Nietzsche received a letter from Meta von Salis. Thanking him for her gift copy of *The Case of Wagner*, she said not another word about the book, either for or against.

This casual thank-you note must have nettled the hypersensitive Nietzsche, who with the passage of the years had grown increasingly avid for fame and recognition – not least of all from critical friends like Erwin Rohde. Or, for that matter, from his 'highly revered' 'Aunt Malwida'. Towards the end of July he had written to her from Sils-Maria that nothing written about him during the past ten years had truly 'reached' him, even though he had given mankind 'the most profound book it possesses [presumably *Zarathustra*], a book compared to which books in general are merely literature . . . In my dear Vaterland . . . I am treated like somebody who belongs in a lunatic asylum: this is the form that "comprehension" of me has taken. Moreover, the cretinism of Bayreuth stands in my way. Even after his death the old seducer Wagner has been taking away from me the rest of the men whom I could influence. But in *Denmark* – absurd to say! – I was celebrated during this past winter!! The brilliant Dr Brandes dared to deliver a long series of lectures about me at the University of Copenhagen!' etc. Something similar was brewing in New York. Enough to move Nietzsche to proclaim: 'I am the *most independent* mind in Europe and the *only* German writer – now that's something!'

Malwida von Meysenbug would probably have dismissed this piece of bombast as the pathetic confession of an all too solitary soul had Nietzsche, in a defiant postscript, not felt the need to flex his muscles once again: 'It requires *greatness* of soul to endure my writings. I have the good fortune to vex and set against me everything that is weak and virtuous.' Replying ten days later from Versailles, where she had gone to spend the summer with her foster-daughter Olga Herzen Monod and her family, the good Malwida treated Nietzsche to a little lecture. It was either an error or a paradox to declare that one had the good fortune to have everything that is 'weak and virtuous against one. The *truly* virtuous are by no means weak, rather they are the truly strong, as the original concept of *virtù* also says. And you yourself are the living contradiction thereof, for you are truly virtuous and I believe that your example, if human beings really knew it, would be more convincing than your books.'

Nietzsche, who disliked being lectured to, particularly on questions of virtue and the 'virtuous', did not bother to reply. But on 4 October, after asking his publisher, Naumann, to send three copies of *The Case of Wagner* to Malwida von Meysenbug's address in Versailles, he followed up with a letter in which he explained that 'disposing of Wagner' had been the hardest task of his life. He had just completed the first book of his projected *Umwertung aller Werte* (*Revaluation of all Values*), destined to be the 'greatest philosophical event of all time, with which the history of mankind breaks into two halves'.

Letters such as these, and they were soon to increase dramatically, make sad reading – as symptoms of self-infatuation and rampant megalomania. The more he shrank from tackling his daunting magnum opus (*The Revaluation of all Values*) head-on, the more he felt the need to proclaim it, *urbi et orbi* and even before it had been written, as destined to be the most epoch-making book to have been written since the New Testament. And woe to anyone who might be tempted to doubt it or to treat his opinions with a cavalier indifference! When his once fervent admirer, Hans von Bülow, now director of the Hamburg Symphony Orchestra, failed to answer a letter recommending Peter Gast's *Lion of Venice* opera, Nietzsche wrote to him peremptorily on 9 October: 'You have not answered my letter. You will once and for all be left in peace, that I promise you. I think you have some notion thereof, that the foremost mind of the age has expressed a wish to you. Friedrich Nietzsche.' Life, with an implacable sense of irony, was proving him right in having invented a parable (in the early pages of *Zarathustra* I) about the three basic stages of human existence: the camel stage, the lion stage and finally the stage of the child. But what the child in him was now exhibiting was not a state of 'innocence', untainted by any trace of moral guilt; it was an infantile petulance and tendency to tantrums whenever he felt thwarted or opposed. When Malwida, after reading *The Case of Wagner*, wrote that she disapproved of the way he had treated the man he had so deeply loved – even going so far as to call not only Wagner but also Liszt a *Hanswurst* (a 'clown' or 'buffoon'), which she had found 'utterly revolting' – Nietzsche slammed the door on this old friendship by writing on 18 October, three days after his forty-fourth birthday: 'These are not things about which I permit contradiction. I am, in questions of *décadence* [thus written in French], the highest instance there is on earth . . . '

The arrogant truculence of this language was symptomatic of the combative mood in which Nietzsche had written *Der Antichrist (The*

*Anti-Christian)* – the first salvo in the offensive he intended to launch against the '*décadent*' values of the West, insidiously perverted by close to two millennia of Christian 'corruption'. Although its most shocking thesis – that Christianity had triumphed because it was the product of a 'slave morality' – had already been unveiled in *The Genealogy of Morals* and though it was marred towards the end by tendentious exaggerations, Nietzsche was certainly close to the truth in thinking that, in terms of psychological insight and analysis, this was one of the most devastating books ever to have been written about the origins and triumph of Christianity, and indeed about the very nature of theocracy.

The three main thrusts of this new work were Nietzsche's contentions that Christianity, far from representing a radical 'break' with official Judaism, was essentially a morbid perpetuation of Jewish 'defeatism'; that its founder, Jesus Christ, remained a baffling psychological enigma; and that what seems to have been his teaching was from the outset vulgarized and distorted by his insufficiently sophisticated disciples and, with the help of the former rabbi, Paul, transformed from an incipient form of neo-Buddhism into a seditious instrument of social agitation against the Roman Empire.

Let us take each of these three basic strands – for as in all of Nietzsche's works they were interwoven with many others – and examine each in turn. The ancient Jews were originally a vigorous, healthy people, possessed – Nietzsche claimed in a deliberate effort not to sound antisemitic – of 'the toughest national will-to-life that has ever been seen on earth'. Their god, Jahweh (Jehovah), the rainbringer, the God of Victory and Justice, was the expression of their national pride, of a healthy sense of power and self-confidence during the luminous period of the kings of Israel. But this happy state did not last long and, as a twofold result of anarchy at home and of an Assyrian menace from the outside, culminating in the supreme humiliation of the Babylonian captivity, the triumphant kings disappeared and their power was assumed by priests and prophets, who gradually transformed Jahweh from a victorious god able to 'deliver the goods' to a proud, conquering people, into a disgruntled, vindictive, calculating god, a god of business reckoning who granted good fortune as a reward, and dispensed misfortune as a punishment for 'sins' and 'sinfulness'. What in modern meteorological or scientific terms would be called 'natural phenomena' brought about by 'natural causes' were thus given a religious coloration, the capricious element of luck or chance in life was robbed of its innocence, while misfortune was fatally sullied by an increasingly pervasive, oppressive sense of guilt and sin. As the years passed every happening came to be regarded as a manifestation of the 'will of

God' – the interpreters of this 'will' being an ever more pervasive and omnipresent priesthood, whose presence was prescribed for every sort of ceremony: for births, deaths, marriages, and even meals, where the food had to be blessed and sanctified.

It was from the religiously 'polluted' soil of a theocracy directed by cringing bigots, a 'totally unnatural ground', that Christianity arose – like a blighted plant. A revolt against a fatally corrupted, decadent form of religion is apt itself to be flawed in its very origins, and this, Nietzsche argued, was what happened with Christianity. The revolt against the established order, against the dominant priesthood, assumed a wildly utopian form, in the course of which the humblest and poorest elements of society were explicitly exalted (the reference here is to Christ's 'Sermon on the Mount'), while the key collective notion of a 'chosen people', which had hitherto provided the people of Israel with a strong residual sense of identity and cohesion, was allowed to evaporate into a totally unrealistic notion of individual perfection ('the Kingdom of God is within you').

But what of this 'holy anarchist', whose seditious teachings were destined to transform the Mediterranean world? What exactly was the psychology of this so-called 'Redeemer'? The sections devoted to this question are with little doubt the most penetrating and incisive in this relatively short, explosive book. Here Nietzsche confessed himself baffled by this mysterious, contradictory personality – an astonishing mixture of the sublime, the sickly and the childish – whose teachings, dispensed in a language of parabolic metaphors and symbols, were subsequently distorted by disciples of an infinitely rougher, cruder sort. After praising the young David Strauss for his valiant efforts (in *Das Leben Jesu*) to disengage the basic facts from the clinging vines and underbrush of hyperbolic fancy, Nietzsche ridiculed Ernest Renan ('that buffoon in psychologis') for having, in his *Vie de Jésus* (which had created an uproar in Paris when first published in 1863), claimed that Jesus was an exemplary 'hero' and 'genius'. Nothing, Nietzsche retorted, could have been more profoundly 'unheroic' than a religious creed of non-violence which in effect proclaimed, 'Resist not evil.' For what after all was the essence of Jesus's 'glad tidings' (in Greek *euaggelion* – whence our 'evangel' and 'evangelical')? Nietzsche's answer:

> True life, eternal life is found – it is not promised, it is here, it is *within you*: as life lived in love without deduction and exclusion, without distance. Everyone is a child of God – Jesus definitely claims nothing for himself alone – as a child of God everyone is equal to everyone else . . . To make a *hero* of Jesus! And what a misconception is the very word 'genius'! Our

> entire concept, our culture-concept of 'spirit' has no meaning whatsoever in the world in which Jesus lived. To speak with the precision of the physiologist, a quite different word would here be appropriate: the word idiot.

In writing these devastating sentences Nietzsche was clearly referring to Dostoevsky's novel, *The Idiot* – the pathetic story of a kindly, mystically inclined Russian prince (Myshkin), who ends up looking like a simpleton in trying to be kind-hearted and benevolent, in trying to love and live like a genuine Christian. And indeed, a little further on, Nietzsche explicitly regretted that there should not have existed among Jesus's contemporaries a man of Dostoevsky's acute psychological insight, capable of fathoming the baffling complexities of his personality and exposing the crude näiveté of his followers. What Jesus really was, Nietzsche suggested, was a supreme irrealist, quite possibly the greatest irrealist the world has known and, for that very reason perhaps, the only absolutely genuine Christian there has ever been. For, unlike Moses or Mohammed, who had their feet firmly planted on the ground and who were quite specific in their social recommendations, Jesus brought a message of 'glad tidings' that belonged to no specific time or place, that was atemporal and asocial. Any 'Christian', eager to follow in the footsteps of the Master in the naïve belief that the Kingdom of God is within one, ends up living in a religio-autistic world, totally severed from everyday reality. This inner world is inherently 'subversive' in that it owes allegiance to no established institution, whether Church or other. In this way the human individual is partly 'deified', divinized, delivered from the 'normal, natural' bonds of society. This was the basic Christian element underlying Rousseau's political philosophy. Man is born free (because the 'Kingdom of God' is within him), but in the wicked world of everyday reality, he is everywhere in chains. Normal, collective 'society' is thus demonized.

When it became a faith, Christianity was transformed into something radically different: not a life of 'blessedness' as it is actually experienced here and now, as much as a belief in life as it ought to be lived with an eye to future rewards and punishments to be distributed in a radiantly celestial or darkly hellish future. The work of transformation began from the very moment of the crucifixion, as was bound to happen with relatively uncouth disciples who lacked their master's sense of symbolism and intellectual subtlety. Jesus Christ had to be pulled down to their level of comprehension, as a rebel against the existing social order. He had to be recast in the familiar image of the unheeded prophet, of the long-awaited Messiah, of the future Judge-who-is-to-be. The shock experienced by those simple souls, on seeing their beloved master arrested, nailed to a cross and casually left to die, was traumatic. What an indignity! To suffer a fate reserved for common criminals!

All sectarian veneration, Nietzsche pointed out, tends to blur the truly original traits and idiosyncracies in any form of teaching: it even fails to see them. What had characterized Jesus above all was his sublime ability to rise above every form of hatred and resentment. But this was altogether too altruistic for his much simpler, rough-hewn disciples. Jesus's death – which he himself had conceived as the supreme symbol of his commitment to the truly 'good', non-violent life he had preached and practised – was a crime that had to be avenged and atoned for. And so the latent popular conception of the advent of a Messiah once again came to the fore, and with it a sobering vision of God sitting in judgement on His enemies. However, the agonizing question remained: how could God have permitted such an outrage, such a monstrous crime as that of Jesus's death? In their shocked confusion his disciples came up with (in Nietzsche's words) a 'downright terrifyingly absurd answer':

> God gave his son for the forgiveness of sins, as a *sacrifice*. All of a sudden it was all over with the Gospel! The *guilt sacrifice*, and furthermore in its most repulsive, barbaric form, the sacrifice of the *innocent one* for the sins of the guilty! What atrocious paganism! For Jesus himself had done away with the notion of 'guilt' – he had denied any chasm between God and Man, he had *lived* this unity of God and Man as *his* 'glad tidings' . . . And *not* as a prerogative! From now on, step by step, there seeped into the type-notion of the Redeemer, the doctrine of a Judgement and of a Second Coming, the doctrine of his death as a sacrificial death, the doctrine of the *Resurrection*, with which the entire concept of 'blessedness', the whole and sole reality of the Evangel is juggled away – in favour of a state [of personal immortality] *after* death!

What might have become, as imagined by its visionary founder, a serene, deeply spiritual, authentically non-violent 'peace movement', comparable to Buddhism, with an actually lived and not merely promised 'happiness on earth', was thus nipped in the bud and transformed into a kind of religious 'fraud'. In Nietzsche's words: 'For this remains – I have already emphasized it – the basic distinction between the two *décadence* religions: Buddhism makes no promises but keeps them, Christianity promises everything, but *keeps nothing*.'

The moving spirit in this labour of reinterpretation was Saint Paul, whom Nietzsche again attacked here with a ferocity equal to his earlier assault in *Morgenröte*. What Paul managed to do was to impose his own wilful vision of a watchful God of Punishment, a God recast in the old 'arch-Jewish' (*urjüdisch*) mould of an all-seeing, omnipresent God of Judgement. 'What was the only thing Mohammed later borrowed from Christianity? Paul's invention, his means of establishing a priestly tyranny, for forming herds: the belief in immortality – *that is to say the doctrine of 'Judgement"*.'

Possessed, moreover, of a hatred of the present which was not shared by Christ or Mohammed, Paul proceeded to poison the incipient Christian faith by imbuing it with his own personal preference for celibacy – even going so far, in his First Epistle to the Corinthians, as to denounce fornication as a sin against the body, as a sin 'against the temple of the Holy Ghost which is in you'. It only remained for the later Fathers of the Church to carry this anti-carnal vilification to its logical conclusion: first, by inventing an 'Amphitryon-figure' (God assuming the shape of the Holy Ghost to 'visit' Alcmene-Mary, the wife of the unsuspecting Joseph) in order to explain the supernatural 'virginity' of Jesus's mother; and much later – as late as 1854 – by promulgating the no less 'sullying' dogma of the Virgin Mary's 'immaculate conception'.

The human body, so honoured by the ancient Greeks, was not the only thing that Paul set out to denigrate. Equally potent was his hostility towards the 'good' philologists and physicians of Alexandria, in whose scientific studies he perceived a mortal threat to his highly personal, theocentric and supposedly 'God-inspired' faith. In this respect too Paul, the 'cosmopolitan' Paul so long (and wrongly) revered by generations of Christian theologians, proved himself to be arch-Jewish.

Nietzsche then went all the way back to the start of the Old Testament, inventing a parable of his own to expose the priestly taboo underlying the story of the Creation, as told in the Book of Genesis. An aged God, a kind of heavenly High Priest, is strolling in his garden. He is bored, as even a god can be in his hastily created 'paradise'. To overcome his boredom, he invents Man, who is entertaining. But soon Man too grows bored. To relieve him of this distress, God creates other animals – in vain. Man does not find the animals entertaining; he insists on dominating them, he is even unwilling to be regarded as an 'animal'. In despair, God then creates Woman. That put an end to boredom! But let us listen to Nietzsche's own words:

> Woman was God's *second* blunder. 'Woman is in her essence serpent, Heva' – every priest knows that. 'From Woman comes *every* mischief in the world' – every priest knows that too. *Consequently science* too comes from her . . . It was from Woman first of all that Man learned to taste of the Tree of Knowledge. What had happened? The old God was gripped by a mortal

> terror. Man himself had become God's *greatest* blunder, he had created for himself a rival, science makes one *equal to God* – for priests and gods the game was up if Man becomes scientific! Moral: science is the . . . *first* sin, the germ of all sins, *original* sin. *This alone is morality* – Thou shalt *not* know – the rest follows.

What Nietzsche did not say, perhaps because he thought it too obvious, was that in the comparable cautionary tale in Greek mythology, when Pandora, the sister-in-law of Prometheus, yields to insatiable curiosity and opens the forbidden jar, a host of ills – sickness, old age, the pains of pregnancy, etc. – escape to plague mankind, but knowledge was not one of them.

For this, as now became apparent, was the very root and heart of Nietzsche's dislike of Christianity. From the very outset it had been a wilfully stupid, anti-intellectual religion. And the most stupefying aspect of this millennial exercise in mental stupefaction had been the willingness of 'erudite' theologians to promote and propagate a 'gospel' of collective stupidity.

> The way in which a theologian, whether in Berlin or in Rome, interprets a 'word of the Scriptures', or an experience, or a victory of one's home-country's army, for example, under the higher illumination of the Psalms of David, is always so *audacious* as to drive a philologist up every wall in sight. And what on earth is he to do when Pietists and other cows from the flatlands of Swabia dress up the wretched routine and smoky stuffiness of their existence by having the 'finger of God' transform it into a miracle of 'grace', of 'providence', of 'experience of salvation'! Even the most modest expenditure of intelligence, to say nothing of *propriety*, should suffice to make these interpreters realize how thoroughly childish and unworthy is such an abuse of divine dexterity. With even the smallest dose of piety inside us we should feel that a God who promptly cures a head-cold, who has one climb into a carriage when the rain begins to pour, is so absurd a god that he should be done away with even if he existed. A God as domestic servant, as postman, as red-letter-day almanac-maker . . . 'Divine Providence', in which even today one person in every three still believes in 'cultivated Germany', would be a stronger objection to God than anything else that could be thought up. And in any case an objection to the Germans!

CHAPTER 38

# The Collapse

> *– God is a crude, two-fisted answer, an indelicacy towards us thinkers.*

The sixty-two extant sections of *Der Antichrist (The Anti-Christian)* may well have been left unfinished. Nietzsche, who was in no hurry to have it published, did not send the manuscript to Leipzig. For on the occasion of his forty-fourth birthday (15 October 1888) he was suddenly 'visited' by a new, irresistible inspiration. Would it not be wise, he wondered, before launching his morals-overturning offensive with this explosive book, to have it preceded by a kind of autobiographical 'primer', aimed at combating the many misconceptions about his philosophy that had arisen among those who had taken the trouble to read his books? And since he was in a zestful as well as combative mood – 'I am warlike by nature. Attacking is one of my instincts' – he decided to entitle his new work *Ecce homo* (*Behold the man*): the words that Pontius Pilate, the Roman governor of Judea, was alleged (in the Gospel of St John) to have uttered in presenting Jesus Christ to his orthodox Jewish accusers.

Such a title, chosen by an author who had boldly proclaimed himself an anti-Christian, was bound to sound provocative. America's foremost Nietzsche scholar, Walter Kaufmann, argued (not altogether convincingly in my opinion) that in choosing this title Nietzsche was not trying 'to suggest any close similarity between himself and Jesus; more nearly the opposite. *Here* is a man! Here is a new, a different image of humanity: not a saint or a holy man any more than a traditional sage, but a modern version.' True enough. But a 'modern version' of what? And the answer I think we have to give to this question is: of a philosophical rebel, of an intellectual *enfant terrible*, of an iconoclastic, wilfully destructive, anti-ecclesiastical 'prophet' who (in his letters) had made no secret of his wish to found a new morality destined to last for one thousand years or even two.

The very speed with which this new opus was completed – begun on 15 October, it was finished in first-draft form on 4 November – attests the ebullient, swift-winged spirit in which it was written. Here, with certain qualifications, one can, I think, agree with Walter Kaufmann, who in an introduction written in 1967, declared: '*Ecce Homo* is one of the treasures of world literature. Written in 1888 and first published in 1908, it has been largely ignored or misunderstood. Yet it is Nietzsche's own interpretation of his development, his works, and his significance; and we should gladly trade the whole vast literature on Nietzsche for this one small book. Who would not rather have Shakespeare on Shakespeare, including the poet's own reflections on his plays and poems, than the exegeses and conjectures of thousands of critics and professors?'

This was a courageous affirmation, coming from one of these critics and professors: one whom Thomas Mann regarded as superior to all the other 'authorities' he had encountered. This symbolic act of critical *hara-kiri* could only come from someone who appreciated Nietzsche's sense of ironic introspection as well as his stylistic mastery in serving up pithy formulations. As in this tongue-in-cheek assertion in the Preface:

> I am, for example, not at all a bogey, no moral-monster – I am indeed by nature the very opposite of the type of man who has so far been revered as virtuous . . . I am a disciple of the philosopher Dionysus; I would even rather be a satyr than a saint.

The entire book was spiced with tart remarks of this kind, designed to shock and provoke the reader. The headings chosen for the first three chapters – 'Why I am so Wise', 'Why I am so clever', 'Why I write such Good Books' – were outrageous and designed to prove that the author was the opposite of a virtuously 'objective' pedant indulging in false modesty.

Here for the first time were publicly exposed many of Nietzsche's physiological characteristics, hitherto known only to close friends and acquaintances: his unusually low pulse rate, his poor eyesight, which improved every time his 'vitality' increased, his never having suffered a fever – he quotes a doctor who, after examining him, remarked, 'No, it's not a question of your nerves, it's only I who am nervous' – and his discovery that sickness can be an 'energetic stimulus' to life.

What distinguishes *Ecce homo* above all else is its fresh, uninhibited tone, and the careless ease with which, in describing his personal experiences and his highly idiosyncratic likes and dislikes, Nietzsche managed to give them a universal, but also, alas, easily misunderstood significance. For example:

> My experiences entitle me to be generally distrustful of so-called 'selfless' drives, of all 'love of one's neighbour' so ever ready to help with word and deed. It seems to me inherently a weakness, a particular case of being incapable of resisting charming incitations – only with décadents is *compassion* regarded as a virtue. I reproach the compassionate for easily losing

> a sense of modesty, of respect, of a discreet feeling of distances, for in the twinkling of an eye compassion begins to smell of the mob and seems barely distinguishable from bad manners.

Taken literally – and how could Nietzsche reasonably expect a more subtle interpretation from 'average' readers? – this could not but sound like a wholesale condemnation of all charitable impulses: which is how Nazi Germans, those who took the trouble to read Nietzsche's works (they were always a minority), later chose to interpret this and similar passages, casually overlooking the 'anti-mob' anathema expressed in the final sentence. For the exaltation of 'pitilessness' as a public programme for the masses would, for that very reason, have condemned it in Nietzsche's eyes had he lived to see his 'hard-hearted' philosophy translated into policy. What is good for the Zarathustran *Übermensch* is not necessarily good for ordinary individuals. But therein lies the hidden danger in the 'gospel of compassion'. For what his mercurial 'sixth sense' made him foresee and fear as likely to happen in the future was the industrial exploitation of tearjerking sentimentality and the emotional hysteria which in our day have become the stock-in-trade of television channels throughout the Western world, generating collective climaxes of mawkish exhibitionism – as happened not so long ago after the death of Diana, Princess of Wales.

Here is another example of a 'general truth' derived from an acutely personal experience: the reproachful silence so many of Nietzsche's friends had maintained after the publication of *Human, All Too Human* and the books that had followed:

> It also seems to me that the rudest word, the rudest letter are yet more good-natured, more honourable than silence. Those who remain silent are almost always lacking in delicacy and courtesy of the heart. Silence is an objection; swallowing things necessarily makes for a bad character [Freud would have said, 'creates a neurosis'] – it even upsets the stomach.

*Ecce homo*, as has been noted, was written in a combative mood by a thinker who did not hesitate to define himself as being 'warlike by nature. Attacking is one of my instincts.' Nietzsche now proved it with a reiteration of his 'resistentialist' philosophy:

> Being *able* to be an enemy, being an enemy – that perhaps presupposes a strong nature; in any case it is a condition of every strong nature. It needs elements of resistance, consequently it *seeks* resistance: the *aggressive* pathos belongs just as necessarily to strength as a feeling of revenge, of rancour

> belongs to weakness. Woman, for example, is vengeful: that is determined by her weakness, just as much as is her sensibility to the distress of others.

Rare are the writers today who would dare for an instant to sound so uncompromisingly virile and '*macho*'. But if Nietzsche could do so, it was because, as a philosophical swordsman, he had always respected a self-imposed, four-point code of honour. He had never attacked a cause that was not already or about to become victorious (by which he meant 'fashionable'). He had always attacked alone – whence (though he did not add this) his consistent refusal to contribute articles or essays to periodicals – and he had always been careful to compromise no one but himself. He had never attacked individuals as such – not even David Strauss, singled out because he was the author of a 'senile' bestseller that was symptomatic of a calamitous drift in German 'taste' and 'culture'. The same went for Wagner; what Nietzsche had attacked in his case was the falseness, the 'blurred instinct' of a culture which tended to mistake opulence for refinement, 'late' art for 'great' art. Similarly, in attacking Christianity, it was not from any personal grudge. 'When I wage war against Christianity, I can do so because I have experienced no mishaps or impediments from that quarter – the most serious Christians have always been well disposed towards me. I myself, an opponent *de rigueur* of Christianity, am far from blaming individuals for a calamity of millennia.'

Sometimes, in *Ecce homo*, the provocative bravado sounds too good to be true. Thus, in going back to his earliest years at Röcken and Naumburg, at the start of 'Why I am so clever', Nietzsche bluntly declared that he had never experienced any 'genuinely *religious* difficulties. It has completely escaped me in what I was supposed to be "sinful".' Since from the very start he was an unusually gifted, studious boy, was brought up by a doting mother and, from the age of four years on, lacked a possibly censorious father, it is just possible that during his youth he never seriously suffered from a sense of being a 'sinner'. If so, this was a quality he could claim to share with Jesus Christ – a being so pure that (according to Nietzsche) he did not even know what 'sin' was. But the ironic tone of the next sentence – 'Likewise, I lack any reliable criterion for what a pang of conscience is: from what one *hears* of it, a bite of conscience [*Gewissensbiss*] is not something respectable' – suggests that here Nietzsche was imposing on his youth the *de post facto* image of a precocious unbeliever.

> 'God', 'immortality of the soul', 'redemption', the 'beyond' are merely concepts to which I devoted no attention, no time, not even as a child – for that perhaps I was never childish enough? I have no knowledge at all of

> atheism as an outcome, still less as an event . . . I am too curious, too *questioning*, too exuberant to put up with a crude, two-fisted [*faustgrobe*] answer. God is a crude, two-fisted answer, an indelicacy towards us thinkers – at bottom merely a crude, two-fisted *prohibition*: you should not think!

One of the charms of *Ecce homo* – for despite its strident imperfections (glaringly apparent towards the end) this is a charming book – is its rambling character. It is a peripatetic monologue in which the author takes the reader on a guided tour through his past, paying little heed to strict chronology but much to matters of geography, climate, food and drink. As, for example, in this appraisal of German cooking:

> What doesn't it have on its conscience! Soup *before* the meal (in Venetian cookbooks of the sixteenth century this is still called *alla tedesca*); overcooked meats, vegetables made fat and floury, the degeneration of pastries into paperweights! Add to this the positively bovine drinking needs of the ancient, and by no means solely *ancient* Germans, then one can understand the origin of the *German spirit* – from distressed intestines . . . The German spirit is an indigestion, it is never finished with anything.

There followed some uncharitable remarks about British cooking – as ponderous (according to Nietzsche) as the 'feet of English women'. Then – 'No meals between meals, no coffee,' he arbitrarily decreed, 'coffee spreads darkness. *Tea* is wholesome only in the morning. A little, but strong: tea is very detrimental and can indispose one for a whole day if it is too weak by a single degree' – an assertion that would have made a connoisseur like Lin Yutang shake his head in bewilderment.

And what is an unprejudiced reader to think when he encounters a passage like this one?

> The German climate alone is enough to discourage strong, even heroically disposed intestines . . . List the places where keen-brained men live or have lived, where wit, refinement, malice were part of happiness, where genius made itself at home, almost of necessity: they all of them have an excellent dry air. Paris, Provence, Florence, Jerusalem, Athens – those names mean something: genius is *conditioned* by dry air, clear skies.

Even if what he said about Jerusalem, Athens and Provence is climatically correct, the man who wrote these ridiculous lines had never been to Paris and had only once made a brief stopover in Florence – two hill-surrounded cities where the air is neither excellent nor dry, nor the skies unclouded. And if one were to register the geniuses who have managed to thrive in places where the air was often damp and the sky overcast, the list – headed by Shakespeare, Molière, Rembrandt, Bach, Mozart, Beethoven and Goethe, to name but those – would fill half a dozen pages.

Even as ardent an admirer as Walter Kaufmann had to admit that Nietzsche in his Teutonophobia for once had overdone it, burying the Germans under repeated shovelfuls of ridicule, disparagement and abuse. And, once again, he added insult to injury by unfavourably comparing his ponderous countrymen to the more cultivated, more graceful, more light-footed French.

> The few cases of high culture that I have encountered in Germany were all of them of French origin, above all Frau Cosima Wagner, far and away the foremost voice in matters of taste I have ever heard.

What follows is no less fascinating – as an example of how 'open-minded' Nietzsche could be in judging someone whose religious reasoning he regarded as thoroughly pernicious:

> That I do not read but *love* Pascal, as the most instructive victim of Christianity, slowly murdered, first physically, then psychologically, the entire logic of this gruesome form of inhuman cruelty; that in my spirit, who knows? perhaps in my body too, I have something of Montaigne's sprightliness; that my artist's taste defends the names of Molière, Corneille, Racine, not without a certain wrath against a wild genius like Shakespeare – all that does not keep me from finding the most recent Frenchmen charming company.

Having paid homage to a number of his French 'favourites' – including Guy de Maupassant and Stendhal (an 'honest atheist' and inventor of the best atheistic quip he had yet heard: 'God's only excuse is that he does not exist') – Nietzsche felt the need to sing the praises of two great Germans whose genius owed little to pure air and clear skies, even though both of them spent some time in Paris. The first was Heinrich Heine, of whom he had written, in *Twilight of the Idols*, that, like Goethe, like Hegel, like Schopenhauer, he was not a local, not a national, but a European event. And so, immediately after honouring Stendhal, Nietzsche laid an equally flattering bouquet at the feet of Germany's most emphatically lyrical poet.

> I vainly seek in all the realms of millennial history for an equally sweet and passionate music. He possessed that divine malice without which I cannot imagine perfection: I estimate the worth of men, of races according to the

> need they feel of conceiving the god unseparated from the satyr. And how he handles the German language! One day it will be said that Heine and I have been far and away the foremost artists of the German language – at an incalculable distance removed from everything mere Germans have done with it.

That the others were 'merely' German was a subtle allusion to Nietzsche's proudly vaunted 'Polish' ancestry and to Heine's Jewish origin. Heine, moreover, like Nietzsche, had preferred to exile himself from his native land, even if his genius had first manifested itself long before he settled in Paris. But what of Richard Wagner – the other German genius Nietzsche wished to hail, lest he be accused of petty animosity for what he had written in *The Case of Wagner*?

> . . . Here, where I speak of the relaxations of my life, I must say a word to express my gratitude for what most profoundly and cordially enabled me to recover. This beyond any doubt was my personal rapport with Richard Wagner. I would gladly part with the rest of my human relationships; but for no price on earth would I be willing to omit from my life the days of Tribschen – days of trust, of jollity, of sublime accidents, of *profound* moments.
>
> I do not know what others have experienced with Wagner: over our sky there never passed a cloud. And with that I return once more to France. I have no grounds, I have merely a curled lip of disdain for Wagnerians . . . who think they are honouring Wagner by finding him similar to *themselves* . . . Such as I am, so alien in my deepest instincts to everything German that the merest proximity of a German retards my digestion, the first contact with Wagner was also the first deep breath of my life: I experienced him, I revered him as a *foreign land*, as an antithesis, as a protest incarnate against all 'German virtues'.

In short, Richard Wagner had to leave Germany and go to Paris in order to learn how to become the great genius he became. Not as the creator of *The Flying Dutchman*, of *Tannhäuser*, of *Lohengrin*, but as the composer of *Tristan und Isolde* – an irresistible 'poison' the young Nietzsche had imbibed with all his senses as feverishly as an opium-addict does hashish.

> From the moment on when there was a piano score of *Tristan* – my compliments, Herr von Bülow! – I was a Wagnerian. Wagner's earlier works I deemed beneath me – still too vulgar, too 'German' . . . But to this day I have been looking for a work of the same dangerous fascination, of the same sweet and shuddering infinity such as *Tristan* is, and have been

looking in all the arts in vain. All the strangenesses of Leonardo da Vinci lose their spell at the first note of *Tristan*. This work is absolutely the *non plus ultra* of Wagner; he recuperated from it with the *Meistersinger* and the *Ring*. Becoming healthier – that is a *retrogression* for a nature like Wagner's.

f all of *Ecce homo* had been on this superior level, this little book of ungent reminiscences would have been a masterpiece. But of a sick enius this is probably asking too much. And the sad truth of the matter that, as the book progressed, Nietzsche's worst habit – for a habit it had ecome – became stridently apparent. This was his self-infatuation, ubterraneanly nourished by frustration at having so long been ignored by erman readers who refused to recognize his philosophical significance. is observations about the successive books he wrote, the reasons why he vrote them, the responses they elicited (all too briefly suggested) are full f fascinating insights and valuable information; but every now and then e yielded to his inner demon and indulged in exaggerations unworthy of thinker who detested histrionic exhibitionism (whence his dislike of arlyle) and histrionic ostentation (one of his chief complaints against Vagner). Thus, in discussing the third and fourth of his 'Untimely Meditations', he wrote, in a paragraph that outraged Wagner's iographer, Ernest Newman:

Now that I look back from a certain distance at the circumstances to which these writings bear witness, I would not wish to deny that basically they speak only of myself. The essay, 'Wagner in Bayreuth', is a vision of my future; whereas in 'Schopenhauer as Educator' my innermost history, my *becoming* are inscribed. Above all, the *promise* of my future!

Vhile there was an element of truth in both these observations, the first oncerning Wagner) would best have been left unsaid. But it was when ietzsche undertook to discuss that nemesis of a book, *Thus Spake arathustra* – accorded twelve times as many pages as its precedecessor, *he Joyous Science* – that once again he lost all sense of restraint. dmittedly, his vivid description of the hallucinating moments of spiration during which he felt powerless and 'possessed' merits a place any good anthology of mystical experiences.

Anyone with the slightest residue of superstition left in him can hardly rid himself of the impression of simply being mere incarnation, mere mouthpiece, a mere medium of overpowering forces. The notion of revelation, in the sense that suddenly, with unspeakable certainty and subtlety, something becomes *visible*, audible, something upsets and shakes

> one to the depths, simply describes the facts. One hears, one does not seek; one takes, one doesn't ask who gives; like lightning, a thought flashes up, of necessity, with no hesitation as to form – I was never given a choice [etc.].

But after briefly describing various places where he had experienced suc 'unforgettable moments' of inspiration – it was during a long uphill clim to the old-walled, anti-Saracen mountain village of Eze (near Nice) th he conceived the twelfth chapter ('On Old and New Tablets') c *Zarathustra* III – Nietzsche could not help piling up the superlatives in lamentable display of poor taste:

> This work stands altogether apart. Let us leave aside the poets: nothing perhaps has ever been wrought from such a comparable excess of strength. My concept of the 'Dionysian' here became a *supreme deed*; compared to it, all the rest of human activity seems poor and limited. That a Goethe, a Shakespeare would be unable to breathe even for a moment in this prodigious passion and height, that Dante, compared with Zarathustra, is merely a believer and not one who first *creates* truth, a *world-governing* spirit, a destiny – that the poets of the Vedas are priests and not even worthy of unlacing the sandals of a Zarathustra – all that is minor and gives one no idea of the distance, of the *azure* solitude in which this work lives . . . Let anyone add up the spirit and goodness of all great souls into one: all of them together would not be capable of producing one of Zarathustra's discourses . . .

Such passages make sad reading, coming from a thinker who, as he ha boasted in *Ecce homo*, preferred pure fountain-water to wine or spirits. Bu every time he opened one of his *Zarathustra* volumes, he was, by his ow admission, reduced to tears. To tears of rapture and self-intoxicatio What the French so picturesquely term '*la folie des grandeurs*' had, i Nietzsche's case, become a '*folie des hauteurs*' – a madness of the heights.

On 30 October, five days before completing *Ecce homo*, Nietzsche wro in an ebullient mood to Heinrich Köselitz that never had he experience such an autumn – 'splendid foliage in glowing yellow, sky and the bi river [Po] a tender blue, the air of the highest purity – a Claude Lorrai such as I never dreamed of seeing. Fruits, grapes in brownish sweetness and cheaper than in Venice!' He had found an excellent tailor, who w making him suits that would enable him to be everywhere received as 'distinguished foreigner'. He was eating like a horse, in particular veal an unprecedented tenderness. He had ordered a stove to carry hi rough the winter, having decided not to return to all-too 'chalky, oorly wooded' Nice; and he had asked the manager of the Pension de enève to have the books he had left behind crated and dispatched to his ew address in Turin. In a word, Turin was paradise! Never had he felt so ell and slept so soundly, and viewing himself in the mirror he had been rprised to see a genial, well-fed face looking 'ten years younger than is ermissible'.

All of this had inspired him to write another book – this time about imself and his writings, which he wanted to have published in order to st freedom of expression in Germany; for he was haunted by the fear that e first volume of his *Revaluation of all Values* series *(Der Antichrist)* would e banned as 'sacrilegious' and seized by the moral watchdogs of ismarck's *Reich*. This new book, *Ecce homo*, written in a merry mood and ll of psychological 'canniness', would help to dispel the impression that e was a 'prophet, brute, and moral monster' and perhaps keep people om portraying him as the very opposite of what he really was.

On 6 November Nietzsche sent the text to Naumann in Leipzig, xplaining that he had written *Ecce homo* in less than three weeks (between 5 October and 4 November), as a 'long preface' to the major work (*The nti-Christian* and the volumes that were to follow) which he wanted to ave published some time later. An exchange of letters followed regarding chnical details (the kind of paper and page-format to be used), and then, ree weeks later, not altogether satisfied with what he had written, ietzsche asked his publisher to return the second half of the text, and, ur days later, on 1 December, he asked Naumann to send back the entire xt for last-minute revisions. These were rapidly completed, and on 6 ecember Nietzsche sent the entire manuscript to Leipzig with the surance that no further changes would be made.

Swept off his feet by his literary virtuosity, Nietzsche had persuaded imself that *Ecce homo* would outstrip all of his previous publications and e a sensational bestseller. And not only in Germany! This belief was ncouraged by an astonishing letter he received in early December from friend of Georg Brandes – the iconoclastic Swedish playwright August trindberg, who, after narrowly escaping forcible confinement as a nadman' in a Swedish psychiatric hospital, had found refuge in a little own near Copenhagen. 'Without doubt,' the letter began in French, ou have given mankind the most profound book it possesses' – he was ferring to *Thus Spake Zarathustra* – 'and, not least of all, you have had e courage, and perhaps the royalties, [needed] to spit out those superb ords into the face of the rabble!' There was no point, Strindberg went n in reply to Nietzsche's query, in trying to have his book translated into reenlandese' (i.e. into Swedish and Danish), but why not into French or English? After declaring that he was now ending all his letters, 'Reac Nietzsche: he is my *Carthago est delenda*!' the misanthropic playwrigh added these prophetic words of caution: 'However, at the moment wher you are known and understood, your greatness is diminished, and the holy and unholy riff-raff [*canaille*] will start treating you familiarly as one of thei ilk. Better preserve a distinguished solitude and let us ten thousanc superior beings make secret pilgrimages to your sanctuary in order tc refresh ourselves as we please. Let us preserve the esoteric doctrine ir order to keep it pure, and let us not divulge it without the intermediatio of devoted catechumens, among whom I sign myself – Augus Strindberg'.

This extraordinary letter – no one, not even Georg Brandes, had eve expressed his enthusiasm for *Zarathustra* so unreservedly – led Nietzsche to believe that Strindberg, who had translated one of his plays into French for its première in Paris, might be the talented soul he was looking for tc translate *Ecce homo* into French. Its markedly anti-German tone would ensure it wide acclaim in Paris. But, as he wrote to Strindberg in an eage thank-you letter, what did he think about an English translation? 'An anti German book in England? . . . '

Here there was an obvious candidate: the German-born Helen Zimmern, whose intelligent company Nietzsche had so much enjoyed a Sils-Maria and who had introduced Schopenhauer to English readers. He immediately dashed off a letter to her, explaining, as he had done with Strindberg, that *Ecce homo* had to appear, more or less simultaneously, in German, English and French. He needed a first-class translator capable o seizing all of the nuances in a book which, in strictly literary terms, was an unprecedented masterpiece. This was merely a beginning. Over the nex two years he planned to launch an '*Attentat*' (a 'bomb attack') agains Christianity, so loaded with dynamite that it would blow Bismarck's '*Reich*', the 'Triple Alliance', and other geopolitical 'splendours' sky-high 'We will alter the time reckoning, I swear to you!' he exulted, meaning that the AD 0 date of Jesus Christ's birth would soon be supplanted by new calendar beginning. 'Never has a m[an] had more right to destruction than I have!' Inflammatory words which so scared the expatriate spinste that she did not know how to reply.

Flushed though he was by the heady prospect of epic battles and earth convulsing victories, capable of 'breaking the history of mankind into two halves' (as he had put it to Strindberg), Nietzsche was still lucid enough to realize that the task of rounding up enough translators to hav *Ecce homo* appear more or less simultaneously in half a dozen languages would require much time and effort. In the meantime the Swiss poet and novelist Carl Spitteler had written a laudatory article on *The Case* c

*Wagner* for *Der Bund*, Bern's leading newspaper, while Peter Gast (Heinrich Köselitz) had managed to place an equally enthusiastic review in the Dresden periodical *Der Kunstwart* (*The Custodian of the Arts*). To make amends to Nietzsche, who several months before had berated him in an angry letter for failing to defend the maligned memory of Heinrich Heine, its Jewish editor, Ferdinand Avenarius, had even added an elogious article of his own. Nietzsche immediately wrote to Avenarius to express his delighted surprise. It was a mistake to suppose that the 'deepest' kind of mind (i.e. his own) could not live side by side with the 'most frivolous' (one capable of writing a piece of 'tomfoolery' like *The Case of Wagner*).

Nothing annoyed Nietzsche more than the widespread impression that his 'break' with Wagner was the result of a recent 'change of heart'. Even his admirers had clearly not read his past works with sufficient care and attention. Had they done so, they would have noticed that his earliest criticisms of Wagner had already been expressed in *Human, All Too Human*. The time had come to 'set the record straight'. Again working at the same extraordinary tempo, Nietzsche was able four days later (5 December) to surprise Naumann with yet another text – the fifth in the space of nine months! Inasmuch as *The Case of Wagner* was a 'small piece of tomfoolery', it was time to add a dash of seriousness, for what he and Wagner had personally experienced had been essentially tragic for both of them. He wanted this new text (eight brief sections, drawn from *Human, All Too Human*, *The Wanderer and His Shadow*, *The Joyous Science*, *Beyond Good and Evil* and *The Genealogy of Morals*) to have priority over everything else, in order to give him time to arrange for at least one translation of *Ecce homo* into French. (In a typically witty reply Strindberg had already indicated that his 'somewhat picturesque' French style was that of the boulevards, and that a native Frenchman would have to revise his translation. He had also warned Nietzsche that it was quite simply impossible to find a French translator who did not 'unsalt the style, nor deflower the virginity of expression, according to the rules of the École Normale *rhétorique* . . . ')

On 17 December Nietzsche wrote again to Naumann, giving him the title – *Nietzsche contra Wagner* – for this new opus. But three days later – not having heard from Helen Zimmern nor from Jean Bourdeau, the 'editor' (in stricter fact a mere contributor) of the *Journal des Débats* and the *Revue des Deux Mondes* – Nietzsche sent Naumann a two-word telegram ('*Ecce vorwärts*') instructing his publisher to proceed immediately with the printing of *Ecce homo*. As he explained on 22 December to Heinrich Köselitz, he and Naumann had decided to shelve *Nietzsche contra Wagner* for the time being, since *Ecce homo* included everything essential that needed to be said about his extraordinary friendship with Richard Wagner.

This did not keep him, three days later, from devoting part of his Christmas Day to a very brief preface for *Nietzsche contra Wagner*. In it he explained that he and Wagner had been 'antipodes', and that he had written this 'essay' (he used the English word) 'for psychologists, but not for Germans . . . I have my readers everywhere, in Vienna, in St Petersburg, in Copenhagen and Stockholm, in Paris, in New York – I do not have them in Europe's flatland, Germany . . . And I should perhaps also whisper a word into the ears of the Italian *signori* whom I love as much as I do myself . . . *Quousque tandem*, Crispi [the Italian prime minister who had recently signed a pact with Bismarck's Germany, thus joining Austria] . . . *Triple Alliance*: with the 'Reich' an intelligent people can never make more than a *mésalliance* . . . '

The Christmas and New Year season – associated in his mind with the annual 'going-under' (*Untergang*) of the dying year and rich with nostalgic memories of Naumburg celebrations with the Krug and Pinder families, and, most irretrievable of all, of the unforgettable *Siegfried Idyll* surprise staged for Cosima's birthday in 1870, and, one week later, the *Sylvesternacht* (31 December) concert, when Friedrich Hegar and three other violinists had come from Zürich to play Beethoven quartets for the Wagner household at Tribschen – had always been a difficult period for Nietzsche. This one was no exception. But for quite different reasons. Seldom had he felt so well. For once he was riding the crest of a wave which kept rising ever higher in a steady, giddying ascent. In the space of ten months he had completed five books, and at long last, after years of frustration as a spurned author in Germany, he was becoming a philosophical force to be reckoned with. His fame had spread to the salons of Petersburg, to Paris, where Hippolyte Taine was now trying to find a good translator for the much appreciated *Twilight of the Idols*, to Denmark (thanks to Georg Brandes) and even to Sweden, where the 'scandalous' playwright August Strindberg was now saying to all his friends, 'Read Nietzsche. He is my "*Carthago est delenda*".' But this belated recognition had gone to Nietzsche's head, unleashing the floodgates of self-infatuation and megalomaniacal fantasies which had begun to manifest themselves in 1884.

The first sign that all was not well with the normally calm, studious, affable *professore* was the fits of rage which now occasionally seized him and which surprised Davide Fino's two daughters, who saw him several times angrily tearing up letters he had received. Nietzsche, who had so far maintained a rigorous régime, with regular hours for work in the early morning and part of the afternoon, now spent more time downstairs, improvising music which sometimes sounded Wagnerian and at other times jarringly discordant, as though he was determined to vent his personal anger on the family piano.

No less alarming were the 'internal' symptoms of a growing irrationality and delusions of grandeur evident in Nietzsche's letters (of which the Fino family knew nothing). In early December he wrote to his Danish admirer, Georg Brandes, to announce the forthcoming publication of *Der Antichrist* – 'a destructive blow against Christianity' which should enable them, with the aid of intelligent and understandably anti-Christian Jews, to launch the 'greatest decisive war in history': one that should be naturally attractive to army officers, instinctively ready to understand that to be a Christian was 'to the highest degree dishonourable, cowardly, impure'. He, Nietzsche, was psychologically astute enough to know how to handle 'brown idiots' like the German Kaiser. To prove that he really meant it, he wrote a letter to Kaiser Wilhelm II, in which he annonced as impending the 'deepest conscience-collison' in the history of mankind, explained that he was neither a fanatic nor a prophet – all prophets had hitherto been liars! – but a proponent of the *Truth*, whose fate it was to have looked down 'more profoundly, more courageously, more *uprightly* into the questions of all times' than any man who had yet lived. He contradicted, to be sure, but he was 'the opposite of a nay-saying spirit . . . For when this volcano goes into action, we shall have convulsions on the earth such as have never been . . . ' etc.

This was merely a beginning. A day or two later, or possibly on the very same day, he wrote to the German Chancellor, Prince Otto von Bismarck, that, in sending him the first copy of *Ecce homo*, he had the honour of 'announcing my enmity . . . to the first statesman of our time . . . [signed] The Anti-Christian Friedrich Nietzsche'. On or around 8 December he prepared a letter for Meta von Salis, meant to accompany two gift copies of *Der Antichrist* (one to be sent to Malwida von Meysenbug), calling this new work 'stupendous', and from which his friend Meta would have little trouble guessing that 'the old god is abolished, and that I myself will henceforth rule the world'.

No less bizarre was a letter he began on Christmas Day, addressed to Cosima Wagner, in which he called her 'the only woman I have revered . . . May it please you to receive the first copy of this *Ecce homo*. In it basically all and everything are badly treated, Richard Wagner excepted – and also Turin. Malvida appears in it as Kundry . . . [signed] The Antichrist.'

The next day he informed Franz Overbeck in Basel that he was working on a memorandum destined to be sent to all the courts of Europe with the idea of forming an anti-German league. 'I want to straitjacket the '*Reich*' into an iron jacket and provoke it into a war of desperation. I won't have a free hand until I have the young Kaiser, *with all* the accessories, in my grip. Below us! Far below us! Complete ocean-calm [*Windstille*] of the soul! Slept ten hours non-stop!'

On 29 December he wrote a perfectly reasonable letter to Naumann, agreeing with him that the first print order for *Ecce homo* should not exceed 1,000 copies, and that even this might be 'a bit mad' for a 'work of a lofty style' – one which in France, speaking 'in all seriousness', he estimated would sell from 80,000 to 300,000 copies! The next day – by which time the bright blue skies of autumn had been replaced by wintry fog – he wrote, in what Heinrich Köselitz may briefly have thought was a facetious style, that in a moment of 'heroic-Aristophenesian exuberance' he had penned a proclamation for the royal courts of Europe calling for the 'destruction of the House of Hohenzollern, this race of red-faced idiots and criminals' which for more than 100 years had lorded it over the throne of France and of Alsace too. In the meantime he had named 'Victor Buonaparte, the brother of our Laetitia, Emperor, made my friend Ms Bourdeau, editor-in-chief of the *Journal des Débats* and the *Revue des Deux Mondes*, ambassador to my court.' After which he had enjoyed a midday lunch with his 'cook', auspiciously named de la Pace (of Peace).

On New Year's Eve – for once he had marked the date – he wrote a short note to August Strindberg: 'You will receive an answer to your novelette – it sounds like a *gun-shot.* I have ordered an assembly-day of princes in Rome, I will have the young Kaiser shot. Auf Wiedersehen! For we shall see each other again . . . Une seule condition: Divorçons. [signed] Nietzsche Caesar.' To which the Swedish playwright promptly replied with a witty letter, which began ('θέλω, θέλω μανῆναι!' 'Willing, frenziedly willing!') and, after a few lines in Latin, ended, '*Interdum juvat insanire!* (It sometimes helps to be mad!) Strindberg (*Deus, optimus maximus*).'

But, alas, it was no joking matter. As Meta von Salis realized after receiving this short note, written on 3 January 1889: 'The world is transfigured, for God is on earth. Do you not see how the heavens are overjoyed? I have just taken possession of my Empire, I am throwing the Pope into prison and having Wilhelm, Bismarck and Stöcker shot. Signed *Der Gekreuzigte*' (the crucified one – i.e. Nietzsche the spurned and repudiated prophet who, like Jesus Christ, had been not without honour save in his own country).

No less than three short letters were written that same day to Cosima Wagner. The longest, addressed to 'Princess Ariadne, my beloved', read: 'It is a presupposition that I am a man. But I have already often lived among men and know everything that men can experience, from the lowest to the highest. I have been Buddha among Hindus, Dionysos in Greece – Alexander and Caesar are my incarnations, as well as Shakespeare's poet Lord Bakon [so spelled]. Finally, I am Voltaire and Napoleon, perhaps too Richard Wagner . . . But this time I come as the victorious Dionysos, who will make a festival of the earth . . . The heavens rejoice that I am there . . . I have also hung on the Cross . . . ' [unsigned].

The same, psychologically revealing signature – *Der Gekreuzigte* (the crucified one) – was used over the next few days in short letters sent to Georg Brandes in Copenhagen, to Heinrich Köselitz at his parents' home near Dresden, to Cardinal Mariani, to King Umberto I of Italy and to Malwida von Meysenbug in Rome (in a particularly tender note, 'forgiving' her everything because she had loved him much). Others, signed 'Dionysos', were sent to Erwin Rohde in Heidelberg, to Paul Deussen in Berlin, to Hans von Bülow in Hamburg, to Franz Overbeck and Jacob Burckhardt in Basel. As a special mark of respect – he was the only professor in the entire German-speaking world he genuinely admired – Nietzsche sent Burckhardt a second, far longer letter, in which charming glimpses of the Torino he had come to love were intermingled with fond fantasies about the persons who in his diseased imagination he now imagined himself to be or to have known – beginning with Vittorio Emmanuele, in whose Palazzo Carignano he had been born. This weird letter is too long to be quoted *in extenso*, but here is the postscript: 'Tomorrow my son Umberto is coming with the kindly Margherita [the musically minded Queen to whom Köselitz had once thought of dedicating his *Matrimonio segreto* opera], but I can only receive her here in shirtsleeves. *The rest* for Frau Cosima . . . Ariadne . . . From time to time will be bewitched . . . I go everywhere in my student's gown, here and there I slap someone on the shoulder and say: *siamo contenti? son dio, ho fatto questa caricatura* . . .' (Are we contented? I am god, I have made this caricature).

'I have had Caiaphas placed in chains; last year too I was crucified by German doctors in a very tedious way. Wilhelm [and] Bismarck and all antisemites eliminated. You can make whatever use you wish of this letter, provided it does not diminish me in the eyes of the inhabitants of Basel.'

Even before this letter was sent, Nietzsche's behaviour had become increasingly eccentric. One day he informed his landlord and the Fino family that the oil paintings adorning the walls of his bedroom had to be removed. It had to look 'like a temple', since he was expecting a visit from the King and Queen of Italy during a day of great festivity, when the streets of Torino would be brilliantly illuminated. When the post office employees refused to accept letters addressed to the King and Queen, he asked Davide Fino if he could post them for him, and his landlord, realizing that the professor had momentarily taken leave of his senses, nodded but quietly hid them away.

The climax in his odd behaviour was soon reached with a strange incident that took place on one of Turin's streets. On seeing a cart-driver furiously beating his lagging nag, Nietzsche ran forward and flung his arms around the horse's neck. Exactly what happened thereafter we shall probably never know, for the first printed account of this incident did not appear until thirteen years later in an Italian newspaper. But someone, it seems, hurried over to 6 Via Carlo Alberto to inform Davide Fino that something had happened to *il professore tedesco*, that a crowd had gathered, and could he come as quickly as possible and bring him 'home'?

The curious thing about this incident is that Nietzsche, during the previous May in Turin, had imagined something of the sort as happening in the dead of winter. Suddenly, in the middle of a letter to Reinhart von Seydlitz, he wrote that he had just imagined a tear-jerking scene, worthy of the *moralité larmoyante* Diderot had so rightly scorned, in which an old, brutal cart-driver stubbornly refused to give his thirsty horse the water it craved. And the poor, maltreated horse, instead of protesting, had looked around and indicated that it was grateful, very grateful. Just what inspired this suddenly imagined scene, it is not easy to say. Nietzsche may have been giving an ironic twist to the story of Buridanus's legendary ass, which, when presented with a haystack to the left and another to the right, let itself die because it was unable to make up its mind in which direction to turn. What could be more 'noble' for a maltreated horse than to scorn the water it had been refused! One thing at any rate is certain. In throwing his arms around the sorry nag on a Turin street, Nietzsche, who had endured so many humiliating slights and physical sufferings, was clearly identifying himself with this poor, maltreated creature.

Brought back to the house on the Via Carlo Alberto, Nietzsche was persuaded to go to bed, while a member of the Fino family went to fetch Turin's leading neurologist, Carlo Turina. But the moment the doctor appeared in his bedroom, Nietzsche protested vehemently, '*Pas malade! Pas malade!*' Not until later, when Turina was presented to Nietzsche as a 'friend', did the increasingly deranged 'patient' consent to receive him.

By the time Franz Overbeck reached Turin several days later, *il professore*'s behaviour had grown increasingly irrational. Not satisfied with playing for hours on the piano, he had taken to singing in his bedroom and to ordering bottles of Barbera wine, which the doctor had immediately forbidden. At one point, when Overbeck went upstairs to his bedroom to calm him, he was confronted by an appalling spectacle. A totally naked Nietzsche was leaping and whirling aound in a dance of Dionysian frenzy.

Night, the dark night of madness he had so long feared, had finally descended on Friedrich Nietzsche, blotting out the bright sunshine of Reason he had so much wanted to extol.

CHAPTER 39

# The Aftermath

*– 'With me a catastrophe is being prepared, whose name I know but shall not utter.'*

When, in the early afternoon of Tuesday, 8 January 1889, Franz Overbeck finally reached the corner house on the Via Carlo Alberto, he was greeted by the wife of Davide Fino who, at his wits' end as to what to do about his obstreperous tenant, had gone to see the German consul. When he walked into Nietzsche's bedroom, Overbeck found him slumped in one corner of the sofa trying to read the proofs of *Nietzsche contra Wagner*, which Naumann had just sent to him from Leipzig. Springing to his feet, Nietzsche flung his arms around his friend's neck, convulsively sobbing and repeating his name. He was trembling all over and Overbeck had some trouble keeping his balance as gently he led him back to the sofa. Nietzsche continued to twitch and groan until somebody had him swallow a bromide-water solution, which had been prescribed by Professor Carlo Turina.

Exactly what happened thereafter we shall probably never know; for Overbeck in later years was reluctant to discuss the subject. A German doctor named Baumann, who came to see Nietzsche, noted in a brief report that the 'patient' was ceaselessly upwrought and excited, ate a great deal, wanted even more, and was constantly demanding 'females'. In a letter written one week later to Heinrich Köselitz, Overbeck described Nietzsche as singing and 'raving' on the piano, shifting abruptly from loud *crescendi* as he imagined himself (as Dionysus) being torn to pieces, to indescribably soft notes, conjuring up 'sublime, wonderfully clear-sighted and unspeakably ghastly things' – each improvisation being followed by a convulsive fit. But what most saddened Overbeck was to hear this master of the German language no longer able to express 'his transports of gaiety other than through the most trivial phrases or through ludicrous dancing and leaping'.

One thing was painfully apparent. Nietzsche had lost his mind, probably for ever. Before leaving Basel, Overbeck had hurried out to a recently opened clinic for mentally deranged patients run by Professor Ludwig Wille, who for more than a dozen years had been teaching psychiatry at the university. After being shown the long letter Nietzsche had written to Jacob Burckhardt and the shorter one (ending 'I am having all antisemites shot . . . Dionysos') that Nietzsche had sent to Franz and his wife Ida on 4 January, Wille told Overbeck that there was not a moment to be lost: he must reach Turin as fast as possible and bring Nietzsche back to Basel before the Italian authorities had the 'crazy German' interned as a madman in a lunatic asylum.

In this crisis Overbeck was aided by the German consul, who recommended a German dentist named Bettmann, well known for his talent in calming hysterical patients. Bettmann, who turned out to be Jewish – as though Fate or Fortune had intervened to help the vehemently anti-antisemitic Nietzsche in this moment of distress – lived up to his reputation. While Overbeck spent a hectic Wednesday morning cramming many of his friend's manuscripts, letters and notebooks into several trunks, Nietzsche obstinately refused to leave his bed. But when Bettmann told him that he had to get up to take part in the festivities that were being prepared in Torino, Nietzsche, as docile as a child, obeyed him and got dressed. There was a tearful farewell with Davide Fino, to whom Nietzsche had become most attached, but also a comic moment when the departing tenant insisted on 'borrowing' his landlord's *papalina* – the Italian word for 'nightcap' probably suggesting something ludicrously 'papal'.

There was further trouble at the Turin railway station, where Nietzsche wanted to embrace every passer-by. Bettmann again rose to the occasion, pointing out that such behaviour was unseemly on the part of a *grand seigneur*. As the train pulled out of the station, the now totally uninhibited professor broke into a Venetian gondoliers' song. During the all-night trip to Basel, Overbeck and Bettmann kept feeding Nietzsche sedatives to calm him. Here again the astute dentist proved his extraordinary competence by explaining the need for this nerve-racking trip: a festive crowd had gathered in Basel to offer the 'returning hero' a triumphant welcome.

At the Basel railway station Nietzsche was persuaded without too much difficulty to climb into a cab, which took him and his two travelling companions to Dr Ludwig Wille's psychiatric clinic near the Alsatian border. For the first few days he was an unruly patient, repeatedly bursting into songs and unnerving howls and displaying a 'continuous motorial agitation' (as was noted in the official medical report). His appetite, to the surprise of his new wardens, was gargantuan.

Three days after Nietzsche's 'internment' Franziska turned up in Basel, where she was lodged in the Overbecks' house. At first, the meeting between the worried mother and her beloved 'Fritzchen' went off well. He embraced her warmly, seemed very calm and was able to discuss family matters as though nothing had happened and his mind was as clear as ever. But then, suddenly, he shouted: 'Behold in me the tyrant of Turin!'

Convinced that her son had suffered a momentary collapse due to overwork, and that with God's aid he could be restored to sanity, Franziska insisted that he be removed forthwith from Dr Wille's care and transferred to another psychiatric clinic, run by a Professor Otto Binswanger in Jena, conveniently close to Naumburg. On the 17th Franz Overbeck said goodbye to Friedrich Nietzsche at the Basel railway station. The philosopher's formerly brisk gait was now stumbling and uncertain, his entire bearing had become stiff, and in the harsh light of the gaslamps Nietzsche's once mobile features resembled a mask. Overbeck's lectures made it impossible for him to accompany his friend to Jena, but he and his wife Ida had found a competent replacement: Dr Ernst Mähly, one of Nietzsche's former *Pädagogium* students and the son of his former colleague in Latin studies, Professor Jacob Mähly.

The train journey from Basel (via Frankfurt) to Naumburg proved far more turbulent than the one from Turin to Basel, despite the presence of Fritz's mother. Dr Ernst Mähly had wisely insisted that Professor Wille's clinic provide him with someone to help him; but the strapping twenty-five-year-old medical assistant (Jacob Brand) lacked Bettmann's soothing ingenuity. Several times Nietzsche succumbed to fits of maniacal fury, even turning wildly against his mother, who had to move to another compartment, leaving the two men to cope with the him.

At Jena Mähly and the young medical assistant took Nietzsche to Professor Binswanger's asylum, while his mother was driven to their home by Professor Heinrich Gelzer and his wife Clara (the same who in August 1882 had briefly received Lou Salomé). Franziska Nietzsche then went to the clinic to take care of the financial details. Because of the high cost (5 marks and 50 pfennigs per day) of 'first-class' bed and board, Nietzsche had to be downgraded to a 'second-class' status (2 marks 50). In addition to a thorough physical examination, he was questioned about his past and replied with astonishing frankness. In the brief biographical notice recorded on 18 January in the asylum's daily register, it was noted that Nietzsche had been appointed professor at the University of Basel on the recommendation of Ritschl. This was followed by these words: '1866: syphilis through contagion'. Years later, a young medical student named Simchowitz, who frequently visited this 'Institution for the Cure of the Insane' during the month of January 1889, claimed that Nietzsche had told Binswanger that he had contracted syphilis while serving as a medical orderly during the Franco-Prussian War of 1870.

For Nietzsche's anxious mother the weeks and then the months that followed were particularly painful. To avert new outbreaks of maniacal fury on the part of the hyper-emotional patient, visits by friends or relatives were strictly forbidden. Not until mid-May, after weeks of sedatives and 'soothing' medication had brought about an improvement in his condition – with less wild yelling and fewer pompous declarations, often made in Italian or French to his principal attendant (sometimes called 'Prince Bismarck') that he was the 'Duke of Cumberland', 'King Frederick IV', 'the Kaiser', that he had been brought here by his 'wife Cosima Wagner', etc. – was Franziska Nietzsche finally allowed to see her son.

From the very outset both Ludwig Wille and Otto Binswanger were convinced that Nietzsche had but one or two years to live. But, as the months passed, thanks to his robust constitution, there was no sign of any further physical deterioration. In mid-January of 1890 Heinrich Köselitz, whose finally completed neo-Cimarosan opera, renamed *Die heimliche Ehe* (*The Secret Marriage*), was soon to be staged in Danzig, passed through Naumburg on his way to Jena. He told the delighted 'Frau Pastorin' that, having several weeks to spare, he would take her son out for long walks every day. Twenty-seven months had passed since Köselitz had last seen him. When he turned up at the Jena asylum on 21 January, he was immediately recognized by Nietzsche who, overjoyed, flung his arms around his 'devoted disciple', hugged him and repeatedly squeezed his hand. 'He did not look at all unwell,' Köselitz reported to the Danzig *Kapellmeister* Carl Fuchs. 'I would say that his present mental disorder consists merely in an accentuation of the humorous side of his nature . . . We talked a lot about Venice, and, curiously enough, what his memory had most vividly retained were several comic remarks I had made on the subject.'

Ten days later Köselitz wrote again to Fuchs to say that he was astounded by the 'improvement' he had noted in Nietzsche's health. He had gone upstairs to a large hall, where he had found him among a number of madmen. From there they had gone into the asylum's music-room. Köselitz had offered him six small cakes, but Nietzsche had refused: 'No, dear Friend, I don't want to have sticky fingers, first I want to play a bit.' Sitting down before the keyboard, he had begun to improvise. 'Oh, if you could but have heard him! Not one false note. A tissue of sounds of a Tristanian sadness. *Pianissimi*, then choruses and trumpet fanfares, Beethovenesque rage and shouts of triumph, and then again softness and dream-like reverie, it was indescribable. If only I had had a phonograph!'

On 16 February Franziska Nietzsche arrived from Naumburg. Biswanger's illustrious patient now had two companions to accompany him on his walks, to take him to lunch in various inns, and to entertain him in the afternoons and evenings in Franziska Nietzsche's rented room. They were joined one week later by Franz Overbeck, who took advantage of the Mardi Gras (*Fastnacht*) holidays to make a three-day visit to Jena. More lucid in his judgements than the devout Franziska, who kept reiterating her belief that the 'Good Lord' would finally answer her prayers and restore her beloved Fritz to sanity, Overbeck quickly grasped the limited extent of his friend's 'recovery'. Nietzsche could still talk about his life in Basel, but Overbeck's questions concerning the mental breakdown in Turin and what had happened since then elicited puzzled silence.

In early March Köselitz returned to Danzig to oversee the final rehearsals for the première of his neo-Cimarosan opera. Franziska Nietzsche remained in Jena, where for the next nine weeks, bravely defying rain, sleet and snow, she trudged out to Biswanger's asylum to pick up her son, taking him from there to the Stern (Star) – later it was the Paradies – where, before and after lunch, Fritz played on the *Gasthaus*'s piano. Later, in her rented apartment, his mother would read to him slowly, occasionally stroking his forehead. By the end of March Nietzsche, now usually as docile as a child, had grown so used to this routine that Franziska was able to lodge him in her apartment and to remove his clothes from Binswanger's asylum. Only once during the next five weeks was there a moment of crisis, when Nietzsche, who insisted on going to the public baths three times a week, disappeared, to the consternation of his mother, and wandered around Jena for several hours. To save her son from forcible 'reincarceration' in Biswanger's Institute, Franziska hurriedly packed Fritz's belongings and went to hide for several days in Professor Gelzer's spacious house. Early on 13 May 1890, accompanied by a young student friend of the Gelzer family, she 'smuggled' her son out to the railway station and on to a 6 a.m. train bound for Naumburg, where they were greeted by the faithful housemaid-cook Alwine, overjoyed to see the 'Herr Professor' in such surprisingly good health.

During the next few months, thanks to a daily régime of long walks in the morning and again, after a siesta, in the late afternoon, Nietzsche's outward appearance seemed to improve. He could walk more briskly, no longer needing to lean on his mother's arm, and he could still play the piano beautifully. But these external improvements were deceptive. When, in September, Paul Deussen stopped at Naumburg to see him, he noticed that Fritz could not take the initiative in conversations, every now and then interjecting some incongruous remark.

Although less grieved by the news of Nietzsche's mental breakdown than Heinrich Köselitz, who had felt like throwing himself out of the window of his Berlin apartment, the Leipzig publisher Constantin Naumann was understandably upset by this misfortune. On 14 January (1889) he wrote to Franz Overbeck to express his surprise, since right up until the end of December there had been no trace of insanity in Nietzsche's letters. The *Twilight of the Idols* 'pamphlet' had been ready since early November, and he was now sending out copies to booksellers. In accordance with the author's instructions, he had had *Nietzsche contra Wagner* typeset, but no copies had been printed. The third work of Nietzsche's he had in hand was a brief 'history of his life' entitled *Ecce homo*. Shortly thereafter Heinrich Köselitz made a quick trip to Leipzig. Naumann let him take the manuscript of *Ecce homo* back with him to Berlin. Köselitz was appalled by the alterations Nietzsche had made, particularly in the final chapter ('Why I am a Destiny'), which, in their bombastic outbursts, struck him as being radically different in tone from the far milder opening sections. On 22 January he informed Overbeck that he had read *Ecce homo* and was going to make a new handwritten copy. The text struck him as being a '*fire-belching* preface to the "Revaluation"'. 'This work must in any case be brought out, even if somewhat later,' he added, not realizing that this 'somewhat later' would drag on for another eighteen years.

Meanwhile, among the papers brought back from Turin, Overbeck had discovered the manuscript of *Der Antichrist* – intended to be the first volume of Nietzsche's repeatedly announced *Magnum opus, The Revaluation of all Values*. To guard against its possible disappearance, Overbeck followed Köselitz's example by laboriously writing out a second, far more legible copy of this explosive manuscript.

A major problem confronting Naumann, Overbeck and Köselitz was that of the publishing rights, since Nietzsche was no longer in a mental condition to defend his interests as an author. His mother, as the principal 'guardian', should normally have assumed this responsibility, but this was way beyond her intellectual capacities. If Franz Overbeck (whose sound judgement she trusted) had been teaching theology in nearby Jena, she would almost certainly have made him her principal adviser and co-guardian. Basel being too distant, she decided in early January 1890 to entrust this responsibility to her brother, Edmund Oehler, the vicar of Gorenzen, in whose pleasant home his nephew, Friedrich Nietzsche, had composed his *Silvesternacht* (New Year's Eve) cantata for violins and piano in 1863–4. This choice, to Naumann's intense annoyance, simply froze the situation. For a pious, simple-minded Lutheran like Edmund Oehler there could be no question of bringing out as heretical a work as *Der Antichrist*, the very title of which sounded like a blasphemous provocation. A similar veto was imposed on any immediate publication of the fourth *Zarathustra* volume and nine 'Dionysus-Dithyrambs' (free-verse lamentations and 'thundering ecstasies'), which Köselitz wanted to have appended as a kind of poetic 'coda' to the four-part *Zarathustra* 'symphony'.

Such was the situation in December 1890 when, shortly before Christmas, Fritz's sister Elisabeth turned up in Naumburg. In June of the previous year her despondent husband, Bernhard Förster, who had misled the settlers of the Nueva Germania colony by selling them plots of land that had been conditionally 'lent' to him by the Paraguayan government, had committed suicide. For more than a year his widow Elisabeth had struggled to carry on as the wilful 'manageress' of a hopelessly debt-ridden 'colony'. She had finally returned to Germany to raise more funds from 'patriotic' sponsors and to contest a scathing exposé of Bernhard Förster's deceitful practices and his arrogant wife's lordly lifestyle (four cooks, eight servants!).

Franziska Nietzsche was waiting at the Naumburg station to greet her daughter, along with Fritz, who was carrying a bouquet of roses. Although he immediately recognized his sister, calling her by his favourite nickname of 'Llama', his mother had to nudge her son to get him to hand her the bouquet. After which Fritz began to babble about his experiences in the Prussian army. While Elisabeth was distressed to find her previously articulate brother reduced to this pathetic condition, her mother was shocked to discover that her daughter had returned to Germany not to help her look after Fritz, but to raise money to repay debts rashly incurred with Paraguayan banks during the development of the Nueva Germania colony. Between hurried trips to Chemnitz, Leipzig, Berlin, frantic letter-writing, and the preparation of a book defending the Nueva Germania enterprise, Elisabeth found time to read 'The Last Supper', the 'Ass Festival', and other chapters parodying the New Testament, which struck her as dangerously sacrilegious. She concurred with Uncle Edmund Oehler that the publication of *Zarathustra* IV would not be opportune. As Köselitz wrote to Overbeck in Basel: 'It's really enough to make one die of laughter, to see two God-fearing women and a country parson sitting in judgement on the publication of the writings of one of the most downright of anti-Christians and atheists. But for the moment I'm in no mood to laugh.'

In September of 1891 Edmund Oehler unexpectedly died, and his duties as 'co-guardian' were thereafter assumed by his son Adalbert, a municipal councillor in Halle. Constantin Naumann now decided that he had been kept waiting long enough. Acting on his own, he brought out a second edition (with print orders of 1,000 copies) of *Beyond Good and Evil*, *The Genealogy of Morals*, and *The Case of Wagner*, to satisfy a demand which was steadily growing. Elisabeth was incensed by this 'unauthorized' initiative and decided to start legal proceedings against the Leipzig publisher.

In mid-October, when Köselitz turned up in Naumburg on the occasion of Nietzsche's forty-seventh birthday, he found that his condition had drastically deteriorated. Whereas one year before he could still play beautiful chords and arpeggios on the piano, now he kept hitting false notes and pounding out excruciating discords. The atmosphere in the house was one of unpleasant tension, marked by long arguments between the timorous Franziska, anxious to avoid running up huge debts in legal fees, and her combative daughter Elisabeth, determined to defend her brother's literary interests tooth and nail. All the available 'documents' – exchanges of letters and so on – were turned over to a local lawyer, who threatened Naumann with a lawsuit. The ageing publisher sent his nephew to negotiate with the energetic 'Frau Doktor' Förster and her lawyer. Some hard bargaining ensued. Finally, in early February of 1892, Naumann was granted the right to publish a new, second edition of all Nietzsche's books, including those for which Fritzsch had obtained the first-edition rights. In exchange, Naumann agreed to pay the family an advance of 50 marks for each sixteen pages of printed text – ten more than Nietzsche had been getting when he was still sane.

During the summer Elisabeth returned by ship to Paraguay, while Heinrich Köselitz, again installed in his parents' home near Dresden, took over the job of editing this new edition of Nietzsche's 'Complete Works'. This, he felt, was the debt of gratitude he owed to the man who had encouraged his efforts as a composer, even going so far as to honour 'Pietro Gasti' publicly – first in *Ecce homo*, then again in *Nietzsche contra Wagner* – as a maestro of 'southern' music, comparable to Rossini!

In mid-October, when Köselitz came to Naumburg to examine the contents of five crates filled with books, notebooks and miscellaneous papers which Davide Fino had dutifully shipped from Turin to Franz Overbeck in Basel, he was shocked by the further deterioration in Nietzsche's mental condition. The 'patient' no longer recognized him. At breakfast (which he now took in bed) and also at lunch he had to be personally fed by his mother or Alwine. At night he often kept everyone in the house awake by carrying on long, incoherent monologues, endlessly repeating, for example, 'I am dead because I am stupid,' or, obversely, 'I am stupid because I am dead.'

Taking a number of notebooks and manuscripts back to his parents' home near Dresden, Köselitz continued his job of editing, writing explanatory prefaces (under the pseudonym of 'Peter Gast') for the new second editions of the four 'Untimely Meditations' and all four parts of *Thus Spake Zarathustra*, now published (in 1892) for the first time in their entirety (as Volume VII of this 'Complete Edition' series).

In September 1893 Elisabeth returned from Paraguay, where she had managed to find a buyer for her 'Försterhof' home. Her brother's increasing listlessness and immobility – he now spent more than half of each day in bed or stretched out on a *chaise-longue* – had obliged their mother to pierce a doorway through one wall of his bedroom, so that he could be wheeled into the vine-covered verandah. The early morning walks had been abandoned, so embarrassingly obstreperous in his greetings to strangers and in sudden bursts of song had Fritz become.

Having so ignominiously failed in her colonizing venture in South America, Elisabeth was all the more determined to succeed at home. Leaving her mother and Alwine to look after her brother, she took personal charge of his finances and the future publication of his books – one of which, the at last complete *Zarathustra*, had broken all records with a sale of 1,000 copies in eight months. She was, however, startled to discover that Constantin Naumann had launched the *Gesamtausgabe* (*Complete Edition*) series with a volume numbered II, and even more outraged to learn that 'Peter Gast' had volunteered to 'open' the series with a short biography of Friedrich Nietzsche. What did Köselitz know about Nietzsche's youth and adolescence? Virtually nothing. If anyone was going to write a biography about him, it was going to be his sister, who had now 'distinguished' herself as an author of articles in the *Bayreuther Blätter* and of a book about the Nueva Germania colony in Paraguay. At a tense meeting in Leipzig Elisabeth told Köselitz that a 'scholarly' and less disorderly edition of her brother's works would now have to be published – with the help of another editor. And to make it quite clear who from now on was going to run the show, she obtained permission to keep her maiden name and to call herself Elisabeth Förster-Nietzsche: a glaring *mésalliance* of names (the antisemite coupled with the anti-antisemite) which shocked Köselitz and Overbeck.

This was merely the beginning of a 'new règime'. In Berlin Elisabeth recruited Fritz Koegel, a fervent admirer of her brother's works, the proud possessor of a doctorate of philosophy from Jena, and something of a piano-playing poet. One of the vacant downstairs rooms of the corner house on the Weingartenstrasse, which the financially hard-pressed Franziska used to rent out to lodgers, was turned into a 'Nietzsche Archives' room for the careful assembling and itemizing of the philosopher's notebooks, manuscripts and papers. An inner wall was knocked down, and two other ground-floor rooms were transformed into a 'grand' reception-room for visitors who, it was hoped, could be spared the sound of Nietzsche's occasional shouts on the floor above.

Initially captivated, like her daughter, by Fritz Koegel's 'salon-charmer' manners, Franziska Nietzsche soon began to have misgivings about the long tête-à-tètes Elisabeth was having with her 'chief editor' in the downstairs Archives room, while, aided by the faithful Alwine, she was left to cope upstairs with an increasingly passive or incoherent Fritz. The pious mother was even more shocked by the sounds of joyful piano-playing and singing which were now frequently heard downstairs when, to impress the leading citizens of Naumburg, the snobbish Elisabeth organized 'soirèes' for the most socially significant among them.

One of Fritz Koegel's first assignments was to launch a literary 'counter-attack' against Lou Andreas-Salomé (as she now called herself, having casually added her inert husband's name to her own), whose successive articles on Nietzsche (whose 'intimate' friend she had once been) had created a stir in Berlin. The reopening of hostilities against the 'detestable' Lou galvanized Elisabeth's literary energies. Working at a furious tempo, she completed most of the first volume of the biography of her brother by the end of 1894. In the process the 'traitor' Heinrich Romundt, who had dared to praise Lou Salomé's ten essays, received a 'well-deserved' comeuppance by being eliminated from the story of Friedrich Nietzsche's life!

Elated by the realization that with each passing month her brother's works were arousing new controversies and attracting more and more readers, the forceful Elisabeth browbeat Naumann into signing a contract which obligated the publisher to make her an annual advance of 4,000 marks, more than two-thirds of which were earmarked as an annual salary payment for Fritz Koegel. Elisabeth could now work alone with the charming Fritz Koegel, unchaperoned and undisturbed, on the preparation of a new, large-page edition (later called the *Grossoktav Ausgabe*) of Nietzsche's *Complete Works*. This 'shocking' situation alarmed Franziska Nietzsche – what a bonanza for the smug gossipers of Naumburg! There were angry scenes between mother and daughter. In a huff Elisabeth removed herself from the corner house on the Weingarten-strasse to more spacious quarters on a nearby street, taking with her Fritz Koegel and the Nietzsche Archives.

The tense relations between mother and daughter were not improved when, in April 1895, Elisabeth brought out the first volume of her biography of Friedrich Nietzsche. Franziska was mortified to discover that her role in the upbringing of her son had been repeatedly played down, while that of his grandmother, Erdmuthe Nietzsche, had been deliberately exaggerated.

In September 1895 Elisabeth, reluctantly realizing that she would need his assistance, met Franz Overbeck in Zürich. He agreed to supply her with a few biographical facts, but, like Erwin Rohde, he refused to be involved in the 'evaluation' of unpublished material which Nietzsche, over the years, had jotted down in scores of notebooks. At Franziska Nietzsche's urgent request he made a detour via Naumburg before returning to Basel. For Overbeck too it was a shattering experience to see the piteous condition to which his once sturdy friend had been reduced. 'Not once did he leave his sick-chair,' he later recalled, 'only occasionally did he shoot a fleeting, semi-hostile glance at me, and he gave me the overall impression of being a mortally wounded, noble animal, which has withdraw into its cranny and now thinks only of perishing.'

Flushed by the success her biography was enjoying, Elisabeth felt increasingly irked by her mother's strenuous opposition to the publication of *Der Antichrist* as the eighth volume of Nietzsche's *Complete Works*. To put an end to this ambiguous situation, she boldly decided to buy out her mother's rights to future royalties from Naumann by offering her the enormous sum of 30,000 marks! This could only be done with a bank loan underwritten by several sponsors. Fritz Koegel was sent to Berlin to contact friends and Nietzsche admirers. He returned to Naumburg with the news that he had recruited three sponsors: a lawyer friend named Hermann Heckel, a 'philanthropist' from Leipzig, Raoul Richter, a well-to-do lover of the arts, Count Harry Kessler. Elisabeth, for her part, had written to her brother's friend Meta von Salis with whom she had been corresponding about the future of the 'Nietzsche Archives'.

By the terms of a contract drawn up in December 1895 with the connivance of Nietzsche's second 'guardian' and Elisabeth's first cousin, Adalbert Oehler, the 'Nietzsche Archives' were recognized as being the sole repository of his manuscripts and papers. She was formally declared to be its overseer. All of his author's rights for present and future editions, with Naumann or with publishers in other countries, were transferred from Nietzsche's two official guardians to his sister Elisabeth. In exchange, Elisabeth was granted little more than six weeks in which to provide her mother with the sum of 30,000 marks. The intimidated Franziska was given no time to have second thoughts. On 18 December, after receiving the complete contract text from her nephew Adalbert Oehler, she was informed by Elisabeth that an appointment had been made with a Naumburg notary, who was coming to her house that very afternoon! And it was thus, in fear and trembling before her strong-willed daughter, that a miserable, browbeaten Franziska Nietzsche appended her 'sour-blood' (*blutsauer*) signature to what struck her as being a 'blood-sucking' (*blutsaugende*) contract.

It was now up to Elisabeth to fulfil her part of the bargain – by producing the 30,000 marks before 1 February 1896. Thanks to Koegel's invaluable spadework, the three Berlin 'admirers' agreed to guarantee the bank loan, each to the tune of 6,000 marks. So did the affluent Meta von

Salis. The remaining 6,000 marks were provided by the Berlin banker Robert von Mendelssohn, great-grandson of the famous eighteenth-century philosopher, who did not even ask to be included among the Board of Overseers of the Nietzsche Archives. The next 'logical' step was taken five months later when, to free herself completely from maternal 'interference', Elisabeth moved from 'provincial' Naumburg to more 'cosmopolitan' Weimar, which still boasted a ducal 'court', complete with castle, several palaces and an exquisite baroque library. The Nietzsche Archives were now installed in new quarters on the Wörthstrasse, near the centre of the prestigious town.

While this translocation permitted the snobbish Elisabeth to move up one notch higher on the social ladder to a more 'glittering' society, it put an unexpected end to her flirtatious friendship with Fritz Koegel. Introduced in nearby Jena to Professor Gelzer and his wife Clara, Fritz Koegel, the handsome salon charmer, proceeded to fall in love with their daughter Emily. Elisabeth then hired a new assistant – a bright young scholar named Rudolf Steiner (the later founder of 'Anthroposophy'). He proved his competence not only by working more expertly than Koegel, but by offering to give Elisabeth private lessons in philosophy.

Meanwhile, from Christmas 1896 on, Franziska Nietzsche's health deteriorated dramatically. Emotionally exhausted by the constant quarrels with her daughter, humiliated and saddened by her departure for Weimar, physically worn out by the daily and often nocturnal care she had to provide for her '*Herzenssohn*' Fritz, she no longer had the strength to resist the onset of a '*Darmkataarh*' (intestinal 'catarrh' or flu), which may well have been a malignant cancer. On 20 April 1897 – a day fateful because it happened to coincide with the eighth birthday of a man who was destined to fulfil her son's worst fears to a diabolical degree, an Austrian named Adolf Hitler – Franziska Nietzsche died, tended to the last by the faithful cook Alwine, and her Naumburg doctor, while a few yards away her mindless Fritz remained blissfully ignorant of what was going on.

Faced with a new crisis, Elisabeth appealed once again to Meta von Salis. In the little house on the Wörthstrasse there was simply no room for her brother. Something bigger was needed. Meta von Salis made a quick trip to Weimar, where, to the south, near the summit of a barren hill 'graced' by an antiquated windmill which had lost its weatherbeaten sails, she found a vacant three-storey villa. Though nondescript in appearance, it had one shining virtue, charmingly enshrined in its name: Villa *Silberblick* (Silver view). It commanded a fine view over the little city, with its ducal *Schloss* and dark tower, its ochre-hued houses, the spire of the Peter-and-Paul church, where the erudite Johann Gottfried Herder had once preached, and the soft, green-leafed willows, birches and ashes bordering the gently flowing Ilm, along which Goethe, Schiller and so many others had enjoyed strolling. Meta von Salis agreed to buy the Villa Silberblick for 39,000 marks – as a fitting home for the rest of his lifetime for the soft-spoken philosopher who, nine years before, had let himself be rowed over the luminous waters of Lake Sils.

In June Fritz Koegel was dismissed as editor-in-chief of the stalled *Grossoktav* edition, while Rudolf Steiner, who had abandoned the hopeless task of trying to teach the pig-headed Elisabeth the rudiments of philosophy, gave up his work at the Archives. On 20 July Elisabeth had the archives moved from the Wörthstrasse, in the centre of Weimar, and trundled up the long hill to the Villa Silberblick. On closer inspection, it struck her as not being grand enough to be a suitable home for her brother – particularly since it lacked a verandah, like the one in Naumburg, where Fritz had spent so many sun-blessed afternoons. Seized by the kind of *folie des grandeurs* she had already displayed as the self-crowned Queen of the Nueva Germania colony in Paraguay, Elisabeth recruited a small army of masons, carpenters, roofers, plumbers and painters and had a verandah added to the villa, a new bathroom installed, and the 'guest-room' doubled in size. Trees were also planted around the villa, to provide Nietzsche with shade for his eyes.

Belatedly informed of these 'urgently needed' improvements – the costs of which were to be covered by the villa's owner – Meta von Salis was furious. She sent Elisabeth a stinging letter, accusing her of having wanted to turn the Villa Silberblick into her own luxurious home rather than into one for her brother. This of course was the truth. But since Elisabeth had now cast herself in the role of high priestess in a Trinity composed of her brother, his works and herself, she pleaded not guilty to any serious wrong-doing.

Nietzsche was hardly installed in his new home, along with the archives and the 'staff', when the Villa Silberblick received its first visitor: another of the four *Nietzsche Archiv* sponsors, Count Harry Kessler. The son of a rich Hamburg banker who had been ennobled by Kaiser Wilhelm I, Harry Kessler had been brought up in Paris and sent to school in England before attending the universities of Bonn and Leipzig. At this time a dapper young man of twenty-nine, he was the very model of the *Vornehmheit* (superior distinction) Nietzsche had praised in his writings. His cosmopolitan background also made him a polished European polyglot who deplored the rising tide of nationalistic hatreds which, as Nietzsche had predicted, were likely to tear the Old World to pieces.

Kessler, to his surprise, was met at the Weimar railway station by a liveried manservant, before being driven in a carriage through the old town and on up the hill to the Villa Silberblick. Inside, he was impressed by the amount of ground-floor space that was available for the storing of the archives, and by the long reception-room, with windows looking out over Weimar and its little valley. Kessler's guest-room was on the second floor, above the private apartments of Elisabeth and her brother. 'Everything,' he noted in his diary, 'is solidly furnished, but without regard to more refined tastes. It is the home of a well-to-do university professor or civil servant.'

On the evening of his arrival, Kessler was treated for several hours to a long-winded account of Elisabeth's personal feuds with Koegel and Rudolf Steiner. 'When Frau Förster talks of her brother,' he noted in his diary, 'it sounds as though he were a tiny child, just beginning to speak. She seems to have become so used to regarding her brother as a babbling infant that she does not comprehend the awful tragedy of it all.'

The next morning, after breakfast, Elisabeth took her house-guest in to meet her brother. When they entered Nietzsche's room they found him asleep on a sofa. 'His mighty head had sunk halfway down to the right of his chest, as if it were too heavy for his neck. His forehead was truly colossal; his mane-like hair is still dark brown, like his shaggy, out-thrusting moustache . . . In his lifeless, flabby face one can still see deep wrinkles dug by thought and will power, but softened, so to speak, and being smoothed out. There is an infinite weariness in his expression. His hands are waxen, with green and violet veins, and slightly swollen, as with a corpse.'

Far from wishing to conceal her witless brother, Elisabeth now turned the Villa Silberblick into a kind of shrine, where 'pilgrims' were received in a long drawing-room, heated in winter by a monumental green porcelain stove, while handsome copies of Nietzsche's books were exposed in various bookcases. The most admiring and socially significant of these visitors were taken upstairs to see the mute 'thinker,' who, to simplify the irksome problem of dressing and undressing him, now spent much of his time in a white linen gown, which made him look like a guru. The fashionable, prize-winning painter Curt Stöving – whom Elisabeth had already lured to Naumburg to paint a portrait of her brother (which showed him, pathetically stoop-shouldered, looking like a 'sick, caged bird') – was invited to the Villa Silberblick, this time to execute a bust. He was followed in May 1898 by another sculptor, Max Kruse. The next summer (1899) the noted painter Hans Olde was invited to spend two months in Weimar, during which he churned out seven oil paintings, one pen drawing, seventeen pencil or charcoal drawings, five etchings, and took sixteen photographs – several of which 'immortalized' the massive forehead and the bushy moustache for posterity (in countless magazine and newspaper reproductions, on book covers, etc.).

Elisabeth meanwhile had been having trouble finding competent scholars capable of carrying on the work begun by Fritz Koegel and Rudolf Steiner. Putting her pride in her pocket, she began making overtures to Heinrich Köselitz, whom she had so summarily dismissed several years before. Flattered though he was by this change of heart, Köselitz could not help noticing that the editors of the *Grossoktav* edition had been coming and going at an average rate of one per year. As he reported to Overbeck in Basel, 'Naumann is once again being sued by a lawyer for this angelic lady. Almost all she knows how to do is to upset, torment, maltreat people and to pass judgement with the most blatant unfairness.'

After his mother's death in April 1900, Köselitz finally yielded to Elisabeth's entreaties. In announcing the news to Franz Overbeck, who was invited to come to Weimar with his wife to visit him in his new lodgings on the Lisztstrasse, Köselitz added: 'To imagine that Frau Förster could intrude on our privacy is out of the question. She never takes a step in the town, she only travels by carriage with a coachman and liveried footman seated on the box.'

It is quite possible that in pulling Köselitz back into her editorial web, Elisabeth was counting on him not only to edit manuscripts but also to keep her brother musically entertained. For in June 1900, when Isabella von der Pahlen – now happily married, the mother of several children, and a well-known graphologist – visited the Villa Silberblick, wishing to examine samples of Nietzsche's handwriting during different periods of his life, she was struck by the fact that he remained extraordinarily sensitive to music. After Elisabeth had explained to her 'darling' Fritz that this was somebody he had once known, Isabella von der Pahlen took Nietzsche's thin, emaciated hand in both of hers and gently reminded him that years ago they had travelled in the same train to Genoa and met again in Pisa (in the autumn of 1877, when he was on his way to Sorrento). Nietzsche looked at her, puzzled, and then, shaking his head, he turned and looked questioningly at his sister. But a moment later, when from the corridor came the sound of rippling notes and rolling chords, as 'Peter Gast' danced with his fingers up and down the keyboard, Nietzsche's body suddenly responded with a feverish spasm of excitement and his 'transparent hands' came together to signal his applause.

Little could Isabella guess that this was one of the last times Friedrich Nietzsche would thrill to the sound of piano music. A few weeks later he succumbed to an attack of influenza, which turned into a pneumonic inflammation of one lung. During the night of Friday to Saturday, 24–25 August, he suffered a heart attack. He died a few hours later, shortly before noon of the saint's day of St Louis – 25 August, which, again by a most curious coincidence, had been the birthday of King Ludwig II of Bavaria and, for that reason, the day on which a grateful Richard Wagner had chosen thirty years before to marry Cosima Liszt (von Bülow).

Alerted by telegram at his Berlin home, Harry Kessler reached Weimar the next day. Since there was not time enough to call in a professional sculptor, he satisfied Elisabeth's request by personally fashioning a death-mask with the assistance of a local plasterer. Nietzsche's corpse was then stretched out inside a stout oak coffin on a 'bed' of white linen and damask.

At five o'clock on the afternoon of Monday, 27 August, a bizarre funeral service was held in the jam-packed Archives Room of the Villa Silberblick, amid lit candles, potted palms and heaps of flowers. The musical arrangements, hastily improvised by 'Peter Gast', included a Brahms cantata based on a poem of Claus Groth's (one of the young Fritz's favourites) and a five-voice 'Miserere' which Köselitz had personally composed in the style of Palestrina – both sung by women friends of Elisabeth. Ernst Horneffer (one of the archivists) had been asked to deliver the valedictory, but, feeling that this was insufficiently grand for the occasion, Elisabeth had asked the celebrated art historian Kurt Breysig to prononce a funeral oration. Standing awkwardly by the window, he had trouble reading his lengthy text until, after a bit of hasty scrambling, he was able to place his pages on a sewing-box which, propped up against the window-sill, served as a lectern. It was an interminable oration, which bored most of the listeners and exasperated one of them, the architect Fritz Schumacher, who later wrote: 'The same sterile scholasticism against which Nietzsche had fought throughout his life followed him to the grave. If he had arisen, he would have thrown the lecturer out of the window and chased the rest of us out of his temple.'

Even more grotesque was the burial ceremony, which, at Elisabeth's insistence and in spite of the protests of the vicar (who boycotted the proceedings), was held the following afternoon in the graveyard of the Röcken parish church – so that Friedrich Wilhelm Nietzsche could be laid to rest next to the coffins of his father, Pastor Ludwig, and his little brother, Joseph. A male choir, hastily recruited by Köselitz from the mass of Nietzsche and Oehler relatives who converged on the Thuringian village, provided the musical accompaniment. The solemnity of the occasion was enhanced by the ringing of the old bells which, fifty-six years and 318 days before, had joyously announced the entry into the world of Pastor Ludwig's and his wife Franziska's baby son, and which, four years later, had tolled the death-knell for the piano-playing pastor's premature demise.

This time the funeral oration was delivered by Nietzsche's first cousin, Adalbert Oehler, now mayor of Halberstadt. It was followed by three brief 'parting words' uttered by Nietzsche's former Pforta tutor and later Basel colleague, Professor Max Heinze, who declared that from his sickroom the spirit of his works had conquered a 'large part of the intellectual world'; by Carl von Gersdorff, who altered the traditional Latin farewell greeting from '*Have cara anima!*' to '*Have anima candida!*' (Hail to you, brilliant spirit!); and by Carl Fuchs, the normally long-winded musicologist and *Kapellmeister* from Danzig, who managed for once to compress his thoughts into an eleven-line poem, in which Nietzsche's '*Morgenröte*' (morning glow) was transformed into his final '*Morgenglanz*' (morning brilliance).The *Bekenntnis* ('Confession of Faith' or 'Statement of Loyalty', depending on the listeners' religious or agnostic interpretation) was delivered by 'Peter Gast' (Heinrich Köselitz) who, after comparing Nietzsche's fate to Spinoza's, concluded: 'Hallowed be thy name to all coming generations!' After which, in a culminating masterpiece of unintended satire – which would have provoked a burst of 'cosmic laughter' from Nietzsche – nine admirers quoted brief verses from that most sacrilegious of modern anti-Christian scriptures, *Thus Spake Zarathustra.*

Of Nietzsche's four close, truly intellectual friends (all of them university professors), not one was present to witness the tragicomic ceremony staged by Elisabeth and Köselitz at Röcken. Jacob Burckhardt had died three years before in Basel. Erwin Rohde had followed him to the grave in January 1898, worn out by academic drudgery and the painstaking research that had preceded the writing of his *magnum opus*, *Psyche* – in which he had developed a basically anti-Nietzschean interpretation of the Greek 'soul'. Paul Deussen, again travelling with his wife, could not be reached. As for Franz Overbeck, whom Köselitz tried vainly to alert, he was off vacationing in the French Vosges mountains with his wife Ida – to the secret relief of Elisabeth Förster-Nietzsche, who cordially detested both of them for having once shown sympathy towards Lou Salomé.

# Epilogue

It is difficult to avoid superlatives in dealing with Nietzsche's philosophy, in which so much is incandescently hot or chillingly cold, breathtakingly high or abysmally deep. But I hope I may be forgiven for declaring, at the start of this brief Epilogue, that never, in the history of modern thought, did a philosophy that was largely spurned during the first forty-four years of the thinker's life enjoy such a spectacular 'take-off' during the last decade of his existence, or go on to exert such a powerful (and, alas, baleful) influence during the four decades that followed.

The reasons for this are complex: so complex indeed that entire books have been written to explain this extraordinary phenomenon. Richard Frank Krummel, who made a systematic attempt to investigate every aspect of Nietzsche's colossal influence in his homeland (*Nietzsche und der deutsche Geist – Nietzsche and the German Spirit*) needed two volumes (published in 1974) to deal with the subject. Interested readers unfamiliar with the German language need not despair, however. For since then the subject has been admirably treated by Stephen Aschheim in *The Nietzsche Legacy in Germany, 1890–1990*, first published by the University of California Press in 1992. Like Stendhal, Nietzsche was persuaded that his genius would not be properly recognized until forty years after his death. In this he turned out to be mistaken. Already in March 1887, twenty-one months before his mental breakdown, he was struck by the 'comic fact' (as he put it in a letter to Franz Overbeck) that his books had begun to exert a curiously 'subterranean' influence. 'Among all radical parties (Socialists, nihilists, antisemites, Christ[ian] Orthodox, Wagnerians) I enjoy a wondrous and almost mysterious repute.' To which he added with singular lucidity: 'The extreme sincerity of the atmosphere in which I have placed myself, seduces. I can even misuse my frankness, I can scold, as has happened in my most recent books – people suffer therefrom, some may perhaps "abjure" me, but they cannot rid themselves of me.'

Nietzsche, in this last sentence, had put his finger on one major cause of the 'mysterious' esteem he had acquired: his fearless candour in a late Victorian age of multiple hypocrisies, his refreshing refusal to beat about the bush, his unflinching determination to call a spade a spade, no matter how unfashionable and unpopular his trenchant assertions and anathemas might seem. What he did not say, at any rate in this letter, was that his uncompromising candour was expressed with a poetic force and polemical verve (the two often go hand in hand) at least equal to Henrich Heine's, while the 'open-endedness' (Aschheim's apt term) of his protean philosophy – at once radical and aristocratic, nostalgic and futuristic, rational and sub-rational, romantic and anti-romantic, 'post-modern' and anti-modern, anti-Gothic and neo-Gothic – made it irresistibly attractive to persons from the most varied walks of life and political persuasions – except, significantly, diehard conservatives of the Throne-and-Altar species.

The rise of 'Nietzscheism' – for an -ism it soon became – during the last decade of the nineteenth century happened to coincide with the advent of a new style in architecture, internal decoration, glassware and ceramics, significantly called in German *Jugendstil* ('young style') and in French, more prosaically, *Art nouveau*, whose distinctive features – intertwining vines, flowing curves, leafy patterns – all paid symbolic homage to a 'rediscovery' of Nature and of Life, away from and in opposition to the Triumph of Mechanics and those material 'things' which, as Emerson had noted, were now 'in the saddle and ride mankind'. Perhaps nobody has more vividly expressed the mystico-religious spell cast by Nietzsche's books during this crepuscular *fin de siècle* than his polyglottic admirer, Harry Graf Kessler:

> There grew within us a secret Messianism. The desert, to which every Messiah belongs, was in our hearts; and suddenly, like a meteor, Nietzsche appeared . . . The way in which Nietzsche influenced, or more precisely possessed, us cannot be compared with the effect of any other thinker or poet. He did not merely speak to reason and fantasy. His impact was more encompassing, deeper, and more mysterious. His ever-growing echo signified the irruption of *Mystik* into a rationalized and mechanized age. He bridged the abyss between us and reality with the veil of heroism. Through him we were tranported out of this ice age, re-enchanted and enraptured.

It was precisely this irruption of a sub-logical, irrational mystique into the smug, philistine, bourgeois world of the Wilhelmian *Kaiserreich* which explains what otherwise would be inexplicable: the extraordinary attraction exercised by Nietzsche's books on fervent feminists who should have been repelled by his outspokenly macho and anti-feminist philosophy.

Dazzled by the effulgence of his 'liberating' message, so softly, subtly, poetically, defiantly and yet wistfully expressed in the 'Old and New Tablets' chapter of *Zarathustra* III – 'O thou my will! Thou end of every plight, thou my necessity! Preserve me from all small victories! Thou fate-stroke of my soul, which I call destiny! Thou in-me! Over-me! Preserve and save me for one great destiny!' – one of these charmed creatures, Hedwig Dohm, answered the captivating challenge in 1894 by bringing out a novel boldly entitled *How to Become Women – Be What You Are*, in which the heroine called Nietzsche the 'greatest living philosopher'. Not to be outshone, another fervent feminist, Käthe Schirrmacher, followed up the next year with another novel, in which the New Woman of this still stiffly corseted *fin de siècle* was made to proclaim:

> We want to be modern! That means a break with misunderstood Greek and Roman ideas – a break with orthodox religion – freedom, use of our energy, nature – independence, experimentation rather than abstraction and stereotype – a triumphant ego! In such a transition the weak may succumb, those transitional types that are no longer very old and not yet very new – but we, we will make it!

That is, the *Überfrauen*, the over- or super-women of the looming twentieth century!

Paradoxically, it was his vehement critics, even more than his fervent fans – writers like the Kant-inspired Socialist Kurt Eisner (author of a book aggressively entitled *Psychopathia spiritualis*), or like the renowned Hungarian-Jewish pathologist Max Nordau, who contributed most to Nietzsche's notoriety and fame by portraying him as mentally deranged. In Nordau's bestselling book, *Entartung* (*Degeneration*), Nietzsche was lumped together with Baudelaire, Oscar Wilde, Maurice Maeterlinck, Ibsen, Zola and Walt Whitman as a prototypically 'decadent' author. The book created such a sensation that it was soon translated from German into half a dozen European languages, including English. In it Nietzsche's 'ecstatic prophecies' were likened to the 'senseless stammering and babbling of deranged minds', while his philosophy was denounced as the crazy work of a sadist with whom 'no image of wickedness can arise without arousing him sexually'.

There is not space here to describe the multiple ramifications of what by the turn of the century had become not simply a philosophico-religious cult but, as Steven Aschheim has so well described it, a 'kitsch industry', actively promoted by his sister's 'Nietzsche Archives' in Weimar, in which heroic busts, drawings and paintings – all of them emphasizing the massive forehead, the thick eyebrows, the downward-curling bush of a moustache (soon become as famous as Bismarck's) – were popularized on postcards, magazine illustrations and even bookplates, like the one portraying the philosopher, his forehead bound by a Christ-like crown of thorns, above the Zarathustran words: 'Of all that is written, that alone I love which one writes with one's blood.'

Nietzsche's death during the summer of 1900, tragically terminating ten years of superannuated 'longevity' (of the kind he himself had so forthrightly condemned), merely enhanced his status as the 'martyr of deep thought' he had been made to resemble in countless photographs and pictures. The 'event' unleashed a small avalanche of eulogies and elegiac essays, as well as some 'heroic' verses by Germany's foremost poet, Stefan Georg, who for some years past had been encouraging the members of his literary 'circle' to carry on the élitist work of cultural renovation and personal self-ennoblement Nietzsche had so courageously begun.

Elisabeth Förster-Nietzsche chose to celebrate her brother's death in her own high-handed manner by soon bringing out a thick anthology of his hastily jotted but so far unpublished notes under the inflammatory title *The Will to Power*, brazenly proclaiming it to be her brother's *Hauptwerk* (*magnum opus*) and philosophical 'testament'.

Long before this, the Nietzsche cult had crossed the English Channel – partly thanks to Max Nordau's vitriolic denunciation (a British bestseller in 1895), partly to the untiring efforts of a Scotsman, Thomas Common, so smitten by the author of *Thus Spake Zarathustra* that he had abandoned the idea of becoming a Protestant clergyman. The story of how a galaxy of Anglo-Irish authors were, for shorter or longer periods, fascinated by Nietzsche – they include Havelock Ellis, William Butler Yeats, George Bernard Shaw, H.G. Wells, James Joyce, John Davidson, Alfred R. Orage, Wyndham Lewis, Edwin Muir, Herbert Read, D.H. Lawrence, J.C. Powys and two expatriate poets, T.S. Eliot and Ezra Pound – has been well told in at least two books I can heartily recommend: David Thatcher's *Nietzsche in England – 1890–1914* and Patrick Bridgwater's *Nietzsche in Anglosaxony* (which also describes the impact made by Nietzsche's philosophy on American journalists and authors such as Henry L. Mencken, Jack London, Theodore Dreiser and Eugene O'Neill). And I might add, for literary connoisseurs interested in matters of similarities (rather than of direct influences), Stephen Donadio's *Nietzsche, Henry James, and the Artistic Will.* (All three of these books are listed in the Bibliography.)

Now, after this brief transoceanic 'digression', let us leapfrog our way forward towards the grim, grotesque, all too *Götzen-Dämmerung* finale. From 1908 on, when it became clear that turmoil in the Balkans was likely to plunge the great powers of Europe into a fratricidal war, Max Nordau's earlier fulminations against the blaspheming, God-denying 'German madman' surfaced again with redoubled force. In English newspaper and magazine articles Nietzsche was denounced as a dangerous warmonger and his name was linked to that of General Friedrich von Bernhardi, who in a bellicose book had extolled war as the 'noblest form of human activity'. A rabidly anti-Nietzschean prelate, Canon E. McClure, let loose with a savage indictment, *Germany's War Inspirers, Nietzsche and Trietzschke* – the super-patriotic, antisemitic historian with a 'bandaged head' whom Nietzsche had so witheringly denounced in *Beyond Good and Evil.* In October 1914 Thomas Hardy, who had once been enough impressed by Nietzsche's wit to regard him as a 'first-class Swiftian in disguise', blamed the German army's shelling of Reims Cathedral on Nietzsche and 'his followers [sic!] Treitschke, Bernhardi, etc.' To his everlasting credit as a model of British 'fair play', the orchestral conductor Thomas Beecham immediately replied: 'To me, an old student of Nietzsche, it is only too evident that Mr Hardy's criticisms of this remarkable man are founded on the most superficial knowledge . . . '

In Germany, where the bellicose atmosphere of '*Deutschland! Deutschland über Alles!*' hysteria had been growing steadily more heated – prompting one of the country's keenest philosophical minds, Max Scheler, to write a stupid book on *The Genius of War* – Nietzsche, who had repeatedly denounced the nationalistic 'stupidification' (*Verdummung*) of his countrymen, was annexed by the super-patriots he so loathed and brandished as the poet-prophet of heroic manliness. To the delight of Elisabeth, a particularly compact edition of *Thus Spake Zarathustra* was prepared and 150,000 copies printed up, at the High Command's request, for distribution (along with Goethe's *Faust* and the New Testament) to German soldiers in the field. What Aschheim has called the 'sanitized' version of her brother's philosophy was thus popularized as never before – not least of all by the tireless Elisabeth herself, who in newspaper articles presented her once Prussian-hating brother (the anti-Bismarckian Nietzsche of 1876–88) as the noble embodiment of everything that was finest in the Prussian tradition of good breeding, strict self-discipline, respect for authority and order, sense of duty, etc.

In the volatile post-Versailles Germany of 1919 – a once proud *Reich* that had lost its Kaiser, been stripped of its overseas colonies, wrenched from its traditional moorings and left to drift on the muddy waters of a hastily improvised Republic – there was enough political dynamite in Nietzsche's works to satisfy the appetite of crestfallen souls in desperate search of radical solutions to deal with a revolutionary situation. Dangerous affirmations like the Zarathustran exhortation, 'It is not the good cause that makes a good war, but the good war that makes the good cause,' were ready-made to transform the cult of violence into a heady political philosophy. It was with bayonets and rifles that Trotsky's 'proletarians' had invested Petrograd's Winter Palace in November 1917; so too it was by the virile exercise of brute force, not through 'effeminate' negotiations, that the many Soviet-inspired 'Workers' and Soldiers' Councils' which had mushroomed all over post-war Germany were gradually suppressed by *Freikorps* veterans of the Great War and the *Reichswehr* troops of General von Seeckt. War, as a 'school for manliness and courage', was extolled by recently demobilized veterans like Ernst Jünger – whose *Stahlgewitter* (*Thunderstorms of Steel*) went through twenty-six editions and sold 240,000 copies in 1920. In a book highly praised by Thomas Mann, Ernst Bertram, an influential member of the élitist Stefan Georg 'circle', argued that what was needed to save the country was the kind of *Überdeutschtum* (Super-Germanness) Nietzsche had so stoically incarnated – with the qualities of will power, courage and endurance exalted and enveloped in an aura of heroic myth. On a more popular and cruder level, reliance on the 'will to power' encouraged the development of a nihilistic, crypto-Nietzschean cult of destruction, preached and practised by *Freikorps* 'minstrels' (Aschheim's description) like Ernst von Salomon (one of the instigators of the murder of the Weimar Republic's Jewish foreign minister, Walther Rathenau, in 1922): 'What we wanted, we did not know, and what we knew we did not want. War and adventure, insurrection and destruction, an unknown, agonizing yearning . . .' For what? The answer, filling this agonizing void, was provided a year or two later by a recently released jailbird, in a book seething with all the pent-up hatreds and jealousies of a frustrated misfit, of a resentful 'underdog', and entitled *Mein Kampf*.

In the midst of the prevailing anarchy extraordinary feats of intellectual gymnastics were needed to reconcile Nietzsche's detestation of the 'herd' with twentieth-century Socialism – with the help of quotations from *The Will to Power*. 'Workers should learn to feel like soldiers,' proclaimed Werner Sombart, the famous historian of capitalism. 'An honorarium, an income, but no pay!' (a quotation from *The Will to Power*). 'Socialism in the grand style' – that of King Frederick William I – decreed Oswald Spengler, 'was not a system of compassion, peace, and kindly care, but one of will-to-power'. And in a polemical pamphlet – *Preussentum und Sozialismus* (*Prussianness and Socialism*) – published in 1920, the doomsday prophet of *The Decline of the West* appealed to young Germans: 'Become men! We do not need ideologies any more, no speeches about *Bildung* and the spiritual mission of the Germans. We need toughness, we need fearless scepticism, we need a class of socialist mastermen [*Herrenmänner*]. Once again: Socialism means power, power, yet again power!'

Since this was the kind of action that the once ardently socialistic Benito Mussolini was now energetically applying in Italy, it is not surprising that Spengler should have been one of his earliest German admirers. In October 1927, when Harry Graf Kessler was invited by

Elisabeth Förster-Nietzsche to attend a three-day Nietzsche Symposium in Weimar, he came close to refusing when he learned that Oswald Spengler was to be the main speaker. He found the famous author's lecture so insipid that he dismissed him in his diary as a 'half-educated charlatan . . . Perhaps he is the foremost Nietzsche-priest. But God preserve us from this species.'

Worse, far worse was soon to come. In February 1932, thanks in large part to Elizabeth's behind-the-scenes exertions, the German première of a play about Napoleon's 'Hundred Days', co-authored by Benito Mussolini, was staged at Weimar's National Theatre. Hitler turned up in Weimar with a retinue of stormtroopers, and when he heard that Nietzsche's sister was also attending the performance, he came to her box and offered her a huge bouquet of roses.

By this time the Nazi worm had bored its way into the very core of the Nietzsche Archives apple. Six months later, when Harry Kessler again visited the Villa Silberblick in Weimar, he was appalled to learn that Frau Förster-Nietzsche had picked a Nazi law professor from the University of Jena to be chairman of the board and to help her cousin, the equally Hitler-admiring Major Max Oehler, run the archives. At the Villa Silberblick, as Kessler noted in his diary, 'everything from the footman all the way up to the major domo is a Nazi'. The vengeful 'tarantulas' Nietzsche had castigated in *Zarathustra* II were now burrowing into every nook and cranny of German national life, egged on by 'connoisseurs' like Ernst Horneffer (who had also worked for years in the Weimar archives), who swore by all the gods in the Nordic pantheon that Nietzsche's was by no means a purely individualistic philosophy, and that the *Übermensch* was 'not a singular concept but a species-and-generic concept' and thus destined to become 'the fruit of an immense, uninterrupted human breeding project'.

Alfred Bäumler, soon to be rewarded by the Nazis with a chair of philosophy at the University of Berlin, had already published a book impudently titled *Nietzsche: the Philosopher and Politician* – (a greater insult could not have been hurled at him during his lifetime!) – in which he claimed that Nietzsche's philosophy, as anyone could realize by reading *The Genealogy of Morals*, was based on race, on class, on *Volk*! Thus, even before Adolf Hitler was appointed Chancellor of the soon-to-be-proclaimed Third *Reich* in late January of 1933, Nietzsche's philosophy had been nationalized, collectivized, massified and made 'respectable' by the same process of ideological *Gleichschaltung* (social 'levelling') which the Nazi steamroller was soon to impose on every sector of national activity.

Barely two weeks after his surprise appointment, Chancellor Adolf Hitler made another visit to Weimar to attend a gala performance of *Tristan und Isolde*, staged to commemorate the fiftieth anniversary of

Richard Wagner's death. Once again, to Elisabeth Förster-Nietzsche's rapturous delight, the now omnipotent Führer made a point of visiting her theatre box.

Three more visits to Weimar were made by Germany's new *Übermensch* during 1934 – one of them with Hitler's favourite architect, Albert Speer, who was asked to oversee the erection, next to the *Nietzsche Archiv*, of a splendid monument honouring the great German thinker whom the new régime had now annexed and made its own. Before she died in early November of 1935 – her grandiose funeral too was 'graced' by the presence of the Führer – the eighty-eight-year-old Elisabeth Förster-Nietzsche was gratified to learn that a handsomely bound copy of *Thus Spake Zarathustra*, now become a bible for the goose-stepping, straight-arm-saluting adolescents of the *Hitler-Jugend*, had been solemnly placed, alongside *Mein Kampf* and Alfred Rosenberg's *Myth of the Twentieth Century*, in the vault of the Tannenberg Memorial (commemorating the Germans' decisive victory over the Russians in the autumn of 1914) as one of the three ideological pillars of Germany's Third *Reich*.

# Notes

The following abbreviations have been used for Nietzsche's published works and correspondence:

| | |
|---|---|
| *AC* | *Der Antichrist* (*The Anti-Christian*) |
| *ADB* | *Allgemeine Deutsche Biographie* |
| *AsZ* | *Also sprach Zarathustra* (*Thus Spake Zarathustra*) |
| *Beg.* | *Begegnungen mit Nietzsche* (ed. by S.L. Gilman) |
| *BW* | *Briefwechsel* (*Correspondence* – Walter de Gruyter ed.) |
| *Dok* | *Friedrich Nietzsche, Paul Rée, Lou von Salomé – Die Dokumente ihrer Begegnung* (ed. by E. Pfeiffer) |
| *Eh* | *Ecce homo* |
| *FW* | *Die fröhliche Wissenschaft* (*The Joyous Science*) |
| *GdT* | *Die Geburt der Tragödie* (*The Birth of Tragedy*) |
| *GM* | *Zur Genealogie der Moral* (*The Genealogy of Morals*) |
| *GW-Mus* | *Gesammelte Werke – Musarionausgabe* |
| *G-D* | *Götzen-Dämmerung* (*Twilight of the Idols*) |
| *JGB* | *Jenseits von Gut und Böse* (*Beyond Good and Evil*) |
| *KGA* | *(FN Werke) Kritische Gesamtausgabe* |
| *KSA* | *(FN Werke) Kritische Studienausgabe – dtv* (paperback edition, Deutscher Taschenbuch Verlag) |
| *MAM* | *Menschliches, Allzumenschliches* (*Human, All Too Human*) |
| *MR* | *Morgenröte* (*Morning Glow, Daybreak, Dawn*) |
| *NF* | *Nachgelassene Fragmente* (*Posthumous Fragments*) |
| *NNH* | *Vom Nutzen und Nachteil der Historie* |
| *NW* | *Nietzsche Werke – Kritische Gesamtausgabe* (de Gruyter) |
| *SBKSA* | *Sämtliche Briefe – Kritische Studienausgabe* (*Complete Collection of Letters* – Critical Students' ed.) |
| *UB* | *Unzeitgemässe Betrachtungen* (*Untimely Meditations*) |
| *WuS* | *Der Wanderer und sein Schatten* (*The Wanderer and his Shadow*) |
| *WdB* | *Werke in drei Bänden* (3-volume ed. of FN's works, edited by Karl Schlechta, Carl Hanser Verlag) |
| *WzM* | *Der Wille zur Macht* (*The Will to Power*) |

And these abbreviations for Nietzsche, his relatives, friends, etc.:

| | |
|---|---|
| CvG | Carl von Gersdorff |
| CosB | Cosima von Bülow |
| CosW | Cosima Wagner |
| *CWD* | *Cosima Wagner Diaries* |
| EF-N | Elisabeth Förster-Nietzsche |
| Eli | Elisabeth Nietzsche (sister) |
| ER | Erwin Rohde |
| FN | Friedrich Nietzsche |
| FrN | Franziska Nietzsche (mother) |
| JBur | Jacob Burckhardt |

| | |
|---|---|
| Kös | Heinrich Köselitz (alias 'Peter Gast') |
| Lou | Lou Salomé |
| MvM | Malwida von Meysenbug |
| Naum | Constantin Naumann |
| N | Nietzsche |
| Ov | Franz Overbeck |
| RvS | Reinhart von Seydlitz |
| Schm | Ernst Schmeitzner |
| Schop | Arthur Schopenhauer |
| RW | Richard Wagner |

For reasons of convenience I have, for the first chapters, used the standard Walter de Gruyter edition of FN's correspondence (*BW*) rather than the 8-volume (*dtv*) paperback edition (*SBKSA*), which does not include letters written to Nietzsche. In both editions each letter is numbered and, when used here, is placed in parentheses. Ordinary numbers (without parenthetic brackets) indicate page numbers. Many of FN's letters and postcards were undated; in such cases the probable date appears in parenthesis. Year figures in dates have usually been reduced to 2 digits (59, instead of 1859, for example).

The translations from Nietzsche's letters and published works are my own throughout.

## 1. A Strongly Pastoral Tradition

*Page*

1 The details concerning FN's ancestors and parents were obtained from Max Oehler, *Nietzsches Ahnen*, Adalbert Oehler, *Nietzsche's Mutter*, Elisabeth Förster-Nietzsche's *Das Leben FNs* (vol I), and Curt Paul Janz's biography (vol I).

4 On the principality of Altenburg, Richard Blunck, *FN, Kindheit und Jugend*, 25 – all the page numbers from here on are taken from the the French translation (see Bibliography). On the fragmented state of Germany, Franz Schnabel, *Deutsche Geschichte im neunzehnten Jahrhundert*, vol I, 83–100.

5 On David Ernst Oehler and Pobles, A. Oehler, 1ff; EF-N, *Das Leben FN's*, 12–13. 'her father's efforts to teach her French' – Oehler, *op. cit.*, 9. On Ludwig N's talent for improvising on the piano, see FN, '*Aus meinem Leben Die Jugendjahre 1844 bis 1858', WdB* III, 13.

6 Ludwig N's marriage to Franziska, A. Oehler, pp. 36–39. On Erdmuthe N, EF-N, *Das Leben* I, 25–26. On FN – 'he was even slow to learn to speak', EF-N, *Leben* I, 27;

6–7 'FN's adolescent recollections' – '*Aus meinem Leben Die Jugendjahre*', *WdB* III, 13–14.

7 'nicknamed *Papperlieschen*' – Gustav Adolf Oswald, writing to FN 15 Oct 1851, *BW* I/1, p. 305. 'The "monstrous" February Revolution' – briefly described by FN in '*Mein Lebenslauf II (1861)*' – *WdB* III, 91.

8 'black clouds billowed up' – '*Jugendjahre*', *WdB* III, 15. Ludwig N's 'softening of the brain' – Janz I, 45–46; FN, '*Jugendjahre*', *WdB* III, 16. 'The ceremony began . . .' – *ibid.*, 16. FN's premonitory dream – *ibid.*, 17.

9 'His last evening at Röcken' – *ibid.*, 17.

## 2. Naumburg

10 Naumburg in 1850 – EF-N, *Leben* I, 22. Other details obtained from a visit to Naumburg made in Oct 1994. 'unfamiliar sight of townsfolk', FN, '*Jugendjahre*', 18.

11 On Knabenbürgerschule – EF-N, *Leben* I, 30; on Candidate priest Weber, FN, *'Jugendjahre'*, 19–20; on Schönburg Schloss, *ibid.*, 11–12. On Wilhelm Pinder and Gustav Krug – *ibid.*, 19–25. On FN's winter passion for sledding – Ernestine N, letter to FN, 28 Feb 1853, *BW* I/1, 316.

11–12 On Crimean War, FN, *'Jugendjahre'*, 20, *'Aus den Hundstagsferien'*, *WdB* III, 73.

12 'summer spent near Halle' – Erdmuthe N to FN, August 1854, *BW* I, 318. On Domgymnasium and *Ordinarius* Silber – FN, *'Jugendjahre'*, 29–30. On deaths of Aunt Auguste and Grandmother Erdmuthe, *ibid.*, 28–29. On change of residence, *ibid.*, 30; Janz, *FN* I, 65. New bedroom and rapiers – FN>Eli, 27 April 56, *BW* I/1, 6.

13 On FN's piano lessons – A. Oehler, *op. cit.*, 60; Janz I, 53. Mozart's *Requiemn* etc. – FN, *'Jugendjahre'*, 27. 'uncles playing Beethoven sonatas' – FN>Krug, *BW* I/1 (12). 'thirteenth birthday on 15 October 1857' – FN>Ernst Oehler, *ibid.* (16). 'blinding headaches' – FrN>FN, 10 Aug 57, *ibid.*, 322. 'vineyards of the Spechzart' – FN, *'Jugendjahre'*, 46.

13–14 *'Die Götter von Olymp* – EF-N, *Leben* I, 46–47.

14 *Orkadal* – FN, *'Jugendjahre'*, *WdB* III, 37–38. 'By working overtime' – FN>Rosalie N, *BW* I/1, p. 13. 'Grandfather Oehler's 71st birthday' – *ibid.* (18), p. 14. *'Aus meinem Leben'* – FN, *WdB* III, 13–34.

14–15 Christmastime and birthdays – *ibid.*, p. 33.

15 'A thought-lacking poem' – *ibid.*, p. 35. On *Zukunftsmusik* – Janz I, 57; David Cairns, *Hector Berlioz* Eleanor Perenyi, *Liszt*, 285–96.

15–16 FN's detestation of *Zukunftsmusik*, as opposed to 'classical' music – FN, *'Jugendjahre'*, 34–35.

## 3. A Formidable Scholastic Fortress

17 FN's admission to Pforta – EF-N, *Leben* I, 89–90; Janz I, 64. On Latin schools in Saxony and Pforta – *ibid.*, 65–70; Madame de Staël, *De l'Allemagne*, Part I, ch. XIV; EF-N, *Leben* I, 98–100; Richard Blunck, *FN – Kindheit und Jugend*, 56–58.

18 FN on his scholastic 'prison' – FN>Pinder, Feb 1859, *BW* I/1 (55), 47–48. 'The daily programme' – Paul Deussen, *Mein Leben*, 63–66; FN, Pforta 'diary', 9, 12 Aug 1859 entries, *WdB* III, 44–45, 48–49. Pforta curriculum as 'far stricter' than Domgymnasium, FN>FrN (9 Oct 58) 17, 18; to Pinder (early Nov 58), *BW* I/1 (30), p. 24.

19 On F.L. Jahn and his *Turnjacken*, F. Schnabel, *op. cit.* I, 306; Georg Brandes, *Main Currents in Nineteen Century Literature*, vol VI, 3–4; P. Viereck, *Metapolitics*, 64, 68, 75, 80–87.

19–20 'To judge by his letters' – notably (23) to his mother and (32) to his grandfather, David Ernst Oehler, *BW* I/1, 18, 26.

20 On the 'proximity of Naumburg' and meetings with his mother, aunts, and sister – FN>FrN, 11 and (16 Oct), *BW* I/1 (24, 25); Deussen, *Leben*, 66; EF-N, *Leben* I, 106. 'forced to give up Homer' – FN>Pinder, *BW* I/1 (30), p. 24. 'Pinder's answering letter' – Pinder>FN, *ibid.*, 328–9. 'requests for Christmas gifts' – *ibid.*, 32–36. 'onset of a mid-winter thaw' – FN to Aunt Rosalie, *ibid.*, 40. 'wrote again to W. Pinder' – *ibid.* (54), pp. 46–47. 'Prometheus myth' – FN>Pinder, *ibid.* (70), pp. 60–61.

20–21 'tramp of marching feet' – FN>FrN (mid-May, 20–23 June 59), 64, 68.

21 'May Song' madrigal – *NW-Mus* I,11. Trip to Jena described in *'Aus den Hundstagsferien'*, *WdB* III, 67–70; FN letters to Emil Schenk, *BW* I/1 (84, 85). 'diary he began keeping' – *WdB* III, 42–63. FN on *Don Quixote*, *ibid.*, 58; FN>FrN, *BW* I/1 (87). Sept 59 exam results – FN>FrN, *ibid.* (95); FN>Pinder (96).

22 'biography of Alexander Humboldt' – birthday gift from his Aunt Rosalie, FN>RN, *BW* I/1 (109), p. 82; its impact on him, *WdB* III, 73; on *Kosmos*, W. Langer, *Political and Social Upheaval – 1832–1852*, p. 535. 'Heinrich von Kleist' etc. – FN to Rosalie N, *BW* I/1, p. 86. David Oehler's death – Eli>FN, 15 Dec 59, *ibid.*, 339–40; FN>FrN, (124); FN's 'disturbing dream' – EF>N, *Leben* I, 156.

## 4. Three Naumburg Bards

23 'blinding headaches' etc. – FN>FrN, 8 Jan 60 (124); FN>Rosalie N, 13 Jan 60 (125); FN>FrN (126), BW I/1, 89–91. 'having to keep order' – FN>Pinder, *ibid.*, 104; Deussen, *Leben*, 69–70. Trip to Gorenzen and Eisleben described in FN, '*Meine Ferienreise*', Pforta 1860, *WdB* III, 78–88.

24 Decision to found 'Germania' Society, etc. – EF-N, *Leben* I, 132–6; and, farther on, a complete list of contributions made by FN, Krug, Pinder from Aug 60 to June 63, pp. 144–9. 'less primitive washroom' – FN>Rosalie N, *BW* I/1 (164). On Professor Corssen, Deussen, *Leben*, 69; and FN's later tribute in *G-D* ('What I owe to the Ancients', notably to Sallust and Horace), *KSA* 6, 154; Penguin ed., 105.

24–25 'long letter from Gustav Krug' – *BW* I/1, 342–8.

25 Wagner and third act of *Tristan und Isolde* – Ernest Newman, *The Life of RW*, vol II, ch. 28. King Frederick William IV's death – Deussen, *Leben*, 69. On birthday fireworks – FN>FrN, 20 Oct 60, *BW* I/1 (188). Newspapers allowed at Pforta – FN>FrN, *ibid.* (202). FN's 'Christmas oratorio' – FN to Krug and Pinder (14 Jan 61), (203).

25–26 FN an 'ardently Christian believer' – Deussen, 70.

26 FN's confirmation – B. Dächsel to FN, 1 March 61, *BW* I/1 (35), 350–1 Edmund Oehler to FN, 5 March 61 (36), pp. 351–2. FN's 'rheumatism of the neck' – FN>FrN, *ibid.* (205). 'leeches were applied' – FN>FrN, 16 Feb 61 (214). 147. 'head of his class' – FN to Edmund Oehler, April 61, *ibid.* (223). Krug and overture to *Tristan*, his '*Barbarossa*', FN's 'Serbian Folk-Songs' etc. – Krug>FN (April 61), *BW* I/1, 353–6. 'best and most *Lisztian*' – Krug>FN, 30 April, *ibid.*, 357.

27 'spoiled by Franz Liszt's cancellation' – see Krug>FN, *ibid.*, 357; 'heatwave temperatures of 35°' – FN>FrN, *BW* I/1, (255). Robert Buddensieg's death – FN>FrN, *ibid.* (257); FN>Pinder (258). Buddensieg's specialty was Biblical and Hebraic studies – FN, August 59, *WdB* III, 57. 'an able Latinist named Max Heinze' – FN to Max Heinze, Aug-Sept 61, *BW* I/1 (260–3); and his good opinion of Heinze – FN>Pinder (mid-May 60 (147). 'The September exams' – FN>FrN/Eli, *ibid.*, 179.

27–28 On Hölderlin – Pinder>FN, (late May 61), *ibid.*, 360; FN>FrN (12 Oct) p. 181; FN, '*Brief an meinen Freund . . .*', dated 19 Oct 61, *WdB* 111, 95–98; Janz I, 78–80; Charles Andler, N: *Sa vie et sa pensée*, vol I, 47–56; G. Brandes, *Main Currents in Nineteenth Century Literature* vol II, 44–48; on Empedocles, Freeman, *Ancilla to the Pre-Socratic Philosophers*, 51–69; E. Brehier, *Histoire de la Philosophie*, vol I, 67–70; W. Kaufmann, *N – Philosopher, Psychologist, Antichrist*, 306.

28 '*Allein zu sein . . .*', Hölderlin, *Sämtliche Werke*, vol II 'Empedocles's death . . .', *GW-Mus* I, 34–35, or *WdB* III, 97–98. On August Koberstein, Deussen, *Leben*, 77; FN>FrN (mid-Nov 59), *BW* I/1, 84; Krug>FN (late Nov 60), *ibid.*, 348. 'I would nevertheless . . .' – Janz I, 80. 'Schumann's *Paradies und Peri*', FN>Eli (late Nov), *BW* I/1, 188.

29 'Barrau's History of French Revolution', etc. *ibid.* (289). 'Krug's efforts . . .' etc. – Krug>FN, late May 61, *ibid.*, 361–2. also (46), 369–72. 'Wilhelm Pinder's

contribution' and FN on Byron – EF-N, *Leben* I, 137–8; *GW-Mus* I, 37–51.

29–30 FN's 'positive appraisal of Louis Bonaparte's . . .' – *GW-Mus* I, 52–57; Pinder's reaction – EF-N, *Leben* I, 139, 146. 'another quarterly "synod"' (March 62) – *ibid.*, 147–9; FN's summing up (22 Sept 62) – *WdB* III, 99–101.

## 5. The Final Years at Pforta

31 'once again he was bled by leeches' – FN>FrN, *BW* I/1 (294). A complete list of FN's illnesses at Pforta can be found in R. Blunck, *Kindheit*, 113–5. 'Fate and History' – *GW-Mus* I, 60–66.

32 'Freedom of the Will and Fate' – *ibid.*, 67–69. 'That God should have become man' – FN>Pinder, Krug, Apr 62, *BW* I/1 (301), p. 202. Emerson's essays are mentioned in FN's '*Meine literarische Tätigkeit*', 1862, *WdB* III, 101, 106–7, 112. Pinder's nonchalant reply (22 May 62) – *BW* I/1, 381–2.

32–33 On Ermanarich saga and FN's 'symphony' – *WdB* III, 101–5; Janz I, 94–96. 'first sketch entitled "Serbia", "Hungarian sketches"' etc., *ibid.*, 95.

33 IIa mark for Ermanarich 'saga' – FN>FrN, June 62, *BW* I/1, (313). FN's essay on Cicero – *ibid.*, (313), p. 209.

33–34 'In early July' – FN>FrN, 24 June 62, *ibid.* (322), 213–4; on his vacation at Gorenzen – FN>Eli, *ibid.* (323, 325), FN to Raimund Granier (324), pp. 214–20; Janz I, 110–12.

34 'He also wrote a few poems' – *GW-Mus* I, 73–75. 'To consider Jesus' – '*Für die Ferien*', *WdB* III, 106. '*Still, mein Herz*' – EF-N, *Leben* I, 148. 'new bout of violent headaches' – FN>FRN, *BW* I/1, p. 222. FN as *Primaner* and *Primus*, *ibid.* (333), p. 223.

34–35 'wild "Wagner orgy"' – EF-N, *Leben* I.

35 'to dismay of . . . Gustav' – Krug>FN, 15 Oct, *ibid.*, p. 386. 'complete works of Byron' – FN>FRN, *ibid.* (339), 228. FN a 'trenchant "idealist"' – Deussen, *Leben*, 74. On *Dreibund*, Guido Meyer – Deussen, *Leben*, 70–71; FN>FrN, 1 March 63, *BW* I/1, (343); Meyer>FN, 25 March, *ibid.*, 397–403.

35–36 FN, as tipsy *Primaner* – FN>FrN, 16 April 63, *ibid.* (350).

36 FN ending Germania Society, EF-N, *Leben* I, 149. Plato's *Symposium* – from '*Mein Leben*', *WdB* III, 118. FN and Anna Redtel – FN>FrN (29 Aug 63), *BW* I/1, 252; EF-N, *Leben* I, 176–7; Janz I, 125–6; Anna Redtel>FN (Sept 63), *BW* I/1, p. 403; Pinder>FN, 13 Oct, 406. FN passing September (63) exams – FN>FrN, *ibid.* (382), 256. 'presents he requested' – *ibid.*, p. 257.

36–37 On Pforta 'Music Room' and Carl von Gersdorff – Janz I, 96.

37 Ermanarich 'treatise', *GW-Mus* I, pp. 136–69. Koberstein praising FN's treatise – Janz I, 96. 'end-of-semester exams' March 64 – EF-N, *Leben* I, 177.

37–38 Pinder and Krug praising Heidelberg – *BW* I/1, 418–21, 421–3.

38 FN's thesis on Theognis of Megara – *GW-Mus* I, 209–53. 'I have just finished lunch' – FN>Pinder, 4 July 64, *BW* I/1 (432). 'a musical *Morgengruss*' – FN>Deussen (8 July 64), *ibid.* (434).

38–39 'According to his sister Elisabeth' – *Leben* I, 187–8; Janz I, 124.

39 'Great . . . was the rejoicing' – EF-N, *Leben* I, 188, 192–3; 'brief valedictory speech' – Deussen, *Leben*, 80; EF-N, *Leben* I, 194–5; 'wreath-festooned carriage' – *ibid.*, 195.

## 6. With the Beer-Drinkers of the Rhine

40 'The once refractory Rhinelander' – Deussen, 80–81. Trip from Naumburg to Bonn – *ibid.*, 81–82; FN>FrN/Eli, 27 Sept 64, *SBKSA* (*dtv*) II, 3–5; and, from

Oberdreis, *ibid.* (446). On FN's lodgings in Bonn, FN>FrN/Eli, *ibid.* (448); meals with Deussen, (449), 16; Deussen, *Leben*, 82. 'beneath a portrait of his father' – FN to F. Dächsel and Rosalie N, *SBKSA* II (454), 27.

41 'Without 30 thalers a month' – FN>FrN/Eli, 17–18 Oct, *ibid.*, 12–13. 'In his next letter' – FN>FrN/Eli (24–25 Oct), *ibid.*, 14. On the *Burschenschaften* – F. Schnabel, *op. cit.* II, 234–258; F.B. Artz, *Reaction and Revolution*, 139–41; Viereck, *Metapolitics*, 80, 84–87, 94. Deussen on 'patriotic fooling around' – *Leben*, 84; FN an 'ardent German patriot' – FN to FrN/Eli, *SBKSA* II (449) 14; (451) 19–20. On the 'Franconia' and its *Kneipe* – Deussen, *Leben*, 84–85; FN>FrN/Eli, *SBKSA* II (449), 14–15. 'outing to nearby Plittersdorf' – *ibid.*, 14–15.

41–42 On Otto Jahn – *ADB* vol 13, pp. 668–86; Deussen, *Leben*, 82, and English tr. of *Beg.* (Conversations with N), 21.

42 On Friedrich Ritschl – Deussen, 83; *ADB* vol 28. 'excursion to Sieburg' – FN>FrN/Eli, *SBKSA* II (451), 19–20, to Rolandseck (11–12 Dec) – *ibid.* (453), 23–24. 77. 'Accompanied by his landlady' – *ibid.* (449), 15. 78. 'local *Gesangverein*' and 'a dozen Schumannesque *Lieder*' – Dec 64, FN>FrN/Eli, *ibid.* (455), FN>Eli (456). '*Die Franconen im Himmel*' – Janz I, 136; 'nickname of "Gluck"' – FN>FrN, *SBKSA* 2, 22; 'Meister' for Deussen, *Leben*, 85. 'Christmas holidays in Bonn' – FN>FrN/Eli, Dec 64, *SBKSA* 2, (455), and (457). 'Weber's *Freischütz*' – FN>FrN/Eli, *ibid.*, 34–35.

42–43 'first New Year resolution' – FN>Rosalie N, 11 Jan 65, *ibid.* (459).

43 'Schumann's *Manfred*' – *ibid.*, p. 36. 'Jenny Bürde-Ney' – FN>FrN/Eli (18 Feb 65), *ibid.*, 43. 'Karl Devrient' – FN>Rosalie N (11 Jan 65), *ibid.*, 36–37. 'Friederike Gossmann' – FN>FrN/Eli (2 Feb 65), *ibid.*, 39. '55 thalers deep in debt' – *ibid.*, 39; 'philistines', 40. 'carnal homage to the Devil' – Deussen, *Erinnerungen an FN*, 23ff, also included in Sander L. Gilman's *Begegnungen mit N*, and the shorter English version, *Conversations with N*, 23–24. Richard Blunck, who had once studied under Deussen, claimed in FN – *Kindheit und Jugend*, 123–4, that he could not conceivably have invented this story. Janz (I, 137–8) agreed, pointing out that this brothel experience later inspired Zarathustra's poem, '*Die Wüste wächst*' (The Wilderness Grows). 'he desperately needed 80 thalers' – FN>FrN/Eli (18 Feb 65), *SBKSA* 2 (461).

44 'stern reprimand' – FrN's letter has been lost, but not FN's 'indignant' reply (late Feb 65), *ibid.* (462). 'Deussen home at Oberdreis' – *ibid.* (463), 46. 'Fritz's puffy cheeks' – EF-N, *Leben* I, 208–9; Blunck, *Kindheit* 130; Janz I, 146. 'The devout Franziska' etc. – see her letter to FN, 25 Nov 64, *BW* I/3 (90), 21; Rosalie N>FN, 15 Oct 64, (88); A. Oehler, *FN's Mutter*, 80; Janz I, 146–8. On David F. Strauss's *Leben Jesu*, see Albert Schweitzer, *The Quest for the Historical Jesus*, partic. ch. 7. On Pierre Bayle – Paul Hazard, *Crise de la conscience européenne*, ch. 5.

45 On Johann Christian Wolff, Schweitzer ; Paulus, *ibid.*, ch. V 'Lessings's contention' – *ibid.*, 15–16.

46 'The novelty of Strauss's *Das Leben*' – Schweitzer, ch.8. 'The new *Das Leben Jesu*', judged by Schweitzer – 193–5.

46–7 'The preface alone' – *ibid.*

47 'the debate was surely long, heated, bitter' – A. Oehler, *N's Mutter*, 84–88. 'His sister Elisabeth . . .' – *BW* I/3 (97), 44–45. 'As far as your basic principle' – FN>Eli, *BW* I/2 (469), 60 'become an *Überkluge*' – Eli>FN, 26 May 65, *BW* I/3 (97), 44. FN shifting to Philology – FN>FrN (10 May 65), *SBKSA* 2, 53.

47–48 Bonn 'at its loveliest' – FN>FrN/Eli, *ibid.* (465), 49–50.

48 FN 'gave up his piano' – *ibid.*, 50. 'tailor-made suit' – *ibid.*, 50; 'new plea for

funds' – 52. 'early hour of seven' – *ibid.*, 51. 'a moving letter' from Gersdorff – CvG>FN, *BW* I/3 (95). FN 'replying on Ascension Day' – FN>CvG, *BW* I/2 (467), 54–55 'speech on Germany's patriotic poets', *ibid.*, 56.

48–49 'On the 2nd' – FN>Eli (11 June 65), *ibid.*, 61–63.

49 'certainly the finest thing' – FN>FrN, *ibid.* (470), 65. 'distinctly cool welcome' and 'we, that is the Franconians' – *ibid.*, 66. FN accosting member of 'Allemann' fraternity, and the subsequent duel – Deussen, *Leben*, 84–85; Gilman, 22–23.

49–50 FN's 'decision to leave Bonn' – FN>CvG, *BW* I/2, 55–56; FN>FrN/Eli, 29 May 65, *ibid.*, 58.

50 'Carl von Gersdorff's wish' – CvG>FN (17 May 5 65), *BW* I/3, 37. On Ritschl's quarrel with Otto Jahn and decision to move to Leipzig – FN>FrN/Eli (3 May 65), *BW* I/2, 49; FN>CvG (25 May), *ibid.*, 55–56. 'headaches, induced by drenching downpours' – FN>Friederike Dächsel (after July 10). 'N's final weeks in Bonn', rheumatic pains – FN>FrN/Eli, *BW* I/2, 78; to CvG (4 Aug), *ibid.* (476), 76. 'frenzy of letter-writing' – FN>FrN/Eli, *ibid.* (477), 78. 'accompanied . . . by a new friend . . . Hermann Mushacke' – according to FN, '*Rückblick auf meine zwei Leipziger Jahre*', *in WdB* III, 128; although Deussen claimed (years later) to have accompanied FN to the 'night steamship' – Gilman, 25. 'letter from Mushacke' – 24 Aug, *BW* I/3 (99), 51–52. 'There I transgressed' – FN to Mushacke (30 Aug), *BW* I/2, 79–80.

## 7. Arthur Schopenhauer's Fateful Spell

51 'visit to Mushacke's family' and trip to Leipzig – FN, '*Rückblick* . . .' *WdB* III, 128–9; Reiss's restaurant and student lodgings on the Blumengasse – *ibid.*, 130. 'illustrious predecessor, Goethe' – *ibid.*, 130–1; also FN to Eduard Mushacke, 19 Oct 65, *BW* I/2 (481), 88. 'This unexaltedness . . .' – FN to Raimund Granier, *ibid.*, 82–83.

51–52 FN letter to Franconia fraternity – 20 Oct 65, *ibid.* (482).

52 Ritschl's inaugural address – FN, '*Rückblick*', 131. FN's discovery of Schopenhauer – *ibid.*, 133–4. 'Who knows what kind of folly' – *ibid.*, 134. 'swamp-air of the fifties' – FN in *Eh*.

53 On Descartes' hostility to Aristotelian empiricism, see Ortega y Gasset's brilliant lectures in *La idea de principio en Leibniz y la evolución de la teoría deductiva*, in vol VIII of his *Obras Completas* (1958–59); and in particular ch. 24 (*El nuevo 'modo de pensar' y la demagogía aristotélica*'). Ortega had already stressed the essentially deductive (as opposed to empirical) basis of Galileo's theorems regarding the velocity of falling bodies, in *En torno a Galileo* (*Obras Completas*, vol V, written in 1933). On the *a priori* conviction, held by so many astronomers, that the sun revolves around the Earth, see A. Koestler's fascinating study in *The Sleepwalkers*. Even Copernicus, who first challenged this conviction, was persuaded *a priori* that the planets revolve around the sun in *perfect* circles. 'The second fatal legacy of the Aristotelian school' – brilliantly dealt with by Ortega in ch. 18 ('*El sensualismo en el modo de pensar aristotélico*') of his *Leibniz*.

53–54 'The logic he created . . .' – Ortega, *op. cit.* (ch. 17), 145–54.

54 'so the four sciences that were recognized by the Greeks' – Ortega, *op. cit.*, On the 'kindergarten' character of Greek arithmetic – Ortega, *ibid.* ch. 7, partly based on H.G. Zeuthen's *Geschichte der Mathematik im XVI. und XVII. Jahrhundert*. 'Aristotle being, as Descartes pointed out' – *Discours de la Méthode*, Part VI (Etienne Gilsen ed., p. 70). On the neglected importance of the principle of contradiction, see Bertrand Russell's first work, devoted to Leibniz.

55 'post-Aristotelian dialectics . . . an intellectual Tower of Babel' – *op. cit.*, ch. 19.

I have greatly simplified Ortega's subtle critique of Aristotle's unwillingness to accept anything resembling a 'principle of contradiction', and the subsequent development of a 'logic' essentially based on hybrid syllogisms reposing on empirically induced (rather than on mathematical or geometric) notions: the result being a 'system' of thinking that was not only approximative and lacking in rigor but even, strictly speaking, illogical and conceptually fruitless. '*mathesis universalis*' – Descartes, *Discours*, *Regulae ad directionem ingenii* (Gilson, 217), XIV – on the posthumous fate of these primordial 'rules', see Pierre Frédérix's *Monsieur Descartes en son temps.*

56 'The most significant of these principles' – Ortega (*op. cit.*, ch. 1) lists ten basic principles formulated by Leibniz in vol II of his *Philosophischen Schriften*, 56, the principle of 'sufficient reason' occupying the fourth place, after the Principle of Identity and the Principle of Contradiction.

56–57 On Hume's critique of the principle of 'sufficient reason', see Part III, sections 1–6, of his *Treatise of Human Nature.*

57 'When Newton formulated the laws of universal gravitation' – Hume, in section 6, of his *Treatise*, had rashly written: 'We cannot penetrate into the reason of the conjunction . . . of contiguous events.' But this is precisely what Newton did by explaining why objects fall to the ground. What is truly astounding is that Hume, a professed admirer of Newton's 'empirical' methods, should have written this between 1735 and 1736, more than forty years after Newton had published his *De Motu Corporum and Philosophiae Naturalis Principia Mathematica.*

57–58 All philosophizing from the point of view of 'God' – Leibniz, in his epistolatory duel with Newton's advocate, Clarke, had rejected the notion that the simultaneity of all events in the universe was guaranteed by the 'consciousness of God' (*censorium Dei*) on the grounds that this was merely a theological assumption, not something that had been empirically or scientifically proved. Kant in effect extended this critique to all realms of human knowledge and experience, notably in his Introduction to *Kritik der reinen Vernunft*, vol III of his *Sämmtliche Werke.*

58 'human "apprehension" . . . involves intellection' – admirably summed up by Kant in a single sentence in the introduction to his 'Transcendental Logic': 'Thoughts without content are empty, apprehensions without concepts are blind.' *ibid.*, 82. 'human understanding was the "legislator of the universe" ' – *ibid.*,

59 'Kant, who was not a Newtonian for nothing' – see Gottfried Martin's excellent treatment of this subject in sections 11–14 of his small but valuable book, *Immanuel Kant – Ontologie und Wissenschaftstheorie.*

60 On Karl Leonhard Rheinhold, see biographical essay in *ADB*, vol 28, p. 83. 'Fichte . . . then outdid Rheinhold' – notably in his *Wissenschaftslehre* (1801). See Johannes Hoffmeister's Introduction to Hegel's *Phänomenologie des Geistes.*

61 'Kant, in his *Critique of Judgement*' – no less than one third of this third *Critique* was devoted to questions of teleology. On the 'purposiveness' of Nature, sections 61–66, in particular. Logic as the 'forecourt of the Sciences' – Kant, *Vernunft* F. Schnabel on Hegel's 'spiritual monism', *op. cit.* III, 4–5.

61–62 On Altenstein and Frederick William III, *ibid.*, 18–19, and vol II, 342–3.

62 On the collapse of Hegelianism – Karl Löwith, *From Hegel to Nietzsche*, Part I, ch. 2; on Karl Rosenkranz and his quarrel with Rudolf Haym, 54–60. On the 'principle of substitution' – Hegel, Preface to *Phänomenologie des Geistes*, I (second paragraph).

64 'The starting point in Schopenhauer's treatise' – chs. 1–5 of *The World as Will*

*and Representation*, vol I, translated by E.F.J. Payne (for all future page references).

65 'For logic . . . can never be of practical use' – *ibid.*, ch. 9, p. 45; see also his denigration of mathematics, 121, 188–9. 'All this . . . follows from the nature of Reason' – *ibid.*, ch. 16, 86. 'pathological hatred of his mother' – biographical details here are drawn from Friedrich Krummer's essay in *ADB*, vol 32.

65–66 'The scientist was thus compared' –

66 'Spinoza had once observed' – *ibid.*, 126. 'Thus everywhere in nature we see contest' – *ibid.*, 146–7.

67 'Schop's mighty impact' – FN>FrN/Eli, *BW* I/2 (486), 95–96.

67–68 'In her letter of reply' – FrN>FN, 12 Nov, *BW* I/3 (106), 62–64.

68 'on the very Sunday' – FN>FrN/Eli, *BW* I/2 (487), 97. On Carl Riedel – *ibid.*, 96. 'After one of these concerts' – Eli>FN, *BW* I/3 (109), 67–68; FN>Eli, *BW* I/2 (489), 99–100. 'founding of a Philological Club' – FN to FrN/Eli, *ibid.* (489), 100; FN>Rosalie N, 12 Jan 66, *ibid.* (490), 102; FN>FrN/Eli, 12 Jan 66 (491), 194; FN's description, in *WdB* III, 134–5, mentioning the *Bierstube* and the *Löwe* restaurant; H.W. Wisser's and H. Süremberg's reminiscences, in Gilman's *Conversations with FN*, 26–30.

69 'lunch to Mahn's restaurant' etc. – FN, *WdB* III, 136–7. On Friedrich Ritschl's encouragement – *ibid.*, 139. 'The twenty-one-year-old student' – *ibid.*, 135.

## 8. Philologist and Cannoneer

70 'Shortly after the Easter holidays' – FN>FrN/Eli, *BW* I/2 (22 April), 124. 'F . . . was frankly bored' – FN to Mushacke, *ibid.* (27 April), 126–9. 'Karl Devrient' – FN>FrN/Eli, 29 May, *ibid.*, 132–3; Theodor Wachtel, 132.

70–71 On Prussia's war with Austria – Robert Brinkley, *Realism and Nationalism*, 267–72.

71 W. Pinder, in Berlin – Pinder>FN, 9 July 66, *BW* I/3 (127), 114–5. 'at Tübingen . . . Paul Deussen' – Deussen, *Leben*, 90. Carl von Gersdorff in Berlin – CvG>FN, *BW* I/3, 116–23. 'and even a 'rabid Prussian' – FN>FrN/Eli, early July, *BW* I/2, 135. FN doubting Bismarck's ability to found a 'united German state' – FN>FrN/Eli (early July 66), *ibid.*, 134–5. 'City Commandant hoisted the black-and-white Prussian colours' – *ibid.*, 136.

72 Leipzig's packed theatres, compared to Dresden's – *ibid.*, 136, and FN>CvG (512), p. 144, re Hedwig Raabe's theatrical success. Gersdorff, irked by anti-intellectual prejudices of Prussian army officers – CvG>FN, 17 Aug 66, *BW* I/3, 136–8. 'That one can live pleasantly in Leipzig' – FN>CvG, *BW* I/2, 150. 'certain terrors' – the question of just where and when FN contracted syphilis may never be solved. Richard Blunck (*op. cit.*, 180–1) devoted two pages to the question, quoting the 'testimony' of three doctors – Paul Möbius, who was living in Leipzig in 1865–6, the noted psychiatrist, W. Lange-Eichbaum, and an unnamed 'pathologist' who, in 1930, confirmed what he had learned about this 'hush-hush' matter from Möbius's brother. At some point two compromising letters, which might have solved the mystery, were apparently destroyed. See also Janz I, 202–3. 'another cholera epidemic . . . FrN's groundfloor tenants' etc. FN>Mushacke, 10 Oct 66, *BW* I/2, 165–6. Bad Kösen, RW's *Walküre* – FN>CvG, 11 Oct 66, *ibid.*, 174.

72–73 FN's discovery of F.A. Lange's *Geschichte des Materialismus* – FN>CvG, *BW* I/2 (517), 159–60. On Lange – R.C. Brinkley, *op. cit.*, 53; Hermann Cohen's Preface to *GdM.*

73 On Jacob Moleschott, Brinkley, 22, 54; Lange, 456.

73–74 'When worm, chafer, man' – *ibid.*, 456 (vol III, 280 in E.C. Thomas's English translation).

74 On Ludwig Büchner, Brinkley, 8, 12, 22; Lange, 445–9. 'Philosophical expositions . . .' – *ibid.*, 445 (Eng.tr., 267). 'Darwin's *Origin of Species*' – Lange, 570–8 (Eng.ed., 267).

74–75 'The struggle for a spot on earth' – *ibid.*, 577 (Eng., 34).

75 'When N returned to Leipzig" – FN>FrN/Eli, *BW* I/2, 178. 'One day . . . Ritschl asked N' – FN>Mushacke, *ibid.*, 182–3.

76 'At Naumburg . . . Christmas' – FN>Mushacke, *ibid.*, 193. 'When, in April 1867' – Deussen>FN, *BW* I/3, 171–2. 'Are you really determined' – FN>Deussen, 4 Apr 67, *BW* I/2 (539), 206. On Erwin Rohde, FN to Mushacke (July 66), *BW* I/2, 140; FN>CvG, August 66, *ibid.* (517), 158, in which he described ER as being a 'very bright, but stubborn and opinionated (*eigensinniger*)' fellow; see also paragraph about ER in '*Rückblick auf meine zwei Leipziger Jahre*', *WdB* III, 145–6. 'a joint veneration for Schop' – FN>CvG, *ibid.*, 238. 'The two "Prussian patriots"' – ER>FN, 10 Sept 67, *BW* I/3 (170), 213; and the 'shaking-up' of the 'underbelly' – FN>FrN/Eli, *BW* I/2, 218–9. 'Having completed his Diogenes L. prize essay' – (6 Aug 67), *ibid.*, 223.

76–77 'he was informed by a lieutenant' – FN>Mushacke (4 Oct) *ibid.* (549), 225–6; 'duty with the 2nd Battery' – FN to Deussen, *ibid.* (551), 228.

77 'On 5 October he made a quick trip to Berlin' – FN to Mushacke (4 Oct), *ibid.*, 225–6. 'reported for duty with the 2nd Battery' – FN>Rudolf Schenkel, 5 Nov, *ibid.* (553). 'The day's training began' etc. – FN>ER, 3 Nov, *ibid.*, 232–4; and FN>CvG (554), 240–1. 'Schopenhauer, help me!' – FN>ER, *ibid.*, (552), 233.

77–78 'As the ablest rider' and the subsequent accident – FN>ER (3 April 68), *ibid.* (565), 261–2.

78 'One day in late May . . . a tiny piece . . . of bone' – FN to Ritschl, 26 May 68, *ibid.* (572), 280; FN>CvG (576), 292–3. 'a famous surgeon named Volkmann' – FN>Deussen, 22 June, *ibid.*, 290; FN>CvG, 293. FN having himself photographed in 'mock military pose' – EF-N, *Leben* I, 273; *Beg.*, 72; FN>ER, *BW* I/2 (583) 307. 'From Naumburg N . . . travelled to Leipzig' – FN>FrN/Eli, (1 July) *BW* I/2 (577), 295–6. FN in Bad Widdekind to see Volkmann – *ibid.*, 295–7; FN to Sophie Ritschl, 2 July 68, *ibid.* (578), 298–9.

78–79 'N's cure at Bad Widdekind' etc. – FN>Eli (10 July), *ibid.* (579); FN>FrN/Eli (29 and 30/31 July), 300–2. '*Parerga und Paralipomena*' – FN>FrN/Eli (1 July), *ibid.* (577) 295; Eli>FN (13 July), *BW* I/3 (189), 274.

79 'Schop was an intellectual demi-god' – FN>Deussen, *BW* I/2 (588), 316. Wagner's *Meistersinger* – FN>ER, *ibid.* (583), 306. 'Female influences' – FN>ER, *ibid.*, 306. 'essay on Diogenes Laërtius' – FN>ER (3 Nov 67); FN>CvG, 1 Dec 67, *ibid.* (552) 230; (554) 237. Zarncke and his *Litt. Centralblatt* – FN>ER, *ibid.*, 265; FN to Zarncke (15 April), *ibid.* (566), 266. 'on the Hesychianum' – FN to Deussen, *ibid.* (573), 283. 'Simonides of Chios' – FN to Ritschl, *ibid.* (571), 279; FN>ER (6 June), 289.

## 9. A Momentous Encounter

80 'idea of spending a year in Paris' – for ex. FN>ER (3 April 68), *BW* I/2, 264; FN>Deussen, 2 June 68, 282. 'to bring the Schop gospel' – FN>CvG (8 Aug), 309. 'Should he go to Berlin' – for ex. FN>Mushacke (15 July) *ibid.* 220. Ernst Windisch – often mentioned in FN's letters, for ex. to Deussen (2 June 68), *ibid.* 283; to ER (6 June), 286–7; and Windisch>FN (2 May 68), *BW* I/3, 249–54. 'In June, during a brief trip to Naumburg' – FN>ER (8 Oct 68), *ibid.*, 321–2.

81 On Karl Franz Brendel and the *Neue Zeitschrift für Musik* – Ernest Newman, *Life of RW*, vol II, 185–6, 218, 223–5, 301, 368–9; E. Perenyi, *Liszt*, 287–8. On *Die Grenzboten* – Newman, *RW* II, 242, and 399fn, re an article 'of a quite monumental stupidity' written by FN's former professor of Philology, Otto Jahn, described by FN (8 Oct) to ER as a 'Grenzboten-hero', *BW* I/2, 322. 'Years before, Wagner . . .' – Newman, *RW* II, 224. '*Judentum in der Musik*' – *ibid.*, 218. Mary Whittall translated this as *Jewry in Music* in Curt von Westernhagen's biography of *RW* (153, 407): a slight improvement on the standard mistranslation, *Judaism in Music.* Munich première of *Meistersinger* – Newman, *RW* IV, 140–2.

81–82 FN's enthusiam for *Meistersinger* – FN>ER (27 Oct), *BW* I/2, 332; Liszt on its 'incomparable sap' – Newman, *RW* IV, 112.

82 E. Windisch and Lessingstrasse lodgings – FN>FrN/Eli *BW* I/2 (Oct 68), 325–6; on Biedermann and the *Deutsche Allgemeine Zeitung*, FN>ER (27 Oct), *ibid.*, 330–2; FN>FrN/Eli, 30 Oct (597). 'the bright-eyed Suzanne Klemm' – FN>ER (27 Oct), *ibid.* 332 (described as, in Greek letters, *glaukhidion*).

82–85 'evening of November 5, 1868' and FN's first meeting with Wagner – all described in great detail in long FN letter to ER (9 Nov) – *ibid.* (599), 335–41.

## 10. From Leipzig to Basel

86 'Homer and Hesiod were contemporaries' – FN>Deussen, (April-May 68), *BW* I/2, 271; FN>ER (9 Dec 68), 349; ER> FN, 20 Dec 68, *BW* I/3, 317–9. V. Rose's 'porcupine style' – FN>ER (8 Oct) *BW* I/2, 324.

86–87 '*Kleinkrämer* . . . triviality' – for ex. FN>Deussen, *ibid.* (595), 327–9; to ER (20 Nov), 344–5.

87 'sudden, "leap-like comparison"' – FN>ER (9 Dec), 350. Rohde's 'stagnant swamp' – ER>FN, 3 Jan 69, *BW* I/3, 325. 'Hermann Brockhaus' – FN>FrN/Eli, *BW* I/2, 347. 'Heinrich Laube' – FN>FrN/Eli, *ibid.*, 334, 336, 361; FN>ER (9 Dec 68), 351. 'Suzanne Klemm' – FN>FrN/Eli, *ibid.*, 347; FN>ER (9 Dec), 351. 'his *Habilitation* exams' – FN>ER (9 Nov), *ibid.*, 337. 'to Paris for a year of scholastic dissipation' – FN>ER, *ibid.*, 358. 'incredible news that . . . Adolf Kiessling' – FN>ER, (16 Jan 69), *ibid.* (608), 358–60. Ritschl on FN, 'so mature, so early' – Janz I, 254–5, quoting from Johannes Stroux's *N's Professur in Basel.*

87–88 'Professor Wilhelm Vischer' – FN>ER, *BW* I/2, 359.

88 'Richard Wagner had recently sent him' – *ibid.*, 360. 'singing *Tannhäuser* melodies' – *ibid.*, 359. 'It was six days' – FN>ER, 10–16 Jan 69, *ibid.*, 356–60 FN letter of Jan 17, *ibid.* (609), 361–2. *Meistersinger* première – FN>FrN/Eli, *ibid.*, 361. 'supreme artistic indulgence' – FN>ER, (22, 28 Feb 69) *ibid.*, 379. 'On 12 February' – Vischer's letter is mentioned in FN's note to Gersdorff – FN>CvG, *ibid.* (614); also in FN's letter to Vischer (13 Feb 69), 372. 'dozen visiting cards' – *ibid.* (614–9), 368–71.

89 'The good tidings' etc. – FrN>FN, Eli>FN, 13–14 Feb 69, *BW* I/3 (213, 214), 336–9. 'Overnight N became . . . a social lion' – FN>FrN/Eli, *BW* I/2, 373–4; FN>ER (22, 28 Feb 69), 377–8. 'May Zeus and all the Muses' – FN>CvG (11 April 69) *ibid.*, 385–6. 'On 19 April' – FN>FrN/Eli (20 April 69), *BW* II/1, 3–4. During the train trip south from Heidelberg FN got off at Karlsruhe to enjoy a performance of *Die Meistersinger.* 'hideous hole in the wall' – FN>Eli, (late June or early July), 20.

89–90 On the Münsterplatz and Basel – Janz I, 278–84, 290; Karl Baedeker, *Die Schweiz* (Leipzig, 1893).

90 'Recher's . . . restaurant' – FN>FrN/Eli, *BW* II/1, 4. 'seven registered philologists' – FN>Ritschl, 10 May 69, *ibid.*, 7. On Wilhelm Vischer, Franz Gerlach, and Jakob Mähly – Janz I, 306–13; FN>ER (16 June), *BW* II/1, 16–17. N's 'work day began' – FN>Ritschl, *BW* II/1, 7. 'His inaugural address' – FN>Eli, *ibid.* (5), 10–11.

90–91 N's 'social obligations' inspiring 'various degrees of boredom' – FN>FrN (7), 14–15; to Sophie Ritschl (16) 30.

91 On Jacob Burckhardt – FN>ER, *ibid.* (6), 13; FN>Deussen, (10), 22. Basel, as 'hostile to the Theatre-Graces' – FN>ER, 11 Nov 69, *ibid.* (40), 72. FN's 'anti-social solitude', compared to Kiessling's love of boyish company, FN>ER, *ibid.* (15), 28.

## 11. Tribschen

92 Wagner's 'New Year's greeting card' – FN>ER, 16 Jan 69 *BW* I/2 (607), 360. 'Long live free Switzerland' – *ibid.* (618), 371. 'a paddle-steamer trip' – Janz I, 293–5. 'repeating the same plaintive chord' – *ibid.*, 295, quoting from FN notebook; FN's later reminiscence in letter to RW, 15 Oct 72, *BW* II/3 (260), 62.

92–93 Details on FN's trip around the Vierwaldstätter lake were obtained, with the help of a local resident (Joseph Gwerder), from photocopies of a timetable brochure, '*Navigation à vapeur sur le Lac des Quatre Cantons*', published in July 1869, and from Baedeker's *Die Schweiz*; FN's jolly evening at Flüelen and his return to Lucerne from FN's notebook, Janz I, 295–6.

93 'more beautifully located house' – description based on a trip I made to Tribschen in 1992. 'vegetable and flower garden' etc. – frequently mentioned in Cosima Wagner's invaluable diary: for ex. 'sun, buds, blossoms, for the first time the sound of cowbells' (14 April 69).

93–94 This description of the house's interior is based on RW's own description in letter written on 22 March 1869, quoted in the '*Zeittafel*' section of the Piper Verlag edition of Cosima W's *Tagebücher*, 874–5; also Judith Gautier, *Auprès de RW*, 33–115.

94 RW's 'estranged wife' – Minna (Christine Wilhelmine Planer), had died in January 1866 – Newman III, 530. 'two younger of her four daughters': Isolde (born in April 65), Eva (in Feb 67) – *ibid.*, 262; IV, 51. 'her elder sister Blandine' etc. – on Cosima's youth and upbringing, Jacques Vier, *La Comtesse d'Agoult et son temps*, vol I; Newman III, 279–80.

94–95 Cosima's 'soft blue eyes, golden hair' – so described by Judith Gautier (*Auprès de RW*, 109), who visited Tribschen in July 69; 'deep, resonant voice' – much appreciated by RW: for ex. *CWD*, 7 March 1870 entry.

95 'exquisitely mannered poise' – Newman III, 280. 'used the term *gescheuten*' – FN>ER, *BW* II/1 (6), 13. FN quoting from RW's *Opera and Drama* – *CWD* I, 17 May. 'two performances of *Meistersinger*' – for Dresden, *BW*/I, 365; for Karlsruhe stop-over, during train trip to Basel – FN>FrN/Eli, *BW* II/1 (1), 3–4. 'a thorough knowledge of R's works' – *CWD* I, 17 May.

96 Mannheim première of *Meistersinger* – *ibid.*, 11 March. 'recent publication . . . of *Das Judentum in der Musik*' – Newman IV, 179–81; also *ibid.* III, 197–9. The full title of the 'updated' version was *Aufklärungen über das Judentum in her Musik*. Published by Weber in March 69 – *CWD* I, March 9 – it was later included by E.W. Fritzsch in RW's *Gesammelte Schriften*. 'obtrusive Jewry' – FN>RW, 22 May 69, *BW* II/1, 9. 'little-known photograph' – FN>FrN, *BW* II/1 (13), 26. leave-taking at Rössli inn – RW>FN, *BW* II/2 (6), 14.

96–97 'a note from Cosima von Bülow' – CosB>FN, *BW* II/2, 11.

97 FN cursing 'loathsome' chains – FN>RW, *BW* II/1, 9; inability to accept invitation – FN>Eli, *ibid.*(5), 10. FN's 'ecstatic "bread-and-butter" letter' – *BW* II/1 (4) 'made a most favourable impression at Tribschen' – *CWD*, 23 May 69. 'Many blissful experiences' – RW>FN, 3 June, *BW* II/2 (6). 'A few days before, Cosima' – *CWD* I, 26 May; also 24th and 25th ('*viel Tapezierer-Nöte*' – trouble with wallpapering), and RW entry, June 3 (p. 102). 'Professor N had arrived' – *ibid.*, June 5 entry.

97–98 'The governess' – Hermine, *ibid.*, May 26.

98 'neophyte-confusion' – CosB>FN, 7 June, *BW* II/2 (7). 'At 1 o'clock in the morning', etc. – Sunday, June 6 entry (in RW's handwriting), *CWD* I, 103–4. 'The very next day' – CosB>FN, *BW* II/2 (7), 15. 'into little two-storey house' – FN>Eli, *BW* II/1, 20.

98–99 FN at Interlaken – FN>Sophie Ritschl, *ibid.*, 29–30.

99 'letter written the next day' – FN>Eli, 27 July, 32–33. FN 'again turned up at Tribschen' – *CWD* I, 31 July. 'batch of manuscripts' – FN>G. Krug, 4 Aug, *BW* II/1, FN to Gustav Krug ('this man . . .') – *ibid.*, 37. 'After lunch on this . . . Sunday' – *CWD* I, 1 Aug entry.

99–100 'Early the next morning' – CosB>FN, *BW* II/2, 29–30.

100 'The spectacular view' – FN>Ritschl, 2 Aug, *BW* II/1 (18). 'Tuesday the skies cleared again' – CosB>FN, *ibid.*, 30; On Eduard von Hartmann – FN>CvG, 4 Aug, *BW* II/1, 36. 'Ah, dear Friend' – FN>ER (17 Aug), *ibid.* (22), 41. 'A single, second-class train fare' – FN>Eli, *ibid.* 33. 'On Friday, 27 August' etc. – *CWD* I, 141; RW>FN (telegram), *BW* II/2 (17). 'Cosima, in a recent letter' – (26 Aug) *BW* II/2, 36.

100–1 On week-end commotion in Tribschen household – *CWD* I, 141–2; Judith Gautier, *Auprès de RW*, 181–2; on *Rheingold* première, Newman IV, 202–17.

101 '*immer angenehm*' – *CWD*, 146 (Piper ed.), 142 (Harcourt Brace ed.). 'the greatest genius' – FN>Deussen, 25 Aug, *BW* II/1, 46. 'Schop and Goethe . . .' – FN>ER, 3 Sept, *ibid.* (28), 52. 'eyes "as blue as the Lake of Lucerne"' – Judith Gautier, *Auprès de RW*, 75. Liszt on RW, 'shriek of a young eagle' – Liszt, *Briefe* IV, 140, 145; quoted by Newman, *W as Man and Artist*, 173.

101–2 Edouard Schuré, *Souvenirs sur RW* , 76 – quoted by Newman, *ibid.*, 172–3.

102 Hans von Bülow: 'This century' – in Newman III, 556. 'for nothing in the world' – FN, *Eh*, 'Why I am so clever', section 5.

## 12. An Intoxicating Friendship

103 'remuneration for services rendered' – FN>Eli, 27 *BW* II/1, 'sell a state bond' – *ibid.* (late Aug), 48. 'which brought in 81 thalers', and his mother's 'pained' letter – *BW* II/2 (19), 40. 'scheduled trip to Lake of Geneva was cancelled' – FN>FrN, *BW* II/1 (26), 49; FN>Eli (25 Sept)), 53–54; FN>FrN/Eli (late Sept), 56. 'completing the indexing' of the *RMfP* – FN>FrN, *ibid.*, 56. 'some pleasant hours with G. Krug' – *ibid.* (41). 'with his intelligent wife, Sophie' – Ritschl>FN, 14 Aug, *BW* II/2, 58.

104 'his cosy lodgings' – FN>FrN/Eli (27 Oct), *BW* II/1, 70. 'worn horsehair rug' – FN>Eli (23 Nov) *ibid.*, 77. 'three *dumb* students' – FN>Ritschl, *ibid.*, (39) 71; and for Latin grammar – FN>ER, 11 Nov, 72. 'On Saturday, 13 November' – *CWD* I, 164. '(A few days before, Wagner . . .)' – *CWD* I, 5 Nov entry. 'Sunday was undisturbed' – *ibid.*, Nov 14 entry. 'Of social gregariousness' – FN>FrN, *BW* II/1 (44),79. 'two pictures of Schop' – FN>ER (11 Nov), *ibid.*, 73. 'without isolation' – FN>Krug (17 Nov), *ibid.*, 75.

104–5 Christmas at Tribschen – details from *CWD* I, entries for Friday, 24 Dec, 1869 to Monday, 3 January, 1870.

105 'W's Uncle Adolf': on efforts to obtain this portrait, see three letters to FN from Cosima, 29 Sept,19 Oct, 2 Nov (*BW* II/2, 49, 61, 69); *CWD* I, Nov 7; Eli>FN undated fragment (late Oct), *BW* II/2 (35a), 619–20; FN>FrN/Eli (27 Oct), *BW* II/I, 69, and (29 Nov), 45; CosB>FN (30 Nov), *BW* II/2, 85 (mention of Doris Brockhaus). 'rare Schop photograph' – FN>FrN/Eli (27 Oct), *BW* II/1, 69; with 'Wagner coat of arms' – *ibid.* (29 Nov) 80. FN's Christmas gift for Cosima – *CWD* I, 24 Dec entry. 'Herr Nützsche' on frozen lake: CosB>FN, 17 Jan 70, *BW* II/2, 118, and 5 Feb (72), 144. 'upstairs . . . *Denkstube*' – *CWD* I, 5 Nov 69 entry; FN> FrN/Eli (20 Dec), *BW* II/1, 85.

105–6 'Ancient Music Drama' lecture – FN>CvG, *BW* II/1 (first mention, 28 Sept 69), 60–61; FN>ER (late Jan, 15 Feb), 94; FN's preparatory notes in *NF, N-KSA* 7, pp. 7–49; '*Das griechische Musikdrama*' – text in *GW-Mus* V, 5–22. 'delivered on Jan 18, 1870' – CosB>FN, *BW* II/2, 120. 'before a "mixed public"' – FN>ER, *BW* II/1, 94. 'of middle-aged "mothers"' – FN's letter has disappeared, but not RW's amused reply 27 Jan 70, *BW* II/2 (65).

106 'second lecture' ('*Socrates und die Tragödie*') – FN>FrN, Feb 70), *BW* II/1, 96 – was 'more provocative' – FN>Deussen, *ibid.*, 98–99; 'arousing . . . varying degrees of "hatred and fury"' – FN>ER (58) 95,(69) 112. Text in *NW* III/2 (*Nachgelassene Schriften 1870–1873*), 25–40. Gustav Teichmüller (*ADB*, vol 37, 543–4) and his angry reaction – 'Both Wagner and Cosima' – *CWD* I, 3 Feb 70; RW's remonstrance, 4 Feb 70, *BW* II/2, 137–8; CosB>FN, 5 Feb, 138–40; '*The Acharnians*' – *CWD* I, Feb 6.

106–7 'I now have nobody' – RW>FN, *BW* II/2, 145–6 (correct date, 7 Feb 70 – cf. CosW diary entry).

107 'Professor Ordinarius' – FN>FrN/Eli, *BW* II/1, (72). Mother and Elisabeth reaching Basel – FN>Frn/Eli, *BW* II/1, 113; 'good Friday service': Eli>FN, *BW* II/2, 186. 'chalet-pension . . . above Montreux' – FN>FrN/Eli, *BW* II/1, 107; 'unusually cloud-free Mont Blanc' – FN>Ritschl, (74).

107–8 'Fritz cut short his vacation' – *ibid.* (75), 117.

108 'from nine to fourteen' philologists – FN>ER, *ibid.*, 119. On Mähly's ill health – FN>ER (6 May), *ibid.*, 121; FN>Ritschl (early June), 123. 'dozen rose-bushes' – FN>RW, *ibid.* (79); CosB>FN (23 May), *BW* II/2, (103), 212. Erwin Rohde in Basel – ER>FN, *BW* II/2 (24 May) 214–6. 'three-day Pentecostal excursion' – FN's visit to Tribschen with Rohde – *CWD* I, June 11, 12. 'members of the "third generation"' – *CWD* I, 24 May 70. 'as was Carl von Gersdorff' – FN>CvG (11 March), *BW* II/1 (65, 66); CvG>FN, 4 April, *BW* II/2, 188–93; CvG letter to RW, received 4 April – CosB>FN, *ibid.*, 187, and *CWD*, 4 April entry.

108–9 Rohde's 'manly earnestness' – CosB>FN, 24 June, *BW* II/2, 224–5.

109 'Dürer engraving' – *CWD* I, 11, 14 June entries; and Cosima's profound appreciation – CosB>FN, 24 June, *BW* II/2, 225. 'Wagner took immediate exception' – *CWD* I, 11 June. 'At luncheon, the next day' – 12 June (*CWD*). On Wüllner rehearsing for *Die Walküre* première in Munich, Newman IV, 267–8. Wagner's 'discovery' of Bayreuth – *CWD* I, 5 March 70.

109–10 FN's 'thank-you letter to Cosima' – *BW* II/1 (19 June), *BW* II/1, 125; and her reply, 24 June 70, *BW* II/2, 224.

## 13. A Bitter Taste of Warfare

111 'On 6 July 1870' – CvG>FN, *BW* II/2 (113), 231. 'Like Sophie Ritschl' –

SR>FN, *ibid.* (15 July), 232. 'Our whole threadbare culture' – FN>ER, *BW* II/1, 130–1. 'the "*Zeitverflachung*"' – FN>CvG, *ibid.*, 2 July, 126.

112 'crammed with French and German tourists' – EF-N's reminiscences, in *Beg.* (78), 145 (20 July 1870). 'top of the Axenstein cliff' and FN's tormented state of mind – FN>Sophie Ritschl, *BW* II/1, 132–3. 'On 28 July' – *CWD* I entry ('Visit from Prof N'). 'Taking leave of his sister' – in her book of reminiscences, *Wagner und Nietzsche zur Zeit ihrer Freundschaft*, written in 1914, when she was almost 70 years old, Elisabeth forgot to mention the week-long stay at the Axenstein hotel, as having preceded her stay with the mother of one of FN's professorial colleagues – *Beg.* (77), 144.

112–3 'All of W's francophobic resentments' – see *CWD* I entries of 17, 18, 19 July, among others.

113 On the visit of RW's three French admirers, *CWD* I, 28, 29, 30 July entries. Judith Gautier, recalling this visit to Tribschen in *Auprès de RW*, p. 225, sought to conceal the prevailing tension, declaring that she would have liked RW less if he had been less of a German patriot! 'N and . . . Hans Richter' – EF-N, in *Beg.* (77), 144–5. Eli 'as being a nice, modest girl' – *CWD* I, July 29.

113–4 FN 'with his sister in the Maderanerthal' – EF-N, *Leben* II/1, 31–32; *Beg.*, 145–6.

114 'robust name of 'Alpenklub'' – Janz I, 372–3. 'Two days later N wrote to W. Vischer' – 8 August, *BW* II/1 (89). 'Cosima immediately wrote' – CosB>FN, 9 Aug, *BW* II/2 (118). FN and his sister leaving Basel – *Beg.* (80), 146–7. 'were lodged in a Hôtel Wallfisch' – details drawn from FN notebook, 4(1), under heading '*Erlangen Samstag den 20. August*', in *dtv* ed. of *FN Nachlass 1869–1874, N-KSA*, vol 7, pp. 87ff; FN>Eli, *BW* II/1 (20 Aug) 135–6; FN>FrN (20 Aug), 136–7.

114–5 'On 22 August' etc – detailed account in FN's long letter to W. Vischer (11 Sept 70) from Erlangen, *BW* II/1 (99); also FN>CvG (20 Oct), 148–9; Janz I, 376.

115 'battlefield of Wörth' – FN>FrN (29 Aug), *BW* II/1 (95). 'In each Alsatian village' – *ibid.*, 138. 'From Haguenau . . . Bischweiler' – FN>Ritschl, 29 Aug, *ibid.* (96) 'Lorraine capital of Nancy' – FN>Eli, 2 Sept, *ibid.* (97). FN letters to Tribschen – *CWD* I, 29 Aug, 1 Sept, and others mentioned in CosW letter to FN, 2 Sept, *BW* II/2 (121). Cosima writing that 'she and Richard Wagner had been married on 25 August' – CosW>FN, 2 Sept, *ibid.* Whereas all of her previous letters had been signed 'C. von Bülow' or 'CB', this one was signed 'Cosima Wagner, geb: Liszt'.

115–6 'colleague from Basel' etc. – FN>Vischer (11 Sept), *BW* II/1 (99); RW (also 11 Sept), 142–3; FN>CvG, 20 Oct, 148–9.

116 'By 19 September' – FN>CvG, *ibid.* 'letter to . . . Ritschl' – 21 Sept 70, *ibid.* (101), 145.

## 14. Wild Hopes and Fantasies

117 'On 21 October' – FN>W. Vischer (from Naumburg, 19 Oct 70), *BW* II/ 1, 146. 'recurring fits of vomiting' – FN>FrN/Eli, *ibid.*, 150. 'end-of-term exam papers' – *ibid.*, 150; FN>Ritschl, 152. 'lecture courses' – on Hesiod's *Days* (11 students), on 'metric schemes' of Greek poets (5 students only): figures given by Johannes Stroux, *N's Professur in Basel*, 96. 'In late October' – FN>Ritschl, *BW* II/1, 152.

117–8 'Nine days later' – FN>CvG, *ibid.*, 155, answering CvG's long letter of 10 Oct, *BW* II/2 (125).

118 'the same incorrigible Pio Nono' – see Cosima's comment on the dogma of

'Papal infallibility', recently proclaimed at the conclusion of the Vatican Council, which had begun its deliberations in December 1869 – CosB>FN, 16 July 1870, *BW* II/2, 233. 'The clearest expression of N's misgivings' – CvG>FN, *BW* II/2, (132, 23 Nov), 268–9. See also CvG's letters of 10 Oct (125), 25 Oct (126), 247–56; and FN's delighted response, 12 Dec, *BW* II/1, 162. 'another weekend trip to Tribschen' – *CWD* I, 26, 27 Nov 70.

118–9 '*Nicht kapituliert*' – later changed to '*Die Kapitulation*': Newman, IV, 277–8.

119 'Two weeks later' – FN>FrN/Eli (12 Dec), *BW* II/1, 163–4. 'a new Rector (Heusler)' – *ibid.*, 164. 'blood and ever more blood' – ER>FN, 11 Dec, *BW* II/2, 280–1. 'prompt reply from N' – FN>ER (15 Dec), *BW* II/1, 165–6.

119–20 'Heinrich Romundt' – FN's letter later disappeared, but was answered on 1 Jan 71 (*BW* II/2, 301–5). 'playwright turned philologist' – see FN>CvG, 22 June 68 (*BW* I/2, 293–4), and FN>ER, 6 Aug 68, *ibid.*, 306, mentioning HR's 'tragedy', *Marianne und Herodes*.

120 'tutoring refractory son of a professor of Physiology' – Ritschl to FN, 17 Nov 69, *BW* II/2, 78–79; FN>Ritschl (after 23 Nov 69), *BW* II/1, 77–78; HR>FN, 14 Dec 69, *BW* II/2, 93–94, and other HR letters. 'When N left Basel for Tribschen' – invited by RW, 3 Dec, by Cosima, 9 and 21 Dec, *BW* II/2 (45, 46, 51); first mention of 'Tribschen symphony' – FN>FrN/Eli (12 Dec), *BW* II/1, 163. 'last-minute telegram' – RW>FN, 23 Dec 70, *BW* II/2 (143), and FN>FrN/Eli, 23 Dec, *BW* II/1, 170. 'fifteen instrumentalists' and Richter – Newman IV, 273; Janz I, 392–4. 'Cosima . . . was not inordinately surprised' – *CWD* I, 24 Dec 'the house-guest's gifts' – FN>FrN/Eli (23 Dec), *BW* II/1, 170.

120–1 'Cosima's surprise was thus total' – *CWD* I, Dec 25.

121 FN's 'Genesis of Tragic Thought' – *ibid.*, Dec 26. RW's enthusiasm for Apollinian vs. Dionysian – *ibid.*, Jan 3, 4, 5 (1871) entries; CosW>FN, 4 Jan 71, *BW* II/2, 308–9. 'first blow to his . . . hopes' – ER>FN, *ibid.*, 294–6. Gustav Schönberg to FN, 30 Dec 70, *ibid.* (148). Heinrich Romundt to FN, 1 Jan 71, *ibid.* (150).

122 'On or around 21 January' – FN>FrN/Eli, *BW* II/1 (119). 178–9. 'letter . . . to W. Vischer' – *ibid.* (118).

123 'scholar named Franz Overbeck' – on his background, see C.A. Bernouilli, *Franz Overbeck und FN*, vol I; Janz I, 358–63. 'lodgings in Schützengraben . . . house' – ('*unsere Residenz*') Ov>FN, 17 April 71, *BW* II/2 (178), 358. 'Kuno Fischer's scintillating lectures' – significantly overlooked in Bernouilli's coverage of Ov's Jena years. 'On 6 February' – FN>FrN/Eli, *BW* II/1 (122). 'terse telegram to his sister' – *ibid.* (123). 'this epistolatory and telegraphic wrangling' – FrN>FN (7 Feb 71), *BW* II/2 (161); Eli>FN (162); FN (telegram) to Eli, *BW* II/1 (124); Eli>FN (8 Feb), *BW* II/2 (164). 'Lisbeth duly boarded the unheated train' – EF-N, *Leben* II, 55–56. 'in a fur overcoat . . . Overbeck' – FN>Ov, *BW* II/1, 186.

123–4 'At Lucerne they moved', and on to Flüelen – EF-N, *Leben* II, 56; on Mazzini, EF-N, *Beg.*, 153–60.

124 'For most of their stay' – FN>Ov, *BW* II/1, 186–7; FN to Julius Piccard, 25 March 71 (129); FN>ER (29 March), 189–91. 'On 1 March' – FN>FrN, *ibid.* (127). 'The Origin and Aim of Tragedy' – so called in FN letter to ER, 29 March 71, *ibid.*, 189. 'On 2 April' – FN>Eli, *ibid.* (131); 'little snakes and lizards' mentioned in FN>Ov (128), 187. 'Leaving his sister at Weggis' – *CWD* I, April 3 entry.

124–5 On RW's *Kaisermarsch* and other offerings, *ibid.*, April 3, 4 entries, Newman IV, 274–80.

125 'About W's and Cosima's reactions' – *CWD* I, April 5, 6, 7. 'On Easter Eve N left Tribschen' – *ibid.*, April 8. 'After two more sleepless nights' – FN>ER, 10 April 71, *BW* II/1 (132), 193. 'Rudolf Eucken, a former pupil of Teichmüller's' – see his *Lebenserinnerungen*, 59; studying under Trendelenburg, 70, 77; doctoral dissertation on use of prepositions in Aristotle's Metaphysics, 80; also Janz I, 400–5. 'What idiocies I committed!' – FN>ER, *BW* II/1 (132),193.

## 15. The Birth of Tragedy

126 'To lighten N's academic burden' – Stroux, *op. cit.* 96. 'On April 20th' – FN>W. Engelmann, *BW* II/1, 193–4. 'elicited no response' – FN>ER (7 June), *ibid.*, 197; Romundt>FN, 22 May, *BW* II/2 (186), 373. 'continued to be plagued by insomnia' – FN>ER (7 June), *ibid.* (135). 'tour of German cities ' – Nürnberg, Bayreuth, Leipzig, Dresden, Berlin, Darmstadt, Heidelberg, *GWD* I, 15 April to 14 May.

126–7 'evening' spent with RW and Cosima – *ibid.*, 15 May; FN>ER (7 June), *BW* II/1, 198; on Bayreuth theatre – *CWD* I, April 19; Newman IV, 300.

127 '300,000 thalers', *ibid.*, 306–9. 'The date being 22 May' – *CWD* I, 22 May; 'Reformation-Journal' – FN>ER (7 June), *BW* II/1, 198. 'Two days later the "Professor"' – *CWD* I, May 24.

127–8 On the *Communards*' uprising – Brinkley, *op.cit*, 119–20.

128 'The news left N . . . shattered' – FN>CvG, *BW* II/1, 204. 'What does it mean to be a scholar' – FN>Vischer, *ibid.* (134). 'At noon on this same Saturday' – *CWD* I, May 27 entry. 'W went to the Lucerne post-office' – *BW* II/2 (telegram, facetiously signed 'Familie Lindhorst'), (187). 'The next day Fritz and his sister' – *CWD* I, May 28. 'a little hotel at Gimmelwald' – FN>CvG (21 June), *BW* II/1, 205; FN>ER (12 July), 209. 'Here they were joined by . . . CvG' – CvG>FN, *BW* II/2. 'most honourably released' – FN>ER (19 July), *ibid.*, 212.

128–9 'letter from Heinrich Romundt' – HR>FN (14 July), *BW* II/2, 400–1; FN ordering Engelmann to give ms. to HR, *BW* II/1 (28 June), 205–6.

129 'shower of illuminating thoughts' – FN>ER, *BW* II/1, 210. 'noble and earnest chacteristics of the North German' – *CWD*, 30 July. 'a not quite natural reserve makes his behaviour' – *CWD* I, 3 Aug entry. 'Seven weeks later N took . . . train' – FN>Eli, *BW* II/1, 223; FN>FrN, 15 Sept, 225. 'the "merry" city of Basel' – Eli>FN, *BW* II/2 (1 Sept), 417. 'During the second week of October' – FN>ER, 6 Sept, *BW* II/1 (151); FN>CvG (156), 227; ER>FN (5 Oct), *BW* II/2 (226); FN>Deussen (16 Oct), 231. 'state of sagging ebriety' – FN>ER (accompanying photo of the jolly trio), *ibid.* (20 Oct), 233; FN>CvG (163).

129–30 Goethe verses: *im Ganzen, Guten, Schönen* – had been quoted to FN by Mazzini when they had met at Flüelen in February, before crossing the Saint Gotthard Pass; FN>FrN/Eli (13 Nov), *ibid.*, 240; FN>CvG (18 Nov) 242.

130 'Gersdorff and Rohde . . . were accordingly exhorted' – FN>CvG (20 Oct), *ibid.*, 234; FN>ER (162), 234. 'Erwin Rohde, having no open window' – ER>FN, 27 Nov, *BW* II/2, 446. 'Gersdorff's performance' – CvG>FN (3 Nov), *BW* II/2, 450. 'N . . . hied himself to house of . . . J. Burckhardt' – FN>CvG (18 Nov), 244.

130–1 'a shadowy figure . . . Paul Deussen' – *ibid.*, 244–5; FN>FrN/Eli (13 Nov) 240. 'Deussen had obtained' – FN>Deussen, *ibid.* (12 Sept), 221–2; (24 Sept) 230; also PD, *Leben*, 128–30.

131 'six university students' – FN>FrN/Eli, *BW* II/1, 240; Stroux, 96: the nine students mentioned in FN's letter to his mother had chosen a course in Latin

epigraphy (1 hour per week only). 'During the jolly week' – FN>Deussen, *BW* II/1, 16 Oct, 231; FN>CvG (18 Nov), 243. 'Ernst Wilhelm Fritzsch' – RW>FN, 16 Oct, urging him to offer ms. to Fritzsch, *BW* II/2, 446. FN replied on Oct 21 (*CWD* I entry), requesting RW's endorsement, which RW sent to Fritzsch that same day. 'Fritzsch was frankly baffled' – FN>RW, *BW* II/1, 245. 'On 18 November' – Fritzsch>FN, *BW* II/2 (233), dated 16 Nov, but received by FN on the 18th, FN>Fritzsch, *BW* II/1 (167); FN>RW (169). 'ten new sections' – FN>Fritzsch (18 Nov), *ibid.* (167). 'Not until the second week of December' – FN>CvG, *ibid.* (176); FN>ER (177), 255–7; too late to be a Christmas gift: Fritzsch>FN, 21 Dec, *BW* II/2 (246).

131–2 'Emil Heckel' – *CWD* I entries for 19 May, 6 Oct, 8 Nov, 22 Nov, 132.

132 'Cosima, after writing three times' – *BW* II/2 (26 Nov, 237), (6 Dec, 242), (13 Dec, 243), also RW>FN, 26 Nov (238) and 'last-minute telegram' – 16 Dec (245). 'Tears that our communion in music' – *CWD* I, Monday, 18 Dec 'N was given a room' – FN>FrN/Eli, *BW* II/1 (23 Dec), 262. 'he was introduced to W's friends' – *CWD* I, Dec 20 entry; FN>CvG (23 Dec), *BW* II/1, 259–60. 'two glorious days, compared to which' – FN>ER, *ibid.* (177), 256–7. 'he and F. Brockhaus' – *CWD* I, Dec 21 entry. 'new festival opera-house . . . "*Richardshöhe*"' – FN>CvG (23 Dec), *BW* II/1, 260.

133 'six public lectures' – FN>FrN/Eli (23 Dec), *BW* II/1, 262. 'New Year's Eve Echo' – FN>ER (23 Nov), *ibid.*, 247 and (21 Dec) 257; FN>FrN/Eli, 261. 'inspired by . . . Gustav Krug' – who, with Pinder, had joined FN in Leipzig during the jolly five days with ER and CvG: Krug>FN, 21 Dec, *BW* II/2 (248). 'one copy . . . for his mother' – Eli>FN (25 and 27 Dec) *BW* II/2, 483–4. 'second copy delivered to Cosima' – *CWD* I, Dec 25 entry. 'she graciously wrote' – CosW>FN (30 Dec), *BW* II/2 (254); see also Wagner's somewhat embarrassed reaction: RW>FN (10 Jan 72), *ibid.*, 505 'nervous stomach upsets' – RW>FN, *ibid.*, 504–5; FN>CvG (10 Jan 72), *BW* II/1, 273; to FrN>Eli (24 Jan 72), 277. 'first batch of printed copies' – FN>RW (2 Jan 72) *ibid.*, 271–2.

133–4 'By noon of that day' – *CWD* I, Jan 3, 1872 entry.

134 'Bonaventura Genelli' – see FN's later reference to this influence in letter to ER, (16 July 72), *BW* II/3, 25.

136 Schop's 'Metaphysics of Sexual Love' – *WWR* II, ch. 44.

136–7 'a malevolent demon' – *ibid.* 534; 'character inherited from the father', etc., 537.

137 Schop: 'it might appear more suitable for the text' – 143 FN – 'lyric poetry of Ancient Greece' – *GdT*, section 6. 'the orally declaiming chorus' – *GdT*, § 7. 'Sadness is not made for men' – FN>Krug, *BW* II/1, 268.

137–8 'The ancient Greek, "knew and felt the terrors . . . of existence"' – *GdT*, § 3.

138 'an "Olympian divine order of joy"' – *GdT*, § 3 (Kaufmann, 43). 'Thus do the gods justify the life of man' – *ibid.*

138–9 'The satyr, as the Dionysian chorist' – *GdT*, § 8 (Kauf, 58–59). 'singing and dancing crowds' – *GdT*, § 1 (K 36–37). 'Man, rising to Titanic stature' – *GdT*, § 9: '*Götterdämmerung*' – p. 68 in *KSA* I. 'A lovelier book than this' – RW>FN, *BW* II/2 (256).

139 'The evening reading session' – *CWD* I, Jan 4, 1872 entry.

139–40 'denunciation of contemporary shallowness', etc. – *GdT*, § 22.

140 'panegyric to the "glorious, intrinsically healthy"' – *GdT*, section 23 in particular. RW, discovering Schop – Newman II, 291, 430–2. 'copy of *BdT* to Ludwig' – CosW>FN, *BW* II/2 (3 Jan 72), 493; FN>CvG (10 Jan 72), *BW* II/1, 273. 'Other copies were dispatched' – *ibid.* (CosW); for Marie von Schleinitz (in Berlin), FN>CvG (10 Jun 72), *BW* II/1, 273, and CvG's reply, 12 Jan 72, *BW* II/2 (263); for Captain Max von Baligand, a particularly active

member of Munich's Wagner Club, FN>CvG (23 Dec 71), *BW* II/1, 259. On Marie Mukhanoff's 'incomparable violet eyes', see Judith Gautier (whose father was one of her 'victims'), *Auprès de RW*, 104–5, 134. Marie Mukhanoff, a former pupil of Chopin's, was also a gifted pianist (E. Perenyi, *Liszt*, 226–7). 'Still other copies were sent'(to Hans von Bülow and Franz Liszt) – FN>Bülow, Jan 72, *BW* II/1 (187); FN>Fritzsch, 16 Jan, *ibid.* (asking copy for Liszt and Max von Baligand). 'The first, writing . . . from Dresden' – HvB>FN, 27 Jan 72, *BW* II/2, 519. 'The second let a month go by' – Liszt>FN, 29 Feb 72, *ibid.* (292).

141 'About the response of the "creatively inclined"' – see, for example, Marie Mukhanoff's ecstatic response to FN's book, as reported to him by his arch-Wagnerian admirer, Max von Baligand (15 Feb, *BW* II/2, 544).

## 16. The End of an Idyll

142 'another visit to Tribschen' – *CWD* I, 20 Jan 72. 'a discussion of N's plans for extending the spirit of this cultural Renaissance' – FN>ER, 2 Jan 72, *BW* II/1 (183); FN>CvG (10 Jan), 273. 'six public lectures' – FN>FrN/Eli, 3 Dec 71, *ibid.*, 250. N 'played his *Sylvesternacht* composition' – *CWD* I, 20 Jan 72.

142–3 'delegation of students from four university fraternities' – text of their joint statement of thanks, in *BW* II/2 (266); also FN>FrN/Eli (24 Jan 72) *BW* II/1, 277–8, his rejection of Greifswald offer.

143 'On January 23' – CvG>FN, *BW* II/2 (268). 'unexpectly Wagner turned up in Basel' – FN>RW (24 Jan), *BW* II/1 (190 'a Baron Loën from Weimar, a Baron Cohn from Dessau' – *CWD*, 22 Jan FN 'with a hurried note to Gersdorff' – (24 Jan), *BW* II/1 (189).

143–4 'In Basel N's little book' – FN>FrN/Eli (24 Jan), *ibid.*, 277.

144 'What I have had to hear about my book' – FN>ER, (28) Jan 72, *ibid.*, 279. 'Rohde . . . had not been idle' – ER>FN, 29 Jan, *BW* II/2, 524–5. 'the review article was rejected' – ER>FN, 26 Feb, *ibid.*, 554. 'Hermann Hagen . . . fan letter' – HH>FN, 1 Feb 72, *ibid.* (277). 'A war to the knife?' – FN>ER, 28 Jan, *BW* II/1, 279–80.

144–5 'On 30 January' – FN>Ritschl, *ibid.* (194). '*geistreiche Schwiemelei*' – Janz I, 470.

145 'So decidedly do I belong by my entire nature' – Ritschl>FN, *BW* II/2 (285). Hans von Bülow, in Basel – FN>ER (11 April or shortly thereafter), *BW* II/1, 306; FN>FrN/Eli (after 15 April), 307. FN: 'the tendency to use the theatre' – *GdT* § 23 (K 133–4).

148 'in his first (*Bildungsanstalt*) lecture' – delivered on 16 January 1872: German text in *WdB* III, 177–95.

148–9 'In the second lecture' – *ibid.*, 196–213.

149 'In the third public lecture' – *ibid.*, 214–28.

149–50 'In the fourth public lecture' – *ibid.* (5 March), 229–46.

150 'On Sunday, 18 February' – *CWD* I, Feb 18 entry. 'the "indispensable" CvG' – CosW>FN, 31 Jan, *BW* II/2, 526. On Bernhard Löser, see RW's dictated account of his trip to Berlin, inserted after 9 Feb 72 entry in *CWD* I, 456. On the banker Friedrich Feustel – *CWD* I, 8 Jan 72 entry; also his surprise visit to RW in Berlin, *ibid.*, 457. 'One month later, the Thursday before Palm Sunday' – *CWD* I, March 23, 24, 25. 'fifth public lecture' – *WdB* III, 247–63. 'success of his lectures' – FN>Fritzsch, 22 March, *BW* II/1 (104).

150–1 'Jacob Burckhardt' – quoted in Janz I, 447.

151 'Carl Riedel's choral ensemble' – *CWD* I, March 16 entry. 'BFT "was going to cost 900,000 thalers"' – *CWD* I, March 26. 'ready for printing as a second book' – FN>Fritzsch, *BW* II/1, 300; FN planning 'a tour of the "German fatherland"'

– FN>ER, *ibid.* (207) 'N's latest "*combinazione*" – ER>FN, *BW* II/2 (mid-April), 584–5. 'head-cold and . . . weariness' – FN>FrN/Eli, *BW* II/1, 307. 'his Leipzig publisher did not . . . think' – Fritzsch>FN, 1 April, *BW* II/2 (301), replying to FN's 22 March letter (*BW* II/1, 300).

152 'Dr. Hermann Immermann' – Janz I, 448, 450. 'At Vernez, near Montreux' – FN>Ov, *BW* II/1, 311; also Pinder>FN, 16 April, *BW* II/2 (304). 'stage-scenery expert, Karl Brandt' – *CWD* I, April 20. 'Wagner sent a telegram' – relayed by Ov (*BW* II/2, 586). 'His letter did not reach Tribschen until Monday afternoon' (April 22) – see *CWD*, 21, 22 April. 'In Basel he was much put out' – RW telegram to Cosima, received late evening of Monday, *ibid.*, April 22. Before leaving Lucerne, RW had sent FN a telegram proposing a 3-hour meeting in Basel – RW>FN, 22 April, *BW* II/2 (308). Ov, realizing that it was now too late, sent the telegram with a letter to FN at Vernex, and telegraphed FN's exact address to Cosima at Tribschen – 22 April, *ibid.* (309).

152–3 'Two days later' – CosW>FN, 24 April, *BW* II/2 (310).

153 FN 'reached Tribschen the next evening' – *CWD* I, Thursday, April 25. 'The potted palms were still there' – because the gardener had said they were too delicate and would not survive the train trip to Basel, *ibid.* (390), 591. 'The trees in the garden' etc. – description based on Cosima's diary entries, April 24, 25, 26 in particular. 'Tribschen has ceased to be' – FN>CvG, 1 May, *BW* II/1, 317.

## 17. Future-Philosophy and After-Philology

154 'seven-word Latin telegram' – ER>FN, 30 April, *BW* II/2 (312). 'one of the 700 seats' – FN>Krug, 4 May, *BW* II/1, 320. 'places for "his" two professors' – FN>ER, 4 May, *ibid.* (218); CosW>FN, 9 May, from Bayreuth, *BW* II/2 (318). FN 'made it to Bayreuth' – *CWD* I, Saturday, May 18 entry.

154–5 'The next day it began to rain' – *ibid.*, May 19 entry;

155 'Erwin Rohde did not reach Bayreuth' – ER>FN, *BW* II/2 (322). Max von Baligand hugging FN – as told by Gustav Krug to Elisabeth N – Eli>FN (25 May), *BW* II/4 (323), 3. MvB had met FN at the Mannheim concerts of December 1971, and had shared a railway-carriage compartment with him on return trip (FN>CvG, *BW* II/1, 259). 'On Monday morning' – the description of this and the following two days is based on Cosima's diary entries and Ernest Newman's account (vol IV, ch. 17). 'N . . . was granted a seat in W's carriage' – Newman, *ibid.*, 359, quotes from a pertinent passage in FN's fourth 'Untimely Meditation', *Richard Wagner in Bayreuth* (*KSA* I, 434).

156 'Erwin Rohde returned to Kiel' – ER>FN (26 May), *BW* II/4 (324), 4. FN's 'two fine thank-you letters' – mentioned by Cosima, *CWD* I, May 29 entry. The complete text of ER's article in the *Norddeutsche Allgemeine Zeitung*, and of the first version rejected by Zarnke, can be found in Karlfried Grunder's *Der Streit um Nietzsches 'Geburt der Tragödie'*, 15–26: referred to from here on as *Streit*. 'Cosima Wagner, who read' – *CWD* I, May 26 entry; to FN she complained that ER's article was 'more difficult to understand than the book itself.' (29 May, *BW* II/4, 6–7.)

156–7 'Friend, Friend, Friend' – FN>ER, 27 May, *BW* II/3 (223).

157 'he dashed off a letter' – FN>Fritzsch, *ibid.* (224), 4–5. 'the pamphlet . . . *Zukunftsphilosophie*' CvG>FN, *BW* II/4, 9–10. On Wilamowitz-Möllendorff – Janz I, 464–7. 'In it he mocked' – text of Wilamowitz-M's pamphlet in (*op. cit.*) *Streit*, 27–55. 'angry cry of the theoretical man' – CvG>FN, 31 May, *BW* II/4, 10. 'Rohde . . . dismissed W's diatribe' – ER>FN, 5 June, *ibid.*, 12. RW: 'newest example of nastiness' – *CWD* I, June 9 entry.

157–8 RW: 'Open Letter' to FN – *BW* II/4 (328), 13–21; in *Streit*, 57–64.

158 'Cosima . . . found it quite masterly' – *CWD* I, June 11 entry. RW 'then sent it to' – CvG>FN, 22 June, *BW* II/4, (332), 28. 'Its appearance' (in the *NAZ*) delighted FN: FN>CvG, 24 June, *BW* II/3, 13–14. 'as it did his sister' – on FN's elegant and Eli's gaily coloured mode of dress, see interesting recollection of Walther Siegfried, in *Beg.* (119), 197. Heinrich Romundt, after 9 months spent as a tutor in Nice, reached Basel in mid-June 1872 – letters (218), (232), (288), (295), (307), (12 May 72, 320) to FN, in *BW* II/2; FN>ER, *BW* II/3 (7 July), 20; FN>CvG (2 Aug), 42.

159 '*tödlich falschen Zucht*' – *BW* II/4, p.14, line 37. 'on the pre-Platonic philosophers' – FN>ER (12 May) *BW* II/1, 323; (11 June), *BW* II/3, 10. On '*Gifthütte*' – Janz I, 483.

160 'When he learned that . . . Bülow' – CvG>FN, 22 June, *BW* II/4, 28; FN>CvG, 24 June, *BW* II/3, 14; to Bülow, 24 June (232); FN>RW (after receiving favourable telegram from Bülow) (233) 16. 'the two performances of Tristan' – FN>ER (7 July), *BW* II/3, 19–20. 'pleasant hours . . . spent with Malwida von Meysenbug' – FN>ER (mentioning a 'circle of Florentine friends'), (7 July), *ibid.*, 20; FN>MvM, 24 July, (243). Ov and '*Afterphilogie*' – FN>ER (16 July), *BW* II/3, 22–23. 'Wilam-ohne-Witz' – FN>Krug, 24 July, *ibid.*, 30. '"half-arsed" exercise' – FN>ER (2 Aug), *ibid.*, 43.

160–1 'Just four days after Overbeck' – FN>Bülow, *ibid.* (240).

161 'Replying . . . by return post' – Bülow>FN, 24 July, *BW* II/4 (347). 'N's musical talents were negligible' – Newman IV, 'This was neither RW's nor Cosima's opinion' – CosW>FN, 15 Oct, about FN's 'Manfred Meditation' *BW* II/4, 94; RW>FN (24 Oct), 105. 'Franz Liszt too was impressed': he found Hans von Bülow's judgement '*sehr desperat*' – a Frenchified German way of saying 'very despair-inducing'. As for FN's 'Manfred Meditation', it struck RW as expressing the violent clash between 'two oddities' (*zwei Absonderlichkeiten*) – *ibid.*, 105. 'In late August Malwida von M' – MvM>FN, *ibid.*, 70–71. 'can with equal propriety be called "maternal"' – as FN himself declared, later (14 April 76) writing to MvM that, thanks to her, he had discovered that 'mother-love without the physical bond of mother and child is one of the finest revelations of caritas.' (*SBKSA* 5, 14 April 76, 149.)

161–2 'The last but one of ten children' – these details on MvM's youth are drawn from her *Mémoires d'une idéaliste*, with preface by Gabriel Monod, and from Janz I, 675–85.

162 On Giuseppe Mazzini, MvM, *Le Soir de ma vie*, 31–32. 'During MvM's brief stay in Basel' – (Saturday, 31 Aug 72) MvM>FN, *BW* II/4 (355), 70; MvM>FN, 29 Aug (357). 'Alexander Herzen's . . . memoirs' – FN>MvM (27 Aug), *BW* II/3, 49. '*Mémoires d'une idéaliste*' – MvM>FN, 4 Sept, *BW* II/4 (358). 'where the short-sighted Fritz' – FrN>FN, 8 Oct, *BW* II/4, 79.

162–3 'But on the 27th he suddenly changed his mind' – FN>FrN, *BW* II/3 (255), Friday noon (27 Sept) announcing his arrival, Sunday evening; FrN>FN (8 Oct) describing preparations for FN's arrival in Naumburg, followed instead by express letter (brought by postman) from Eli, explaining that FN would not be coming to Naumburg, her bitter maternal shock, *BW* II/4 (361); also Eli>FN (14 Oct, *BW* II/4, 91) on his apologetic telegram, probably sent from Zürich.

163 'The trip began auspiciously' – FN>FrN (from Splügen, 1 Oct), *BW* II/3 (257), describing the train-trip, the stop at Chur, the Ragiusa torrent and thermal spa, and on to Splügen.

163–4 'This high-Alpine valley' – *ibid.*, 55; also FN>CvG (from Splügen, 5 Oct), 57.

164 'The rest of the trip' – FN>Krug (from Chiavenna, 5 Oct), *BW* II/3 (259);

FN>Eli (18 Oct), *ibid.*, 67; FN>CVG (trip to Bergamo), 68; 'He was back in Basel on 11 October – FN>FrN, 16 Oct, *BW* II/3, 65. 'reproachful letter from . . . mother' – FrN>FN, 8 Oct, *BW* II/4 (361). 'ER's *Afterphilologie* rebuttal' – Fritzsch finally agreeing to publish it (to FN, 20 July), *BW* II/4 (344); Teubner (printer) predicting that it would not sell 100 copies, FN>ER (25 July), *BW* II/3, 35; publication around 24 Oct (FN>Eli, *BW* II/3, 73–74); text (48 pages in Fritzsch edition) can be found in *Streit*, 65–110. FN among RW's 'literary lackeys' – FN>RW (15 oct), *BW* II/3, 63. 'Wagner . . . was also delighted' – *CWD* I, Oct 25 entry. Hermann Usener on FN – FN>ER, 25 Oct, *BW* II/3, 70. 'At the start of the winter semester' – FN>ER (undated), *ibid.*, 85.

165 'fifty-three students had enrolled for . . . Burckhardt's lectures', etc. Janz I, 489. 'forty students had signed up for Rudolf Eucken's lecture course on Aristotle', Eucken, *Lebenserinnerungen*, 54. 'twenty students registered' for one of Romundt's courses – FN>Krug (15 Nov), *BW* II/3, 93. 'But only two students' – FN>ER, *ibid.*, 85; Stroux, *op. cit.*, 97. 'His projected course on Homer' – FN>RW (mid-Nov 72), *BW* II/3, 89.

## 18. A First Essay in Polemics

166 'Fritz decided to spend . . . Christmas' – FN>FrN/Eli (20 Dec) *BW* II/3, 106. 'to whom he had sent copies of his Basel lectures' – FN>MvM, 7 Nov, *ibid.* II/3, 83; MvM>FN (22 Nov), initially enthusiastic commentary, *BW* II/4, 135–6. 'On reading this, one has . . .' – FN>MvM, (20 Dec) *BW* II/3, 104. 'Schop had instinctively understood' – see, for ex, *Parerga und P*, vol I, 'On Philosophy at the Universities' (Payne tr.), 173, 176. vol II, 'On Jurisprudence and Politics', 258; 'On Authorship and Style', 540–2; 'On Reading and Books', 560.

166–7 'N sent a note of birthday greetings' – *CWD* I, Dec 25 entry. 'Prefaces to Five Unwritten Books' – FN>CvG, 23 Dec 72, *BW* II/3, 108. FN>ER, 4 Jan 73, 111; CosW>FN, 12 Feb 73, *BW* II/4, 207.

167 'Prof N's manuscript' – *CWD* I, Jan 1–4. 'hurried trip to . . . Weimar' – FN>ER, *BW* II/3, 4 Jan 73, 111. 'important meeting with . . . Fritzsch', who obtained permission to bring out a second ed. of *GdT*, *ibid.*, 111. 'More difficult to fathom': FN had asked CvG to join him briefly in Bayreuth, after 3 Jan 1873, during his return trip to Basel – 23 Dec 72, *ibid.*, 108; but CvG could not leave his grief-stricken father until later, late Dec, *BW* II/4, 159. 'RW took N's *Nichtkommen*' – CosW>FN, 12 Feb 73, *BW* II/4, 207. RW: 'Strictly speaking, you are, after my wife' – 25 June 72, *ibid.*, 29.

167–8 RW: 'I now look at my son, my Siegfried' – *ibid.* (372), 104.

168 FN, 'having Rohde replace him' – *BW* II/3 (276), 95–96; 'strenuously rejected' by ER – *BW* II/4 (8 Dec), 145–6. 'neither RW nor Cosima were at all eager' – RW made this quite clear to CvG after Foundation-Stone ceremony in Bayreuth, CvG>FN, 31 May 72, *BW* II/4, 9. RW: 'to discuss what kind of periodical' – on Friday 22 Nov, FN had travelled to Stuttgart to see RW and Cosima, spending the next two days with them in now German-ruled Strassburg; but there had been scant opportunity for serious discussions (*CWD* I, Nov 22–24 entries, and CosW>FN (4 Dec, from Cologne), *BW* II/4, 144.

168–9 'CvG unexpectedly arrived' – *CWD* I, Jan 7, 1873 entry.

169 'CvG sensed from the tone of their voices' – CvG>FN, (later explanation, 9 March 73), *BW* II/4, 224. 'In mid-January RW and Cosima' – *CWD* I, 11 Jan to 8 Feb entries. During their stay in Hamburg, they saw ER and even invited him to lunch (21 Jan 73 entry). ER mentioned the 'Prefaces to Five Unwritten

Books', and a conscience-stricken Cosima sent FN a telegram, apologizing for her silence – *BW* II/4, 23 Jan, (403). ER, in describing this meeting, said that it had been impossible to discuss the Bayreuth enterprise seriously with a harassed RW, and suggested that FN and he visit Bayreuth during the summer holidays – *ibid.* (26 Jan 73), 187. 'Not until 12 February' – CosW>FN, *ibid.* (412). The German text of the 'Five Prefaces for Five Unwritten Books' can be found in *WdB* III, 265–99. FN 'letter . . . in early March to Gersdorff' – *BW* II/3, 131. 'G lost no time' – CvG>FN (9 March), *BW* II/4, 224–5. 'W in the meantime had written' – RW>FN, 27 Feb, *ibid.*, 216.

169–70 'relatively obscure pre-Socratic philosophers of Ancient Greece' – which developed into 'Philosophy in the Tragic Age of the Greeks': first mentioned in letter to FrN/Eli (15 Feb 73), *BW* II/3 (295); then to ER (21 Feb), 124; to MvM (late Feb), 127; to CvG (5 April), 139.

170 'Heraclitus, in particular' – § 5–8 of *Die Philosophie im tragischen Zeitalter der Griechen, WdB* III, 353–413. 'whereas the ice-cold Parmenides' – §s 9, 10. 'rejected everything . . . that was "incipient, lush"' – § 10 (*WdB* III, 388; *N Werke, Nachgelassene Schriften*, III/2, 337–8.

171 '*Der Philosoph als Artz der Cultur*' – FN>CvG (2 March), *BW* II/3, 132; FN>ER (22 March), 136. gift for 'RW's sixtieth birthday' – FN>CvG (5 April), *BW* II/3, 139. 'thrown off his stride' – ER>FN, 23 March, *BW* II/4, 228. 'N replied with a telegram', etc. – FN>CvG (5 April), *BW* II/3, 138. 'The two friends reached Bayreuth' etc. – *CWD* I, April 6 and ensuing entries.

172 'they shared Schop's contempt for *Jetztzeit* . . . journalism' – see FN's idealistic conception of a truly 'instructive' *Kulturzeitung*, needed to further the Bayreuth cause, FN>ER (20–21 Nov 72), *BW* II/3, 95.

173 'That evening' – Good Friday, 11 April (*CWD*). '*Monodie à deux*' – FN letters to ER (21 Feb 73) *BW* II/3, 124; FN>MvM (end Feb), 126; FN>CvG (2 March), 132; FN>ER, 136. *BW* II/3, 124, 126, 132, 136. 'We are a little vexed' – *CWD* I, April 11. 'humble letter of apology' – FN>RW, 18 April, *BW* II/3, (304). 'recently published book . . . *Der alte und der neue Glaube*' – CosW>FN, 12 Feb, *BW* II/4, 209.

173–4 'rotten product of a "putrefying brain"' – FN>CvG (5 April), *BW* II/3, 139.

174 'As he wrote to Wagner' – *ibid.*, 145. 'One week later' – FN>RW (26 April), *ibid.*, 146–7. On Overbeck's *Die Christlichkeit der Theologie*, see K. Löwith, *From Hegel to Nietzsche*, 377–88. 'As regards your Straussiana' – RW>FN, 30 April, *BW* II/4, 248. 'Like a hungry dog' – FN>FrN/Eli (29 April), *BW* II/3, 148. 'By 5 May' – FN>ER, *ibid.* (307).

174–5 'blinding headaches' – FN>RW, 20 May, *ibid.*, 154.

175 'brief stop-over in Florence' – MvM>FN, *BW* II/4, 252. 'had contracted malaria' – CvG>FN, 9, 10 May, *ibid.*, 249–51. FN 'could no longer read or write' – *CWD* I, 1 June entry (after being notified by CvG); ER>FN, 20 June, *BW* II/4, 263. 'It was also the selfless Gersdorff' – Fritzsch>FN, *ibid.* (442); and (444), 29 June 73. 'On or around 7 July' – Eli>FN (13 July), *ibid.* (446).

175–6 'Perched on a hillside' – this description of Flims is largely based on two letters written by CvG to Eli on 18 July, and on 9 August to ER, lengthily quoted by Janz (I, 541–4); 'and (for a while) Heinrich Romundt' – HR>FN (10 Aug), *BW* II/4 (451). 'the first long letter he could write' – FN>RW, 18 Sept, *BW* II/3, 156–8; *DS* had stirred up 'an "indescribable" uproar' – *ibid.*, 157.

176–7 German text of the first *UB* (*Unzeitgemässe Betrachtung*) *David Strauss – der Bekenner und der Schriftsteller*, can be found in *KSA* I, 157–242. The English translation, here as elsewhere, is mine.

178 'a kind of hybrid centaur dubbed the *Bildungsphilister*' – *DS*, § 2.

179 'For the worm a corpse is a lovely thought' – *ibid.*, § 6, 188.

180 'Germany's philistine culture' – *ibid.*, § 12, 241.

## 19. The Uses and Abuses of History

181 'headaches . . . so blindingly acute' – FN>ER, *BW* II/3, 166. 'from Emil Heckel's Wagner Club' – FN>Heckel (19 Oct), *ibid.* (320). FN>ER, 18 Oct, *ibid.*, 166–7. 'the rough draft of an "Appeal"' – FN>ER (31 Jan 73), *BW* II/3, 121. 'On Wednesday, Oct 22' – FN>ER, 25–26 Oct, *ibid.*, (322). 'A copy was . . . dispatched' – FN>RW (25 or 26 Oct), *ibid.* (323); FN>CvG (27 Oct), 173.

181–2 'We want to be heard' – '*Manruf an die Deutschen*', *WdB* III, 303–7.

182 'Even for Erwin Rohde' – ER>FN (29 Oct), *BW* II/4 (473). 'I swear to God' – RW>FN (21 Sept), *ibid.*, 295. 'But, as W had learned from experience' – *CWD* I, Oct 28. 'On his way to the Wagners' house' – *ibid.*, Oct 30 entry. 'The next morning' – *ibid.*, Oct 31 entry. 'Overnight the pure blue sky' etc. – FN>CvG (7 Nov), *BW* II/3 (325); *CWD* I, Oct 31, Nov I entries. On the rejection of FN's bellicose text, see also FN>Eli (14 Nov), *BW* II/3, 178.

183 'crazy widow . . . Rosalie Nielsen' – letter to FN (17 June) in *BW* II/4 (440). CvG, during his stay in Basel, had forcibly ejected her from the Schützengraben house (CvG>FN, 1 Nov, *BW* II/4, 334). Other mentions in ER>FN (14 Oct), *ibid.*, 325; FN>CvG (27 Oct), *BW* II/3, 174: 'the snout-specter (*Rüsselgespenst*) is back again, and not merely in one's head!'; and FN>Eli (14 Nov), 178.

183–4 'nine verses of . . . doggerel' – in *BW* II/4 (476).

184 'was almost permanently unwell' – FN>Eli (14 Nov), *BW* II/3, 178; FN>H von Senger (20 Nov), 179–80; FN>Pinder, 13 Dec, (334). Immermann: 'Be more stupid' – ER>FN, 23 Dec, *BW* II/4, 358. 'birthday . . . to "celebrate" in bed' – FN>ER, 18 Oct, *BW* II/3, 166. 'On 10 December CvG' – FN>Eli, *ibid.* (333). 'after completing a three-month . . . tour' – CvG to FN, *BW* II/4 (457, Genoa), (460, Florence), (463, Siena), (464, Florence), (471, 475 Venice), (479, Padua), (482, Brescia). 'this excellent man, who is . . . lacking' – *CWD* I, Dec 19. 'he had finished the recopying' – CvG>FN, 26 Dec, *BW* II/4, 362. 'began the . . . final chapter' – FN>CvG, *BW* II/3, 184. 'quick trip to Leipzig' – FN>Ov (31 Dec), *ibid.* (337).

185 'long letter written in Nice' – Romundt>FN, 16 Feb 72, *BW* II/2, 548–9. 'In the brief foreword' – German text of *Vom Nutzen und Nachteil der Historie für das Leben*, in *KSA* I, 245–334. '*Höhenzug*' – *ibid.*, § 2, 229.

186 'Such petty beings "want only one thing"' – *ibid.* § 2, 259–60. Emerson: 'negligent of expense' – *Essays*, 'Heroism', 177–8. 'Fame, in this most transfigured form' – *NNH*, § 2, 260. 'one hundred truly productive souls' – § 2, 260–1.

187 'restless cosmopolitan searching' – § 3, 266. 'it is not Justice that sits in judgement' – § 3, 269.

188 'Then is the past regarded critically' – § 3, 269. 'A great scholar and a great blockhead' – § 6, 294.

189 'atmosphere of pious illusion' – § 7, 296. 'needs to be enveloped in an aura of mystery' – § 7, 298. 'quick, get down on your knees' – § 8, 309.

190 'Oh, excessively proud European' – § 9, 313. 'they live like the Republic of Geniuses' – § 9, 317. 'the goal of Humanity' – § 9, 317.

190–1 '*Begriffsbeben*' – § 10, 330.

191 'shopworn "party words" and hackneyed notions' – § 10, 331.

## 20. Forging a Philosophical Hammer

192 'half frozen from hours spent' – FN>FrN/Eli, *BW* II/3, 189. 'gave up his habit of lunching' – (14 Jan 74) *ibid.*, 190; the 'nearby tavern' was called *Der Kopf* (The Head). 'corrected galley proofs' – ER>FN, 9 Jan 74, *BW* II/4 (498). 'Jacob Burckhardt responded' – to FN, 25 Feb 74, *ibid.* (512).

192–3 'Cosima and RW were put off' – *CWD* I, Feb 22 entry. 'We continue with our friend's book' – *ibid.*, Feb 23.

193 'On the 27th W wrote to N' – *BW* II/4 (513). 'Not until 20 March' – CosW>FN, *ibid.* (523). 'ER . . . was more critical' – ER>FN, 24 March 74, *ibid.* (525). 'W . . . had reached . . . the same conclusion' – *CWD* I, April 9.

193–4 'tedious Pädagogium classes . . . would make it impossible' – FN to Vischer (9 March 73), *BW* II/3 (350); FN>FrN/Eli (9 March), 207.

194 'letter of congratulation' FN>RW – *CWD* I, April 4 entry. 'Cosima's later reply' – to FN (20 April), *BW* II/4 (536). RW: 'He should either marry' – *CWD* I, April 4 entry.

194–5 RW: 'brutally frank . . . letter' – to FN (6 April), *BW* II/4 (529a) 654–6.

195 'N did not immediately reply' – 20 May, *BW* II/3 (365). Written as a birthday-greeting letter commemorating FN's first visit to Tribschen five years before, this was as beautifully phrased and moving a letter as FN ever wrote. On Wilhelmina Planer, see Newman, vol I.

195–6 'In late May . . . Gersdorff' – to FN, *BW* II/4 (544).

196 'Fritz thanked his friend' – FN>CvG, 1 June, *BW* II/3 (367). 'warm, fruitful rain' – FN>ER, *ibid.* (363). 'In the rough plan – for thirteen 'UMs' – see *Nachgelassene Fragmente, Herbst 1873 Winter 1873–1874, KGA* III/4, pp. 354–5, 30 (38); *KSA* 7, pp. 744–5, 30 (38). 'That I am somewhat dilettantish' – FN>ER (19 March), *BW* II/3, 210. For similar statements about his desire to get the 'negative-polemical stuff' out of his system – see FN>Carl Fuchs, 28 April, *ibid.*, 220–1, in which he mentions his '13 *Unzeitgemässen*'; also FN>Emma Guerrieri-Gonzaga,10 May, (362), 224. 'Schop among the Germans' – FN>ER (14 May), *ibid.*, 227.

196–7 'Wilhelm Vischer died' – FN>CvG, 9 July, *ibid.*, 241. 'only four university "cripples"' – FN>ER (26 Sept), *ibid.*, 259.

197 'letter from . . . Fritzsch' – *BW* II/4, 10 July, 509–11. 'letter from Ernst Schmeitzner' – *ibid.*, 8 July, (553). 'On 19 July' – FN>Ov (from Bergün), *BW* II/3 (379). FN and Romundt may even have left Basel on 18 July. 'At the Hôtel Lukmanier' – FN>Eli (22 July), *ibid.*, 245. 'pretty girl, Berta Rohr' – *ibid.*, 246; FN>CvG (26 July), 247–8.

197–8 'price of 6 francs per night' – FN>Eli, *ibid.*, 245. 'chloritic and weak-nerved folk' – FN>FrN, *ibid.*, 248–9.

198 'intelligent letter from . . . Schmeitzner' *BW* II/4, (557). 'letter from Overbeck' – 26 July, *ibid.*, 518–9. 'It is truly wondrous how two souls' – Ritschl to Vischer, 2 Feb 1873, quoted in Janz I, 511–2.

199 'When a great thinker scorns' – *Schop als Erzieher, KSA* I, § 1, 338.

199–200 'Nobody can build for you the bridge' – *ibid.*, § 1, 340.

200 'The answer was Cromwell' – in 'Circles', *Essays*, 227. ' These are the voices we hear in solitude' – *Essays*, 35. FN: 'What up till now' – *SaE, KSA* I, § 1, 340.

201 'the mightiest furtherance of life' – § 3, 362. 'had ridiculed as the 'chair-professor' – notably in 'On Philosophy at the Universities', in *Parerga and Paralipomena* I, 137–97. 'excessively silvered pseudo-Frenchiness' – in German

'*übersilberte Scheinfranzosentum*' – § 2, 347. 'From time to time they avenge themselves' – § 3, 354.

202 Kant, as 'too much of a conformist' – § 3, 351. 'only men of bronze' – § 3, 352. 'with the receding waters of religion' – § 4, 366. 'The first and most popular was Jean-Jacques Rousseau', § 4, 369. Goethe, 'a contemplative man in the grand manner' – § 4, 370 'He who would like to live in a Schop manner' – § 4, 371–2.

202–3 'books that "have no fire in them"' – § 4, *KSA* I, 364.

203 'the *Erwerbenden*' – § 4, 368; repeated, § 6, 387. 'the most sublime order of philosophers, artists and saints' – § 5, 383.

203–4 'These failings and foibles' – § 6, 395–9.

204–5 'pushed the rabbit back' – § 6, 399–400.

205 'the hair of every presently living person' – § 6, 401. 'anyone possessed of a genuine *furor politicus*' – § 7, 409. 'six qualities . . . of . . . genius' – § 8, 411. 'abolish all academic chairs of philosophy' – § 8, 421–2.

206 'Beware when the great God lets loose a thinker' – from 'Circles', Emerson, *Collected Works* (first series), 105.

## 21. A Tense Apotheosis

207 'On 2 August' – a Sunday, see FN>Eli, *BW* II/3 (383). 'At Glarus . . .' – FN>Ov (30 July), *ibid.*, 252; the meeting had been preceded by exchange of letters: from Emma G-G>FN (18 July), *BW* II/4, 514; FN>CvG (26 July), *BW* II/3, 247. 'exasperating afternoon under pelting rain' – in late October, FN wrote to Emma G-G, describing wretched stop-over in Glarus, *ibid.* (400). 'This first contre-temps' – FN>CvG (24 Sept), *ibid.*, 258. 'acute stomach pains and colic' – FN>Ov (7 or 8 Aug), *ibid.* (385). 'Informed by a hotel attendant' – *CWD* I, August 5 entry.

208 'both N and Prof Overbeck' – *ibid.*, August 6. Brahms's *Triumphlied*, heard by FN in Zürich (FN>F. Hegar, early April, *BW* II/3 (355); then in Basel FN>ER, 14 June, 236); Janz I, 579–80. RW on Brahms's *Triumphlied*: 'Handel, Mendelssohn, and Schumann, wrapped in leather' – *CWD* I, August 8.

209 'N's unusual epistolatory silence' – FN>CvG, *BW* II/3 (390); see also FN's brief note to Ov (7 or 8 August), urging him to come to Bayreuth to see for himself what was going on, *BW* II/3 (385). FN's critical comments on RW and his music: extracts from *Nachgelassene Fragmente, Anfang 1874 bis Frühjahr 1874, KGA* III/4, pp. 370–91, 403–8; *KSA* 7, pp. 756ff. 'If Goethe was a transplanted painter' – 32(8); in *KSA* 7, p.756. 'None of our great musicians' – 33(13); *KSA* 7, 791. 'In *Tannhäuser* he sought' – 32(15); *KSA* 7, 759. 'In *Meistersinger* and in parts of . . . *Nibelungen*' – 32(15). 'As an actor he wanted to imitate Man' – 32(16); *KSA* 7, 760. 'Not to be forgotten: . . . a *theatrical* language' – 32(22); *KSA* 7, 761.

210 'The tyrant acknowledges no individuality' – 32(32); *KSA* 7, 765. 'After describing W's lack of finesse' – *ibid.*, 380, 32(39); *KSA* 7, 766. 'W's art is overflowing and transcendental' – 381, 32(44); *KSA* 7, 767. 'Worn out by weeks of . . . tension' – FN>CvG, *BW* II/3, 258; FN>ER (26 Sept), 259. 'a two-week hiking-tour in the mountains' – FN>ER, 7 Oct, *ibid.*, 262. Adolf Baumgartner used to come every Wednesday to FN's study in the Schützengraben house, to take dictation, help him to write letters, read for him, etc: FN>ER (15 Feb 74), *ibid.* (346); in November FN called him his 'arch-disciple', FN>ER (403), 276.

211 'On 6 October' – FN>ER, *ibid.*, 261–2. 'completely new course' on Greek literature – FN>RW (10 Oct?), 265; also *CWD* I, August 15 entry (Ov bringing

RW and CosW news about FN). 'kept busy from 8 a.m. till 11 p.m' – FN>CvG, 16 Nov, *ibid.* (404). 'joyfully celebrated in the "Baumann cavern"' – named after the landlady of the Schützengraben house. 'thirty author's copies' – Schm>FN, *BW* II/4, 581. 'E. Schmeitzner had . . . travelled to Bayreuth' – *CWD* I, Aug 20 entry. 'It came from Marie Baumgartner' – *BW* II/4, 19 Oct (596). RW telegram: 'Deep and great' – *ibid.*, (598). 'Five days later Cosima' – *ibid.*, 26 Oct (599). 'From London . . . Hans von Bülow' – *ibid.* (603).

212 'the best twelvemonth . . . in years' – FN>FrN/Eli, 3 Dec, *BW* II/3, 277. 'he left his academic books' – FN>ER, 21 Dec 74, *ibid.*, 284. 'his musical compositions' – notably his 'Hymn to Friendship', which he completed, and a 'Hymn to Solitude', which he began: FN>MvM, 2 Jan 75, *BW* II/5, 7. 'His return trip . . . from Naumburg' – FN>Eli (17 Jan 75), *ibid.* (416). 'he had finished with Greek poetry' – FN>ER, *ibid.*, 17. On the *Nibelungen* rehearsals, see FN>Krug, 31 Oct 74, *BW* II/3 (399); FN>C. Fuchs, 21 Dec 74 (408); FN>MvM, 2 Jan 75, *BW* II/5, 8; FN>Eli, 26 Jan 75, 12–13. 'at Cosima's request . . . Elisabeth' – CosW>FN, 16 Jan 75, *BW* II/6/1, 15–16; FN>Eli, 17 Jan, *BW* II/5 (416); see also *CWD* I, Jan 23 (Eli's acceptance), Feb 15 (Eli's arrival at 'Wahnfried'), Feb 16–19 (Eli's initiation as children's supervisor, Feb 20 (departure of RW and Cos).

212–3 'Mardi Gras . . . in a Lucerne hotel' – FN>RW, *ibid.*, (427).

213 'earthquake of the soul' – FN>ER (28 Feb 75), *ibid.*, 27–28. The doctrine of 'Papal infallibility' had finally been proclaimed, after seven months of wrangling in the Vatican Council, in July 1870, almost simultaneously with the outbreak of the Franco-Prussian War.

214 'Work, nothing but work!' – FN>Eli, 19 April, *BW* II/5, 43 (which includes a violent attack against a recent invasion of American gospel-brandishing evangelists; on Eli's sojourn in Bayreuth, see Eli>FN, 13 March, 20 March (from Bayreuth), *BW* II/6/1 (649), (655); 2 April (from Naumburg), 91–93. 'after a brief "Easter vacation"' – FN>FrN/Eli (5 May), *BW* II/5 (442). 'letter from E. Schmeitzner' – 14 May, *BW* II/6 (668). 'agreement of previous July' – FN>Schm, 15 July 74, *BW* II/3 (378); Schm>FN, 21 July 74, *BW* II/4 (557). 'despite . . . presence of his sister' – FN>Eli (9 May 75), *BW* II/5 (444), (11 May), 51. 'convulsive stomach upsets' – FN>CvG (21 May), *ibid.* (447). 'Professor Immermann' – FN>ER (14 June) *ibid.* (455); FN>C. Fuchs (end June), 66. 'sinister "Höllenstein solution"' – FN>CvG (26 June), 64–65.

214–5 'I don't wish to shake your confidence' – CvG>FN, *BW* II/6/1, 136–7.

215 'Black-Forest town of Bonndorf' – FN>CvG, 12 July, *BW* II/5, 72; FN>Ov (14 July), 77–79. 'An amiable septuagenarian' – FN>FrN/Eli, 17 July, *ibid.* (468). FN to Marie Baumgartner (19 July) – *ibid.*, 82–83. 'blood-sucking leeches' – FN>CvG (19 July), *ibid.* (470).

216 'N finally told the doctor' – FN>CvG, 21 July, 86–87. FN's letters to: FrN/Eli, 25 July, *ibid.*, 89–90; ER, 1 Aug (474); M Baumgartner, 2 August (475). 'A swimming-pool had been built' – FN>CvG, *ibid.*, 86. 'letters from enthusiastic friends' – CvG, 13 Aug, *BW* II/6/1 (706); ER>FN, 13 Aug (707). FN 'suffered an intense half-hour spasm' – FN>Ov, *BW* II/5 (481). 'when N returned to Basel' – *ibid.*, 106. 'to live with his high-strung nervous system' – FN>ER, *ibid.* (485); 110; FN>CvG, 114. 'in all, six rooms' etc. – Eli>FN (after 10 Aug), *BW* II/6/1 (705); FN to H. Romundt, 26 Sept, *BW* II/5, 116.

216–7 'In persuading "Lieschen" to keep house' – FN>CvG, 26 Sept, *ibid.*, 112.

217 CvG 'had been vainly wooing' – CvG>FN, 28 July, *BW* II/6/1, 178 (Gottlieb von Wulften's daughter). 'infatuation for a young girl' – ER>FN, 12 June, *ibid.*, 124; FN>CvG, 26 Sept, *BW* II/5, 113; FN's warning words about being

dragged down by an 'inferior creature', FN>CvG, 8 May 75, 48; and FN's description of himself as someone not 'racked by passions' – FN>ER, 125–6. 'of Walter Scott novels' – FN>ER, 8 Dec, *ibid.*, 126. 'pouring pitcher-fulls' – FN>CvG (18 Jan 76), *ibid.*, 132. 'In early January of 1876' – FN>Carl Burckhardt, 2 Jan 76, *ibid.* (496); Kuratel's reply, 6 Jan, *BW* II/6/1 (735). 'I am training myself to unlearn' – FN>CvG (13 Dec 74), *BW* II/5, 128. 'ER appointed full Professor' – ER>FN, *BW* II/6/1, 278; 'his "unlucky" damsel', 14 Feb 75, 277. 'so paralysingly painful' – FN>ER, 18 Feb, *BW* II/5 (501).

218 'Shortly afterwards CvG turned up' – CvG>FN, 3 March, *BW* II/6/1 (747). 'the widowed mother was saddened' – Eli>FN, 11 March, *ibid.* (748). 'in the village of Veytaux' – FN>FrN/Eli (8 March), *BW* II/5 (507). 'The weather' etc. – FN>Eli (13 March), *BW* II/5 (508); 'frothing waters' – FN>FrN/Eli (16 March), 142. 'heedless of the rain' – FN>FrN/Eli, 20 March (510). 'with Manzoni's *I Promessi Sposi*' – FN>Eli (13 March), (508). 'On 29 March' – FN>Eli (28 March), *ibid.* (512). 'the less than cheering news' – FrN>FN, 1 April, *BW* II/6/1, 300–1; Eli>FN, 2 April, 302–3. 'So concerned was Gersdorff' – Ov>FN, 4 April, *ibid.*, 307–8. 'Overbeck's betrothal' – CvG>FN, 23 Jan, *ibid.*, 275. 'I can only say to you" – Ov>FN, *BW* II/6/1 (760). 'shortly before he left Veytaux' – FN>Ov (5 April), *BW* II/5 (515). 'a Countess Diodati' – first mentioned to FN by Hugo von Senger, 10 July 72, *BW* II/4, 39. FN had met Senger in Munich, where both heard Hans von Bülow conduct RW's *Tristan und Isolde* – FN>Senger, 25 July 72, *BW* II/3 (245).

218–9 'The Countess had . . . lost her mind' – FN>Eli (8 April, from Geneva), *BW* II/5 (516).

219 On Mathilde Trampedach and her sister, Janz I, 629–32, with details drawn from an unpublished ms. (*Geschichte der Familie von Senger*) – Janz III, 397.

219–20 'Gather together all the courage of your heart' – FN to M. Trampedach, 11 April, *BW* II/5, 147.

220 'You are sufficiently magnanimous' – FN>MT, 15 April, *ibid.* (517). 'The six days N spent in Geneva' – FN>ER (14 April), *ibid.* (519). 'When we see each other again' – FN>CvG (15 April), *ibid.* (520).

221 'to a young musician . . . Heinrich Köselitz – see Schmeitzner to FN, 9 Oct 75, *BW* II/6/1, 232. For Köselitz's own account of how he befriended FN, see his Introduction (under the pseudonym 'Peter Gast') to vol IV of FN's *Gesammelte Briefe*, which he helped EF-N to publish in 1908 (Insel-Verlag, Leipzig). 'By the time Kös had finished' – just as he had done with *GdT*, FN added some more material at the end, which was not sent to Schm until 11 June, FN>Schm, *BW* II/5 (532). 'two luxuriously bound *Festexemplare*' – Schm>FN, *BW* II/6/1 (792). These deluxe copies of the fourth *UB*, titled *Richard Wagner in Bayreuth*, reached the '*Wahnfried*' villa on 10 July and were gratefully-acknowledged by Cosima as 'the only refreshment and uplifting' she had been granted during the hectic preparations – CosW>FN, 11 July, *ibid.* (793). 'Your book is prodigious!' – RW>FN, 13 July, *ibid.* (797). 'Similar advice was offered' – MvM>FN, *ibid.* (796).

221–2 'high number of students' – FN>CvG, 26 May, *BW* II/5, 163.

222 'a year of absence' – Kuratel>FN, *BW* II/6/1 (791). 'how the great composer would react' – the letters to RW and Cosima, accompanying the deluxe copies, were each rewritten once: see *Entwürfe*, *BW* II/5 (535), (536), and the final versions (537), (538). 'once again, for the past 3–4 weeks' – FN>ER, *ibid.* (534). 'to announce his engagement' – ER>FN, 17 July, *BW* II/6/1 (800). 'Nietzsche immediately responded' – (18 July), *BW* II/5 (542). '*Es geht ein Wandrer*' – *ibid.*, 177.

223 'On Saturday, 22 July' – Overbeck's surprise at FN's abrupt departure, in Ov>FN, 2 Aug, *BW* II/6/1, (803). 'R and C Wagner, who only learned of his arrival' – *CWD*, 24 July. 'by a well-to-do Bayreuther' (Carl Giessel) – FN>Eli (25 July), *BW* II/5, 179. '*fast habe ich's bereut!*' – FN>Eli, *ibid.* (544). 'Three days later' – FN>Eli, *ibid.*, 179–80. 'the entire loafing riff-raff of Europe' – *Eh.*

223–4 'enduring headaches' etc. – FN>Eli (1 Aug), *BW* II/5 (546).

224 'Not until Monday, 7 August,' – FN>Eli (from Klingenbrunn), *ibid.* (547). 'after receiving a plaintive letter' – Eli>FN, *BW* II/6/1 (804). 'eye-soothing sprays and lotions' – *ibid.*, 370. 'To judge from two letters' – Eli>FN, 30 August (from Bayreuth), *ibid.* (807); 4–7 Sept, from Naumburg, (813). On CvG's infatuation for Nerina Finochietti Eli>FN, 30 Aug, *ibid.*, 376, 378; CvG>FN, 31 Aug (from Bayreuth), 380–1; and 5 Sept (from Gotha), 390.

225 'another lovely blonde creature . . . Louise Ott' – mentioned by Eli (to FN, *ibid.*, 379); Janz I, 727–8. 'Everything was dark around me' – FN>Louise Ott, 30 Aug, *BW* II/5 (549). 'To this Louise answered' – L. Ott to FN, 2 Sept, *BW* II/6/1 (810).

## 22. Winter in Sorrento

226 'accompanied by . . . Albert Brenner' – on his adolescent moodiness and his stay in Rome, Brenner>FN, 23 Dec 75, *BW* II/6/1 (731); 13 Jan 76 (739); and MvM>FN, 12 Jan 76 (738). MvM had personally financed Brenner's trip to Bayreuth – MvM>FN, 13 July, *BW* II/6/1, 362. 'atropine eye-drops' etc. – FN>FrN/Eli (4 Sept), *BW* II/5 (550) and (11 Sept), 185; to Louise Ott (22 Sept), 185–6; to ER (553). 'serious relapses . . . eight to ten days' – FN>MvM, 189. 'Ov had taken his young bride' – Ov>FN, 8 Sept, *BW* II/6/1 (815). Paul Rée, mentioned twice by FN in letters to ER: 5 May 73, *BW* II/3, 150; 20 May 73, 154; and highly praised as a 'dear newly-won friend' in FN>Rée, 3 March 76, *BW* II/5 (505). Biographical details in *FN, Paul Rée, Lou von Salomé – Die Dokumente ihrer Begegnung* (*Dok* from here on), ed. by Ernst Pfeiffer, 365–6. At Bayreuth his first small book, *Psychologische Beobachtungen*, had created quite a stir among FN's friends – Eli>FN, *BW* II/6/1, 31 Aug, 375, 377–9.

226–7 'On 26 September' – FN>MvM, *BW* II/5 (555).

227 'followed his friend to Montreux' – Rée>FN, *BW* II/6/1 (820). 'spent two restful weeks' – at the Hôtel du Crochet, FN>Frn/Eli (9 Oct), *BW* II/5 (558); FN>A. Baumgartner (12 Oct, 559); FN>FrN (16 Oct, 560). 'sent a postcard to his sister' – FN>Eli (18 Oct), *ibid.* (562). 'not the prophet of a future' – *RWB*, *KSA* I, 510. FN's concluding sentence was particularly bold, since in his essay on *Jewishness in Music*, RW had written: 'The thinker is a poet who looks behind him, but the true poet is the prophet and herald of the future.'

228 '*Drang nach Macht und Ruhm*' – *ibid.*, § 8.

229 Schop's 'anti-historical, essentially static' view of the world – quite rightly criticized by Georg Simmel in Part 6 of his *Schopenhauer und Nietzsche*. '*Die Pflugschar*' – see FN>Mathilde Maier, (15 July 78) according to which one third of this planned fifth 'Untimely Meditation' was written during his flight from Bayreuth to Klingenbrunn: *BW* II/5, 338. 'removal of all the weeds, the rubbish, the vermin' – *SaE*, § 1, *KSA* I, 341.

230 'Claudine von Brevern' etc. – this train-trip later described by Isabella von der Pahlen, in ch. 2 of her graphological analysis of FN, published under her married name of Ungern-Sternberg), *Nietzsche im Spiegelbild seiner Schrift*. 'In a hurriedly written note' – 23 Oct 76, *BW* II/5 (564). See also FN's postcard to Eli, same page (563), in which he speaks of headaches and vomiting, lasting 44

hours. 'At Bayreuth, where the question had been seriously discussed' – in his 6 August letter from Klingenbrunn, FN begged his sister not to give up the idea of Basel and Arlesheim, the latter being a village south of Basel where they were hoping to acquire a property capable of housing a community of kindred souls (FN>Eli, *BW* II/5, 182–3). Six weeks later Eli wrote to FN that MvM had been almost lyrical in envisaging 'a kind of monastery [*Kloster*] in which each lives personally free and yet in a beautiful togetherness.' (Eli>FN, 18 Sept, *BW* II/6/1, 399.) 'school for teachers' – in an unpublished note written during the spring of 1875, FN listed seven categories of persons who might compose a 'School for Teachers': the doctor, the natural scientist, the economist, the historian of culture (the model here being Jacob Burckhardt), the 'connoisseur' (*Kenner*) of Church History (obviously Franz Overbeck), the connoisseur of the (ancient) Greeks (FN himself), and the 'connoisseur of the State': presumably some kind of modern Machiavelli, whose present equivalent FN had yet to find – *N Werke* (*KGA*) IV/1, *Nachgelassene Fragmente*, 116, 4(5); *KSA* 8, p. 40.

230–1 'to the captivating Louise Ott' – (22 Sept), *BW* II/5 (552).

231 ' the steamboat voyage . . . lasted three days' – 8 days from Bex to Sorrento, FN>Eli, 28 Oct, *ibid.* (565). 'At Livorno . . . N and Albert Brenner' – Isabella von Ungern-Sternberg, *op.cit*, 30–32 (a highly fanciful account, though the meeting did take place: confirmed by Claudine von Brevern's later letter to FN, 15 Dec 75 (from Rome), *BW* II/6/1, 452. 'I also prefer this way' – FN>Eli, 28 Oct, *BW* II/5 (565). 'That evening, to cheer him up' – MvM, *Le Soir de ma vie* (third volume of her *Mémoires d'une idéaliste*), 38–39. 'large high-ceilinged bedroom' – FN>Eli, *BW* II/5 (565).

231–2 'The previous afternoon' – *CWD* I, Oct 27 entry.

232 'The week-long stay in Venice' – *CWD* I, Sept 17–28 entries; bad news from Feustel, Sept 23 entry. 'a terse telegram from Venice' – RW>FN, *BW* II/6/1 (821) 'In the long reply' – FN>RW, 27 Sept, *BW* II/5 (556). 'four severe seizures' – FN>Ov, (11 Nov), *ibid.* (568). 'unnaturally stiff N seemed' – MvM, *Le Soir*, 40.

233 'I believe there is in N' – CosW>MvM, 17 April 1887, quoted in Richard Du Moulin Eckart's *Cosima Wagner* I (pp. 794–5 of French ed.), quoted by Newman IV, 547.

233–4 'After the (breakfast) tea' – *op. cit.*, same Paul Rée letter.

234 'a longish letter to his now orphaned mother' – FN>FRN, *BW* II/5 (576). 'very efficient *Krankenwärterin*' – a *Krankenwärter* is the term normally used for 'medical orderly': more or less what FN had been in 1870. But FN and Paul Rée also liked the term because it had been used by Goethe who, during his first trip to Italy (Naples, 27 May 1787) had been moved by the sight of so much beggary to predict that 'humanity' would finally triumph, but that he much feared that at the same time 'the world will become a huge hospital and each (man) the humane nurse (*Krankenwärter*) for the other.' FN's later attacks on the cult of 'humanity' and 'humane' sentimentaility were greatly influenced by this Goethean prediction. 'Seated on one side' – MvM, *Le Soir*, 39–40. 'Jacob Burckhardt's lectures' – A. Baumgartner>FN, 10 Oct 76, *BW* II/6/1, 415. 'never has this most glorious' – MvM, *Le Soir*, 40–41. 'readings from Xenophon' etc. – *Dok*, 376.

235 'Paul Rée, while reading' – MvM, writing to Olga Herzen, quoted in *Dok*, 373–4. 'Christmas, in particular' – Rée>Eli, 25 Dec, *Dok*, 20. 'The many letters she had been receiving' – MvM, *Le Soir*, 48–49. 'that . . . Köselitz . . . be appointed "Perpetual Secretary"' – FN>Eli, 29 Sept, *BW* II/5 (557).

236 'but not in order to sell these men' – FN>Reinhard von Seydlitz (RvS from

here on), 24 Sept, *ibid.* (554). 'Albert Brenner . . . recoiled in horror' – Brenner>FN (14 March 76), *BW* II/6/1, 291–2. 'letter from Claudine von Brevern' – *BW* II/6/1 (847). FN 'asked his publisher' – FN>Schmeitzner (18 Dec), *BW* II/5 (580). 'that Ernst Schmeitzner had agreed' – Kös and P. Widemann to FN, *BW* II/6/1, 476. On Hans von Wolzogen, Newman IV, 574–5. Initially delighted, RW and Cosima were later irritated by HvW's *Der Nibelungen-mythos Sage und Literatur: CWD* I, 11 Oct 76 entry. 'R.W has not learned to fear' – FN>Kös and Widemann (8 Jan 77), *BW* II/5 (586).

236–7 'Louis Keltenborn, the most musically gifted' – see his detailed account of his friendship with FN during his years as a Basel Univ student – *Beg.* (70), especially 115–23.

237 'a birthday-greetings letter' – FN>CosW (19 Dec 76), *BW* II/5, 1. 'Every doctrine, even the most sublime' – CosW>FN, 1 Jan 77, *BW* II/6/1, 472–3.

237–8 'On 1 Feb, Paul Rée' – *Dok*, 21.

238 'At the suggestion of . . . Heinrich Schiess' – 7 Feb 77, *BW* II/6/1, 495. 'Professor Schrön had subjected him' – FN>FrN (18 Feb 77), *BW* II/5, 222. 'The Mediterranean sun had by this time' – FN>FrN/Eli (12 March) *ibid.*, (600). 'If only I could believe' – FN>FrN, *ibid.* (601). 'Reinhard von Seydlitz' – FN>RvS, late Feb, *BW* II/5 (599); and RvS replies, 5, 8 March: *BW* II/6/1 (879, 880). 'welcome additions to M's "convent of free spirits" – see FN's postcard to Eli (20 Jan 77, *BW* II/5 (589); Eli>FN, 8, then 16 Feb *BW* II/6/1, 501–2, 507 ('*Idealcolonie*'). 'while Paul Rée headed for Jena' – Rée>Ov, *Dok*, 23. 'On 10 April' – FN>FrN/Eli (17 April), *BW* II/5, (605). MvM had developed a 'maternal fondness' – *Dok*, 374.

239 'Several days in bed' – FN>Rée, *BW* II/5 (606). 'kind of woman N should marry' – Eli>FN, 18 Sept 76 (FrN hoping that Fritz would find himself a wife in Italy) *BW* II/6/1, 400. 'Fritz's busybody sister' – Eli>FN (notably advocating Berta Rohr as a possible wife for FN (22–24 March 77), *ibid.*, 522. 'possibility of marrying . . . Natalie Herzen' – FN>Eli, *BW*II/5, 227. 'Even a marriage based on "reason"' – among the preparatory notes for a (finally unwritten) 'Untimely Meditation' entitled 'We Philologists', we find this comment: 'Just how little Reason, and how greatly Chance rules the lives of human beings is shown by the almost regular incongruity between the so-called life-vocation and one's disposition thereto: the luckiest cases are exceptions, like the luckiest marriages, and these are not brought about by Reason. (*N Werke* IV/1, *KGA*, pp. 95–96, 3(19); *KSA* 8, 19–20. 'In her answering letter' – Eli>FN, *BW* II/6/1, 536–8.

239–40 'Good, *but* rich!' – FN>Eli, 5 April, *BW* II/5, 230–1.

240 'Dearest Friend' – FN>Rée, *ibid.* (613). 'The trip from Sorrento to Naples' – FN>RvS (11 May, from Genoa), *ibid.* (614).

240–1 'The voyage up the Tyrrhenian coast' – FN>MvM (13 May, from Lugano *ibid.*, 235–6; including FN's arrival in Genoa.

241 'He had *aes triplex*' – FN>RvS (11 May), *ibid.* (614).

241–2 'The next morning' and the rest of the journey from Genoa to Lugano are related in the same FN letter to MvM, *ibid.* (13 May), 236–8.

## 23. A Book for Free Spirits

243 'From Lugano . . . to . . . Bad Ragaz' – FN>ER (20 May 77), *BW* II/5 (616). 'On Whitsunday (May 20)' – FN>FrN/Eli (postcard), *ibid.* (617); (28 May), 240. 'A decision of this gravity' – ER>FN, 20 May, *BW* II/6/, 560–1.; Ov>FN, 3 June, 568–9; and (29 June), ER>Ov, in *BW Franz Overbeck – Erwin Rohde*,

21. FN 'agreed to postpone his decision' – FN>Eli (2 June), *BW* II/5, 620. 'The three and a half weeks . . . at Ragaz' – FN>Ov (1 and 6 June), *ibid.*, (619, 622). 'Helvetian name of Rosenlauibad' – FN>MvM, *ibid.* (621).

244 'In Florence . . . Natalie Herzen' – MvM>FN, 12 June (from Florence), *BW* II/6/1 (914); 25 June, from Chiavenna, (920). 'Another of Malwida's candidates' – MvM>FN, 5 June, from Sorrento, *ibid.*, 578. 'the luckless Malwida' – MvM>FN, 28 June, *BW* II/6/1 (922). 'disastrous trip to London' – *CWD* I, May 1 to June 2 entries; the financial and other disappointments of the trip being followed by little Siegfried's falling ill of tonsilitis in Heidelberg (July 5–9). 'In the end, Olga Herzen Monod' – FN>FrN (from Rosenlauibad, 10 Aug), *BW* II/5 (647); FN>Eli, 648); FN>MvM (28 Aug) 276. 'the ill-planned "rendez-vous" at Äschi' – planned at Sorrento and mentioned by MvM>FN, 5 June, *BW* II/6/1, 578. 'The talented Albert Brenner' – Kös>FN, 31 July, *ibid.*, 647; MvM> FN, 31 July, 649–50. 'Paul Rée had to hurry off' – Eli>FN, 22 June, *ibid.*, 586. 'When MvM reached Äschi' – MvM>FN, from Thun (10 July), *ibid.*, (931). 'a couple of months left to "win a wife"' FN>MvM (1 July), *BW* II/5, 250. 'Fritz spent two ruinously expensive days' – FN>MvM, 27 July, *ibid.*, 258–9. 'a Frankfurt doctor, Otto Eiser' – see his letter to FN, asking him to come give a talk in Frankfurt to members of a recently formed Wagner Club, *BW* II/6/1, 14 April 77 (887).

244–5 'At Meiringen . . . Otto Eiser' – FN>MvM, 27 July, *BW* II/5, 260. Eiser>FN, 21 July, *BW* II/6/1 (936); 'whose books he had brought along' – FN>Eli, *BW* II/5 (638). 'After . . . questioning him' – FN>Eli, *BW* II/5 (641); Eiser>FN, 26 July *BW* II/6/1 (938); FN>MvM (4 Aug), mentioning 4-day stay at Rosenlauibad of Dr. Eiser and his wife, *BW* II/5, 268; on Prof Schrön's treatment being too 'homoeopathic', FN>Ov (28 Aug) *ibid.* (654).

245 'The most enjoyable moments at Rosenlauibad' – Irene vS>FN, 17 Aug, RvS>FN, *BW* II/6/1 (957, 958); FN>RvS (20 Aug, 22 Aug), *BW* II/5 (649, 650); on Irene vS's agility, *ibid.*, 273. 'Too penniless to be able' – RvS>FN, 10 Aug, *BW* II/6/1 (953); FN>RvS (22 Aug), *BW* II/5 (650). 'new apartment on the Gellertstrasse' – Eli>FN, 28 Aug, *BW* II/6/1 (962); FN>MvM (3 Sept), *BW* II/5, 283; EF-N, *Leben* II/1, 327. 'A private "house-warming"' – MvM>FN, *BW* II/6/2 (971); Janz I, 784–5 (quoting from MvM's description to Olga Herzen Monod). 'But why, why, was it so wonderul' – RvS>FN, *BW* II/6/2 (973). 'Like "Aunt Malwida" . . . much upset' – RvS>FN, *ibid.* (969).

245–6 'Thanks to F. Overbeck's intervention' – EF-N, *Leben* II/1, 327; 'academic work load' – Stroux, *op. cit.*, 100.

246 'roughly one-and-a-half hours of eyesight' – FN>Ov, *BW* II/5, 275. 'In early October' – Eiser>FN, 31 August, *BW* II/6/2 (964); 1 Sept (966); 13 Sept (976); FN>RvS (27 Sept), *BW* II/5 (666). 'The gist of the report' – Eiser>FN, 6 Oct, *BW* II/6/2 (988). 'a major paroxysmic relapse' – Eiser>FN, 11 Oct, *ibid.* (991). 'In the covering letter' – FN>Carl Burckhardt, 17 Oct, *BW* II/5 (670). 'the faint glimmer of eyesight' – FN>CosW, *BW* II/5 (669).

246–7 'In her answering letter' – CosW>FN, 22 Oct, *BW* II/6/2 (1004).

247 For FN's opinion of Hans von Wolzogen, see FN>Fuchs (29 July), *BW* II/5, 262. 'three excellent doctors' – one of them was Prof Erb, an ophthalmologist and expert in electrotherapy whom FN probably saw at Heidelberg, on his way back from Frankfurt: Ov>FN, 23 Sept, *BW* II/6/2 (980); FN>Ov (25 Sept), *BW* II/5, 286. 'Wagner's proximity' – FN>Eli (29 June), *ibid.*, 248. 'Hans von Wolzogen was asked' – RW's correspondence with Dr. Eiser was first published as an annex to Curt von Westernhagen's biography of RW, in 1956 (see note to Oct 23, 77 entry in *CWD* I, 1157). See also Janz I, 788–90.

247–8 RW to Cosima: 'He will more likely listen' – *CWD* I, 23 Oct entry.

248 MvM 'had gently scolded him' – *BW* II/6/1, 668. 'Schopenhauerian parody': '*Pues el delito mayor / Del hombre es de haber nacido*' – quoted by Schop in Section 51 of *WWR* I (p. 254). 'Nietzsche's version' – FN>CvG, 21 Dec, *BW* II/5 (674). On the revelations leading up to FN's ultimatum to CvG: MvM>FN, 24 Sept, *BW* II/6/2 (981); FN>Ov (25 Sept), *BW* II/5 (665); CvG>FN, 25 Sept, 21 Oct, *BW* II/6/2 (977, 1002).

249 'In his reply' – CvG>FN, *BW* II/6/2, 781. 'with the help of H. Kös' – FN>Schm, 3 Dec 77, *BW* II/5, 293–4. 'A Book for Free Spirits' – FN>Schm, *ibid.* 'Schm, who had already heard from Kös' – Schm>FN, 19 Oct, *BW* II/6/2, 741. 'while I have a shimmer of eyesight left' – FN>Schm, 3 Dec, *BW* II/5, 293.

249–50 'in an apologetic letter' – FN>R/CosW, *ibid.* (676).

250 'no more than "a chemical combination of atoms"' – MvM, *Lebensabend einer Idealistin*, 59.

252 'the crisis of (his) life' – FN>MvM (11 June 78, *BW* II/5 (725). 'Each of its aphorisms . . . is like a finely polished diamond' –

253 Kaufmann, *Nietzsche*. See also Erich Heller's encomium: 'the most brilliant and inspired document that nineteenth century positivism, and indeed any kind of positivism has brought forth' – *The Disinherited Mind*, 311. 'the *Gedankenbaum*' – MvM, *Le Soir*, 55. In German a *Gedankenblitz* means a 'brainstorm'.

253–4 'plan for thirteen "Untimely Meditations"' – in *FN Werke, KSA* 7, *Nachlass* 1869–1874 (Autumn 1873 – Winter 1873–1874), pp. 744–5, item 30 (38); later modified early in 1875: *KSA* 8, p.9, § I (3), I (4).

259 '*impose on it a legality that it does not from the outset have*' – § 111, *Origin of the Religious Cult, MAM* I, *KSA* 2, 115.

## 24. The Wanderer and his Shadow

262 'On 30 December' – RvS>FN, *BW* II/6/2 (1022). 'Four days later' – RW>FN (1 Jan 78), *ibid.* (1025). 'More Liszt than Wagner' – FN>RvS, 4 Jan 78, *BW* II/5 (678).

263 'new Professor . . . Rudolf Massini' – Janz I, 796. 'obtained the . . . Governing Council's consent' – FN>Carl Burckhardt, 11 Feb 78, *BW* II/5 (680). 'another major relapse' – FN>Eli, *BW* II/5 (683). 'that Fritzsch had quietly sold' – Schm>FN, 7 March 78 (announcing Fritzsch's bankruptcy) and March 8, *BW* II/6/2 (1039, 1040); FN>Schm (8 March), *BW* II/5 (687). 'His long walks' etc. – FN>Eli (16 March), *ibid.* (696). 'Reluctantly declining' – RvS>FN, 3 Nov, 5 Dec 77, *BW* II/6/2 (1008, 1015); FN>FrN, 2 April, *BW* II/5 (703); FN>Ov (3 April), 315–6. 'On 16 April – FN>Schm, 14 April, *ibid.* (709), warning that their meeting should not exceed a half-hour. 'followed . . . by another nervous relapse' – FN>Schm (19 April), *ibid.* (713); FN>Rée (23 April), 323.

263–4 'Tuesday had been a real "*Feiertag*"' – Schm>FN, 20 April, *BW* II/6/2, 835.

264 'W and his editorial factotum' – Schm>FN, *BW* II/6/2. 'On 20 April' – Schm>FN, *BW* II/6/2 (1056). '27 privileged recipients' – FN>Schm, *BW* II/5 (712). 'Writing from Salzburg' – RvS>FN, *BW* II/6/2 (1060).

264–5 'first meeting with RvS' during Bayreuth Festival, when FN told RvS that he could write to him – RvS>FN, 3 Sept 76, *BW* II/6/1 (811); and FN's reply, 24 Sept 76, *BW* II/5 (554).

265 'In his letter of reply' – FN>RvS, 13 May 78, *BW* II/5 (721). 'The second person' – Marie Baum>FN, *BW* II/6/2 (1061) 'The single paragraph' – MvM>FN, *BW* II/6/2 (1063). 'In early May' – Schm>FN, dated 9 (more

probably 10) May, *ibid.* (1065). 'Cosima's diary' – *CWD* II, 17, 25, 30 April ('N's pitiable book), 23 May 78.

265–6 'Radically different' – Rée>FN, *BW* II/6/2 (1066); FN's hand-written compliment – FN>Rée (24 April), *BW* II/5 (717).

266 'N immediately replied' – FN>Rée, 12 May, *ibid.* (720). 'small bust' (of Voltaire) – announcement card (Le Vaillant et Cie): '*Vous recevrez*' etc., in *BW* II/6/2 (1076). '*l'âme de Voltaire*' – *ibid.* (1077). This 'surprise' was probably arranged by Paul Rée. 'E. Schmeitzner's relations with W' – Schm>FN, *BW* II/6/2 (1078). 'In a remarkable letter' – MvM>FN, *ibid.* (1083).

266–7 'the *crisis* of life' – FN>MvM (11 June 77), *BW* II/5 (725).

267 'The idea that . . . Rée had led N astray' – RvS>FN, 19 June, *BW* II/6/2 (1084). 'The same charge' – ER>FN, *ibid.* (1082).

268 (Schop) – '*Handeln or operari*' – *WWR* I, ; 'wisdom . . . isolates the wise man' – ER>FN (1082), 898. 'uncorroded by any Réeish rumination' – *ibid.*, 898.

269 '"rickety platform" of friendship' – FN>ER, *BW* II/5 (727). Mathilde Maier, vainly asking FN to help her launch a Women's Wagner Club in Mainz: MM>FN, *BW* II/4 (517, 522).

269–70 'long letter she now wrote to him' – MM>FN, *BW* II/6/2 (1091).

270 'To this extraordinary letter' – FN>MM, *BW* II/5 (734). 'two more reproachful letters' – MM>FN, 28 July, 14 August, *BW* II/6/2 (1098), (1104). 'Few can be as surely convinced' – FN>MM (postcard fragment, sent from Grindelwald, around 6 Aug), *BW* II/5 (741). 'as though he had "emptied the milk-pot"' – FN>Rée (late July), *ibid.* (737).

270–1 On Carl Fuchs – Janz I, 667–75; as a good example of Fuchs's long letters, CF>FN, 30 June–20 July 78, in which he expressed doubts about RW's *Ring* operas, and also *Parsifal*, *BW* II/6/2 (1093); and FN's comment on his 'long, very intelligent letters' – FN>Eli, *BW* II/5 (739).

271 'They all stink of church air' – Schm>Kös, in Janz I, 824–5. 'But on 1 July' – Schm>FN, *BW* II/6/2 (1089). FN's aversion for any kind of *Parteiblatt* – see his stern rebuke to Fuchs in late July 78, *BW* II/5, 340. 'yielding to FrN's . . . pleas' – Eli>FN, 19 July, *BW* II/6/2, 917; FN>Rée (late July), giving his new address at 11, Bachlettenstrasse, *BW* II/5 (737). 'Most of the furniture' – E. Bessiger>FN (20 June 78), *BW* II/6/2 (1085); FN>FrN, 8 July, *BW* II/5 (733).

271–2 'he left the sultry city' – FN>Eli (late July), *BW* II/5 (739).

272 'Alpine hotel . . . 6,600 feet' – FN>FrN/Eli, 2 Aug, *ibid.* (740). 'when . . . the skies cleared' – FN>Rée (10 Aug), *ibid.*, 345; wretched weather – FN>FrN/Eli (13 Aug), 346. RW, 'The Public and Popularity' ('*Publikum und Popularität*') in vol X ('*Bayreuther Blätter*') of RW's *Gesammelte Schriften und Dichtungen*, 61–90. Schm>FN, 1 Aug, *BW* II/6/2 (1101). 'By the end of the third week' – FN>FrN/Eli (25 Aug), *BW* II/5, (746). 'he had regained his appetite' – (3 Sept) *ibid.* (750) 'That same day' – FN>Schm, *ibid.* (751). FN 'sent another postcard to Schm' – (10 Sept), *BW* II/5 (754); 'who for financial reasons was forced' – Schm>FN, *BW* II/6/2 (1106).

272–3 'Most disown me three times' – FN>Marie Baum, *ibid.* (755).

273 'on the Bachlettenstrasse' – Janz I, 802–3. 'An even longer walk' – FN>Marie Baum (23 Oct), *BW* II/5 (764) 'telegram to Franz Overbeck' – FN>MB, 28 Oct, *ibid.* (765). 'in the luxurious villa' (Falkenstein) – FN>FrN/Eli (21 Sept), *ibid.* (759). 'his exquisite manners' – Ov>FN, *BW* II/6/2, 984–5. 'While N was full of praise' – *ibid.* 'corner-house on the Weingartenstrasse' – 'N continued to be plagued by headaches' – FN>FrN/Eli (21 Oct), *BW* II/5 (763); 23 Nov (773); (30 Nov) 'every three days' (777). 'fortitude . . . to continue his university lectures' – EF-N, *Leben* II/1, 327; Janz I, 804–5. 'Ah, if only you knew what a

blessing' – FN>FrN/Eli (30 Nov) *BW* II/5, 368.

273–4 'The first days of December' – *ibid.* (778); (21 Dec) 373.

274 'with one paroxysmic seizure' – FN>Marie Baum (29 Dec), *ibid.* (787). 'spells of composition . . . 15 minutes' – FN>Eli, *ibid.* 'he appealed to . . . Marie Baumgartner' – 15 Nov, *ibid.*, 363; MB>FN *BW* II/6/2 (1124), 17 Nov (1127); FN>MB (26 Nov), *BW* II/5, 366. 'The work was completed' – FN>Schm, 31 Dec 78, *ibid.* (789). 'N's intention was to have them added' – FN>Schm (postcard fragment, 23 Nov), *BW* II/5 (774); Schm>FN, 25 Nov, *BW* II/6/2 (1128). 'The good news that H. Kös' – Schm>FN, 3 Jan 79, *BW* II/6/2 (1140); FN's pleased response – to Schm (5 Jan 79), *BW* II/5 (792), adding 7 new aphorisms, to total 400. 'From early February of 1879 on' – FN>FrN/Eli, *ibid.* (802). 'In early March . . . major shock' – FN>Schm, *ibid.* (819). 'forcing him to cease all his lectures' – FN>Ov (17 March), *ibid.* (820) 'after informing his "so-ready-to help" comrade' – FN>Kös, *ibid.* (822). 'On 22 March . . . N left Basel' – FN>FrN/Eli; FN>Ov (23 March), (824, 825) 'He had intended to cross the Savoy mountains' – FN>Ov (23 March), *ibid.* (825).

274–5 'He was retrained . . . by the fear of putting too great a distance' – FN>Ov (23 March), *ibid.* II/5 (825).

275 'at a lakeside hotel' – Hôtel Riche-Mont; see FN>Kös, FN>FrN/Eli, FN>Ov (all 26 March), *ibid.* (826, 827, 828). '*more torture* than recovery' – FN>FrN/Eli, *ibid.* (830).

275–6 'He had . . . intended to cross Savoy mountains' – FN>Ov (23 March), from Geneva, *ibid.* (825). 'privileged recipients' – headed by Marie Baum, Kös, Paul Rée, Ov, FN>Schm (28 Feb), *ibid.* (807), and 15 others (early March, 810).

276 'at a lakeside hotel' – Hôtel Riche-Mont, FN>Kös, FN>FrN (26 March), *ibid.* (826, 827). '*more torture* than recovery' – FN>FrN/Eli, *ibid.* (830). 'phantasies of many Christian saints' – *MAM*, § 141.

277 'I call classic what is healthy' – Goethe, *Gespräche mit Eckermann*, 2 April 1829. '*Mitfreude*' – FN praising CvG's 'splendid capacity for *Mitfreude*' (13 Dec 75), *BW* II/5, 129; also used four years later in letter to Marie Baum – '*mitfreunde Freundin*' (6 April 79), *ibid.*, 405. 'The I is always detestable' – Pascal, *Pensées*.

277–8 RW essay, '*Was ist deutsch?*' – *Ges. Schriften* X (Bay Bl), 36–53.

278–9 'Schmeitzner regarded this "*Hadesfahrt*"' – to FN, *BW* II/6/2 (1157).

279 'You are heading upwards' – MvM>FN, 28 March, *BW* II/6/2 (1170). 'fifth-floor room overlooking the lake' – FN>Ov (30 March), *BW* II/5 (831); FN>FrN/Eli (830).

279–80 'If only I were blind!' FN>Ov, *ibid.* (831).

280 'His Palm Sunday' – FN>Marie Baum (6 April), *ibid.* (835). 'I, as is well known' – JBur>FN, 5 April, *BW* II/6/2 (1176). 'his "Basilophobia"' – FN>Ov (3 April), *BW* II/5, 402. 'I have opinions of all sorts' – *ibid.* (837). 'abominable, detrimental Basel' – FN>FrN/Eli (12 April), *ibid.*, 407. 'with one paroxysmic fit following another' – (25 April), *ibid.* (845). 'unable to deliver his first lecture' – FN had asked Ov to have his first lecture officially announced for Saturday, April 26 – FN>Ov (from Geneva, 18 April), *ibid.* (843). 'On 2 May' – FN>Carl Burckhardt, *ibid.* (846). 'The request was endorsed' – Rud. Massini to C. Burckhardt-B, 3 May, in Stroux, *op. cit.*, 88; and retirement granted by Dr. Paul Speiser (Education Council), 16 June, *BW* II/6/2 (1199). 'Alerted by a telegraphic dispatch' from Ov – EF-N, *Leben* II/1, 323, Eli replied on May 6 with telegram, urging FN to go to Baden-Baden rather than to some mountain resort, where it would still be too cold – *BW* II/6/2 (1192). 'to a castle near Bern' etc. – EF-N, *Leben* II/1, 329–31.

280–1 'N, heading in the opposite direction' – Louise Rothpletz>FN (mid-June), *BW*

II/6/2 (1197); 'mansard bedroom-study' mentioned by Ov>FN, 7 April *ibid.* (1179).

281 'to help the "errant fugitive"' – FN's description of himself as 'fugitivus errans': FN>Rée (end July), *BW* II/5, 431. 'J.S. Mill's autobiography' had been sold out, but Louise Rothpletz sent FN a copy of Gibbon's *Decline and Fall, op. cit.* (1197). 'next destination was Wiesen' – FN>Eli (30 May), *BW* II/5 (849). 'recommended by . . . Paul Widemann' – FN>Schm (8 June), *ibid.* (855). 'Pain, loneliness, walks' – FN>Ov, *ibid.* (854). '120 copies of *Human, A T Human* sold' – FN>Ov, *ibid.*, 419. 'upper Engadine . . . fear of being engulfed' etc. – FN>Eli (7 June), 416. 'Basel's Governing Council' – R. Falkner>FN, 14 June, *BW* II/6/2 (1198). 'the city's Academic Society' – Ov>FN, 19 June, *ibid.* (1202). 'left Davos on June 21st' – arrival date in St. Moritz indicated in FN>Schm, 18 Dec 79, *BW* II/5 (915). 'a trunk, full of clothes and books' – Ov>FN, *BW* II/6/2, 1120. 'But now I have taken possession' – FN>Ov, *BW* II/5 (859).

281–2 'on 24 June, "Dear Sister,"' – FN>Eli, *ibid.* (860).

282 'outrageous "*highland*-prices"' – FN>Eli, 6 July, *ibid.* (862). 'woods, lakes, the finest footpaths' – FN>FrN, *ibid.* (863). 'cloudiest, rainiest . . . summer' – FN>Eli (24 July), *ibid.*, 430. 'he had filled six small notebooks' – 'Sustained by the dried plums' etc. – L.Rothpletz>FN, 19 June, *BW* II/6/2 (1203); 28 June (1207; 10 July (1209). 'a pathetic postcard to Overbeck' – (12 Aug), *BW* II/5 (872). Ov 'journeyed all the way to St. Moritz' – Ov>FN, *BW* II/6/2 (1220). 'He found N lodged in a tiny room' – where (FN>FrN, 21 July) he lived off milk, eggs, tongue, dried plums, bread and Zweiback, never once going to a restaurant or hotel (*ibid.*, 428). 'could not accompany Overbeck on his walks' – FN>Eli, *ibid.*, 437. FN later described his habitat in St. Moritz as being 'a tiny room with bed, the meals of an ascetic', FN>Kös, *ibid.*, 442–3.

282–3 'special endowment fund' – Heusler Foundation: Janz I, 848.

283 'He strongly advised . . . Fritz' – Ov>FN, 27 Aug, *BW* II/6/2, 1152. 'On hearing the bad news from Chemnitz' – Ov>FN, 17 June, *ibid.*, 1120. FN 'had decided not to go to Venice' – Kös trying to lure FN to Venice with 'idyllic description' of the Lido: Kös>FN, 13 May, 19 June, *BW* II/6/2 (1195, 1196); FN>Ov, on Kös as 'Lidograph', *BW* II/5, 420. 'On 11 Sept he sent Kös a long letter' – *BW* II/5 (880); Ov had informed FN that Kös could devote 2–3 hours a day to his new ms – 2 Sept, from Zürich, *BW* II/6/2 (1224). 'sent from Venice on 12 Sept' – Kös>FN, *ibid.* (1229). 'On 22 Sept' – FN>Kös, *BW* II/5 (883). 'had completed . . . half the ms' – Kös>FN (24 Sept), *BW* II/6/2 (1232). 'by 4 Oct everything' – FN>Kös, *BW* II/5 (888). 'You will not believe' – FN>Kös (5 Oct), *ibid.* (889).

283–4 'That same day' – FN>Schm, *ibid.* (890).

## 25. From *Morgenröte* to Messina

290 'Like the good "Eris" imagined by Hesiod' – *WuS*, § 29.

293 '*We shatter the sword*' – *WuS*, § 284.

295 'On 18 October' – FN>Schm, *BW* II/5 (892); 'and his friend Paul Widemann' – FN>Kös (21 Oct), *ibid.* (893). 'But so mentally stimulated' – FN>Ov, *ibid.*, 456; FN>Schm (895). 'On 12 December' – Schm>FN, *BW* II/6/2 (1262). 'It seemed to him incredible' – FN>Schm, *BW* II/5 (915).

295–6 'The first to express gratitude' – Marie Baum>FN, 20 Dec, *BW* II/6/2 (1266).

296 'To Erwin Rohde' – *ibid.*, 22 Dec 79, 1246–8. 'Writing from distant Rome' – MvM>FN, 27 Dec, *ibid.* (1269). 'Meanwhile Fritz's health' – FN>Kös, 28 Dec, *BW* II/5 (917). 'His sister Elisabeth' – see her letters from Tamins and Chur:

*BW* II/6/2 (1228), (1233), (1239), (1245). 'Never have I observed' – FN>Eli, *BW* II/5 (918). '*118 serious* nervous-attack days' – *ibid.* (922).

296–7 'In early January of 1880' – FN>Eiser, *SBKSA* 6 (1).

297 'for in his thank-you note' – Eiser>FN, 13 Jan 80, *BW* III/2 (7). FN 'Frau W(agner) . . . is the most sympathetic woman I have met' – FN>MvM, 14 Jan 80, *SBKSA* 6, 5–6. 'by reading him German translations' – FN>Ov, 14 Nov, *SBKSA* 5, 464. 'Here . . . he found . . . a lakeside hotel' – FN>Eli (14 Feb 80), *SBKSA* 6 (6). 'with, nearby, an olive orchard' – FN>FrN, *ibid.* (11, 12). 'On 23 February . . . Heinrich Kös' – FN>Eli (24 Feb), *ibid.* (10). 'after receiving a bank order' – Kös to a friend, 27 Jan 80, *Dok* 74. 'Here Kös found N a room' – FN>FrN (15 March 80), *SBKSA* 6, (16).

298 'My room . . . is 22 feet high' – (27 March 80), *ibid.* (18). 'After a long, bracing walk' – (2 April), *ibid.* (20). 'By adopting a simple diet' – FN>Eli (3 May), *ibid.* (26). '*L'Ombra du Venezia*' – *Nachlass 1880–1882 KSA* 9, 47. 'the inexpensive food' – FN>Eli (28 May), *SBKSA* 6 (29).

298–9 'wooded hills of Carinthia' – FN>Ov (22 June), *ibid.* (33). 'dismal drizzle' – FN>Kös (5 July, from Marienbad) *ibid.* (35).

299 'hostellery, the Hermitage' – FN>FrN (5 July), *ibid.* (36). 'hideously expensive prices' – FN>Eli (19 July), *ibid.* (42). 'the spa's "fatal waters"' – FN>Kös (18 July), *ibid.*, 28. 'two valuable studies . . . Jacob Wackernagel' – FN>Ov, *ibid.*, 23; on Wackernagel, Janz I, 522–3. 'Sainte-Beuve "portraits"' – FN>Ida Ov (18 Aug), *SBKSA* 6 (48). 'harvest-festival mood' – FN>Kös (20 Aug), *ibid.* (49). On Kös's difficulty in establishing a 'sympathetic rapport' with other human beings, see Kös>FN (15 Aug), *BW* III/2 (45). FN on Wagner: 'with nobody perhaps have I ever laughed so much' – FN>Kös, *SBKSA* 6, 36. 'they take me absolutely for a Pole' – *ibid.*, 37.

300 'On 31 August' – FN>Eli (23 August, announcing soon arrival in Naumburg, *ibid.* (51). 'unusually sullen and morose' – FN>FrN/Eli, 25 Dec, *ibid.*, 54. 'not once . . . did he dip his quill' – FN>Kös (20 Oct), *ibid.*, 40. 'another nerve-wracking trip' – FN>FrN/Eli (14 Oct, from Stresa), *ibid.* (52); stop-over in Basel, Gotthard Tunnel fit, *ibid.* and FN>Ov (53). 'In Stresa . . . three fretful weeks waiting for trunk' – FN>Eli (31 Oct), *ibid.* (57); (7 Nov, trunk's arrival), (61); his 'deep melancholie' in Stresa – FN>Kös (17 Nov), 47. 'a jumble of nervous seizures' – FN>FrN/Eli (16 Nov, from Genoa), *ibid.* (63). 'humble mansard room . . . 164 steps to reach' – FN>Eli, *ibid.* (69). 'The cobblestones were so unworn' – *ibid.*

300–1 'never has the dawn (*Morgenröte*)' – FN>Ov, *ibid.*, 49–50.

301 'with a dormer-window view' – FN>FrN/Eli (24 Nov), *ibid.* (68). 'it had no stove' – FN>FrN/Eli (15 Dec), *ibid.* (71). 'so unbelievably mild' – FN>FrN/Eli, 25 Dec, *ibid.* (73). 'To his amazement, the busy seaport' – FN>FrN/Eli (24 Nov), 51. 'sun-warmed "like a lizard"' – FN>FrN/Eli (8 Jan 81), *ibid.*, 57. 'launching of his "Genoese ship"' – FN>Kös (25 Jan 81), *ibid.* (77). 'the happiest of men' – Kös>FN, 26 Jan 81, *BW* III/2, 134–5. 'working at a furious tempo' – Kös>FN (6 Feb), *ibid.* (56). 'To see the beauty and . . . gracefulness' – FN>Kös, *SBKSA* 6, (80). 'one of N's shortest aphorisms' – see FN *KSA* 9, p. 413, 9(17). 'to scrap . . . *Die Pflugschar*' – FN>Kös (9 Feb), *SBKSA* 6, (80); Kös>FN, 10 Feb 81, *BW* III/2, 137; and in *Nachlass* notes, *KSA* 9, 409. 'more simply – *Morgenröthe*' (using the old spelling) – FN>Kös, 20 March, *SBKSA* 6, 73.

301–2 'On 23 February' – FN>Schm, *ibid.* (85).

302 'The first pages of the manuscript' – Kös>FN, *BW* III/2, 145. 'had met and befriended CvG' – see Kös letters to FN: *ibid.*, 26 Jan 81, 135; 10 Feb, 138; 23

Feb, 141–2; 10 March, 144. 'Eager though N was to see his old friend again' – FN>Kös (13 March), *SBKSA* 6, 68; in this and later letter of 20 March (94), FN even asked Kös to find out if CvG would be willing to accompany him to Tunis in the autumn. 'impossible to maintain a normal conversation' – FN>Kös (6 April) *ibid.* (98). 'Recoaro . . . recommended . . . by a . . . pharmacist' – Kös>FN, 8 April, *BW* III/2, 158–9; FN>Kös (10 April), *SBKSA* 6, 82. 'At Recoaro N had a hard time' – FN>FrN/Eli (18 May), *ibid.* (109). 'a musician of the *first rank*' – FN>Ov, *ibid.* (110). 'a new Leipzig printer (Teubner)' – FN>Schm (16 and 19 April), sent from Genoa, before departure for Recoaro, *ibid.* (104, 105). 'absence of nearby forests' – FN>Ov (31 May), *ibid.* (111). 'Kös, for his part' – FN>FrN/Eli (5 June), *ibid.* (113). 'Not until 17 June' – Kös>FN, *BW* III/2 (77).

302–3 'thunderstorms caused by . . . Adriatic air' – FN>Kös, *SBKSA* 6 (115).

303 'On 19 June' – FN>Schm, *ibid.* (117). 'Where is the land . . . ?' – FN>Kös (23 June), *ibid.*, 96. 'suffering from paroxysmic seizures' – FN>Eli (7 July), *ibid.* (121) 'Once again the trip was agony' – FN>Kös (8 July), *ibid.* (122). 'When he finally reached St. Moritz' etc. – FN>Eli, *ibid.*, 98–99. 'in the Engadine . . . the best on earth' – *ibid.*, 98. 'the most delightful corner of the earth' – FN>Kös, *ibid.*, 100.

304 'On 15 July' – FN>Marie Baum, *ibid.* (128). 'casual . . . nibbling stage' – JBur>FN, 20 July, *BW* III/2 (80). *Morgenröte: Dawn*, translation used by Walter Kaufmann, in his *Nietzsche*, 484; *Daybreak*, title used for R.J. Hollingdale's translation. I have used the German word because none of the English equivalents has a comparable poetic force (through the juxtaposition of 'morning' and 'redness') – not even the French *Aurore*. 'make the "not so lovely name"' – FN>FrN/Eli, *SBKSA* 6 (114).

305 'Just as *Sittlichkeit*' – *MR*, § 9.

309 'the Old Testament prophets – "great haters"' – *MAM* I, ; *MR*, § 38; also (later) § 377.

310 'At the Death-Bed of Christianity' – *MR*, § 92. 'what Europe must sometime also do' – *MR*, § 96.

311 'July, by Engadine standards' – FN>FrN/Eli, *SBKSA* 6 (129). 'suffered a chilblained finger' – FN>FrN/Eli (30 July), *ibid.* 110; FN>FrN (18 August), 114; FN>FrN/Eli (2 Sept), 126; FN>FrN (21 Sept), 130–1.

311–2 'big Electricity Exposition' – FN>Kös (21 Aug), *ibid.*, 119.

312 'September brought little relief' – FN>Ov, *ibid.*, 127. 'abandoned by his friends' – FN>Kös, 14 Aug, *ibid.*, 112–3. 'and a plateful of polenta' – FN>FrN (24 Aug), *ibid.*, 121. '*Never* theatre concerts, etc.' – *ibid.*, 121. 'was a book Kuno Fischer' – FN>Ov (30 July), *ibid.*, 111.

312–3 '*Death* stared down on me' – FN>Kös, *ibid.*, 131.

313 'The uncomfortable downhill trip' – FN>FrN/Eli, *ibid.*, 155. 'sheer "cruelty to animals" . . .': in German '*Thierquälerei*', 'animal torture', often used by FN to describe his physical sufferings – FN>FrN/Eli (8 Oct), *ibid.* (157). 'Genoa, the most 'unmodern' city' – FN>Ov (14 Oct), *ibid.* (158). 'the month of October blew and blustered' – FN>Kös (27 Oct); FN> Ov (28 Oct), *ibid.* (162, 163). 'The weather was now so mild' – FN>Kös (6 Nov), *ibid.* (165). 'Eager to show . . . *Morgenröte* II' – *ibid.*, 138. 'Köselitz . . . now trying . . . to write another comic opera' – Kös>FN, 26 Aug, *BW* III/2, 181. During the first months of 1881 Kös had wanted to put a Goethean *Singspiel* fantasy, *Scherz, List, und Rache* (Joke, Cunning and Revenge) to music – see Kös>FN, 10 March, *ibid.* (61); but even before their stay at Recoaro and FN's subsequent visit to Venice, in May and June, FN had drawn his 'disciple's attention to Stendhal's essays on Italian

composers, and his admiration for Cimarosa's *Matrimonio segreto*: FN>Kös (21 March), *SBKSA* 6 (95); Kös>FN, 22, 26, 31 March, *BW* III/2 (63, 65, 66); and on his own *Matrimonio*, Kös>FN, 8 Nov, *ibid.* (89). 'A truly French talent for comic opera' – FN>Kös, *SBKSA* 6 (172).

314 'a . . . signed betrothal card' – CvG>FN, 15 Dec, *BW* III/2 (94). 'Martha Nitzsche' – FN>Kös (18 Dec), *SBKSA* 6 (180). 'for having in such a *grandiose* manner' – FN>CvG, *ibid.* (179). 'Wish me good luck' – FN>Kös, *ibid.*, 150. 'badly needed typewriter . . . from a Copenhagen manufacturer' – see FN>Ov (20/21 Aug, from Sils-Maria), *ibid.*, 117; FN>Eli (21 Aug), 120. 'Köselitz's prompt response' – Kös>FN, 20 Dec, *BW* III/2 (95). 'happiest find in terms of health' – FN>FrN/Eli, *SBKSA* 6 (181). 'A miserable Christmas' – FN>Kös (28 Dec 81), *ibid.* (182). 'no wind, no clouds, no rain!' – FN>Kös (17 Jan 82), FN>Ida Ov (mid-January), FN>FrN (late Jan 82)), *ibid.* (187, 188, 194). 'One Genoese old-timer' – FN>FrN, *ibid.*, 164. 'Buoyed by the splendid weather' – FN>Ida Ov (19 Jan), *ibid.*,156. 'On 28 January he sent the ms' – FN>Ov (29 Jan 82), *ibid.*, 162. '*fresh* strength for it' – *ibid.*, 162.

315 'On 4 February Paul Rée' – Rée>Eli, 5 Feb 82, in *Dok*, 92–3. 'A Genoese mechanic was summoned' – FN>FrN/Eli, 10 Feb, *SBKSA* 6, 169. 'The "Sarah" in question' – *ibid.*, 169. 'the all too familiar symptoms' – *ibid.*, 168.

315–6 'This severe attack' – Rée>Eli (17 March, from Rome), *Dok*, 98–99.

316 'Rée at least did not lose' – FN>FrN/Eli, *SBKSA* 6 (206). 'Paul Rée was so "strapped"' – FN>Rée (21 March), thanking him him for a money-order of 30 Swiss francs; and FN>Rée (23 March), protesting that Rée had sent him 20 lire too many, *ibid.* (215, 216). 'problem of his next "refuge"' – FN>Kös (4 March), FN>Ov (17 March); FN>Rée (23 March), *ibid.* (205, 210, 216). 'The Danish typewriter' – FN (typed letters) to FrN/Eli (late Feb), to Ov (early March), to Kös, FrN/Eli (4 March), to G. Krug (10 March), *ibid.* (203, 204, 205, 206, 207). 'This machine . . . is as delicate' – FN>Ov (17 March), *ibid.* (210).

317 'But Köselitz . . . had made it quite clear' – Kös>FN, 19 Jan 82, 12 March, *BW* III/2 (100,110), among others. 'From the moment Paul Rée reached Rome' – see FN>Rée (21 March), *SBKSA* 6 (215). '"Aunt Malwida", who received Rée' – MvM>FN, 27 March, *BW* III/2 (115). 'Malwida recommended Pieve di Cadore' – FN>MvM (21 March, *ibid.* 185; and MvM's reply (27 March, from Rome), *BW* III/2, 248. 'She was a talented young poetess' named Lou Salomé. For these details on her youth, I am indebted to Rudolph Binion's excellent biography.

318 'On 21 March Nietzsche' – FN>MvM, *SBKSA* 6 (214). 'Give this Russian lady my greetings' – FN>Rée, *ibid.* (215). 'Ah, this damned cloud-electricity!' – *ibid.* (23 March), (216). 'Thank God – you will say' – FN>Kös (24 March), *ibid.* (217). 'I will write . . . summer domicile' – FN>Eli (27 March), *ibid.* (218).

318–9 'His next postcard . . . from . . . Messina' – FN>FrN/Eli (1 April), *ibid.* (219).

## 26. Lou Salomé

320 'We know little about N's voyage' – FN>Ov (8 April from Messina), *SBKSA* 6 (221). 'Disconcerting to his friends' – Ov>ER, in *FO-ER*, 20 April, 61. 'The . . . biographer, Curt Paul Janz' – Janz II, 98–102; and FN>Kös, late Feb, *SBKSA* 6 (202). FN 'gripped by a powerful *Wanderlust*' – see FN>Kös, 14 Aug 81 (in which he talked of going to Mexico); FN>Ov (28 Oct 81, also to Mexico); FN>Kös (4 March 82, going to Biskra, southern Algeria, with Paul Rée), *SBKSA* 6, 113, 137, 174. 'a small brig, *Das Engelchen*' – FN>Kös (15 March), *ibid.*, 178–9. 'in an aphorism ('Well prepared men') – *FW*, § 283: in

German '*Vorbereitende Menschen*' suggests 'men who are preparing themselves' for future challenges. Walter Kaufmann's translation, in *The Gay Science* – 'Preparatory human beings' – is not exactly felicitous, though technically accurate. *Vorbereiten* – 'to prepare' – is derived from *reiten* (to ride), and the entire context of this key section makes it clear that for FN these 'preparatory human beings' were 'fore-riders' (i.e. forerunners) or harbingers of a hardier, more courageous generation of human beings, ready to defy mind-numbing prejudices and conventions in their 'fearless' pursuit of knowledge.

320–1 'fully resembled sea-sickness' – FN>FrN/Eli, *ibid.* (219).

321 'Of the three-and-a-half weeks N spent in . . . Messina' – during which FN was narrowly saved from drowning in an offshore whirlpool by a helpful dog: see his account, given to Meta von Salis in 1888: in *Beg.*, (299), 594–5. 'had reached the "rim of the earth"' – FN>Kös, *ibid.* (220). 'Reason has *triumphed*' – FN>Ov (8 April), *ibid.* (221). 'postcard sent to Paul Rée, who immediately replied from Rome' – the postcard has disappeared, but Rée's reply can be found in *BW* III/2, 20 April 82, (118). 'half-Punic zone' – Ov>FN, 20 April, *ibid.*, 249.

322 'The bewitching siren' – these details on Lou Salomé's temperament and youthful upbringing are taken from Rudolph Binion's excellent biography, *Frau Lou*, Part I.

323 'Gottfried Kinkel's letter of introduction' – included in Ernst Pfeiffer's *FN, Paul Rée, Lou von Salomé – Die Dokumente ihrer Begegnung* (*Dok* from here on), 17 Jan 82, pp. 91–92. 'The good Malwida responded' – *ibid.*, 9 Feb, (9 March), 94–95.

323–4 'one of these exquisitely refined soirées' – Lou's description in her *Lebenserinnerungen*, included in *Dok*, 96–98, with long explanatory note, 412–5. March 17th was specifically designated as the day of their first encounter, in letter addressed to Paul Rée on 17 March 1888: *ibid.*, 415–6.

324 'This funny, sensational prelude . . .' – Lou, *ibid.*, 97.

325 'Rée . . . had emerged "disgusted" from his first love-affair' – Rée>FN, 2 July 1877, *BW* II/6/1, p. 596.

325–6 'Malwida treated him to a stern lecture' – MvM>Rée, 30 March 82, *Dok*, 105.

326 'Lou's indignant response' – *Dok*, 102–3. '*frisch, fromm, fröhlich*' – On Jahn, see Viereck's *Metapolitics*.

326–7 MvM 'was overjoyed to greet the "vagabond son"' – MvM>Olga Herzen-Monod, 26 April 82, *Dok*, 420.

327 Lou's description of this first meeting in Saint Peter's, in *Lebenserinnerungen*, quoted in *Dok*, 107–10. For a description of Lou, see Binion, 31–32.

327–8 'For the superficial observer . . .' – Lou's description in *FN* in *Erläuterungen zum Lebensrückblick*, reproduced in *Dok*, 422–3.

328 'had decided to send them to Ernst Schmeitzner' – FN>Schm, *SBKSA* 6 (227); Schm's later payment, 25 May, *BW* III/2 (122a), p. 498.

329 'Rée was asked by the "High-Commanding Fräulein Lou"' – Lou>Rée, *Dok*, 108 (probably on April 25).

329–30 '"Aunt Malwida" confessed' – MvM>Lou, in *Dok*, 111–4.

330 'both men were preceded' – Rée>Lou (16 May 82) spoke of a 'two-day separation in Rome', *Dok*, 115.

330–1 On the 'pilgrimage' to the summit of the *Monte sacro*, see Lou's brief account in *Lebenserinnerungen* (*Dok*, 109–10), and Binyon, p. 54; also fn. 72 (p. 513), based on Lou's diary entry for 18 Aug 82.

331 'Host and hostess were amazed' – Ov>ER, in *Briefwechsel zwischen Overbeck und Rohde*, 63–64; Ov>Kös, 25 June, in *Dok*, 149–50.

332 'as Ida Overbeck observed years later' – *Beg.* (234), 425. 'The future is completely sealed . . .' – FN>Rée, *SBKSA* 6 (223). 'Both she and Paul Rée

were waiting' – FN>Ov (15 May), *ibid.* (226) On the Löwengarten, Janz II, 128–9.

332–3 'Lou's biographer Rudolph Binion' – *op. cit.*, 55.

333 On the 'bad' Lucerne photograph – see FN>Lou, *SBKSA* 6, 198. 'a copy of *Schopenhauer as Educator*' – FN>Ida Ov, *ibid.*, 196. 'on the cover of her knick-knack box' – Binion, 56. 'From half-measures weaned' etc. Goethe's verses in German: '*Uns vom Halben zu entwöhnen/ Und im Ganzen, Guten, Schönen/ Resolut zu leben*' – see FN>Lou (28 May), *SBKSA* 6 (234). 'A poem entitled 'To Pain' – in German, *An den Schmerz*: six four-verse stanzas, which FN later copied out and sent to Kös in Venice, around 1 July 82 – *SBKSA* 6 (252). 'get rid of her persistent cough' – Rée>Lou (16 May), *Dok*, 115–6.

334 'On 16 May N boarded the train . . .' – FN>Ov, *SBKSA* 6 (226). 'when he reached the Overbecks' house' – FN>Ida Ov, *ibid.* (233). 'an unmistakably amorous letter' – Rée>Lou, in *Dok*, 115–6. 'in the almost daily letters': in fact, four – *Dok*, 115–8.

334–5 'One of the suggestions . . . in Lucerne' – Rée>Lou (22 May), *Dok*, 118; FN>Lou (24 May), *SBKSA* 6, pp. 194–5.

335 'N began to get cold feet' – FN>Rée, FN>Lou, *ibid.*, 194–5. 'how jolly the "Herr Professor"' – Eli>Ida Ov (5 June), *Dok*, 131–2. 'entitled 'Idylls from Messina' – FN>Schm, *SBKSA* 6 (227); Schm> FN (22 May 82), *BW* III/2 (122). Text in *KSA* 3, 335–42. 'The title, *Die fröhliche Wissenschaft*' – FN>Schm (8 May, from Basel), *SBKSA* 6 (224); Schm>FN, *BW* III/2 (10 May), 254. 'Elisabeth's "girlish" handwriting' – EF-N, *Das Leben FNs*, II/2, 395–6; included in *Beg.* (237), 431–2; FN>Rée, *SBKSA* 6 (230). 'The nightingales have been singing' – FN>Lou, *ibid.* (231).

336 'a copy of the Lucerne photograph' – FN>Lou (28 May), *ibid.*, 198. 'a wedding celebrated by some German cousins' – Binion, 58. Louise Salomé's father, Siegfried, was the son of a Hamburg baker who had eloped to Petersburg with a Danish bride in 1813 and had later made a fortune in sugar refining – *ibid.*, 5. 'Nietzsche wrote to Ida Overbeck' – *SBKSA* 6 (233).

336–7 'N next wrote to his "dear friend"' – (28 May) *ibid.* (234).

337 'To Paul Rée, N wrote the next day' – *ibid.*, (235). 'while continuing to bombard Lou Salomé' – Rée>Lou, undated letters probably sent on 22, 24, 25 or 26, 28, and near the end of May, in *Dok*, 118–24. 'a lecture by Jacob Burckhardt' – Lou>Ov (30 May), *ibid.*, 128.

337–8 'Franz Overbeck was so intrigued' – FN>Ov, *SBKSA* 6, (236).

338 'Writing on 4 June from Hamburg' – Lou>FN, *BW* III/2 (125). 'In his reply N mentioned the 8-page letter' – *SBKSA* 6, (237). 'On or around 9 June' – Rée's letter has disappeared, but is mentioned in his letter to Lou (8 June?), *Dok*, 137–8. 'In his letter of reply' – FN>Rée (10 June?), *SBKSA* 6, (238). 'Malwida von Meysenbug had just sent her' – *Dok*, 133–4.

339 'To this suggestion Nietzsche reacted negatively' – *SBKSA* 6 (239). FN: 'I am in all matters of action' – *ibid.*, 203. 'dreadful existence of *renunciation*' – FN>Lou, *ibid.* (240). 'Lou immediately sent him a letter intended to cheer him up' – this is one of the many letters Lou sent to FN which have disappeared. Its contents may be surmised from FN's reply.

339–40 'For the past half-hour' – FN>Lou (15 June?), *ibid.* (241).

340 'The trip was made on Friday, 16 June' – FN>Lou (18 June), *ibid.* (243). 'A Swiss forester had once assured N' – FN>Kös, *ibid.* (244). 'The next morning the sun was shining' – FN>Lou (26 June?), *ibid.*, 211: 'The Grunewald was much too sunny for my eyes.' 'teeming with boisterous holiday-makers' – EF>N, *Das Leben FNs* II/2, 396. Also in *Beg.*, 431.

340–1 'The next day he wrote to Paul Rée' – (18 June), *SBKSA* 6 (242).

341 'the little, apparently very silly trip' – *ibid.* (243).

342 'on 19 June he wrote to Heinrich Köselitz' – *ibid.*, (244). 'the imperious "dice-toss" of Fate' – cf. FN>Rée, *ibid.*, 205.

## 27. *Incipit tragoedia*

343 'On 22 June, when they met' – FN>Schm (21 June telegram), *SBKSA* 6 (246) '63 tongue-in-cheek "aphorisms"' – '*Scherz, List und Rache*', in *KSA* 3, 353–67; and, in English translation, 'Joke, Cunning and Revenge", Walter Kaufmann's version of *The Gay Science*, 39–69.

343–4 '*Ja! ich weiss, woher ich stamme!*' – *KSA* 3, § 62, p. 367.

344 'all the proof-reading troubles' – see FN>Eli (5 July 82), *SBKSA* 6, (260); and Arthur Egidi's testimony, in *Beg.*, 446, 448. 'little castle of Dornburg' – *Dok*, 433, fn to p. 151. 'to accompany the poetically minded Lou' – FN>Lou (26 June?), *SBKSA* 6 (249). 'three beautiful romantic poems' – '*Der Brautigam*', '*Früh, wenn Tag, Gebirg und Garten*', '*Dem aufgehenden Vollmond*'. 'Fräulein Lou was going to spend' – Rée>Lou (13 June?), in *Dok*, 140–1. 'Since Elisabeth was planning to attend' – FN>Lou, *SBKSA* 6 (249).

344–5 Elisabeth had 'long thrilled at the idea of helping to found a "colony" or *Kloster*' – for example, in the village of Arlesheim, south of Basel: see EF-N, *Das Leben FNs* II/1, p. 261; FN>Eli (6 Aug 1876), *SBKSA* 5 (547); Rée>Eli (end January 1880), *Dok*, 73–74.

345 'The cosy single-windowed room' – Arthur Egidi's description, in *Beg.*, 447, 450. 'overtures were made to the parish priest' – FN>Eli, *SBKSA* 6, (254, 255, 257, 266), between 1–14 July. 'The day after his arrival N wrote' – FN>Lou (26 June), *SBKSA* 6, (249). 'after suffering another severe seizure' – FN>Eli, *ibid.*, (254). 'this time to thank Lou' – *ibid.* (256).

346 'plaintive letters to his mother' – FN>FrN, *ibid.*, (259, 261). 'the members of a local 'Embellishment Club' – *ibid.*, 221. 'friend Lou . . . daughter of a Russian general' – FN>Kös, *ibid.* 222.

347 'recently published tenth book' – FN>MvM (13 July?), *ibid.* (264). 'and yet, if I could quite spectrally' – FN>Lou, *ibid.*, (269).

348 'she could not . . . read a music score' – FN>Kös, *ibid.* (272); and Lou's own admission about her 'music-deaf ear', in her *Lebenserinnerungen* (*Dok*, 165–6). 'He was a Berliner named Arthur Egidi' – see his account of his encounters with FN, in *Beg.*, 443–6. 'pick up Lou Salomé in Leipzig and accompany her to Bayreuth' – MvM>Lou (13 July), *Dok*, 158–9; FN>Eli (16 July), *SBKSA* 6, 227.

349 'the painter Paul Zhukovsky' – his father had met his mother, *née* von Rentem, in Baden-Baden, where he had settled after leaving Petersburg in 1841. There are many references to Paul von Joukowsky (the 'von', unknown in Russia, was as phoney as the 'von' in Lou von Salomé's name) in the fourth volume of Newman's *The Life of RW*. See in particular pp. 623–5, 633. 'after finishing a huge family portrait' – mentioned in Lou's memoirs (*Lebenserinnerungen*, *Dok*, 165) as the work of 'Count Joukowsky'. See also Rée's jealous reaction to Lou's letters to him about this 'admirer' – *ibid.*, 171–2. 'Heinrich von Stein . . . the erudite tutor of . . . Siegfried Wagner' – often mentioned in the second volume of Cosima's diary, from Oct 1879 to summer of 1880; also in Newman IV, 621. 'after being told off by Paul Rée' – Rée>Lou (1 or 2 Aug), *Dok*, 168–9; 'in such vigorous discussions' – *ibid.*, 172–3 'During their "privatissime" audience' – FN>Kös, *SBKSA* 6, (276); 'even a deaf man would have been enthused' – *ibid.*, 234.

350 'On 28 July' – FN>Eli, *ibid.*, (273). 'she stunned Ida Overbeck by the

vehemence' – Ida Ov, in reminiscence of FN, in *Beg.*, 426. 'hair-splitting sophistry' – Resa v Schirnhofer in *Beg.*, 474. 'the "amusing" Lucerne photograph' Resa v Schirnhofer, *Beg.*, 474. '"The old wizard", he added' – FN>Kös, *SBKSA* 6, (276). 'felt tempted to accompany the young Berliner' – Arthur Egidi, in *Beg.*, 448, 450. 'Elisabeth minced no words' – see her long letter to Clara Gelzer (24 Sept to 2 Oct 82), in *Dok*, 251–3.

350–1 'Fritz immediately sent Lou a telegram' – the telegram has disappeared, but is mentioned in Lou's August 2nd reply.

351 'In her letter of reply' – Lou>FN, *Briefe an N*, III/2 (133). 'Ida Overbeck . . . had been sharply rebuffed' – Lou>Ida Ov, *Dok*, 160–1. 'Malwida von Meysenbug, for her part' – MvM>Lou, *Dok*, 179–80. 'better if they simply forgot their plans' – Eli>Clara Gelzer, *Dok*, 253.

351–2 'I wanted to live alone' – FN>Lou, *SBKSA* 6, (279).

352 'One day a bird flew past me' – FN>Kös (4 Aug), *ibid.* (278). 'eighteen other presentations' – Newman IV, 689–93. 'On the 5th' – Egidi's account, in *Beg.*, 450. 'a two-paragraph letter to Jacob Burckhardt' – *SBKSA* 6, (277).

354 'had . . . scoffed at the idea that human beings might be descended from apes' – see Raimund Granier to FN, 13 Sept 65, *BW* I/3, 5; and FN's reply, *BW* I/2, 84.

355 '"Natural selection" – a terminological misnomer' – as pertinently pointed out by L. Harrison Matthews, in his Introduction to the Everyman's University Library edition of Darwin's *The Origin of Species* (J.M. Dent, 1971).

356 'the mass perpetuation of idiots' – see FN's critical comments on Herbert Spencer, in *Nachgelassene Fragmente* (Spring to Autumn of 1881, *Nietzsche KSA* 9: 11(40), pp. 455–6; 11(42), 11(43), 11(44) *Die Vorwegnehmenden*, 11(46), beginning *Rudimentäre Menschen* pp. 455–9; and, on the Chinese: 11(34), p. 454.

358 'the ploughshare of evil' – in German, *die Pflugschar des Bösen* – *KSA* 3, p. 376.

359 'N anticipated not only Freud – see Paul-Laurent Assoun's interesting book, *Freud et Nietzsche*. 'Examine the lives of the finest and most productive' – § 19.

362 '*noblesse du coeur*' – repeated in FW, § 55, '*Der letzte Edelsinn*'

365 'Well preparing human beings' (*Vorbereitende Menschen*) – re this title, see explanatory note to p. 320.

## 28. Storm and Stress

367 'their good friend, Heinrich Gelzer,' – see Janz I, 401–2; Binion, 76. On Malwida von Meysenbug not liking idea of Lou spending two weeks alone with N, see MvM>Lou, 18 Aug 82, *Dok*, 179. 'any more than did . . . Paul Rée' – Rée>Lou, (3/4 August) *Dok*, 171.

367–8 'Lou turned on Elisabeth' etc. – a long, detailed account of this furious row was later written by Eli for Clara Gelzer (24 Sept – 2 Oct 82), *Dok*, 251–8. Its authenticity was personally guaranteed by Heinrich Gelzer when he turned the letter over to Franz Overbeck's (and Nietzsche's) biographer, C.A. Bernouilli.

368 'Nietzsche, who turned up in the early afternoon' – FN>FrN, *SBKSA* 6, (280).

369 'Nietzsche was allowed to climb the stairs' – Monday, 14 August instalment, sent to Paul Rée in Stibbe: *Dok*, 181. 'Nietzsche began to take long walks' etc. – *ibid.* 'While Elisabeth disappeared into the woods' – *ibid.*, 183. 'much to the annoyance of Herr Hahnemann' – according to the later (1939) recollections of his widow, in *Dok*, 442–3. 'rough draft of an essay on "Woman"' – Lou's 'diary', *ibid.*, 182.

369–70 'memorandum entitled "The Theory of Style"' – *ibid.*, 212–3; also *SBKSA* 6, (288).

370 'including (no. 12) the condition of pregnancy' – *Dok*, 215–6. On the 'Stibbe Nest-Book' – see long note, *ibid.*, 444–8. 'having become for his *Schneckli*' – Rée>Lou (6 Aug), *ibid.*, 175. 'To keep life from becoming a burden' – *Dok*, 195 (aphorism 21). 'He added six aphorisms of his own' – *SBKSA* 6 (8–24 Aug), 242–3. 'The immense expectation with regard to sexual love' – In § 114 of *Beyond Good and Evil*, this became: 'The immense expectation with regard to sexual love, and the shame in this expectation, from the outset spoils all of women's perspectives.' 'the *intelligentest of all women*' – FN>Kös, *SBKSA* 6, 239. 'was immediately dispatched to Köselitz' *ibid.*, 238. '*Gebet an das Leben*' – FN>Kös (1 Sept 82), *ibid.* 249.

370–1 'In a letter to Paul Rée' – it has disappeared, but Lou's longing to see more of the world was sympathetically treated in Rée's reply from Helgoland, *Dok* (17–18 Aug), 219.

371 Nietzsche 'behaving like a "bridegroom"' – Rée>Lou (15–16 August), *Dok*, 217. 'You do not need to befriend him *more*' – Rée>Lou (19 or 20 Aug), *Dok*, 221. 'a proposal . . . warmly approved by Malwida von Meysenbug' – MvM>Lou, 23 August, *Dok*, 221–2. 'the day after Lou Salomé's departure' – FN>Lou, *SBKSA* 6, (291). 'His sister Elisabeth flatly refused to accompany him' – Eli to Clara Gelzer, *Dok*, 256–7. 'Fritz argued with her briefly' – FN>Lou, *SBKSA* 6, 247. 'To Paul Rée, . . . he asked if he had received his gift copy' – FN>Rée, *ibid.*, 247. 'the new popping-up specter' – FN>Lou, *ibid.*, (293). '*chain-sickness*' – in German *Kettenkrankheit*, a variation of *Kettenträger* (chain-bearers), the title of § 227 in *Morgenröte*, where clever women living in an oppressive, narrow-minded environment were likened to angry dogs, ready to snap at everything unexpected.

372 'torn to shreds by a plaintive letter' – Eli>Clara Gelzer, *Dok*, 257–8. 'had she been a Catholic, she would have retired . . . to a convent' – FN>Ov (9 Sept), *SBKSA* 6, 256. 'In a rage Fritz went upstairs' – *ibid.* 'From Leipzig Fritz wrote . . . to Elisabeth' – *ibid.*, (300). 'Our intelligences and tastes' – FN>Ov, *ibid.*, (301).

373 'The next day N sent a postcard to his mother' – *ibid.*, (302). 'had found time to write to Lou' – FN>Lou (8 Sept) *ibid.* (298); Kös>FN, *BW* III/2, 4 Sept 82, p. 282. 'The second-floor room' – see reminiscences of Janicaud's son Walter, in *Beg.* (242), pp. 451–3. 'Max Heinze . . . one of the few members of Leipzig's academic community' – on FN's bitterness over the way he was snubbed, see FN>Hans von Bülow (early Dec 82), *SBKSA* 6, 290; FN>Ov (20 Jan 83), 319.

373–4 'four letters of congratulation' – *BW* III/2, from Gersdorff (142), M. Baumgartner (143), Burckhardt (144), Gottfried Keller (146).

374 'On the last day of September' – FN>FrN (1 Oct), *SBKSA* 6 (314); FN>Kös (2 Oct), (315). 'Max Heinze's wife' – FN>Lou (26 Sept), *ibid.*, 266. 'so Malwida von Meysenbug claimed' – MvM>Lou, *Dok*, 221–2. 'Carl Riedel' – FN>Kös (16 Sept), *SBKSA* 6, (307). 'the performance was such . . . hocus-pocus' – FN>Kös (2 Oct), *ibid.* 268–9.

374–5 'On 18 October the "trinitarians"' – FN>FrN/Eli, *ibid.* (319).

375 'N had been told by Arthur Nikisch' – FN>Kös, *ibid.* (318). 'philosophy of the knights of the Holy Grail' – Kös>FN, 20 Sept, *BW* III/2, 294. 'close, attentive reading of *Human, All Too Human*' – Binion, 89; so intensive that it affected Lou's eyesight – FN>Lou, *SBKSA* 6 (26 Sept), 265. 'Although I am a protection' – Rée>Lou, 12 Sept, *Dok*, 226–7.

376 'No, certainly not!' – *ibid.*, 227. 'I am scared of this Fräulein Lou' – Kös>FN, 20 Sept, *BW* III/ 2, 294.

377 'The sensual moment is the last word of love' – *Dok*, (46), p. 210. 'The greater

the intensity' – (unnumbered), *Dok*, 205. 'Spiritual proximity' – (37), *Dok*, 208. 'Just as Christian (like every) mysticism' – *Dok*, 239.

378 'In Leipzig Heinrich Köselitz was struck by N's habit' etc. – Kös to a woman friend in Vienna (16 Oct), *Dok*, 237. 'She is truly a genius' – (7 Nov), *ibid.*, 242. 'this "Peter Gast" was a new Italo-German . . . Mozart' – see, for ex, fragment of a letter from FN to Hermann Levi in Munich, *SBKSA* 6, (326). 'One such was Ludwig Hüter' – Lou>Hüter (14 Oct), *Dok*, 236–7; Binion, 66–67. 'beautiful and emotionally bewitching' – Binion, 112–3.

378–9 'Heinrich von Stein . . . the "blond, imposing . . . German"' *CWD*, 25 Oct 1879 entry. 'in the name of our trinity' – Lou>Heinrich von Stein, 24 Oct, *Dok* 239.

379 'Stein found the invitation too tempting' – HvS>Lou, 27 Oct; HvS>Rée, 1 Nov, in *Dok*, 240, 241. 'Unfortunately . . . Nietzsche was absent' – FN>HvS, *SBKSA* 6 (322). 'his mother . . . had sent him a fancy cake' – FN>FrN, *ibid.* (319). 'In his letter of "forceful" recommendation' – FN's letter to Louise Salomé has unfortunately disappeared, but it is mentioned in FN>Lou (8 Nov), *SBKSA* 6, (325). 'the glowing picture N painted' – Louise Salomé to FN, 10 Nov, *BW* III/2, (154).

379–80 'Lou's state of health struck him as so "pitiable"' – FN>Ov (10 Nov), *SBKSA* 6, 276.

380 'What melancholy!' – FN>Lou, *ibid.*, (325). 'that Genoa, with all the implicit perils' – FN>Ov, *ibid.*, 275.

380–1 '*Freundin – sprach Columbus*' – *ibid.*, (321); and Binion, 94.

## 29. *Finita è la commedia*

382 'On 7 November or thereabouts' – FN>Louise Ott, *SBKSA* 6 (323). 'to a Basel jurist, Dr. August Sulger' – *ibid.*, (324). 'Louise Ott was so overjoyed' – LO>FN, 10 Nov, *BW* III/2, (153). The flowers were mentioned in FN>CvG (15 Nov), *SBKSA* 6, (331). 'But on 15 November' – FN>LO, FN>Sulger, *ibid.* (328, 329). 'where the first wintry snows' – later recalled, FN>Ov, (9 March 83), *ibid.* (388). 'vainly waiting for letters' – Ida Ov, in *Beg.* (234), 426. 'He told his Basel hosts' – Ida Ov reminiscence, *ibid.*, 426–8. 'But you are describing Daniel Deronda!' – FN>Rée (23 Nov), *SBKSA* 6, 280.

383 'They were the only persons in Basel' – the Overbecks were also the only persons who had been given some inkling of the rows that had broken out between Lou and Elisabeth in Jena and at Tautenburg, since Elisabeth, in her long letter to Clara Gelzer, had specifically asked Clara to read it to Ida and Franz Overbeck. *Dok*, 258. 'Genoa, where . . . he found that in his absence' – FN>Ov (23 Nov), *SBKSA* 6, (333); FN>Kös (332). 'postcard to Paul Rée, who replied' – FN>Rée, *ibid.* (334). Rée's 'reproachful note' later disappeared, like all of his and Lou's letters to FN, possibly destroyed by FN's sister Eli, to keep their counter-arguments and accusations from becoming known to posterity. 'A hundred times during the past year' – FN>Rée (23 Nov), *ibid.*, (334).

383–4 'Nietzsche was on his way to the post-office' – FN>Lou (24 Nov) *ibid.*, (335); 'Take this as a token of trust . . .' etc.

384 'he never wanted to relive what he had gone through' – FN>Kös, *ibid.*, (343).

384–5 'M[y] d[ear] L[ou]' – FN>Lou (mid-December 82), *ibid.* (347).

385 'Yes, I was angry with you' – FN>Lou, *ibid.*, (348). FN 'poured out his heart in a litany of grievances' – *ibid.*, letters (350–5).

385–6 'Save for a single remaining fragment of a page' – FN to Lou and Rée (around 20 Dec 82), *ibid.*, (361).

386 'Malwida von Meysenbug, who had written to N' – MvM>FN, 13 Dec 82, *BW* III/2 (162). 'You wanted to know what I think of Fräulein Salomé?' – FN>MvM; the first (rough draft) version of this letter is in *SBKSA* 6, (357), the second (actually sent) is (358).

386–7 'Whether I have suffered much' etc. – (rough draft), *ibid.* (351) also, in a somewhat different version, in *Dok*, 262–3.

387 'Religion as a spiritual release' – FN *NF*, Summer–autumn 1882, § 322, *KSA* 10, p. 92.

388 'I have never doubted that somewhere' – FN>Rée (rough draft, mid-December 82), *SBKSA* 6, (353). 'a reference to Lou's frail state of health' – see FN's notes, dating from late November, 'Compassion my weak point' and similar comments condemning compassion as 'unmanly': *NF KSA* 10, [3] 334, 386, 4[34], pp. 94, 100, 117. When Lou said: 'I will soon die etc.' *SBKSA* 6 (336), 283. 'My sole reproach against you today' – FN>Lou, *ibid.* (352). 'But L[ou], what sort of letters are you writing!' – FN>Lou (rough draft, mid-Dec), *ibid.*, (355).

389 'A dreadful compassion, dreadful disillusionment' – FN>Rée/Lou, *ibid.* (360). 'After taking a huge dose of opium' – FN>Lou/Rée, *ibid.* 'Fritz was so furious with his mother' – FN>FrN/Eli, *ibid.* (363).

389–90 'To Fr Ov he wrote on Christmas Day' – FN>Ov, *ibid.*, (365).

390 'a letter that had expressed higher praise for *The Joyous Science*' – ER>FN, 26 Nov 82, *BW* III/2, 307. 'Overbeck, who had long been urging Erwin Rohde' – for ex. Ov>ER 7 Feb 82, in *BW FO-ER* (31), p. 53. 'The friend gives, the lover demands' – *Dok*, 209, § 46. 'Just as in love we idealize the loved one' – *Dok*, 210.

390–1 'In the meantime all I see' – FN>Rée, *SBKSA* 6, (362).

## 30. The Birth of Zarathustra

392 'dark depths of the "abyss"' – *Abgrund*: word used by FN>Ov, (1 Feb 83), *SBKSA* 6, 324. 'of *Selbstüberwindung*' (self-overcoming) – used by FN>Ov (25 Dec 82), *ibid.*, 312. 'the "watch-spring" of his overly tensed' – *ibid.* 'never . . . had Nietzsche felt so frozen' – FN>Ov (31 Dec 82), 313. 'blinding headaches and fits of vomiting' – FN>Ov (20 Jan 83), *ibid.*, 319. 'that he had "disgraced his father's tomb"' – FN>Ov, *ibid.*, 326. 'who used ideas as others use crossword puzzles' – FN>MvM (1 Jan 83), *ibid.*, 315. 'But then suddenly the skies cleared' – FN>Kös (1 Feb 83), *ibid.* (370); FN>Ov (372), 326. 'his spirits cheered by a friendly letter' – MvM>FN, *BW* III/2, (169). 'the first draft of which was completed in ten days' – FN>Ov (1 Feb 83), *SBKSA* 6, 324.

392–3 'finished a "quite small book"' – FN>Kös, *ibid.*, (370).

393 'a few days of fine "tuning"' – FN>Ov, *ibid.* 324. 'persuaded that he had not long to live' – FN>Ov (10 Feb 83), *ibid.*, 326. 'It is a "work of poetry"' – FN>Schm (13 Feb 83), *ibid.* (375). 'N's books were not written for the "general public"' – see FN>Kös (20 Aug 82), *ibid.*, 238. 'N . . . dashed off a postcard to Köselitz' – *ibid.*, (378). 'In his lengthy reply' – Kös>FN, *BW* III/2, (174).

393–4 'the best-esteemed woman' – '*bestverehrte Frau*', FN>CosW, *SBKSA* 6, (380). Thrice repeated – pp. 330–2.

394 'It was hard for six long years' – FN>Kös, *ibid.* (381). 'W offended me to a *deadly* degree' – FN>MvM (21 Feb), *ibid.*, 335. 'his old lodgings on the Salita delle Battestini' – 'far and away the *most complete man*' – FN>Ov (22 Feb),337. 'migraine, stomach upsets and insomnia' – *ibid.* (6 March), 338.

394–5 'severe attack of influenza' – FN>Kös (7 March), 340.

395 'I do not like my mother' – FN>Ov (6 March) *ibid.*, 385. 'By 9 March a heavy snowfall' – FN>Ov, *ibid.*, 341. 'the intelligent letters . . . from Heinrich Köselitz' – see Kös>FN, *BW* III/2, 3 Dec 82 (160); 12 Dec 82 (161); 6 Jan 83 (165); 13 Jan (166); 21 Jan 83 (168); 3 Feb (171); 16 Feb (174); 22 Feb (176). 'Was not one of the three Muses named Meleti . . . ?' – FN>Deussen, *SBKSA* 6, (389). 'he was filled with a "black melancholy"' – FN>Ov, *ibid.* (393). 'he sent Schmeitzner a furious letter of reproach' – *ibid.* (395). 'elicited an apologetic reply' – letter has been lost, but was mentioned by FN>Schm (1 April), *ibid.* 396. 'the Leipzig printer, Teubner' – FN>Kös (2 April), *ibid.*, 353; and FN>Ov, 354.

395–6 'five nervous "weeks of fever"' – FN>Schm (1 April), *ibid.* (396).

396 'The first rapturous response' – Kös>FN, 2 April, *BW* III/2 (184). 'Markedly different was the reaction of the type-setters' – FN>Schm (2 April), *SBKSA* 6, (399), which includes FN's prediction: 'I *foresee* European anarchies and earthquakes . . .' 'Do you want a new name for me?' – FN>MvM (3/4 April), *ibid.*, 400.

396–7 'The good Malwida . . . wrote back immediately' – MvM>FN, 6 April 83, *BW* III/2 (186).

397 'Towards the end of April N found a conciliatory letter' – the letter has disappeared, but FN had already heard from Kös, who had seen Eli in Venice, that she was on her way to Rome, and from MvM, who had found her lodgings near her villa: MvM>FN, 6 April, *ibid.* 363. 'In his reply Fritz said he was pleased' – FN>Eli, 27 April, *SBKSA* 6, (408). 'the . . . mountain crests were still powdered' – FN>FrN, *ibid.*, (416). 'His sister had found him a quiet, spacious top-floor room' – EF-N, *Das Leben FNs*, II/2, 433; *Beg.*, (247), p. 463. 'One of them was Franz von Lenbach' – see Theo Schücking's reminiscences of FN in Rome, *Beg.*, 459. Lenbach was so busy painting members of the German colony in Rome that he could find no time for FN: Lenbach>FN, *BW* III/2, 24 May (196). 'in which Ernst Schmeitzner referred . . . to the financial "perplexities of the publisher"' – Schm's letter has disappeared, but not FN's reply: *SBKSA* 6, (417). 'temperature had now begun to rise' – FN>Ov (20 May), *ibid.*, 379.

398 'the only objects that had spoken to his soul' – *ibid.* 'He and Elisabeth kept searching for mountain resorts' – EF>N, *Das Leben FN's* II/2, 452–3; *Beg.*, (248) 463. 'a quick exploratory trip to Aquila and Terni' – FN>Kös (1 July), *SBKSA* 6, 388. 'the flaming sword of the sirocco' – FN>Eli (10 June), *ibid.* (422). 'Fritz, in a merry mood, amused himself' – EF-N, *Leben FN's*, I 221–5; *Beg.*, 465–6. 'The grey, pitted waters were barely visible' – FN>Eli (15 June), *SBKSA* 6, (423). 'I now almost shrink from solitude' – *ibid.* 'There was no let-up in the rain' etc. – FN>FrN/Eli, 21 June, *ibid.*, (425).

398–9 'the good Naumburg ham and sausages' – FN>FrN, *ibid.* (426).

399 'In a long letter to Carl von Gersdorff' – (end June), *ibid.*, (427) 'beloved Sils-Maria in the Engadine . . .' – FN>Kös, *ibid.*, (428).

399–400 '*schwebend*' – the sentence begins: '*Ich bin im* Ganzen *merkwürdig schwebend, erchüttert*" – *ibid.*, 388–9.

400 'Zarathustra – or Zoroastes' – according to Curt Paul Janz (II, 222), FN was first 'struck' by the figure of Zarathustra while reading Georg Friedrich Creuzer's *Symbolik und Mythologie der alten Völker*: a four-volume work which seems to have fascinated more than one member of FN's Philological Club in Leipzig because of the 'off-beat' originality of its views.

401 'its archaic Biblical style' – Janz (II, 223–4) aptly links this to the neo-Gothic 'vogue' which exercised such influence in nineteenth century architecture and literature. 'his new work was a "*ya-sagend*" (yes-saying) book' – FN>Deussen

(16 March 83), *SBKSA* 6, 343. 'For, N felt, if one must believe in gods, let them at least dance' – see in *Thus spake Zarathustra* I, Z's seventh speech, entitled 'On reading and writing': 'I would believe only in a god who knew how to dance.' (*KSA* 4, p. 49.) 'The believing human being is the opposite of the religious human being.' – *Nachgelassene Fragmente*, July–August 1882, 1(77), *KSA* 10, p. 30.

403 'But lo! This goblet again wishes to be empty' – Zarathustra's Prologue, *AsS* I, § 1, *KSA* 4, p. 12; p. 122 in Walter Kaufmann's *Portable Nietzsche*. All the translations, here as elsewhere, are mine. '*I teach you the Overman.*' – *AsS* I, § 3, *KSA* 4, p. 14.

404 'which . . . Walter Kaufmann rightly translated . . . as "overman"' – in his valuable Introduction to the French translation of *Ainsi parlait Zarathustra*, the German scholar, Peter Putz, pointed out that the *über* in *Übermensch* more closely denoted 'trans' (*hinüber*) than 'over' – as in 'transcend'. The *Übermensch* is the 'overman' who can transcend himself. 'Bouquins' edition (Robert Laffont), II, 275–6.

404–5 'Man is a rope' etc. – *AsZ*, *KSA* 4, § 4.

405 '*der letzte Mensch*' – *ibid.*, § 5. 'Your soul will be dead even before your body' – *ibid.*, § 6. 'where the grave-diggers mock him' – *ibid.*, § 8. 'Yet who, verily, was this "breaker, this criminal"' – *ibid.*, § 9.

406 '*das klugste Thier unter der Sonne*' – *ibid.*, § 10. 'Would that I could be more clever!' – *ibid.*

407 'In Zarathustra's tenth discourse' – not numbered, but titled.

407–8 'On War and Warriors' (*Vom Kriege und Kriegsvolke*).

409 'You are going to women? Do not forget the whip!' This now famous exhortation had been suggested by a novelette of Turgenev entitled 'First Love', EF-N, *Leben*, II/1, pp. 559–61; *Beg.*, 428–9. 'The next to the last of the prophet's twenty-one "speeches"' – is entitled, 'On free death' – *AsZ*, *KSA* 4, pp. 93–96. 'each of which ends with the same sentence, "Thus spake Zarathustra"' – as Janz (II, 223) pointed out, the 'Thus spake' formula was also inspired by the ritual opening of the writings of the pre-Socratic philosophers of ancient Greece.

409–10 'Many die too late, and a few die too early.' On FN's fear of not having long to live, see his letter to Ov (from Rapallo, 10 Feb 83) *SBKSA* 6 (373); FN>Eli (10 July 83), 395; FN>Kös (13 July) 397.

## 31. 'Oh, my son Zarathustra!'

412 'despite erratic variations in the weather' – FN>Eli (6 July 83), *SBKSA* 6, 391. 'He beseeched Elisabeth to intervene' – *ibid.*, 392. 'at having so swiftly given birth to a second *Zarathustra* "child"' – FN>Eli (10 July), *ibid.*, 394–5; FN>Kös (13 July), 397. 'Its main accusation' – see FN>Rée (mid-July 83), *ibid.* (434). Elisabeth's letter to Rée's mother has disappeared. Eli sent a sent a copy to FN (see FN>Ida Ov (29 July), *ibid.*, 410).

413 'the "sublime" ability to rise above praise and blame' – see FN's unhappiness over Eli's lust for revenge: FN>Eli, *ibid.*, 406, 407. 'The letter to Frau R(ée) is . . . your finest performance yet' – FN> Eli (10 July), *ibid.*, 395–6. 'In a fit of rage he now wrote Rée a furious letter' – *ibid.* 'This sterile, dirty, evil-smelling she-ape' – FN>Georg Rée, *ibid.*, (435). Only the rough draft has survived, but we have FN's word for it that he actually sent the letter – FN>Eli, *ibid.*, 406. 'What . . . infuriated N was to discover . . . that his sister' – FN>Ida Ov (29 July), *ibid.* 410. Ida Ov 'who had . . . sent him some tea and vegetable soups' –

FN>Ov, (9 July), *ibid.*, 393. 'My sister wants to get her revenge' – FN>Ida Ov (mid-July), *ibid.* 405–6.

414 'Quite apart from the idealistic light' – FN>Ida Ov (14 Aug), *ibid.*, 423–4. 'It was so extremely cold' – FN>Eli (end July), *ibid.*, 416. 'Fritz remarked wrily that his misguided publisher' – *ibid.*, 414–5. 'had endured a "day of hell"' -*ibid.*, 416. 'by sending off his insulting letter to Georg Rée' – *ibid.*, 'Paul Rée and Lou Salomé had decided to spend a few weeks at Schuls' – Binion, 116–7.

415 'a letter of friendly admonition . . . he had overstepped 'every *accepted* mean' – FN>Eli (end July), *SBKSA* 6, 416. 'the most beautiful book of post-Christian times' – Kös>FN, 20 May, *BW* III/2, 377. 'I am delighted that Zarathustra's mood' – 24 July, *ibid.*, 383–4. 'N's response to this down-to-earth criticism' – FN>Kös, (3 Aug 83), *SBKSA* 6, 417–8.

415–6 'The first proofs of *Zarathustra* II' – FN>Kös, *ibid.*, (447).

416 'Schmeitzner was by now so debt-ridden' – FN>Ida Ov, *ibid.*, 424. 'had developed a "veritable hatred" for his sister' – *ibid.*, 437. 'it has bowled me over' – Kös>FN, 21 Aug, *BW* III/2, 391.

418–9 '("The Night-Song"), which he had composed one night in May' – see *Eh*, § 4 of '*Thus Spake Zarathustra*', *KSA* 6, 341; Kaufmann's *Ecce homo* (paperback), 302.

421 'Where I found the living . . . the Will to Power' – *KSA* 4, 147–8.

424 'The Now and the Past on earth' – *ibid.*, 179.

## 32. 'Midday and Eternity'

427 'Every word of my Zarathustra' – FN>Eli (29 Aug 83), *SBKSA* 6, 439–40. 'belated distribution of printed copies of Zara I' – FN>Kös, *ibid.* 442. 'What a path from *The Birth of Tragedy*' – CvG>FN, 7 Sept, *BW* III/2 (206).

428 'Among Franziska N's friends in Naumburg' – see FrN>FN, 10 April 1877, *BW* II 6/1, 528; 26–27 Aug, *BW* II 6/2, p. 1150; Janz I, 38. 'occasionally visited by her two sons, Paul and Bernhard' – see FN's ref. to Bernhard Förster in FN>Eli, 20 Jan 77, *SBKSA* 5, 216. 'instructor at the famous Friedrich Gymnasium' – details derived from H.F. Peters, *Zarathustra's Sister*, 41–42. 'intellectual heroes were Ernst Hasse' – on Hasse, see Carlton Hayes, *A Generation of Materialism*, 244, 276; George Mosse, *The Nationalization of the Masses*, 91–94. 'and Adolf Stöcker' – Hayes, *op. cit.*, 199, 200, 244, 258, 261; Janz II, 575–6. 'Heinrich von Treitschke' – Hayes, *op. cit.* 242–4; P. Viereck, *Metapolitics*, 203–6. 'we talked and talked like two books' – Eli>FN, *BW* II 6/1, 480–1. 'this "kindly" Berliner' – FrN>FN, 10 April 77, *BW* II 6/1, 528. Bernhard Förster 'as a vehement anti-Semitic agitator' – FrN>FN (31 May 1880), *BW* III/1, 72.

428–9 RW: 'I am like a phantom' – *CWD*, 17 April 1881.

429 'wrote to Wagner, asking him to sign' – *CWD*, 19 April 82. Peters, *Zarathustra's Sister* (p. 51), claims that Förster asked Elisabeth to collect signatures in Naumburg for this petition. Förster 'involved in a bloody brawl' – Peters, *op. cit.*, 51. 'wilfully "egotistical" philosophy, which . . . she herself found detestable' – Eli>Clara Gelzer, 24 Sept to 2 Oct 82, *Dok*, 151–2.

429–30 'been completely wrenched from the path of my life' – Eli>Kös (Peter Gast), 7 Jan 83, *Dok*, 284.

430 'I sincerely congratulate Dr. Förster' – FN>Eli (late July 83), *SBKSA* 6, 415.

430–1 'To be a good German means to de-Germanize oneself' – *MAM* II ('Mixed Opinions and Maxims'), § 323.

431 On the heated arguments with 'Lieschen' at Naumburg, see EF-N, *Leben FNs* II/2, 469–70; *Beg.* (251), 467–8. 'There now reigns in our lovable Germany' – FN>Schm, *SBKSA* 6, 446. 'Schmeitzner . . . promptly replied' – *BW* III/2, 21

Sept 83, (209). 'Early in October Fritz said good-bye . . .' – FN>FrN/Eli, *SBKSA* 6 (463).

431–2 'his old lodgings . . . had been rented out' – *ibid.*, (464).

432 'Informed that Malwida vM . . . La Spezia', FN>MvM, *ibid.*, 453. 'his nervous seizures were recurring' – FN>Kös, *ibid.* (467). 'Italy, from Spezia southward' – FN>FrN/Eli, *ibid.* (468). 'that Barcelona had a sunnier climate than Genoa' – FN>Paul Lanzky (13 Oct 83), *ibid.* (466). 'the stubbornly Italianophilic Köselitz' – Kös>FN, 'two rapturous letters from a romance-language scholar' – Paul Lanzky to FN, 19 Oct 83, *BW* III/2 (212). On Lanzky, see Janz II, 250–3; and Lanzky's own account of his friendship with FN, in *Beg.*, 508ff. 'inviting N to visit him at Vallombrosa' – Lanzky>FN, *BW* III/2 (219).

432–3 'He vented his ill-humour on his sister' – FN>Eli, *SBKSA* 6, (471).

433 'All the experiences of the past year . . .' – FN>MvM, *ibid.* (472). 'The same plaintive note . . . was sounded' – FN>Ov (9 Nov), *ibid.* (473) 'struck by many lofty beauties' – Ov>FN, *SBKSA* 6, 13 Nov (215).

433–4 'This time it is no long fixed individual observations' – JBur>FN, 10 Sept 83, *BW* III/2 (207).

434 'as far as the fortified fishing village of Villefranche' – FN>Kös, *SBKSA* 6, (474). 'Nietzsche was at first put off by this large seaside resort' – FN>FrN/Eli (4 Dec), *ibid.*, (475). 'Nizza, as a *French* city' – FN>Kös, *ibid.*, 457.

435 'sharing meals in the dining-room with a Prussian general' – FN>FrN/Eli, *ibid.*, 459. 'he urged Köselitz to leave Venice' – FN>Kös, *ibid.*, 457. 'Köselitz . . . replied that he was more penniless than ever' – Kös>FN 7 Dec 83, *BW* III/2, (217). 'good-bye to the "colourful dinner-table company"' – FN>Ov (24 Dec from Villa Mazzoleni), *ibid.* (477). 'if not the pleasure of warmth' – FN>FrN/Eli, *ibid.* (478). 465. 'On 18 January 1884 N surprised his publisher' – FN>Schm, *ibid.* (479). 'strictly speaking in . . . 3x2 weeks.' – FN>Ov (25 Jan 84), *ibid.* 466. 'row with his German landlady' – *ibid.*, 467.

435–6 'You now have the most future-rich book' – FN>Schm, *ibid.* (485).

436 'freer form of presentation' – ER>FN, 22 Dec 83, *BW* III/2 (218). 'The "confession" that followed' – FN>ER (22 Feb 84), *SBKSA* 6 (490).

437 'Never had his health been better' – see, for ex., FN>Kös (25 Feb 84), *ibid.*, (491); and *ibid.* (493). 'somewhere along the "Canale Grande"' – FN>Kös (5 March), 484. 'Zarathustra is ever more magnificent' – Kös>FN, 25 March, *BW* III/2, 428–9.

438 'He who has always spared himself much' – *KSA* 4, p. 194. 'Oh you loving fool, Zarathustra' – opening section ('*Der Wanderer*' *ibid.*, 196.)

440 'the human beings, like the houses, have all grown smaller' – '*Von der verkleinernden Tugend* (Of virtue that makes small) -*ibid.* 211. 'Their ideal is *Mittelmässigkeit*' – *ibid.*, 215. 'reaches the gateway to a "great city"' – in section titled *Vom Vorübergehen* (On passing by) – *ibid.*, 222–5.

441 'unstable Viennese poet named Siegfried Lipiner' – on Lipiner, see Janz I, 781–3; his letters to FN, in *BW* II/6/2; FN>Ov (7 April 84), *SBKSA* 6, 494; and several mentions in CosW's diary, Sept 1878. 'An entire essay could be written' – it would include the older David Strauss, betrayer (in the name of conventional facility) of the upright youthful critic he had once been; the once liberal and now arch-Catholic exponent of Christian mysticism, Joseph von Görres; cult-forming practitioners of 'spiritism', like the renowned Leipzig professor, Zöllner; and even the former libertine and now fervently Catholic Franz Liszt. 'For a father, he doesn't worry . . .' – *KSA* 4, 229. 'How I would like to *laugh* with you' – *SBKSA* 6, 475.

442 'These are: *Wollust* (voluptuous lust) . . .' – section entitled 'Of the three evils'

(*Von den drei Bösen*, *KSA* 4, 235–40).

443 'Everything goes, everything returns . . .' – § 2 of 'The Convalescent' (*Der Genesende*), *KSA* 4, 272–3.

444 'It was not to this torture-cross . . .' – *ibid.*, 274–5.

## 33. Knights and Ladies of the *Gaya Scienza*

446 'sent a postcard to Henrich Köselitz' – FN>Kös, *SBKSA* 6, (499). 'he had to write another one' – *ibid.*, (501). 'N's response was prompt and sympathetic' – *ibid.*, (500). 'the 29-year-old Resa von Schirnhofer' – see her account of this first encounter in her reminiscences, in *Beg.* (256), 473ff; also Janz II, 268–81.

448 'On 21 April N finally left Nice' – FN>Kös (telegram), *SBKSA* 6 (506). 'in the San Canciano district' – FN>Ov, *ibid.*, (507). 'disruptive force of a whirlwind' – FN>Ov, 21 May, *ibid.*, (513). On Joseph Paneth, see Janz II, 254–7; also pp. 35–36 of Paul-Laurent Assoun's *Freud et Nietzsche*, which deals with Paneth's friendship with Freud, who was both fascinated and curiously paralyzed by FN's books. 'Regard me rather as someone who has unfurled his flag' – FN>Paneth, *SBKSA* 6, (511).

449 'Who knows how many generations . . .' – FN>MvM, *ibid.*, 499. 'My task is immense' – FN>MvM (early June), *ibid.* (516). 'The two weeks N spent in Basel' – later described by FN>Ov (12 July), *ibid.*, (518). 'as though I was living among cows' – FN>Kös, *ibid.* (522). 'the old "colony of kindred souls" idea' – FN>Ov (12 July), 512.

450 'From Basel N moved on to . . . Zürich' – with a brief stop-over at Lucerne and a longer one in a hotel above Airolo, near the southern end of the St. Gothhard tunnel – see FN>Ov, *ibid.* (518). A cholera epidemic in Chiavenna had made it impossible to reach Sils-Maria by the shorter Italian route. On Meta von Salis, see FN's letter (from Airolo, 12 July), *ibid.* (519), and Janz II, 297–305. 'first meeting with N had been a "halcyonic" moment' – so described in her reminiscence, *Beg.* (258), 485–8. 'the first (336) from *Morgenröte*' – wrongly numbered as 335 in Meta's reminiscences, *ibid.*, 487.

451 'he was glad to leave the torrid . . . city of Zürich' – FN>Kös (from Sils-Maria, 25 July), *SBKSA* 6, 522. 'with a small library of books which had been carefully preserved for his return' – see Eugénie Galli's touching description of Herr Durisch's grocery shop, modest house, and the books FN used to leave with him, for use the following summer, in *Beg.* (263), 500–2. 'my theory that the world of Good and Evil . . .' – FN>Ov (23 July), *SBKSA* 6, 514. 'With a spartan rigor' – Durisch's description, to Galli, *op. cit.* 'in a long . . . threadbare brown jacket' – Emily Fynn, in *Beg.*, 495.

452 'The first was Helen Zimmern' – see her reminiscence in *Beg.*, (262). 'an elderly Russian spinster, Mademoiselle de Mansuroff' – FN>FrN (2 Sept 84), *SBKSA* 6, 527. 'the dark green lake, the nearby wood' – Resa v S, in *Beg.* (260), 489. 494; FN's invitation, *SBKSA* 6 (25 July), (523); her reply (28 July) *BW* III/2 (236).

452–3 'Leaning against the door-jamb' – *Beg.*, 492–4.

453 'the visit to Sils-Maria of Heinrich v Stein' – HvS>FN, 17 May 84, *BW* III/2 (232); FN>Kös (3 Dec 82), *SBKSA* 6, 289, on Stein being 'dumbfounded by *The Joyous Science*' 'the Law that is over me, my task' – FN>Stein, *ibid.*, (514). 'When Heinrich von Stein reached Sils-Maria' – FN>Stein (20 Aug), *ibid.*, (527); FN>Kös, 2 Sept 84, *ibid.* 525; FN>Ov, 14 Sept, 531; FN>Kös, 20 Sept, 535; Stein>FN, 24 Sept, *BW* III/2 (241). 'no more than twelve sentences in the *Zarathustra* trilogy' – FN>Ov, 14 Sept, *SBKSA* 6, 531.

454 'Knights and Brothers Fraternity of the *gaya scienza*' – FN>Kös, 2 Sept, *ibid.*, 524. 'at last a man with a . . . *heroic* disposition' – FN>Resa v S (2 Sept), *ibid.*, 528. FN's health: 'it was better in Venice' – FN>Kös, *ibid.*, 525. 'His sister Elisabeth had just written to say' – FN>FrN (20 Sept), *ibid.*, 536. 'if *Der Löwe von Venedig* . . . was to be staged' – Kös>FN, 22 Aug 84, *BW* III/2, (237); Kös>FN, 5 Sept, *ibid.*, 238. 'Realizing . . . that the despondent Köselitz' – FN>Ov, 14 Sept, *SBKSA* 6, 532.

454–5 'Nietzsche began by writing to F. Hegar' – FN>Kös (20 Sept) *ibid.*, 534.

455 'the score of . . . "Jest, Ruse, and Revenge"' – *ibid.* 'his *Singspiel* extravaganza was "absurdly orchestrated"' – Kös>FN, 23 Sept, *BW* III/2 (239). 'cart away 104 kilograms of books' – FN>FrN (4 Oct), *SBKSA* 6, 538. 'uninterrupted "Nizza-like" succession' – FN>Kös (30 Sept), *ibid.* 537; FN>Ov, 4 Oct, 539. 'Hegar offered him a "festive" welcome' – FN>Kös, *ibid.*, 537. On Robert Freund, friend of the Rothpletz (Ida Overbeck's) family, see Ov>FN, 4 April 76, *BW* II/6/1, 307–8. 'went to call on Gottfried Keller' – see FN>Keller, from Sils-Maria 20 Sept, *SBKSA* 6, (535). '*Ich glaube, dä Kerl ischt verruckt*' – Freund's account of their meeting in *Beg.*, 506. 'had been joined by his sister Elisabeth' – FN>Ov, 4 Oct, *SBKSA* 6, 539.

456 'Fritz in such a merry mood', EF-N, *Leben* II/2, 537–8; *Beg.* (268), 507 'Whoever sees you as I have' – Eli>FN, 20 Oct, *BW* III/2, 467; Also, FrN on Eli's admiration for her brother, *ibid.*, 471. 'preliminary copying-out of the orchestral score' – FN>Kös, *SBKSA* 6, (541). 'Köselitz's "Lion" overture had been granted' – FN>Kös, *ibid.* (546). 'showed N's "victory letter" to his . . . father' – Kös>FN, 20 Oct, *BW* III/2 (250). 'his orchestral assistant Weber' – Kös>FN, 25 Nov, *ibid.* (260).

456–7 'reasonably assured that his protégé' – On FN introducing Kös to Hegar and others, see FN>FrN (30 Oct), *SBKSA* 6, 549; FN>Ov (551).

457 'without a single acquaintance to talk to' – FN>FrN/Eli (14/15 Nov), *ibid.*, 556; (28 Nov) 561; 'without a theatre or concert hall', 556. '*Mistral-Wind, du Wolken-Jäger*' – FN>Kös (22 Nov), *ibid.* (557). 'the "community of kindred souls" idea' – FN>Stein, 18 Sept, *ibid.* (534). 'Stein understood this well' – Stein>FN, 24 Sept, *BW* III/2, (241). See, in *SBKSA* 6, (562), FN's doleful poem of regret, 'Hermit's Longing' over Stein's negative response.

457–8 'On 26 November N left Menton' – FN>Paul Lanzky, *ibid.* (559).

458 'Paul Lanzky, who had left his hotel at Vallombrosa' – FN>FrN/Eli (4/11 Dec 84), *ibid.*, 568. '*Geht die Welt nicht schief* . . .' – FN>Resa v S, *ibid.*, (561). 'whom N met at the Nice dockside' – FN>Lanzky, *ibid.* (559). 'He has a notion of who I am' – FN>FrN/Eli, *ibid.*, 568. 'Someone get me a cook!' – FN>FrN/Eli (early Jan 85), *SBKSA* 7, 3.

459 Stein's response to N's poem – Stein>FN, 7 Dec 84, from Berlin, *BW* III/2, 484–6 – 'was a *dark* letter' – FN>FrN/Eli, *SBKSA* 7, 4. On FN's desperate longing to be surrounded by disciples, and his wild hope that some day a philanthropic well-wisher would offer him a castle in which to lodge a 'circle of high-minded and brave persons', see Paul Lanzky's testimony in *Beg.*, 514–5.

## 34. 'Very Black and Squid-like'

460 'marked in January 1885 by below-zero temperatures' etc. – FN>FrN/Eli (14 Jan 85); 'furious three-day storm' – FN>FrN (29 Jan), *SBKSA* 7, (570, 571). 'Except we turn back and become as cows' – 'with a "sublime finale"' – FN>CvG, 12 Feb 85 *SBKSA* 7, (572); 'in the form of a "divine blasphemy"' – FN>Kös (14 Feb, 573). 'Did He not create the World in his own image' – *AsZ*

IV ('The Awakening') *KSA* 4, 389. 'the word "publicity" and "public"' – FN>CvG, *SBKSA* 7, 9.

460–1 'privately produced by C Naumann' – FN>Naum, 12 March, *ibid.* (579).

461 'to extract some 6,000 francs' worth' – FN>CvG, *ibid.*, (572). 'In Basel both the Academic Society' – Ov>FN, 15 Feb, *BW* III/4 (268). Paul Lanzky 'increasingly . . . getting on N's nerves' – FN>FrN/Eli, (14 March), *SBKSA* 7, 22. 'highly limited edition of 20 copies' – FN>Naum, 12 March, *ibid.*, (579). 'Kös . . . had just left Zürich' – Kös>FN (12, 26 March), *BW* III/4 (271, 274). 'Although put out by this sudden . . . "flight"' – FN>Kös (14 March), *SBKSA* 7 (580); Ov>FN, 28 March, *BW* III/4 (275). 'N finally decided to join his . . . "disciple" in Venice' – FN>Kös (30 March), *SBKSA* 7, (588). 'His eyes were now constantly watering' – FN>Ov, 31 March; FN>H. Schiess (late April); FN>FrN (end April), *ibid.* (589, 597, 598). 'Venice . . . proved a bitter disappointment' – FN>Ov, 7 May, *ibid.*, (599). 'Oh Genoa and Nizza!' – FN>Eli (7 May), *ibid.*, (600). 'now that thickly forested Vallombrosa' – Lanzky>FN (early June) *BW* III/4 (281).

461–2 'Elisabeth . . . had been bombarding him with letters' – Eli>FN (3 May), *ibid.* (278).

462 'This of course was wishful thinking' – FN>Eli, 20 May; FN>FrN (end May), *SBKSA* 7, (602, 604). 'knowing who he really was' – FN>Eli (mid-March), *ibid.*, (583). 'persuading their uncle, Bernhard Dächsel,' – Eli>FN, 3 May, *BW* III/4, (278). 'to print forty . . . copies of *Zarathustra* IV' – FN>Naum (19 March), *SBKSA* 7, (585). 'On 6 June N left Venice' etc. – FN>FrN, 5 June, *ibid.*, 56. 'the entire Engadine steamed and stewed' – FN>FrN (26 June), (606). 'lady named Luise Röder-Wiederhold' – FN>FrN, *ibid.*, 55; L. Röder-W to FN, 30 May 85, *BW* III/4 (280); Kös>FN, 26 March, *ibid.*, 15. 'At times the impenitent idealist' – FN>Resa v S, *ibid.* (607).

463 'finally felled by a week-long seizure' – FN>Ov (13 July), *ibid.*, 66. 'After the "angelically" patient Frau Röder' – L. Röder>FN, 7 July, (from Chur), *BW* III/4 (284). 'But worst of all: she has no manners' – FN>Kös, 23 July, *SBKSA* 7, 70. 'above all because she appreciates good manners' – FN>Eli, *ibid.*, 65–66. 'a widow, Mrs Emily Fynn' – see her reminiscences of FN in *Beg.*, (280); also her letters to FN, 19 Sept, 4 Oct, *BW* III/4 (295, 298) and FN>EF, *SBKSA* 7, (627). 'her "swan-like" poise and movements' – praised in *Beyond Good and Evil*, § 252 (*KSA* 5, 196), as a rare virtue possessed by the 'most beautiful Englishwomen', in marked contrast to the loutish raucousness of their (Methodist) hymn-singing menfolk.

464 'Distinguished, for example' – FN>Kös, 23 July, (613). 'In August the oppressive heat' – FN>Kös, 21 August, *ibid.*, (624). 'With the conclusion of the harvest' – FN>Eli, 21 Aug, *ibid.*, 88. 'another visit to "cloud-covered" Germany' – FN>FrN/Eli, *ibid.*, 92.

464–5 'his mother's repeated pleas' – FrN>FN (9 June, end Aug), *BW* III/4 (282, 293).

465 'He was also nagged by a sense of guilt' – FN>FrN/Eli, 6 Sept, *SBKSA* 7, (629). 'who no longer had a publisher' – FN>Eli, *ibid.*, (621, 625); FN>Kös, 21 Aug, (624). 'reaching Naumburg the next day' – FN>Kös (22 Sept); FN>Ov (6 Oct) *ibid.*, (630, 632). 'alternately *ranting* and riding' – FN>Ov, *ibid.*, 97. 'to have him married to the daughter' – *ibid.* 'Schmeitzner had . . . been "bending with the wind"' – FN>Ov (early Dec) *ibid.*, 117–8. 'The price Schmeitzner was demanding' – FN>Eli, 21 Aug, FN>Schm, 20 Oct, *ibid.*, (625, 637). 'hired the services of a clever Jewish lawyer' – Kaufmann>FN, 23 Oct, *BW* III/4 (304). 'to celebrate his forty-first birthday' – FN>Ov, 17 Oct, *ibid.*, (636). 'privately he shared his mother's misgivngs' – FN>Eli (7 Feb 86), *ibid.*, (669). 'On 1

November Fritz was accompanied' – FN>FrN, *ibid.*, (640).

465–6 'In gloomily overcast Munich' – FN>Eli (7 Nov), *ibid.*, (641).

466 'where an aging star-gazer with snow-white hair' – FN>RvS (24 Nov) *ibid.*, (647). 'From Florence, now shepherded by Paul Lanzky' – FN>FrN (7 Nov) *ibid.*, (642). 'Hardly pausing for breath' – FN>Lanzky (9–10 Nov), *ibid.*, (643). 'It was *highly worthwhile*' – FN>Eli (11 Nov), *ibid.* (644). 'to a "perfect" second-storey bedroom' – FN>FrN, (10 Dec), 125. 'over the square des Phocéens' – FN>Kös, 24 Nov 85, *ibid.*, 114. 'The air . . . is incomparable' – FN>Kös, *ibid.* 'none of the three *Zarathustra* volumes' – FN>Ov, *ibid.*, 117–8.

466–7 'a bottle of Munich's Kindl-Bräu beer' – FN>Eli 20 Dec, *ibid.* (653).

467 'On Christmas Day' etc. FN to Bernhard/Eli Förster, *ibid.*, (654). 'Stimulated by an "everlasting" succession of bright . . . days' – FN>RvS, 2 Jan 86; FN>FrN (5 Jan); FN>Ov (9 Jan), *ibid.*, 133, 135, 138. 'a second, follow-up volume to *Morgenröte*' – FN>Credner (mid-Jan 86), *ibid.*, (663). 'Credner's response . . . was not unfavourable' – Credner>FN, 26 Jan 86, *BW* III/4 (339). 'an advance of 40 marks for every sixteen pages' – Cr>FN, 6 Feb, (342). 'On the 15th N's sister left Hamburg' – FrN>FN, 11 Feb, *ibid.* (345); Bernhard and Eli Förster to FN, (shortly before 15 Feb, 346). 'after receiving a melancholy letter from Fritz' – FN>EF-N (7 Feb) *SBKSA* 7, (669). 'Instead she sent a note to Irene von Seydlitz' – IvS>FN, 19 Feb, *BW* III/4 (348). 'Thanks to two woollen shirts' – FN>Eli, 12 March, *SBKSA* 7, 159–60.

467–8 'On 27 March he informed Hermann Credner' – FN>Cr, *SBKSA* 7, (679).

468 'a second letter of explanation' – FN>Credner, *ibid.*, (682). 'like "very black, almost squid-like" ink' – FN>Kös (21 April), *ibid.* 181. In German: '*sehr schwarz, beinahe Tintenfisch*' – a pun on the German word for 'inkwell', *Tintenfass*. 'sent the manuscript to his old Pforta tutor' – FN>FrN (28 April), *ibid.* (692). 'he occupied the composer's apartment' – Kös>FN, 1 April, *BW* III/4, 152. 'After nine lonely days' – FN>Kös (7 May), FN>Max Heinze (7 May), *SBKSA* 7, (695, 696). 'Irene von Seydlitz had written to N' – 19 Feb 86, *BW* III/4 (348). 'stretched taut in his problem' – FN>Irene vS, 7 May, *SBKSA* 7 (699). 'Reinhart and his wife had left for Berlin' – RvS>FN, 16 May, *BW* III/4 (379). 'When . . . Fritz reached Naumburg on 12 May' – FN>FrN, *SBKSA* 7 (700). 'visited by a Chemnitz "editor" named . . . Erlecke' – FrN>FN, 9 May, *BW* III/4, 170; Erlecke>FN, 8 May (374). 'that Erlecke was a disreputable scoundrel' – FN>Erlecke (shortly after 18 May), *SBKSA* 7, (701).

468–9 'Credner, who had not bothered to answer' – FN>Credner (shortly before 25 May; FN>Credner (presumably on 25 May, mentioning telegram, sent from Naumburg), *ibid.* (702, 703).

469 'In early June N moved to Leipzig' – FN>Kös, 5 June, *ibid.*, (706). 'He had already asked . . . Naumann to provide him' – FN>Naum, 3 June, *ibid.*, (705). 'The estimate was more than what he had expected' – FN>Naum, *ibid.* (705). 'On 5 June he sent a telegram to Kös' – *ibid.*, (706). 'he asked Paul Widemann to join them' – *ibid.*, (707). 'reduce the "outrageous" price . . . 12,000 marks' – FN>Ov, 20 June, 196. 'the temperature soared to 30 degrees Celsius' – FN>Eli and Bernard Förster, 2 Sept, *ibid.*, 240. 'rented from the schoolteacher . . . Janicaud' – FN>Widemann, *ibid.* (707). 'distraught behaviour of Erwin Rohde' – FN>Eli/B.Förster, *ibid.*, 240. 'On 27 June Nietzsche could at last leave Leipzig' – FN>Kös, *ibid.*, (714). 'to perform "Peter Gast's" latest brainchild' – FN>Ov, 20 June, *ibid.*, 196. 'When Fritzsch heard that Nietzsche' – FN>Fritzsch, 5 July, *ibid.*, (718). 'after making a two-nights stop-over in Chur' – FN>FrN, *ibid.* (717).

470 'Schmeitzner . . . sent N an itemized listing' – Schm>FN, 1 July, *BW* III/4

(387). 'Nietzsche's irritated response' – FN>Ov (14 July), *SBKSA* 7 (rough draft) 203, (sent letter) 208. 'N's "absolute blindness for . . . business matters"' – Schm>FN, 3 April 86, *BW* III/4 (363). 'all things considered, RW was the only one' – FN>Ov, *SBKSA* 7, 207–8.

470–1 '"intellectually frustrated" and exhausted' – FN>FrN, *ibid.*, 209, 214–5.

471 'the now inseparable Anglo-Russian "trio"' – *ibid.*, 215. 'Refuse to admit Women's Emancipation as one may' – FN>Kös, *ibid.*, 213–4. 'that Naumann's competent printers' – FN>Naum, *ibid.*, (728). ' a telegram from Ernst . . . Fritzsch' – FN>Ov, *ibid.*, (729). 'not to be "embittered and estranged"' by what he read' – *ibid.*, 223.

471–2 'print order of 1,250 copies' – Credner>FN, 6 Feb, *BW* III/2 (342).

472 'goldsmith's art and expertise' – *MR*, preface, § 5, *KSA* 3, 17. 'a scathing "critique of modernity"' – *Eh*, § 2 of '*Beyond Good and Evil*', *KSA* 6, 350.

473 '"stillest hour" of solitude' – see final chapter, '*Die stillste Stunde*', in *Zarathustra* II, *KSA* 4, 187–90.

477–8 'I have yet to meet a German' – *JGB*, § 251, *KSA* 5, 193.

478 '*Genie des Geldes und Geduld*' – *ibid.*, 194. 'the English . . . as not being a "philosophical race"' – *ibid.*, § 252. 'N's quarrel with Hobbes' – explained in *JGB* § 294, and based on Hobbes's criticism of laughter when indulged in at the expense of others, in *Leviathan* I, ch. 6. 'gloomier, more sensual, more strong-willed' – *JGB*, § 252, 195. 'English clumsiness and peasant seriousness' – *ibid.*, 196.

479 'three "respectable but mediocre Englishmen"' – *ibid.*, § 253, 196. '"damnable Anglomania" for modern ideas' – *ibid.*, 197. 'European *noblesse*' – *ibid.*, 197. 'a "long ladder in the Order of Rank"' – *JGB*, § 257, 205. '"more completely beasts"' – in German '*die ganzeren Bestien*': *ibid.* 206.

480 'N had not yet read Alexis de Tocqueville's' – the only reference to Tocqueville in FN's letters was made later, in Feb 87, FN>Ov, *SBKSA* 8, 28, in which he explained that he had not finished reading Tocqueville and Taine; this presumably included T's *L'Ancien Régime*. 'Madame de Rémusat's reminiscences' – mentioned in his books and in letter to Overbeck, July 84 (*SBKSA* 6, 514).

481 'Life itself is *essentially* appropriation' – *JGB*, § 259. 'because life is precisely will to power' – *ibid.*, *KSA* 5, 208.

483 'Walter Kaufmann, in his commentary' – *Beyond Good and Evil*, Vintage Books edition, fn., p. 228.

## 35. The Genealogy of Morals

484 'Nietzsche's Dangerous Book' – *Der Bund* article first mentioned by FN to Naumann, 19 Sept 86, *SBKSA* 7 (749); FN>Kös (20 Sept), *ibid.* (751). 'included ten university professors' – FN>Eli/B.Förster, 2 Sept, *ibid.*, 240–1. 'It is entirely in this sense . . .' – quoted by FN>MvM (24 Sept), *ibid.* 258. 'one cannot think of a greater enticement' – FN>Naum, *ibid.* (749). 'There are truths . . . "spoken into one's ear"' – (20 Sept) *ibid.*, 253. 'how Man can be "made greater"' – 22 Sept, *ibid.* (754).

485 'Replying a few days later' – JBur>FN, 26 Sept, *BW* III/2 (403). 'more impressed by Taine's reaction' – Taine>FN, 17 Oct, *ibid.* (411); FN>Ov, *SBKSA* 7, 265; FN>FrN (26 Oct), 269; FN>RvS (767). 'To help Fritzsch sell' – FN>Fritzsch, 7 Aug, *ibid.* (730). 'stigmatized it as "badly written, ponderous"' – *GdT*, '*Versuch einer Selbstkritik*', § 3, *KSA* I, 14. 'had completed the first two prefaces' – FN>Fritzsch, *SBKSA* 7 (740). 'already preparing a third for

*Morgenröte*' – FN>Kös, 2 Sept, *ibid.*, (742). 'unexpected arrival of Meta von Salis' – see *Beg.* (291), 553–7.

485–6 'Heaven have mercy on European understanding' – 19 Sept, *SBKSA* 7 (750).

486 'N on 25 September' – FN>MvM, 24 Sept, *ibid.*, 256. 'at Ruta Ligure' – FN>Emily Fynn, 2 Oct; FN>Naum, 4 Oct; FN>Kös , 10 Oct; FN>FrN (10 Oct); FN>Ov, 12 Oct; FN>G. Keller, 14 Oct – *ibid.*, (757, 758, 760, 761, 763). 'where his disappointing "disciple"' – FN>FrN, *ibid.* (760); also Lanzky's account in *Beg.*, 515–6, 521–2. 'living quarters at the Pension de Genève' – FN>Gen. Simon (20 Oct?), *SBKSA* 7 (764). 'What a melancholy autumn!' – FN>RvS, 26 Oct, *ibid.* (768); RvS>FN, 22 Oct, *BW* III/4 (412). 'had completed his preface to *Morgenröte*' – FN>Fritzsch, early Nov, *ibid.* (772). 'both being "friends of the lento"' *MR*, Preface, § 5. 'preface for . . . new edition of *The Joyous Science*' – FN>Ov, 14 Nov, *SBKSA* 7, 282.

487 'could not penetrate the windowpanes' – Pension's south-facing rooms were more expensive: see FN>Ov, 25 Dec, *ibid.*, 294. 'encouraged his "ice-cold thoughts"' – FN>MvM, 13 Dec, *ibid.*, 290. 'In late December . . . N sent the fifth book of *The Joyous Science*' – FN> Fritzsch, *ibid.* (784).

491 'the toad-like croackings, the tomb-stone voices' – Epilogue (§ 383) of *The Joyous Science*. '*Ich wohne in meinem eignen Haus*,' etc. *FW*, *KSA* 3, 343. 'finally found . . . a sunny, south-facing room' – FN>Ov, *SBKSA* 8 (788).

491–2 FN in Monte Carlo, to hear *Parsifal* overture: FN>Kös (21 Jan 87): 'the very highest psychological awareness' – *ibid.*, 12.

492 'The instinct of kinship' (with Dostoevsky) – FN>Ov (23 Feb 87), *ibid.* (804). 'Encouraged by Overbeck' – Ov's letter has disappeared, but is mentioned in FN>Kös (7 March 87), *ibid.*, 41–42.

493 On Nice earthquake, FN>Kös, *ibid.* (805); FN>FrN (806); FN>RvS (807). 'only sixty-five copies (of *Beyond Good and Evil*) had . . . been sold' – Naum>FN, 22 Feb 87, *BW* III/6 (436). 'by a kind of slow, "subterranean" process' – FN>Naum, 2 March, *SBKSA* 8 (810). 'By the third week of March' – FN>FrN (22 March), *ibid.* (818).

493–4 'villa run by a reliable Swiss couple' – FN>Ov, 24 March, *ibid.* (820).

494 'The train trip . . . was a nightmare' – FN>Ov, 14 April, *ibid.*, 58. 'eyes . . . to react with a plaintive "No"' – FN>Kös (4 April), *ibid.*(827) 'This spot . . . is lovelier than any spot on the Riviera' – FN>Kös, 55. 'He was fed up with Sils-Maria' – FN>Ov, 14 April, *ibid.* (831). 'with me a *catastrophe* is being prepared' – *ibid.*, 57–58. 'in Venice, where there was not a free room to be rented' – see FN> Kös (15 April), *ibid.* (832); again (19 April), (834); Kös>FN, 22 April, *BW* III/6 (453). On FN's despair at not being able to go to Venice, see FN>Kös (26 April), then postcards indicating he was going instead to Zürich, *ibid.* (835, 836, 837).

494–5 FN reaching Zürich in state of prostration – FN>Fritzsch, 29 April, *ibid.* (838); pathetic letter to Overbeck, (839).

495 'one of the few pleasant moments . . . during ten dismal days' – FN>Kös (4 May); FN>Ov (4 May); FN>FrN (10 May), *ibid.* (842, 843, 844). 'He called on Friedrich Hegar' – FN>Eli, 5 June, *ibid.*, 84. 'Meta von Salis was . . . in Zürich' – FN>Eli, *ibid.*; and Meta's later reminiscence in *Beg.* (291), 575. 'The year she had spent in Paris – FN>MvM, 12 May, *SBKSA* 8, 71; and Resa von Schirnhofer's reminiscence in *Beg.* (295), 571–4. Natalie Herzen had been a personal friend of Turgenev, who had died four years before in his country-house near Paris. 'cheaply lodged in a schoolteacher's suburban house' – FN>Ov, 13 May from Rosenhügel, *SBKSA* 8 (847), in which FN also described the shameless behaviour of Heinrich Adams.

495–6 'nothing to console him, "neither man, nor book, nor music"' – *ibid.*

496 '"*old* men, such as J. Burckhardt or H. Taine"' – FN>ER, 12 May, *ibid.* (846). 'Taine was vastly overrated' – Rohde's two letters to FN have unfortunately disappeared, but their tenor can be judged by FN's replies: FN>ER, 19 May, praising Taine as a 'brave pessimist', then (23 May) apologizing for his angry outburst, *ibid.* (849, 852). 'the corrected page-proofs of "We Fearless Ones"' – FN>Fritzsch, *ibid.* (853). 'Sils-Maria, now too "popular"' – FN>Kös, 20 May, 8 June, *ibid.*, 79, 86; 'and to go to Celerina' – FN>Lendi, *ibid.* (857). 'warmly welcomed by the grocer-mayor' – FN>FrN, *ibid.* (862). 'the mountainsides were still beautifully clothed' – *ibid.*

496–7 'Beset by headaches' – FN>Ov, 17 June, *ibid.*, 93.

497 '114 copies of *Beyond Good and Evil*' – FN>Eli, 5 June, *ibid.*, 84–5; FN>Naum, 24 June (866). 'state of "literal décadence"' – FN>Kös (22 June), *ibid.*, 95. 'hymn designed to be sung "in memoriam"' – FN>Fritzsch, *ibid.*, 97–8. News of Heinrich von Stein's death – FN>Ov, 30 June, *ibid.*, 103.

497–8 'I really loved him' – FN>Kös, 27 June, *ibid.* (868).

498 'Sils-Maria's two hotels were completely filled' – and for details in next two paragraphs, see Meta von Salis's reminiscence, *Beg.* (296), 575–87 (also full of fascinating information about FN's literary tastes and his admiration for enterprising women. 'Emily Fynn, her daughter' – FN>Ov (17 July), *SBK.* 8, 110.

499 'in his "bad news" letter of 22 February' – *BW* III/6 (436). 'had completed a small *Streitschrift*' – FN>Naum, *SBKSA* 8 (877).

500 'the truly great haters in the history of the world' – *GM*, § 7, *KSA*, 267. 'had called the Jews "great haters"' – *MAM*, ; similar statements in *MR*, § 38, 377.

501 'All that has been done on earth against "the nobles"' – *GM*, § 7. '"The masters" have been disposed of . . .' – § 9, *KSA* 5, 269.

502 'the witches' cauldron of unsatisfied hatred' – § 11, *KSA*, 274. 'the beast of prey, the magnificent *blond beast*' – *ibid.*, 275.

503 'Walter Kaufmann, in commenting this passage' – in *Nietzsche – Philosopher, Psychologist, Antichrist*, 225. 'this "western tip of Asia"' – in German, '*Asien und sein vorgeschobenes Halbinselchen Europa*', in § 52 of *Beyond Good and Evil.*

505 'The last form of political gentility' – *GM*, § 16, *KSA* 5, 287–8. 'God sacrificing himself for the guilt of mankind' – *ibid.*, § 21. 'whose Olympian gods were mirror-images of "nobler . . ."' – § 23.

507–8 'the notion of "sin" was a pernicious invention of semitic thought' – *MAM*; and again in *FW*, § 135.

## 36. The Marvels of Turin

509 'when his old Pforta friend, Paul Deussen' – FN>Kös, 30 Aug, *SBKSA* 8, 138; FN>FrN (4 Sept), 141; FN>E. Fynn, 7 Sept, 142; FN>Kös (8 Sept), 143–4. 'since the two philologists had last seen each other' – FN>RW (10 Oct 1874), *SBKSA* 4, 265. 'For N it was a joy to take his visitors' – see Deussen's description in *Beg.*, (297a), 587–8; and Meta von Salis, *ibid.*, 579. 'after adding a fascinating third essay' – 'What is the meaning of ascetic ideals?'; 'and sending the amplified text' – FN>Naum, 28 Aug, *SBKSA* 8, (897). 'On 20 September' – FN>Kös, telegram, *ibid.*, (915).

510 'Despite an electrifying thunderstorm' – FN>Ov (24 Sept), *ibid.* (918) 'he found his favourite *maestro*' – FN>FrN (10 Oct), *ibid.*, 164. 'correct the proofs of his new book' – FN>Naum (15 Oct), *ibid.* (926). 'Nightmarish . . . was the next train trip' – FN>Kös, 23 Oct, *ibid.* (937). 'the "intoxicating" air of Nice' –

FN>Kös, 27 Oct, *ibid.*, 179–80. 'N suffered "blue fingers" in the morning' – *ibid.*, 178. 'Heeding his mother's sensible advice' – FrN>FN, 25 Oct, *BW* III/6, 95; FN>FrN, 31 Oct, (23 Nov), *SBKSA* 8 (941, 956). 'a "fire-idol" around which' – FN>Kös, 24 Nov, *ibid.* (958). 'filled with "nut-cracking" problems' – FN>JBur, *ibid.* (952).

510–1 'moving letter of thanks . . . from Georg Brandes' – Brandes>FN, 26 Nov, *BW* III/6 (500).

511 'the intellectually most brilliant Dane' – FN>Kös, 20 Dec, *ibid.*, 213 'In his long reply, written on 2 December' – FN>Brandes, *SBKSA* 8 (960). 'Ernst Wilhelm Fritzsch was asked' – FN>Fritzsch, 2 Dec 87, 6 Jan 88, *ibid.* (961, 972); FN>Kös, 15 Jan 88, *ibid.*, 232. 'take a copy of *Zarathustra* IV' – FN>Kös, 6 Jan 88, *ibid.*, 226. 'The four months N spent in Nice' – FN>FrN, 20 March 88, (1005). 'benevolence of his "fire-idol" stove' – FN>Ov, 3 March, *ibid.*, 266. 'improvement in the quality of the food' – FN>FrN (17 Feb), 257. 'was a Baroness Plänckner' – FN>FrN, 20 March, *ibid.*, 273.

511–2 'frail health of . . . Crown Prince Friedrich' – FN>FrN, 5 March, 269. On FN's sadness over the illness and death of the Crown Prince, see FN>FrN, 5 March 88, *ibid.*, 269; FN>Kös, 20 June, 338–9.

512 'no wine, no beer, no alcoholic spirits' – FN>FrN, 20 March, 272. 'he was a "brave" but "sick animal"' – FN>FrN, (17 Feb – rough draft, then posted fragment), *ibid.* (995, 996). 'shamelessly superficial reviews of his books' – see, for ex., FN to Carl Spitteler, 10 Feb (preliminary draft, then posted letter), *ibid.* (987, 988); FN>Kös, 13 Feb, *ibid.*, 252; FN>Josef Viktor Widmann (editor of *Der Bund*), 13 Feb, *ibid.* (992); as well as hostile reviews, accusing him of being 'eccentric', 'pathological', 'psychiatric' – FN>RvS, 12 Feb, *ibid.*, 248–9. '"unbearable tension" from which he suffered' – FN>FrN (17 Feb), 256. 'the completion of a four-volume work' – in its initial form, outlined by FN on 17 March 1887 (while he was in Nice), the first volume was supposed to deal with 'European Nihilism', the second was to be a 'Critique of the highest values', the third elaborated the 'Principle of a new Establishment of Values', while the fourth and final volume investigated 'Cultivation and Breeding' (*Zucht und Züchtung*), *NF*, *KSA* 12, 318. '*Zarathustra* "trilogy" was merely an ornamental "entrance-hall"' – FN>MvM, (early May 1884), *SBKSA* 6 (509), 49. 'This new series, as later planned,' (in late August 1888) – see *NF*, *KSA* 13, 537–8.

513 'A "History of European Nihilism"' – already mentioned in the third essay of *GM*, *KSA* 5, § 27, 408–9. '"The anarchism of Prince Krapotkin"' – Brandes>FN, 15–17 Dec, *BW* III/ 6, 131. 'he kept altering the initial outline' – *NF*, *KSA* 12, 318, dated 17 March 1887; modified in autumn, *ibid.* § 10 (58) (186), pp. 490–1; in early 1888, plan for 4-book work first entitled *Umwerthung der Werte*, then (underneath) *Umwerthung aller Werte* (*KSA* 13, 194), immediately followed by 372 planned aphorisms for the first two books, 195–211. 'I have readied the first draft of my "Attempt . . ."' – FN>Kös, *SBKSA* 8, 252. 'Zürich, despite the friendships' etc. – FN>Kös, *ibid.*, 277.

514 'Replying on the 30th' – Kös>FN, *BW* III/6, 183. 'Turin was a clean, quiet city,' – FN>FrN (31 March), *ibid.* (1012). 'the most confused and catastrophic' (trip) – FN>Kös, 7 April, *ibid.*, 284–5; for an excellent description of this chaotic trip, see Lesley Chamberlain's *Nietzsche in Turin*, 11–12. 'Fortunately the heavy trunk' – FN>Ov,10 April, *SBKSA* 8, 291. '"But *Turin*!" he began ecstatically' – FN>Kös, *ibid.*, 285–6.

515 'in a corner-house belonging to . . . Davide Fino' – details from L. Chamberlain, *N in Turin*, 21–23. On Davide Fino's reminiscences of FN, as garnered by German 'scholars', see Karl Strecker (author of a book on FN and

Strindberg), and his two contributions to *Beg.*, (310a, 310b), 614–8; Victor Helling, *Beg.*, 618–20. 'usually a *minestra* (soup)' – FN>Ov, *SBKSA* 8, 292. 'dry Alpine air was so "sublimely clear"' – FN to C. Fuchs, 14 April *ibid.*, 294. 'A few paces from his frontdoor' – FN>Resa von Schirnhofer, 14 April, *ibid.* (1019). 'arcades and vaulted passageways' – FN>FrN (20 April), *ibid.*, 301. 'exchange of letters with Georg Brandes' – FN>Brandes, 27 March, *ibid.* (1009); Brandes>FN, 3 April, *BW* III/6 (533).

515–6 'Astonished that a non-German' – FN>Brandes, 10 April, *SBKSA* 8, (1014).

516 'a fascinating discussion of the conflicting opera styles' – Kös>FN 4 Nov, *BW* III/6 (492); FN>Kös, 10 Nov, *SBKSA* 8 (948); Kös>FN, 12 Nov, *BW* III/6 (495); FN>Kös, 24 Nov, *SBKSA* 8 (958); Kös>FN, 23 Dec 87, *BW* III/6 (508); Kös>FN, 9 Jan 88 (511); FN>Kös, 15 Jan 88, *SBKSA* 8, 233; Kös>FN, 24 Jan, *BW* III/6 (515); FN>Kös, 13 Feb, *SBKSA* 8, 251; Kös>FN, 17 Feb, *BW* III/6 (519); FN>Kös, 26 Feb, *SBKSA* 8 (1000); Kös>FN, 8 March, *BW* III/6 (528); FN>Kös, 21 March, *SBKSA* 8, 275. 'I am in a good mood,' – FN>Kös, *ibid.* (1022). 'in one more rhapsodic letter' – FN>Kös, 1 May, *ibid.* (1025). 'a packed auditorium of 300 listeners' – Brandes>FN, 29 April, *BW* III/6, (537). '*Sic incipit gloria mundi*' – FN>Deussen, 3 May, *ibid.* (1026).

516–7 'hanging a "tiny tail of buffoonery"' – FN>Brandes, 4 May, *ibid.* (1030).

517 'keep the temperature from rising to a hot 31°C' – FN>FrN, 10 June, *ibid.*, 328. 'His beloved valley seemed to be steaming' – FN>Meta von Salis, 17 June, *ibid.*, 335. 'they had suffered twenty-six avalanches' – *ibid.*, FN>FrN, 328. 'shocked by the "sky-high" prices' – FN>FrN (16 June), *ibid.*, 334. '*a perla perlissima* of beauty' – FN>Kös, 14 June, *ibid.*, 331. 'it began to snow, and then to rain' – FN>Kös, 20 June, *ibid.*, 338. 'no let-up in the wet weather' – FN>FrN, 25 June, *ibid.*, 342; FN>Ov, 4 July, 347; FN>FrN (7 July), 348–9; FN>Ov, 11 July (1058); FN>Naum, 12 July (1059); FN>Kös, 17 July, 354. 'manuscript of his new book on 26 June' – FN>Naum, *ibid.* (1052). 'the text was so disorderly' – Naum>FN, 6 July, *BW* III/6 (551). 'asked him to send back the ms.' – FN>Naum, *SBKSA* 8, (1059).

518 'That same night the temperature dropped below zero' – *ibid.*, 350. 'the rewritten text back to Naumann' – FN>Naum, 16 July, *ibid.* (1060) 'to carry the title: *Der Fall Wagner*' – FN>Kös, *ibid.*, 355. 'Köselitz's response was . . . ecstatic' – Kös>FN, *BW* III/6 (560).

## 37. The 'Cave-bear' of Sils-Maria

519 'During the second week of August' – FN>Emily Fynn, 11 Aug, *SBKSA* 8, 386; FN>Kös, 11 Aug, *ibid.*, 389. 'the most beautiful colours' – FN>FrN (13 Aug), *ibid.*, 392. 'Meta von Salis chose this auspicious moment' – see FN's invitation, 17 June, *ibid.*, 335; Meta's response, in *Beg.* (299), 593; arrival date at Sils (2 August), FN>FrN, *SBKSA* 8, 381. 'the first woman ever to obtain a degree' – according to Janz II, 304–5; her doctor's dissertation for Zürich University's Faculty of Philosophy was devoted to Agnès de Poitou, wife of the German Emperor Henry III, who ruled the Empire as regent from 1056–1062, during the youth of her son, Henry IV – FN>MvM, 30 July 87, *SBKSA* 8, 119. 'and even volunteered to row her curious mentor' – MvS, in *Beg.* (299), 593–7. 'After ten days of fine weather the rains returned' – FN>FrN, 22 Aug, *SBKSA* 8, 394. 'Proud though he was of his anti-Wagner "pamphlet"' – FN to Meta vS (22 Aug), *ibid.*, 396–7.

519–20 '*Umwertung aller Werte*' – on FN's constantly changing schemes regarding form and contents, see *NF, KSA* 13, 503, 508, 515–6, 519–20, 535–8.

520 '"driven by the spirit" (of inspiration)' – FN>Meta v Salis, *SBKSA* 8, (1102). '"far and away the cleanest" manuscript' – FN>Naum, *ibid.* (1103). 'Naumann's heart-warming response' – 11 Sept, *BW* III/6 (577). 'In 4 days alone 220 millimeters' – FN>Kös, *SBKSA* 8, 416. 'almost inundating the highway from Silvaplana' – *ibid.* (1106).

520–1 '"the meeting-place of Italy and Finland"' – quoted by L. Chamberlain, *N in Turin.*

521 'who had shamefacedly admitted that he was not musically talented' – Brandes>FN, 29 April, *BW* III/6 (537). 'as a "Herr Cosmopoliticus"' – FN>Brandes, 13 Sept, *SBKSA* 8 (1107). 'The movement is now more than ever haloed' – FN>JBur, 13 Sept, *ibid.* (1108).

521–2 'The little church of Sils-Maria' – FN>RvS, 13 Sept, *ibid.* (1110).

522 'to make a joint donation of 2,000 marks' – FN>Deussen (22 July), *ibid.* (1068); FN>FrN, 24 July, 366; and Deussen's account in *Erinnerungen an FN*, 94–98, and in *Beg.*, 588–9. 'subtle expression of my entire *philosophical heterodoxy*' – FN to Deussen, 14 Sept, *ibid.* (1111). 'On 20 September N was at last able to say goodbye' – FN telegram to Naumann 18 Sept, *ibid.* (1120). 'near the flooded town of Como' – FN>Kös, 27 Sept, *ibid.*, 444. 'Nothing, to his delight, had changed' – *ibid.*

522–3 'This new book . . . was "roughly twice as strong"' – FN>Kös, *ibid.*, 417–8.

523 'he had left his parents' home near Dresden' – Kös>FN, 11 Sept, *BW* III/6. (576). 'You have brought your artillery up' – Kös>FN, 20 Sept, *ibid.* (581) 'he was choosing *Götzen-Dämmerung*' – FN>Kös, 27 Sept, *SBKSA* 8, 443.

524 'Can an ass be tragic?' – *G-D, Sprüche und Pfeile*, § 11. 'unfavourably compared to Heraclitus's courageous acceptance' – *ibid.*, '*Die "Vernunft" in der Philosophie*', *KSA* 6, 74–79. 'Christianity, growing from Jewish roots' – *ibid.* § 4, 101; Penguin Classics, 58. 'Sample: "Learning to think:"' – § 7, *ibid.*, 65; *KSA* 6, 109. 'Excursions of an Untimely Man' – Penguin Classics, 67–104; *KSA* 6, 111–53. 'Thomas à Kempis' – § 4, '*The Imitatio Christi*'. 'Schopenhauer' – § 21, 22; 'Immanuel Kant' – § 29.

525–6 'overjoyed by the "cold stream of cognition"' – CvG>FN, 23 Sept, *BW* III/6 (582).

526 'for her gift copy of *The Case of Wagner*' – Meta vS>FN, 30 Sept, *ibid.* (583). 'though he had given mankind "the most profound book"' – FN>MvM, *SBKSA* 8 (1078).

526–7 'The *truly* virtuous . . .' – MvM>FN, 12 August, *BW* III/6 (565).

527 'after asking . . . Naumann to send three copies' – *SBKSA* 8 (1125). 'the greatest philosophical event of all time' – FN>MvM, 4 Oct, *ibid.* (1126). 'When . . . Hans von Bülow . . . failed to answer a letter' – FN>Bülow, 10 Aug, *ibid.* (1085). 'You have not answered my letter.' – FN>Bülow, *ibid.* (1129). 'not only Wagner but also Liszt a *Hanswurst*' – MvM>FN (fragment, mid-Oct), *BW* III/6 (591). 'These are not things about which I permit contradiction' – FN>MvM, *SBKSA* 8 (1131).

528 'The ancient Jews were originally a vigorous healthy people' – *AC*, § 25. 'the toughest national will-to-life' – *AC*, § 24, 27. 'the capricious element of luck or chance' – § 24.

529 'a theocracy directed by cringing bigots' – § 26. 'A revolt against a fatally corrupted, decadent form of religion' – § 27. 'But what of this "holy anarchist"' – § 27, 28. 'Here N confessed himself baffled' – § 28, 29. 'an astonishing mixture of the sublime, the sickly and the childish' – § 31. 'After praising the young David Strauss' – § 28. 'Ernest Renan ("that buffoon in psychologis")' – § 29. 'True life, eternal life is found . . . it is *within you.*' – § 29.

530 'a man of Dostoevsky's acute psychological insight' – § 31. 'the only absolutely genuine Christian there has ever been' – § 39. 'a message of "glad tidings" that belonged to no specific time or place' – § 32. 'When it became a faith, Christianity' – § 40.

530–1 'familar image of the . . . long-awaited Messiah' – § 40.

531 'a downright terrifyingly absurd answer: God gave his son for the forgiveness of sins' – § 41. 'What might have become . . . a serene . . . authentically non-violent "peace movement"' – § 42. 'Buddhism makes no promises' – § 42.

531–2 'What Paul managed to do' – § 42, 43.

532 'What was the only thing Mohammed later borrowed from Christianity?' – § 42. 'to denounce fornication as a sin against the body' – *First Epistle to the Corinthians*, ch. VI, 18–20. 'by inventing an "Amphitryon-figure"' – *AC*, § 34. Paul's 'hostility towards the "good" philologists and physicians of Alexandria' – § 47.

532–3 'Woman was God's *second* blunder' – § 48.

533 'From the very outset it had been a wilfully stupid, anti-intellectual religion' – § 51, 52. 'The way in which a theologian' – § 52.

## 38. The Collapse

534 'The sixty-two extant sections of *Der Antichrist* . . . may well have been left unfinished.' In a letter to Ov, 18 Oct (*SBKSA* 8, 453), FN simply indicated that this first of four books of his *Umwertung aller Werte* (Revaluation of all Values) series was now ready for the printer, and that each volume would appear separately. 'on the occasion of his forty-fourth birthday . . . he was suddenly "visited"' – see the short 'Ode to Happiness' FN composed to celebrate 'this perfect day, when everything is ripening and not only the grape turns brown', when he had decided to relate for himself the story of his life: placed between the Preface and the first chapter of *Ecce homo*. See also FN>Naum, 6 Nov, *SBKSA*, 464, in which he explained that, thanks to an 'incomparable feeling of well-being' and a wonderful autumn, he had managed between 15 Oct and 4 Nov to complete the story of his life, his books, and his opinions in a 'fragmentary fashion'. 'I am warlike by nature' – *Eh*, 'Why I am so wise', § 7. 'the words that Pontius Pilate' – Gospel of St. John, 19:5. 'Walter Kaufmann, argued' – in combined paperback ed. of *The Genealogy of Morals* and *Eh*, Vintage Books (1967), 204. 'finished in first-draft form on 4 November' – FN>Naum, 6 Nov, 464.

534–5 Kaufmann: '*Ecce homo* is one of the treasures' – *op. cit.*, 201.

535 'one whom Thomas Mann regarded as superior' – as quoted on jacket-cover of Kaufmann's *Nietzsche – Philosopher, Psychologist, Antichrist* 'I am, for example, not at all a bogey' – Preface to *Eh*, § 2. 'No, it's not a question of your nerves' – 'Why I am so wise', § 1.

535–6 'My experiences entitle me' – in 'Why I am so wise', § 4.

536 'that the rudest word, the rudest letter' – *ibid.*, § 5.

536–7 'Being *able* to be an enemy' – *ibid.*, § 7.

537 'When I wage war against Christianity' – *ibid.* 'had never experienced any "genuinely *religious* difficulties"' – 'Why I am so clever', § 1.

537–8 '"God", "immortality of the soul"' etc. – *ibid.*

538 'German cooking: "What doesn't it have on its conscience!"' – *ibid.* 'The German climate alone' – *ibid.*, § 2. 'Even as ardent an admirer as Walter Kaufmann' – in 'Editor's Introduction' to Vintage paperback ed. of *Genealogy of Morals* and *Eh*, 205.

539 'The few cases of high culture' – *Eh*, 'Why I am so clever', § 3. 'That I do not read but *love* Pascal' – *ibid.*

539–40 'I vainly seek in all the realms of . . . history' – *ibid.*, § 4.

540 'Here, where I speak of the relaxations of my life' – § 5.

540–1 'From the moment on when there was a piano score of *Tristan*' – § 6.

541 'a paragraph that outraged . . . Ernest Newman' – 'Now that I look back from a certain distance' – *Eh*, 'The Untimely Ones', § 3.

541–2 'Anyone with the slightest residue of superstition' – *Eh*, '*Thus Spake Zarathustra*', § 3.

542 'This work stands altogether apart' – *ibid.*, § 6. 'preferred pure fountain-water' – *Eh*, 'Why I am so clever', § 1.

542–3 'On 30 October, five days . . .' – FN>Kös, *SBKSA* 8 (1137); and 1 Nov reply of B. Savornin, manager of the Pension de Genève, *BW* III/6 (598

543 'On 6 November N sent the text . . .' – FN>Naum, *SBKSA* 8 (1139). 'An exchange of letters followed – Naum>FN, 15 Nov, *BW* III/6 (604); FN>Naum, 19, then 25 Nov, *SBKSA* 8 (1149, 1156); Naum>FN, 28 Nov, *BW* III/6 (617); FN>Naum, 26 Nov, *SBKSA* 8 (1158); Naum>FN, 28, then 29 Nov, *BW* III/6 (617, 618). 'not altogether satisfied . . .' N asked Naum to return second half of ms. – 27 Nov; 'and . . . asked Naum to send back the entire text' – 1 Dec, *SBKSA* 8 (1161, 1167). *Ecce homo* would 'be sensational best-seller' – FN>Naum, 25 Nov, *ibid.* 487.

543–4 'astonishing letter . . . from . . . August Strindberg' – AS>FN, *BW* III/6 (early Dec 88), *BW* III/6 (621). 'in reply to Nietzsche's query' – FN's letter to Strindberg has been lost. It was at the suggestion of Georg Brandes, a personal friend of Strindberg (16 Nov, *BW* III/6, 353), that FN had written to the Swedish playwright.

544 Strindberg, 'who had translated one of his plays into French' – FN>Brandes, 20 Nov, *SBKSA* 8, 483: written after reading AS's play, *Les Mariés* – praised in FN letter to Strindberg, 27 Nov, *ibid.* (1160). 'But, as he wrote to Strindberg . . .' – FN>AS, 8 Dec, *ibid.* (1176). 'He immediately dashed off a letter' to Helen Zimmern – FN>HZ (8 Dec) *ibid.* (1180).

544–5 'Carl Spitteler had written a laudatory article on *The Case of Wagner*' – Spitteler>FN, 6 Nov, *BW* III/6 (600).

545 'while Peter Gast had managed to place' – Kös>FN, 7 Dec (including mention of Avenarius's laudatory 'coda'), *ibid.*, 373; FN's anger over Avenarius' shabby treatment of Heine, FN>Ov, 20 July 88, *ibid.*, 362. 'FN immediately wrote to Avenarius' – (10 Dec), *ibid.*, 516–7. 'Again working at the same . . . tempo' – FN>Naum (15 Dec), *ibid.* (1191). 'In a . . . witty reply, Strindberg' – AS>FN, 11 Dec, *BW* III/6 (625). 'giving him the title – *Nietzsche contra Wagner*' FN>Naum, *ibid.*, 530. 'having not heard from . . . Jean Bourdeau' – FN>JB (17 Dec), *ibid.* (1196); mentioned by FN as editor of *Journal des Débats* etc. in letter to Naum, (17 Dec), 529; Bourdeau's reply, 27 Dec 88, *BW* III/6 (636). 'a two-word telegram (*Ecce vorwärts*)' – FN>Naum (20 Dec), (1201).

545–6 'he had decided to shelve *Nietzsche contra Wagner*' – FN>Kös (1207).

546 'very brief preface for *N contra W*' – dated 'Turin Christmas 1888', *KSA* 6, p. 415. Still unsure if *Ecce homo* should be given absolute priority, FN now foresaw publication of *Nietzsche contra Wagner* in 1889, FN>Naum, 27 Dec 88, (1213). 'His fame had spread to the salons of Petersburg' – thanks, notably, to a feminine admirer, Princess Anna Dimitrievna Tenischeff, whose 2 Dec 88 'thank-you' letter (for a gift copy of *Der Fall Wagner*) can be found in *BW* III/6 (609); rough draft of FN's reply in *SBKSA* 8, 510. 'Paris, where Hippolyte Taine' – who had recommended Jean Bourdeau, a better connoisseur of German literature than

himself: HT>FN, 14 Dec *SBKSA* 8 (627). 'He is my "*Carthago est delenda*"' – Strindberg>FN (early Dec), *BW* III/6 (621).

546–7 'fits of rage which now occasionally seized him' – see Anacleto Verrecchia, 'Nietzsche's Breakdown in Turin' (extracts translated from his *La catastrophe di Nietzsche a Torino*), included in Robert P. Harrison's *Nietzsche in Italy*, p. 105–12. 'Davide Fino's two daughters' – Giulia, whom FN did not particularly like, and Irene, with whom he liked to play four-hand pieces on the family piano: *ibid.* 'angrily tearing up letters' – also bank-notes, *ibid.*, 112. The letters torn up may have included a nasty 40th-birthday letter that his anti-Semitic sister had written to him from Paraguay, reproaching him for consorting with Jewish riff-raff ready to help themselves from every pot, like Georg Brandes: a letter that so angered FN that he mentioned it in an otherwise cheerful Christmas letter to Overbeck, *SBKSA* 8 (1210). Discussed by Lesley Chamberlain in her remarkable *Nietzsche in Turin*, 172–3.

547 'the "internal" symptoms of a growing irrationality' – brilliantly treated by L. Chamberlain in the eleventh and final chapter ('Collapse into the Beyond') of *N in Turin*. 'a destructive blow against Christianity' – FN>Brandes, rough draft, *SBKSA* 8 (1170). 'the "deepest conscience-collision" in the history of mankind' – FN>Kaiser Wilhelm II, *ibid.* (1171). 'he wrote to the German Chancellor' – FN>Bismarck (rough draft), *ibid.* (1173). 'the old god is abolished,' – FN>Meta von Salis, rough draft, (1177). 'the only woman I have revered' – FN>CosW, rough draft, (1211).

547–8 'I want to straitjacket the "*Reich*"' – FN>Ov (26 Dec), (1212).

548 'On 29 December . . . perfectly reasonable letter' – FN>Naum, (1220). 'the "destruction of the House of Hohenzollern"' – FN>Kös, rough draft (30 Dec 88), *ibid.* (1227). 'On New Year's Eve' – FN>Strindberg, *ibid.* (1229). 'Willing, frenziedly willing!' (in Greek, *thelo thelo manimai*!) Strindberg>FN, *BW* III/6 (645).

548–9 'three short letters . . . to Cosima Wagner' – *SBKSA* 8 (1240, 1241, 1242). 'It is a presupposition that I am a man' – *ibid.* (1241). Lesley Chamberlain, *N in Turin*, is particularly good in analyzing the symbolic significance of these oneirico-psychopathic transmogrifications, in ch. 11, already referred to, and in dealing frankly with the syphilitic roots of these megalomaniacal hallucinations. 'in short letters sent to Georg Brandes' etc – thus numbered in *SBKSA* 8, Brandes (1234); Kös (1247); Cardinal Mariani (1254); King Umberto I (1255), MvM (1248).

549 'Others, signed "Dionysus"' – FN to: ER (1250); Deussen (1246); Bülow (1244); Ov (1249); JBur (1245). 'N sent Burckhardt a second, far longer letter' – 6 Jan 89, (1256). FN's bedroom 'had to look "like a temple"' – Verrecchia, *op. cit.*, 105.

550 'On seeing a cart-driver' etc. – discussed at some length by Verrecchia, *op. cit.* 'The curious thing about this incident' – FN>RvS, 13 May 88, *SBKSA* 8, 314. '*Pas malade! Pas malade!*' – Verrechia, *op. cit.*, 106. etc. – 'Professor Carlo Turina', who, according to Janz III, 40, came to see FN four times: details obtained from a collection of F. Overbook's papers preserved in Basel University's library (fn. 187, *ibid.*, 395). 'Not content with playing for hours on the piano' – Verrecchia, *op. cit.*, 111–2.

550–1 'a totally naked Nietzsche' – Verrecchia, 107–8, basing his account on information provided by Kurt Liebmann in *Nietzsches Kampf und Untergang in Turin*. This was apparently not the first time that FN had indulged in such 'Dionysian' antics; for Davide Fino's wife had once seen him in action while peeping through the keyhole of his bedroom door. Franz Overbeck was always extremely reluctant to describe exactly what he had seen, even to a close friend like Kös. On FN's obsession with the Dionysus-Zagreus myth, a penetrating analysis in the tenth chapter of L. Chamberlain's *N in Turin*.

## 39. The Aftermath

552 'When . . . Overbeck finally reached the corner house' – Janz III, 38–9. 'Ov found him slumped in one corner of the sofa' – so described by Ov in long letter to Kös, written one week later, on 15 Jan 1889, *ibid.*, 39; see also Ov's later account, '*Erinnerung an Friedrich Nietzsche*', published in the *Neue Rundschau*, in 1906, and included in *Beg.*, (105), 644–8. 'Overbeck in later years was reluctant' – Janz III, 41–42, quoting from C. A. Bernouilli, *Franz Overbeck und Friedrich Nietzsche*, vol II, 251. 'A German doctor named Baumann' – Janz III, 45, appendix (13), 308, based on E. Podach, *Nietzsches Zusammenbruch*. 'Ov described N as singing and "raving" on the piano' – quoted in Janz III, 39. 'Ov had hurried out to a recently opened clinic' etc. – Janz III, 37–38.

552–3 'I am having all antisemites shot' – FN>Ov/Ida (4 Jan 89), *SBKSA* 8, (1249).

553 'a German dentist named Bettmann' – Janz III, 40–41, 43–45. 'borrowing his landlord's *papalina*' – Verrecchia, in Harrison's *N in Italy* , 112. 'broke into a Venetian gondoliers' song' – and not a Neapolitan fishermen's song, as had been claimed: Janz III, 45. 'At the Basel railway station' – *ibid.*, 46–47; and Ov's report to Kös of his trip to Dr. Wille's psychaitric clinic' – *ibid.*, 49–50. 'For the first few days he was an unruly patient' – first page of chapter entitled 'Jena' in E. F. Podach's *Nietzsches Zusammenbruch*. 'Three days after N's internment Franziska' – Janz III, 51–52.

554 'Franziska insisted that he (FN) be . . . transferred to another psychiatric clinic' – *ibid.* 'N's once mobile features resembled a mask' – *ibid.*, 53. 'The train trip from Basel' – see Professor Mähly's description of his son's ordeal and his remark, after his return to Basel that he felt lucky to have come home in one piece: *Beg.* (315), 648–9. Jacob Brand identified in Janz III, 82. 'to take care of the financial details' – *ibid.*, 83. '1866: syphilis through contagion' Podach, *FNs Zusammenbruch*, 174–8 'a young medical student named Simchowitz' – S. Simchowitz, art. '*Der kranke Nietzsche*', in *Frankfurter Zeitung*, 7 Aug 1900; reprinted in *Beg.* (317a), 650–1; also a second reminiscence published for the 25th anniversary of FN's death, '*Der sieche Dionysus . . .*', in the *Kölnische Zeitung*, 29 Aug 1925; reprinted in *Beg.* (317b), 652–5. See also the testimony of the psychiatrist, Dr. Theodor Ziehen, extract from an unpublished interview with Richard Oehler in 1938, *Beg.* (318), 655–6. Ziehen, who later was appointed professor of Philosophy at Halle, was Professor Binswanger's assistant in 1889, and kept Overbeck informed of 'progress' made in FN's condition – Janz III, 84–85.

554–5 'to avert new outbreaks of maniacal fury' – Janz III, 85. Paul Deussen and his wife were among those who were not allowed to see FN, after visiting Franziska N in Naumburg.

555 'that he was the "Duke of Cumberland"' etc. – Janz III, 88–89. 'that N had but one or two years to live' – Podach, *op. cit.*, 139–40. 'neo-Cimarosan opera . . . *Die heimliche Ehe*' – Janz III, 102, 109. 'he was immediately recognized by N' – Kös>Ov, quoted in Janz III, 109. 'He did not look at all unwell' Kös>Carl Fuchs, Podach, *op. cit.*, 139–40, 19 (page refs from French edition). 'Ten days later Kös wrote again to Fuchs' – *ibid.*, 148–9, 181 (fn. to p. 148 – Kös letter to Fuchs, 1 Feb 1890, as publ. in *Der Tag*, 19 Sept 1924. On N having retained all of his musical sensitivity, see also the interesting testimony of an anonymous witness who was struck by the fact that every time a fellow inmate, a certain

Baron X, played the zither, FN would spring to his feet and begin dancing, *Beg.* (316). 'On 16 Feb Franziska N arrived' – Janz III, 109.

555–6 'They were joined one week later by Franz Overbeck' etc. – Janz III, 110–2.

556 'In early March Kös returned to Danzig' – *ibid.*, 113. 'Fritz played on the *Gasthaus*'s piano' – *ibid.*, 114–5, 117. 'Only once . . . was there a moment of crisis' – *ibid.*, 117–8. 'When, in September, Paul Deussen' – PD's account in *Erinnerung an FN*, included (but wrongly dated as 'April' 89) in *Beg.* (320a), and again in *Mein Leben*: *Beg.* (320b), pp. 658–60; Janz III, 124. Kös 'had felt like throwing himself out of the window' – *ibid.*, 80.

557 '*Twilight of the Idols* "pamphlet"' etc. – Naum>Ov, full text, *ibid.*, 310–11. 'Kös was appalled by the alterations' – Kös>Ov, 27 Feb 89, *ibid.*, 132. '*fire-belching* preface to the "Revaluation"' – Kös>Ov, *ibid.*, 311. 'Ov had discovered the ms of *Der Antichrist*' – 'A major problem confronting Naum, Ov and Kös' etc. – *ibid.*, 128–31. 'was way beyond her intellectual capacities' – FrN's nephew, Richard Oehler, even claimed that she had never read her son's books: art. in *Zukunft* 58 (1907), extract in *Beg.* (336), 683. 'to entrust this responsibility to . . . Edmund Oehler' – Janz III, 130.

558 'In June of the previous year . . . B. Förster' – ch. 11 in H. F. Peters' *Zarathustra's Sister*, also Janz III, 125–8, based on Podach, *Gestalten um Nietzsche*. 'Franziska N was waiting at the Naumburg station' – *ibid.*, 113, but Peters cites no source. 'Elisabeth found time to read "The Last Supper"' etc. – Janz III, 135–6. 'It's . . . enough to make one die of laughter' – Kös>Ov, *ibid.*, 131. 'In Sept of 1891 Edmund Oehler . . . died' – *ibid.* 'a second edition . . . of *Beyond Good and Evil*' etc. – *ibid.*, 144. 'Elisabeth . . . decided to start legal proceedings' – *ibid.*, 148–9.

559 'when Kös turned up in Naumburg' – *ibid.*, 143. 'All the available documents . . . were turned over to a local lawyer' named Wilde: *ibid.*, 146–7. 'Finally, in early February of 1892 – *ibid.*, 148–50. 'Elisabeth returned by ship to Paraguay' – *ibid.*, 151. 'I am dead because I am stupid' etc. – *ibid.*, 153–4.

560 'In Sept 1893 Elisabeth returned from Paraguay' – *ibid.*, 159. 'where she had managed to find a buyer' – Peters, *ZS*, ch. 13. 'had obliged their mother to pierce a doorway' – *ibid.*, 155–6, 167. Naum 'had launched the *Gesamtausgabe* series' – *ibid.*, 168–9. 'At a tense meeting in Leipzig' – graphically (perhaps too graphically) described by Peters (with imprecise letter references) as having taken place on 23 Oct 1893. 'In Berlin Elisabeth recruited Hans Koegel' – also written Kögel, notably by Janz, *ibid.*, 160. 'turned into a "Nietzsche Archives" room' – *ibid.*, 162–7. Janz, with admirable impartiality, gives Elisabeth due credit for her determination to establish an 'archive' for her brother's manuscripts (*ibid.*, 164). What she did with it thereafter is, of course, another matter. For added details on how this 'Nietzsche Archives' room was decorated, see Peters, *ZS*, 132. 'In Berlin Elisabeth recruited Fritz Koegel' – also written Kögel, as in Janz III, 160. 'N's occasional shouts from the floor above' – *ibid.*, 167. 'Initially captivated by Fritz Koegel's "salon charmer" manners' Peters, 134–5.

561 'launch a literary 'counter-attack' against Lou Andreas-Salomé' – already begun by 'Peter Gast' (Kös), as editor-in-chief of the *Gesamtausgabe* ed.: Janz III, 169–70; and Binion, *Frau Lou*, 162–4. 'Working at a furious tempo' – Janz III, 170. 'Heinrich Romundt, who had dared to praise' – *ibid.*, 169.

561–2 'Elisabeth . . . met Franz Overbeck in Leipzig' – *ibid.*, 177.

562 'a shattering experience . . . piteous condition' – *ibid.*, 177–8. 'mother's strenuous opposition to . . . *Der Antichrist*' – *ibid.*, 189. 'boldly decided to buy out her mother's rights' – *ibid.*, 194ff. Fritz Koegel was sent to Berlin' etc. – *ibid.*, 202. 'her brother's friend Meta von Salis' – who had already lent 500 marks to

EF-N to help her buy a compromising letter regarding some shady transactions in Paraguay: *ibid*. 'contract drawn up in December 1895' – *ibid*., 194–6; full text, 337–41. 'The intimidated Franziska was given no time' – *ibid*., 194–5. 'appended her "sour-blood" signature' – *ibid*., 196.

562–3 'the three Berlin "admirers"' – including the Leipzig 'philanthropist', Raoul Richter. Composed of three articles, the 26 Jan 1896 text mentioned only the total 'loan' sum of 30,000 marks, but Meta von Salis had volunteered to raise her share of the loan to 10,000 marks, if needed: *ibid*., 202–3; text, 341–3.

563 'The next "logical" step was taken' – *ibid*., 208–9. 'Koegel . . . proceeded to fall in love with . . . Emily' Gelzer – Peters, *ZS*, ch. 17. 'a bright young scholar named Rudolf Steiner' – 209. 'Meanwhile, from Christmas 1896 on' – hardly mentioned by Janz, who did, however, describe the bitter altercations between EF-N her mother's doctor, Oscar Gutjahr: *ibid*., 177. See also Peters, 160. 'Meta von Salis made a quick trip to Weimar' – *ibid*., 209–11. 'In June Fritz Koegel was dismissed' etc. – *ibid*., 209; and on Rudolf Steiner's withering opinion of EF-N's philosophical capacities, 173. 'Seized by the . . . *folie des grandeurs*' – *ibid*., 210; Peters, 161.

564–5 'the villa Silverblick received its first visitor' – 7 Aug 1897. On Kessler's origins and schooling, *ibid*., 165–6; on the villa Silverblick, EF-N and her brother, 166–7; quotations from a *Sonderdruck . . . der deutschen Schiller Gesellschaft*, 1968, vol XII, 72.

565 'heated in winter by a monumental green porcelain stove' – as I noticed during a visit to this dismally empty house made in May 2000. For safe-keeping even FN's books had been removed and were at that time stored in the cellars of Weimar's Stadtschloss. 'The most . . . socially significant of these visitors' – for ex. Resa von Schirnhofer, Nov 1897: in *Beg*. (343), 695–7. 'in a white linen gown' – and tended, as of old, by the FrN's servant-cook, Alwine: see Philo vom Walde's account of his visit, made in 1898: '*FN in Weimar', Wiener-Familien-Journal* 145 (1898), incl. in *Beg*. (345), 700–4, where Alwine is twice mentioned. 'The fashionable . . . painter Curt Stöving' – Janz III, 211; and on previous visit to Naumburg, 174 fn. 'looking like a "sick, caged bird"' – Peters's apt description, in *ZS*, 143. 'by another sculptor, Max Kruse' – Janz III, 215; marble bust, now in Nietzsche-Haus, Sils-Maria, *ibid*., 363. 'the noted painter Hans Olde' – *ibid*.; see also Steven Aschheim, *The Nazi Legacy in Germany*, 112–3.

566 EF-N 'began making overtures to H. Kös' – Janz III, 217. 'Naum is once again being sued' – Kös>Ov, 14 April 98, *ibid*., 217. 'To imagine that Frau Förster could intrude' – Kös>Ov, *ibid*., 220. 'when Isabella von der Pahlen' – description of her visit to Weimar in her book on FN's handwriting, *N im Spiegelbild seiner Schrift*, 42–45, publ. under her married name, v. Ungern-Sternberg; also in Janz III, 215–7.

566–7 'he succumbed to an attack of influenza' etc. – *ibid*., 221.

567 'Harry Kessler reached Weimar the next day' etc. – Peters, *ZS*, 171–3. Photo of FN's death-mask on p. 172. 'The same sterile scholasticism' – *ibid*., 173; and a longer description of the proceedings by Fritz Schumacher in his memoirs, *Stufen des Lebens: Erinnerungen eines Baumeisters*, included in *Beg*. (347), 707–8. 'Even more grotesque was the burial ceremony' – Janz III, 222–3.

568 'funeral oration . . . by Adalbert Oehler' – text in *Beg*., 760–2. 'brief "parting words" by Max Heinze' – *ibid*., 763. 'by Carl von Gersdorff . . . "*Have anima candida!*"', *ibid*. 'by Carl Fuchs' – *ibid*., 763–4. 'The *Bekenntnis* . . . delivered by "Peter Gast"' – *ibid*., 764–5. 'nine admirers quoted brief verses' – *ibid*., 765–6.

'Jacob Burckhardt had died three years before' – 8 Aug 97, Janz III, 210. 'Erwin Rohde had followed him' – 11 Jan 98, *ibid.*, 171. 'As for Franz Overbeck' – *ibid.*, 223–4.

## Epilogue

Most of the information in this Epilogue is derived from Steven Aschheim's meticulously researched *The Nietzsche Legacy in Germany 1890–1990*. Since this book, now available in paperback, contains an excellent index, I have often omitted exact page references for the 'sources' used, when they come from his valuable book.

569 'Among all radical parties (Socialists . . .)' – FN>Ov, *SBKSA* 8, 48. 'while the "open-endedness"' Aschheim, 14–15, 45.

570 'There grew within us a secret Messianism' – from *Geschichte und Zeiten: Erinnerungen* (1962), extract in Aschheim, 23.

570–1 'O thou my will! Thou end of every plight' – *AsS* III, *KSA* 4, 268–9.

571 'a "kitsch industry", actively promoted by . . . "N Archives"' – Aschheim, 34–7, 46–49.

572 FN's 'status as the "martyr of deep thought"' – *ibid.*

573 'Canon E. McClure, let loose with a savage indictment' – *ibid.*, 130–1. 'Thomas Beecham immediately replied' – P. Bridgewater, *N in AngloSaxony*, 147. 'compact edition of *Thus Spake Zarathustra* . . . 150,000 copies' – Aschheim, 135–6, 142.

574 '*Freikorps* minstrels' etc. – *ibid.*, 156–7.

574–5 'In October 1927, when Harry Graf Kessler . . .' *Tagebücher 1918–1937*, 5,12,13, and especially the 15 Oct entry, with Spengler's speech being dismissed as the work of a '*halbgebildeten Scharlatan*', pp. 543–6.

575 'Napoleon's "Hundred Days", . . . Benito Mussolini' – Peters, *ZS*, 218–9 'everything from the footman . . . to the major domo is a Nazi' – Kessler, *Tagebücher*, 7 Aug 32 entry, p. 681. 'like Ernst Horneffer' – Aschheim, 249.

575–6 'gala performance of *Tristan und Isolde*' – Peters, *ZS*, 220.

576 'with Hitler's favourite architect, Albert Speer' – Aschheim, 240. 'her grandiose funeral too was "graced" by . . . the Führer' – *ibid.*; also Peters, *ZS*, 224.

# Bibliography

Nietzsche's Works (in chronological order)


*Die Geburt der Tragödie* (The Birth of Tragedy) 1872

*Unzeitgemässe Betrachtungen* (Untimely Meditations)

1. *David Strauss, der Bekenner und Schriftsteller* (David Strauss, the Confessor and Writer) 1873

2. *Vom Nutzen und Nachteil der Historie für das Leben* (On the Utility and Disadvantage of History for Life) 1874

3. *Schopenhauer als Erzieher* (Schopenhauer as Educator) 1874

4. *Richard Wagner in Bayreuth* 1876

*Menschliches, Allzumenschliches* (vol I) (Human, All Too Human) 1878

2. *Vermischte Meinungen und Sprüche* (Mixed Opinions and Maxims) 1879

3. *Der Wanderer und sein Schatten* (The Wanderer and his Shadow) 1880

*Morgenröte* (Morning Glow) 1881

*Die fröhliche Wissenschaft* (The Joyous Science) 1882

Book V – '*Wir Furchtlosen*' ('We Fearless Ones') added in 1887

*Also sprach Zarathustra* (Thus Spake Zarathustra)

Part I (May), Part II (November) 1883

Part III 1884

Part IV (limited edition) 1885

*Jenseits von Gut und Böse* (Beyond Good and Evil) 1886

*Zur Genealogie der Moral* (The Genealogy of Morals) 1887

*Der Fall Wagner* (The Case of Wagner) 1888

*Götzen-Dämmerung* (Twilight of the Idols) 1888

*Der Antichrist* (The Anti-Christian) 1888

*Ecce homo* (written in 1888), posthumously published in 1908

*Nietzsche contra Wagner* (written in 1888) – 1895
*Der Wille zur Macht* (The Will to Power), (compiled by his sister), posthumously – – 1901

***

## Editions Used for this Biography

*Nietzsche Werke, Kritische Gesamtausgabe* – edited by Giorgio Colli and Mazzino Montinari. Berlin, Walter de Gruyter, 1967 ff.

*Nietzsche Werke, Nachgelassene Aufzeichnungen*, 4 vols (continuation of the *KGA* series by Johann Figl, H.G. Hödl, Ingo Rath, Wolfgang Müller-Lauter, Karl Pestalozzi, and others. Berlin, New York, Walter de Gruyter, 2000.

*Friedrich Nietzsche* (Collected Works), *Kritische Studienausgabe* – ed. by Giorgio Colli and Mazzino Montinari: Deutsche Taschenbuch Verlag (*dtv*), 15 vols Munich, 1999 (new ed.).

*Friedrich Nietzsche, Gesammelte Werke* (23 vols) – ed. by Richard Oehler, Max Oehler, Friedrich-Christian Würzbach. Munich, Musarion Verlag, 1922–1929.

*Nietzsche Briefwechsel* (Correspondence) – ed. by Giorgio Colli and Mazzino Montinari. Berlin, New York, Walter de Gruyter, 1975ff.

*Friedrich Nietzsche, Sämtliche Briefe: Kritische Studienausgabe* (FN's letters, paperback edition), 8 vols Munich, Deutscher Taschenbuch Verlag (*dtv*), 1986.

*Friedrich Nietzsche, Werke in drei Bänden* – ed. by Karl Schlechta. Munich, Hanser Verlag, 1960.

*Friedrich Nietzsche, Frühe Schriften* – ed. by Hans Joachim Mette and Rüdiger Schmitt, 5 vols Munich, C.H. Beck, 1994.

*Friedrich Nietzsche, Oeuvres,* 2 vols (Bouquins Collection) – edited by Jean Lacoste and Jacques Le Rider, with introductions provided by Peter Pütz, and a postscript by Georges Liébert on "Nietzsche et la musique". Paris, Robert Laffont, 1993.

Books concerning Nietzsche, his Life, Times, Historical, Musical, and Philosophical Context.

ANDLER, Charles. *Nietzsche: sa vie et sa pensée.* Paris, Bossard, 1920-1931.

ANDREAS-SALOMÉ, Lou. *Friedrich Nietzsche in seinen Werken.* Vienna, Carl Konegen, 1894.

——— *Erläuterungen zum Lebensrückblick: Grundriss einiger Lebens-*

*erinnerungen. Aus dem Nachlass* – ed. by Ernst Pfeiffer. Zürich, M. Niehan, 1951.

ARTZ, Frederick B. *Reaction and Revolution: 1814–1832*. New York, Harper Torchbooks, 1963.

ASCHHEIM, Steven A. *The Nietzsche Legacy in Germany: 1890–1990*. Berkeley, London, University of California Press, 1994.

ASSOUN, Paul-Laurent. *Freud et Nietzsche*. Paris, Presses universitaires de France, 1980.

BARZUN, Jacques. *Berlioz and the Romantic Century*. New York, Columbia University Press, 1969.

——— *Darwin, Marx, Wagner*. Boston, Little, Brown & Co, 1947.

——— *From Dawn to Decadence – Five Hundred Years of Western Cultural Life*. New York, Harper/Collins, 2000.

BERNOUILLI, C.A. *Franz Overbeck und Friedrich Nietzsche: eine Freundschaft*, 2 vols Jena, Diederichs, 1908.

BERTHOLD, Arthur. *Bücher und Wege zur Büchern*. Berlin & Stuttgart, Speermann, 1900.

BERTRAM, Ernst. *Nietzsche: Versuch einer Mythologie*. Berlin, Bondi, 1918.

BINION, Rudolph. *Frau Lou: Nietzsche's Wayward Disciple*. Princeton University Press, 1968.

BLUNCK, Richard. *Friedrich Nietzsche: Kindheit und Jugend*. Munich and Basel, Ernst Reinhardt, 1953; the page references in my Notes are based on Eva Sauser's French translation, *Enfance et Jeunesse*, (Paris) Corréa – Buchet Chastel, 1955.

BRANDES, Georg (George Morris Cohen). *Main Currents in Nineteenth Century Literature* (partic. vol VI, 'Young Germany'). London, William Heinemann, 1924.

BREHIER, Emile. *Histoire de la Philosophie*, vols I-IV. Paris, Félix Alcan, 1934.

BRIDGEWATER, Patrick. *Nietzsche in Anglosaxony*. Leicester University Press, 1972.

BRINKLEY, Robert. *Realism and Nationalism – 1852–1871*. New York London, Harper Torchbooks, 1963.

CAIRNS, David. *Hector Berlioz*, 2 vols London, Penguin paperback, 1999.

CHAMBERLAIN, Lesley. *Nietzsche in Turin – The End of the Future*. London, Quartet Books, 1997.

COWAN, Marianne. *Philosophy in the Tragic Age of the Greeks*. (Translation of FN's *Philosophie im tragischen Zeitalter der Griechen*). South Bend, Indiana, Gateway Editions, 1962.

DARWIN, Charles. *The Origin of Species*. (Introduction by L. Harrison

Matthews) Everyman's University Library. London, Melbourne, Toronto, Dent 1972.

DEUSSEN, Paul. *Erinnerungen an Friedrich Nietzsche*. Leipzig, Brockhaus, 1901.

——— *Mein Leben* (publ. by Erika Rosenthal-Deussen), Leipzig, Brockhaus, 1922.

DONADIO, Stephen. *Nietzsche, Henry James and the Artistic Will*. New York, Oxford University Press, 1978.

DU MOULIN ECKART, Richard Graf. *Cosima Wagner, ein Lebens- und Charakterbild*, vol I. Munich-Berlin, Drei Masken Verlag, 1929.

ECKERMANN, Johann Peter. *Gespräche mit Goethe in den letzten Jahren seines Lebens* (ed. by Fritz Bergemann). Frankfurt, Insel Verlag (Taschenbuch), 1955.

EMERSON, Ralph Waldo. *Essays* (with Introduction by Irwin Edman). Apollo Editions Paperback. New York, Thomas Crowell, 1951.

——— *Essays*, 11 vols Boston, Riverside edition, 1887.

EUCKEN, Rudolf. *Lebenserinnerungen – Ein Stück deutsches Lebens*. Leipzig, Koehler, 1921.

FAYE, Jean-Pierre. *Le vrai Nietzsche – Guerre à la guerre*. Paris, Hermann, 1998.

FÖRSTER-NIETZSCHE, Elisabeth. *Das Leben Friedrich Nietzsches*. Leipzig, C.G. Naumann: vol I (1895); vol II/1 (1897); vol II/2 (1904).

——— *Der junge Nietzsche*. Leipzig, Kröner, 1912.

FREEMAN, Kathleen. *Ancilla to the Pre-Socratic Philosophers* (Complete translation of Diehls' *Fragmente der Vorsokratiker*) Oxford, Basil Blackwell, 1948.

GAUTIER, Judith. *Auprès de Richard Wagner – Souvenirs 1861–1882*. Paris, Mercure de France, 1943.

GILMAN, Sander L. (in collaboration with Ingeborg Reichenbach). *Begegnungen mit Nietzsche*. Bonn, Bouvier Verlag Herbert Grundmann, 1981. (Condensed version in English, *Conversations with Nietzsche*, translated by David J. Parent. New York, Oxford, Oxford University Press, 1987.)

GILSON, Etienne. *La Philosophie au Moyen Age*. Paris, Payot, 1947.

——— *René Descartes – Discours de la Méthode. Texte et commentaire*. Paris, Librairie philosophique J. Vrin, 1947.

GRAVES, Robert. *The Greek Myths*, 2 vols Harmonsworth, Penguin Books, 1957.

GREGOR-DELLIN, Martin. *Richard Wagner – Sein Leben. Sein Werk. Sein Jahrhundert*. Munich, Piper, 1980.

GRUNDER, Karlfried. *Der Streit um Nietzsches 'Geburt der Tragödie'* (including texts by E. Rohde, Richard Wagner, U. von Wilamowitz-

Möllendorff). Hildersheim, Georg Olms, 1969.

HARRISON, Thomas. *Nietzsche in Italy* (with contributions from Mazzino Montinari, Giorgio Colli, Michel Serres, Giorgio Agamben Anacleto Verrechia, and others). Stanford University, Saratoga, California, 1988.

HAYES, Carlton J.H. *A Generation of Materialism – 1871–1900*. New York, London, Harper, 1941.

HAYMAN, Ronald. *Nietzsche – A Critical Life*. London, Weidenfeld and Nicolson, 1980.

HAZARD, Paul. *La Crise de la conscience européenne – 1680–1715*. – Paris, Fayard, 1961.

HEIDEGGER, Martin. *Nietzsche*, 2 vols Pfullingen, Neske, 1961.

——— '*The Word of Nietzsche: "God Is Dead"*' – Part II of *The Question Concerning Technology and Other Essays*, trans. William Lovitt. New York, Harper & Row, 1977.

HELLER, Erich. *The Disinherited Mind – Essays in Modern German Literature and Thought*. London, Bowes & Bowes, 1975.

HILLEBRAND, Karl. *Zeiten, Völker und Menschen* (particularly vol II, three essays on FN's 'Untimely Meditations'). Berlin, 1875, Strassburg, 1892.

HILLESHEIM, James W. and SIMPSON, Malcolm R. *Schopenhauer as Educator* (Translation of FN's *Schopenhauer als Erzieher*. Introduction by Eliseo Vivas.)

HIMMELFARB, Gertrude. *Darwin and the Darwinian Revolution*. New York, 1959.

——— *One Nation, Two Cultures*. New York, Random House, Vintage Books 1999.

HÖLDERLIN, Friedrich. *Sämtliche Werke* (particularly vols 12 and 13, on Empedokles), ed by D.E. Sattler. Basel & Frankfurt, Stoernfeld/Roter Stern, 1985.

HOLLINGDALE, R.J. *Beyond Good and Evil* (translation of FN's *Jenseits von Gut und Böse*, Hammondsworth, Penguin Books, 1990.

——— *Daybreak* (translation of FN's *Morgenröte*). Introduction by Michael Tanner. Cambridge University Press, 1982.

——— *Human, All Too Human* (translation of *Menschliches, Allzumenschliches*). Introduction by Richard Schacht. Cambridge University Press, 1996.

——— *Twilight of the Idols* and *The Antichrist* (translation, with Introduction and Commentary, of *Götzen-Dämmerung* and *Der Antichrist*). Penguin Books, 1977.

——— *Untimely Meditations* (FN's four *Unzeitgemässe Betrachtungen*) translated by P. J. Hollingdale, with Introduction by J.P. Stern.

Cambridge and New York. Cambridge University Press, 1980.

——— *A Nietzsche Reader.* Translated selections, with Introduction. Harmondsworth, Penguin Classics, 1977.

——— *Schopenhauer Essays and Aphorisms.* (Selected and translated, with Introduction). Harmondsworth, Penguin Books, 1976.

HOWALD, Ernst. *Friedrich Nietzsche und die klassische Philologie.* Gotha, Andreas Perthes, 1920.

JANZ, Curt Paul. *Friedrich Nietzsche – Biographie.* 3 vols Munich, Vienna, Carl Hanser, 1993. (An indispensable, even though woodenly written, biography for all FN scholars.)

JASPERS, Karl. *Nietzsche: Einführung in das Verständnis seines Philosophierens.* Berlin and Leipzig, de Gruyter, 1947. English translation by Charles F. Wallraff and Frederick J. Schmitz, *An Introduction to the Understanding of his Philosophical Activity.* Tucson, University of Arizona Press, 1965.

JUNG, Carl Gustav. 'Apollinian and Dionysian' – from vol VI of his *Collected Works* (pp. 136–46). Bollingen Series. Princeton University Press, 1974.

——— *Two Essays in Analytical Psychology* (particularly ch. 3, 'The Other Point of View: The Will to Power'). New York, Meridian Books, 1956. (Extracted from vol VII of his *Collected Works.*)

——— *Nietzsche's Zarathustra: Notes of the Seminar given in 1934–1939.* 2 vols, ed. by James L. Jarrett. Princeton University Press, 1988.

KANT, Immanuel. *Sämmtliche Werke,* 10 vols G. Hartenstein edition. Leipzig, Leopold Voss, 1867.

KAUFMANN, Walter. *Nietzsche. Philosopher, Psychologist, Antichrist.* Princeton University Press, 1974. (Regarded by Thomas Mann as superior to all previous attempts at critical interpretation.)

——— *The Birth of Tragedy* and *The Case of Wagner* (translation, with commentary, of *Die Geburt der Tragödie* and *Der Fall Wagner*). Vintage Books. New York, Random House, 1967.

——— *The Portable Nietzsche* (*Thus Spake Zarathustra, Twilight of the Idols, The Antichrist, Nietzsche contra Wagner,* and brief extracts from other works, translated and edited, with critical prefaces). Harmondsworth, Penguin Books, 1977.

——— *The Gay Science, With a Prelude in Rhymes and an Appendix of Songs.* (English translation, with commentary, of *Die fröhliche Wissenschaft.*) Vintage Books. New York, Random House, 1974.

——— *Beyond Good and Evil* (translation of *Jenseits von Gut und Böse,* with commentary by WK). New York, Vintage Books, 1966.

——— *The Genealogy of Morals* (translated by WK and R.J. Hollingdale) and *Ecce homo* (translated, with commentary, by WK). New York,

Vintage Books, 1989.
——— *The Will to Power* (translation, by WK and R.J. Hollingdale, of *Der Wille zur Macht*, with Introduction and commentary by WK). New York, Random House, Vintage Books, 1968.
KESSLER, Harry Graf. *Tagebücher: 1918–1937* (a fascinating diary by a great FN admirer). Published with a Preface by Wolfgang Pfeiffer-Belli. Frankfurt-am-Main, Insel Verlag, 1961.
——— *Gesichter und Zeiten*. Berlin, S. Fischer, 1962.
KOESTLER, Arthur, *The Sleepwalkers*.
KOFMAN, Sarah. *Nietzsche et la métaphysique*. Paris, Galilée 1983.
——— *Nietzsche et la scène philosophique*. Paris, Galilée, 1986.
——— *Le Mépris des Juifs. Nietzsche, les Juifs, l'antisémitisme*. Paris, Galilée, 1994.
KRUMMEL, Richard Frank. *Nietzsche und der deutsche Geist*. 2 vols Berlin, Walter de Gruyter, 1974, 1983.
LANGE, Friedrich Albert. *Geschichte des Materialismus – und Kritik seiner Bedeutung in der Gegenwart*. With Preface by Hermann Cohen. 3 vols Iserholm, J. Baedeker, 1882 (4th ed.). (English translation by Ernest C. Thomas (3 vols), London, 1881.
LANGER, William. *Political and Social Upheaval 1832–1852*. (Part of 'The Rise of Modern Europe' series.) New York, London, Harper Torchbooks, 1969.
LÖWITH, Karl. *Von Hegel zu Nietzsche. Der revolutionäre Bruch im Denken des neunzehten Jahrhunderts*. Zürich, 1941, Europa Verlag. English translation by David E. Green, *From Hegel to Nietzsche: The Revolution in 19th Century Thought*. London, Constable, 1965.
MARTIN, Gottfried. *Immanuel Kant – Ontologie und Wissenschaftstheorie*. Cologne, Kölner Universitätsverlag, 1951.
MEYSENBUG, Malwida von. *Mémoires d'une idéaliste*. 2 vols Préface de Gabriel Monod. Paris, Fischbacher, 1900.
——— *Lebensabend einer Idealistin*, Berlin, Schuster & Loeffler, 1900.
——— *Le Soir de ma vie* (volIII of *Mémoires*), Paris, Fischbacher, 1908
——— *Memoiren einer Idealistin*. 3 vols Berlin, Schuster & L, 1905.
——— *Im Anfang war die Liebe: Briefe an ihre Pflegetochter* (Letters to her foster-daughter, Olga Herzen). Munich, C.H. Beck, 1926.
MOSSE, George L. *The Nationalization of the Masses* – Political Symbolism and Mass Movements in Germany from the Napoleonic Wars through to the Third Reich. New York, Howard Fertig, 1975.
NEWMAN, Ernest. *The Life of Richard Wagner*. 4 vols London, Cambridge, Melbourne, Cambridge University Press, 1976 (paperback).
NIETZSCHE, Friedrich. *Friedrich Nietzsche, Paul Rée, Lou von Salomé. Die*

*Dokumente ihrer Begegnung*. Edited by Ernst Pfeiffer, on the basis of work previously accomplished by and with Karl Schlechta and Erhart Thierbach. Frankfurt/Main. Insel-Verlag, 1970.

NIETZSCHE STUDIEN. *Internationales Jahrbuch für die Nietzsche Forschung*. (Yearbook series of 'Nietzsche Studies' launched by Mazzino Montinari, Wolfgang Müller-Lauter, Heinz Wenzel.) Berlin, New York, Walter de Gruyter, from 1972ff.

NOLTE, Ernst. *Nietzsche und der Nietzscheanismus*. Frankfurt/Main, Berlin, Propyläen, 1990.

OEHLER, Adalbert, *Nietzsches Mutter*. Munich, C.H. Beck, 1940.

OEHLER, Max. *Nietzsches Ahnen*. Weimar, Wagner, 1938.

ORTEGA Y GASSET, José. *Obras completas*. (In particular, vol V, '*En torno a Galileo*', and vol VIII, '*La idea de principio en Leibniz y la evolución de la teoría deductiva*' – probably the profoundest analysis yet made of Descartes' battle with Aristotelian scholasticism.)

PATZER, Andreas. *Franz Overbeck – Erwin Rohde – Briefwechsel* (Correspondence of Overbeck and Rohde, edited by Patzer, with an Introduction by Uvo Holsche.) Berlin, Walter de Gruyter, 1990.

PERENYI, Eleanor. *Liszt – The Artist as Romantic Hero*. Boston, Atlantic Monthly Press, 1974.

PETERS, Heinz Frederick. *Zarathustra's Sister. The Case of Elisabeth and Friedrich Nietzsche*. New York, Crown Publishers, 1977.

PFEIFFER, Ernst. *Friedrich Nietzsche, Paul Rée, Lou von Salomé. Die Dokumente ihrer Begegnung* (listed above, under Nietzsche). A useful reconstitution of the extraordinary Nietzsche-Rée-Lou Salomé embroglio, based on letters exchanged, diary entries, etc. Frankfurt/Main, Insel-Verlag, 1970.

PODACH, Erich F. *Gestalten um Nietzsche*. Weimar, Erich Lichtensteig, 1932.

——— *Nietzsches Zusammenbruch*. Heidelberg, Kampmann, 1930.

——— *Der kranke Nietzsche. Briefe seiner Mutter an Franz Overbeck*. Vienna, Bermann-Fischer, 1937.

RÉE, Paul. *Der Ursprung der moralischen Empfindungen*. Chemnitz, Schmeitzner, 1877.

——— *Die Entstehung des Gewissens*. Berlin, C. Duncker, 1885.

——— *Die Illusion der Willensfreiheit*. Berlin, Heymans, 1885.

RIEDEL, Manfred. *Nietzsche in Weimar*. Leipzig, Reclam Verlag Leipzig, 2000.

ROHDE, Erwin. *Der griechische Roman und seine Vorläufer*. Leipzig, Breitkopf & Härtel, 1876.

——— *Psyche – Seelenwelt und Unsterblichkeitsglaube der Griechen*. Freiburg, Siebeck, 1894.

ROSS, Werner. *Der ängstliche Adler – Friedrich Nietzsche Leben*. Stuttgart, Deutsche Verlags-Anstalt, 1980.

SAFRANSKI, Rüdiger. *Nietzsche. Biographie seines Denkens*. Munich, Carl Hanser Verlag, 2000.

SALIS-MARSCHLINS, Meta von – *Philosoph und Edelmensch: Ein Beitrag zur Charakteristik Friedrich Nietzsches*, Leipzig, C.G. Naumann, 1897

SALOMÉ, Lou – see above, under Andreas-Salomé.

SCHLECHTA, Karl. *Der Fall Nietzsche*. Munich, Hanser, 1975.

SCHNABEL, Franz. *Deutsche Geschichte im neunzehnten Jahrhundert*. 4 vols Freiburg, Herder Verlag, 1929–1937.

SCHOPENHAUER, Arthur. *Sämtliche Werke* (5 vols). Frankfurt/Main, Cotta-Insel, and Suhrkamp Taschenbuch, 1994. *Die Welt als Wille und Vorstellung* (vol I): English translation *The World as Will and Representation* (2 vols) by E.F.J. Payne. New York, Dover Publications, 1969. *Parerga und Paralipomena* (vol V of *Sämtliche Werke*): translated under identical title by E.F.J. Payne, Oxford University Press,1974.

SCHURÉ, Edouard. '*L'individualisme et l'anarchie: Nietzsche et sa philosophie*'. Long essay in *La Revue des Deux Mondes*, 15 Aug 1895, (pp. 775–805).

SCHWEITZER, Albert. *The Quest for the Historical Jesus*. English translation by W. Montgomery from 1906 German text, *Von Reimarus zu Wrede*. Preface by H.C. Burkitt; Introduction by James M. Robinson. New York, Macmillan, 1961 (paperback).

SIMMEL, Georg. *Schopenhauer und Nietzsche*. Leipzig, Duncker & Humblot, 1907.

STEINER, George. *The Death of Tragedy*. New York, Alfred Knopf, 1961.

(An enthralling study of the development of modern tragedy, from Shakespeare to the 'anti-drama' of Samuel Beckett, with several interesting pages devoted to Wagner and Nietzsche.)

STERN, J.P. *Nietzsche*. London, Fontana/Collins, 1978.

——— *A Study of Nietzsche*. Cambridge University Press, 1979.

STROUX, Johannes. *Nietzsches Professur in Basel*. Jena, Frommann (Walter Biedermann), 1925.

THATCHER, David S. *Nietzsche in England 1890–1914. The Growth of a Reputation*. Univerity of Toronto Press, 1970.

UNGERN-STERNBERG, Isabella Freifrau von (born von der Pahlen). *Nietzsche im Spiegelbild seiner Schrift*. Leipzig, C.G. Naumann 1902

VERRECHIA, Anacleto. *La catastrophe di Nietzsche a Torino*. Turin, Einaudi, 1978.

VIER, Jacques. *La Comtesse d'Agoult et son temps*. 6 vols (The first volume describes the social, and particularly Parisian milieu in which Cosima Liszt was brought up.) Paris, Armand Colin, 1958–1963.

VIERECK, Peter. *Metapolitics – From the Romantics to Hitler.* New York, Alfred Knopf, 1941.

WAGNER, Cosima. *Die Tagebücher.* Munich, Piper, 1976 (vol I), 1977 (vol II). English version: *Cosima Wagner Diaries, Volume I, 1869–1877; Volume II, 1878–1883.* Edited and annotated by Martin Gregor-Dellin and Dietrich Mach; translated with an Introduction by Geoffrey Skelton. A Helen and Kurt Wolff Book. New York and London, Harcourt Brace Jovanovich: vol I, 1977; vol II, 1978.

WAGNER, Richard. *Gesammelte Schriften und Dichtungen.* Leipzig, E.W. Fritzsch, 1898.

WESTERNHAGEN, Curt von. *Wagner.* Eine Biographie. 2 vols Zürich, Atlantis Musikbuch Verlag, 1978. English version: *Wagner. A Biography.* 2 vols Translated by Mary Whittall. London, New York, Melbourne. Cambridge University Press, 1978.

# Index

**C**

NORTH COUNTRY LIBRARY SYSTEM
0 11 01 0318081 3